# Routledge Handbook of Media Law

Featuring specially commissioned chapters from experts in the field of media and communications law, this book provides an authoritative survey of media law from a comparative perspective. The handbook does not simply offer a synopsis of the state of affairs in media law jurisprudence; rather it provides a better understanding of the forces that generate media rules, norms and standards against the background of major transformations in the way information is mediated as a result of democratization, economic development, cultural change, globalization and technological innovation.

The book addresses a range of issues including:

- media law and evolving concepts of democracy;
- network neutrality and traffic management;
- public service broadcasting in Europe and the United States;
- theories and approaches in media governance;
- cultural development, diversity and protection.

A variety of rule-making institutions are considered, including administrative and judicial entities within and outside government, but also entities such as associations and corporations that generate binding rules. The book assesses the emerging role of supranational economic and political groupings as well as non-Western models, such as China and India, where cultural attitudes toward media freedoms are often very different.

**Monroe E. Price** is Director of the Center for Global Communication Studies at the Annenberg School for Communication at the University of Pennsylvania and Joseph and Sadie Danciger Professor of Law and Director of the Howard M. Squadron Program in Law, Media and Society at the Cardozo School of Law.

**Stefaan G. Verhulst** is Chief of Research at the Markle Foundation. Previously, he was the co-founder and co-director, with Professor Monroe Price, of the Programme in Comparative Media Law and Policy (PCMLP) at the University of Oxford, as well as Senior Research Fellow at the Centre for Socio-Legal Studies.

**Libby Morgan** has been the Associate Director of the Center for Global Communication Studies at the Annenberg School for Communication at the University of Pennsylvania.

"In our digital age, understanding the landscape of media law is essential not just to legal experts, but to companies, policy makers, and the public at large. This is simply the best book on the market – informed, rich, elucidating and full of insights. Highly recommended!"

Viktor Mayer-Schönberger, Professor of Internet Governance and Regulation, University of Oxford

"Media law is a key aspect of the fast increasing role of the media in our ever more interconnected world. Understanding the rapidly evolving legal frameworks that govern the media across the globe is vital. Researchers, policymakers, and activists alike could not wish for a better resource than the *Routledge Handbook of Media Law.* Its first-rate contributors provide a comprehensive and authoritative tour d'horizon of a fascinating field. The comparative and multi-disciplinary perspective is thoroughly compelling and enables us to understand how media law, society and politics constitute each other."

Wolfgang Reinicke, Founding Dean, School of Public Policy, Central European University, Budapest and President, Global Public Policy Institute, Berlin

# Routledge Handbook of Media Law

*Edited by Monroe E. Price, Stefaan G. Verhulst and Libby Morgan*

Routledge
Taylor & Francis Group
LONDON AND NEW YORK

First published in paperback 2015

First published 2013
by Routledge
2 Park Square, Milton Park, Abingdon, Oxon OX14 4RN

and by Routledge
711 Third Avenue, New York, NY 10017

*Routledge is an imprint of the Taylor & Francis Group, an informa business*



*British Library Cataloguing in Publication Data*
A catalogue record for this book is available from the British Library

*Library of Congress Cataloging in Publication Data*
A catalog record has been requested for this book

ISBN: 978-0-415-68316-6 (hbk)
ISBN: 978-1-138-85888-6 (pbk)
ISBN: 978-0-203-07457-2 (ebk)

Typeset in Bembo
by RefineCatch Limited, Bungay, Suffolk

Printed and bound in the United States of America by Publishers Graphics, LLC on sustainably sourced paper.

# Contents

# Contributors

**Joan Barata** is Professor of Communications Law and Vice Dean for International Relations at the Blanquerna Communications School at the Universitat Ramon Llull in Barcelona. Previously, he was Head of the President's Cabinet and Secretary General for the Catalonia Audiovisual Council. He earned his doctorate at the University of Barcelona, where his thesis was on television, democracy and the notion of public service.

**Antonios Broumas** is a technology lawyer, an independent researcher and a digital rights activist. He studied law at the University of Athens, Greece. He holds LL.M. degrees in philosophy of law from the University of Athens and in information technology and electronic communications law from the University of Strathclyde, UK. His main areas of interest, research and writing focus on the interaction between law, technology and society. Antonios currently practices law in the electronic communications industry, especially in the fields of telecoms and personal data regulation.

**Mira Burri** is Senior Research Fellow and Lecturer in Law at the World Trade Institute of the University of Bern, Switzerland. Her present research focuses on the interaction between digital technologies and the law, in particular in shaping new media and cultural policies. She is the co-editor of, among other publications, *Trade Governance in the Digital Age* (Cambridge University Press, 2012), *Governance of Digital Game Environments and Cultural Diversity* (Edward Elgar, 2010), *Intellectual Property and Traditional Cultural Expressions in a Digital Environment* (Edward Elgar, 2008) and *Free Trade versus Cultural Diversity* (Schulthess, 2004).

**Richard Collins** is Visiting Professor in the Centre for Law, Justice and Journalism at City University London. He has held university posts in Australia and the UK, and fellowships or professorial appointments in Australia, Canada, South Africa and the United States. He co-founded the Communication Policy Research Program at the Institute for Public Policy Research and he directed its media policy program through the early and mid 1990s. He has been Specialist Adviser to three House of Lords' Select Committee enquiries on media issues (BBC Charter Review, public service broadcasting and digital switchover). He has published widely, in the UK and overseas, and his books include *Three Myths of Internet Governance* (Intellect, 2009), *Media and Identity in Contemporary Europe: Consequences of Global Convergence* (Intellect, 2002), *From Satellite to Single Market: New Communication Technology and European Public Service Television 1982–1992* (LSE Books/Routledge, 1998) and *New Media, New Policies* (with Cristina Murroni, Polity Press, 1996).

**Rogier Creemers** is Postdoctoral Research Officer at the Programme for Comparative Media Law and Policy (PCMLP) at the University of Oxford. He received his Ph.D. from Maastricht University, where his thesis was on the relationship between media piracy in China, intellectual property law and media regulation, and globalization. His main research interests include the nexus between media policy and political change in China.

**Karen Donders** is Lecturer in European Media Policy and European Information Society at the Vrije Universiteit Brussel. She is Senior Researcher at the Center for Studies on Media Information and Telecommunication (SMIT), which is a partner of the Interdisciplinary Center for Broadband Technology (IBBT), and is a Post-Doctoral Fellow with the Research Foundation Flanders (FWO).

**Thomas Gibbons** is Professor of Law at the University of Manchester, where he formerly served as Dean of the School of Law. He was a specialist adviser to the UK's (Puttnam) Joint Committee on the Draft Communications Bill 2002 and has frequently acted as an expert adviser to the Council of Europe.

**Ellen P. Goodman** specializes in information policy law at Rutgers University School of Law—Camden, where she is co-director and co-founder of the Rutgers Institute for Information Law and Policy. Her research interests include media policy, spectrum policy, the use of information as a policy tool, advertising law and the informational aspects of sustainability policy. She recently served as Distinguished Visiting Scholar at the Federal Communications Commission and contributed substantially to the agency's seminal report on the *Information Needs of Communities*.

**Lesley Hitchens** is Professor of Law at the University of Technology Sydney. Prior to taking up an academic position, she practiced as a commercial lawyer in Sydney with Allens and in London with Herbert Smith. She holds degrees from Macquarie University and the University of NSW in Australia, and the University of London (London School of Economics). Her research in media and communications law and regulation has a particular focus on the relationship between broadcasting policy and regulation, and, more recently, the impact of new media on traditional regulatory approaches.

**Bernd Holznagel** is Director of the Institute for Information, Telecommunication and Media Law (ITM) at the University of Münster in Germany, where he teaches constitutional law, administrative law, European law and administrative sciences. He studied law and sociology in Berlin, pursued postgraduate LL.M. studies at McGill University in Montreal, Canada, and received his Ph.D. at the University of Hamburg (1990). His research interests include regulatory law and state aid law, as well as media and data protection law. He is a member of the Academic Advisory Council of the German Regulatory Authority.

**Karol Jakubowicz** is an international expert in broadcasting. He is a member of the Independent Media Commission in Kosovo and of the Intergovernmental Council of the UNESCO "Information for All" Program, and heads Working Group 2 of the COST A30 ACTION "East of West: Setting a New Central and Eastern European Media Research Agenda" of the European Science Foundation. He holds a Ph.D. degree in Sociology of Mass Communications from the University of Warsaw, Poland. Jakubowicz has worked as a journalist and executive in the Polish press, radio and television for many years. He has been Vice-President, Chairman of the Supervisory Board and Head of Strategic Planning and Development at Polish Television, and was Director of the Strategy and Analysis Department at the National Broadcasting Council of Poland. He has taught at the Institute of Journalism, University of Warsaw, and has been a Visiting Professor at the Institute of

Journalism, University of Dortmund, and at the Amsterdam School of Communications Research, University of Amsterdam.

**Natascha Just** is Senior Research and Teaching Associate in the Division on Media Change & Innovation, Institute of Mass Communication and Media Research (IPMZ), University of Zurich, Switzerland. She is also a Fellow of the Stanford-Vienna Transatlantic Technology Law Forum (TTLF). She holds an M.A. in Communication Science/Romance Philology and a Ph.D. in Communication Science from the University of Vienna. Her current research centers on the transformation of statehood in the convergent communication sector, with a special emphasis on changing governance structures, competition policy and market power control. She is co-author of *Self- and Co-regulation in the Mediamatics Sector: Alternative Regulation between State and Market* (2002, in German).

**Christian Katzenbach** is Researcher in Media and Communication Studies and Governance at the Alexander von Humboldt Institute for Internet and Society (HIIG). His research and teaching focuses on media regulation and governance, online communication and social media, media change and innovation. Before joining the HIIG, he was Research Associate and Lecturer at the Institute for Media and Communication Studies at the Freie Universität Berlin.

**Raminder Kaur** is Senior Lecturer in Anthropology at the University of Sussex. She was awarded her Ph.D. at SOAS. She has held postdoctoral research positions at Brunel University (ESRC-funded project 'Reconsidering Ethnicity'), University of East Anglia (Getty Research Fellow) and at the University of Manchester (Simon-Marks Fellow). She was previously Lecturer at the University of Manchester. Her publications include *Censorship in South Asia* (co-edited with William Mazzarella, 2009), *Diaspora and Hybridity* (co-authored with Virinder Kalra and John Hutnyk, 2005), *Bollyworld* (co-edited with Ajay Sinha, 2005), *Travel-Worlds: Journeys in Contemporary Cultural Politics* (co-edited with John Hutnyk) and *Performative Politics and the Cultures of Hinduism* (2003, 2005).

**Michael Latzer** is Professor of Communications at the Institute of Mass Communication and Media Research (IPMZ), University of Zurich, Switzerland, where he chairs the Division on Media Change & Innovation. Latzer is an expert on media convergence and European information society issues, eCommerce, digital economy, telecommunications and media governance (self- and co-regulation). He is the author of more than 100 publications including *European Public Sphere and Media Change, The State of Europe: Transformation of Statehood from a European Perspective, The Economics of eCommerce, Mediamatics: The Convergence of Media, Telecommunications and Information Technologies, Technology Governance and Self- and Co-Regulation in the Mediamatics Sector.*

**Eva Lievens** is a member of the Communications Law Department at the Interdisciplinary Centre for Law and ICT (ICRI) at the Katholieke Universiteit Leuven and a Postdoctoral Research Fellow of the Research Fund Flanders. She obtained her Ph.D. in law with a thesis entitled 'Regulatory instruments for content regulation in digital media: A prospective study on the protection of minors against harmful content' in June 2009. She holds a law degree from the University of Ghent and a Masters degree in Transnational Communications and Global Media from Goldsmiths College, London.

**Jan Loisen** is Lecturer in Media, Culture and Globalization Theories and Introduction to Communication Science at the Vrije Universiteit Brussel. He is Senior Researcher with the Center for Studies on Media Information and Telecommunication (SMIT), which is a partner of the Interdisciplinary Center for Broadband Technology (IBBT).

**Nicola Lucchi** is EU Marie Curie Research Fellow at the Catholic University of Louvain, Belgium. His research and teaching focus on information law and policy, and the interaction between law and innovation. He was previously Research Associate at the Department of Legal Studies of the University of Ferrara.

**Daithí Mac Síthigh** is a graduate of Trinity College Dublin, Ireland, and Lecturer in Digital Media Law at the University of Edinburgh. Previously, he was Lecturer at the UEA Law School, University of East Anglia (2008–2012) and Director of its LL.M. Information Technology and Intellectual Property. His research interests include content regulation, telecommunications policy, new media and international law, and his doctoral thesis was entitled 'Convergence and the right to communicate: Assessing the application of media law to the Internet.' He is the convenor for media and communications in the Society of Legal Scholars and an associate editor of *SCRIPTed: A Journal of Law and Technology*.

**Paolo Mancini** is Full Professor at the Faculty of Political Science at the University of Perugia. His research interests focus on the relationship between mass communication systems and the political system, and on the study of electoral campaigns, in which he has considerable comparative research experience. His principal English-language publications include *Between Commodification and Lifestyle Politics: Does Silvio Berlusconi Provide a New Model of Politics for the Twenty-First Century* (Oxford, 2011), *Comparing Media Systems Beyond the Western World* (with Daniel Hallin, Cambridge, 2012) and *Comparing Media Systems: Three Models of Media and Politics* (with Daniel Hallin, Cambridge, 2004).

**Robin Mansell** is Professor of New Media and the Internet at the London School of Economics and Political Science. Her current research focuses on the social, political and economic influences of media and communication policy and regulation, with a special interest in governance arrangements for new media and the Internet. Recent publications include *Imagining the Internet: Communication, Innovation and Governance* (Oxford, 2012) and *Handbook of Global Media and Communication Policy* (edited with Marc Raboy, Wiley-Blackwell, 2011).

**Aysha Mawani** is completing a Ph.D. in Communication Studies from McGill University, for which she was awarded an SSHRC Doctoral Fellowship. Her dissertation research focuses on UNESCO's policies in support of cultural diversity, and examines their relationship with the intersection of globalization and governance.

**William Mazzarella** is Professor of Anthropology at the University of Chicago. He is the author of *Shoveling Smoke: Advertising and Globalization in Contemporary India* (2003) and *Censorium: Cinema and the Open Edge of Mass Publicity* (2013). He is also the co-editor, with Raminder Kaur, of *Censorship in South Asia: Cultural Regulation from Sedition to Seduction* (2009).

**Helmi Noman** is Senior Researcher at the Citizen Lab, Munk School of Global Affairs, University of Toronto, and Research Affiliate of the Berkman Center, working on the OpenNet Initiative. He leads the research on Internet, media and telecommunications laws, and issues surrounding filtering and censorship in the Middle East and North Africa. His research also explores the impact of information and communication technologies on the Arab information societies, the Arabic web content, how the use of the Internet defies the social and political structures in the region, and the potential systemic changes that cyberspace can bring to real space in the Arab world.

**Rónán Ó Fathaigh** is Researcher and Ph.D. candidate at Ghent University, where his research focuses on 'The chilling effect on freedom of expression and information.' He holds a Master of Laws (Public Law), Bachelor of Laws and Bachelor of Arts from the National University of Ireland, Galway. He is a former Legal Researcher at RTÉ Solicitors' Office, Dublin.

**Caroline Pauwels** is Lecturer in Encyclopedia to Communication Sciences, Media Policy and European Media Policy at the Vrije Universiteit Brussel. She is Director of the Center for Studies on Media Information and Telecommunication (SMIT), which is a partner of the Interdisciplinary Center for Broadband Technology (IBBT).

**Monroe E. Price** serves as Director of the Center for Global Communication Studies at the Annenberg School for Communication, University of Pennsylvania, and Professor of Law and Director of the Howard M. Squadron Program in Law, Media and Society at the Cardozo School of Law, where he served as Dean from 1982 to 1991. With Stefaan Verhulst, he was Founding Director of the Programme in Comparative Media Law and Policy (PCMLP) at Wolfson College, Oxford. Among his many books are *Media and Sovereignty, Television, The Public Sphere and National Identity* and a treatise on cable television.

**Marc Raboy** is Full Professor and Beaverbrook Chair in Ethics, Media and Communications in the Department of Art History and Communication Studies at McGill University. He is the author or editor of seventeen books and more than 100 journal articles or book chapters. His current research looks at media and communication governance issues in light of increasing globalization. From 2001 to 2003, he served as Expert Adviser to the House of Commons Standing Committee on Canadian Heritage for its study of Canadian broadcasting. He is a founding member of an international advocacy campaign for Communication Rights in the Information Society.

**Katharine Sarikakis** holds the Chair of Media Industries, Media Organisation and Media Governance in the Department of Communication at the University of Vienna, where she also serves as Vice Director of the Ph.D. programs of the Faculty of Social Sciences. Her research centers on the political processes and political economic dimensions of media and communications governance. She is currently working on a research monograph that explores issues of control over citizenship through commercial and political surveillance and communication and cultural policies of copyright, labor and ownership. She is the founding co-editor of the *International Journal of Media and Cultural Politics* and is the founder of the Communication Law and Policy Section of ECREA. Her publications include *Feminist Interventions in International Communication* (co-edited with Leslie Regan Shade, Rowman & Littlefield, 2008), *Media and Cultural Policy in the European Union* (Rodopi, 2007) and *Media Policy and Globalisation* (with Paula Chakravartty, Edinburgh University Press, 2006).

**Florian Saurwein** is Research and Teaching Associate in the Division on Media Change and Innovation at the Institute of Mass Communication and Media Research (IPMZ) of the University of Zurich, Switzerland. He studied Communication Science and Political Science at the University of Vienna and holds an M.A. in Communication Science. Among others, he is co-author of the book *Self- and Co-regulation in the Mediamatics Sector: Alternative Regulation between State and Market* (2002, in German). His current research interests focus on interrelations between media change and democracy.

**Nicole Stremlau** is Coordinator of the Program in Comparative Media Law and Policy (PCMLP) at the University of Oxford and Research Fellow in the Center of Socio-Legal Studies. Her research interests include media policy in postwar situations, and her current research focuses on information flows in Somaliland and Somalia, examining how they affect the nation- and state-building process. She has conducted extensive research in Ethiopia and lived there for several years, during which time she worked at a local newspaper in Addis Ababa. She holds a Ph.D. in Development Studies from the London School of Economics and Political Science.

**Dimitris Tsapogas** is a doctoral student and Research Assistant for Media Governance, Media Organization and Media Industries at the Department of Communication at the University of Vienna. His main interests are in the ethical, social and political aspects of digital communications: specifically, the possible barriers that privacy and surveillance concepts pose to users' online participation and engagement.

**Joseph Turow** is Robert Lewis Shayon Professor of Communication at the University of Pennsylvania's Annenberg School for Communication. His research focuses on digital cultural industries, especially at the intersection of the Internet, marketing and society. Recent publications include *The Daily You: How the New Advertising Industry is Defining Your Identity and Your Worth* (Yale University Press, 2012) and *Media Today: An Introduction to Mass Communication* (Routledge, 2011).

**Peggy Valcke** is Research Professor at the University of Leuven, where she currently heads the Interdisciplinary Centre for Law & ICT (ICRI—IBBT) at the Faculty of Law. She is Visiting Professor at the University of Tilburg and teaches media law at the University of Brussels and in the Florence School of Regulation (European University Institute). In 2006, she was Visiting Professor at Central European University in Budapest. Her research focuses on media, communications, IT and competition law, with a particular emphasis on media pluralism. She is the editor of the *International Encyclopedia for Media Law* (Kluwer Law International) and is a member of the editorial boards of, among others, *The Journal of Media Law* (Hart Publishing), *Computer, Law and Security Review* (Elsevier) and *Journal of Information Policy* (Fordham University). She is one of the five members of the General Chamber of the Flemish Media Regulator and is part-time member of the Belgian Competition Council.

**Hilde van den Bulck** is Professor of Communication Studies and head of the Research Group Media, Policy and Culture at the University of Antwerp (UA) in Belgium. She obtained a degree in Communication Studies at the Katholieke Universiteit Leuven (Belgium), an M.A. in Mass Communications at the CMCR, University of Leicester (UK), and a Ph.D. in Social Sciences at the Katholieke Universiteit Leuven with a thesis on public service broadcasting and its cultural and programming policy as a project of modernity. In her research, she combines expertise in media structures and policy with expertise in media culture.

**Nico van Eijk** is Professor of Media and Telecommunications Law and Director of the Institute for Information Law (IViR), Faculty of Law, University of Amsterdam. He studied law at the University of Tilburg and received his doctorate on government interference with broadcasting in 1992 from the University of Amsterdam. He also works as an independent legal adviser. He is chairman of the Dutch Federation for Media and Communications Law, a member of the supervisory board of the Dutch public broadcasting organization (NPO) and chairman of two committees of the Social and Economic Council of the Netherlands (SER). His more recent work includes studies and publications on topics such as file sharing, net neutrality and duties of care on the Internet.

**Stefaan G. Verhulst** is Chief of Research at the Markle Foundation and Senior Research Fellow at the Center for Global Communication Studies, Annenberg School for Communication, University of Pennsylvania. He is also Adjunct Professor in the Department of Culture and Communication at New York University, and Senior Research Fellow for the Center for Media and Communication Studies, Central European University in Budapest. Previously, he was the co-founder and Co-Director, with Professor Monroe Price, of the Programme in Comparative Media Law and Policy (PCMLP) at the University of Oxford, as well as Senior Research Fellow at the Centre for Socio-Legal Studies. In that capacity, he was appointed Socio-Legal Research Fellow at Wolfson College at Oxford, and served as the UNESCO Chairholder in Communications Law and Policy for the UK.

**Dirk Voorhoof** is Professor at the Faculty of Political and Social Sciences and the Faculty of Law at Ghent University, Belgium, where he teaches courses in media law, copyright law and journalistic ethics. He is a member of the Flemish Regulator for the Media. He recently published a *Handbook on Media Law* (Larcier, 2011), a textbook on *European Media Law* (Knops Publishing, 2012) and a book on protection of journalistic sources (Die Keure, 2008), and he regularly publishes in *Auteurs & Media, Mediaforum* and in IRIS-Legal Observations of the European Audiovisual Observatory, Strasbourg. Together with Hannes Cannie, he published "The abuse clause and freedom of expression under the European Human Rights Convention: An added value for democracy and human rights protection?" *Netherlands Quarterly for Human Rights* (2011) 27(1): 54–83.

**Rolf H. Weber** is Professor of Civil, Commercial and European Law at the University of Zurich Law School in Switzerland. He studied at the University of Zurich, where he was admitted as attorney, wrote his doctoral thesis and obtained his doctoral degree in 1979. He teaches and publishes in civil, commercial and European law, with special topics in Internet, media and competition law, international finance and trade regulation. He is a member of the Steering Committee of the Global Internet Governance Academic Network (GigaNet), the European Dialogue on Internet Governance (EuroDIG), and the High-level Panel of Advisers of the Global Alliance for Information and Communication Technologies and Development (GAID).

**Guobin Yang** is Associate Professor at the University of Pennsylvania's Annenberg School for Communication and the School of Arts and Sciences' Department of Sociology. He was previously Associate Professor in the Department of Asian and Middle Eastern Cultures and the Department of Sociology at Barnard College, Columbia University. He has published on a wide range of social issues in China. His books include *The Power of the Internet in China: Citizen Activism Online* (Columbia University Press, June 2009), *Re-Envisioning the Chinese Revolution: The Politics and Poetics of Collective Memories in Reform China* (edited with Ching-Kwan Lee, 2007) and *Dragon-Carving and the Literary Mind* (Library of Chinese Classics in English translation, 2003).

**Christopher S. Yoo** is Professor of Law, Communication, and Computer and Information Science at the University of Pennsylvania's School of Law, where he also serves as Director of the Center for Technology, Innovation and Competition. His research focuses on exploring how the principles of network engineering and the economics of imperfect competition can provide insights into the regulation of the Internet and other forms of electronic communications. He is the author of *The Dynamic Internet: How Technology, Users, and Businesses Are Transforming the Network* (AEI, 2012), *Networks in Telecommunications: Economics and Law* (with Daniel F. Spulber, Cambridge, 2009) and *The Unitary Executive: Presidential Power from Washington to Bush* (with Steven G. Calabresi, Yale, 2008).

# Introduction

*Stefaan G. Verhulst and Monroe E. Price*

The demand for a more comparative and socio-legal analysis of media law and policy has increased greatly. Geopolitics, technology, business developments and a more nuanced understanding of the interrelationships between these forces have all contributed to a resurgence in the field. One might, of course, argue that all research is in essence comparative, even if comparisons are merely drawn unconsciously; an exercise that seeks to define and focus on a singular entity can be said to be comparative (if by default) in its exclusion of other entities.

This handbook is founded on the assumption that deliberate, conscious comparative research is necessary and has major benefits. As such, it tries to capture existing and new scholarship on the dynamics of media law and policy developments across technologies, societies and time in a way that transcends day-to-day changes in this fast-moving field.

The handbook begins from the premise that the laws and policies governing the media are deeply socially embedded, and represent the values, patterns and processes of control as they relate to mediation, freedom of expression and access to information. Media laws and policies are the result of forces—institutional, technical and cultural—acting toward a particular notion of social order. They are social artefacts embedding both technical and symbolic properties.[1] They signal a country or society's commitment to democracy, they speak to a notion of identity and they are symbolically representative of social cohesion. Media laws and policies offer a window, too, onto globalization and its changing meaning over time.

Any media law and policy handbook, therefore, requires an analytic framework that goes beyond the "letter of the law"—applying instead a more encompassing socio-legal and interdisciplinary methodology. It also requires adapting existing theories to new contexts, as well as the generation of new abstract models that can explain how and why certain rules and standards are promoted and advocated. Finally, it requires a comparative perspective: The values, patterns and processes associated with media laws and policies and the forces that perpetuate them often do not fully reveal themselves unless compared across societies or when confronted with new developments that question their validity and effectiveness.

1 For an exploration of the concept of "law as social artefact," see Suchman 2003.

Such comparisons can lead to fresh, exciting insights and to a deeper understanding of issues that are of central concern in different countries. They can identify gaps in knowledge and policies, and may point to possibly new directions that can be followed by researchers, businesspeople, policymakers or legal reformers. Comparisons can also sharpen the focus of analysis of the subject under study by suggesting new, contrasting perspectives. In addition, comparative media law and policy research can give us a better understanding of how one country or medium borrows from the traditions and conventions of another, how intellectual property migrates across various media over time and where best practices exist in the world for the regulation of new communications technologies. Moreover, comparative research can give us an improved knowledge as to whether specific media patterns and structures are causally conditioned by social, political, economic, historical and geographic circumstances. Only by examining relationships across media forms, across national and regional boundaries, across cultures, institutions and environments, and over time can a full picture of the processes of change and globalization be created.

Our approach and interest in establishing a comparative and socio-legal perspective of media law and policy stems from our work at the Centre for Socio-Legal Studies at Oxford University, where we both were co-founders of the Programme in Comparative Media Law and Policy in 1996. As such, this handbook of media law and policy reflects the lessons learned and the body of work developed and reviewed in this field of the past fifteen years—explaining and speculating upon the *actual relationship* between media law and the ordering of mediation and communications in modern societies, emphasizing the norms, narratives and arrangements that underpin media law, and examining the various and often contradictory forces that characterize twenty-first-century communications policy.

This includes the tension and debate among different societies on what constitutes freedom of expression and how, if at all, norms should reflect a mix of public goals, including security and human dignity. A comparison of the importance of human rights in media law doctrine can not only reveal different notions of information control, but also can illuminate different narratives of democracy and political legitimacy. At the same time, approaching media laws and policies simply as artifacts that can be compared across nations helps to demystify them, allowing researchers to bring new insights and evidence of social and political processes otherwise hidden.

A particular tension in current debates pertains to the appropriate role of different actors, within and outside of government, in determining and enforcing regulations—and whether there is a need for a new governance model, articulated as co-regulation, "new governance," or some other way. Finally, technological transformations and new communications practices are challenging existing conventions of media oversight. Several years after the arrival of "cyberlaw" as a newly significant way of organizing thought, the capacity of law to steer certain Internet practices in accordance to existing values and expectations is being questioned.

To address these various issues and questions, this handbook is ordered into the following five sections.

## Media policy and institutional design

In this section, we aim to provide a better understanding of the institutional forces, actors or networks that generate media rules, norms and standards, and that either perpetuate them or foster change. Socio-legal and comparative questions the contributors seek to address in this session include: how to analyze media policy processes through a stakeholder analysis; what is the impact of "rational legal authority" embedded in media policy institutions and mechanisms on the structure of the news media and the performance of journalists; how to understand the concept of independence in both media regulation and practice, including through the lens of "club government," a culture of appointment and consensus; and what rationales international, intra-governmental and non-state organizations use to approach media policy, and how this impacts the sovereign capacities of nation-states in governing their domestic mediating ecologies.

## Media policy, freedom of expression and citizenship

Our contributors revisit the foundational concepts and principles that inform much of media policy and law in democratic societies (i.e. freedom of expression, notions of citizenship and the public interest). Various recent political and technological trends, as well as changes in court interpretations, have challenged existing constitutional perspectives on freedom of expression. In addition, the broad adoption of the Internet has opened up a scholarly debate on the meaning of "access," "freedom" and "rights" within a digitally mediated environment, and how to expand these from an advocacy point of view. Similarly, other areas of media policy—in particular those that are related to the concepts of public interest and citizenship—are re-examined, with multiple implications for approaching and defining "public media" in the twenty-first century.

## Media policy and comparative perspectives

This section seeks to interrogate alternate ways of conceptualizing media law and policy, including competing narratives or rationales that exist in various regions and jurisdictions of the world. Geopolitical shifts away from the unipolar mean that varying perspectives on the organization of society and the role of media within it gain salience or rejection. Engaging in comparative study becomes an exercise in power as well as an intellectual pursuit. To document these comparative media law transfers and differences, we selected various case studies that illustrate approaches not often considered nor analyzed: the use of customary law (*xeer*) in media-related disputes in the Horn of Africa (illustrating the importance of an understanding of local context prior to engaging in policy transfer); the role of faith-based censorship in majority Muslim countries (offering different perspectives on the way in which societies think about Internet control); the development of a rigorous formal and informal information control regime within China (combining both hard and soft methods of control); and the importance of "cultural regulation" in South Asia (illustrating the self-reflective and performative nature of such regulation).

## Media policy and media governance

In this section, our contributors focus on new theories and approaches to "media governance" as a response to a changing mediating and policy ecology at various levels: the identity of those governing; the law and policy mechanisms used; and the geographical reach of the governance models chosen. New administrative understandings; critical perspectives on independence; shifts in public service aspirations; altered theories of the state: all of these have implications for taken-for-granted perspectives on media governance. In particular, novel modes of control, enabled through code and technology, have evolved wholly or partially outside conventional media law, providing for alternative regulatory institutions and tools. The essays place the issue of "independence" in a more complex set of considerations, including questions of the need for global governance in an increasingly interdependent and interconnected world, and the strengths and weaknesses of such an approach.

## Media policy and technological transformation

Finally, we have encouraged the authors to grasp the technological and related industrial transformations that have taken place in the media field, and their impact on how information is being mediated and controlled, as well as the narratives used to describe public interest objectives associated with technological changes. Comparative insights help to guide the extent to which objectives, assumptions and models for one world of technology can or cannot be adapted to another. In particular, our curatorial efforts have focused on the three most salient policy issues that have emerged as result of advances in technology: the impact of social media and networks on traditional notions of "media;" the impact of increased information disclosure and use on rights and expectations of privacy; and how to approach new mechanisms of control at the infrastructure level that have implications for information flows and control. The authors reflect on whether, and how, the current response or lack of response to the growing blurring between media, telecommunications and the Internet will impact the goals of democracy, economic growth and social justice.

## The value proposition behind a comparative approach to media law and policy

Despite the growth of the use of comparative research and the increased need as well as demand, for it, there persists a certain reluctance and narrowness of scope within existing scholarship. Perhaps this stems from a lack of knowledge or understanding of different cultures and languages, or from insufficient awareness of the research traditions and processes operating in different national contexts.

One purpose of this introduction to the handbook is therefore to address such shortcomings by analyzing the needs, possibilities, limitations and pitfalls of comparison, and to probe problems of definition, methodology and presentation.

Over the last few decades, many developments have led to a growing awareness of the value of comparative analysis and a call for greater comparative research. These developments include the rise of globalization, the end of the Cold War, the rise of Asian economies and the growing geopolitical importance of the Middle East (particularly as a result of the "Arab Spring"). In addition, the emergence of social media and online governance structures has enabled new platforms for communication, protesting and mobilizing.

The increased transnational connection and flow of people and information has also clearly challenged the universality of Western theoretical models and concepts, and has forced scholars to look beyond their borders and disciplines (Curran and Park 2000). Amidst a growing homogeneity and uniformity, the emphasis of academic research has shifted from seeking uniformity among variety to studying the preservation of enclaves of uniqueness. Anthony Giddens has, for instance, observed that "globalisation today is only partly westernisation. Globalisation is becoming increasingly decentered" (Giddens 1999). Indeed, while some cultural differences are diminishing as a result of globalization, others are becoming more salient. Only comparative research succeeds in capturing this rich variety across nations, institutions and cultures.

The need for more comparative media law research is clearly driven in large part by this broader context of globalization. But comparative media law has also emerged in response to a complicated mix of other forces. Technological transformations, political transitions, and institutional and market restructuring are among the most important pressures. In addition, advanced telecommunications and the worldwide expansion of media markets have created an urgent need to understand our emerging "global media culture."[2] The world is engaged in a vast remapping of the relationship of governments, corporations and societies to the images, messages and information that course within and across traditional boundaries. States, governments, public international agencies, multinational corporations, human rights organizations and billions of individuals are all involved in this process. All is under construction, yielding, as it were, a thorough shaking and remodeling of media and communications systems. The result, at the moment, is a teeming experiment in the reconstruction of existing media laws and policies. The various players are seeking a vocabulary of change and a set of laws and institutions that provide legitimacy, continued power or the opportunity to profit from the ongoing change. Only with a comparative and interdisciplinary grasp of the massive changes taking place can there be a more sophisticated and nuanced understanding of the impact on democratic values and economic development.

Among the various forces driving comparative media law, technological change is, clearly, one of the most important. The introduction of a new medium is often met with both utopian visions of a more perfect society and apocalyptic anxieties about the collapse of an old order. In much the same way, the emergence of new media forces us to rethink relationships and regulatory assumptions that governed previous communication technologies. It brings into question the applicability and value of older models within a new environment. To understand the true complexity of technological convergence—one of the most salient features of the new media environment—we must improve our understanding of the interrelationships among many different technologies and media environments. We must therefore compare and think across media. A fully comparative insight into the meaning of convergence and technological change across nations, its importance for regulators over time and the different perspectives with which to assess its impact are clearly among the most important issues that require understanding. Without such understanding of the broader, comparative perspective it will be impossible to consider more localized regulatory responses—for instance, at a pan-European or national level.

Moreover, the massive transformations in the media sector, brought about by technological convergence, economic liberalization and globalization of manufacturing processes, have resulted in major changes to media ownership patterns throughout the world. Media ownership, once bounded by the geographical limitations of the nation-state, has become transnational. Transparency of media ownership structures and guarantees of pluralism are challenges for every government and institution. The need for global mapping of media ownership and control patterns has become a major motivator behind much comparative media research.[3]

All of these transformations are changing the global regulatory ecology for the communications sector. New forms of regulation are emerging, marked by a move away from traditional command-and-control regulation and toward more responsive regulatory systems.

2 For detailed comparative reports from sixty countries on "the global opportunities and risks that are created for media by the following developments: the switch-over from analog broadcasting to digital broadcasting; growth of new media platforms as sources of news; [and] convergence of traditional broadcasting with telecommunication," see The Open Society's "Mapping Digital Media Project."

3 As, for example, in Price 2002.

Self-regulation has, for instance, been suggested as a possible solution for many of the current problems on the Internet. Clearly, in order to analyze self-regulation on the Internet, the scope of study has to be transnational and comparative. Moreover, in order to examine, for instance, codes of conduct as effective responsive mechanisms to content concerns on the Internet, the units of analysis have to be the major transnational Internet content, service and network providers (e.g. Facebook, MSN, Yahoo, Twitter, Google). Cross-institutional and cross-instrument research is therefore a new and important field of comparative media law research.

In addition to these technological and institutional transitions, a growing demand for comparative data exists in transitional societies that are (re-)considering the balance between state regulatory prerogatives and the freedom of media outlets. Both the post-Cold War period and more recently the media revolution resulting from the "Arab Spring" (McMahon 2012) have not only opened previously inaccessible countries for a comparative media law perspective, but have also demonstrated that the shaping of media laws and administrative agencies are key determinants in the emergence of stable democracies. Much has been learned during these periods of transition about styles of preparing laws, needs of groups involved in improving the process and entities dedicated to establishing a media sphere that includes independent newspapers, television and radio stations (Price and Krug 2000; Krug and Price 2002). Some societies have faced the challenge of inventing a media law where none existed before. In other societies, where a government or regime has been discredited and where control of the press was characteristic of a regime's excesses, revision of the media law is often necessary. In a third group of societies, such as those in the post-Soviet transition, there are difficulties in providing technical assistance in implementing media laws and revising flaws in a first generation of legislative reforms. In all of these societies, problems exist because of a lack of reliable information about regulatory models, legal and societal changes within a given state, challenges of new technologies, and changes in the international scheme of trading and regulation with respect to the media. Often, groups participating in the process of media law improvement do not have an adequate sense of the Western or neighboring models available, and how they might be interpreted and adjusted for the local context.

The demand for comparative media law research is dispersed over time. It may be most intense while a statute is being drafted or debated, or a new technology is being introduced, but it is equally valuable during implementation, even though the requirement for discourse and alternatives may not be so evident. To be responsive, media law research must be able to react to these rhythms of demand, providing solutions at various stages of the drafting, adoption and implementation of media laws.

## Models and categories of comparative media law and policy

As mentioned earlier, comparisons are an integral part of most sciences. Many scholars would therefore argue that the very nature of their method is comparative and that thinking in comparative terms is inherent to their research. In truth, no phenomenon can be isolated and studied without comparing it to other phenomena. The question may therefore be posed whether comparative media law and policy research presents a different set of theoretical, methodological and epistemological challenges, or whether this kind of analysis must be treated just as another variant of the (comparative) problems already embedded in traditional law and/or media research.

One could take the view that conducting comparative research across countries is no different from conducting any other kind of media or legal research. Our view is that it is necessary to be aware of the many problems of conducting comparative research in a world of complex interdependencies. Without becoming paralyzed in the face of these complexities, it is important to go ahead, opting for compromise and trying to use existing tools for new insights. To advance our knowledge about comparative media law research it is necessary to consider some distinctive characteristics of comparative studies.

Not all comparative studies are alike. One can, for instance, distinguish two broad types of research in comparative media law research. Exponents of *micro-comparison* analyze the laws belonging to the same legal family, within a single jurisdiction. Researchers pledged to *macro-comparison*, on the other hand, investigate laws in different jurisdictions in order to gain insight into alien institutions and thought processes. For some legal scholars, concerned mainly with legal technicalities, micro-comparison holds the greater attraction, whereas macro-comparison is the realm of the political scientist or legal philosopher, who sees law as a social science and is interested in its role in government and the organization of the community.

Within comparative media law, both types of investigation are often employed (Verhulst, Goldberg and Prosser 1999). In analyzing regulatory responses to the changing media, micro-comparison takes priority when a range of regulatory challenges and problems, such as data protection, competition, content control and others, are examined within a specific nation and described by a country expert. Macro-comparison follows when the research project managers compare the selected jurisdictions and their detailed descriptions.[4]

Many similar distinctions can be made.[5] Another particularly useful distinction is between vertical and horizontal comparison (Ferrari 1990). Vertical comparison concerns social and legal contexts showing different levels of economic and technological development, such as Internet penetration or take-up of digital television. Horizontal comparison is concerned with contexts sharing a relatively similar level of economic and technological development, but largely differing in their development, their production organization, their political and legal regime and other relevant characteristics (Hitchens 2006).

## Paradigms of comparative media law and policy

Another way of considering comparative media law and policy research as a distinctive method is to look at the paradigm field in which it operates. At least four conflicting models and poles underpin most comparative media law projects, as follows.

### *Uniformity and diversity paradigm*

Because of globalization and the creation of free markets, it is predicted that media laws and policies will present a considerable measure of similarity and uniformity, at least with respect to communications infrastructure and economic regulation. Yet, owing to the endurance of social traditions or cultural preferences that are still quite different in many parts of the world,

4 For examples of macro research, see Dent 2004, Chesterman 1997 and Klik 1988. For an example that includes both macro and micro research, see Suominen (2003).

5 Kohn (1989) identifies, for instance, four kinds of comparative research on the basis of the different intent of the studies. Countries can be: (1) the object of the study—the interest of the researcher lies primarily in the countries studied; (2) the context of the study—the interest is mainly vested in testing the generality of research results concerning social phenomena in the countries compared; (3) the unit of analysis—where the interest is chiefly to investigate how social phenomena are systematically related to characteristics of the countries researched; and (4) transnational—namely, studies that treat nations as components of a larger international system.

there is and will be much less harmony between the rules dealing with content. Moreover, a diversity of media law within one country may also exist on an ethnic, religious or federalist basis, such as among the *Länder* of Germany.

Comparative media law considers the benefits and burdens of uniformity and plumbs the contexts demanding diversity, trying to establish a terminology that enables comparison. Comparative research has moved from justification for uniformity to studying the uniqueness and variety among homogeneity.[6]

### *Rhetoric and reality*

One interesting challenge for comparative research is to face the "grass is greener on the other side" syndrome, or in some cases "dark side of the moon" comparisons. Indeed, comparisons are often used by vested interests (e.g. incumbent operators) to prove, for reasons of political or rhetorical expediency, the effectiveness or harmfulness of a specific foreign policy. Comparative data, in particular, are sometimes utilized in a deliberately muddled way to advance a particular agenda. One key task of comparative media law research, as with all methodologies, is to put legal and policy practices within their appropriate contexts to create a better understanding of reality rather than ammunition for exchanges of heated rhetoric.

### *Metaphors and models*

During the process of comparative thinking about the global restructuring of the media and when conceptualizing regulatory responses, two specific techniques are often applied: the methods of model and metaphor (Price 2002). First, comparing the experience of others, proponents of one system or another invoke what they deem to be a "model" for imitation, such as looking at the BBC for public broadcasting, the "newspaper model" for regulation, or a hybrid of both for new media policy (Brevini 2010).

The second technique for conceptualization involves the use of metaphors to simplify the task of articulating the path of change, such as the metaphors of the "information superhighway," "cyberspace" or "killer applications." Metaphors and models are useful and common tools. They can help to guide researchers and policymakers through uncharted territory (Verhulst and Price 2000; Price 2000; Price 1997). But there are limitations. Metaphors can be poetic devices that wrap complex ideas in appealing words, used to persuade even when acceptance is not wholly warranted. Both metaphors and models can be short cuts that avoid more complex reasoning.[7]

### *Transfer and exclusion*

Comparative media law research provides the evidence for the use of models and metaphors in policy or law transfer debates. The basic thrust of current theories of policy and law transfer is the idea that law and policy diffusion is a process explained by imitation, copying and adaptation on the part of policymakers.[8] Comparative media law and policy plays a crucial role

6 See Holznagel 1999 and Eko 2001.
7 For a further analysis of the role of metaphors, see Gozzi, Jr. 1999.
8 For an overview of the policy transfer literature, see Dolowitz and Marsh 1996. The law transfer process has been described in Gardner 1980.

within this process of identifying "success policies" and best practices that can then be exported to other countries via a process of learning, interpretation and even translation. Lesson drawing, as a process of interpretation and translation, is a major goal of comparative media law. In some exceptional cases, comparative media law has also been used for "forced" policy and law transfer, by conditioning financial assistance or other incentives, or even to determine exclusion from membership to specific international authorities, such as the Council of Europe, on the adoption of certain media policies.[9]

## Functions of comparative media law

From the above, it may be obvious that comparative media law research serves multiple aims and functions. In general and at a more epistemological level, one could define comparative research as an *école de vérité*, a methodology that seeks to supply comparative solutions and a better international understanding. More concretely, at least four key uses for comparative media law research can be identified: the further study of historical and cultural components; commercial application; legislative assistance; and international law and harmonization.

### *Historical and cultural relativism*

We may view comparative media law from the standpoint of its value to the historical and cultural study of legal and policy decision-making in the field of communications (including the political economy of policymaking). Ideas regarding the place of law in society, the nature of the law itself and its relationship with new communications technologies become appreciably clearer when comparative law is joined to historical research. Indeed, to some extent, historical background may aid in forecasting the future of certain national systems and the applicability of existing law to new tendencies. A closely related consideration prompts many Western jurists, political scientists and sociologists to acquaint themselves with non-Western methods of reasoning. For example, comparative studies can reveal that sources and conceptions of free speech or fairness and its role vary widely (Carmi 2005). The notions of a rule of law and of rights of the individual—fundamental to Western civilization—are not wholly recognized by societies more faithful to the principle of conciliation and concerned primarily with harmony within the group. These differences may be used as a justification for authoritarian rule, but they also may reflect important variances in structuring the relationship of the individual and society.

### *Commercial uses*

Comparative media law may be used for essentially practical ends. Industry leaders, for instance, need to know what benefits they can expect, what risks they may run and generally how they should invest capital or run businesses abroad. This practical aspect has encouraged the growth of comparative law in the United States, where the essential aim of law school has been usually to turn out practitioners—and one need hardly mention the strong link in Germany between big industry and the various institutes of comparative law. Sometimes it is said that studies with such a focus should not be considered a part of comparative media law,

9 For a good discussion of policy transfer within the new EU accession states, see Harcourt 2003.

but practical considerations certainly have helped to finance and promote the development of comparative legal studies in general.[10]

### Aid to legislators

The remapping of communications structures because of all kinds of transitions (from planned economies to free markets, from analog to digital, from war to peace) requires an ongoing reform of legal systems. When considering new regulatory frameworks, policymakers and legislators quite often have a desire to identify foreign models that already have been tested, instead of framing a new, revolutionary system. Seeking foreign inspiration for a number of legal rules or institutions is a well-known phenomenon—sometimes so all-embracing that one speaks of "reception" or "transfer."[11] The study of comparative media law is therefore used by legislators to identify "transferable models" and has found a special place among scholars in those countries where such a reception or transfer has occurred (Syprelli 2003/4).

### Use in international law

Globalization of communications and the growth of the Internet have led to calls for more international and regional efforts to harmonize the regulatory framework of specific transactions. Those engaging in cross-border communications, for instance, do not know with certainty which national law will regulate their content, since the answer depends to a large extent on a generally undecided factor—namely, which national court will be called upon to decide the questions of competence. The sole lasting remedy appears to be the development of a more harmonized international system. The development of the TV without Frontiers Directive in 1989 (revised in the Audio-Visual Media Services Directive) was, for instance, a regional answer to a similar call from transnational satellite broadcasters. Harmonization can succeed only through the medium of comparative law. Regional authorities are highly dependent on comparative material in order to identify policy issues and monitor the implementation of existing multilateral agreements, or to highlight the need for action in certain areas.

## Methodological challenges behind comparative media law and policy

Despite growing demand and multiple benefits, comparative media law and policy studies are still at the pioneering stage, and are both difficult and risky.[12] It is therefore necessary to examine the limitations and potential pitfalls of such studies. Livingstone, reflecting on cross-national comparative media research, described comparative research as "exciting but difficult, creative but problematic . . . cross-national comparisons are both attacked as impossible and defended as necessary" (Livingstone 2003: 478).

10 For examples of comparative legal research with business applicability, see Gasser *et al.* 2004 and Lucchi 2005.

11 For a summary of the literature on policy transfer and its applicability, see, e.g., Marsh and Sharman 2009.

12 For some notable contributions comparing media laws, see Barendt 1993, Hoffman-Riem 1996, and Hallin and Mancini 2004.

Comparative research in general poses certain well-known problems, such as accessing comparable data (Stacey 1969) and comparing concepts and research parameters (Hantrais and Mangen 1996; Frank and Hanitzsch 2011). Additionally, when comparing different jurisdictions and legal systems, researchers may be subject to further pitfalls: (1) clashing linguistic and terminological perspectives; (2) cultural differences between legal systems; (3) potential arbitrariness in the selection of objects of study; (4) difficulties in achieving "comparability" in comparison; (5) the desire to see a common legal pattern in legal systems (the theory of a general pattern of development); (6) the tendency to impose one's own (native) legal conceptions and expectations on the systems being compared; and (7) dangers of exclusion/ignorance of extralegal rules (Zweigert and Kötz 1989).

As for comparative media law specifically, one might observe three additional sources of limitations, as we explored in Verhulst and Price (1998): (1) inadequate availability of statutory and secondary material for those engaged in comparative research; (2) the quick "expiration" of information as a result of the rapid and constant change of communications law (a process itself driven by rapid technological change); and (3) the possibility that information, even if available and correct, may not be easily summarized, compressed or reduced to elements that are comparable. These are questions of organization, terminology and presentation. Each of these potential difficulties is worth discussing briefly.

## *Limitations on availability of statutory and other regulatory sources*

Despite researchers' expertise and experience in the field, the absence of ready, comprehensive and up-to-date material remains a definite limitation on the capacity to undertake meaningful comparative media law and policy research. This shortcoming restricts the way in which advocates and legislators can use comparative research in their process of reform. But, even if the statutes and decisions are available, formal language and legal terminology within statutory or regulatory material are potentially misleading as the exclusive source of law.[13] Words alone do not convey the manner in which concepts are variously carried out and enforced. In some societies, a formal prohibition may be quite strict, but the practice may be quite lenient. A similar divergence may exist when interpreting constitutional principles, such as freedom of speech.

## *The speed of change of regulation and law within the communications sector*

A second potential difficulty has to do with the pace of change. Comparative research usually provides only a snapshot of regulatory formations when a motion picture is required. While this is a problem of research generally, and certainly of research that depicts the way in which the world is organized as of a certain date, it is particularly true in the area of telecommunications and broadcasting, where technological innovation often outstrips legal developments. Thus the need to keep up to date with fast-moving technological change often muddles the waters for would-be comparativists. In particular, convergence, a favorite doctrine of regulation analysts, suggests that existing categories for regulation are being confounded.[14]

13 A fairly extensive literature acknowledging the importance of language as a factor in comparative research and law exists. See e.g. Grossfeld 1990, ch. 13.

14 For two good discussions of the interaction between legal and technological change, see Kohl 1994 and Lessig 1999.

### Limitations based on selection, comparability and simplification

The comparability of regulatory regimes depends on a number of factors, some constant, many transient. Some commentators list the following determinative factors: the cultural, political and economic components of a society; the particular relationships that exist between the state and its citizens; and a society's value system and its particular conception of the individual (see, e.g., de Cruz 1993). Other general factors include the homogeneity of the society in question and its geographical situation, language and religion. It is indeed difficult to find countries that have achieved a similar stage of development in those areas.

Even more difficult than the problem of selection is the problem of simplification and definition: Almost all forms of comparison require the articulation of similarities so that resemblance and differences can be noted (Blumler, McLeod and Rosengren 1992). Therefore, a related problem to be addressed in any comparative study is one of context. In terms of media law and policy, for example, it is important to understand the reasons why a comparison is being made—reasons that may not have to do with the law itself, but with the objectives of law. Often the goal of a broadcast regulatory structure is to increase the diversity of voices, or to enhance the right of a citizen to receive or impart information. A restriction on foreign ownership may have an impact in a society rich in broadcast signals that is totally different from that in one in which such signals are few and competition is just beginning.

## Conclusion

The primary purpose of this introduction, as we stated at the outset, was to examine the benefits, challenges and current approaches in comparative media law and policy studies—the rationale that provided the impetus behind this handbook. The demand has been growing at a dramatic rate in recent years. In the coming years we can expect that some of the conceptual and theoretical vagueness that afflicts the field will gradually solidify.

Yet a major obstacle will remain: the difficulty of encouraging institutions and their researchers to break free of prevailing restraints, often a combination of the organizational and the ideological. Comparative research is particularly essential when existing institutions are in decline and the paradigms that supported them are in question. The architecture of information and its relationship to society is very much in play. The consensus on the public functions of the media and the powers to be wielded by the state—all of these are in flux. This is a period of long transitions and extensive shifts. We do not know, fully, how to crawl within diverse social and political systems, and we seek to understand the implications of approaches in one society for the benefit of another. Globalization produces its discontents and it is a task of comparative research to extricate ourselves.

## References

Barendt, E. (1993) *Broadcasting Law: A Comparative Study*, Oxford: Oxford University Press.

Blumler, J. C., McLeod, J. M. and Rosengren, K. E. (eds.) (1992) *Comparatively Speaking: Communication and Culture Across Space and Time*, London: Sage Annual Reviews of Communication Research, vol. 19.

Brevini, R. (2010) 'Towards PSB 2.0? Applying the PSB ethos to online media in Europe: A comparative study of PSBs' Internet policies in Spain, Italy and Britain,' *European Journal of Communication*, 25(4): 348–365.

Carmi, G. E. (2005) 'Comparative notions of fairness: comparative perspectives on the fairness doctrine with special emphasis on Israel and the United States,' *Virginia Sports & Entertainment Law Journal*, 4: 275–308.

Carter, B. (2011) 'Court overturns F.C.C. cross-ownership rule,' *New York Times*, 7 July.
Chesterman, M. (1997) 'OJ and the dingo: How media publicity relating to criminal cases tried by jury is dealt with in Australia and America,' *The American Journal of Comparative Law*, 45(1): 109–147.
Curran, J. and Park M. J. (2000) *De-Westernizing Media Studies*, London: Routledge.
de Cruz, P. (1993) *A Modern Approach to Comparative Law*, Oxford: Oxford University Press.
Dent, C. (2004) 'Defamation law's chilling effect: A comparative content analysis of Australian and US newspapers,' *Media & Arts Law Review*, 9(2): 89–112.
Dolowitz, D. and Marsh, D. (1996) 'Who learns from whom: A review of the policy transfer literature,' *Policy Studies*, 44: 343–357.
Eko, L. (2001) 'Many spiders, one World Wide Web: Towards a typology of Internet regulation,' *Communication Law and Policy*, 6(3): 445–484.
Esser, F. and Hanitzsch, T. (eds.) (2011) *Handbook of Comparative Communication Research*, London/New York: Routledge.
Ferrari, V. (1990) 'Socio-legal concepts and their comparison,' in E. Oyen (ed.) *Comparative Methodology: Theory and Practice in International Social Research*, London: Sage.
Gardner, J. A. (1980) *Legal Imperialism: American Lawyers and Foreign Aid in Latin America*, Madison, WI: University of Wisconsin Press.
Gasser, U., Bambauer, D., Harlow, J., Hoffmann, C., Hwang, R. and Krog, G. (2004) 'iTunes: How copyright, contract, and technology shape the business of digital media—A case study,' *Berkman Center for Internet & Society*, Harvard Law School.
Giddens, A. (1999) 'The Reith Lecture Series: New world without an end,' *The Observer*, 11 April.
Gozzi Jr., R. (1999) *The Power of Metaphor in the Age of Electronic Media*, Cresskill, NJ: Hampton Press.
Grossfeld, B. (1990) *The Strength and Weakness Of Comparative Law*, New York: Oxford University Press.
Hallin, D. C. and Mancini, P. (2004) *Comparing Media Systems: Three Models of Media and Politics*, Cambridge: Cambridge University Press.
Hantrais, L. and Mangen, S. (1996) *Cross-National Research Methods in the Social Sciences*, London: Pinter.
Harcourt, A. (2003) 'The regulation of media markets in selected EU accession states in Central and Eastern Europe,' *European Law Journal*, 9(3): 316–340.
Hitchens, L. (2006) *Broadcasting Pluralism and Diversity: A Comparative Study of Policy and Regulation*, Oxford: Hart Publishing.
Hoffmann-Riem, W. (1996) *Regulating Media: The Licensing and Supervision of Broadcasting in Six Countries*, New York: The Guilford Press.
Holznagel, B. (1998–99) 'New challenges: Convergence of markets, divergence of the laws? Questions regarding the future communications regulation,' *International Journal of Communications Law and Policy*. Online. Available HTTP: http://ijclp.net/old_website/2_1999/ijclp_webdoc_5_2_1999.html (accessed 30 May 2012).
Klik, P. (1998) 'Mass media and offers to the public: An economic analysis of Dutch civil law and American common law,' *American Journal of Comparative Law*, 36(2): 235–278.
Kohl, U. (1994) 'Legal reasoning and legal change in the age of the Internet: Why the ground rules are still valid,' *International Journal of Law and Information Technology*, 7(2): 123–151.
Kohn, M. (1989) *Cross-National Research in Sociology*, Newbury Park, CA: Sage.
Krug, P. and Price, M. E. (2002) 'A module for media intervention: Content regulation in post-conflict zones,' Cardozo Law School, Public Law Research Paper No. 58.
Laughlin, A. (2011) 'Jeremy Hunt asks Ofcom to review UK cross-media ownership rules,' *DigitalSpy*, 12 September. Online. Available HTTP: http://www.digitalspy.com/media/news/a339877/jeremy-hunt-asks-ofcom-to-review-uk-cross-media-ownership-rules.html (accessed 20 May 2012).
Lessig, L. (1999) *Code and Other Laws of Cyberspace*, New York: Basic Books.
Livingstone, S. (2003) 'On the challenges of cross-national comparative media research,' *European Journal of Communication*, 18(4): 477–500.
Lucchi, N. (2005) 'Intellectual property rights in digital media: A comparative analysis of legal protection, technological measures and new business models under E.U. and US law,' *Berkeley Electronic Press*. Online. Available HTTP: http://law.bepress.com/cgi/viewcontent.cgi?article=3040&context=expresso (accessed 30 May 2012).
Marsh, D. and Sharman, J. C. (2009) 'Policy diffusion and policy transfer,' *Policy Studies*, 30(3): 269–288.

McMahon, R. J. (2012) 'The Arab media's shaky awakening,' Council on Foreign Relation's *Foreign Service Journal*. Online. Available HTTP: http://www.afsa.org/FSJ/0512/index.html#/19/zoomed (accessed 30 May 2012).

Price, M. E. (1997) 'Market for loyalties and the uses of comparative media law," *Cardozo Journal of International and Comparative Law*, 5: 445–459.

—— (2000) 'Privatization and self-regulation as tropes of global media restructuring,' Cardozo Law School, Public Law Working Paper No. 010, New York.

—— (2002) *Media and Sovereignty: The Global Information Revolution and Its Challenge to State Power*, Cambridge, MA: MIT Press.

Price, M. E. and Krug, P. (2002) *The Enabling Environment for Free and Independent Media: Contribution to Transparent and Accountable Governance*, Washington, DC: USAID.

Spyrelli, C. (2003–04) 'Regulating the regulators? An assessment of institutional structures and procedural rules of national regulatory authorities,' *International Journal of Communications Law and Policy*, 8. Online. Available HTTP: http://ijclp.net/old_website/8_2004/pdf/spyrelli-paper-ijclp-page-neu.pdf (accessed 30 May 2012).

Stacey, M. (1969) *Comparability in Social Research*, London: Heinemann.

Suchman, M. C. (2003) 'The contract as social artifact,' *Law & Society Review*, 37(1): 91–142.

Suominen, K. (2003) 'Access to information in Latin America and the Caribbean,' *Comparative Media Law Journal*, 2: 29–68.

Verhulst, S. G. and Price, M. E. (1998) 'A methodological perspective on the use of comparative media law,' in M. E. Price and S. G. Verhulst (eds.) *Broadcasting Reform in India: Media Law from a Global Perspective*, Oxford: Oxford University Press.

—— and —— (2000) 'In search of the self: Charting the course of self-regulation on the Internet in a global environment,' Cardozo Law School, Public Law Working Paper No. 015, New York.

——, Goldberg, D. and Prosser, T. (1999) *Regulating the Changing Media: A Comparative Study*, Oxford: Clarendon Press.

Zweigert, K. and Kötz, H. (1989) *An Introduction to Comparative Law*, Oxford: Oxford University Press.

# Part I

# Media policy and institutional design

# 1

# Tracing media policy decisions

## Of stakeholders, networks and advocacy coalitions

*Hilde van den Bulck*

## Introduction: the complexity of media policy processes

In recent decades, the area of media policy has become increasingly complex as a result of a number of trends and processes. First, digitization and the ensuing convergence has opened up traditional media markets to new players, most notably those from the once-distinct sector of telecommunications and their spin-offs. Convergence has also led to new configurations between old and new players. Together, this has resulted in new stakeholders to be identified and analyzed in their attempts to influence media policy (d'Haenens and Brink 2001). Second, the growing economic importance of media and information and communication technologies (ICT) as an industry has led to the emergence of new policy actors having a stake, and therefore interfering, in media policy decisions (Hendriks 1995; Neff 2005). This has been encouraged, politically, by what Freedman (2005: 6) calls "the hegemony of market-led approaches to the provision of goods and services."

Third, the political landscape has evolved considerably. Media policy was never restricted to one political locus of decision-making. Yet recent decades have witnessed a move towards increased multilevel governance (Hamelink and Nordenstreng 2007; Collins 2008). Broadly defined, this refers to policymaking responsibilities being shared by various policy actors at the regional, national and inter- or supranational levels (Hooghe and Marks 2001). In Europe, this was pushed by the growing interest and involvement of the European Union (EU) in media and ICT (Donders and Pauwels 2008). This resulted in a growing homogenization of national media laws and policies through EU directives. What is more, the EU, and particularly the European Commission, has proven to be susceptive to lobby work from other media policy stakeholders, pushing governments to include an ever-wider range of stakeholders into the policymaking process. At a global level, discussions within the World Trade Organization (WTO) about the status and position of media in the context of the General Agreement on Trade in Services (GATS) and the Agreement on Trade-Related Aspects of Intellectual Property Rights (TRIPS) aim to impact on media and ICT policies worldwide (Puppis 2008; Freedman 2008). Many authors (e.g. Moe 2011; Brevini 2010) maintain that, despite these increased European and global interferences and homogenization tendencies, media policies are still mainly a national affair. Yet there is no denying that these trends have widened and complicated the scale and scope of media policy formation, as old and new stakeholders work to influence policies at different levels.

Finally, the introduction of Web 2.0 and social media and thus of audiences not just as consumers but as active producers—the so-called "prosumers"—has resulted in hard-to-pinpoint, non-traditional, non-institutional and non-industrial stakeholders with, at times, substantial power to mobilize and lobby.

As a result, analyzing media policy has become much more complex. It is increasingly difficult to identify all relevant stakeholders; "the traditional 'subsystem' of dedicated civil servants, legislators and select industry players" (Freedman 2005: 6) has expanded to include a much wider range of stakeholders. Governments have come to recognize this trend and show an increasing reliance on multi-stakeholder negotiations (cf. Donders 2011). Many other partners, not yet openly recognized, also push the boundaries for attention and impact. What is more, the policy process has become a much more complicated web to disentangle, and this has made it harder for scholars to study and understand it.

This complexity of the media policy process is in sharp contrast to the attention that is paid to its conceptual and methodological dimensions by scholars working on media and ICT policy. With a few notable exceptions (e.g. Chin 2011; Freedman 2008; Parker and Paranta 2008; Puppis and Just 2012), most books, chapters and articles dealing with shifting media policies limit themselves to a mere mention of key methodological tools (e.g. interviews or document analysis) and rarely go into the conceptual clarifications necessary to understand the key components of a policy process (e.g. demarcation of stakeholders, views on change as brutal paradigm shift or incremental). However, inspiration can be found in study areas within political sciences and sociology that focus more explicitly on a conceptual understanding of the key components of policy processes.

This chapter aims for a better understanding of the growing complexity of the media policy process by providing a discussion of concepts that are central to the analysis of such processes. It illustrates these conceptual insights by analyzing actual policies regarding Flemish public service broadcasting and other cases of media policy as they evolve towards multi-layered, multi-stakeholder processes. The chapter starts with a discussion of stakeholder analysis as a way in which to understand different actors, their arguments and logic, their visibility and power, all impinging on a policy decision. Yet while stakeholder analysis is an excellent tool to identify policy actors and their views, it cannot tell us much about their impact on the actual process through which certain policies came about. This chapter also discusses different conceptual tools to understand exactly how certain policies are achieved. Throughout, conceptual clarification is combined with a discussion of key methodological tools and illustrated with contemporary cases of media policy processes. As such, this chapter aims to contribute not only to a better understanding of the ever-more-complex and multilayered policy process, but also to good practices in media policy process analysis.

## Identifying and analyzing the spiders in the media policy web

Media policy analysis seeks to "examine the ways in which policies in the field of communication are generated and implemented, as well as their repercussions or implications for the field of communication as a whole" (Hansen *et al.* 1998: 67). Most critical academic media policy research is conducted *ex post*, tracing how certain policy outcomes came about, why certain policy outcomes became dominant, what parties were involved in the decision-making process and how power was distributed amongst them (Freedman 2008; Fischer 2003). However, as governments move to multi-stakeholder decision-making in media policy, in recent years a growing amount of *ex ante* or forward-looking policy-oriented research has been set up to contribute to future media policies. Reference can be made to the European Commission's consultations of stakeholders regarding Green Papers on media and ICT-related issues,[1] the BBC Trust public consultations regarding the 2010 BBC Strategy Review,[2] or the public hearing contracted by the Norwegian Ministry of Culture, inviting comments from stakeholders regarding the proposed manifesto of NRK, the Norwegian public service broadcasting institution (Øvrebo and Moe 2009). Both *ex ante* and *ex post* stakeholder research implicitly or explicitly considers a policy decision as the result of a process characterized by the formulation of different views and interests, expressed by actors or stakeholders who adhere to a particular logic, engage in debate and work towards a policy decision in relevant fora (Hutchinson 1999; Blakie and Soussan 2001). As such, media policy analysis starts with stakeholder analysis.

## *Stakeholders in the policy arena*

While stakeholder analysis is applied but rarely identified as such in media and communication policy studies, it has a considerable tradition in other fields of enquiry, including business management (e.g. Mitchell *et al.* 1997), health care (e.g. Brugha and Varvasovsky 2000), and development and environmental studies (e.g. Prell *et al.* 2009). Even though "each [policy] sector poses its own problems, sets its own constraints, and generates its own brand of conflicts" (Freeman 1985: 469), and although institutions and loci of power to influence policy outcomes differ across sectors (Howlett 2004), these studies provide conceptual tools applicable to, and useful in, the field of media policy.

Trying to understand the media policy process by means of stakeholder analysis involves a number of analytical steps. It starts from a broad understanding of the main structures and processes of decision-making in a specific country, region, or media and ICT subfield, as well as a study of relevant conceptual–theoretical insights and positions regarding the policy issue under study. The next step involves the identification of all relevant stakeholders (i.e. individuals, groups, organizations and institutions with a vested interest in a particular policy or its outcome). These can include politicians, regulatory institutions, media organizations, citizens and other representatives of civil society, as well as providers of communications services and the advertising industry. Identifying stakeholders is usually a dynamic, iterative, process because unexpected parties may surface during data collection and analysis. Interestingly, the category of stakeholders does not entirely overlap with that of policy actors. Certain stakeholders with a distinct interest in a certain outcome may not actually take part in the policy process (with large sections of media audiences as a typical example), while policy actors with no explicit stake (e.g. academics and civil servants) can considerably influence the outcome of the process.

The next and crucial step is concerned with the identification of actors and stakeholders: who they are; who they represent or belong to; their stake or visibility; and their impact or power. They can further be characterized on the basis of their attitude towards the policy issue and of the main logic they adhere to. The latter relates to the perception of the situation, and the structure of goals and means in a certain situation (Van den Bulck 2008). Within the field of media policy, arguments are formulated mainly within a technological, economic,

1 For example, http://ec.europa.eu/internal_market/consultations/2011/audiovisual_en.htm
2 For example, https://consultations.external.bbc.co.uk/departments/bbc/bbc-strategy-review/consultation/consult_view

political and/or cultural logic. Two stakeholders can be in favor of a certain policy outcome (e.g. no product placement in public service broadcasting content) but can argue this on the basis of a different logic (e.g. the economic logic of profit maximization in the case of commercial competitors and a cultural logic of protecting program quality in the case of certain groups in civil society). A shared logic does not necessarily result in the same policy preference. This approach to stakeholder analysis fits in with a recent trend in media policy studies advocating a focus on the role of ideas. Incorporating such an "ideational" view can overcome a too-strong focus on what stakeholders want by also looking at "their worldviews, values and cognitive frames or intellectual paradigms—which may themselves shape actors' interests" (Parker and Parenta 2008: 4).

A final step involves the mapping of all relevant fora in which each stakeholder can be seen to present and debate their arguments (e.g. a minister's cabinet, parliamentary committees, political or protest rallies). While in many sectors the media are an important forum, in the case of media policy analysis this forum can be seen to overlap—or at least to have considerable ties—with a number of stakeholders (Freedman 2008).

Data collection in stakeholder analysis typically is based on two complementary methodological tools involving written and oral sources: document analysis (cf. Altheide 1996; Van den Bulck 2002) and elite in-depth interviews (Aberbach and Rockman 2002; Bogner *et al.* 2009; Dunn 2004; Seldon and Pappworth 1983; Van Gorp 2011). Primary and secondary sources[3] in media policy document analysis typically include published and internal policy documents and White and Green Papers, annual reports and other documents of key informants (government, key media institutions, advisory committees, etc.), and communications from stakeholders on relevant fora. Such document analysis is best complemented by in-depth interviews with privileged witnesses who have been part of, or have special insight into, the policymaking process and who can help in the reconstruction of meaning, beliefs or patterns of action.

## Case: Multi-stakeholder policymaking for Flemish public service broadcasting

To illustrate the usefulness of stakeholder analysis in untangling the increasingly complex web of actors involved in media policy processes, an analysis is made of the Flemish government's policy with regards to Public Service Broadcasting (PSB), reflective of trends elsewhere in Europe. As a public institution, public service broadcasting across Europe was traditionally regulated and evaluated by the government, which set the regulatory framework that stipulated the rules of the game, including the scope of the remit, the financial constraints, internal and external hierarchies and control, and criteria with which to evaluate the institution's legitimation. In terms of accountability, PSB answered only to government in some way or another. This close relationship to the state was often ensured through a considerable politicization of the institution, for instance through politically appointed board of governance members, journalists and other key figures (Bardoel and Lowe 2007; Van den Bulck 2007). This changed over the course of the late 1980s and 1990s following the break-up of public service monopolies and shifting views on accountability, influenced by growing

3 Primary sources include original documents (e.g. a policy paper), contemporary records (e.g. a newspaper article at the time) and records in close proximity to an issue or event (e.g. the diary of a key stakeholder). Secondary sources are based on primary sources (Startt and Sloan 1989: 114; see also Altheide 1996; Bryman 2001; Deacon *et al.* 2007; Van den Bulck 2002).

interference of a common European policy framework and the "new public management" doctrine (Hood 1991). This led to new forms of governance, seen in the contractualization of relations with political principals, and the externalization of policy and watchdog roles from government to independent agencies (Pollitt and Bouckaert 2004).

In the case of Flemish PSB—today called VRT—the loss of its monopoly in 1989 resulted in a near-terminal crisis that was resolved by a considerable make-over. This included, amongst other things, the introduction of a management contract, renewable every five years, that stipulated the organization's financial framework and content goals, and introduced benchmarks based on viewing (and later on) appreciation figures (Van den Bulck 2007). Focusing on negotiations in the run-up to the third (2007–11) and fourth (2012–16) management contract stakeholder analysis enables us to understand the policy outcome as the result of the involvement of a growing range of policy actors.

### *Reconstructing negotiations towards the VRT 2007–11 management contract*

When formal negotiations towards the 2007-11 management contract between the public service broadcasting institution VRT and the Flemish government started in 2005, the existing contract had helped VRT to secure a strong position in the media landscape. This led to both national and international praise for VRT as a prime example of successful public service broadcasting reorientation. However, the cultural and commercial sector criticized VRT, stating that it had regained its success at the expense of some of its core objectives, such as quality and universalism, and had become indistinguishable from its commercial competitors, creating a market imbalance (Donders 2011). Commercial competitors further believed that this imbalance would increase if VRT were given free rein in the field of digitization and new media applications. It is against this backdrop that negotiations started. Administrative procedure (Verhoest and Legrain 2005) stipulates that a management contract is negotiated between the government (i.e. then Media Minister Bourgeois) and an organization (VRT).[4] However, a comparison of the original views and ideas of these two key actors and the eventual contract shows a considerable shift, suggesting the involvement of other actors in the policy process. A stakeholder analysis was conducted (see Van den Bulck 2008) to understand the trajectory and outcome of this particular policy decision.

Research started by building a theoretical framework, identifying viewpoints regarding the role of PSB in new digital media, as well as potential arguments and logics (for relevant literature, see Van den Bulck 2008).[5] Next, the research period was determined. The end of

4 The official scenario (cf. Verhoest and Legrain 2005: 27ff) stipulates preparatory activities and talks in which—on the basis of an evaluation of the current contract—both partners draw up a new deal. VRT is invited to draw up a five-year plan and budget, while cabinet workers prepare an advice to the minister (Uyttendaele and Braeckevelt 2007). Following negotiations, the propositions are being discussed and debated on the wider political forum, where it is finalized and voted (Verhoest and Legrain 2005).

5 This resulted in a number of normative-ideological positions regarding the position of PSB in digitization: everything is legitimate (L1); attrition model/arrested development (L2a); attrition model/harmless role (L2b); attrition model/superfluous (L2c); and obsolete model (L3). Possible arguments were clustered around four types: technological determinism (TD); technological nationalism (TN); technological democracy (TDc); and technological relativism (TR). Potential logics were originally expected to be either of an economic, cultural or political nature, and, after a first round of analyses, were expanded to include an audience logic.

the relevant period was quite straightforwardly identified as the signing of the management contract (July 2006)—the policy outcome. The start was less easily pinpointed, because media policy is an ongoing process. It was decided to start with the publication of the original policy statement by the Flemish media minister, one of the key informants, released at the start of his mandate in 2004 and including his original viewpoints on PSB and digitization.

The crucial next step was the identification of all relevant stakeholders. A first set of stakeholders was identified by the media minister himself, who initiated a public survey—a first in Flemish media policy—inviting the general public to answer three open-ended questions regarding the relevance and goals of public service broadcasting. The minister also asked a number of civil society institutions to express their views. Other stakeholders were identified based on prior knowledge of Flemish media structures, processes and policymaking, and on preliminary expert interviews. Subsequently, all relevant published and internal documents from stakeholders and documents, transcripts, and media coverage of discussions in relevant fora were collected. Documents were checked for authenticity and for references to further relevant sources and actors. In-depth interviews with privileged witnesses were conducted. Both resulted in the identification of additional stakeholders. It also became clear that commercial competitors could not be considered as one stakeholder, but as a series of actors with different stakes, views and arguments. Documents and transcripts were analyzed, looking for viewpoints and logic, which were brought together in a matrix (cf. Table 1.1).

Comparing and contrasting views of all identified stakeholders with the original views of the key informants—each proposing the continuation of a strong VRT, including in the area of new media—and to the eventual policy decision indicated that policy ideas had moved in the direction of views expressed by the commercial competitors and by the cultural sector. This is reflected in the stipulation in the eventual contract that VRT was allowed to start one

*Table 1.1* Management-contract stakeholders and their logic, view on technology, view on PSB and relevant forum

| *Actor* | *Forum* | *Logic* | *View on technology* | *View on PSB* |
|---|---|---|---|---|
| Media minister | cabinet, gvmt, media | cultural logic<br>audience logic<br>economic logic | TD/TN/TDc | L2a&b/ L1 |
| VRT CEO | cabinet, media, audience | cultural logic<br>audience logic<br>economic logic | TD/TDc/TN | L1 |
| PUBLIC | referendum, media | cultural logic | | L1 |
| Civil Society Culture | referendum, media | cultural logic | TD | L1/L2a |
| POF* | cabinet, media | economic logic | TD | L2b/L3 |
| VMMa** | cabinet, media "politicians" | economic logic | TR | L1/L2b |
| SBS*** | cabinet, media | economic logic | TD | L2b/L3 |
| Media Council | cabinet | cultural logic<br>audience logic | TD/TDe | L2b/L3 |

* (Lobby) Organization representing commercial television in Flanders
** Flemish media conglomerate (AV and print media)
*** Flemish branch of German/Swedish company ProSiebenSat.1 (commercial television)

digital channel— rather than the requested eight—of a cultural nature, excluding initiatives in the field of sports or children's programming. While this seems to indicate a strong impact of the cultural sector favoring more attention to the arts, it also echoes the idea of commercial competitors that digitization should not lead to market disruption by allowing public service broadcasting to run digital television channels that could compete with commercial initiatives.

### *A multi-stakeholder approach towards the VRT 2012–16 management contract*

While negotiations towards the 2007–11 management agreement suggest considerable informal involvement of a range of stakeholders based on ad hoc initiatives of the media minister and unsolicited lobby work, by the time of negotiations for the 2012–16 contract much of this involvement had been formalized.

This formalization was influenced by the growing Europeanization of media policy. Indeed, following complaints in 2004 lodged by Flemish commercial media companies with the European Commission against various aspects of VRT's public funding, the EU started procedures against the Flemish government, involving a number of consultation rounds (2004-08) and focusing, among other issues, on a vague definition of the remit and a lack of formal control mechanisms. As a result, the Flemish Media Bill of 2008 stipulates that, in the run-up to each new management contract of VRT, a public survey "about the extent of the public service remit and the operationalization hereof" (Art. 20. § 1) and a stakeholder inquest regarding the future role and position of public service broadcasting are to be executed (Van den Bulck 2011). This is to be done by the Flemish Media Council, a policy advice committee set up in 2007 and composed of a number of independent experts and the representatives of all main stakeholders in the field of media including VRT, private television stations, private radio stations, daily and weekly press, professional journalists, electronic communication networks (providers), independent members of the audiovisual production sector, copyright organizations and media users. As such, EU interference in the field of media can be seen to have actively stimulated the recognition of a wide range of stakeholders to be included in the policymaking process.

One result of the formalization of stakeholder involvement was the set-up of the first systematic academic *ex ante* stakeholder inquest in the history of Flemish media policy (Donders *et al.* 2010). The study started from a theoretical contextualization, identifying a continuum of five theoretical positions on the future role of PSB and fourteen indicators or aspects stakeholders could position themselves against. The former included the position of "no PSB," the PSB Light model, on evidence-based model, the public media institution, and a digital commons model (Donders *et al.* 2010: 11-14). The latter included six central indicators—core (with eight subindicators), cross-media, cost, clarity, control and command, and checks and balances (Donders *et al.* 2010: 14-18). Next, all relevant stakeholders were identified. Following the government and the Council's stress on a multi-stakeholder approach, a wide range of sectors was included, including those from the broadcasting industries, the distribution sector, journalists and the print media, the cultural arena, regulators, government and civil society. International and European players were originally included, but were later dropped for reasons of feasibility. One of the main difficulties in stakeholder identification was the fact that, increasingly, individual actors (e.g. cable distributors) are active in several sectors (e.g. both distribution and broadcasting), while one sector can incorporate a considerable diversity of individual stakeholders (e.g. civil society) (Donders *et al.* 2010). Because of the forward-looking nature of this study, methodologically it was based on individual and round table expert interviews rather than documents, which often provide a backward-looking perspective. The interviews were guided by the indicators identified in the theoretical framework. Analysis of these data resulted in a number of policy solution clusters, set out in their relative strength on an ideological-normative axe (see Figure 1.1) and positioned in relationship to the five-point continuum (see Figure 1.2) (Donders *et al.* 2010; for a

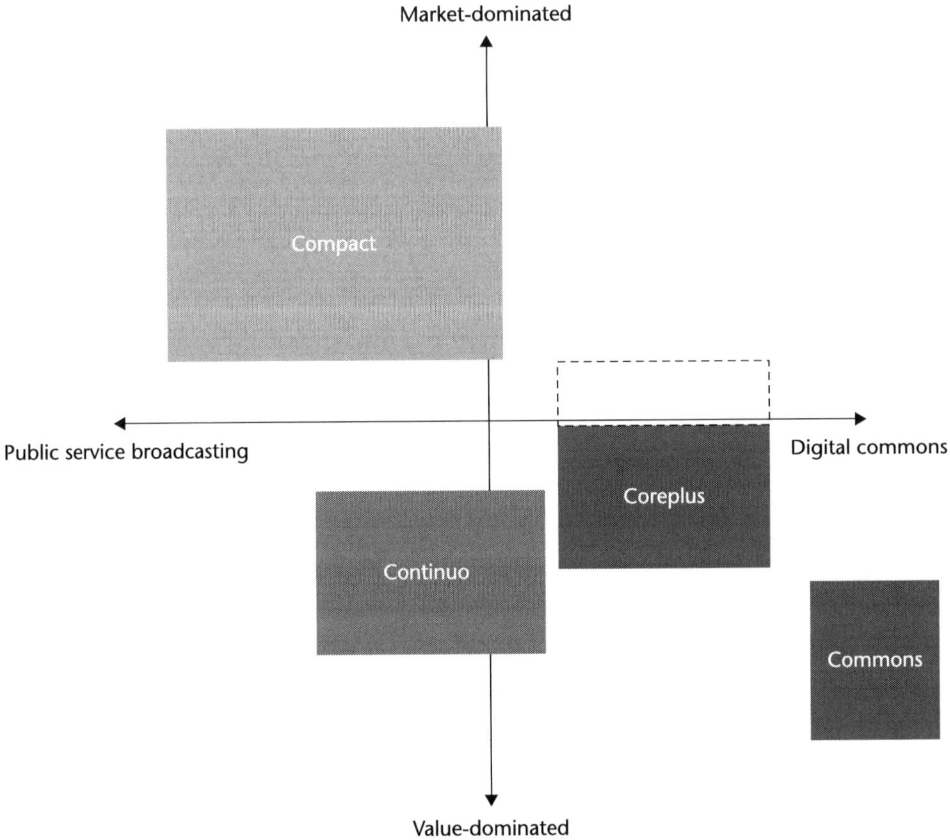


*Figure 1.1* Stakeholders' position on market-dominated/value-dominated and PSB/digital commons axes (Donders *et al.* 2010: 122)

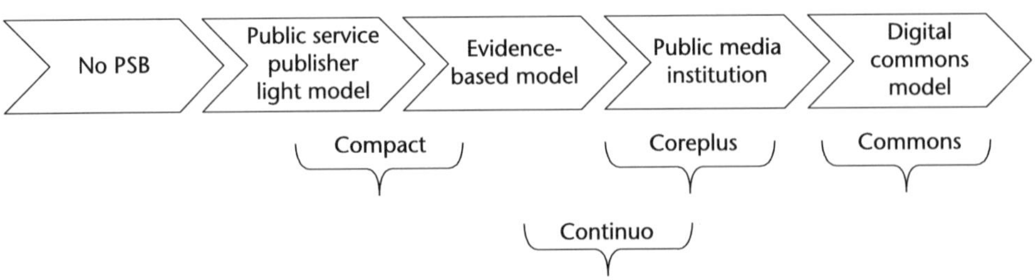


*Figure 1.2* Stakeholder positioning on continuum (Donders *et al.* 2010: 122)

discussion of the results, see Donders 2011). While, at the time of writing, the impact of this stakeholder analysis on the eventual contract is unclear, it shows a clear move by the Flemish government towards the formal recognition of a range of interested parties.

## The limits of stakeholder analysis

### *Conceptual blind spots*

Although stakeholder analysis is essential to understanding how particular media policies take shape, it has a number of shortcomings, resulting in blind spots in policy process mapping. First, it tends to be inspired by an "institutional" view of the media policy process, focusing on formal and visible points of decision-making and on institutional arrangements (Parker and Parenta 2008). This may result in a failure to identify key non-institutional and informal policymaking fora, in which stakeholders lobby outside "official" policy channels (Freedman 2008; Kingdon 1995). In the above mentioned analysis of the 2006 contract negotiations (Van den Bulck 2008), commercial competitors' lobby work outside formal meeting points (media council and cabinet) was detected, but could not be sufficiently mapped on the basis of documents and interviews with key informants. Second, this may lead to an inability to detect all relevant actors and stakeholders, including civil servants and small or relatively invisible informal actors (e.g. certain pressure groups) in the policymaking process. Researchers thus miss out on interesting informants who can help to explain certain steps in the process. There is a need for a more complex view of all those involved in the policy process, their positions and interrelations. Third, because most stakeholder analyses focus on a specific issue, they quickly become "outdated" as actors and their views, arguments and logics are likely to shift from one case to the next. This, according to Weible (2007: 97), makes it difficult to get a long-term, systematic stakeholder map.

Finally, there is a need for a better conceptual understanding of the dynamics of the policy process as a means to identify who gets something on the policy agenda, how different stakeholders relate to one another and to the central policymaker (e.g. media minister), and how the decision-making process works formally and informally. There is also a need for "a wider subsystem scope, recognizing that stakeholders typically are not concerned with just one policy venue or alternative but with the outcomes of an entire policy subsystem over long periods of time" (Weible 2007). These new understandings have methodological implications.

### *Methodological shortcomings*

Indeed, the conceptual problems are complemented by shortcomings inherent in the methodological tools. With regard to document analysis, first, the adequacy and/or completeness of the collected materials can prove problematic. For instance, an overly institutional view of stakeholders and policy can blind researchers to bottom-up and other alternative forces (e.g. Facebook protest groups) and crucial written or other sources that may provide evidence of these ideas and efforts (cf. Murphy 1980). Second, documents can reveal only part of the evolution of the policy process as they cannot always account for changes in positions of stakeholders. For instance, in the analysis of the 2006 management contract negotiations, the considerable shift in views from the media minister's original policy statements to his subsequent annual policy papers could not be accounted for on the basis of the available documents. Neither can document analysis relate the content of a document directly to the actual policy outcome, because documents cannot account for intervening variables such as the relative impact of different stakeholders on the policy outcome. In the same case study, the media minister's shifting views seem to indicate a recognition of the claims of stakeholders other than VRT. Yet available documents could not reveal which stakeholders were key in this: was it commercial media eager to move into digital markets and lobbying to avoid public service competition? Or was it the cultural sector pushing for additional attention to the arts? In other words, documents are static and usually reflect only one stakeholder's views, while the policy process is dynamic and complex, with a variety of stakeholders and views struggling over a period of time to influence the policy outcome.

The shortcomings of document analysis are partly overcome by complementing this method with expert interviews. In the first study of the negotiations towards the 2007–11 contract, interviews confirmed the impact of the commercial competitors rather than the cultural sector on the eventual decision. Expert interviews, however, pose their own problems, which can hamper an understanding of the dynamics and causality of the policy process (Bogner *et al.* 2009; Van Audenhove 2010; Van den Bulck 2002). Interviewees may exaggerate or downplay their own role. In the above case study of the 2006 policy process, for example, in a two-hour in-depth interview with two civil servants (Uyttendaele and Braekeveld 2007) the intervieweers were eager to show their professionalism and therefore continuously downplayed the role of informal relationships or lobby work from non-institutional stakeholders, in favor of a picture of the policy process close to the official guidelines. Interviewees' answers may also be inspired by grudges or other personal feelings that taint their memories or lead them to adjust their accounts. An in-depth interview with VRT's CEO (sacked six months after signing the management contract) was tainted by his desire for vindication and to clear his name. In other words, interviewees' stakes in and experiences with the policy process affect the information they provide. What is more, informants often do not know "the whole story," because they are locked up in their own particular part of that story or are stakeholders who were on the sidelines of the process (possibly without realizing it themselves). Conceptual and methodological shortcomings indicate a need for models and tools that can help us to understand the complexities of the policy process.

## From actor to process: Policy communities, advocacy coalitions and networks

To fully grasp the complexity of media policymaking, it is necessary to extend the above-explained focus on the policy actors with a focus on the policy process: *how* do the policy decisions come about? Laswell (1956) saw the policy process as consisting of four stages: agenda setting; formulation; implementation; and evaluation. This so-called "stages" heuristic framework, however, has been criticized for its unrealistic assumption of a linear process of clearly demarcated stages and its lack of understanding of causal relationships. John (2003) contends that, regardless of a pluralist consensus, a critical conflict, or a mixed position, the policy process must be considered as complex, involving a multitude of sources of causation and feedback, a wide variety of actors and institutions, and a complex web of relations between them.

### *Policy communities and advocacy coalitions*

A good point of departure is Paul Pross's (1986) notion of "policy communities," which embraces all of the actors with an interest in a broad policy area such as media or a subarea such as public service broadcasting. This concept can help to account for how and where actors or stakeholders attempt to exert influence. Pross makes an analytical distinction between actors located in the "sub-government" and actors that are part of the "attentive public." The first consists of key governmental institutions that develop and implement public policy. Other stakeholders, interest and lobby groups can be expected to try and exert a strong influence on these bodies. The "attentive public" refers to all other actors interested in this policy area, "monitoring and criticizing prevailing policy and outcomes" (Lindquist 2001: 6).

A further development on the notion of policy networks is Sabatier and Jenkins-Smith's (1993; 1999) "advocacy coalition framework" (ACF). This framework is based on the assumption that there are sets of core ideas about causation and value in public policy. The relationships between actors who share similar values and beliefs result in advocacy coalitions. These can be tight or loose, and cut across governmental and non-governmental boundaries, as well as across Pross's distinction between sub-government and attentive audiences. What links them all is a shared set of beliefs and a general agreement on the best solution to a certain policy issue. According to Sabatier and Jenkins–Smith typically two to four advocacy coalitions can be found in every policy community with regard to a particular issue and it is possible to identify these networks of actors within a policy sector. Different coalitions fight it out until one coalition emerges as the dominant one controlling the key instruments of policymaking and implementation.

Elaborating on the analysis of the 2006 policy process leading up to the 2007–11 management contract for VRT, it is possible, first, to distinguish between Pross's two main categories. The "sub-government" includes, among others, the media minister, his/her cabinet members, the Flemish civil service media administration and others such as the Flemish Media Policy Council, the Flemish Media Regulator (VRM) and the parliamentary media committee. The public service broadcasting institution itself can also be seen to reside in this subset. The "attentive public" includes competing media as stakeholders and/or lobby groups, but also others, including the local radio federation, advertisers, academics, consultants, civil society organizations representing audience groups, think tanks, journalists and prominent individuals. Second, by analyzing the available material, it is possible to distinguish between two main advocacy coalitions based on the core beliefs about the position and future of PSB in the Flemish media landscape: those in favor of a strong public service broadcaster, including in the area of new digital media platforms, and those in favor of a more modest public service broadcasting institution to ensure a "level playing field." Inspired by Pross, this can result in the chart for the Flemish case illustrated in Figure 1.3.

## *Policy networks*

A somewhat different, but possibly complementary, approach to understanding the policy process can be found within network studies. While policy communities refer to an understanding and mapping of stakeholders according to their overlapping interests and views, the concept of policy networks focuses on relationships among political actors: how do these relationships come about? How do they develop and change? How do stakeholders use these relations to deal with and influence the policy process? What impact do these relations have on the policy process and outcome? The term "network" (rather than "community" or "coalition") focuses the attention specifically on the connections between different actors in the policy process. The meaning and relevance or influence of an actor is thus primarily determined by his position in the network and not just by his views and goals, and the analysis focuses not so much on the policy outcome as on the patterning of relations within a network and the process of influence to reach this particular outcome (Wasserman and Faust 2008; Roldan Vera and Schupp 2006).

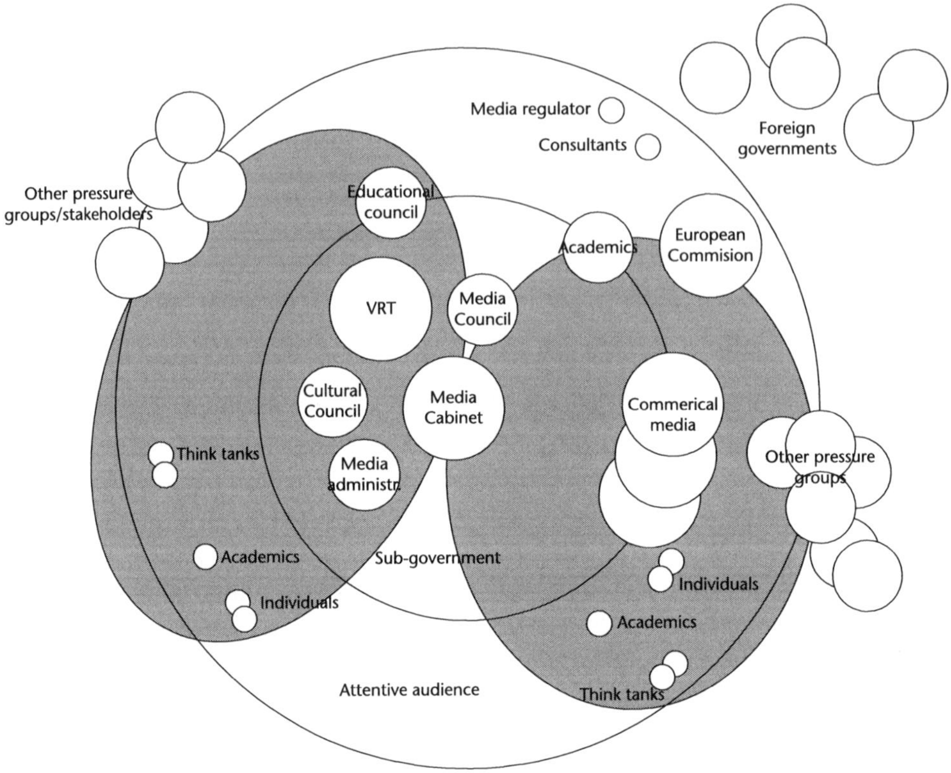


*Figure 1.3* Policy communities and advocacy coalitions for the 2006 Flemish PSB contract-renewal policy process

No systematic network analysis of the policymaking process regarding the Flemish public service broadcasting management contract has been performed. An interesting example within media studies, providing guidance in executing such analysis, is Löbisch and Pfaff-Rüdiger's (2012) network analysis of the German youth protection system. Löbisch and Pfaff-Rüdiger consider a network to be a specific pattern of social relations between individual, collective or corporative actors that are interdependent rather than independent. The ties between actors can differ in strength, with intense and frequent ties being maintained with actors dealing with similar issues and holding similar views. Strong ties can be positive, but also counterproductive or negative (e.g. peer pressure between civil society organizations with historical ties). Relations can be symmetrical or asymmetrical, and conflicts can occur, resulting in clusters and factions within a network structure. Löbisch and Pfaff-Rüdiger explain how these conflicts result in structural holes, which in turn provide space for brokerage roles for actors that are in a unique position to connect different clusters of relationships. This provides certain actors with an additional advantage and leverage power.

## Modifications

Three important caveats are necessary with regards to policy communities, advocacy coalitions and networks. First, Kingdon (1995) and Sabatier and Jenkins-Smith (1993) confirm the above mentioned need to pay attention to the influence exerted through informal relationships, which are often quite invisible and subtle, but nevertheless can create considerable leverage within the policymaking process. Lindquist (2001: 13) refers to them as "epistemic communities." Interviews for the analysis of the 2007–11 management contract negotiations revealed, for instance, frequent contacts between commercial media players and certain political parties. Second, both the position of an actor in a coalition and its force in a network may depend on the specific issue at hand, because different coalitions and networks can be found within one field such as media policy. Stakeholders active in one media policy subarea (e.g. PSB) may differ considerably from actors involved in another (e.g. telecommunications). Some actors within the broad area of media policy may limit their activities to one specific issue (e.g. local radio), while others can be seen to operate in many different subareas. One stakeholder can adhere to different (even opposing) views and positions, and its position and influence in the network can differ depending on the issue. For instance, while public service and commercial broadcasters were shown to hold opposing views regarding the position of VRT in the Flemish media market, they hold similar views and have lobbied together at government level when it comes to the position of distribution networks and providers within that same market. Third, Rhodes (2007) stresses the need to pay attention to the agency of individuals within the policy process. Such a decentered approach recognizes "that the actions of these individuals are not fixed by institutional norms [. . .] but, on the contrary, arise from the beliefs individuals adopt against the background of traditions and in response to dilemmas" (Rhodes 2007: 1252). Lindquist (2001) refers to these individuals as "policy entrepreneurs": advocates of certain policy causes or solutions, experienced in understanding policy environments and spotting policy windows. Accordingly, policy process analysts need to identify which individuals are pivotal in bringing about policy change.

### Accounting for policy changes

A further conceptual issue is how to account for more or less radical shifts in policies. Kingdon's (1995) multiple streams theory assumes that policy issues "flow along" in independent streams and can be picked up (or not) by politicians to be turned into policies. This view has been criticized for the high level of randomness it attributes to the policy process. Network analyses such as the one mentioned above focus, in terms of change, mostly on how the structure of networks alters owing to changes in its environment (Adam and Kriesl 2007). Löblich and Pfaff-Rüdiger (2012) found in this regard that the network around youth protection and media was considerably influenced by legislative changes (resulting in the arrival of a new player, the *Kommission für Jügendmedienschutz*) by the growth of online media and by youth's changing media use. In the case of the network around the Flemish public service broadcasting policymaking, between the 2007–11 and the 2012–16 contract negotiations, following lobby work from commercial channels, VRT was no longer allowed to broker an exclusivity contract with its main program provider Woestijnvis, resulting in a cut of the ties between both actors. This pushed Woestijnvis to buy the Flemish SBS stations VT4 and 5TV, promising heightened competition between television stations. This changed the relative positions and relationships between the different commercial channels. As a result, by the time the 2012–16 contract negotiations started, the network had changed.

In Pross's model of policy communities, the push for change comes mainly from the attentive audience, as its members have no real stake in preserving the status quo and are more likely to come up with creative ideas for new policy approaches. The sub-government is expected to have an interest in maintaining the status quo. This may account for certain changes in media policy, for instance showing the influence of academics and equal-opportunity groups in pushing certain solution paradigms for a more balanced gender or ethnic minority portrayal in media content and advertising. Yet there are many other examples in media policy that point to changes originating from within the sub-government, core policymaking circle.

Sabatier and Jenkins-Smith's advocacy coalition (ACF) model provides a more complex view on change. At the macro level, policymaking (and policy change) is influenced by stable, exogenous factors such as the characteristics of the problem (e.g. Flanders as a small media market), institutional structures (e.g. multilevel governance) and socio-cultural phenomena (e.g. digital age gap). It is further influenced by dynamic exogenous factors such as changes in socio-economic circumstances (e.g. the move away from the welfare state), shifts in governmental structures (e.g. the transfer of media competences from the federal state to the regions resulting in new media regulatory frameworks), and policy decisions in other subsystems and policy areas (e.g. liberalization of the telecommunications market). In general, a policy community maintains the status quo as it is built around deep core beliefs, such as longstanding traditions of social responsibility in broadcasting or of liberalism in the press.

Change can further be seen to appear through policy-oriented learning or shocks in the system. In the case of policy-oriented learning, the evaluation and lessons learned from one policy implementation affect a subsequent policy decision. An interesting illustration of this can be found in Chin's (2010) analysis of policy learning and regional media in China. Policies can also change as the result of a shock to the system that originates externally or internally, as acknowledged in more recent adjustments to the advocacy coalition model (Weible *et al.* 2009). The larger economic crisis that started late in 2008, for example, led to the failure of the traditional business model of the press, a crisis that, in turn, influenced views of certain stakeholders on the role and position of PSB in online news provision. These shocks can cause actors to shift advocacy coalitions, if only for tactical reasons. It may also cause coalitions to adapt their arguments to new situations and even to move across coalition divides. The balance of power in policy networks changes, and the structure and memberships of coalitions alter (John 2003).

Not unlike the proponents of the advocacy coalition framework, Rhodes (2007) analyzes consistency and change in terms of "traditions" and "dilemmas." Traditions explain how rule, power, order and norms arise and become sustained patterns of policymaking. Change is caused by a dilemma that "arise[s] when a new idea stands in opposition to existing beliefs or practices and so forces a reconsideration of the existing beliefs and associated tradition" (Rhodes 2007: 1253). This suggests that, in order to understand changes in media policy, we need to look for the relevant dilemmas. Rhodes further specifies that the power to change is contingent and relational, relative to the power of other actors and stakeholders.

### *Methodological implications*

At first glance, models focusing on communities, coalitions and networks do not seem to generate distinctly new methodologies. Network analysis as such has a long tradition of using survey instruments or quantitative data to provide a detailed reconstruction of a particular network (e.g. Butts 2008), yet several case studies, such as that of the German youth and media protection network, are executed within a qualitative, interpretative tradition. An analytical overview of eighty applications of the ACF (Weible *et al.* 2009) indicates that one in four are based on in-depth interviews and one in eight on a combination of interviews and document analysis.

The conceptual attention to the process aspect of media policy leads to interesting new ways of using the "traditional" policy methods of document analysis and elite or expert interviews. With regard to documents, it involves an additional or complementary coding of the documents to look for relationships, coalitions and changes over time. A number of advocacy coalition studies have opted for a quantitative approach to document analysis, using time-series analysis and/or cluster analysis on expressed policy positions to prove the existence of advocacy coalitions, indicating long-term development of actors' beliefs and showing changes in both the polarization between advocacy coalitions and the relative stability of beliefs of different coalitions (Bandalow 2006). Qualitative document analysis can likewise incorporate such a focus.

Apart from identifying shared core beliefs, such document analysis does not allow the researcher to prove a link between advocacy-coalition members. This is relevant in a case in which, for instance, two members may share the same beliefs, but have a competitive interest in not cooperating. This adds to the importance of expert interviewing, in which experts can be asked explicitly and elaborately about cooperation and polarization with other actors, the relative strength and density of these relationships, and the position and latitude of the interviewee compared to the other actors, among others (John 2003).

Finally, Rhodes endorses complementing document analysis and interviews with observation and other ethnographic methodologies that "can take full measure of the processional, network and coalition aspects as well as of individual agency" (Rhodes 2007: 1252). One way for a researcher to engage in participant observation is through the actual membership of a policymaking body, for instance a media policy council. A more feasible approach available to all researchers is that of transient observation—without "disguise" and mainly as an outsider (Murphy 1980: 110). This can allow for a form of triangulation of the data obtained through documents and interviews, and can provide additional information without relying on "the potentially unreliable reports of others" (Murphy 1980: 113).

## Conclusion

Focusing mainly on recent policymaking in the area of (Flemish) public service broadcasting, this chapter has combined discussion of an observed shift in media policymaking towards a multi-stakeholder approach with a conceptual and methodological underpinning of media policy analysis.

As the Flemish case study illustrates, media policy has increasingly become multilayered and complex, with more actors being involved—formally or informally, invited or uninvited—in the shaping and reshaping of media policies. In the case of public service broadcasting in Flanders, indicative of trends elsewhere in Europe, the growing interference of the European Union, through its efforts to create a single common market through directives and regulation, went hand in hand with, and was even strengthened by, a growing push of other than the key policy actors to become involved in media policymaking. As the specific analysis of the policy process towards the 2007–11 management contract of VRT indicates, this not only results in a much more crowded and intricate web of stakeholders in the policy process, but results in a shift in the locus of governance power. In the case of public service broadcasting, it makes these institutions accountable to stakeholders other than the government representing the public interest.

Looking for good practices in media policy process analysis, it appears that, conceptually, a combination of an actor and a process perspective proves fruitful. Systematic stakeholder analysis helps to identify all relevant stakeholders, their views, their power and the fora in which they defend their "stakes." Advocacy coalition analysis—possibly complemented with network analysis—enables us to understand how stakeholders relate to one another, how they work together or fight each other in the policy arena, and how they influence the policy outcome. This combination further guides a renewed handling of the traditional methodological tools of document analysis and in-depth interviews. These tools better equip communication scholars to study the media policy process. Indeed, the continued trend toward media convergence and concentration, the rise of new industrial and private media players, and most of all the interference of the EU and other transnational institutions promise to push media policymaking further in the direction of multi-stakeholder formations.

## References


Aberbach, J. D. and Rockman, B. A. (2002) 'Conducting and coding elite interviews,' *Political Science and Politics*, 35(4): 673–676.

Adam, S. and Kriesl, H. (2007) 'The network approach,' in P. Sabatier (ed.) *Theories of the Policy Process*, Boulder, CO: Westview Press.

Altheide, D. L. (1996) *Qualitative Media Analysis*, Qualitative Research Methods Series, London: Sage.

Bandelow, N. C. (2006) 'Advocacy coalitions, policy-oriented learning and long-term change in genetic engineering policy: An interpretist view,' *German Policy Studies*, 3(4): 747–805.

Bardoel, J. and Lowe, G. F. (2007) 'From public service broadcasting to public service media: The core challenge,' in G. F. Lowe and J. Bardoel (eds.) *From Public Service Broadcasting to Public Service Media RIPE@2007*, Göteborg: Nordicom.

Blakie, P. and Soussan, J. G. (2001) *Understanding Policy Processes*, Leeds: University of Leeds.

Blutts, C. T. (2008) 'Social network analysis: A methodological introduction,' *Asian Journal of Social Psychology*, 11: 13–41.

Bogner, A., Littig, B. and Menz, W. (2009) *Interviewing Experts*, Basingstoke: Palgrave Macmillan.

Brevini, B. (2010) 'Towards PSB 2.0? Applying the PSB ethos to online media in Europe: A comparative study of PSB's Internet policies in Spain, Italy and Britain,' *European Journal of Communication*, 25(4): 348–365.

Brugha, R. and Varvasovszky, Z. (2000) 'Stakeholder analysis: A review,' *Health Policy and Planning*, 15(3): 239–246.

Bryman, A. (2001) *Social Research Methods*, Oxford: Oxford University Press.

Chin, Y. C. (2011) 'Policy process, policy learning and the role of the provincial media in China,' *Media, Culture and Society*, 33(2): 193–210.

Collins, R. (2008) 'Hierarchy to homeostasis? Hierarchy, markets and networks in UK media and communications governance,' *Media Culture and Society*, 30(3): 295–317.

Deacon, D., Pickering, M., Golding, P. and Murdock, G. (2007) *Researching Communications: A Practical Guide to Methods in Media and Cultural Analysis*, London: Hodder Arnold.

d'Haenens, L. and Brink, S. (2001) 'Digital convergence: The development of a new media market in Europe,' in L. d'Haenens and F. Saeys (eds.) *Western Broadcasting at the Dawn of the 21st Century*, Berlin/New York: Mouton de Gruyter.

Donders, K. (2011) 'Public service media in Flanders: A long way to heaven?' *International Journal of Electronic Governance*, 4(1/2): 27–42.

—— and Pauwels, C. (2008) 'Does EU policy challenge the digital future of public service broadcasting? An analysis of the Commission's state aid approach to digitization and the public service remit of public broadcasting organizations,' *Convergence*, 14(3): 295–311.

—— Raats, T., Moons, A. and Walravens, N. (2010) *De toekomstige plaats en rol van de openbare omroep in Vlaanderen: Stakeholderbevragin i.o.v. De Sectorraad Media*, Brussel: VUB.

Dunn, W. N. (2004) *Public Policy Analysis: An Introduction*, Upper Saddle River, NJ: Pearson Prentice Hall.

Fischer, F. (2003) *Reframing Policy Analysis: Discursive Politics and Deliberative Practices*, Oxford: Oxford University Press.

Freedman, D. (2005) *How Level is the Playing Field? An Analysis of the UK Media Policymaking Process: Report on Research into Media Policy-making in the UK funded by the Economic and Social Research Council*, London: Goldsmith.

—— (2008) *The Politics of Media Policy*, Cambridge: Polity Press.

Freeman, G. P. (1995) 'National styles and policy sectors: Explaining structured variation,' *Journal of Public Policy*, 5(4): 467–496.

Hamelink, C. and Nordenstreng, K. (2007) 'Towards democratic media governance,' in E. De Bens, C. Hamelink and K. Jakubowicz (eds.) *Media Between Culture and Commerce: An Introduction*, Bristol: Intellect.

Hansen, A., Cottle, S., Negrine, R. and Newbold, C. (1998) *Mass Communication Research Methods*, London: Macmillan.

Hendriks, P. (1995) 'Communications policy and industrial dynamics in media markets: Toward a theoretical framework for analysing media industry organisation,' *Journal of Media Economics*, 8: 61–76.

Hood, C. (1991) 'A public management for all seasons,' *Public Administration*, 69(1): 3–19.

Hooghe, L. and Marsk, G. (2001) *Multi-Level Governance and European Integration*, Oxford: Rowman & Littlefield.

Howlett, M. (2004) 'Administrative styles and regulatory reform: Institutional arrangements and their effects on administrative behaviour,' *International Public Management Journal*, 7(3): 317–333.

Hutchinson, D. (1999) *Media Policy: An Introduction*, London: Blackwell.

Jansen, D. and Wald, A. (2007) 'Netzwerktheorien,' in L. Benz, S. Lütz, U. Schimank and G. Simonis (eds.) *Handbuch Governance: Theoretische Grundlagen und empirische Anwendungsfelder*, Wiesbaden: VS.

John, P. (2003) 'Is there life after policy streams, advocacy coalitions, and punctuations? Using evolutionary theory to explain policy change,' *The Policy Studies Journal*, 31(4): 481–498.

Kingdon, J. (1995) *Agendas, Alternatives, and Public Policies*, Boston, MA: Little Brown.

Laswell, H. (1956) *The Decision Process*, College Park, MD: University of Maryland Press.

Lindquist, E. A. (2001) *Discerning Policy Influence: Framework for a Strategic Evaluation of IDRC-supported Research*, Victoria (BC): University of Victoria. Online. Available HTTP: http://www.idrc.ca/uploads/user-S/10359907080discerning_policy.pdf (accessed 17 November 2010).

Löblich, M. and Pfaff-Rüdiger, S. (2012) 'Qualitative network analysis: An approach to communication policy studies,' in M. Puppis and N. Just (eds.) *Trends in Communication Policy Research: New Theories, Methods and Subjects*, Bristol: Intellect.

Mitchell, R., Agle, B. and Wood, D. (1997) 'Towards a theory of stakeholder identification: Defining the principle of who and what really counts,' *Academy of Management Review*, 22(4): 853–886.

Moe, H. (2011) 'Defining public service beyond broadcasting: The legitimacy of different approaches,' *International Journal of Cultural Policy*, 17(1): 52–68.

Murphy, J. T. (1980) *Getting the Facts: A Fieldwork Guide for Evaluators and Policy Analysts*, Santa Monica, CA: Goodyear Publishing.

Neff, G. (2005) 'The changing place of cultural production: The location of social networks in a digital media industry,' *Annals, AAPSS*, 597: 134–152.

Øvrebo, O. A. and Moe, H. (2009) 'Nettmedier og offentlicheten Vox Publicas nethring om NRK-plakaten,' *Norsk Mediantidsskrift*, 17(1): 4–25.

Parker, R. and Parenta, O. (2008) 'Explaining contradictions in film and television policy: Ideas and incremental policy change through layering and drift,' *Media, Culture and Society*, 30(5): 609–622.

Pollitt, C. and Bouckaert, G. (2004) *Public Management Reform: A Comparative Analysis*, Oxford: Oxford University Press.

Prell, C., Hubacek, K. and Reed, M. (2009) 'Stakeholder analysis and social network analysis in natural resource management,' *Society and Natural Resources*, 22(6): 501–518.

Pross, P. (1986) *Group Politics and Public Policy*, Toronto, ON: Oxford University Press.

Puppis, M. (2008) 'National media regulation in the era of free trade the role of global media governance,' *European Journal of Communication*, 23(4): 405–424.

—— and Just, N. (eds.) (2012) *Trends in Communication Policy Research: New Theories, Methods and Subjects*, Bristol: Intellect.

Rhodes, R. A. W. (2007) 'Understanding governance: Ten years on,' *Organization Studies*, 28(8): 1243–1264.

Roldan Vera, E. and Schupp, T. (2006) 'Network analysis in comparative social sciences,' *Comparative Education*, 42(3): 405–429.

Sabatier, P. and Jenkins-Smith, H. (1993) *Policy Change and Learning: An Advocacy Coalition Approach*, Boulder, CO: Westview.

—— and —— (1999) 'The advocacy coalition framework: An assessment,' in P. Sabatier (ed.) *Theories of the Policy Process*, Boulder, CO: Westview.
Seldon, A. and Pappworth, J. (1983) *By Word of Mouth: Elite Oral History*, London: Methuen.
Startt, J. D. and Sloan, W. D. (1989) *Historical Methods in Mass Communication*, Hillsdale, MI: Lawrence Erlbaum.
Uyttendaele, C. and Braeckevelt, D. (2007) Personal interview with media specialists of the Cabinet of Flemish Media Minister Bourgeois, Brussels, October.
Van Audenhove, L. (2010) 'Expert interviews and interview techniques for policy analysis.' Online. Available HTTP://www.ies.be/files/060313%20Interviews.vanAudenhove.pdf (accessed 21 September 2012).
Van den Bulck, H. (2002) 'Tools for studying the media,' in C. Newbold, O. Boyd-Barrett and H. van den Bulck (eds.) *The Media Book*, London: Edward Arnold.
—— (2007) 'Old ideas meet new technologies: Will digitisation save public service broadcasting (ideals) from commercial death?' *Sociology Compass*, 1(1): 28–40.
—— (2008) 'Can PSB stake its claim in a media world of digital convergence? The case of the Flemish PSB management contract renewal from an international perspective,' *Convergence*, 14(3): 335–350.
—— (2011) '*Ex ante* test in Flanders: Making ends meet?' in K. Donders and H. Moe (eds.) *Exporting the Public Value Test: The Regulation of Public Broadcasters' Media Services across Europe*, Göteborg: Nordicom.
Van Gorp, J. (2011) 'Inverting film policy: Film as nation builder in Post-Soviet Russia, 1991–2005,' *Media, Culture and Society*, 33(2): 243–258.
Verhoest, K. and Legrain, A. (2005) *Handleiding beheersovereenkomsten. Deel 1: processen en actoren*, Leuven, Steunpunt Bestuurlijke Organisatie Vlaanderen, Report D/2005/10106/021.
Wasserman, S. and Faust, K. (2008) *Social Network Analysis: Methods and Applications*, Cambridge: Cambridge University Press.
Weible, C. M. (2007) 'An advocacy coalition framework approach to stakeholder analysis: Understanding the political context of California marine protected area policy,' *Journal of Public Administration Research and Theory*, 17(1): 95–117.
—— Sabatier, P. A. and McQueen, K. (2009) 'Themes and variations: Taking stock of the advocacy coalition framework,' *Policy Studies Journal*, 37(1): 121–140.

# 2

# Rational legal authority, formal and informal rules in the news media

*Paolo Mancini*

## Rational legal authority and rule of law: Differences and similarities

Formal law is certainly important in determining the structure and the performance of the news media. At the same time, law is inserted within a cultural framework that very often either contradicts the existing law or makes it ineffective through transformations and ad hoc adaptations. We know, too, that very often formal and informal law are intertwined. This chapter focuses on the fundamental questions raised by this mixture of law and culture, and of formal rules and informality, as these realities are reflected into the structure and mostly into the performance of news media and their professionals.

In my examination of how the culture of a country, and specifically the political culture of a country, is able to transform and to adapt the existing law, I use the term "rational legal authority" in preference to the much more often used phrase "rule of law." For a number of reasons, the idea of rational legal authority seems to me much broader than that of "rule of law" so prevalent in the Anglo-Saxon world in sociology, politics and, of course, in legal studies and in socio-legal studies. Obviously, the field for application of these principles is mainly law, but if we take the definition that Martin Krygier proposes for rule of law—("socially patterned behaviors, shared and internalized norms, and so on" (Krygier 2011: 69)—we are not far away from what sociologists state as to the importance of the rules in defining the existence of a community of people: "Ordered interaction is achieved when a high probability exists that a significant number of actors in a given context will orient their behavior to the same norm" (Spencer 1970: 124).

The idea of rational legal authority comes directly from Max Weber, the German sociologist, and represents a third type of authority (after traditional and charismatic authority). Rational legal authority derives from the increasing need of the society "for order and protection" (Weber 1980: 74).

This interpretation, adopted in much of sociology, may prove useful in the field of media studies as well. Indeed, as every textbook of sociology teaches, the sharing of reciprocal expectations is the basis of society. Laws, and respect for laws, represent the most institutionalized form of reciprocal expectations. A society exists when people respect "socially patterned behaviors, shared and internalized norms," as in Krygier's definition, and, of course, the media are an important part of the society.

In Weber's definition, the most important feature of rational legal authority is the existence of rules, the rational character of which represents "the validity of power" (Weber 1980: 56). In contrast, traditional and charismatic authorities were based on the existence of rooted habits and procedures, and on single figures of leaders able to establish, legitimize and maintain such authorities. Rational rules represent, in Weber's view, the core of modern societies, linking people together through the expectation of reciprocity: the need for order and protection.

The second defining feature of rational legal authority is the objectivity of the rules. Rules are characterized by universality: they are the same for everybody; they work the same way for everybody; and in doing so they oppose subjectivity and abuse that are observable in those societies in which rational legal authority either does not exist or is very low.

Specialization (conceived essentially as specialized education carefully checked through a system of examinations) is what mainly distinguishes rational legal authority from rule of law. Indeed, with the idea of specialization we progressively move from the field of law to the field of society—its structure, its proceedings and its historical evolution. Specialization is the legitimizing base of rational legal authority and, in Weber's view, it represents the distinguishing feature of bureaucracy—the social body in charge of fastening rational legal authority. Weber writes that "professional examinations and specialized preparation are progressively more essential to modern bureaucracy" (Weber 1980: 97). In different parts of his writings, Weber insists on the need for education—university education in particular—and regular and patterned examinations to ensure a sufficient level of knowledge, skills and specialization to legitimate the bureaucracy. Specialization through education and hard examinations is the necessary precondition for the rational character of the rules.

Weber's interpretation of rational legal authority implies the existence and the importance of the state, or, using his word, "power." Rational legal authority is both a consequence of and precondition for a unifying state; indeed, it implies that an authority (power) exists, and that the main goal of rules and bureaucracy is to legitimate the existence of such an authority. In this view, rational legal authority and therefore the construction of the state go together with the process of "bourgeois rationalization" (Hallin and Mancini 2004: 57)—that is, the birth, and then the development, of professionalization and rationalization in many fields of the society that took place in some countries in Europe and North America in the eighteenth and nineteenth centuries at the time when modern states were under construction (Anderson 1983). In these years, a dramatic process of social change took place: liberal institutions were established thanks to specific and differentiated routines and procedures. Shefter (1977) has convincingly demonstrated that this process of rationalization—characterized by the development of a strong and well-rooted bureaucracy, universal rules and a diffuse practice of examinations to enter civil service—prevented the development of party patronage in Germany and other countries. In particular, he underlines how civil service was closely linked with other institutions in German society, most notably with the legal profession and universities.

In this sense, the idea of rational legal authority is connected to particular patterns of social change that foster a process of differentiation among social systems, each of which features specific rules having universal character. This prevents particularistic and clientelistic attitudes determining a higher level of involvement with the idea of common good, as citizens perceive that there exists a corpus of shared norms that they can rely on. In the Western world, there has been a historical moment in which different corpuses of specialized rules, institutions and procedures have been created, giving birth to different and specialized systems.

In this regard Jeffrey Alexander (1981) has argued that the birth of journalism, as a system autonomous from other social systems, occurred at the beginning of the liberal era and was characterized by the need to provide information of universal character available to different social systems and actors without any bias. In his view, journalism was in charge of spreading news "of universal character" to a plurality of different and often competing actors.

In many other countries beyond (but also within) the Western world, this has not happened, and the corpus of rules, habits and procedures that features journalism as an independent and autonomous system able to provide news following specific rules, procedures and routines was not established. The absence of such a corpus of specific rules has favored the opening of journalism to external pressures and interests.

Indeed, there is a second observation that derives from Weber's thesis: is it possible to transfer the idea of rational legal authority to the level of *single social systems*? Here, I use the term "social system" referring to Talcott Parsons and other functionalists. Following Alexander's thesis, it seems possible to assume that just as a society is constructed through the existence of a framework of rational rules, so the shared rules of a profession, mostly deriving from professionals themselves, are "patterned behaviors" that are important for what Weber calls a better "satisfaction" of the entire society (1980: 74) as well as the specific community under observation (professional journalists). In terms of institutionalization, law is what legitimizes modern states and their authority, just as, more generally, rules legitimate (and differentiate) all of the organized systems, constructing and reinforcing their identity.

As noted earlier, sociologists have supposed that the existence and the respect of norms are preconditions for the constitution of a "society." It seems possible to assume that ordered interactions constitute the basis of each community, including a community of professionals. Rational legal authority implies the existence of a community of people that shares the same rules, respect for which depends on their rational character fastened by a body and a framework of specialized procedures. Journalism can be such a community or a system. Pierre Bourdieu's "field theory" is not too far away from this possible approach when he talks of journalism as a microcosm that obeys "its own laws, its own nomos" (Bourdieu 1993: 33). In other words, journalism can be conceived as an autonomous field with specific rules, procedures and routines that make it different from other social fields.

## *Rational legal authority and the news media*

Although the concepts of rule of law and rational legal authority are not much used in media studies, the idea of rational legal authority can be very important for the study of news media, because it may indicate how, and how much, news media represent a body or a "system" in itself, distinguished and separated from other systems and operating following a specific set of shared rules and routines. It may also help to explain what constitutes the dominant culture of a society and how news media fit within it.

In *Comparing Media Systems* (Hallin and Mancini 2004), we used the idea of rational legal authority to feature and evaluate four possible variables in comparative analysis:

- the autonomy of news media from government and, more generally, political pressures;
- the level of professionalization of those acting within the media system;
- the level of media instrumentalization (the possible interference of external forces on the media system); and
- the fair distribution of resources to news media (public subsidies, etc.) as opposed to clientelism.

Our first idea was that the existence and the respect of "formal and universalistic rules of procedures" (Hallin and Mancini 2004: 54) could deeply affect the structure and the performance of the media system, defining its level of independence from other systems; therefore it could represent an interesting and useful dimension to be used in comparative analysis. Rational legal authority could help to deter the interference of government and other social and economic forces over the media, and allow it to be governed by clear, independent rules and procedures established by professionals themselves and often controlled by self-regulatory bodies. In this way journalism is able to express its own specific "professionalism" different and separated from that of other professions. Looking comparatively it is possible to observe very different situations: In some countries the journalistic profession is very weak and open to external influences, while in others, there exists a more mature and rooted tradition of professional identity that helps limit interference with reporters.

Rational legal authority can also elevate the level of media professionalization, as recruitment and career advancement are governed by the adhesion to fixed and universalistic parameters of evaluation. Usually, this is what we find in those countries where, in the society at large, the development of a strong bureaucracy is rooted in a continuous practice of examinations and specialized education. Typically, each system of this society (not just journalism) is characterized by a high level of professionalism, specific tracks of career advancement, and universal, transparent and merit-based forms of recruitment.

Such a clear, well-rooted professionalism, determined by this system of recruitment and career improvement, could help professional journalists (and other professionals) resist external pressures and external interference. This is the lesson we learn from Shefter's examination of how the existence of a strong, autonomous bureaucracy built on a system of specialized education has prevented the diffusion of party patronage and party interference with recruitment and career advancement in the state apparatus.

Finally, the distribution of resources following universalistic criteria and precise rules could discourage clientelism and particularism. Indeed, the instrumental use of news media (that is, the likely use of the news media to support particular and often contingent interests) is diminished when clear rules exist as to the distribution of resources among different news outlets and different bodies of the society.

In short, my point on the relationship between rational legal authority and news media is the following: Enlarging Weber's definition, different levels of rational legal authority could have significant impacts on the performance (and also on the structure) of the news media system, just as they do on other social systems. The existence of professional rules with universal value and application, the codification of procedures, the existence and the respect for universal professional norms (as well as recruitment based on shared values and a shared system of evaluation) could ensure the development of a news media system that is independent from other social systems, in particular government.

Other scholars have similar views. Addressing the relationship between clientelism and news media, Natalia Roudakova proposes a use of the concept of rational legal authority in a similar way: "clientelism can be seen as a cultural feature: a belief that formal universalistic rules are less important than personal connections. The exact reverse is true, in political science, of clientelism's analytical opposite, rational legal authority, defined as a form of socio-political order where access to public resources is transparent, impersonal, and merit-based, where the notion of public good is strong and where adherence to formal, universalistic rules of procedures overrides particularistic interests and personal connections" (Roudakova 2008: 42). Hallin and Papatahanassopoulos have studied the diffusion of clientelism in the news media of Southern Europe and South America, connecting the diffusion of clientelism both to the low level of rational legal authority, and to the late development of democratic institutions in these countries (as compared with other countries) as a response to the breakdown of traditional structures (Hallin and Papatahanassopoulos 2002).

## *Rational legal authority and political culture*

My understanding of rational legal authority cannot be separated from the idea of political culture. Indeed, citizens and professionals act within a complex and often contradictory set of attitudes, perceptions and practices that connect them to society at large and direct their everyday behaviors regarding their fellow citizens and political institutions. Corruption, particularism, identification with one's fellow citizens, trust in institutions and their rules, and cooperativeness with institutions are undoubtedly part of the political culture of a country (Almond and Verba 1963; Verba 1965). Blumler and Gurevitch have applied their idea of political culture to the field of mass communication in this way: "Political culture may be defined as the values, norms, beliefs, sentiments and understandings of how power and authority operate within a particular political system. Generally political culture sets informal and unwritten ground rules as to how the political process is to be performed" (Blumler and Gurevitch 2004: 335). Their insistence on "norms" stresses the strict relationship that exists between rational legal authority and political culture.

It is impossible to abstract journalism (or any profession) from political culture: Political culture affects citizens in their private behaviors but also, importantly, in their relationship with the system of rules of each society and problems of general interest. Engineers have to follow the rules established to start building a house—there are procedures they have to follow, applications to complete, permissions to be obtained. Are these procedures generally applicable and valid for every engineer? Or are there common ways to overcome the expected procedures, or personal (and political) links and relationships that may facilitate the process? My point is very simple: In those countries where engineers are accustomed to following patterned behaviors and procedures, journalists too share (more or less formal) common habits that help to ensure a sufficient level of professional autonomy. There is a sufficient and clear perception of living together within a community that shares the same rules and general attitudes. Therefore the involvement with common good is also high.

This is even more important when we face a profession, such as journalism, that does not have a very clear professional status: Its rules are not particularly technical; they are relatively vague and uncertain. Precise and detailed routines and techniques do not exist; indeed, many speak of journalism as a craft more than as a profession. This makes journalism even more dependent on the surrounding cultural and political context.

Michael Schudson has developed further Richard Hoggart's (1981) idea: "the most important filter through which news is constructed is the cultural air we breathe, the whole ideological atmosphere of our society, which tells us that some things can be said and that others are best not to be said. That cultural air is one that in part ruling groups and institutions create but it is in part one in whose context their own establishment takes place" (Schudson 2005: 189). Some years before, Schudson himself had already pointed out the importance of the cultural environment within which journalists behave, stating that "the news then is produced by people who operate often unwittingly within a cultural system, a reservoir of stored cultural meanings and patterns of discourse . . . news as a form of culture incorporates assumptions about what matters, what makes sense, what time and place we live in, what range of considerations we should take seriously" (Schudson 1995: 14). The idea of the "overall cultural mix" proposed by Blumler and Gurevitch is not much different. The two authors wrote: "All political systems generate principles derived from the tenets of their political cultures, for regulating the political role of the mass media" (Blumler and Gurevitch 1995: 19). They continue: "In the end the central issue in the relationship between media and political institutions revolves around the media's relative degree of autonomy and to what extent and by what means this is allowed to be constrained. Thus, it is the overall cultural 'mix' in a given society that will tend to fix the position of the media on the subordination-autonomy continuum and determine which constraints are permitted some degree of control over them" (Blumler and Gurevitch 1995: 20). Autonomy and constraints that are determined by the existence of rules, their respect and the level of specialization are central.

## *Some empirical evidence*

In this section I try to offer some empirical examples of my understanding of rational legal authority and its connection to political culture at large. The starting point is an article by Marina Kurkchiyan titled "Russian Legal Culture: An Analysis of Adaptive Response to an Institutional Transplant." I take this article as an illustration of problems and practices that are possible to observe in many other countries, particularly in Central and Eastern Europe but also in some Mediterranean countries such as Italy. Kurkchiyan describes the results of research conducted in two Russian cities on the establishment of a journalism self-regulatory body modeled after the United Kingdom's Press Complaints Commission. She found "considerable differences both in quality and scale" between the British original and the Russian transplant (Kurkchiyan 2009: 360). Most of the differences are not related to rules themselves, but rather to their application and understanding; The observed differences have to do with the surrounding "air we breathe" of the two societies, Russian and British.

Reading this article I was struck by the many similarities between what Kurkchiyan observes in Russia and the news media situation in Italy and other Mediterranean countries, despite their very different cultural and political contexts. These similarities have much to do with the political culture of the two geographical areas and with their level and kind of rational legal authority. The starting point for this comparison can be the topic of formalism. In both Russia and Italy, legal culture has a very high level of formalism. Formalism has a double face: First of all it is a defense (very often unsuccessful) to a lack of respect for existing rules. Formalism is an attempt to foster respect, but at the same time it is a superstructure to hide the missing respect. As Kurkchiyan writes, quoting the work of McBarnet and Whelan, there seems to exist in Russia a "two sided nature of law, as a means of controlling and a means of escaping control" (Kurkchiyan 2009: 355). Olessia Koltsova has a very similar view: "the severity of Russian Laws is compensated by their non-observance" (Koltsova 2006: 54).

The other face of formalism is informality. As Kurkchiyan states, "in Russian legal culture, there seems to be a paradox: a powerful demand for formality exists alongside an equally powerful instinct to solve actual problems informally" (Kurkchiyan 2009: 355). The severity of law, Kurkchiyan observes in her research, opens up significant space to informal negotiations and adjustments.

The Italian situation is similar. Writing about the Italian state, Paul Ginsborg, a British historian of Italian society, writes that "formalism and particularism were strictly bound within a spiral from which it was impossible to escape. As much in detail the State was trying to regulate and guarantee its relationship to citizens, in the same measure its decisions were becoming complex and unproductive and citizen's attitudes were becoming particularistic" (Ginsborg 1998: 407). Kurkchiyan's statement that "people and politicians alike design ways to impose one control system over another but without actually trusting anyone else to implement them" (Kurkchiyan 2009: 356) describes very vividly two main aspects of this culture, which apply equally to the field of mass media: formalism (new rules over old rules), along with mutual distrust (and therefore particularism).

Italian journalism offers many examples of this. The *Ordine dei Giornalisti* (Journalists' Guild) is a professional association, established by law, which all professional journalists must join after passing an examination. Such an obligatory association does not exist in any other Western democracy. The *Ordine dei Giornalisti* is run by a committee that is seated at the Ministry of Justice; The committee in charge of professional examinations to become a member of the *Ordine dei Giornalisti* is composed of two members appointed by the Court of Appeal. These are clear indications of a high level of formalism, but at the same time strong connections between professional journalism and government; indeed, the National Committee of the *Ordine dei Giornalisti* is officially seated at the Ministry of Justice and evaluates the candidate journalists.

But in spite of formal examinations and the formal appointments of judges as members of the examination committee, the professional identity of Italian journalists is very weak: There is not a strong and independent professional journalism sector, and there are often overlaps with other professions and social fields (Hallin and Mancini 2004). It is not by chance that a famous Italian journalist described the Italian journalist as "*Il giornalista dimezzato* [The halved journalist]" (Pansa 1977). By this, he meant that half of each journalist is the property of someone else: businessmen, corporations, or political parties. One of the conditions of Weber's definition of rational legal authority (specialization) seems to be satisfied: to become a journalist, it is necessary to pass a formal exam. In everyday practice, however, the recruitment of journalists does not follow a merit-based system. The recruitment system essentially depends on the links between the owners of the media outlets and candidates: familial links (sons and daughters of journalists become journalists themselves), political links (recruitment is based on common political affiliation) or other links (friendship, etc.). Indeed, to pass the exam one needs to have been hired for two years by a news outlet; this is mostly based on particularistic links, not on merit and professionalism (Bechelloni 1980, 1995).

The fact that formal training at university level started late in Italy compared to other Western democracies, despite the existence of a formal exam to become a journalist, is a clear indication of how recruitment was, and in large part continues to be, based on criteria other than merit, professionalism and specialized education. Of course, there are exceptions to this and new tendencies are emerging. Indeed, recruitment increasingly passes through the filters of university and professional education, which imposes some limitations on external pressures and clientelistic links.

Particularism and clientelism are historical heritages; They are deep-rooted, national attitudes. Almond and Verba concluded that "the picture of Italian political culture that has emerged from our data is one of relatively unrelieved political alienation and of social isolation and distrust . . . Italians are particularly low in national pride, in moderate and open partisanship, in the acknowledgement of the obligation to take an active part in local community affairs, in their ability to join with the others in situations of political stress, in their choice of social forms of leisure-time activity, and in their confidence in the social environment" (Almond and Verba 1963: 402).

Before Almond and Verba, Edward Banfield (1958) had reached very similar conclusions in his study in the south of Italy. He observed "amoral familism" (the extreme defense of family interests, with little regard for moral values) as opposed to the sense of belonging to a wider community. Robert Putnam (1993) confirmed this vision thirty years later, stressing the difficulty that individuals and groups had in acting together for the common interest that he observed in many Italian regions, especially in the south. In 1998, a well-known Italian historian, Ernesto Galli della Loggia, discussing the characteristics of national identity, wrote: "Individualism, but also a very well-rooted familism: these are the two main characters of the Italian social being that are most often pointed out by foreign observers, but also by a long tradition of national self-consciousness" (Della Loggia 1998: 87).

Particularism struggles with the universality of rules, and informality bends and contradicts their formality. The consequence, as to our topic, is the low level of journalists' professional identity; as "the halved professionals" suggested above, they are unable to promote a universally accepted self-regulation. As a consequence, it is government and parliament (not journalists) that are often the initiators of laws regarding the autonomy and the work of journalists. This low level of professional identity is not too far away from what Kurkchiyan observes in Russia, where journalists are involved with a number of activities that have nothing to do with news reporting, as understood in most Western democracies: "The publications contain a great deal of distorted information, engage in smear campaigns, and routinely print what are known as "ordered" or paid for articles consisting of stories intended to discredit rivals and opponents of the proprietor or whoever supports the outlet financially" (Kurkchiyan 2009: 347). *Blat, black PR*, and *kompromat* are the words most frequently used when Russian journalism is discussed (Ledeneva 2004; Koltsova 2006; Roudakova 2008): They indicate activities in which journalists are often involved that have nothing to do with news reporting. Pasti also writes about the weak professional identity of Russian journalists: "Like ordinary people, journalists must manage through common sense and effort to find a niche in the new prosperous Russia. Therefore they serve the interests of those who possess political and economic capital, i.e. the state and business elite" (Pasti 2005: 109). Similar tendencies are also found in many other Central Eastern European countries: Discussing post-socialist democracies, Alina Mungiu Pippidi writes: "In societies based on particularism rather than free competition . . . media outlets are not ordinary business ventures. Rather, investors use their channels for blackmail or for trading influence" (Mungiu Pippidi 2010: 126).

Italian journalists do not arrive at the extreme of Russian journalists, but their overlap with politics and business is a deep-rooted tradition (Mancini 2000) that has developed, as discussed above, from a low level of rational legal authority that prevents the development of an autonomous body of professionals and a tendency for journalists to have other "commitments" beyond the diffusion of news.

Journalism is permeated by external pressures and reporters become instruments in the hands of external powers. Indeed, because of the nature of their work, journalists have more opportunities to get involved with decision-makers; they have connections in many different fields and consequently are more exposed than other professions to opportunities to mix their expertise with the needs of other social actors. A study published in 2011 showed that, in Italy, more than 12 percent of members of parliament either are journalists or are former journalists; in the United Kingdom, this number decreases to 6.5 percent, and in Germany, to 3.9 percent (Ciaglia 2011).

A clear example of "of one control system over another" and the diffusion of informality is the Italian practice of *lottizzazione*. Rai, the Italian public service broadcaster, is known for this well-rooted practice, which can be defined as the sharing of positions of major power and prestige, of a company or institution, that is brought about by agreement of the parties that have direct or indirect control over the people who are given appointments by them, based on choices that are mainly of a political nature and not always motivated by specific technical abilities (Padovani 2005; Mancini 2009). This practice works not only for Rai, but also for all of the institutions that are placed under the control of the state; or have some connections to the state, yet it is not formalized anywhere: There is no rule that distributes decision-making positions among the political parties or other power groups.

Following the logic of *lottizzazione,* the editors of the three newscasts of Rai are informally "appointed" by each of the major political parties of both the majority and the opposition, and all of the other major positions within the structure of public service broadcasting are divided among these parties. Every time a new editor of public television newscasts has to be appointed, there is a long and complex process of negotiation among the different parties and within the competing factions of each party. Negotiation becomes even more complex and difficult when the moment arrives to appoint the members of Rai's board of directors. This process receives substantial coverage in the printed press (although less coverage on television), but political parties do not admit any official involvement.

One of the reasons for such a *lottizzazione* is that of mutual control: Sitting at the table where the important decisions are taken is the way in which political parties can control the other competing parties. Indeed, despite the existence of rigid rules (for instance as to the allotment of air time to the competing parties), their respect for each other is very low; therefore mutual control is a way in which to reach an agreement with the other parties about the issues to be debated. Informal negotiations are continuously carried on at the table where representatives of different and competing parties sit. Rules exist, yet they are not respected and do not have universal character. As a result, reciprocal control, carried out in an informal way, is a necessary process.

Of course, such informality and the entire practice of *lottizzazione* also indicate a diffused clientelism that accompanies the low level of rational legal authority: Through *lottizzazione,* political parties distribute the resources they are able to control (jobs, responsible positions, etc.) to their "clients." This allows political parties to ensure their own survival and growth.

The practice of *lottizzazione* is similar to what Kurkchiyan observes in her experiment in the two Russian cities: "In practice, people connected to the councils held an extremely instrumentalist attitude to law. The way that individual members of councils interpreted the law depended either on the political orientations of the conflicting sides or on an openly acknowledged desire to support friends and to keep up personal relationships" (Kurkchiyan 2009: 352).

## *Some possible explanations*

Returning to the four interpretive dimensions proposed in *Comparing Media Systems* (Hallin and Mancini 2004), it could be said that both in Italy and in Russia (as well as in a large number of Mediterranean, Central and Eastern European countries, and elsewhere), news media are not independent from government, the level of professionalization is low, the levels of media instrumentalization and clientelism are high, and the level of rational legal authority is generally low. At a formal level, rules and professional specialization exist, but they do not have universal validity and they are not respected.

Which components of the "air we breathe" make the Italian and Russian situation so similar? Why does the level of rational legal authority appear to be so poor in the Italian and Russian news media? Why is there such a high level of informality that often contrasts with formal proceedings? Some possible explanations may be proposed.

In both countries, the level of identification with the idea of community appears to be very low. Particularism prevails over universalism and the idea of common good is weak or absent. This is one of the findings of Kurkchiyan's study: "The research data could be interpreted as evidence of a broken social consensus on meanings and shared beliefs in the society" (Kurkchiyan 2009: 358). The body that is supposed to be the entity in charge of fastening either rational legal authority or rule of law—the state—is not recognized and legitimized as such. Rational legal authority implies that an authority exists: it is the state, the community. In the cases that have been observed, the absence of rational legal authority means that a state (a shared community) "does not exist," or at least it is not recognized as such (Ginsborg 1998).

This is a very strange paradox in both Italian and Russian history. On the one hand, the state is very important: It is an actor in many different fields; it distributes an enormous amount of resources; and it deeply affects the life of its citizens. On the other hand, its level of legitimation is very low; in Italy, citizens deeply distrust all public institutions (Cassese 1998) and Italy has been described as a "statist society and a society without state" (Malatesta 1996: xix). The diffused distrust in state institutions depends also on the importance of all those networks of particularism, mostly informal networks, which feature the activities of the state itself: These informal networks undermine the identification into a more formal community of people sharing the same rules.

In the same way, a universally recognized community of professionals does not exist in the field of news media. The community of professional journalists does not share a common framework of rules: Even if these rules exist, their universalism is not recognized and particularism prevails. The idea of rational legal authority is low both in society at large and in its constituting systems.

In Russia and Italy, there is no trust in common institutions and the behavior of the elected leaders, and there exists a long history of political polarization. Similar polarization exists within the field of professional journalism. As a result, reporters tend to feel more like advocates than neutral providers of news; They have a high level of partisanship that prevents professionals from identifying themselves with their own community and with the state.

A second component of the "air we breathe" has to do with the professional identity of journalism, which is very weak. The absence or the weakness of professional rules, the fact that informality prevails over formality, and the overlap between professional journalists and other professions (particularly politicians, businessmen, and lobbyists) prevents journalists from feeling a common bond. Italian journalists do not orient their behavior to common norms.

## Conclusion

I have tried to place certain dimensions of media law and governance in comparative perspective and within the discourse of rational legal authority. My intention has been to take into account both formal and informal mandates, and to demonstrate how they can be placed (and explained) within specific social and political cultures. Very often, formalism masks a deeper understanding of the modes by which a profession is structured and governed, and how it is governed. Insight can be gained into significant aspects of law, media and society, including four primary areas of concern for the relationship of the news media to society: the autonomy of news media from government and, more generally, political pressures; the level of professionalization of those acting within the media system; the level of media instrumentalization (the possible interference of external forces on the media system); and the fair distribution of resources to news media (public subsidies, etc.) as opposed to clientelism. By exploring these options further, we could achieve a better understanding of media and democratic practices.

## References

Alexander, J. (1981) 'The mass news media in systemic, historical and comparative perspective,' in E. Katz and T. Szecsko (eds.) *Mass Media and Social Change*, Beverly Hills, CA: Sage.

Anderson, B. (1983) *Imagined Communities*, London: Verso.
Almond, J. G. and Verba, S. (1963) *The Civic Culture. Political Attitudes and Democracy in Five Nations*, Princeton: Princeton University Press.
Banfield, E. (1958) *The Moral Basis of a Backward Society*. Chicago: The Free Press.
Bechelloni, G. (1980) 'The journalist as political client in Italy,' in A. Smith (ed.) *Newspaper and Democracy*. Cambridge: MIT Press.
Bechelloni, G. (1995) *Giornalismo e Post-Giornalismo*, Napoli: Liguori.
Blumler, J. and Gurevitch, M. (1995) *The Crisis of Public Communication*, London: Routledge.
Bourdieu, P. (1993) *The Field of Cultural Production*, New York: Columbia University Press and Cambridge: Polity.
Cassese, S. (1998) *Lo Stato Introvabile*, Roma: Donzelli.
Ciaglia, A. (2011) 'Democrazie in primo piano. Un'analisi comparata del rapporto tra politica e sistema dei media in tre democrazie europee,' Unpublished thesis, Sum, Firenze.
Ginsborg, P. (1998) *L'Italia Del Tempo Presente*, Torino: Einaudi.
Gurevitch, M. and Blumler, J. (2004) 'State of the art of comparative political communication research,' in F. Esser and B. Pfesch (eds.) *Comparing Political Communication*, Cambridge: Cambridge University Press.
Hallin, D. and Papathanassopoulos, S. (2002) 'Political clientelism and the media: Southern Europe and Latin America in comparative perspective,' *Media, Culture and Society*, 24(2): 175–195.
Hallin, D. and Mancini, P. (2004) *Comparing Media Systems. Three Models of Media and Politics*, Cambridge: Cambridge University Press.
Hoggart, R. (1981) 'Foreword,' in Glasgow University Media Group, *Bad News*, London: Routledge and Kegan Paul.
Koltsova, O. (2006) *News Media and Power in Russia*, Abingdon: Routledge.
Krygier, M. (2011) 'Four puzzles about the rule of law: Why, what, where? And who cares?' in J. Fleming (ed.) *Getting to the Rule of Law*, New York and London: New York University Press.
Kurkchiyan, M. (2009) 'Russian legal culture: an analysis of adaptive response to an institutional transplant,' *Law and Social Inquiry*, 34(2): 337–364.
Ledeneva, A. (2004) *How Russia Really Works: The Informal Practices That Shaped Post Soviet Politics and Business*, London: Cornell University Press.
Malatesta, M. (1996) 'Professioni e professionisti,' in M. Malatesta (ed.) *Storia d'Italia. Annali10, I professionisti*, Torino: Einaudi.
Mancini, P. (2000) *Il Sistema Fragile*, Roma: Carocci.
—— (2003) 'Between literary roots and partisanship: journalism education in Italy,' in R. Frohlich and C. Holtz-Bacha (eds.) *Journalism Education in Europe and North America. An International Comparison*, Cresskill: Hampton Press.
Mungiu Pippidi, A. (2010) 'The other transition,' *Journal of Democracy*, 21(1): 120–127.
Ornebring, H. (2009) *The Two Professionalisms of Journalism. Journalism and the Changing Context of Work*, Oxford: Working Paper, The Reuters Institute for the Study of Journalism.
Padovani, C. (2005) *Fatal Attraction. Public Television and Politics in Italy*, Lanham: Rowman and Littlefield Publishing Group.
Pansa, G. (1977) *Comprati e venduti*, Milano: Bompiani.
Pasti, S. (2005) 'Two generations of contemporary Russian journalists,' *European Journal of Communication*, 20(1): 89–115.
Putnam, R. (1993) *Making Democracy Work*, Princeton: Princeton University Press.
Roudakova, N. (2008) 'Media-political clientelism: lessons from anthropology,' *Media, Culture and Society*, 30(1): 41–59.
Schudson, M. (2005) 'Four approaches to the sociology of news,' in J. Curran and M. Gurevitch (eds.) *Mass Media and Society*, London: Hodder Arnold.
Shefter, M (1977) 'Party patronage: Germany, England and Italy,' *Politics & Society*, 7(4): 403–451.
Spencer, M. (1970) 'Weber on legitimate norms and authority,' *The British Journal of Sociology*, 21(2): 123–134.
Verba, S. (1965) 'Comparative political culture,' in L. Pye and S. Verba (eds.) *Political Culture and Political Development*, Princeton: Princeton University Press.
Weber, M. (1980) *Economia e Società*, Torino: Edizioni di Comunità (Italian translation of Wirtschaft und Gesellschaft, Mohr, Tubingen, 1922).

# 3

# "Club government" and independence in media regulation

*Thomas Gibbons*

## Introduction

Independence is a major theme in the contemporary discussion of regulation in general. Indeed, the presence of independent regulators is a defining characteristic of the modern regulatory state. For the media, independent regulation has long been associated with the value attributed to media independence itself and, because that is strongly associated with the democratic process, there has been heightened sensitivity to attempts to manipulate regulation for partisan purposes. This chapter examines the current developments in independent regulation of the media, and its purpose and rationale. In describing the history of media regulation in the United Kingdom, what has been called "club government" becomes significant: a mode of describing the culture of appointment and consensus, and its relationship to independence. Drawing on the UK experience of media regulation, the chapter discusses the tension between independence and accountability in the democratic process. In the light of developments in new media and the general trend towards decentered regulation, it asks whether there is a continued role for independent regulation, and concludes that there is, but not necessarily in its traditional guise. Instead, independent regulation should be considered as a set of principles that should be applied to all media sectors.

## Regulation and independence: The current context

Regulatory independence entails a degree of separation between the enactment of policy and its implementation, by means of institutions that have exclusive responsibility for certain decisions, in the absence of bias on their part, and in the absence of threats or incentives to act differently. The standard rationale for independent regulation, for what is essentially a delegation of power by government, is that the execution of the relevant policy requires expertise, and that it is more efficient to create a special scheme to allow a specialist body, the regulator, to carry it out (Baldwin, Cave and Lodge 2011; Shapiro 2002). In addition, the rise of the so-called "regulatory state" in the 1980s and 1990s, including in Europe and the United Kingdom (Majone 2000; Moran 2003; Baldwin, Cave and Lodge 2011), has been partly characterized by concern with the process of regulation itself; that has included an emphasis on the presence of an independent regulator as a symbol and a reflection of even-handed application of policy. Independent regulatory agencies may be regarded as a demonstration of a credible commitment to a policy, by showing that it will not be vulnerable to short-term changes of political direction (Majone 2000; Thatcher and Stone 2002; Magetti 2007; Harker 2011; Rittberger and Wonka 2011). Regulatory independence provides transparency, professionalism and accountability, which encourages investment and stability.

Independence in regulation is not synonymous with complete autonomy, however, because it has to be understood in terms of the relevant regulatory policy or mandate; these depend on political choices. No regulatory scheme is policy-neutral; its purpose is to shape behavior to achieve public interest goals. Of course, an administrative arrangement for implementing a legislative program may be described in similar terms and the distinction between the two is not always easy to draw. The differences seem to be based on levels of policy detail, the time frame for political change, the range of interests to be balanced and the extent of objectivity in applying the policy. For example, a media policy to promote, say, regional production might be considered to be part of a regulatory scheme if: the relevant legislation reflected the general principle without specifying exactly what was to count as regional production; decisions to allocate resources to such production did not reflect short-term political advantage; action was tailored to particular circumstances; and decision-making was evidence-based and fair. The very use of regulation can be seen, therefore, as the outcome of a "mega-level," virtually constitutional undertaking by politicians to exercise restraint over involvement in policy implementation.

To secure legitimacy and political acceptance for its independent elements, an ideal regulatory scheme has to have a number of attributes: the mandate has to be clear; the regulator's expertise, whether it is technical proficiency in economics and competition (antitrust) or knowledge and experience of an industry, must be evident; appropriate procedures need to be followed; the outcome must be successful; and, importantly, all of those factors must be rendered accountable (Baldwin, Cave and Lodge 2011). As will been seen, whichever methods are adopted to balance these qualities, they often appear to turn on distinguishing the formulation of policy or strategy, which may be regarded as general and political, from day-to-day operational practice, which may be regarded as particular and regulatory. However, the distinction is not clear-cut, and may not even be desirable (see Prosser 2010b). Politicians may set a policy agenda and enshrine it in a legislative mandate, but the success of the policy may well depend on the way in which the mandate is interpreted and applied by the regulator. Politicians will want sufficient scrutiny of the regulator's activities to enable them to retain control over the broad direction of policy. All of these points suggest that the central values of an independent regulatory scheme emphasize process rather than substance. Independence indicates that policy will take effect according to the fair application of established rules by specialists in the field. It does not mean that the rules cannot be reviewed and amended. This, in turn, means that regulatory independence is ultimately precarious and vulnerable to radical political revision.

## Independent media

In addition to the rationales based on expertise and detachment from short-term political influences, independent regulation has been considered to be important because it supports the idea of the independence of the media themselves from government control. Such independence is widely regarded as essential to the well-being of democratic culture: although the media are largely concerned with providing entertainment in the pursuit of commercial success, they also provide a significant channel for disseminating information, conveying opinion and enabling exchanges between individuals and groups. Their potential influence on opinion forming and behavior—whether real or perceived—goes to the core of policy formation, and has a potential impact far beyond the media sector itself. From a democratic perspective, these capacities—to circulate information and to influence opinion—suggest that government should not be able to control media content and should acknowledge that the media have a valuable function in calling government to account.

These ideas are related to two sets of constitutional features associated with Western liberal democracies (see Gibbons 1998). One is the doctrine of freedom of speech (Barendt 2007; Schauer 1982), which holds that, even if speech causes harm, special justification is required for interfering with the exercise of expression. To a greater or lesser extent, the doctrine is incorporated into institutional arrangements, such as the US Constitution's First Amendment or the European Convention on Human Rights, which is enforced in the UK under the Human Rights Act 1998 (Nicol, Millar and Sharland 2009). While the media do not have a privileged status as such—while acknowledging the debate about the meaning of the "free press" clause in the First Amendment (see Schauer 1982)—journalists' contributions are typically given great weight in legislation and adjudication about free speech issues, often resulting in preferential treatment.

The other relevant constitutional dimension is the separation of powers. Under that familiar doctrine, it is held that the principal organs of the state—the legislature, the executive and the judiciary—should be institutionally separated so that they can check and balance each other's exercise of power. However, the doctrine applies to the media only by analogy, on the premise that the media can then be regarded as the "Fourth Estate" of the constitution. That role was asserted for the press only in the nineteenth century (Hampton 2010) and arguably came to fruition in the early twentieth century, in an era of "press barons" who were economically independent of the political parties that had previously dominated the newspaper industry (Curran and Seaton 2009). While it has no institutional basis, the idea of the press as the Fourth Estate has a strong rhetorical appeal, conjuring an image of journalists who are critical "watchdogs" on behalf of society, scrutinizing the exercise of public power and exposing abuse.

This rhetoric has provided a significant political defence against attempts to intervene in press behavior and publishing that go beyond the basic requirements of the general law. For the press, independence has traditionally been associated with the absence of formal regulation. Its existence as financially and corporately separate from government means that it cannot be an unwilling mouthpiece of government. Where special public interests in press activity have been conceded (for example, in relation to accuracy or respect for privacy) a scheme of self-regulation has been regarded as the very badge of separation. Media independence is also highly valued in broadcasting, yet the necessity of total separation from state involvement has not been recognized, because broadcasting serves so many public purposes in which there is a strong democratic interest. As a result, elaborate structures of regulation are required to prevent the government from exerting undue political control over content.

In many ways, the arguments for independent media regulation are little different from those for independent regulation in any sector. In addition to having specialist knowledge of the sector—in this case, the technicalities of communications and the peculiarities of communications markets—the media regulator must have an additional level of expertise: an acute awareness of the democratic significance of media independence and the constitutional implications of regulating the media. Precisely because the media are both a tool of communication and such an inherent part of our cultural and political life (Silverstone 2007), there is a reflexive dimension to media policy: its very shaping can alter the terms of debate about its substance. The dilemma is to know whether a media regulator can be trusted to promote media policies while maintaining a sufficient degree of media independence.

## The evolution of independent media regulation in the UK

The difficulties in achieving an appropriate balance between independence and accountability are well illustrated in the early regulation of public service broadcasting in the United Kingdom and its gradual development into the system of (almost, but not fully) independent regulation that now exists. When the British Broadcasting Corporation (BBC) was established in 1926, it was based on the standard institutional mechanism of the time: the public board—what might be considered an early twentieth-century precursor to the modern regulatory agency. The public board represented public ownership of what was considered public property—namely, the airwaves—which were to be managed in the national interest (see Gibbons 1998). Such boards were not so much regulatory as administrative, reflecting a civil service culture, but they were independent in day-to-day decisions and subject to little formal political supervision. Earlier, the Sykes Committee was concerned that the BBC (at that time a private company) should be completely independent from politics and the Crawford Committee had recommended that its establishment as a public corporation should take place under statute to reflect that. In fact, the government decided to incorporate the BBC under a royal charter, to signal that it was not a "creature of Parliament and connected with political activity" (Briggs 1961: 352–3). Although the government retained control of the underlying policy, by licensing the BBC through a formal agreement to transmit only public service broadcasting, it did not directly interfere with editorial policy.

These arrangements should be interpreted as illustrations of the "club government" approach that characterized much British public administration until the 1980s (see, generally, Moran 2003). Rather like members of a club, politicians and administrators tended to share similar backgrounds and outlooks that were reflected in common understandings about appropriate action—here, how to run a public broadcasting service. As it happened, one person had a major role in shaping those understandings: John Reith, the first Director-General of the BBC. During the General Strike in 1926, he persuaded the government not to use the BBC as a propaganda machine (which it was technically empowered to do), but to allow it to act as a conciliatory force by means of even-handed reporting of both sides to the dispute (Curran and Seaton 2009). That neutral stance developed into undertakings to deal with controversial matters only on an impartial basis and not to editorialize on current affairs or matters of public policy (Gibbons 1998). While it is true that editorial independence was one of the BBC's founding principles, with its journalism based on impartiality and objectivity (Born 2004), that impartiality represented a constraint that it imposed on itself as a defence against political interference.

Nevertheless, Reith was able to consolidate the BBC's practical independence in other ways. The charter placed formal responsibility for programming in the hands of the BBC's board of governors, who were supposed to represent the public interest in the BBC's activities. However, Reith secured an agreement in 1932 (the "Whitley agreement") that the governors' remit would be general and not particular; the execution of policy and general administration of the broadcasting service was to reside with him and his executive (Burns 1977). As a result, although some chairmen of the governors did try to assert a supervisory role, much of the BBC's day-to-day operations were immune to effective internal accountability up to the 1970s.

At the same time, the BBC was frequently subject to political pressure from governments and politicians, who often expected the corporation to behave "responsibly" in representing official interpretations of the public interest (Scannell and Cardiff 1991). Although the BBC successfully defended its position at the time of the Suez crisis (Briggs 1979), the club government style of public administration, in the absence of a full regulatory framework, created uncertainty about its role and obligations, even if that lack of external regulation was also a mark of its independence. During the 1980s, there were a number of disagreements between the government and the BBC over the organization's impartial treatment of sensitive issues such as the Falklands war, the civil unrest in Northern Ireland, and the US air raid on Tripoli in 1986 (Gibbons 1998). In these cases, what protected the BBC's stance was a broad political consensus that the independence of broadcasting should be respected. Where such a consensus does not exist, public service broadcasters are obviously vulnerable to political pressure, recent examples being found in both France and New Zealand (Benson and Powers 2011; Gibbons and Humphreys 2012).

The BBC's institutional independence was, and still is, regarded as an essential element of its editorial autonomy. But that independence had the effect of deflecting scrutiny of its delivery of its public policy goal, public service broadcasting. As indicated, independence may be accepted as legitimate only if adequate systems of accountability are in place. The BBC governors' ability to hold the executive to account was increasingly questioned in the 1990s, a period during which the *raison d'être* for public service broadcasting was challenged by commercial rivals and competition regulators. Following the 2004 Hutton Inquiry, which sharply criticized the BBC's internal supervision and accountability process, the Charter and Agreement of 2006 (Department of Culture, Media and Sport 2006a, 2006b) introduced substantial reform. The governors were replaced with a board of trustees, which sets the overall strategic direction and resources, and an executive board, which has responsibility for delivery of services and operational management. Through the agreement with the government, the BBC Trust issues "service licenses" for programming, establishing the criteria against which the BBC can be judged. The agreement also makes provision for the BBC to submit to Ofcom's jurisdiction in respect of broadcasting standards, except in relation to its editorial independence and impartiality (Gibbons 2012). The result of these changes is that, although the BBC formally retains its institutional independence and, substantively, its editorial independence, it is now effectively regulated by Ofcom. Its board of trustees duplicate many of Ofcom's duties and their role is more symbolic than essential to the BBC's remit. That symbolism should not be underestimated, since it emphasizes the importance of the BBC's editorial values and its public service obligations. But, in terms of this discussion, the point is that the presence of an independent regulator does not compromise the BBC's public purposes, reflecting as they do the media policy commitment to public service broadcasting.

Independent regulation in the UK's commercial sector (known as "independent" television and radio) came much earlier. Initially, a hybrid broadcaster–regulator model was adopted, with the Independent Television Authority (ITA), subsequently the Independent Broadcasting Authority (IBA), being modeled on the BBC, and technically being the broadcaster responsible for programming commissioned from a set of regional production companies. The ITA has been described as the first UK agency based on the US experience with independent regulatory commissions (Baldwin, Cave and Lodge 2011; Prosser 1997), with elements of independence from government in adjudication and in regulation, as well as policy development. But the idea of the ITA as broadcaster really had more features of club government, enabling control over program content (hence taking on an editorial role and enhancing editorial independence) and depicting the supply of programming as a matter of administration (through contracts with the production companies). It was a public corporation, charged with implementing public service broadcasting policy through commercial funding by advertising.

The statutory basis for the ITA underpinned its independence from government. But the novel aspect of commercial television was precisely the presence of the industry in the regulatory landscape and the ITA's independence from that was less clear. At first, the public law implications—that the ITA and IBA were actually allocating public resources as a regulator—were not appreciated (see Lewis 1975). The agency understood its mandate as extending the public service approach of the BBC to the private sector, and that explains the relationship between it and the production companies. In times of financial crisis in the industry, the agency was sometimes depicted as being unwilling to regulate, preferring instead to accommodate companies' demands for concessions (Gibbons 1998). But, rather than seeing itself as being captured by the industry, the agency's emphasis was on doing whatever was necessary to keep the program schedules filled for the benefit of the audiences. From the industry's perspective, this was achieved through the exercise of a very wide discretion to choose (although without sufficient transparency) who would make programs (Prosser 1997; Lewis 1975).

During the mid-1980s through to the early 1990s, the utilities industries in the UK were privatized, with considerable reform of regulation. Because the perceived legalism of the US "commission-style" agency was not wanted (Prosser 1997), individuals were appointed as directors of regulatory agencies (Graham 2000). However, this model was not extended to the media, and the IBA was replaced in 1990 with two similar committee-style agencies, the Independent Television Commission (ITC) and the Radio Authority (RA). Although they appeared similar and had some continuity of approach, regulation of the media changed to more closely reflect the characteristics of a modern regulatory state. The ITC and the RA were quite different in being independent regulators, with the responsibility for delivering programming being placed on the broadcasting companies; the regulators ceased to be their editors and had a more "hands-off" relationship with them in administering the regulatory scheme. The policy mandate for that scheme was much more fully articulated in the relevant statutes, moving away from the club government approach to public service broadcasting policy and reflecting the erosion of a commonality of interest between commercial rivals. The regulators continued to issue codes of practice, as the IBA had done, but they were more detailed and less discretionary. In addition, the regulators were much more clearly amenable to judicial review, and indeed successfully defended a number of challenges to their early licensing decisions, demonstrating their more formal, even legalistic, approach to regulation (Gibbons 1998).

Nevertheless, change was gradual: the early ITC and RA continued the informal and supportive contact with program companies that characterized traditional public service broadcasting, although, by the end of the 1990s, it had become much more formal. The establishment of Ofcom in 2002, with a remit to be a "super-regulator" for all communications industries, under the Communications Act 2003 (Gibbons 2012) consolidated the incremental shift to independent media regulation in the UK. Subsuming the previous regulators for broadcasting, telecommunications and spectrum, Ofcom's statutory basis insulates it from political criticism. The legislation enjoins it to follow what are now accepted to be principles of good regulation: namely, proportionality, consistency, transparency, targeting and accountability (Better Regulation Task Force 2005: Annex B). Ofcom consults widely, and provides generally clear and comprehensive policy direction. Anecdotally, it is widely respected within the industry as an exemplar of good practice. From a commercial perspective, it appears to support the "credible commitment" rationale for independence, but its parallel commitment to freedom of expression in the application of its Broadcasting Code also seems to demonstrate that it values media independence. The latter point is important because, given its apparent success in independent regulation, it might be asked why its remit should not fully extend to the BBC and why a similar model of regulation should not be contemplated for other areas of media activity currently outside its jurisdiction—namely, the press and the Internet. In relation to the BBC, its relationship with Ofcom is exceptional and not exactly logical: It has been able to secure significant institutional autonomy from the standard regulatory scheme by convincing politicians that oversight by a regulator could compromise its editorial independence. Before dealing with possible extensions of the regulator's role, however, a number of pressures against maintaining regulatory independence need to be examined.

## *Indicators of independence*

Independent regulation is desirable because it enables a measured, long-term approach to policy to be developed and it enables specialist expertise to be applied in implementing policy. In the media industries in the UK, the principal areas of policy encompass, broadly, the promotion of: public service broadcasting; media pluralism; the UK content production industry; an effective digital infrastructure; and consumer protection. The regulator's expertise covers the technical aspects of these areas, but, importantly, it also includes a legacy of experience in dealing with problems over a number of decades. In many ways, Ofcom is the sum of its predecessors and that gives it considerable authority. At the same time, that legacy exposes it to charges of institutional inertia and unwillingness to challenge path-dependent evolution of policy. There will naturally be pressure to resist an independent regulator's direction of travel and the important issue to assess is whether attempts to introduce change are effected in a proper way. As already indicated, that requires some balancing of independence against proper accountability. Only in one field of regulatory action is independence generally accepted to be overriding—in the impartial and objective awarding of licenses and adjudication of complaints, grievances and disputes.

Gilardi and Maggetti (2011) have summarized a set of widely recognized indicators that can be used to quantify the degree of independence enjoyed by regulators. Criteria of formal independence include matters such as: the terms of office of the chair and management boards, and the procedures for appointing, renewing and dismissing them; their formal relationship with politicians, including the latter's powers to overturn the regulator's decision; the regulator's organization and finances, including the source of its budgets; and the regulator's formal powers to make rules and to apply sanctions. Observers of regulatory activity have long recognized that the formal position may not reflect the reality of the relationships between regulators, politicians and other stakeholders. As a set of informal indicators of independence from both politicians and "regulatees," Gilardin and Maggetti suggest criteria that include: influence on the size of budgets and the regulator's organization; the frequency of contact between the regulator and politicians or regulatees; the incidence of the "revolving door" (the movement of individuals between the regulatory institution and activity in politics or positions in the industry, and vice versa); and the partisanship of nominations to the chair or management board.

These criteria can assist with empirical quantification of practical understandings and intuitions about the conditions for regulatory independence. However, they must be seen in the context of the regulator's mandate and the amount of discretion which that allows. In addition, and perhaps just as significant—albeit much more difficult to measure—the regulator's freedom of thought and judgement may determine the working relationship with key stakeholders. Whether the regulatory style exhibits features of "club government" (Moran 2003) or of an "epistemic community" (Braithwaite and Drahos 2000), the regulator's ability and willingness to maintain a critical distance from demands about the scope and purposes of regulation—derived respectively from cultural background and education, or from informed consensus in policy circles about preferred solutions—may determine whether independence is enhanced or undermined. Those considerations may suggest why some research finds that a formal structure of independence is likely to be a prerequisite for de facto independence (Hanretty 2011), whereas other work indicates that it is not as important as factors such as the age and maturity of agencies, the presence of many "veto" players in markets (so that no single interest can dominate policy), and the relationship between domestic agencies and international networks of regulators (who may provide external validation of policy) (see Maggetti 2007). In the UK, the factors of particular interest in assessing independence are the exercise of patronage in appointing regulators and their financing, relationships with the industry, interpretation of the regulatory mandate and political influence.

## *Patronage and finance*

The attitudes and values of a regulator are likely to have a significant influence on the way in which a regulatory scheme is implemented in practice. Ultimate responsibility for the appointment of individuals to a regulatory body usually rests with government ministers and that might well be thought appropriate in a democracy. The problem with such a power of patronage is the suspicion that the appointment to office carries with it a set of understandings about the way in which the job will be carried out and that those understandings will favor particular interests. While terms of office may be limited, typically to five years, they may be renewed, so the opportunity for longer-term influence is not diminished. Although the appointment of BBC Governors, and now trustees, has tended to reflect a balance of prominent persons in public life, the political connections of the chairman with the government that appointed him has been of interest and has sometimes been controversial (see Gibbons 1998). Currently, public appointments of this kind in the UK are made through an independent appointments process. There are similar procedures in, for example, Germany and the Scandinavian countries (Bensen and Powers 2011); by contrast, in France, power to appoint the director of the main public service broadcaster has recently been transferred back from the regulator to the president of the republic (Kuhn 2011), signalling a reassertion of political control over the scope of public service in media policy. Politicization of the media continues to exist in Central and Eastern Europe, as much through appointments to regulatory posts as by direct interference in decisions (Martin, Scheuer and Bron 2011).

An independent process has the effect of removing direct political favor from the appointment decision. However, it may be difficult to exclude basic predispositions concerning policy directions: An economically liberalizing government is likely to select regulators who are broadly sympathetic to that approach, other personal attributes and expertise being equal; an interventionist government might do the opposite. Given the highly structured nature of decision-making in an independent regulator, the influence of such predispositions might be difficult to detect. When Ofcom was being established, it appeared to have a high proportion of members with a background in economics and competition regulation (see Smith 2006). Its early pronouncements often reflected a "consumer" rather than "citizen" perspective (Livingstone, Lunt and Miller 2007; Gibbons 2005), leading to concerns that it was not sufficiently committed to the public interest goals within its remit. Arguably, it now has a more balanced approach, but it is difficult to judge whether that is attributable to subsequent changes in personnel or its own self-awareness of the requirements of its mandate. Here, one factor that should be borne in mind is the working culture of the regulator and the influence of its traditional values and procedures: it may not be easy for a new appointment to introduce change.

However they are appointed, regulators' scope for independent action is constrained by their budget. The size of the budget will determine the priorities and extent of regulatory activity. At one end of a spectrum, a regulator may be confined to "firefighting" and reacting only to major complaints. At the other end, a regulator may be able to conduct research, plan strategically and operate a sophisticated enforcement process. In the UK, although it is a system of self-regulation, the underfunding of the Press Complaints Commission by the industry is cited as a major reason for its ineffectiveness; in contrast, Ofcom has the resources to maintain a comprehensive oversight of the communications sector. The predictability of funding is also very important: to be independent, a regulator cannot be vulnerable to frequent changes to allocated budgets, especially if these are in response to critical reviews by politicians or stakeholders. Analogous, although it is not directly a matter of regulation, the predictability of the license fee as a stable source of the BBC's funding has long been regarded as being critical to the longevity of public service broadcasting as a policy. The license fee is not a tax (even if it is perceived to be so by many), so is distanced from direct political determination, and is typically settled over a period of five years or more. As a regulator, Ofcom's position is safeguarded through a statutory requirement to ensure that its revenue fully covers the costs of regulation, and to raise from each of the television, radio and networks and services sectors its best estimate of the cost of regulating each sector for the year ahead. It is therefore self-financing, with its level of finances being directly related to the scope of the activity that it wishes to pursue, constrained only by its policy to administer its tariffs fairly and equitably and with the minimum burden on stakeholders.

### *Independence from industry*

The principal rationale for having a separate regulatory agency is its expertise and knowledge of the industry. But that very closeness to the industry makes the agency vulnerable to "capture" (Baldwin, Cave and Lodge 2011; Magetti 2007), whereby it aligns itself with those it is supposed to regulate (Stigler 1971). While there is much speculation about this possibility, the evidence for capture is equivocal, both generally (Carrigan and Coglianese 2011) and in relation to media regulation (on the FCC, see Napoli 1998). Apart from the existence of formal oversight and accountability mechanisms, the political salience of media policy and the varied nature of the media landscape, with so many different firms and institutions pressing for their own agendas, mean that it is unlikely that any one interest could dominate policy. Although there may be no evidence of systematic capture, however, the possibility of a regulator being influenced by a particular industry concern remains (Magetti 2007).

Still, that is more likely to be explained by a coincidence of viewpoint rather than capture. As indicated above, the early presence in Ofcom of individuals sympathetic to liberalizing economic theory (see Redding 2006) was thought to have made the regulator more amenable to "lighter touch" approaches from the industry. That appeared to manifest itself in its early analysis of the public service broadcasting brief (Gibbons 2005). Under a different chief executive, Ofcom has appeared more sensitive to public service arguments (Ofcom 2009). However, in both circumstances, any tendency to an ideological stance could only have an impact on the tone of policy, because the sustainability of public service content is built into the Ofcom mandate. Anticipation of the possible conflicts within the organization between the liberalizing trend in telecommunications and spectrum regulation, on the one hand, and interventionism in public service and standards regulation, on the other, led to a structural mechanism (the content board) to be created as part of Ofcom's constitution. More generally, "viewpoint" capture may be a greater risk than industry capture. A regulator such as Ofcom inevitably has close connections with the "policy community" both in the UK and at European level. There is indeed an "epistemic" community (Braithwaite and Drahos 2000) of lobbyists, policymakers and academics, who regularly meet at conferences and consultation events. Ofcom is more likely to be a leader than a follower in contemporary policy direction, but the risk is that a consensus of received wisdom may become dominant in that community and thereby influence the regulator.

Prior to Ofcom, the ITC and the RA were sometimes accused of having been captured by the industry when they made decisions that appeared to be weak (for example, when companies experienced financial difficulties, the ITC and the RA often were willing to alter license conditions to reduce public service commitments rather than to enforce the original terms). It is also possible to see this as an example of pragmatism rather than capture: Regulators have paid genuine attention to structural problems in the industry and have decided to prioritize the continued provision of a slightly reduced service rather than force a company to cease trading.

In the UK, the best evidence of capture is not found in the formal system of communications regulation, but in the self-regulated scheme operated by the press. Indeed, as will be discussed below, the lack of independence of the self-regulator has been a significant factor in the failure of the scheme to be effective in dealing with serious breaches of law and ethics.

## *Interpreting the mandate*

Independent regulation implies that the regulator has the discretion to determine how policy is implemented. The breadth of that discretion depends on the policy mandate in the relevant legal framework. In the UK, as indicated, the institutional responsibility of the BBC to define public service broadcasting was transferred to the early broadcasting regulators. Their interpretation of that mandate was articulated a little more explicitly for the ITC and RA, and was much more comprehensively laid out in Ofcom's remit, coinciding with a much sharper description of the BBC's duties in its current charter and agreement. Essentially, what legislators have done is to incorporate the practice and experience of earlier regulation into the current scheme: they have ratified the original discretion into a set of precepts and criteria from which the regulator would be unlikely to dissent. For Ofcom, the legacy broadcasting mandate has been supplemented by requirements for telecommunications and spectrum allocation (largely derived from the EU's Communications Framework), together with various principles of good regulation. The effect has been to increase Ofcom's discretion because its remit includes a wide range of duties, some of which are in tension, and it has to prioritize and resolve that conflict. They all flow from Ofcom's principal duty: "to further the interests of citizens in relation to communications matters" and "to further the interests of consumers in relevant markets, where appropriate by promoting competition." Thus, in carrying out its functions under the Communications Act 2003, Ofcom is required to secure the following general objectives:

i. the optimal use of wireless spectrum;
ii. the availability throughout the UK of a wide range of electronic communications services;

iii. the availability throughout the UK of a wide range of television and radio services of high quality and appealing to a variety of tastes and interests;
iv. the maintenance of a sufficient plurality of providers of different services;
v. the application of standards to protect the public from offensive and harmful material and from unfair treatment or intrusions into privacy; and
vi. the best regulatory practice.

These substantive criteria are supplemented by a duty to "have regard in all cases" to the desirability of having public service broadcasting, competition in relevant markets, facilitating self-regulation, encouraging investment and innovation, guaranteeing freedom of expression, protecting the vulnerable and preventing crime (see Gibbons 2012). In implementing these duties, Ofcom has adopted the practice, in some cases enjoined by the statute, to consult stakeholders and to publish the principles under which it will operate. Discretion is tempered, therefore, with the assurances about reasonable expectations.

Ofcom's function is to act both as an external constraint on industry activities and to promote particular social policies. This follows the longstanding tradition of UK media regulation (Gibbons 1998). Prosser has recently described these functions as, respectively, "control" and "enterprise" roles, and as actually being characteristic of regulation more generally (Prosser 2010a). To take up a point made earlier, it may not be appropriate for a regulator to be independent, in the sense of being completely detached from policy; a regulator must be enterprising, in Prosser's sense, to carry out its mandate. The problem is deciding how to do that without crossing the line into what politicians consider to be their responsibility for original policy creation.

The difficulty was illustrated by reactions to Ofcom's Public Service Broadcasting Review in 2009, mentioned earlier. Taking a broad view, Ofcom realized that media convergence and digital switchover would lead to major changes in the public service broadcasting market with important implications for the way in which it would have to be funded in the future. It therefore suggested options for reform in addition to analyzing the contemporary situation. This was apparently not well received at the Department of Culture, Media and Sport, which set up a convergence think tank to explore broadly similar issues, albeit without the prospect of discovering anything new about an already well-explored topic. The episode was considered by many to be a warning to Ofcom that it was exceeding its remit. In fact, it showed that Ofcom was indeed the expert and that political initiative was lacking. However, it also illustrated the delicate nature of the independent regulator's position, underscoring the politicians' view that the regulator's proper role, when thinking creatively, is only to give advice (on this point, see also Hanretty 2010). Yet it would be inappropriate for a regulator to withhold its expert judgement out of undue deference to politicians' sensitivities. Ofcom may well agree because, in some of its more recent interventions, it has finessed the dilemma by analyzing the problem and the need for policy change, but then explicitly and publicly referring it to the minister (for example the need to revisit media pluralism rules, in the course of an assessment of News Corporation's proposed complete purchase of BSkyB: Ofcom 2010).

By contrast, a clear mandate to exercise discretion can have the effect of undermining politicians' desired outcomes. When the ITC implemented a then-radical scheme to award commercial broadcasting licenses by competitive tendering in the early 1990s, it adopted a broad interpretation of the minimum qualification threshold, to secure that public service would not be compromised. As a result, a number of companies that had hoped to take advantage of the newly liberalized regulatory regime did not obtain franchises. This caused much discontent amongst politicians, including the prime minister, but the ITC's methodology and decisions proved to be robust when challenged for judicial review (see Gibbons 1998). On one view, this could be seen as non-democratic, but there was no attempt by politicians to alter the outcomes by retrospective legislation.

### Political involvement in decisions

There has been relative freedom from interference in the regulator's activities in UK regulation. At a briefing to the Leveson Inquiry, which was established in 2011 to examine the culture, practice and ethics of the press in the UK, the chief executive of Ofcom emphasized that the regulator's statutory independence is supported by political acceptance of its status. "That independence in my experience is guarded jealously by everybody at the top of Ofcom. Indeed, the entire senior management cohort regard it as something that is a matter of absolute integrity . . . My experience has been . . . that both current government and the previous government have studiously honoured our independence on all matters. And in fact it has only ever required me to mention independence and the Government will say, 'Yes, you are absolutely right.' " (Leveson 2012). For all that, both formally and informally, some anomalies remain. Politicians cannot bring themselves to withdraw all means of control over the media, most likely because they continue to believe strongly that the media have the power to shape their destinies.

One of the most remarkable residual measures is a direct power of censorship. Under the Communications Act 2003 (s. 336) and the BBC's agreement (BBC 2006b, clause 81), a minister may impose a direction to include an announcement in a service or to refrain from including specified material. The broadcaster's only form of resistance is that it may include an announcement that material has been included or excluded at the minister's insistence. While such a provision, which dates back to early broadcasting regulation, would now be very controversial, and is justified as being for use only in situations of emergency, it clearly has considerable symbolic significance.

Less surprising, because it does not directly affect editorial responsibility, but also contentious, because it seems to be inconsistent with independent regulation, is a series of provisions, under the Communications Act 2003 (and also in the BBC's agreement), which require ministers to be consulted or to approve decisions about regulatory matters. To provide a flavor, the range of powers includes appointments to Ofcom committees, intervention in spectrum allocation for national security or public health reasons, oversight of compliance with international obligations, designation of universal service obligations and what counts as significant market power, certain appointments to Channel 4, European programming and independent production quotas, the extension of Channel 3 licenses in connection with the digital switchover, the scope of regulation of the BBC by Ofcom, aspects of advertising regulation, and approval of media mergers. Of course, there may be arguments in favor of ministerial oversight. The interests of democracy and government may extend beyond the core issues in the particular sector (for example, the survival of an industry embodies issues of industrial and regional policy as well as cultural policy (see Dabbah 2011)). But the list of retained powers in the UK seems rather long and may be interpreted not so much an indication of the need for accountability, as a political lack of trust in the regulator.

In practice, the existence of such powers may create a more insidious risk. This is because they imply that the regulator should consult with the minister in the course of regulating in the relevant area (see also Graham 2000). There is the opportunity, therefore, for informal pressure to be exerted. Arguably, this reflects only the tradition of club government in the UK, for there have long been informal liaison meetings that bring together regulators and government departments. Despite the creation of Ofcom, old habits linger on, but the difference is that the regulator is sufficiently independent to be a much more equal partner in such dialog. Indeed such channels of communication may favor the regulator. During the passage of the Broadcasting Act 1990, the IBA and the ITC (in "shadow" form, whereby the organization had been set up in advance, in anticipation of legislative ratification) had an important role in shaping the legislation. The same was true of the "shadow" Ofcom when the Communications Act 2003 was being discussed. Politicians may be content to defer to expert views about the feasibility of their ideas.

The most controversial role for politicians in the UK in recent years has concerned the approval of media mergers. This has historically been a politician's reserved power (Gibbons 1998) and similar provision was made in a scheme introduced by Part V of the Communications Act 2003. Although that assimilated media mergers to the general mergers regime, under which the competition regulators determine relevant competition issues, it also made provision for discretionary ministerial intervention if it is believed that a merger raises public interest matters relating to pluralism. Following such a public interest intervention, Ofcom is asked to report on the circumstances, but it has only an advisory role. The minister has a further discretion whether to refer the case to the Competition Commission and, if so, whether to accept its recommendations. Given the formalizing of the competition rules and the general trend towards independence in regulation, it was widely considered that ministers would routinely refer such cases to the regulators. That is what happened when BSkyB was required to reduce the size of its significant interest in the main commercial terrestrial broadcaster ITV (see Craufurd Smith 2009). However, in another case involving News Corporation's wish to take full ownership of BSkyB, Ofcom reported that the proposed acquisition could operate against the public interest. Controversially, the minister did not refer the matter to the Competition Commission and allowed an informal process of negotiation to take place to accommodate pluralism concerns. It seems certain that the takeover would have been approved, but for the revelation that the *News of the World* newspaper, owned by News International and in turn controlled by News Corporation, had been involved in systematic telephone hacking to obtain stories. In the wake of that revelation, and the establishment of the Leveson Inquiry into press standards, News Corporation withdrew its bid.

As the Leveson Inquiry proceeded, details of connections between politicians and News Corporation emerged. They included a link between the company and the minister who had declined to make the BSkyB public interest referral. Ironically, he had earlier mused whether "it is appropriate for politicians to have the final say" (Hunt 2011). Not all politicians disagree: A parliamentary report recommended that ministers should be removed from the process (House of Lords Select Committee on Communications 2008). Yet it seem likely that the government will resist such a move, arguing that the problem is not that a politician is involved in media pluralism decisions, but that the process should be transparently free from bias.

A subsequent development suggests that, even if politicians were to remove themselves from media merger decisions, there will continue to be political pressure on such issues and the regulator will have to take the brunt of that. As a consequence of the *News of the World* telephone-hacking scandal, Ofcom decided under the Broadcasting Act 1990 to investigate whether BSkyB is a "fit and proper person" to own a broadcasting license, given that News Corporation has a 39 percent stake in it. Keen to make political capital, two political parties expressed the hope that the investigation would be expedited. But Ofcom indicated that its review, which has now decided in BSkyB's favour, would take "as long as it takes" (BBC 2012; Ofcom 2012).

While the removal of most political oversight may be desirable, one side effect may be to pass supervision on to the courts. As already indicated, recent reform of the UK competition law regime removed the minister's role in competition enforcement. It has been suggested that this may serve as an invitation to the courts to impose a high level of scrutiny on the regulator to ensure that it is fulfilling its mandate (see Harker, Peyer and Wright 2011). In the broadcasting field in the UK, however, judicial review has tended to be deferential to the regulator's expertise (Gibbons 1998). At the same time, regulators have been keen to ensure that they comply with administrative law procedures. Judicial review may be a mixed blessing: it may substitute process values for substantive expertise, but it may also prevent abuse of power (Shapiro 2002) and may help to rein in agencies with political appointees, such as in the litigation following the Federal Communication Commission's attempts to reform ownership regulation in the United States (Gibbons and Humphreys 2012)).

## New media and new forms of regulation

Even as the value of independence has become accepted as a key characteristic of media regulation, developments in the industry have challenged the continued relevance of the traditional model. Convergence between media platforms, transnational distribution of content and a shift in relationships with content producers, from audience to "user" behavior, have led to a greater emphasis on choice and interactivity in media engagement. The presence of a regulatory agency, exercising "command and control" regulation, no longer seems appropriate to such developments. There has been a strong trend towards experimenting with "hybrid" models of regulation (Murray and Scott 2002) that draw on self-regulation, education and the architecture of content distribution. This trend is a reflection of a much wider movement towards "decentered regulation" (Black 2001) or "new governance" (Carrigan and Coglianese 2011). The implications of this movement are not necessarily deregulatory; rather, that new ways of protecting public policy concerns about industry activity must be found.

From the perspective of independent regulation, the difficulty with this tendency towards less structured regulation is that it invariably requires greater trust to be placed on the relevant industry to fulfill public purposes. For the media, it appears to reinforce the unregulated position of the press, and it counsels against extending regulation to new areas of activity such as the Internet or mobile applications. In the UK at least, experience of press self-regulation has not proven to be entirely effective. One of the principal reasons for the failure is the lack of independence in the current scheme operated by the Press Complaints Commission (PCC). The PCC is financed by the publishing industry, and consists of a panel of editors and members of the public who apply a code of practice drawn up by a committee of editors. It does not have any powers of sanction, but can request a newspaper to publish an adverse adjudication, and it generally attempts to resolve complaints through mediation. Rather than being a regulator, the PCC is little more than a presentational arrangement to forestall statutory intervention.

The PCC's lack of independence has been heavily criticized (Media Standards Trust 2009). In the light of the telephone-hacking scandal and the review of the press by the Leveson Inquiry, it seems desirable and likely that it will be replaced by a new scheme. If that is a self-regulatory scheme, whether it will be properly independent will depend on whether the industry is willing to submit itself to a set of principles that are largely opposed to its own interests; given the decline in newspaper circulation, expenditure on good journalism may not be a priority. The success of a self-regulatory scheme is closely related to the coincidence of interest between industry goals and public purposes. That is one reason why the UK advertising industry's approach, implemented by the Advertising Standards Authority, which celebrated its fiftieth anniversary in 2012, is highly respected: Both advertisers and the public have an interest in advertising being "legal, decent, honest and truthful" (Advertising Standards Authority 2012). In the case of the press, introducing a strong measure of independence in its regulation would go some way towards rebuilding public trust in it.

Having industry involvement in regulation does have advantages: The industry has information and experience; its processes can be more flexible; it can legitimize regulatory constraints on firms' behavior; and it can identify effective sanctions and ensure compliance. One way of securing those benefits, whilst guarding against unwillingness or inability to secure public policy objectives, is to adopt a scheme of co-regulation, whereby an independent regulator oversees the sector's participation (see Hans-Bredow-Institut 2006). In the UK media, there are two main examples in which Ofcom has delegated its powers, but retained the ability to intervene: broadcast advertising regulation, which is operated by the Advertising Standards Authority; and video-on-demand regulation, which is operated by the Authority; for Television On-Demand (ATVOD). In both areas, however, co-regulation represents a modification of the traditional model, a gradual relinquishing of control. To extend it to new areas of media would entail a level of intervention that may be politically unacceptable and practically difficult. In that case, the outcome is likely to be a relatively uncoordinated set of piecemeal measures. An example, albeit relating to child protection, would be the EU's Safer Internet Programme, which attempts to combine national criminal laws with industry codes of practice, technical initiatives such as content filtering and media literacy.

## Independence as a regulatory value

Before the development of highly structured independent media regulation in the UK, the club government approach to broadcasting regulation reflected a broad consensus about regulatory objectives. The rise of the regulatory state, with its characteristic presence of independent regulators, was connected to a breakdown in that consensus and the need formally to mediate between competing interests. But one value that has endured is the importance of independence in regulating media. In the past, that value has been associated with particular institutional frameworks for particular sectors of the media, a trait that is less apposite for the more fragmented setting of new forms of media. However, if it is acknowledged that there are public interests in new media activity, perhaps coinciding with a new recognition of such interests in traditional media, is there scope for securing them independently in ways that do not require traditional formal arrangements, but which are not defined by the industry?

As an idea and a practice, independent regulation is now sufficiently well established to be able to draw a number of principles from it. It should provide expert consideration, in a measured way, of the best way in which to implement politically agreed policies, free from self-serving pressures from both politicians and the industry. One way of thinking about independent regulation in any media context is to focus on such underlying principles and not their institutional manifestation. While they apply to any form of regulation, those principles are especially important for the media because of their close association with policy formation. The importance of an independent assessment of issues and policy options does not entail that a regulator such as Ofcom should take direct responsibility for them, but a focus on independent media regulation suggests that the system has to have the attributes of a good regulator.

One can envisage different areas of decentered regulation, perhaps with different combinations of media industry groups responding to users' concerns. However, some form of coordination would be desirable, to ensure common practice and to share experience, and, ultimately, to ensure the independence of different schemes. Indeed, one of the implications of accepting that good regulation is independent regulation is that the decentering of regulation cannot go too far. It hardly seems appropriate to leave coordination to the political process; equally, some control over self-regulatory initiatives seems necessary. Ofcom's chief executive has recently suggested a set of core features that should be part of any regulatory system that is effective and has public trust in the new media environment. They include clearly defined regulatory objectives, independence from political influence and those regulated, independent budgetary control, genuine powers of investigation, clear and transparent processes, effective powers of enforcement and sanction, clear public accountability and accessibility to the public (Richards 2012). Few might quarrel with these features, but the difficulty is to enforce those precepts while recognizing the value of hybrid solutions to substantive problems. For them to be recognized as legitimate, and to be effective, they require at least a framework in law. To implement that, analogous to the idea of enforced self-regulation (Ayres and Braithwaite 1992), an approach of "enforced independent regulation" might be an appropriate way of enabling legal intervention in all areas of media activity, but only for the purpose of requiring the establishment of independent schemes to protect relevant public interests (as accepted in articulation of policy through the political process). In such an approach, an overarching regulator would be needed, but its role would evolve to one that is different from, say, Ofcom's in the UK, with a greater emphasis on stipulating good practice and a greater concern with independence in good governance and process. At the same time, there would still be a role for an independent body that could identify the substance of the public interest in media, whether it be the promotion of free speech, pluralism of content, protection of the vulnerable, cultural experience, connectivity, access to services, or media literacy.

The idea of independent media regulation has matured to the stage at which it can now provide considerable confidence that regulation itself need not be a threat to the media's editorial independence. That does not mean that interference in media activity should become any easier. But where there are public aspirations for that activity, whether in the traditional media or in the new, the principles of independent regulation can provide some assurance that they will be respected.

## References


Advertising Standards Authority (2012) *CAP Code*. Online. Available HTTP: http://www.cap.org.uk/The-Codes/CAP-Code.aspx?q=CAP%20Code%20new_General%20Sections_01%20Compliance#c6 (accessed 25 May 2012).

Ayres, I. and Braithwaite, J. (1992) *Responsive Regulation*, Oxford: Oxford University Press.

Baldwin, R., Cave, M. and Lodge, M. (2011) *Understanding Regulation: Theory, Strategy and Practice*, 2nd edn., Oxford: Oxford University Press.

Barendt, E. (2007) *Freedom of Speech*, 2nd edn., Oxford: Oxford University Press.

Benson, R. and Powers, M. (2011) 'Public media and political independence: Lessons for the future of journalism from around the world,' *Free Press*. Online. Available HTTP: http://www.savethenews.org/sites/savethenews.org/files/public-media-and-political-independence.pdf (accessed 25 May 2012).

Better Regulation Task Force (2005) *Regulation—Less is More: Reducing Burdens, Improving Outcomes* (the Arculus Report). Online. Available HTTP: http://www.bis.gov.uk/files/file22967.pdf (accessed 25 May 2012).

Black, J. (2001) 'Decentring regulation: Understanding the role of regulation and self-regulation in a "post-regulatory" world,' *Current Legal Problems*, 54 (1): 103–147.

Born, G. (2004) *Uncertain Vision: Birt, Dyke and the Reinvention of the BBC*, London: Secker & Warburg.

Braithwaite, J. and Drahos, P. (2000) *Global Business Regulation*, Cambridge: Cambridge University Press.

Briggs, A. (1961) *The History of Broadcasting in the United Kingdom, Vol. I: The Birth of Broadcasting*, Oxford: Oxford University Press.

—— (1979) *The History of Broadcasting in the United Kingdom, Vol. IV: Sound and Vision*, Oxford: Oxford University Press.

British Broadcasting Corporation (2012) 'Ofcom "won't be rushed" on BSkyB licence decision.' Online. Available HTTP: http://www.bbc.co.uk/news/uk-17919134 (accessed 25 May 2012).

Burns, T. (1977) *The BBC: Public Institution and Private World*, London: Macmillan.

Carrigan, C. and Coglianese, C. (2011) 'The politics of regulation: From new institutionalism to new governance,' *Annual Review of Political Science,* 14: 107–129.

Craufurd Smith, R. (2009) 'Media ownership and the public interest: The case of Virgin Media, British Sky Broadcasting and its ITV shares,' *Journal of Media Law,* 1: 21–36.

Curran, J. and Seaton, J. (2009) *Power without Responsibility: Press, Broadcasting and the Internet in Britain*, 7th edn., London: Routledge.

Dabbah, M. M. (2011) 'The relationship between competition authorities and sector regulators,' *Cambridge Law Journal*, 70(1): 113–143.

Department for Culture, Media and Sport (2006a) *Copy of Royal Charter for the continuance of the British Broadcasting Corporation*, Cm. 6925, London: HMSO.

—— (2006b) *An Agreement between Her Majesty's Secretary of State for Culture, Media and Sport and the British Broadcasting Corporation*, Cm. 6872, London: HMSO.

Doyle, G. (2002) *Understanding Media Economics*, London: Sage.

Gibbons, T. (1998) *Regulating the Media*, 2nd edn., London: Sweet and Maxwell.

—— (2005) 'Competition policy and regulatory style: Issues for OFCOM,' *info*, 7(5): 42–51.

—— (2012) *Media Law in the United Kingdom*, The Hague: Kluwer Law International.

—— and Humphreys, P. (2012) *Audiovisual Regulation under Pressure: Comparative Cases from North America and Europe*, London and New York: Routledge.

Gilardi, F. and Maggetti, M. (2011) 'The independence of regulatory authorities,' in D. Levi-Faur (ed.) *Handbook on the Politics of Regulation*, Cheltenham: Edward Elgar.

Graham, C. (2000) *Regulating Public Utilities: A Constitutional Approach*, Oxford: Hart Publishing.

Hampton, M. (2010) 'The Fourth Estate ideal in journalism history,' in S. Allan (ed.) *The Routledge Companion to News and Journalism*, London: Routledge.

Hanretty, C. (2010) 'Explaining the de facto independence of public broadcasters,' *British Journal of Political Science*, 40(1): 75–89.

Hans-Bredow-Institut (2006) *Final Report: Study on Co-regulation Measures in the Media Sector*, Study for the European Commission, Directorate Information Society and Media, Brussels. Online. Available HTTP: http://ec.europa.eu/avpolicy/docs/library/studies/coregul/final_rep_en.pdf (accessed 25 May 2012).

Harcourt, A. (2005) *The European Union and the Regulation of Media Markets*, Manchester: Manchester University Press.

Harker, M., Peyer, S. and Wright, K. (2011) 'Judicial scrutiny of merger decisions in the EU, UK and Germany,' *International & Comparative Law Quarterly,* 60(1): 93–124.

House of Lords Select Committee on Communications (2008) *The Ownership of the News, Volume I: Report*, HL Paper 122-I, London: HMSO. Online. Available HTTP: http://www.publications.parliament.uk/pa/ld200708/ldselect/ldcomuni/122/122i.pdf (accessed 25 May 2012).

Hunt, J. (2011) 'Boldness be my friend', Speech to Royal Television Society Cambridge Convention, 14 September. Online. Available HTTP: http://www.culture.gov.uk/news/ministers_speeches/8428.aspx (accessed 25 May 2012).

Leveson Inquiry (2012) 'Briefing Session 3: Regulatory Systems', Regulatory Systems Briefing 5 October 2011, 29. Online. Available HTTP: http://www.levesoninquiry.org.uk/news-and-events/briefing-sessions/briefing-session-3-regulatory-systems (accessed 25 May 2012).

Lewis, N. (1975) 'The IBA contract awards,' *Public Law*, 20: 317–340.

Livingstone, S., Lunt, P. and Miller, L. (2007) 'Citizens and consumers: Discursive debates during and after the Communications Act 2003,' *Media, Culture and Society*, 29(4): 613–638.

Maggetti, M. (2007) 'De facto independence after delegation: A fuzzy-set analysis,' *Regulation and Governance,* 1(4): 271–294.

Majone, G. (2000) 'The credibility crisis of community regulation,' *Journal of Common Market Studies*, 38(2): 273–302.

Martin, B., Scheuer, A. and Bron, C. (eds.) (2011) *The Media in South-East Europe: A Comparative Media Law and Policy Study*, Sofia: Friedrich Ebert Stiftung. Online. Available HTTP: http://www.fes.bg/files/custom/library/2011/The%20Media%20in%20South-East%20Europe.pdf (accessed 25 May 2012).

Media Standards Trust (2009) *A More Accountable Press, Part 1: The Need for Reform: Is Self-Regulation Failing the Press and the Public?* Online Available HTTP: http://mediastandardstrust.org/projects/press-self-regulation (accessed 25 May 2012).

Moran, M. (2003) *The British Regulatory State: High Modernism and Hyper-Innovation*, Oxford: Oxford University Press.

Murray, A. and Scott, C. (2002) 'Controlling the new media: Hybrid responses to new forms of power,' *Modern Law Review*, 65(4): 491–516.

Napoli, P. (1998) 'Government assessment of FCC performance: Recurring patterns and implications for recent reform efforts,' *Telecommunications Policy*, 22(4/5): 409–418.

Nicol, A., Millar, G. and Sharland, A. (2009) *Media Law and Human Rights*, 2nd edn., Oxford: Oxford University Press.

Ofcom (2009) *Putting Viewers First: Second Public Service Broadcasting Review*. Online. Available HTTP: http://stakeholders.ofcom.org.uk/binaries/consultations/psb2_phase2/statement/psb2statement.pdf (accessed 25 May 2012).

—— (2010) *Report on Public Interest Test on the Proposed Acquisition of British Sky Broadcasting Group plc by News Corporation*. Online. Available HTTP: http://stakeholders.ofcom.org.uk/binaries/consultations/public-interest-test-nov2010/statement/public-interest-test-report.pdf (accessed 25 May 2012).

—— (2012) *Fit and Proper Assessment of BSkyB*. Online. Available HTTP: http://stakeholders.ofcom.org.uk/broadcasting/tv/fit-and-proper/BSkyB/ (accessed 26 September 2012).

Prosser, T. (1997) *Law and the Regulators*, Oxford: Oxford University Press.

—— (2010a) *The Regulatory Enterprise*, Oxford: Oxford University Press.

—— (2010b) 'Models of economic and social regulation,' in D. Oliver, T. Prosser and R. Rawlings (eds.) *The Regulatory State: Constitutional Implications*, Oxford: Oxford University Press.

Redding, D. (2006) 'The non-democratic regulator: A response to Sylvia Harvey,' *Screen*, 47(1): 107–111.

Richards, E. (2012) 'Speech to the Oxford Media Convention', 25 January 2012. Online. Available HTTP: http://media.ofcom.org.uk/2012/01/25/speech-to-the-oxford-media-convention/ (accessed 25 May 2012).

Rittberger, B. and Wonka, A. (2011) 'Introduction: Agency governance in the European Union,' *Journal of European Public Policy*, 18(6): 780–789.

Rizzuto, F. (2010) 'Reforming the "constitutional fundamentals" of the European Union telecommunications regulatory framework,' *Computer and Telecommunications Law Review*, 16(2): 44–56

Scannell, P. and Cardiff, D. (1991) *A Social History of British Broadcasting, Vol. I 1922–1939: Serving the Nation*, Oxford: Basil Blackwell.

Schauer, F. (1982) *Free Speech: A Philosophical Enquiry*, Cambridge: Cambridge University Press.

Shapiro, M. (2002) 'Judicial delegation doctrines: The US, Britain and France,' *West European Politics*, 25(1): 173–199.

Silverstone, R. (2007) *Media and Modernity: On the Rise of the Mediopolis*, Cambridge: Polity.

Smith, P. (2006) 'The politics of UK television policy: The making of Ofcom,' *Media, Culture & Society*, 28(6): 929–940.

Stigler, G. (1971) 'The theory of economic regulation,' *The Bell Journal of Economics and Management Science*, 2(1): 3–21.

Thatcher, M. and Stone Sweet, A. (2002) 'Theory and practice of delegation to non-majoritarian institutions,' *West European Politics*, 25(1):1–22.

4

# Mainstreaming EU cultural policies internally and externally

## Caught between subsidiarity and global subsidiarity?

*Jan Loisen, Caroline Pauwels and Karen Donders*

### Introduction

Global media policy is a contentious domain of policymaking, especially in the European Union, where one seeks to balance cultural and economic aspects of audiovisual goods and services. The EU and its member states have struggled to deal with the treatment of hybrid cultural and economic policy domains such as the audiovisual sector along subsidiarity lines. Equally, they have struggled to balance powers of the EU member states, and the European Commission, Courts and Parliament along the same subsidiarity lines.

Internally, the EU pushed a process of liberalization through harmonization—for example in the realm of television regulation (Katsirea 2008)—and by applying competition rules to constrain film subsidies and support public service broadcasting (Donders 2012). These actions have provoked member state resistance: they have argued that media is a competence of the member states. In this context, and as a response to fears of a dramatic increase of competences and power of the European Community, the subsidiarity principle was introduced in the 1992 Maastricht Treaty. Put simply, the subsidiarity principle means that policy actions and decisions should be taken at the lowest policy level possible; the EU shall take action only when the proposed action cannot be realized by member states. Needless to say, subsidiarity implies a difficult balancing act in the case of trade and culture issues, where EU competences meet those of the member states. Although subsidiarity at first sight seems straightforward—member state action is the rule and EU intervention the exception—its articulation in practice is ambiguous and uncertain (Carozza 2003). Subsidiarity can be seen as both a rule and a principle. The "rule," in terms of a direct and formal reference to subsidiarity, was defined in Article 3b of the Maastricht Treaty as follows:

> The Community shall act within the limits of the powers conferred upon it by this Treaty and of the objectives assigned to it therein.
>
> In areas which do not fall within its exclusive competence, the Community shall take action, in accordance with the principle of subsidiarity, only if and in so far as the

> objectives of the proposed action cannot be sufficiently achieved by the Member States and can therefore, by reason of the scale or effects of the proposed action, be better achieved by the Community.
>
> Any action by the Community shall not go beyond what is necessary to achieve the objectives of this Treaty.

To only focus on a narrow interpretation of subsidiarity in terms of exactly allocating competences at either EU or member state level would, however, possibly render the concept empty. In cases of overlapping policy domains and competences, there is no clear line to be drawn with regard to the question of where competences of involved actors start or end. For media policy, Garnham argues that it "is not and can never be the tidy creation of ideal situations. Compromises and trade-offs are endemic" (Garnham 1998: 210). In fact, the Court of Justice of the European Union (formerly the European Court of Justice) has refrained from invoking subsidiarity in disputes between the EU and the member states over the division of competences (Barber 2005), indicating subsidiarity's deeply political nature. This was acknowledged by the European Commission in 1993:

> subsidiarity cannot be reduced to a set of procedural rules; it is primarily a state of mind which, to be given substance, presupposes a political answer to the fundamental questions which application of the principle will undoubtedly raise once the Treaty on European Union enters into force.
>
> (*European Commission 1993: 2*)

Therefore, subsidiarity understood as a principle promises to be more useful "in the search for ways of resolving the tensions and balancing the interests of integration and differentiation, of harmonisation and diversity, of centralisation and localisation or devolution. The notion of subsidiarity can be seen as yet another conceptual space in which this balance can be negotiated, as a language through which the ongoing debate is channelled" (de Búrca 1998: 10).

Whereas internally the EU itself pushes for liberalization and harmonization, and tries to find a balance with the member states along subsidiarity lines, externally it has been far more defensive, guarding (sometimes protectionist) internal cultural policies in trade liberalization agreements in, most importantly, the World Trade Organization (WTO) (Pauwels and Loisen 2003). The adoption of the UNESCO Convention on the Protection and Promotion of the Diversity of Cultural Expressions (hereafter "the Convention" or "the Convention on Cultural Diversity")—a Convention negotiated by the European Commission, which exceptionally represented the EU member states in a cultural policy domain—can be seen as an attempt to mainstream the EU's internal balancing exercises between cultural and economic values on the international scene (although the latter often prevail in EU internal market policies) (Michalis 2007).

The reference to mainstreaming culture via the Convention is explicitly put forward by the European Commission in stating that, "concerned to ensure a broader consideration of cultural diversity in the development of State policies, it could be argued that in effect, the Convention replicates the cultural mainstreaming obligation of Article 167(4) at the international level" (EC 2010a: 3). Article 167(4) of the Treaty on the Functioning of the European Union (TFEU), which replaces Article 151(4) of the Treaty establishing the European

Community (TEC),[1] prescribes that "the Union shall take cultural aspects into account in its action under other provisions of the Treaties, in particular in order to respect and to promote the diversity of its cultures." When the European Commission takes action in trade negotiations (for which it has an exclusive competence) and these negotiations touch upon culture, the Commission should take into account cultural issues (for which the member states, in principle, have an exclusive competence). The cultural mainstreaming clause essentially transposes the principle of subsidiarity into the cultural realm (Barnett 2001; Psychogiopoulou 2006).

In arguing that the Convention replicates the cultural mainstreaming obligation of Article 167(4) at the international level (EC 2010a), the application of subsidiarity in trade and culture issues therefore takes on a global dimension. However, no principle, let alone rule, of "global subsidiarity" exists in international law. Nonetheless, the concept has been introduced in academic literature (Howse and Nicolaïdis 2003). Inspired by the EU's subsidiarity principle, it has been extended to deal with policy issues in which trade objectives need to be reconciled with social, environmental and cultural goals.

Against this background, the chapter's aim is threefold. First, it explores the concepts and regulatory transposition of subsidiarity and global subsidiarity in relation to global media policy. In so doing, it seeks to further global media policy research, which remains an under-conceptualized field of study (Raboy and Padovani 2010). Second, at a more empirical level, the chapter studies the ways in which several institutions interact when dealing with trade and cultural issues in external trade negotiations. It will focus on the so-called "Protocols on Cultural Cooperation" negotiated by the European Commission and concluded by the EU on a bilateral basis with trade partners. Negotiation and conclusion of the Protocols reflect the EU's attempt to mainstream its approach to trade and culture issues along subsidiarity lines worldwide. The Protocols on Cultural Cooperation indeed link up to several other developments[2] that the EU and its member states contribute to. The Commission's strategy is not undisputed, however. Finally, the chapter seeks to reflect on the "usability" of subsidiarity and global subsidiarity as concepts to frame policy discussions and broader policy developments: do regulatory and political practices do justice to the consensual and democratically oriented conceptualizations of subsidiarity and global subsidiarity in literature?

1 The two principal treaties on which the EU is based are the Treaty on European Union (TEU), also known as the Maastricht Treaty (in effect since 1993), and the Treaty on the Functioning of the European Union (TFEU), which sets the conditions of the EU's operation in greater detail. The TFEU entered into force after the ratification of the Treaty of Lisbon on 1 December 2009 and is the amended successor of the Treaty establishing the European Community (TEC), also known as the Rome Treaty of 1958. Articles 167(4) TFEU and 151(4) TEC on culture have remained the same and are very similar to Art. 128 of the Maastricht Treaty, which introduced cultural mainstreaming.

2 The Protocols are the first concrete implementation of provisions in the Convention (which is supposed to replicate the cultural mainstreaming obligation of Art. 167(4) TFEU at international level). In addition, they are used as a tool to implement (within the EU) the Audiovisual Media Services (AVMS) Directive, and, via Art. 1(n) of the Directive (to clarify that it does not refer to the Convention), to contribute to cultural diversity by extending the definition of "European works" to include audiovisual co-productions with certain non-European countries in particular. Furthermore, the Protocols are negotiated in parallel with bilateral free trade negotiations between the EU and selected trade partners. Therefore the analysis will also shed light on how the sensitive relationship between trade and culture may be approached in the near future–at least by the European Commission, which takes the lead in negotiating the Protocols.

Methodologically, the chapter is based on a literature study, document analysis and expert interviews with stakeholders (including the European Commission, EU member states, sector representatives and interest groups) in the negotiation of the Protocol on Cultural Cooperation with Korea. The main argument of the chapter is that subsidiarity, and global subsidiarity in particular, offer theoretical and political, yet rarely powerful legal, grounds to incorporate cultural considerations into international trade and culture policies. However, and this is a second argument, the translation of theory into practice is difficult. Subsidiarity raises empirical problems in terms of adequately operationalizing the concept. Moreover, it generates power plays between different actors when trying to implement it in concrete policy practices. Both the Convention on Cultural Diversity and the Protocols on Cultural Cooperation show that subsidiarity is too often used as a mere power play between institutions, each struggling for their own legitimacy. Only a few examples of processes can be discerned where subsidiarity is used in a broad way, stimulating international trade and culture negotiations on the basis of multi-stakeholder discussions that, in turn, can contribute to compromise and a shared understanding of the way forward for the multilevel governance of trade and culture issues.

## A conceptual and regulatory exploration of subsidiarity and global subsidiarity

### *From subsidiarity . . .*

In the 1980s and 1990s, the process of European integration deepened. This triggered concerns about the shared competences between EU institutions and EU member states and those that are exclusively tied to the EU, or member state, level. In particular, some analysts feared an overextension of Community powers (Colombo 2004). For that reason, Article 5 of the Treaty establishing the European Community (TEC) mentioned that no Community action shall be taken for the attainment of objectives going beyond the realization of the Treaty. Subsidiarity was introduced as a formal, procedural and hence mainly legal principle into Community law. At the same time, the principle also had a clear political meaning, acknowledging that all are playing a part in EU integration and should pay due respect to each other's parts. Subsidiarity as a managing principle in the EU has two dimensions: first, the Community has to refrain from intervention when member states can more efficiently or appropriately achieve objectives; and second, it must act effectively when necessary (that is, when goals can be achieved through European intervention). Hence the Community institutions (most notably the European Commission) are bound by both abstention and intervention (Pauwels 1995). There was, and remains, an element of complementarity at the core of the subsidiarity principle: actions of the different actors within the EU have to complement each other and all have to take responsibility where they are needed and allowed to (Schütze 2009). The principle of subsidiarity was not formally recognized in Community law until 1992, with the adoption of the Maastricht Treaty, although traces can be found in the earlier European Coal and Steel Community Treaty (1951).[3]

Subsidiarity is not a new concept: it was mentioned in the works of Aristotle, Alexis de Tocqueville and John Stuart Mill, and was part of the Christian-democratic social doctrine

3 Article 5 of this treaty mentioned that the Community shall take action only when necessary for the functioning of the internal market.

and the 1931 papal encyclical *Quadragesimo Anno* on the reconstruction of the social order (by Pius XI), aiming to protect individual citizens from rising totalitarianism and exploitation (Commission des Communautés Européennes, Cellule de Prospective 1992). The earlier approaches to subsidiarity share a desire to limit the influence of the state where smaller communities or individuals themselves can take care of their own interests. Indeed, society consists of different spheres in which sovereignty reigns that should be fulfilled and respected (Pauwels 1995). With the emergence of the EU—arguably one of the most, if not the most, relevant integration projects of the twentieth and twenty-first centuries—the subsidiarity concept gained significant political and legal importance.

With regard to cultural and media policy, the subsidiarity principle is of particular importance. Culture is an area in which member states hold exclusive powers and the Community can, as made explicit in Article 6 of the Treaty on the Functioning of the European Union (TFEU), only "support, coordinate or supplement Member States' policies." Article 167 TFEU (*ex* 151 TEC) reaffirms the special status of culture within the Community order and reserves this domain for the EU member states in principle. However, when taking action under its exclusive competences (for example competition, functioning of the internal market, trade), the Community might affect culture; it is bound by Article 167(4) TFEU to take into account cultural considerations (Psychogiopoulou 2006). One of these cases in which cultural considerations have to be taken into account is trade policy. While the latter is an exclusive competence of the Community, in matters where trade policies concern culture and audiovisual services and might "risk prejudicing the Union's cultural and linguistic diversity," the European Commission is obliged to share its powers with the member states and unanimity in decision-taking is required (paragraph 4(3) (a) in Article 207 TFEU, *ex* 133 TEC).[4] Articles 167(4) and 207 TFEU embody the difficult balance between abstention and intervention. Indeed, while the European Commission considers Article 167(4) TFEU a legitimate basis for supplementary action in cultural policy domains and refers to it on a regular basis for sustaining its actions in exclusive policy domains such as competition, others criticize such a "complementary" approach for constituting an overextension of Community competences in practice (Barnett 2001) and for

4 Article 207(4)(3)(a) TFEU explicitly stipulates that "[t]he Council shall also act unanimously for the negotiation and conclusion of agreements: (a) in the field of trade in cultural and audiovisual services, where these agreements risk prejudicing the Union's cultural and linguistic diversity." Such a phrasing is an awkward compromise between the former "pre-Lisbon" and current "post-Lisbon" practice for negotiating and concluding trade agreements that relate, among other things, to culture. Before the Lisbon Treaty, Art. 133 TEC, which set out the procedures for action in the framework of the Common Commercial Policy, provided for an automatic sharing of competences when trade policies concerned culture and audiovisual services. Notwithstanding that external trade policy was ordinarily dealt with exclusively by the Union, Art. 133(6) TEC stated that agreements that include provisions regarding cultural and audiovisual services fall within the shared competence of the Union and its member states. Consequently, decisions in the Council needed to be taken by unanimity and such mixed agreements were to be concluded jointly by the Union and the member states (Krajewski 2005). After Lisbon, Art. 207 TFEU (*ex* Art. 133 TEC), stipulates that EU trade policy is an exclusive EU competence for all sectors. Following the Lisbon Treaty's entry into force, sectoral carve-outs, shared competences or mixed agreements have been dispensed with to both streamline and simplify the EU's Common Commercial Policy. Notwithstanding the abolition of sectoral carve-outs, the specificity of audiovisual goods and services remains acknowledged in the above-mentioned Art. 207(4)(3)(a) TFEU. A specific approach is conditional, however, as the Article in question prescribes a sharing of competences only when a risk is demonstrated.

being willingly ignorant of member states' exclusive competences on culture (Harcourt 2002).

In a similar vein, the current vague phrasing of Article 207(4)(3)(a) TFEU is ambivalent in the sense that it is difficult to interpret and appears to possibly serve both the interests of parties inclined more to a culture protectionist stance and of those wishing to engage in deeper trade liberalization commitments in the cultural sector. How can one judge and measure that a risk exists for cultural and linguistic diversity—a concept that is not defined in the TFEU—and how will the provision function (Loisen and De Ville 2011)? How can one define the threshold indicating that a risk exists for linguistic diversity (for example in the case of minority languages such as Welsh or Gaelic)? How few people have to speak a minority language to speak of such a risk? Can this risk, moreover, be linked to the predominantly English-speaking media system or the vast inflow of American media content? If so, does this warrant protective measures of the minority language, and to what extent? In the context of the Protocol on Cultural Cooperation with Korea, fears were expressed by, among others, Flemish animation sector representatives (Bouckaert *et al.* 2009). They claimed that a Flemish tradition in high-quality and distinctively European animated audiovisual content would be thwarted if co-productions between companies from large EU member states and low-cost Korean animation companies were to be facilitated by the Protocol. Would Belgium, then, have a case to argue that the EU–Korea Protocol would constitute a risk for cultural diversity?

Two options seem plausible with respect to Article 207(4)(3)(a) TFEU. The Council of the EU could opt to continue the pre-Lisbon practice to decide unanimously in the case of agreements that include cultural and audiovisual services (de Witte 2008). Alternatively, in the post-Lisbon context, the member state(s) requesting unanimity should demonstrate that a risk actually exists. Should other member states represented in the Council of the EU not follow the argument made, the normal qualified majority vote would hold, and the Court of Justice of the European Union would become the last recourse of parties that claim the agreement poses a risk to cultural and linguistic diversity (Leal-Arcas 2010; Krajewski 2005).

Needless to say, such vague treaty Articles result in manifold conflicts between the European Commission and the EU member states when dealing with media and culture. These conflicts resurface now that the European Commission uses both Articles 167(4) and 207 TFEU to form the basis of external policies. Indeed, the European Commission seeks to mainstream the Convention on Cultural Diversity by encouraging trade partners to ratify and implement the Convention, in a parallel process of bilateral trade negotiations. The application of the cultural mainstreaming clause of Art. 167(4) TFEU is not straightforward, however. Notwithstanding the inextricable link between market and cultural issues, this transversal concern has led to different interpretations (Psychogiopoulou 2006) and appraisals of its implementation. Fisher (2007), in a note requested by the European Parliament's Committee on Culture and Education, evaluates the Article as a neglected obligation, the implementation of which represents both a failure to ensure coordination across Commission Directorates and a "failure of resolve" indicating culture's subordination to other Commission concerns. Others remain hopeful that the cross-sectional clause will realize its full potential in the delicate balancing act for different goals to be sustained and complemented on various related policy levels (Psychogioupolou 2006). Nonetheless, a general and returning criticism on the concept of mainstreaming is how it will eventually be concretely implemented and monitored.

From a global media policy perspective, the export of subsidiarity to other parts of the world is not necessarily a good idea. The most general point of criticism relates to the rather blurry nature of subsidiarity. Even though enshrined in the Treaty and hence of a legal nature, one can indeed argue that subsidiarity "is too imprecise and soft, and therefore entirely open to disagreement" (Carozza 2003: 78–9). Constantin (2008) finds the apparent lack and even impossibility of legal operationalization of subsidiarity a major weakness. Next to the vagueness of the concept, and the uneasy accord between its legal and political dimension, two competing narratives are at the basis of its function: subsidiarity as "a shield against EU powers" versus "a dynamic principle, a double-edged sword which the two legal worlds can use when it seems to fit the political bill" (Constantin 2008: 152). For the critics, the vague concept of subsidiarity has, in practice, been embraced by the European Commission as an instrument for justifying dominant economic action, to the detriment of cultural and public interest objectives in the domain of media and culture.[5] Another critique refers to the instrumental and ad hoc character of subsidiarity: it has been used to argue both for and against Community action.

Notwithstanding the introduction of the cultural Article in the Maastricht Treaty in 1992, its transposition in terms of evocation or implementation by the member states or in the legal practice of the European Courts has been minimal at best (Psychogiopoulou 2006). Despite the existence of Article 167(4) TFEU and the importance attached to subsidiarity in member state rhetoric, subsidiarity has not been "used" when regulatory actions and policy initiatives of the European Commission in exclusive competence domains such as trade and competition may harm the cultural objectives of member states' audiovisual policies. Member states and other stakeholders do not seem to invoke the Article, and refrain from asking the Court of Justice of the EU to interpret it, which could serve to clarify the delineation of competences between the EU and the member states, and the balance of economic and cultural considerations such as pluralism or cultural diversity. With an eye on possible precedents, member states are apparently hesitant to invoke subsidiarity in legal and policy practices that impact cultural policy.

On the positive side, however, subsidiarity has provided a legal basis for the European Commission to take into account cultural considerations in its application of internal market rules. Moreover, it has allowed the European Commission to speak with one voice in forums like UNESCO—which are normally reserved for EU member states—when deemed necessary by both the European Commission and the member states. In other words, it is precisely because subsidiarity is ambivalent (Van Kersbergen and Verbeek 2007), fluid (de Búrca 2000) and not a "hard" concept (Carozza 2003) that it can be adapted in a flexible way to very specific circumstances. This made it possible for the member states to argue more forcefully for the adoption of the Convention, which was for some of them a marker of a more balanced treatment of audiovisual services in international trade negotiations. Finally, the political value of the subsidiarity concept should—even though understandable given the instrumental use of the concept—not be swept under the carpet too easily. Subsidiarity is not exclusive, it is inclusive—a characteristic that should be at the core of democratic processes in society:

> The European principle of subsidiarity is important because it is one of the key constitutional principles that serve to set the character of the EU. As a legal principle, a justiciable

5 See, e.g., Barnett 2001, Harcourt 2002 and Holtz-Bacha 2005.

> constraint on the power of the Community Institutions, subsidiarity has had little obvious effect. Perhaps daunted by the complicated political assessments the principle entails, or, less charitably, perhaps disinclined to develop a principle that limits the centralisation of power, the European Court of Justice has not made use of the principle. The degree to which subsidiarity has indirectly affected the measures advanced by the Community is unclear. But *the principle stands as a declaration of how the EU perceives itself,* and as the sort of political community the authors of the Treaties intended it to be. In particular, *it represents a commitment to democracy, to de-centralised power and, most importantly, opposition to nationalist ideals of state legitimacy.*
>
> *(Barber 2005: 324–5; emphasis added)*

## *. . . to global subsidiarity*

Whereas the European concept of subsidiarity is politically and legally grounded, the concept of global subsidiarity is conceptualized predominantly by academics with the aim of re-establishing a form of post-World War II embedded liberalism[6] in vastly more complex international (trade) relations (Lang 2006; Schofield 2004). In that sense, global subsidiarity is far less part of a fight between competing narratives. From the outset, it is situated within a normative, democratic and open-ended perspective on how institutions interact. Consequently, global subsidiarity relates not that much to subsidiarity as a rule, but rather to subsidiarity as a general principle and practice. Instead of a clear definition, Howse and Nicolaïdis (2003) explain global subsidiarity in terms of having three essential features—institutional sensitivity, political inclusion and top-down empowerment—that can recover the spirit of embedded liberalism. This may be very relevant for global media policy, as tensions between cultural and economic aspects of media transcend the European level, and are omnipresent in the international policy arena. Indeed, "the stalemate among the 149 members [now 157] of the WTO regarding the relationship between trade and culture [. . .] has dogged the organization from the days of the General Agreement on Tariffs and Trade (GATT) of 1947 to the present" (Voon 2007: 2).

The EU has continuously tried to exclude its audiovisual sectors from progressive liberalization agreements. This strategy has met with varying success: the EU and its member states have retained the right to impose quotas and grant subsidies, but have not been able to exempt the audiovisual sector from the World Trade Organization's action radius and the General Agreement on Trade in Services (GATS) (1994) in particular. Whereas the EU itself has refrained from making commitments to liberalize its audiovisual sectors, other trade partners can, and have done so within the WTO (Pauwels and Loisen 2003). In addition, the United

6 The concept of "embedded liberalism" refers to the fusion of countries' power with a shared purpose to open markets and trade, but with due respect and policy space for domestic stability. This compromise between dominant economic interests and wider social contract objectives guided international economic relations after World War II (Ruggie 1982). From the 1980s onwards, the compromise has come under strain and embedded liberalism appears to have disintegrated, while neoliberal ideology flourished. The appropriation of audiovisual services in the commercially oriented World Trade Organization seems to illustrate that the balancing act inherent in the embedded liberalism compromise became skewed to the detriment of national and cultural media policy objectives. Nonetheless, in the new millennium, so-called "trade and" issues have increasingly challenged the WTO's pivotal role in global governance.

States increasingly pressures other states to include the sector in its bilateral trade and investment agreements (Wunsch-Vincent 2003).

A counter movement to the opening of the audiovisual market, led by France and Canada, has pushed for the adoption of the Convention on Cultural Diversity, which recognizes the rights of member states to develop, implement, defend and protect cultural policies (Pauwels *et al.* 2006). More specifically, the Convention stresses the rights of sovereign states to adopt measures aimed at the protection and promotion of the diversity of cultural expressions within their territories (Articles 2.2 and 6.1 of the Convention).

The Convention's impact is debatable, however, and has certainly not ended the discussion on the treatment of audiovisual goods and services in international trade forums such as the WTO, nor has it been conclusive about nations' rights and duties in developing and implementing cultural policies. There seems to be an "incompleteness of the trade and culture discourse" (Burri-Nenova *et al.* 2011), with a lack of appropriate and legally enforceable solutions for cultural diversity opposed to strong legal commitments on trade liberalization.

The "incompleteness" of discussions on the relation between trade and other policy domains, commonly referred to as "trade and" issues, is not unique to culture and media. Frustration on the supremacy of economic objectives over other, often public interest, considerations has stalled the progressive liberalization of global markets and induced a legitimacy crisis of the WTO (Dunoff 1999). The never-ending Doha Round, which commenced in 2001, exemplifies this. Some see a stronger WTO institutional architecture (Jackson 2001), the stressing of individual economic rights (Petersmann 2001), or the WTO dispute settlement mechanism (Cass 2005) as drivers toward "constitutionalization" of the WTO to overcome its crisis. In turn, critics of constitutionalization discourses (e.g. Dunoff 2006) argue that such discourses essentially aim for less political "meddling" with trade liberalization and more independent, expert input to put the process of trade liberalization back on track. In the critics' view, constitutionalization is non-democratic and possibly dangerous because it forecloses debate among a wide variety of stakeholders and reinforces the club-like character of the WTO (Keohane and Nye 2002). Clearly, constitutionalization discourses also run counter to the principle of subsidiarity that aims to open up a conceptual space for reflection and discussion among a series of stakeholders.

In response to the constitutionalization discourse regarding the WTO, Howse and Nicolaïdis (2003) have argued for a model of global subsidiarity inspired by the European subsidiarity concept—as a principle or practice, not as a clear rule. They claim that global subsidiarity is a suitable concept to organize discussions on "trade and" issues, to incentivize equitable discussions about these issues and to revitalize the WTO:

> Imposing the constitutionalist spirit on the World Trade Organization is not the answer. Rather, the spirit of embedded liberalism needs to be recovered and reinterpreted under the new conditions of globalization. Again inspiration can come from the European Union, not in its constitutional guise, but by incorporating some of the institutional and political features associated with subsidiarity.
>
> (*Howse and Nicolaïdis 2003: 86*)

The features referred to are institutional sensitivity, political inclusion and top-down empowerment. First, institutional sensitivity relates to the flexible treatment of issues by organizations, which need to realize that some domains belonging to their competences are better dealt with by other, competing, institutions, possibly at another level of governance (Howse and Nicolaïdis 2003). In the case of global media policy, developments surrounding the protection and promotion of cultural diversity question the primacy of trade law and liberalization commitments. The Convention calls for a different treatment of trade and culture issues under international trade and national cultural and media law. This variable treatment has to be developed by all involved stakeholders, while the WTO should refrain from dealing with these sensitive issues independently (Krajewski 2001; Steger 2007). Second, political inclusion is necessary to enhance public support for international policy and law. The requirement of political inclusion is mainly concerned with involving as many stakeholders in debates on "trade and" issues and making these as transparent as possible. For example, even though civil society cannot have a legal vote in WTO dispute settlement procedures, it should be heard (Howse 2002). Such inclusion can only trigger political and societal discussion, which is, according to Pauwelyn (2005) too often absent from overly legal discussions on international policy and law. In a way, the feature of political inclusion is similar to the quest for multi-stakeholder, and hence equitable discussions on global media policy (Padovani and Pavan 2011). Third, international institutions have to play a role in empowering local actors such as non-governmental organizations that might be overlooked at the national level. In so doing, these institutions, and the WTO in particular, might restore their "global democratic deficit" (Howse and Nicolaïdis 2003: 90) and create accountability of actors other than nation-states.

Whereas subsidiarity in EU terms is more a multilevel governance balancing exercise, delineating competences between the higher and lower levels, it should be clear that global subsidiarity is broader in the sense that it encourages multi-stakeholder discussions in the first place. Global subsidiarity remains, for now, a primarily academic concept that needs to be elaborated further. It is not entrenched in international trade law and has only been marginally taken up in practice. In that sense, one could argue that global subsidiarity is a utopian idea. Nonetheless, the concept is relevant because it offers a frame and angle to balance competences and shifting power relations, on the one hand, and diverging values, on the other. Global media policy should be inclusive and equitable in terms of stakeholders and of goals (Loisen 2009).

## Protocols on Cultural Cooperation: Mainstreaming EU cultural policies

With the development of the Convention on Cultural Diversity, the global subsidiarity model became increasingly relevant for the "trade and culture" issue of global audiovisual policy. Albeit usually considered a weak international legal instrument (Hahn 2006), the Convention may have great significance in political terms, although one needs to "make it work" (referring to the title of Obuljen and Smiers 2006). This was also envisaged by Pascal Lamy, current Director-General of the WTO, when he was European Commissioner for Trade:

> To remain credible, we need to be aware that the promotion of cultural diversity is not limited to each Member state protecting its national industry. Otherwise, this would be, as some say, some sort of disguised protectionism which would not convince anybody. We can better persuade, in particular developing countries, of the legitimacy of our discourse if we can show our real opening up to diversity.
>
> (*Lamy 2003, author's translation*)

Interestingly, this is precisely what the EU aims to achieve—at least in its discourse—with the implementation of the Convention. In various documents, the ambition is outlined to build a global cultural pillar in governance on the basis of the Convention (EC 2007a). The Council of the EU therefore calls upon the member states and the Commission to, *inter alia*, strengthen the role of culture within the framework of external relations, to promote the Convention, to stimulate cooperation with third countries and international organizations, and to draw up a European strategy for incorporating culture consistently and systematically in the external relations of the Union, with due regard for complementarity between the Union's activities and those of the member states. In this context, a Commission staff working document articulated its intention to "mainstream" at the international level the subsidiarity and culture-related Article 167(4) TFEU (EC 2009a: 9). In other words, mainstreaming subsidiarity in cultural trade matters reveals the goal to set up a global subsidiarity framework for culture. It is an open question, however, whether the EU's approach is in line with the global subsidiarity concept, as elaborated by Howse and Nicolaïdis and other scholars (that is, institutional sensitivity, polical inclusion, top-down empowerment), and with the understanding of subsidiarity, as exemplified by Barber (that is, a commitment to democracy, decentralized power, and opposition to nationalist ideals of state legitimacy). These approaches to subsidiarity are united in their call for fundamental debates on the European integration project and the division of competences among stakeholders.

With respect to the Protocols on Cultural Cooperation, the question then becomes whether, in their elaboration, not the rule, but the principle, of subsidiarity was respected. In an increasingly complex multilevel governance context of policy issues for which many actors have competences, these debates are indispensable to overcome a mere power play between institutions clinging on to exclusive competences that frustrate other relevant parties. Subsidiarity's principal advantage in providing a conceptual space in which a balance between competing views can be negotiated and ongoing debate is channelled (de Búrca 1998) is not only acknowledged by scholars. With the introduction of the subsidiarity principle in the Maastricht Treaty, the Commission itself advanced a similar concern in stating that subsidiarity cannot be reduced to a set of procedural rules (European Commission 1993). Neat solutions for complex policymaking are rare, and political and democratic debate can only be to the benefit of policy's endemic compromises and trade-offs. In a similar vein, exchange and debate between academic analysis and actual policymaking can be instructive for both theory and practice: both engage in a permanent process of trial and error, or verification and falsification.

## *The European Commission's take on the Protocols on Cultural Cooperation*

Notwithstanding the impact that the Convention has had on the level of political discourse, implementation is only beginning. Aware of the challenge for the EU—one of the driving forces behind the succesful conclusion of the Convention—to lead by example in the implementation of the new instrument, the European Commission has begun to develop a new approach to the treatment of cultural activities and industries in its bilateral and regional agreements (EC 2009a). The instrument of a Protocol on Cultural Cooperation aims to promote the principles of the Convention within the context of bilateral trade negotiations. It serves the purpose of enforcing the principles of the Convention (Articles 12, 16 and 20 of the Convention in particular) and transposing them into more concrete commitments.

The First Protocol (2008), agreed with the Caribbean Forum (CARIFORUM), mentions the preferential treatment[7] for cultural goods, services and practitioners of developing countries, thereby implementing Article 16 ("Preferential treatment for developing countries") of the Convention on Cultural Diversity. A Second Protocol with Korea, which is not a developing country, yet implements Article 12 of the Convention ("Promotion of international cooperation"), was agreed in 2009. The European Commission's proactive attitude with regard to the negotiation and adoption of the Protocols on Cultural Cooperation has provoked resistance from various stakeholders[8] arguing that such a stance was neither welcome nor legitimate in light of the competence divisions between the European Commission and the EU member states in the cultural domain. Although both Protocols offer examples of the way in which the European Commission seeks to externalize its treatment of cultural policy objectives at the international stage, the Protocol with Korea was particularly contentious (see European Coalitions for Cultural Diversity 2009; French Ministry for Foreign and European Affairs 2009). For that reason, it is the subject of analysis here.

Legally speaking, it is not that clear whether the European Commission had the authority to act as it did within its exclusive competencies on trade, nor that some member states (especially France and, to a lesser extent, Belgium, Germany and Italy) legitimately claimed exclusive competence over culture. Although it was clearly a question of subsidiarity, the principle was not explicitly introduced into the debate on how competences should be divided between the Commission and the member states in this particular trade and culture issue.

Nonetheless, the European Commission put forward several reasons for pursuing the Protocols on Cultural Cooperation. First, it argued the conclusion of the Protocols was a mere implementation of the Convention. Second, and related, the Protocols would ensure a fast ratification of the Convention by trade partners. This would strengthen the Convention and the EU's position that audiovisual goods and services should be treated with caution in the World Trade Organization (EC 2009a). Third, the commitments made in the Protocols would facilitate the exchange in cultural goods and services between the trade partners, while still acknowledging the dual nature of these goods and services. The latter goal is to be achieved by dealing with the very sensitive audiovisual sector only within the framework of a protocol. In other words, any provision relating to the audiovisual sector is to be

7 "Important differences exist between the concept of preferential treatment / special and differential treatment as used within the WTO and in Article 16 of the Convention. The special and differential treatment as defined by the WTO is inherently restricted in scope. Actually it was designed as an exception to a general rule, aimed at bringing a temporary solution to a given situation. Preferential treatment as defined by Article 16 of the Convention, and more generally in issues related to cultural cooperation, necessarily implies sustainable and structural effects on cultural exchanges" (author's translation).

8 For the member states, France in particular has been vigilant. See, e.g., its Ministry of Foreign and European Affairs' Communication on a new European external cultural strategy (2009). As regards the professional sector, the European Coalitions for Cultural Diversity sent letters to different EU officials of the Commission and its relevant Directorates-General (i.e. to Mr. Barroso, Baroness Ashton, Mr. Figel and Ms. Reding) expressing concern about the proceedings with the EU-Korea Cultural Cooperation Protocol (ECCD 2009). Different national coalitions for cultural diversity and sectoral organizations followed suit and targeted similar letters to their national representatives—e.g. a letter from several audiovisual sector representatives in Flanders to the Flemish government (Bouckaert *et al.* 2009).

disconnected from trade and market access provisions that are part of the trade agreement that is negotiated in parallel (European Commission 2007b). With respect to the goal of facilitation of exchanges in audiovisual services, the European Commission advocates that the Protocols are a tool to implement the Audiovisual Media Services (AVMS) Directive. In the 2007 AVMS Directive, the definition of "European works" is broadened—in comparison with the AVMS Directive's forerunner, the Television without Frontiers (TwF) Directive of 1989—to include co-productions between EU member states and third countries that meet certain criteria as stipulated in agreements between the EU and non-EU countries.[9] The EU–Korea Protocol would make it possible for certain Euro–Korean co-productions to be defined as "European works" in the EU market and as "Korean works" in the Korean market, which would make them eligible to be included in the quota provisions that both entities have installed to protect and support their audiovisual industries.[10] Indeed, since the adoption of the TwF Directive in 1989, EU member states have had to ensure a majority proportion of programming of European works on television (Pauwels and Donders 2011). The European Commission stresses, however, that nothing in the Protocols on Cultural Cooperation text prevents the parties from retaining their capacity to develop public cultural policies that target the protection and promotion of the diversity of cultural expressions. With regard to the latter, the member states remain the first responsible parties, with the EU acting in a complementary fashion. These goals underlie the development of a global framework and strategy for future cultural cooperation agreements.

Finally, the Protocols allowed for a case-by-case approach to deal with the significant diversity of third countries and, admittedly, the different levels of economic and cultural interests of the EU (EC 2009a). With regard to developing countries, the Protocols acknowledge an asymmetrical relationship: the European market is more open towards importing goods, services and people from developing countries in order to ensure that the stronger economic situation of the EU does not harm the audiovisual industries of the partner countries (EC 2008; EC 2009a). For developed countries such as Korea, a logic of strict reciprocity of benefits and cooperation should be followed in light of the sensitivity of cultural issues negotiated. In any case, audiovisual goods and services, which are highly sensitive, should be excluded from the bilateral trade agreement provisions that are negotiated in parallel (EC 2007b). This creates a somewhat paradoxical situation. On the one hand, a bilateral free trade agreement (FTA), and the Protocol on Cultural Cooperation that is appended to it, are

9 The TwF Directive aimed to create an internal market for broadcasting activities and to stimulate, simultaneously, the national production of broadcasting services. To this end, it was agreed that broadcasters should program at least 50 percent of "European works." Article 6.1 TwF Directive defined "European works" as works originating from EU member states, or, dependent upon a series of conditions, from European third states party to the European Convention on Transfrontier Television of the Council of Europe or even other European countries. In short, (co-)productions targeted in the TwF Directive had to originate in Europe. With the AVMS Directive, the definition has been broadened by adding to the TwF list "works co-produced within the framework of agreements related to the audiovisual sector concluded between the Union and third countries and fulfilling the conditions defined in each of those agreements" (Art. 1 (n)(iii) AVMS).

10 Article 16 of the AVMS Directive stipulates, for example: "Member States shall ensure, where practicable and by appropriate means, that broadcasters reserve for European works a majority proportion of their transmission time, excluding the time allotted to news, sports events, games, advertising, teletext services and teleshopping. This proportion, having regard to the broadcaster's informational, educational, cultural and entertainment responsibilities to its viewing public, should be achieved progressively, on the basis of suitable criteria."

negotiated in parallel and monitored in the EU context by the Trade Policy Committee of the European Union.[11] On the other hand, the Commission repeatedly stresses that the audiovisual sector will be dealt with in the Protocol, yet is systematically excluded from the scope of trade provisions (e.g. in the FTA's chapter on services) (EC 2007b; EC 2009b).

A first, technical, reason for this strategy, peculiar at first sight, is that the Protocol appended to the FTA would allow for possible discriminatory measures in the Protocol vis-à-vis other partners (e.g. the United States) because of its compatibility with Article V GATS ("Economic integration"). This Article allows for an exception to the WTO's most favored nation (MFN) principle as applied to trade in services if a non-multilateral economic integration agreement (such as the EU-Korea FTA) is concluded that meets certain conditions in terms of substantial sectoral coverage and does not exclude *a priori* certain sectors. Because Korea has taken on commitments under GATS for audiovisual services and did not exempt it from MFN application, linking the Protocol to the FTA is necessary to achieve substantial sectoral coverage that at the same time allows some preferential (between the EU and Korea) and thus discriminatory (for other countries) treatment (Loisen and Pauwels 2010).

Second, strategic considerations have played a role. Swift action is seen as essential to stress the EU's leadership in promoting the implementation of the Convention as the cultural pillar in global governance, and as a counterbalance to (future) developments in other institutions that could possibly harm cultural diversity. In this respect, moreover, the Protocols can be seen as a response to the United States' bilateral strategies to further audiovisual trade liberalization.[12] Developing partnerships with third countries by means of a protocol could broaden and strengthen the alliance in support of the Convention. The Protocol with Korea could be an instrument to align an important Asian partner to the EU's position regarding the inter-institutional dialectics between the WTO and UNESCO in the case of cultural diversity (Loisen and Pauwels 2010).

### *Criticisms of the Protocols on Cultural Cooperation*

In spite of the European Commission's efforts to convince member states and the European cultural sectors who fear liberalization of trade in culture and media that it aims to consolidate the EU's traditional approach of disconnecting culture from trade, several points of criticism have been made. In particular, France, the European Coalitions for Cultural Diversity and sector representatives protested against the Protocols.

A first cluster of criticisms revolved around the division of competences between the European Commission and the EU member states, echoing the issue of institutional sensitivity within a global subsidiarity model. In particular, the parallel treatment of bilateral free trade agreements and cultural cooperation has been criticized, with French Minister of Culture Chrisine Albanel stating that "the Brussels Commission has no mandate to sign this agreement under conditions that threaten cultural diversity" (French Minister of Culture Christine Albanel in Berretta 2009, authors' translation). Several stakeholders feared that the

11 The Trade Policy Committee is better known as the (former) Article 133 Committee, which was named after the Treaty of Amsterdam's Art. 133 on the Common Commercial Policy. It assists the European Commission in trade matters, and provides an internal negotiation forum and link between the Commission and the Council of the EU.

12 For more information on the US bilateral trade strategies with regard to the cultural sector, the audiovisual sector in particular, see Bernier 2004 and Wunsch-Vincent 2003.

specific character of culture and audiovisual goods and services were downgraded in the negotiations that were led by the Directorate-General for Trade, and made inferior to the success of reaching an agreement on the bilateral FTA. The fact that the Protocols were discussed in the Trade Policy Committee of the European Union, while, for example, the Directorate General for Education and Culture played a secondary role, reinforced this impression (Loisen and De Ville 2011).

The second cluster of criticisms concerned the consistency of the European Commission's approach. The adoption of Protocols on Cultural Cooperation in parallel to bilateral trade agreements may seem to be at odds with the intention of the Convention, to counterbalance an economically focused approach to trade and culture. In any case, the different views illustrate that different parties interpret the tools at hand very differently. The European Commission takes on the obligation to implement the Convention by developing a new approach in the relation between trade and culture; others see the Convention primarily as an instrument to separate culture and trade altogether. The French Ministry of Foreign and European Affairs was particularly worried about a trend-setting effect of the Protocols, which "run the risk of allowing a *de facto* reintroduction of audiovisual services into trade negotiations" (2009: 5). Whereas the European Commission (2009b) speaks of a mere facilitation of exchanges in audiovisual goods and services, critics argue that the "facilitation of exchanges" mimics market access provisions that can be found in bilateral trade agreements and WTO contracts (Thiec 2009).

A final, and more technical, point of criticism made by some countries and sector stakeholders concerns the classification of Euro–Korean co-productions as "European works." Sector stakeholders argued that such a beneficial treatment of co-productions is acceptable only when they concern cooperation with developing countries. Because Korea is not a developing country, they regarded the benefit as a threat to European domestic production and not in line with the goal of reciprocity that the Commission put forward. The European Commission countered that it would conduct a study on the effects of the provision on European domestic production (2009b). An *ex ante* study would be difficult, however, owing to speculation on parameters and actor behavior, and one may ponder whether a negative outcome of an *ex post* study would turn back the Protocols on Cultural Cooperation.

The European Commission has countered the concerns addressed above, arguing that interservice consultations (that is, formalized consultations between relevant and interested Directorates-General), including the Directorate-General for Education and Culture, have taken place and that, certainly in the negotiation of the Korea Protocol, stakeholders were consulted. Sector stakeholders and some member states nonetheless lament the limited impact that their cultural experts could have on the process, as well as the timing (too late) to express their views. An analysis of the changes made in the development of the EU–Korea Protocol indicates, however, that the European Commission did change certain parts of the protocol as a consequence of stakeholder critiques (see Loisen and De Ville 2011; Loisen and Pauwels 2010).

First, for the Protocol with CARIFORUM countries to enter into force, the Carribean countries were obliged only to "be committed" to the Convention (that is, to plan to sign it in the future), but Korea's actual ratification of the Convention is necessary for the Protocol to start. Second, a Committee for Cultural Cooperation was established to monitor the Protocol with Korea, consisting of senior officials with experience and expertise in cultural affairs, which is independent from the Trade Committee monitoring the EU–Korea FTA. The latter committee does not have any competences with regard to the Protocol on Cultural Cooperation. Third, the EU–Korea Protocol established a disconnect between arbitration procedures, dispute settlement and sanctions of the Protocols on Cultural Cooperation, on the one hand, and the bilateral trade agreement, on the other. Moreover, members of the dispute settlement body for the Protocols on Cultural Cooperation are not only lawyers, but also cultural experts. Finally, with regard to the contentious issue of co-productions, stricter financial and artistic criteria were introduced in the Protocol's development, so EU-Korean co-productions could benefit from quota regulations. In addition, this system will be regularly monitored and evaluated. Should a party (that is, Korea, the EU or an EU member state) wish to end the preferential treatment system for co-productions, it can do so unilaterally. Although it remains to be seen whether one party can turn over a system supported by all others, this important concession to the critical stakeholders—certainly in light of a possible future protocol with India, which has a strong audiovisual sector—helped to appease the earlier quarrels within the EU (Loisen and Pauwels 2010).

## Conclusion: Caught between legal, political and theoretical conceptions of global subsidiarity

### *Subsidiarity and (global) subsidiarity: Prospects and pitfalls*

A first conclusion with regard to the conceptual exploration of subsidiarity and global subsidiarity is that both concepts are difficult to operationalize in legal terms. A main criticism of subsidiarity, as enshrined in the Treaty on European Union, is indeed its legal vagueness, even though it is part of one of the most important legal texts on which the EU rests. The same applies for global subsidiarity, which has no legal basis, and its legal operationalization whenever included in an international trade law context seems difficult at best. The legal vagueness of both subsidiarity and global subsidiarity might impair their effectiveness in terms of being used by members of an organization; such members, fearing the unpredictability of the concepts, may simply refrain from referring to subsidiarity. The fact that EU member states choose not to invoke Article 167(4) TFEU—requiring the Commission to take cultural aspects into account in its action under other provisions of the TFEU, in particular to respect and promote the diversity of its cultures—in cases in which they consider the intervention of the European Commission as too fargoing, such as in European State aid control of public service broadcasting (Donders 2012), is a case in point.

The concepts of subsidiarity and global subsidiarity are much clearer from a political perspective. Both concern the political and democratic deliberation of the levels on which decision-making and decision-taking should take place. Indeed, the assumption underlying subsidiarity and global subsidiarity is that the most suitable policy level should be in charge of decision-making and taking. Complementarity, responsibility and accountability are at the heart of subsidiarity and global subsidiarity.

Legal vagueness and complexity can be traced through to the implementation of subsidiarity; although one might agree on the main (political) idea of subsidiarity and, by extension, global subsidiarity, implementing it in concrete situations is challenging. The process of implementing the Convention can regress in down-to-earth power play (that is, clinging on to competences without engaging in fundamental discussions on the adequate level to pursue policies beneficial to cultural diversity). It should be noted, for example, that, in the implementation of the Convention by the EU and the member states, the goal of a worldwide diversity of cultural expressions may be minimized owing to inward-looking or short-term EU or member state specific interests. If developing countries remain between a rock and a hard place—caught either in a liberalization scenario, or with minimal access to other markets and state support for which many third parties countries do not have the resources and with which they cannot compete—the implementation of the Convention could result in failure. Challenges also arise because of the vagueness of concepts that might legitimize action on one policy level, yet make action on another level illegitimate. When invoking subsidiarity in the EU for cultural matters, one needs to define and delineate complex and normative concepts and principles that are difficult to operationalize. For example, how can a member state fully establish a risk of a Protocol on Cultural Cooperation when it can make use only of vague and ill-defined concepts such as pluralism, cultural identity and linguistic diversity? Hypothetically speaking, could and would the Flemish government, which in Belgium has competence over cultural and media policy, try to demonstrate that the EU–Korea Protocol on Cultural Cooperation threatens cultural diversity or Flemish cultural identity because of possible repercussions on its animation sector? It would seem very difficult to establish and prove a link between increasing Euro–Korean co-productions in the European market, a setback of Flemish audiovisual animations, and a risk for Flemish cultural identity and cultural diversity at large.

Even when a consensus can be found on who is to do what, the level of actual implementation is still problematic. For example, in the case of the Protocols on Cultural Cooperation, one needs to monitor, measure and evaluate how the agreements are transposed into practice and affect member states and their audiovisual sectors. But measurement is not easy, because of vague concepts and a lack of measurement tools. At what point is cultural diversity guaranteed or, alternatively, at risk in a given member state or the whole of the EU? Moreover, once conclusions are reached, subsidiarity questions on who is to take action resurface. In that regard, subsidiarity and global subsidiarity require constant negotiation and the involvement of different government authorities. They are concepts that refer to processes and not so much to a given practice at one moment in time. Hence the difficulty of legally and empirically operationalizing them.

No clear answers on who is responsible at which policy level for audiovisual policy issues can therefore be given *a priori*. The subsidiarity principle, understood as a commitment to democracy and decentralized power, and further elaborated for a worldwide multilevel governance context in the global subsidiarity model, provides a valid and valuable framework with which to engage. Nevertheless, subsidiarity and global subsidiarity frameworks need to be elaborated further and tested in order to go beyond academic discussions; this is particularly true for global subsidiarity, which has been until now mostly a theoretical construction.

### *Institutional sensitivity, political inclusion and top-down empowerment: The way forward*

The analysis of the Protocol on Cultural Cooperation between the EU and Korea might be considered a first practical test of the global subsidiarity concept: the EU's goal of mainstreaming subsidiarity in cultural trade matters reveals the goal to set up a global subsidiarity framework for culture. Yet it is an open question whether the EU's approach is in line with the main principles of the global subsidiarity framework, as elaborated upon by Howse and Nicolaïdis (2003). The Protocol on Cultural Cooperation with Korea was only the second protocol negotiated, and the criticisms raised have led DeTrade not to foresee new Protocols in the near future. Hence, it is far from clear whether this new approach will be followed, extended or abandoned in the future. However, the analysis can give some indications with regard to this open question and allows for making policy recommendations to future cultural cooperation agreements—whichever from these may take.

In terms of institutional sensitivity, there appears to be an ongoing learning process regarding how to allow for differentiation with regard to the EU's trading partners, on the one hand, and how to balance cultural diversity concerns with regional, national or supranational policy initiatives and in domains other than trade, on the other hand. Moreover, the European Commission has adapted its approach, gradually giving "cultural voices" from member states and other stakeholders a say in the development of the Protocol on Cultural Cooperation with Korea. During negotiations with Korea, it has created specific institutions responsible for monitoring and evaluating the implementation of the Protocols, instead of entrusting this task to trade-oriented institutions in charge of the associated free trade agreement. The negotiations on the Protocols on Cultural Cooperation also made possible the reflection about and development of new safeguarding mechanisms in the spirit of the Convention. Moreover, these experiences have generated new ideas to differentiate between third parties with which the EU will negotiate. In addition, experiences so far have provided opportunities to strengthen the relationship between policy frameworks that are related to cultural diversity. For example, the relationship between a Protocol on Cultural Cooperation and the rules of the Audiovisual Media Services Directive has been made explicit. Nonetheless, although the European Commission and EU member states were successful in adapting the institutional set-up throughout the process of the negotiations on the Protocol on Cultural Cooperation with Korea, the observed adaptiveness is still limited: the European Commission wants to expand its powers, whereas member states wish to retain their competences. The difficult balance between these two institutional interests gives the impression of a zero-sum game in EU internal and external policies, largely to the detriment of media policy within and outside the EU. In a way, institutional sensitivity goes against organizations' intuitive protection of their own interests. It is, indeed, only after a few member states and representatives of the European audiovisual industries organized themselves and obliged all relevant parties to have a debate on the negotiation of the Protocol with Korea that the gradual adaptation of the institutional set-up started.

Coming to the element of political inclusion, the Protocol on Cultural Cooperation with Korea has proved to be an indispensable learning process for all stakeholders concerned. Early negotiations were quite secretive. As the communication on proceedings in trade and economic negotiations with third parties faltered, anxiety and confusion among stakeholders grew, leading to suboptimal conditions for a constructive debate. The European Commission was forced to allow stakeholders to voice their concerns more clearly in the later stages of the negotiations, and to clarify the relationship between trade and culture more explictly. This had a beneficial effect on the eventual outcome of the negotiations. The strained relationship between cultural and trade objectives remains very pervasive, however, and hampers cooperation between EU institutions, member states and the professional sector, which, in turn, threatens the capacity of the EU to speak with one voice in cultural-diversity-related matters in international negotiations. It is essential to have transparency and adequate communication to relevant stakeholders on the development and implementation of a new strategy for cultural diversity in external relations, and at the earliest stage possible. This is not a substitute for (sometimes endless) consultation exercises, but for genuine deliberative processes underlying decision-taking within the EU, between the EU institutions, national levels and civil society, and within member states (e.g. between trade and cultural ministries). Such an approach will democratize supranational and international governance, and enhance public support as well.

Finally, top-down empowerment is the main bottleneck—in terms of its translation into practice—if one wants to embed global media policy firmly within a global subsidiarity approach. It is the criterion that is the least legal and political in nature, and requires the empowerment of stakeholders beyond policy. In the negotiations on the Protocol on Cultural Cooperation with Korea, this means civil society, producers, script writers, broadcasters, etc.:

all parties that have an interest in future negotiations on cultural cooperation agreements and on the implementation of the Convention on Cultural Diversity in general. The Protocols on Cultural Cooperation have generated a certain momentum, but essentially target only a small number of international partners. How can their implementation, in a similar vein, include more third parties (particularly developing countries) *and* support the goal of a worldwide diversity of cultural expressions? The EU can take on a central role in building capacity and empowering its international partners, and provide for an alternative in dealing with the dual nature of the diversity of cultural expressions, as opposed to, for example, US bilateral liberalization strategies for the audiovisual and cultural sector. The evidence so far demonstrates, however, that the mainstreaming of culture in related EU policies and instruments is catered for extensively in the EU's discourse, but is rather limited in practice.

Mainstreaming of culture in practice requires improving coordination procedures and platforms, dialog and cooperation between stakeholders in a truly bottom-up fashion, and continuous assessment and adjustment. Essentially, if one seeks to transpose the principles of global subsidiarity and the normative aspects of subsidiarity into global media policy, one needs to abandon traditional power politics. Substance, not form, complementarity, not exclusivity, empowerment, not deceit and non-transparency, and accountability and responsibility, not blame-gaming, should be at the core of subsequently: (1) problem definition; (2) policy development; (3) decision-making and taking; (4) policy implementation; and finally (5) evaluation and adaptation. There will never be an ideal policy outcome, but dialog and transparency surely add to the democratic legitimacy of politics, and ultimately impact effective and efficient policymaking.

## References

Barber, N. W. (2005) 'The limited modesty of subsidiarity,' *European Law Journal*, 11(3): 308–325.

Barnett, C. (2001) 'Culture, policy and subsidiarity in the European Union: From symbolic identity to the governmentalisation of culture,' *Political Geography*, 20(4): 405–426.

Bernier, I. (2004) 'The recent free trade agreements of the United States as illustrations of their new strategy regarding the audiovisual sector.' Online. Available HTTP: http://www.diversite-culturelle.qc.ca/index.php?id=133&L=1 (accessed 30 September 2011).

Berretta, E. (2009) 'Albanel proteste contre un accord entre l'Europe et la Corée du Sud,' *Le Point*, 18 March. Online. Available HTTP: http://www.lepoint.fr/archives/article.php/326988 (accessed 30 September 2011).

Bouckaert *et al.* (2009) 'Betreft: Cultureel samenwerkingsprotocol EU/Zuid-Korea,' Letter to the Flemish Government, Brussels.

Bourcieu, E. (2008) 'Annex prepared by E. Bourcieu' in 'UNESCO: Intergovernmental Committee for the Protection and Promotion of the Diversity of Cultural Expressions' (CE/08/2.IGC/8) *Expert Reports on Preferential Treatment for Developing Countries. Article 16 of the Convention on the Protection and Promotion of the Diversity of Cultural Expressions*, Paris: UNESCO.

Burri-Nenova, M., Beat Graber, C. and Steiner, T. (2011) 'The protection and promotion of cultural diversity in a digital networked environment: Mapping possible advances towards coherence' in T. Cottier and P. Delimatsis (eds.) *The Prospects of International Trade Regulation: From Fragmentation to Coherence*, Cambridge: Cambridge University Press.

Carozza, P. G. (2003) 'Subsidiarity as a structural principle of international human rights law,' *The American Journal of International Law*, 97(1): 38–79.

Cass, D. Z. (2005) *The Constitutionalization of the World Trade Organization: Legitimacy, Democracy, and Community in the International Trading System*, Oxford: Oxford University Press.

Colombo, A. (2004) *The Principle of Subsidiarity and European Citizenship*, Milan: Vita e Pensiero.

Constantin, S. M. (2008) 'Rethinking subsidiarity and the balance of powers in the EU in light of the Lisbon Treaty and beyond,' *Croatian Yearbook of European Law and Policy*, 4: 151–177.

Council of the European Union (2008) 'Conclusions of the Council and of the representatives of the governments of the member states, meeting within the Council, on the promotion of cultural diversity and intercultural dialogue in the external relations of the Union and its member states,' (OJ C 320/04), Brussels: European Council.

de Búrca, G. (2000) 'Reappraising subsidiarity's significance after Amsterdam,' Harvard Jean Monnet Working Paper 7/99, Cambridge: Harvard Law School. Online. Available HTTP: http://centers.law.nyu.edu/jeanmonnet/papers/99/990701.html (accessed 30 September 2011).

de Witte, B. (2008) 'The value of cultural diversity in European Union law,' in H. Schneider and P. Van den Bossche (eds.) *Protection of Cultural Diversity from a European and International Perspective*, Antwerp: Intersentia.

Donders, K. (2012) *Public Service Media and Policy in Europe*, Basingstoke: Palgrave MacMillan.

Dunoff, J. L. (1999) 'The death of the trade regime,' *European Journal of International Law*, 10(4): 733–762.

—— (2006) 'Constitutional conceits: The WTO's "Constitution" and the discipline of international law,' *European Journal of International Law*, 17(3): 647–675.

European Coalitions for Cultural Diversity (ECCD) (2009) '*Final Declaration' (on the Draft EU–Korea Protocol on Cultural Cooperation)*, Paris: ECCD, 5 May. Online. Available HTTP: http://www.coalitionfrancaise.org/eng/?p=96 (accessed 30 September 2011).

European Commission (1992) *Formation Intellectuelle de l'Idée de la Subsidiarité*, Brussels: European Commission.

—— (1993) *Commission Report to the European Council on the Adaptation of Community Legislation to the Subsidiarity Principle*, COM(93) 545 def., Brussels: European Commission.

—— (2007a) *Communication from the Commission to the European Parliament, the Council, the European Economic and Social Committee and the Committee of the Regions on a European Agenda for Culture in a Globalizing World*, COM(2007)242 final, Brussels: European Commission.

—— (2007b) *Argumentaire on the Title on Cultural Cooperation in Future EU Trade Agreements*,' Brussels: European Commission. Online. Available HTTP: http://www.efah.org/components/docs/argumentaire%20EN.pdf (accessed 30 September 2011).

—— (2008) *Follow-up Argumentaire on the Cooperation Protocol in Future EU Trade Agreements*, Brussels: European Commission. Online. Available HTTP: http://trade.ec.europa.eu/doclib/docs/2008/february/tradoc_137751.pdf (accessed 30 September 2011).

—— (2009a) *Commission Staff Working Document on the External Dimension of Audiovisual Policy* SEC (2009) 1033 final, Brussels: European Commission.

—— (2009b) *Concept Paper: Cultural Cooperation Protocol with Korea*, Brussels: European Commission. Online. Available HTTP: http://trade.ec.europa.eu/doclib/html/142542.htm (accessed 30 September 2011).

—— (2010a) *European Regional Organization Questionnaire*, Brussels: European Commission, in response to the regional organization questionnaire for the study *Implementing the UNESCO Convention of 2005 in the European Union*, Report requested by the European Parliament's Committee on Culture and Education, 12 February. Online. Available HTTP: http://www.diversitystudy.eu/ros/european_commission_regional_organizations_questionnaire.pdf (accessed 30 September 2011).

—— (2010b) Case No COMP/M.5932: *News Corp/BSkyB*, Brussels: European Commission, 21 December.

Fisher, R. (2007) *Briefing Paper on the Implementation of Article 151.4 of the EC Treaty* (note requested by the European Parliament's Committee on Culture and Education), Brussels: European Parliament.

French Ministry of Foreign and European Affairs (2009) *For a New European Union External Cultural Strategy*, Paris. Online. Available HTTP: http://www.coalitionfrancaise.org/eng/wp-content/uploads/2009/12/comm_fr_strat_culturelle_ext_eng.pdf (accessed 30 September 2011).

Garnham, N. (1998) 'Media policy,' in A. Briggs and P. Cobley (eds.) *The Media: An Introduction*, Harlow: Addison Wesley Longman.

Hahn, M. (2006) 'A clash of cultures? The UNESCO diversity convention and international trade law,' *Journal of International Economic Law*, 9(3): 515–552.

Harcourt, A. (2002) 'Engineering Europeanization: The role of the European institutions in shaping national media regulation,' *Journal of European Public Policy*, 9(5): 736–755.

Holtz-Bacha, C. (2005) 'The EU, the member states and the future of public broadcasting,' *Doxa*, 3: 231–237.

Howse, R. (2002) 'From politics to technocracy—and back again: The fate of the multilateral trading regime,' *The American Journal of International Law*, 96(1): 94–117.

—— and Nicolaïdis, K. (2003) 'Enhancing WTO legitimacy: Constitutionalization or global subsidiarity?' *Governance: An International Journal of Policy, Administration, and Institutions*, 16(1): 73–94.

Jackson, J. H. (2001) 'The WTO "constitution" and proposed reforms: Seven "mantras" revisited,' *Journal of International Economic Law*, 4(1): 67–78.

Katsirea, I. (2008) *Public Broadcasting and European Law: A Comparative Examination of Public Service Obligations in Six Member States*, New York: Wolters Kluwer International.

Keohane, R. O. and Nye, J. S. (2002) 'The club model of multilateral cooperation and problems of democratic legitimacy,' in R. O. Keohane (ed.) *Power and Governance in a Partially Globalized World*, London and New York: Routledge.

Krajewski, M. (2001) 'Democratic legitimacy and constitutional perspectives of WTO law,' *Journal of World Trade*, 35(1): 167–186.

—— (2005) 'External trade law and the constitution treaty: Towards a federal and more democratic Common Commercial Policy?' *Common Market Law Review*, 42(1): 91–127.

Lamy, P. (2003) 'Les négociations sur les services culturels à l'OMC,': Speech given for the European Parliament's Cultural Commission, Brussels, 19 May.

Lang, A. (2006) 'Reconstructing embedded liberalism: John Gerard Ruggie and constructivist approaches to the study of the international trade regime,' *Journal of International Economic Law*, 9(1): 81–116.

Leal-Arcas, R. (2010) 'The European Union's trade and investment policy after the Treaty of Lisbon,' *The Journal of World Investment & Trade*, 11(4): 463–514.

Loisen, J. (2009) 'The audiovisual dossier on the agenda of the World Trade Organization: An institutional and political economic study on the tenor, form and margins of the WTO intervention in audiovisual policy,' Unpublished PhD thesis (in Dutch), Free University of Brussels.

—— and de Ville, F. (2011) 'The EU-Korea Protocol on Cultural Cooperation: Towards cultural diversity or cultural deficit?' *International Journal of Communication*, 5: 254–271. Online. Available HTTP: http://ijoc.org/ojs/index.php/ijoc/article/view/882/522 (accessed 30 September 2011).

—— and Pauwels, C. (2010) 'Study Paper 3c: Protocols on Cultural Cooperation,' in G. Avocats and multidisciplinary research team (eds.) *Implementing the UNESCO Convention of 2005 in the European Union*, Brussels: Report requested by the European Parliament's Committee on Culture and Education. Online. Available HTTP: http://www.diversitystudy.eu/ms/ep_study_long_version_20_nov_2010_final.pdf (accessed 30 September 2011).

Michalis, M. (2007) *Governing European Communications: From Unification to Coordination*, Lanham, MD: Lexington Books.

Obuljen, N. and Smiers, J. (eds.) (2006) *UNESCO's Convention on the Protection and Promotion of the Diversity of Cultural Expressions: Making it Work*, Zagreb: Institute for International Relation.

Padovani, C. and Pavan, E. (2011) 'Actors and interactions in global communication governance: The heuristic potential of a network approach,' in R. Mansell and M. Raboy (eds.) *Handbook of Global Media and Communication Policy*, Boston, MA: Blackwell.

Pauwels, C. (1995) 'Culture and economy: The fields of tensions in the Community's audiovisual policy. An analysis of the limits and possibilities of a qualitative cultural and communications policy in an economically integrated Europe,' Unpublished PhD thesis (in Dutch), Free University of Brussels.

—— and Donders, K. (2011) 'From television without frontiers to the digital big bang: The EU's continuous efforts to create a future-proof internal media market,' in R. Mansell and M. Raboy (eds.) *Handbook of Global Media and Communication Policy*, Boston, MA: Blackwell.

—— and Loisen, J. (2003) 'The WTO and the audiovisual sector: Economic free trade vs cultural horse trading?' *European Journal of Communication*, 18(3): 291–313.

——, —— and Donders, K. (2006) 'Culture incorporated, or trade revisited? How inter-institutional dialectics and dynamic actor positions affect the outcomes of the debate on cultural trade and diversity,' in N. Obuljen and J. Smiers (eds.) *UNESCO's Convention on the Protection and Promotion of the Diversity of Cultural Expressions: Making it Work*, Zagreb: Institute for International Relations.

Pauwelyn, J. (2005) 'The Sutherland Report: A missed opportunity for genuine debate on trade, globalization and reforming the WTO,' *Journal of International Economic Law*, 8(2): 329–346.

Petersmann, E. (2001) 'Human rights and international economic law in the 21st century: The need to clarify their interrelationships,' *Journal of International Economic Law*, 4(3): 3–39.

Psychogiopoulou, E. (2006) 'The cultural mainstreaming clause of Article 151(4) EC: Protection and promotion of cultural diversity or hidden cultural agenda?' *European Law Journal*, 12(5): 575–592.

Raboy, M. and Padovani, C. (2010) 'Mapping global media policy: Concepts, frameworks, methods,' *Communication, Culture & Critique*, (3)2: 150–169.

Schofield, M. (2004) 'Global subsidiarity and the WTO: An analysis using Dworkin's conception of democracy,' *Policy and Society*, 24(3): 45–67.

Schütze, R. (2009) *From Dual to Cooperative Federalism: The Changing Structure of European Law*, Oxford: Oxford University Press.

Steger, D. P. (2007), 'The culture of the WTO: Why it needs to change,' *Journal of International Economic Law*, 10(3): 483–495.

Thiec, Y. (2009) 'The first assessment of the EU-Korea Protocol,' Brussels: INCDEurope. Online. Available HTTP: www.eurocinema.eu/docs/EU_Korea_PCC_Assessment_03.09.pdf (accessed 30 September 2011).

Unesco (2005) 'Convention on the Protection and Promotion of the Diversity of Cultural Expressions,' (CLT-2005/CONVENTION DIVERSITE-CULT REV.), Paris: Unesco, 20 October.

Van Kersbergen, K. and Verbeek, B. (2007) 'The politics of international norms: Subsidiarity and the imperfect competence regime of the European Union,' *European Journal of International Relations*, 13(2): 217–238.

Voon, T. (2007) 'A new approach to audiovisual products in the WTO: Rebalancing GATT and GATS,' *UCLA Entertainment Law Review*, 14(1): 1–32.

Wunsch-Vincent, S. (2003) 'The digital trade agenda of the US: Parallel tracks of bilateral, regional and multilateral liberalization,' *Aussenwirtschaft*, 58(1): 7–46.

# 5

# Commercial content and its relationship to media content

## Commodification and trust

*Lesley Hitchens*

### Introduction

In a 2010 lecture, Alan Rusbridger, editor of the well-known British newspaper *The Guardian*, reminded the audience of the importance of subsidies in media. He was not referring only to public funding for public broadcasters such as the British Broadcasting Corporation (BBC), but also to advertising (Rusbridger 2010). He argued that advertising subsidized the commercial broadcast and print media, and ensured that the public was able to receive the news and information that it was unlikely to be willing to fund fully through direct payment. As Rushbridger reminds us, advertising is at the heart of media, and media occupy a commodified space. Yet despite the intimacy of this connection, the relationship is not without constraints, as commercial interests have not been allowed unrestrained access to these communication channels.

The principle of transparency has served as one important constraint. Although there are major differences in policy and regulatory attitudes to commercial communications, both the United States and the United Kingdom have required commercial communications to be transparent—in other words, the public should know what is commercial speech and what is not. Transparency is important because it enables the public to evaluate the information it is receiving. It provides a means by which the public can know whether the content being broadcast has been produced with the usual journalistic standards and processes, or whether the material is simply promoting a certain commercial or political agenda. Journalistic standards should, at a minimum, require that: facts have been checked and information verified; information has been presented fairly without misrepresentation or the suppression of relevant facts; those involved in the production of content have exercised editorial judgement independent of personal interests or outside influences; and conflicts of interest (real or perceived) have been avoided or disclosed. Such an approach provides a basis for trust and a means for the public to negotiate the vast mass of information and opinion to which it may be exposed—a mediated path.

The United States has maintained a consistent policy and regulatory approach towards the use of paid-for content. Advertising, sponsorship and program integration techniques, such as product placement, are all permissible forms of commercial communication provided that they comply with the rules associated with transparency. The United Kingdom, however, has recently undergone a significant policy and regulatory change. In relation to both commercial radio and television, there has been longstanding caution about commercial communications. While advertising, in the traditional spot form, was permitted, commercial references in programming were prohibited, with limited exceptions.[1] This meant that product placement was prohibited on television and radio, and sponsorship and program-related material were tightly regulated. This arose out of concerns about the potential for commercial interests to interfere with programming and the independence of editorial decisions.[2] In the United Kingdom, in addition to the transparency principle, two other principles have also provided important policy foundations: principles of editorial independence and separation—principles that are not relevant to commercial regulatory policy in the United States. The editorial independence principle is intended to ensure that editorial control is retained over programming and content. The separation principle, which will not be examined in this chapter, requires advertising and program content to be kept separate.[3]

The significant change to UK commercial regulatory policy has been to permit product placement.[4] However, the United Kingdom has retained the principle of editorial independence, distancing itself from the US approach, which relies solely on the transparency principle. The fact that the United Kingdom was not prepared to relinquish the editorial

1 "Spot" advertising features a brief advertising message inserted between radio or television programs or during a break in the program. It is usual for several spot advertisements to be broadcast together. "Commercial references" in UK broadcasting regulations are understood as referring to "product placement," "sponsorship," and "program-related material." In the current Ofcom Code, "commercial references" are defined as "any visual or audio reference within programming to a product, service or trade mark (whether related to a commercial or non-commercial organisation)" (Ofcom 2011a: section 9). Sponsorship also has a specific meaning in the UK and is not used, as it is in the US, to refer to commercial communications generally. In the UK, sponsorship relates to programming that has had some or all of its costs met by a sponsor, the latter with a view to promoting its products, services, trademarks or activities (Ofcom 2011a: section 9). Program-related material refers to material that "consists of products or services that are directly derived from a programme and specifically intended to allow viewers to benefit fully from, or to interact with, that programme" (Ofcom 2011a: section 9). Although there have been some consequential effects, the introduction of product placement has not significantly changed the regulatory arrangements for sponsorship and program-related material.

2 In the UK, these issues arise primarily in relation to commercial interests because political advertising is prohibited (Communications Act 2003, s. 321(2)), although advertising for non-commercial purposes, such as by charities, may also occur. For this reason, this chapter generally refers to commercial interests, although in the US, advertising may be for corporate or political purposes. In discussing the US, some examples of advertising for non-commercial purposes are, however, included because they have raised issues of concern in recent years.

3 With the introduction of product placement, the separation principle is no longer feasible. The rules under this principle required the advertising and program elements of a broadcasting service to be kept separate (Ofcom 2008a: rule 10.2). The separation principle and accompanying rules were linked with both transparency and editorial independence, and were another way of ensuring that commercial references did not creep into programming. With the introduction of product placement into UK broadcasting, the rules that implemented the separation principle have been repealed and replaced by a requirement of "distinctness," so there must be a clear distinction between editorial content and advertising (Ofcom 2011a: rule 9.2)

4 Product placement is referred to as "the inclusion in a programme of, or of a reference to, a product, service or trade mark, where the inclusion is for a commercial purpose, and is in return for the making of any payment, or the giving of other valuable consideration, to any relevant provider or any person connected with a relevant provider, and is not prop placement" (Ofcom 2011a: section 9).

independence principle indicates that there was some disquiet about the introduction of a more relaxed commercial environment. Yet one might question why should this be the case? After all, the media have long operated within a commercial environment and, as Rusbridger indicated, commercial communications have played a key role in media output. Product placement can be viewed as just another example of this commercial, commodified environment. In addition, there has been the longstanding US tolerance of product placement. Nevertheless, the UK relaxation is restrained. It is this disquiet that the chapter seeks to explore. The introduction of product placement in the United Kingdom provides an opportunity to re-examine the relationship between commercial interests and the media. Are the protections that have been put in place sufficient to alleviate disquiet, or do practices such as product placement put at risk at some fundamental level—and in a way that cannot be fully ameliorated by regulatory design—the public's ability to access trusted content?

To consider these questions, the chapter follows two paths. First, it reviews in more detail the two principles that may be seen as protections to mitigate the impact of commercial interests: the transparency principle and the independence principle. It does this by examining how they are reflected in regulatory design, using the United States and the United Kingdom as illustrations. Despite a greater tolerance in the United States for commercial or paid-for content, there have also been concerns there about the practice.

For the second path, the chapter considers the place of commercial interests and the disquiet around such interests by posing three lines of inquiry. The first considers whether there is an inherent limitation in the rules that weaken their effectiveness in constraining the influence of commercial content. The second inquiry reviews the disquiet by considering the principle of access. The ability of the public to access information and ideas has been a longstanding tradition of media policy: Has the principle of access been undermined by more liberal approaches to commercial content? The final line of inquiry examines the problem using Sandel's argument from corruption, which suggests that the value of certain goods is diminished or corrupted by the market (Sandel 2005). The chapter asks whether media content is such a good.

Commercial content is a well-established component (and an important resource) of the media environment: A discussion of its role and even legitimacy may seem irrelevant or pointless. Is it legitimate, especially at a time when traditional media-funding models are under threat, to question the existence of paid-for content? It is, after all, as Rusbridger reminds us, another way of subsidizing the media. At the same time, the media must be responsible participants for their part in public discourse: ". . . the speaker cannot disassociate him- or herself from the possible effects of his or her discourse" (Garnham 1992: 368). Public discourse is vital in a functioning democracy and, as Couldry has written:

> In a mature democracy . . . most people share an orientation to a public world where matters of common concern are, or at least should be addressed. . . . This public connection is partly, even principally, sustained by a convergence in what media people consume, in other words by shared or overlapping media consumption (so 'public connection' is mediated).
>
> (*Couldry 2008: 107*)

The media's responsibility is in the mediation of that connection between the public and governments and public figures. Given these responsibilities, it is appropriate to test and question the placing of commercial content and practices such as paid-for content. Ongoing inquiries that question the relationship between commercial and media content provide a way of testing whether the media are meeting (or are able to meet) their public discourse responsibilities.

The public's orientation and connection through media consumption may be weakened by the fragmented nature of communication in the broadband age but, as suggested in the next section, the need for mediation may be greater. It will be seen also in this chapter that trust is an ongoing theme in policy discussions about the relationship between paid-for and media content. The importance of trust for public discourse will be addressed at the conclusion of this chapter, but its importance also justifies an ongoing inquiry into the role of commercial content and the policy and regulatory constraints on commercial influences.

## Identifying the media

As broadband and digital technologies increasingly enable the public to access information from a wide range of sources and to participate in ways not previously possible, rules about broadcast commercial communications, and a focus on them, may seem irrelevant. Of course, the media environment that is developing with the aid of broadband and digital technologies is not straightforward. The old media are not being replaced by the new in some crude manner; rather, there is a much more fluid situation in which old and new forms of communication may coexist together or merge as old media adapt to accommodate the new technology. The continuing importance of the traditional media should not be underestimated as a source of information and ideas. Further, while the traditional delivery platforms of old media may be losing their dominance, as content providers they are likely to remain significant as they expand into the digital space. It is important not to become too obsessed with possibly artificial concepts of old and new media, and to focus instead on the role that media play in public discourse and how they sustain that role in a changed media environment. Understanding the existing policy and regulatory frameworks for traditional media can contribute to the process of thinking about how to respond to the broadband age and ensure access to trusted content.

Of course, one cannot deny that the media space has changed, and continues to change, dramatically, opening up the public's access to information and other content as well as to a range of voices and formats. However, this new space is often unmediated and the public needs a way in which to navigate through the vast mass of information and opinion available in this environment—a mediated path. Habermas has commented:

> Use of the Internet has both broadened and fragmented the contexts of communication. . . . [T]he less formal, horizontal cross-linking of communication channels weakens the achievements of traditional media. This focuses the attention of an anonymous and dispersed public on set topics and information, allowing citizens to concentrate on the same critically filtered issues and journalistic pieces at any given time. The price we pay for the growth in egalitarianism offered by the Internet is the decentralized access to unedited stories.
>
> (*Habermas 2006*)

The broadband environment will not necessarily reduce the need for trust and systems to enable that trust. As will be seen in the next section, this has been recognized in the new European Union audiovisual regulatory framework.

## The introduction of product placement into the United Kingdom

Before proceeding with the two paths to be considered in this chapter, it may be useful to explain, briefly, the background to the decision to permit product placement in the United

Kingdom, especially as it illustrates the dilemma that policymakers faces in trying to balance commercial imperatives and public interest concerns—a dilemma perhaps heightened as the media industry struggles to develop viable business models in the broadband environment.

## *Audiovisual services*

The catalyst for the change in UK policy was the revision of the EU Television without Frontiers (TwF) Directive. Adopted in 1989, the TwF Directive was designed to provide a common framework of minimum standards across the European Union to ensure freedom of reception of television services. In 2007, the TwF Directive was substantially amended and became known as the Audiovisual Media Services Directive (AVMS Directive). One of the main purposes for amending the TwF Directive was to ensure that the EU media regulatory framework was able to respond to the changing environment in relation to the delivery of television services regardless of the technology used to deliver it. The AVMS Directive now covers on-demand services as well as television services delivered over the Internet or mobile platforms. The AVMS Directive draws a distinction between television services that are delivered at scheduled times and on-demand (television-like) services that can be viewed at the time the viewer chooses. A lighter form of regulation applies to on-demand services, but the rules on product placement apply to both services. It could be said that it was a liberalizing directive because, at the same time, it relaxed quantitative rules on advertising, such as the permitted amount and scheduling of advertising (Valcke 2008). The AVMS Directive explicitly prohibits product placement, but allows a member state to derogate from this prohibition with respect to four specific programming genres: cinematographic works; films and series made for television or on-demand services; sports programs; and light entertainment programs (Article 11).[5] Derogation is expressly prohibited for children's programs (Article 11.3), and the product placement prohibition remains for news.[6]

The UK government's position on product placement underwent something of a sea change in response to the new framework. Initially, it was inclined to continue the prohibition on product placement. The consultation on the implementation of the directive into the UK canvassed the arguments for and against the introduction (Department for Culture, Media and Sport 2008). Although the government found it relatively easy to dismiss most of the arguments offered in favor of product placement, the argument that the additional revenue would assist commercial broadcasters, facing increased competition for audiences and advertising revenue, to meet their public service-like obligations to provide quality and diverse programming was potentially more persuasive (Department for Culture, Media and Sport 2008). As the consultation noted, it was this argument that had been most persuasive in the EU's willingness to relax the product placement rules (Department for Culture, Media and

5 In fact, the AVMS Directive was not as radical as it might at first appear, because the TwF Directive did not expressly prohibit product placement. However, the rules on surreptitious advertising and separation of advertising from programming led most member states to assume that they constituted a de facto prohibition on product placement (Department for Culture, Media and Sport 2008: 47).

6 While the prohibition on product placement clearly applies to news, it left in doubt the status of some other formats such as current affairs, religious and consumer programs, because they may have been captured under the series exception (Bradshaw 2010). "Prop placement" where the product or service is supplied free of charge and no other payment is involved, is also permitted (Art. 11(3)(b)).

Sport 2008).[7] However, initially, the government was willing to weigh up this commercial argument against long-held public interest principles (Department for Culture, Media and Sport 2008). The consultation noted the significance of trust in the success of UK broadcasting:

> An important element of the success of broadcasting in the United Kingdom, and especially of public service broadcasting, has been the trust audiences have been able to have in broadcasters. This has been challenged by recent abuses in premium rate telephone charging and there must be a priority now for broadcasters to re-build audience trust in their integrity and maintain their distinctiveness from other media.[8]
>
> (*Department for Culture, Media and Sport 2008: 52*)

It is noteworthy that the abuse of trust referred to had occurred within a highly regulated environment; clearly, the existence of well-defined rules did not guarantee that trust would not be abused. In any event, the government's initial preferred position was to reject any relaxation. It noted that there was no consensus on the issue, with commercial broadcasters and advertisers in favor of introducing product placement, and consumer and viewer groups strongly opposed (Department for Culture, Media and Sport 2008). Prior to the release of the consultation report, the government's position had already been foreshadowed in a speech given by then Secretary of State for Culture, Media and Sport Andy Burnham, when he also emphasized the importance of the public having trust in what was being seen and heard, and his concerns about the impact of product placement on that trust:

> I can see the arguments and benefits of product placement and understand why people feel it is an inevitability given the pressures they are under. But . . . I can also see the cost and the very high costs that might be paid in the long term. I feel there is a risk that product placement exacerbates this decline in trust and contaminates our programmes. There is a risk that, at the very moment when television needs to do all it can to show it can be trusted, that we elide the distinction between programmes and adverts.
>
> (*Burnham 2008*)

Following further consultation, the government announced its decision not to permit product placement. It acknowledged the economic arguments, but did not consider that these outweighed the detrimental impact that product placement was predicted to have. During the consultation, program makers, broadcasters and advertisers had generally argued in support of product placement because of the revenue-enhancing opportunities it would provide, and

7 Still, the government was not overly persuaded about the estimates of likely revenue from product placement, and did not think that comparisons could be easily drawn with the United States, given the tighter restrictions on product placement that would apply in the United Kingdom by reason of the AVMS Directive (Department for Culture, Media and Sport 2008: 51).

8 During 2006–08, Ofcom conducted a series of investigations into programs that encouraged viewer participation in competitions using premium-rate telephone charging services. The concerns related to whether the programs were disguised advertising and whether the competitions had been operated fairly in accordance with Ofcom rules. The investigations resulted in commercial television broadcasters being fined over £5 million, the highest sanctions ever imposed by Ofcom. For further details see Ofcom(2008b).

emphasized the opportunities for maintaining investment in the quality and diversity of programming (Burnham 2009). However, there is no reason why increased revenue would necessarily be used in this way unless there was an obvious profit return on the increased investment in programming.

Only a few months after reaching this policy position, however, the same government (but with a new Secretary of State for the portfolio) announced a further consultation on product placement, making it clear that it was reconsidering its position (Bradshaw 2009). The outcome of this consultation, announced in February 2010, was to permit the introduction of product placement. There was no significant change in the arguments put forward, but the government now took the view that the commercial benefits of product placement could be adequately balanced with the safeguards that would be in place (Bradshaw 2010).[9]

## *Radio services*

The EU reforms only affected television, but they provided the impetus for a UK review of regulation of radio's commercial content. The outcome has been to permit commercial integration into programming, although some areas such as news, children's programming, and the selection of music to be broadcast are quarantined from commercial arrangements (Ofcom 2011: rules 10.3–10.5). More significantly, the editorial independence principle will not apply to radio. In the review conducted by Ofcom that led to the changed policy position, it was clear that commercial pressures were again driving change. Industry interests wanted a regulatory approach that would provide enough flexibility for the radio industry to generate new revenue (Ofcom 2010c: para. 4.25).

Thus, radio and television in the United Kingdom have now, for the first time, taken very different policy and regulatory approaches. While the television reforms have been constrained by the EU framework, the greater relaxation in the radio sector may foreshadow an inexorable pressure for change in the television sector, especially as multi-platform delivery makes it increasingly difficult to maintain the traditional regulatory silos. Tellingly, the transparency principle, which is stated as the basis for the new rules for commercial references in radio programming, is described ". . . as a means to secure consumer protection" (Ofcom 2011a: section 10). Given the longstanding public interest policy position in the United Kingdom in relation to the protection of programming from commercial distortion, it seems a significant shift to view these new rules as falling simply within the frame of consumer protection. It is this tension between the commercial pressures and public interest concerns that is explored in the final part of this chapter.

## *The regulatory map*

The new rules that apply to television and radio services came into force in February 2011. They are administered by Ofcom and are incorporated into the Ofcom Broadcasting Code. In relation to television, the rules apply to scheduled television services whether they are broadcast by traditional platforms or delivered online. The Authority for Television on Demand (ATVOD) is responsible for the regulation of on-demand television-like services, including the product placement rules (ATVOD 2011). ATVOD is an industry-based

9 Another potential influencing factor was a perceived risk to UK competitiveness, as the other EU member states (with the exception of Denmark) had decided to permit product placement.

regulator that shares regulatory responsibilities for this sector with Ofcom. The EU reforms offer an example of how to respond to the need to promote journalistic standards and trust in a broadband environment. However, the regulatory design is complex, and there are already difficulties in determining the type of content regulated and by whom (Craufurd Smith 2011). Such difficulties will grow as traditional forms of media output such as print and television draw on each other's formats and tools. This discussion is outside the scope of this chapter, but it illustrates the need to develop flexible regulatory mechanisms. For simplicity, references to the product placement rules in this chapter will refer only to the Ofcom rules.

In the next two sections, the chapter pursues the first path of investigation, and reviews the principles of transparency and editorial independence and their role in constraining commercial content. The chapter will mainly refer to the traditional media. The UK rules are not confined to traditional media, but the United States has not addressed the new media environment in relation to advertising regulation. Nevertheless, as noted earlier, understanding the policy that has informed traditional media practice can be important when building policy and regulatory responses in the broadband environment.

## The principle of transparency

Although there are differences in approach to product placement between the United Kingdom and the United States, both jurisdictions adhere to the principle of transparency. The principle requires that the audience has the means to distinguish between commercial and program content, and to be able to know when content has been paid for. Transparency makes clear to the audience what is an advertisement or paid-for content and what is not. Thus UK rules require advertisements to "be obviously distinguishable from editorial content" (BCAP 2010: rule 2.1). Without transparency, the audience may be misled not only about the nature of the content, but also about the production of the content. In the absence of such information, audiences are likely to assume that the content was produced applying usual journalistic standards and processes. A failure of transparency means that the audience is unable to evaluate properly the nature of the information it is receiving. In the United States, the importance of the transparency principle and its link to trust was emphasized by then Federal Communications Commission (FCC) (the US communications regulatory authority) Commissioner Jonathan S. Adelstein and FCC Commissioner Michael J. Copps, in an FCC decision concerning the failure to disclose sponsorship by a US government department:

> Growing abuses of the public trust in recent years are shaking Americans' confidence in the press. When pundits are paid to promote a corporate or government agenda while the public is never told, all commenters and journalists become suspect. The repeated revelations of advertisers paying their way onto news programming without disclosure undercut the credibility of all journalists.
>
> (*Federal Communications Commission 2007b: 12*)

### *Embedding transparency in rules*

Although commercial influence on programming is not objectionable under US policy, the transparency principle is important and a complex regulatory design has been built to draw out the true sponsor of the material being broadcast. This is exemplified in the long-established and oft-repeated principle that audiences are "entitled to know by whom they are being persuaded" (Federal Communications Commission 1963: 1). The United States serves as a useful illustration of how rules might be designed to promote the transparency principle and its application in practice. The regulatory scheme is underpinned by what is known as the "sponsorship identification rule." Section 317(a)(1) of the Communications Act of 1934 requires that, where matter is broadcast by television or radio for which some monetary or in-kind benefit has been provided, the fact of that payment must be disclosed at the same time. Although described as the "sponsorship identification rule," the rule covers the traditional spot type of advertisement, as well as sponsorship and product integration practices. For the traditional spot advertisement, transparency presents no such difficulty, since the purpose of the advertisement is normally to identify the corporate brand, and so such a mention would usually constitute compliance (47 CFR §73.1212(f)). Where the paid-for content is in a different format from the spot advertisement, such as a sponsored program or product placement, the licensee at the time of the broadcast must announce the fact of the sponsorship or paid-for content and the identity of the person who has provided the monetary or in-kind benefit, or upon whose behalf the payment was provided (47 CFR §73.1212(a)). There is a strong emphasis on disclosure of the true identity of the "sponsor"; the rules are also designed to ensure that the licensee uses reasonable diligence to obtain relevant information from employees and any other person with whom it deals in relation to program matter, so that the appropriate sponsorship identification announcement can be made (47 CFR §73.1212(b)). Hence a licensee's information-gathering obligations could, for example, extend to independent contractors, such as radio or television presenters, and even those persons who deal with the licensee on behalf of the presenters.

While the sponsorship identification rule is concerned with monetary or in-kind benefits paid to the licensee, a second rule, the "payment disclosure rule," aims to bolster the other rule and capture payments to third persons. It imposes an obligation on any employee or person involved with the production or preparation of program content and who receives a payment in relation to the provision of content to be broadcast to disclose the fact of acceptance or payment to the licensee (Communications Act of 1934, §507). The rule applies to a number of parties: an employee receiving the payment; the person making the payment; a person involved with the production or preparation of the program who receives payment; and a person who supplies a program or program matter and who has relevant information. The "payment disclosure rule" is designed to ensure that the relevant information passes through the chain of production and distribution up to the licensee (Federal Communications Commission 2005: 3). Once a licensee receives this disclosure, it will have an obligation to comply with the sponsorship identification rule and to make disclosure as if the licensee had itself received the monetary or in-kind benefit (Communications Act of 1934, §317(b)).

It should be noted that the US rules are not limited to commercial corporate sponsors; they also cover sponsorship from political, government, advocacy and lobbyist sources. Further, if the matter is political or relates to a controversial issue of public importance, then disclosure must be made even if no payment has been made (47 USC §317(a)(2)). Even in relation to commercial content, careful judgement is needed to determine whether a monetary or in-kind benefit has been provided, as demonstrated by two recent FCC decisions. Both concerned video news releases (VNRs)[10] provided to the broadcasters: in one instance, by car manufacturer

10 VNRs are "essentially prepackaged news stories, that may use actors to play reporters and include suggested scripts to introduce stories. These practices allow such externally prepackaged news stories to be aired, without alteration, as broadcast or cable news" (Federal Communications Commission 2005: 1).

General Motors (Federal Communications Commission 2011a); in the other, by the maker of a cold remedy, Zicam (Federal Communications Commission 2011b). The broadcasters in each case argued that no monetary or in-kind benefit had been received for the VNRs, and that they fell within the proviso to § 317(a)(1), which removes the sponsorship identification obligation if no, or only nominal, payment has been provided, or if the product or service in question is used in a manner that is reasonably related to the use of such product or service in the broadcast. In both cases, the FCC rejected the argument because the portrayal of the products in question was disproportionate to the subject matter of the broadcast (Federal Communications Commission 2011a: para. 14; Federal Communications Commission 2011b: paras. 11–12). In the matter concerning General Motors, a supposed news report on consumer demand for convertible cars included only images of, and references to, General Motors cars. The FCC decided that these images were not fleeting or transient, but disproportionate to the needs of the report, and therefore the public should have been informed as to the true source of the VNR material. The example of this news report illustrates the potential harm in this type of paid-for content: How is one to know if a report is providing information about a genuine increase in demand for convertible cars, or is merely a promotional item in which the information presented about demand may not be especially robust? In both matters, the FCC also held that valuable benefits had been provided in the provision of the VNRs themselves. It was not necessary for a monetary payment to be made (Federal Communications Commission 2011a: para. 11; Federal Communications Commission 2011b: para. 9).

### *Transparency and codes of conduct*

As the rules show, it is the failure to disclose who is paying for the airtime that is objectionable under US regulatory policy. This does not mean, however, that there are no principles in place about how to deal with paid-for content and its influence on program content. The Code of Ethics and Professional Conduct of the Radio Television Digital News Association (RTDNA) emphasizes the responsibility of electronic journalists in the process of gathering and reporting of news to the public: They should do so "without fear or favor, and vigorously resist undue influence from any outside forces, including advertisers, . . . powerful individuals, and special interest groups" (RTDNA 2000). Journalists are also required to "determine news content solely through editorial judgement and not as a result of outside influence." The RTNDA has separate guidelines to deal with VNRs and audio news releases that again emphasize the importance of protecting the editorial integrity of the video and audio that they air, especially in relation to news, suggesting that such integrity might come into question if broadcasters rely on packaged news material (RTNDA n.d.). These principles of editorial integrity are not unlike those that apply in the United Kingdom, as will be seen in the review of the editorial independence principle, but it may be questioned how effective they are in practice.

### *Transparency in practice*

Despite these codes of ethics and guidelines and the comprehensive statutory rules on transparency and disclosure, there have been ongoing concerns in the United States about the influence on programming of both commercial and non-commercial interests. An extensive inquiry in 2005 revealed widespread music payola practices in the radio sector (Federal Communications Commission 2007a). The FCC initiated the inquiry only after the New York Attorney-General had commenced an investigation into the same practices, which prompted an FCC Commissioner to suggest that the FCC had become lax in enforcing the sponsorship rules (Federal Communications Commission 2007a). VNRs, as illustrated by the Zicam and General Motors decisions, are examples of commercial product integration that are affecting both news and current affairs content. As a result of pressure from the public and public interest groups, such as Free Press, the FCC issued a public notice reminding broadcasters of their responsibilities to comply with the sponsorship identification rules when using VNRs (Federal Communications Commission 2005). Consistent with the US acceptance of paid-for content, the FCC was not concerned about the fact of the VNRs, but rather the possibility that disclosure responsibilities may not have been met.

Yet there seems something intrinsically at odds with the notion that paid-for content, even with the requisite sponsorship identification, can nevertheless be presented in the guise of news, using actors as "reporters". If the sponsors think this is worth their investment, even with identification, this may suggest that the public, even with disclosure, may not fully understand the nature or the extent of the paid-for content. And if it is disguised, or disclosure is not effective, it suggests that the sponsors value association with content that apparently adheres to journalistic standards, even though the integration undermines the very values with which association may be sought.

The 2005 Public Notice led to further investigations into the use of VNRs and whether there had been compliance with the sponsorship identification rules. Comcast Corporation was fined a total of US $20,000 in relation to five VNRs that were broadcast without disclosure of the sponsors (Federal Communications Commission 2007c, 2007d). While the Comcast breaches related to commercial products, VNRs have been used by both government and public bodies. For example, in 2007, the FCC issued notices of fines against two television licensees for failing to broadcast sponsorship identification. The matter concerned a political commentator, Armstrong Williams, who was paid by the US Department of Education to promote a particular government program, known as "No Child Left Behind." The licensees had broadcast programs produced by Williams and his media company promoting the government program (Federal Communications Commission 2007b).[11]

The ongoing concerns about VNRs and other embedded advertising practices led the FCC to instigate an inquiry in 2008 into the continued effectiveness of the sponsorship identification rules (Federal Communications Commission 2008). Despite evidence (including the recent Zicam and General Motors matters) that the FCC is willing to impose fines where the rules are breached, the 2008 inquiry has not advanced. In a recent discussion paper produced by FCC staff on the information needs of communities in a broadband environment, there was quite extensive consideration of the commercial arrangements in play and the manner in which these may be affecting news and current affairs as the separation between news and advertising sales departments dissolves (Federal Communications Commission 2011c). This discussion paper was unconnected to the 2008 inquiry, but it is an indication that concerns remain about the relationship between paid-for content and program content, even within the FCC, especially as we move into a very different media environment. The experience in the United States shows also that extensive rule design will not guarantee that the public is properly informed about the nature of the information it is receiving.

11 In relation to one of the broadcast programs, the licensee had received no payment—monetary or in-kind—but this was irrelevant because the broadcast concerned "a controversial issue of public importance." In such situations, the sponsorship identification rule still had to be complied with (Federal Communications Commission 2007b).

## The principle of editorial independence

It is the principle and regulatory requirement of editorial independence that sets the UK approach apart from that of the United States. The editorial independence principle is intended to ensure that the broadcaster retains editorial control over program content and that programs are not distorted for commercial purposes. In the United Kingdom, prohibition of product placement and strict control over sponsorship arrangements and program-related material were always viewed as being integral to the maintenance of this principle. With the prohibition on product placement now being relaxed, the role for editorial independence might be viewed as redundant, as one might question the feasibility of trying to maintain such a principle when paid-for content can now be integrated into programming.

The EU regulatory framework sets the parameters for the UK product placement reforms for television services and requires the principle of editorial independence to be retained. The United Kingdom has imposed a prohibition on some genres that were not clearly covered by the EU reforms. Hence product placement is prohibited in religious, consumer advice and current affairs programming (Ofcom 2011a: rule 9.12).[12] However, documentaries and other factual programs that do not fall within the consumer advice or current affairs genres can carry product placement. When Ofcom was consulting about the new rules, it proposed excluding documentaries and factual programs as well, because it was concerned about the impact of product placement on programs designed to investigate serious issues and the threat to the integrity of such programs. It considered that a prohibition could help to "maintain audience trust in serious factual programming" (Ofcom 2010b: paras. 4.52–4.59). However, this proposal did not proceed. Ofcom acknowledged the difficulties in trying to classify such programming and the risk of regulatory uncertainty, and considered that there were sufficient safeguards embodied in the editorial independence principle. Nevertheless, given the exclusion of product placement from news and current affairs, it is difficult to see why the safeguards are apparently sufficient for other types of factual programming when they are not considered so for news and current affairs.

The Ofcom 2011 Code rules for commercial references in television programming are framed to support the principle of editorial independence (and transparency) and the Code states that it is mindful that the inclusion of commercial references in programs "creates a particular risk that the key principles may be, or appear to be, undermined" (Ofcom 2011a: section 9). Hence, in relation to all forms of "commercial references," broadcasters must "maintain editorial control over programming" and "ensure that editorial content is distinct from advertising" (Ofcom 2011a: rules 9.1–9.2). The imperative to ensure that programming is not distorted by commercial content can be seen in additional rules that prohibit the promotion of products, services and trade marks in programming (Ofcom 2011a: rule 9.4) or which

12 The UK product placement regime will be explained only in broad detail. Some aspects of the regime are derived from the AVMS Directive and the UK government has imposed some additional obligations, such as additional programming genres. Another example of an additional obligation is a prohibition on product placement of foods that are high in fat, salt and sugar. Additional restrictions imposed by the United Kingdom will apply only to programs produced under the UK jurisdiction. It should also be noted that, although the Ofcom 2011 Code refers to "commercial" references in programming, the rules apply to product placement for non-commercial purposes, for example where a charity may wish to pay for the inclusion of references. Ofcom considered that such situations should be covered by the rules to provide regulatory consistency and to safeguard the editorial independence principle (Ofcom 2010a: paras. 4.21–4.24).

give undue prominence to products, services and trade marks (Ofcom 2011a: rule 9.5). Undue prominence may arise where a product appears without editorial justification or by reason of the degree of prominence that is given to it (Ofcom 2011b: paras. 1.31–1.34).

Broadcasters are also required to ensure that product placement does "not influence the content and scheduling of a programme in a way that affects the responsibility and editorial independence of the broadcaster" (Ofcom 2011: rule 9.8). Where product placement is used, the transparency principle also comes into play. The Code requires the product placement to be signalled to the audience (Ofcom 2011a: rule 9.14). This is to occur at the start and end of the program, and at the recommencement of the program after each advertising break. The format of the signal is prescribed and takes the form of a black-and-white "P" (Ofcom 2011b). Ofcom considered that a universal and neutral signal, rather than one tailored to an individual broadcaster's brand, was essential because product placement in UK-produced programs would be new to audiences: The use of a universal signal would reduce confusion (Ofcom 2010d).

The introduction of product placement into UK radio and television services represents a substantial cultural and policy shift. The protections built into the new policy, such as the maintenance of the editorial independence principle and the exclusion of certain genres, are in themselves an acknowledgement of the risks that product placement creates for public discourse. The final section of this chapter examines whether such concerns might be justified by considering the disquiet around commercial interests.

## Testing the disquiet

It was suggested early in this chapter that the presence of paid-for content integrated into the usual program content might cause some disquiet. Certainly in the United Kingdom, with its decision to permit product placement after a long history of opposition to such practices, the presence of safeguards betrays some anxiety about the impact of the practice. The transparency principle has been at the core of the US regulatory framework for paid-for content, resulting in comprehensive and wide-reaching rules. However, here too disquiet is evident. There is a sense that the transparency principle and the rules exemplifying it have not been enough to resist commercial imperatives. Ethical standards also seem to have been unable to persuade the public that it can be sure about the nature of the content that it is receiving. Nevertheless, it might be thought that, with the maintenance of the editorial independence principle, the UK public will be able to have confidence in the nature of the content, especially in relation to news and current affairs programming. Whether that confidence is well placed is what this last section sets out to examine. Accordingly, this chapter considers the practice of paid-for content from the perspective of the effectiveness of rules and rights of access, and then by looking at whether program content is corrupted through commodification. The discussion is speculative and does not reach any firm conclusions, but there is a need for such ongoing inquiries.

### *The limits of rules*

Will the UK rules work? Will they achieve the principles embodied within them? The US rules rely on the principle that the public is entitled to know who is trying to persuade them, and so the sponsorship identification rules focus on knowing what content has been paid for and by whom. Thus, provided that the appropriate identification information has been given to the viewer or listener, it becomes irrelevant that the so-called program may be almost entirely, or indeed completely, commercial content. A regime based on transparency relies upon the audience to make the appropriate connection between the identification information and the actual impact that has on the content. This is not necessarily a logical connection. Knowing that a program is being sponsored does not always mean that the audience will understand that the sponsor may also have had an influence over the program content. That doubt and the awareness of the growing use of embedded advertising led the FCC to launch its inquiry into the effectiveness of its sponsorship identification rules in 2008 (Federal Communications Commission 2008).

By contrast, it may be assumed that such risks will not be present in the United Kingdom because of the retention within the rules of the editorial independence principle: the audience will be aware that product placement is being used and they will not be confused about the impact of the commercial content because the rules guarantee editorial independence. How the rules will function in practice is something that will only be determined over time, and there may well be pressure points, especially on the degree of prominence (for example that a commercial reference receives within a program). However, regardless of the rules and compliance with them, the introduction of product placement may so condition the environment that it will inexorably, even if invisibly, have an impact on programming and editorial decisions. Will program commissioners and makers have in mind that the ability to attract revenue could be affected by the treatment of products within the story line? Apple, for example, expects that its products will be shown only in a positive light (ABC 2010). None of this needs to happen in concert with potential sponsors, nor even consciously within the broadcasting organization; it would need only to form part of the unspoken—even unconscious—assumptions about the relationship between editorial decisions and revenue raising through product placement. It is, in essence, another version of the "chilling effect."

In this sense, rules will have limits. They will have a role only in those transactions, consciously arrived at, in which a product placement arrangement is being put, or is already, in place.

## *The concept of access*

The suggestion that the introduction of product placement may condition the environment to influence editorial decisions connects with a broader concern: namely, the impact of product placement on the public's ability to access the receipt of information and ideas. The principle of access has long informed media policy, although the degree to which it is built into regulatory arrangements varies between the United States and the United Kingdom (Hitchens 2006). Quantitative and scheduling rules about advertising are one way of seeking a balance between corporate (and other) sponsors' interest in communicating via the media and the public's interest in accessing information and ideas, although these rules are largely absent in the United States—with some exceptions (Hitchens 2006).

Product placement that promotes certain interests (commercial and, in the United States, political) arguably threatens the integrity of access principles. In the United Kingdom, the product placement rules that maintain editorial independence and protect certain forms of programming, especially news and current affairs, might be viewed as preserving access. But that would be to ignore the contribution that all types of programming could make to informing the public and providing understanding. This has been recognized by the United Kingdom:

> Whether arts or sciences, fiction or documentaries, entertainment or news, the subjects of television and radio are central to how we live our lives and how we understand each other. They allow our community to talk to itself.
>
> (*Department of Trade and Industry and Department for Culture, Media and Sport 2010: para. 5.3.11*)

Increasing the opportunities for sponsors to utilize communication channels, especially if the nature of the paid-for content is not clear to the audience, may unduly shift the balance between public access and the sponsor's access, undermining the public's access to program content and to information and opinion.

### *The limits of markets: The argument from corruption*

The disquiet occasioned by product placement and related practices can be examined from another perspective. Michael Sandel, writing on the moral limits of markets, suggests that the argument from corruption forms the basis of one objection to the reach of the market (Sandel 2005). It can be argued that certain goods are "diminished or corrupted if bought or sold for money" (Sandel 2005: 122), citing the "moral importance of the goods at stake" (Sandel 2005: 123). For Sandel, this is not just about getting the right rules in place:

> The argument from corruption is intrinsic in the sense that it cannot be met by fixing the background conditions within which market exchanges take place. It applies under conditions of equality and inequality alike.
>
> (*Sandel 2005: 123*)

If the argument from corruption is to apply here, then it must be because of "the character of the particular good in question" (Sandel 2005: 124). Can it be said that media content is of such a character that commodification should be resisted? Is it a good that has a moral or civic value or role, the character of which would be diminished or corrupted by market valuation or exchange? Is "the assumption that all goods are commensurable, that all goods can be translated without loss into a single measure or unit of value," an assumption that can apply here (Sandel 2005: 124)? A number of objections are apparent with this argument. First, there is the obvious fact that media content, regardless of rules on product placement and paid-for influence, already exists in an advertising-conditioned environment; advertising subsidizes the media, as Rusbridger (2010) reminds us, and programming is driven by the need to deliver audiences to advertisers. Second, the production and distribution of media content clearly operates within a market environment that must deliver to shareholders. Third, those who create the content rely on markets to communicate that content, or at least to enable that content to be communicated. These objections may undermine the argument that media content has a value that cannot be subject to market exchange.

The reality is that media content is already a marketable and well-entrenched commodity, and news programming, as the US experience has shown, is certainly a commodity. Hirst refers to the "duality of the news commodity, the contradiction between the informational use-value of journalism and its commercial exchange-value in a capitalist economy" (Hirst 2011: 178). Clearly, the use of VNRs in the United States demonstrates the exchange-value attractiveness of this informational use-value of news, even though the very exchange may destroy the value of the news product if its credibility is weakened. Thus, notwithstanding Sandel's objection, is the solution simply to put in place "the background conditions within which [the] market exchanges take place" (Sandel 2005: 123)? In the United Kingdom, the background conditions include the quarantining of news and current affairs from product placement (but not factual programming generally), although the rules may be limited in responding to the chilling effect that may arise in the broader commodified program environment. And, indeed, the very background conditions are an acknowledgement of the risk. The fact is that, until very recently, product placement has been prohibited in the United Kingdom. The prohibition was itself an acknowledgement that there was something about the nature of media content that was intrinsically valuable and should not be exposed to the risk of corruption by the intrusion of paid-for content. Although programs and their production may have operated within a market environment, the core, the essence, of that programming—the content itself—was something that was viewed to have existed outside of that market.

As a result, there is an air of unreality in any suggestion that media is of such a character that commodification should be resisted because of its corrupting nature. Further, the commercial media have a place in the public sphere: They add another voice and dimension to public discourse (Hitchens 2006). As Keane reminds us:

> Market-influenced media can also function as important countervailing forces in the process of producing and circulating opinions; they are not only economic phenomena but sites of signification that often run counter to opinion-making monopolies operated by churches and states. But contrary to the claims of market liberalism, that does not mean that civil society and its media must be ruled by "market forces."
>
> (*Keane 1991: 152–3*)

However, this does not mean that it should not be possible to distinguish between the media as an operation and the content itself, and to define the limits of the market somewhere between the two. Product placement may be an example of the market reaching too far. Despite the well-entrenched US position and the newly established UK position, it is legitimate to keep under review the reach of the market and the nature of that reach—to question what might be the appropriate degree of commodification:

> One thing is nevertheless clear: the maximum feasible *decommodification* and "re-embedding" of communications media in the social life of civil society is a vital condition of freedom from state and market censorship.
>
> (*Keane 1991: 153*)

The disquiet that has marked the introduction of product placement in the United Kingdom and the evident disquiet in the United States around commercial practices in the media may signal that the degree of commodification is already excessive. That will have implications for the background conditions—the policy and rules—that have been put in place. Despite a lack of progress on the 2008 inquiry into the sponsorship identification rules, it is evident that the FCC has doubts about the effectiveness of the rules in the United States. It is too early to tell in the United Kingdom, but the introduction of product placement and the different regulatory approach will offer scope for reviewing the degree of commodification and its impact on the media environment.

## Conclusion and the importance of trust

Despite the differences in policy approach between the United States and the United Kingdom, one idea has been common to both jurisdictions: the importance of trust. The public must be able to trust media and journalists. That trust resides in the knowledge that media adhere to journalistic standards and are transparent about the nature of the content being delivered. Trustworthiness is central to the credibility of the media process and to the responsibility media have for their part in the public discourse. In a commodified environment, ethical standards of journalism—and hence trust—are put at risk. If public discourse is to thrive, trust will be central:

> If the media mislead, or if readers cannot assess their reporting, the wells of public discourse and public life are poisoned. The new information technologies may be anti-authoritarian, but curiously they are often used in ways that are also anti-democratic. They undermine our capacities to judge others' claims and to place our trust.
>
> (*O'Neill 2002*)

In relation to broadcast media, the degree of commodification still needs scrutiny and the "background conditions" that can provide protection for the public and enable trust must also be kept under scrutiny. In the broadband environment, new ways will have to be found of equipping the public to test the communications being accessed. Voices in the broadband environment will need to earn the trust of the public. If the media seeks to retain a role as trusted mediators in this new space, then they must acknowledge their responsibility for the quality of public discourse.

## References


ABC (2010) 'An apple a day keeps the bill away,' *Media Watch,* 21 June. Online. Available HTTP: http://www.abc.net.au/mediawatch/transcripts/s2932976.htm (accessed 30 June 2010).

Authority for Television on Demand (ATVOD) (2011) *Rules and Guidance: Statutory Rules and Non-Binding Guidance for Providers of On-Demand Programme Services (ODPS).* Online. Available HTTP: http://www.atvod.co.uk/rules-and-guidance

Broadcast Committee of Advertising Practice, (BCAP) (2004) *Television Advertising Standards Code.* Online. Available HTTP: http://www.cap.org.uk/The-Codes/~/media/Files/CAP/Codes/BCAPTVAdCode.ashx

—— (2010) *Code of Broadcast Advertising.* Online. Available HTTP: http://www.cap.org.uk/Advertising-Codes/Broadcast-HTML.aspx

Bradshaw, B. (2009) Speech delivered to the Royal Television Society, 16 September.

—— (2010) Written ministerial statement on television product placement, 9 February.

Burnham, A. (2008) Speech delivered to the Convergence Think Tank, 11 June.

—— (2009) Written ministerial statement on the implementation of the Audiovisual Media Services Directive, 11 March.

Couldry, N., Livingstone, S. and Markham, T. (2008) '"Public connection" and the uncertain norms of media consumption,' in K. Soper and F. Trentmann (eds.) *Citizenship and Consumption,* Basingstoke: Palgrave Macmillan.

Craufurd Smith, R. (2011) 'Determining regulatory competence for audiovisual media services in the European Union,' *Journal of Media Law,* 3(2): 263–285.

Department for Culture, Media and Sport (2008) *The Audiovisual Media Services Directive: Consultation on Proposals for Implementation in the United Kingdom,* July, London: HMSO.

Department of Trade and Industry and Department for Culture, Media and Sport (2000) *A New Future for Communications,* Cm. 5010, London: HMSO.

European Union (1989) *The Television without Frontiers Directive,* OJ L 298, 17 October: 23.

—— (2007) *The Audiovisual Media Services Directive,* OJ L 332, 18 December: 27.

Federal Communications Commission (1963) *In re Applicability of Sponsorship Identification Rules,* Public Notice 40 FCC 141, 6 May.

—— (2005) *Commission Reminds Broadcast Licensees . . . of Requirements applicable to Video News Releases Rules,* Public Notice FCC 05-84, 13 April.

—— (2007a) *Citadel Broadcasting Corporation,* Order, FCC 07-28, 13 April.

—— (2007b) *In the matter of Sonshine Family Television and Sinclair Broadcast Group,* Notice of Apparent Liability for Forfeiture FCC 07-152, 27 August.

—— (2007c) *In the matter of Comcast Corporation,* Notice of Apparent Liability for Forfeiture 22 FCC 17030, 21 September.

—— (2007d) *In the matter of Comcast Corporation,* Notice of Apparent Liability for Forfeiture 22 FCC 17474, 26 September.

—— (2008) *In the matter of Sponsorship Identification Rules and Embedded Advertising,* Notice of Inquiry and Notice of Proposed Rule Making FCC 08-155, 26 June.

—— (2011a) *In the matter of Fox Television Stations,* Notice of Apparent Liability for Forfeiture DA 11-521, 24 March.

—— (2011b) *In the matter of Access.1 New Jersey License Company,* Notice of Apparent Liability for Forfeiture DA 11-523, 24 March.

—— (2011c) *The Information Needs of Communities: The Changing Media Landscape in a Broadband Age,* June.

Garnham, N. (1991) 'The media and the public sphere' in C. Calhoun (ed.) *Habermas and the Public Sphere,* Cambridge, MA: MIT Press.

Habermas, J. (2006) 'Towards a United States of Europe', *Sign and Sight.com,* 27 March. Online. Available HTTP: http://www.signandsight.com/features/676.html (accessed 15 September 2011).

Hirst, M. (2011) *News 2.0: Can Journalism Survive the Internet?* Crows Nest, NSW: Allen & Unwin.

Hitchens, L. (2006) *Broadcasting Pluralism and Diversity: A Comparative Study of Policy and Regulation,* Oxford: Hart Publishing.

Keane, J. (1991) *The Media and Democracy,* Cambridge: Polity Press.

Ofcom (2008a) *The Ofcom Broadcasting Code,* October.

—— (2008b) 'Ofcom fines ITV plc for misconduct in viewer competitions and voting,' New release, 8 May.' Online. Available HTTP: http://media.ofcom.org.uk/2008/05/08/ofcom-fines-itv-plc-for-misconduct-in-viewer-competitions-and-voting/

—— (2010a) *Broadcasting Code Review: Commercial Communications in Radio Programming—Consultation,* 28 June.

—— (2010b) *Broadcasting Code Review: Commercial References in Television Programming—Consultation,* 28 June.

—— (2010c) *Broadcasting Code Review: Commercial Communications in Radio Programming—Statement on the Ofcom Broadcasting Code,* 20 December.

—— (2010d) *Broadcasting Code Review: Commercial References in Television Programming—Statement on the Ofcom Broadcasting Code,* 20 December.

—— (2011a) *The Ofcom Broadcasting Code,* 28 February.

—— (2011b) *Guidance Notes, Section Nine: Commercial References in Television Programming,* 28 February.

O'Neill, O. (2002) 'A question of trust,' Reith Lectures No. 5. Online. Available HTTP: http://www.bbc.co.uk/radio4/reith2002/lecture5.shtml (accessed 3 September 2011).

Radio Television Digital News Association (RTDNA) (2000) *Code of Ethics.* Online. Available HTTP: http://www.rtnda.org/pages/media_items/code-of-ethics-and-professional-conduct48.php (accessed 12 October 2011).

—— (n.d.) *Guidelines for Use of Non-Editorial Video and Audio.* Online. Available HTTP: http://www.rtdna.org/pages/media_items/rtnda-guidelines-for-use-of-non-editorial-video-and-audio250.php (accessed 20 September 2011).

Rusbridger, A. (2010) 'The 2010 Andrew Olle media lecture: The splintering of the fourth estate,' Lecture delivered at the Australian Broadcasting Corporation, Sydney, 19 November. Online. Available HTTP: http://www.abc.net.au/local/stories/2010/11/19/3071359.htm (accessed 14 February 2011).

Sandel, M. J. (2005) 'What money can't buy: The moral limits of markets,' in M. E. Ertman and J. C. Williams (eds.) *Rethinking Commodification,* New York: New York University Press.

Valcke, P. *et al.* (2008) 'Audiovisual media services in the European Union: Next-generation approach or old wine in new barrels?' *Communications and Strategies,* 71(3): 103–118.

# Part II

# Media policy, free speech and citizenship

# 6

# The European Court of Human Rights, media freedom and democracy

*Rónán Ó Fathaigh and Dirk Voorhoof*

## Introduction

One of the great engines for defining and shaping the relationship between journalism and democracy has been the European Court of Human Rights (ECtHR). The Court engages in this process through interpreting the right to freedom of expression and information as guaranteed under Article 10 of the European Convention of Human Rights (ECHR),[1] and determining whether a state's interference with the right to express, impart and receive information and ideas is consistent with Article 10. Generally, and reflecting the jurisprudence of the Court's first fifty years, the story told has been one of the Court as a steady and significant champion of such rights, as an institution that has played a great role and had a positive influence on global understanding of free expression and the media.[2] Many of its leading judgments are routinely cited by superior courts throughout the world, including the Constitutional

1 The ECHR has been ratified by the forty-seven member states of the Council of Europe. For a list of member states: Online. Available HTTP: http://www.coe.int (accessed 28 September 2011). See generally Harris *et al.* 2009.

2 It has long been held as a matter of principle by the European Court that the right to freedom of expression and information is one of the fundamental characteristics of a democratic society and indispensable for maintaining freedom and democracy in a country. See, e.g., *The Sunday Times* v *United Kingdom* (1979), and, more recently, *Axel Springer AG* v *Germany* (2012) and *Tuşalp* v *Turkey* (2012). In its case law related to journalism and media freedom, the Court has also emphasized the essential function that the press fullfils in a democratic society, with the press playing its vital role as a "public watchdog" in a democracy. This correlation between greater press freedom and a well-functioning democracy has been well documented by non-governmental organizations (NGOs) that conduct press freedom and human rights indices, such as Reporters sans Frontières and Freedom House. See also Voorhoof 2009.

Court of South Africa,[3] the Supreme Court of Canada,[4] the High Court of Australia,[5] and the Inter-American Court of Human Rights.[6]

However, institutions and their environments change. This chapter takes two areas—the protection of reputation and the definition and deployment of journalistic ethics (or the consequence of their discovered absence)—to explore how the Court appears to be changing and what influences affect judicial decision-making. Too little attention has been paid to these processes of change as the Court interprets and applies the ECHR, and determines whether a state's interference with freedom of expression is consistent with Article 10.

As a preliminary issue, it is important to note the distinction between the European Court of Human Rights and the Court of Justice of the European Union. The European Court of Human Rights is an institution of the Council of Europe, an international organization comprising forty-seven member states, including Russia and many former Soviet countries, committed to the maintenance and further realization of human rights (Statute of the Council of Europe, Article 1(c)). The Court of Justice is an institution of the European Union, which is a political and economic union of twenty-seven member states.[7] Importantly, the European Union is now obliged to accede to the ECHR (a Council of Europe document),[8] and this process of accession is in its final stages.[9] This will mean that, in the future, acts of the European Union will be subject to review by the European Court of Human Rights in light of the European Convention.[10]

The first part of this chapter will describe the high level of protection historically afforded to freedom of expression, and the application of these principles to many new areas of

3 See, e.g., *The Citizen 1978 (Pty) Ltd.* v *McBride*, citing *Bladet Tromsø and Stensaas* v *Norway* (1999), *Bergens Tidende and others* v *Norway* (2000) and *Tønsberg Blad AS and HauKom* v *Norway* (2007).

4 See, e.g., *Bou Malhab* v *Diffusion Métromédia CMR Inc.* (2011), citing *Bladet Tromsø and Stensaas* v *Norway* (1999) and *Colombani and others* v *France* (2002).

5 See, e.g., *Theophanous* v *Herald & Weekly Times Ltd.* (1994), citing *Lingens* v *Austria* (1986), *Barfod* v *Denmark* (1989) and *Handyside* v *United Kingdom* (1976).

6 See, e.g., *Herrera-Ulloa* v *Costa Rica* (2004), citing *Lingens* v *Austria* (1986) and *Castells* v *Spain* (1992).

7 See the Consolidated version of the Treaty on European Union and the Treaty on the Functioning of the European Union. See generally Craig and de Búrca 2011.

8 See European Union (2012: Art. 6 (2)). The Council of Europe has also facilitated the accession of the European Union: see Article 17 of Protocol No. 14 to the Convention, amending the control system of the Convention.

9 The Council of Europe Steering Committee for Human Rights submitted a report to the Council of Europe Committee of Ministers on a draft legal instrument for the accession of the European Union to the European Convention on Human Rights. Online. Available HTTP: http://www.coe.int/t/dghl/standardsetting/hrpolicy/CDDH-UE/CDDH-UE_MeetingReports/CDDH_2011_009_en.pdf (accessed 6 March 2012). The EU will accede to the European Convention once the accession agreement has entered into force, which requires ratification by all state parties to the European Convention, in addition to the European Union itself.

10 The Court of Justice of the European Union already applies the Charter of Fundamental Rights of the European Union, which guarantees freedom of expression and the media (Art. 11: "(1) Everyone has the right to freedom of expression. This right shall include freedom to hold opinions and to receive and impart information and ideas without interference by public authority and regardless of frontiers. (2) The freedom and pluralism of the media shall be respected"). The Court of Justice has also integrated the rights and freedoms of the European Convention in its jurisprudence, including the right to freedom of expression and information. See *Elliniki Radiophonia Tiléorassi AE and Panellinia Omospondia Syllogon Prossopikou* v *Dimotiki Etairia Pliroforissis and Sotirios Kouvelas and Nicolaos Avdellas and others* (1991); *Schmidberger, Internationale Transporte and Planzüge* v *Austria* (2003); *Scarlet* v *SABAM* (2011); and *SABAM* v *Netlog NV* (2012).

expression will be highlighted. The second discusses a recent wave of jurisprudence that has arguably eroded long-developed principles under Article 10 ECHR. The final part will attempt to offer a tentative explanation for the somewhat divergent approach that the Court is adopting in some Article 10 jurisprudence.

## Democracy, freedom of expression and media freedom

In its seminal judgment on freedom of expression and media freedom, the European Court in *Lingens* v *Austria* (1986) firmly rooted the notion of freedom of expression as an indispensable tenet of democracy. The Court laid down the principle that freedom of expression was one of the essential foundations of a democratic society, and one of the basic conditions for its progress (*Lingens* v *Austria* (1986), [41]). Moreover, in *Özgür Gündem* v *Turkey*,[11] the Court emphasized the key importance of freedom of expression as one of the preconditions for a functioning democracy (*Özgür Gündem* v *Turkey* (2000), [43]), with democracy thriving on freedom of expression (*Manole and others* v *Moldova* (2009), [95]).

While such principles may seem self-evident, the consequence of free expression being viewed as a prerequisite for a functioning democracy was that the Court adopted a particularly high standard of scrutiny whenever restrictions were imposed: holding that any restriction on freedom of expression must be narrowly interpreted and the necessity for any restrictions must be convincingly established (*Observer and Guardian* v *United Kingdom* (1991), [59]).

Moreover, the Court has demonstrated its preference for a certain concept of democracy, which is based on pluralism, public debate and robust speech.[12] It follows that, in a pluralist democracy, many diverging views must be accommodated, with the Court finding in many judgments that freedom of expression not only applies to information and ideas that are favorably received, but also includes those that offend, shock or disturb.[13] Pluralism demands that such views are tolerated; otherwise there is no democratic society (*Lingens* v *Austria* (1986), [41]).

### *The role of the media in a democracy*

The Court views the media as similarly indispensable to democracy. It has long recognized the preeminent role of the media in a state governed by the rule of law (*Castells* v *Spain* (1992), [43]). Thus, according to the Court, the media adopt an essential function in a democratic society and play a vital role of "public watchdog" (*Sunday Times* v *United Kingdom* (1991), [50]) and "purveyor of information" (*Barthold* v *Germany* (1985), [58]). Moreover, the media have a duty to impart information and ideas on all matters of public interest (*Jersild* v *Denmark* (1994), [31]).

Importantly, the Court has also held that the public has the right to receive information and ideas from the press on all matters of public interest (*Lingens* v *Austria* (1986), [41]). When

11 See also *Castells* v *Spain* (1992), [43]).

12 See *Manole and others* v *Moldova* (2009): "[The Court] takes as its starting point the fundamental truism: there can be no democracy without pluralism. One of the principal characteristics of democracy is the possibility it offers of resolving a country's problems through dialogue, without recourse to violence, even where they are irksome. Democracy thrives on freedom of expression."

13 See, e.g., *Thorgeir Thorgeirson* v *Iceland* (1992); *Feldek* v *Slovakia* (2001); *Gündüz* v *Turkey* (2003); *Giniewski* v *France* (2006).

a speaker's right to expression is curtailed, the public is also denied information to which it is entitled and democracy is thus weakened.

The Court has also elaborated upon the degree to which journalists may engage in provocative expression and exaggeration (*Prager and Oberschlick* v *Austria* (1995), [38]). Furthermore, the Court has held that if national courts apply an overly rigorous approach to the assessment of journalists' professional conduct, the press could be unduly deterred from discharging their function to keeping the public informed (*Kasabova* v *Bulgaria* (2011)).

Based on the foregoing principles, the Court has developed certain standards of scrutiny in relation to the media in a variety of circumstances.

First, the Court will apply the most careful scrutiny when sanctions imposed are capable of discouraging the press in debates over matters of legitimate public concern (*Tønsbergs Blad AS and Haukom* v *Norway* (2007)). Second, the punishment of a journalist for assisting in the dissemination of statements made by another person in an interview seriously hampers the contribution of the press to discussions on matters of public interest and should not be envisaged unless there are particularly strong reasons for doing so (*Jersild* v *Denmark* (1994)). Third, the dangers inherent in prior restraints are such that they call for the most careful scrutiny; news is a perishable commodity and to delay its publication, even for a short period, may well deprive it of all its value and interest (ibid., [60]).

## *Protection of journalistic sources*

One of the major consequences of the Court's view on the preeminent role of the media in a democracy is that the Court has developed a considerable jurisprudence on protection of journalistic sources.[14] In its influential judgment in *Goodwin* v *United Kingdom* (1996), the European Court held that the protection of journalistic sources was a "basic condition for press freedom" (*Goodwin* v *United Kingdom* (1996), [39]). Again, the Court anchored the principle of source protection as a necessary component of a functioning democracy, stating:

> Without such protection, sources may be deterred from assisting the press in informing the public on matters of public interest. As a result the vital public-watchdog role of the press may be undermined and the ability of the press to provide accurate and reliable information may be adversely affected.
>
> (Ibid.)

With such attention to protection of sources, the Court has adopted a strict standard of scrutiny whenever an order for source disclosure was made; a disclosure order is compatible with Article 10 only where it is justified by an overriding requirement in the public interest (ibid.). The Court recognized the chilling effect that such an order has on press freedom generally. Searches and confiscations of journalistic material or other coercive measures in order to reveal the identity of an informant can hardly be justified from this perspective.

Building upon the principle of protection of journalistic sources established in *Goodwin*, the Court held in *Financial Times Ltd.* v *United Kingdom* (2009) that an order for disclosure will arise only in exceptional circumstances in which no reasonable and less invasive

14 See *Goodwin* v *United Kingdom* (1996); *De Haes and Gijsels* v *Belgium* (1996); *Ernst* v *Belgium* (2003); *Voskuil* v *Netherlands* (2007); *Tillack* v *Belgium* (2007); *Financial Times Ltd.* v *United Kingdom* (2009); *Sanoma Uitgevers B.V.* v *Netherlands* (2010); *Martin and Others* v *France* (2012); and *Ressiot and others* v *France* (2012).

alternative means of averting the risk posed are available, and the risk is sufficiently serious and defined (*Financial Times Ltd.* v *United Kingdom* (2009), [69]). Moreover, the Court treated as irrelevant the fact the source was anonymous, holding as a matter of principle that an order of disclosure, even where the source was anonymous, would have a chilling effect on other potential sources (ibid., [70]). Moreover, in *Tillack* v *Belgium* (2007), the European Court emphasized that journalists' right not to reveal their sources could not be considered a mere privilege to be granted or taken away depending on the lawfulness or unlawfulness of their sources, but was part and parcel of the right to information, to be treated with the utmost caution (*Tillack* v *Belgium* (2007), [65]).

These powerful principles that the European Court has developed throughout the past two decades has led to the recent influential Grand Chamber[15] judgment in *Sanoma Uitgevers B.V.* v *Netherlands* (2010), concerning an order on the press to surrender a disk containing photographs from an illegal street race, which may arguably be the standard-setting judgment applicable to jurisdictions throughout the Council of Europe. The European Court found that the order was not permissible, given that there had been no domestic legislation setting out the circumstances in which source disclosure could be ordered. The Court held that, in order to comply with Article 10 ECHR, there must be an independent assessment mechanism as to whether the interest in criminal investigation overrode the public interest in source protection (*Sanoma Uitgevers B.V.* v *Netherlands* (2010), [100]).

The Grand Chamber's judgment requires that the right to protect journalistic sources should be safeguarded by sufficient procedural guarantees, including the guarantee of prior review by a judge or an independent and impartial decision-making body, before the police or the public prosecutor have access to information capable of revealing such sources. It is particularly noteworthy that the Court described the principle of protection of journalistic sources as a "right" of journalists that was a cornerstone of press freedom (ibid., [50]).

## *Whistleblowing and democracy*

A unanimous Grand Chamber of the European Court delivered an impressive judgment concerning the rights of whistleblowers and the media, and their importance to democracy. In *Guja* v *Moldova* (2008),[16] the Court started from the premise that, in a democratic system, the acts or omissions of government must be subject to the close scrutiny of the media and public opinion. It followed that the interest that the public has in particular information may be so strong as to override a legally imposed duty of confidence (*Guja* v *Moldova* (2008), [74]). The applicant in *Guja* had been dismissed from his position in the Public Prosecutor's Office for providing a newspaper with two letters addressed to the Prosecutor's Office from a member of Parliament urging the Prosecutor General to "get personally involved" in a case that had been taken against four police officers.

The European Court held that the public interest in having information about undue pressure and wrongdoing within the Prosecutor's Office was so important in a democratic society that it outweighed the interest in maintaining public confidence in the Prosecutor's Office (*Guja* v *Moldova* (2008), [91]). The Court concluded that the dismissal was a violation

15 The European Court usually sits in Chambers of seven judges. However, in cases raising a serious question affecting the interpretation or application of the Convention, or a serious issue of general importance, the Court sits in a Grand Chamber of seventeen judges (Article 43, ECHR).

16 See also *Peev* v *Bulgaria* (2007), *Kudeshkina* v *Russia* (2009) and *Heinisch* v *Germany* (2011).

of Article 10 of the Convention, holding that disclosure by a civil servant of illegal conduct or wrongdoing in the workplace can enjoy the protection of Article 10 (*Guja* v *Moldova* (2008), [72]).

Again, it is evident from *Guja* how the European Court has developed expansive principles for the protection of freedom of expression rooted in the concept of democracy: open discussion on topics of public concern is essential to democracy, and members of the public should not be discouraged from voicing their opinions on such matters (*Guja* v *Moldova* (2008), [91]).

### *Access to information and democratic scrutiny*

Notwithstanding earlier case law indicating that Article 10 ECHR may not include an individual right of access to information,[17] the European Court, in a series of recent judgments, has moved towards recognizing such a right as essential in a democracy. In *Társaság a Szabadságjogokért (TASZ)* v *Hungary* (2009), the applicant (the Hungarian Civil Liberties Union) made an application to the European Court over a refusal by the Hungarian Constitutional Court to release a complaint made to it by a parliamentarian over the constitutionality of the Criminal Code. The European Court held that there had been a violation of Article 10 because the Constitutional Court's monopoly on information amounted to a form of censorship.

In reaching its conclusion in *TASZ*, the Court held that a state's obligation in matters of freedom of the press include eliminating barriers to the exercise of press functions where such barriers exist solely because of information monopolies held by the authorities (*TASZ* v *Hungary* (2009), [36]). In developing this expansive principle, the Court stated that the applicant non-governmental organization (NGO) was exercising a similar function to the press as a "social watchdog" in a democracy (ibid.), and its activities warranted similar Convention protection to that afforded to the press (ibid., [27]).

Furthermore, in *Kenedi* v *Hungary* (2009), a historian was refused access by the Ministry of Interior to material held in its possession on the state security service, in defiance of a domestic court order. The European Court held that the refusal was in defiance of Hungarian law and amounted to arbitrariness, resulting in a violation of Article 10. Crucially, the Court held that freedom of expression included a right of access to original documentary sources for legitimate historical research (*Kenedi* v *Hungary* (2009), [43]).

What may be gleaned from the European Court's jurisprudence on access to information is that any hindrance on access to information that may prevent public watchdogs (including the media and non-governmental organizations, or NGOs) from disclosing information to citizens is a denial of the public's right to receive information on matters of public interest.

## A divergence in Article 10 jurisprudence

Having regard to the foregoing, it is more than evident that the European Court, through its case law on Article 10 ECHR, has significantly strengthened the protection of freedom of expression throughout the Council of Europe by guaranteeing pluralism, transparency and media freedom. However, there is growing recognition that the European Court, through

17 See *Leander* v *Sweden* (1987); *Guerra and others* v *Italy* (1998); *Loiseau* v *France*(2003); *Roche* v *United Kingdom* (2005). See also Hins and Voorhoof (2007).

certain controversial judgments, has been contributing to an erosion of long-established Article 10 principles.[18] What is now most alarming is the tone and veracity of notable dissenting opinions in a series of freedom of expression cases[19] that may provide an insight into the level of judicial debate within the European Court itself regarding media freedom.

There are two issues that may have a profound impact on the future protection of media freedom as interpreted by the European Court: the recognition of a right to protection of reputation under Article 8 of the Convention; and the importance of the principle of adherence to journalistic ethics.

### *The unenumerated right to protection of reputation*

One the most significant developments that has affected the manner in which the European Court interprets and applies freedom of expression principles has been the recognition by the Court of a right to protection of reputation under Article 8 ECHR, a provision that guarantees a right to respect for private and family life. Reputation is not explicitly mentioned in Article 8 and was deliberately deleted during the drafting of the European Convention.[20] However, in a series of recent judgments,[21] the European Court has taken it upon itself to read a right to protection of reputation into Article 8, which culminated in the Grand Chamber recognizing this right in *Cumpănă and Mazăre* v *Romania* (2004).

Following the recognition of reputation as an autonomous right, the Court has now taken a further step forward, holding that, where a litigant in a domestic court fails in defamation proceedings against another person, including a media organization, the unsuccessful litigant may make an application to the European Court to determine whether the domestic courts adequately protected the right to reputation (*White* v *Sweden* (2006), [20]). This ground-breaking principle has led to a significant increase in applications to the European Court under Article 8.[22]

An important judgment in this regard is that of *Pfeifer* v *Austria* (2007), which concerned a failed defamation action by the applicant against an ideologically rightwing magazine. The magazine article had described the applicant as belonging to a "hunting society" that drove a conservative political scientist to suicide. The Austrian courts found that the statements in the newspaper article had been value judgements, and dismissed the action. The European Court, however, reviewed the statements and concluded that the value judgements lacked a factual basis (*Pfeifer* v *Austria* (2007), [48]), thus concluding that there had been a violation of the applicant's right to protection of its reputation. Moreover, the Court held that a person's

18 See Millar 2009; Sottiaux 2009; Lester 2009.

19 See, e.g., *Flux* v *Moldova (No. 6)* (2008): "I fear this judgment has thrown the protection of freedom of expression as far back as it possibly could. Journalists have been told what to expect if they publish anything disturbing to the authorities, however pressing the social need and sufficient factual basis are, if their professional behaviour leaves anything to be desired" (*per* Bonello J, dissenting opinion, joined by Thór Björgvinsson and Šikuta JJ).

20 *Preparatory Work on Article 8 of the European Convention on Human Rights*, Council of Europe, Strasbourg, 9 August 1956, para. 7, ff. 1, "Deletion of the words: 'nor to attacks upon his honour and reputation'. Online. Available at HTTP: http://www.echr.coe.int/library/colentravauxprep.html (accessed 29 September 2011).

21 See, e.g., *Radio Francee* v *France* (2004, [70]); *Chauvy and others* v *France* (2004); *Abeberry* v *France* (2004).

22 See, among others, *White* v *Sweden* (2006); *Pfeifer* v *Austria* (2006); *Petrina* v *Romania* (2008); *Karakó* v *Hungary* (2009); *Petrenco* v *Moldova* (2010).

reputation was protected even where the criticism against a person occurs in the context of a public debate (ibid., [35]).

The European Court has now taken another step forward by accepting applications where it is claimed that a member state should impose criminal proceedings against a media organization, in circumstances in which civil proceedings were already available. A case in point is that of *Sipoş* v *Romania* (2011), in which an applicant claimed that the acquittal of a broadcaster for criminal defamation was a violation of the right to reputation. A majority of the European Court agreed, holding that the domestic courts, by acquitting the defendant broadcaster, had failed to strike a fair balance between the right to reputation and freedom of expression (*Sipoş* v *Romania* (2011), [39]). This result is quite striking given that the Court in *Sipoş* recognized that civil proceedings would have been more appropriate than criminal proceedings (*Sipoş* v *Romania* (2011), [38]).

The conclusion in *Sipoş* is all the more curious when one considers that the Parliamentary Assembly of the Council of Europe has adopted a Resolution urging member states to decriminalize defamation.[23] The European Court itself has held that criminal sanctions have a chilling effect on the exercise of journalistic freedom of expression in a number of judgments, in particular its Grand Chamber judgment in *Cumpănă and Mazăre* v *Romania* (2004), at [91]).

The recognition of the right to protection of reputation as a right under the European Convention has resulted in fundamental shifts in jurisprudence in some member states of the Council of Europe. The most telling example is that of the United Kingdom, where, in the judgment of *Reynolds* v *Times Newspapers Ltd* (2001), the House of Lords developed a new "public interest" defense in defamation actions. In arriving at this conclusion, the House of Lords stated:

> Above all, the court should have particular regard to the importance of freedom of expression. The press discharges vital functions as a bloodhound as well as a watchdog. The court should be slow to conclude that a publication was not in the public interest and, therefore, the public had no right to know, especially when the information is in the field of political discussion. *Any lingering doubts should be resolved in favour of publication.*
>
> (Reynolds v Times Newspaper Ltd. *2001: 205; emphasis added*)

The above statement of principle reinforced the breathing space available to the media in publication on matters of public interest. However, following the *Cumpănă and Mazăre* v *Romania* and *Pfeifer* v *Austria* judgments recognizing the protection of reputation to be an autonomous right under Article 8, the Court of Appeal in the United Kingdom decided, in *Flood* v *Times Newspapers Ltd.* (2010), that the final sentence in the passage quoted above from *Reynolds* no longer stands, and that the right to reputation and the right to freedom of expression now have equal weight (*Flood* v *Times Newspapers Ltd.* (2010), [21]).

23 See Resolution 1577 (2007) towards decriminalisation of defamation, adopted by the Parliamentary Assembly on 4 October 2007. Online. Available HTTP: http://assembly.coe.int/Mainf.asp?link=/Documents/AdoptedText/ta07/ERES1577.htm (accessed 30 September 2011). See also Resolution 1123 (1997) on the honouring of obligations and commitments by Romania, adopted by the Parliamentary Assembly on 24 April 1997. Online. Available HTTP: http://assembly.coe.int/Mainf.asp?link=/Documents/AdoptedText/ta97/ERES1123.htm (accessed 30 September 2011).

Notwithstanding the above case law, certain elements of the European Court have not followed this trend. For example, in *Karakó* v *Hungary* (2009), a Chamber of the Court held that reputation had only been deemed to be an independent right "sporadically" and questioned whether it should be recognized under Article 8 (*Karakó* v *Hungary* (2009), [23]). Moreover, the Court in *Karakó* sought to introduce a threshold requirement for engaging Article 8, only where the allegations affecting reputation are of such a serious interference as to undermine a person's personal integrity (ibid.).[24]

Reputation is mentioned in Article 10 ECHR as a legitimate interest justifying a permissible restriction on freedom of expression. However, it is not listed as a fundamental "right" in the Convention. The Court has long held and still reiterates that any restriction on freedom of expression must be construed strictly, and the need for any restriction must be established convincingly.[25] The elevation of protection of reputation to the status of a Convention right has resulted in the European Court delivering judgments that effectively overturned failed defamation proceedings against the media, and will send mixed signals to domestic courts throughout the Council of Europe on how to properly balance media freedom with protection of reputation. Such an inconsistent approach by the Court could result in difficulties for domestic courts in applying Article 10 jurisprudence.

However, in 2012, the Grand Chamber of the Court was presented with an opportunity in *Axel Springer AG* v *Germany* (2012) to clarify the uncertainty surrounding the right to reputation. The case concerned a permanent injunction granted by the German courts prohibiting the *Bild* newspaper from publishing an article detailing the arrest and conviction of a well-known actor for possession of cocaine. The Grand Chamber held that there had been a violation of the right to freedom of expression and stated that, while Article 8 included the right to protection of reputation, "in order for Article 8 to come into play, however, an attack on a person's reputation must attain a certain level of seriousness and in a manner causing prejudice to personal enjoyment of the right to private life" (*Axel Springer AG* v *Germany* (2012), [83]). Thus there is now a threshold requirement of "seriousness" before Article 8 may be relied upon and this may signal an overruling of cases such as *Sipoş*. It remains to be seen how the Court will further develop this threshold requirement and seek to temper the importance attached to the unenumerated right to reputation when balanced with freedom of expression.

## *Adherence to journalistic ethics*

A second recent restrictive trend in the interpretation of Article 10 ECHR principles has been the importance that the Court now places on adherence to journalistic ethics in determining whether there has been a violation of the right to freedom of expression. Article 10 explicitly states that freedom of expression carries with it "duties and responsibilities." However, the historical jurisprudence of the European Court had always subscribed to the view that it was not for the Court, or domestic courts, to substitute their own views for those of the press as to what technique of reporting should be adopted by journalists (*Jersild* v *Denmark* (1994)). This principle was premised on the proposition that Article 10 protected not only the substance of the ideas expressed, but also the form in which they are conveyed (*Oberschlick* v *Austria* (1991), [57]).

24 This reasoning was also approved in the subsequent case of *Polanco Torres and Movilla Polanco* v *Spain* (2010).

25 See, e.g., *Lindon, Otchakovsky-Laurens and July* v *France* (2007).

Indeed, in many cases the consideration that a journalist had acted in accordance with professional journalistic ethics was often held to be decisive in order to hold that freedom of expression prevailed over other rights or interests invoked by a member state. This was the finding in cases including *De Haes and Gijsels* v *Belgium* (1997), *Fressoz and Roire* v *France* (1999), and *Bladet Tromsø and Stensaas* v *Norway* (1999). In *Fressoz and Roire*, for example, the European Court held that the conviction of a journalist for publishing confidential tax documents of the director of the Peugeot company was a violation of Article 10. The Court referred to the fact that the applicant journalist had verified the authenticity of the tax documents and "acted in accordance with the standards governing his profession as a journalist" (*Fressoz and Roire* v *France* (1999),[55]).

This approach is mirrored in jurisdictions around the world where superior courts have developed new defenses to defamation actions by creating the defense of "responsible journalism" on matters of public interest. Such an approach is evident in courts such as the Supreme Court of Canada,[26] the House of Lords,[27] the High Court of Australia,[28] and the Constitutional Court of South Africa.[29] The common thread running through this case law is that superior courts recognize that free expression should prevail even where an honest error is made resulting in a defamatory publication, provided that the journalist adhered to responsible journalistic practices.

In stark contrast to the international trend, the European Court has recently been tending in the opposite direction. This new approach is most evident in the case of *Flux* v *Moldova (No. 6)* (2008), in which the applicant newspaper had been ordered to apologize and pay damages for alleging bribery on the part of a school principal, which had been based on an anonymous letter. The applicants had produced three witnesses who had testified to the bribes, but the domestic courts had held that the evidence had not been sufficient to overturn the presumption of innocence.

The European Court concluded that the newspaper had acted in "flagrant disregard" of the duties of responsible journalism by making no attempt to contact the school principal and conducting no investigation into the matters raised in the letter (*Flux* v *Moldova (No. 6)* (2008), [29]). Thus there had been no violation of Article 10. The judgment of the Court was divided by a 4:3 vote, with a stinging dissent being delivered criticizing the majority over its assessment of journalistic ethics:

> I fear this judgment has thrown the protection of freedom of expression as far back as it possibly could. Journalists have been told what to expect if they publish anything disturbing to the authorities, however pressing the social need and sufficient the factual

26 *Grant* v *Torstar Corp.* (2009), creating a new defense of "responsible communication on matters of public interest" with "journalistic standards [providing] a useful guide to evaluate the conduct of journalists and non-journalist alike."

27 See *Reynold* v *Times Newspapers Ltd.* (2001), creating a new defense of "responsible journalism," and *Jameel* v *Wall Street Journal Europe* (2007).

28 See *Lange* v *Australian Broadcasting Corp.* (1997).

29 See *N.M.* v *Smith* (2007: § 203), in which the Court approved a new defense of reasonable publication, stating: "But to pre-empt the undue chilling effect of huge potential claims for damages following on honest error, it added that even if aspects of a publication turned out to be untrue, a showing that the media concerned had taken reasonable steps to ensure the veracity of the relevant information would establish a good defence to the unlawfulness of the publication. What mattered was the reasonableness of the publication in the circumstances."

> basis are, if their professional behaviour leaves anything to be desired. Even if alarming facts are sufficiently borne out by evidence, in the balancing exercise to establish proportionality, disregard for professional norms is deemed by Strasbourg to be more serious than the suppression of democratic debate on public corruption . . . in the Court's view the social need to fight poor journalism is more pressing than that of fighting rich corruption.
>
> (Ibid.: *dissenting opinion, [18]*)

This approach has been mirrored in *Stoll* v *Switzerland* (2007), in which the Court held that there had been no violation of Article 10 following the criminal conviction of a journalist for the publication of a confidential report by the Swiss ambassador to the United States relating to the strategy to be adopted with the World Jewish Congress on compensation for Holocaust victims and assets in Swiss bank accounts. The European Court decision lambasted the journalist, stating that the "chief intention was not to inform the public on a topic of general interest but to make [the ambassador's] report the subject of needless scandal" (*Stoll* v *Switzerland* (2007), [151]). The Court held as a matter of principle that journalistic ethics play a particularly important role nowadays, given the influence wielded by the media in contemporary society, with the Court being of the view that monitoring journalistic ethics had now taken on an added importance (ibid., [104]).

The dissent admonished the position that was taken by the majority in *Stoll*, stating in the strongest terms possible:

> [This judgment is] a dangerous and unjustified departure from the Court's well established case-law concerning the nature and vital importance of freedom of expression in democratic societies . . . the Court should be tending in the opposite direction, particularly at a time when a series of episodes in the democratic world has shown that, even in the sphere of foreign policy, democratic scrutiny is possible only after confidential documents have been leaked and made public. . . .
>
> [This judgment] introduces an element of censure regarding the form chosen by the journalist and leads the Court to endorse the wholly different position of a private body concerned with journalistic ethics . . . In any event, the majority's criticism concerning the form of the applicant's articles is not relevant from the Court's perspective.
>
> (Ibid.)

With these decisions, it appears that the European Court may be adopting a position on adherence to journalistic ethics that is inconsistent with freedom of expression principles throughout the world, which have sought instead to broaden the breathing space for media by developing new defenses based on responsible journalism. The European Court, in contradistinction, is using non-adherence to its conception of journalistic ethics to reduce the protection of media freedom generally.

However, there are signs that the Court may be aware of the dangers involved in according too much importance to considerations of journalistic ethics. In *Bozhkov* v *Bulgaria* (2011), at [51]),[30] a journalist had been convicted of criminal defamation following the

30 See also *Kasabova* v *Bulgaria* (2011) and *Lewondawska-Malec* v *Poland* (2012).

publication of an article alleging corrupt practices on the part of four school inspectors in the admission of students to certain elite secondary schools in Bulgaria. The Court held that there had been a violation of Article 10, and underlined the principle that an overly rigorous approach to the assessment of journalists' professional conduct may lead to the press being unduly deterred from discharging their function to keeping the public informed (*Kasabova* v *Bulgaria* (2011),[55]). It is yet to be seen whether this principle will take center stage in future jurisprudence.

## Explaining a divergent approach

It is clear from the foregoing that while, on the one hand, the European Court has contributed immensely to developing strong protection for media freedom,[31] it has also demonstrated a tendency for restrictive interpretation of freedom of expression principles. The puzzle to be solved is the cause of this shift in jurisprudence. Two issues seem to be instructive: the ideology of individual judges; and growing political pressure on the Court.

### *Ideology of individual judges*

First, it may be argued that there has been an ideological shift occurring in the European Court, with certain judges holding personal views on the relative importance of freedom of expression vis-à-vis other interests and rights. Evidence for such a proposition is exemplified in the concurring opinion of Judge Zupančič in the case of *Von Hannover* v *Germany* (2004), a judgment that developed the right to privacy of public persons:

> Moreover, I believe that the courts have to some extent and under American influence made a fetish of the freedom of the press . . . It is time that the pendulum swung back to a different kind of balance between what is private and secluded and what is public and unshielded.
>
> (Von Hannover v Germany *2004 per Zupančič J*)[32]

The hostility toward press freedom is also echoed in the concurring opinion of Judge Loucaides in *Lindon, Otchakovsky-Laurens and July* v *France* (2007):

> [T]he case-law on the subject of freedom of speech has on occasion shown an excessive sensitivity and granted over-protection in respect of interference with freedom of expression . . . one should not lose sight of the fact that the mass media are nowadays commercial enterprises with uncontrolled and virtually unlimited strength . . . they should be subject to certain restraint out of respect for the truth and for the dignity of individuals.
>
> (Lindon, Otchakovsky-Laurens and July v France *2007 per Loucaides J*)

31 See Voorhoof and Cannie 2010.

32 See also *Vejdeland and others* v *Sweden* (2012), concurring opinon of Judge Zupančič: "For my controversial concurring opinion in *von Hannover* v *Germany*, I have been repeatedly attacked for the phrase mentioning the fetishisation of the freedom of the press under American influence. Recent events in the United Kingdom, where serious abuses on the part of the Murdoch press have been uncovered, tend to vindicate the position taken in the *von Hannover* case."

There are many examples of similar sentiments being expressed by various judges of the European Court.[33] At the same time, there has been an increase in dissenting opinions, which raises alarm about the direction that the Court has been taking. For instance, in *Lindon, Otchakovsky-Laurens and July* v *France* (2007), those dissenting were of the view that the finding of a non-violation of Article 10 ECHR following the successful criminal defamation action by a politician against an author and newspaper represented "a significant departure from our case-law of the ECtHR in matters of criticism of politicians" and ran "counter to the Court's case-law concerning the duties and responsibilities of the press."

Also, in *Barata Monteiro da Costa Nogueira and Patricio Pereira* v *Portugal* (2011), a majority of the Court held that there had been no violation of Article 10 in circumstances in which two politicians were criminally convicted for defaming a political opponent during a press conference. The dissent was of the view that the judgment "contributes to the weakening of the philosophy of freedom of expression itself . . . At a time when the winds are changing, we think that our Court more than ever is there to reinforce freedom of expression as a key element in democracy" (*Barata Monteiro da Costa Nogueira and Patricio Pereira* v *Portugal* (2011)).

It is clear that some elements within the Court have lost sight of the fact that public watchdogs such as the media "are not meant to be peaceful puppies; their function is to bark and to disturb the appearance of peace when a menace threatens" (*Saygili and Falakaoğlu* v *Turkey (No. 2)* (2009)).

## *Growing political pressure on the European Court*

Second, there has recently been a concerted effort by certain political leaders in Europe not only to criticize certain judgments of the European Court, but also to question the very legitimacy of the Court itself. This criticism was most severely demonstrated following the Chamber judgment in *Lautsi* v *Italy* (2009), in which the European Court found that the display of crucifixes in state schools was a violation of the Convention.

There was an unprecedented critical political response to the Chamber judgment in *Lautsi* (McGoldrick 2011: 470). There was widespread criticism of the judgment in Italy, with Italian politicians roundly denouncing the judgment. One Minister stated: "No one, not even the ideologically motivated European Court, will succeed in rubbing out our identity" (Hooper 2009). The Italian government announced that it would appeal the judgment, and requested a referral to the Grand Chamber. In March 2011, a unanimous Grand Chamber

33 See, e.g.: "[Ethical considerations] play a particularly important role nowadays, given the influence wielded by the media in contemporary society: not only do they inform, they can also suggest by the way in which they present the information how it is to be assessed. In a world in which the individual is confronted with vast quantities of information circulated via traditional and electronic media and involving an ever-growing number of players, monitoring compliance with journalistic ethics takes on added importance" (*Stoll* v *Switzerland* (2007), [104]); "Such an elevation of the public interest in the freedom of the press at the expense of the private individuals caught up in the seal hunting story in this case pays insufficient attention to the national laws on defamation and the balanced freedom of the press-conscious judgments of the domestic courts" (*per* Palm, Fuhrmann and Baka JJ, dissenting, *Bladet Tromsø and Stensaas* v *Norway* (1999)); "We no longer live in a world in which the press can always assume the position of a victim. More and more often, the press abuses its powerful position and, deliberately and malevolently, undermines the good name and integrity of other persons. We have no alternative but to address this new situation" (*per* Garlicki and Vučinić JJ, concurring, *Wizerkaniuk* v *Poland* (2012)).

reversed the finding of a violation of the European Convention, concluding that the decision to display crucifixes in classrooms was within the limits of the margin of appreciation left to member states (*Lautsi* v *Italy* (2011)).

This political reaction to *Lautsi* is mirrored in another controversial series of judgments issued by the European Court, this time concerning the United Kingdom. In *Hirst* v *United Kingdom (No. 2)* (2004), the Court held that a blanket ban on voting for convicted prisoners was a violation of the right to vote.[34]

The *Hirst* judgment was followed by *Green* v *United Kingdom* (2010), in which a unanimous Court found that the United Kingdom had continued to violate the right to vote by failing to legislate to repeal the blanket ban on prisoners' voting. The United Kingdom requested a referral to the Grand Chamber, which was refused.[35]

The British Prime Minister described the ruling in *Green* as making him feel "physically ill" (Mulholland and Stratton 2011). Former Labour Party Lord Chancellor Jack Straw remarked, "in attempting to overrule British law on prisoner voting rights the unelected judges in Strasbourg have exceeded the limits of their authority" (Chapman 2011). A senior Conservative Party member David Davis stated that there was a "crisis here which has been brought about by the court extending its own power, trying to overrule in effect a parliament" (*The Guardian* 2011). Consequently, in a symbolic action, a non-binding parliamentary vote was organized, with MPs voting by 234: 22 to support the motion that the blanket ban on prisoners' voting rights should continue (Watt and Travis 2011).

A political storm erupted in the United Kingdom over its relationship with the European Court and, in 2011, the UK government went so far as to establish a commission to investigate the creation of a British bill of rights that would build upon the obligations under the European Convention,[36] and to consider reforms of the European Court of Human Rights.[37] During its chairmanship of the Committee of Ministers of the Council of Europe (November 2011 to May 2012), the United Kingdom sought to prioritize reform of the European Court, placing particular emphasis on enhancing the margin of appreciation afforded to member states in applying the Convention. However, in the Brighton Declaration on reform of the Court agreed between member states in April 2012, the substantive relationship between the Court and member states was maintained.[38]

34 See ECHR Protocol No. 1, Art. 3.

35 See *Press Release issued by the Registrar of the Court*, No. 377, ECtHR, 28 April 2011. Available online at http://cmiskp.echr.coe.int/tkp197/view.asp?action=open&documentId=884719&portal=hbkm&source=externalbydocnumber&table=F69A27FD8FB86142BF01C1166DEA398649 (accessed 27 September 2011).

36 See *Discussion Paper: Do We Need a UK Bill of Rights?*, Commission on a Bill of Rights, September 2011. Online. Available HTTP: http://www.justice.gov.uk/downloads/about/cbr/cbr-discussion-paper.pdf (accessed 27 September 2011).

37 See *Interim Advice to Government: Reform of the European Court of Human Rights*, Commission on a Bill of Rights, July 2011. Online. Available HTTP: http://www.justice.gov.uk/downloads/about/cbr/cbr-court-reform-interim-advice.pdf (accessed 27 September 2011).

38 It was agreed that a reference to the margin of appreciation would be placed in the Preamble to the Convention only, with no elevation in its importance: "[The Conference] [c]oncludes that, for reasons of transparency and accessibility, a reference to the principle of subsidiarity and the doctrine of the margin of appreciation as developed by the Court's case law should be included in the Preamble of the Convention . . . " (High Level Conference on the Future of the European Court of Human Rights, Brighton Declaration, 19 and 20 April 2012. Online. Available HTTP: http://www.coe.int/en/20120419-brighton-declaration/ (accessed 20 March 2012)).

In addition to the growing political opposition to the European Court, there has been notable academic and judicial criticism of it. Lord Hoffmann, a former British Law Lord, made a blistering attack on the European Court in a paper delivered in 2009 (Hoffmann 2009),[39] commenting that some judgments from the European were akin to "teaching grandmothers to suck eggs," and that the European Court "lacks constitutional legitimacy" (ibid.: para. 38). Lord Hoffmann also criticized the Court for utilizing the "living instrument" doctrine as a "banner under which the Strasbourg court has assumed power to legislate what they consider to be required by 'European public order'" (ibid.: para. 36). Similar criticisms have manifested themselves in other European states, in particular the Netherlands,[40] and also in Belgium and Denmark.

The judges of the European Court are not oblivious to this context of immense political pressure surrounding the legitimacy of the European Court. This context may go some way towards explaining the shift in direction surrounding the protection of freedom of expression and press freedom by the European Court.

However, two Grand Chamber judgments delivered in 2012 may signal that a majority of the Court will not take heed of external pressure and debate, at least in terms of freedom of expression. In *Axel Springer AG* v *Germany* (2012),[41] the Court held that there had been a violation of Article 10 following the fining of a German newspaper for breach of privacy for publishing articles detailing the arrest and conviction of a well-known actor. The most significant aspect of this judgment is the affirmation by the Grand Chamber that the Court requires only "strong reasons" to substitute its view for those of the domestic courts (*Axel Springer AG* v *Germany* (2012), [88]). The dissenting judges disagreed with such an approach, being of the view that the Court should interfere with domestic courts' determination only where it has been "manifestly unreasonable" (ibid.).

A similar preference for freedom of expression over privacy rights is evident in *Von Hannover* v *Germany (No. 2)* (2012), which concerned a claim for breach of privacy following the publication of photographs of the Monegasque royal family on a skiing holiday. A unanimous Grand Chamber held that the refusal of the German courts to prevent the publication of the photographs had not represented a violation of the right to privacy under the European Convention (*Von Hannover* v *Germany* (2012), [126]).

## Conclusion

The European Court of Human Rights has manifestly contributed to the development of media freedom and freedom of expression in member states throughout the Council of Europe, with its judgments applicable to the more than 800 million people living in those member states (Voorhoof 2009). Its influence in the new democracies of the former Soviet states has been particularly strong, and it has become a crucial instrument to motivate or even compel national authorities to abstain from interferences in freedom of speech and press freedom, and to respect freedom of public debate, political expression and critical journalism to a higher degree.

39 See also the Foreword by Lord Hoffmann in Pinto-Duschinsky, *Bringing Rights Back Home* (Hoffmann 2011).

40 See, amongst others, Baudet 2010 and Murray 2010.

41 See also *Lahtonen* v *Finland* (2012), in which the Court held that conviction of a journalist and publisher for publishing an article detailing criminal proceedings against a police officer for car theft was a violation of Article 10 ECHR.

While there have been some restrictive trends and interpretations of freedom of expression, there are recent signs of the European Court correcting the path taken. Certain judges of the European Court have engaged in a public dialog with others in raising the alarm over the dangerous direction that the Court may have taken, and it is hoped that the result of such a dialog is a realignment in favor of free expression, transparency, protection of investigative journalism, and the role of media and NGOs in nourishing public debate.

## References


*Abeberry* v *France* (2004) Application no. 58729/00, Admissibility Decision, ECtHR.

*Axel Springer AG* v *Germany* (2012) Application no. 39954/08, Grand Chamber Judgment, ECtHR.

*Barata Monteiro da Costa Nogueira and Patricio Pereira* v *Portugal* (2011) Application no. 4035/08, Chamber Judgment, ECtHR.

*Barfod* v *Denmark* (1989) Application no. 11508/85, Chamber Judgment, ECtHR.

*Barthold* v *Germany* (1985) Application no. 8734/79, Chamber Judgment, ECtHR.

Baudet, T. (2010) 'Het Europees Hof voor Rechten van de Mens vormt een ernstige inbreuk op de democratie' ['The European Court of Human Rights constitutes a serious infringement of democracy'], *NRC Handelsblad*, 13 November.

*Bergens Tidende and others* v *Norway* (2000) Application no. 26132/95, Chamber Judgment, ECtHR.

*Bladet Tromsø and Stensaas* v *Norway* (1999) Application no. 21980/98, Grand Chamber Judgment, ECtHR.

*Bou Malhab* v *Diffusion Métromédia CMR Inc.* (2011) 1 SCR 214.

*Bozhkov* v *Bulgaria* (2011) Application no. 3316/04, Chamber Judgment, ECtHR.

*Castells* v *Spain* (1992) Application no. 11798/85, Chamber Judgment, ECtHR.

Chapman, J. (2011) 'Day we stood up to Europe: In an unprecedented move, MPs reject European Court's ruling that prisoners must get the vote,' *Daily Mail*, 11 February.

*Chauvy and others* v *France* (2004) Application no. 64915/01, Chamber Judgment, ECtHR.

*Colombani and others* v *France* (2002) Application no. 51279/99, Chamber Judgment, ECtHR.

Craig P. and de Búrca, G. (2011) *EU Law: Text, Cases and Materials*, 5th edn., Oxford: Oxford University Press.

*Cumpănă and Mazăre* v *Romania* (2004) Application no. 33348/96, Grand Chamber Judgment, ECtHR.

*De Haes and Gijsels* v *Belgium* (1997) Application no. 19983/92, Chamber Judgment, ECtHR.

*Elliniki Radiophonia Tiléorassi AE and Panellinia Omospondia Syllogon Prossopikou* v *Dimotiki Etairia Pliroforissis and Sotirios Kouvelas and Nicolaos Avdellas and others* (1991) C-260/89, ECR I-02925, ECJ.

*Ernst* v *Belgium* (2003) Application no. 33400/96, Chamber Judgment, ECtHR.

*Feldek* v *Slovakia* (2001) Application no. 29032/95, Chamber Judgment, ECtHR.

*Financial Times Ltd.* v *United Kingdom* (2009) Application no. 821/03, Chamber Judgment, ECtHR.

*Flood* v *Times Newspapers Ltd.* (2010) EWCA Civ 804.

*Flux* v *Moldova (No. 6)* (2008) Application no. 22824/04, Chamber Judgment, ECtHR.

*Fressoz and Roire* v *France* (1999) Application no. 29183/95, Grand Chamber Judgment, ECtHR.

*Giniewski* v *France* (2006) Application no. 64016/00, Chamber Judgment, ECtHR.

*Goodwin* v *United Kingdom* (1993) Application no. 17488/90, Grand Chamber Judgment, ECtHR.

*Gant* v *Tarstar Corp.* (2009) SCC 6.

*Greens and M.T.* v *United Kingdom* (2010) Application nos. 60041/08 and 60054/08, Chamber Judgment, ECtHR.

*Guerra and others* v *Italy* (1998) Application no. 14967/89, Grand Chamber Judgment, ECtHR.

*Guja* v *Moldova* (2008) Application no. 14277/04, Grand Chamber Judgment, ECtHR.

*Gündüz* v *Turkey* (2003) Application no. 35071/97, Chamber Judgment, ECtHR.

*Handyside* v *United Kingdom* (1976) Application no. 5493/72, Plenary Court Judgment, ECtHR.

Harris, D. J., O'Boyle, M., Bates, E. P. and Buckley, C. M. (2009) *Law of the European Convention on Human Rights*, 2nd edn., Oxford: Oxford University Press.

*Heinisch* v *Germany* (2011) Application no. 28274/08, Chamber Judgment, ECtHR.

*Herrera-Ulloa* v *Costa Rica* (2004) IACHR 3.

Hins, W. and Voorhoof, D. (2007) 'Access to state-held information as a fundamental right under the European Convention on Human Rights,' *European Constitutional Law Review*, 3: 114–126.

*Hirst* v *United Kingdom (No. 2)* (2004) Application no. 74025/01, Chamber Judgment, ECtHR.
Hoffmann, L. (2009) 'The universality of human rights,' Judicial Studies Board Annual Lecture, Online. Available HTTP: http://www.judiciary.gov.uk/Resources/JCO/Documents/Speeches/Hoffmann_2009_JSB_Annual_Lecture_Universality_of_Human_Rights.pdf (accessed 23 September 2011).
—— (2011) 'Foreword,' in M. Pinto-Duschinsky *Bringing Rights Back Home: Making Human Rights Compatible with Parliamentary Democracy in the UK*. Online. Available HTTP: http://www.policyexchange.org.uk/publications/publication.cgi?id=225 (accessed 23 September 2011).
Hooper, J. (2009) 'Human rights ruling against classroom crucifixes angers Italy,' *The Guardian*, 3 November.
*Jameel* v *Wall Street Journal Europe SPRL* (2007) 1 AC 359.
*Jersild* v *Denmark* (1994) Application no. 15890/89, Grand Chamber Judgment, ECtHR.
*Karakó* v *Hungary* (2009) Application no. 39311/05, Chamber Judgment, ECtHR.
*Kasabova* v *Bulgaria* (2011) Application no. 22385/03, Chamber Judgment, ECtHR.
*Kenedi* v *Hungary* (2009) Application no. 31475/05, Chamber Judgment, ECtHR.
*Kudeshkina* v *Russia* (2009) Application no. 29492/05, Chamber Judgment, ECtHR.
*Lahtonen* v *Finland* (2012), Application no. 29576/09, Chamber Judgment, ECtHR.
*Lange* v *Australian Broadcasting Corp* (1997) HCA 25.
*Lautsi* v *Italy* (2009) Application no. 30814/06, Chamber Judgment, ECtHR.
*Lautsi* v *Italy* (2011) Application no. 30814/06, Grand Chamber Judgment, ECtHR.
*Leander* v *Sweden* (1987) Application no. 924/81, Chamber Judgment, ECtHR.
Lester, A. (2009) 'The European Court of Human Rights after 50 years,' *European Human Rights Law Review*, 4: 461.
*Lewandowska-Malec* v *Poland* (2012) Application no. 39660/07, Chamber Judgment, ECtHR.
*Lindon, Otchakovsky-Laurens and July* v *France* (2007) Application nos. 21279/02 and 36448/02, Grand Chamber Judgment, ECtHR.
*Lingens* v *Austria* (1986) Application no. 9815/82, Plenary Court Judgment, ECtHR.
*Loiseau* v *France* (2003) Application no. 46809/99, Admissibility Decision, ECtHR.
McGoldrick, D. (2011) 'Religion in the European public square and in European public life: Crucifixes in the classroom?' *Human Rights Law Review*, 11(3): 451–502.
*Manole and others* v *Moldova* (2009) Application no. 13936/02, Chamber Judgment, ECtHR.
*Martin and others* v *France* (2012) Application no. 30002/08, Chamber Judgment, ECtHR.
Millar, G. (2009) 'Whither the spirit of Lingens?' *European Human Rights Law Review*, 3: 277–288.
Mulholland, H. and Stratton, A. (2011) 'UK may be forced to give prisoners the vote in time for May elections,' *The Guardian*, 1 February.
Murray, D. (2010) 'Laten we ons bevrijden van het Europese Hof' ['Let us free ourselves from the European Court'], *de Volkskrant*, 20 November.
*N. M.* v *Smith* (2007) ZACC 6.
*Observer and Guardian* v *United Kingdom* (1991) Application no. 13585/88, Grand Chamber Judgment, ECtHR.
*Özgür Gündem* v *Turkey* (2000) Application no. 23144/93, Chamber Judgment, ECtHR.
*Peev* v *Bulgaria* (2007) Application no. 64209/01, Chamber Judgment, ECtHR.
*Petrenco* v *Moldova* (2010) Application no. 20928/05, Chamber Judgment, ECtHR.
*Petrina* v *Romania* (2008) Application no. 78060/01, Chamber Judgment, ECtHR.
*Polanco Torres and Movilla Polanco* v *Spain* (2010) Application no. 34147/06, Chamber Judgment, ECtHR. (Judgment available in French only)
*Pfeifer* v *Austria* (2006) Application no. 12556/03, Chamber Judgment, ECtHR.
*Prager and Oberschlick* v *Austria* (1995) Application no. 15974/90, Chamber Judgment, ECtHR.
*Radio France* v *France* (2004) Application no. 53984/00, Chamber Judgment, ECtHR.
*Ressiot and others* v *France* (2012) Application nos. 15054/07 and 15066/07, Chamber Judgment, ECtHR.
*Reynolds* v *Times Newspapers Ltd.* (2001) 2 AC 127, HL.
*Roche* v *United Kingdom* (2005) Application no. 32555/96, Grand Chamber Judgment, ECtHR.
*SABAM* v *Netlog NV* (2012) (not yet reported) ECJ.
*Sanoma Uitgevers B.V.* v *Netherlands* (2010) Application no. 38224/03, Grand Chamber Judgment, ECtHR.
*Saygili and Falakaoğlu* v *Turkey (No. 2)* (2009) Application no. 38991/02, Chamber Judgment, ECtHR.

*Scarlet* v *SABAM* (2011) (not yet reported) ECJ.
*Schmidberger, Internationale Transporte and Planzüge* v *Austria* (2003) E.C.R. I-56694, ECJ.
*Sipoş* v *Romania* (2011) Application no. 26125/04, Chamber Judgment, ECtHR. (Judgment available in French only)
Sottiaux, S. (2009) '*Leroy* v *France*: Apology of terrorism and the malaise of the European Court of Human Rights' free speech jurisprudence,' *European Human Rights Law Review*, 3: 415–427.
*Stoll* v *Switzerland* (2007) Application no. 69698/01, Grand Chamber Judgment, ECtHR.
*Társaság a Szabadságjogokért (TASZ)* v *Hungary* (2009) Application no. 37374/05, Chamber Judgment, ECtHR.
*The Citizen 1978 (Pty) Ltd.* v *McBride* (2011) ZASC 11.
*The Guardian* (2011) 'Straw and Davis united against prisoners' voting right,' 18 January.
*The Sunday Times* v *United Kingdom* (1979) Application no. 6538/74, Plenary Court Judgment, ECtHR.
*The Sunday Times* v *United Kingdom (No. 2)* (1991) Application no. 13166/87, Plenary Court Judgment, ECtHR.
*Theophanous* v *Herald & Weekly Times Ltd.* (1994) HCA 46.
*Thorgeir Thorgeirson* v *Iceland* (1992) Application no. 13778/88, Chamber Judgment, ECtHR.
*Tillack* v *Belgium* (2007) Application no. 20477/05, Chamber Judgment, ECtHR. (Judgment available in French only)
*Tønsberg Blad AS* v *Norway* (2007) Application no. 510/04, Chamber Judgment, ECtHR.
*Tuşalp* v *Turkey* (2012) Application nos. 32131/08 and 41617/08, Chamber Judgment, ECtHR.
*Vejdeland and others* v *Sweden* (2012) Application no. 1813/07, Chamber Judgment, ECtHR.
*Von Hannover* v *Germany* (2004) Application no. 59320/00, Chamber Judgment, ECtHR.
*Von Hannover* v *Germany (No. 2)* (2012) Application nos. 40660/08 and 60641/08, Grand Chamber Judgment, ECtHR.
Voorhoof, D. (2009) 'Freedom of expression under the European Human rights system: From *Sunday Times (No. 1)* v *UK* (1979) to *Hachette Filipacchi Associés ("Ici Paris")* v *France* (2009),' *Inter-American and European Human Rights Journal*, 1–2: 3–49.
—— and Cannie, H. (2010) 'Freedom of expression and information in a democratic society: The added but fragile value of the European Convention on Human Rights,' *International Communication Gazette*, 72(4–5): 407–423.
*Voskuil* v *Netherlands* (2007) Application no. 64752/01, Chamber Judgment, ECtHR.
Watt, N. and Travis, A. (2011) 'MPs decide to keep blanket ban on prisoners' vote,' *The Guardian*, 10 February.
*White* v *Sweden* (2006) Application no. 42435/02, Chamber Judgment, ECtHR.
*Wizerkaniuk* v *Poland* (2012) Application no. 18990/05, Chamber Judgment, ECtHR.

# 7

# The different concepts of free expression and its link with democracy, the public sphere and other concepts

*Joan Barata*

## Introduction: Free expression as an essential right

Freedom of speech and information are first-generation essential rights that were envisaged and protected for the first time in the early times of the Enlightenment. Since then, they have been conceived by constitutional texts as *sine qua non* founding conditions for modern states. Article XI of the French Declaration of the Rights of Man and of the Citizen of 1789, for example, states that "The free communication of ideas and opinions is one of the most precious of the rights of man. Every citizen may, accordingly, speak, write, and print with freedom, but shall be responsible for such abuses of this freedom as shall be defined by law." The very famous wording of article XVI establishes very clearly that "A society in which the observance of the law is not assured" ... has no constitution at all.[1]

This first recognition of what is broadly known in constitutional law as freedom of expression includes two major trends that form the bedrock on which further constitutional provisions in this area are built (including the First Amendment of the US Constitution[2]): first, that freedom of expression is a fundamental essential right, directly linked to a citizen's capacity to live and participate within a modern society; and second, that the exercise of these rights by citizens should be adequately guaranteed by the state.

The wording and the core elements of constitutional provisions regarding the protection of freedom of expression have not substantially changed during the last 200 years on either side of the Atlantic Ocean. However, the communications environment (in other words, the public sphere) of the twenty-first century is dramatically different to that which existed 150, or even fifty, years ago. Historically, freedom of expression was an individual right that was primarily aimed to protect the activities of the very small *bourgeoise* political elite. These activities essentially used written and oral means of communication, and protection was understood as lack of state interference in individual autonomy. After this seminal moment, the universalization of civil and political rights implied that free expression rights formally

1 English translation from http://avalon.law.yale.edu/18th_century/rightsof.asp
2 "Congress shall make no law respecting an establishment of religion, or prohibiting the free exercise thereof; or abridging the freedom of speech, or of the press; or the right of the people peaceably to assemble, and to petition the Government for a redress of grievances."

covered all communicative activities by any single citizen, not just those undertaken by relevant sectors of society. Apart from this, the increasing presence and role of different media, from the written press onwards, has created a communications environment that is probably very far from the minds of thinkers and politicians who provided a first solid conceptual and legal background for freedom of expression. The explosion of press and especially broadcast media changed the original idea of a free society of free people discussing the public interest, to a landscape in which the focus was no longer securing free individual autonomy, but rather informing the general public about public issues.[3]

As Jack M. Balkin has clearly pointed out, the great tension in the twentieth century in terms of freedom of speech was between the "passive" rights of the mass public and the practical and effective rights of a very few (Balkin 2008). At the same time, during the twentieth century, states have consequently assumed a more active role in the regulation of free expression, particularly in the area of audiovisual communications: As it will be shown later, most countries have approved legislative frameworks for the provision of audiovisual media services, which include, to some extent, provisions such as licensing requirements, protection of pluralism and direct provision of content to citizens through public service schemes. Of course, these regulatory schemes go beyond the original liberal idea of lack of state interference, putting in the hands of public institutions the remit to create and foster the conditions for a fair and equal access to information by any citizen[4] (Balkin 2008).

The digital era and especially the Internet have introduced new kinds of communicative instruments that have continued to change and decentralize the structure of the public sphere, as well as the communications market.

At the same time, the abovementioned process of decentralization has also led to something that might be seen as the seminal start of a real international public sphere. This development represents an important legal challenge, to the extent that, until now, freedom of expression has been granted at the national level by territorial public institutions. Transnational market forces are powerful and technology is eliminating the physical barriers that made this type of territorial definition possible. In this context, the national regulatory processes of speech may easily become artificial and ineffective.

Yet states are likely to be reluctant to relinquish their role as regulators of alliances and loyalties that take place in the public sphere (Price 2002), and interests of all kinds—ranging from control of obscenity, to protection of minors or national security, to the importance of local markets for advertising—press strongly for the maintenance of important instruments of state control.

It is true, moreover, that there is an undeniable and strong economic and corporate incentive and pressure towards the standardization of mass public opinion at a global level. Great conglomerates are becoming increasingly aware of the fact that a key element for the effective penetration of communication markets at a supranational level is global production and supply of "*Friends*-type" content packages—that is, content commercial products that are politically neutral, unrelated to local issues and aimed at reaching those segments of the

3 See John Meiklejohn's famous statement that what is important and should be protected is the fact that "everything worth saying shall be said" (Meiklejohn 1948: 25).

4 For example, in the United Kingdom, section 3 of the Communications Act 2003 establishes that one of the principal duties of Ofcom (as regulatory public entity) is to "further the interest of citizens in relation to communications matters," or "the maintenance of a sufficient plurality of providers of different radio and television services."

audience that are attractive to advertisers in developed Western markets, or even in certain emerging economies such as China or India.

This is a time of significant stress between different poles of power. Private global actors try to erode the classical state position of influence on the dynamics of the public sphere. Transnational institutions like the European Union try to foster the creation of regional markets in which certain values and principles are enforced and specific cultural products are protected and promoted. At the same time, individual nodes of the Internet push to create new allegiances and communities, crossing borders and circumventing in some cases the excess of government control. This has implications for how we protect free expression and where the possible restrictions may come from. It is a debate about globalization, cultural identity, market power, technology and, of course, individual autonomy. The debate provides an opportunity to see how freedom of expression as classical liberal right, conceived originally to fit in a typographic and discursive society can adjust to and accommodate the complexities of our twenty-first-century public spheres.

This text first provides a general vision of the definition and scope of freedom of information and freedom of expression. This overview will expose the differences existing between the US constitutional liberal tradition, and the principles that inspire the legal systems of most European countries (and Canada). While it is not the main objective of this chapter to undertake such comparative analysis, this might be of interest in terms of understanding how such freedoms are viewed according to different parameters in different democratic environments.

A second and more important objective of the following pages consists of showing how, nowadays, this constitutional perspective should be complemented by a more sophisticated analysis. In particular, the chapter will discuss the way in which the new communications value chain of the Internet era has introduced new technological and regulatory constraints that directly affect the free flow of ideas at both the national and global levels. These new elements are key in properly explaining and understanding the level of protection of freedom of expression that exists within a certain legal system and/or technology.

## (Free) Expression

Expression should be understood as an individual communicative conduct that occurs within the public sphere with the aim of transmitting ideas, opinions or sentiments. The free expression of people, therefore, is a main element of modern constitutionalism to the extent that it contributes to individual self-determination and to full development of personality, creating the conditions for participation in public discussion processes and social and political change. In addition, expression and communication are basic elements of democracy to the extent that they are a fundamental prerequisite for the effectiveness of citizen control and accountability of public powers. Communication in democracy, in short, is more than words (Baker 1994), and it should be understood from both an individual and a "collective" perspective.

A more specific definition of "free expression" would explain the concept as a process taking place within a specific market: the marketplace of ideas.[5] According to this theory, the exercise of freedom of expression in the form of a robust and comprehensive discussion deserves maximum protection to the extent that is the only channel through which "the

5 This metaphor should be attributed to US Supreme Court Justice Oliver Wendell Holmes in *Abrams v United States*, 250 US 616, 630 (1919).

truth" can end up rising. This emergence of truth is the result of the public confrontation of different points of view, no matter how offensive, wrong or inadequate they may be. Framed in this way, debate should not be subject to any form of regulation or state intervention apart from those specifically intended to prevent interference in the exercise of individual rights. In this sense, any negative consequence or externality that may arise from the exercise of one person's right to free expression finds its proper correction in the simultaneous exercise of this same freedom by other "speakers." In the marketplace of ideas, different expressions compete to most convincingly reach participants in the debate.

The marketplace of ideas theory basically links the protection of freedom of expression to the emergence of truth. According to some views, this connection will even justify the adoption of certain specific regulatory measures in those cases in which it might be considered that the market has some kind of "failure" and it is necessary to guarantee adequate or equal access for all viewpoints. These measures can even include some specific restrictions to individuals' freedom of speech.[6] The US case of the now-abandoned "fairness doctrine" is a very illustrative example of a regulatory effort to guarantee a certain degree of equilibrium and lack of bias within the public sphere.[7]

Despite the importance that the notion of the marketplace of ideas (with or without failures) has for many communication scholars (especially in the United States[8]), it does not adequately capture all of the implications of the creation, development and preservation of a fully democratic, pluralistic and deliberative public sphere.

As has already been pointed out, freedom of expression guarantees, on the one hand, a sphere of self-determination and self-fulfillment for every individual: The open expression of ideas, thoughts or sentiments should be adequately guaranteed within a free society. On the other hand, free expression is also an instrument that facilitates deliberation, the exchange of ideas, exposition to shocking and unexpected points of view, political discussion and citizens' decision-making processes in several important social areas, including of course (but not limited to) voting decisions.[9] These are significant important objectives that justify and define the scope of the protection provided by the free expression clause in most Western constitutions.

The realization of these objectives and principles goes far beyond the search for the truth within the marketplace of ideas. Indeed, the abovementioned elements are closely connected to values such as human dignity, pluralism, cultural diversity, and deliberative and participative democracy, which also appear as fundamental rights in most constitutional texts.

To take a very clear example, those values, among others, inspire the wording of Article 10 of the Convention for the Protection of Human Rights and Fundamental Freedoms (commonly known as the European Convention on Human Rights, or ECHR). The ECHR is the flagship treaty of the Council of Europe, as the legal instrument that guarantees a European system (from Portugal to Russia and Turkey) for the common establishment and

6 For a more in-depth analysis of the different market failure theories, see Baker 2002.

7 A very complete description of the rise and decline of the fairness doctrine can be found in Fiss (1996).

8 See Coase 1974 and Fowler and Brenner 1982.

9 In the same sense, Baker (1989) refers to the two key First Amendment values: self-fulfillment and participation in change.

protection of basic human rights.[10] The maximum interpreter of the ECHR, the European Court of Human Rights (ECtHR), has formulated the "argument of democracy" as one of the most important rationales that legitimate the right to freedom of expression.[11] In one of the Court's most famous decisions in the area of free expression, *Handyside* v *United Kingdom* (1976), the Court stated:

> The Court's supervisory functions oblige it to pay the utmost attention to the principles characterising a 'democratic society'. Freedom of expression constitutes one of the essential foundations of such a society, one of the basic conditions for its progress and for the development of every man. Subject to paragraph 2 of Article 10 (art. 10-2), it is applicable not only to 'information' or 'ideas' that are favourably received or regarded as inoffensive or as a matter of indifference, but also to those that offend, shock or disturb the State or any sector of the population. Such are the demands of that pluralism, tolerance and broadmindedness without which there is no 'democratic society'.
>
> (Handyside v UK *1976*.)

In this context, the specific free press clause plays a very central role. As it is well known, most modern constitutions protect two different fields of free expression: speech and the press, which is understood as a specific protection of the role of the media. In this sense, the ECtHR has an important case law doctrine that clearly establishes the crucial role that media and journalists play as public watchdogs of government performance, and in the promotion of open and effective debate on matters of public interest. Although Article 10 of the ECHR does not recognize the right of citizens to seek and obtain information, the ECtHR has stated that the effective protection of the rights of those that assume the responsibility to impart information and ideas cannot be separated from the (derived) right of the public to receive them (*The Sunday Times* v *The United Kingdom* 1979). At the same time, the ECtHR has established with particular emphasis that the wording of such provisions protects journalistic activities and practices from restrictive state interference, but also imposes some positive obligations to public institutions in order to safeguard media freedom and to create the conditions for a real and effective exercise of free expression rights (*Özgur Gündem* v *Turkey* 2000). In this same sense, the ECtHR, and more broadly the Council of Europe as a regional institution, have been declaring the importance of the adoption of national public policies able to create and to guarantee a plural structure of media outlets in order to allow the widest range of information sources and independent viewpoints.[12]

10 Article 10 ECHR states: "Everyone has the right to freedom of expression. This right shall include freedom to hold opinions and to receive and impart information and ideas without interference by public authority and regardless of frontiers. This article shall not prevent States from requiring the licensing of broadcasting, television or cinema enterprises. 2. The exercise of these freedoms, since it carries with it duties and responsibilities, may be subject to such formalities, conditions, restrictions or penalties as are prescribed by law and are necessary in a democratic society, in the interests of national security, territorial integrity or public safety, for the prevention of disorder or crime, for the protection of health or morals, for the protection of the reputation or rights of others, for preventing the disclosure of information received in confidence, or for maintaining the authority and impartiality of the judiciary."

11 More in-depth explanation of such rationale is provided in McGonagle 2009.

12 See the different recommendations and other documents approved by the Council of Europe in this field. Online. Available HTTP: http://www.coe.int/t/dghl/standardsetting/media/Themes/Div_en.asp

If we now focus on the US system, it should be noted that the abovementioned ideas are not far from what is established in the First Amendment, especially if we look at it from a historical perspective. As Monroe E. Price (1989) has written, the scope of individual freedom that embraces the First Amendment has its original meaning in a social and political system in which a community's survival was guaranteed through the existence of different equilibrated forces (religious groups, families, local governments) that could manage a balance between the forces of tradition and the urge towards creativity in dissent. That is to say that, in the eighteenth century, the checks and balances were quite different, which explains why the framers of the US Constitution could only glimpse the possibility of negative interfere in the social processes of formation of values: the federal instances of government. Thus it is clear that the democratic aspirations of the framers are linked to the existence of a particular social process of emergence and contrast of collective values, thoughts and opinions within a structure that, at any rate, would be far from a consumerist model or a marketplace that merely maintains and reinforces the existing dominating structure in terms of economic and communicative power (Price 1989; Fiss 1986). According to this interpretation of the ideological background of the US Constitution, C. Edwin Baker (1989) has affirmed that an individual's right to free speech does not extend to a right to use property to suppress other people's freedom to speak; as a result, economic regulations that tend to alleviate compensate, or even to restrict such power would be fully in line with constitutional principles (Baker 1989).

The dominant academic and judicial interpretation of the First Amendment, however, takes a different, more "absolutist" approach that believes all categories of expression (political speech, hate speech or commercial speech) should be treated in the same way, and the same legal treatments applied no matter whether expressions come from an individual or a large corporate entity or association. This approach has been adopted by a wide range of actors among which we can find the Supreme Court, prestigious First Amendment scholars and powerful litigators, such as the American Civil Liberties Union.[13] In short, even if the Supreme Court has accepted that the First Amendment requires effective speech protection for every individual, it only accepts this idea as a major rationale to restrict government intervention in the communications industry, whereas the imposition of restrictions on private entities in order to protect others' rights and to create the conditions for a more open, plural and diverse public sphere have been considered very restrictively.[14]

Thus, if we try to make a broad definition of freedom of expression that encompasses the ethical and political values that have inspired most Western constitutions, we might say that free speech is protected to the extent that it facilitates and guarantees access to the public sphere for any form of communication that is intended to disseminate beliefs, principles, values and human feelings, no matter its political, social or cultural value or importance (Cohen 1998). According to this, it should be outlined that, although free speech is directly connected to the idea of deliberation within a democratic society, it is too narrow a view to then understand that such freedom is protected only when its exercise is directly connected with political discourse and matters of public interest. Constitutional texts tend to protect all

13 A good general overview of these issues can be found at Shipan 1998, Robinson 1998, Geller 2003, Weinberg 1993 and Bernstein 2004.

14 See more on this critical approach in Sunstein 2009.

kind of expressions, including minor public conducts that do not aspire to generate any relevant public debate or to influence thinking and behavior of others. Thus constitutional protection of free expression does not only cover, in principle, those cases in which individuals intentionally seek to contribute to some form of discussion or deliberation of public interest, but also any externalization of individual thoughts and feelings. In other words, freedom of expression is at the service of something named by Balkin (2004) as "democratic culture"—that is, the free participation of every individual in the various forms of cultural production, in the broad sense of the term, and in the development of the different communities and subcommunities that may exist in a complex, plural and diverse democratic society.

Even more importantly, such constitutional protection is justified because freedom of speech serves values such as democracy, human dignity and pluralism in an acceptable manner, which is to say, non-violently and non-coercively (Baker 2009). The inverse also holds true: Any form of expression, whatever the social, political, economic or cultural field to which it may relate, that is directly and inextricably linked to an interference, coercion or direct attack upon the freedom and rights of others is not deserving of protection according to the constitutional provisions of basically all European countries. Understandably, an expressive conduct of this nature does not fit in with the rules of democratic civility.

Despite the constitutional similarities on this point, there is a significant contrast between the US legal system and the constitutional schemes for the protection of essential rights in Europe and Canada, regarding how such interference or coercion should be understood and defined.

In particular, public and intense expression of certain attitudes of racial hatred, as well as political ideologies historically linked to the violation of essential human rights, raise special challenges in drawing a clear line between what can be considered truly antidemocratic conducts and merely offensive expressions.

Even if the latter generate negative reactions (often intense), by definition they do not involve any form of interference in self-determination and capacity for free social participation. In this line, Baker argues that if we consider communication as a structural element of democracy, it is not possible to exclude those forms of expression that, in some way, may contribute to the effective realization of a collective plural dialog, even when such expressions may eventually be harmful for others, to the extent that they disseminate points of view that strongly contradict the very intense principles and beliefs. The ECtHR in Europe (as shown of *Handyside* v *United Kingdom*) has been very clear in this sense, stating that the protection of freedom of expression also applies to those ideas that "offend, shock or disturb the State or any sector of the population."

Regarding some forms of what can strictly be called "hate speech," the solution articulated by American jurisprudence should be seen as inspired in the marketplace of ideas theory. Briefly, the doctrine stated by the Supreme Court in most of these cases claims that the benefits linked to the public expression of a non-repressed point of view outweigh the harm likely to be caused by certain expressions of hatred, if such damage does not involve a very direct and immediate threat or attack to the rights of individuals, particularly in regard to their physical integrity.[15]

This US liberal approach to such an issue can, however, hide important matters that should not be neglected in the context of modern democracies. In this sense, it is pertinent to ask to

15 See a very complete description and analysis in Baker 1997.

what extent the presence in the public sphere of certain expressions of racial hatred, or hatred with regard to gender or sexual orientation, affects social cohesion and effective political participation. At the same time, it is also worth questioning whether any attack on the elements that form the basic status of human dignity should be accepted in a democracy that is based on such pillars. If we bear in mind, on the one hand, the increasing ethnic, social and cultural diversity that characterizes our societies and, on the other hand, the difficulties that some minority groups are facing to achieve an adequate level of integration within society, it would seem appropriate that public institutions assume a responsibility to limit what can become, under the guise of mere expression, substantial and real constraints to free participation, and dominance of certain groups or individuals over others.

In this last sense, the ECtHR has developed a very clear case law that does declare a violation of Article 10 ECHR in those cases in which the expressions used may lead to a feeling of rejection and antagonism, for example if the language points at certain communities (such as Islamic communities), as "the enemy" or "occupants" of one European territory that should be "re-conquered" (*Soulas and others v France* (2008)). In *Leroy v France* (2008), the Court analyzed a cartoon providing a satirical depiction of the 9/11 attacks on New York as a way to show, in the words of its author, the decline of American imperialism. In this case, the Court considered that the cartoon glorified the violent destruction of certain models of society and diminished the dignity of the victims, creating a feasible risk of public disorder, so that this kind of expressive conduct could not possibly fall under the scope of Article 10 ECHR as well. (It has to be underlined that the cartoon was published in the Basque country, where at that point the terrorist group ETA was still active.)

The audiovisual sector would be another very good example of this contrast between the two sides of the ocean. In this sense, the US Supreme Court has taken a very strict approach to broadcasting regulation, in particular those cases in which the restrictions imposed on media can be considered to be "content-based."[16] The Supreme Court has even refused to take into consideration the positive effects of some specific regulations that may have emerged from a content-based analysis.[17] At any rate, it should be noted that this approach has only become a consolidated case law doctrine after the 1980s, together with the emergence of a political vision of freedom of speech completely separated from the idea of the public interest.[18] Indeed, this is one of the fields in which the tension between the rights of citizens as members of an open and really participative public sphere, and the position of "active" big media companies is not contemplated as such in terms of First Amendment protection scope. This constitutional provision is applied, with basically no distinction, to entities that are very far from the original notion of individual voices that participate in communitarian and plural debates. As it has already been pointed out, recent First Amendment cases have focused on

16 Even if differences between content-based (subject to a strict scrutiny by the judge) and content-neutral regulations (subject to a non-strict scrutiny) are blurry in some cases. See the analysis made on this issue by Stone 2009.

17 The most important example of this kind of rationale can be found in *Turner Broadcasting System, Inc. v FCC* (I and II), 512 US 662 (1994) and 520 US 180 (1997), in which the Supreme Court analyzed the constitutionality of cable must-carry rules, stating that commercial and non-commercial beneficiaries of such regulations should be seen in equal terms without taking into consideration the differences that may exist in terms of type of content provided and vis-à-vis the interests of viewers, thus adopting a content-neutral approach. See the analysis of those decisions in Lutzker 1994, Price and Hawthorne 1994, and Robinson 1998.

18 A very clear presentation of this approach can be found in Fowler and Brenner 1982. See also Zaragoza, Bodorff and Emord 1988.

judicial protection of media corporations; very few Supreme Court decisions have taken into consideration the interests of citizens and the promotion of democratic deliberation processes when considering audiovisual regulations that may limit in some way the economic freedom of those entities. Finally, and as it is very well known, there is an area, the protection of the so-called "decency" (or avoidance of "indecent" content) on broadcast media, in which regulations and administrative decisions have been more intrusive in terms of content restriction. Here, courts have generally applied specific and exceptional scrutiny criteria (for example the test of whether government regulation advances a compelling governmental interest by the least restrictive means) that can hardly be found in decisions affecting other areas of speech.[19]

The European approach to audiovisual regulation is slightly different. Article 10(1) of the ECHR establishes that the protection of freedom of expression does not prevent states from regulating the audiovisual media by means of licensing schemes. Of course, this is a common scope of regulation not only in Europe and the United States, but also for most developed countries, at least regarding audiovisual services that are provided through the spectrum.

In addition, the ECtHR jurisprudence regarding restrictions of freedom of expression follows the wording of Article 10(2) ECHR, which states that the exercise of this freedom cannot only be seen from an individual and positive perspective, because it carries duties and responsibilities. The same paragraph mentions a set of grounds on which some formalities, conditions, restrictions and penalties can be imposed—among others, national security, public safety, prevention of disorder or crime, and protection of the reputation and rights of others. Such restrictions must be specifically prescribed by law in the respective national legal system and must be necessary in a democratic society. The ECtHR has constantly interpreted these provisions quite narrowly, in order to guarantee that national authorities apply, in every single case, the least possible restrictive means. However, it is clear that this opens the door to different national legal regimes in which some content-based restrictions may be established if they meet such requirements, in particular regarding media formats that might be particularly influential vis-à-vis public opinion, such as broadcasting services.

The European Union has approved a general legal instrument that establishes a common basic framework for every member state in the regulation of television and on-demand audiovisual media services. Commonly known as the "Television without Frontiers" (TwF) Directive, the original directive was approved in 1989 as the Directive "on the coordination of certain provisions laid down by law, regulation or administrative action in Member States concerning the pursuit of television broadcasting activities." The latest revision was approved in 2007, incorporating on-demand services under its scope and becoming the Audiovisual Media Services (AVMS) Directive.[20] In order to justify the need for a common basic EU regulation, the AVMS Directive stresses that:

> [T]raditional audiovisual media services—such as television—and emerging on-demand audiovisual media services offer significant employment opportunities in the Union, particularly in small and medium-sized enterprises, and stimulate economic growth and investment. Bearing in mind the importance of a level playing-field and a true European

19 See *FCC* v *Pacifica Foundation* 438 US 726 (1978) and the criticisms expressed in Baker 1996 45.

20 For the text of the AVMS Directive, Online. Available HTTP: http://eurlex.europa.eu/LexUriServ/LexUriServ.do?uri=CELEX:32010L0013:EN:NOT

> market for audiovisual media services, the basic principles of the internal market, such as free competition and equal treatment, should be respected in order to ensure transparency and predictability in markets for audiovisual media services and to achieve low barriers to entry.
>
> (*AVM Directive, Recital 10*)

At the same time, Recital 5 states very clearly:

> Audiovisual media services are as much cultural services as they are economic services. Their growing importance for societies, democracy—in particular by ensuring freedom of information, diversity of opinion and media pluralism—education and culture justifies the application of specific rules to these services.

Thus European media law understands the provision of audiovisual media services as a modality of the exercise of freedom of speech, and acknowledges the impact that such services have on important values, principles and citizens' rights within a modern democratic society (such as protection of human dignity, protection of minors, restrictions to harmful commercial content in both quantitative and qualitative terms, protection of the European audiovisual industry, and local culture and language).

In line with the abovementioned Recitals, the specific Articles of the AVMS Directive modulate the legitimate activities of European audiovisual media, bearing in mind that member states keep a certain amount of discretion in how they design their own specific legal framework for the audiovisual sector. These provisions (and the way in which they will be enforced by national authorities) are not only subject to the scrutiny of the ECtHR in "constitutional" terms, but also to the supervision of the Court of Justice of the European Union in much broader terms, in particular regarding the basic requirements for the preservation of an internal European market for the provision of the mentioned services. At any rate, the different legislative frameworks that have been approved by all EU member states introduce, following the provisions of the Directive, a regulatory regime in which restrictions such as quantitative time limits for advertising content or compulsory language and European content quotas are widely imposed. These restrictions do not actually exist in the US legal system, and they would probably be rejected by the Supreme Court and lower federal courts, according to their current restrictive vision of content-based limits and the way in which corporate media interests are directly connected with the constitutional scope of freedom of speech, as it has just been shown.

## Free expression and (private) censorship

The growing social importance of the Internet is forcing a profound reconsideration of the industrial model of broadcast mass media, as well as the terms in which it conditions the process formation of public opinion.

More particularly, it is interesting to outline the progressive introduction of a communications model based on the so-called "peer production." As stated by Internet scholar Yogchai Benkler (2003, 2006), this idea describes a process of production of information or culture by a potentially large number of individuals whose actions are not subject to the influence or coordination, either by capital or by dynamics of the market of communication corporations. The radical distinction between senders and receivers, especially marked during the second half of the twentieth century, has started to crumble, as well as the still-existing dominance of commercial media discourses compared to those who might be regarded as non-commercial. Thus, despite the continuing influence and power of traditional broadcast media, many modalities of communication of this post-industrial age will no longer be subject to centralized manufacturing, ultimately developing unprecedented mechanisms of democratic civic discourse.

In a very similar sense, communications scholar Manuel Castells (2009) uses the term "mass self-communication" to define communication systems or networks organized strictly horizontally, established by a myriad of individual subjects and of multimodal nature, covering areas such as photo sharing, joint creation of online encyclopedias, the circulation of music and movies, the deployment of networks of political activists, and also the creation and dissemination of audiovisual content. Such networks are in contrast to those that organize conventional radio and television, in which communication flows strictly from the top down. It seems thus that we are entering an era of decentralization of communications and culture in which new opportunities for any individual to receive content, as well as to speak, are emerging. At the same time, old powerful actors are losing their oligopoly over information control and distribution. However, these changes do not seem to bring us to an ideal situation in which a general clause of freedom of expression alone would be sufficient as a legal framework to guarantee the complete absence of any danger of censorship or, more broadly, the exercise and abuse of certain domination powers. The key issue, however, will be the fact that this danger of domination or censorship would now mostly come from private corporations instead of state powers.

The new Internet landscape would seem to provide citizens with powerful new tools that might alleviate in some way the need for direct public intervention to protect or preserve freedom of expression. However, as some authors have pointed out, the Internet also brings with it new difficulties, in particular in areas such as searching, exercising choice and trust, and gaining access under fair and affordable conditions (Helberger 2008). In this sense, specific matters such as fairness of contractual conditions, the guarantee of fair and non-discriminatory use of competing and interoperable applications and devices, and the access to reliable, fair and non-biased sources of information or search instruments are related to very important regulatory challenges (for example net neutrality) that are now in the midst of important public policy debates. In this context, it is not clear whether a reasonable degree of autonomy and literacy from every individual consumer, together with the general protection brought by consumer and competition law,[21] will be sufficient to guarantee not only a free content market, but also the protection of many relevant public values in the relation between citizens and companies, including free access to a wide range of information sources, the right to accurate information and the protection of minors.

For example, looking at the most popular formats and offers of Internet on-demand content, it is evident that, in almost all of them, the power of individual consumers and citizens is not as wide as common perceptions might suggest. Device manufacturers, content aggregators and managed networks of Internet service providers are the most common intermediaries who grant consumers access to content. In these cases, the range of choice and the conditions under which a specific search will be managed depend on the criteria and the decisions previously taken by media/telecom/device companies. Thus, despite a superficial vision of a free, open, on-demand audiovisual market with unlimited access

21 That is, rules that are applied to every economic sector to protect market competition and a fair treatment of consumers.

to material of a consumer's choice, the reality is that the most relevant systems for the provision of these kinds of services are managed according to the interests of only a few powerful gatekeepers. As it has been pointed out, the distortions that could result from this dominant position not only would seriously impair the rights and expectations of individual consumers, but may also erode the principles of pluralism, free access and diversity that apply to citizens, both as individuals and as a part of the public opinion, who participate in the public sphere in modern democracies. What is at stake, once again, is not only the capacity of each individual to choose among different services within a competitive market, but also the real access for citizens to an offer of content that is fair, with a diverse range of different and plural voices, non-harmful, and varied enough to guarantee an open public sphere and the protection of rights, principles and values that are beyond the specific interests of its participants.

On the other hand, it is also necessary to look at these matters from a different perspective. Individuals are not only consumers of on-demand or Internet content, but also for the first time they have the possibility of becoming content producers: "audiovisual voices." This second perspective raises many different regulatory problems, particularly if we accept that most of the user-generated content is not placed on private individual websites, but in popular and profitable distribution platforms, managed by big media and Internet companies. It is clear that, in such cases, the owner of the platform becomes in some way the "regulator" (and even may become the "censor") of the content that will finally be made available to the general public. Its privileged position as a reliable and well-known provider of user-generated content plays a key role. Should this regulatory power (and possible political power as well)[22] remain in private hands without public regulatory—and, of course, democratic—supervision, according to the principles that we have been mentioning here? Is it reasonable to move, in a very few decades, from the terrain of statutory regulation to the land of essentially private-based control of content that is distributed through electronic networks, portals and search engines?

In this wide, problematic context for analysis, an additional (and in some ways paradoxical) regulatory tendency is evident.

If we were to look at authoritarian regimes that clearly impair free expression (for example China or Iran), we would notice that, instead of trying to directly control the networks, these political regimes have been focusing on guaranteeing that most important intermediaries will filter content in line with their directives. A sensitive issue in this area in recent years has been the fact that many Western Internet intermediary companies (Google, Yahoo!, etc.) have been gaining positions and seeking business opportunities in those countries and are reluctant to directly accept certain requirements of traffic monitoring of the content provided. Such requirements would be considered by those same companies as unacceptable in their original democratic countries (primarily, the United States). The seriousness and importance of this problem led a group of US congressmen to propose in 2006 the Global Online Freedom Act, which would prohibit portals and search engines of the United States from accepting restrictions imposed by non-democratic regimes.

22 Think, for example, of the content criteria that apply to YouTube videos, which the company established and enforces itself. These rules affect and limit in different ways the exercise of freedom of expression and information, and are applied following a "private" procedure with no administrative and judicial control. Online. Available HTTP: http://www.youtube.com/t/terms

Moreover, the United States and the European Union (and its member states) have adopted or promoted certain measures to foster the cooperation of intermediaries in the effective control of what is being distributed through their networks, applications or services. It is true, however, that such measures have generally been connected to the protection of very general and non-controversial values or principles, especially in the prevention of child abuse and pornography (OSCE 2004), although in some cases (such as preventing terrorism and protecting national security and defense after 9/11 in the United States) such regulations have not been free of controversy either.[23] In countries such as France and Germany there have been important debates on judicial decisions that broaden the scope of liability of intermediaries in cases that involve the transmission of Nazi content or other harmful and illegal content (Kreimer 2006). And in Italy, in the famous Google case, a court held the company directly responsible for a video posted by a third party on YouTube (Wong 2010).

As a matter of fact, both the United States and the EU have established, during the last decade, a regulatory model of intermediary liability based on two main principles: notice and takedown; and liability exemption. Any Internet intermediary that performs typical non-editorial functions (housing, storage, conduit, etc.) is generally exempt from liability and from the duty to monitor the content it provides. It would become liable only if it were effectively warned about the possible presence of illegal content. At the same time, US and European legal regimes had generally established the need for a fair process as a condition for the hypothetical removal of any piece of illegal content. These are the primary directives that inspired texts like the Digital Millennium Copyright Act of 8 October 1998 in the United States, and various EU directives in this matter.[24] However, a very progressive tendency of traditional state regulatory powers towards placing a higher degree of responsibility and monitoring capacity in private hands can be detected, in particular in the case of the Internet intermediaries. In line with what has been explained here, intermediaries are easily "reachable" by legislative and administrative national powers (at least, much more reasonable than some original creators of content), and the imposition of duties and restrictions over their activities can be presented as a measure that does not imply a direct and immediate interference in expressive activities. At the same time, though, this new legal understanding of intermediaries' roles and capacities would obviously alter the original idea of liability exemption.

A very good example of what has just been mentioned is the case of two legislative projects discussed within the US Congress and the Senate: the Stop Online Piracy Act (SOPA); and the Protect Intellectual Property Act (PIPA). At the time of writing, these two projects have not been approved and appear to have stalled for political reasons. However, it is worth pointing out here that the current wording of such legal proposals establishes, among other things, the power of copyright owners to stop online advertisers and credit card processors from doing business with a website merely by filing a unilateral notice that the site is "dedicated to theft of US property"—even if no court has actually found any infringement. Moreover, and according to the critical analysis undertaken by relevant

23 This is clearly the case of the United States Patriot Act of 26 October 2001.

24 See Directive 2001/29/EC of the European Parliament and of the Council of 22 May 2001 on the harmonization of certain aspects of copyright and related rights in the information society, and Directive 2000/31/EC of the European Parliament and the Council of 8 June 2000 on certain legal aspects of information society services, in particular electronic commerce in the internal market. This last directive is now under revision. Online. Available HTTP: http://ec.europa.eu/internal_market/e-commerce/communication_2012_en.htm

First Amendment scholars such as Lawrence H. Tribe, the new and more generous immunity provisions in the Bill create an immense incentive for advertisers and payment processors to comply with such a request immediately upon receipt (Tribe 2011). A key factor in this sense is that SOPA and all of its legal instruments are based on concepts as vague as "theft of US property," which, for example, may put outside the law websites that take actions "to avoid confirming a high probability of . . . use" for infringement (SOPA, §§ 102–3). This would seem to require private monitoring actions that have been deliberately avoided to this point. Moreover, criticisms point at the fact that many sites will be reluctant to offer some kinds of controversial, but at the same time fully protected and lawful, speech (for example links to foreign websites if they might be offering creative content that may raise intellectual property controversies), for fear that they might be accused of a SOPA violation and suffer a cut-off of revenue from online advertising or credit card payments for transactions.

Technologies do not change or privatize the importance and the role of the public sphere. Democratic institutions should avoid excessive domination powers coming from the convergent and progressively concentrated world of device manufacturers, distributors, content aggregators and telecom companies. Openness and real diversity are still necessary, in particular in a world in which many walled gardens have emerged in territories seen by private interests as the Promised Land. As Balkin (2008) has convincingly pointed out, protecting free speech values in the digital age will be less a problem of constitutional law and more and more a problem of technology and administrative regulation, so that free speech values increasingly depend on policies that promote innovation and keep incumbent businesses from blocking new ideas, services and applications. As we have just seen, sometimes the incentives for intermediaries to restrain third parties' expressive freedom may derive from a direct imposition or a burden established by the legal framework, so that the legitimate aim to protect important values and interests such as intellectual property will create a very dangerous "chilling effect" for the free dissemination of ideas and creations.

In this context, co-regulation and self-regulation have become the trending topics of content public policy issues in the Web 2.0 era. However, apart from the relief that these concepts may provide, both to those who are worried about the end of statutory regulation and those who are concerned about a possible excess of it, the discussion about possible schemes that would realistically be accepted and applied by all of the actors involved still has to bring concrete and feasible conclusions.

## References

Baker, C. E. (1989) *Human Liberty and Freedom of Speech*, New York and Oxford: Oxford University Press.

—— (1994) 'Of course, more than words,' *University of Chicago Law Review*, 61: 1181–1211.

—— (1996) 'The evening hours during Pacifica Standard Time,' *Villanova Sports & Entertainment Law Journal*, 3: 45–60.

—— (1997) 'Harm, liberty and free speech,' *Southern California Law Review*, 70: 979–1020.

—— (2002) *Media, Markets, and Democracy*, Cambridge: Cambridge University Press.

—— (2009) 'Scope of the First Amendment: Freedom of speech,' in V. D. Amar (ed.) *The First Amendment: Freedom of Speech—Its Constitutional History and the Contemporary Debate*, New York: Prometheus Books.

Balkin, J. M. (2004) 'Digital speech and democratic culture: A theory of freedom of expression for the information society,' *New York University Law Review*, 79: 1–55.

—— (2008) 'The future of free expression in a digital age,' *Pepperdine Law Review*, 36: 101–119.

Benkler, Y. (2003) 'Freedom in the Commons: Towards a political economy of information,' *Duke Law Journal*, 52: 1245–1276.

—— (2006) *The Wealth of Networks. How Social Production Transforms Markets and Freedom*, New Haven, CT: Yale University Press.

Burskin, M. J. (2004) 'Towards a new standard for First Amendment review of structural media regulation,' *New York University Law Review*, 79: 1030–1070.

Castells, M. (2009) *Communication Power*, New York: Oxford University Press.

Coase, R. H. (1974) 'The market for goods and the market for ideas,' *American Economic Review*, 64: 384–391.

Cohen, J. (1998) 'Democracy and liberty,' in J. Elster (ed.) *Deliberative Democracy*, Cambridge: Cambridge University Press.

*Federal Communications Commission* v *Pacifica Foundation* 438 US 726 (1978).

Fiss, H. (1986) 'Free speech and social structure,' *Iowa Law Review*, 71: 1405–1425.

—— (1996) *The Irony of Free Speech*, Cambridge, MA: Harvard University Press.

Fowler, M. S. and Brenner, D. L. (1982) 'A marketplace approach to broadcast regulation,' *Texas Law Review*, 60: 207–257.

Geller, H. (2003) 'Promoting the public interest in the digital era,' *Federal Communications Law Journal*, 55(3): 515–520.

*Handyside* v *United Kingdom* (1976) Application no. 5493/72, ECtHR.

Helberger, N. (2008) 'From eyeball to creator: Toying with audience empowerment in the Audiovisual Media Services Directive.' Online. Available HTTP: http://www.ivir.nl/publications/helberger/From%20eyeball%20to%20media%20literate%20viewer.pdf (accessed 20 April 2012).

Kreimer, S. F. (2006) 'Censorship by proxy: The First Amendment, Internet intermediaries, and the problem of the weakest link,' *University of Pennsylvania Law Review*, 155(1): 11–101.

*Leroy* v *France* (2008) Application no. 36109/03, ECtHR.

Lutzker, G. S. (1994) 'The 1992 Cable Act and the First Amendment: What must, must not, and may be carried,' *Cardozo Arts & Entertainment Law Journal*, 12: 467–498.

McGonagle, T. (2009) 'Free expression and respect for others,' in *Living Together: A Handbook on Council of Europe Standards on Media's Contribution to Social Cohesion, Intercultural Dialogue, Understanding, Tolerance and Democratic Participation*, Strasbourg: Council of Europe.

Meiklejohn, A. (1948) *Free Speech and Its Relation to Self-Government*, New York: Harper.

—— (1965) *Political Freedom: The Constitutional Powers of the People*, Oxford: Oxford University Press.

Möller C. and Amouroux A. (eds.) (2004) *The Media Freedom Internet Cookbook*, Vienna: OSCE. Online. Available HTTP: http://www.osce.org/fom/13836?download=true (accessed 20 April 2012).

*Özgur Gündem* v *Turkey* (2000) Application no. 23144/93, ECtHR.

Price, M. E. (1989) *Shattered Mirrors: Our Search for Identity and Community in the AIDS Era*, Oxford: Oxford University Press.

—— (2002) *Media and Sovereignty: The Global Information Revolution and Its Challenge to State Power*, Cambridge, MA: MIT Press.

Price, M. E. and Hawthorne, D. (1994) 'Saving public television: The remand of Turner Broadcasting and the future of cable regulation,' *Hastings Communication and Entertainment Law Journal*, 17: 65–95.

Robinson, G. O. (1998) 'The electronic First Amendment: An essay for the new age,' *Duke Law Journal*, 47: 844–970.

Shipan, C. R. (1998) 'Keeping competitors out: Broadcast regulation from 1927 to 1996,' in B. Noll and M. Price (eds.) *A Communications Cornucopia: Markle Foundation Essays on Information Policy*, New York: Brookings Institute.

*Soulas and others* v *France* (2008) Application no. 15948/03, ECtHR.

Stone, G. F. (2009) 'Content regulation and the First Amendment,' in V. D. Amar (ed.) *The First Amendment: Freedom of Speech—Its Constitutional History and the Contemporary Debate*, New York: Prometheus Books.

*Sunday Times* v *United Kingdom* (1979) (1979–80) 2 EHRR 245.

Sunstein, C. S. (2009) 'Free speech now,' in V. D. Amar (ed.) *The First Amendment: Freedom of Speech—Its Constitutional History and the Contemporary Debate*, New York: Prometheus Books.

Tribe, L. (2011) 'The Stop Online Piracy Act (PIPA) violates the First Amendment.' Online. Available HTTP: http://www.net-coalition.com/wp-content/uploads/2011/08/tribe-legis-memo-on-SOPA-12-6-11-1.pdf (accessed 20 April 2012).

*Turner Broadcasting Systems, Inc.* v *Federal Communications Commission and others* 512 US 622 (1994).

Weinberg, J. (1993) 'Broadcasting and speech,' *California Law Review*, 81: 1101–1204.

Wong, C. (2010) 'Don't blame the messenger: Intermediary liability and protecting Internet platforms,' *eJournal USA*, 15(6): 19–21.

Zaragoza, R., Bodorff, R. and Emord, J. W. (1988) 'The public interest concept transformed: The trusteeship model gives way to a marketplace approach,' in J. T. Powell and W. Gair (eds.) *Public Interest and the Business of Broadcasting*, New York: Quorum Books.

# 8

# Internet freedom, the public sphere and constitutional guarantees

## A European perspective

*Bernd Holznagel**

### Introduction

The Internet is the biggest communications innovation of the last decades (Disselkamp 2005; Münker 2009). Hardly any other innovation has brought change that is so varied, so directly noticeable, and constantly transforming and developing for individuals, businesses, and also for politics. The judicial system in Europe has found it difficult to keep up with the speed with which the Internet has developed, and to consider whether there are different regional approaches to the regulation of Internet and society. The premise of this chapter is that the European perspective is different because of its: (a) particular pre-existing structure and approach to communications technology; (b) fundamental aspects of constitutional rights to free expression; and (c) longstanding traditions embodied in the national constitutions, as well as the European Charter of Fundamental Rights (CFR).

Mass communication, which through press, radio and television addresses the general public, is subject to particular protection under European law. The reasons for this lie in the particular meaning that these media have in the forming of political engagement and thereby in the shaping of a democratic public awareness. Constitutional law, above all, strives to prevent government institutions or powerful commercial interests from exerting an undue influence. A reason frequently given for this position is the particular responsibility that the media carry, for example, during an electoral campaign.

In this context, the question arises whether, and to what extent, the Internet as a means of mass communication should be subject to the same legal protection, but also to the same responsibilities, as are older, "legacy" media, including print and broadcasting. The idea of Internet services being a fundamental right, of the same quality as press and broadcasting, is quite new. Internet freedom is still a fundamental right in the process of being created and defined. This chapter is part of that process.

* The author wishes to thank Stella Renk-Berry and Pascal Schumacher for their assistance with this chapter.

First, we must settle to what extent Internet services participating in mass communication are entitled to protection under constitutional law. Our position is that these services should not be dealt with under the laws regulating the freedom of the press or of broadcasting. Instead, the definition of the "mass media" should be further diversified and an independent concept of freedom in Internet services should be recognized. We will then deal with the possibilities that the law has to restrict the freedom of Internet services. We will explain what actions we can expect when we accept that the duty of the state is to support and encourage the shaping of democratic public awareness on the Internet. When important community values are at risk, it is the clear duty of the state to protect them.

## Publicity as a condition of a democratic society

Publicity mediates between the people, other forces in society and the political decision-making system (Jarren and Donges 2006). This mediation works both ways: from the public to the politicians, and from the politicians to the public. There is political publicity in both social and totalitarian systems. It becomes democratic publicity when it is in alignment with the concept of democracy. This means that the relationship in the fields of responsibility and its delegation from the people to the government bodies must be kept transparent, accessible, rational and controlled. Thus publicity becomes the precondition for a free and functioning democracy.

Mass media, especially press and radio, play a vital role in influencing public opinion. They play a central role in gathering, processing and interpreting information. Individual citizens would, in today's world, find it difficult to process and make sense of a multiplicity of events. These events are processed and presented by the journalists. They offer the public information that allows them to develop scale of values (Hoffmann-Riem 2002). Journalistic activity is, for the most part, safeguarded by particular media freedoms. They are a part of the general basic right to freedom of opinion and the freedom to express those opinions, but, as a rule, they also are privileged through constitutional jurisdiction. Recently, this function—of processing and interpreting information—has also been taken over by some Internet services.

## Constitutional classification of Internet services

From a European perspective, allocating a particular Internet service to the particular basic right of communication is crucial. Unlike the United States, European constitutional law distinguishes between individual and mass communication, and attaches different legal consequences to them. For instance, because of their significance in the production of a democratic public awareness, freedoms enjoyed by the media are particularly important and are often given preference when they clash with other values and freedoms that could also claim protection (Jarass 2010).

The legal starting point for a proper characterization (whether a right or not and what kind of right) is the wording of the respective Article in the EU Charter of Fundamental Rights (CFR). The Charter, which first came into effect under the Lisbon Treaty in 2009, applies to all bodies of the European Union (the European Commission, the European Council, etc.), as well as for the member states in their implementation of EU law—for example, in the enforcement of the many guidelines and regulations. The European Court in Luxembourg is responsible for the interpretation of the Charter.

For the various Internet services, the point of contact to their legal status as basic rights in Europe is Article 11 of the CFR. This distinguishes between the freedom to express opinions and the freedom of the media. The differences between individual and mass communications, and the different protective guarantees that are linked to their different value as fundamental rights are made clear. Article 11 states:

> (1) Everyone has the right to freedom of expression. This right shall include freedom to hold opinions and to receive and impart information and ideas without interference by public authority and regardless of frontiers.
> (2) The freedom and pluralism of the media shall be respected.

### *Individual or mass communication?*

The wording of Article 11 2(1) gives the freedom of the media its own particular guarantees, which are different from those accorded to the more general freedom to an expression of opinion. In order to choose the appropriate sphere of protection, it must be determined whether Internet services are considered to be individual or mass communication. However, the Internet is a typical "hybrid" medium. Some of its services, such as email, have communication between individuals as a primary purpose. Other services, such as web pages, blogs, YouTube or Internet protocol television (IPTV) (Ricke 2011), as well as social media forums, including Facebook and Twitter or Google+, are aimed at an indefinite number of users. These services can only be regarded as a means of mass communication.

Large segments of Internet services, especially those that are suitable to influence public opinion, are a form of mass communication. Their special role in shaping public awareness overstrains individual freedom of speech. Rather, they should be categorized as being part of the freedom of the media. However, there are noticeable differences between traditional mass media and Internet services that require consideration and affect their legal classification, as we will see later in this chapter.

### *Changes and development in democratic publicity on the Internet*

By its very nature, publicity through personal contact and through assembly reaches only a limited number of people. To reach a lot of people, it used to be necessary to distribute one's information through the mass media—through television, radio and the press. However, it is very difficult for an individual to get access to the world of mass media. Access is carefully controlled by powerful gatekeepers, for example publishers and editors; terrestrial frequencies and cable channels are few in number and require a permit (Holznagel and Kibele 2011); the costs of producing programs are high; and starting a daily newspaper is difficult. In such an environment, editors and owners decide what to publish. Decision-makers from the higher circles of the state and the economy have a much greater potential influence here than the general public. They have advertising budgets and public relations departments to procure favorable attention for their interests and their projects. In addition, media users have little possibility to give feedback. Their role remains passive; they are merely consumers of information.

These conditions, under which public awareness was produced, led to the constitutional courts in Europe striving to curtail the gatekeepers' power to influence both individual and collective opinion and decision-making. They set up obstacles to prevent monopolies from influencing public opinion and provided tools to guarantee diversity in the information and opinion market (BVerfGE 57: 295, 323; 163, 172). In addition, they strove to prevent the state from exerting excessive influence over the gatekeepers (Hoffmann-Riem 2001). The mass media have a duty to ensure diversity of opinion, thus enabling each individual citizen to draw on a wide range of information and to take part in the forming of the political will

(Holznagel 2008). Another important principle is that the gatekeepers must keep their distance from the state and from advocacy or lobbying groups. The media must not place themselves at the mercy either of the state or of particular groups or businesses.

With the Internet, this situation has changed. Communication has developed from being one-sided and centralized to being decentralized and interlinked. The World Wide Web (WWW) has grown into an extremely complex structure that is comprehensive, cross-linked, and combines and connects different services, offers and websites with each other. Anyone can communicate and obtain information at very low cost (Anderson 2007). This serves to weaken the traditional gatekeepers of the old analog communication (Neuberger 2009). Journalism loses its monopoly of power to filter and to evaluate information. Although the tide of information is rising continuously, journalists and editors are losing their position of authority as the quality controllers of information and communication. Evaluation platforms and search engines offer orientation. They are the powers that now determine what information the user takes notice of. Here originate the new possibilities of manipulating the process of decision-making and developing opinions (Dankert and Mayer 2010).

This also means that, in the world of Internet communication, a potentially unlimited number of people find themselves in the position of both communicator and recipient. Everyone has the same potential, under "best effort" conditions, to influence decision-making and the formation of political opinion. Attention, as a prerequisite for successful communication, is, under these conditions, a particularly rare and valuable commodity (Franck 2000). Thus it is possible to "tip the scales" in the melee of conflicting opinions by accelerating or decelerating the transport of communications, something that online management techniques like "deep packet inspection" make perfectly feasible. Thus arise new dangers for the principle of equal opportunities in communication (Schulz 1998). If using such techniques means that part of the population is excluded from using the Internet and does not have access to e-commerce and e-government services, the mandate of providing basic services is at risk (Holznagel 2010). These two principles—equal opportunities and basic services—are decisive in the legal classification of Internet communication.

## *Need to reflect the particularities of Internet communication in the constitutional discussion*

Under these circumstances, the European constitutional debate seeks ways in which to appropriately reflect the differences between classical mass media and Internet services in the application of the fundamental rights. Our proposition is to abandon rigid classifications and to recognize a third category of "freedom of Internet services," alongside the freedoms of broadcasting and of the press. This freedom must be distinguished from the freedom of Internet access, which is intended to ensure broadband Internet access for everyone (Baer 2011). The advantage of such a classification is that the separate groupings of the present forms of communication—a separation that, in reality, has already long taken place—can be mirrored in constitutional law much more precisely.

A characteristic of the European fundamental rights protection system is that fundamental rights—including freedom of Internet services—also influence the legal system. Fundamental rights have a specific constitutional function. On the one hand, they define the subjective right of individuals to defend themselves against the powers of the state. On the other hand, they also constitute objectively and legally an evaluation by the constitution, which is valid for all fields of the legal system and for all guidelines pertaining to legislation, administration and adjudication (BVerfGE 49: 89, 141). From this character of fundamental rights, we can conclude that the legislator is under a primary obligation to protect the contents of the fundamental rights from injury and endangerment, so that the laws he draws up differentiate and substantiate these rights. He is under this obligation even when the injuries and endangerments in question do not emanate from the state, or when the state is not even partially responsible for them—an obligation known in German law as duty of protection (*Schutzpflicht*). In addition, the objective-legal aspect of the fundamental rights means that, when simple law is being interpreted, the evaluations of the constitution must be taken into account. These principles are valid in all fields of law (Jarass 2010), but they come into effect when private third parties threaten a fundamental right.

## Internet freedom as a subjective right

### *Interference*

Interference in Internet freedom results when the protected activity is regulated in a stressful or burdensome manner. Furthermore, interference is given when the protected activity is hampered indirectly or de facto in a qualified way (Jarass 2010). Among other measures, the searching of editorial rooms or the confiscation of information can be defined as interference. Other interference of a more Internet-related kind would be the blocking or delaying of data traffic for the network operator, or a blacklisting decree, or forbidding a link aimed at the access provider (Schumacher 2011).

### *Justification of interference*

#### Possible justifications

Each exercise of a fundamental right brings limitations and boundaries. It is part of the European tradition of fundamental rights that interference is permissible only when it is based on law and has a legitimate aim. In addition, this limitation of a fundamental right must be in accord with the principle of commensurability (i.e. the measure of interference must be necessary, appropriate and fair).

#### Legitimate subjects of protection

The protection of minors in general is classed as a legitimate aim under the protection of morals (*Handyside* v *UK* 1976: § 49). This would mean a restriction on the dissemination of pornography, but also of other content that could endanger minors. Protection of identity and of personal honor is covered by protection of reputation, as far as defamatory expressions and libel are concerned (*Bergens Tidende* v *Norway* 2000: § 51). Protection of data privacy (the right to informational self-determination) can be enforced as a means of "preventing the disclosure of information received in confidence," which is aimed at protecting privacy, as well as national and public security (Grabenwarter 2008). It can also be inferred that the state is obliged objectively and legally to maintain media diverse media (*The Observer and Guardian* v *UK* 1991; *Informationsverein Lentia* v *Austria* 1993: § 32). The principle of pluralism may be enforced here so that the "others," whose rights may be protected, can also make use of their communication and freedom of information. Limiting hate speech, racist expressions or other illegal content (e.g. in the case of someone using the Internet to prepare terrorist attacks) can be justified in the interests of "national or public safety" and territorial integrity, or the "prevention of disorder or crime." It all depends on the particular case in question.

## The commensurability of individual measures

*Internet kill switch*

To prevent cases of severe threats to public order that are organized and spread through the web, politicians have discussed ways to shut down all of the Internet communication in a country at once. The concept is called an Internet kill switch. Such a mechanism would allow a previously specified authority to deactivate Internet traffic in a quick and effective way. Recent draft US legislation also see it as a possible counter-strategy in cyberwarfare. On a worldwide basis, however, the idea is largely criticized, particularly since several North African regimes controlled and obstructed Internet-access in order to stifle civil uprisings during the Arab Spring.

Such a measure represents a very serious interference in a multitude of fundamental rights (among others, freedom of information, of communication and of Internet services), and not only for those members of the public taking part in the riots. The entire public would be cut off completely from the Internet, which today is an indispensable tool for coping with everyday life. The damage that this Internet shutdown would cause could be substantial—resulting not only in monetary losses, but lack of access to vital information. When we consider these objections, an Internet kill switch cannot be actively considered (KOM 2010). There are much less drastic means that can be used to restore order.

*Three strikes (and you're out)*

Another method of fighting illegal Internet offers in general and of downloads in particular is what is known as the "three strikes" approach (Anderson 2008; Fink 2009), under which Internet users who repeatedly download illegal content find their Internet access blocked. As far as the user in question functions as a provider of Internet services (e.g. a blogger or a Facebook user), this means that his freedom to use Internet services is being interfered with. For other users, however, freedom of information is what is being limited.

This measure was first introduced in France with the so called "Loi HADOPI."[1] This law stipulates that, in the case of pirate copying, the courts could, after two warnings, block Internet access for up to a year. Similar laws have now been introduced in New Zealand (Copyright and Infringing File Sharing Amendment Act 2011), South Korea (Korean Copyright Act 2009), Taiwan and the United Kingdom (Digital Economy Act 2010).

The "three strikes" principle represents a serious interference in the freedom of Internet services, as well as other freedoms. An individual is completely cut off from Internet communication for a certain length of time. The goal that this measure is pursuing—in effect, the "protection of the rights of others"—could be achieved just as effectively by other measures, such as traffic management. In addition, the access blockade should not spring into action automatically, but should be approved by a judge (Greve and Schärdel 2009). The fact that the law has been infringed three times should not be the only determining factor. In the long run, this measure could have an intimidating effect on Internet communication in general. Users could be held back from downloading content from the Internet (even legal content), thus waiving their right to freedom of information, because they are afraid of being cautioned or of losing their Internet access. The "three strikes" approach can therefore be regarded as incommensurable (Fink 2009).

1 HADOPI stands for *Haute Autorite pour la Diffusion des Oeuvres et la Protection des Droits sur Internet* [The High Authority for the Dissemination of Works and for the Protection of Rights on the Internet].

*Measures against anonymity*

After the terror attacks in Oslo and on the Norwegian island of Utöya in summer 2011, demands to restrict anonymity on the Internet grew. This would mean that criminal offences could be more easily discovered and prevented. The German Minister of the Interior, Hans-Peter Friedrich, hopes that with this measure political communication will be more civilized, of a better quality: "Normally people stand behind what they say and what they believe, with their names. Why isn't it a matter of course in internet as well?" (Friedrich 2011: 25). Facebook also supports efforts in this direction (Lischka 2011). The underlying assumption is that someone who is active on the Internet under his own name is less likely to insult other users or to be involved in illegal activities.

On the other hand, communicating on the Internet anonymously or under a pseudonym generally ensures that debates are lively and animated. When we consider platforms where talks center on very personal topics—for example political forums or discussion groups for victims of abuse—it is often only under anonymous conditions that users are able to participate undisturbed and unthreatened. If it were forbidden to take part in these discussions anonymously or under a pseudonym, this would mean that any other user, with a single click on Google, could find out what had been said in this group and identify the person who had said it. At the same time, he would be able to piece together countless other scraps of private data, freely available on the Internet, the sum total of which would be an extremely threatening invasion of privacy. Especially in dictatorial regimes, people debating on political platforms would have reason to fear serious reprisals if they were forced to reveal their identity. Any political participation would be very quickly stifled under these circumstances. The wish that manners may improve in Internet political communication is certainly no justification for introducing the obligation to name names.

If the reason for prohibiting anonymity is to discover or prevent criminal offences (i.e. if investigative authorities have access to the identity data stored by Internet service providers), the seriousness of the interference is the criterion in judging its commensurability. In this case, the interference is serious: the author of a simple user commentary, for example, could be traced back years later and associated with the current contents of the communication. A general disclosure of identity in all online activities would therefore be unsupportable. At any rate, this measure should be limited to particular, individual cases involving serious crime.

*Blocking certain content*

If the protection of fundamental values of major importance is involved, as, for example, in the fight against child pornography, a measure in great demand is the blocking of access. This would have been put into effect by a court order addressed to the provider, if he were subject to the national jurisdiction. In Germany, a law to hinder access was initially approved, but the protests of the cyber community ensured its ultimate failure. Since both access and host provider are under the protection of the freedom of the Internet, it is this fundamental right that sets the standard of scrutiny. When questioning if the measure can be sustained, it must first be determined what protected value is here being discussed. We are not just dealing with the censorship of Internet content; rather we are striving to destroy the market for child pornography and also to protect children from sexual abuse. When we consider how vitally important this protected value is, an access block must be available only as a last resort (Holznagel and Schumacher 2011; Schumacher 2004). Also with regard to other protected values—such as the protection of minors, protection of copyright and prevention of illegal gambling—then, when we consider the international nature of the provider and the market, and how the host of laws and regulations clash and contradict, there are no other measures equally effective and with fewer "by-effects." There is little hope of effective supranational agreements or of self-regulation in the foreseeable future (cf. Sieber and Nolde 2008). If we consider whether these measures are commensurable, it must be taken into account that first, providers in their function as carriers are under the strict obligation to provide the necessary services, even, potentially, over and above the range of products they offer. Second, this measure would tend to intimidate providers, and thus obstruct and hinder them in their democratic function as distributor of opinions. In addition, these measures cannot be targeted precisely enough, and it is relatively easy to circumvent them if one has a reasonable knowledge of the appropriate technologies. The sustainability of access blockades must be regarded with some skepticism, and should always be accompanied by a thorough weighing up of the conflicting interests and by a strict adherence to the individual points of law (Süme 2009; Marbberth-Kubicki 2009).

*Liability of the provider*

In Europe, host providers are not exempt from every liability for illegal contents (Marly 2010). The European guidelines decided early on a policy of "notice and take down" (Articles 14 and 15 of the E-Commerce Directive). Once a host provider has noticed illegal content, they must remove it; otherwise they are liable. This policy has, on the whole, been successful. It is an appropriate compromise between the interests of Internet freedom and the interests of other third parties (Holznagel 2007).

Further measures, such as requiring that the providers are licensed, something that we are familiar with from broadcast law, is not necessary. There are so many providers that opinion pluralism is automatically protected: a permit is completely unnecessary. It is no problem to identify a specific provider: all that is necessary are the obligatory information and notification formalities. In addition, as experience in countries such as China shows, a licensing requirement can very quickly become an instrument to control and suppress unwelcome opinions.

*Deleting specific content*

When illegal content on the Internet is directly deleted, the verdict in constitutional law is relatively straightforward. The accuracy is much greater here and only the service and host providers (who are responsible for the content) are affected. The measure is more effective, because the possibilities of evasion are smaller. Of course, the international character of this misdemeanor also limits the scope of the countermeasures. However, this cannot justify rejecting a measure that has turned out to be the best possible way of fighting illegal contents (Schumacher 2004). In addition, the deletion measures used at the national level (the German Federal Bureau of Criminal Investigation, industrial federations, etc) and at the international level (Inhope) have shown a high success rate (Greif 2011). Compared to blocking, deletion is a much milder countermeasure, and is, with regard to its commensurability, much less of a problem.

*The state deployment of filter programs and deep packet inspection*

There is a very wide range of filter, blocking and evaluation systems. For the most part, however, these systems are employed by users and operate mostly with "black lists" containing forbidden addresses, as well as also partially with "white lists" containing permissible content. In some countries, a state-certified evaluation program has been considered. Turkey has gone a step further: since August 2011, each user has to choose from a range of Internet access packages with different degrees of filter intensity (Küper-Busch 2011). There is a package for children, one for the family, one for standard access and one for the international Internet. In all packages, sites glamorizing violence and those with pornographic content are filtered out.

The problem with this filtering system from a legal perspective is that certain filters are mandatory—for example in schools and libraries. This can quickly develop into something reminiscent of "thought control" and of "overblocking." The Turkish government agencies have even compiled a list of forbidden words for web addresses and Internet portals (Küper-Busch 2011). It is not clear what criteria was used to choose these words. This measure is undeniably an excessive interference in the freedom of the Internet. Not only does it negatively affect the culture of constructive debate and have a chilling, intimidating effect on a public discussion forum, but it also suffers from a lack of transparency. Government sanctions in this field should be documented, made public and explained (OSCE 2011). This is the case for all government measures that affect the communication infrastructure.

Using new network management techniques, it is possible, depending on motivation and accessibility, to monitor, filter and coordinate the data transport much more closely than has been the case up to now (KOM 2010; Sietmann 2011). These techniques make it possible to affect and influence the transported data in many ways (Chirico *et al.* 2007). Thus it is now possible, by means of deep packet inspection (DPI), to get into the data packages of an email, to read the content and even to change it (Kettering and Köhler 2011). As a result, videos can be examined to ascertain whether or not they contain specific words. It is also increasingly easy either not to transmit specific services or to transfer them at specific times. With reference to the freedom of the Internet, it must be ensured that the state does not take over these new techniques to prevent the dissemination of opinions that it does not like, or to preferentially distribute information of which it approves.

## Objective judicial dimensions of the freedom of the Internet

### *The state's duty of protection*

As mentioned above, the state is not just concerned with any intervention in Internet freedom; the legislator and the authorities are also under a positive obligation to protect the contents of the fundamental rights from injury and endangerment. This duty plays a special role in the following situations.

### The derivation and scope of government structuring powers

The state is authorized and, in part, obliged to take steps to guarantee and protect the process of democratic publicity (BVerfGE 83: 238, 296; 90: 60, 87; Schüller 2011; Hermann and Lausen 2004). In this regard, its activities are aimed at securing pluralism and opinion diversity.

The legislator is allowed significant latitude in how he fulfills these obligations. Because of the conditions for communication on the Internet and the absence of the gatekeepers of the old media, there would be no justification for him to establish a dual system of communication—private and public providers side-by-side—a system that has a long tradition in the broadcasting sector of nearly all European countries (Holznagel 1996). It is, however, his task to protect the process of free and open communication on the Internet. State measures here enhance, where appropriate, the communication chances of those entitled to it. This function is particularly important in mass communication, because it is comparatively difficult to attract attention for the issues to be discussed. For this reason, the legislator has limited the Internet activities of the public broadcasting stations, for example, by banning advertising and comprehensive, area-wide local news coverage. Thus the electronic press is allowed certain advantages to even out the competition.

## *Responsibility of Internet services during election campaigns*

In a representative democracy, parliamentary elections are the most important instrument of legitimation. For the voter to vote for the party that best represents his views and his interests, he must be adequately informed about the political objectives that the party has and its performance record in the past elections. It is also important to motivate him—to persuade him to vote at all. At present, a trend towards reduced voter turnout is observed in the Western democracies; indifference towards political parties and political topics is something that is difficult to reconcile with the ideal of a "rule of the people."

During election campaigns, it is the mass media that decide which topics are discussed and when. If a topic is particularly relevant for the supporters of one party, widespread discussion about this will result in increased mobilization and participation of their own voting public. The top candidates go to great lengths to stay in the media spotlight and to be portrayed in the best light. During election campaigns, it is very important that the media coverage of the different candidates and parties is fair and unbiased. The legal system therefore incorporates a series of precautionary measures, so that mass media acts responsibly and appropriately during an election campaign. This is especially valid for the broadcast media, where we see, for example, how minutely the transmission times for the electoral advertising of each party are regulated. The press, which in general is assumed to be self-regulated, is subject to the regulations of fairness, such as the separation of advertising and editorial opinion, or the imperative to correction or rectification.

In complete contrast to broadcasting and press, the Internet is not regulated during election campaigns. In Europe, the problem has been perceived as serious enough to demand a solution. At the moment, political watchdogs regularly monitor the websites of broadcasters during election campaigns. Most of the journalists working here share the journalistic ethos and are bound by an obligation to exercise due care. The media observe each other very closely, so that any offense against this ethos is quickly discovered and becomes a source of lively discussion. The regulatory model now in existence, however, is beginning to fray at the edges. In practice, there is considerable uncertainty in the case of blogs and wikis as to whether the present regulations can work for the electronic press.

A legislative clarification would provide an increased certainty of law. Completely new challenges are encountered when we consider the Web 2.0 services, which are in extensive use, especially by the younger generation. These types of communication are to be perceived partly as individual communication; in many cases, however, especially when we consider Twitter and Google+, they must be defined as mass communication. In some cases, such as Facebook, the question as to individual or mass communication is answered entirely by the privacy settings chosen by the user. Journalistic standards, however, are neither required nor expected here. Another problem is that, on Facebook and Twitter, data can be sent anonymously or under pseudonym. At the same time, these services can be used by political movements and parties, as shown in the case of the American presidential campaign or the protests in the Middle East and North Africa, to mobilize and to inform supporters. Especially during election campaigns, these services have strong potential for manipulation. Politicians are seldom the ones issuing their own newscasts and bulletins; it is done for them by a task force thickly sown with public relations advisers.

With such staged "grassroots movements," the controlling function of publicity can be manipulated. The idea that elections are decided by rational debates over the candidates and party programs that are on offer is steadily being eroded. At the moment, we cannot foresee a viable solution, any way in which to resist these developments, especially during electoral campaigns. On the other hand, the cyber community has proven itself to be extremely vigilant and critical, especially in the political field. The activities of the McCain task force did not remain a secret very long in the strongly interlinked online community. Within a very short time, McCain's astroturfing had come to light; not only did the campaign fail to achieve its goals, but McCain lost credibility, even among his own supporters.

Together with the traditional mass media, cyber publicity can make an important contribution to exposing political misinformation. Exactly because the social media system is so transparent, it is particularly difficult to initiate and to sustain a faked grassroots movement. Admittedly though, until now, the net citizens had a head start when it came to information and technology; the politicians had less experience with social media and were often very clumsy in handling issues such as Facebook. Political public relations work, however, is catching up fast. In the future, Internet campaigns will be much more professionally managed and it will be more and more difficult to expose disinformation.

If Twitter and Facebook are to be used by government ministries or heads of state, the limits and boundaries in force for government public relations must also be observed. The limits are there with election advertising. It would also be helpful if the vigilance with which the cyber community checks up on anything suspicious in the net were encouraged, so that transparency is ensured. One possibility could be the setting up of a Watch Blog during election campaigns. This could, for example, be run by the same bodies that organize the self-regulation of the media, or it could be a platform accessible to all and any users. This sort of platform has already been initiated with great success by the German Ministry for Consumer Protection. At www.lebensmittelklarheit.de, clients can name products whose packaging and presentation they feel is deceptive. Ministry officials check the information. The manufacturer is given seven days to formulate a response, which is put online together with the complaint, the comment of the ministry official and a photo of the product.

### *Orientation and navigation on the Internet*

In the flood of information on the Internet, search engines control which information the user notices. This gives rise to the possibility for manipulation and the danger posed to diverse opinion is great.

There is no sector-specific regulation for navigation and search engines on the Internet. This is also true for the provider that dominates the market (Dankert and Meyer 2011). Recently, the European Commission has been examining whether Google is abusing its almost absolute control of the market. In most European countries, Google has more than 90 percent of the market. The company stands accused of manipulating search results, giving a number of businesses an unjustified competitive advantage. We will have to wait and see how this turns out.

Financial incentives to establish a European search engine have had no success. European member states have initiated some level of guidance in a regularly issued code of conduct, which has been adopted by the providers of search engines. Where necessary, it is the duty of public institutions (centers for consumer protection, public broadcasting stations) to assist the user in choosing from a dizzying range of offers. In the future, a seal of approval could be introduced that would evaluate the reliability of the information search. The search engine providers could be kept under observation; if manipulation were discovered, the state would have a duty to inform the Internet community and, if need be, to take the necessary measures to put a stop to it.

### *Internet offers of the public broadcasting station*

Public broadcasting has a long tradition in Europe, the British Broadcasting Corporation (BBC) being a shining example. Public broadcasting is not to be mistaken for government-run broadcasting. Its independence is usually guaranteed by a committee, composed of members of different political persuasions, who operate independently of the orders or the authority of the government. Public broadcasting in Europe became actively involved in the Internet at an early stage. The broadcasters did not want to lose contact with youth and wanted to keep the acceptance of their viewers. Politicians shared these concerns and were ready to support the broadcasters financially, using the broadcasting licensing fees.

Under constitutional law, public broadcasting enjoys special protection in Europe. The state has the duty to provide for and to ensure pluralism and diversity of opinion, and public broadcasters are given the task of providing basic services in the fields of news and communication. Private broadcasting companies are regarded as less willing and able to do this, because the source of their revenue means that their orientation must follow the lowest common denominator, the taste of the majority. In order to allow for the interests of the electronic press and competitors in the private broadcasting sector, the activities of public broadcasting are tightly confined. Thus public broadcasting companies exercise their basic supply task, for which they receive licensing revenues, and are only allowed to offer online services that are initiated and formulated by a journalistic-editorial team. Advertising and sponsoring are not permitted. They are also not permitted to buy up films and episodes of television series (unless they are specially ordered productions) and then offer them on demand.

On the whole, it remains to be seen whether public broadcasting has any kind of future on the Internet, especially when we consider the number of services already offered there. Publishers especially are against the "public Internet," since they fear the loss of further revenue. On the other hand, public broadcasting stations should not be too narrowly restricted. It will only be possible for them to acquire and keep younger viewers if they offer new and exciting products. Media law has the task of bringing the publishers' freedom of the Internet and the public stations' freedom of broadcasting into an appropriate balance.

## *Protecting net neutrality*

Private entities ensure that they have an advantage in the competition of conflicting opinions when they use techniques such as deep packet inspection. In so far as the basic supply mandate and the equality of each competitor's chances are at risk, it is the legislator's duty, as guarantor of the freedom of Internet services, to take action and ensure a free and unimpeded Internet connection. The focal point of this freedom is the protection of intellectual debate, of the free exchange of opinions. The state cannot allow this free competition to be influenced by economic or any other kind of pressure or compulsion (BVerfGE 25: 156).

On the whole, the freedom of Internet services makes it now easier to define those specific phenomena that ensure the neutrality of data transport. For example, in the context of the present freedom of broadcasting, the principle of freedom of transport has a very minor significance (Eifert and Hoffmann-Riem 2011). However, it plays a major role in the context of the freedom of Internet services, not only with regard to the blockade of data, but also with regard to the deliberate delay of a data package, as well as the manipulation of its contents.

The European states are all approaching this problem differently. In the Netherlands and in Belgium, the government has decided on a categorical ban on any kind of inequality in the treatment of data, so as to secure the strictest judicial protection of net neutrality (Dürr 2011). In Germany, the legislator has recently passed amendments to the telecommunications act, which also affect net neutrality. The new provisions primarily aim at establishing transparency: the consumer must be informed as to whether or not the net provider adheres to the principle of net neutrality (Sec (2) no. 1, 43a, 45n, 45o TKG). The consumer can then pick out the provider he prefers. This assumption is often criticized, largely owing to the high cost involved in a change of provider. It would be helpful if the legislator were to build in a special right for the consumer to terminate the contract if the provider were found to violate the principles of net neutrality. In addition, Sec 41a of the new telecommunications act now authorizes the government to determine in a statutory order fundamental requirements to assure indiscriminatory data transfer and access to contents and applications. According to the stated grounds, this provision aims at "preventing an arbitrary deterioration of services as well as unjustified retardations of data traffic in the networks." This framework provision is a good starting point for preventing infringements to net neutrality. A prohibition of discrimination in data traffic is the only way to deal with such threats. However, Sec 41a only "allows" the government to provide a statutory order—there is no obligation to do so. Nor is the provision concrete enough as far as possible justifications for net neutrality infringements. It is therefore important that the government makes use of the provision in a timely manner and orders specific and concrete provisions that assure equal chances and the protection of a basic supply in communication. In setting the minimum standards, therefore, care must be taken that at least one "best-effort basis" service is kept. Fixing the standards of quality should ensure that, in the service classes, communication takes place under equal conditions. If necessary, it must be stipulated that communication within these classes is to be transported service- and provider-neutral.

### Ensuring the communicative basic supply: Broadband for everyone

In the end, efforts will be needed to ensure that as much of the public as possible has access to the Internet. One of the conditions of a functioning democracy is that the procurement of the media can be easily accessed anywhere and everywhere (Ricke 2009). This is reflected in the concept of an EU-wide basic supply of communication under the Universal Services Directive (Directive 2002/22/EC Article 87f para. 1 GG). The member states have set ambitious goals (BMWi 2009) and have, using many new instruments, pressed ahead with the improvement and the extension of the net. Just how far the concept of the universal applicability of the TKG can be stretched to include the goal of access to broadband Internet is something that is being widely discussed at the moment (Krempl 2011). Finland has actually guaranteed the right to broadband Internet access as a new fundamental right. Since the middle of 2010, every household there has the right to a minimum connection speed of 1 Mbps (Mossdorf 2010). Many regions and communities in Germany and France (see European Commission 2004a; European Commission 2004b) have gone to considerable lengths to improve the Internet supply of their citizens.

## *Applying private law*

Both the German Federal Constitutional Court and the European Court for Human Rights emphasize that, although fundamental rights do not apply in the relationship between two private persons, they do have what is known as an "indirect third-party effect." This means that private law can also be construed and interpreted in the light of the fundamental right which is relevant in that particular case. Since agglomeration of power in the field of media often arises without any intervention from the state, this "objective-legal" function of the fundamental rights has an important significance. However, this must be analyzed and evaluated separately for each of the problem areas that have already been mentioned.

Private schools and libraries, for example, are only allowed to apply filter systems as long as they are not used to influence or control the opinions of the end-user. With regard to data transport, there must be limits set for the provider of a telecommunications network. There can be no question that the blockade of specific opinions or the deliberate delaying of specific content is inexcusable. If net neutrality is interfered with, the authorities must be very careful to distinguish between unjustifiable aims and innocuous, pragmatic goals, such as the avoidance of overload situations, and then to harmonize such goals with the demands of Internet freedom.

## Conclusion

European constitutional debate needs to recognize the freedom of Internet services as a self-reliant fundamental right. Recognizing a third category of media freedoms outside the freedom of the press and broadcasting allows those network phenomena (for example, neutral data transport) that have up to now been ignored in the context of the freedom of broadcasting or of the press to be dealt with and defined in a custom-made way. On this basis, juridical-political solutions can be worked out and can be better brought into line with the distinctive features of the Internet. Recognizing the freedom of Internet services would also mean that the Internet activities of public broadcasters could be put on a new legitimate footing. The usual dogmatic ramifications of freedom of broadcasting in some European states are now meeting with little sympathy or acceptance, especially from the younger generation. Here, in constitutional law, modernizing processes are essential if we are to further guarantee democratic publicity under the changing conditions sparked by the arrival of Internet communication.

## References

Anderson, C. (2007) *The Long Tail* [Der lange Schwanz, Nischenprodukte statt Massenmarkt. Das Geschäft der Zukunft], Munich: Hanser.

Anderson, N. (2008) 'IFPI: "Three strikes" efforts hit worldwide home run,' *Ars Technica*, 20 August. Online. Available HTTP: http://arstechnica.com/tech-policy/2008/08/ifpi-three-strikes-efforts-hit-worldwide-home-run/ (accessed 21 August 2012).

Baer, S. (2011) 'Braucht das Grundgesetz ein Update? Demokratie im Internetzeitalter,' *Blätter für deutsche und internationale Politik*, 90–100.

*Bergens Tidende* v *Norway* (2000) Application no. 26132/95, ECtHR.

BMWi (2009) *Breitbandstrategie der Bundesregierung*. Online. Available HTTP: http://www.bmwi.de/Dateien/BBA/PDF/breitbandstrategie-der-bundesregierung,property=pdf,bereich=bmwi,sprache=de,rwb=true.pdf (accessed 21 August 2012).

Chirico, F., van der Haar, I. and Larouche, P. (2007) 'Network neutrality in the EU,' Tilec Discussion Paper No. DP2007-030, Tilburg University.

Disselkamp, M. (2005) *Innovationsmanagement*, Wiesbaden: Gabler.

Dürr, B. (2011) 'Niederländisches Parlament will Netzneutralität per Gesetz festschreiben,' *Spiegel-Online*, June. Online. Available HTTP: http://www.spiegel.de/netzwelt/web/internetpolitik-niederlaendisches-parlament-will-netzneutralitaet-per-gesetz-festschreiben-a-767682.html (accessed 21 August 2012).

Eifert, M. and Hoffmann-Riem, W. (2011) 'Telekommunikations- und Medienrecht als Technikrecht,' in M. Schulte and R. Schröder (eds.) *Handbuch des Technikrechts*, Berlin: Springer.

European Commission (2004a) *Commission Decision N 381/04—France, Projet de réseau de télécommunications haut debit des Pyrénées-Atlantiques*. Online. Available HTTP: http://ec.europa.eu/eu_law/state_aids/comp-2004/n381-04.pdf (accessed 1 June 2012).

—— (2004b) *Commission Decision 382/04—France, Mise en place d'une infrastructure haut débit sur le territoire de la région Limousin (DORSAL)*. Online. Available HTTP: http://ec.europa.eu/eu_law/state_aids/comp-2004/n382-04.pdf (accessed 1 June 2012).

Farhi, P. (2008) 'Win points for McCain!,' *Washington Post*, 7 August. Online. Available HTTP: http://www.washingtonpost.com/wp-dyn/content/article/2008/08/06/AR2008080603589.html (accessed 21 August 2012).

Fink, U. (2009) 'Internet-Zugangssperren: Wäre "Three-Strikes" in Deutschland verfassungsgemäß?,' Online. Available HTTP: http://carta.info/13113/zugangssperren-three-strikes-verfassungsgemaess/ (accessed 21 August 2012).

Fischer-Lescano, A. and Maurer, A. (2006) 'Grundrechtsbindung von privaten Betreibern öffentlicher Räume,' *NJW*, 20: 1393–1396.

Franck, G. (2000) 'Die Ökonomie der Aufmerksamkeit,' in U. Keller (ed.) *Perspektiven metropolitaner Kultur*, Frankfurt/Main: Suhrkamp.

Friedrich, H.-P. (2011) 'Klare Kante ohne viel Radau,' *Der Spiegel*, 32: 24–26.

Grabenwarter, C. (2008) *EMRK*, München: C. H. Beck.

Greif, B. (2011) 'Löschen statt sperren: Bundesregierung kippt Zugangserschwerungsgesetz,' *ZDNet*, 6 April. Online. Available HTTP: http://www.zdnet.de/41551361/loeschen-statt-sperren-bundesregierung-kippt-zugangserschwerungsgesetz/ (accessed 21 August 2012).

Greve, H. and Schärdel, F. (2009) 'Internetsperren wegen Urheberrechtsverstößen: Three strikes and You're out!' *ZRP* 54.

*Handyside* v *UK* (1976) Application no. 5493/72, ECtHR.

Hoffmann-Riem, W. (2002) *Kommunikationsfreiheiten*, Baden-Baden: Nomos.

Hoffmann-Riem, W. and Schulz, W. (1998) 'Politische Kommunikation: Rechtswissenschaftliche Perspektiven,' in O. Jarren, U. Sarcinelli and U. Saxer (eds.), *Politische Kommunikation in der demokratischen Gesellschaft*, Opladen: Verlag für Sozialwissenschaften.

Holznagel, B. (1996) *Rundfunkrecht in Europa*, Tübingen: J. C. F. Mohr.

—— (2001) 'Regulierte Selbstregulierung im Medienrecht,' *Die Verwaltung*, Supplement 4: 81.

—— (2008) 'Erosion demokratischer Öffenltichkeit?,' *VVDStRl*, 67: 382.

—— (2010) 'Netzneutralität als Aufgabe der Vielfaltssicherung,' *K&R*, 5: 95–100.

—— (2011) 'Meinungsbildung im Internet,' *NordÖR*, 205.

Holznagel, B. and Kibele, B. (2011) '§ 20 RStV,' in G. Spindler and F. Schuster (eds.) *Recht der elektronischen Medien*, München: C. H. Beck.

Holznagel, B. and Schumacher, P. (2011a) 'Netzpolitik Reloaded,' *ZRP*, 3: 74.

Holznagel, B. and Schumacher, P. (2011b) 'Die Freiheit der Internetdienste,' MIND—Collaboratory Discussion Paper Series No. 1. Online. Available HTTP: http://www.collaboratory.de/w/Die_Freiheit_der_Internetdienste (accessed 21 August 2012).

Holznagel, B., Dörr, D. and Hildebrand, D. (2008) *Elektronische Medien*, München: Vahlen.

Holznagel, D. (2007) 'Zur Providerhaftung: Notice and Take Down in § 512 US Copyright Act,' *GRUR Int.*, 971ff.

*Informationsverein Lentia* v *Austria* (1993) Application no. 37093/97, ECtHR.

Jarass, H. D. (2011) 'Art. 5,' in H. D. Jarass and B. Pieroth (eds.) *GG*, München: C. H. Beck.

Kettering, E. and Köhler, L. (2011) 'ZDF befürwortet gesetzliche Regelungen zur Sicherung der Netzneutralität.' Online. Available HTTP: http://www.unternehmen.zdf.de/fileadmin/files/Download_Dokumente/DD_Das_ZDF/Publikationen/2011-03-22_ZDF_Netzneutralitaet.pdf (accessed 27 August 2012).

Kloepfer, M. (2010) 'Netzneutralität und Presse-Grosso in der Informationsgesellschaft,' *AfP*, 120–144.

Köhler, G. M. and Dürig-Friedl, C. (2001) *Demonstrations- und Versammlungsrecht*, München: C. H. Beck.

KOM (2010) *Report on the Public Consultation on the Open Internet and Net Neutrality in Europe*, 9 November 2010. Online. Available HTTP: http://ec.europa.eu/information_society/policy/ecomm/doc/library/public_consult/net_neutrality/report.pdf (accessed 21 August 2012).

Koreng, A. (2010) *Zensur im Internet*, Baden-Baden: Nomos.

Krempl, S. (2011) 'Schwarz und Grün streiten über Breitband für alle,' *heise online*, 5 April. Online. Available HTTP: http://www.heise.de/newsticker/meldung/Schwarz-und-Gruen-streiten-ueber-Breitband-fuer-alle-1222457.html (accessed 27 August 2012).

Lischka, K. (2011) 'Googles private Meldestelle.' Online. Available HTTP: http://www.speiegel.de/netzwelt/netzpolitik/eric-schmidt-ueber-soziale-netzwerke-googles-private-meldestelle-a-783042.html (accessed 29 August 2011).

Marberth-Kubicki, A. (2009) 'Der Beginn der Internet-Zensur: Zugangssperren durch Access-Provider,' *NJW*, 25: 1792–1796.

Marly, J. (2010) 'Art. 14,' in E. Grabitz and M. Hilf (eds.) *Das Recht der Europäischen Union*, 41st edn., München: C. H. Beck.

Mecklenburg, W. (1997) 'Internetfreiheit,' *ZUM*, 7: 525.
Meyer, J. (2010) *Charta der Grundrechte der Europäischen Union*, Baden-Baden: Nomos.
Meyer-Ladewig, J. (2011) *Europäische Menschenrechtskonvention*, Baden-Baden: Nomos.
Michel, E.-M. (2009) 'Senden als konstitutiver Bestandteil des Rundfunkbegriffs,' *ZUM*, 6: 453.
Mossdorf, K.-J. (2010) 'Finnland erstes Land der Welt mit Recht auf schnelles Internet,' *Teltarif*, 1 July. Online. Available HTTP: http://www.teltarif.de/finnland-breitband-internet-dsl-grundsicherung/news/39284.html (accessed 27 August 2012).
Münker, S. (2009) *Emergenz digitaler Öffentlichkeiten: Die sozialen Medien im Web 2.0*, Frankfurt/Main: Suhrkamp.
Neuberger, C. (2009) 'Versuch über das Internet,' in V. Diemand, U. Hochmuth, C. Lindner and P. Weibel (eds.) *Ich, Wir und Die Anderen: Neue Medien zwischen demokratischen und ökonomischen Potenzialen II*, Hannover: Heise.
—— and Lobigs, F. (2010) *Die Bedeutung des Internet im Rahmen der Vielfaltssicherung (Schriftenreihe der Landesmedienanstalten Band 43)*, Berlin: Vistas.
——, Nuernbergk, C. and Rischke, M. (2007) 'Weblogs und Journalismus: Konkurrenz, Ergänzung oder Integration?' *Media Perspektiven*, 2: 96–112.
*The Observer and Guardian* v *UK* (1991) Application no. 13585/88, ECtHR.
Ory, S. (2011) 'Herausforderungen der Medienfreiheit—oder: Der Rundfunk als Endpunkt der Konvergenz?,' *AfP*, 1: 19.
OSCE (2011) *Report: Freedom of Expression on the Internet—Study of Legal Provisions and Practices Related to Freedom of Expression, the Free Flow of Information and Media Pluralism on the Internet in OSCE Participating States*. Online. Available HTTP: http://www.osce.org/fom/80723 (accessed 27 August 2012).
Papier, H.-J. and Schröder, M. (2010) 'Gebiet des Rundfunks,' *epd* medien, *60*, 4 August: 17–33.
Ricke, T. (2009) 'Der Digital Divide aus medienrechtlicher Sicht: Informationelle Grundversorgung durch Medienkompetenzförderung,' in D. Aufderheide and M. Dabrowski (eds.) *Internetökonomie und Ethik*, Berlin: Duncker & Humblot.
—— (2011) *IPTV und Mobile TV*, Baden-Baden: Nomos.
Rücker, D. (2005) 'Notice and take-down Verfahren für die deutsche Providerhaftung,' *C&R*, 5: 347–354.
Schmidt, J. (2008) 'Was ist neu am Social Web? Soziologische und kommunikationswissenschaftliche Grundlagen,' in A. Zerfaß, M. Welker and J. Schmidt (eds.) *Kommunikation, Partizipation und Wirkungen im Social Web, Bd. 1*, Köln: Herber von Harlem.
Schmitt-Glaeser, W. (2005) *HStR, Bd. III*, Heidelberg: C. F. Müller.
Schüller, V. (2011) 'Die Kommunikationsfreiheiten in der Verfassung,' in D. Dörr, J. Kreileand and M. Cole (eds.) *Handbuch Medienrecht,* 2nd edn., Frankfurt/Main: Verlag Recht und Wissenschaft.
Schulz, W. (1998) *Gewährleistung kommunikativer Chancengleichheit als Freiheitsverwirklichung*, Baden-Baden: Nomos.
Schulze-Fielitz, H. (2000) in G. F. Schuppert and Ch. Bumke (eds.) *Bundesverfassungsgericht und gesellschaftlicher Konsens*, Baden-Baden: Nomos.
—— (2010) 'Art. 5,' in H. Dreier (ed.) *Kommentar zum Grundgesetz*, 2nd edn., Tübingen: Mohr Siebeck.
Schumacher, P. (2004) 'Fighting illegal Internet content: May access providers be required to ban foreign websites? A recent German approach,' *IJCLP*, 8.
—— (2009) *Innovationsregulierung im Recht der netzgebundenen Elektrizitätswirtschaft,* Baden-Baden: Nomos.
—— (2011) 'BGH stärkt der Europäischen Pressefreiheit den Rücken.' Online. Available HTTP: http://www.jurablogs.com/de/bgh-staerkt-europaeischen-pressefreiheit-ruecken (accessed 27 August 2012).
Sieber, U. and Nolde, M. (2008) *Sperrverfügungen im Internet*, Berlin: Duncker and Humblot.
Sietmann, R. (2011) 'Schmalspur: Der Kampf gegen die Netzneutralität zielt auf die Vereinnahmung des Internet,' *c't*, 8: 158.
Sokolov, D. (2011) 'Österreich bereitet "Kill Switch" für das Internet vor.' Online. Available HTTP: http://www.heise.de/newsticker/meldung/Oesterreich-bereitet-Kill-Switch-fuer-das-Internet-vor-2-Update-1181448.html (accessed 27 August 2012).
Stammler, J. (1995) 'Paradigmenwechsel im Medienrecht,' *ZUM*, 2: 104.
Süme, O. J. (2009) 'Kinderpornographie: Accesssperren als Ausweg,' *MMR*, 1: 1.
Uecker, P. (2009) 'Host-Provider, Content-Provider, Access-Provider oder was? Zur rechtlichen Abgrenzung dieser Provider-Typen,' *DFN-Infobrief Recht*, 6: 5–6.

# 9

# Freedom of expression and the right of access to the Internet

## A new fundamental right?

*Nicola Lucchi*

## Introduction

Technological developments in communication have brought revolutionary opportunities and changes in the landscape regarding how people obtain, process and exchange information. One of the emerging challenges for the legal and regulatory regime is in shaping a modern interpretation of the right to freedom of thought and expression (Dutton *et al.* 2011). The rapidly evolving media revolution has generated a number of new regulatory initiatives designed to reduce systemic risks associated with this means of communication, "ranging from risks to children, to privacy, to intellectual property rights, to national security, which might more indirectly, and often unintentionally, enhance or curtail freedom of expression" (Dutton *et al.* 2011: 8).

The "game" of Internet regulation has found itself at the center of a geopolitical clash being played at international level and involving multiple actors and interests. All of the world's superpowers (the US, Russia, Continental Europe, China and Japan), as well as countries with low levels of democracy or authoritarian regimes, seem to intend to retain control of this new communication dimension (Nye 2011). In this context, the World Conference on International Telecommunications—held in Dubai in December 2012—has offered very different views on the future model of governance of new media. This conference's plans were to renegotiate the treaty of 1998 that gave birth to the International Telecommunications Regulations.[1] Currently, these regulations do not specifically concern technical standards, infrastructure or content, but some states are supporting an expansion of the criteria to include some form of legislative provisions on Internet regulation with the potential to have direct adverse effects on fundamental rights and freedoms (Gross and Lucarelli 2011; Mainoldi 2012).[2]

This chapter explores the relationship between modern communication technologies and constitutional freedoms. In particular, it takes a closer look at a range of Internet and freedom-of-expression-related issues. Attention is given to the need to rebalance the current culture of

1 See Final Acts of the International Telecommunication Union 1989.
2 See also Center for Democracy & Technology 2012.

"rights" characterized by exclusionary and divisive attitudes, mainly oriented towards control (Elkin-Koren and Netanel 2002: viii). Networked digital communications are now considered crucial components of a democratic system because they are a vehicle for moving "information, knowledge, and culture," which are key elements to develop "human freedom and human development" (Benkler 2006: 1).

As so eloquently expressed by Yochai Benkler in *The Wealth of Networks*:

> A series of changes in the technologies, economic organization, and social practices of production in this environment has created new opportunities for how we make and exchange information, knowledge, and culture. These changes have increased the role of nonmarket and nonproprietary production, both by individuals alone and by cooperative efforts in a wide range of loosely or tightly woven collaborations. Together, they hint at the emergence of a new information environment, one in which individuals are free to take a more active role than was possible in the industrial information economy of the twentieth century. This new freedom holds great practical promise: as a dimension of individual freedom; as a platform for better democratic participation; as a medium to foster a more critical and self-reflective culture; and, in an increasingly information-dependent global economy, as a mechanism to achieve improvements in human development everywhere.
>
> (*Benkler 2006: 2*)

In this context, the relevance of networked communication as a tool of mass democracy is increasingly evident. In some countries, the Internet is the one of very few sources of pluralistic and independent information (Mendel and Salomon 2011; Deibert *et al.* 2010). The events of the Arab Spring have served to highlight how important new communication and information technologies have become (Moglen 2011). Using a mix of blogs and social networking sites, the new medium has demonstrated its power to support spontaneous democratic mobilization from below: a concrete and participatory form of democracy (Balkin 2009). The result of these online movements was surprising, with hundreds of thousands of people being summoned to action. Up to now this kind of influence was a prerogative that belonged only to political and union organizations. The impact that digital communication tools can have on public opinion and decision-making is therefore enormous. This is true not only in developing countries, but also in Western liberal democracies. Empirical evidence of the mobilizing and political potential of the Internet is also provided by the recent viral movements such as "Occupy Wall Street" in the United States or the trans-European "Indignados" protesters, both tangible examples of the features and potentialities provided by new horizontal communication channels. The Internet has revivified "the notion of freedom of expression as an individual liberty" (Zencovich 2008: 100) so that it is no longer constrained by institutional or organizational elements. According to a recent document published by the UN Human Rights Council, this latest wave of demonstrations:

> . . . has shown the key role that the Internet can play in mobilizing the population to call for justice, equality, accountability and better respect for human rights. As such, facilitating access to the Internet for all individuals, with as little restriction to online content as possible, should be a priority for all States.
>
> (*United Nations General Assembly et al. 2011: 4*)

Despite the new opportunities provided by the Internet (or perhaps because of them), Internet filtering, content regulation and online surveillance are increasing in scale, scope and sophistication around the world, in both democratic countries as well as in authoritarian states (Deibert *et al.* 2010: xv). The most troublesome aspect of this new trend is that "the new tools for Internet controls that are emerging go beyond mere denial of information" (Deibert *et al.* 2010: 6). We are facing a strategic shift away from direct interdictions of digital content and toward control of Internet speech indirectly through the establishment of a form of cooperation with Internet service providers (Szuskin *et al.* 2009). Law enforcement policies such as the so-called "graduated response" (also known as "three strikes") proposed in different countries put in place a system for terminating Internet connections for repeat online infringements (Strowel 2010).

The practical effect of this method of control is that the freedom of the networked environment is increasingly squeezed between security needs, market-based logic and government interventions (Rodotà 2006). As in the past, innovations in communications technology have upset the previously established balance of power. But now the situation has gone beyond the normal interaction between opposing players. With respect to security needs, it should be necessary to pass through an effective democratic control to ensure that restrictions of fundamental rights are kept to a minimum and freedoms of individuals are respected. It is thus necessary that each country identifies proper avenues of control in conformity with their democratic principles. On the contrary, the logic of the market is inclined to shape the network as an increasingly close-meshed tool within which democratic citizenship is gradually reduced. Furthermore, within this setting, there are significant threats to rights and freedoms posed by increasing government intervention, as well as by private regulation as a complementary mechanism to public regulation. This new environment has opened a new animated discussion about a possible "institutional translation" of the meanings, values and scope attached to communication sent over the network (Jørgensen 2006; United Nations General Assembly *et al.* 2011; Dutton *et al.* 2011; Horner *et al.* 2010; Akdeniz 2010). In particular, there is a wide-ranging debate on the question of equal, public and fair access to network services.

In light of these factors, we want to focus on the vexing and controversial question of "Internet access" as a basic human right (Best 2004: 24). In this sense, it is first important to explain that the right of access to the Internet may be understood in terms of: (i) access to network infrastructure; (ii) access at the layer of transport and services; and (iii) access to digital content and applications. While the right to Internet access can be analyzed on various levels, this chapter will focus on the right to access digital content and applications. At the same time, it is important to remember that access to network infrastructure is essential; without this it is not possible to gain access to the transport and content layers.

The purpose of this contribution is to discuss in which way constitutional rules concerning freedom of expression and information can play a role in the adoption of particular regulatory limitations pertaining to the media sector. The following chapter will examine some recent cases that deal with the dilemma of online content regulation. In particular, consideration will be given to two main aspects: first, the relevance and role of computer-mediated communication and its potential impact on the democratization of freedom of expression and the problem of conflicting rights; and second, the debated question of the regulation of digital content and Internet-based applications in general. In this regard, the investigation considers the US Supreme Court's First Amendment approach toward computer-mediated communication through a brief review of two leading cases: *Reno* v *ACLU* (1997) and *Denver Area Educational Telecommunications Consortium, Inc.* v *FCC* (1996). The analysis then reveals the ramifications of the French Constitutional Council's Decision no. 2009-580DC (Conseil Constitutionnel 2009), highlighting the Court's reasoning about the fundamental role of access to information.

The aim of this part of the contribution is to discuss how access to network services is increasingly perceived as being worthy of elevation to the rank of a fundamental right.

## Reshaping the boundary of freedom of expression in the digital age

The Internet is undoubtedly the most widely recognized and utilized digital communication technological tool employed to propagate information. Individuals have new opportunities to exchange and share knowledge and ideas, to release their creativity and to participate in social and political life. It represents a new medium of communication that gives people a range of alternative ways of making and using information resources and services, and it is thus perceived and proved to be a fundamental instrument to guarantee effective freedom of expression (Zencovich 2008). In fact, the Internet has commonly been seen as providing a technological enrichment of individual freedom of expression (Deibert and Rohozinski 2008). For this reason, digital rights defenders and digital libertarians "have raised growing concerns over how legal and regulatory trends might be constraining freedom of expression" over the new medium (Dutton 2011: 8).

The Internet has the potential to strengthen freedom of expression by providing, developing and facilitating new mechanisms for exchanging data and, as a consequence, ensuring a more intense flow of information (Zencovich 2008). At the same time, however, such conditions are used as a justification for content regulation targeted in part at trying to counteract the pervasiveness and anarchic nature of the medium (Holoubek *et al.* 2007; Zencovich 2008). The potential impact of the Internet and new media on democratization is stronger than that of the traditional media. Digital networked communication has completely changed the way in which people access, interact and contribute to the flow of information and knowledge.

The Internet has also entered and transformed democratic institutions at large. It has opened new means of communication and expanded access to different sources of information. It has disrupted traditional modes of social and political communication, of scholarly publishing and knowledge dissemination, as well as long-standing business models. It is also changing interactions and organizational dynamics between both states and citizens. A full range of human activity is now intimately and inevitably connected to online services: finding and applying for a job; doing research; completing education; taking part in social communication; participating in politics; finding legal information; enjoying entertainment; or just buying and selling. It is therefore clear that access to the Internet is becoming a fundamental instrument for a full participation in public life. For these reasons, there is a growing trend among civil liberties groups, human rights activists and legal scholars to argue that "Internet access has become so essential to participation in society—to finding jobs and housing, to civic engagement, even to health—that it should be seen as a right, a basic prerogative of all citizens" (Tuhus-Dubrow 2010). At the same time, another issue that we are facing is the conflict between the democratic function performed by the digital communication and the commercial enclosures driven by its services. Up to now, the Internet has grown into a mature medium with little government regulation (Robinson and Nachbar 2008). But an increasing change of perspective is evident in the policy debate where the question of Internet regulation is currently an emerging and controversial argument. This change, of course, is based on the understanding that all of the traditional media are converging around the Internet and it is now becoming both a telecommunications medium and a mass medium (Robinson and Nachbar 2008). For this reason, there are growing political and economic pressures to extend some forms of regulation to it. But the problem is that regulating the

Internet would mean regulating all media, restricting the flow of information, as well as its exchange.

In almost all democratic systems, the use of both new and old forms of information media has not only posed problems of boundary definition, but have often also resulted in attempts to contain and control information flow (Castells 2010; Couch 1990). The key point is that computer-mediated communication is beyond the control of the nation-state (Castells 2010). The problem of information control has thus become amplified by the phenomenon of new media (Foray 2004). It is recognized that the economic problem of information is essentially its protection and disclosure—that is, a problem of public goods (Foray 2004).

In order to contain information and maintain control over access, a number of countries, including the United States, the United Kingdom, Canada and Australia, have made legislative attempts to regulate and monitor digital content. Virtually every industrialized country and many developing countries have passed laws that expand "the capacities of state intelligence and law enforcement agencies to monitor internet communications" (Deibert and Rohozinski 2008: 138). The number of regulations designed to monitor and control the flow of information on the Internet has increased, in particular since 11 September 2001 (Deibert and Rohozinski 2008; Benkler 2006; Goldsmith and Wu 2006). Online media face a massive increase in regulation at transnational and national levels. Legislation that has already been introduced and enacted (e.g. the so-called "Sinde law" in Spain and the HADOPI law in France) directly threatens the Internet as a free, egalitarian and democratic way of communicating. The same sort of issues come up with proposed legislation such as the international Anti-Counterfeiting Trade Agreement (ACTA) 2010 or the Stop Online Piracy Act (SOPA) of 2012 and the Protect Intellectual Property Act (PIPA) of 2012 discussed in the United States. The aim of these new pieces of legislation is often justified to fight online piracy and digital copyright, as well as newer forms of cyber-crime and cyber terrorism. But Internet activists and defenders of freedom of expression fear that similar legal instruments can also be used to establish a surveillance regime that allows restrictions on freedom of movement over different access network technologies. Such ongoing attempts to regulate the Internet "reflect the natural maturation process that previous media, such as print, radio, and television, all experienced as they evolved out of unrestrained and experimental to tightly controlled and regulated environments" (Deibert and Rohozinski 2008: 137).

The experience of democratic countries with provisions designed to monitor and control the flow of information on the Internet reveals that restriction of the freedom of the media may not withstand constitutional scrutiny. The degree to which the different constitutional protections in each nation can interact in this area varies across both the medium and the nature of content. In particular, constitutional scrutiny of media access regulation has traditionally varied significantly by the predefined category of technology (print, radio and television), but constitutional debates surrounding modern digital platforms continue to be perceived in traditional terms (Blevins 2012). Media freedom is usually guaranteed or limited by media laws, but the advent of the Internet has highlighted how the traditional regulation and control policy can go beyond the regulatory mechanisms used in the traditional media. In particular, the global dimension of the Internet requires a shift from conventional media regulation. The promotion of freedom, access to information and pluralism of the media, including unrestricted media regulation, are all key aspects for supporting a concrete implementation of freedom of expression, which represents one of the basic elements of all democratic societies.

Regulations on the global medium of the Internet have often been criticized for their inability to reconcile technological progress with protection of economic interests, as well as other conflicting interests; essentially, these policy measures "alter the environment within which Internet communications take place" (Deibert *et al.* 2008; Sustein 2001). Illustrative examples are given by the controversy over the constitutionality of the US Communications Decency Act of 1996 in *Reno* v *American Civil Liberties Union* (1997), invalidating certain provisions of a proposed law designed to regulate indecent and obscene speech on the Internet; or by the ruling of the Supreme Court of the United States in *Ashcroft* v *American Civil Liberties Union* (2002), holding that the enforcement of the Child Online Protection Act should be enjoined because the law likely violated the First Amendment; or by the French case of the "Loi Fillon," in which the French Constitutional Council censored most of the dispositions of the Fillon amendment concerning regulation of the Internet and the related power given to the Conseil Supérieur de l'Audiovisuel (Conseil Constitutionnel 1996). Another interesting example is provided by the decision regarding the so-called "HADOPI Law,"[3] partially censored by the French Constitutional Council also on the ground of its inconsistency with Article 11 of the 1789 Declaration of the Rights of Man and of the Citizen. The following paragraphs analyze these representative judicial decisions.

Any discussion on this matter inevitably leads to two classic questions: what restrictions and safeguards should be imposed on the fundamental freedom of expression in a democratic society, and under which conditions and guarantees are these restrictions and safeguards feasible?

## Digital networks: Regulation and free speech

Freedom of expression is constitutionally protected in many liberal and democratic countries. It is considered one of the cornerstones of the United Nations Declaration of Human Rights (Article 19) and is recognized as a fundamental right under Article 10 of the European Convention on Human Rights. The justification for the protection of freedom of expression is to enable the self-expression of the speakers (Sadurski 1999). The multimedia revolution has affected not only habits of thought and expression, but also economics, science and law, thereby involving issues concerning fundamental freedoms and access to knowledge in a global debate (Kapzcynski 2008). The rules governing the world of information and communication are now subject to profound change. This has inevitably caused tension in the delicate balance that underpins fundamental rights and basic democratic principles. Regulatory policies should not interfere or restrict freedom of expression. However, freedom of expression is not an absolute right, and consequently some limitations and restrictions may apply under certain legitimate circumstances (Verpeaux 2010; Zencovich 2008; Emerson 1963). In this regard, it is also necessary to distinguish between the right to freedom of expression and right of access to the medium: The nature of the two rights are different and their two profiles do not necessarily match (Emerson 1963; Sustein 2001; Blevins 2012). For example, nobody can prevent a person from creating a newspaper, but that does not mean that I am entitled to write a column in any newspaper: The two limits are differently modulated. Similarly, the grant of a right to use the means of dissemination of thought cannot be justified on the basis

3 Law 2009/669 of 12 June 2009. HADOPI stands for *Haute Autorité pour la Diffusion des Oeuvres et la Protection des Droits sur Internet* [The High Authority for the Dissemination of Works and for the Protection of Rights on the Internet].

of the US doctrine of the "public forum."[4] On this point, the US Supreme Court has tended to interpret this doctrine narrowly, rejecting the application of the forum analysis to any medium (Sunstein 2001; Packard 2010).[5]

In almost all democratic societies, new media, besides incurring definitional problems, have led to attempts to restrict and control online information (Sunstein 2001). The advent of the Internet has had a profound and revolutionary impact on the general framework of media regulation and on the government of the broadcasting sector in general (Price 2002; DeNardis 2009). This has often led to the adoption of legislative measures criticized for their inability to reconcile technological progress with economic and other interests. In particular, no area of law has been more affected by the digital media revolution than intellectual property (Packard 2010). Our society and economies have become increasingly dependent upon the availability, exchange and sharing of digital information. The emergence of digital technology and computer networking has drastically changed commercial and regulatory development in the media sector. While digital media products have experienced incredible market success, they are given inadequate and disproportionate protection under existing and emerging legislation.

In recent years, there have been several attempts by states to regulate content on the Internet. One of the most famous, and certainly one of the most debated, was the United States Communications Decency Act (CDA) of 1996. It was the first important effort by the United States Congress to control pornographic content on the Internet. It also represents one of the first "Internet blocking or filtering" attempts capable of interfering with basic democratic principles. In the landmark 1997 case of *Reno* v *ACLU*, the US Supreme Court held that the Act violated the freedom of speech provisions of the First Amendment (*Reno* v *ACLU* (1997); Godwin 2003). In an effort to protect minors from Indecent" and "patently offensive" materials, the Act had the effect, *inter alia*, of restricting access to material that was not harmful to adults:

> In order to deny minors access to potentially harmful speech, the CDA [Communications Decency Act] effectively suppresses a large amount of speech that adults have a constitutional right to receive and to address to one another. That burden on adult speech is unacceptable if less restrictive alternatives would be at least as effective in achieving the legitimate purpose that statute was enacted to serve.
>
> (Reno v ACLU *(1997), 874*)

The case generated significant international press coverage, as well as heated legal debate over freedom of expression on the Internet and with regards to developing technologies, and many of the findings and conclusions are still relevant today. Among the essential findings,

4 The "public forum" doctrine dictates that restrictions placed upon speech are typically subject to higher scrutiny when the speech occurs in areas historically associated with First Amendment activities such as streets, sidewalks and parks. At the same time, the privilege of a US citizen to use the streets and parks for communication of views on national questions is not absolute: see *Hague* v *C.I.O.* (1939). In fact, the First Amendment does not guarantee the right to communicate one's view at all times and places or in any manner that one desires: see *Heffron* v *International Society for Krishna Consciousness* (1981).

5 See *United States* v *Am. Library Ass'n* (2003) (refusing to apply public forum analysis to Internet terminals in public libraries) and *Denver Area Educ. Telecomm. Consortium* v *FCC* (1996) (refusing to apply public forum analysis to public access cable channels).

the Court had the ability to set out the nature of cyberspace, the techniques of accessing and communicating over digital networks and alternative means of restricting access to the Internet (Jacques 1997). In this ruling, for the first time, the Supreme Court introduced a sort of legal recognition to have unrestricted access to the Internet through a broad interpretation of the First Amendment. In other words, the Court extended free-speech rights to the Internet. The rationale expressed by the Supreme Court confirmed the opinion of the District Court. In particular, the Opinion, as written by Justice Stevens, reported one of the District Court's conclusions: "As 'the most participatory form of mass speech yet developed'. . . [the Internet] is 'entitled to the highest protection from governmental intrusion' " (*Reno* v *ACLU* (1997), 863). The decision concluded by arguing that:

> The record demonstrates that the growth of the Internet has been and continues to be phenomenal. As a matter of constitutional tradition, in the absence of evidence to the contrary, we presume that governmental regulation of the content of speech is more likely to interfere with the free exchange of ideas than to encourage it. The interest in encouraging freedom of expression in a democratic society outweighs any theoretical but unproven benefit of censorship.
>
> (Reno v ACLU (*1997), 885*)

In other words, the constitutional protection of freedom of expression implies a constitutional protection of the access to information through the Internet. The US Congress responded to the Supreme Court's decision by passing new legislation, the Child Online Protection Act (COPA), but this second attempt to regulate Internet content did not fully resolve the constitutional issues presented by the provision of the CDA (Deibert *et al.* 2008). The new regulatory instrument "essentially incorporated the traditional standards of obscenity law (which in theory deny any protection to speech that is found to be 'obscene')" (Robinson and Nachbar 2008: 33). However, after three separate rounds of litigation, the Supreme Court held the statute invalid on the ground that the government had not shown COPA to be the least restrictive means of regulating indecent content on the net.

The CDA case seems to be connected with a red thread to the current debate over Internet access and regulation of illegal material. Today, as in the past, the need to find the most appropriate balance between the protection of individual rights and the general interests of the community is still a very complex issue.

## A right to Internet access?

In recent years, there have been various speculations as to whether access to the Internet can be addressed from a fundamental rights perspective. If this view were accepted, it would have a substantial impact on any possible restriction of an individual's Internet access. Discussing the Internet's communication potential requires an evaluation of the preconditions that facilitate or inhibit the effective use of information resources. One of these preconditions is the right to access the network or, as already defined, a right to freedom of connection (Dutton 2011). In this perspective, the fundamental question concerning access to network services is emerging from the right to freedom of expression. If the value of freedom of expression rests primarily on the ability of every individual to communicate and exchange ideas, the Internet must be considered a key instrument for the implementation of this freedom, and access to this medium represents an essential precondition of the freedom to communicate. By similar reasoning, it should also represent an element of the "freedom of expression" guaranteed by most democracies. For these reasons, the Internet has been described "as the most participatory form of mass speech yet developed," deserving "the highest protection from government intrusion" (*ACLU* v *Reno* (1996), 883).

Across Europe, some countries seem to have taken clear steps towards a recognition of the right to "Internet access." Following these initial actions, there is now a growing debate amongst governments, policymakers and civil society regarding the legal status of the access to network services (United Nations General Assembly *et al.* 2011; Lucchi 2011; Dutton *et al.* 2011; Horner *et al.* 2010; Akdeniz 2010).

Such discussion first emerged after a decision of the French Conseil Constitutionnel, adopted on June 22 2009. For some commentators, this decision supports the pursuit of legal recognition of "access to the Internet" as a fundamental right. In fact, by reviewing the constitutionality of laws under article 61(2) of the French Constitution (Hamon and Troper 2009; Berman and Picard 2008), the Court declared partially unconstitutional a law—referred to as "HADOPI 1"—aimed at preventing the illegal copying and redistribution over the Internet of digital content protected by copyright (Conseil Constitutionnel 2009).[6]

With the HADOPI anti-piracy legislation, France became the first country to experiment with a warning system to protect copyrighted works on the web. Pursuant to this law, Internet usage is monitored to detect illegal content sharing and suspected infringers are tracked back to their Internet service providers (ISPs). The legislation provides for gradual intervention (the so-called "three strikes" procedure); three email warnings are sent before a formal judicial complaint is filed (HADOPI, Article L. 331–25, al. 1). The email warnings are sent directly by the ISPs at the request of the HADOPI Authority. If illegal activity is observed in the six-month period following the first notification, the HADOPI Authority can send a second warning by registered mail (HADOPI, Article L. 331–25, al. 2). Should alleged copyright infringement continue thereafter, the suspected infringer is reported to a judge, who has the power to impose a range of penalties, such as Internet disconnection (HADOPI, Article L. 335–7).

When called to evaluate the constitutionality of the procedural aspects of the law, the Conseil Constitutionnel highlighted a sort of "fundamental right" of access to computer networks (Marino 2009: 245). At the same time, arguments put forth by the conseil referred also to the need for a balancing analysis by a jurisdictional authority before any sanctions are applied. In fact, in countries where the judicial authority is independent from the legislative and executive powers, only a judge has the authority to decide whether a particular content, communication or action is illegal or not. This debate over the control of information and digital communication platforms has not been restricted to France. In fact, similar laws and policies have been adopted, considered, or rejected by Australia, Hong Kong, Germany, the Netherlands, New Zealand, South Korea, Spain, Sweden, Taiwan and the United Kingdom (Yu 2010).

The framework set up by French law anticipates further developments in the relationship between the use of networks and fundamental rights, as well as unavoidable adverse effects within other European countries and European Union legislation. For example, in the United Kingdom, the Digital Economy Act 2010 addresses the problem of online copyright infringement by the introduction of the same graduated response regime, and an analogous system is in use or being considered in New Zealand, Taiwan and South Korea (Santoro 2010). The

6 See the 1958 French Constitution, Art. 61(2). According to this provision: "Acts of Parliament may be referred to the Constitutional Council, before their promulgation, by the President of the Republic, the Prime Minister, the President of the National Assembly, the President of the Senate, sixty Members of the National Assembly or sixty Senators."

same concerns have arisen with regard to the proposed Anti-Counterfeiting Trade Agreement (ACTA) (Kaminsky 2009; Bridy 2010), which is also focused on the implementation of a "graduated response" regime.[7] Many European countries have refused to ratify ACTA, mentioning privacy and human rights issues.[8] The European Commission has also submitted its request for an opinion on ACTA to the European Court of Justice in order to examine its compatibility with the treaties and in particular with the Charter of Fundamental Rights of the European Union.[9] However, after much controversy, the proposed agreement was definitively rejected by the European Parliament on 4 July 2012, and therefore it cannot become law in the EU.[10] Finally, another similar example is offered by the so-called *Ley Sinde* ("Sinde's Law"),[11] which represented the first legal instrument introduced in Spain to address the illegal downloading of copyrighted content on the web (Law 2/2011 on Sustainable Economy). The provisions included in Spain's Sustainable Economy Act of 2011 contain a set of norms to establish a special commission designed to review requests submitted by copyright holders against websites for suspected infringement activity. This special commission—recently appointed—has the authority to shut down the website as the result of any violations and also to take action against content intermediaries (Royal Decree 1889/2011 of 30 December 2011 Regulating the Intellectual Property Commission).[12] Spain's Supreme Court has recently agreed to hear a complaint against the law filed by a web users group.[13] However, at the beginning of May 2012, the Court denied the request of temporary suspension of the challenged rules because of the lack of any clear reasons to be granted.[14]

In this uncertain setting, the decision of the French Conseil Constitutionnel triggered a debate about Internet access as a possible constitutional or fundamental right (Banisar 2006). In fact, one the most troublesome issues that the Conseil Constitutionnel had to address concerned the right of access to online networks. The Conseil Constitutionnel based its discussion of this issue on Article 11 of the 1789 Declaration. According to Article 11:

> The free communication of ideas and opinions is one of the most precious of the rights of man. Every citizen may, accordingly, speak, write, and print with freedom, but shall be responsible for such abuses of this freedom as shall be defined by law.
>
> (*Declaration of the Rights of Man and the Citizen 1789*)

The judges of the Conseil Constitutionnel concluded that this right also includes the freedom to access online networks, given the diffusion of such services and their growing importance to the participation in democratic life and consequently to freedom of expression (Verpeaux 2009). Specifically, the relevant paragraph in the Court's opinion reads as follows:

7 The term "graduated response" refers "to an alternative mechanism to fight Internet piracy (in particular resulting from P2P file sharing) that relies on a form of co-operation with the Internet access providers that goes beyond the classical 'notice and take down' approach, and implies an educational notification mechanism for alleged online infringers before more stringent measures can be imposed (including, possibly, the suspension of termination of the internet service)" (Strowel 2009: 77).

8 See BBC 2012 and *The Guardian* 2012.

9 Statement by John Clancy (2012).

10 See European Parliament 2012.

11 Named after former Minister of Culture, Ángeles González-Sinde.

12 The Royal Decree also sets down the administrative procedure—with a formal and limited judicial review—for the sanctioning of illegal distribution of copyrighted content.

13 See *El Pais* (2012).

14 See Tribunal Supreme Español 2012.

> In the current state of the means of communication and given the generalized development of public online communication services and the importance of the latter for the participation in democracy and the expression of ideas and opinions, this right implies freedom to access such services.
>
> (*Conseil Constitutionnel 2009: para. 12*)

In other words, the Court determined that the law at issue—which contemplates forcibly disconnecting an individual from the Internet without any type of judicial oversight—is in conflict with Article 11 of the 1789 Declaration of the Rights of the Man and of the Citizen, which still enjoys constitutional value in France (Berman and Picard 2008). The Conseil Constitutionnel recognized that access to the Internet is closely related to, and safeguarded by, freedom of expression. The freedom of communication—which enjoys a particular *status* as a protected right—certainly deserves strengthened protection with respect to Internet access. In fact, this type of communication—as opposed to other forms of access to information—necessarily relates to each individual. The Conseil Constitutionnel, in applying its jurisprudence on the assessment of proportionality, has established that the freedom of communication, as applied to the right of access to network services, assumes a peculiar importance (Conseil Constitutionnel 2008: para. 22). Consequently, the restrictions imposed by the sanctioning of the public authorities' power must be limited. On this issue, the Conseil Constitutionnel stated that "violations of freedom of access to the Internet can be analyzed, under the Constitution, as invasions of the liberty guaranteed by the Article 11 of the Declaration of 1789" (*Cahiers du Conseil Constitutionnel* 2009: 7). Access to such an important tool of communication has become, for millions of citizens, an integral part of their exercise of many other constitutionally protected rights and freedoms (Benkler 2006). Therefore inhibiting access to such a source of information would constitute a disproportionate sanction, in the sense that it would also have a strong and direct impact on the exercise of those constitutional rights and freedoms (Marino 2009). In fact, the Internet, as opposed to other forms of media, allows for the exercise of the freedom of communication not only in a passive way, but also in an active way, because the user can be both a producer and consumer of information (Perritt 2001; Murray 2010). Thus individuals on the Internet are "active producers of information content, not just recipients" (Balkin 2009: 440): These new features provide unexpected options for communication that the traditional media has never offered before.

The conclusion of these arguments implies that Internet disconnection represents a disproportionate penalty for minor offenses. However, despite several press announcements to the contrary, the Court did not mention that Internet access constitutes a fundamental right in itself or that it should be actively guaranteed.

On the same point, the European Parliament has recently stated that the right to Internet access also constitutes a guarantee of the right to access education. Specifically, on 22 March 2009, the European Parliament declared that granting all citizens Internet access is equivalent to ensuring access to education, reasoning on the ground that such access should therefore not be denied or used as a sanction by governments or private companies:

> . . . whereas e-illiteracy will be the new illiteracy of the 21st Century; whereas ensuring that all citizens have access to the Internet is therefore equivalent to ensuring that all citizens have access to schooling, and whereas such access should not be punitively denied by governments or private companies; whereas such access should not be abused in pursuit of illegal activities; whereas it is important to deal with emerging issues such as

network neutrality, interoperability, global reachability of all Internet nodes, and the use of open formats and standards.

(*European Parliament 2009: Q*)

## The international debate around the right to "Internet access"

As discussed earlier, there is an ongoing debate among scholars, policymakers and civil rights activists around the recognition of a fundamental right to Internet access. As pointed out above, a preliminary question concerns the determination of the meaning of "access," which encompasses different functional meanings: access to network infrastructure; access at the transport layer; and access to digital content and applications. Generally speaking, when we talk about "Internet access," we refer to the access to network infrastructure, which essentially includes the other two functional meanings.

In order to position the analysis of the issues in the global context, an overview of the different legal approaches to this question is set out below. Indeed, legislation from other countries has come into effect or is proposed to cover much the same ground. In addition to France, Finland and Estonia, Greece and Costa Rica have also taken important actions concerning the question of access to the Internet (Long 2010). In Finland, Decree no. 732/2009 of the Ministry of Transport and Communications on the Minimum Rate of a Functional Internet Access as a Universal Service sets provision on the minimum rate of a functional Internet access. The Decree does not mention an explicit right of individuals to access the network infrastructure, but rather contemplates a civil right to broadband. In particular, it states that access to broadband Internet is a universal service, similar to other public utilities like telephone service, water supply, electricity, etc. That is, according to Finnish law, the Internet is considered to be a staple commodity to which every consumer and company must have access. This also means that Finnish telecommunication companies are required to provide all Finnish citizens with an Internet connection that runs at a reasonable connection speed. In Estonia, according to section 33 of the Public Information Act 2000, as amended, "every person shall be afforded the opportunity to have free access to public information through the Internet in public libraries, pursuant to the procedure provided for in the Public Libraries Act (RT I 1998, 103, 1696; 2000, 92, 597)." Moreover, according to Estonian legislation on telecommunications, Internet access is also considered a universal service. In particular, the paragraph number five of the Act provides a list of universal services including also the Internet realm, stipulating that they are to be made available to all subscribers regardless of their geographical location and at an identical price (Republic of Estonia, 2000: § 5(2)). Finally, as far as Greece is concerned, the Constitutional Reform of 2001 has amended the Hellenic Constitution introducing—among other novelties—an explicit right for all citizens to participate effectively in society. In particular, the second paragraph of article 5A stipulates that the state is obligated to facilitate access to information transmitted electronically, as well as the exchange, production and dissemination of information "un instrumento básico para facilitar el ejercicio de derechos fundamentales" [a basic tool to facilitate the exercise of fundamental rights and democratic participation].[15] More recently, the Constitutional Court of Costa Rica explicitly declared Internet access to be a fundamental right (*Andres Oriedo Guzman* v *Ministerio de Ambiente* (2010)).

15 Author's translation.

On the question of "Internet access" as a fundamental right, it is interesting to also mention the provocative proposal to add a new article 21 *bis* to the Italian Constitution. In the Italian legal system, article 21 of the Constitution stipulates that anyone has the right to freely express their thoughts in speech, writing, or any other form of communication. The proposal officially presented, and proposed by Professor Stefano Rodotà and *Wired* magazine, sparked a lively debate in Italy between supporters and opponents. In December 2010, a group of members of the Italian Parliament submitted a Constitutional amendment to introduce this new provision in the Italian Constitution. However, at the time of writing, the prevailing opinion is that, in this context, there is no need for a specific constitutional provision designed explicitly to protect the right of access to the Internet. Such a principle can instead be easily derived from existing standards on freedom of speech or of expression through an interpretation of the same principle in a contemporary way. A practical example is given by the interpretive approach adopted by the French Conseil Constitutionnel in the evaluation of the HADOPI Law (Conseil Constitutionnel 2009).

The overall impression gained from all of these discussions indicates a tremendous amount of misunderstanding concerning the substantial difference between civil rights and fundamental rights (or human rights). The question concerns the legal nature of these information rights. These confusing and misleading discourses about "a right to Internet access" have led to a simplistic categorization of the Internet as a fundamental right. In reality, this definition is much more complex and multifaceted than the simple wording suggests. In the contemporary media scenario, access to the Internet is a necessary condition for a concrete achievement of some fundamental human rights such as freedom of speech, communication and expression of thought. These observations may lead us to interpret recent court decisions and regulatory interventions not as a recognition of a new fundamental right, but rather as an opportunity to give an updated meaning to already recognized fundamental legal rights. To a certain extent, defining violations does not imply an automatic creation of new rights, but serves as a remedial or a redefinition of existing rights. All of these considerations address the fact that Internet access is essentially an enabler of rights. It could be also considered an instrument with which to enjoy rights and freedoms already granted, rather than a specific right itself (Cerf 2012).

## Conclusion

The advent of the Internet has placed in front of lawyers the important question of how to interpret the right to participate in the virtual society (Frosini 2002): in other words, how to assess, from a legal perspective, the optimal setting of the freedom to use Internet communication tools both to provide and obtain information. It is no longer just a mere exercise of the traditional right to freedom of thought and expression. It is increasingly perceived as a constitutional dilemma and the courts are more often asked to resolve this dispute concerning the evolutionary interpretation of law.

This context has been employed to review the controversy over the constitutionality of the US Communications Decency Act of 1996, as well as more recent disputes over control of Internet access, including the legal arguments over the constitutionality of the French HADOPI Law, the controversy stemming from the Spanish "Sinde" anti-piracy law, and other internationally debated cases that raise questions of whether the Internet could be considered a fundamental human right. Using these cases as examples, we have reflected on the importance of fundamental rights as an institutional safeguard against the expansionary tendency of market powers and on the increasing role of the courts in expanding and adapting the frontiers of fundamental legal rights. We have also observed how the Internet has effectively returned more power to individuals with a radical redistribution of control on information flow and a completely new approach to the way in which society operates.

In particular, we have illustrated how, for the first time, the constitutional principle of freedom of expression has been formally expanded to include Internet access as part of freedom of speech. The rationale for this expansion is based on the idea that the right of each individual to access digital network services is an essential ingredient in the freedom of communication and expression. In particular, inability to access Internet networks negatively affects other rights. While some judicial opinions recognize the freedom to connect to the Internet, this does not imply that Internet access is a fundamental right; rather, it is the constitutional guarantee of freedom of expression that includes a constitutional guarantee of Internet access. A prerequisite for the realization of the effective exercise of freedom of expression and access to information is uninhibited access to Internet network infrastructure. As a consequence, limitations on the right of Internet access can be imposed only under strict conditions as with limitations imposed on other forms of expression and communication (Strowel 2009).

So, retuning to our initial question: is Internet access a fundamental right? The problem with answering this query is that:

> There is no freedom lost forever or freedom secured forever. History is a dramatic combination of freedom and oppression, new freedoms reflecting new oppressions, old suppressed oppressions, new re-joined freedoms, new imposed oppressions and old lost freedoms. Each period is characterized by its forms of oppression and its struggles for freedom.[16]
>
> (*Bobbio 1995: 75*)

This statement may be taken as a useful reference point in defining new rights. In this light, the debated classification of Internet access as a fundamental right may be seen under a different perspective: It is not necessary to rigidly define a new right, but rather to ensure new freedoms against new forms of control and restriction.

## References


Akdeniz, Y. (2010) *OSCE Report: Freedom of Expression on the Internet*, OSCE. Online. Available HTTP: http://www.osce.org/fom/80723 (accessed 14 September 2012).

*American Civil Liberties Union et al.* v *Janet Reno* 521 US 844 (1997).

*Andres Oviedo Guzman* v *Ministerio de Ambiente* (2010) Sentencia No. 2010-012790, Sala Constitucional de la Corte Suprema de Justicia de Costa Rica, Energia y Telecomunicaciones. Online. Available HTTP: http://bit.ly/9MyR81 (accessed 14 September 2012).

*Ashcroft, J. Attorney General* v *American Civil Liberties Union* 535 US 564 (2002).

Balkin, J. M. (2009) 'The future of free expression in a digital age,' *Pepperdine Law Review*, 36: 427–444.

Banisar, D. (2006) 'The right to information in the age of information,' in R. F. Jørgensen (ed.) *Human Rights in the Global Information Society*, Cambridge, MA: MIT Press.

BBC (2012) 'ACTA: Germany delays signing anti-piracy agreement,' 10 February. Online. Available HTTP: http://www.bbc.co.uk/news/technology-16980451 (accessed 28 May 2012).

Benkler, Y. (2006) *The Wealth of Networks: How Social Production Transforms—Markets and Freedom*, New Haven, CT: Yale University Press.

Berman, G. A. and Picard, E. (eds.) (2008) *Introduction to French Law*, The Hague: Kluwer Law International.


16 Translation by the author.

Best, M. L. (2004) 'Can the Internet be a human right?' *Human Rights and Human Welfare*' 4(1): 23–31.

Blevins, J. (2012) 'The new scarcity: A First Amendment framework for regulating access to digital media platforms,' *Tennessee Law Review*, 79: 353–416.

Bobbio, N. (1995) *Eguaglianza e Libertà*, Torino: Einaudi.

Bridy, A. (2010), 'ACTA and the specter of graduated response,' American University, Washington College of Law, PIJIP Research Paper No. 2. Online. Available HTTP: http://digitalcommons.wcl.american.edu/cgi/viewcontent.cgi?article=1002&context=research&sei- (accessed 14 September 2012).

*Cahiers du Conseil Constitutionnel* (2009) 'Commentaire de la décision n. 2009-580 DC du 10 juin 2009,' 27: 1–19. Online. Available HTTP: http://www.conseil-constitutionnel.fr/conseil-constitutionnel/root/bank_mm/commentaires/cahier27/cccc_580dc.pdf (accessed 14 September 2012).

Castells, M. (2010) *The Power of Identity*, 2nd edn., Malden, MA: Wiley-Blackwell.

Center for Democracy and Technology (2012) 'ITU move to expand powers threatens the Internet: Civil society should have voice in ITU Internet debate.' Online. Available HTTP: https://www.cdt.org/files/pdfs/CDT-ITU_WCIT12_background.pdf (accessed 28 May 2012).

Cerf, V. G. (2012) 'Internet access is not a human right,' *New York Times*, 5 January, A25.

Clancy, J. (2012) 'EU Trade Spokesman,' 11 May. Online. Available HTTP: http://trade.ec.europa.eu/doclib/press/index.cfm?id=799 (accessed 28 May 2012).

Conseil Constitutionnel (1996) *Décision no. 96-378DC du 23 juillet 1996*. Online. Available HTTP: http://www.conseil-constitutionnel.fr/conseil-constitutionnel/root/bank/pdf/conseil-constitutionnel-10818.pdf (accessed 14 September 2012).

—— (2008) *Décision no. 2008-562DC du 21 février 2008*. Online. Available HTTP: http://www.conseil-constitutionnel.fr/conseil-constitutionnel/root/bank_mm/anglais/a2008562dc.pdf (accessed 14 September 2012).

—— (2009) *Décision no. 2009-580DC du 10 Juin 2009, relative à la loi favorisant la diffusion et la protection de la création sur internet*. Online. Available HTTP: http://www.conseil-constitutionnel.fr/conseil-constitutionnel/root/bank/download/cc-2009580dc.pdf (in French). Online. Available HTTP: http://www.conseil-constitutionnel.fr/conseil-constitutionnel/root/bank_mm/anglais/2009_580dc.pdf (in English) (accessed 14 September 2012).

Couch, C. J. (1990) 'Mass communications and state structures,' *Social Science Journal*, 27: 111–128.

Deibert, R. J. (2008) 'Black code redux: Censorship, surveillance, and the militarisation of cyberspace,' in M. Boler (ed.) *Digital Media and Democracy: Tactics in Hard Time*, Cambridge, MA: MIT Press.

—— and Rohozinski. R. (2008) 'Good for liberty, bad for security? Global civil society and the securitization of the Internet,' in R. J. Deibert *et al.* (eds.) *Access Denied: The Practice and Policy of Global Internet Filtering*, Cambridge, MA: MIT Press.

——, Palfrey, J., Rohozinski, R., Zittrain, J., and Gross Stein, J. (eds.) (2008) *Access Denied: The Practice and Policy of Global Internet Filtering*, Cambridge, MA: MIT Press.

——, Palfrey, J., Rohozinski, R., Zittrain, J. and Haraszti, M. (eds.) (2010) *Access Controlled: The Shaping of Power, Rights, and Rule in Cyberspace*, Cambridge, MA: MIT Press.

DeNardis, L. (2009) *Protocol Politics: The Globalization of Internet Governance*, Cambridge, MA: MIT Press.

*Denver Area Educational Telecommunications Consortium, Inc.* v *Federal Communications Commission et al.* 518 US 727 (1996).

Dutton, W. H., Doptatka, A., Hills, M., Law, G. and Nash, V. (2011) *Freedom of Connection, Freedom of Expression: The Changing Legal and Regulatory Ecology Shaping the Internet*, Paris: UNESCO. Online. Available HTTP: http://unesdoc.unesco.org/images/0019/001915/191594e.pdf (accessed 14 September 2012).

*El Pais* (2012) 'Top court will review Sinde Download Law,' 8 February. Online. Available HTTP: http://elpais.com/elpais/2012/02/08/inenglish/1328729926_874644.html (accessed 28 May 2012).

Elkin-Koren, N. and Netanel, N. W. (eds.) (2002) *The Commodification of Information*, The Hague: Kluwer Law International.

Emerson, T. I. (1963) 'Toward a general theory of the First Amendment,' *Yale Law Review Journal*, 72: 877–956.

European Parliament (2009) *Recommendation of 26 March 2009 to the Council on Strengthening Security and Fundamental Freedoms on the Internet*. Online. Available HTTP: http://www.europarl.europa.eu/sides/getDoc.do?pubRef=-//EP//TEXT+TA+P6-TA-2009-0194+0+DOC+XML+V0//EN (accessed 14 September 2012).

—— (2012) Press release, European Parliament rejects ACTA. Online. Available HTTP: http://www.europarl.europa.eu/news/en/pressroom/content/20120703IPR48247

Frosini, V. (2002) 'L'orizzonte giuridico dell'Internet,' *Il Diritto dell'Informazione e dell'Informatica*, 2: 271–280.
Gibbons, T. (2009) *Free Speech in the New Media*, Aldershot: Ashgate.
Godwin, M. (2003) *Cyber Rights: Defending Free Speech in the Digital Age*, Rev. edn., Cambridge, MA: MIT Press.
Goldsmith, J. and Wu, T. (2006) *Who Controls the Internet? Illusions of a Borderless World*, New York: Oxford University Press.
Gross, D. A. and Lucarelli, E. (2011) 'The 2012 World Conference on International Telecommunications: Another brewing storm over potential UN regulation of the Internet," *Who's Who Legal*, November. Online. Available HTTP: http://www.whoswholegal.com/news/features/article/29378/the-2012-world-conference-internationaltelecommunications-brewing-storm-potential-un-regulation-internet/ (accessed 26 May 2012).
*Guardian* (2012) 'ACTA loses more support in Europe,' 15 February. Online. Available HTTP: http://www.guardian.co.uk/technology/2012/feb/15/acta-loses-moresupport-europe (accessed 28 May 2012).
*Hague* v *C.I.O.* 307 US 496 (1939).
Hamon, F. and Troper, M. (2009) *Droit Constitutionnel*, 31st edn., Paris: LGDJ.
*Heffron* v *International Society for Krishna Consciousness* 452 US 640 (1981).
Holoubek, M., Damjanovic, D. and Traimer, M. (eds.) (2007) *Regulating Content: European Regulatory Framework for the Media and Related Creative Sectors*, The Hague: Kluwer Law International.
Horner, L., Hawtin, D. and Puddephatt, A. (2010) *Information and Communication Technologies and Human Rights*, Brussels: European Parliament. Online. Available HTTP: http://www.europarl.europarl.europ arl.europa.eu/activities/committees/studies/download.do?language=it&file=31731 (accessed 14 September 2012).
Inter-American Court of Human Rights (1985) *Advisory Opinion OC-5/85 of November 13, 1985*, Inter-Am. Ct. HR (Ser. A) No. 5.
International Telecommunication Union (1989) 'Final acts of the World Administrative Telegraph and Telephone Conference—Melbourne 1988,' in *International Telecommunication Regulations* 3-8. Online. Available HTTP: http://itu.int/dms_pub/itus/oth/02/01/s02010000214002PDFE.pdf (accessed 27 May 2012).
Jacques, S. C. (1997) '*Reno* v *ACLU*: Insulating the Internet, the First Amendment and the marketplace of ideas,' *American University Law Review*, 46: 1945–1992.
Jørgensen, R. F. (ed.) (2006) *Human Rights in the Global Information Society*, Cambridge, MA: MIT Press.
Kaminski, M. (2009) 'Recent development: The origins and potential impact of the Anti-Counterfeiting Trade Agreement (ACTA),' *Yale Journal of International Law*, 34: 247–256.
Kapzcynski, A. (2008) 'The access to knowledge mobilization and the new politics of Intellectual Property,' *Yale Law Journal*, 117: 804–885.
Long, D. E. (2010) 'Three strikes and you are off the Internet,' *Chicago Daily Law Bulletin*, 29 October. Online. Available HTTP: http://www.jmls.edu/news/Long%20CDLB%2010%2010%2 029.pdf (accessed 14 September 2012).
Lucchi, N. (2006) *Digital Media and Intellectual Property: Management of Rights and Consumer Protection in a Comparative Analysis*, Berlin: Springer.
—— (2011) 'Access to network services and protection of constitutional rights,' *Cardozo Journal of International and Comparative Law*, 19: 645–679.
Mainoldi, L. (2012) 'I padroni di Internet,' *Limes "Media come Armi"* 1: 9–16.
Marino, L. (2009) 'Le droit d'accès à Internet, nouveau droit fondamental,' *Recueil Dalloz*, 30: 2045.
Mendel, T. and Salomon E. (2011) *Freedom of Expression and Broadcasting Regulation*, Paris: UNESCO.
Moglen, E. (2011) 'Why political liberty depends on software freedom more than ever,' Speech given at the 2011 FOSDEM Conference in Brussels, 5 February. Online. Available HTTP: http://www.softwarefreedom.org/events/2011/fosdem/moglen-fosdem-keynote.html (accessed 27 April 2012).
Murray, A. (2010) *Information Technology Law*, Oxford: Oxford University Press.
Nye, J. S. (2011) *The Future of Power*, New York: PublicAffairs.
Packard, A. (2010) *Digital Media Law*, Malden, MA: Wiley-Blackwell.
Perritt, H. H., Jr. (2001) *Law and the Information Superhighway*, 2nd edn., Gaithersburg, MD: Aspen Law and Business.
Price, M. E. (2002) *Media and Sovereignty: The Global Information Revolution and Its Challenge*, Cambridge, MA: MIT Press.

*Reno, Attorney General of the United States, et al.* v *American Civil Liberties Union et al.* 521 US 844 (1997).
Republic of Estonia (2000) Telekommunikatsiooniseadus of February 9, 2000 (RT I 2000, 18, 116). Online. Available HTTP: https://www.riigiteataja.ee/a kt/71844 (accessed 27 April 2012).
Robinson, G. O. and Nachbar, T. B. (2008) *Communications Regulation*, St. Paul, MN: Thomson/West.
Rodotà, S. (2006) *La Vita e le Regole: Tra Diritto e Non Diritto*, Milan: Feltrinelli.
Sadurski, W. (1999) *Freedom of Speech and Its Limits*, Dordrecht: Kluwer Academic Publishers.
Santoro, P. (2010) 'Progressive IP strategies for European clients,' in E. Baud *et al.* (eds.) *IP Client Strategies in Europe*, Boston, MA: Aspatore.
Strowel, A. (2009) 'Internet piracy as a wake-up call for copyright law makers: Is the "graduated response" a good reply?' *World Intellectual Property Organization Journal*, 1: 75–86.
Sunstein, C.R. (2001) *Republic.com*, Princeton, NJ: Princeton University Press.
Szuskin, L. F. de Ruyter, S. and Doucleff, J. (2009) 'Beyond counterfeiting: The expanding battle against online piracy,' *Intellectual Property and Technology Law Journal*, 21(11): 1–12.
Tuhus-Dubrow, R. (2010) 'One nation, online: The push to make broadband access a civil right,' *Boston Globe*, 20 June. Available online at: http://www.boston.com/bostonglobe/ideas/articles/2010/06/20/one_nation_online/_ (accessed 28 May 2012).
Tribunal Supremo Español [Spanish Supreme Court], Sala de to Contencioso-Administrative (2012) Petition n.48/12, 11 May. Online. Available HTTP: http://ibercrea.es/wp-content/uploads/2012/05/Auto-Supremo-Cautelar-LS.pdf (accessed 1 October 2012).
United Nations Economic and Social Council, Commission on Human Rights (2000) *Report by the Special Rapporteur on the Promotion and Protection of the Right to Freedom of Opinion and Expression*, UN Doc. E/CN.4/2000/63, 18 January. Online. Available HTTP: http://www.unhchr.ch/Huridocda/Huridoca.nsf/0/16583a 84ba1b3ae5802568bd004e80f7/$FILE/G0010259.pdf (accessed 14 September 2012).
United Nations General Assembly, Human Rights Council, Commission on Human Rights (2011) *Report by the Special Rapporteur on the Promotion and Protection of the Right to Freedom of Opinion and Expression*, UN Doc. A/HRC/17/27, 16 May. Online. Available HTTP: http://www.unhchr.ch/Huridocda/Huridoca.nsf/0/16583a84ba1b3ae5802568bd004e80f7/$FILE/G0010259.pdf (accessed 14 September 2012).
*United States* v *Am. Library Association* 539 US 194: (2003).
Verpeaux, M. (2009) 'La liberté de communication avant tout: La censure de la loi Hadopi 1 par le Conseil Constitutionnel,' *La Semaine Juridique Generale*, 39: 46.
—— (2010) *Freedom of Expression*, Strasbourg: Council of Europe.
Yu, P. K. (2010) 'The graduated response,' *Florida Law Review*, 62: 1373.
Zencovich, V. Z. (2008) *Freedom of Expression: A Critical and Comparative Analysis*, London: Routledge-Cavendish.

# 10
# From freedom of speech to the right to communicate

*Daithí Mac Síthigh*

## Introduction

The concept of communication rights forms an important part of current debates on media and the Internet. This chapter explores several sources for the concept: the "right to communicate" as a human right, the project for a New World Information and Communications Order (NWICO), and the medium-focused scholarship of Harold Innis, among others. The right to communicate is reviewed as a more appropriate approach to the regulation of media and technology than existing concepts of freedom of expression, particularly as incorporated in the First Amendment to the US Constitution. The reasons for the "failure" of the NWICO and UNESCO's MacBride Commission are considered, as are alternative approaches to the First Amendment itself, including Barron's "access" reasoning and the use of common carriage obligations.

Questions of international treaty law are then considered, tracing the fate of communication rights in instruments regarding trade, telecommunications and cultural diversity across a number of different organizations. Only then do we look at the 1990s and 2000s in more detail, the time of "globalization" and the first "dot-com" boom, with accompanying legal and institutional debates regarding Internet governance, cultural diversity and more. Here, it is suggested that reinvigorated international debates on communication rights provide an opportunity to address the problems of global communications law in a new way. Building upon these observations, the outlook for the right to communicate, whether directly or through expansion of existing rights, is considered.

## The context for communication rights

### *Rights, reform and regulation*

Feintuck and Varney (2006) note that media regulation can be understood through analyzing how a regulatory system and polity responds to challenges such as convergence, globalization and horizontal and vertical integration. The introduction of new media also provides new challenges, but here the response of governments can often be to develop new forms of restriction, provoking a discussion of new (or reformulated) rights (Chalaby

2000). Policy reform is an opportunity for campaigners and researchers to evaluate the relationship between media and society and the appropriate legal measures that are necessary (Curran 2010). As such, the way in which rights are articulated and engaged and regulatory approaches considered or reconsidered is a particular preoccupation of this chapter.

In one analysis, the advocacy of media reform has been explained as taking place through five different frames: "free press," "media democracy," "media justice," and the "mental environment" (i.e. media ecology), as well as the right to communicate (Hackett and Carroll 2006: 78–9). The main international human rights instruments, and some non-governmental organizations (such as Article 19), have historically relied on a free press "frame" as a preferred approach. In this chapter, I argue that "the right to communicate" is especially useful as a frame within the debate on international law, as it refers to and builds on a rich heritage of international cooperation, and has become quite relevant as the information society is debated. While it has proven to be difficult to separate human rights relating to expression or communication from the "free press" argument in a US context, the right to communicate as a trope is more rewarding in the case of public international law. There, the historical power of the idea of the free press as the driver is not so obviously embedded. The debate on whether or how free speech can be justified by liberal or democratic considerations, and with what implications (so important within First Amendment scholarship), can also be transcended, because the concept of communication rights values from conception both individual and collective exercises of communicative freedoms.

Communication rights have also been argued to have the characteristics of "third generation" human rights (Hicks 2007; Cammaerts and Carpentier 2007)—where first generation are civil and political rights, and second generation are social and economic rights. This emerging area of human rights law is an exciting one, and one that has seen both academic and legislative interest, with, for example, the European Union Charter of Fundamental Rights attempting to go beyond the hierarchy of the three generations and to classify rights in a more thematic fashion. In addition, there is a useful parallel with other rights considered to be in the third generation, such as environmental and heritage questions, in that they can be understood as demanding a supportive culture and structure for the achievement of quite far-reaching goals, rather than a defense against state oppression of vulnerable or troublesome individuals.

## *The medium matters*

A valuable approach to the development of a theory of the right to communicate is that of what can be termed the "Toronto School" (de Kerckhove 1989; Watson and Blondheim 2007). While the work of Marshall McLuhan is most widely known, the writers associated with this approach, in particular Harold Innis, put forward an idea that the development of new technologies of communication is associated with the development of societies and civilizations more generally, paying particular attention to the differences between different media of communications (Innis 1950; Innis 1951a). Such writings are important, however, not only for their specific object of attention, but also for the approach that is taken to questions of media and communication and how communication studies relate to social, economic and historical studies, and ultimately (when viewed from the present day) to legal and institutional arrangements.

Innis reports on how print and print culture developed in opposition to the control of knowledge and information by religious orders where parchment alone was used for the dissemination of information (Innis 1950). In contrast, legal support for printing through the First Amendment and associated legal instruments (such as postal regulations) has contributed to print technology's move from being an alternative or a technology of opposition to forming a part of the "mainstream media" and a potential technology of control. Carey, who noted his debt to Innis, argues that if lawmakers refuse to look beyond the mantra of "freedom of the press," they overlook the importance of communication and the way in which such freedom can be manipulated to restrict access to media and to information by granting and defending monopolies (Carey 1989). We will return to this problem in due course.

As is now widely understood, much early work in communication studies assumed a linear, transmission model that was based on the communication of messages from sender to receiver. Innis, Carey and others challenged this assumption and provoked a widening of the debate, looking at the implications of technological change and the relationship between media and society (Babe 2000; Czitrom 1982). This broad approach remained marginal in the earlier days of the electronic media (which was a time of growth in international law), outside the mainstream of American research that focused on the "effects" of media in a behavioral rather than a social or economic sense. Scholars influenced by the Toronto School built on the work of Innis in the development of a "medium theory" approach to communication (Meyrowitz 1985), more sensitive to disparities in power than the dominant approaches in "mainstream American" media scholarship (Babe 2009: 117). Innis's exploration of the recurring problem of the "monopoly of knowledge" is based on the historical evidence for this phenomenon. He discusses the way in which successive elites have controlled the dissemination and construction of knowledge by regulating or restricting access to a medium of communication, for example the restriction on dictation in the fourteenth-century University of Paris (Innis 1950).

## The right to communicate

The early period of the right to communicate runs from 1969 (its proposal by Jean d'Arcy) to 1984 (the report of the MacBride Commission), although this section will consider events before and after this period. The purpose of this discussion is to identify some of the key "roots" of the right and how it influences discussions at international organizations in particular.

The international dimension is important; those who supported it saw the right to communicate as more comprehensive than existing rights and freedoms, such as freedom of the press, and more accommodating of the claims of groups and nations than existing, distributed provisions of international law on communication (Fisher and Harms 1982). The reaction to d'Arcy's proposal is first considered, followed by the closely related matter of the work of UNESCO on a New World Information and Communications Order (NWICO).

To some extent, the right also came to be the embodiment of "the positive" in the oft-stated relationship between "negative" and "positive" media regulation, which is an issue for many domestic systems of human rights protection too. Therefore I will also discuss two other aspects of media regulation that can be linked with the right to communicate: "access" rights and the regulation of "common carriers."

### *Jean d'Arcy and defining the right to communicate*

The first advocate of this right was Jean d'Arcy, a UN official, who, in a paper provoked by the then-controversial issue of direct broadcasting by satellite (a topic we return to below), suggested that it was time to reconsider the treatment of information in the Universal Declaration of Human Rights, so as to bring together and extend disparate provisions in the context of global communication (Anawalt 1983). Until his death in 1983, d'Arcy continued to develop and advance this theory in a number of fora, suggesting in his introduction to a 1982 collection of papers that the right was by now a matter of some agreement.

Despite d'Arcy's efforts to champion the right, however, the pace of development slowed, and its visibility diminished somewhat in subsequent years. The right to communicate became associated with dialog over monologue, and viewed as potentially contributing to breaking the deadlock of "free flow" discussions, by adding to existing rights rather than replacing them. This "change of outlook" would involve resources and access, but not as an end for its own sake, instead contributing to the building of genuine non-hierarchical democratic dialog.

An earlier illustration of the use of the concept of the "right to communicate" is in the discussions surrounding the 1971 *Instant World* report prepared for the Canadian government. The report suggested that assembly and free speech were an inadequate setting for the "impending age of total communications," adding that the development of communication systems would be governed by political decisions, which could be designed so as to protect and promote a right to communicate (Department of Communications 1971: 38). The report argues that freedom of knowledge and of speech are part of the privileges of a democratic society, with the right to communicate being referred to as an objective for a democratic society and an international communications environment (Department of Communications 1971). *Instant World* is also important as a signal for later developments, and recent scholarship points to a renewal of interest in its role in the Canadian contribution to the right to communicate (e.g. Raboy and Shtern 2010; Dakroury 2008).

It is rare that we find constitutional considerations of the right at a national level. One exception may be that of the Constitution of Ireland, where a 1984 case, *Paperlink* v *Attorney General*, noted an unenumerated right to communicate (in a situation in which the textual guarantee of freedom of expression was found to be inapplicable). However, more recent cases have taken a less limited approach to expression and (possibly) collapsed the distinction between the two rights, despite the unrealized potential of developing the right to communicate (O'Dell 2007).

Despite the lack of an adequate definition of the right to communicate, its notable aspects can be identified as emphasizing participation and multidirectional communication and on redressing imbalances or biases in media systems. We might also note the more prosaic task of joining issues such as freedom of information and the concept of cultural diversity to the conventional right of freedom of expression. These two working definitions facilitate the discussion of related concepts in this section, and are revisited in the discussion of the Internet below.

## *New order*

Between 1965 and 1978, UNESCO moved away from an initial concern with more technical (although undoubtedly important) agreements (Dutt 1995) towards an overtly political interpretation of international communications. A culmination was the 1978 Mass Media Declaration, the result of years of negotiation, which set out a range of principles for the "contribution" of the mass media to international peace (Hanjal 1983). With this idea in mind, alongside fears regarding North–South imbalances in communication and the increasing power of transnational media enterprises, a wide-ranging agenda began to be set out. The result was the concept of a New World Information and Communications Order (NWICO). The idea for an NWICO, elaborating the importance of a free *and balanced* flow of information, is attributed to the Tunisian Mustapha Masmoudi, who was the chair of the information council of the Non-Aligned Movement. The NAM was a key player in the formulation of new approaches to dominance in culture and information (Schiller 1989), despite criticism from the USSR (Singh 1988), as well as the later skepticism from the United States.

The discussion of NWICO reached its height with the 1980 publication of *Many Voices, One World*, the final report of the UNESCO International Commission for the Study of Communication Problems, also known as the "MacBride Commission" after its chair, Seán MacBride. The Commission was made up of a group of communication experts from around the world, and was expected to make a contribution to a debate in UNESCO on the global regulation and promotion of communication, a debate that had already become quite divided by the time the Commission was established. We are most interested here in the sections of this wide-ranging report that dealt with the regulation of the media and the relationship between law, technology and society in a global context. The Commission recommended measures including the reform of trade law, the development of cultural policies by nation-states, and a range of measures that would assist developing nations in getting their "voice" across to a global audience. It took a holistic approach to the role of the state in media, looking at both national measures and international cooperation, at a time when international law was at a relatively weak point and international trade law far from the force it is today. In addition, some have suggested that workable proposals for a less market-driven approach to projects such as telecommunications liberalization were included in the report, with an attempt to focus these efforts on the creation of public spaces over markets rather than furthering state control over individual liberties (Mansell and Nordenstreng 2007).

Although much of the report is (valuably) descriptive, a key passage set out the concerns of flows and dominance, presented a theory of the democratization of communication, and discussed specific issues relating to presentation of the world and the role of public opinion (MacBride Commission 1980). The right to communicate was the dominant legal–philosophical concept in this section on democratization. The report echoed comments of d'Arcy that set out the historical evolution of rights and media technologies, arguing that with new opportunities to communicate come new challenges to communication rights, which should be seen as opportunities to give further recognition to the rights of man (MacBride Commission 1980). The report added a rights-based dimension to the more detailed (but less legally focused) work of Innis, by considering the relationship between changes in the medium of communication and social and economic development.

The report was the subject of much criticism, particularly from some Western states who argued that it was a blueprint for censorship and state control. Many see the ensuing debate as central in the decision of the United States and United Kingdom to withdraw from UNESCO in 1984, although there were, of course, other factors and the United Kingdom's withdrawal was the subject of internal division (Dutt 1995). The controversy was undoubtedly a significant setback for the organization and for the right to communicate.

The media's response to the report deserves attention, particularly because the critique that it favored censorship of the press is an enduring feature of the period. In fact, journalists' associations (the "Western" International Federation of Journalists and the "Soviet" International Organisation of Journalists) took a careful approach, attempting to organize joint discussions of the report. However, these associations experienced hostility from the organizations of editors and owners, the International Press Institute and the Federation of International Editors of Journals (Hamelink 2008). These organizations, along with others, led the World Press Freedom Committee (Morris and Waisbord 2001), which condemned the entire NWICO project in its Declaration of Talloires (World Press Freedom Committee 1981). Herman argues, however, that, at the crucial conference where this declaration was agreed, few journalists were present and NWICO supporters were not permitted to speak (Herman 1989). The distinction between the interests of the media (particularly proprietors) and the right to communicate became very apparent, although this tension was already visible within US law on speech, as we now discuss.

## *The right to communicate and the First Amendment*

The right to communicate can be compared with a US-focused "First Amendment" approach to speech. The First Amendment, owing to its position in a list of protections against the power of the nascent US federal government at the end of the eighteenth century, is a text that is both broad and narrow. It is broad in that it appears to forbid any interference with free speech and freedom of the press. However, it is narrow in being addressed to Congress alone. Of course, in practice, media regulation has been possible in the United States—often by defining certain actions as not constituting "speech." However, the limits of free expression—and how it is to be "balanced" with other fundamental rights—are not to be found in the Constitution. There is little scope for state action in defense of the right to communicate, particularly where doing so might interfere with the rights of "the press" and its owners. This is why Innis, from the point of view of the historian of communication, doubted its scope.

First Amendment jurisprudence has been criticized by some legal scholars on the grounds that it has become more of a defense of the rights of editors and corporations against the state than a broad, pluralist vision of the media (Sunstein 1993; Anderson 1999; Fiss 1998). Attempts to build on the First Amendment as a broader guarantee of "access to the press" do exist, associated in particular with Jerome Barron (1967; 1969). The Supreme Court has at times issued bold statements in favor of a diversity of information sources. The high-water mark was surely the 1945 *Associated Press* v *US* case (Cooper 2005), which noted that "the widest possible dissemination of information from diverse and antagonistic sources is essential to the welfare of the public" (*Associated Press* v *US* (1945)), but the influence of this case is limited. More importantly, Barron's access arguments were explicitly rejected in the "right to reply" case of *Miami Herald* v *Tornillo* (1974).

Criticism of the prevailing approach to the First Amendment continues in some academic precincts; there, views are more consistent with the key aspects of the right to communicate, whether it be a proposed "collectivist approach" to the First Amendment (Napoli and Sybblis 2007: 13–14), or the critique that mainstream judicial approaches to the First Amendment are too focused on the power of government and not sensitive enough to the links between the purpose of constitutional protection and present-day threats from private bodies (Sunstein 1993). Similar debates are happening in relation to European human rights law, where there is scope for the consideration of positive obligations and horizontal rights. For example, the European Court of Human Rights has taken a generous approach to the right of the public to access official information (e.g. *Timpul Info-Magazin* v *Moldova* (2007)), but the jurisprudence on information comes down to the duty of a government "not to interfere with communication of information between individuals, be they legal or natural persons" (Council of Europe 2011: 24). The Court had a crucial opportunity to consider communication rights in the *Appleby* v *UK* (2003) case regarding the exclusion of protestors from a privately owned shopping center, but set a high threshold for future positive obligations regarding the Convention rights of expression and assembly, particularly because of the implications for property rights (defended by Sluijs 2011). Critics (Layard 2010; Mac Síthigh 2012) argue that the interpretation deprives individuals, in an increasingly bordered world, of opportunities to communicate.

### *Common carriage*

One feature of media and telecommunications law (including that of the United States) that could be a useful corrective to a narrow speech approach and benefit from a right to communicate approach is that of the common carrier. This enables some control of private action in the public interest, noting the special status of particular classes of private bodies and adopting appropriate legal principles. Common carrier laws pre-date the presentation of the right to communicate by d'Arcy, and still exist in the present day. A common carrier has historically carried goods or people, or in some cases provided services to the public, but the doctrine is also a very important one in US telecommunications law (Nunziato 2009; Marsden 2010). The most important aspect of a legal principle of this nature is that there is, in general, a linked obligation and benefit, or a package of obligations and benefits. For example, a common carrier might be required to carry all goods, or to follow sector-specific rules in how it deals with customers—obligations that interfere with absolute concepts of commercial freedom or property rights. But these obligations confer status or benefits, such as privileged participation in a regulated sector not open to other businesses, or immunity from certain types of liability.

The focus of common carrier law is on the regulation of technology. Its existence acknowledges the value of the approach of the Toronto School, and Innis's warnings regarding control of communications as a means for wider control. Attempts to extend common carrier principles to the media have frequently been unsuccessful. For example, the consideration of radio broadcasters as common carriers in the 1920s (Benjamin 2006), a debate between "newspaper" and "telegraph" models (Schmidt 1976), did not result in common carrier status. Instead, broadcasters were required to comply with limited obligations (such as a certain degree of impartiality), which were later whittled away by First Amendment litigation.

Similarly, with the introduction and development of cable in the late 1960s, hopes were expressed that it would be pluralist, decentralized, diverse, non-homogenous and welcoming to public access services (Schmidt 1976). In *FCC* v *Midwest Video* (1979), however, the US Supreme Court declined to consider cable networks as common carriers. This experience, therefore, is not a suitably encouraging template for the treatment of some Internet actors as public forums or common carriers (Stein 2006). The rhetoric of the "free Internet" is not new, but the use of telecommunications law to maintain an open, neutral Internet (in proposals regarding "net neutrality") demonstrates that the idea continues to be a powerful one.

## Communication rights and media regulation in international law

International treaties in relation to communication have, for most of the twentieth century, focused on technical coordination. "Politicizing" institutions that have technical mandates, or taking a rights-based approach, can prove controversial. In this section, we explore some key treaties, including their engagement with rights and the social consequences of technologies. In spite of the essentially municipal nature of the greater part of the regulation of media and communication, international instruments do affect the options available within a given state. Therefore the call for an international right to communicate is properly assessed as one for a more rights-aware type of international law; this is particularly important as it may mean that there is an existing institutional framework within which the right can be articulated. The areas first discussed are telecommunications, satellite broadcasting, and the law on trade in goods and services. Subsequently, developments in relation to the Internet are considered, in so far as they differ from previous forms of international media law, but also illustrate how the right to communicate has re-emerged; relevant too is the new instrument on cultural diversity, which (in part) advances a right to communicate agenda, as a response to the success of the establishment and effectiveness of the multilateral instruments on trade.

## *Telecoms, satellites and trade*

The International Telecommunications Union (ITU), a specialized agency of the UN, traces its roots to the International Telegraph Convention signed in Paris in May 1865 and the International Telegraph Union that was founded to manage it and subsequent developments. Since 1934, the Union has also been responsible for a similar convention on radio of 1906—an early example of "convergence," although the functions remained quite separate for some time and still do to some extent. An important and enduring role of the Union is to convene the regular World Radiocommunication Conferences, which are responsible for spectrum allocation. This has always had an impact on broadcasting and on content more generally; the ITU is charged with balancing competing claims to spectrum, including for Internet-related services (Touré 2008). It is impossible to imagine a global spectrum system without some sort of control; "spectrum scarcity" is a phrase that is relevant in terms of the availability of broadcast channels, but because developments so far have not enabled us to change the laws of physics, the efficient use of spectrum still requires some form of allocation or coordination at an international level.

Early debates on spectrum allocation at an international level tended to focus on high-level allocations (i.e. blocks for broadcast, aviation, shipping, etc.). While issues arose in relation to interference, therefore, they were easy to resolve as compared with the dispute over direct broadcasting by satellite (DBS). DBS was the result of technological innovation (in the public and private sectors), but its success or failure would also depend on the legal aspects of its deployment. In particular, DBS would entail broadcasts that would, when the technology was used to its full extent, be available across a wide region, including a greater number of states than would have been the case with other broadcast technologies. Not surprisingly, this proved controversial. At first, the matter was framed as a subset of the law on the use of outer space, including a 1972 UNESCO Resolution (sponsored by the USSR) that contained a strong non-commercial (but potentially very restrictive) vision of the role of satellites in global media (UNESCO 1972). Subsequent debates (in UNESCO and elsewhere) showed three "blocs" emerging. One, led by the United States, was skeptical of any legal role other than coordination of frequencies. This view was based on the United States' constitutional approach to free speech. A second group of states, associated with the USSR, favored a strong principle of "prior consent" for broadcasts received via DBS in a given state, which we can attribute to particular concerns about broadcasting that had arisen in a Cold War context, including the activities of the US government in broadcasting via analog radio to eastern European states from friendly territory. Finally, Sweden and Canada tried (but failed) to establish a compromise, which expressed concern about the impact of commercially powerful "spillover," suggesting bilateral agreements and a principle of international cooperation (Thompson 1982; Preston, Herman and Schiller 1989). None of these three blocs prevailed; the lack of a resolution is said to have meant that media corporations were able to act in an area of weak legal control and to prepare the ground for a similar approach to the Internet (Ó Siochrú and Girard 2002).

The other key area for communication, slower to emerge than technical coordination, is that of the law of trade. Some suggest that this constitutes a new phase in global media governance (Puppis 2008; Ó Siochrú and Girard 2002). Before this, the post-war 1949 General Agreement on Tariffs and Trade (GATT) was a key moment in the development of trade law, and, to a limited extent, engaged with media and communication issues. Article 4 allows parties to reserve time for "films of national origin," and Article 20 allows the protection of both public morals and "national treasures of artistic, historic or archaeological value." Although there is no general "cultural exemption," as was later adopted in the Canada-United States Free Trade Agreement and North American Free Trade Agreement (NAFTA), the consequences of this lacuna are limited. GATT was limited to products, not services, while the focus of present-day cultural policy is in the domain of the regulation of services. Nonetheless, some areas of media are clearly within the ambit of the GATT, even where there are cultural consequences. Examples are foreign-language books (Driessen 1999) and postal subsidies for magazines (Grant and Wood 2004; Jeffrey 1999).

The GATT is, of course, now part of the World Trade Organization (WTO) system of international trade law. It is therefore important to consider how the cultural "issue" is dealt with in more recent instruments, such as the General Agreement on Trade and Services (GATS). Regardless of whether states see media in trade terms or cultural terms, the WTO has provided a key focal point for debate and negotiation regarding the media (Choi 2008; Wunsch-Vincent 2003). The organization itself has avoided full engagement with the issue, through its structure of requiring parties to GATS to make offers or "commitments" in particular areas. Very few states have done so with respect to audiovisual services; of those that have, the majority are limited in scope to pre-existing commitments (European Commission n.d.). No EU states have made commitments, and states have also continued to exempt audiovisual matters from most-favored nation (MFN) status (i.e. conditions as good as other trading partners). The United States, meanwhile, has taken an approach of seeking often-controversial bilateral agreements (Wunsch-Vincent 2003; Calabrese and Briziarelli 2011), where media and culture have become troublesome battlegrounds in the process of approval, particularly in the partner state. In these cases, and indeed at the WTO, the US approach appears to be a willingness to make some concessions on core media issues such as local content in the established media (TV/radio broadcasting or printed materials) but not on issues classified as electronic commerce, and in particular to seek liberalization of Internet media even without doing so for traditional media (Freedman 2008; Delegation of the United States 2000). The status of "digital products" has caused controversy in successive WTO rounds (Puppis 2008), and it is likely that the ongoing development of non-linear forms of media and new web-based services mean that this debate will continue. These events have demonstrated the ways in which distinctions between different forms of communication are used by states to pursue policy goals, but where does the right to communicate sit within discourses of trade and new technologies? The answer, it seems, lies in new institutional and legal developments, which we now discuss.

## *Internet governance*

UNESCO continues to play a role in the debate on communication rights and shows great interest in the communicative capabilities of new technologies. As discussed above, it was a major actor in the debate on the development of a NWICO, as well as regarding direct broadcasting by satellite. With regard to the "information society," however, it is clear that UNESCO does not occupy the field alone. Another UN body—the ITU—wishes to play a major role in Internet governance, and has taken many steps in this direction, including taking a key role in discussion of domain name regulation in the late 1990s (Mueller 2002). It also passed the initial resolutions that led to the two World Summits on the Information Society (WSIS) in 2003 and 2005, and provided logistical support for both summits. In exploring the current position of the right to communicate, therefore, we must consider both UNESCO and the ITU, as well as new structures like WSIS.

In 1992, Pekka Tarjane, then-Secretary General of the ITU, floated the idea that the Universal Declaration on Human Rights should be amended to recognize a right to communicate (Hamelink 2008). It was not until later in the decade, particularly in the context of the emerging mainstream Internet, that the right to communicate made its fully fledged reappearance in global debate and academic literature. There has been a resurgence in references to a distinctive right to communicate under international law, and the concept has also developed in the light of the experiences of the reaction to NWICO and MacBride, as well as the challenges and opportunities that relate to emerging technologies.

There remains some opposition to the use of communication-based ideas in these debates, not least from organizations like the World Press Freedom Committee (WPFC), discussed above as a critic of NWICO. Others dismiss the case for the right to communicate as a "reincarnation of NWICO," in that it appears to support government regulation of commercial markets for cultural or political reasons (Hackett and Carroll 2006: 81). Supporters of the right to communicate respond that the WPFC is pursuing an argument in favor of private enterprise, but framing it as a defense of journalistic freedom (McIver *et al.* 2003). Nonetheless, it is also argued that the power of the doctrine comes not only from the formulation of specific rights, but also the democratic ideology and ideals that underpin it (Cammaerts and Carpentier 2007). Conscious attempts to "update" the arguments of the 1980s have been made (e.g. Thussu 1998), which in turn influence the contribution of civil society actors to WSIS (Mueller, Kuerbis and Pagé 2007). It is both possible and appropriate to apply the essential elements of the 1970s and 1980s debate on the right to communicate to new media and the Internet. The problems diagnosed in the MacBride report have not been swept away by new technology, and there continue to be imbalances and a need for careful regulation that protects against corporate and/or Western domination (McIver *et al.* 2003). Furthermore, in the later context of "Web 2.0," there is an opportunity to link the participative aspects of contemporary web culture to more general arguments about media democracy and the construction of transformative social movements (Birdsall 2007).

It is therefore possible to express some optimism regarding the use of the right to communicate in the context of the debate on how the Internet should be treated under public international law and intergovernmental processes. However, the changed institutional context cannot be ignored, because UNESCO's move towards individual communication and empowerment (in the second half of the 1980s) could inhibit the development of a NWICO for the digital age (Leye 2009). Nonetheless, the WSIS "brought back to the table" the unresolved business of NWICO, including an opportunity to readdress some of the conflicts within civil society (Raboy 2004: 355), such as those between associations of journalists and communication rights advocates discussed in this chapter.

Civil society organizations, albeit primarily those from the global North, played an important role in articulating a "distinct normative vision about the role of communication in society" at WSIS (Chakravartty 2007: 299). A particularly influential role has been played by the Communication Rights in the Information Society (CRIS) group (Chakravartty 2007; Cammaerts and Carpentier 2007). The group put forward a challenge to the role of the nation-state, but also attempted to frame a rights-based argument. It was a somewhat unexpected opportunity for older discussions on information flows to be presented, although the summit itself turned out to be dominated by discussions of domain name management (ICANN, etc.) and extremely general considerations on for development and the digital divide. Both of these points are important to the communication rights agenda, but were presented from different starting points: a desire for national control regarding the former; and a putative North–South dialog on the latter. Hurley's self-professed "rallying cry" laid out the range of issues that WSIS and other fora were set to discuss, arguing that these disparate developments could be brought together in a World Commission on the Information Society, which would be charged with recommending norms and institutions with human rights as a starting point (Hurley 2003). The use of the right and the building of support for it at these important international fora can serve as a template for further developments. Nonetheless, the outcome has been discursive (such as the Internet Governance Forum that now meets annually), rather than legal. For legal developments, we must return to UNESCO and its work on cultural diversity.

## *Cultural diversity*

UNESCO has indeed succeeded in putting issues of communication on the international legal agenda, through a new instrument: the Convention on the Protection and Promotion of the Diversity of Cultural Expressions (also known as the Convention on Cultural Diversity). This is the closest that international law has ever come to the right to communicate, albeit indirectly and in an incomplete fashion. The early supporters of such a convention were Canada and a number of developing nations, recalling the middle-ground approach to DBS (discussed above). On this occasion, the proposal gained the early support of the European Union, although the United States (which by now had rejoined UNESCO) was an opponent, along with other states including Taiwan, Japan and Chile. The Convention was agreed in October 2005 and has been in force since March 2007, with 121 states parties (and the European Union) as of May 2012. Eighty states have ratified the Convention. Great hopes are placed on it, with the European Commission arguing that it should play the same normative role for cultural diversity as World Intellectional Property Organization (WIPO) conventions and WTO agreements have in their own areas (European Commission 2006).

Many key concerns of communication rights are included within the scope of the Convention. Article 6, on the rights of parties within their own territories, sets out measures that may be adopted in order to protect and promote cultural diversity. Paragraph 2(b) refers to opportunities for the creation, distribution and enjoyment of domestic "cultural activities, goods and services"; paragraph 2(h) refers to media diversity and public service broadcasting. Article 8 builds on this and purports to permit all appropriate measures, consistent with the Convention, where there is a threat that particular cultural expression risks becoming extinct. The paragraphs on development in Articles 14 and 18 refer to some of the issues raised in the report of the MacBride Commission, and can be argued to be a belated recognition of those principles. Also capable of inclusion here is the commitment to facilitating access to developed countries for the cultural work of developing countries, and an International Fund for Cultural Diversity.

However, the key legal provision must surely be Article 20, on the relationship between the Convention and other treaties. The Article clearly is the product of difficult negotiations, with two possibly contradictory impulses reflecting different approaches. Paragraph 1 is a commitment to "mutual supportiveness" between the Convention and other treaties, and a further commitment to take the Convention into account either when interpreting and applying other treaties, or when signing new treaties (with a related undertaking in Article 21 to promote the Convention in international fora). Paragraph 2 of Article 20, however, states that the Convention does not modify rights and obligations under any other treaties. Proposed language that the Convention would prevail over other treaties, and that there would be a role for the International Court of Justice, did not make it into the final version. However, a dispute resolution procedure is established in Article 25 and the Annex. There is an emerging scholarly consensus (Puppis 2008; Choi 2008; Craufurd Smith 2007) that the next steps will depend on whether the WTO, particularly in dispute resolution panels, will take the Convention into account, either through development of the law or a formal amendment to relevant treaties. For now, we note that it introduces rights (other than trade and property) into the resolution of disputes. This may be a reaction to the way in which the principles of trade law have become significant through strong enforcement mechanisms, rather than an avowed, positive statement of the right to communicate, but even a reaction represents a new opportunity to develop international legal principles in relation to communication and culture.

## The future for the right to communicate

Although a direct, enforceable right to communicate remains a goal rather than a provision of human rights law, the development of the rights of freedom of expression and information demonstrate some progress in line with the objectives of supporters. We can see this in particular regarding Article 10 of the European Convention on Human Rights and Article 11 of the European Union Charter of Fundamental Rights, which already mark themselves out in textual terms, through references to receiving and imparting information and, in the case of the latter, the importance of media pluralism. At an international level, UNESCO commissioned a report (as a reflection on the implication of the Internet) on "freedom of connection" (Dutton *et al.* 2011). While not as extensive as its work on NWICO or the right to communicate, this does demonstrate a willingness to expand existing rights in a way that understands the opportunities and limitations of technological development.

The recent report of the UN Special Rapporteur on Freedom of Expression, Frank La Rue, is a remarkable one. In the report, the Internet is noted as supporting "access to information and knowledge that was previously unattainable" through the cross-border exchange of information and ideas. La Rue concludes that international human rights law is "equally applicable to new communication technologies" and that the Internet facilitates the realization of other fundamental rights (La Rue 2011: 7). The Council of Europe has also issued careful recommendations on search engines and social networking sites, recognizing the need to scrutinize private control and to promote communication in a rights-aware environment.

The European Court of Human Rights had already moved in this direction, finding that "in light of its accessibility and its capacity to store and communicate vast amounts of information, the Internet plays an important role in enhancing the public's access to news and facilitating the dissemination of information generally" (*Times Newspapers Ltd.* v *United Kingdom* (2009)). In an earlier case, *Autronic AG* v *Switzerland* (1990), regarding the right to receive information broadcast from foreign nations by satellite, the Court had taken a very generous approach to what constitutes expression, and was prepared to disregard the corporate status of the applicant and its "economic and technical" motives. Subsequently, the Court considered the right of a tenant to install a satellite dish (for the purpose of receiving foreign broadcasts), confirming that state action preventing individuals from receiving transmissions infringed upon the rights protected by Article 10(1) and required justification under Article 10(2).

The Canadian approach of taking a very broad approach to what constitutes expression for the purposes of Article 2(b) of the Charter of Rights and Freedoms (and resolving cases through the proportionality test of Article 1), has provoked a debate on what Anderson calls "liberal" and "constitutive" theories; the latter includes the notion that "it is not necessarily the state, but imbalances in communicative power, perhaps through relative economic or social advantages, that may cause blockages in the expressive relationship" (Anderson 1999: 60). This tracks closely both to the right to communicate and the NWICO, and even echoes (probably not deliberately) the Innisian reading of communications history.

Even in the United States, the promotion of an expansive interpretation of the First Amendment in relation to "access to audiences" in respect of the regulation of ISPs and search engines (Chandler 2007) can be linked with the international developments discussed in this chapter. A distinction has been observed as between "speaking opportunities" and "speech rights," with the Internet well served for the former, but not so obviously for the latter (Stein 2006: 83). The current work of the Special Rapporteur suggests that the difference is beginning to be understood. It is also greeted by scholars of Internet rights as a significant development of relevance to US users and regulators (e.g. MacKinnon 2011).

## Conclusion

As much of the information on the Internet emerges from a context free of the elaborate structures and editorial controls of traditional media, one could be forgiven for assuming that rights-based arguments, formulated at a time of more restricted access to the media, no longer have much relevance. It is certainly a positive feature of online communication that individuals and audiences can choose from a very wide range of sources (Balkin 2009), and that the non-corporate, non-professional individual can participate in the production of content through less expensive technologies of production.

Even if this rosy picture is accurate, Innis's warnings about "new monopolies" (Innis 1950; Innis 1951b) are echoed in reviews of the various practices of intermediaries and hosts in new media (York 2010; Laidlaw 2010; Mac Síthigh 2008). As such, while the *specific* remedies put forward and sometimes adopted in past decades may no longer be appropriate or necessary, the fundamental *premises* underlying the critique of media power and calls for a NWICO remain relevant. Indeed, given the persistence of possible chokepoints of control on the Internet (and elsewhere in electronic media), attention is essential. The default "law" of new media to date has been influenced by the location of the early Internet systems in the United States and the approach taken by its government, influenced by the First Amendment and a generally non-directive approach to the control of key infrastructure. However, the right to communicate requires an understanding that media regulation goes beyond the context of mere freedom from government control.

International media law in the twenty-first century is not simply a footnote to the Internet and the First Amendment. An internationally derived alternative would therefore be of particular assistance, especially if it could draw in concepts of the protection of culture and the promotion of non-commercial expression. In that context, the time may have come for the right to communicate, informed by the earlier work of the Toronto School and the MacBride Commission, and to some extent the subaltern "access" and "common carrier" discourses in US law, to play a role in the development of global media governance.

## References

Anawalt, H. (1983) 'The right to communicate,' *Denver Journal of International Law & Policy*, 13: 219–236.

Anderson, G. (1999) 'Understanding constitutional speech: Two theories of expression,' in G. Anderson (ed.) *Rights and Democracy: Essays in UK–Canadian Constitutionalism*, London: Blackstone.

*Appleby* v *UK* (2003) Application no. 44306/98, ECtHR.

*Associated Press* v *United States* 326 US 1 (1945).

*Autronic AG* v *Switzerland* (1990) Application no. 12726/87, ECtHR.

Babe, R. (2000) *Canadian Communication Thought: Ten Foundational Writers*, Toronto: University of Toronto Press.

—— (2009) *Cultural Studies and Political Economy*, Lanham, MD: Lexington.

Balkin, J. (2009) 'The future of free expression in a digital age,' *Pepperdine Law Review*, 36(12): 427–444.

Barron, J. (1967) 'Access to the press: A new First Amendment right,' *Harvard Law Review*, 80: 1641–1678.

—— (1969) 'An emerging First Amendment right of access to the media,' *George Washington Law Review*, 37: 487–509.

Benjamin, L. (2006) *Freedom of the Air and the Public Interest: First Amendment Rights in Broadcasting to 1935*, Carbondale, IL: Southern Illinois University Press.

Birdsall, W. (2007) 'Web 2.0 as a social movement,' *Webology*, 4. Online. Available HTTP: http://www.webology.org/2007/v4n2/a40.html (accessed 30 March 2012).

——, McIver, W. and Rasmussen, M. (2003) 'Translating a right to communicate into policy,' Online. Available HTTP: http://centreforcommunicationrights.org/component/content/article/36-debate/90.html?layout=citation (accessed 30 March 2012).

Calabrese, A. and Briziarelli, M. (2011) 'Policy imperialism: Bilateral trade agreements as instruments of media governance,' in R. Mansell and M. Raboy (eds.) *Handbook of Global Media and Communication Policy*, London: Blackwell.

Cammaerts, B. and Carpentier, N. (eds.) (2007) *Reclaiming the Media: Communication Rights and Democratic Media Roles*, Bristol: Intellect.

Carey, J. (1989) *Communication as Culture: Essays on Media and Society*, Boston, MA: Unwin Hyman.

Chakravartty, P. (2007) 'Governance without politics: Civil society, development and the postcolonial state,' *International Journal of Communication*, 1: 297–317.

Chalaby, J. (2000) 'New media, new freedoms, new threats,' *International Communication Gazette*, 62(1): 19–29.

Chandler, J. (2007) 'A right to reach an audience: An approach to intermediary bias on the Internet,' *Hofstra Law Review*, 35: 1095–1137.

Choi, B. (2008) 'Trade barriers or cultural diversity? The audiovisual sector on fire,' in W. Drake and E. Wilson (eds.) *Governing Global Electronic Networks*, Cambridge, MA: MIT Press.

Cooper, M. (2005) 'Reclaiming the First Amendment,' in R. McChesney, R. Newman and B. Scott (eds.) *The Future of Media*, New York: Seven Stories.

Council of Europe (2011) *Internet: Case-Law of the European Court of Human Rights*. Online. Available HTTP: http://www.echr.coe.int/NR/rdonlyres/E3B11782-7E42-418B-AC04-A29BEDC0400F/0/RAPPORT_RECHERCHE_Internet_Freedom_Expression_EN.pdf (accessed 30 March 2012).

Craufurd Smith, R. (2007) 'The UNESCO Convention on the Protection and Promotion of the Diversity of Cultural Expressions: Building a New World Information and Communication Order?' *International Journal of Communication*, 1: 24–55.

Curran, J. (2010) 'Media reform: Democratic choices,' in J. Curran and J. Seaton (eds.) *Power Without Responsibility: Press, Broadcasting and the Internet in Britain*, 7th edn., London: Routledge.

Czitrom, D. (1982) *Media and the American Mind: From Morse to McLuhan*, Chapel Hill, NC: University of North Carolina Press.

Dakroury, A. (2008) 'Present at the Creation: The Telecommission Studies and the Intellectual Origins of the Right to Communicate in Canada,' Ph.D. thesis, Carleton University.

de Kerckhove, D. (1989) 'McLuhan and the "Toronto School of Communication",' *Canadian Journal of Communication*, 14(4): 73–79.

Delegation of the United States (2000) *Communication from the United States: Audiovisual and Related Services*. Online Available HTTP: http://www.jmcti.org/2000round/build-in-agenda/service/S_CSS_W_021.pdf (accessed 30 March 2012).

Department of Communications (1971) *Instant World: A Report on Telecommunications in Canada*, Ottawa, ON: Information Canada.

Driessen, B. (1999) 'The Slovak state language law as a trade law problem,' in M. Kontra (ed.) *Language: A Right and a Resource*, Budapest: CEU Press.

Dutt, S. (1995) *The Politicization of the United Nations Specialized Agencies: A Case Study of UNESCO*, Lewiston, NY: Mellon.

Dutton, W., Dopatka, A., Hills, M., Law, G. and Nash, V. (2011) *Freedom of Connection: Freedom of Expression*, Paris: UNESCO.

European Commission (2006) *UNESCO Convention on Cultural Diversity: A New Instrument of International Governance*. Online. Available HTTP: http://europa.eu/rapid/pressReleasesAction.do?reference=MEMO/06/500 (accessed 30 March 2012).

—— (n.d.) *The General Agreement on Trade in Services (GATS) and the Doha Development Agenda*. Online. Available HTTP: http://ec.europa.eu/avpolicy/ext/multilateral/gats/index_en.htm (accessed 30 March 2012).

*FCC* v *Midwest Video Corp*. 440 US 689 (1979).

Feintuck, M. and Varney, M. (2006) *Media Regulation, Public Interest and the Law*, 2nd edn., Edinburgh: Edinburgh University Press.

Fisher, D. and Harms, L. S. (1982) *The Right to Communicate: A New Human Right*, Dublin: Boole.

Fiss, O. (1998) *The Irony of Free Speech*, Harvard: Harvard University Press.

Freedman, D. (2008) *The Politics of Media Policy*, London: Polity.

Grant, P. and Wood, C. (2004) *Blockbusters and Trade Wars: Popular Culture in a Globalized World*, Vancouver, BC: Douglas & McIntyre.

Hackett, B. and Carroll, B. (2006) *Remaking Media: The Struggle to Democratize Public Communication*, London: Routledge.

Hamelink, C. (2008) 'The global governance of mass media content,' in W. Drake and E. Wilson (eds.) *Governing Global Electronic Networks*, Cambridge, MA: MIT Press.

Hanjal, P. (1983) *Guide to UNESCO*, London: Oceana.

Herman, E. (1989) 'US mass media coverage of the US withdrawal from UNESCO,' in W. Preston, E. Herman and H. Schiller (eds.) *Hope and Folly: The US and UNESCO, 1945-1985*, Minneapolis, MN: University of Minnesota Press.

Hicks, D. (2007) 'The right to communicate: Past mistakes and future possibilities,' *Dalhousie Journal of Information & Management*. Online. Available HTTP: http://ocs.library.dal.ca/ojs/index.php/djim/article/viewArticle/25 (accessed 30 March 2012).

Hurley, D. (2003) 'Pole star: Human rights in the information society.' Online. Available HTTP: http://www.ichrdd.ca/english/commdoc/publications/globalization/wsis/PoleStar-Eng.html (accessed 30 March 2012).

Innis, H. (1950) *Empire and Communications*, Oxford: Clarendon.

—— (1951a) *The Bias of Communication*, Toronto, ON: University of Toronto Press.

—— (1951b) 'The concept of monopoly and civilization,' reprinted in D. Drache (ed.) (1995) *Staples, Markets and Cultural Change*, Montreal, QC: McGill-Queen's University Press.

Jeffrey, L. (1999) 'The impact of technological change on Canada's affirmative policy model in the cultural industry and new media sectors,' *Canada–United States Law Journal*, 25: 379–388.

La Rue, F. (2011) *Report of the Special Rapporteur on the Promotion and Protection of the Right to Freedom of Opinion and Expression*,' A/HRC/17/27. Online. Available HTTP: http://www2.ohchr.org/english/bodies/hrcouncil/docs/17session/A.HRC.17.27_en.pdf (accessed 30 March 2012).

Laidlaw, E. (2010) 'A framework for identifying Internet information gatekeepers,' *International Review of Law, Computers & Technology*, 24(3): 263–280.

Layard, A. (2010) 'Shopping in the public realm: The law of place,' *Journal of Law & Society*, 37(3): 412–441.

Leye, V. (2009) 'UNESCO's communication policies as discourse,' *Media, Culture & Society*, 31(6): 939–956.

Mac Síthigh, D. (2008) 'The mass age of Internet law,' *Information & Communications Technology Law*, 17(2): 79–94.

—— (2012) 'Virtual walls: The law of pseudo-public spaces,' *International Journal of Law in Context*, 8(3): 394–412.

MacBride Commission (1980) *Many Voices, One World*, London: Kogan/UNESCO.

Mansell, R. and Nordenstreng, K. (2007) 'Great media and communication debates: WSIS and the MacBride report,' *Information Technology and International Development*, 3(4): 15–36.

Marsden, C. (2010) *Net Neutrality: Towards a Co-regulatory Solution*, London: Bloomsbury.

McIver, W., Birdsall, W. and Rasmussen, M. (2003) 'The Internet and the right to communicate,' *First Monday*, 8. Online. Available HTTP: http://firstmonday.org/htbin/cgiwrap/bin/ojs/index.php/fm/article/view/1102/1022 (accessed 30 March 2012).

Meyrowitz, J. (1985) *No Sense of Place*, Oxford: Oxford University Press.

*Miami Herald* v *Tornillo* 418 US 241 (1974).

Morris, N. and Waisbord, S. (2001) *Media and Globalization: Why the State Matters*, Lanham, MD: Rowman & Littlefield.

Mueller, M. (2002) *Ruling the Root: Internet Governance and the Taming of Cyberspace*, Cambridge, MA: MIT Press.

——, Kuerbis, B. and Pagé, C. (2007) 'Democratizing global communication? Global civil society and the campaign for communication rights in the information society,' *International Journal of Communication*, 1: 267–296.

Napoli, P. and Sybblis, S. (2007) 'Access to audiences as a First Amendment right: Its relevance and implications for electronic media policy,' *Virginia Journal of Law and Technology*, 12(1): 1–31.

Nunziato, D. (2009) *Virtual Freedom: Net Neutrality and Free Speech in the Internet Age*, Palo Alto, CA: Stanford University Press.

O'Dell, E. (2007) 'Couriers, communications and the Constitution,' Conference paper, *The Constitution at 70*, Trinity College Dublin, May.

Ó Siochrú, S. and Girard, B. (2002) *Global Media Governance*, Lanham, MD: Rowman & Littlefield.

*Paperlink* v *Attorney General* [1984] ILRM 373.

Preston, W., Herman, E. and Schiller, H. (eds.) (1989) *Hope and Folly: the US and UNESCO, 1945–1985*, Minneapolis, MN: University of Minnesota Press.

Puppis, M. (2008) 'National media regulation in the era of free trade,' *European Journal of Communication*, 23(4): 405–424.

Raboy, M. (2004) 'The WSIS as a political space in global media governance,' *Continuum: Journal of Media and Cultural Studies*, 18(3): 347–361.

—— and Shtern, J. (2010) 'Introduction,' in M. Raboy and J. Shtern, *Media Divides: Communication Rights and the Right to Communicate in Canada*, Vancouver, BC: University of British Columbia Press.

Schiller, H. (1989) 'Is there a United States information policy?' in W. Preston, E. Herman and H. Schiller (eds.) *Hope and Folly: The US and UNESCO, 1945–1985*, Minneapolis, MN: University of Minnesota Press.

Schmidt, B. (1976) *Freedom of the Press* v *Public Access*, New York: Praeger.

Singh, S. (1988) *The Rise and Fall of UNESCO*, Ahmedabad: Allied.

Sluijs, J. (2011) 'From competition to freedom of expression: Introducing Article 10 ECHR in the European network neutrality debate,' TILEC Discussion Paper 2011-40. Online. Available HTTP: http://ssrn.com/abstract=1927814 (accessed 30 March 2012).

Stein, L. (2006) *Speech Rights in America: The First Amendment, Democracy, and the Media*, Chicago, IL: University of Chicago Press.

Sunstein, C. (1993) *Democracy and the Problem of Free Speech*, New York: Free Press.

Tambini, D., Leonardi, D. and Marsden, C. (eds.) (2007) *Codifying Cyberspace: Communications Self-Regulation in the Age of Internet Convergence*, London: Routledge.

Thompson, E. (1982) 'Technological overview of current issues in the communications and information society,' in Canadian Council on International Law (ed.) *Communication and Information: International Legal Aspects*, Ottawa, ON: CCIL.

Thussu, D. (1998) 'Introduction,' in D. Thussu (ed.) *Electronic Empires: Global Media and Local Resistance*, New York: Hampton Press.

*Times Newspaper Ltd.* v *United Kingdom* (2009) Application nos. 3002/03 and 23676/03, ECtHR.

*Timpul Info-Magazin* v *Moldova* (2007) Application no. 42864/05, ECtHR.

Touré, H. (2008) 'Sharing finite resources,' *ITU News*. Online. Available HTTP: http://www.itu.int/itunews/manager/display.asp?lang=en&year=2007&issue=08&ipage=editorial&ext=html (accessed 30 March 2012).

UNESCO (1972) *Declaration of Guiding Principles on the Use of Satellite Broadcasting for the Free Flow of Information, the Spread of Education and Greater Cultural Exchange*. Online. Available HTTP: http://unesdoc.unesco.org/images/0000/000021/002136eb.pdf (accessed 30 March 2012).

Watson, R. and Blondheim, M. (eds.) (2007) *The Toronto School of Communication Theory: Interpretations, Extensions, Applications*, Jerusalem: Hebrew University Press.

World Press Freedom Committee (1981) *Declaration of Talloires*. Online. Available HTTP: http://www.wpfc.org/DeclarationofTalloires.html (accessed 30 March 2012).

Wunsch-Vincent, S. (2003) 'The digital trade agenda of the US: Parallel tracks of bilateral, regional and multilateral liberalization,' *Aussenwirtschaft: Swiss Review of International Economic Relations*, 58(1): 7–46.

York, J. 'Policing content in the quasi-public sphere,' *OpenNet Initiative*. Online. Available HTTP: http://opennet.net/sites/opennet.net/files/PolicingContent.pdf (accessed 30 March 2012).

# 11

# Public service media narratives

*Ellen P. Goodman*

The emergence of public service media in the mid-twentieth century on both sides of the Atlantic was a response to particular technological realities and market structures. Public media systems manifested theories about the function of media in a democracy, the sources of cultural authority and innovation, the limitations of the market, and the values of social cohesion and inclusion.

In the early twenty-first century, the underlying theories and justifications for public service media are now in flux. Those who defend continued public funding of legacy and new non-commercial media services, and work to reform their operations, have struggled to untangle the contingencies of twentieth-century organizational structures from the enduring values that spawned their creation. In other words, policymakers and commentators have recognized that legacy public broadcasting systems must be updated for a post-broadcasting world, or wither away. But the values and purposes of a new, multi-platform, multi-actor public media system are not yet clearly articulated.

Controversy over the function of US public media demonstrates distinct, and sometimes competing, narratives of the role of public media in a digital, social and data-soaked information environment. The US public media experience is in some ways *sui generis*, and certainly different from the experience of correlate systems in Europe. Whereas the British Broadcasting Corporation (BBC), for example, has dominated British broadcasting, American public media networks National Public Radio (NPR) and Public Broadcasting Service (PBS) have had relatively small audience shares. Whereas European public broadcasters pre-dated commercial broadcast media, American public media entities were interventions in well-established commercial markets.

It may very well be the outlier status of American public media institutions, however, that makes their experience particularly relevant to those seeking new modes of public media service. The American model of public broadcasting—and the narratives that shaped it—in some ways map well onto the demands of a digital age. This model includes diverse funding sources, distributed ownership and citizen engagement. And it is grounded in narratives of community service, innovation and democratic participation, as well as in those of market failure and canonical excellence.

This chapter will begin by identifying the narratives that shaped the twentieth-century public media systems in the United States and discussing the contemporary challenges to those narratives. It will then argue that a new narrative of *innovation* captures central public media traditions and evolving aspirations for the twenty-first century.

## Principal narratives for public service media

It must be stated at the outset that, at a general level, most public service media narratives can be framed as a response to market failure. At least this is true wherever a neoliberal market discourse holds sway, as it does in the United States. We start with the basic and generally accepted view that public and other forms of non-market support may be necessary to supplement the market's production and distribution of media content. That public media manifest a response to market failure has long been the dominant justification for these services in the United States (Carnegie Commission 1979; Hoynes 1994; Goodman 2004; Balas 2003). The power of this idea spread and in recent years has become important in the UK as well, crowding out other justifications for public service media (Barnett 2004; Collins 2004; Ofcom 2008; Ofcom 1999).

The market failure argument was quite simple in the early days of broadcasting. At the time of the establishment of United States and other public media systems, it was assumed, and in fact observed, that commercial media were not interested in producing the kinds of programming that fueled democratic discourse; nor were they interested in engaging consumers with matters of citizenship. Over time, theorists such as C. Edwin Baker (2006; 2002) used basic economic principles to identify the market mechanisms that motivated commercial media entities to produce what they did, and why it was folly to expect them to provide all of the media that informed citizenship requires.

In brief, the argument goes like this: consumers lack the incentive to demand, and commercial media producers lack the incentives to produce, the optimal amounts of socially valuable news, information and content (Institute for Policy Integrity 2010). It is a general tenet of economics that individual willingness to pay for a product will typically fail to reflect the spillover value of that product to society (Frischmann and Lemley 2007; Yoo 2007). The spillover value that public interest media produce includes a better informed and educated public, more accountable government and business sectors, more robust cultural and artistic production, more social cohesion and more innovation in the informational sphere. This mismatch between market production and public needs leads to an underproduction of content that is valuable for democratic and civic thriving (Ofcom 2008; van Dijk, Nahius and Waagmeester 2006; Hargreaves Heap 2005).[1]

The promotion of spillover value is a classic justification for government investment generally. This is certainly true for public subsidies for basic research in the sciences. Public service media is the equivalent in the informational sphere (along with arts and cultural grants programs). Indeed, public media advocates have invoked "public good" economics language in this context. *Atlantic* editor Derek Thompson writes that "news isn't like flowers or sausages." Because it is a public good, the government "can and should close the gap between the individual value and the social value" of news by funding public media's in-depth news reporting (Thompson 2011).

Digital networks started to challenge the market failure justifications for public media in the first decade of the twenty-first century. It seemed that innumerable media options on digital platforms would cater to every niche interest and satisfy every informational need. It

1 For a more thorough discussion of economic rationales behind public broadcasting, see Goodman and Chen 2010.

became harder to see where the information gaps were, and harder to question the ability of both commercial and new amateur mass media activity to produce optimal value. Theorists responded by refining the market failure narrative for public service media. In particular, they identified more precisely the areas in which commercial and amateur media were likely to fall short in their production, focusing especially on high-cost journalism and high-cost niche content (Goodman 2004; van Dijk, Nahuis and Waagmeester 2006; Hargreaves Heap 2005).

These articulations of the public good value of certain forms of media content and service also advert to a more transcendent contribution of public service media. This contribution has been described in terms of the motivation and intention of public service media practitioners. In other words, the most important distinction between public and commercial media content lies not in genre, format, production value, inclusiveness, or in any other objective parameter. It is a distinction of motive. Public media practitioners, it is said, are committed to addressing audiences as citizens rather than as consumers. This commitment infuses every choice through the production and distribution of every work (PBS 2012; Clark and Schardt 2010; Jakubowicz 2007 and 2008; Ofcom 2008).

Attempts to articulate this mission orientation of public media abound. For example, the opening paragraph of the 1970 founding mission statement for NPR states that the network:

> . . . will promote personal growth; it will regard the individual differences among men with respect and joy rather than derision and hate; it will celebrate the human experience as infinitely varied rather than vacuous and banal; it will encourage a sense of active constructive participation, rather than apathetic helplessness.
>
> (*Richter 2006: 107*)

Remarking on the founding ideology of the Public Broadcasting Act of 1967, a commentator observes that the market to be addressed was "characterized not as a market of consumers, to be captured for profit, but rather as a public of citizens, to be 'served' " (Stavitsky 1993: 11).

To say that market failure is the principal narrative for public service media is too true and broad to be of much use. The question is what particular kinds of market failures have been most significant in the development of public media narratives and activities and how the responses have been framed. This chapter focuses on three distinct kinds of informational functions that US public media entities have served, noting similarities in Europe. These functions are the promotion of democratic discourse, the delivery of universal service, and educational and cultural elevation.

## Democratic discourse

Public media supporters hail the ability of these services to promote citizen competency to participate in democratic discourse. Perhaps the most graphic representation of this idea is Jürgen Habermas' notion of the "public sphere"—an idealized space in which citizens are able to participate critically in the formation of public opinion. Although published decades after the formation of the US public broadcasting system, Habermas' *The Structural Transformation of the Public Sphere* (1989) has provided a useful vocabulary to talk about the democratic goals that have long animated American and other public media systems (Goodman 2004; Engelman 1996).[2]

2 For a more in-depth discussion of theoretical rationales underlying public broadcasting, see Goodman 2004.

Habermas (1989) posited that democracies require a public sphere in which people can communicate on equal footing and engage in rational dialog about matters of shared importance (Boggs 1997; Bohman 1996). The public sphere exists as an aspirational space outside of the state and the market in which individuals engage, either directly or through mediators, in "communicative action." This is a pure form of communication resulting from dialogic exchanges among people with no motive to manipulate for the sake of profit or other ends. While all forms of media can contribute to the public sphere, Habermas posited that commercial media threatened the "colonization of the public sphere by market imperatives" (Habermas 2006: 422). The "intrusion of the functional imperatives of the market economy into the 'internal logic' of the production and presentation of messages" means that the commercial media cannot always be trusted to support the ideal public sphere (Habermas 2006: 422).

Theorists on both sides of the Atlantic have argued that public media entities are freer and more inclined to foster communicative action than their commercial counterparts. They have credited public broadcasting institutions with creating mediated public spheres for the formation of rational opinion (Ramsey 2010; Splichal 2006; Balas 2003; Curran 1991; Scannell 1989; Garnham 1986). James Curran has mapped public media goals onto Habermas' theory of communication. There is a good fit, he says, between what the BBC does and the conception of the public sphere "with its ideology of disinterested professionalism, its careful balancing of opposed points of view and umpired studio discussions" (Curran 1991: 42). Nicholas Garnham argues that public service broadcasting creates a public sphere because "it (a) presupposes and then tries to develop in its practice a set of social relations which are distinctly political rather than economic, and (b) at the same time attempts to insulate itself from control by the state" (Garnham 1986: 49).

Those who designed the US public broadcasting system deployed language very much in keeping with this narrative of democratic discourse. Indeed, the system arose out of calls for the reinvigoration of democracy at a time when "democracy was perceived to be breaking down, partly due to commercial television" (Ouellette 1999: 66). In 1961, Federal Communications Commission (FCC) Chairman Newton Minow gave what would become a very famous speech excoriating commercial media for becoming a "vast wasteland" that failed to serve up the kind of programming citizens required (Minow 1961). There was growing concern that existing public interest standards failed to optimize the democratic, cultural and educational value of broadcasting (Varona 2009).

Congressman Samuel N. Friedel, who introduced the 1967 Public Broadcasting Act, hoped that public broadcasting could remedy this democratic deficit. He asserted that "a successful democracy depends on enlightened and well-informed citizens," and that "public television can contribute to this end" (Friedel 1967: 108). The Act built on the vision of the foundational Carnegie Commission Report for a public television system that could host "debate and controversy" and "provide a voice for groups in the community that may otherwise be unheard" (Carnegie Commission 1967: 92).

Around the world, advocates for public service media continue to use the democratic narrative—one specifically rooted in notions of deliberative discourse—to build a case for continued support. Starting in the 1990s, public service media organizations felt the pressure to articulate their objectives. In doing so, they returned again and again to the goal of improving democratic accountability (McQuail 1992).

The BBC, for example, stresses its role in "sustaining citizenship and civil society" by engaging a wide audience, encouraging conversation and debate about current affairs, and building a greater understanding of political processes and institutions governing the UK (BBC 2012). As the BBC chief operating officer recently stated, "Our first and most important public purpose is our civic purpose, our role in supporting a democracy" (Thomson 2010). Implicitly, the BBC links the fostering of democratic discourse to the provision of programming that is accurate and impartial. Studies show that the qualities the BBC values are the very same ones that audiences say they value, with nearly 90 percent of the BBC audience averring that impartiality "should always be at the heart of what the BBC stands for" (BBC 2011b: 3) and 70 percent saying they value BBC programs because they "help me understand what's going on in the world" (Ofcom 2011: 3). The BBC has emphasized the informational quality of its content as one reason why, although it produces only 27 percent of total television news hours in Britain, it attracts up to 72 percent of total viewing (BBC 2011a; Ofcom 2011; Thomson 2010).

In the United States, in the face of repeated efforts to ax funding for public broadcasting, advocates have also stressed the role of public media in supporting citizen needs. These advocates are less likely to use the terms "impartial" and "accurate" than they are to focus on subject matter and tone. This emphasis draws directly on the transcendent mission orientation of public media discussed above. Public media outlets, their defenders claim, focus sustained attention on issues of importance to democratic governance and offer a forum for reasoned debate in a media environment characterized by hyperbole and ideological polarization.

The Corporation for Public Broadcasting (CPB), for example, recently affirmed that its first objective is to "promote an educated and informed civil society" by making available information citizens need to be "active, participating members of our democratic society" (CPB 2012). CPB has also emphasized the citizenship-building function of local public stations that strengthen civil society through their local service (Harrison 2011). PBS uses similar language, calling its services "uniquely different from commercial broadcasting" because they "treat audiences as citizens, not simply consumers" (PBS 2012: 2).

Others have emphasized the willingness of public media entities to invest in newsgathering in the face of secular declines. Several influential reports on the decline of US journalism at the end of the first decade of the twenty-first century looked to public broadcasters to plug the information holes left by closing newspapers (Federal Communications Commission 2010; Downie, Jr. and Schudson 2009; Knight Commission 2009).[3] A resurgent public media sector, they thought, could provide the sort of accountability reporting and reasoned discourse that was being squeezed out of commercial media.

The notion that public media systems can foster democratic discourse is not always rooted in a well-defined or thoroughly articulated conception of democracy. Most of the invocations of democratic discourse focus on public media as suppliers of content that is informative and balanced.[4] Public media entities can be counted on to provide the accountability journalism and other kinds of high-quality content necessary to support informed democratic participation (Clark and Aufderheide 2010). The BBC's editorial stance, for example, is characterized by its seriousness and impartiality. It prides itself on giving a "full ventilation of the facts" and being "tough and rigorous, testing each side of [a] debate" (BBC 1996: 53, as cited in Debrett 2010: 34). This conception of "discourse," at least when it comes

3 For additional sources calling for public media to step into the information gap in journalism, see Goodman and Chen 2010.

4 Section 396(g)(1)(A) of the Communications Act of 1934, for example, authorizes public broadcasters to develop programs "with strict adherence to objectivity and balance in all programs or series of programs of a controversial nature" (47 USC § 396(g)(1)(A) (1934)).

to the media's role, is fairly top-down. Public media supplies content, which then feeds public discourse. It does not itself convene the public in conversation.

There are other ways in which to conceive of the role of media in supporting democratic discourse. C. Edwin Baker (1998) placed Habermas' theory of the public sphere along a spectrum of theories about the media's role in a democracy. Baker called Habermas' theory a species of "complex democracy" theory. It is one that idealizes the power of democratic discourse to cultivate common public interests through the hashing out of competing interests. To perform this function, the public sphere would have to expose differences while also fostering recognition of commonalities. As many scholars have noted, such mediated spaces are disfavored by market forces, since these forces reward conflict, customization and self-referential echo chambers (Pariser 2011; Sunstein 2010). Thus, advocates of the public sphere usually see a role for non-commercial media.

Whatever specific theory of democracy one brings to the analysis, it seems fairly clear that, for true discourse to take place, the public sphere must be a space that actually engages citizens in the conversations that it hosts. The aspiration that public media would foster engagement and debate is part of the democratic discourse story. But it is a very different vision from the top-down, dispassionate delivery of news and information to a waiting public. This different vision casts the public media entity as a forum for, and fomenter of, democratic engagement. The media entities that create the spaces also have to be active agents of citizen involvement. This is the vision of public media set out in *Public Media 2.0* (Clark and Aufderheide 2009). It is a narrative that emphasizes in particular the role of public media in providing voice to the underrepresented and bringing that voice into the mainstream. It calls on public service media to be active in developing and amplifying distinct voices in the community.

This populist and participatory strand in the democratic discourse narrative is evident in the founding documents of the American system. The Public Broadcasting Act of 1967 states that "public television and radio stations and public telecommunications services constitute *valuable local community resources for . . . solv[ing] local problems through community programs and outreach programs*" (47 USC § 396(a)(8) 2001; emphasis added). Another goal was to create "public telecommunications services which will be responsive to the interests of people both in particular localities and throughout the United States, . . . and which will constitute a source of alternative telecommunications services for all the citizens" (47 USC § 396(a)(5) 2001). Indeed, the aspiration for a public media system that represents diverse interests and voices, in addition to one that provides high-quality content, is embedded in the structure of US public broadcasting. There are currently more than 350 public television stations and 820 radio stations that are financed by and accountable to their local communities (PBS 2011; NPR 2012).

At the same time, the participatory-focused argument for public service media draws on traditions that have often been at odds with the elite national public broadcasting brands of PBS and NPR in the United States, and the BBC in the UK. Indeed, this argument resonates more powerfully with the community media movements that have supported low-power radio, cable access channels and other forms of populist media (Breitbart *et al.* 2011; Waldman *et al.* 2011). The concept of "engagement," at least in twentieth-century public media entities, was not necessarily harmonious with the ideals of objective journalism and high production values.

One of the most engaged, community-focused forms of journalism came out of the public journalism movement of the 1980s and 1990s, which sought public participation in solving community problems (Rosen 1996). This movement encouraged journalistic practices that privileged community engagement over objectivity, impartiality and journalistic distance. The hope was that citizen journalists and professional journalists together could tackle problems such as environmental degradation or public corruption. Journalistic engagement with the community was not a departure from objectivity, but an acknowledgement of the longstanding claim that journalistic objectivity is impossible (Gans 1980; Breed 1955).

The digital age has broken down the clear distinction between elite, top-down information delivery and bottom-up engagement around information. Professional journalists and other media producers now routinely rely on crowd-sourcing and citizen journalism, and seek to maximize public engagement through social media (Jarvis 2011; Shirky 2008; Nisenholtz 2008; Gillmor 2004). The move to incorporate new voices into even the most elite public media productions is also pronounced. For example, American Public Media founded the Public Insight Network, which has developed a network of more than 150,000 citizen experts for reporting purposes (http://www.publicinsightnetwork.org). Many US public broadcasting stations are staking their futures on models of engagement much more rooted in community, local content, and traditions of community and public journalism (Station Resource Group 2011; Clark and Schardt 2010; Jakubowicz 2008).

The movement of public media institutions into a more dynamic relationship with the publics they serve raises questions about what exactly these institutions have to contribute to the welter of information. Many and varied institutions are involved in community media and civic engagement. Many and varied voices are participating in information exchanges through digital and social networks. What seems to be emerging is a role for public media institutions in curating information—that is, providing a platform, amplification, or context for information or voices as trusted intermediaries. This role is in addition to, and sometimes integrated with, the traditional role of providing high-quality content.

To oversimplify, the job of public media in supporting an analog public sphere was to produce certain kinds of democracy-enhancing content and to bring new voices and publics into the mix. In the digital public sphere, these tasks continue, even if on a smaller scale. This distinction between market and public media actors—centered as it is on mission and motive—is impervious to technological change. But added to this task of content production is something more amorphous: creating connective tissue among voices, contextualizing them and generally helping the public to make meaning from information that public media institutions do not themselves generate.

## Universal service

"Universal service" is a term usually associated with the build-out of telecommunications to rural and impoverished areas, rather than with public media (Nuechterlein and Weiser 2005). The discourse on universal service has, until recently, centered on telecommunications infrastructure and the challenge of providing basic telephone connectivity to rural areas. In the past several years, the focus has shifted to broadband infrastructure in recognition of the reality that basic connectivity entails access to the high bandwidth services that drive our digital lives (Goodman and Chen 2010; Federal Communications Commission 2011).

In a sense, public service media infrastructure was the original broadband public infrastructure, providing high bandwidth service to all. Public broadcasting in the United States was intentionally structured to further universal service goals—a broadcast signal transmitting out of every sizable community and controlled by locals. The system of American public broadcasting was built on top of a distributed network of radio and television stations often affiliated with state universities and other local institutions. One of the goals of the public broadcasting system was to interconnect these distributed stations so that they could take advantage of national economies of scale, while still maintaining locally controlled telecommunications infrastructure (Waldman *et al.* 2011; Rowland 2002; Somerset-Ward 1993; Avery 1979; Burk 1979).

Naturally, given the prevalence of commercial media in the larger metropolitan areas, the existence of local public media was especially important in rural markets unprofitably served by commercial media. Thus public media policy has shared in the more general telecommunications policy support for programs to provide service to underserved (usually rural) areas. As a wide array of public media, media advocacy and governmental organizations point out, US federal funding of public media helps to support rural stations whose communities rely on them for access to news and public safety information (Current Public Media Blog 2011; NPR 2011; Dawidziak 2011; Tady 2011; APTS 2011a, 2011b; Healey 2011; Office of Management and Budget 2011). In these less populated areas, especially where broadband service is spotty, public broadcasting is often the only source of free local, national and international news, public affairs, and cultural programming (170 Million Americans n.d.c; Minow 2011).[5] Public funding is more critical to these rural public stations than it is to urban stations with larger memberships. Indeed, public broadcasters call federal government funding in these rural areas the "lifeblood" for their services (Walker and Sallee 2011).

As is evident from the discussion above, the universal service narrative for public media deals not only with the distribution of communications, but also with its content. In this context, universal service is more frequently framed as a "diversity interest." The Carnegie Commission Report called for an American public broadcasting system that would give voice to the marginalized (Engelman 1996). Public television programming had the potential, the report stated, to "deepen a sense of community in local life," to "be a forum for debate and controversy," and to "provide a voice for groups in the community that may otherwise be unheard" (Carnegie Commission 1967: 92). Similarly, in the UK, one of the aspirations for public media is that it will "[represent] diversity and alternative viewpoints," to increase awareness of different cultures and outlooks (Ofcom 2011: 4).

In the 2011 battle to save public media funding in the United States, journalist Farai Chideya and National Black Programming Consortium board member Eric Easter emphasized the role of public media in hosting minority and independent voices, thereby empowering diverse audiences. Chideya (2011) argued that what is at stake in the battle for public media is "our own access to information and community." The threatened loss of funding, Easter (2011) said, would hit "the people on the ground—minority and independent filmmakers and digital storytellers for whom public grants are often their sole source of funding," adding that "public media could be Black America's most promising frontier for distribution of serious, non-commercial content—the kind we say we want but never seem to get."

5 As former FCC, PBS and Carnegie Foundation Chairman Newton N. Minow put it: "[I]n many communities [public radio and television] are essential sources of local news and information—particularly public radio, which is relatively inexpensive to produce and distribute and is a valuable source of professionally reported news for millions of Americans. There is virtually nothing else like it on the air" (Minow 2011).

Public media advocates consistently point out that musical forms in short supply on commercial radio, such as jazz, classical, opera and local music, find a home on public radio stations (170 Million Americans n.d.b). Local station managers report that their outlets are often the only ones to give a significant amount of airplay to local musicians (Yasko 2011). There is a longstanding connection between local public broadcasting stations and niche musical tastes—sometimes considered subversive by the majority. From the start, public stations were designed to be places for experimental forms of communication (Eichholtz 1967).

As frequently as the universal service theme is used to defend public media institutions, it is used to critique them. For decades, US public broadcasting critics have pointed out that the system serves only a small slice of American audiences (Silver *et al.* 2010; Balas 2003; Artz 2003; Starr 2000; Horowitz and Jarvik 1995; Somerset-Ward 1993). Some of these critiques seem to be well founded. For example, African Americans are about 80 percent, and Hispanics only 42 percent, as likely to listen to public radio as the population as a whole (CPB 2010a). On the other hand, PBS's television audience reflects "the overall US population with respect to race/ethnicity, education and income" (Waldman *et al.* 2011: 168). Relying on third-party studies, the FCC reports that, as of 2008, 11.8 percent of the PBS audience in the United States was African American (compared to 12.1 percent in the overall population), and 10.9 percent of its audience identified as Hispanic (compared to 10.8 percent in the overall population). Moreover, African Americans, Asians and Hispanics were all over-indexed on PBS's online platforms (Waldman *et al.* 2011). Nevertheless, it is clearly the case that attracting more diverse audiences with more diverse content is of central importance to today's US public media institutions (Station Resource Group 2010; Silver *et al.* 2010; AIR media works n.d.; PBS 2008).

The universal service narrative for public media is robust and broad, covering both infrastructure and content. But it contains within it no clear prescriptions about what service should be provided. Moreover, the institutional supports for fulfilling a universal service mission are terribly scant given the prerequisites for universal service in the digital age.

Consider streaming and digital applications. For public service broadcasters to translate their universal service mission into the digital age, they need to stream content over all platforms that all people use. This means maintaining broadcast signals on television and radio, as well as streaming content on mobile and broadband platforms and making it available in the cloud. This is an expensive proposition, especially because the costs of streaming increase with the number of users, while broadcast transmission scales without added cost (Waldman *et al.* 2011). There is no provision in US public media funding instruments to support these costs and it is not yet clear how membership models can be built to sustain them.

There is also the question of what "free" and "universal" entails. Public media institutions in the United States have had a great deal of success with digital applications. NPR especially has made a big splash with its podcasts and iPad applications (Waldman *et al.* 2011). So far, these are all available without charge. However, as digital media and media platforms mature, more and more content goes behind paywalls (Reisinger 2011; Sonderman 2011; Peters 2011). There will be financial pressure on public media entities to charge for their content. The regulations governing public broadcasting in the United States say nothing about whether or not public media content distributed online has to be free to the public. Nor, for that matter, is there any prohibition on advertising on a non-broadcast platform.

The meaning of free and universal service in the digital environment, and the translation of the public service media mission to a world with different cost structures and business models, all have to be worked out if the universal service narrative is to persist. Perhaps most centrally, the universal service narrative for public media work out the significance of a non-commercial alternative in the broadband world. There are no non-commercial set-asides of "channels" in broadband as there are in broadcasting. It is not at all clear whether there could be any or what form they would take. What is becoming clear is that commercial broadband infrastructure providers (e.g. cable and telephone companies) and intermediaries (e.g. Google and Facebook) erect controls on information that are not entirely comfortable. These come in the form of access controls or tolls, privacy intrusions, algorithm manipulations, or in many other forms. There may well be new utility for a non-commercial alternative in digital infrastructure and service to allow unfettered and affordable access to information, without compromising privacy. But this vision for non-commercial infrastructure and networked services in broadband has not yet been articulated or connected with public service media traditions.

## Educational excellence

Another central narrative for public media, also spawned by market failure theory, is that public media educates. In the United States, public broadcasting was explicitly and narrowly educational from the start. European public broadcasting traditions also emphasize education, along with information and culture (Lukács 2007). The UK, Sweden and the Netherlands, for example, all explicitly identify education as a major function of public service media (Lukács 2007). As the origins of US public broadcasting reveal, however, the US system has made education and educational institutions much more central.

Most of the first US public broadcasting stations were licensed to educational institutions and a sizable percentage still are (Waldman *et al.* 2011). In 1917, the first public radio station—known as a non-commercial educational station—aired adult education programming in Madison, Wisconsin (Witherspoon and Kovitz 1987). Four years later, the Latter Day Saints' University in Salt Lake City, Utah, was the first educational institution granted an official license by the federal government (Witherspoon and Kovitz 1987). The station broadcast educational lectures, as well as basketball games and musical concerts (Frost 1971).

By the mid-1930s, there were hundreds of such stations. Many of these were operated by land-grant universities in the Midwest, which sought to extend the services of state universities to all citizens (Slotten 2006). Radio broadcasting was thought to be another tool to diffuse agricultural innovations and scientific research out into the hinterlands. The objective was both to improve the economic status of farmers and to elevate their social and cultural levels by giving them "access to the general educational and cultural contributions of universities" (Slotten 2006: 256). According to Hugh Richard Slotten, "the public service tradition established by university radio stations gave the tradition in the USA a distinct identity, especially compared to the paradigmatic British model. The educational connection was crucial" (Slotten 2006: 267). These stations viewed themselves as serving a specialized audience with educational content not provided by the commercial market, as opposed to serving a mass audience.

In 1948, the FCC introduced a new class of lower-powered non-commercial radio licenses, which made radio more affordable to many non-profit institutions. The number of stations grew throughout the 1950s and 1960s, becoming laboratories for journalism schools and classrooms for colleges and universities (Richter 2006; Burk 1979).

In 1951, the FCC set aside the first 242 channels for non-commercial television broadcasting, declaring "The public interest will be clearly served if these stations contribute significantly to the educational process of the Nation" (Avery 1979: 147). This channel reservation culminated a campaign by the FCC's first female Commissioner, Frieda Hennock, to promote non-commercial broadcasting. Hennock made it her principal mission for several years to evangelize the public benefits of non-commercial television, emphasizing in particular its educational value. It would be a "tragic waste from the standpoint of the public interest," she preached to educators, "if, at the outset of development in this field, adequate provision were not made for the realization of the almost limitless possibilities of television as a medium of visual education" (Brinson 2002: 120).

Hennock's early conception of educational television, shared with many practitioners, was of classroom instruction delivered to the school and home, as well as elevated cultural programming. The problem with this vision is that university television licensees with relatively small audiences and funding sources had difficulty achieving the scale required to produce high-quality programming. By the mid-1960s, there were many critics of American educational broadcasting. It had produced lots of instruction, but too little excellence.

Dissatisfaction with the quality of the programming, particularly on television, led to a presidential commission to examine the future of "educational television." This became the Carnegie Commission on Educational Television, whose seminal 1967 report broadened the notion of "educational." Picking up on this broad and ambitiously aspirational view of education through media, President Johnson's speech on the Public Broadcasting Act of 1967 announced that the time had come "to enlist the computer and the satellite, as well as television and radio . . . in the cause of education." The aspiration was for a "network for knowledge" (Johnson 1967).

American public media entities today still emphasize their educational function, both as providers of excellent children's programming and digital applications, and of purpose-built audiovisual classroom curricula. Eighty-five percent of PBS member stations offer educational content to their communities that are designed to fit applicable education standards, and 95 percent offer structured learning as part of their educational services. PBS is ranked among the top three sources of online K–12 content and has been ranked by teachers as a top source of video in the classroom (Waldman *et al.* 2011).

This stress on education is in no small part a result of the fact that education is politically safe. Partisans across the political spectrum value public broadcasting's educational content ("Awards" 2011). Public support of educational media content can be framed as—and in many ways is—simply an extension of state investment in a system of free public education and libraries. Such investments are fairly non-controversial elements of proactive policy to promote democratic values through knowledge (Balkin 2004).

The politically anodyne nature of education leads advocates for public media funding to point to the fact that public media produces award-winning educational programming that is used heavily in both the classroom and the home (170 Million Americans n.d.a). In speaking out against defunding public media, documentary filmmaker Ken Burns highlighted the "critical services" that are exclusively available through public media and that serve to "supplement studies in schools from Oklahoma to Alaska, West Virginia to Arkansas" (Fleischer 2011). The FCC, in its review of public media's contribution to the informational needs of communities, also emphasized educational content and services (Waldman *et al.* 2011).

In many ways, the educational narrative for public service media dovetails with its other narratives. An educated citizenry is a necessary ingredient to a highly functioning democracy. In that sense, educational content is an input into the public sphere that public service media is designed to maintain and nourish. And the provision of educationally rich material is an element of universal service. It is part of the "why" of universal service and part of the "what" of diverse content.

At the same time, however, the educational mission of public media is in tension with other public media goals in at least four ways. First and most simply, educational content costs a lot of money. Money spent on developing content to fit into a school curriculum or to educate adults is money that is not spent on other content, such as journalism.

Second, to have an educational agenda is to have a substantive vision of what the public (and its various parts) needs to learn. All content choices require some conception of the good, but educational content choices may embed a more developed and systematic set of value judgements. In the past, the exercise of these judgements has led to claims that public media is foisting on the public an elitist vision of the "canon" (Ouellette 1999: 63).

Third, as with the other non-market functions of public media, its educational mission is in tension with the goal of broad adoption. Public broadcasters rely on relatively popular programming, or at least programming that appeals to larger donors, in order to fuel pledge drives and to grow member funding (Silver *et al.* 2010). The most high-minded educational programming may not fall into this category and, naturally, school-oriented programming is designed for a very niche market.

Finally, an institution acting as a vendor of audiovisual material to schools is functioning in a very different capacity from one that is developing entertainment or journalism for distribution over mass media platforms—or from one that is curating and contextualizing content in the middle space between distributed voices and high-cost content. Where educational materials are purpose-built for use in schools, the public media entities have to partner with the state (in the United States, usually individual states) to identify and satisfy needs. This kind of partnership puts public media entities in a very different relationship with the state from the oppositional one that journalists cultivate. The development of an educational agenda, at least in its formal sense, is at odds with the more "procedural" model of public media as a forum or public sphere for the voice of diverse value systems.

The aspiration to "educate," in its broadest sense, is really not much different from the aspiration to "promote democracy" or provide "universal service," and is entirely consistent with the emerging functions of public media in digital networks. However, the narrower function of providing digital artifacts for the classroom and other formal learning environments moves public media in a different direction—one that is both less ambitious and more politically palatable in the United States.

To the extent that the educational, universal service and democratic discourse narratives compete with each other, there is a need for a meta narrative that can be deployed in all of the areas in which public media operates and can be used to defend decisions to abandon functions that are no longer necessary.

## Towards a new narrative for public media: Innovation

I have suggested above that the principal narratives for public service media can all be characterized as market failure stories. This is certainly true in the United States, where public policy and private funders created public broadcasting as an intervention into a commercial market. It is less true of British and other European public service broadcasting models that pre-dated commercial media and that have more explicitly pro-active cultural agendas. Yet in European systems too, scholars recognize that increasingly "public media must legitimate itself more explicitly according to market-based sensibilities" (Lowe and Bardoel 2007: 14; see also Lukács 2007).

The difference between market failure rationales and cultural impact rationales for public service media is really one of focus. The narrowly focused market failure rationale posits a role for public media where consumers cannot get the media they seek. If we widen that focus, we comprehend that consumers may not seek all of the media that would be good for them or with which, on reflection, they might wish to be provided. This broad view of market failure converges on the cultural rationale for public media. It has become an aridly academic project to parse market failure from other rationales for public media, recognizing that, in all cases, proponents seek interventions into media markets in order to provide a good that increases social welfare (Foster 2004).

The kinds of media market failures that public service media have aimed to address are markedly diverse. In some cases, they are products, such as educational content. In other cases, the failures are systems or technology failures, such as the failure to provide a universal communications service. And in other cases, they are mixtures of products and process, such as the failure to engage citizens in reasoned democratic debate.

Market failures endure in the twenty-first century, and with them market failure narratives. However, the contours of market failure are different and swiftly evolving in the digital world. Opportunities for commercial and non-commercial media content are legion (e.g. blogs, wikis, video and audio uploads), although the platforms for this expression tend to be commercial (e.g. social networking sites). Massive amounts of public and private data are now available for educational use and democratic discourse, albeit in unsifted and unnarrated form. New digital applications and tools are becoming available every day, although many are neither optimized for the mission of public media nor financially sustainable. Finally, the functions of media, as well as the modes of engagement with media products and services, are changing rapidly. What all this means is that the precise shape of market failure in this environment is much harder to discern and predict.

In this environment, the structures and narratives of the twentieth century are deficient. It made sense, then, when broadcasting was the dominant medium of mass communications and barriers to entry were high, to situate public service media in a broadcast frame. By this, I mean not only the technologies of broadcasting, but also broadcasting models of large institutions, high-cost content and one-to-many distribution. Commentators and practitioners are now casting about for new models that relate optimally to digital technologies and that recognize shifting communications needs in a digital world (Steenfadt 2011). Sometimes, these narratives seem to be constructed to rescue incumbent public media institutions and, at worst, are self-justifying defenses of troubled models. But, at best, the search for new narratives is grounded in the recognition that the functions of public media remain important even as the institutions that perform these functions evolve and shift.

A central narrative to emerge from these attempts to redefine and restructure public media is one of innovation. This final section describes varied uses of the term "innovation" in the context of US public media. As everywhere in media, the term is used in the transitive as an aspiration for breakthrough products and services. First, all media entities aspire to be "innovative." In that usage, innovation is not a narrative so much as a survival strategy. Second, the term "innovation" can be used to recast the traditional narratives of democratic discourse, education and universal service. Contributions to these longstanding public interest goals are inputs to social and economic innovation. Viewed this way, public media services are components of and complements to other policy interventions to promote innovation.

Third, and most interestingly, the term "innovation" can be used to refer to a new conception of public media entities as collaborators and facilitators in the emerging non-commercial media ecosystem. In this sense, public media products and services are not only inputs into societal innovation more generally (as in the traditional narratives); nor are public media entities, working alone and set apart, merely the authors of media innovation (as in the internal innovation strategy). Instead, public media entities provide critical components of collaborative systems for the innovative creation and distribution of information, and engagement with it. The value of these particular kinds of collaborative innovations is related to their being non-commercial and mission-driven. This cluster of innovation narratives has the potential to advance central values contained within older narratives, while embracing and adapting to digital realities.

## Product and service innovation: Innovation within

At the most basic level, legacy public media institutions recognize that innovation in their products and services is necessary to adapt their missions to digital networks. The UK regulator Ofcom observes:

> There is a long history of renewal and reinvention in delivering public service as technologies change—major museums were founded to inform and educate citizens in the nineteenth century; public service radio and television reached the whole UK in the twentieth century; and now a new approach is needed for the digital media world of the twenty-first century.
>
> (*Ofcom 2007: 2*)

American public media networks have all embraced the language of innovation to announce new initiatives that seize on digital distribution, social networking, crowd-sourcing and other new modalities of communication. The Corporation for Public Broadcasting has articulated innovation as one of its core goals, specifically calling for more "innovative use of technology, online distribution, and broadcast and multicast channels to reach audiences wherever and whenever they use media" (CPB 2011). In a recent report, a task force of local and national public radio leaders stated that its sector must do more, innovating in the form and content of our work to reflect a changing media environment (Station Resource Group 2010: 91). PBS has likewise launched a PBS "Engage" website with an "Innovation Showcase" to help PBS, member stations and programs to use new technologies to serve the public better (http://www.pbs.org/engage/).

We can situate these initiatives in a public media tradition of experimentation—a process of innovation as distinct from the supply of products that filled a non-market niche. It was this spirit of experimentation in the United States that resulted in new genres, such as children's programming (*Sesame Street*), new modes of political coverage (e.g. gavel-to-gavel coverage of the Watergate proceedings) and content delivery systems (e.g. communications satellites for program distribution), and the first telecasts of live arts performances (*Dance in America*) (Somerset-Ward 1993; CPB 2010b). Public broadcasting started the genre of long-form investigation (*Frontline*), historical documentary (*American Experience*) and quirky cultural explorations (*This American Life*). Public television was also the first to develop video description services for the blind and closed captioning for the hearing impaired (Witherspoon and Kovitz 2000). And its early experiments in fostering community dialog on race pioneered a model of sustainable, diversified community engagement practices now common in public broadcasting, and in documentary filmmaking more generally (Abrash 2007).

In Europe, too, those engaged in redefining the purpose and function of public media have drawn on the language of innovation. According to Johannes Bardoel and Leen d'Haenens (2008), "there is a new emphasis on [public service broadcasting's] contribution to the national audio-visual production market, and as a breeding ground for innovation and talent" (Bardoel and d'Haenens 2008: 343).

At the same time, existing public media entities face criticism for their sluggishness to innovate (McKibbon 2010; Knight 2009). These institutions are not immune from the general reluctance of established organizations to deconstruct themselves. As Clay Christensen observed in *The Innovator's Dilemma* (2008), it is not usually to entrenched institutions that we look first for innovation-friendly disruptive technologies. The ability of smaller firms to catalyze innovation grows stronger as twenty-first-century diffusion of innovations accelerates and access to innovations increases. With respect to scientific innovation, the Organisation for Economic Co-operation and Development (OECD) notes that, "the innovation process of the 21st century is radically different to that of the preceding one. Perhaps the most important difference is the new or renewed importance of new and small firms" (OECD 2010: 25).

If smaller firms and entities at the edges of digital networks are an important source of innovation, the question of how their innovations can scale and be sustained remains. Increasingly, this is where public media entities are finding a role. In the United States, large public media institutions have overcome inertia and institutional skepticism to reconceive of themselves as partners, investors and platforms for smaller innovators. This will be addressed below.

## Public media as input: Driving social and technological innovation

Before turning to the role that public media entities are trying to forge for themselves as partners in chains of innovation, I will touch briefly on another relationship that they have with innovation. This is the role of public media as inputs into general social and technological innovation. The use of the term "innovation" in this context is a new way of casting the traditional narratives discussed above. One can conceive of democratic engagement, education and universal service as themselves innovations or pro-innovation forces. Public media serve to advance these social innovations that are themselves external to media products and practices.

It is in this way that public media appeared in one of the most important contemporary US communications policy conversations: the 2010 National Broadband Plan. That document set forth a communications policy agenda for the next decade focused on spreading the availability and adoption of broadband technologies in order to further progress and innovation in healthcare, energy, employment and other broad swaths of public life.

Because the focus of the Broadband Plan was on telecommunications and broadband connectivity, the inclusion of public media as a component, albeit small, of the Plan was not foreordained. The Plan emphasized the historic and potential role of public media in promoting innovation as part of a "digital public media ecosystem" (FCC 2010: 304). There was discussion of the traditional educational and other functions that public media entities play. But there was also recognition of new ways in which public media might support social innovation. One of the specific public media applications that the Plan commended, and thought should be extended, was the creation of a public media application programming interface (API). In the first few years of its existence, NPR's API, or open platform, allowed public broadcasters and third parties to access a huge trove of public broadcast content and curate and distribute it.

The Plan expressed hope that public media entities might serve this function for vast amounts of archived materials and become part of a "national archive" for the distribution of digital and digitized materials. According to the Plan, public media's "archival content could provide tremendous educational opportunities for generations of students and could revolutionize how we access our own history" (FCC 2010: 304). This aspiration echoes the hopes of the BBC's "Creative Archives" pilot project, which made available archival BBC content over an open platform. Copyright clearance problems ended that particular effort in 2006, and also pose challenges to American archival platforms.

These ventures imagine public media entities performing traditional roles, making high-quality content available in the public interest. The framing, however, is new: public media entities as platforms for follow-on innovation. Commentators foresaw the public media API as a potential "engine of innovation" (Tenore 2010). Public media officials, in petitioning the government for archive funding, described a role for themselves as information platforms. They sought to rectify the problem of "[b]illions of dollars worth of content assets . . . [that] are effectively lost to educators, inventors, government officials and private citizens because they have not been indexed and stored on accessible digital media" (Harrison *et al.* 2009). The API and archive projects have both moved slowly from their beginnings, undoubtedly in part because of funding shortages, intellectual property concerns and coordination difficulties. Whatever the future of these specific projects, they suggest a role for public media entities in developing electronic public parks—spaces for creativity that these entities neither sponsor nor manage.

## Public media as central nodes in networks of media innovation

A third narrative of innovation emerges to describe the role of public media as a partner in a distributed mesh of public service media innovation. According to the National Broadband Plan, "public media must continue expanding beyond its original broadcast-based mission to form the core of a broader new public media network that better serves the new multi-platform information needs of America" (FCC 2010: 303). This network includes non-profit digital journalism ventures, as well as information providers such as Wikipedia and open-source software providers such as Mozilla. There are no analogues to these entities in the twentieth-century broadcast world and so no established conceptions of their relationship with traditional public media entities.

When used by entities outside of the large public media institutions, the innovation narrative of the new public media network involves creative destruction (Schumpeter 1943). It stresses the creation of fundamentally new platforms and modes of product and service development that challenge the status quo—that challenge, in a sense, the failures of public media institutions themselves to nurture new forms and new voices. The catchwords are "incubation" and "collaboration." Digital networks, by their nature, support innovation in content (at least low-cost content), and provide easy access for new entrants experimenting in new digital applications. But innovations that serve public media objectives of democracy, education and inclusion do not necessarily scale or have staying power. The function of incubating innovations is critical and often underperformed. According to the OECD, speaking generally about the role of incubator, there is a need to:

> . . . bring together the skills and expertise necessary to help sustain and develop [an] enterprise; provide a space to experiment and assess new ideas in practice; allow fast learning across a community of innovators; and, establish clear pathways for scaling up

> the most promising models. The absence of intermediaries . . . is a key reason why too few innovations succeed.
>
> (*OECD 2010: 208–209*)

The vision of public media as intermediaries or nodes in a web of public service media producers and distributors is shared in Europe and the UK. One of the most far-reaching ideas for restructuring public media in Britain, for example, is Phil Redmond's to remake the BBC as a "patron of the tele-visual arts across all digital platforms." Rather than produce and distribute its own content, it would perform the role of stimulating and helping to scale content production of others. It would "plug into every school, college and university to help stimulate and exhibit media training and practitioners." The license fee that currently supports public broadcasting in Britain would instead "be developed as both a cultural and economic regeneration fund, embedded within the regions, seeking out, nurturing and feeding talent" (Redmond 2004: 82).

Those most active in developing models for public media incubation and collaboration in the United States are at the periphery of the public media system, working with assets at the system's core. Some of these efforts seek to open up the existing public broadcasting system, rather than to pursue Redmond's more ambitious shake-up. The head of the Association of Independents in Radio, for example, has been pushing for public media to provide more service to underserved communities, to innovate in media genres and voices, and to function as a platform for experimentation. The Association recently designed and administered the "Public Radio Makers Quest 2.0" competition, which tasked radio producers with inventing new formats for public media and new approaches that blended traditional broadcast with new digital media tools and platforms (Clark and Schardt 2010). This project developed into a CPB-funded experiment in 2012: "Localore" tries to scale innovations in content by placing new producers with mentors at existing public radio stations to grow local capacity, and to support new voices and experiments in combined radio and digital distribution (AIR mediaworks n.d.).

The Public Radio Exchange (PRX) is a successful start-up incubated by public media institutions in order to provide a platform and distribution network for new radio voices (http://www.prx.org/). It is now working with the Knight Foundation on the "Public Media Accelerator" designed to target strategic innovation by identifying and accelerating ideas with the potential to transform the field (http://publicmediax.org/). It plans to incubate these ideas by using a mentorship-driven technology start-up accelerator model. According to Jake Shapiro, head of PRX, the goal is an exchange of relative competencies between the public media and tech sectors: "The tech sector will gain from public media's high-quality content, commitment to community, and public service mission; and public media will gain from technology's network efficiencies, professional and social connections, and radical new distribution paths" (Shapiro 2012).

New forms of collaboration are also arising in journalism, involving the largest players in the American public media universe. Commentators favorably cite the role that public broadcasting stations can play in supporting new local journalistic start-ups (Waldman *et al.* 2011; Downie and Schudson 2009; Knight Commission 2009). These collaborations mesh the energy of digital start-ups with the reach and institutional stability of public broadcasting. For example, a public broadcasting station provides a digital journalistic enterprise with physical support (office space, technical support) and a broadcast platform; the digital start-up provides the public broadcaster with new content and, possibly, expertise in digital networking and applications.

These efforts to make public media more porous and conducive to mission-oriented innovations find support in the literature on public media, which stresses the need for adaptation and disruption (Steenfadt 2011; Aslama and Syvertsen 2007; Jakubowicz 2006). Such efforts are also consistent with proposals that government's central role in media policy, as in other policy areas, is to support innovation. In addressing journalism deficiencies, Geoffrey Cowan and David Westphal argue that the government should "focus on innovation" (Cowan and Westphal 2011: 137).

Indeed, one of the criticisms of US innovation policy is that it has historically failed "to provide government support during the critical period when a new technology has to be ramped up for mass production or mass deployment" (Block 2011: 14). Currently there is little federal support for technical innovation in media, whether in the established public broadcasting world or among native digital ventures (Waldman *et al.* 2011: 320). Indeed, the provision of federal support to journalistic start-ups or public interest applications would almost surely raise intractable free speech problems connected with government intervention into speech markets. That is another reason why the use of public media assets to support new ventures is attractive. These established entities are already conduits for at least minimal federal support.

The calls to sustain and increase funding for public media in the United States acknowledge the nascent innovation narrative (Clark 2011; Current Public Media Blog 2011; NPR 2011). But they do not develop it. One of the reasons is that, to the extent that innovation for public media means opening up established institutions to new entrants, it unsettles the very notion of who are public media. In the past, even as the mission of public media was protean and contested, its constituency was static and clear: select broadcast institutions. The new innovation narrative raises questions about who should be considered a public media participant and how existing platforms can support new entrants and disruptive technologies. Funding structures would have to be remade to map onto these new conceptions of public media. It is unclear whether there is a political constituency to advocate for new funding structures, since incumbent public media institutions could face losses as resources are spread among more players.

These political realities may constrain the full flowering of the innovation narrative. At the same time, other political realities—namely, skepticism about the need for traditional public media services—counsel for the further development of the narrative and its implementation. This chapter has identified some of the strengths and limitations of traditional public media narratives. The innovation narrative has the potential to revive what works in these conceptions (and implementing practices) and deemphasize those aspects that are rooted in twentieth-century media practices.

The term "innovation" is usually used in the context of technological innovation and economic growth. Deliberate intervention in the market to support technological innovation is, of course, a market failure story. Government steps in to provide "a public or quasi-public good—the technology infrastructure itself—that leverages the ability of firms and other actors in a national innovation system to participate efficiently in the innovation process" (Link and Link 2009: 19). This rather thin notion of innovation fits well with what may be the evolving role of public media in the universal service realm: to provide infrastructure (whether broadband or other) that the market does not, in order to promote access to communications and communicative power. Education is part of the essential scaffolding on which innovative practice is built (Waldman *et al.* 2011; Marshall 2010; Office of Science and Technology Policy 2009). Where public media has special competency in providing educational services, the value can be understood in terms of innovation infrastructure.

More robust conceptions of innovation go beyond the technical and the economic to include innovations for the sake of democratic and social flourishing (Bielefeld 2009; Murray *et al.*, 2010; Kerr 2007). These innovations include communicative forms and strategies that engage publics in democratic discourse. Public media efforts to use new technologies to create informative and trusted journalism, and to curate and contextualize third-party information, could all be framed as market interventions to introduce or scale these innovations. Experiments with business models and with engagement techniques that do not require sacrificing consumer privacy or surrendering to commercial appeals similarly fit within an innovation frame.

While pliable, the innovation frame is not endlessly elastic. There are many public media activities that are not innovative or pro-innovation and that would have to be shed if innovation were taken seriously as a principal test of value. Some of what public media currently does is derivative or duplicative of other services. Public media structures are not optimized for innovation and public media entities are not assessed by innovation metrics. Indeed, much of the criticism of American public media is that it is not sufficiently innovative or supportive of the innovation of others. Were public media entities willing, or required, to take on the innovation narrative seriously, their political fortunes and their service might improve significantly.

## References


170 Million Americans for Public Broadcasting (n.d.a) 'Education.' Online. Available HTTP: http://170millionamericans.org/education (accessed 8 May 2012).

—— (n.d.b) 'Impact.' Online. Available HTTP: http://170millionamericans.org/impact (accessed 8 May 2012).

—— (n.d.c) 'What is public broadcasting?' Online. Available HTTP: http://170millionamericans.org/what-public-broadcasting.

Abrash, B. (2007) 'The view from the top: P.O.V. leaders on the struggle to create truly public media.' Online. Available HTTP: http://aladinrc.wrlc.org/bitstream/1961/4606/1/pov.pdf (accessed 8 May 2012).

AIR mediaworks (n.d.). 'Localore.' Online. Available HTTP: http://airmediaworks.org/localore (accessed 8 May 2012).

Artz, B. L. (2003) 'The public and its problems: Race, class, and media access,' in M. P. McCauley, E. E. Peterson, B. L. Artz, and D. Halleck (eds.) *Public Broadcasting and the Public Interest*, New York: M. E. Sharpe.

Aslama, M. and Syvertsen, T. (2007) 'Public service broadcasting and new technologies,' in E. de Bens (ed.) *Media Between Culture and Commerce*, Brighton: IntellectBooks.

Association of Public Television Stations (2011a) 'APTS presented champion of public broadcasting award to Senator Thad Cochran,' Press release, 15 April. Online. Available HTTP: http://www.apts.org/news/press-release/apts-presented-champion-public-broadcasting-award-senator-thad-cochran (accessed 8 May 2012).

—— (2011b) 'Public media association condemns House NPR vote,' Press release, 17 March. Online. Available HTTP: http://www.apts.org/news/press-release/public-media-association-condemns-house-npr-vote (accessed 8 May 2012).

Aufderheide, P. and Clark, J. (2010) 'Comments in re FCC launches examination of the future of media and information needs of communities in a digital age,' 6 May, GN Docket No. 10–25.

Avery, R. K. and Pepper, R. (1979) *The Politics of Interconnection: A History of Public Television at the National Level,* Washington DC: National Association of Education Broadcasters.

Baker, C. E. (1998) 'The media that citizens need,' *University of Pennsylvania Law Review*, 147: 317–408.

—— (2002) *Media, Markets, and Democracy*, New York and Cambridge: Cambridge University Press.

—— (2006) *Media Concentration and Democracy*, New York and Cambridge: Cambridge University Press.

Balas, G. R. (2003) *Recovering a Public Vision for Public Television*, Lanham, MD: Rowman and Littlefield.

Balkin, J. M. (2004) 'Digital speech and democratic culture: A theory of freedom of expression for the information society,' *New York University Law Review*, 79: 1–58.

Bardoel, J. and d'Haenens, L. (2008) 'Reinventing public service broadcasting in Europe: Prospects, promises and problems,' *Media, Culture & Society*, 30(3): 337–355.

Barnett, S. (2004) 'Which end of the telescope? From market failure to cultural value,' in D. Tambini and J. Cowling (eds.) *From Public Service Broadcasting to Public Service Communications*, London: Institute for Public Policy Research.

BBC (1996) *BBC Annual Report*, London: BBC.

—— (2011a) *BBC Response to Ofcom's Invitation to Comment on Measuring Media Plurality*. Online. Available HTTP: http://stakeholders.ofcom.org.uk/binaries/consultations/916359/responses/bbc.pdf (accessed 8 May 2012).

—— (2011b) *Public Opinion on the BBC and BBC News*. Online. Available HTTP: http://stakeholders.ofcom.org.uk/binaries/consultations/916359/responses/bbc-annex2.pdf (accessed 8 May 2012).

—— (2012) 'Public purposes: Sustaining citizenship and civil society.' Online. Available HTTP: http://www.bbc.co.uk/aboutthebbc/insidethebbc/whoweare/publicpurposes/ (accessed 8 May 2012).

Bielefeld, W. (2009) 'Issues in social enterprise and social entrepreneurship,' *Journal of Public Affairs Education*, 15(1): 69–86.

Block, F. (2011) 'Innovation and the invisible hand of government,' in F. Block and M. R. Keller (eds.) *State of Innovation: The US Government's Role in Technology Development*, Boulder, CO: Paradigm Publishers.

Boggs, C. (1997) 'The Great Retreat: Decline of the public sphere in late twentieth-century America,' *Theory and Society*, 26(6): 741–780.

Bohman, J. (1996) *Public Deliberation*, Cambridge, MA: MIT Press.

—— and Regh, W. (eds.) (1997) *Deliberative Democracy*, Cambridge, MA: MIT Press.

Breed, W. (1955) 'Social control in the newsroom: A functional analysis,' *Social Forces*, 33(4): 326–335.

Breitbart, J., Glaisyer, T., Ninan-Moses, B. and Losey, J. (2011) 'Full spectrum community media.' Online. Available HTTP: http://newamerica.net/publications/policy/full_spectrum_community_media (accessed 8 May 2012).

Brinson, S. L. (2002) *Personal and Public Interests: Frieda B. Hennock and the Federal Communications Commission*, Westport, CT: Praeger Publishers.

Brown, A. (1996) 'Economics, public service broadcasting, and social values,' *Journal of Media Economics*, 9(1): 3–15.

Burk, J. E. (1979) *An Historical-Analytical Study of the Legislative and Political Origins of the Public Broadcasting Act of 1967*, New York: Arno Press.

Carnegie Commission on the Future of Public Broadcasting (1979) *A Public Trust: The Report of the Carnegie Commission on the Future of Public Broadcasting*, Boulder, CO: Paradigm Publishers.

Chideya, F. (2011) 'Why to save public media: It's yours,' *Huffington Post*. Online. Available HTTP: http://www.huffingtonpost.com/farai-chideya/why-to-save-public-media-_b_823255.html (accessed 8 May 2012).

Christensen, C. (2003) *The Innovator's Dilemma*, New York: HarperCollins.

Clark, J. (2011) 'Defunding public media would stifle digital innovation,' *PBS MediaShift*, 21 March. Online. Available HTTP: http://www.pbs.org/mediashift/2011/03/defunding-public-media-would-stifle-digital-innovation080.html (accessed 8 May 2012).

—— and Aufderheide, P. (2009) *Public Media 2.0: Dynamic, Engaged Publics*. Online. Available HTTP: http://www.centerforsocialmedia.org/documents/whitepaper.pdf (accessed 8 May 2012).

—— and Schardt, S. (2010) *Spreading the Zing: Reimagining Public Media through the Makers Quest 2.0*, Boston, MA: Association of Independents in Radio and Center for Social Media.

Collins, R. (2004) 'Public service broadcasting: Too much of a good thing?' in D. Tambini and J. Cowling (eds.) *From Public Service Broadcasting to Public Service Communications*, London: Institute for Public Policy Research.

Cowan, G. and Westphal, D. (2011) 'The Washington-Madison solution,' in R. McChesney and V. Pickard (eds.) *Will the Last Reporter Please Turn out the Lights: The Collapse of Journalism and What Can Be Done to Fix It*, New York: The New Press.

CPB (2009) 'CPB/PBS Diversity and Innovation Fund.' Online. Available HTTP: http://www.pbs.org/producing/difund/ (accessed 8 May 2012).

—— (2010a) *Public Radio in the New Network Age: Wider Use, Deeper Value, Compelling Change—Report and Recommendations of the Public Radio Audience Growth Task Force*. Online. Available HTTP: http://www.srg.org/GTA/Public Radio in the New Network Age.pdf

—— (2010b) 'Comments in re the future of media and information needs of communities in a digital age,' GN Docket No. 10-25, 7 May.

—— (2012)'Goals and objectives,' 4 June. Online. Available HTTP: http://www.cpb.org/aboutcpb/goals/goalsandobjectives (accessed 5 October 2012).

Curran, J. (1991) 'Rethinking the media as a public sphere,' in P. Dahlgreen and C. Sparks (eds.) *Communication and Citizenship: Journalism and the Public Sphere in the New Media Age*, London: Routledge.

Current Public Media Blog (2011) 'CPB, APTs NPR, and PBS react to House Appropriations Bill to zero out pubcasting support,' 12 February. Online. Available HTTP: http://currentpublicmedia.blogspot.com/2011/02/cpb-and-apts-react-to-house.html (accessed 8 May 2012).

Dawidziak, M. (2011) 'Public broadcasters in Northeast Ohio says loss of federal funding would be devastating,' 26 February. Online. Available HTTP: http://www.cleveland.com/tv-blog/index.ssf/2011/02/public_broadcasters_in_northeast_ohio_says_loss_of_federal_funding_would_be_devastating.html (accessed 8 May 2012).

Debrett, M. (2010) *Reinventing Public Service Television for the Digital Future*, Chicago, IL: Chicago University Press.

Downie Jr., L. and Schudson, M. (2009) 'The reconstruction of American journalism.' Online. Available HTTP: http://www.journalism.columbia.edu/system/documents/1/original/Reconstruction_of_Journalism.pdf (accessed 8 May 2012).

Easter, E. (2011) 'Your take: Why black America should fight for public media,' 19 February. Online. Available HTTP: http://www.farai.com/why-to-save-public-media-for-you/ (accessed 8 May 2012).

Eichholz, G. C. (1967) Remarks on the Public Television Act of 1967, Hearings on H.R. 6736, 90th Congress.

Engelman, R. (1996) *Public Radio and Television in America: A Political History*, Thousand Oaks, CA: Sage.

Federal Communications Commission (FCC) (2010) *Connecting America: The National Broadband Plan*. Online. Available HTTP: http://download.broadband.gov/plan/national-broadband-plan.pdf (accessed 8 May 2012).

—— (2011) 'Connect America Fund *et al.*' WC Docket No. 10-90 *et al.*, Report and Order and Further Notice of Proposed Rulemaking, FCC 11-161, 2011 FCC LEXIS 4859 (USF/ICC Transformation Order), 18 November. Online. Available HTTP: http://transition.fcc.gov/Daily_Releases/Daily_Business/2011/db1122/FCC-11-161A1.pdf (accessed 8 May 2012).

Fiedel, S. N. (1967) Remarks on the Public Television Act of 1967, Hearings on H.R. 6736, 90th Congress.

Fleischer, M. (2011) 'Ken Burns sticks up for public media,' 15 February. Online. Available HTTP: http://www.mediabistro.com/fishbowlla/ken-burns-sticks-up-for-public-media_b22610# (accessed 8 May 2012).

Foster, R. *et al.* (2004) 'Measuring public service broadcasting, from market failure to cultural value,' in D. Tambini and J. Cowling (eds.) *From Public Service Broadcasting to Public Service Communications*, London: Institute for Public Policy Research.

Frischmann, B. M. and Lemley, M. A. (2007) 'Spillovers,' *Columbia Law Review*, 107: 257–301.

Frost, S. E. (1971) *Education's Own Stations*, New York: Arno Press and The New York Times.

Gans, H. (1980) *Deciding What's News*, New York: Vintage Books.

Garnham, N. (1986) 'Media and the public sphere,' in P. Golding, G. Murdock and P. Schlesinger (eds.) *Communicating Politics*, Leicester: Leicester University Press.

Gillmor, D. (2004) *We the Media*, Sebastopol, CA: O'Reilly Media.

Goodman, E. P. (2004) 'Media policy out of the box: Content abundance, attention scarcity, and the failures of digital markets,' *Berkeley Technology Law Journal*, 19: 1389–1472.

—— and Chen, A. H. (2010) 'Modeling policy for new public media networks,' *Harvard Journal of Law and Technology*, 29: 111–170.

Habermas, J. (1989) *Structural Transformation of the Public Sphere*, Cambridge, MA: Polity.

—— (2006) 'Political communication in media society: Does democracy still enjoy an epistemic dimension? The impact of normative theory on empirical research,' *Communication Theory*, 16(4): 411–426.

Hargreaves Heap, S. (2005) 'Television in a digital age: What role for public service broadcasting?' *Economic Policy*, 20(41): 111–157.

Harrison, P. (2011) *2011 Annual Report: President and CEO's Report*'. Online. Available HTTP: http://www.cpb.org/annualreports/2010/about/president-ceo-report.html (accessed 8 May 2012).

——, Kerger, P. and Haarsager, D. (2009) 'Letter to President-Elect Barack Obama,' 2 January. Online. Available HTTP: http://www.current.org/pbpb/documents/stimulus-request-Jan09.pdf (accessed 8 May 2012).

Hawthorne, D. W. and Price, M. E. (1994) 'Rewiring the First Amendment: Meaning, content and public broadcasting,' *Cardozo Arts and Entertainment Law Journal*, 12: 499–520.

Healey, J. (2011) 'The House swings at NPR, hits every radio programmer,' *Los Angeles Times*, 17 March. Online. Available HTTP: http://opinion.latimes.com/opinionla/2011/03/the-house-swings-at-npr-hits-every-radio-programmer.html (accessed 8 May 2012).

Horowitz, D. and Jarvik, L. (1995) *Public Broadcasting and the Public Trust*, Los Angeles, CA: Center for the Study of Popular Culture.

Hoynes, W. (1994) *Public Television for Sale: Media, the Market and the Public Sphere*, Boulder, CO: Westview Press.

Institute for Policy Integrity (2010) 'in re FCC launches examination of the future of media and information needs of communities in a digital age,' GN Docket No. 10-25, 7 May.

Jakubowicz, K. (2006) 'Keep the essence, change (almost) everything else: Redefining PSB for the 21st century,' in I. Banerjee and K. Seneviratne (eds.) *Public Service Broadcasting in the Age of Globalisation*, Kuala Kumpur: AMIC.

—— (2007) 'Public service broadcasting in post-communist countries: Finding the right place on the map,' SPRY Memorial Lecture, University of Montreal, Montreal, Canada, 27 November.

—— (2008) 'Participation and partnership: A Copernican revolution to reengineer public service media for the 21st century,' Conference on *Public Service Media in the 21st Century: Participation, Partnership and Media Development*, Mainz, Germany, 8–11 October.

Jarvis, J. (2011) *Public Parts: How Sharing in the Digital Age Improves the Way We Work and Live*, New York: Simon and Schuster.

Johnson, C. (2000) 'Federal support of public broadcasting: Not quite what LBJ had in mind,' *CommLaw Conspectus*, 8: 135–147.

Johnson, L. B. (1967) 'Remarks on signing the Public Broadcasting Act, 1967,' Washington, DC, 7 November. Online. Available HTTP: http://current.org/pbpb/legislation/pba67-LBJremarks.html (accessed 8 May 2012).

Johnson, S. (2010) *Where Good Ideas Come From*, New York: Riverhead Books.

Kerr, J. E. (2007) 'Sustainability meets profitability: The convenient truth of how business judgment rule protects a board's decision to engage in social entrepreneurship,' *Cardozo Law Review*, 29: 623–668.

Knight Commission (2009) *Knight Commission on the Information Needs of Communities in a Democracy, Informing Communities: Sustaining Democracy in the Digital Age*. Online. Available HTTP: https://secure.nmmstream.net/anon.newmediamill/aspen/kcfinalenglishbookweb.pdf (accessed 8 May 2012).

Link, A. and Link, J. (2009) *Government as Entrepreneur*, New York: Oxford University Press.

Lowe, G. F. and Bardoel, J. (2007) 'From public service broadcasting to public service media: The core challenge,' in J. Bardoel and G. F. Lowe (eds.) *From Public Service Broadcasting to Public Service Media*, London: Sage.

Lukács, M. (2007) 'Education in the transition to public service media,' in J. Bardoel and G. F. Lowe (eds.) *From Public Service Broadcasting to Public Service Media*, London: Sage.

Marshall, S. P. (2010) 'STEM talent: Moving beyond traditional boundaries,' *Science News*, 177(1): 36.

McKibbon, B. (2010) 'All programs considered,' *New York Review of Books*, 11 November. Online. Available HTTP: http://www.nybooks.com/articles/archives/2010/nov/11/all-programs-considered/?pagination=false (accessed 8 May 2012).

McQuail, D. (1992) *Media Performance: Mass Media and the Public Interest*, London: Sage.

Minow, N. (1961) 'Television and the public interest,' Speech delivered to National Association of Broadcasters, Washington, DC. Online. Available HTTP: http://www.americanrhetoric.com/speeches/newtonminow.htm (accessed 8 May 2012).

—— (2011) 'A vaster wasteland,' *The Atlantic*. Online. Available HTTP: http://www.theatlantic.com/magazine/archive/2011/04/a-vaster-wasteland/8418/2/ (accessed 8 May 2012).

Murray, R., Caulier-Grice, J. and Mulgan, G. (2010) *The Open Book of Social Innovation*. Online. Available HTTP: http://jokkolabs.net/uploads/Documents/Open_Book_of_Social_Innovation.pdf (accessed 8 May 2012).

Nisenholtz, M. (2008) 'The hyperlinked news organization,' in J. Turow and L. Tsui (eds.) *The Hyperlinked Society*, Ann Arbor, MI: University of Michigan Press.

NPR (2011) 'NPR statement regarding H.R. 1076.' Online. Available HTTP: http://www.npr.org/about/press/2011/031711.NPRStatementRegardingHR1076.html.

—— (2012) 'NPR stations and public media.' Online. Available HTTP: http://www.npr.org/about/aboutnpr/stations_publicmedia.html (retrieved 8 May 2012).

Nuechterlein, J. E. and Weiser, P. J. (2005) *Digital Crossroads: American Telecommunications Policy in the Internet Age*, Cambridge, MA: MIT Press.

Ofcom (1999) 'Annex 8: Market failure in broadcasting,' in *The Future Funding of the BBC: Report of the Independent Review Panel*. Online. Available HTTP: http://www.culture.gov.uk/images/publications/reviewcobbc.pdf (accessed 8 May 2012).

—— (2007) 'A new approach to public service content in the digital media age.' Online. Available HTTP: http://stakeholders.ofcom.org.uk/consultations/pspnewapproach/ (accessed 8 May 2012).

—— (2008) 'Annex 11: Market failure in broadcasting,' in *The Digital Opportunity: Ofcom's Second Public Service Broadcasting Review*. Online. Available HTTP: http://www.ofcom.org.uk/consult/condocs/psb2_1/annex11.pdf (accessed 8 May 2012).

—— (2011) *Ofcom Public Service Broadcasting Annual Report*. Online. Available HTTP: http://stakeholders.ofcom.org.uk/broadcasting/reviews-investigations/public-service-broadcasting/annrep/psb11/ (accessed 8 May 2012).

Office of Management and Budget (2011) 'Statement of administration policy: H.R. 1076—Prohibition of federal funding of National Public Radio,' 17 March. Online. Available HTTP: http://www.whitehouse.gov/sites/default/files/omb/legislative/sap/112/saphr1076h_20110317.pdf (accessed 8 May 2012).

Office of Science and Technology Policy (2009) *A Strategy for American Innovation: Driving towards Sustainable Growth and Quality Jobs*. Online. Available HTTP: http://www.whitehouse.gov/assets/documents/SEPT_20__Innovation_Whitepaper_FINAL.pdf (accessed 8 May 2012).

Organization for Economic Co-operation and Development (OECD) (2010) *SMEs, Entrepreneurship, and Innovation*, Paris: OECD.

Ouellette, L. (1999) 'TV viewing as good citizenship? Political rationality, enlightened democracy and PBS,' *Cultural Studies*, 13(1): 62–90.

Pariser, E. (2011) *The Filter Bubble: What the Internet is Hiding from You*, New York: Penguin Press.

PBS (2008) 'PBS Diversity Task Force announces members of the leadership development program class of 2009,' 1 July. Online. Available HTTP: http://www.pbs.org/aboutpbs/news/20080701_diversitytaskforce.html (accessed 8 May 2012).

—— (2011) 'PBS overview.' Online. Available HTTP: http://www.pbs.org/about/background/ (accessed 8 May 2012).

—— (2012) *Today's PBS: America's Largest Classroom, The Nation's Largest Stage, A Trusted Window to the World*. Online. Available HTTP: http://www.pbs.org/about/media/about/cms_page_media/146/PBS_Fact_Sheet_Jan2012.pdf (accessed 8 May 2012).

Peters, J. W. (2011) '*The Times* announces digital subscription plan,' *The New York Times*, 17 March. Online. Available HTTP: http://www.nytimes.com/2011/03/18/business/media/18times.html?pagewanted=all (accessed 8 May 2012).

Ramsey, P. (2010) 'Public service broadcasting and the public sphere: Normative arguments from Habermasian theory,' *Networking Knowledge: Journal of the MeCCSA Postgraduate Network*, 3(2). Online. Available HTTP: http://ojs.meccsa.org.uk/index.php/netknow/article/view/51/51.

Redmond, P. (2004) 'Public service content: The conditions for creativity,' in D. Tambini and J. Cowling (eds.) *From Public Service Broadcasting to Public Service Communications*, London: Institute for Public Policy Research.

Reisinger, D. (2011) '*NYTimes*: Consumer pay wall response "Positive",' *CNet News*, 21 July. Online. Available HTTP: http://news.cnet.com/8301-13506_3-20081371-17/nytimes-consumer-pay-wall-response-positive/ (accessed 8 May 2012).

Richter, W. A. (2006) *Radio: A Complete Guide to the Industry*, New York: Peter Lang Publishing.

Rosen, J. (1996) *Getting the Connections Right: Public Journalism and the Troubles in the Press*, New York: Twentieth Century Fund.

Rowland, W. D. (2002) 'Public broadcasting in the United States,' in *Encyclopedia of Communication and Information*. Online. Available HTTP: http://www.centerforsocialmedia.org/future/docs/pbintheusa.pdf (accessed 8 May 2012).

Scannell, P. (1989) 'Public service broadcasting and modern public life,' *Media, Culture and Society*, 11(2): 135–166.

Shapiro, J. (2012) 'Why PRX, Knight created an accelerator for public media,' 19 January. Online. Available HTTP: http://www.pbs.org/idealab/2012/01/why-prx-knight-created-an-accelerator-for-public-media018.html (accessed 8 May 2012).

Schumpeter, J. A. (1943) *Capitalism, Socialism and Democracy*, London: Allen and Unwin [originally published in the USA in 1942; reprinted by Routledge, London in 1994].

Shirky, C. (2008) *Here Comes Everybody*, New York: Penguin Books.

Silver, J., Clement, C., Aaron, C. and Turner, S. D. (2010) *New Public Media: A Plan for Action*. Online. Available HTTP: http://www.freepress.net/press-release/2010/5/10/free-press-releases-emnew-public-media-plan-actionem (accessed 8 May 2012).

Slotten, H. R. (2006) 'Universities, public service radio and the "American system" of commercial broadcasting,' *Media History*, 12(3): 253–272.

Somerset-Ward, R. (1993) 'Public television: The ballpark's changing,' in *Quality Time? The Report of the Twentieth Century Fund Task Force on Public Television*, New York: Twentieth Century Fund Press.

—— (1998) 'American public television: Programs—now, and in the future,' in E. M. Noam and J. Watermann (eds.) *Public Television in America*, New York: Bertelsmann Stiftung.

Splichal, S. (2006) 'Public media in service of civil society and democracy,' in C. Nissen (ed.), *Making a Difference: Public Service Broadcasting in the European Media Landscape*, Eastleigh: John Libbey.

Starr, J. M. (2000) *Air Wars: The Fight to Reclaim Public Broadcasting*, Boston, MA: Beacon Press.

Station Resource Group (2010) *Public Radio in the New Network Age: Wider Use, Deeper Value, Compelling Change*. Online. Available HTTP: http://www.srg.org/GTA/Public_Radio_in_the_New_Network_Age.pdf (accessed 8 May 2012).

—— (2011) *Toward Wider Use and Deeper Value*. Online. Available HTTP: http://www.srg.org/GTA/GTA_OrganizationReport.pdf (accessed 8 May 2012).

Stavitsky, A. G. (1993) 'Listening for listeners: Educational radio and audience research,' *Journalism History*, 19(1): 11–18.

Steenfadt, O. (ed.) (2011) *Future or Funeral? A Guide to Public Service Media Regulation in Europe*. Online. Available HTTP: http://www.mediapolicy.org/wp-content/uploads/Future-or-Funeral-11-11-2011-final-WEB.pdf (accessed 8 May 2012).

Sunstein, C. (2010) *Republic.com 2.0*, Princeton, NJ: Princeton University Press.

Tady, M. (2011) 'What you need to know about the assault on NPR and PBS,' *In These Times*, 24 February. Online. Available HTTP: http://www.inthesetimes.com/article/7001/what_you_need_to_know_about_the_assault_on_npr_and_pbs/ (accessed 8 May 2012).

Tenore, M. (2010) 'Public media API could be "engine of innovation" for journalism,' 9 September. Online. Available HTTP: http://www.poynter.org/how-tos/digital-strategies/e-media-tidbits/105504/public-media-api-could-be-engine-of-innovation-for-journalism/ (accessed 8 May 2012).

Thomson, C. (2010) 'The next big thing: How public media innovation is changing journalism,' Opening speech, 18 October, Washington, DC. Online. Available HTTP: http://www.savethenews.org/blog/11/10/19/panel-tackles-innovation-public-media (accessed 8 May 2012).

Thompson, D. (2011) 'The case for government-funded journalism,' *The Washington Post*, 4 February. Online. Available HTTP: http://voices.washingtonpost.com/ezra-klein/2011/02/the_case_for_government-funded.html (accessed 8 May 2012).

van Dijk, M., Nahuis, R. and Waagmeester, D. (2006) 'Does public service broadcasting serve the public? The future of television in the changing media landscape,' *De Economist*, 154(2): 251–276.

Varona, A. E. (2009) 'Toward a broadband public interest standard,' *Administrative Law Review*, 61: 1.

Waldman, S. *et al.* (2011) 'The information needs of communities: The changing media landscape in a broadband age.' Online. Available HTTP: http://reboot.fcc.gov/futureofmedia/ (accessed 8 May 2012).

Walker, L. R. and Sallee, J. (2011) 'The argument for funding public media,' *The Washington Post*, 3 February. Online. Available HTTP: http://www.washingtonpost.com/wp-dyn/content/article/2011/02/03/AR2011020305170_pf.html (accessed 8 May 2012).

White, H. A. (1994) 'Fine tuning the federal government's role in public broadcasting,' *Federal Communications Law Journal*, 46: 491–519.

Witherspoon, J. and Kovitz, R. (1987) *The History of Public Broadcasting*, Washington, DC: Current Publishing.

Yasko, S. (2011) 'Federal funding of public radio pays dividends,' *The Baltimore Sun*, 28 February. Online. Available HTTP: http://articles.baltimoresun.com/2011-02-28/news/bs-ed-public-broadcasting-20110228_1_federal-funding-public-radio-wtmd (accessed 8 May 2012).
Yoo, C. S. (2007) 'Copyright and public good economics: A misunderstood relation,' *University of Pennsylvania Law Review*, 155: 635–715.

# 12

# Accountability, citizenship and public media

*Richard Collins*

## Introduction

Recent changes in the structure and funding of UK media reflect both a general trend in "developed" economies and a (partial) realization of the vision put forward in the 1986 UK Peacock Report on the financing of the British Broadcasting Corporation (BBC) (Peacock 1986). The change is away from free-to-air broadcasting towards subscription funding, with a consequential "emancipation" (at least from a Peacockian perspective) of the viewer (the story for radio listeners is different), who is now able to signal preferences through prices. Advertising revenues are migrating from television to the Internet: Ofcom's[1] most recent International Communications Market study tracked sharp rises in online advertising revenues between 2003 and 2009 in 13 countries (Ofcom 2010: 214). In the United Kingdom, Internet advertising spend grew by 10 percent during this period, achieving a share of the UK advertising market of 24.3 percent (search advertising accounted for 56 percent of UK Internet advertising), outpacing the overall recovery in the advertising market and thus signaling a loss of revenues by "legacy" media and a corresponding growth of Internet advertising revenues.[2] In contrast, broadcasting subscription revenues have risen—in the United Kingdom, by 5.8 percent (Ofcom 2010: 9).

This signals a widely generalized commercial media response to the changes in the advertising market: the adoption of a different funding model—namely, subscription finance.

In 1986, the Peacock Committee, charged by the UK government with assessing the future funding of the BBC, argued that technological change would enable viewers to express their preferences through the price system (subscription funding), and thus ensure that supply and demand in broadcasting would be more and more perfectly coordinated and that market failure in broadcasting would be mitigated. Peacock's argument rested on two propositions: first, that viewers and listeners are well able to identify their own needs and interests and thus should be sovereign; and second, that, once created, well-functioning broadcasting markets

1 Ofcom, the Office of Communications, is the integrated regulator of electronic communications which replaced five former agencies and which was created under the Communications Act 2003.

2 See IAB 2010.

would enable viewers and listeners effectively to hold broadcasters to account through the price system, which would express their preferences and the intensities of their preferences.

Peacock's arguments, their adoption by governments and their growing realization through technological change, exemplify Moran's (2003) identification of a general shift in modes of institutional governance and social coordination—away from hierarchical ("command and control") governance towards market governance and coordination. Markets have been embraced both for their putative efficiency gains and also (as Peacock insisted) because they are assumed to improve users' (consumers') sovereignty and capacity to hold suppliers to account. In theory, this trend towards greater responsiveness to demand, through subscription finance (market governance), is well fitted to empowering users. In practice, however, it tends to both undersupply the "merit goods" (e.g. news) on which free and democratic societies depend, and has not emancipated users as much as theory would suggest. Subscription broadcasters tend to offer a bundle of services rather than individual services, meaning that, to get what they want, consumers often have to purchase what they do not want and also have to defray the higher transaction costs intrinsic to subscription finance. Poorer potential consumers are excluded by unaffordable prices and dominant firms have been able to exercise market power in any or all areas of a complex supply chain (including content, encryption, electronic program guides, subscription management, platform control) to chill and/or foreclose entry to broadcasting markets to the detriment of consumers (see, *inter alia*, Cox 2004: 50–53) and competitors. Nonetheless, there is some evidence that Peacock's rosy vision has been realized: users can decide whether they wish to pay or not, because they are not required to pay a compulsory subscription (a license fee) nor must they bear the costs of advertising whether or not they consume the media services funded, in whole or part, by advertising.

It is not surprising, therefore, that the growth of subscription-financed media[3] has engendered a skeptical scrutiny of publicly funded media. Not only does subscription broadcasting evidently provide the merit goods (HBO dramas, Sky Arts' concerts and opera, Discovery documentaries, etc.), which commercial broadcasting was deemed, historically, to undersupply, but also, unlike public service broadcasting, it enables viewers to signal their preferences and to hold suppliers to account through the price system. A number of historically well-established rationales and practices for and of public intervention in broadcasting have thus been put in question: notably, their efficiency, their accountability and the degree to which historically established levels of intervention were proportionate to the extent to which markets failed.

## Accountability

The last major test of public attitudes in the United Kingdom towards broadcasting (during the run up to BBC Charter renewal in 2006) revealed "clear evidence of a general desire for greater accountability to viewers and listeners, for ensuring that the interests of licence fee payers are properly represented, and for greater transparency in the way that the BBC operates": Jonathan Zeff, head of broadcasting policy at the Department for Culture, Media and Sport (DCMS), referring to findings from its 2005 public consultation on the terms under which the BBC's royal charter should be renewed, at "The Future of the BBC," Westminster

3 It is possible to exaggerate these trends: in terms of consumption, there has been scant change. Free-to-air broadcasting still dominates viewers and listeners' time budgets (see Ofcom 2011: 141, 178), but in terms of revenue, subscription broadcasters have overtaken free-to-air broadcasters (see Ofcom 2011).

Media Forum Consultation Seminar, June 2005. Ubiqus, the company undertaking the consultation to which Zeff referred, summarized respondents' concerns:

> The majority of respondents answering this question [i.e. about governance] wanted the Governors to be more directly accountable to and representative of the general public. This was the key recommendation from the public, and was often coupled to a reduction in Government influence and authority over the Governors and the BBC.
>
> (*Ubiqus 2004: 33*)[4]

In the discussion that follows, I consider how far changes in broadcasting finance and organization are consonant with the public attitudes expressed in the course of the Charter Review consultation of 2005. I draw on Warnock's (1974) notion of two-part accountability (provision of information and ability to exercise sanctions), and on both Hirschman's (1970) and Thompson's (2003) triadic distinctions (respectively, between exit, voice and loyalty, and hierarchical, market and network forms of governance). With a focus on the role of trust (drawing on O'Neill 2002), I ask: how are the accountability requirements of giving an account and holding to account exercised in the contexts defined by Hirschman and Thompson? I argue that the conservatism (and weakness) in the mechanisms and practices of BBC accountability arise from the prevailing normative framing of the relationships between the BBC and its viewers and listeners. In contrast with the "strong" framing of a sovereign *consumer* (see Peacock 1986; Potter 1988) as an active user able to hold institutions to account in a well-functioning market, the *citizen* in broadcasting is constructed (following Marshall 1981a) as a welfare recipient.

The UK debate about BBC accountability has taken place in a context in which, for the past two-and-a-half decades, institutional coordination and governance through markets has greatly increased (liberalization and privatization) and hierarchical "command and control" governance has correspondingly diminished. At the same time, significant attention has been given to the accountability of a substantial number of public-sector institutions (although broadcasting, exceptionally, has received less attention) that remain subject to hierarchical governance and organization. Kelly and Muers (2002), in an influential paper for the UK Cabinet Office, referred to a wider trend towards "a more rounded accountability which faces outwards towards users and citizens, as much as upwards towards departments and inspectorates" (Kelly and Muers 2002: 35). This trend is prevalent in the UK public sector, where police, health and education services have all been reorganized to bring them closer and make them more accountable to their users,[5] as well as more widely internationally (see, *inter alia*, Moore 1995).

Broadcasting, and the BBC, is an exception to both these trends. The governance and accountability of the BBC, despite the replacement of the time-honored board of governors

4 See also Ubiqus 2005.

5 For example, patient and public involvement forums (PPIFs) were established for all NHS trusts, statutory bodies made up of local volunteers and representatives of voluntary organizations (see Department of Health 2003). Trusts must provide information to PPIFs on demand and a PPIF has a statutory right to enter and inspect premises where either NHS trusts or primary care trusts provide services. In another relevant domain, neighbourhood policing policies charge the police with the duty to engage and involve communities in crime reduction and priority setting, and to work with citizens more closely (see Home Office 2004).

by a BBC Trust under the BBC Charter and Agreement of 2006,[6] is based on a handing down of funding and remit by government although the Trust (appointed by government), like the BBC board of governors that preceded it, has responsibility (with some duties remitted to Ofcom) for regulation and governance.

The Trust has also been charged with improving accountability to users—notably by making the BBC more transparent and by consulting license fee payers. It has built on the precedents set by its predecessor, the BBC governors, and there is no doubt as to the improvement of the quality and quantity of data about the BBC that is now available in the public domain—not least through its public value tests and service licenses authorizing BBC management to undertake specific activities on defined terms.[7] Parliamentary attention—notably, through select committees of both the House of Commons and House of Lords, the National Audit Office and the eliciting of information from the BBC under Freedom of Information entitlements—have also done much to improve the extent to which the BBC *gives an account* of itself. However, viewers' and listeners' powers *to hold the BBC to account*, either directly or indirectly through their representatives in Parliament, have hardly changed.

## Hierarchy or market? Accountability through voice and exit

The distinction between giving an account and holding to account was, to my knowledge, first made in a broadcasting context by Mary, now Baroness, Warnock.[8] She argued that accountability consists of two elements—an entitlement to knowledge and a power to impose sanctions—and stated:

> A is accountable to B where B has entrusted to A some duty (especially in regard to the spending of money) and where, if A fails to fulfill this duty, B has some sanction which he may use against A. This is one necessary part of it. But it follows that B has a *right* to be exactly informed of what A has done towards fulfilling his duty.
>
> (*Warnock 1974: 2*)

Warnock's model could be restated as a duty to *give an account* (to provide information) and to *be held to account* (to be subject to sanction). Under the tutelage of the BBC Trust, license fee payers are better informed, but the ability of license fee payers to exercise sanctions (to hold the BBC to account) has changed little, although one element of Warnock's definition is better satisfied (i.e. provision of information—powers of sanction remain with the government, Ofcom and the Trust, rather than with the license fee payer).

As to the terms "hierarchy" and "markets": governance, or control, of institutions may be exercised through a variety of different forms of coordination, notably hierarchies (command and control), markets or networks (Thompson 2003), or a combination thereof. Accountability under hierarchical governance is generally upward, whereas accountability in market governance is usually downward. Under network governance, accountability is customarily exercised through collaborative relationships and practices characterized by trust between the parties; one might call this "horizontal accountability."

6 The text of the Charter and Agreement are available online at http://www.bbc.co.uk/bbctrust/about/how_we_govern/charter_and_agreement/ (accessed 1 January 2012).

7 For discussion of these important initiatives, which have resonated across Europe, see Donders and Moe 2011.

8 Warnock is a member of the House of Lords, a philosopher of established reputation and served as a member of the Independent Broadcasting Authority.

It is a truism to observe that one of the "grand narratives" of UK public sector governance over the last quarter of a century has been a rebalancing towards market and away from hierarchical governance (see e.g. Moran 2003). This has been manifested both through a re-engineering of the internal relationships of public sector bodies to embody the precepts of "new public management" (NPM) on private sector lines (Osborne and Gaebler 1992), as well as through liberalization and privatization that reshaped public bodies' outward-facing relationships. The growing salience of market, rather than hierarchical, governance in the media and communications sector has been shaped both by technological change and by government policy. Government policy has shifted from inhibiting entry, by licensing of firms, to general authorization and promotion of entry; in both broadcasting and telecommunications, monopoly (or duopoly) has given way to competition between hundreds of firms. Technological change has delivered falling prices and intensified competition between wired (fiber optic cables and digital compression) and wireless (satellite) transmission and in information storage and processing capacity. These, together with the general adoption of Internet protocol standards, have made hierarchical control, whether of market entry or the content and character of services, more difficult to exercise.

This is not to state that markets have completely displaced hierarchy, but rather that the straightforward command-and-control systems of hierarchical governance that existed fifty years ago for broadcasting, post and telecommunications have given way to a complex intersection of different governance systems, with market and network governance assuming a much greater role than before. This is particularly prevalent in the Internet sector. In broadcasting, the shift has been slower and less pronounced, but as advertising revenues decline and subscription funding grows, the non-market elements in the UK broadcasting system, and the BBC in particular, have come increasingly to be measured against a market template.

## Exit, voice and loyalty

In 1970, Albert Hirschman published his *Exit, Voice and Loyalty*, in which he identifies three ways in which stakeholders can hold institutions to account—through exercise of what he called "exit," "voice," and "loyalty." Different governance systems provide different means for stakeholders to signal their preferences by **exit**ing from the relationship (through market governance by ceasing to buy products and services), making their **voice** heard (through hierarchical governance by voting) or by demonstrating their **loyalty**.

If "loyalty" is regarded as a null option (if one is loyal, then one does not exercise voice or exit), exit is exercised through price and voice through politics. True, "voice" may be exercised in market systems (e.g. via complaints) and "exit" may be exercised in hierarchical systems (e.g. by leaving the jurisdiction in question), but "voice" remains a form of accountability principally exercised in political systems and "exit" a form of accountability principally exercised in market or commercial systems.

Applying Hirschman's model to broadcasting shows that there are significant imperfections in both market and hierarchical accountability mechanisms. In advertising-financed market systems, viewers and listeners have few opportunities to hold broadcasters to account and broadcasters are seldom required to give an account to users: users lack the means to effectively exercise the sanction of voice (although they may write, phone in, or formally complain), but they do have an exit sanction. Although viewers and listeners do not directly fund advertising-financed broadcasting, viewer and listener exit has adverse (indirect) financial consequences for the broadcaster. In subscription-funded systems, viewers and listeners also have few opportunities to hold broadcasters to account (and nor are broadcasters characteristically required to give an account to users) through the exercise of voice (although they too may write, phone in or formally complain), but they too are effectively able to exercise the sanction of exit—and their exit has direct and adverse financial consequences for subscription-financed broadcasters.

For the BBC and other public service broadcasters like it, funded neither by advertising nor subscription, viewers and listeners have few opportunities either to exercise voice or to exit.[9] Viewers and listeners are unable to directly and effectively represent their preferences to the BBC—that is, to exercise voice—because the BBC lacks the institutional forms of either joint stock companies (shareholders' meetings, election of directors, reporting requirements defined by stock exchanges and financial regulators) or democratic politics (notably the election of representatives) through which "voice" can be expressed. Nor are viewers, license fee payers, able to lawfully exit from their relationship with the BBC (other than by abstaining from *all* television consumption).[10] In Hirschman's terms, the public is unable effectively to hold the BBC to account because it is unable either to exercise voice or to exit.

Such public disenfranchisement appears increasingly anomalous as the very devices, such as computers and mobile phones, which empower the public more effectively to control its general viewing experience trigger a liability to pay for BBC services whether or not they are used and independent of how much they are used, without a corresponding ability to hold the BBC to account. Loyalty, rather than being chosen, is made compulsory. The price of loyalty has also increased: public funding of the BBC rose by 63 percent between 1997 and 2010. However, the BBC has been required to give an account of itself to viewers and listeners to a greater degree than have commercial broadcasters.

## The BBC and horizontal accountability

In spite of the growth of market governance, the UK broadcasting sector is less subject to market governance, and thus accountability through exit, than are other communication sectors. The BBC enjoys a very special status as a publicly owned body that, in important respects, is not subject either to external hierarchical governance and upward accountability or to market governance and downward responsibility to users. The importance of the BBC's editorial and journalistic independence has secured significant measures of exemption for the BBC from the formal scrutiny of Parliament and from comprehensive regulation by Ofcom.[11] These exemptions qualify the extent to which the BBC is hierarchically subject to a requirement either to give an account of itself and to be held to account by an external authority.

Viewers and listeners (formally, the license fee is a charge only on television viewers, but most radio listeners are also television viewers and thus license fee payers) are unable lawfully to exit from their obligation to fund the BBC. Yet the BBC is not upwardly, hierarchically,

9 True, viewers and listeners may cease to consume BBC programs, but this has no obvious financial impact on the BBC (BBC funding has risen over the last decade, although its share of television, but not radio, consumption has fallen). However, it seems likely that there is a "tipping point" at which compulsory license fee funding would cease to have legitimacy because too few were watching or listening to BBC services. That point has yet to be reached.

10 The license fee is a charge only on television viewers; currently, there is no radio license in the United Kingdom. The license fee is formally classified as a tax by the Office of National Statistics (ONS 2006).

11 Although at the price of significant measures of government control of BBC finance, remit and governance.

accountable in respect of its funding as are other tax-funded public sector and public service institutions. The BBC's license fee/tax funding is not subject to parliamentary scrutiny,[12] as is other tax-funded activity, and only in 2011 was the BBC made formally subject to audit by the National Audit Office (NAO). The BBC's self-regulating and self-authorizing status has been thought necessary to secure the editorial and journalistic independence that is both a major *raison d'être* of the BBC and is regarded widely as among its most significant and valuable achievements. In turn, its self-regulatory and self-authorizing status has rested on public trust in the BBC rather than on the ability of the public to hold the BBC to account. How widely is the BBC trusted and how well founded is that trust?

## Trust

In a poll conducted in January 2005, YouGov found[13] that the BBC is "still the most trusted for news" (though Sky News is more trusted than the BBC's News 24) (YouGov 2006). However, the BBC's trustworthiness has come into question in a number of instances. Lord Hutton's probe (Hutton 2004) into the "Gilligan affair" revealed how some aspects of the BBC's journalistic and editorial procedures had fallen short of the high standards on which public trust has been based.[14] Others have observed that the BBC's procedures fall short of those adopted by other highly reputed news organizations (e.g. BBC 2006 and O'Neill 2004: 12). Different aspects of BBC conduct, such as those revealed in the PKF Report on BBC funding (DCMS 2006b) and National Audit Office (NAO) reports on value for money[15] provided by the BBC, have also given rise to concern. Further, enquiries into specific aspects of BBC journalism (such as the BBC's reporting of the European Union, the Israel–Palestine conflict and intra-UK affairs; see BBC 2005b, 2006 and 2008) have found grounds for criticism. Most damaging, though, was the fact that Ofcom fined the BBC £400,000 for eight separate breaches of the Ofcom program codes. Ofcom commented: "In each of these cases the BBC deceived its audience by faking winners of competitions and deliberately conducting competitions unfairly" (see Ofcom 2008). A year earlier, Ofcom had fined the BBC £50,000 for falsifying the results of a competition on the iconic children's program *Blue Peter.*[16] Moreover, the sheer volume of recent studies and enquiries into the BBC suggest some generalized disquiet about aspects of its performance and grounds to probe whether the pervasive public trust in the BBC is wholly well founded.[17]

12 Parliament can only approve or reject, but not amend, the government's proposals for the BBC license fee.

13 See also BBC 2004a: 45.

14 The BBC's own reflections on its journalistic and editorial practices, the Neil Report (BBC 2004b), constructively acknowledged that the BBC had a case to answer and that its procedures and training should be improved.

15 See BBC n.d.a.; n.d.b.

16 The BBC Trust stated that these "were particularly serious as they resulted in children being misled to participate in a competition they had no chance of winning and in a child in the studio being involved in deceiving the audience" (BBC 2007).

17 To invoke the findings of National Audit Office studies of the BBC's operational performance and the findings of enquiries into the quality and character of BBC journalism may suggest that the BBC is damned if it does and damned if it does not. There can be no doubt that the commissioning, formally by the governors, and publication of such studies betokens a laudable transparency in BBC governance and perhaps a healthy institutional culture of self-criticism.

We have, then, a complex series of (incomplete) systems of holding the BBC to account, but which exist in a context of accumulating evidence that the BBC's self-authorizing practices may not be worthy of public trust. O'Neill's proposition that "traditional approaches to compliance relied heavily on cultures of trust" (O'Neill 2005: 1) does much to explain both why formal systems of holding the BBC to account have been patchy and underdeveloped and why there are now unprecedented levels of demand for more formality in the mechanisms used to hold it to account.

## Accountability or obligation?

The changes to the BBC's governance arising from the Charter review around 2005–06, notably the rebadging of the BBC's board of governors as the BBC Trust, did little to strengthen viewers' and listeners' power to hold the BBC to account. Rather, in varying degrees, they have nominally, rather than substantively, remodeled the established system of upward, hierarchical, accountability in contrast with a general social trend (see Blaug, Horner and Lekhi 2006) towards greater user and citizen participation in the policy and practice of public sector institutions.

Why should the BBC be an exception to this trend? Essentially, because viewers and listeners are not thought to be competent judges of their own needs and interests. In part, this reflects a general relationship between experts and non-experts: it is appropriate and customary for non-experts to defer to experts (e.g. in education, medicine, law and other domains). In part, it reflects the BBC's sedulous guardianship of its independence, recently exemplified in its rejection (on the grounds that the electoral process might be subject to capture) of election of members of its advisory committees.[18] In part, it is a legacy of Reith's notion of users of BBC services as incompetent to judge their own needs[19]—a notion that the Pilkington Committee eloquently restated as "Those who say they give the public what it wants begin by underestimating public taste and in the end by debauching it" (Pilkington 1962: para. 47). And in part it is an aspect of the BBC's role as provider of "merit goods":[20] individuals are likely to "under demand" merit goods—those goods and services beneficial to society as a whole—when greater benefits accrue to society than accrue to the individuals making the demand decisions. In such cases, supply will reflect the lower levels of demand expressed by individuals acting in their individual interests rather than the levels optimal for society as a whole. In consequence, society should step in to collectively supplement the inadequate levels of individual demand for such "merit goods"—see, *inter alia*,

18 All of the BBC's (and BBC-appointed) advisory bodies have refused to brook election of their members (BBC 2005a: 94, 97, 100, 103). And the BBC, perhaps rather ventriloquistically, supported them (BBC 2005a: 59).

19 Reith's comment provides a representative flavor of this sentiment: "In earliest years accused of setting out to give the public not what it wanted but what the BBC thought it should have, the answer was that few knew what they wanted, fewer what they needed" (Reith 1949: 101).

20 "Merit goods," in the language of neoclassical economics, are goods that confer long-term benefits, but for which no individual thinks it is worth paying. Examples include high culture, scientific research, education, etc. Because free markets tend to undersupply merit goods, it is generally accepted that there is a legitimate role for the state in providing them; hence public funding for education, the arts, research and public service broadcasting. Without the justification afforded by its provision of merit goods, the legitimacy of both public funding and a system of governance offering those who pay few opportunities either to "exit" or exercise their "voice" is compromised (see Hirschman 1970).

Graham's (1999) and Davies' (2005) "standard defence" of public service broadcasting as a provider of merit goods.

A view of individual users of broadcasting services as incompetent to decide leads necessarily to a rejection of viewer and listener sovereignty over the BBC. But such a conception of the viewer and listener risks leaving the BBC marooned as an isolated relic of "club governance" and underdeveloped downward accountability at a time both when other public sector bodies have strengthened their accountability to users and when consumer sovereignty is more and more salient as an objective in markets (see Department of Health 2003; Home Office 2004).

## The consumer and the citizen in broadcasting

Both the growth in salience of the market sector in communications and the impact of new public management (NPM) and its doctrines on the public sector (Kelly and Muers 2002; Moore 1995; Osborne and Gaebler 1992) has thus led some to intensified scrutiny and criticism of the BBC. Reciprocally, it has been defended as a public sector bastion that, because of its importance for "citizenship" should not be subjected to the market and NPM norms. In this context, the term "citizenship" has been categorically distinguished from the term "consumer," with different accountability (and other) entitlements and expectations attaching to each identity.

Accountability to consumers, normatively, is to be realized by enabling consumers to make (or not make) purchases from one or more of a number of competing providers (see also Potter 1988). Within this sort of normative schema, public service broadcasting, and the BBC in particular, looks at best somewhat odd and at worst appears as a major obstacle standing in the way of a well-functioning market through which consumers are able to hold producers and providers accountable through the price system.

Accountability to citizens, on the other hand, is both more difficult to define (but see Calabrese and Burgelman 1999; Hartley 1999; Murdock 1999a, 1999b, and 2004; Stevenson 2003) and to realize. Moreover, the term "citizen" has been given a particular inflection in discussions of UK broadcasting policy and this inflection has marginalized accountability questions. The notion of citizenship as a power to share in decision-making (see, *inter alia*, Brinckmann 1930) or, in Hirschman's terms, to exercise voice has scarcely been considered, much less implemented. Perhaps the fear of what Heller (1978: 2) wittily identified as the unwelcome possibility of a "Hobbesian state of anarchy and disruption," which might attend the exercise of a "public right to intervene in the management of services," is the reason for this absence. Fear of Hobbesian horror, rather than fear of "public service bureaucracies that are insulated from public or parliamentary scrutiny and effectively independent in their pursuit of organizational objectives and growth" (Heller 1978: 2), has been the stronger force in public policy and practice.

Instead of either a market system of accountability, in which users can exercise the sanction of exit, or a hierarchical system, in which users can exercise the sanction of voice, the BBC is governed by a kind of trust-based horizontal system of network accountability based on mutual obligation. These reciprocal obligations consist in the broadcaster's obligation to provide the information and education (sweetened with entertainment) that viewers and listeners require to participate fully in social and political life, and in viewers' and listeners' obligation to provide the funding necessary for broadcasters to do so. If trust, on which such relationships of mutual obligation depend, erodes (as trust in the BBC has begun to erode), and if more formalized and effective accountability arrangements of voice and/or exit are established in other domains (as they are being and have been), then the institutions and relationships of a trust-based order tend to lose legitimacy. This relationship of mutual obligation is consonant with the dominant version of citizenship mobilized in the UK broadcasting discourse that is strongly indebted to the work of T. H. Marshall.

## Citizenship

There are a host of definitions of "citizenship," but Brinkmann's (1930: 471) usefully identifies two components to citizenship: notably, "the notion of liberty . . . and membership of a political unit involving co-operation in public decisions as a right and sharing of public burdens . . . as a duty." Interestingly, neither of these normative conceptions has much figured in UK accounts of broadcasting and citizenship, and this may be explained by the remarkable salience of the work of T. H. Marshall in such discussions. Marshall is the most-cited author[21] in the index to Calabrese and Burgelman's 1999 collection of essays on citizenship and communications, and Marshall's thought is the source of the "welfarist" move characteristically evident in contemporary scholarly discussion of broadcasting and citizenship. The welfarist move, I argue, constitutes broadcasting as one of a bundle of welfare rights and thereby extends Marshall's triad of rights (civic, political and social) to encompass additional putative broadcasting-related rights.

Calabrese usefully summarizes Marshall (Calabrese and Burgelman 1999: 261) as having defined "citizenship" as consisting in three elements, each realized at a distinct historical moment: first, civic rights (secured in Western Europe in the eighteenth century); second, political rights (secured in Western Europe at the end of the nineteenth century); and third, welfare rights (secured in Western Europe in the twentieth century).[22] Marshall's triadic bundle of rights (civil, political and social) provides a template for a number of influential accounts of citizenship and the media. Murdock (1999), for example, extends Marshall's bundle to include a fourth type of right—information and cultural rights—and has argued that "the core rationale for public service broadcasting lies in its commitment to providing the cultural resources required for full citizenship" (Murdock 2004: 2). Hartley (1999) further extends the definition of citizenship to include a fifth form: "DIY"—"do it yourself"—citizenship.

Marshall and his successors thus offer a notion of citizenship as an onion: each bundle of citizenship entitlements/attributes surrounds the others concentrically, and in complementary and non-rival fashion. But all layers of the onion must putatively be present if the entitlements of citizenship are to be fully realized. Marshall added a third layer (social rights) to a pre-existing two-layer onion (civic and political rights), and Murdock, Hartley and others have added further layers (notably the cultural and/or informational, and the DIY, layers).

But Marshall's extension of the concept of citizenship constructs citizenship *passively*, as a series of entitlements—or as he puts it "rights and legitimate expectations"—rather than as an active, participatory and creative practice. Marshall refers to "welfare" as an "integral part of the whole apparatus that includes social security, education, public health, the

21 Castells and Habermas score the same number of citations in the index.

22 We may pass over this occidental perspective as not unreasonable when addressing so Western a phenomenon—the notable oriental instances of, *inter alia*, Indian, Japanese, Taiwanese and Thai public service broadcasting notwithstanding.

medical services, factory legislation, the right to strike, and all the other rights and legitimate expectations which are attached to modern citizenship" (Marshall 1981a: 81). Citizenship is thus a condition of competence legitimately to make claims on others within a polity. It does not include the power to hold authority to account or to participate in making decisions.

## Consumer and citizen concepts in action

The terms "consumer" and "citizen" were embedded in UK broadcasting law for the first time in the Communications Act 2003 (CA 2003), which defines "citizen" as "all members of the public in the United Kingdom" (section 3(14), but does not define "consumer" (although the Act attributes particular importance to consumers' interests, notably "in respect of choice, price, quality of service and value for money"—section 3(5)). The Act requires Ofcom:

> (a) to further the interests of citizens in relation to communications matters; and
> (b) to further the interests of consumers in relevant markets, where appropriate by promoting competition.
>
> (*CA 2003*, s. 3(1))

The term "consumer," although found in the Telecommunications Act 1984, effectively entered the UK broadcasting policy discourse in the Peacock Report (Peacock 1986). The report, formally a consideration of BBC funding, argued for stronger and more effective consumer sovereignty realized through a greater use of markets.

Broadcasting markets have changed in different ways from those Peacock envisaged, and UK pay television is far from a consumer arcadia, but though the Peacock Report's predictions have yet to be fully borne out, the Report marked a decisive conceptual break with established doctrines that constituted viewers (and listeners) as vulnerable and in need of protection.[23] Opposition to the Peacockian vision (and notably to the reduction in the size and scale of public service broadcasting that Peacock foreshadowed) and its flagship notion of the sovereign consumer crystallized (as discussed above) around the rival, and somewhat numinous, term "citizen." This term, although never articulated in a formal and official report, as was the term "consumer" by Peacock, was inserted into the CA 2003 as one of the two fundamental interests that Ofcom was charged to serve. The term "citizen" entered the text of the Act thanks to successful lobbying of Parliament by broadcasting activists concerned by the possible effect that Ofcom's duty only to secure the consumer interest would have on broadcasting.

Since the CA 2003 came into effect, the BBC, the government and Ofcom have all put forward accounts of broadcasting and citizenship (see BBC 2004; DCMS 2006a; Ofcom 2004), but none include an active notion of citizenship that comprehends citizens' power to hold institutions to account. Rather, in so far as viewers' and listeners' ability to hold broadcasters to account figures in such discussions, it is in their capacity as consumers that they are empowered. See, for example, Ed Richards'[24] statement that:

23 This "guardianship" mentality was exemplified in the Pilkington Report (1962). For discussion, see, *inter alia*, Collins, Garnham and Locksley 1988: 114–117.

24 Given when Richards was Ofcom's Senior Partner for Strategy and Market Developments. He subsequently became Chief Executive of Ofcom (and, at the time of writing, continued to hold that post).

> As consumers, our concern is that we are supplied with what we as individuals, or perhaps on behalf of our families, *want to watch or what we want to have an option to watch.*
>
> (*Ofcom 2004*)

Richards further claimed (as the Peacock Committee in 1986 had envisaged) that:

> Post analogue switch off we will see the evolution of something approaching a reasonably well functioning market in broadcasting . . . consumers, through *their own* choices will be able to express their preferences—through what they choose to watch, what they choose to subscribe to or what they choose to buy on a per view basis.
>
> (*Ofcom 2004*)

In the elaboration of policy norms (BBC 2004; DCMS 2006a; Ofcom 2004, etc.) we see broadcasting's role in respect of the citizen defined (whether broadly or narrowly) as the provision of socially desirable content by broadcasters, whereas the relationship between broadcasting and the consumer is conceived as one in which consumers are able to express and realize their preferences. The rhetorical construction of the broadcasting citizen and the broadcasting consumer is that being a citizen is to have provided by an authority—*control resides outside the citizen*—whereas being a broadcasting consumer is to be in control of what one watches (or listens to)—*control resides with the consumer.*

## Conclusion

The debate about the future of the BBC that took place in the United Kingdom throughout 2004–06 was remarkable for its range and intensity, although finally resulting in something very like the status quo ante for the BBC. The accountability of the BBC, although a matter on which both the public expressed its concern in the government's consultations and parliamentary and other enquiries expressed views in the wealth of commentaries and reports that appeared during Charter review, remains much as it was before. True, the BBC Trust is charged to give viewers and listeners a better and fuller account of the BBC than were, and did, the governors. True, the Trust is more clearly distinguished from the BBC management than was its predecessor (and may therefore be better able to hold the BBC to account). But little has changed in the crucial relationship between the user and the broadcaster. Whether as consumer or citizen, the viewer and listener disposes of few powers to hold the BBC to account.

The viewer and listener's relationship to the BBC is conceptually constructed as a relationship of citizenship (rather than of consumption); second, there is a clear normative rhetoric in both scholarly and policy domains that constructs citizenship as a derivative of the content that broadcaster(s) provide for viewers and listeners—content the consumption of which, it is assumed, will foster citizenship properties in viewers and listeners.[25] This, then, is a *passive* conception of citizenship. In contrast, the consumer of broadcasting is, normatively at least, able to exercise choice: s/he is constructed as an *active* agent. In consequence, viewers and listeners are compelled to trust; they have neither voice nor exit and thus enjoy no alternative to loyalty. At best, there is only an account of the BBC given by an unchosen representative,

25 There is, of course, no necessary correspondence between the normative and the empirical.

the Trust, rather than an ability to hold to account that, normatively, a citizen not fated to a Marshallian passivity as a client of top-down welfare might enjoy.

## References


BBC (n.d.a) 'Value for money reviews.' Online. Available HTTP: http://www.bbc.co.uk/bbctrust/our_work/vfm/index.shtml (accessed 8 December 2011).

—— (n.d.b) 'BBC Governor's reviews: Value for money reviews.' Online. Available HTTP: http://www.bbc.co.uk/bbctrust/our_work/other/govs/vfm.shtml (accessed 8 December 2011).

—— (2004a) 'The BBC's contribution to informed citizenship.' Online. Available HTTP: http://www.bbccharterreview.org.uk/pdf_documents/BBC_submission_informed.pdf (accessed 16 February 2006).

—— (2004b) *The BBC's Journalism after Hutton: The Report of the Neil Review Team*, London: BBC. Online. Available HTTP: http://www.bbc.co.uk/info/policies/pdf/neil_report.pdf (accessed 26 February 2006).

—— (2005a) *Review of the BBC's Royal Charter: BBC Response to a Strong BBC, Independent of Government*, London: BBC. Online. Available HTTP: http://www.bbc.co.uk/thefuture/pdfs/green_paper_response.pdf (accessed 28 December 2005).

—— (2005b) *BBC News Coverage of the European Union: Independent Panel Report*. Online. Available HTTP: http://www.bbcgovernors.co.uk/docs/reviews/independentpanelreport.pdf (accessed 11 July 2006).

—— (2006) *Report of the Independent Panel for the BBC Governors on Impartiality of BBC Coverage of the Israeli–Palestinian Conflict*. Online. Available HTTP: http://www.bbcgovernors.co.uk/docs/reviews/panel_report_final.pdf (accessed 25 June 2006).

—— (2007) 'Premium rate telephony and related editorial issues: BBC trust statement,' 29 May. Online. Available HTTP: http://www.bbc.co.uk/bbctrust/news/press_releases/2007/may/29_may.shtml (accessed 29 May 2012).

—— (2008) *The BBC Trust Impartiality Report: BBC Network News and Current Affairs Coverage of the Four UK Nations*, London: BBC Trust. Online. Available HTTP: http://downloads.bbc.co.uk/northernireland/archive/chronicle/pdf/2000s_archival/2_King.pdf (accessed 21 September 2011).

Blaug, R., Horner, L. and Lekhi, R. (2006) *Public Value, Politics and Public Management: A Literature Review*, London: The Work Foundation.

Brinkmann, C. (1959 [1930]) 'Citizenship,' in E. Seligman and A. Johnson (eds.) *Encyclopedia of the Social Sciences*, New York: Macmillan.

Calabrese, A. (1999) 'The welfare state, the information society, and the ambivalence of social movements,' in A. Calabrese and J.C. Burgelman (eds.) *Communication, Citizenship, and Social Policy: Re-thinking the Limits of the Welfare State*, Lanham, MD: Rowman & Littlefield.

—— and Burgelman J.-C. (eds.) (1999) *Communication, Citizenship and Social Policy*, Lanham, MD: Rowman and Littlefield.

Collins, R., Garnham, N. and Locksley G. (1988) *The Economics of Television: The UK Case*, London: Sage.

Cox, B. (2004) *Free for All? Public Service Television in the Digital Age*, London: Demos. Online. Available HTTP: http://www.demos.co.uk/media/freeforall_page378.aspx (accessed 29 March 2005).

Davies, G. (2005) 'The BBC and public value,' in D. Helm (ed.) *Can the Market Deliver? Funding Public Service in the Digital Age*, Bloomington, IN: Indiana University Press.

Donders, K. and Moe H. (eds.) (2011) *Exporting the Public Value Test*, Gothenburg: Nordicom.

Department for Culture, Media and Sport (DCMS) (2006a) *A Public Service for All: The BBC in the Digital Age*, London: DCMS. Online. Available HTTP: http://www.bbccharterreview.org.uk/have_your_say/white_paper/bbc_whitepaper_march06.pdf (accessed 7 April 2006).

—— (2006b) *Review of the BBC Value for Money and Efficiency Programmes* (the PKF Report). Online. Available HTTP: http://www.bbccharterreview.org.uk/pdf_documents/pkfreport_bbcfundin0406.pdf (accessed 21 May 2006).

Department of Health (2003) *Briefing Note*. Online. Available HTTP: http://www.dh.gov.uk/assetRoot/04/07/42/88/04074288.pdf (accessed 14 August 2006).

Graham, A. (1999) 'Broadcasting policy in the multimedia age,' in A. Graham *et al.* (eds.) *Public Purposes in Broadcasting*, Luton: University of Luton Press.

Gripsrud, J. (ed.) (1999) *Television and Common Knowledge*, London: Routledge.
Hartley, J. (1999) *Uses of Television*, London: Routledge.
Heller, C. (1978) *Broadcasting and Accountability*, London: British Film Institute.
Helm, D. *et al.* (2005) *Can the Market Deliver? Funding Public Service Television in the Digital Age*, Eastleigh: John Libbey.
Hirschman, A. (1970) *Exit, Voice and Loyalty: Responses to Decline in Firms, Organizations, and States*, Cambridge, MA: Harvard University Press.
Home Office (2004) *Building Communities, Beating Crime: A Better Police Service for the 21st Century*, Cm 6360, London: HMSO. Online. Available HTTP: http://police.homeoffice.gov.uk/news-and-publications/publication/police-reform/wp04_complete.pdf?view=Binary (accessed 14 August 2006).
Internet Advertising Bureau UK (IAB) (2010) 'UK online ad spend rises 10%,' 5 October. Online. Available HTTP: http://www.iabuk.net/news/uk-online-adspend-rises-10 (accessed 21 December 2011).
Kelly, G. and Muers, S. (2002) *Creating Public Value: An Analytical Framework for Public Service Reform*, London: Strategy Unit, Cabinet Office. Online. Available HTTP: http://www.e-democracy.gov.uk/documents/retrieve.asp?pk_document=22&pagepath=http://www.e-democracy.gov.uk:80/knowledgepool/ (accessed 3 January 2006).
Lord Hutton (2004) *Report of the Inquiry into the Circumstances Surrounding the Death of Dr David Kelly CMG*, HC 247, London: HMSO. Online. Available HTTP: http://www.the-hutton-inquiry.org.uk/content/report/index.htm (accessed 29 March 2005).
Mackay, H. and O'Sullivan T. (eds.) (1999) *The Media Reader: Continuity and Transformation*, London: Sage.
Marshall, T. (ed.) (1981a [1972]) *The Right to Welfare*, London: Heinemann Educational.
—— (1981b [1972]) 'Welfare in the context of social policy,' in T. Marshall (ed.) The Right to Welfare, London: Heinemann Educational.
Moore, M. (1995) *Creating Public Value: Strategic Management in Government*, Cambridge, MA: Harvard University Press.
Moran, M. (2003) *The British Regulatory State: High Modernism and Hyper-Innovation*, Oxford: Oxford University Press.
Murdock, G. (1999a) 'Rights and representations: Public discourse and cultural citizenship,' in J. Gripsrud (ed.) *Television and Common Knowledge*, London: Routledge.
—— (1999b) 'Corporate dynamics and broadcasting futures,' in H. Mackay and T. O'Sullivan (eds.) *The Media Reader: Continuity and Transformation*, London: Sage.
—— (2004) 'Building the digital commons: Public broadcasting in the Age of the Internet,' The 2004 Graham Spry Memorial Lecture. Online. Available HTTP: http://www.com.umontreal.ca/spry/spry-gm-lec.htm (accessed 12 January 2005).
Ofcom (2004) Speech of 25/5/2004 to the Westminster Media Forum by Ed Richards, Senior Partner, Strategy & Market Developments, Ofcom on Ofcom's Review of Public Service Television Broadcasting. Online. Available HTTP: http://media.ofcom.org.uk/2004/05/25/speech-to-westminster-media-forum-ofcom-review-of-public-service-broadcasting/ (accessed 8 December 2011).
—— (2008) 'Ofcom fines the BBC for unfair conduct of viewer and listener competitions,' 30 July. Online. Available HTTP: http://media.ofcom.org.uk/2008/07/30/ofcom-fines-the-bbc-for-unfair-conduct-of-viewer-and-listener-competitions/ (accessed 8 December 2011).
—— (2010) *International Communications Market Report 2010*, London: Ofcom. Online. Available HTTP: http://stakeholders.ofcom.org.uk/binaries/research/cmr/753567/icmr/ICMR_2010.pdf (accessed 21 September 2011).
—— (2011) *Communications Market Report UK*, London: Ofcom. Online. Available HTTP http://stakeholders.ofcom.org.uk/binaries/research/cmr/cmr11/UK_CMR_2011_FINAL.pdf (accessed 31 December 2011).
Office of National Statistics (ONS) (2006) 'Classification of public sector television,' News release 20 January. Online. Available HTTP: http://www.statistics.gov.uk/pdfdir/cpst0106.pdf (accessed 17 February 2006).
O'Neill, O. (2002) *A Question of Trust*, Cambridge: Cambridge University Press.
—— (2004) *Rethinking Freedom of the Press*, Dublin: Royal Irish Academy.
—— (2005) 'Justice, trust and accountability' [Text provided to the author in English as personal communication; published in German as "Gerechtigkeit, Vertrauen und Zurechenbarkeit"], in

O. Neumaier, C. Sedmak and M. Zichy (eds.) (2005) *Gerechtigkeit: Auf der Suche nach einem Gleichgewicht*, Frankfurt: Ontos Verlag.

Osborne, D. and Gaebler, T. (1992) *Reinventing Government: How the Entrepreneurial Spirit is Transforming The Public Sector*, Reading, MA, and Wokingham: Addison Wesley.

Peacock, A. (1986) *Report of the Committee on Financing the BBC*, Cmnd 9824, London: HMSO.

Pilkington, Sir H. (1962) *Report of the Committee on Broadcasting 1960*, Cmnd. 1753, London: HMSO.

Potter, J. (1988) 'Consumerism and the public sector: How well does the coat fit?' *Public Administration*, 66: 149–164.

Reith, J. (1949) *Into the Wind*, London: Hodder and Stoughton.

Stevenson, N. (2003) *Cultural Citizenship*, Maidenhead: Open University Press.

Thompson, G. (2003) *Between Hierarchies and Markets: The Logic and Limits of Network Forms of Organization*, Oxford: Oxford University Press.

Ubiqus (2004) *BBC Royal Charter Review: An Analysis of Responses to the DCMS Consultation*. Online. Available HTTP: http://www.bbccharterreview.org.uk/pdf_documents/ubiques_analysis_bbccr_responses.pdf (accessed 26 February 2006).

—— (2005) *BBC Royal Charter Review: Green Paper Public Consultation—An Analysis of Responses to the DCMS Consultation*. Online. Available HTTP: http://www.bbccharterreview.org.uk/pdf_documents/ur_analysis%20of%20gpresponses.pdf (accessed 20 April 2006).

Warnock, M. (1974) 'Accountability, responsibility—or both?' *Independent Broadcasting*, 2: 2–3.

# Part III

# Media policy and comparative perspectives

# 13

# Customary law and media regulation in conflict and post-conflict states

*Nicole Stremlau*

In the process of drafting new media laws for states emerging from violent conflict, or transitioning towards more democratic governments, the role of customary law is often overlooked. While "best practices" or international standards draw on widely accepted norms of international human rights law, they also focus on the experience of media regulation that has emerged in Western countries promoted by non-governmental organizations (NGOs) and international actors in the name of "freedom of expression." The adoption of these norms and regulatory institutions is encouraged, often wholesale, with little attention to the local context. After laws are adopted, the emphasis then tends to shift to their uptake or to teaching relevant legal authorities about how to apply the provisions and raise awareness, particularly among journalists, about the new media legislation.

This chapter argues that even if customary law has not been sufficiently developed to address questions of information communication technologies (ICTs) or the mass media, it can have a role in ensuring the rule of law and may also hold important examples and relevance for the drafting of new media legislation. The focus in this chapter is on examples from Somalia and Somaliland, but there is undoubtedly resonance across other societies with customary law regimes in Sub-Saharan Africa, such as the Dagomba in Northern Ghana, the Luo in Western Kenya, and the Oromo in Southern Ethiopia. Further afield, countries struggling to build state institutions and to emerge from war, such as Iraq and Afghanistan, have rich traditions of customary law. While dictatorships and international conflict can erode and strain local social order, customary law is often extraordinarily resilient and it can have an important role in peacemaking.

Despite recent trends towards "hybridity" in the criminal justice sector, as notably seen in the transitional justice debates, the role of customary law has received little international attention. This is particularly the case when compared with Sharia law, or Islamic law, which has been included in recent lawmaking processes in countries that are instituting democratic practices in the aftermath of the "Arab Spring." "States," with their artificial boundaries in much of Africa and the Middle East, might have multiple customary law regimes that may differ significantly, but customary law is often outward-looking, with provisions governing relations and interactions between neighboring clans, tribes or groups. Additionally, in urban areas, group-based social contracts, which are a common characteristic of customary law, may be less potent among fragmented families and diverse communities, further reducing customary law's relevance. At the same time, the very nature of customary laws can help to identify common ground. For lawmaking to have legitimacy and resonance in many post-war societies, it must be in dialog with, if not directly drawing on, customary law. This is particularly true for the Somali-speaking region of the Horn of Africa.[1]

Somalia has been without a functioning government since early 1991, when the Soviet-backed government of President Siad Barre fell, and it is commonly described as "lawless" or "the world's most failed state" (Messner 2011). This conceptualization not only overlooks public authority and governance more generally, but it also obscures the way in which law and governance actually works in Somalia. Prevailing analyses of the media environment often have a similar focus—emphasizing what is not working. Despite common perceptions, media across Somalia are vibrant and have expanded significantly since the fall of Barre's regime. There are dozens of radio stations broadcasting across South-Central Somalia. Weekly newspapers roll off the presses in Somaliland's capital of Hargeysa, mobile phones are pervasive and Somali satellite television channels are beamed into teahouses across the region. Despite the growth of media and ICTs, parts of Somalia remain among the most dangerous in the world for a journalist. While the violence and challenges faced by local media are comparatively well documented,[2] the focus in this chapter is on an often-overlooked aspect: namely, how the media function in the absence of a state and without the formal governance and regulations that accompany state institutions.

The three main regions of Somalia, including the self-declared independent Republic of Somaliland in the north, the self-governing region of Puntland, and the region referred to as South-Central Somalia (where the Transitional Federal Government, or TFG, is striving to establish a government despite continued conflict with the extremist group Al Shabaab), all have media laws on the books. Yet to fully understand media "law" in this region, we must move beyond a state-centric approach that emphasizes formal laws, judiciaries and the role of governments, and consider the role of *xeer* (or *heer*). *Xeer* is analogous to a customary law regime, but more far-reaching, in that it serves as an overall social contract not only providing legal precedents, but also a broader agreement for governing relations between clans and the role of the individual within society. It is typically a bilateral agreement between two groups; it is neither static nor uniform and the "laws" vary on the agreements reached between groups.

This chapter will focus on the distinctiveness of *xeer*, and the role of the elders, or traditional leaders, and communities that implement it, in providing a legal framework for the media and rule of law in Somalia more generally. Through the mediation and enforcement of cultural norms on the part of elders, the media across the Somali-speaking region have been able to flourish. At times, elders have provided recourse for common legal challenges faced by media outlets, such as accusations of libel or slander. *Xeer* has also offered mechanisms for protecting property, such as technology and infrastructure, and opportunities for businesses to recover stolen funds or overdue payments lawfully. The ways in which some contemporary media issues have been and continue to be resolved reflect both the legacy and current reality of the importance of *xeer*.

Two cases will be used to illustrate the enduring relevance of *xeer* in regulating the media. The first examines issues around defamation and insult by discussing the 2007 case of the *Haatuf*

1 The Somali-speaking region of the Horn of Africa includes the regions of Somalia as well as the Ogaden region of Ethiopia, Northern Kenya and parts of Djibouti, all of which are primarily populated by Somalis with significant cross-border movement.

2 See, e.g., the latest Freedom House 2001 or Reporters sans Frontières 2009b reports on Somalia.

newspaper in Somaliland. Here, several journalists were jailed for insulting the then-president's wife, and the editor was arrested for resisting the police during a search of *Haatuf*'s offices. The case was resolved with traditional mediation. A precedent for handling such cases can be found in how *xeer* has been applied to speech more generally, and historically, to poetry.

The second case addresses the protection of media infrastructure, with a focus on the thriving telecoms industry. The endurance and expansion of telecoms, which continues to be one of Somalia's most vibrant and profitable business sectors, raises questions about how these competitive companies manage to coexist, as well as how they are regulated and made accountable with little or no government intervention. Again, by tracing the way in which *xeer* has provided a degree of protection for property, particularly livestock, and the resolution of disputes, historical precedence can be identified and applied to this modern issue.

The cases presented in this chapter are indicative of how *xeer* may be used to resolve media disputes or protect the development of the media sector. Neither *xeer* nor the examples themselves are entirely generalizable. As will be described in greater depth later in this chapter, *xeer* is essentially a contract between two groups. The exact nature of it may differ between groups, across clans and regions; it is constantly evolving, and not all Somalis continue to respect its relevance. While *xeer* is seen as legitimate among most Somalis, and indeed as a foundation of their society, it remains one instrument among several for enforcing the rule of law, including Sharia law and government laws. Given this variability and the fluid nature of the legal system, we can only offer examples that are indicative of how *xeer* has addressed some of the issues faced by the media and may continue to remain relevant in the future.

## The media in Somalia

Since the early 1990s, after the fall of Siad Barre, the media have grown exponentially across the Somali-speaking region. While mobile phones and poetry are uniformly pervasive, the mass media landscape varies.

In Somaliland, more than ten papers regularly publish in the capital city, Hargeysa. Some of the most notable papers, including *Jaamuriyaa* and *Hatuuf*, and their English counterparts *The Republican* and *The Somaliland Times*, were launched more than ten years ago by former Somali National Movement (SNM) veterans who liberated Somaliland from the rest of Somalia. As a consequence, these papers have adopted a strong pro-Somaliland and independence agenda. More recently, newspapers published by a younger generation of journalists have emerged, such as *Ogaal* and *Geeska Afrika*, which have positively impacted the publishing industry by offering a greater diversity of content and promoting competition that has encouraged higher standards of professionalization.

Even with limited levels of literacy, newspapers have played a significant political role and contributed to Somaliland's democratic process by providing a forum for political parties to debate, sometimes coopt and often wholesale "buy out" papers to serve as their platforms. They have also offered an opportunity to further connect the homeland with the diaspora, as popular papers typically have online versions as well. Despite the relatively vibrant newspaper industry, there are no private radio stations. Citing concerns of national stability and drawing on examples from South-Central Somalia, the Somaliland government has been reluctant to liberalize the radio sector, leaving the airwaves to rogue local broadcasters (sometimes streaming through the Internet), international stations such as the Voice of America or BBC Somali Service, or the Somaliland government's station, Radio Hargeysa.

The environment in South-Central Somalia and in Puntland is significantly different. Particularly in Mogadishu and the surrounding area, private radio stations have proliferated, while newspapers are rare. Over the past ten years, dozens of stations have been launched by various interest groups, including diaspora members with political aspirations, warlords seeking to consolidate power over a particular region, and Al Shabaab aiming to promote and extend its ideology. Some of the more recognized stations include Radio Shabelle, launched by Canadian-Somalis, the TFG's Radio Mogadishu and Al Shabaab's Al Andalus. Radio stations have a central role in the South, both reflecting and at times contributing to the conflict. As one Somalilander noted in reference to the media environment in South-Central Somalia:

> You hardly see a radio which is operating impartially, but each and every radio station or newsletter is based on individual and clan interests, which is really contributing to the current problems in South Somalia. The media in Somalia is in such a chaotic manner, no editing, no ethical journalists are working there and they are contributing to the problem.
> (*Anonymous 2009*)

The media in Puntland are less dynamic than in the other two regions; while private radio stations are allowed, there are fewer of them and there are no newspapers currently publishing, although there have been local newspapers in the past. All regions share access to satellite television stations, which have a central role in shaping political debate, projecting different views of "the nation" and connecting the diaspora with national politics. Universal TV and Horn Cable TV are the two largest and most influential stations; the former focuses on events in the South and the latter addresses perspectives from Somaliland, reflecting differing agendas and visions of Somalia's development.

Most recently, mobile phones have proliferated exponentially, serving as purveyors of information and news. This is not surprising given the rich oral culture of the Somalis, as well as the premium placed on reliable and first-hand information during times of crisis and conflict when people are willing to use scarce resources to stay connected to enhance their security. While mobile phone penetration in Somalia lags behind neighboring Kenya's estimated 70 percent, lack of regulation has led to some of the lowest rates on the continent for both domestic and international calls. The easy access to mobiles, at a reasonable cost, has made them an important tool for remittances and money transfers, particularly in the absence of formal banking institutions.

Media law in Somalia falls under at least three separate formal jurisdictions, including the Somaliland Constitution, the Puntland Constitution and the current draft Constitution of the TFG, which ostensibly prevails across all of Somalia.[3] All three constitutions include protections for freedom of expression and press freedom. Somaliland has a separate press law and a press code of conduct. There is no broadcasting law; the broadcasting sector has not been liberalized and remains constrained by a Ministerial Decree banning private radio stations (Minister of Information and Guidance 2002). Puntland also has a media law on the books, and the Ministry of Information issues directives to the media depending on the political climate (IFEX 2010). At the time of writing, the TFG is considering a new draft Communications Act to replace an earlier version from 2007. These laws have received significant support and input from international organizations active in the media support sector.

3 There are other self-governing regions. including the Galmudug State, which sees itself as an autonomous region in part of a federal Somalia, and the SSC Somalia, which includes the Sool, Sanag and Cayn regions, which is seeking separation from Somalia and advocates for Somali unity.

## The role of *xeer* in providing law and order

In the absence of a viable state, communities across the Somali-speaking territories have relied on alternative systems for establishing public authority, providing security and delivering services, many of which are rooted in the foundations of traditional governance and institutions (Menkhaus 2008). There are several options for legal recourse: the "modern" legal system, in which disputes are resolved in "formal courts" by judges; Islamic or Sharia courts run by religious leaders; and traditional "courts," in which clan leaders or elders mediate, either formally or informally. For many Somalis, the formal courts are simply not an option, particularly outside of Somaliland. Even when it is possible to use the formal courts in one of the three regions, the systems are all regarded as the most easily and frequently corrupted, and lack capacity for dealing with cases in a timely manner.[4] It is often a choice of last resort for the aggrieved parties, and is sometimes used when other approaches fail to reach a settlement. Sharia courts are particularly popular in South-Central Somalia, but prevalent across the region. Most Sharia courts are led by highly reputable religious leaders who will adjudicate a case and deliver a verdict quickly for a small fee. However, for many Somalis, traditional leaders who draw on *xeer* are the preferred and most accessible option.

Rooted in traditions of mediation, and an understanding of the delicate challenge to balance relations both between and within complex clan affairs, *xeer* involves the community in a form of collective accountability and restitution. Clans have served as the basis for law and security, both social and physical, and as the most important economic unit.[5] But such structures are fluid, as clans may merge with others and allegiances shift through alliances such as marriage. Ties of friendship and partnership matter too: Trust and reputation may be as high between two men who went to university together as they are between clans. Families are increasingly and exceptionally transnational. Disputes that occur in Mogadishu have the potential to be continued in London, or a well-respected elder in Ohio might be called on to mediate a case of stolen property in Kisamayo.

*Xeer* has demonstrated that it is not only remarkably adaptable, but also highly relevant in dealing with the most serious of contemporary crimes. For many businessmen, families and even diasporic communities, *xeer* is the first point and preferred approach to resolving disputes. The ability of *xeer* to adapt is partly embedded in the institution itself; it is not formally codified and it is not rules-based.[6] While *xeer* is based on precedent, it is unwritten and depends on agreements between each clan. Elders who adjudicate are the keepers of oral codes and what is effectively *xeer*'s equivalent of "case law" that have been passed down over generations. Judges and victims frequently refer to the ways in which other cases were resolved, often authenticating the precedent by stating that they were present and witnessed the earlier judgment being passed down.

Attempts to resolve disputes start at the lowest level. Elders, as long as they are not immediate family members or have grievances against a party, act as judges and legal advisers for

4 This was a complaint made by several individuals interviewed in the course of research. The debate is also captured in several articles in the *Somaliland Times*: see, e.g., *Somaliland Times* 2002.

5 The six major clans comprise the Hawiye, Dir, Isaaq, Darood, Rahanwyn and Digil.

6 *Xeer* was traditionally communicated orally, but some records have been kept. In the British Protectorate in Somaliland, for example, district commissioners would keep files of local clan and lineage-group treaties. These files were often written in Arabic or English; for the British colonizers, *xeer* thus became "a source of law, since the collective responsibility of the Government is that defined in [x]eer agreements" (Lewis 1959: 286).

the clans involved. Religious leaders and politicians are unable to adjudicate. After a judge hears a case, witnesses are called and a decision for compensation may be reached. The amount, or penalty, depends on the pre-existing contract between the clans involved, as *xeer* is based on these distinct agreements between clans, amounts may vary. Compensation will also depend on the nature of the crime—for example, general categories include homicide (*dil*), wounding (*qoon*), which not only includes physical wounding, but also to damage to property, and insult (*dalliil*), which often applies to a breach of contract, such as marriage, or slander (van Notten 2005).

The focus on collective responsibility, including interests of "family" or "clan" units prevailing over the individual, is a distinctive characteristic influencing not only how Somalis think about the rule of law, but also significantly differentiating *xeer* from modern legal systems. Thus notions of "collective property" or "clan interests" take precedence over "private property" or "individual interests," with the clan taking collective responsibility for the transgressions of an individual. When it comes to considering cases of slander or the protection of property, concerns about the "collective" would consider how an insult, or the damage of one member's reputation, affects the group as a whole. Similarly, clan elders view it as their responsibility to maintain the respect of the entire clan and will thus do their best to resolve the wrongdoings of wayward members to maintain the clan's good standing in the broader society.

This emphasis on the collective is not unique to Somali custom and is a common feature in customary law in Sub-Saharan Africa. Family members, clans or tribes may be liable for the crimes, particularly torts, of other members. This is a far more expansive view of liability than in a common law system (Deng 1996). In Somali culture, the focus on the collective differs from other customary law regimes in Africa in the extent to which it is democratic. Hereditary chiefs, which are historically a principal organizational feature of government on much of the continent, do not have the same role among Somalis. Instead, despite the nominal leadership of Sultans, elders collectively make decisions and control clan affairs, contributing to a far more decentralized, horizontal and democratic society (Muhammad 1967; Lewis 1961). This democratic ethos has played a role in shaping the strong culture of debate and discussion that characterizes Somali society.

*Xeer*, which is thought to have emerged in the seventh century, evolving and adapting locally over the centuries, has been weakened considerably over the last hundred years. To varying degrees, European colonizers introduced their own legal systems and sought to override *xeer* as well as to coopt it, along with Sharia law, as a way of managing and controlling the colonies.[7] The subsequent government of Siad Barre, which aspired to "scientific socialism," followed by decades of ongoing violence in the South, have weakened customary institutions considerably. However, *xeer* has demonstrated its exceptional adaptability and has melded and coexisted with Sharia law and modern law (Muhammad 1967). It functions differently across the Somali-speaking territories, retaining the greatest influence in Somaliland, despite the presence of a relatively stronger central government. This is partially attributable to historical factors: Britain had little interest in ruling the region directly, while Italy sought to fully integrate and colonize the South and eroded the influence of local institutions in its effort to consolidate power. Additionally, the reach of Barre's socialist

7 Both the UK and Italy established codified and secularized Western law for significant criminal matters and Sharia for family matters. *Xeer* was tolerated for matters that seemed comparatively minor.

dictatorship, which also manipulated local institutions, was weaker in the North. After the civil war, Somalilanders have been able to achieve sufficient peace to embark on a major state reconstruction project, in which *xeer* has been an important component.

Despite the demonstrated ability of *xeer* to adapt and its positive role in Somaliland, it has been strained. Particularly in recent years, some elders have been seen as corruptible, politicized and have lost legitimacy as neutral arbiters. This has encouraged the growth of Sharia courts to deal with matters beyond the family. While difficult to generalize, businessmen, particularly in the South, have tended to seek recourse in Sharia courts rather than the traditional courts. Nevertheless, and despite the scant data on where and how disputes are mediated, *xeer* has retained its relevance, with various degrees of importance. Those that do seek recourse through the system very carefully select the elders involved, recognizing that any satisfactory conclusion would be entirely dependent on the legitimacy of the judges.

When discussing *xeer* in the context of a specific case, or crime, it difficult to generalize about the process or even whether *xeer* would take precedence over "modern" or Sharia courts. It may depend on many factors, including where the crime or offence occurred, who was involved ("Do they have strong clan ties and respect the system?"; "Are they from a powerful clan or weak clan?") and what the grievance actually is. In some cases, for example, there may be an attempt to resolve a conflict in the formal court system, but if the judges reach a decision that is unacceptable to the person who has brought the grievance, the parties might turn to traditional leaders. In other cases, the opposite may occur: The first attempt to resolve the dispute will be according to *xeer*, but the aggrieved party may later take it to the courts. If, however, one of the parties requests that the conflict be taken to the Islamic or Sharia courts, where religious leaders will adjudicate, it is generally difficult for the other party to refuse because to do so would suggest that they are either "un-Islamic" or that the grievance or defense is not solid enough.

In understanding how *xeer* can be relevant for the new challenges present in contemporary Somali society, it is helpful to look at historical precedent for lessons. While decades of war have eroded and destroyed much of the social fabric and institutions, certain core values or concepts continue to be identified.

## Poetry as a precedent for regulating the modern media

The eminent scholar of Somalia, Ioan Lewis, has referred to northern Somalia as a "pastoral democracy" in which freedom of expression and freedom of movement have been essential to the survival and security of nomadic groups (Lewis 1961). The exchange and importance of news is such an integral part of Somali life that it is common for two people to greet each other with *"Iska warran"* which means "Do you have news with you?"

News is often conveyed through poems that are memorized and transmitted orally. Poetry is produced and consumed constantly, and many Somalis are able to easily memorize a poem and recite it perfectly, because ensuring its accuracy can be a matter of life or death. Poems, which often form chains known as *silsilad*, not only allow for contrasting perspectives on an event, but are also "technically definitive, whereby they cannot be altered but must be recited verbatim" (Barnes 2006: 108). This unwritten copyright serves to ensure accuracy, but also has the important role of creating a historical record. Even without the aid of modern technology such as radio, the Internet or cassettes, within weeks or days of their first recital, poems spread so rapidly that Somali lore suggests that supernatural agents facilitate them (Barnes 2006).

Poetry is seen as a highly trusted source of information. When passing information orally, it is expected that the messenger will say whether they saw it or heard it; if they heard it, they have to mention whether it came from someone who is seen as "totally reliable" and who would not exaggerate. Individuals who are deemed as untrustworthy can be ostracized and are unable to be called as witnesses. Poets themselves are highly influential and are often called on as elders or judges when resolving disputes. They have held, and to some degree continue to hold, prominent positions in the political sphere, and are regarded as intellectuals with the ability to interpret and convey the urgency and importance of current events.

While the rich oral culture of Somalis has been well documented, the mechanisms for regulating speech have received far less attention. Poetry has had a significant role in both mediating and agitating conflicts, which make questions of regulation all the more pertinent.[8] Although it is difficult to distill "norms," and because *xeer* is an agreement between two clans that differ according to each pact, there are still some cases that can be seen as indicative of how an insult has been mediated. Precedents for the application of *xeer* to address insult, slander and untruthfulness in poetry are important for understanding its contemporary relevance.

There is little written record of how *xeer* has been used to adjudicate issues such as slander or insult, so we must rely on oral records. Isman Ibrahim Warsame, the brother of the well-known poet Mohamed Ibrahim Warsame Hadraawi, narrated an important case for setting precedents that he estimates took place in the 1930s. Warsame hails from the Togdheer region of Somaliland and is a traditional leader—an elder, poet and judge—who has resolved many disputes according to *xeer.*

According to Warsame (2011), a man from the Haber Younis clan was married to a woman from the Haber Jalo clan, whom he wanted to divorce. The husband insulted the woman through a poem that referred to her personality and her body. When the man recited the poetry, men from her clan seized guns and said that they were going to kill him. Elders intervened and told the clan not to kill the husband; they first wanted to listen to the poem to judge its severity. The elders concluded that the poem was so insulting that it essentially "killed" the woman and they declared that the man's clan must pay fifty camels for her (relatively standard compensation for murdering or killing a woman), and twenty camels for her mother, who also suffered from the insults (in contrast, compensation for murdering a man might be double, at 100 camels). The man was asked to divorce the woman and, with fifty camels to her name, the woman quickly remarried.

The elders also declared that the man could never make or recite poems anywhere in the region. This was a very severe penalty, given the isolation of telling the community not to listen or believe someone. As Warsame noted:

> When a decision has been made that this person should not be listened to or do any poetry, [the elders] will bring the whole community together. It will be a public event. Traditional leaders will impose an embargo on the man and say that he should never

8 Under Siad Barre's rule, poetic contests were launched by poets in Somalia and in the diaspora, to challenge the dictator and to spread the word of an alternative future. For example, in December 1979, ten years after Siad Barre took power, the renowned poet Gaarriye launched a challenge to the government in the form of a poem entitled "Tribalism is worthless." Another poet, Hadraawi, followed with a poem of his own. For more than six months, a furious poet battle that came to be known as "Deelley" (because every poet had to alliterate in "d"), swept the Somali territories, involving more than fifty poets from the region and in the diaspora. Many were critics of the government, but some defended it. The circulation of the poetic contest was enhanced by the use of cassettes and clandestine radio. For some commentators, this experience had a decisive influence in uniting dissenters of the regime, leading to the development of organized liberation movements (Ducaale 2005).

> make any poetry. After [the embargo] the person can do it privately, it is his business but in public he is banned. It is priceless. Because the leaders are well respected, the community will respect them and will not believe him.

Drawing a contemporary parallel, Warsame noted that "asking him not to do poetry anymore, was like the *News of the World* closing down" (Warsame 2011).

Typically, insults and defamation are considered to "harm one's individual dignity" and some form of compensation from the offender is usually required—either a verbal apology, a pledge to not repeat the insult, or material compensation. It has been increasingly common for compensation to be settled with monetary payments rather than camels, but some groups will still estimate costs based on the value of a camel. Rituals may also be involved: for example, the perpetrator may visit the insulted person with his clan leader (*oday*) and offer a small gift, while the *oday* places his turban on the head of the aggrieved, thereby effacing the insult (van Notten 2005).

One factor that cuts across different *xeer* pacts is the importance of social structure in determining the extent (or not) of the damages. If a young man insults an old man, for example, it is considered an insult, but if an old man insults a young man, it is not. This custom is also common across customary law regimes in Sub-Saharan Africa; among the Kamba in Kenya, it is an offense to insult a person of a superior age-grade, and among the Akan people of Ghana, slander against a chief is considered to threaten his officers and "public order" in the community (Matson 1953: 48).

The role of *xeer* in mediating slander or insult in verbal confrontations or poetry has set important precedents, or even what could be considered to be standards, about how media such as newspaper journalists must consider such issues.

## The controversial case of the *Haatuf* newspaper

One of the most significant tests for Somaliland's press law, and for its legal system more generally, has been the 2007 case of the *Haatuf* journalists in Somaliland's capital, Hargeysa. This relatively recent example highlights the limits of the modern legal system and the enduring relevance of *xeer* in addressing instances of what one side may perceive to be insult or slander.

In January 2007, the Somaliland police arrested and imprisoned several *Haatuf* journalists, including Yusuf Abdi Gabobe, Ali Abdi Dini, Mohamed Omar Sheikh Ibrahim and Ibrahim Mohamed Rashid Farah, on accusations of inciting inter-community tension. The Hargeysa Regional Court found the journalists guilty of "insulting the good name and honor of the Head of State, for inciting the national forces of Somaliland to rebel against the state and encouraging the general public to riot and engage in acts of public disorder against the state" (*Somaliland Times* 2007b).

The allegations arose from a series of articles published from November to January concerning then President Dahir Rayale Kahin's handling of a land dispute in Borama and alleged corruption on the part of his wife, Huda Barkhad.[9] An article published on 10 December 2006 clearly framed the corruption in clan terms and alleged that President Rayale was favoring "Adwalians" (those from the Adwal region), from where Rayale hails.

9 The series of articles is entitled "How different is President Rayale's style of governance than that of the late President Egal."

Even more specifically, it suggested that a disproportionate number of individuals from his wife's sub-clan, the Reer Nuur, had been recruited for government jobs and benefits (*Somaliland Times* 2007a). There were also allegations that the First Lady's mother was involved in corruption and the confiscation of government land.

Amidst significant controversy and public protests supporting the journalists, the Supreme Court of Somaliland upheld the Regional Court's decision to try the *Haatuf* journalists for insult and sedition under the 1962 Penal Code of Somalia, rather than the more recent, and far more lenient, 2004 Press Law of Somaliland, arguing that the press law was not robust enough to handle the gravity of the accusations. The Press Law stipulates that media offences must be dealt with in accordance with the civil law, which does not provide for the imprisonment of journalists in libel cases and explicitly prohibits criminal sanctions (Jama 2007).

The Court suspended *Haatuf's* license (Reporters sans Frontières 2007), and Yusuf Abdi Gabobe was sentenced to two years' imprisonment, primarily for resisting arrest, while the other three journalists received two years and five months. *Haatuf* was also fined five million Somaliland shillings (approximately US $800) (EHAHRDP 2006). The three detainees were released on 29 March 2007, after having been pardoned by the President (Reporters sans Frontières 2009a).

Despite the findings of the Supreme Court, in what would quickly become a deeply contested process challenging both the role of courts and the role of traditional mediation, elders from the Sa'ad Mussa clan (to which Yusuf Abdi Gabobe and Mohamed Omar Sheikh Ibrahim, the primary author of the articles, belonged) met with Rayale's clan over a period of days at the Maansoor Hotel. During this series of meetings, Sa'ad Mussa elders expressed regret over the publication of articles that defamed the president and his wife. The mediation was reportedly organized by the government—specifically, by senior government officials from the Sa'ad Mussa clan—along with an estimated 150 attendees. Surrounded in controversy, the government-backed meeting at the Maansoor was soon followed by a meeting at the Rasun Hotel, at which some leaders from the Sa'ad Mussa sought to disassociate themselves from the Maansoor meeting, reflecting tensions as to which court should adjudicate such contemporary issues dealing with the mass media and the highly politicized nature of the dispute.

Eventually, the case was solved with the mediation of traditional elders according to *xeer*. Around ten meetings took place; a formal apology was made on behalf of Mohamed Omar's family to the first lady's family, including her brothers and sisters, and two girls were given for marriage. This conclusion, and the mediation, was apparently reached without the consent or participation of the journalists themselves. The journalists resisted the role of the elders and stressed that their case should first be resolved according to the Press Law, which the journalists not only had a strong role in drafting, but which also was clearly in their favor. At the very least, the journalists were insistent that theirs was an issue for the courts, not for clans. Yet there is precedent for such an outcome: if clan elders determine that it is necessary to resolve a dispute and to apologize on the behalf of a clan for the sake of the entire clan's reputation, they may do so even without the acquiescence of those involved.

While the case was successfully resolved, it raised contentious issues about the limits of *xeer*, particularly in urban settings, and its application to contemporary issues such as the mass media. Reflecting the views of the journalists and their allies, Mohamed Abdi Araby, a participant at the Rasun meeting, argued that "*Haatuf* is an independent national newspaper that doesn't represent any tribe and is not accountable to any clan." He accused the president of "corrupting the clan system" (*Somaliland Times* 2006). In essence, these critics argued that because *xeer* is based on agreements between clans, and the newspaper is not intended to speak on behalf of a clan or to represent a particular clan, it should not be susceptible to the same legal framework. Instead, they argued, that it is the role of more "modern" institutions such as the government's court system to judge the merits of a case pertaining to journalists—not traditional elders.

For a society that has long been structured by collective clan relations and engagements, these arguments posed significant challenges not least because of who was involved. As a well-known veteran of the armed struggle and the Somali National Movement, Yusuf Gabobe is a respected member of the community. Because the articles implicated the president's wife, and not simply the president, the allegations were regarded as more severe and defamatory. Thus, despite the efforts on the part of the journalists to argue that it was not a clan affair, owing to the gravity of the allegations traditional mediation emerged as the forum of choice for the aggrieved, rather than the courts. According to one Somalilander who followed the case closely, precisely because a woman was involved, the case necessitated traditional mediation; The adjudication with traditional elders was a "healing process" that could offer a more "lasting" result.

## *Xeer*, property and new technology

The challenges surrounding the applicability of *xeer* to the mass media also extend to issues of new technology—telecoms in particular—which are rapidly evolving and transnational, making it difficult for legal regimes to keep pace. Despite these complexities, *xeer* has been exceptionally adept at adjusting and has been central to supporting Somalia's unique and booming telecoms businesses. While this section will focus on the development of new technology companies, rather than mass media companies, there are implications for all media companies.

Somalia is the only country on the continent where telecoms investments and companies are owned and initiated entirely by national entrepreneurs. In other countries, government telecom ministries and international corporations such as MTN, Celtel and Vodacom have established the networks and leveraged large-scale investment. They have been reluctant to engage in a country that appears to have little rule of law and weak central governments with which to negotiate. This has allowed space for smaller Somali companies to grow and to use local knowledge to their advantage. International capital from the diaspora has been forthcoming, and transnational networks based on trust and governed by *xeer* have allowed markets to flourish with unusually fierce competition between corporations, even for this sector.

With no formal banking services, money transfer businesses have provided the foundation for the telecommunications infrastructure. It is not surprising that expanding into telecoms as a means of enhancing remittance transfer would be seen as a way in which to raise profits. Money transfer companies emerged from the more informal *xawilaad*, a system analogous to the *hawala* transactions across the Islamic world that are built on trust, reputation and strong networks.[10] Dahabshiil, for example, is the largest Somali remittance company and owns Somtel in Somaliland; Al Barakat, the remittance company that was forced to close after 11 September 2001 under US government pressure, owns Telesom in Somaliland, Golis in Puntland and Hormuud in South-Central Somalia. The diaspora has had a central role in

10 *Hawala* is an informal system across much of the Middle East and Asia. Built on trust, migrants give money to a local agent, who then calls up a colleague in the home country instructing him on the amount to be passed on to the family or friends, with the understanding that he will be reimbursed and paid a small fee in the future.

both financing business ventures and in creating the market for growth. The importance of clan and family ties extends beyond borders and includes the need not only to stay connected, but also to provide social welfare for those who remain in Somalia.[11]

*Xeer* has been instrumental in providing what could almost be considered to be a legal framework, or unwritten contract, that has enabled these businesses to grow. While the companies often have major offices in tax-friendly locations such as Dubai, from which they direct their international operations, they are largely reliant on traditional leaders or Islamic courts for mediating problems that arise in Somalia. Just as *xeer* has addressed questions of defamation or slander, as seen in the previously discussed cases, it has provided protection for the property of the companies offering security for investments and mechanisms for recovering losses from debt or theft.

The role of *xeer* in the telecoms sector is related to its historical use to regulate the livestock trade, in which, as Peter Little has so eloquently documented, it continues to retain influence (Little 2003). There is a strong tradition of clans providing security and support for other clans that might be passing through their territory in caravans. Referred to as *abbaan*, the custom is for certain powerful sub-clans or leaders to host, and attach their names to, caravans, essentially making any attack on the guest caravan an attack on the clan family (Lewis 1961). For caravans, this has often meant paying, or giving presents to, a local leader to ensure safe passage.

In the contemporary context, telecoms or money transfer companies, or indeed virtually any company that operates across the Somali-speaking region, employ individuals to work in local offices based on their clan to ensure that their property and interests will be protected and that there will be sufficient recourse in the event of difficulties. Local guards are also hired to protect the premises from vandals or warlords, but the real security comes from specific agreements with clan leaders, which primarily cover infrastructure and equipment, but do not typically extend to individual security. For example, if equipment were stolen from an office in the Southern town of Kisamayo, owned by businessmen from Hargeysa, the owners would work closely with the local clan that is protecting the infrastructure to engage local elders to mediate and recover the stolen goods. However, if a person were working in Kisamayo for a family-owned company based in Puntland, and if that employee were to be attacked in the office, it would be a matter for the clan of the victim and the clan of the perpetrator.

While security is a major problem, there remains significant respect among much of the population to protect and support the property of local businesses. This is certainly not to say all of the population: violence and vandalism are pervasive, and some individuals clearly do not abide by clan contracts. And, as with any society, there have long been wayward members, which is very much the case in an area that has been affected by decades of violence. Nevertheless, despite the fierce competition within this sector, technology and infrastructure are rarely stolen. Companies have largely agreed to respect one another and there is a shared understanding that trade in stolen goods would not only lead to reprisals, but would also seriously damage the reputations of the businesses involved (Allen 2009). Thus there is little market for locally stolen equipment from these companies. This contrasts with the equipment and investments from international organizations or corporations, particularly the United

11 Remittances are the first contribution towards gross domestic product, with the World Bank estimating an average inflow of US$ 1 billion annually, the most significant contribution on the continent (World Bank 2006: 5).

Nations, of which theft is more common and the capture of which is more likely to be seen as a "political payoff" (Nurhussein 2008: 70).

Precedent within *xeer* differentiates theft (*tuugo*) and vandalism (*xoolo*). Businesses will invest significantly in protection from security guards drawn from the local clans to prevent vandals or looters, but if, for example, funds are embezzled by an employee, traditional leaders will often be called on as the first point of contact to resolve the dispute, even in Somaliland where the government is stronger. It is expected that the person will return the stolen goods; if that is not possible, compensation will be paid.

Since reputation and trust are central to successful and sustained businesses in the Somali economy, clan leaders will vigorously seek to guard both. The wayward actions of one member can damage the standing of the collective, so families are typically eager to resolve disputes quickly. When a clan's traditional leaders are approached with the crime, it can be a significant gesture in shaming the individual charged by exposing his or her actions, which will tarnish the family name. At a minimum, even if the stolen property is not recovered, approaching the traditional leaders with evidence makes them aware of the problem and provides an opportunity for the aggrieved party to put forward his or her version of a story.

The protection of reputation is also at the core of debt recovery. For customers to have access to phone accounts that are paid monthly rather than prepaid, there is an informal credit check. Most telecoms companies will usually judge a customer on the reputation of his or her father (this is similar to the way in which money transfer companies issue loans). If the father has a poor reputation, it is difficult for his children to establish an alternative one. This is why it is not uncommon for children or grandchildren to pay the debts of a family member who has passed away. While making a person's debtor status publicly known or accusing someone of theft is one financial recovery mechanism, it is not an approach with which companies take liberties. Initial attempts to resolve minor debts typically involve elders negotiating repayments, encouraging the person who owes money to settle the account, or collecting money from the family or clan to repay the debt (Allen 2009). This is a delicate balance and one of which the businesses are keenly aware; to be reckless with the reputations of customers would threaten a business's own reputation for trust and fairness. As with all disputes, identifying the leaders who mediate is key. As one businessman noted: "Not all [traditional leaders] are reputable, but some are. Some you can buy. You have to find someone who will know it very well, whose words are his deeds" (Anonymous Somaliland businessman 2012).

## Conclusion

This chapter has offered a frequently overlooked perspective on the importance of considering media law in its context by moving beyond the overwhelming focus on formal legal institutions and infrastructure to local legal traditions and processes. While the examples discussed here have sought to illuminate the ways in which *xeer* remains relevant for regulating media and new technology, it is important to caution against generalizations, particularly given that the political, economic and social situation is subject to significant fluctuations in much of the Somali-speaking region.

Over the past two decades of ongoing conflict, *xeer* has demonstrated its adaptability. Its relevance reaches far beyond mediating in media disputes, and it offers unique opportunities to provide governance and security in Somalia. It has, for example, provided a basis for Somaliland's successful peacemaking, and what could also be called "state-making," process. During Somaliland's Boroma Conference of 1993, a national peace charter was established based on the principles of *xeer*. The role of elders, who enforce *xeer*, was institutionalized to "encourage and safeguard peace [and] create a new or enforcing existing Code of Conduct [*xeer*] among the clans" (Bradbury 1997: 22). Thus elders were tasked with resolving disputes and conflicts and ensuring security, while politicians and the government were to manage, develop and administer the state. A national *Guurti* (unelected upper house of parliament consisting of elders) was later included in the first Constitution of Somaliland. Combined with a democratically elected lower house of parliament, this innovative system has sought to meld traditional authority and government with more modern democratic principles. For almost twenty years, this hybrid arrangement has managed to hold despite significant pressures and regional instability. In 2010, Somaliland held presidential elections, widely considered to be "free and fair," in which the opposition party defeated that of the incumbent president (AFP 2010). While the reach of the government beyond the capital city of Hargeysa and other major cities is relatively weak, Somaliland's democratic credentials are an exception on the continent.

Despite the evidence suggesting that *xeer* may have a fundamental role in providing what are normally considered to be "state services," such as justice and security, it has largely been overlooked by external aid organizations, which remain focused on promotion of the rule of law and state-building in the context of formal state structures. Since the civil war and the fall of Siad Barre's government in the early 1990s, Somalia has experienced dozens of attempts by international actors at state-making, which emphasize supporting and installing internationally backed governments that have largely faltered. A conflagration of various domestic groups, some with strong financial or ideological interests, in combination with the agendas of regional powers and international actors, has hindered, and at times even derailed, the potential for grassroots peacemaking and the establishment of viable institutions of governance.

In this vein, much of the media development and media for governance programs in Somalia, similar to those across the developing world, have focused on the role of the mass media in holding governments to account. The emphasis is on the ability of citizens, through the media, to make public institutions more responsive, while governments are held responsible for the degree to which media "thrive" or are "suppressed" predominantly by state actors. But different forms of accountability coexist—public authority may be an Imam, or services may be provided by a local NGO. Similarly, as this chapter has argued, media and voice may be effectively regulated with a variety of legal instruments.

In contexts such as Somalia, it is often misplaced to focus on the role of the state in both regulating and protecting media. As Ken Menkhaus has argued, "the evolution of informal systems of governance and security has largely been invisible to external aid agencies engaged in promotion of rule of law and state-building, most of whose energies are devoted strictly to formal state structures" (Menkhaus 2008: 37). Although external actors typically advocate or encourage the internationally recognized government to adopt a particular legal template for the media, a more local approach, building on local concepts (including customary laws) to regulate speech and media outlets, may not only have more resonance, but may also be more likely to be successful.

## References

AFP (2010) 'Somaliland election free and fair: Observers,' 28 June. Online. Available HTTP: http://www.google.com/hostednews/afp/article/ALeqM5hPOQSDOSIy7VmRt2QHOrxBFVn1uw (accessed 30 May 2012).

Allen, G. (2009) 'Connected: Developing Somalia's telecoms industry in the wake of state collapse,' Ph.D. thesis, University of California Davis.

Anonymous (2009) Interview, Hargeysa.

Anonymous Somaliland Businessman (2012) Interview, London.

Barnes, C. (2006) 'Gubo-Ogadeen poetry and the aftermath of the Dervish wars,' *Journal of African Cultural Studies*, 18(1): 105–117.

Bradbury, M. (1997) *Somaliland: CIIR Country Report*, London: Catholic Institute for International Relations.

Davies, J. and Dagbanja, D. (2009) 'The role and future of customary tort law in Ghana: A cross-cultural perspective,' *Arizona Journal of International and Comparative Law*, 26(2): 303–333.

Deng, F. M. (1966) 'The family and the law of torts in African customary law,' *Houston Law Review*, 4(1): 1–44.

Ducaale, B. Y. (2005) 'The role of the media in political reconstruction,' in Academy for Peace and Development (ed.) *Rebuilding Somaliland: Issues and Possibilities*, Lawrenceville, NJ: Red Sea Press.

East and Horn of Africa Human Rights Defenders Project (EHAHRDP) (2006) *Mission Report on the Trial Observation of Detained Human Rights Defenders in Somaliland*, 4 March. Online. Available HTTP: http://www.somalilandtimes.net/sl/2006/273/76.shtml (accessed 30 May 2012).

Elias, O. (1954) 'Insult as an offence in African customary law,' *African Affairs*, 53(210): 66–69.

Freedom House (2011) *Somalia*. Online. Available HTTP: http://www.freedomhouse.org/report/freedom-press/2011/somalia (accessed 1 June 2012).

Haji, N. A. and Noor, M. (1967) 'Civil wrongs under customary law in the Northern regions of the Somali Republic,' *Journal of African Law*, 11(2): 99–118.

Höhne, M. (2008) 'Newspapers in Hargeysa: Freedom of expression in post-conflict Somaliland,' *Africa Spectrum*, 43(1): 91–114.

Human Rights Watch (2009) *Hostages to Peace: Threats to Human Rights and Democracy in Somaliland*. Online. Available HTTP: http://www.hrw.org/sites/default/files/reports/somaliland0709web.pdf (accessed 30 May 2012).

IFEX (2010) 'Puntland Information Ministry issues new directives for independent media,' 28 June. Online. Available HTTP: http://www.ifex.org/somalia/2010/06/28/puntland_censorship_edict/ (accessed 30 May 2012).

Jama, I. H. (2007) 'Using insult laws is an insult to the Somaliland media and public: The detention and trial of *Haatuf* journalists,' *Somaliland Law*, 20 January. Online. Available HTTP: http://www.somalilandlaw.com/Insult_Law___the_Press_in_Somaliland.pdf (accessed 30 May 2012).

Lewis, I. M. (1959) 'Clanship and contract in Northern Somaliland,' *Journal of the International African Institute*, 29(3): 274–293.

—— (1961) *A Pastoral Democracy*, Oxford: Oxford University Press.

Little, P. (2003) *Somalia: Economy Without State*, Oxford: James Currey.

Menkhaus, K. (2008) 'Understanding state failure in Somalia: Internal and external dimensions,' in A. Harneit-Sievers and D. Spillker (eds.) *Somalia: Current Conflicts and New Challenges—A Publication on Promoting Democracy under Conditions of State Fragility*, Berlin: Heinrich Böll Stiftung.

Messner, J. J. (2011) 'Somalia tops the failed states index,' *The Fund for Peace*. Online. Available HTTP: http://www.fundforpeace.org/global/?q=node/123 (accessed 30 May 2012).

Minister of Information and Guidance (2002) *Ministerial Decree Banning the Importation and Operation of Privately Owned Radio Stations*, Somaliland. Online. Available HTTP: http://www.somalilandlaw.com/broadcasting__law.html#Radiobandecree (accessed 30 May 2012).

Nurhussein, S. (2008) 'Global networks, fragmentation, and the rise of telecommunications in stateless Somalia,' M.A. Thesis, Department of Geography, University of Oregon.

Reporters sans Frontières (2007) 'Heavy sentences for four journalists working for Somaliland daily,' 5 March. Online. Available HTTP: http://www.rsf.org/Heavy-prison-sentences-for-four.html (accessed 26 August 2009).

—— (2009a) 'Three *Haatuf* journalists freed after being held for three months,' 30 March. Online. Available HTTP: http://www.rsf.org/Three-Haatuf-journalists-freed.html (accessed 26 August 2009).

—— (2009b) *Somalia*. Online. Available HTTP: http://en.rsf.org/report-somalia,43.html (accessed 1 June 2012).

*Somaliland Times* (2002) Issue 25, July. Online. Available HTTP: http://somalilandtimes.net/Archive/Archive/00002500.htm (accessed 30 May 2012).

—— (2006) 'Elders accuse Rayale of corrupting the clan system,' 27 January. Online. Available HTTP: http://www.somalilandtimes.net/sl/2006/262/1.shtml (accessed 30 May 2012).

—— (2007a) 'How different is President Rayale's style of governance than that of late President Egal?' 27 January. Online. Available HTTP: www.somalilandtimes.net/sl/2006/262/3.shtml (accessed 30 May 2012).
—— (2007b) 'Haatuf journalists sent to prison,' 10 March. Online. Available HTTP: http://www.somalilandtimes.net/sl/2006/268/1.shtml (accessed 1 June 2012).
Van Notten, M. (2005) *The Law of the Somalis*, Trenton, NJ: Red Sea Press.
Warsame, I. I. (2011) Interview, London.
World Bank (2006) 'Remittances and economic development in Somalia: An overview.' Online. Available HTTP: http://siteresources.worldbank.org/INTCPR/Resources/WP38_web.pdf (accessed 30 May 2012).

# 14

# In the name of God

## Faith-based Internet censorship in majority Muslim countries

*Helmi Noman**

Few of the chapters in this book directly deal with the role that religion plays in media policies—especially in states where religion strongly influences government and the cultural trends that are shaped by media are strongly contested. In this chapter, the impact of religion—particularly on information delivered through the Internet—becomes the analytic focus. The structure of Internet-related debates, and the themes raised through religious influences, reorder the way in which societies think about media and regulation.

Religion-based Internet censorship bars the free flow of information in many majority Muslim countries by means of regulatory restrictions and Internet service provider (ISP)-level technical filtering that blocks objectionable web content. When regimes implement and enforce faith-based censorship, they create borders around certain content. Such boundaries can produce a peculiar Internet culture among users whose browsing behavior is confined within these limits. The flow of information in cyberspace in majority Muslim countries mirrors, to a large extent, the flow of information in "real" space in these nations. For example, many majority Muslim countries criminalize the promotion of non-Islamic faiths among their Muslim citizens offline. Thus we see technical filtering and legal restrictions on the same activity online. Similarly, because homosexual relationships are considered taboo in the majority of Muslim countries, online homosexual content is also banned in many of these countries.

* This chapter was originally written as an OpenNet Initiative occasional paper. The author would like to thank Ronald Deibert and Rafal Rohozinski for guidance, Masashi Crete-Nishihata, Adam Senft, James Tay and Greg Wiseman for research assistance, and Jacqueline Larson for editorial assistance. The OpenNet Initiative (ONI) is a collaborative partnership of three institutions: the Citizen Lab at the Munk School of Global Affairs, University of Toronto; the Berkman Center for Internet and Society at Harvard University; and the SecDev Group (Ottawa). The ONI's mission is to investigate, expose and analyze Internet filtering and surveillance practices in a credible and non-partisan fashion. I intend to uncover the potential pitfalls and unintended consequences of these practices, and thus help to inform better public policy and advocacy work in this area. For more information about ONI, please visit http://opennet.net

While a number of rationales for censoring objectionable online content are put forward by non-Muslim states, the censorship policies of majority Muslim countries are primarily based on the Islamic faith and interpretations of its instructions. Majority Muslim countries collectively adhere to a legal framework that is heavily based on religious concepts in the Cairo Declaration of Human Rights in Islam, which in many ways is in conflict with the religion-neutral Universal Declaration of Human Rights that was adopted in 1948 by the General Assembly of the United Nations as a common standard for rights such as freedom of expression and belief. Moreover, the constitutions of many majority Muslim countries sanction the Islamic faith in one way or another, which constitutes a built-in limitation on freedom of speech. For some, that limitation is holy and unquestionable.

Faith-based censorship is a by-product of a Qur'anic concept known as the promotion of virtue and the prevention of vice. It is practiced in some countries under that explicit religious term, but, in other countries, under broad religious mandates. Thus state religious authorities in some countries play a direct role in developing censorship policies. Some civic groups even promote the culture of censorship, pressuring political authorities and using the court system to enforce it. In fact, a number of religious scholars have a dogmatic approach to the Internet and have produced research and opinions concluding that the Internet is detrimental to the Islamic faith and society; they propose different measures to combat access to, and dissemination of, questionable content. While some of these scholars recommend that users avoid "un-Islamic" content, others take a more aggressive stand and recommend compromising websites with content deemed blasphemous. There is no local consensus on faith-based censorship; some groups oppose it and question the legitimacy of the practice and the censors' agendas.

## Faith-based censorship: The legal and regulatory frameworks

In August 1990, the fifty-seven member states of the Organization of the Islamic Conference (OIC) adopted the Cairo Declaration on Human Rights in Islam (CDHRI), which diverted from the Universal Declaration of Human Rights (UDHR) on key issues.[1] The CDHRI provides an overview of human rights in Islam and serves as a general guidance for member states of the OIC, an intergovernmental organization that describes itself as "the collective voice of the Muslim world and ensuring to safeguard and protect the interests of the Muslim world."

Unlike the UDHR, the CDHRI makes significant references to God and faith as part of the legal framework for human rights in Islam. It stipulates that all rights and freedoms in the CDHRI are subject to the Muslim code of religious law known as *Sharia*, and that Sharia is the only source of reference to explain or clarify any of the CDHRI articles. In addition, the CDHRI affirms in its preamble that "fundamental rights and universal freedoms in Islam are an integral part of the Islamic religion and that no one as a matter of principle has the right to suspend them in whole or in part or violate or ignore them in as much as they are binding divine commandments." Rather than a secular approach to human rights, the CDHRI derives the rights from the "revealed books of God" and the messages that were sent through "the last of His Prophets" (i.e. Mohammed).

1 The Cairo Declaration on Human Rights in Islam was adopted by the Nineteenth Islamic Conference of Foreign Ministers in Cairo, Arab Republic of Egypt, which took place between 31 July and 5 August 1990. English translation of the full Arabic text is available on the website of the Organization of Islamic Conference at http://www.oic-oci.org/english/article/human.htm

On the issue of freedom of expression, the CDHRI says that everyone shall have the right to express his opinion freely, but only if the opinions are not contrary to the principles of Islamic Sharia. Although the CDHRI recognizes that information is vital to society, it says in Article 22 that information "may not be exploited or misused in such a way as may violate sanctities and the dignity of Prophets, undermine moral and ethical values or disintegrate, corrupt or harm society or weaken its faith." Although the CDHRI gives everyone the right to enjoy the fruits of their scientific, literary, artistic, or technical production and the right to protect the moral and material interests stemming from it, the document stipulates that such content should not be contrary to the principles of Islamic Sharia.

With this heavy emphasis on religion, majority Muslim countries have criticized the UDHR for not taking into consideration the cultural and religious context of non-Western countries (Europe News 2007). At the same time, the CDHRI has been criticized by international legal experts for falling short of international human rights standards by recognizing human rights in accordance with Islamic Sharia only, and for restricting freedom of speech to the limits of Islamic principles (ibid.).

In addition, the OIC has, since 1999, been a proponent of the United Nations Defamation of Religions Resolutions, which seek to "codify a right for religions, especially Islam, not to be offended" (Grahamm 2009). Since 1999, the UN has annually adopted resolutions stressing protectionism towards religions, particularly Islam per se, rather than Muslims, a matter that raises the concern that this amounts to exceptionalism from legitimate scrutiny (Ghanea 2007).

The OIC renewed its call for a global ban on offending the Prophet Mohammad and Islam in September 2012 following a wave of protests that swept Muslim countries after the film *Innocence of Muslims*, which ridiculed Prophet Mohammed, was posted on YouTube. The group equated the film with religious hatred and violence, and called member states of the UN to "introduce and/or implement adequate measures, including legislations, against acts of hate crimes, discrimination, violence, and intimidation caused by negative stereotyping and incitement to religious hatred, violence, discrimination on the basis of religion, in particular for Muslims, and in accordance with their obligations under the international human rights instruments" (Organization of Islamic Cooperation 2012).

Efforts to enhance and reform human rights frameworks in majority Muslim countries have also been criticized by legal experts for not conforming to the UDHR. The League of Arab States (LAS) adopted the Arab Charter on Human Rights of 2004, which came into force in March 2008 and was ratified by ten of the twenty-two LAS member states (Algeria, Bahrain, Jordan, Libya, Palestine, Qatar, Saudi Arabia, Syria, the United Arab Emirates and Yemen). Although the Charter recognizes key rights that are in line with international human rights law as reflected in treaties, jurisprudence and opinions of UN expert bodies, "it also allows for the imposition of restrictions on the exercise of freedom of thought, conscience, and religion far beyond international human rights law," and it leaves many important rights to national legislation (Rishmawi 2009).

These national legislations include the constitutions themselves. The constitutions of almost all of the Arab countries mention Islam as the official religion of the state (Latify 2010). Moreover, Islamic law influences the legal code in most Muslim countries, or is a source for laws (Johnson 2010). As a result, questioning Islamic beliefs is not constitutionally accommodated or legally tolerated across most of the Muslim world, and most of the states have strict laws that censor objectionable religious content (OpenNet Initiative n.d.). These laws include press and publications acts and penal codes that criminalize making references to Islam that are considered insulting (Noman 2009). In May 2012, Kuwait's parliament approved an amendment to the penal code to stipulate the death penalty for anyone who insults God, Prophet Mohammed, or his relatives. This followed an increase in online Arabic postings that allegedly were offensive to the Prophet Mohammad and his wife Aysha (Toumi 2012).

Legal boundaries on permissible religious content have been extended to legislation beyond regional regulatory frameworks, constitutions and media laws, and have been incorporated into recently introduced Internet laws that were crafted to criminalize "abusing" holy shrines, the Islamic faith and religious values (e.g. UAE's 2007 Federal Cyber Law and Saudi Arabia's 2008 Law on the Use of Technology) (ibid.). Even Internet service providers' (ISP) terms and conditions mandate that users shall not use Internet services to contradict the religious values of the pertinent countries (e.g. Oman's Omantel and Yemen's Y.net) (ibid.). Hence faith-based restrictions on freedom of expression in majority Muslim countries have been long practiced on traditional media and have been applied to online activities. States have imprisoned citizens who express views critical of Islam in print media or online. For example, in January 2007, a court in Morocco shut down a monthly magazine for two months and gave a reporter and an editor a three-year suspended prison sentence each for publishing jokes about Islam (BBC News 2007). In Yemen, a journalist was convicted in December 2006 for reprinting the Danish cartoons of Prophet Mohammed. The newspaper's license was revoked and it was closed down for three months (OpenNet Initiative 2007a). In Egypt, a blogger was sentenced in February 2007 to four years in prison for "incitement to hatred of Islam" and for insulting the president on his blog (OpenNet Initiative 2007a).

## Faith-based censorship: The religious root

Faith-based regulation and censorship of the Internet is rooted in the Islamic religious concept known as *Hisbah* in Arabic. Sharia-oriented political scientists define *Hisbah* as "the duty of enjoining good when it is neglected and forbidding evil when it is prevalent in society" (Al-Halawani 2009). The role of a *Muhtasib*, the one who practices *Hisbah*, can be assigned by the political leadership or a volunteer can perform *Hisbah* duties without political assignment. The individual who practices *Hisbah* "serves as the eye of the law on both state and society. In other words, this person supervises the application of the law in society" (ibid.) The majority of Muslim countries collectively subscribe to the concept of *Hisbah*. The Cairo Declaration of Human Rights in Islam refers to the concept of *Hisbah* in Article 22b, which reads: "Everyone shall have the right to advocate what is right, and propagate what is good, and warn against what is wrong and evil according to the norms of Islamic Sharia" (Organization of the Islamic Conference 1990).

Some countries have institutionalized the concept of *Hisbah*. For example, in Saudi Arabia, *Hisbah* is a state-sponsored institutionalized operation called the Committee for the Promotion of Virtue and the Prevention of Vice, a religious police in charge of enforcing Sharia law with an Internet presence at www.pv.gov.sa. The group has published on its website a lengthy study in Arabic entitled *The Moral Vice of the Internet and How to Practise* Hisbah, which establishes a link between censorship in general and faith-based censorship in particular and the Qur'anic concept of *Hisbah*. The paper proposes the following broad *Hisbah* practices for both states and individuals to exert in *Hisbah* efforts: implementing state- and family-level faith-based censorship; developing awareness programs to educate the public about the danger and potential threat of "immoral" websites; providing religious advice to the operators of these websites; compromising and eliminating websites that contain objectionable content; and increasing the quantity of beneficial web content (Committee for the Promotion of Virtue and Prevention of Vice 2010).

Faith-based censorship in the form of practicing *Hisbah* has also been extended to social-networking websites. Some 300 *Hisbah* volunteers from Saudi Arabia's Committee for the Promotion of Virtue and the Prevention of Vice have been trained to exercise *Hisbah* on Facebook and in chat rooms, and more program volunteers from around the country are expected to receive the same type of training (*Emirates 24/7* 2010).

State Internet censors in Sudan explicitly refer to the concept of *Hisbah* as the rationale for filtering Internet content in the country. The censorship body, the National Telecommunication Corporation (NTC), publicly acknowledges filtering the Internet and explains that its Internet censorship regime is not a violation of personal rights nor a form of religious fanaticism, but rather an implementation of the religious Qur'anic duty of "promotion of virtue and prevention of vice." NTC argues that it censors the Internet "to protect the doctrine of the 'Ummah' [Islamic nation] and its moral values, and to strengthen the principles of virtue and chastity" (National Telecommunication Corporation 2010).

Individual citizens have also invoked *Hisbah* to push for the implementation of Internet censorship in some countries. In Egypt, for example, a lawyer filed a suit in a Cairo court in May 2009 demanding the government block access to pornographic websites because they are offensive to religion and society. Although the court ruled in his favor (BBC News 2009), ONI testing conducted afterwards found no evidence that the court order had been enforced. User groups around the theme of virtual *Hisbah* emerged on the Internet in the past few years. For example, Hisbah Net (http://hesbahnet.com) is a discussion forum dedicated to the "promotion of virtue and the prevention of vice" online. The forum makes available user-developed recommendations on how to best fight "immorality" and anti-Islam content online. On the same theme, a group of Egyptian anti-pornography activists organized an online campaign demanding the government block access to pornography— they had reportedly written to the then prime minister of Egypt in 2008 seeking his support and "reminding" him that Egypt is an Islamic country (Islam Web 2008).

User-organized campaigns in Egypt emerged in 2011 after the 25 January revolution. Examples include the "Campaign to Block Pornographic Content Online."[2] Other less-organized campaigns are also found in other countries such as Algeria, where ONI found no evidence of technical filtering of social sites.[3]

Although the concept of promoting virtue and preventing vice takes different forms and has different features when applied to Internet censorship, demands for Internet censorship in the Muslim world have also emerged under different pretexts and are not always faith-driven.[4]

## Role of religious authorities in enforcing faith-based censorship

Given the religious nature of this type of censorship, it is not surprising that religious authorities in several majority Muslim countries have played a key role in developing and enforcing faith-based censorship, sometimes directly as part of a government initiative to control access to the Internet and sometimes as independent individual or group efforts. In Iran, the Ministry of Islamic Culture and Guidance has served as part of a government body whose responsibility is to rid the web of "illicit and immoral" content (OpenNet Initiative 2009b). In Kuwait, the

2 See http://www.no-xsite.com

3 See, e.g., the web forum 4 Algeria, Online. Available HTTP: www.4algeria.com/vb/showthread.php?t=93655 (accessed 25 March 2011).

4 ONI individual country studies cover some of these issues. See the country studies. Online. Available HTTP: http://opennet.net/country-profiles

Minister of Communications, who was also the Minister of Religious Endowment and Islamic Affairs, took part in a February 2008 government plan to monitor and regulate Internet content (OpenNet Initiative 2009c). In Pakistan, the Ministry of Religious Affairs is part of a committee set up by the Ministry of Information Technology to enforce the blocking of content perceived as anti-state or anti-Islam (Imtiaz 2010). And in Indonesia, Islamic parties heavily backed an anti-pornography law that was passed in 2008 and upheld by the constitutional court in 2010 (Vaswani 2010). The controversial law was used to develop Internet filtering policy (Reuters 2010) and, as a result, the government ordered ISPs to start blocking access to pornography websites on 11 August 2010, the start of the holy month of Ramadan (Reporters sans Frontières 2010). The timing of this stresses the religious dimension of the policy.

In Indonesia, a group of Muslim clerics from the country's largest Islamic organization recommended creating rules to govern how Muslims use Facebook, out of concern that the site could facilitate illicit affairs (Gelling 2009). In Saudi Arabia, the religious police (Committee for the Promotion of Virtue and the Prevention of Vice) have started to receive training on monitoring social networking and chat sites (*Emirates 24/7* 2010). They also have expressed an interest in accessing blocked websites so that they can practice surveillance on online discussion that takes place on those sites. The chairman of the Saudi Shura (Consultative) Consul, however, rejected their demand (OpenNet Initiative 2009d). A Saudi-based religious scholar once demanded that ISPs in Saudi Arabia place Qur'anic verses prohibiting the consumption of pornography on block pages (Al-Arabiya 2011), apparently as a religious warning to those who try to access banned content. An April 2011 Saudi telecom regulatory proposal recommended that anyone who produces, sends, receives, or stores web content that contradicts Islamic values should be publicly defamed.[5] The proposal, developed by a committee that included religious authorities, also recommended that the Saudi government should work with international search engines to introduce mechanisms that would delist pornographic results for Internet users in Saudi Arabia.

## The Internet as a destructive force

Although Muslim religious establishments acknowledge the many positive aspects of the Internet and have used it to disseminate their own content and to promote their agendas, some Islamic authorities and research circles consider it a destructive force that can potentially erode religious values, moral systems, and the fabric of social and family life. The Internet's presumed detrimental impact on faith and society is partly behind the religious demands to regulate it and to implement technical barriers and draw legal dividing lines. Interestingly, some apprehensive attitudes go as far as suggesting that the Internet was developed to distort Muslim identity and that Muslims manage to use it to fire back at the "enemies of God" (Al-Khatib 2004). Others hold a pragmatic approach and see the Internet as a parallel world with positive opportunities that should be explored to advance the interests of Muslims. The two groups agree, however, that creating an "Islamic" Internet is a religious mandate (ibid.).

Religiously oriented research papers and articles tend to have a negative attitude towards the Internet. An Islamabad-based think-tank paper that discusses *Hisbah* in Pakistan and the demand for its revival says: "The culture of dish antenna and unchecked Internet services promoted liberal and sometimes quite immoral attitude [sic] from Islamic perspectives that started to reflect in society through different means from national media to roadside

5 The full text of the telecom regulatory proposal was published in April 2011 by several Saudi newspapers, including *al-Madina* at http://www.al-madina.com/node/299792

billboards" (The Institute of Policy Studies 2010). Similarly, an article published by a Saudi-based religious media institution endorses the government implementation of technical filtering because it concludes that the Internet can destroy moral values, the individual, the economy and the entire society, and that the Internet is "destructive to our religion, especially after the appearance of websites that threaten and defame our faith" (Al-Mohammed 2010).

The presence of Christian evangelist websites has also fuelled calls to regulate and censor the Internet. An article published on several Arabic websites warned of foreign efforts to Christianize Muslims through the use of "thousands" of websites, which have allegedly increased by 1,200 percent recently (Ismael 2008). Other articles encourage Muslims to "combat online Christianization efforts,"[6] citing as a threat the establishment of the Internet Evangelism Coalition (www.webevangelism.com), an initiative set up by the Billy Graham Center in 1999 to "stimulate and accelerate web-evangelism within the worldwide Body of Christ." Different religious scholars and establishments propose different means to "combat" such online Christian evangelical efforts. While some demand that governments block access to these websites, others go as far as to issue *fatwas* (religious edicts) that permit attacking and compromising these sites (Al-Hamad 2010). Radical groups have tried not only to implement Internet filtering regimes, but also to ban the Internet altogether. The Taliban, for example, banned it in July 2001 when it was the ruling body in Afghanistan because it believed that the Internet disseminates obscene, immoral and anti-Islam material (OpenNet Initiative 2007c). Religious extremists have attacked Internet cafes in Gaza under the pretext that the Internet corrupts the moral values of Palestinian youth (OpenNet Initiative 2007b).

## *Fatwas* as religious dividing lines on web activities

Since the introduction of the Internet in many majority Muslim countries, a number of Internet-specific *fatwas*, mostly restrictive, have added a layer to the regulatory boundaries on acceptable web activities at the end-user level. For example, one *fatwa* stated that browsing YouTube is forbidden by Islam because of the objectionable material found on the site (Bin Ali al-Mashaikih 2009), while another *fatwa* allowed access to YouTube on the condition that the user self-censors his or her browsing behavior (Islamic Web Fatwa Center 2009). No matter how virtual, online activities have been subject to scrutiny and *fatwas*, and questions about the Islamic legality or religious permissibility of different aspects of the Internet have emerged in the past few years from both Internet users and entrepreneurs. For example, Saudi Arabia's Standing Committee for Issuing Fatwas was asked a question about whether operating Internet cafes is Islamically acceptable "knowing that there are some harmful and *haraam* [Islamically forbidden] things" in these venues.

The answer was:

> If this equipment can be used for false and evil ends, which will harm Islamic beliefs or enable people to look at permissive pictures and movies, or news of immoral entertainment, or to have dubious conversations and play *haraam* games, and the owner of the café cannot prevent these evils or control the machines, then in that case it is *haraam* for him to deal in that, because this is helping in sin and *haraam* things.
>
> (*Islam Question and Answer* n.d.)

6 See for example an Arabic article entitled 'Christianization over the Internet' by Ahmed Abu Zaid, which appeared on 14 November 2010 on several Islamic websites, including at http://www.salmajed.com/node/9826

Some scholars even object to women using emoticons—the facial expressions pictorially represented by punctuations and letters (e.g. :-), and :D), when chatting with male users who are not their *mahram*, a legal terminology used for an unmarriageable kin with whom sexual intercourse would be considered incestuous. One Saudi religious scholar said:

> A woman should not use these images when speaking to a man who is not her *mahram* because these faces are used to express how she is feeling, so it is as if she is smiling, laughing, acting shy and so on, and a woman should not do that with a non-*mahram* man. It is only permissible for a woman to speak to men in cases of necessity, so long as that is in a public chat room and not in private correspondence.
>
> (*Islam Question and Answer* n.d.)

The development and sale of circumvention software was also deemed *haraam* by a religious *fatwa* issued in March 2011 by the Islamic Web Fatwa Center, which is run by Qatar's Ministry of Religious Endowments and Islamic Affairs. The *fatwa* said that it is Islamically forbidden to code and sell proxy software and tools that enable users to access objectionable content—and this applies even if the coders and sellers put conditions on the use of such tools (Islam Web Fatwa Center 2009).

In addition, there are religious *fatwas* objecting to engaging in online intellectual discourse that discusses freedom from religious rules and teachings. For instance, the Grand Mufti of Dubai demanded that state authorities should prevent the spread of secular and atheistic content online, which he labeled a ruinous phenomenon. The Grand Mufti argued that secular and atheist content is destructive, and does not fall within freedom of opinion. He argued that freedom of expression and human rights are compatible with Islamic Sharia, and that "man is capable of discussing ordinarily worldly matters, but faith is beyond the limited capacity of man, because he does not know the unknown, neither does he know the beneficial from the harmful" (Tokan 2008; author's translation).

## The Islamic Internet

The religious calls to create Islamic content, concern about objectionable online material and religious *fatwas* against browsing forbidden websites have prompted some individuals and groups to develop websites that would presumably make the user's online experience compatible with Islamic Sharia. As a result, the "Islamic Internet" has emerged in the past few years in the form of faith-based censored and Islam-friendly, or "Sharia-compliant," websites that imitate popular video-sharing sites, search engines and social-networking websites. For example, video-sharing website NaqaTube.com (*Naqa* is Arabic for "pure") promises its users a Sharia-compatible YouTube surfing experience. The site takes religiously "pure" video clips from YouTube and posts them to NaqaTube. Other examples of video-sharing websites include Islamic Tube Muslim Video, HalalTube and FaithTube. There are also Islamic search engines such as "I'm Halal" and Taqwa, both of which censor objectionable keywords and results. In addition, a Facebook-style social networking website called "Ikhwan Book" was developed by the Egypt-based Muslim Brotherhood. "Islamic" erotica has also emerged on the Internet as an alternative to the "non-Islamic" variety. For example, there is a "Sharia-compliant" online store that sells erotica items and care products and information. In addition, there are "Islamic" Google gadgets, browser toolbars and plug-ins that are meant to return, and facilitate access to, preapproved and preselected Islamic content.[7]

A radical form of faith-based content and technical censorship can potentially materialize if Iran goes ahead with its plan to create a Halal Internet. In April 2011, Iran's head of economic affairs with the Iranian presidency announced that Iran would develop an "Islamic Internet" that will conform to Islamic principles. The official said that this planned Internet will operate parallel to the present World Wide Web, but will eventually replace the Internet in Muslim countries (AKI 2011). Evidence emerged in 2012 suggesting that Iran has created a nationwide, private Internet that is widely accessible inside the country but hidden from the outside world (Anderson 2012). It is not clear whether this network is itself the Halal Internet, but if such a project is indeed developed and widely used, it could potentially be an extreme manifestation of faith-based censorship because it would likely be a network or an Intranet of preapproved content and closely monitored online user behavior.

## *Faith-based technical filtering*

OpenNet Initiative research and empirical test results reveal that Internet censorship in general has been on the rise in many majority Muslim countries as part of a worldwide trend. Censorship regimes in several majority Muslim countries, especially in the Middle East and North Africa, are found to pervasively filter online political dissidence, but also to target content deemed offensive for religious, moral and cultural reasons.

Government-mandated Internet filtering in many majority Muslim countries is implemented at the ISP level, giving citizens no option to exercise their own judgement on what is appropriate to access. Technical filtering is made even more intrusive because the filtering regimes also target Internet tools that can be used to bypass ISP-level filtering.

State-imposed censorship is made possible by filtering technology built by Western companies that provide the technology infrastructure, as well as access to millions of URLs in various potentially undesirable categories (Noman and York 2011). Governments then mass-block websites by activating categories that they deem offensive, but they also create their own categories and manually add more objectionable websites.

Content categories typically provided by commercial filtering software providers include art and culture, dating, entertainment, fashion, gambling, history, humor, incidental nudity, advocacy groups, nudity, online shopping, politics, pornography, portal sites, profanity, provocative attire, proxies, recreation, religion and ideology, sexual materials, software, sports, travel and violence.

Based on ONI in-field research and technical testing conducted since 2006, we can categorize faith-based Internet censorship-targeted content into the following key categories: content perceived blasphemous, offensive or contrary to the Islamic faith; websites with content considered prohibited by Islamic Sharia; websites belonging to religious groups whose ideologies are not in line with the official state-sanctioned religion or specific sect of religion; and liberal, secular and atheistic content (see Table 14.1). Each is discussed in turn.

7 See the following websites: http://www.islamictube.com; http://www.muslimvideo.com; http://www.halal-tube.com; http://www.faithtube.com; http://www.imhalal.com; http://ikhwanbook.com; http://www.elasira.eu

*Table 14.1* Faith-based technical filtering in majority Muslim states

| | *Considered prohibited by Islamic Sharia* | *Perceived as blasphemous, offensive, or contrary to the Islamic faith* | *Websites belonging to non-state-sanctioned religions or sects* | *Liberal, secular and atheistic content* |
|---|---|---|---|---|
| Bahrain | X | X | X | X |
| Bangladesh | | X | | |
| Gaza Strip | X | | | |
| Indonesia | X | X | | |
| Iran | X | X | X | X |
| Jordan | | X | | |
| Kuwait | X | X | X | X |
| Morocco | X | | | |
| Oman | X | X | | |
| Pakistan | X | X | X | |
| Qatar | X | X | | |
| Saudi Arabia | X | X | X | X |
| Sudan | X | X | | |
| Tunisia | X | X | | |
| Turkey* | | | | X |
| United Arab Emirates | X | X | | X |
| Yemen | X | X | | X |

* Based on verified secondary reports and not ONI field tests

## Content perceived blasphemous, offensive or contrary to the Islamic faith

This category includes websites containing "blasphemous" content—that is, content providing unfavorable or critical reviews of Islam, or that attempts to convert Muslims to other religions, mostly Christianity. Examples include the websites http://www.thekoran.com, http://www.islamreview.com and http://www.islameyat.com. Also in this category are sites such as the "Everybody Draw Mohammed Day" page on Facebook and YouTube clips that contain "un-Islamic" content. Saudi Arabia, Kuwait, Bahrain, Yemen, Qatar, Oman, the UAE, Pakistan, Bangladesh, Jordan, Indonesia, Iran, Sudan and Tunisia are among the countries that block content in this category, to varying degrees.

## Websites with content considered prohibited by Islamic Sharia

This content category includes pornography, nudity, photos of women in provocative attire, homosexuality, dating, gambling and alcohol-related websites. Saudi Arabia, Kuwait, Bahrain, Yemen, Qatar, Oman, the UAE, Gaza Strip, Iran, Tunisia, Morocco, Sudan, Pakistan and Indonesia have been found to block content in this category, again by varying degrees.

## Websites belonging to religious groups whose ideologies are not in line with the official state-sanctioned religion or specific sect of a religion

This category includes the websites of minority faith groups such as Shi'i Muslims, Bahá'is, and Hindus. Countries that block-selected websites in this category include Saudi Arabia,

Iran, Kuwait, Bahrain and Pakistan. The Sunni regimes of Saudi Arabia and Bahrain block Shi'i content, and the Shi'i regime of Iran blocks Sunni content. It is also worth noting that some of the websites in this category are also related to political activism (e.g. Shi'i sites in Bahrain), so content in this category can thus be considered political.

### Liberal, secular and atheistic content

This category includes websites containing leftist literature, secular ideologies, atheist groups and bloggers, and content about Darwinism and evolution. Bahrain, Kuwait, Saudi Arabia, Iran, the UAE, Turkey and Yemen are among the countries that target this content category at varying degrees.

In addition to ISP-level filtering, some governments have expanded their national Internet filtering policies to Blackberry Internet Services (BIS). Limited manual testing by ONI found evidence that Saudi Arabia, Oman and the UAE implement Internet filtering on BIS. ONI found that content categories blocked by ISPs are also blocked via BIS connections. Also, limited testing on Indonesian telecommunications provider XL revealed evidence that limited content critical of the Islamic faith was blocked.

## Censoring *Innocence of Muslims* movie trailer

In September 2012, as this chapter was ready to go to press, many countries around the world began censoring, to varying degrees, the controversial American-made anti-Islam movie trailer, *Innocence of Muslims*, which is available on YouTube. While some countries have censored the film from their end by technically blocking its URLs at national ISP levels (e.g., Afghanistan, Sudan, UAE, Pakistan and Yemen), other countries have passed on the burden to YouTube and requested that it make the film inaccessible from their respective countries (e.g., India, Jordan, Lebanon, Indonesia and Malaysia). Some countries, like Saudi Arabia, have taken both measures.

YouTube has decided to leave the video on its website, saying it did not violate YouTube policy, but has "temporarily restricted access" to it in Egypt and Libya, citing "exceptional circumstances" and "the very difficult situation" in these two countries. The exceptional circumstances refer to the violent protests that took place in Egypt and Libya and the killing of the US ambassador to Libya and three members of his staff.[8]

## Intricacies surrounding faith-based censorship

There are a number of intricacies surrounding faith-based censorship as it is implemented in many majority Muslim countries. First, the policies are wholesale regulations imposed on a supposed community of the faithful, but such national-level unified policies do not accommodate the not-so-faithful, let alone the faithless. Second, censorship policies target not only that which is perceived un-Islamic, but also that which does not conform to the state-sponsored version of Islam. Third, there are inconsistencies between policies that regulate cyberspace and those that tolerate similar activities in real space. For example, an Internet user in Dubai cannot access escort websites, but the same person can easily solicit a prostitute from some of

8 See YouTube's statement given to the Associated Press on 12 September 2012 at http://www.google.com/hostednews/ap/article/ALeqM5grO5ODkwZqo33PZ7Wwo6J_Z8RXg?docId=67afe1f7288e4d64918e6f94d0adac9b

the notorious bars and streets of the city. This inconsistency suggests that social considerations, such as appeasing conservative families browsing the Internet at home, and economic factors, such as keeping the money-generating hotel rooms and bars busy, play a role in developing those policies. Thus censorship regulations are likely to change as authorities weigh the multiple political and socioeconomic factors that shape the policies. Fourth, technical censorship is unevenly implemented by different regimes and there is no region-wide unified policy. For example, a traditionally socially liberal country such as Tunisia implemented pervasive ISP-level social filtering during the regime of Ben Ali, and some local groups have been pressing the interim government to continue to filter such content, while other less liberal countries or at least equally liberal countries, such as Jordan, have no ISP-level social filtering.

## Faith-based censorship contested

Faith-based censorship in majority Muslim countries is such a contentious issue that it has become part of the identity of politics and the debate on the role of religion in public life, the limits of free speech, and the rights of non-Muslim minority groups. The culture of faith-based censorship, the restrictive laws, and the pretexts used by regimes and religious authorities have been fiercely criticized by various intellectual groups, especially those that embrace and promote liberal or secular ideologies. A 2009 Arabic book entitled *Censorship: Its Various Faces and Disguises* (Buaziz *et al.* 2009) is one of the recent notable intellectual arguments against religious and political censorship. Written by mostly liberal Arab writers, the book exposes, denounces and resists censorship because, as contributor Omar Kadour puts it, "censorship rapes our intellect" in the name of God and society (author's translation). Another contributor, Hamid Zannar, notes that regimes in the Arab world have indeed succeeded in forming and enforcing a culture of political and religious censorship. "When the regimes say that Islam is the religion of the state, then faith-based censorship eradicates one's free and individualistic identity. One then lives in exhausting secrecy" (Kadour 2009; author's translation).

Faith-based censorship has been blamed by Kuwaiti intellectuals for the deterioration of once-vital intellectual life in their country. The intellectuals reject the "increasing oppressive religious guardianship" on freedom of creativity that amounts to "intellectual terrorism" (Al-Shimiri 2010; author's translation). In Egypt, a group of anti-censorship intellectuals describe efforts by the religious authorities to confiscate objectionable literary and artistic works as a fierce attack on the mind, intellect and art, and say such efforts resemble the work of the medieval inquisition tribunals. They also criticize the religious establishment's attempts to have the final word on intellectual freedom (Al-Sayed 2004). In April 2011, the Cairo-based advocacy group called the Arabic Network for Human Rights Information condemned the first post-25 January revolution *Hisbah* case filed by lawyers against a storybook entitled *Where is Allah?* for allegedly insulting religious beliefs (The Arabic Network for Human Rights Information 2011). The advocacy group expressed deep concern about the return of religious and political *Hisbah* cases to Egypt after the 25 January revolution that aimed to advance freedom of expression in Egypt. The group said that making artwork subject to religious assessment is an assault on freedom of expression, and that dragging artwork into courtrooms is not acceptable (ibid.).

Moreover, free-speech advocates have argued that faith-based censorship has been used by regimes to disguise political filtering. In Bahrain, for example, rights groups maintain that the regime has introduced faith-based Internet censorship supposed to target pornographic content as a pretext to block local political and human rights websites, and that, in practice, the regime has treated oppositional content and pornographic websites the same (Sandels 2009).

Opposition to faith-based censorship takes other shapes and forms that range from bloggers individually or in groups organizing online campaigns, to free political prisoners, activists demanding political and legal reform, free-speech groups advocating the adoption of internationally accepted human rights standards, to politically minded individuals with technical skills developing or promoting Internet circumvention tools to help users to bypass state Internet filtering regimes.

## Conclusion

There is an ongoing struggle among state and non-state actors who want to regulate the Internet to protect and even strengthen the "Islamicity" of their countries, and those who see the Internet as an alternative information tool with which to bypass the undesirable guardianship of the religious authorities—between those who see the Internet as a potential threat to religious identity, and those who strive to bring to censored real space some of the qualities of the Internet: openness, freedom and neutrality. Opponents of faith-based censorship seem to have the tougher task, because some of the authorities derive their legitimacy from implementing Islamic Sharia and acting as the guardians of Islamic values. The debate about faith-based censorship is therefore part of the much-talked-about larger issue: Internet censorship and human rights. But when it comes to faith-based censorship, there is another problematic dimension to the argument. Because proponents of faith-based censorship consider it a non-negotiable divine policy, violators are labeled sinners rather than rights advocates, which leaves little room for democratic debate. The assassination of Pakistan's Punjab Governor Salman Taseer by one of his own bodyguards in January 2011 shed light on the extent to which some people will go to silence those who have different opinions on faith-based issues. While some considered the slain governor a true promoter of Islamic tolerance because of his calls for amendments to Pakistan's stringent blasphemy laws that discriminated against non-Muslim citizens, others hailed the assassin as a hero and a true protector of Islamic values, and even questioned the legitimacy of the laws—considered secular—that criminalized the assassination.[9]

The climate of intimidation imposed by radical elements and movements, and the fear of serious repercussions, are likely to keep liberal voice's demands so soft that they cannot make significant policy shifts in the near future. Moreover, if conservative religious authorities and their political allies continue to have the upper hand in developing and enforcing Internet regulatory policies, we are more likely to see a fractured Internet that is physically part of the global network, but increasingly bordered by religiously driven regulatory boundaries and technical filtering blockades that confine the user's online experience. The chilling effect of censorship can further thicken these boundaries, because users will be more likely to self-censor their online behavior and avoid the use of Internet circumvention tools for fear of being penalized. Another layer can yet be added to the boundaries if online content hosts like YouTube continue to, unilaterally or under pressure from religious and political censors, geographically limit access to materials though they fall within their terms of service. Faith-based filtering reflects not only rejection of certain websites, but also ideological intolerance towards issues such as alternative views on Islam, non-Islamic faiths, secular content and sexual orientation.

It remains to be seen whether the recent popular uprisings and revolutions in the region will ultimately produce Internet governance dynamics that will reverse, lighten, or simply

9 For details, see Nagiana 2011 and Khan 2011.

tighten the current Internet restrictions. Immediate developments indicate, however, that while there has been a reduction in political censorship in some of these countries, faith-based censorship has remained the same. After the president of Yemen relinquished power in November 2011, political filtering targeting opposition content was reduced, but faith-based censorship stayed the same. In post-revolution Tunisia, courts twice ordered the country's Internet agency to restore Internet filtering of pornographic content on Islamic religious ground. In Morocco, a new Constitution guaranteeing press freedom and prohibiting any form of prior censorship was ratified in July 2011, but the country's press code continued to outlaw making "offensive" comments about Islam and the king. In addition, the fact that Islamist parties won a majority of the seats in the first post-revolution legislative elections in Egypt and Tunisia, and in Morocco after the ratification of the new Constitution, raises the question of whether they will impose stricter interpretation of Islamic Sharia laws and try to challenge the universality of the UDHR. In fact, one of the first demands put forth by the Egyptian Salafist Nour Party after winning seats in parliament in the 2011–12 elections was a block on all pornographic websites in Egypt's Internet network (Ahram Online 2012).

Faith-based censorship, as practiced in many majority Muslim countries, will continue to be legally problematic because there are compatibility issues between two conceptually different frameworks: the collectively adopted religious approach to human rights and the internationally accepted secular human rights standards. The tension between the two frameworks will continue as long as international human rights norms are not reflected in national legislation or there is no mechanism, within a region or internationally, for a review of national decisions against binding, more encompassing, standards.

## References

Ahram Online (2012) 'Salafist MP demands Egypt ban on porn sites,' 20 February. Online. Available HTTP: http://english.ahram.org.eg/NewsContent/1/64/34976/Egypt/Politics-/Salafist-MP-demands-Egypt-ban-on-porn-sites.aspx (accessed 22 May 2012).

AKI (2011) 'Iran: Tehran announces new "halal" Islamic internet,' 13 April. Online. Available HTTP: http://www.adnkronos.com/IGN/Aki/English/CultureAndMedia/Iran-Tehran-announces-new-halal-Islamic-internet_311908244227.html (accessed 22 May 2012).

Al-Arabyia (2008) 'Da'ia yotalib ibdal safahat hajb mawaqi alinternet biayat quraniyah [A religious preacher demands replacing the text on the Internet blockpages with verses from the Qur'an],' 24 October. Online. Available HTTP: http://www.alarabiya.net/articles/2008/10/24/58842.html (accessed 9 January 2011).

Al-Halawani, A. (2009) 'Islamic duty of enjoining good and forbidding evil,' *Islam Online*, 29 December. Online. Available HTTP: http://www.islamonline.net/servlet/Satellite?c=Article_C&cid=1260258457931&pagename=Zone-English-Living_Shariah%2FLSELayout (accessed 14 November 2010).

Al-Hamad, K. (2010) 'Aldawa alislamiyah ala alinternet: Tikrar amibtikar? [Promotion of Islam via the Internet: Repetition or innovation?],' *Islam Today*, 23 February. Online. Available HTTP: http://islamtoday.net/bohooth/artshow-86-128253.htm (accessed 14 November 2010).

Al-Khatib, M. (2004) 'Alinternet alislami, ayna alkhalal [Islamic Internet: Where is the problem?],' *Al-Jazeera.net*, 3 October. Online. Available HTTP: http://www.aljazeera.net/NR/exeres/AB26DC74-F13F-41EC-902D-69238D12AB36.htm (accessed 14 November 2010).

Al-Mohammed, F. 'Indama yakhdish alinternet haya almojtama [When the Internet damages the shyness of society],' *Islamic Promotion Media Foundation*. Online. Available HTTP: http://www.aldaawah.com/?p=1085 (accessed 14 November 2010).

Al-Sayed, A. (2004) 'Muthaqafo masr dhida ashorta alazhariya [Egypt's intellectuals are against the al Azhar's police],' *alarabiya.net*, 17 June. Online. Available HTTP: http://www.alarabiya.net/articles/2004/06/17/4412.html (accessed 2 December 2010).

Al-Shimiri, L. (2010) 'Muthaqafoon: narfod wisayat aljamaat aldiniyah wa royataha alohadiya almota'sifah [Intellectuals: We reject the guardianship of the religious groups and their oppressive one-sided vision],' *Aafaaq Center for Research and Studies*, 26 August. Online. Available HTTP: http://aafaqcenter.com/post/344 (accessed 1 January 2011).

Anderson, C. (2012) 'The Hidden Internet of Iran: Private Address Allocations on a National Network' Cornell Univesity Library, 28 September. Online. Available HTTP: http://arxiv.org.abs/1209.6398 (accessed 6 October 2012).

Arabic Network for Human Rights Information (2011) 'First Hesba case after the Glorious Revolution of January 25th: The Arabic network condemns the communiqué submitted by the Neo Actio Popularis against the storybook *Where is Allah?*' 28 April. Online. Available HTTP: http://www.anhri.net/en/?p=2464 (accessed 28 March 2012).

*BBC News* (2007) 'Journalists fined over Islam joke,' 15 January. Online. Available HTTP: http://news.bbc.co.uk/2/hi/6262919.stm (accessed 28 March 2012).

—— (2009) 'Egyptian court "bans porn sites",' 12 May. Online. Available HTTP: http://news.bbc.co.uk/2/hi/middle_east/8046787.stm (accessed 28 March 2012).

Bin Ali al-Mashaikih, K. (2009) *Fatwa*, 23 August. Online. Available HTTP: http://www.islamlight.net/almoshaiqeh/index.php?option=com_ftawa&task=view&id=32919 (accessed 28 March 2012).

Buaziz, S. *et al.* (eds.) (2009) *Alrkabah boujouhha wa'kna'tha almkhtlfah* [*Censorship: Its Various Faces and Disguises*], Damascus: Petra.

Committee for Promotion of Virtue and Protection of Vice (2010) 'The moral vice of the Internet and how to practise Hisbah.' Online. Available HTTP: http://www.pv.gov.sa/SiteTree/Pages/books.aspx?View=Tree&NodeID=8681&PageNo=1&BookID=1 (accessed 14 November 2010).

*Emirates 24/7* (2010) 'Saudi Arabia to monitor Facebook chatting,' 10 October. Online. Available HTTP: http://www.emirates247.com/news/region/saudi-arabia-to-monitor-facebook-chatting-2010-10-10-1.301947 (accessed 14 November 2010).

*Europe News* (2007) 'Cairo Declaration of Human Rights in Islam: Diverges from the Universal Declaration of Human Rights in key respects,' 1 December. Online. Available HTTP: http://europenews.dk/en/node/3847 (accessed 28 March 2012)

Gelling, P. (2009) 'Does Facebook lead to adultery?' *Global Post*, 28 May. Online. Available HTTP: http://www.globalpost.com/dispatch/indonesia/090528/does-facebook-lead-adultery (accessed 14 November 2010).

Ghanea, N. (2007) '12 "phobias" and "isms": Recognition of difference or the slippery slope of particularisms?' in N. Ghanea, A. Stevens and R. Walden (eds.) *Does God Believe in Human Rights?* Leiden: Martinus Nijhoff.

Grahamm, L. (2009) 'Defamation of religions: The end of pluralism?' *Emory International Law Review*, 23: 69–84. Online. Available HTTP: www.law.emory.edu/fileadmin/journals/eilr/23/23.1/Graham.pdf (accessed 28 March 2012).

Imtiaz, H. (2010) 'Hate on the Internet,' *Dawn.com*, 8 October. Online. Available HTTP: http://criticalppp.com/archives/25353 (accessed 28 March 2012).

Institute of Policy Studies (2010) 'The institution of Hisbah and demand for its revival.' Online. Available HTTP: http://www.ips.org.pk/pakistanaffairs/politics/1185.html (accessed 14 November 2010).

Islam Question and Answer (n.d.) 'He has an Internet café and is asking about his income.' Online. Available HTTP: http://www.islam-qa.com/en/ref/82873/internet (accessed 28 March 2012).

Islam Web (2008) 'Shabab misr: La lilmawaqi alibahiya [Egyptian youth: No to pornographic websites],' 25 December. Online. Available HTTP: http://www.islamweb.net/media/index.php?page=article&lang=A&id=148161 (accessed 14 November 2010).

Islam Web Fatwa Center (2009) *Fatwa*, 16 May. Online. Available HTTP: http://www.islamweb.net/fatwa/index.php?page=showfatwa&lang=A&Id=151229&Option=FatwaId (accessed 14 November 2010).

Ismael, M. (2008) 'Tasallul waba altanseer ala alwatan alarabi [The infiltration of the epidemic of christianization to the Arabic World],' *Islam Way*, 11 November. Online. Available HTTP: http://ar.islamway.com/article/4804 (accessed 14 November 2010).

Johnson, T. (2010) 'Islam: Governing under Sharia,' *Council on Foreign Relations*, 10 November. Online. Available HTTP: http://www.cfr.org/religion/islam-governing-under-sharia/p8034 (accessed 14 November 2010).

Kadour, O. (2009) 'Censorship: The other that rapes our intellect,' in Samir Buaziz *et al.* (ed.) *Alrkabah boujouhha wa'kna'tha almkhtlfah* [*Censorship: Its Various Faces and Disguises*], Damascus: Petra.

Khan, M. I. (2011) 'Salman Taseer murder: Is Pakistan past tipping point?' *BBC News*, 7 January. Online. Available HTTP: http://www.bbc.co.uk/news/world-south-asia-12136274 (accessed 30 May 2012).

Latify, A. (2010) 'Ikhtilaf mawqi alislam fi aldasatir alarabiya [The various positions of Islam in the Arabic constitutions],' 8 August. Online. Available HTTP: http://www.aljazeera.net/analysis/pages/8b203415-d898-4461-a1a8-8232232a0c88 (accessed 14 November 2010).
Nagiana, U. (2011) 'Scores of lawyers gather showing support for "assassin",' *The Express Tribune*, 6 January. Online. Available HTTP: http://tribune.com.pk/story/99746/scores-of-lawyers-gather-showing-support-for-assassin/ (accessed 29 May 2012).
National Telecommunication Corporation (2011) 'Censorship policy,' Published in Arabic. Online. Available HTTP: http://web.archive.org/web/20100918071703/http://www.ntc.gov.sd/index.php?n=b3B0aW9uPWNvbV9jb250ZW50JnZpZXc9YXJ0aWNsZSZpZD0xNDUmSXRlbWlkPTImbGFuZz1hcg%3D%3D (accessed 14 November 2010).
Noman, H. (2009) 'Overview of Internet censorship in the Middle East and North Africa,' *OpenNet Initiative*, 6 August. Online. Available HTTP: http://opennet.net/research/regions/mena (accessed 31 March 2012)
and York, J. C. (2011) 'West censoring East: The use of Western technologies by Middle East censors, 2010–2011,' *OpenNet Initiative*, April. Online. Available HTTP: http://opennet.net/west-censoring-east-the-use-western-technologies-middle-east-censors-2010-2011 (accessed 31 March 2012).
OpenNet Initiative (2007a) 'Internet filtering in Yemen in 2006–2007.' Online. Available HTTP: http://opennet.net/studies/yemen2007 (accessed 31 March 2012).
—— (2007b) 'Gaza and the West Bank.' Online. Available HTTP: http://opennet.net/research/profiles/gazawestbank (accessed 31 March 2012).
—— (2007c) 'Afghanistan.' Online. Available HTTP: http://opennet.net/research/profiles/afghanistan (accessed 31 March 2012).
—— (2009a) 'Egypt,' 6 August. Online. Available HTTP: http://opennet.net/research/profiles/egypt (accessed 31 March 2012).
—— (2009b) 'Iran.' Online. Available HTTP: http://opennet.net/research/profiles/iran (accessed 31 March 2012).
—— (2009c) 'Kuwait.' Online. Available HTTP: http://opennet.net/research/profiles/kuwait (accessed 31 March 2012).
—— (2009d) 'Saudi Arabia country study.' Online. Available HTTP: http://opennet.net/research/profiles/saudi-arabia (accessed 31 March 2012).
—— (n.d.) 'Country profiles.' Online. Available HTTP: http://opennet.net/country-profiles (accessed 31 March 2012).
Organization of Islamic Cooperation (2012) 'OIC Group in New York Condemns the Release of the Anti Muslim Video, and Calls for Collective Action against Provocations and Systematic Incitement to Hatred.' Online. Available HTTP: http://www.oic-oci.org/topic_detail.asp?t_id=7189&x_key= (accessed 22 September 2012).
Organization of the Islamic Conference (1990) 'The Cairo Declaration of Human Rights in Islam.' Online. Available HTTP: www.oic-oci.org/english/article/human.htm (accessed 31 March 2012).
Reporters sans Frontières (2010) 'Government orders ISPs to start anti-porn filtering,' 11 August. Online. Available HTTP: http://en.rsf.org/indonesia-government-orders-isps-to-start-11-08-2010,38118.html (accessed 14 November 2010).
Reuters (2010) 'Indonesia to ask Internet providers to block porn,' 14 July. Online. Available HTTP: http://www.reuters.com/article/2010/07/14/us-indonesia-porn-idUSTRE66D2MQ20100714 (accessed 14 November 2010).
Rishmawi, M. (2009) 'The Arab Charter on Human Rights,' *Carnegie Endowment for International Peace*, 6 October. Online. Available HTTP: www.carnegieendowment.org/2009/10/06/arab-charter-on-human-rights/6cj1 (accessed 31 March 2012).
Sandels, A. (2009) 'Almoaradat tosawa bilebahiyah fi albahrain [Oppositional and pornographic [content] are treated as equal in Bahrain],' *Menassat*, 24 March. Online. Available HTTP: http://www.menassat.com/?q=en/news-articles/6236- (accessed 14 November 2010).
Tokan, H. (2008) 'al-Illhad yaghzo al-Internet al-Arabi wa yothir ghadab rijal al-deen [Atheism invades the Arabic Internet and angers religious scholars],' *CNN Arabic*, 22 August. Online. Available HTTP: http://arabic.cnn.com/2009/entertainment/8/22/athiesm.arab/ (accessed 14 November 2010).
Toumi, H. (2012) 'Kuwait Parliament approves amendment to death penalty,' *Gulf News*, 3 May. Online. Available HTTP: http://gulfnews.com/news/gulf/kuwait/kuwait-parliament-approves-amendment-to-death-penalty-1.1017758 (accessed 22 May 2012).
Vaswani, K. (2010) 'Indonesia upholds anti-pornography Bill,' *BBC News*, 25 March. Online. Available HTTP: http://news.bbc.co.uk/2/hi/8586749.stm (accessed 14 November 2010).

# 15

# Media control with Chinese characteristics

*Rogier Creemers*

## Introduction

It is difficult to underestimate the political importance of media in the People's Republic of China. Since 1949, the media have often been the stage on which intra-Party struggles were fought. In 1966, the Cultural Revolution was launched through an attack on a stage play, written by the Shanghai Leftist Yao Wenyan, because it was considered to be an attack on Mao Zedong (Fisher 1989). In 1979, the contest for the paramount leadership between Deng Xiaoping and Hua Guofeng, reflecting both sides' plans for Chinese development, was manifested through newspaper articles and editorials (Schoenhals 1991). Revolutionary films and operas were a prime tool of propaganda, and films in particular still remain closely controlled by the Party-state.

These aspects of media in China have been particularly well studied in Western literature. However, as China has developed, the role of media has grown much more complex and economically important, requiring a closer look at the conceptualization and structuring of Chinese media governance. Between 2004 and 2010, the cultural industries grew by 23 percent on average annually, and their share of gross domestic product (GDP) reached 2.78 percent in 2010 (HXCI 2012).[1] Cinema box office revenues grew tenfold between 2000 and 2011 (Zheng 2012), and it was announced in April 2012 that China had surpassed Japan to become the second largest film market globally.

Further development of the cultural sector[2] is a high-priority objective of the Twelfth Five-Year Plan, and merited a special plenary session of the Seventeenth Party Congress in October 2011.[3] The resulting Decision concerning Deepening Cultural Structural Reform

1 In comparison, China's entire agricultural sector is estimated at 10 percent of GDP (CIA 2012).

2 As this chapter will expound later, the "cultural sector" encompasses a range of diverse activities, including radio, film, television, news media, performing and fine arts, museums, electronic gaming, etc.

3 This Sixth Plenum of the Seventeenth Party Congress, held 15–18 October 2011, was dedicated to discussing the Party's new cultural policy, summarized in the 2011 Resolution. The Central Committee maintains a website that is dedicated to articles, speeches and documents that "study and implement the spirit of the 6th Plenum of the 17th Party Congress" (Central Committee 2011a).

contains clear objectives for the further development of cultural products, but also indicates ambitions to support the development of public cultural services, increasing personnel training and education, fostering technological innovation and application, raising cultural consumption levels, enhancing funding and investment, and fostering markets and intermediary actors, such as agents and valuators (Central Committee 2011). Politically, this line continues the well-established purpose of enhancing Party-state control and carrying out its ideological project, under the newly constructed concept of the "Socialist core value system" (*shehuizhuyi hexin jiazhi tixi* 社会主义核心价值体系).[4]

These goals are ambitious, and beg the question of how they will be achieved. In other words, the question of which mechanisms exist between policy objectives and outcomes is important. To shed some light on this, this chapter aims to map the most important actors, structures and processes influencing Chinese media governance. First, it provides a brief overview of Chinese media policy since Deng Xiaoping introduced market reforms in 1978. Second, it maps the central-level regulatory authorities dealing with media governance. Third, it outlines the structure of Chinese media law and regulation. Finally, it sketches domestic and international pushback against the extant media regime, and touches upon governance challenges brought on by digital technology and the Internet.

## Chinese media policy since 1978

After the People's Republic of China was established in 1949, the Party leadership progressively tightened control over the circulation of information. Under the leadership of the newly established Ministry of Culture, staffed by rather radical cadres (Amitin 1980), newspapers mandatorily came under the influence of the Party, writers and journalists were grouped in professional associations controlled by the Party, and important sections of the cultural sector were nationalized. As the ideological climate changed during the 1950s and 1960s,[5] artists, authors and journalists were subject to increasing political pressure, culminating in the Cultural Revolution. During this period, the cultural sector came under intense pressure. Permitted entertainment was limited to singing "Red Songs" and performing a canon of eight permitted revolutionary operas.

It became clear in 1978 that a strong shift in cultural and press policy was needed. However, this did not mean full-scale commercialization and liberalization of the media. Rather, the media and the cultural sector would still remain primarily a vehicle to realize Party-state policy. This was made clear in a number of speeches by Deng Xiaoping, in which Deng reacted against increasing calls for democracy centered on Beijing's Democracy Wall, on which increasing numbers of pamphlets were posted. Deng ordered the wall to be torn down (Vogel 2011), and established the Four Cardinal Principles[6] as a foundation for Party policy, including the production of media. In a speech in early 1980, Deng was very clear about the extent to which the regime could be openly criticized: "It is absolutely not permitted

4 This concept was introduced by the Sixth Plenum of the Sixteenth Party Congress as an effort to boost the role of morality in Chinese society and stress social development. See also Saich (2007).

5 This period saw relatively large shifts to and fro between openness and crackdown. The Hundred Flowers Campaign, which had a stated aim of providing better governance through open criticism, evolved into the Anti-Rightist campaign, in which many of the more outspoken voices were persecuted, and the disastrous Great Leap Forward. Another period of relative relaxation in the early 1960s was followed by the fundamental upheaval of the Cultural Revolution.

6 These are: persisting in the Socialist path; persisting in the dictatorship of the proletariat; persisting in CCP leadership; and persisting in Mao Zedong Thought (1979 Four Cardinal Principles speech).

to propagate whatever freedom of expression or publication, and freedom of association and to form organizations that include anti-revolutionaries" (Central Committee 1980). Furthermore, he indicated that, while the absolute fixation on ideological rectitude of the Cultural Revolution would cease:

> Literature and art cannot be separated from politics. No progressive and revolutionary literature and art worker cannot consider the social influence of their works, and cannot consider the interest of the people, the interest of the country, and the interest of the Party. Fostering new Socialist people is politics.

Nonetheless, as Chinese politics focused on economic reforms in the 1980s, the role of culture, media and propaganda became less prominent. In the face of criticism from the cautious planners within the Party, led by Chen Yun, Deng Xiaoping also required the support of intellectuals to push through his ambitious reform agenda. Initiatives were undertaken to start drafting laws for the press, which were to provide a more predictable, less capricious framework for news reporting. Copyright legislation was enacted as a means to support the establishment of a media market. Initial openings were made concerning the import of foreign media products.[7] Nonetheless, conservative factions within the Party, such as Deng Liqun, remained in charge of the media, and used their position to control media policy. As a reaction against concern over the influx of foreign ideas through increasing international contacts, the conservative factions launched the Campaign against Spiritual Pollution in 1983. This campaign proved to be very unpopular, and was ended after two months, but Chen Yun prevented the ousting of Deng Liqun (Vogel 2011).[8] Reform did take place in the economic realm. Hitherto, the Chinese media had been largely financed through either direct subsidies or mandatory consumption from other Party and state institutions, which aimed to produce pure propaganda. The financial burden that this presented caused the impetus for the introduction of market mechanisms.[9] Cultural work units would need to make their activities commercially viable, while television stations and newspapers were permitted to run commercials and advertisements. Nonetheless, the media were deemed to be too crucial to leave to the vagaries of the market. Hence high-level, central Party and state media organs remained on the public payroll, often through subsidies, while most cultural organizations were obliged to be successful in attracting market revenues on the basis of their own merit in order to survive.[10] In order to make it possible for creative works to be sustainable in the marketplace, efforts to draft copyright regulation were increased.[11]

In the aftermath of the protests in Tiananmen Square and more than 400 other cities, economic development suffered deeply as the outside world withdrew business from China, while propaganda and spiritual work again returned to the forefront of the Party. Mindful of the role that newspapers had played in the protest, drafting of the Press Law was stopped, and the progressive head of the drafting committee, Hu Jiwei, was removed from all of his official positions. At the same time, the role that the relaxation of control over the press had played

7 See, e.g., the 1984 Hong Kong and Taiwan Import Report.

8 Hardliners such as Deng Liqun and Hu Qiaomu thereby remained in control of the media and propaganda administration, which would play a critical role in the events of 1989.

9 See also Kraus 2004.

10 Often, this was done through creative means. The Beijing Philharmonic Orchestra, for example, opened restaurants (Kraus 2004).

11 China's first copyright regulations were introduced in 1984 for books and periodicals, and in 1986 for audiovisual products. See also Creemers 2012 and Mertha 2005.

in the end of Communist regimes in Eastern Europe and the dissolution of the Soviet Union (Shambaugh 2008) led the hardline leadership to reassert strict control over all media outlets, and measures were taken to ban books and to control newspapers.[12]

Nonetheless, this did not mean a return to the Cultural Revolution. The economic reforms in the 1980s had built up momentum, which had also crossed into the cultural realm. As living standards increased, especially in the urban and coastal areas, there was more money for leisure, and a market for pirated foreign and Hong Kong films had developed (MRFT, MOFCOM, SAIC 1986). Months before the protests, the Central Committee had first recognized the existence of a market for cultural products. A copyright law had been in the making, and was quickly rushed through after the protests—the 1990 Copyright Law of the People's Republic of China.[13] By 1992, Deng had been able to steer China back in the direction of economic development, although the focus had shifted from small-scale development in the countryside to more centralized, state-guided urban construction, under the name of the Socialist market economy.[14] Similarly, the cultural and propaganda sector increasingly became seen as an opportunity for profit as well as a political tool.

Throughout the 1990s, a new regulatory structure for culture and media was established, with the government taking a different role, more akin to a traditional regulator and gatekeeper. Rather than operating through direct administrative intervention, enterprises became slightly more independent, and different licensing structures and control mechanisms were established. This did not mean a loosening of content control per se. The Party remained in control over broad policymaking, with state organs charged with implementation and practical arrangements. Party organizations within media outlets were maintained, and the regulatory framework included safeguard provisions to ensure that products, personnel and companies going beyond the pale could be brought to order. Between 1994 and 1997, rules were made for audiovisual products (State Council 1994), films (State Council 1996), publications (State Council 1997a), and radio and television (State Council 1997b). Also, a detailed plan for cultural development was laid down for the first time in 1997 (Ministry of Culture 1997), which had a strong focus on grassroots cultural and artistic development.

The new century brought new challenges. China's impending accession into the World Trade Organization (WTO) and the rampant piracy of foreign products painfully emphasized the country's inability to produce cultural products for its own markets, let alone international expansion. Hence culture and media reform was deepened, with an eye to international competitiveness and resistance from a feared invasion of foreign products.[15] During the WTO accession negotiations, China successfully managed to keep nearly its entire media market closed off, with the exception of areas in which it required skills and know-how, such as the cinema sector.[16] In 1999, a major reform of the television sector began.[17] A first major ingredient of this reform was

12 See Wong 2005, ch. 5.

13 See also Zhang 2002.

14 For a deep analysis of this transition, see Huang 2008.

15 For a contemporary evaluation, see Li 2002 and Guan 2001.

16 See WTO Document China, Schedule of Specific Commitments on Services, WT/ACC/CHN/49/Add.2, 1 October 2001. China has since faced three WTO complaints in the media sector: *China—Financial Information Services, China—Intellectual Property Rights* and *China—Audiovisual Goods and Services*. The first ended in a negotiated solution; inconsistency with WTO obligations was found in the two latter cases, but neither significantly dented China's media control regime. See also Creemers 2012.

17 Outlined in the 1999 Radio and Television Network Opinions. See also Yu 2009.

the conglomeration of provincial radio and television channels into large media groups. This allowed for a reduction of costs and an increase in coverage, but also a strengthening of state control. Further policy adjustments were made to expand financial and knowledge input. In spaces where it was deemed acceptable, private and foreign capital investment was permitted, and new types of business transaction were allowed. Copyright, for example, could be used for collateral. At the same time, training programs for skilled culture and media workers expanded, and there was increased support for the establishment of industry bases, for the export of cultural products and for certain media outlets to establish overseas offices; special funding was also granted to ethnic-minority-related art. Most importantly, cultural enterprises were increasingly required to "transform into enterprises." Hitherto, most culture and media entities were considered to be public-interest "undertakings" (*shiye* 事业). This change turned them into commercially run, marketized "enterprises" (*qiye* 企业).

Most of the reforms, however, have taken place in the economic aspects of media and culture. The role that media have in Chinese politics has essentially remained unchanged since the Deng Xiaoping era. In the official parlance, culture has both an economic and ideological function, and both must be grasped firmly.[18] The often mercurial economic policies sometimes obscure the fact that the core of Chinese media control is very stable indeed: books, newspapers, films and television programs are there to carry forward the Party's message. First and foremost, the prime objective of cultural and media policy in China is to maintain and enhance the authority and legitimacy of the Communist Party, by monopolizing the public debate, or, as noted in a number of policy documents, "occupying the ideological battlefield."[19] While culture and media are permitted to be diverse, philosophical or political pluralism is not permitted. In other words, media diversification is aimed to tailor the message of the Party towards different audience groups, divided by ethnicity, locality, gender or age. In contrast with the Soviet Union, which tried to frontload political reform to stimulate economic change, the Chinese leadership considers the maintenance of the political status quo, under the terminology of social stability, to be essential for its economic project. As a result, the objective of media regulation and governance is to ensure that media enterprises carry out Party-state orders. In addition, China's moves towards economic reform and marketization should not be confused with privatization, which has always been limited in this area. In nearly all activities in the culture and media sector in which "non-public capital"[20] is permitted, a controlling state stake is required. Furthermore, there is a lack of clarity about property rights in the media sector. A secret document from 2001 indicated that, in principle, key media outlets were the property of the Party, rather than the state (Zhao 2008). While some of these organizations or their holding groups have been opened for outside investments, it remains unclear what that means in terms of their property or other rights vis-à-vis the enterprise in which they invest.

By the end of the first decade of the twenty-first century, politics moved back to the forefront of media reform. In the retrenchment after the 2008 Olympics, an increasing focus was placed on the ideological side of media. Apart from the international role outlined above, this reflected the increasingly volatile political situation in China, which emerged in the wake

18 See, e.g., Central Committee 2012.

19 See, e.g., GAPP 2011.

20 The Chinese word for "private" (*siying* 私营) is never used with respect to the cultural sector. Rather, terms such as "non-publicly owned" (*feigongyouzhi* 非公有制) and "people-run" (*minying* 民营) are employed.

of the international financial crisis. As the 2012 transition to a new generation of leaders approaches, fault lines in the Chinese Communist Party's (CCP) political structure became increasingly clear, as was illustrated by the ouster of Chongqing Party Chief Bo Xilai in March 2012. Additionally, increasing disaffection with Party leadership and a perceived lack of morality prompted the Party to launch a campaign based on a new concept, the "Socialist core value system." This was demonstrated clearly in the new framework for the cultural sector, which was laid down at the end of 2011. The Sixth Plenum of the Seventeenth Party Congress declared that China had become a "large Socialist culture country," and needed to also become a "strong Socialist culture country" (Central Committee 2011b), led by the Socialist core value system.

In short, the task of the official Chinese media is not primarily to speak the truth to power or to hold governments, businesses and other interest groups to account. Faced with endemic corruption and a perception of misuse of privilege by officials, the leadership has taken measures to raise the credibility of both the news media and government offices. New rules of information transparency oblige government departments to actively provide clearer information concerning their internal activities through different forms of reporting,[21] and they must provide for procedures for citizens to request information. Similarly, increasing measures have been taken to expand "public opinion supervision" (*yulun jiandu* 舆论监督), which means that the news media are to report any alleged misconduct of government departments and enterprises. However, the overarching objective of stability is present in this sphere as well.[22] Government departments still have considerable discretion in deciding which documents they can withhold from public scrutiny, while Party organizations are not covered by access to information measures at all. Similarly, detailed rules on the implementation of public opinion supervision stress that critical media reports must be positive and constructive, and not dwell on negative aspects. Furthermore, the rules prohibit journalists from writing too many public supervision reports or concerning a specific target in a given period, so as not to endanger social stability (Central Committee 2005).

Entertainment and other non-news media, while not as closely controlled as the news media, nonetheless play an important role in the leadership's propaganda strategy. In the film sector, for example, the state supports the production of "main melody films." These films, which typically extol heroic episodes from the Communist past or Chinese history,[23] receive significant amounts of state support: they are directly subsidized, receive policy preferences, for example in the use of land and cultural facilities, and often feature star-studded casts of top actors, who participate at vastly reduced rates. Often, cinemas are obliged to reduce or cease screening of other films while a large government-supported film is being screened. Both on a running basis and to commemorate important festivities or anniversaries, the leadership commissions large publication projects of historical or cultural studies works, documentaries and music collections.

This centralized mode of policymaking has worked relatively effectively regarding the traditional media. In the last few years, however, China's media governance system has been

21 A database of materials pertaining to this is available from the Yale Law School China Center. See online at http://www.law.yale.edu/intellectuallife/openinformation.htm

22 See, e.g., Central Committee 2005 and SARFT 2010.

23 Recent examples include: *Founding of a Republic*, about the period running up to the establishment of the People's Republic; *Aftershock*, about the 1976 Tangshan earthquake; *Founding of a Party*, about the early days of the CCP; and the biographic film *Confucius*.

shaken to the core by the advent of the Internet. In contrast to traditional media, which could be easily controlled through administrative bodies and Party groups, online media have been notoriously difficult to control, manage and coopt into the Party's media strategy. Yet at the same time, the Party-state has astutely recognized the Internet as a medium for further growth and economic development, and a useful tool for guiding public opinion. Hence measures similar to those governing traditional media have been taken to ensure the Party-state's occupation of this "public opinion battlefield." To resist foreign influence and to close down channels of potential international communication, foreign social media and video websites such as You Tube were—and remain—banned from China, while domestic service providers, licensed by and therefore dependent on, the goodwill of the Party-state, were encouraged to develop their businesses. The state has tightened regulation concerning Internet cafes and other surfing venues, including a real-name registration system, often on dubious grounds—for example, a fire in an Internet cafe (Liang and Lu 2010). Similar controls over news content are in place for online news providers, and as individual interaction with the Internet has grown through fora, bulletin board systems (BBSs) services and social media, Internet enterprises have been subject to increasing liabilities for the content that users post on their websites. At the same time, China has directed significant propaganda efforts at the online sphere, including the so-called "Fifty-Cent Party"[24] (*wumaodang* 五毛党), whose members number in the tens of thousands.

## Institutional structure of the Chinese media control apparatus

In order to implement these policies, a complex bureaucratic structure has been developed, which is one of the most important parts of the Party-state apparatus. This administration is organized along Leninist lines of penetration. Before the reform period, this meant that the entire society was subject to dual modes of control: a state structure that was responsible for policy implementation, shadowed by a parallel Party structure, which was in charge of overseeing the state institutions and the economic entities in which they were housed. Although the Party has retreated from a significant number of economic activities since 1979, it has maintained its command over the economy, among other ways through the *nomenklatura* system of appointments (Shambaugh 2008). A crucial tool in the Party's political arsenal, the media are kept very close to the center of political decision-making.

The entire Chinese administration is divided in a number of functional conglomerations, called "systems" (*xitong* 系统). These are pyramid structures that—if important enough—are directly headed by a member of the Politburo. One of these, the propaganda and education *xitong*, contains nearly all modes of media and other cultural activities. The system groups Party and state departments, as well as economic entities engaged in the specific functional field (Saich 2004). At the top level, there are two informal consultation bodies. The first is the Central Propaganda and Ideology Work Leading Small Group (*zhongyang xuanchuan sixiang gongzuo lingdao xiaozu* 中央宣传思想工作领导小组). This leading group comprises the Central Propaganda Department, the Central United Front Department, the Ministry of Foreign Affairs, the Overseas Chinese Office, the Hong Kong Office, the Taiwan Affairs Office, the State Administration of Radio, Film and Television (SARFT), the Ministry of

24 This term refers to the fifty cents members receive for posting pro-government messages on discussion fora and other websites. For detailed information concerning the functioning of this body, see Hung 2010.

Culture, the Ministry of Commerce, the State Tourism Bureau, the General Administration of Customs, and the General Administration of Press and Publications (GAPP) (Shaw 2005). It is also in direct charge of the Central Foreign Propaganda Office, which is better known as the State Council Information Office (Brady 2010). A second group was established in 1997 to govern spiritual civilization construction and its remit partially overlaps with the former group. However, both groups are chaired by the Politburo member overseeing propaganda.

The leading small groups are relatively informal groups that mainly exist to regularize consultation and communication between the different institutions involved. They lay down broad policy guidelines, after building consensus between different interests both inside and outside the *xitong*, and are a direct line of communication between the system and the entire Politburo. They also make it possible to coordinate core propaganda work with the actions of departments from different *xitong*. Sometimes, they may be established for ad hoc purposes; for example, as piracy became a problem, a leading group was established especially to deal with this issue.[25] More recently, the Ministry of Culture, SARFT and GAPP became members of a leading small group to attack counterfeit and inferior goods (China Copyright and Media 2010).

These groups are not responsible for day-to-day governance and overseeing work. That is the task of the main formal institution in the *xitong*: the Central Propaganda Department (CPD, 中宣部 *zhongxuanbu*).[26] This has been an integral part of the Central Party administration since it was founded in the 1920s, and it directly controls all state culture and propaganda-related departments, as well as the Chinese Academy of Social Sciences and the Xinhua Press Agency. It is in direct contact with high-level news outlets to instruct whether, and how, certain matters should be reported.

The close relationship of the CPD with the media administration is underlined by the fact that the heads of the main media-related bodies—the Ministry of Culture, SARFT, GAPP, and the State Council Information Office—serve as deputy chairmen of the CPD. Furthermore, there is a close relationship between the CPD and the official media outlets. Current Chinese Central Television (CCTV) chairman Jiao Li, for example, was a CPD vice-director before assuming his current position. Zhang Yannong, the current editor-in-chief of the *People's Daily*, also came from the CPD. This structure demonstrates that media in China are in effect subject to a dual command structure. On the one hand, state authorities formulate and implement rules and regulations, albeit generally to implement CPD policy, while on the other hand, Party presence within the regulators as well as large media outlets, which generally outranks the state hierarchy, ensures that the Party maintains the final say over what happens.[27]

While the Party structure is in charge of setting objectives and broad policy guidelines, it is up to state institutions to transform these policies into regulations for day-to-day use. The

25 This was called "Sweeping Pornography and Striking Illegality" (*saohuang dafei* 扫黄打非). Primarily, it was aimed at illegal content, rather than infringements of intellectual property rights. See also Mertha 2007.

26 It has changed its official English name into the Central Publicity Department, but its Chinese name was preserved (Hassid 2008).

27 It also means that, apart from administrative punishment, chief personnel in the media sector are subject to potentially very strict Party discipline. For a general introduction, see MacGregor 2010, in particular chapters 3 and 5.

media sector is structured according to departmental and hierarchical lines. Most important in governing the media are SARFT, GAPP, the Ministry of Culture (which governs the cultural market, as well as theatre and the arts), and the Ministry of Information Industry, which is in charge of the hardware side of the Internet. These organs are replicated at provincial and local levels although at lower administrative levels different functions are often combined or amalgamated in one organ.

A similar structure is present in the media industry, particularly in the highly structured broadcasting sectors. For example, the national broadcasters China Central Television (CCTV) and China National Radio (CNR) fall directly under the authority of SARFT, while provincial authorities govern provincial channels, city authorities govern city channels, and local authorities govern local channels. In 2001, a series of measures was taken to centralize local television programming at national and provincial levels.[28] Public access channels are provided where lower administrative levels can insert programs covering local interests. In the newspaper and periodical sector, all media outlets are required to have a sponsoring work unit and a controlling department. The sponsoring work unit is in charge of the editorial line of the publication, while the controlling department ensures that it stays within disciplinary and regulatory boundaries. There are Party cells in all significant media enterprises. In the news media, these are in charge of editorial policy, while in the entertainment media, they make sure that the Party influences which films or television programs are made and distributed (He 2008).

As a result of this highly centralized and bureaucratic system, the media are generally governed through administrative regulation documents and Party and government decrees, rather than law.[29] The purpose of this mode of regulation has been to ensure that Party-state administrative bodies would have ample space for intervention in the media sector, rather than to establish basic and general standards. As a consequence, the basic regulatory framework for the media reflects the top-down nature in the system.

The advent of the Internet has upset this top-down pattern of bureaucratic control. For the first time in the history of the People's Republic, it has become easier for individuals to produce and circulate information on a large scale. Among other things, this has spurred the development of media-related private law, in particular with regards to content.[30] Also, while administrative control is an effective tool when dealing with a relatively small number of media enterprises, it is a very expensive tool to use when controlling hundreds of millions of Internet users. Hence, in recent years, licensing and liability have been increasingly used to ensure that Internet content remains within an acceptable scope. At the end of 2011, Beijing issued a municipal regulation imposing, among other regulations, a real-name system on the popular microblog site Weibo (Beijing Municipal Government 2011). Furthermore, it obliged all microblog operators to individually screen posts from popular members, to provide instant technological access to public security organs, to be able to filter out key words and specific

28 These measures draw from the secret Document No. 17 of 2001, the 2001 Radio, Film and Television Reform Opinions (Central Committee, SARFT, GAPP 2001). For implementation measures, see SARFT 2001.

29 There are two laws that directly deal with media standards: the Copyright Law and the Advertising Law. Furthermore, the recent Tort Law contains basic provisions concerning infringement of civil rights on the Internet. There is also an emerging attention for defamation law, particularly with relation to the Internet, but also the traditional press. About the latter, see Liebman 2006; Josephs 1992; Fu and Cullen 1998.

30 See, e.g., the inclusion of Internet-related civil rights in the 2010 Tort Law.

terms at very short notice, and to preserve the information of specific users. These regulations apply to any microblog service provided in Beijing. Since the majority of the country's microblogs are based there, this effectively means that the regulations have nationwide application.

However, owing to the particular nature of the construction of the Chinese state, a large part of media governance actually takes place outside of the state hierarchy, and these elements are often subject to the parallel structure of Party control. All top-level media professionals and regulators are Party members, and therefore subject to Party discipline. This gives the CCP a tremendous level of control over the actions of individuals, not least because of its power to appoint and dismiss Party members in the entire *xitong*. It is not uncommon, for example, that journalists or editors deemed to not be sufficiently faithful are transferred away to less sensitive positions, for example to academia. In grave cases, they are dismissed or even jailed. In 2004, three top executives of the influential *Southern Metropolitan Daily* were sentenced to jail terms, ostensibly for bribery and economic crimes. However, this was more of a retaliation, as the newspaper had exposed cover-ups of, among other incidents, the SARS epidemic and the death in unlawful detention of Sun Zhigang (Zhao 2008).[31] Conversely, the Party may transfer leaders into media organizations to influence the policy direction of those organizations. In early 2012, for example, the relatively conservative Yang Jian was put in charge of the Nanfang Media Group, which enjoys a strong reputation of independent investigative and critical journalism, ostensibly to bring it closer into the fold (Bandurski 2012). This strict control translates into effective Party control over media policy through non-regulatory means. Party cadres are primarily evaluated on the basis of their fulfilling Party objectives, rather than professional or commercial considerations. In other words, Party members wishing to enhance their career need to be successful in spreading the Party's message.

## Media and foreign intervention

Media control is not limited to the domestic sphere. For a number of reasons, there are strong restrictions in place against foreign content, operators and investment. Politically, nationalism has become perhaps the most important element of CCP legitimacy after the decline of Communist ideology. Constructing an anti-foreign discourse enables the Party to present itself as a heroic force delivering China from a century of national humiliation by foreign powers.[32] Furthermore, after the collapse of the Eastern Bloc regimes, the leadership diagnosed peaceful evolution efforts spearheaded by Western nations and their media outlets as one of the prime catalysts for the overthrow of Communist governments. This fear is still strongly present in Chinese media policies. In January 2012, for example, President Hu Jintao warned against "foreign hostile powers" that were implementing a "long-term strategy to Westernize and divide China" (Hu 2012). Hence, while the "Marching Out" strategy is designed to expand Chinese influence in the rest of the world, at home the domestic objective is very much to keep influence from the rest of the world out.

Political concerns are supplemented by economic issues. Even though foreign films comprise only a small proportion of the total amount of films in Chinese cinemas and are subject to random political intervention, their box office intake vastly outstrips that of their

31 For further discussion of the dangers of being a journalist in China, see He 2008, ch. 9.

32 Generally, see Callahan 2009.

Chinese counterparts, leading to fears about the invasion of foreign culture and the destruction of the domestic media industries. China is particularly wary of the example of Taiwan. In the Taiwanese film market, Hollywood pushed for market liberalization, which was agreed to by the Taiwanese government. A few years later, Hollywood films comprised more than 90 percent of the market, destroying the local film industry and gravely damaging that of Hong Kong, for which Taiwan was the main export market (Curtin 2003).

At the same time, foreign media enterprises do have some attraction for the Chinese leadership. They possess technical expertise in filmmaking, technology and distribution that China lacks. They also have deep pockets and are often eager to expand into China. Hence policy and regulation vis-à-vis these foreign enterprises is a similar balancing exercise to that regarding private capital: attracting and encouraging participation in those specific fields in which Chinese technology, know-how, skills or resources are lacking, and limiting activities elsewhere.

Most attention in this regard has been paid to the film market. After strong lobbying by the United States in the early 1990s, particularly in the context of the trade tensions surrounding intellectual property rights and piracy at that time, SARFT agreed to allow the import and screening of ten foreign films in Chinese cinemas per year, on a revenue-sharing basis. This number was doubled at the time of China's WTO accession (World Trade Organization 2011). By then, China also permitted a small number of foreign satellite television stations to broadcast into high-level hotels and luxury residential compounds aimed at foreigners. The limit on US movie exports remained a thorn in the side of the US film majors until February 2012, when Xi Jinping and Joe Biden reached an agreement to allow for an additional quota of fourteen enhanced-format films, as well as a higher proportion of box office income to be passed to the US side. In May 2012, this was communicated to the WTO as a settlement ending the DS363 case (World Trade Organization 2012), in which it was found that China's denial of import rights to foreign media enterprises constituted an infringement of its WTO obligations. It remains to be seen whether these higher quotas will effectively transpire into higher profits for foreign filmmakers, because a host of other measures relating to foreign film screenings are still in force. In other words, China has incrementally permitted slight increases in foreign film imports, while at the same time maintaining initiative and control as to how the imported films are distributed and marketed.

## Pushback against media policy

Challenges to the current media governance structure do not come exclusively from outside. Within China, a number of factors are weakening the Party-state's hold over the main tools of public communication, as social tensions rise and digital technology progresses. Until the advent of new media, the Party-state propaganda and media system has been very effective in perhaps its most central task: monopolizing the public debate. At least as far as mainstream media are concerned, there are few organized contenders that offer competing discourses, and even social media and the Internet seem to have become progressively captured by the Party-state apparatus. However, this general status is being increasingly buffeted by novel forces brought on through commerce, economic development and technology. Internally, tensions have arisen because of the structuring of, and relationship among, different Party and state departments, and between government and media.

One first major tension engendered by the Chinese media framework is the strife between the central and provincial levels, particularly in the television sector. China Central Television (CCTV), the national broadcaster, is very closely linked to SARFT, as the heads of both departments are members of the Central Propaganda Department. Politically, CCTV is considered to be one of the most important propaganda tools, and all local-level broadcasters are required to transmit its news programming on their first channel. However, CCTV's political clout also has an economic side. The income from all advertising broadcast around and during transmitted CCTV programming directly goes to CCTV, causing complaints about unfair competition. In late 2011, SARFT issued a series of new regulations imposing limits on provincial satellite channels in terms of the programs they could broadcast.[33] Being completely commercial, these provincial channels had developed programs that were very popular, but also very far from the center of ideological rectitude. These included talent competitions such as *Super Girl*, dating shows and gaming programs. Some of these programs were banned outright (Jacobs 2011), while quantitative limits were imposed on the percentage of "entertainment programs" that satellite channels were allowed to broadcast. A number of commentators opined that, apart from the economic concerns, the new regulations might be a consequence of CCTV's losing market share against these nimbler competitors, and lobbying for support.

Second, while media policy is officially aimed at "sticking close to reality, sticking close to life, and sticking close to the masses," making media products that "the people love to see and hear," the top-down mode of deciding on content has alienated a significant portion of the audience, who have looked elsewhere for both news and entertainment. The economic measures and development plans that have been progressively developed after the Sixteenth Party Congress seem to treat media as a homogenous, commodified product, for which better results can be achieved through standardizing and streamlining processes and raising input quality. While the plans pay lip service to encouraging creativity, their space for experimentation and envelope-pushing is severely limited. Uncertainty about exact censorship requirements inclines producers to safer, well-trodden paths, and to look towards the government for content guidance (Demick 2012).[34] Because the media administration can close down programming, cease publication of certain products, or even shutter businesses at very short notice,[35] insecurity about the long-term prospects of media products and enterprises further pulls investors and media outlets towards the official line. The insistence of a particular representation of Chinese culture in media products makes them less attractive to foreign audiences.

Third, vertical administrative fragmentation is limiting the development of converged media services and new media business forms. It also presents tremendous barriers to entry, because media enterprises may be required to navigate different regulatory frameworks and licensing procedures, each of which can be sufficient to keep a new competitor out of the market. This problem is especially grave in the area of the Internet, as the Internet emerged long after the regulatory structure was put in place, and as the lure of high revenues causes turf wars between different government bodies. For example, there was a well-publicized spat between the Ministry of Culture and GAPP concerning Internet games (Creemers 2012). Bureaucratic strife has also hindered the emergence of converged media services. Since the turn of the century, providing "three-network integration" (the integration of

33 This became known as the "Decree Limiting Entertainment" (*xianyuling*) (SARFT 2011).

34 Even the popular CCTV New Year Gala is becoming less popular as a result of this risk avoidance. See Lu (2007) and Zhang (2011).

35 See, e.g., Zhang (2008). In 2009, SARFT also ordered the cessation of *Narrow Dwellings*, a television series reflecting the anxieties of young urban professionals, possibly because it too closely reflected deep social and economic problems (Liu 2009).

telecommunications, radio and television, and the Internet) has been a high priority in China's media reform. By early 2012, however, only a few localized trials had been implemented, because the different administrations involved seem to be unable to come to an agreement.

Fourth, the anti-foreign stance in the media has caused friction with important trading partners, in particular the United States, whose media enterprises have a hard time accessing the enormous and expanding Chinese market. This has led to three nearly averted trade conflicts in the 1990s, termed "cycles of futility" by Peter Yu (2005), and two WTO cases. What is often overlooked, however, is that there is also a domestic constituency that is at the receiving end of these limiting measures, which is the domestic media distribution sector. Foreign media products—to the extent that they can be imported—are distributed by state-owned enterprises, and account for significant amounts of television advertising, box office income, or sales figures. In 2011, despite significant issues with box office income measurement methods, and the Chinese practice of disadvantaging foreign films around important events, holidays and anniversaries, US films still amounted for 46 percent of Chinese box office income (Cain 2012).

Fifth, against the evolving background of economic reform and growth, the framework conditions for the Party's political program have shifted significantly. As material welfare has grown, especially in the cities, the official narrative has been exposed to ever more competition. The Internet has empowered the Chinese citizenry to generate and gain access to content beyond the Party-approved scope. Access to leisure activity and luxury products has blunted the Party's mobilization appeals. Media outlets are tempted by large commercial profits, but this requires having a product that will do well in the marketplace, rather than being effective in currying higher-level favor. As a result, the Party-state faces three very important questions. If income has to be sought in the marketplace, how will the Party-state still be able to control content and make sure that its own interests take precedence over the commercial interests of the media? How can the official message be packaged in such a way that audiences accept it, in the face of increasing competition? If financial input is required into the media sector, where will this come from and what does this mean for Party-state control?

But perhaps the greatest problem that the official media face is that of cynicism. Increasingly, the Party-state is struggling to make its message relevant to China's expanding middle and upper class, which seems to be more concerned with material pursuits than ideological or moral rectitude.[36] Conversely, those left behind by China's widening income gap feel increasingly betrayed by a rhetoric that claims that the first and foremost objective of the Party is to "serve the people." At the time of writing, however, one could argue that the Party is becoming increasingly atrophied in this aspect. The Twelfth Five-Year Plan documents bring back the militaristic, campaign-like language that was part and parcel of ideological documents during the Maoist era. It is also unlikely that the re-emergence of the ideal of Lei Feng[37] will be able to reinvigorate ardor for the Communist project (Jacobs 2012). In other words, the CCP will need to deliver tangible improvement in issues related to rule of law, corruption, environmental protection, labor rights, land use and other matters of concern. However, this may require deep political change, and hence a near-reversal of the Party's direction until now.

36 This has been driven home by the increasing concern about events in which rich or powerful individuals were perceived to act in an overly privileged manner. See, e.g., Bandurski (2011).

37 Lei Feng was a model soldier. During the Cultural Revolution, he was posthumously presented as a sort of modern-day ideal type to inspire and hearten young Chinese. There is considerable doubt about the veracity of Lei Feng's actions—and even his existence. See Shirk (1982).

## Conclusion

The governance structure of Chinese media has seen a combination of atrophy and adaptation. In economic and business aspects, the media have largely transformed into marketized enterprises, financial restrictions have been relaxed, support structures have been put in place, foreign content input has been somewhat increased, and modern technology has made remarkable headway. Comprehensively, the cultural sectors have grown tremendously. At the same time, centralized control has been consolidated and strengthened. The ad hoc mechanisms that governed media and propaganda in the early 1980s have been institutionalized, significantly enhancing central control over public communication. This reflects policy, which has been consistently aimed at enhancing and fostering the propaganda and public relations functions of media and culture simultaneously with economic modernizations.

These efforts are increasingly countered by social, economic, technological and commercial forces, aimed not only at the media and propaganda system itself, but also at the political order of which that system is the mouthpiece. Further change in media, both top-down and bottom-up, both state-driven and initiated by private individuals, will be closely tied to political change in China. The Party-state has the challenge of adapting to the political needs of the Chinese population, before atrophy renders it impossible for the CCP to maintain legitimacy. Its communication channels are vital in that respect. However, the Party-state increasingly needs to confront the increasing participation from society through the Internet, as well as the fact that its own diversification creates challenges for the homogeneity of its message.

## References

Amitin, M. (1980) 'Chinese theatre today: Beyond the Great Wall,' *Performing Arts Journal*, 4(2): 9–26.

Bandurski, D. (2012) 'Change at top media group raises concern,' *China Media Project*, 3 May. Online. Available HTTP: http://cmp.hku.hk/2012/05/03/22310/ (accessed 12 May 2012).

—— (2011) 'China's "symphony" of privilege,' *China Media Project*, 9 September. Online. Available HTTP: http://cmp.hku.hk/2011/09/09/15376/ (accessed 12 May 2012).

Beijing Municipal Government (2011) *Some Beijing Municipal Provisions on Microblog Development and Management*. Online. Available HTTP: http://chinacopyrightandmedia.wordpress.com/2011/12/16/some-beijing-municipal-provisions-on-microblog-development-and-management/

Brady, A. (2010) *Marketing Dictatorship: Propaganda and Thought Work in Contemporary China*, Lanham, MD: Rowman & Littlefield.

Cain, R. (2012) 'A sweet and sour week at the cinema,' *ChinaFilmBiz*, 4 January. Online. Available HTTP: https://chinafilmbiz.wordpress.com/2012/01/04/a-sweet-and-sour-week-at-the-cinema/ (accessed 12 May 2012).

Callahan, W. (2009) *China, the Pessoptimist Nation*, Oxford: Oxford University Press.

Central Committee of the Communist Party of China (1980) 'The present circumstances and tasks,' Speech.

—— (2005) *Opinion Concerning Further Strengthening and Improving Public Opinion Supervision Work*.

—— (2011a) *Central Committee Resolution*. Online. Available HTTP: http://cpc.people.com.cn/GB/67481/94156/231018/index.html (accessed 12 May 2012).

—— (2011b) *Decision Concerning Deepening Cultural Structural Reform*.

—— (2012) *Outline of the Cultural Reform and Development Plan during the National 'Twelfth Five-Year Plan' Period*.

——, SARFT, GAPP (2001) *Opinions Concerning Deepening Press, Publications, Radio, Film, and Television Sector Reform*.

China Copyright and Media (2010) *Notice Concerning the Establishment of a Leading Small Group for the Nationwide Special Campaign Attacking Intellectual Property Rights Infringement and Production and Sale of Fake and Inferior Products*, 26 October. Online. Available HTTP: http://chinacopyrightandmedia.

wordpress.com/2010/10/26/notice-concerning-the-establishment-of-a-leading-small-group-for-the-nationwide-special-campaign-attacking-intellectual-property-rights-infringement-and-production-and-sale-of-fake-and-inferior-produc/ (accessed 1 June 2012).

CIA (2012) *The World Factbook*. Online. Available HTTP: https://www.cia.gov/library/publications/the-world-factbook/geos/ch.html (accessed 30 May 2012).

Creemers, R. (2012) 'Explaining audiovisual media piracy in China,' Ph.D. Thesis, Maastricht University.

Curtin, M. (2003) 'The future of Chinese cinema: Some lessons from Hong Kong and Taiwan,' in C. Lee (ed.) *Chinese Media, Global Contexts*, London: Routledge.

Demick, B. and Lee, J. (2012) 'Must-see Chinese TV becoming a snooze,' *Los Angeles Times*, 20 January.

Fisher, T. (1982) '"The play's the thing": Wu Han and Hai Rui revisited,' *The Australian Journal of Chinese Affairs*, 7: 1–35.

Fu, H. and Cullen, R. (1998) 'Defamation law in the People's Republic of China,' *Transnational Law*, 11: 1–22.

GAPP (2011) *Press and Publication Sector 'Twelfth Five-Year Plan' Period Development Plan*.

Guan, E. (2001) 'WTO yujingxiade Zhongguo dianying weiji yu duice qianxi [A short analysis of the crisis and countermeasures of Chinese film in the WTO context]', *Dianying Pingjia* [*Film Criticism*], 3: 50–51.

Hassid, J. (2008) 'Controlling the Chinese media: An uncertain business,' *Asian Survey*, 48(3): 414–430.

He, Q. (2008) *The Fog of Censorship: Media Control in China*, Hong Kong: HRIC.

Huang, Y. (2008) *Capitalism with Chinese Characteristics*, Cambridge: Cambridge University Press.

Hung, C. (2010) 'China's propaganda in the information age: Internet commentators and the Weng'an incident,' *Issues & Studies*, 46(4): 149–180.

HXCI (2012) *Wenhuabuzhang Cai Wu Jiedu Shiqijie Liuzhong Quanhui Jingshen* [*Minister of Culture Cai Wu deciphers the spirit of the 6th Plenum of the 17th Party Congress*], 2 February. Online. Available HTTP: http://www.hxci.cn/jcck/201202/23/2192.shtml (accessed 12 May 2012).

Jacobs, A. (2011) 'Popularity may have doomed Chinese TV talent show,' *New York Times*, 19 September.

—— (2012) 'Chinese heroism effort is met with cynicism,' *New York Times*, 5 March.

Josephs, H. (1992) 'Defamation, invasion of privacy, and the press in the People's Republic of China,' *UCLA Pacific Basin Law Journal*, 11: 191–220.

Kraus, R. (2004) *The Party and the Arty in China: The New Politics of Culture*, Lanham, MD: Rowman & Littlefield.

Li, Y. (2002) 'The wolf has come: Are China's intellectual property industries prepared for the WTO?' *UCLA Pacific Basin Law Journal*, 20: 77–112.

Liang, B. and Lu, H. (2010) 'Internet development, censorship, and cyber crimes in China,' *Journal of Contemporary Criminal Justice*, 26(1): 103–120.

Liebman, B. (2006) 'Innovation through intimidation: An empirical account of defamation litigation in China,' *Harvard International Law Journal*, 47(1): 33–109.

Liu, Al. (2009) '*Narrow Dwellings*: A TV series that slipped through SARFT's guidelines,' *Danwei*. Online. Available HTTP: http://www.danwei.org/tv/narrow_dwellings.php (accessed 2 October 2010).

Lu, X. (2007) 'Ritual, television, and state ideology: Re-reading CCTV's 2006 Spring Festival Gala,' in Y. Zhu and C. Berry (eds.) *TV China*, Bloomington, IN: Indiana University Press.

MacGregor, R. (2010) *The Party: The Secret World of China's Communist Rulers*, New York: HarperCollins.

Mertha, A. (2005) *The Politics of Piracy: Intellectual Property in Contemporary China*, Ithaca, NY: Cornell University Press.

Ministry of Culture (1997) *Cultural Undertaking Development 'Ninth Five-Year Plan' and Long-term Prospects and Objectives for 2010 Outline*.

Ministry of Radio, Film, and Television (MRFT), Ministry of Commerce (MOFCOM), State Administration for Industry and Commerce (SAIC) (1986) *Notice Concerning Rectification of the Audio and Video*.

Saich, T. (2007) 'China in 2006: Focus on social development,' *Asian Survey*, 47(1): 32–43.

—— (2004) *Governance and Politics of China*, Basingstoke: Palgrave MacMillan.

SARFT (2001) *Implementation Regulations Concerning City (District) and County (City) Radio and Television Broadcasting Organ Duty Transformation Work*.

—— (2010) *Strengthening a Rule of Law Government Construction Plan*.

—— (2011) *Opinion Concerning Further Strengthening Comprehensive Satellite Television Channel.*
Schoenhals, M. (1991) 'The 1978 truth criterion controversy,' *China Quarterly*, 126: 243–268.
Shambaugh, D. (2008) *China's Communist Party: Atrophy and Adaptation*, Washington DC: Woodrow Wilson Center Press.
Shaw, C. (2005) 'Zhonggong zhongyang gongzuo lingdao xiaozu de zuzhi dingwei [The organization and status of the CCP Central Work Leading Small Groups],' *Zhongguo dalu yanjiu* [*Mainland China Research*], 48(3): 1–23.
Shirk, S. (1982) *Competitive Comrades: Career Incentives and Student Strategies in China*, Berkeley, CA: University of California Press.
State Council (1994) *Audiovisual Products Management Regulations.*
—— (1996) *Film Management Regulations.*
—— (1997a) *Publishing Management Regulations.*
—— (1997b) *Radio and Television Management Regulation.*
Vogel, E. (2011) *Deng Xiaoping and the Transformation of China*, Cambridge, MA: The Belknap Press of Harvard University Press.
Wong, Y. (2005) *From Deng Xiaoping to Jiang Zemin: Two Decades of Political Reform in the People's Republic of China*, Lanham, MD: University Press of America.
World Trade Organization (2012) *Joint Communication from China and the United States*, WT/DS363/19, 11 May.
—— (2001) *Report of the Working Party on the Accession of China: Addendum*, WT/ACC/CHN/49/Add.2.
Yu, H. (2009) *Media and Cultural Transformation in China*, Abingdon: Routledge.
Yu, P. (2005) 'Still dissatisfied after all these years: Intellectual property, post-WTO China, and the avoidable cycle of futility,' *Georgia Journal of International and Comparative Law*, 34: 143–158.
Zhang M. (2011) 'Chunqan zenyang cai neng tiejin minzhong? [How can the Spring Festival Gala stick close to the masses?],' 5 February. Online. Available HTTP: http://view.news.qq.com/a/20110205/000004.htm (accessed 12 May 2012).
Zhang, R. (2008) *The Cinema of Feng Xiaogang: Commercialization and Censorship in Chinese Cinema after 1989*, Hong Kong: Hong Kong University Press.
Zhang, Z. (2002) 'Dalu xin gaizheng zhuzuoquanfa gaishu [An overview of the newly revised Copyright Law of Mainland China] 大陆新修正著作权法概述,' *Zhihui caichan quan yuekan* [*Intellectual Property Rights Monthly*] 智慧财产权月刊.
Zhao, Y. (2008) *Communication in China*, Lanham, MD: Rowman and Littlefield.
Zheng, Y. (2012) 'China's movie sector becomes second largest,' *Xinhua*, 13 April. Online. Available HTTP: http://news.xinhuanet.com/english/china/2012-04/13/c_131524655.htm (accessed 12 May).

# 16

# Social dynamics in the evolution of China's Internet Content Control Regime

*Guobin Yang*

The political control of the Internet in China has been an important focus of attention in both the public media and the research communities. Much of current work, however, presents a static image of censorship and control. The emphasis is on the institutional frameworks of control and the empirical testing of what is censored. Yet the Internet has developed rapidly in China for the past twenty years. China's Internet Content Control Regime (ICCR) has not remained static, but has undergone change. This chapter delineates the changing features of China's ICCR and analyzes the conditions that have contributed to these changes. My argument is that, compared with the earlier period, the ICCR in China has become smarter in the twenty-first century, combining both hard and soft methods of control, and both state and non-state institutions and practices. This has happened, I will argue, in response to the rising tide of Internet activism and in the context of a heightened crisis of governance of the Chinese regime.

## Regime and regime change

China's Internet control regime may be defined as the "totality of the institutions and practices of Internet control" (Yang 2009: 47). This concept of regime resembles the Bourdieusian notion of field—namely, "a patterned system of objective forces (much in the manner of a magnetic field), a relational configuration endowed with a specific gravity which it imposes on all the objects and agents which enter it" (Bourdieu and Wacquant 1992: 17).

Similarly invoking the concept of the field, Braman (2004) offers a conceptualization of regime in her study of global information policy regimes. As she puts it, "A field is a structure of possibility and probability that constrains and encourages certain types of choices, though a degree of indeterminacy always remains. Every field is historically specific, dynamic, and affected by both internal and external factors" (Braman 2004: 14). Placing the concept of regime in dialog with Bourdieu's (1992) theory of the field and systems theory in the natural sciences, Braman (2004) argues that regime theory offers a useful solution to challenges facing international relations theory in the age of globalization. It widens the conceptual toolkit beyond the traditional "geopolitical entity of the nation-state" to take account of less formal elements such as non-state actors, discourses and norms.

Although for Braman, regime consists of formal governmental institutions and rules (government), informal, non-state institutions and norms (governance), and the cultural and social context that sustains institutions, rules, and norms (governmentality), she stresses the distinction between state and non-state institutions in the global policy regime. Likewise, I view China's ICCR as a field of state and non-state institutions in the regulation and control of Internet content.

As a complex adaptive system, a regime is dynamic and constantly changing. A regime of information technology policy is subject to the influences of technological developments. Asking whether technology "overwhelms law and the capacity of a state to regulate," Price responds that "New technology changes the frame for negotiation, for decision making and for the formation and application of policy" (Price 2002: 147). Consequently, what happens is a process of adjustment: ". . . norms and institutions that were created for one set of technologies adjust or erode" (Price 2002: 147).

The image of a regime as a changing and adaptive system fits the Chinese reality. In studies of Chinese politics, the concept of "regime" is commonly used to refer to China's political system as a whole—for example, as in the ongoing debates about whether there is a crisis of regime legitimacy, or why the Chinese regime is so resilient. The ICCR is a lower-order policy regime under the Chinese polity. But because it is part of the political system, understanding the nature of the political system as a whole may shed light on the evolution of the Internet control regime.

A key concept in the study of Chinese politics is fragmented authoritarianism. First proposed by Lieberthal and Oksenberg (1988), the concept posits that:

> Policy made at the centre becomes increasingly malleable to the parochial organizational and political goals of various vertical agencies and spatial regions charged with enforcing that policy. Outcomes are shaped by the incorporation of interests of the implementation agencies into the policy itself. Fragmented authoritarianism thus explains the policy arena as being governed by incremental change via bureaucratic bargaining.
>
> (*Mertha 2009: 996*)

Mertha argues that the concept of fragmented authoritarianism continues to capture the nature of the policymaking process in China, but adds that the process has become increasingly pluralized. He finds that new "policy entrepreneurs," especially individuals within government agencies, editors and journalists, and non-governmental organization (NGO) activists, have influenced the policymaking process (Mertha 2009). Arguing that Chinese authoritarianism relies increasingly on rule by law (rather than rule of law), Lee (2007) proposes the alternative concept of fragmented legal authoritarianism to capture the features of the Chinese political system.

After the student protests in 1989, Andrew Nathan (2003) uses the notion of authoritarian resilience to characterize the regime's persistence. For Nathan, the main feature of China's resilient authoritarianism is institutionalization. Nathan shows evidence of institutionalization in four crucial areas—succession politics, selection of political elites, functional specialization of state bureaucracies, and the establishment of institutions for political participation aimed at strengthening CCP legitimacy. Elizabeth Perry concurs about the authoritarian nature of the Chinese regime, but argues that this authoritarianism retains many elements of China's revolutionary heritage. Like the Maoist regime, for example, the current brand of "revolutionary authoritarianism" has mechanisms both for launching and absorbing popular grievances (Perry 2007: 7). More recently, Heilmann and Perry (2011) propose the concept of "adaptive governance" to describe the flexible nature of the contemporary Chinese regime. They trace this ability of creative adaptation to the guerrilla-style decision-making that was formed during China's long revolution under conditions of pervasive uncertainty.

Wang (2008) proposes six policy agenda-setting models in the Chinese polity. These are the "closed door" model, the "inside access" model, the "outside access" model, the top-down "mobilization" model, the "reach-out" model and the "popular pressure" model. He notes, however, that the first five models were common in the past, but the last, more democratic "popular pressure" model did not appear until the late 1990s. Popular pressure has arisen, argues Wang, because Chinese citizens have become more wary of the negative consequences of market reform, such as growing social polarization and environmental degradation.

The above review shows that scholars of Chinese politics recognize the adaptive nature of the Chinese regime and view social forces as an important source of regime adaptation. Similarly, I argue that social forces are an important factor in the evolution of China's ICCR. The crucial condition underlying the expansion of the ICCR is the rising tide of online activism at a time of governance crisis. The increasing difficulty of curtailing online protest, compounded by a sense of governance crisis, compels the Party-state to enlist the support of non-state institutions and practices for Internet content control.

## Governance crisis

In a 2002 *Foreign Affairs* article and later in a book-length study, Minxin Pei (2006) argues that China is suffering from a governance crisis. He attributes the decline of the Chinese Communist Party (CCP) to the shrinkage of its organizational penetration, the erosion of its authority and appeal among the masses, and the breakdown of its internal discipline.

After Pei's article was published, Hu Jintao succeeded Jiang Zemin as Party Chairman, and a major Party plenum was convened in 2004. The plenum passed an unprecedented resolution concerning "the strengthening of the Party's ability to govern" (CCP 2004), essentially acknowledging the governance crisis. In its own words, "The Party's governing status is not congenital, nor is it something settled once and for all" (ibid.). The document does not provide detailed analysis of the causes of this governance crisis. One policy recommendation, however, stresses the importance of managing the Internet because of its influence on public opinion, suggesting that Internet public opinion is putting pressure on the Party-state:

> Attach great importance to the influence of the Internet and other new media on public opinion, step up the establishment of a management institution that integrates legal binding, administrative monitoring and management, industrial self-regulation, and technical guarantee, strengthen the building of an Internet propaganda team, and forge the influence of positive opinion on the Internet.
>
> (*CCP 2004*)

Other scholars have studied the question of governance crisis under the rubric of Party or regime legitimacy. An empirical study of 168 articles on the topic of regime legitimacy in Party school journals, university journals, and public policy journals between 2003 and 2007 finds that 30 percent of the sampled articles warn of a legitimacy crisis (*hefaxing weiji*) looming for the CCP, while 68 percent warn about some form of legitimacy challenge or threat (*tiaozhan, weixie, wenti, ruodian*, and so on) (Holbig and Gilley 2010). The authors conclude that "most participants in the debate believe that the CCP's legitimacy is vulnerable to growing challenges" (Holbig and Gilley 2010: 340).

It is in the context of a heightening crisis of governance that Internet protest becomes especially challenging for the Party authorities, who increasingly approach the regulation and control of Internet content through both state and non-state institutions.

## Governmental institutions and the practice of Internet control

The "government" component of China's Internet content control regime[1] comprises a set of Party-state agencies and laws and regulations. The highest-level Party agency directly in charge of media (and thus Internet content) is the Department of Propaganda of the CCP. The highest-level government agencies directly responsible for Internet content control of one type or another include:

- the State Council Information Office;
- the Ministry of Culture;
- the Ministry of Industry and Information Technology (MIIT);
- the Ministry of Public Security;
- the State Administration of Radio, Film, and Television (SARFT);
- the Ministry of Commerce;
- the State Administration for Industry and Commerce;
- the Ministry of Health (concerning online health-related information);
- the General Administration of Press and Publication (GAPP);
- the State Food and Drug Administration;
- the Ministry of Education; and
- the National Administration of Surveying, Mapping and Geoinformation (related to mapping information).

These agencies have a vertical structure reaching down to the municipal, *xian* (county), and township levels. Lower-level agencies are charged with implementing central policies. Following the promulgation of a central policy, they may issue local-level regulations targeting their own constituencies. Some agencies may introduce their own regulations. For example, in 2011, the News Office of the Beijing Municipal Government, the Beijing Public Security Bureau, the Beijing Telecommunications Management Bureau and the Internet Information Office jointly issued a new regulation requiring microblog service providers in Beijing to verify users' personal identification for the purpose of registering a user account.

With so many government agencies in the business of managing the Internet, it is not surprising that there are numerous regulations. Table 16.1 shows a sample list of the main regulations related to Internet content.

1 The Internet control regime applies to all three layers of the Internet—the physical infrastructure, the code (software), and the content (Benkler 2000; Lessig 2001). Because content is the primary target of control, I refer to the regime as a content control regime.

*Table 16.1* Sample Internet content regulations, 1994–2011

- Regulation on Protecting Computer Information System Security of the People's Republic of China (1994)
- Provisions on Administering the Security and Protection of Computer Information Networks Connected to International Networks (1997)
- Telecommunications Regulations of the People's Republic of China (2000)
- Provisions on Administering Internet Information Services (2000)
- Regulations for Administering Internet Electronic Bulletin Services (2000)
- Interim Provisions on the Administration of Internet Websites' engaging in News Publication Services (2000)
- Provisions on Administering Internet Access Service Venues (2001)
- Interim Provisions on Administering Online Publishing (2002)
- Provisions on Administering Audio and Visual Programs Disseminated on the Internet (2003)
- Provisions on Administering the Filing of Non-Commercial Internet Information Services (2005)
- Provisions on Administering News Services on the Internet (2005)
- Certain Suggestions on Developing and Managing Internet Games (2005)
- Interim Provisions on Administering Internet Games (2010)
- Interim Provisions on Administering Internet Culture (2011)

*Source*: Author's compilation

Table 16.1 shows that the areas and sites of regulation are all-encompassing. They include Internet cafes, bulletin board systems (BBS), text messaging, online news, video and audio sharing websites, online games, and most recently microblogging websites. Many types of information may be carried only with proper licensing. The seemingly common business practice of licensing thus becomes a mechanism of content control. A license may be revoked if a firm is found to have violated the rules. According to China's Telecommunications Regulations promulgated in 2000, Internet content providers (ICPs) (see below for more) must be licensed in order to operate in the Chinese market. They are also required to display their license numbers on their websites. In addition to an ICP license, many other licenses and approvals are required. On 15 January 2012, the first page of Sina's main site, sina.com.cn, displays links to digital images of fourteen licenses, related to the following types of information service respectively:

- Internet publishing, licensed by the GAPP;
- visual and audio information, licensed by the SARFT;
- Internet news service, licensed by the State Council Information Office;
- medical information, approved by the National Food and Drug Administration;
- value-added telecommunications services, licensed by the MITT;
- mapping services, licensed by the State Administration of Surveying, Mapping and Geoinformation;
- telecommunications and information services, licensed by the Beijing Municipal Telecommunications Management Bureau;
- health information services, approved by the Beijing Municipal Health Department;
- radio and television programs, licensed by the Beijing Municipal Bureau of Radio, Film, and Television;

- website filing certificate at the Beijing Public Security Bureau;
- Internet culture, licensed by the Beijing Municipal Cultural Bureau;
- medical information, licensed by the Beijing Municipal Drug Supervision Bureau;
- education information service, approved by the Beijing Municipal Educational Bureau; and
- electronic board services, approved by the Beijing Municipal Telecommunications Management Bureau.

The institutional developments of the ICCR entail the adoption of new practices of censorship and control. In comparison with coercive methods such as the filtering and blocking of websites and the harassment and detention of cyber dissidents, these new practices aim at soft management and proaction. Two relatively recent institutionalized practices are Internet commentators and media campaigns. Internet commentators, with the pejorative nickname of *wumao* (the "50 Cent Party") are a hidden and proactive way of exercising control. They are employees or volunteers recruited by government agencies to participate in anonymous online discussion, with a mandate to publish views in support of state agendas. Since its introduction in 2005, this practice has become institutionalized and routine. Viewed as an important new method of "occupying the ideological battle ground," it has been adopted widely by local governments and constantly emphasized by top Party leaders.[2]

The other institutional practice is state-sponsored media campaigns. Campaigns were a distinct feature of Chinese politics in the Maoist era. Although some scholars argue that China has shifted to a more "rational" bureaucratic mode of governance in the reform period, campaigns continue to be used in modified forms (Perry 2011). In earlier times, political campaigns focused on issues of economic production, ideological work and class struggle (Cell 1977). Today, campaigns are launched to tackle new issues. The prevalent media discourse about the pathologies of online gaming behavior, Internet addiction and the so-called Internet verbal violence, for example, takes on features of a media campaign intended to justify the strengthening of Internet control.[3]

A recent political campaign for Internet content control was the anti-vulgarity "special action" launched in January 2009. A coordinated nationwide campaign, its goal was "to contain the wide spreading of vulgar contents online, further purify the cultural environment on the Internet, protect the healthy growth of the under-aged, and promote the healthy and orderly development of the Internet" (Xinhua 2009). On the day of its launch, the China Internet Illegal Information Reporting Center (CIIRC), founded in 2004 under the sponsorship of the Internet Society of China, publicized the names of nineteen websites allegedly containing large amounts of "vulgar content." These websites included almost every leading commercial site (i.e. Google, Baidu, Sina, Sohu, Tencent, Netease, Mop and Tianya). The CIIRC requested that these websites remove the content. By 24 February, a total of 2,962 websites had been closed down (People.com.cn 2002).

As part of the campaign, major websites set up special sections to publicize information. The official Xinhuanet, for example, publishes lists of websites that carry "vulgar contents"

2 In September 2011, a news release by a county-level department of population and family planning in Hubei province, for example, states that it utilizes seventeen Internet commentators to monitor Internet information. See Xishui County n.d.

3 On the media discourse about Internet addiction, see Golub and Lingley 2008.

as a way of public exposure.[4] The popular website Tencent carries similar information.[5] Sina also has a special section on the campaign. The dull and static design of the section forms a sharp contrast to its regular features, which are aesthetically much more appealing.

Besides closing down websites, it is not clear how effective the campaign was in meeting its goal. As I will point out later in this chapter, however, the campaign met with strong resistance among netizens, who launched their own anti-anti-vulgarity campaign to express their opposition.

The proactive approach of the ICCR entails strengthening the influences of official websites and official viewpoints. While the practice of Internet commentators is a covert way of exerting influence, there are many overt practices as well. One example is the growing trend for government agencies and officials to open accounts on popular microblog platforms. In September 2011, the Ministry of Public Security held a national conference in Beijing on the functions of microblogs, at which a vice minister urged public security officials to use microblogs to publicize information. The vice minister said that there were already more than 4,000 official microblog accounts at the time, while more than 5,000 police officers were using microblogs (*China Daily* 2011a). One such police officer's microblog account, registered as "A Legendary Policewoman" on Sina's Weibo, had more than 1.2 million followers as of early March 2012. Employed at the Department of Public Security in Beijing, this "legendary woman" posts messages regularly on all sorts of topics, from daily chit-chat to advice on network security, reports of traffic conditions and announcements of official regulations. A photograph of her in police uniform smiling at the viewer conveys the kind of image that government officials would like to project of themselves—a friendly police officer ready to offer help to citizens. Parts of these efforts are intended to improve the public image of China's law enforcement authorities, who have become a major target of Internet protest. The assumption is that only by improving their public image can they expect to exert more positive influences in the Chinese cybersphere.

## Non-state institutions and the practice of content control

The "government" component of the control of Internet content described above is relatively well known. Much less well known are the non-state institutions and practices, whose role has expanded considerably since the beginning of the twenty-first century. Non-state institutions of ICCR have two types: (a) non-profit organizations and NGOs; and (b) ICPs.

### *Non-governmental organizations (NGOs)*

The main non-profit, non-governmental Internet organization is the national Internet Society of China (ISC), which was founded in May 2001. There are similar Internet societies and associations at the provincial, municipal and even county (*xian*) levels. A March 2007 news item on the website of ISC shows that, as of then, these Internet societies had around 4,000 membership organizations nationwide, indicating the rapid growth of the size of this sector.

4 See http://www.xinhuanet.com/politics/20090109 (accessed 28 May 2012).

5 See, e.g., http://tech.qq.com/zt/2009/renovate (accessed 28 May 2012).

These organizations often describe their mission as the promotion of Internet culture and economy in China,[6] and have concentrated on helping the government agenda of Internet control by promoting self-regulation among industries and citizens. The chronicle of activities from 2001 to 2011 listed on the ISC website shows that its activities are mainly in these areas. The chronicle includes, for example, public pledges and industry coalitions on self-regulation initiated by the ISC. These public pledges are apparently important enough that the government White Paper on *The Internet in China*, issued in 2010 by the State Council Information Office, devotes a whole paragraph to them. It begins as follows:

> The state proactively promotes industry self-regulation and public supervision. The Internet Society of China (ISC) was founded in May 2001. It is a national organization of the Internet industry with a remit for serving the development of that industry, netizens and the decisions of the government. The ISC has issued a series of self-disciplinary regulations, including the Public Pledge of Self-regulation and Professional Ethics for the China Internet Industry, Provisions of Self-regulation on Not Spreading Pornographic and Other Harmful Information for Internet Websites, Public Pledge of Self-regulation on Anti-malicious Software, Public Pledge of Self-regulation on Blog Service, Public Pledge of Self-regulation on Anti-Internet Virus, Declaration of Self-regulation on Copyright Protection of China's Internet Industry, and other regulations, which greatly promote the healthy development of the Internet.
>
> (*China.org.cn 2010*)

These pledges are typically issued at news conferences attended by high-level government officials and business executives of major websites. The events are then publicized widely through extensive media coverage. For example, the "Blogging Service Self-Regulation Pledge" was issued at a public event on 21 August 2007. Speakers at the event included officials from the MIIT, the Internet Bureau of the Information Office of the State Council, the News Bureau from the Central Propaganda Department and the Ministry of Public Security, as well as representatives from Internet firms (Tencent 2007).

Internet societies clearly fall under the category of government-sponsored NGOs (GONGOs). To the extent that Internet societies like the ISC mainly aim to promote government agendas, they differ from the numerous grassroots NGOs that have appeared in the past two decades, which have a greater degree of political autonomy.[7]

### *Internal content providers (ICPs)*

ICPs can be commercial or non-commercial entities. The Internet Information Service Administration Regulations promulgated by the State Council in 2000 define commercial

6 For example, the mission statement of the Internet Society of China is as follows: "The main mission of ISC is to promote development of Internet in China and make efforts to construct an advanced information society. ISC is expected to be a link among the community to make efforts benefiting the whole industry, to push forward industry self-discipline, to strengthen communication and cooperation between its members, to assist and provide support for policy making, and to promote Internet application and public awareness" (Internet Society of China 2011).

7 On the development of grassroots NGOs in China, see Yang 2005, Watson 2008, and Shieh and Deng 2011.

services as "those services that use the Internet to provide users with information or create websites for a profit." Non-commercial services are defined as "those services that use the Internet to provide users with open and for-share information."[8] Examples include non-profit websites that offer information on education and health.

In reality, it is not always easy to distinguish between commercial and non-commercial entities. The website affiliated with *People's Daily* is ostensibly an official government site. Yet, in 2005, it was incorporated as a business company under the name of People's Daily Online Development Co., Ltd. (*People's Daily Online* n.d.).

The most popular portal websites in China are mostly commercial ICPs. They are directly responsible for censoring their own and user-generated contents. For this reason, it may not be too much of a stretch to talk about the privatization of Internet content control. Through privatization, the Party-state delegates part of the responsibility of control to private firms. Transnational corporations are implicated in this process as well, as the example of Google in China shows (Google Blog 2006). I will confine my discussion here, however, to domestic websites because they have the largest user population.

Government regulations require ICPs to censor certain types of content. For example, the Internet News Information Service Management Regulation promulgated in 2005 by the State Council Information Office stipulates that if a news website finds information on its electronic bulletin boards that is prohibited by the regulation, the information must be immediately removed. The information must then be filed for future investigation by relevant government agencies (Information Office of the State Council 2005).

The actual practice of content control, however, is much more complex and may vary from firm to firm. For example, one large Internet firm that I studied in 2010 had a team of thirty editors monitoring the contents of its website. Some messages posted to the website are published only after being reviewed by members of this team. About 80 percent of the messages are posted after being screened by the firm's filtering software. If the software gives a red light to a certain posting, an editor will immediately block it. After a message is posted, it is up to the editor to monitor it. If it is found to have sensitive content, or if the firm receives a call from government authorities about a specific posting, then it will be deleted.[9]

Another example is Sina, one of the largest Internet firms in China. Its microblog service Weibo, similar to Twitter but with more interactive functions, has become enormously popular since its launch in August 2009. Two years after its launch, Weibo had registered 227 million users. Some of the most important Internet protest events in the past two years happened on or through Sina Weibo (see below on the Chinese Red Cross case), which has caused trepidation among government leaders and resulted in the sporadic tightening of control. In July 2010, for example, the *New York Times* reported that users had difficulty posting messages on Weibo (Ansfield 2010a). Sina's chief editor Chen Tong candidly confessed at a public forum on 13 June 2010 that "controlling content on Sina Weibo is a big headache." He describes a system of content control at work similar to that described above: A team of its editors continuously monitors the content on Weibo (Sina 2010).

In November 2010, Sina set up a special seven-person team charged with the mission of "stopping rumors." These seven individuals work around the clock to monitor the content on Weibo. If they determine a user to be spreading a rumor, that user's account may be temporarily suspended or permanently closed. Weibo also set up a new function to display and

8 For text of the regulation, see State Council 2000.

9 Interview with a marketing executive of a major Internet firm, 9 July 2010, Beijing.

expose rumors on its first page. Around the same time, in September 2010, Sina formed an external monitoring mechanism called "commissioners of self-discipline." These are individuals of some social stature or experience who are invited to help to monitor Sina Weibo, to weed out harmful content, and to build a "civilized Internet" (Sina 2011). Sina frequently publishes notices when it claims to have found rumors being spread on Weibo. On 4 February 2012, for example, Weibo's first page displayed a notice saying: "A Weibo message claims that a couple from Jiangxi was beaten up in Sanya; one was injured and the other killed. This is a rumor. The people who posted it have been penalized." Three individuals were said to be involved in this case. Sina announced that, as a penalty, their accounts were closed for six months.

## Characteristics of online activism

"Online activism" refers to contentious activities associated with the use of the Internet and other new communication technologies. Sometimes, the Internet is used to publicize or mobilize offline protest. More often, protest takes place online. The most common forms include online petitions, the hosting of campaign websites, and large-scale verbal protests. The most radical is perhaps the hacking of websites. These forms of contention happen in blogs, Internet bulletin boards, online communities, YouTube-type websites and, increasingly, microblog websites such as Sina's Weibo.

Online activism first appeared in China in the late 1990s. Only a small number of online protest happened in that period, partly because of the limited diffusion of the Internet then. Since 2000, however, online protest has become more frequent and influential. These cases share a number of features. One feature concerns the issues of contention. Although protest happens concerning numerous issues, the main issues fall into seven categories—namely, (1) popular nationalism, (2) rights defense, (3) corruption and power abuse, (4) environment, (5) cultural contention, (6) muckraking, and (7) online charity (Yang 2009).

Especially notable are issues concerning rights defense and official corruption and abuse of power. In cases concerning these issues, netizens protest because they do not trust official accounts of the events or because government authorities withheld information. These cases reveal a profound lack of trust in government authorities, especially local government agencies and officials.

A second feature of online activism is spontaneity. Although some cases have clear organizational bases, many others are spontaneous responses to offline incidents of injustices or are launched by individuals. These forms of protest depend on the Internet network structures, where an individual may run a campaign website and a single posting can reach a wide circulation. The most influential and widely publicized online protests take spontaneous forms, with large numbers of Internet users participating simultaneously but without coordination. Spontaneous participation reflects the depth of netizens' moral outrage at issues of social injustice.

Third, related to the spontaneity of online protest is the speed and scale of its dissemination. In large online communities like Tianya.cn (which has more than 60 million registered members as of January 2012), a popular posting may easily attract tens of thousands of views within a matter of hours. Because many netizens sign up to multiple online communities, these postings are inevitably cross-posted in other forums, thus leading to wide online dissemination. A study of thirty-four "Internet incidents" found that, on average, it takes about twenty-four hours for an Internet incident to spread in the Chinese cybersphere (Li Biao 2011: 166).

Fourth, compared with large-scale protests in the past, online activism has concrete and modest goals such as fighting for better wages, against discrimination, or simply protesting against official corruption. Online protesters rarely demand radical political change, if only because such demands are unlikely to get past China's Internet censorship system. Fifth, consistent with its goals, the main forms of Chinese online activism are symbolic and discursive. They include setting up campaign websites, online petitions, mass mailing of action alerts, posting and cross-posting messages in BBS forums, blogs and microblogs, downloading posts for offline circulation, online broadcast of offline activities, and so forth. Thus Internet contention is conducted in words and images. Language and symbols have always been an important part of popular revolt, but they have taken on new dimensions in this information age. As Mark Poster (1990) argues, just as material resources are central to the Marxist mode of production in the industrial age, so linguistic resources have become central to the mode of information.

A recent case, concerning online contentious activities aimed at exposing the shady practices of the Red Cross Society of China, serves as an illustration.

Founded in 1904, the Red Cross Society of China (RCSC) is a member of the International Federation of the Red Cross and also a vice-ministerial-level quasi-governmental agency. In June 2011, it became the target of online protest as a result of the microblog postings of a 20-year-old woman. Below is a summary of the event from *China Daily*, the leading official English-language newspaper in China:

> Recently, China's Red Cross Society came under fire after a credibility scandal erupted on the Internet. Netizens were infuriated when a 20-year-old woman named Guo Meimei, who claimed on Sina Weibo (the Chinese version of Twitter) to be the general manager of a company called Red Cross Commerce, boasted about her luxurious lifestyle, showing off her Maserati and Lamborghini cars, expensive handbags and palatial villa.
>
> The furious netizens began to question whether Guo had financed her lifestyle out of money that had been donated to the society. . . Although both Guo and the society publicly denied having any ties to one another, continuous disclosures of inside stories and disputes over this incident flooded the Internet. The Red Cross Society of China was plunged into an unprecedented crisis of trust.
>
> (*China Daily 2011b*)

This is a typical case of digital activism in China. The activities in the protest consist of multiple types. Netizens ask questions, seek and forward information, offer analysis, debate and protest, and interact in many other ways. The goals of the protest were moderate and diverse. Many people participated out of distrust of government-sponsored organizations such as the Red Cross. Others wished to unearth the sources of the young woman's wealth, sensing misdemeanor. Still others took this as an opportunity to express their resentment against social inequality and the growing gap between the rich and poor. Participation was spontaneous and uncoordinated. People tweeted their own messages or retweeted others'. As of 11 August 2011, Sina's microblog website had more than 2 million microblog tweets containing Guo Meimei's name and just under 2 million tweets containing the name of the Chinese Red Cross. These appeared in a matter of about six weeks. Similar interrogations happened in other microblog websites and in China's numerous BBS forums and blog spaces. As the *People's Daily* article cited above puts it, these contentious online activities plunged the Red Cross Society of China into an unprecedented crisis. According to a Reuters report, donations dropped by 80 percent (Reuters 2011).

## The impact of online protest

How has the rising tide of online activism incurred changes in the ICCR? Why is the state susceptible to the influences of online activism? I will first briefly touch on the impact of online protest. Then I will analyze state perception of online activism and netizens' resistance against control.

There is much debate about the political impact of online participation in China and elsewhere. Scholars have emphasized the expansion of political participation and public deliberation, as well as the outcomes on government policy (Zheng 2008; Sullivan and Xie 2009). A recent study finds evidence of a positive impact on political beliefs (Lei 2011). One area of impact that is hard to measure concerns state legitimacy and citizen trust in government. Yet it is precisely in this area that online activism appears to have the most significant impact. This is clear from the targets of online protest. In my collection of fifty-six cases of online protest for 2009 and 2010, most cases target local governments and officials, especially law enforcement authorities. In these cases, netizens protest in defense of their rights or against official corruption and abuse of power. The prevalence of these issues in online protest shows that the ruling Chinese regime may be suffering from a crisis of credibility. In almost all cases, netizens protested either because they did not trust official accounts of the events, or because government authorities withheld information.

My argument is corroborated by a recent report produced by media scholars in China. This report surveys 248 Internet incidents for 2009 and 274 for 2010. In 2009, 34 percent were concerned with social issues and law enforcement authorities. In 2010, 50 percent were about social issues and law enforcement authorities (Yu 2011). These numbers signal the growth of Internet protests related to law enforcement authorities, indicating that the government's credibility is increasingly under challenge. Under these conditions, government authorities are forced to devise new methods of containing Internet protest.

Some may argue that most cases of online protest are within the range of issues allowed by the government. Not only do they not threaten the regime, but they may even help to build stability (Hassid 2012). It may be true that if state authorities handle online protests in such a way as to prevent their escalation, then online protest may not directly threaten the regime. To the extent that Internet forums provide the space otherwise missing, online protest may help government officials to better understand social grievances and to adjust policies accordingly. Yet an analysis of the perspectives of government officials suggests that they tend to consider online protest to be a growing threat to stability and legitimacy.

## The perception of online protest

Regardless of the "objective" or actual impact of online activism on the state, we might gauge the impact from how state agents perceive online protest. In the literature on international relations, the perception of threat is an important determinant of interstate conflict. The literature on state repression in social movement theory similarly stresses the importance of threat perception in determining the level of state repression of protesters (Davenport 1995; Mahoney-Norris 2000).

The Chinese state authorities perceive online protest as a source of influential public opinion as well as a grave threat. As I noted above, a major development of the ICCR is that, around 2004, the Party-state began to emphasize the role of the Internet in shaping public opinion and the urgent need to control and channel online opinion. This was clearly stated in the "Decision concerning Party Governance." Since then, the Internet has been a policy concern at the very top level. Both CCP Chairman Hu Jintao and Premier Wen Jiabao have made multiple public appearances while inspecting online news agencies or holding online chats with netizens.[10] Another government initiative is the establishment of the *People's Daily* Media Opinion Monitoring Office in 2008 and an Internet News Coordination Bureau under the State Council Information Office (Ansfield 2010b). The most recent evidence of this concern is the issuance of the White Paper on the *Internet in China* in 2010.

The work of the Media Opinion Monitoring Office illustrates the importance that state authorities attach to online opinion. Operating as part of the official news organ *People's Daily*, this office has published quarterly reports since July 2009 on local governments' capacity to respond to "Internet mass incidents" (a euphemism for online protest). Analyzing ten incidents in the first half of 2009, the first report ranks local governments according to six parameters: government responsiveness; transparency of information; government credibility; restoration of social order; dynamic responsiveness; and accountability of government officials. Based on the total points accrued, the report assigns one of four color-coded rankings to the local governments concerned: blue means "response is appropriate," yellow means "needs improvement," orange is "clearly problematic," and red indicates "serious and major problems." The municipal government of Shishou in Hubei province earned a red warning because of its poor handling of a riot in June 2009 that prompted online protest. Besides the rankings, the report contains policy recommendations. It states that Chinese netizens have formed a new "pressure group" and that, with multiple online information channels, it is impossible to stop their voices. Therefore it urges government officials to be responsive to online opinion and to learn to handle it in a way that will not intensify social conflict. The report proposes that publicizing information is a better approach than damming it (*People's Daily* Online Media Opinion Monitoring Office 2009).

Threat is another important dimension in the state's perception of online protest. Although state authorities have realized that online opinion may help to improve governance, they are much more worried about online protest as a source of threat. Articles in journals published by police colleges and vocational schools show that police professionals, who may serve as proxies for state authorities, have a strong sense of the threat of online protest. Online protest is considered as a threat to domestic social stability, national security, and the credibility of law enforcement authorities and government. For example, a researcher at the Ministry of Public Security writes:

> In major social incidents, the Internet has become the most critical source of public opinion. Its influence and social organizing and mobilizing power cannot be overstated. . . . It has serious impact on social harmony and stability.
>
> (*Xue 2009: 6*)

The article also discusses the threat to national security and how foreign forces might be involved:

> The new Internet security strategies promoted by western countries view our country as a hypothetical enemy. They will undoubtedly use their superior information and

10 For example, see *China Daily* 2011c.

> technological power to further penetrate, control, attack, and damage our network. This will not only pose a major threat to our military and economic security, but will also be a major threat to our political and cultural security.
>
> (*Xue 2009: 5*)

A deputy chief of a provincial police department highlights the following characteristics of online protest, or what he terms "Internet mass incidents":

- dramatically increasing numbers;
- complicated and multiple types;
- enormous mobilizing power;
- interface with traditional media;
- online and offline interaction;
- penetration by domestic and foreign hostile forces; and
- serious damage to stability.

(*Hong 2010*)

These features demonstrate the difficulty of containing online protest and therefore a heightened sense of fear among state authorities.

## Resistance against Internet control

One last factor that influences the evolution of the ICCR is citizen opposition. Not docile users, Chinese netizens invent all sorts of methods to dodge, crack, mock, or otherwise challenge Internet censorship and control of information (Yang 2009; Meng 2011). These activities of resistance create holes in the control system. Not only do they increase the cost of control, but their prevalence also shows that, as Internet technologies become more sophisticated, it becomes more difficult for the state to maintain absolute control over Internet content. Thus when government authorities who are uneducated about Internet culture attempt bluntly to block or suppress information, they may find themselves in the embarrassing position of having to retract their statements under challenge from netizens.

In the 1990s and early 2000s, the state's response to Internet protest was mostly reactive, often consisting of a flat denial. When denial was no longer tenable, the authorities were forced to admit errors or to make conciliatory statements. In the end, it appears that state authorities have learned the lesson of the difficulty, if not the impossibility, of completely controlling information flows online. As a result, they began to devise new methods of control.

One example is the school explosion in a village in Guangxi in March 2001, which killed forty-two people, including thirty-eight schoolchildren. After the incident, Premier Zhu Rongji said in a statement that the school was blown up by a madman, thus essentially denying that the local school and government officials could have any responsibility. Parents and netizens challenged this explanation. When further investigation revealed that the children were manufacturing fireworks at the school, Zhu publicly apologized for his earlier statement. As a *New York Times* story reports:

> Mr. Zhu's nationally televised apology, highly unusual for a Chinese leader, reflected the extent to which the government's attempts to contain conflicting accounts of the blast had been undermined by citizens' rapidly spreading access to the Internet and other information channels and by an increasingly self-assertive press.
>
> (*Smith 2001*)

Another case concerns a young government employee named Qin Zhongfei in Pengshui County, Sichuan Province. In August 2006, he composed a satirical poem mocking corrupt county officials and text messaged it to friends. On 1 September, Qin was arrested on charges of slander. Online, people protested against Qin's arrest, arguing that he was simply voicing concerns about corruption and that local officials attempted to silence people's voices by illegally arresting him. Under pressure, the local authorities later dropped the charge; Qin was released and paid a small amount in compensation for the time he was held in detention (Yang 2009).

A final example is the Green Dam case. According to a directive issued by China's Ministry of Industry and Information Technology in May 2009, computers in China would be required to be sold with a pre-installed filtering software called Green Dam-Youth Escort. The announcement of this policy met with instant opposition from both Internet users and firms, at home and abroad. The policy was allegedly designed to protect minors from pornography and other "unhealthy contents" online. Although few would object to protecting minors and China undoubtedly has its share of trouble in battling Internet pornography, the new policy raised serious questions about its hidden intent. People protested against an apparently intrusive policy suddenly imposed from above without any process of consultation. On 30 June 2009 (the day before the policy was supposed to come into effect), the MIIT announced its decision to hold off on the policy, essentially cancelling it.

There are many cases like these, in which government agencies have been forced to change their policy or behavior as a result of popular pressure. Over time, this becomes a lesson for learning to adopt new modes of control.

## Conclusion

This chapter delineates the expansion of China's ICCR from state institutions and practices to encompass non-state, commercial institutions and practices, and the expansion from reactive and coercive methods of control to encompass proactive and soft methods of control. My argument is that social forces, specifically online activism, have significantly shaped this evolutionary trajectory. This argument begins to fill a gap in the literature on Internet control in China, in which there is little analysis of how state power refines itself by adapting to social circumstances.

It is in the context of a heightening crisis of governance that Internet protest becomes especially challenging for the party authorities. What are the implications of this argument for forecasting the future of Internet control and Internet activism in China? Barring any major turns of events, there will be no surprises. The Party-state will continue to refine its control strategies and methods to adapt to waves of Internet protest, just as citizens will continue to protest online. Will one become potent enough to smother the other, or will the other completely break free? Neither scenario seems plausible. It is more difficult, however, to weigh the relative effectiveness of state control vs. Internet activism. Some observers maintain that state control of the Internet is effective; yet it is just as true that online activism has not weakened. In crucial ways, answers to this question depend on conditions external to the Internet, such as how the Chinese Party-state tackles current problems of social injustice, corruption, and the abuse of official power. Paradoxically, how it does this may depend to some extent on whether citizens can continue to use the Internet to express dissent and opposition. At least for now, the Party-state seems to be trapped in this double bind.

## References

Ansfield, J. (2010a) 'China tests new controls on Twitter-style services,' *The New York Times*, 16 July.

—— (2010b) 'China starts new bureau to curb web,' *The New York Times*, 16 April.

Benkler, Y. (2000) 'From consumers to users: Shifting the deeper structures of regulation,' *Federal Communications Law Journal*, 52(3): 561–579.

Bourdieu, P. and Wacquant, L. (1992) *Invitation to a Reflexive Sociology*, Chicago, IL: University of Chicago Press.

Braman, S. (ed.) (2004) *The Emergent Global Information Policy Regime*, Houndsmills: Palgrave.

Cell, C. P. (1977) *Revolution at Work: Mobilization Campaigns in China*, New York: Academic Press.

Central Committee of Chinese Communist Party (CCCCP) (2004) *Decision of the Central Committee of the Communist Party of China regarding the Strengthening of the Party's Ability to Govern*. Online. Available HTTP: http://www.people.com.cn/GB/42410/42764/3097243.html (accessed 3 December 2011).

*China Daily* (2011a) 'Police urged to boost use of micro blog,' 27 September. Online. Available HTTP: http://www.china.org.cn/china/2011-09/27/content_23498523.htm (accessed 22 April 2012).

—— (2011b) 'Guo Meimei and the Red Cross Society scandal.' Online. Available HTTP: http://www.chinadaily.com.cn/opinion/2011-07/15/content_12912148.htm (accessed 22 April 2012).

—— (2011c) 'Chinese Premier Wen Jiabao chats online with netizens,' 28 February. Online. Available HTTP: http://news.xinhuanet.com/english2010/video/2011-02/28/c_13753949.htm (accessed 22 April 2012).

China.org.cn (2010) 'Basic principles and practices of Internet administration.' Online. Available HTTP: http://www.china.org.cn/government/whitepaper/2010-06/08/content_20207983.htm (accessed 22 April 2012).

Ching, K. L. (2007) *Against the Law*, Berkeley, CA: University of California Press.

Davenport, C. (1995) 'Multi-dimensional threat perception and state repression: An inquiry into why states apply negative sanctions,' *American Journal of Political Science*, 39(3): 683–713.

Golub, A. and Lingley, K. (2008) 'Just like the Qing Dynasty: Internet addiction, MMOGs, and moral crisis in contemporary China,' *Games and Culture*, 2(4): 59–75.

Google Blog (2006) 'Testimony: The Internet in China,' 16 February. Online. Available HTTP: http://googleblog.blogspot.com/2006/02/testimony-internet-in-china.html (accessed 30 May 2012).

Hassid, J. (2012) 'Safety valve or pressure cooker? Blogs in Chinese political life,' *Journal of Communication*, 62(2): 212–230.

Heilmann, S. and Perry, E. J. (2011) 'Embracing uncertainty: Guerrilla policy style and adaptive governance in China,' in S. Heilman and E. Perry (eds.) *Mao's Invisible Hand: The Political Foundations of Adaptive Governance in China*, Cambridge, MA: Harvard University Asia Center.

Holbig, H. and Gilley, B. (2010) 'Reclaiming legitimacy in China,' *Politics & Policy*, 38(3): 395–422.

Hong, H. (2010) 'A study of how to respond to abrupt Internet incidents,' *Gongan jiaoyu* [*Policing Education*], 8: 8–13.

Hu, J. (2012) 'Jiandingbuyi zou Zhongguo tese shehuizhuyi wenhua fazhan daolu, nuli jianshe shehuizhuyi wenhua qiangguo [Resolutely walk the path of Socialist culture development with Chinese characteristics, strive to construct a strong Socialist culture country],' Qiushi. Online. Available HTTP: http://chinacopyrightandmedia.wordpress.com/2012/01/04/hu-jintaos-article-in-qiushi-magazine-translated/ (accessed 18 September 2012).

Information Office of the State Council (2005) 'Provisions on administering news services on the Internet [互联网新闻信息服务管理规定].' Online. Available HTTP: http://cnnic.net/zcfg/2005/200509/t20050927_14890.html (accessed 28 May 2012).

Internet Society of China (2011) 'About Internet Society of China.' Online. Available HTTP: http://www.isc.org.cn/english/About_Us/Introduction/listinfo-15315.html (accessed 30 May 2012).

Kennedy, J. J. (2009) 'Legitimation with Chinese characteristics: "Two increases, one reduction",' *Journal of Contemporary China*, 18(60): 391–395.

Lee, C. K. (2007) *Against the Law: Labor Protests in China's Rustbelt and Sunbelt*, Berkeley, CA: University of California Press.

Lei, Y. W. (2011) 'The political consequences of the rise of the Internet: Political beliefs and practices of Chinese netizens,' *Political Communication*, 28: 291–322.

Lessig, L. (2001) *The Future of Ideas: The Fate of the Commons in a Connected World*, New York: Random House.

Li Biao, Y. (2011) *Shanyu yulai: wangluo redian shijian chuanbo de kongjian jiegou he shijian jiegou* [*Media Opinion: The Spatial and Temporal Structures of Dissemination of Popular Internet Incidents*], Beijing: Renmin ribao chubanshe.

Lieberthal, K. and Oksenberg, M. (1998) *Policy Making in China: Leaders, Structures, and Processes*, Princeton, NJ: Princeton University Press.

Ma, Q. (2006) *Non-Governmental Organizations in Contemporary China*, London: Routledge.

Mahoney-Norris, K. A. (2000) 'Political repression: Threat perception and translational solidarity groups,' in C. Davenport (ed.) *Paths to State Repression: Human Rights Violations and Contentious Politics*, Lanham, MD: Rowman & Littlefield.

Meng, B. (2011) 'From steamed bun to grass mud horse: E Gao as alternative political discourse on the Chinese Internet,' *Global Media and Communication*, 7(1): 33–51.

Mertha, A. (2009) 'Fragmented authoritarianism 2.0: Political pluralization in the Chinese policy process,' *The China Quarterly*, 200: 995–1012.

Migdal, J. S., Kohli, A. and Shue, V. (eds.) (1994) *State Power and Social Forces: Domination and Transformation in the Third World*, Cambridge: Cambridge University Press.

Nathan, A. (2003) 'Authoritarian resilience,' *Journal of Democracy*, 14(1): 6–17.

OpenNet Initiative (2005) 'Internet filtering in China in 2004–2005: A country study,' 14 April. Online. Available HTTP: http://www.opennetinitiative.net/studies/china/ONI_China_Country_Study.pdf (accessed 24 May 2005).

Pei, M. (2006) *China's Trapped Transition: The Limits of Developmental Autocracy*, Cambridge, MA: Harvard University Press.

People.com.cn (2002) 'Internet campaign action to close illegal websites,' 24 May. Online. Available HTTP: http://news.sina.com.cn/c/2009-02-24/193617279700.shtml (accessed 27 May 2012).

*People's Daily Online* (n.d.) 'About us.' Online. Available HTTP: http://english.peopledaily.com.cn/102840/7560415.html (accessed 22 April 2012).

People's Daily Online Media Opinion Monitoring Office (2009) 'Rankings of local government's abilities to respond to Internet opinion in the first half of 2009 [2009 年上半年地方应对网络舆情能力排行榜],' 23 July. Online. Available HTTP: http://yq.people.com.cn/zt/dz3/index.html (accessed 22 April 2012).

Perry, E. J. (2007) 'Studying Chinese politics: Farewell to revolution?,' *The China Journal*, 57: 1–22.

—— (2011) 'From mass campaigns to managed campaigns: Constructing a new socialist countryside,' in S. Heilmann and E. J. Perry (eds.) *Mao's Invisible Hand: The Political Foundations of Adaptive Governance in China*, Cambridge, MA: Harvard University Asia Center.

Poster, M. (1990) *The Mode of Information: Poststructuralism and Social Context*, Chicago, IL: University of Chicago Press.

Price, M.E. (2002) *Media and Sovereignty: The Global Information Revolution and Its Challenge*, Cambridge, MA: MIT Press.

—— (2010) 'The battle over Internet regulatory paradigms: An intensifying area for public diplomacy,' *The CPD Blog*, USC Center on Public Diplomacy, 3 August. Online. Available HTTP: http://uscpublicdiplomacy.org/index.php/newswire/cpdblog_detail/the_battle_over_Internet_regulatory_paradigms_an_intensifying_area_for/ (accessed 22 April 2012).

Price, M.E. and Verhulst, S. (2005) *Self-Regulation and the Internet*, The Hague: Kluwer Law International.

Reuters (2011) 'Donations to charities in China plunge after scandals,' 8 December. Online. Available HTTP: http://www.reuters.com/article/2011/12/08/us-china-donations-idUSTRE7B70F820111208 (accessed 22 April 2012).

Shieh, S. and Deng, G. (2011) 'An emerging civil society: The impact of the 2008 Sichuan earthquake on grassroots associations in China,' *The China Journal*, 65: 181–194.

Shue, V. (2010) 'Legitimacy crisis in China?' in P. Gries and S. Rosen (eds.) *Chinese Politics: State, Society and the Market*, London: Routledge.

Sina (2010) 'Sina editor-in-chief Chen Tong says monitoring Weibo content is a headache,' 13 June.

—— (2011) 'Sina proposes to invite self-discipline commissioners to help build Internet civilization,' 9 September. Online. Available HTTP: http://news.sina.com.cn/c/2011-09-09/113023132148.shtml (accessed 22 April 2012).

Smith, C.S. (2001) 'China backs away from initial denial in school explosion,' *The New York Times*, 16 March.

State Council (2000) 'Provisions on administering Internet information services [互联网信息服务管理办法].' Online. Available HTTP: http://cnnic.net/zcfg/2000/200310/t20031009_14923.html (accessed 30 May 2012).
Sullivan, J. and Xie, L. (2009) 'Environmental activism, social networks, and the Internet,' *The China Quarterly*, 198: 422–432.
Suttmeir, R. P. (1989) 'Science, technology, and China's political future: A framework for analysis,' in D. F. Simon and M. Goldman (eds.) *Science and Technology in Post-Mao China*, Cambridge, MA: Harvard University Press.
Tenecent (2007) 'Program for the launching of the self-discipline agreement among Chinese blog service providers [中国互联网博客服务自律公约发布会议程],' 21 August. Online. Available HTTP: http://tech.qq.com/a/20070821/000049.htm (accessed 27 May 2012).
Tsui, L. (2003) 'The panopticon as the antithesis of a space of freedom: Control and regulation of the Internet in China,' *China Information: A Journal on Contemporary China Studies*, 17(2): 65–82.
Wang, S. (2008) 'Changing models of China's policy agenda setting,' *Modern China*, 34(1): 56–87.
Watson, A. (2008) 'Civil society in a transitional state: The rise of associations in China,' in J. Unger (ed.) *Associations and the Chinese State: Contested Spaces*, Armonk, NY: M. E. Sharpe.
Xinhua (2009) 'The State Council Information Office and seven other ministries launch campaign against internet vulgarity [国新办等七部委开展整治互联网低俗之风专项行动],' 5 January. Online. Available HTTP: http://news.xinhuanet.com/politics/2009-01/05/content_10606040_1.htm (accessed 27 May 2012).
Xishui County (n.d.) 'Xishui County strengthens the building of news spokesperson and internet commentator systems to guide public opinion [浠水县加强新闻发言人和网评员建设把握舆论导向].' Online. Available HTTP: http://www.hbpop.gov.cn/hbegs/show.asp?id=10939 (accessed 30 May 2012).
Xue, Y. (2009) 'Hulianwang dui gongan gongzuo de tiaozhan yu duice [The challenges of the Internet to public security work and our strategies],' *Jingcha jishu* [*Police Technology*], 11: 4–7.
Yang, G. (2005) 'Environmental NGOs and institutional dynamics in China,' *The China Quarterly*, 181: 46–66.
—— (2009) *The Power of the Internet in China: Citizen Activism Online*, New York: Columbia University Press.
Zheng, Y. (2008) *Technological Empowerment: The Internet, State, and Society in China*, Stanford, CA: Stanford University Press.

17

# Between sedition and seduction

## Thinking censorship in South Asia

*William Mazzarella and Raminder Kaur*

There is something arresting about sedition and seduction—the promise of subversion and the lure of the siren. Both sedition and seduction imply external threats to the stability of a given order. This is also the way in which censorship is typically understood: as a matter of blocking external challenges to political and cultural authority. But as public cultural phenomenon, both sedition and seduction rest on potentials that are immanent to the field in which any polity must legitimate itself. It follows that censorship is a rather more culturally intimate practice than is usually acknowledged. In this chapter, then, we examine what we prefer to call "practices of cultural regulation" as windows onto the formation of societal norms vis-à-vis the media in South Asia.[1] The concept of cultural regulation covers a spectrum of public interventions that would, according to conventional taxonomies, be considered distinct and, at the extremes, diametrically opposed—as in the case of "publicity" and "censorship."[2]

Following notable colonial antecedents (see Pinney 2009; Mazzarella 2009), the last couple of decades have seen a veritable carnival of South Asian controversies over the line between the acceptable and the unacceptable. By way of example, one might point to the uproar in 1994 over the alleged obscenity of Madhuri Dixit's song-and-dance sequence, *Choli*

1 We are fully aware that the term "South Asia" is a slippery terrain, both historically with reference to the impact of colonial rule, the partition of the Indian subcontinent, and subsequent wars that led to the creation of Bangladesh in 1971, and geopolitically, with unclear and often disputed boundaries to the east, west and north. Our ethnographic and archival expertise lies in the territory known as India to whose changing historical contours this chapter owes a certain bias. This is not to overlook ramifications and developments in neighboring regions and, where appropriate, we have referenced the limited literature on the subject for contemporary nations that constitute South Asia.

2 Sanford Levinson writes: ". . . *regulation* is an ambiguous term. We often speak of '*a* regulation' in the sense of a mandatory requirement or prohibition. Yet we also refer easily, especially if we have been influenced even in the slightest by Michel Foucault, to an unarticled 'regulation' as a means of defining what is 'regular' or, ultimately, 'normal' within a given political-cultural order" (Levinson 1998: 197). We extend this insight to accommodate the performative and the affective consequences of regulation (see also Post 1998; Thompson 1997).

*ke peeche kya hai* ("What lies behind the blouse?") in Subhash Ghai's film *Khalnayak* [*The Villain*]; to Shekhar Kapur's *Bandit Queen* (1994), which ran afoul of caste sentiment, the film censor board and its real-life protagonist, outlaw-turned-parliamentarian Phoolan Devi; to Mani Ratnam's feature *Bombay*, whose dramatization of the Bombay riots of 1992–93 managed to offend Hindu groups, Muslim groups and secular intellectuals alike; to the extraordinary intensity of protest (including one self-immolation) and policing that surrounded the Miss World 1996 pageant in Bangalore; to the Bombay ban on Salman Rushdie's *The Moor's Last Sigh* (1995), which, in the wake of the national ban on *The Satanic Verses* (1989), desecrated Indian political idols old and new by featuring a dog named Jawaharlal Nehru and an unflattering, thinly veiled portrait of Maharashtrian strongman Bal Thackeray; to Mira Nair's feature adaptation of the *Kamasutra*, whose Hindi version was, in 1997, subjected to more stringent cuts than its English-language equivalent; to the public burning of a scholarly article, printed by the *Illustrated Weekly of India* in 1994, which dared to call into question elements of the mythical narratives surrounding both the seventeenth-century Maratha ruler Shivaji and the nineteenth-century proto-nationalist heroine the Rani of Jhansi; and to the cinema-smashing, legal challenges and extralegal harassment that greeted Deepa Mehta's *Fire* in 1998, not to mention the direct physical violence that ended the first attempt at filming its successor, *Water*, in Banaras in 2000, before it had even properly begun.[3]

That is just India. In November 2007, former Pakistani President Pervez Musharraf's state of emergency suspended the 1973 Constitution for a third time. Independent news stations were forced off the air, hundreds of protesting journalists and lawyers were arrested, and the Supreme Court was stacked with clients of the regime. This relatively dramatic move—in some ways reminiscent of the much more extended emergency imposed by Indira Gandhi in India in 1975–77—was not Musharraf's first experiment with censorship. Sporadic official interference with the media, as well as "disappearances," had marked his rule since its beginnings in a "bloodless" coup in 1999. As in other parts of the world, the Internet presents wholly new challenges to official regulation. "Cyber-cops" working for the Pakistan Internet Exchange assiduously filter pornography, blasphemy and "anti-Islamic" content from online circuits. More generally, as Asad Ali Ahmed (2009) has shown, Islamic orthodoxy is regularly asserted in the form of blasphemy accusations. Popular culture is by no means immune: Islamist parties have been involved in incidents such as the 2003 provincial banning of music by the pop band Junoon. And in the wake of the murder of three journalists in October of that year, self-censorship has exerted a tighter hold on the press.

Bangladesh grabbed the limelight on the world map of censorship when Taslima Nasreen's novel *Lajja* was banned in 1993. As with Salman Rushdie's *The Satanic Verses*, the banning of *Lajja* only heightened the adulation with which it was greeted in the "liberal" West. Nasreen's later books, *Ka* and *Dwikhandita*, personal memoirs that identify the author's sexual partners in both Bangladesh and West Bengal, have provoked lawsuits and bans in both cross-border regions. In Nepal, two major incidents stand out since 1990 (prior to that year, under the Panchayat regime, strictly enforced press censorship prevailed). First, there was the deafening silence consequent upon the Narayanhiti massacre of 2001, when the editor-in-chief, general manager and publisher of *Kantipur* were arrested for publishing an editorial by Baburam Bhattarai, the second-in-command of the Maoists, alleging that the king's brother Gyanendra was implicated in the deaths (see Lakier 2009). Second, there was the more dispersed regime

3 *Water* was eventually filmed, under the false name *River Moon*, in Sri Lanka in 2003 and released in 2005.

of press censorship imposed along with the state of emergency from November 2001 until August 2002. While not as brutal as other emergencies in the region, it involved comparable restrictions on the press: all pro-Maoist publications were raided and shut down the day before the emergency was declared. As for Sri Lanka, censorship has generally been a function of the battle between the state and the Liberation Tigers of Tamil Eelam (LTTE) that reached its nadir in 2009 when state repression accompanied the brutal decimation of the Tamil people cultures on the island. It remains illegal to report on any proposed operations or military activity by the security forces, or on the acquisition of arms, ammunition or other equipment by the armed forces or the police. Since the defeat of the LTTE in 2009, the regions that were once contested under the banner of Eelam have seen full-blown political repression. The earlier censorial focus on the LTTE has, on the one hand, broadened into an attempt to silence all dissenting voices and evidence of state-led war crimes and, on the other, shifted into a proliferation of media narratives of Sinhalese victimhood.

The very fact that these and other similar controversies were taken up and circulated by the cosmopolitan media establishment in South Asia (and invariably beyond) is itself an important social fact. Superficially, part of what made them compelling as public dramas was the way in which they seemed to stage the contradictions of South Asian public culture in an age of globalization, a period that combined effervescent consumerism with surging religious nationalism and state authoritarianism. From the mid-1980s, and especially after 1991, the deregulation of consumer goods markets joined hands with an explosion in new commercial media. In the 1980s, India saw the expansion of color television (already established in the rest of South Asia) and the coming of video and cable; in the 1990s, South Asians began absorbing the influence of transnational satellite broadcasting and the Internet.

In this context, the relationship between the public interest and the interests of publicity inevitably became more complicated. Marketers, politicians, cultural producers and social movements all sought to establish a presence and a profile, to realize the value-creating possibilities of these new affect-intensive fields of public identification, as well as to proclaim their dangers (Brosius and Butcher 1999; Kaur 2003; Mankekar 1999; Mazzarella 2003; Rajagopal 2001). Structurally, the lure of what one might call "profitable provocation" meant that the boundaries of public civility and decorum were constantly being challenged. Key areas included the public representation of sex, the supposed irrationality of religious appeals in an ostensibly secular democracy, and the line between legal and illegal forms of political action—this last paradigmatically represented by the popular rise of hypermasculinized, often violent, political organizations such as Bombay's Shiv Sena (Eckert 2003; Gupta 1982; Hansen 2001; Katzenstein 1979).

With so much publicity, many of these controversies actually became less, rather than more, intelligible. The media reportage quickly imposed a kind of discursive hardening, a sort of dramaturgical standardization. It was the pre-scripted urban drama of cultural globalization, the overdetermined clash between the cosmopolitans and the localists, between modernity and tradition, iconically fungible and ready-made for nightly summary on CNN. At the same time, it would certainly be a mistake to suggest that we might reach the "truth" of these events by stripping away the "distortions" and "biases" imposed upon them by the media. These were struggles that, in a very fundamental way, lived and breathed in the media, found their distinctive forms and their conditions of possibility in the space provided by a particular configuration of media and publics.

The contemporary moment needs to be placed in historical and regional context. To what extent do the contemporary discourses, practices and conditions of censorship echo and/or reconfigure those of the colonial period? Historical and comparative contextualizations also require us, in turn, to rethink the very category of censorship. To what extent is it an adequate or relevant descriptor for the kinds of public cultural controversies that we invoked above? In what ways might we retheorize censorship vis-à-vis a fuller understanding of the cultural politics of publicity in South Asia?

## From censorship to cultural regulation

As with many social phenomena, the harder one looks at censorship, the stranger it becomes. At the most elementary level, it quickly becomes clear that the common understanding of censorship as the repressive action of states and state-sanctioned institutions will not get us very far. One might even say that there seems to be something of a correlation between the regulation of cultural production and the proliferation of provocative forms.

Repression first: by attending to censorship only as a matter of silencing and of denial, we risk missing what several scholars have identified as its productive aspects. On one level, we are referring here to the relatively obvious point that any kind of utterance or discourse, indeed the very possibility of language, depends upon a kind of constitutive foreclosure (Bourdieu 1991; Butler 1997, 1998). This foreclosure is, as Judith Butler argues, "a kind of unofficial censorship or primary restriction in speech that constitutes the possibility of agency in speech" (Butler 1997: 41). In this sense, censorship does not act upon a sovereign subject from "outside"; rather, it is one of the very preconditions of subjectivity itself.

In practice, the relation between explicit and implicit forms of censorship is often ambiguous. Genevieve Lakier (2009) demonstrates this through an analysis of the self-censorship at work in the (lack of) representations of the massacre of Nepal's royal family in the indigenous media. Tejaswini Ganti (2009) shows how, in the world of Mumbai film production, self-censorship is inextricable from personal dispositions towards controversial themes. An open question—both empirically and theoretically—is the extent to which the positive meanings allowed or encouraged by a certain linguistic or semiotic configuration are "haunted" by the possibilities that they must disavow, but which remain crucial to their intelligibility. By attending to the particular politics of disavowal that structure particular events or sites, we may well understand something important about the dialectic of fascination and loathing that seems to characterize so much in the realm of censorship.

On another level, some have theorized censorship as productive according to a Foucauldian schema. Classically, we imagine the censor, as Dominic Boyer (2003) reminds us, as the very embodiment of the anti-intellectual. The endangered word (lively, inventive, poetic) confronts the complacent philistinism of the censor (sluggish, pedantic, literal-minded) but censorship may also be understood as a generative technology of truth. Far from only silencing, censorship can be read as a relentless proliferation of discourses on normative modes of desiring, of acting, of being in the world. Censorship, then, would be not so much a desperate rearguard action as a productive part of the apparatus of modern governmentality (Foucault 1977, 1981, 1985; Burchell, Gordon and Miller 1991). We find, for example, that the discourses on Indian women's sexuality that emerge out of censorship practices are internally contradictory in interesting ways (Mehta 2001, 2011). Moreover, as many recent public controversies over obscenity in the media have demonstrated, these discourses are routinely brought up against equally normalizing, but quite different, narratives of Indian sexuality—the compulsory invocation, by "cosmopolitan" critics of censorship, of Vatsyayana's *Kamasutra* and the erotic temple carvings at Khajuraho and Konarak as an integral part of the South Asian civilizational heritage is a case in point (Mazzarella 2003).

Then there is the issue of censorship as the action of states or state-sanctioned institutions. This raises two questions. The first is one of location: *where* is censorship? What are its sites? Where should we look for its logic and its motivation? Should we be examining the utterances and ideologies of those individuals authorized by states to intervene into the public field? To what extent does it makes sense to say that the person who enacts censorship is better placed to comment on it than the person who is subjected to it? The Foucauldian commandment would, of course, encourage us, at the very least, to situate the deliberate utterances of practitioners within a wider institutional field. What is the best way to discern the play of censorship in the textual traces left by its operation? How should we read the relationship between the carapace of case law and the relatively ephemeral rhythms of public debate?

The second question is: what "counts" as censorship? Are we stretching the term too far if we force it to accommodate not only the operations of official regulatory authorities (the courts, the police, censor boards), but also various "extralegal" or "extra-constitutional" initiatives and interventions? Some, for example, speak of the "silent censorship" that market forces (or, better, the social relations that are reified as such) exert on the contents of the media (Jansen 1988). Does violent action against the screening of a film count as censorship? Or indeed any of the many "non-violent" tactics by which activists in South Asia often seek to prevent particular events from unfolding—*bandh, hartal, dharna, gherao, morcha* and so forth?

What about the connections between legal and extralegal forms of censorship? Does it matter if violent or non-violent "extralegal" protests are linked, either by alliance or overt sympathy, to those who in fact do control the official machinery of regulation? Such, for instance, was the case at the time of the Shiv Sena's agitations against Deepa Mehta's *Fire* in Bombay and Delhi in 1998. Then recently ousted from political power in the state of Maharashtra, the Shiv Sena's smashing of theatres and intimidation of actors was greeted ambiguously by the national government. National political leaders deplored the "lawlessness" of the violence, but regionally affiliated allies at the center expressed solidarity with and approval of their actions. The then Minister for Information and Broadcasting was, in fact, to the dismay of many, persuaded to return the film to the censor for recertification (a practice that the Indian Supreme Court declared illegal in December 2000).

On occasion, conversely, the Indian Supreme Court has effectively acknowledged the social force of an unofficial ban. In mid-2006, after Aamir Khan, the lead actor in the feature film *Fanaa Destroyed in Love*, publicized his support for the rehabilitation of people displaced by the Narmada dam project in Gujarat, cinemas were subjected to violent, government-supported protests in that state (see Ganti 2009). Constitutionally guaranteed freedom of expression was thus pitted against the repressive practices of a state government claiming to be acting in the interests of the people. The deadlock was only partly resolved when a public interest litigation filed in the Supreme Court yielded the verdict that, while nothing could be done against the unofficial ban, individual theatres would receive protection if they were to decide to screen the film. In this way, in the language of the ruling, "any untoward incident" might be avoided. Certainly, "extralegal" or "extra-constitutional" forms of censorship, particularly when backed by local leaders, often seem to carry more social force than official decrees.

Censorship is not just *in*, but also *of*, the public sphere. The censor's work is generally figured as semi-clandestine, shy of—indeed perhaps structurally opposed to—publicity. We might imagine a nondescript functionary, seated at an anonymous desk in some minor alleyway of the corridors of power, wielding his pen and scissors with smug pedantry (and, yes, it does seem to us that the censor, despite all evidence to the contrary, is generically imagined as a man). But censorship, as we have suggested, often actually courts the full glare of publicity and its agents are by no means always impersonal bureaucrats. Moreover, the censor's work is, it turns out, curiously dependent upon that which it would silence. Not just structurally—a society without obscenity would no longer require censors—but also sensuously: no one pays the provocative word or image as much careful, detailed, even loving, attention as the censor.

We are all familiar with this compulsive dependency from the drama of legal process, where the forbidden word must be aired again and again precisely to establish its unspeakability. We recognize it in marketing strategies: court bans often heighten the desirability of a product by marking it as controversial. Official censors will themselves often dismiss the indignant objections of their "victims" as nothing but publicity stunts. Shekhar Kapur in the field of commercial cinema (*Bandit Queen*; *Elizabeth*) and Anand Patwardhan in that of political documentary (*Father, Son and Holy War*; *War and Peace*) have both been accused of this in recent years.[4]

In this age of liberalization and proliferating media, the singular centralized authority of government film censorship is increasingly coming to be supplemented by self-regulatory councils and professional advisory bodies, such as the Advertising Standards Council of India (Chowdhry 2009) and the Press Council. Such independent organizations respond to and act upon public complaints against images and texts that are already circulating. But when it comes to the cinema, there has long been a sense that pre-censorship is necessary. The Government of India's Central Board of Film Certification retains the tradition established in 1920 when the first regional film-censor boards were founded: moving images are censored before they reach the viewing public.

Richard Burt points out that censorship sometimes even becomes quite flamboyant, as keen and as media-savvy a participant in the great game of publicity as its ostensible quarry. In this mode, censorship competes quite keenly for the conviction and attention of its public: "Censorship not only legitimates discourses by allowing them to circulate, but is itself part of a performance, a simulation in which censorship can function as a trope to be put on show" (Burt 1994: xviii). Book burning, then, is not simply about getting rid of the books, but equally about "staging an opposition between corrupting and purifying forces and agencies" (Burt 1994: xviii). This publicity-seeking side of censorship is evident across the spectrum of regulatory action. Few cultural protests, whether on the left or the right, whether peaceful or incendiary, commence these days before newspaper and television reporters are in place, and before press releases have been distributed. But the official organs of censorship are equally conscious of the need to perform their efficacy and their relevance. When film actor Anupam Kher took over as chairman of the Central Board of Film Certification in India in the autumn of 2003, the Board was quick to promote a new clampdown on indecency in Hindi film song remix videos and film trailers on television.

All of this points to the fact that any claim to authority or power via regulatory action in the field of public culture necessarily involves some kind of active participation in the poetics and politics of publicity. Calculated interventions into the play of publicity—in the name of protecting the sentiments or cultural integrity of a particular constituency—are a standard feature of contemporary South Asian politics. Such forms of "censorship"—calling for the withdrawal of this or that film, book, or newspaper article—are obviously not just silencing tactics; rather they rely, for their political efficacy, on harnessing and mobilizing the public

4 However, as shown by a recent Supreme Court verdict with regards to the documentary *Father, Son and Holy War*, to be aired on Doordarshan after a period of ten years, some of these accusations may simply be a case of government reticence driven by personal politics.

energy of the very artifacts that they appear to be trying to suppress. That such wagers on mass attention should be a matter of some ambivalence is not surprising. The ideal of communicative rationality in public debate frowns upon the affective, spectacular tactics of publicity—the performance of this distinction becomes particularly evident during elections, when candidates' speeches are closely monitored for breaching potential boundaries. Publicity is, by definition, an affect-intensive game. It touches upon the embodied and the intimate; its mode of persuasion is one of resonance rather than reason. It often seems dangerously close to disorder and chaos, to the nightmare transformation of the enlightened democratic public into the rampaging crowd. But this ambivalent aesthetic is, we are suggesting, the condition of any effective appeal to identification and authority. Public culture may be seen, then, as a field of contest between competing experiments, often improvised and volatile, with the profitable/productive harnessing of this volatile substance. That such experiments, sometimes extraordinarily compelling to their constituencies, are always inconclusive, provisional and even dangerous goes without saying.

From one perspective, censorship seems designed to moderate the excessive force or perceived violence that such experiments in public cultural action may involve, as in the case of "hate speech," "obscenity," or—and this is an important one in India—incitement to communal violence (Butler 1997; Douglas 1998; Gates 1997; Heumann, Church and Redlawsk 1997; Strum 1999; Walker 1994). But, from another perspective, censorship also seems to routinize transgression. Michael Taussig, developing Elias Canetti's aphorism about the secret at the heart of power (Canetti 1964: 290), argues that social orders are based on "public secrets"—that is, forms of knowledge and/or representation that are generally, even obsessively, known precisely in so far as they must not be overtly acknowledged (Taussig 1999). Everyday social dynamics, then, depend upon the institutionalization or management of transgression, the normalization of a system of taboos and their breaking. In India, this dynamic has recently become particularly evident around the phenomenon of the screen kiss. For the first fifty years of Indian independence, Indian commercial film-makers rigorously observed an unwritten (but nevertheless incessantly discussed) "ban" on hero–heroine kissing. The prohibition began to be breached with some regularity in the 1990s, but always with a frisson that effectively reinstated the power of the prohibition. One film, *Kwahish* (2003), was marketed primarily on the premise that it contained seventeen kissing scenes; meanwhile, critics complained that Indians looked "unnatural" and "awkward" kissing in films, and actresses, keen to be seen as respectable, made much of their visceral dislike of screen kissing.[5]

Madhava Prasad (1998) has developed an interesting argument about the prohibition on the screen kiss being an index of the impossibility of a bourgeois space of conjugal privacy and intimacy in the context of a social order that continues in large measure to idealize a patriarchal-feudal model of the family and, by extension, of social relations in general. We do think that the question of the intimate and its possible relationship with public culture is crucial. But we are also interested in exploring the ways in which the compulsive assertion and foregrounding of a prohibition serves to routinize a pattern of incitement, a relation of desire and transgression. Here, too, censorship is not only, or even primarily, a mechanism of denial and repression; rather, it serves to articulate a language of the hidden and the sacred in

5 Film critic T. G. Vaidyanathan once remarked, in a commentary on Aparna Sen's *Paroma* (1985), that "Indians look far more convincing when they are not making love. When they are, the whole business looks forced, contrived, and bloodless" (Vaidyanathan 1996: 116).

which everything is "out in the open" even if it is not "shown." We are, of course, well aware of this dynamic when it comes to marketing or to show business: the strategic deployment of the tease, of provocation as a means of focusing attention, realizing profits, and attracting audiences. However, mainstream politics is no less performative, no less dependent upon a volatile calculus of provocation and respectability, defiance and dignity (Hansen 2001, 2004; Kaur 2003).

What we are proposing, then, is to resituate the concept of censorship as a particular (perhaps in some ways privileged) variant of a more general set of practices of cultural regulation. By placing these practices on an analytic continuum from publicity to censorship, we hope to make visible the ways in which both rely on specific (more or less conscious) attempts to generate value (commercial and/or symbolic) out of a delicate balancing of incitement and containment. So whereas the term "censorship" to a greater or lesser extent alludes to the institutionalized frames of a legalistic discourse, the concept of "cultural regulation" points to the performative, the productive and the affective aspects of public culture.

On one level, then, we are interested in calling into question the too-quick equation of state censorship with cultural regulation per se. At the same time, we believe that it is crucial to recognize the reasons and social effects of this equation. If we began with the figure of formal censorship, then it was because state-sanctioned censorship has become the most consciously and conspicuously formalized institution of cultural regulation. It brings the burden and force of state power to bear on its public cultural interventions, even as it claims, often rather complacently, to be acting in the public interest. No wonder it is reviled; no wonder we are tempted to understand the field of public culture as a relentless struggle between the valor of free expression and the cynicism of repressive power.

The fact that state censorship has become such a paradigmatic figure of regulation enables the complementary institutionalization of the discourse of free speech. But the phenomenon of state censorship is also inevitably compelling, because of the seemingly self-evident way in which it expresses a claim to sovereignty in matters of cultural production. One result of this is that almost any would-be authoritative intervention into public cultural controversy at once challenges, and is more or less covertly covetous of, this sovereignty (cf. Das 1995). We are certainly not advocating that the differences between state-sponsored and non-state regulatory initiatives be downplayed. That would obviously be both politically and analytically indefensible. But we are suggesting that it may be analytically productive to examine the extent to which non-state interventions remain entangled in a state-based model of sovereignty and, conversely, the extent to which the state depends on discursive and performative devices whose efficacy is anything but "empty and homogenous" (Anderson 2006). Raminder Kaur (2009), for example, explores how the performance of nuclear politics in India struggles with a tension between authoritarian efficacy and the appearance, at least, of democratic accountability. In a zone such as this, censorship is not so much a matter of outright prohibition or the absence of transparency; rather, it may take the form of an anxiously measured public revelation of information, narratives and images within the spectacular, performative space of publicity.

Although we are inspired by questions of general theoretical significance, the method we are proposing is one of concrete historical and ethnographic engagement. At the same time, taking cultural regulation as an ethnographic object means grappling with discourses and practices that themselves almost invariably make universalizing claims (in relations to rights and/or duties) and particularizing assertions (often in the name of culture or tradition). We see this combination articulated today all over the world in the name of multiculturalism. But it was forged in the crucible of colonization, and the happy hybridity of the multicultural ideal continues to look rather more problematic from a postcolonial vantage point.

## Private lives, public affairs

The distinction between reasoned debate and affective excitability easily gets mapped onto a supposedly constitutive difference between Western and non-Western publics. This understanding has deep colonial roots, of course, but it persists to this day in the self-understanding of South Asian elites (cf. Haynes 1992; Varma 1998). Foreign scholars of cultural regulation in India will often be told something like: "In theory, I am all for freedom of speech and expression. But in a society like ours . . ." Those who staff the formal institutions of cultural regulation (the courts, the censor boards) lean on this combination of cosmopolitan idealism and apparently "pragmatic" particularist vigilance to protect an excitable, indiscriminate and ignorant majority from its own worst tendencies.

So far, so familiar. It is hardly necessary to point to the myriad ways in which this is a flagrantly ideological, self-serving and elitist discourse. Instead, we would like to push the inquiry in a slightly different direction. When is public affective agitation "good" and when is it "bad"? When, for example, does it promise "commitment" or "patriotism," and when does it threaten unrest and chaos? What are the mediations and the forms of social action that harness agitation to given social projects, reactionary and revolutionary alike? What are the imagined locations of the affective as opposed to the deliberative in given public formations? How, in South Asian contexts, have these formations changed from colonial to postcolonial times, and what regulatory strategies have been mobilized to manage them?

We are reminded of Partha Chatterjee's (1993: 6) famous proposition that Indian publics under colonialism were predicated on a constitutive split: between an "outer" or "material" domain of instrumental politics, and an "inner" or "spiritual" domain of cultural identity and sentiment. This split, Chatterjee argues, allowed for the formation of a distinctively Indian modernity under colonialism, one in which Indians could both participate in the public game of power politics, as defined by British conventions and institutions, and yet nurture the sanctity of a civilizational self-identity away from the predations of power. Indeed, it was around the time when this inner domain started becoming an important resource for Indian projects of cultural renewal that the British started losing touch with it. As Bayly points out, after about 1800, the British were on shaky ground when it came to "affective knowledge" of Indian life; they were "weakest in regard to music and dance, the popular poetry of sacred erotics, dress and food, though such concerns are near the heart of any civilization" (Bayly 1996: 55).

Bayly suggests that the kind of model of colonial public life that Chatterjee espouses is flawed in that it misses the existence of pre-colonial spaces of public debate and deliberation. Sandria Freitag, for her part, suggests that we would profit from exploring the debt that contemporary public culture on the subcontinent owes to the meeting between new media technologies and longstanding indigenous practices of display, ritual and performance pertaining to the public life of royal courts, devotional observance and theatrical spectacle (Freitag 1989, 1996, 2001). It is clear that such performative idioms are crucial not only to an understanding of the colonial period, but also to contemporary South Asian public cultures. Yet it seems to us that this line of argument risks overlooking some of the important implications of Chatterjee's model.

First, Chatterjee is careful to specify that his outer/inner division does not, in fact, correspond to the European categories of "public" and "private" (see also Kaviraj 1997). For one thing, the content of the inner domain in colonial India was much more than a private concern: it was the very substance of a shared cultural heritage. Second, while Bayly is right to point to the pre-colonial existence of deliberative publics and elaborate systems of news reporting, the colonial period introduced a normative concept of "publicness" that was quite new, in that it rested on the characteristically modern assumption of the abstract equality of all participants in public debate. The fact that Indian colonial publics obviously did not even approximately approach such a state did not, as Jurgen Habermas might argue, invalidate the normative force of the ideal. Instead, it introduced a new and ambivalent political field, which mirrored that of the inner and outer domains. Claims to justice and recognition could now refer both to the specifics of cultural identity and to the universalizing ideal of human dignity.

As has been extensively documented, British policy grappled at every step with this contradiction. But what we want to stress here is that the very fact that the inner domain of cultural substance was, by definition, much more than a private concern, and meant that the split became unstable as soon as it had been imagined. In so far as "Indianness" (the content of the inner domain) would become a resource for public mobilizations in the nineteenth century and beyond—whether reformist, traditionalist, or nationalist—this inner domain would, as it were, have to be "outed." In other words, Chatterjee's model foregrounds a problem that is crucial to our project: namely, the ambiguity of identifications and solidarities whose basic substance is marked as being off-limits to the cut and thrust of political action, yet, at the same time, has inevitably become a crucial basis for the efficacy of emergent forms of publicity.

In fact, the whole colonial problem of asserting and, in that very assertion, protecting Indian identities exhibits, in textbook form, the ambivalent dynamic of cultural regulation. Again and again, one sees the struggle to find acceptable ways in which to harness deep affect in the service of public agendas, models whereby the volatility and erotics of meaning-that-matters might be legitimated by reference to scientific universality, nationalist transcendence, religious sublimation, or the "natural" truth of aesthetic beauty. Thus the intensity, the affective density, of the "inner" domain might be provisionally connected to the public projects of the "outer" domain without either "polluting" the formal requirements of the outer domain with the intimate excesses of sentiment or—even more fatally—indecently exposing the intimate domain to the impersonal gaze of an anonymous public. Small wonder, then, that woman should have become such a central cipher for this conflicted fusion—woman as nation, woman as embodiment of virtue, woman as aesthetic ideal, woman as locus of dangerous sexual energy (Sangari and Vaid 1990; Thomas 1990; Uberoi 1990). Nor did the end of British rule resolve the tension. Especially with the boom in commercial publicity during the last couple of decades, publicly circulated images of womanhood have become more hotly contested than ever (Bose 2002; Bose 2006; Chanda 2003; John and Nair 2000; Kasbekar 2001; Kishwar 2001; Mankekar 1999).

One might easily be left with the impression that the agonies of ambivalence were the exclusive preserve of the colonized. To be sure, the project of colonialism set up a situation in which, for the colonized, "the *fact of difference* itself is a constitutive moment that structures the experience of modernity" (Gupta 1998: 37; original emphasis). But it is perhaps too easily forgotten that, in so far as the colonies were a kind of laboratory for the norms and forms of a European modernity (Rabinow 1989), the colonizers, as both regulators and administrators, were not simply attempting to contain eruptions of native sentiment within an iron cage of universalizing reason. The British in India also fitfully and ambivalently understood the importance of mobilizing local "affective knowledge" in the service of empire; theirs was also a complex game of incitement and containment, a constant reaching back and forth across the line that divided the intimate and the affective from the formal and the rational.[6] One sees how this awkward oscillation pervaded the tactics of colonial rule in the history of Indian censorship, all the way from the first real regulations at the end of the eighteenth century to the elaborate, paranoid machinery of empire's endgame. By the same token, it is also present in all of the halting British attempts at once to suppress *and* to appropriate "native" idioms of performance, ritual and cultural production for their own ends (Cannadine 2002; Cohn 1983).

The field of cultural regulation, then, emerged at once as both a problem of administration and of defiance. From the beginning, it was defined by a deeply ambivalent relationship to the tension between the sentimental devices of publicity and the instrumental reason of political strategy. This was the ground out of which the legal apparatus of censorship and containment developed. But this apparatus cannot be understood apart from the publics that it was meant to regulate, and thus, inevitably, also to affirm.

## The birth of cultural regulation

As early as the end of the eighteenth century, the potentials of the nascent mass media—at this point, the press—were being registered and regulated. One of the very first newspapers in India, James Hicky's *Bengal Gazette*, was closed down in 1780 after only a few months of operation, on the grounds that invoked both the brittleness of decency and the volatility of public discourse. The censoring order cited "several improper paragraphs tending to vilify private characters, and to disturb the peace of the settlement" (quoted in Jones 2001: 1160).

Looking across the period stretching from the late eighteenth century through to independence in 1947, we might consider the shifting politics of cultural regulation in several ways. First, there is the question of intensity: when was there more and when was there less regulation? What were the spurs and influences on this alternation? Second, there is the matter of regulatory categories and discourse: why and when did specific markers of excess such as "obscenity," "sedition" and "blasphemy" come into play in projects of cultural regulation? What can we learn from their shifting interrelationships? Third, how should we understand the regulatory politics of the changing importance and availability of particular media, if by "media" we mean not only print (textual and visual), cinema and radio, but also specific idioms of performance and public display? Obviously, we are in no position to "answer" these questions here. But we do think it is worth, in a very preliminary way, developing some of the implications of asking such questions for the study of cultural regulation in modern South Asia.

British attempts to regulate the press in colonial India waxed and waned to an awkward rhythm, caught between immediate administrative concerns "on the ground" and more distant—and sometimes more liberal—parliamentary opinion back in London (Barrier 1974; Bhattacharya 2001; Jones 2001; Kaur 2003). As Gerald Barrier puts it, "Caught between a

6 Bose and Jalal note of the century of "Company Raj" (1757–1857): ". . . since the colonial state could establish a semblance of cultural legitimacy only by appropriating symbols and meanings that commanded authority in indigenous society, the distinction between public and private law was never an easy one to maintain" (Bose and Jalal 1998: 74). And for the post-company period: "Although in 1858 the colonial power had announced its intention not to interfere in the private realm of 'religion' and 'custom,' its policies in the late nineteenth century ensured that precisely these concerns had to be bandied about in the 'public' arenas of the press and politics" (ibid.: 108).

tradition that favoured a free press and anxiety over all but the most innocuous criticism, the British swung back and forth from strict controls to virtual freedom of expression" (Barrier 1974: 4). A formal system of press censorship was introduced in 1799, in connection with the war to annex Mysore.[7] During the next 150 years, one sees periods of relative liberality, in which the ideal of the freedom of the press was foregrounded, and periods of panic, in which the power of emergent Indian publics appeared as a threat to the foundations of British rule. Important moments here include the rise of a vernacular press starting in the teens of the nineteenth century, the shock of the 1857–58 Rebellion, and waves of militant nationalist activism in the first decade of the twentieth century, the early 1920s and the early 1930s.

On the basis of a steadily consolidating vernacular press, particularly in North India, the emergent publics of the latter half of the nineteenth century also saw a complex cross-cutting of nationalist, linguistic, communal, and moral-sexual concerns. Publicists, militants, cultural producers and bureaucrats were all becoming increasingly cognizant of the affective efficacy of sexuality and religion as focal points of political mobilization. It is during this period that "obscenity" formally emerged as a category of regulation, and as a category that was understood as implicated in "sedition"—that is, in explicitly political forms of provocation (Bayly 1996; Gupta 2001; Sharma 1968; Mazzarella 2009). On one level, the struggle over erotics in the printed matter of this period is a witness to the striking affective power of the press as a mass medium with a rapidly expanding vernacular audience. On another level, printed "erotic" literature also became a site for an internal struggle over the relative acceptability of "popular" versus "high" forms of cultural production. Charu Gupta has, for instance, effectively juxtaposed the movement to establish a *shuddh* ("pure") literary Hindi public in the very earliest years of the twentieth century against the backdrop of both the denigration of late medieval, overtly eroticized poetic idioms and a contemporary boom in mass-produced sex manuals (Orsini 2002).

These struggles were further complicated by the increasing significance, from the late nineteenth century, of mass-produced visual media: first, gradual improvements in picture-printing, from woodcuts to lithographs; and subsequently, the cinema, which came to India with a representative of the Lumière Brothers in 1896 and had grown into a thriving domestic industry twenty years later. The political effects of print were certainly not restricted to the literate alone, since it was—and still is—quite common for printed texts to be read or performed for wider audiences. Nevertheless, the forging of "national" and sometimes explicitly "nationalist" image-making vocabularies profoundly changed both the social relations and the aesthetics of Indian public culture. It also brought about a closer, mutually amplifying and mutually re-mediating relationship between these new "mass media" and older forms of performance or ritual.[8] Here, too, we see a complex struggle over aesthetic distinction. There is the "high" nationalist painting of the likes of Abanindranath Tagore, developed as part of a literary and scholarly discourse on Indian cultural particularity, self-consciously opposed to

7 Roy (1995) stresses the 1840s in Bengal as the moment when, under the eagle eye of the Irish missionary James Long, the colonial government began to classify all published materials in a synoptic manner. By 1867, in the wake of the 1857 Rebellion, all books in India had to be officially registered.

8 Roy (1995) notes that this amplification also occurred between print and performance. In Bengal, the growth of the press did a great deal to expand the popularity of the *kathakata* genre, as well as the burgeoning "modern" theatre. Hansen (2001) shows how important emergent forms of print publicity—flyers, handbills, newspaper advertising—were to the marketing of the traveling theatre troupes (initially predominantly Parsi) that began traversing the subcontinent in the 1850s.

the "vulgarity" of bazaar prints as well as the imitative banality of "company art" (Guha-Thakurta 1992, 1995; Kapur 2000).

But perhaps the most influential outcome of this historical juncture was the consolidation of a mass-produced middlebrow national aesthetic, typified by the "god poster" lithography of Ravi Varma or, later, C. Kondiah Raju (Smith 1995; Inglis 1995; Pinney 1997a, 1997b; Jain 2007). These visual conventions were, in turn, definitively influential on the depiction of mythological themes in the nascent Hindi cinema and are still popularly perceived as the "correct" visual rendering of Hindu deities, whether in the comic book nationalist pedagogy of *Amar Chitra Katha* or the sensationally successful television series *Ramayana* of the late 1980s (Hawley 1995; Lutgendorf 1995; Mankekar 1999; Rajagopal 2001). In India, where the devotional gaze is often understood as a medium of grace, this visual veracity is as much a matter of efficacy as of verisimilitude (Babb 1981; Eck 1998). Although their social and political functions may have shifted, the forceful efficacy potentially residing in divine images has obviously not been reduced by mechanical reproduction, by their translation into calendar art, cinema, video and television programming (Davis 1997; Little 1995; Smith 1995).

The mobilizing power of such images has also been a constant feature of regulatory anxiety. Although the Indian nationalist leadership was, on the whole, relatively indifferent to the political potential of cinema, the British certainly took it seriously (Chabria and Usai 1994; Chowdhry 2000). The colonial government instituted a comprehensive commission of inquiry into its political economy, its possible social effects and the adequacy of existing regulatory measures in 1927–28 (Arora 1995; Jaikumar 2003, 2006; Mehta 2001; Sarkar 1982; Vasudev 1978). Indeed, post-independence Indian governments have continued this trend. The censorship of film has been rigorously formalized on the basis of the Cinematograph Act of 1952 and the Cinematograph (Censorship) Rules of 1958; as Kumar (1990) points out, the regulation of other media may be just as vociferously pursued, but always on the basis of a much more haphazard and improvisatory legal infrastructure. Of course, the degree of legal routinization is not necessarily a very useful measure of the practical politics of any regime of censorship. As Tejaswini Ganti (2009) shows, the relationship between Bollywood and the Indian state is an ambivalent one, neither dedicatedly adversarial nor straightforwardly complicit.[9]

## Postcolonial conjunctures

Much has been written on the stunning expansion of commercial entertainment-based television in India in the 1980s; how it brought together, in a volatile compact around the affect-intensive television image, a range of new middle-class aspirations, the blandishments of consumerism, and a mass acceptance for an overtly and frequently aggressive religious nationalism (Kumar 2005; Mankekar 1999; Mazzarella 2003; Rajagopal 2001). From a regulatory point of view, these were, in some ways, peculiar days (Farmer 1996). In the form of the state television service, Doordarshan, the government retained sole proprietorship over this boisterously mushrooming medium, constantly striving to reconcile its habituated "fear of the uncontrollable image" (Ohm 1999: 75) with highly profitable content that was often

9 In the interests of space, we are not taking up the issue of audio-only media here. But much remains to be said on the relation between the "official" culture promulgated by All-India Radio (Lelyveld 1995) that doubles as a border-policing device vis-à-vis Sri Lanka and Pakistan. In addition, cassette technology has, of course, made possible forms of grassroots mobilization that few other mass media technologies can equal (Rajagopal 2001; Manuel 1993).

lustily corporeal. With programming increasingly farmed out to the private sector, but control still centralized in the hands of the government, television in the 1980s became a kind of tug-of-war between state and commercial interests (Appadurai and Breckenridge 1995).

It also doubled as a laboratory for new experiments in cultural regulation. By this, we mean not only the often heavy-handed blackouts that Doordarshan imposed on particular news items, but also the doings and sayings of political critics. We are also thinking of experiments in the profitable mass mobilization of affect, whether commercial, religious, or political. Indeed, one of the defining features of this period, as many have noted, was the increasing televisual interpenetration of devotional viewing, political propaganda and consumer goods advertising.

These developments laid the foundations for the media scandals with which we started this chapter. Today, the dawning consumerism and televisual politics of the 1980s are almost invariably read as a prequel to the full-tilt tryst with liberalization that started with the reforms of 1991. In subscribing to this teleology, however, we may miss something equally as, if not more, important about the new televisual dispensation: namely, the ways in which it was a response to the failure of Indira Gandhi's experiment with dictatorship during the emergency of 1975–77. In histories of the media, the emergency has come to stand as the exception that proves the rule of Indian democratic freedom, and an object lesson in the political dangers of censorship. After all, the story goes, was it not precisely Mrs. Gandhi's totalizing approach to information control that isolated her from "public opinion" to such a degree that she mistakenly believed that she would have no trouble winning the national election in 1977?

The style of information management that prevailed during the emergency was exceptionally heavy-handed. Press materials generally had to be submitted for pre-screening under official categories such as "pre-censorship," "news management," and the starkly simple "banned." As Soli Sorabjee (1977) notes, although overt political critique was, of course, almost impossible, the restrictions also extended to such topics as strikes, the nuclear program, reports on family planning/vasectomy follow-up centers and even the arrest of legendary actress Nargis for shoplifting in London. Under the Defense of India Rules and the Maintenance of Internal Security Act, thousands were jailed and silenced, and—in a kind of perfect sovereign recursivity—any reference to censorship in the media was itself banned. Troubling bodies were incarcerated (political opponents, editors, activists) or physically moved (recalcitrant judges), power to newspapers was cut and a comprehensive range of "directives" were issued to the media from Samachar, the central government news agency. Mrs. Gandhi's heir apparent, Sanjay, is said to have personally demanded substantial cash "contributions" in return for permission to premiere new films in the capital.

Although Mrs. Gandhi's second period in office (1980–84) did see some highly controversial blanket bans on media reportage during localized episodes of political turmoil (e.g. in Punjab and in Assam), the crudely repressive measures of the emergency were not repeated in India. But by identifying these crude tactics with censorship per se, there is a risk of losing sight of some of the subtler forms of cultural regulation that were developed in tandem with the expansion of the commercial media in the early to mid-1980s. As Shiv Visvanathan puts it, the emergency was not so much an embarrassing aberration as "a pilot plant, a large scale trial for the totalitarianisms and emergencies that were to come later" (Visvanathan 1998: 45). One could argue that cultural regulation under the sign of liberalization, particularly after Mrs. Gandhi's assassination in late 1984, required a rapid reinterpretation of the kind of state-centric authoritarian populism that the emergency had come to typify.

Emphatically consigning Mrs. Gandhi to a superseded past, mere months after her death, was, of course, never going to be an easy or an uncontested process.[10] As a project, it involved something far more comprehensive than the dismissal of the emergency as a historical anomaly, a dismissal that she herself had already propounded during her last years in office. Rather, what was required was the impression of a more dispersed affective field, one not so tightly grafted onto the singular image of the charismatic leader. The new, liberalized mode of citizenship was one in which the energies of public participation should be seen as coming from below rather than from the "commanding heights" of the planning commission. It located the nation's destiny less in the heroic agency of a leader and more in the embodied and embedded impulses of everyday life. The language of faith and tradition, of consumerist desire, and of regionally chauvinist identifications might still at times trouble the sovereignty of the national project, but they attained, in this period, a new image of authenticity, the dignity of affective truth as compared to the alienating abstractions, the grand schemes of the Nehru years.

Our point is certainly not to suggest that liberalization brought about some kind of authentically democratic revival; rather, what is visible in debates over the media from this period is a diffuse consciousness, expressed in many different idioms by many different interest groups, of a tension between sovereignty and control in public communications and an increasingly complex set of claims on representation and recognition in public culture. At times, the government clamped down and silenced dissent in the old, crude way. At others, however, the myriad voices emerging from inside and around the government seemed to be advocating the possibility of a more subtle cooptation, one in which consumer choice, religious assertion and regional pride might perhaps still be harnessed to a collective national project. By the same token, of course, the legitimacy of the state as the final arbiter in public cultural matters, in matters of value, identity and desire, was increasingly being called into question. When Hindi movie star Manisha Koirala decided that she had been deceived by director Shashilal Nair in the making of *Ek Chhoti Si Love Story* (2002) after he had inserted provocative, partially undressed scenes featuring a body double, her actions reflected a perfect understanding of the ambiguities of the new dispensation. Hedging her bets, she appealed in quick succession to the Censor Board, the Ministry of Information and Broadcasting, and Shiv Sena Chief Bal Thackeray for justice.

We are now in a very different situation from that which prevailed in the 1980s. Strategies of regulation have diversified in proportion to the proliferation of new media. The coming of commercial satellite television in the early 1990s has shifted television away from state control. In response, government has sought to reassert its authority. In addition to making regular—if relatively ineffectual—noises about bringing television directly under the authority of the Central Board of Film Certification, a 2006 decision of the Mumbai High Court made it illegal for any television station broadcasting in India to screen films with "A" censor certificates (for audiences aged 18 and over). The liberalization and globalization of consumer markets has intensified competition in the field of visual publicity, requiring Indian advertisers to "keep up" with international benchmarks in profitable provocation. And the

10 In some sense, it was, of course, this tension that eventually sullied Rajiv Gandhi's "Mr. Clean" image—namely, his inability to transcend the compulsions of the party machinery that had been established during his mother's rule. More immediately, the conflict expressed itself in several incidents of sudden censorship: for example, the sudden cancellation, in February 1986, of a Doordarshan screening of Jack Anderson's documentary *Rajiv's India*, which some members of the Party's old guard apparently felt was insufficiently respectful of Mrs. Gandhi's political legacy.

increasing regionalization of both television and the press has allowed a far wider range of local identities to find their aspirations and their reification in the mass media.

At the time of the television series *Ramayana* in the late 1980s, controversy raged around the fact that Doordarshan, the broadcast medium of a self-avowedly secular state, was both presiding over and profiting from such blatantly "religious" content.[11] In response to this accusation, Philip Lutgendorf (1995) reminds us that recitations and performances of the epics have always enjoyed and depended upon political patronage in India. One could even add that, from a certain perspective, the landscape of the 1990s and after might even look like a return to something like a pre-modern diversity of cultural patrons and publics, each presiding over their own regional turf, their own chosen "traditions." What such an analysis would miss, in its neoliberal enthusiasm, is the tension that persists between a diversity of claimants to cultural sovereignty and the singular regulatory authority represented by the state and, in particular, by the language and institutions of the law. We are all familiar with this tension as it pertains to the antinomies and limits of liberalism. One thinks, for example, of the Shah Bano case of 1986, which pitted a particularist appeal to Muslim law against the putative universalism of a common civil code.

This is also a question of publics and the forms of media that constitute them. It has become de rigueur to insist that we have transcended the age of "the masses," that the diversification of markets and media have consigned the age of standardization and massification to the dustbin of history. In South Asia, however, such a diversification continues to coexist with a developmentalist narrative that constitutes "the masses" as the prime beneficiaries of state action, both redistributive and regulatory. They are the objects (and intended future subjects) of the process of modernization. They may, most typically, be injured or misled by provocative, obscene or seditious public communications. On the one hand, we can sympathize with Ashis Nandy's (1995) call for an approach to Indian politics that captures the messiness, ambiguity and unpredictability that a more rationalist realpolitik elides and an ethnographic approach would certainly seem to be ideally suited to such a pursuit. On the other hand, we would suggest that the politics of cultural regulation are played out at the intersection between such a politics of the concrete and the reified terms of administration.

This tension also plays itself out as a crisis of temporality. Against the perpetual "not yet" of Third World time, the permanent deferral of the full realization of modernity, the big movements of the last couple of decades have all been premised on a big immediacy, on a sensuous immersion. This dream of immediacy is present in the often violent identitarian politics of regional and religious chauvinism, in the promise of instant consumerist gratification, and in the fullness of devotional absorption upon which contemporary political spectacle is so often premised.

## Conclusion

We began with the juxtaposition of censorship and publicity: to ask what it might mean that practices of cultural regulation seem to have become so central to contemporary South Asian public cultures. We hope to have suggested that this is not only a matter of what does or does not "go into" public circulation, but also points to the political centrality of discourses on and

11 As Rajagopal (2001) points out, part of the contested politics of secularism around the televised epics took the form of arguments about whether the material should be understood as "religious" or "cultural."

around practices of regulation. Regulation is self-reflexive: it cannot help but articulate the terms and foundations of its own legitimacy. For this reason, regulation is performative too: the silencing gesture is not only often quite public, but also simultaneously invokes an entire socio-cultural dispensation.

The conventional language that attaches to censorship and its refusal—"security," "freedom of speech," "diversity," "choice," and so forth—must itself be read as a political technology that helps to negotiate what we referred to earlier as the tension between the public interest and the interests of publicity. Naturally, in an era of globalization and rapidly exploding commercial media networks, the stakes of profitable provocation are immeasurably heightened. But it is absolutely crucial that we understand the politics of the relationship between a generalized discourse on censorship and the specificities of longstanding local histories of media and performance. This is never simply a matter of "localizing" abstract or universalizing claims: cultural regulation *is*, in some sense, the attempt to forge an authoritative relationship between the energy of embedded and embodied phenomena and trans-local normative categories.

Typically, mainstream discussions of censorship in South Asia, as elsewhere, are stolidly steadfast in declaring censorship a "bad thing." We would agree that the repressive aspects of censorship do need to be noted. It is perfectly possible to acknowledge, in a Foucauldian mode, the perverse productivity of various forms of cultural regulation while still recognizing that censorship *does* silence even as it speaks. But the interesting question is not "*Censored ke peeche kya hai?*" ("What lies behind the censored?"); rather, what we hope to have shown is that there is nothing self-evident about censorship, nor about the worlds that it makes. Censorship is not merely a constant forge of discourse, nor is it only a ruthless mechanism of silence. As a gamble on publicity, cultural regulation is, for all of its apparently routinized banality, an uncertain and open-ended venture. In that lies its fascination and its importance for cultural analysis.

## References

Ahmed, A. A. (2009) 'Specters of Macaulay: Blasphemy, the Indian Penal Code, and Pakistan's postcolonial predicament,' in R. Kaur and W. Mazzarella (eds.) *Censorship in South Asia: Cultural Regulation from Sedition to Seduction*, Bloomington, IN: Indiana University Press.

Anderson, B. (2006) *Imagined Communities*, 2nd edn., New York: Verso.

Appadurai, A. and Breckenridge, C. (1995) 'Public modernity in India,' in C. Breckenridge (ed.) *Consuming Modernity: Public Culture in a South Asian World*, Minneapolis, MN: University of Minnesota Press.

Arora, P. (1995) 'Imperiling the prestige of the white woman: Colonial anxiety and film censorship in British India,' *Visual Anthropology Review*, 11(2): 36–50.

Babb, L. (1981) 'Glancing: Visual interaction in Hinduism,' *Journal of Anthropological Research*, 37(4): 47–64.

Barrier, N. G. (1974) *Banned: Controversial Literature and Political Control in British India, 1907–1947*, Columbus, MO: University of Missouri Press.

Bayly, C. A. (1996) *Empire and Information: Intelligence Gathering and Social Communication in India, 1780–1870*, Cambridge: Cambridge University Press.

Bhattacharya, S. (2001) 'India: 1900–1947,' in D. Jones (ed.) *Censorship: A World Encyclopedia*, Chicago, IL: Fitzroy Dearborn, 4 volumes.

Bose, B. (ed.) (2002) *Translating Desire: The Politics of Gender and Culture in India*, New Delhi: Katha.

—— (2006) *Gender and Censorship*, New Delhi: Women Unlimited.

Bose, S. and Jalal, A. (1998) *Modern South Asia: History, Culture, Political Economy*, New Delhi: Oxford University Press.

Bourdieu, P. (1991) 'Censorship and the imposition of form,' in J. Thompson (ed.) *Language and Symbolic Power*, Cambridge, MA: Harvard University Press.

Boyer, D. (2003) 'Censorship as a vocation: The institutions, practices and cultural logic of media control in the German Democratic Republic,' *Comparative Studies in Society and History*, 45(3): 511–545.

Brosius, C. and Butcher, M. (eds.) (1999) *Image Journeys: Audio-Visual Media and Cultural Change in India*, New Delhi: Sage.

Burchell, G., Gordon, C. and Miller, P. (1991) *The Foucault Effect: Studies in Governmentality*, Chicago, IL: University of Chicago.

Burt, R. (1994) 'Introduction: The 'new' censorship,' in R. Burt (ed.) *The Administration of Aesthetics: Censorship, Political Criticism and the Public Sphere*, Minneapolis, MN: University of Minnesota Press.

Butler, J. (1997) *Excitable Speech: A Politics of the Performative*, London: Routledge.

—— (1998) 'Ruled out: Vocabularies of the censor,' in R. C. Post (ed.) *Censorship and Silencing: Practices of Cultural Regulation*, Los Angeles, CA: The Getty Research Institute.

Canetti, E. (1964) *Crowds and Power*, New York: Farrar, Straus and Giroux.

Cannadine, D. (2002) *Ornamentalism: How the British Saw Their Empire*, New York: Oxford University Press.

Chabria, S. and Usai, P. (eds.) (1994) *Light of Asia: Indian Silent Cinema, 1912–1934*, New Delhi: Wiley Eastern.

Chanda, I. (2003) *Packaging Freedom: Feminism and Popular Culture*, Kolkata: Stree.

Chatterjee, P. (1993) *The Nation and its Fragments: Colonial and Postcolonial Histories*, Princeton, NJ: Princeton University Press.

Chowdhry, A. (2009) 'Anxiety, failure, and censorship in Indian advertising,' in R. Kaur and W. Mazzarella (eds.) *Censorship in South Asia: Cultural Regulation from Sedition to Seduction*, Bloomington, IN: Indiana University Press.

Chowdhry, P. (2000) *Colonial India and the Making of Empire Cinema: Image, Ideology and Identity*, Manchester: Manchester University Press.

Cohn, B. (1983) 'Representing authority in Victorian India,' in E. Hobsbawm and T. Ranger (eds.) *The Invention of Tradition*, Cambridge: Cambridge University Press.

Das, V. (1995) *Critical Events: An Anthropological Perspective on Contemporary India*, New Delhi: Oxford University Press.

Davis, R. (1997) *Lives of Indian Images*, Princeton, NJ: Princeton University Press.

Eck, D. (1998) *Darsan: Seeing the Divine Image in India*, New York: Columbia University Press.

Eckert, J. (2003) *The Charisma of Direct Action: Power, Politics and the Shiv Sena*, New Delhi: Oxford University Press.

Farmer, V. (1996) 'Mass media: Images, mobilization, and communalism,' in D. Ludden (ed.) *Contesting the Nation: Religion, Community and the Politics of Democracy in India*, Philadelphia, PA: University of Pennsylvania Press.

Foucault, M. (1977) *Discipline and Punish: The Birth of the Prison*, Harmondsworth: Penguin.

—— (1981) *Power/Knowledge: Selected Interviews and Other Writing*, New York: Pantheon Books.

—— (1985) *The History of Sexuality, vol. 2: The Use of Pleasure*, Harmondsworth: Penguin.

Freitag, S. (1989) *Collective Action and Community: Public Arenas and the Emergence of Communalism in North India*, Berkeley, CA: University of California Press.

—— (1996) 'Contesting in public: Colonial legacies and contemporary communalism,' in D. Ludden (ed.) *Contesting the Nation: Religion, Community and the Politics of Democracy in India*, Philadelphia, PA: University of Pennsylvania Press.

—— (2001) 'Vision and the nation: Theorizing the nexus between creation, consumption, and participation in the public sphere,' in R. Dwyer and C. Pinney (eds.) *Pleasure and the Nation: The History, Politics and Consumption of Public Culture in India*, New Delhi: Oxford University Press.

Ganti, T. (2009) 'The limits of decency and the decency of limits: Censorship and the Bombay film industry,' in R. Kaur and W. Mazzarella (eds.) *Censorship in South Asia: Cultural Regulation from Sedition to Seduction*, Bloomington, IN: Indiana University Press.

Gates, H. L. (1997) *Speaking of Race, Speaking of Sex: Hate Speech, Civil Rights and Civil Liberties*, New York: New York University Press.

Guha-Thakurta, T. (1992) *The Making of a New 'Indian' Art: Artists, Aesthetics, and Nationalism in Bengal, c 1850–1920*, Cambridge: Cambridge University Press.

—— (1995) 'Recovering the nation's art,' in P. Chatterjee (ed.) *Texts of Power: Emerging Disciplines in Colonial Bengal*, Minneapolis, MN: University of Minnesota Press.

Gupta, A. (1998) *Postcolonial Developments: Agriculture in the Making of Modern India*, Durham, NC: Duke University Press.

Gupta, C. (2002) *Sexuality, Obscenity, and Community: Women, Muslims and the Hindu Public in Colonial India*, London: Palgrave.

Gupta, D. (1982) *Nativism in a Metropolis: The Shiv Sena in Bombay*, New Delhi: Manohar Publications.

Hansen, K. (2001) 'The *Indar Sabha* phenomenon: Theatre and consumption in Greater India (1853–1956),' in R. Dwyer and C. Pinney (eds.) *Pleasure and the Nation: The History, Politics and Consumption of Public Culture in India*, New Delhi: Oxford University Press.

Hansen, T. B. (2001) *Wages of Violence: Naming and Identity in Postcolonial Bombay*, Princeton, NJ: Princeton University Press.

—— (2004) 'Politics as permanent performance: The production of political authority in the locality,' in J. Zavos, A. Wyatt and V. Hewitt (eds.) *The Politics of Cultural Mobilization in India*, New Delhi: Oxford University Press.

Hawley, J. S. (1995) 'The saints subdued: Domestic virtue and national integration in *Amar Chitra Katha*,' in L. Babb and S. Wadley (eds.) *Media and the Transformation of Religion in South Asia*, Philadelphia, PA: University of Pennsylvania Press.

Haynes, D. E. (1992) *Rhetoric and Ritual in Colonial India: The Shaping of a Public Culture in Surat City, 1852–1928*, New Delhi: Oxford University Press.

Heumann, M., Church, T. W. and Redlawsk, D. P. (1997) *Hate Speech on Campus: Cases, Case Studies and Commentary*, Boston, MA: Northeastern University Press.

Inglis, S. (1995) 'Suitable for framing: The work of a modern master,' in L. Babb and S. Wadley (eds.) *Media and the Transformation of Religion in South Asia*, Philadelphia, PA: University of Pennsylvania Press.

Israel, M. (1994) *Communications and Power: Propaganda and the Press in the Indian Nationalist Struggle, 1920–1947*, Cambridge: Cambridge University Press.

Jaikumar, P. (2003) 'More than morality: The Indian cinematograph committee interviews (1927),' *The Moving Image*, 3(1): 83–109.

—— (2006) *Cinema at the End of Empire: A Politics of Transition in Britain and India*, Durham, NC: Duke University Press.

Jain, K. (2007) *Gods in the Bazaar: The Economies of Indian Calendar Art*, Durham, NC: Duke University Press.

Jansen, S. C. (1988) *Censorship: The Knot that Binds Power and Knowledge*, New York: Oxford University Press.

John, M. and Nair, J. (eds.) (2000) *A Question of Silence: The Sexual Economies of Modern India*, London: Zed Books.

Jones, D. (2001) 'India,' in D. Jones (ed.) *Censorship: A World Encyclopedia*, Chicago, IL: Fitzroy Dearborn, 4 volumes.

Kapur, G. (2000) *When Was Modernism? Essays on Contemporary Cultural Practice in India*, New Delhi: Tulika.

Kasbekar, A. (2001) 'Hidden pleasures: Negotiating the myth of the female ideal in popular Hindi cinema,' in R. Dwyer and C. Pinney (eds.) *Pleasure and the Nation: The History, Politics and Consumption of Public Culture in India*, New Delhi: Oxford University Press.

Katzenstein, M. F. (1979) *Ethnicity and Equality: The Shiv Sena Party and Preferential Policies in Bombay*, Ithaca, NY: Cornell University Press.

Kaul, C. (2003) *Reporting the Raj: The British Press and India, c 1880–1922*, Manchester: Manchester University Press.

Kaur, R. (2003) *Performative Politics and the Cultures of Hinduism: Public Use of Religion in Western India*, New Delhi: Permanent Black.

—— (2009) 'Nuclear revelations,' in R. Kaur and W. Mazzarella (eds.) *Censorship in South Asia: Cultural Regulation from Sedition to Seduction*, Bloomington, IN: Indiana University Press.

Kaviraj, S. (1997) 'Filth and the public sphere: Concepts and practices about space in Calcutta,' *Public Culture*, 10(1): 83–113.

Kishwar, M. (2001) *Off the Beaten Track: Rethinking Gender Issues for Indian Women*, New Delhi: Oxford University Press.

Kumar, G. (1990) *Censorship in India: With Special Reference to* The Satanic Verses *and* Lady Chatterley's Lover, New Delhi: Har-Anand.

Kumar, S. (2005) *Gandhi Meets Primetime: Globalization and Nationalism in Indian Television*, Champaign, IL: University of Illinois Press.

Lakier, G. (2009) 'After the massacre: Secrecy, disbelief, and the public sphere in Nepal,' in R. Kaur and W. Mazzarella (eds.) *Censorship in South Asia: Cultural Regulation from Sedition to Seduction*, Bloomington, IN: Indiana University Press.

Lelyveld, D. (1995) 'Upon the subdominant: Administering music on All-India Radio,' in C. Breckenridge (ed.) *Consuming Modernity: Public Culture in a South Asian World*, Minneapolis, MN: University of Minnesota Press.

Levinson, S. (1998) 'The tutelary state: "Censorship," "silencing," and the "practices of cultural regulation",' in R. C. Post (ed.) *Censorship and Silencing: Practices of Cultural Regulation*, Los Angeles, CA: Getty Research Institute.

Little, J. (1995) 'Video *Vacana: Swadhyaya* and sacred tapes,' in L. Babb and S. Wadley (eds.) *Media and the Transformation of Religion in South Asia*, Philadelphia, PA: University of Pennsylvania Press.

Lutgendorf, P. (1995) 'All in the (Raghu) family: a video epic in cultural context,' in L. Babb and S. Wadley (eds.) *Media and the Transformation of Religion in South Asia*, Philadelphia, PA: University of Pennsylvania Press.

Lyotard, J. (2004) *Libidinal Economy*, New York: Continuum.

Mankekar, P. (1999) *Screening Culture, Viewing Politics: An Ethnography of Television, Womanhood and Nation in Postcolonial India*, Durham, NC: Duke University Press.

Manuel, P. (1993) *Cassette Culture: Popular Music and Technology in North India*, Chicago, IL: University of Chicago Press.

Mazzarella, W. (2003) *Shoveling Smoke: Advertising and Globalization in Contemporary India*, Durham, NC: Duke University Press.

—— (2009a) 'The obscenity of censorship: Rethinking a middle class technology,' in A. Baviskar and R. Ray (eds.) *'We're Middle Class': The Cultural Politics of Dominance in India*, New Delhi: Routledge.

—— (2009b) 'Making sense of the cinema in late colonial India,' in R. Kaur and W. Mazzarella (eds.) *Censorship in South Asia: Cultural Regulation from Sedition to Seduction*, Bloomington, IN: Indiana University Press.

Mehta, M. (2001) 'What is behind film censorship? The *Khalnayak* debates,' *Jouvert*, 5(3): 1–12.

—— (2011) *Censorship and Sexuality in Bombay Cinema*, Austin: University of Texas.

Nandy, A. (1995) *The Savage Freud and Other Essays on Possible and Retrievable Selves*, Princeton, NJ: Princeton University Press.

Ohm, B. (1999) 'Doordarshan: Representing the nation's state,' in C. Brosius and M. Butcher (eds.) *Image Journeys: Audio-Visual Media and Cultural Change in India*, New Delhi: Sage.

Orsini, F. (2002) *The Hindi Public Sphere 1920–1940: Language and Literature in the Age of Nationalism*, New Delhi: Oxford University Press.

Pinney, C. (1997a) *Camera Indica: The Social Life of Indian Photographs*, Chicago, IL: University of Chicago Press.

—— (1997b) 'The nation (un)pictured? Chromolithography and 'popular' politics in India, 1878–1995,' *Critical Inquiry*, 23(4): 834–867.

—— (2004) *Photos of the Gods: The Printed Image and Political Struggle in India*, London: Reaktion Books.

—— (2009) 'Iatrogenic religion and politics,' in R. Kaur and W. Mazzarella (eds.) *Censorship in South Asia: Cultural Regulation from Sedition to Seduction*, Bloomington, IN: Indiana University Press.

Post, R. (ed.) (1998) *Censorship and Silencing: Practices of Cultural Regulation*, Los Angeles, CA: Getty Research Institute.

Prasad, M. M. (1998) *Ideology of the Hindi Film: A Historical Construction*, New Delhi: Oxford University Press.

Rabinow, P. (1989) *French Modern: Norms and Forms of the Social Environment*, Cambridge, MA: MIT Press.

Rajagopal, A. (2001) *Politics after Television: Hindu Nationalism and the Reshaping of the Public in India*, Cambridge: Cambridge University Press.

Roy, T. (1995) 'Disciplining the printed text: Colonial and nationalist surveillance of Bengali literature,' in P. Chatterjee (ed.) *Texts of Power: Emerging Disciplines in Colonial Bengal*, Minneapolis, MN: University of Minnesota Press.

Sangari, K. and Vaid, S. (eds.) (1990) *Recasting Women: Essays in Indian Colonial History*, Piscataway, NJ: Rutgers University Press.

Sarkar, K. (1982) *You Can't Please Everyone! Film Censorship: The Inside Story*, Bombay: IBH.

Sharma, K. M. (1968) 'Obscenity and the law,' in A. B. Shah (ed.) *The Roots of Obscenity: Obscenity, Literature and the Law*, Bombay: Lalvani.

Smith, H. D. (1995) 'Impact of "God posters" on Hindus and their devotional tradition,' in L. Babb and S. Wadley (eds.) *Media and the Transformation of Religion in South Asia*, Philadelphia, PA: University of Pennsylvania Press.

Sorabjee, S. (1977) *The Emergency, Censorship and the Press in India, 1975–1977*, London: Writers and Scholars Educational Trust.
Strum, P. (1999) *When the Nazis Came to Skokie: Freedom for Speech We Hate*, Lawrence, KS: University of Kansas Press.
Taussig, M. (1999) *Defacement: Public Secrecy and the Labour of the Negative*, Stanford, CA: Stanford University Press.
Thomas, R. (1990) 'Sanctity and scandal: The mythologisation of *Mother India*,' *Quarterly Review of Film and Video*, 11: 11–30.
Thompson, K. (ed.) (1997) *Media and Cultural Regulation*, Newbury Park, CA: Sage.
Uberoi, P. (1990) 'Feminine identity and national ethos in Indian calendar art,' *Economic and Political Weekly*, 25(17): 41–48.
Vaidyanathan, T. G. (1996) *Hours in the Dark*, New Delhi: Oxford University Press.
Varma, P. K. (1998) *The Great Indian Middle Class*, New Delhi: Penguin.
Vasudev, A. (1978) *Liberty and License in the Indian Cinema*, New Delhi: Vikas.
Visvanathan, S. (1998) 'Revisiting the Shah Commission,' in S. Visvanathan and H. Sethi (eds.) *Foul Play: Chronicles of Corruption*, New Delhi: Banyan Books.
Walker, S. (1994) *Hate Speech: The History of an American Controversy*, Lincoln, NE: University of Nebraska.

# Part IV

# Media policy and media governance

# 18

# Controlling new media (without the law)

*Mira Burri*

The purpose of this chapter is to explore some emerging modes of control that evolve wholly or partially outside conventional media law. As self- and co-regulatory models have been aptly covered elsewhere in this volume, the focus of this chapter will exclusively be on the entirely novel mechanisms of control enabled through code and technology in general. We compare these new models with traditional regulatory bodies and their decision-making processes and, making reference to the values and interests that are embedded in the design of mediating technologies, ask whether the new tools of control are appropriate for achieving public policy objectives in a complex new-and-old media landscape, or whether in fact they present some dangers. It is then worth considering whether these dangers are perceived as such only because we encounter something previously unknown and are uncertain of its effects, or whether these dangers are real and some additional regulatory action is necessary to address them. When talking about regulation of technology, it is also important to think of the possibilities of mobilizing technologies themselves as tools of intervention, and how these may be built into an existing governance scheme, making it perhaps more efficient and less costly.

In light of this analysis, the chapter also conjectures that media regulation is no longer a self-contained domain of governance; many other domains also become relevant. The linkages grow only stronger as new media consumption is more deeply integrated in everyday cultural, political and social life. The governance challenge here stems from the often very different regulatory histories, rationales for intervention and institutional structures of these previously separated domains, and renders regulatory design appropriate for the achievement of the core media policy objectives extremely complex (Kalimo and Pauwels 2009). A related phenomenon that can be observed is the growing "messiness" of regulation, as it not only draws together horizontally different domains, but is also unevenly vertically spread along a multilayered structure that mobilizes various actors at the local, national, regional and international levels.

This chapter does not seek to question the conventional media policy objectives in themselves, although research has shown that there is substantial fuzziness and ambiguity as to how these objectives are framed and implemented, and how the framing itself impacts on discourse and policymaking (Karppinen 2010). To reduce the analytical complexity, we take it for granted that the key public interest rationales for media regulation have remained unchanged and are still valid today. For such rationales, Flew has compiled a helpful list, including:

- concerns about the impact of media content, particularly on children and other "vulnerable" individuals;
- the capacity to use media for citizen formation and the development of a national cultural identity;
- implied rights of public participation associated with the broadcasting spectrum being a common resource with competing public and private uses;
- "public good" aspects of the media commodity, including non-rival and non-excludable elements of access and consumption;
- tendencies toward monopoly or oligopoly in media markets, with resulting entry barriers for new competitors and lack of content diversity; and
- the potential relationship between economic power and political power arising from concentration of ownership of the means of public communication (Flew 2011: 63).

Reflecting these rationales of public interest intervention in the media space, Napoli offers a taxonomy of media regulation. He classifies it as either: (i) structural—directed at the structure of media organizations and markets; or (ii) behavioral—directed at the behavior of media outlets. Media ownership regulation is a clear representative of the first type, encompassing rules that limit foreign ownership or horizontal and vertical integration within media industry sectors, or regulations seeking to promote ownership by minority or other groups. Behavioral regulations, on the other hand, are meant to control the activities of media outlets and are most often directed at media content. Restrictions on violence, sexuality and adult language are common examples, but such regulations also include positive prescriptions for certain types of content, such as the minimum amount of nationally produced content, or a certain mixture of public affairs, news and educational programming (Napoli 2011).

As Napoli clarifies, however, there is no one match between a tool and the goal it is meant to attain:

> As should be clear, structural and behavioral regulations often overlap in terms of the goals they seek to achieve. Both often are directed at preserving and promoting principles such as diversity and pluralism. They simply go about pursuing these goals differently.
>
> (*Napoli 2011: 75*)

When assessing the technologically enabled controlling mechanisms in the remainder of this chapter, it is these two objectives that we will also single out—not only for purposes of simplification, but also because these objectives are deeply rooted in national constitutions and in the international human rights regime.

While we will not be questioning the public interest rationale for media regulation, some of our thoughts on new media developments will admittedly raise doubt about the means of achieving these goals, as it should not be forgotten that public media were established and entrusted with specific objectives in a particular time period. That was a time marked by analog communications, spectrum scarcity, high entry costs and very few media outlets—all conditions that have now changed. A very important characteristic of this "older" system to be borne in mind is that it permitted centralized oversight and control through a single point of entry. Control was also embedded in the democratic mechanisms of the nation-state and secured through a complex network of institutions, which balanced the free flow of information against the protection of other essential values and interests, such as privacy, national security and public order (Keller 2011).

## The new media landscape (and what old media law has to do with it)

Television is still the number one media outlet for the average citizen on this planet. Yet few would dispute that the media landscape has utterly changed in the last decade. While the effects are not equally distributed across nations, generations and classes (Palfrey and Gasser 2008; Burri 2012), the patterns of media use have been profoundly modified (Naughton 2006). Television itself is not as it used to be; in most industrialized countries, it has departed from the traditional point-to-multipoint, often state-influenced or controlled, source of news and entertainment operating under scarce spectrum (Bennett and Stange 2011).

Beyond television, the technological, economic and societal changes triggered by digitization have led to a decidedly different information and communication environment (Benkler 2006; Castells 2009). While we distance from technological utopianism and web-determinism, some real changes in the media environment can already be identified, although their implications are not all definitive and more scholarly work is needed to explore these effects. Particularly relevant to the present discussion are three following aspects.

i. *The abundance of content and its different organization* Blogs, social networking sites, virtual worlds and many other forms of information and communication made available over the Internet have proliferated and turned into viable media outlets, coexisting next to traditional ones, offering a new way of accessing information and/or entirely new information. The sheer amount of information that is available at all times from any point connected to the Internet is plainly mind-blowing. What is also worth noting and is often forgotten when describing the new digital media environment is the different way in which information is organized in it. The fact that any type of data can be expressed in digital format has completely changed the rules for organizing information (Weinberger 2007) and knowledge (Weinberger 2012). Whereas the Dewey decimal classification was used for organizing libraries, and alphabetical order for name registers and genre categories in CD shops, the digital environment enables an encompassing, global, miscellaneous, dynamic and interlinked information archive that can be searched through a single entry point according to virtually unlimited criteria.
ii. *New ways of distributing, accessing and consuming content* Enabled through multiple devices over an almost ubiquitous Internet, the patterns of handling information have changed. Instantaneous distribution to millions of people, pulling content instead of passively receiving it, simultaneous consumption from many sources, are but a few of the (television-unlike) features of contemporary online communication. These naturally have serious repercussions for users, businesses and for the entire markets for information goods and services, which have been broadly known under the "long tail" theory—one over the validity of which we cast some doubt later in this chapter.
iii. *New modes of content production, in which the user is not merely a consumer, but is also an active creator* Reduced thresholds to participation, as well as the (ever greater) affordances of digital technologies, have allowed individuals and groups of individuals to create new content, to play around and to remix existing content (Benkler 2006; Jenkins 2006). This type of creativity, interactivity and cooperation is unique to digital media and radically departs from the conventional image of massive and passive audience, of the "couch potatoes" only slightly empowered by their television remote controls.

So, what are the implications of all of these, often transformative, changes of the media environment? How do they impact on the media policy toolkit as a means of attaining diversity and pluralism? To be sure, media law has not so far addressed these implications comprehensively. It is only struggling to appropriately accommodate some, while others simply do not fall within the scope of media law, as traditionally defined and alluded to above. One example from the European experience is the reform of the central piece of the European Union (EU) media law framework—the 1989 Television without Frontiers (TwF) Directive (Directive 89/552/EEC). After lengthy and highly politically charged debates that were supposed to charter the path of EU media regulation into the future, little has changed. The new Audiovisual Media Services (AVMS) Directive (Directive 2007/65/EC) now covers the so-called "on demand" or "non-linear services," as well as television programs.[1] These are subject to somewhat "lighter" regulatory obligations,[2] including some cultural diversity prescriptions. The AVMS Directive extended in effect the cultural quota system, which traditionally prescribed TV channels operating in the EU to broadcast a majority of European works, to digital media outlets (European Parliament and Council of the European Union 2007).[3] Concretely, the Directive created a soft-law obligation for member states to ensure that non-linear media service providers under their jurisdiction "promote, where practicable and by appropriate means, production of and access to European works" (Article 13(1). The Directive further clarifies that such promotion could relate to the financial contribution to the production and rights acquisition of European works or to the share and/or prominence of European works in the catalog of programs.

Overall, there has been no innovation in legal design, which—considering the new circumstances—could have put in place new tools to ensure the attainment of the core media policy objectives, such as pluralism and diversity. Nor has there been a careful assessment of the effects of extending quota mechanisms online—for example, to assess whether they create artificial demand for European productions, (unnecessarily) burden digital businesses, or whether indeed the scheme actually serves its goals (i.e. the real consumption of European works and ultimately, the promotion of cultural diversity—Burri-Nenova 2007). Admittedly, media and cultural policies are still within the scope of competence of the EU member states (Craufurd Smith 2004, 2011), which prevents decisive and comprehensive EU action. But, even at the national level, little has happened because most efforts to meet the challenges of digital technologies have been narrowly focused on reinventing the institution of public service broadcasting (PSB) under the existent constraints of EU competition law (Iosifidis 2007 and 2010; Donders 2011) particularly in the field of state subsidies (Katsirea 2008).

In the meantime, as Web 2.0 hype grows and captures the hearts and minds of academics and policymakers alike, there have been suggestions that the new media environment and the innate potential of free markets are so powerful that they will naturally lead to the achievement of many conventional media policy goals, such as diversity, because the market, through the mechanisms of supply and demand, will create a digitally empowered mix of commercial and non-commercial, professional and amateur, mainstream and niche content.

1 On-demand or non-linear services are offers of audiovisual content "for the viewing of programmes at the moment chosen by the user and at his individual request on the basis of a catalogue of programmes selected by the media service provider" (AVMS, Art. 1(g)).

2 Non-linear services must satisfy only a basic tier of rules. These rules cover: the protection of minors and human dignity; the right of reply; the identification of commercial communications; and minimum qualitative obligations regarding commercial communications.

3 "European work" is defined in a complex way (AVMS, Art. 1(n)(i)–(iii)). Ultimately, it is content produced with European money without any particular requirements regarding quality, exclusivity, originality or cultural distinctness (Burri-Nenova 2007: 1705–10).

Much hope for naturally generated diversity has been, for instance, voiced under the "long tail" theory. This theory maintains that reduced barriers to entry allow new market players to position themselves and make use of niche markets that are economically viable in the digital ecosystem owing to the dramatically falling storage, distribution and search costs (Anderson 2006; Brynjolfsson *et al.* 2006). Supply and demand meet then not only for "mainstream" products available in the "head" of the snake, but also for many other products, now available in the ever longer "tail." Even greater has been the promise of user-created content (UCC) as a powerful tool of democratization of content production and distribution. Indeed, UCC, generated through the new type of "commons-based peer production" (Benkler 2006: 59–90), can be said to bear the key media policy components of diversity, localism and non-commercialism (Goodman 2004), and in this sense could cater for public interest objectives without additional intervention. Going even further, it has been argued that Internet-facilitated communication without intermediaries or other substantial access barriers has created the vibrant "marketplace of ideas" (Lessig 2006: 245) that media policy always aspired to.[4]

Current practices have put both the long tail theory and the democratizing power of the Internet in doubt. As for the long tail, as Napoli aptly summarizes, "it does indeed seem to be unclear at this point whether a media environment of unprecedented choice and sophisticated tools for identifying and accessing relevant content genuinely helps or hurts the prospects for content that has not traditionally resided in the 'head' " (Napoli 2010, 2012). As global media corporations merge, both horizontally and vertically, in the pursuit of better utilization of all available channels and platforms, diversity may in fact be lost. The positivism for user creativity is still strong and its long-term effects on legal modeling may be far-reaching (Benkler 2006 and 2011), at least in the field of copyright (Hargreaves 2011). Yet, in the narrower sense of grassroots content production and its impact on democratic discourse, a number of skeptics have stressed the dangers of fragmentation of the public discourse (van Alstyne and Brynjolfsson 2004; Sunstein 2007). The question of diversity exposure is also vexed, as it appears that citizens' real consumption remains limited to a handful of mainstream online sources that are, as a rule, professionally produced by white, educated males (Hindman 2009). As Verhulst points out, new technologies have even introduced new types of scarcity as the control over information changes from old to new intermediaries, who may control the flow of, and access to, information (Verhulst 2007).

A more careful, finer-grained assessment is necessary. It seems that, in some cases, the features of the digital media environment may hint at opportunities for better, more efficient and flexible accommodation of public policy goals. In other cases, they may equally be viewed as challenges, perhaps calling for additional regulatory intervention (Karppinen 2009; Napoli 2012), of both a structural and a behavioral nature (Napoli 2010). Various enquiries have explored this regulatory challenge in the context of convergence as the gradual coming together of broadcasting, telecommunications and information technology (IT) services, companies and sectors (see e.g. Pauwels *et al.* 2009). The gist of these enquiries is on how the environment evolves and challenges current forms of regulation, necessitating certain adaptations in law. The point we make is somewhat different and underscores that digital technologies have also had profound impact on governance forms, which depart from the conventional notion of law and shift towards more complex, heterogeneous and uncoordinated

4 The concept of the "marketplace of ideas" is not attributed to Lessig, but is traced back to Justice Oliver Wendell Holmes Jr.'s dissenting opinion in *Abrams* v *United States* (1919) (Krotoszynski 2006: 14–15).

mechanisms. One area that seems particularly important is the increasingly critical role of technology as a method of control, existing on top of law or beyond law's scope. The next sections seek to thematize and describe some of these new tools. Necessarily in this discussion, we will enter into domains of regulation other than media law, such as cyberlaw, intellectual property law and telecommunications law.

## Technologies of control

### *Technology as a tool of enforcement*

#### Internet filtering

Internet filtering is the most commonly discussed technologically enabled form of control. Although it has existed for quite some time now, it has evolved significantly in terms of its scope and the extent of intervention, targets and methods. In 1998, then US President Bill Clinton spoke of the "revolutionary democratizing potential of the Internet"; in 2010, Secretary of State Hillary Clinton stressed that, "[e]ven as networks spread to nations around the globe, virtual walls are cropping up in place of visible walls" (Clinton 2010). It is the reality now that, despite all of the talk about the Internet's ability to "route around" censorship, many governments (and not only undemocratic ones) have proven adept at extending state control into cyberspace for a variety of reasons, such as public morality, cultural integrity and political control (Deibert *et al.* 2008, 2010 and 2011a).

The manner of exercising control varies in practice. As Palfrey explains:

> Sometimes the law bans citizens from performing a particular activity online, such as accessing or publishing certain material. Sometimes the state takes control into its own hands by erecting technological or other barriers within the state's confines to stop the flow of bits from one recipient to another. Increasingly, though, the state is turning to private parties to carry out the online control. Often, those private parties are corporations chartered locally or individual citizens who live in that jurisdiction.
>
> (*Palfrey 2007: 70*)

As Palfrey further explains, it is now commonly the case that the state "requires private parties—often intermediaries whose services connect one online actor to another—to participate in online censorship and surveillance as a cost of doing business in that state" (Palfrey 2007: 70).

The evolutionary trajectory of Internet filtering is evident, moving towards more and more sophisticated control mechanisms: from "open net" (from the Internet's birth to 2000) through "access denied" (2000–05), where crude filters and blocks were installed, towards "access controlled" (2005–10), where mechanisms are multiple and varied, entering at different points of control to limit access to knowledge and information (Palfrey 2010; Deibert *et al.* 2011b: 6–15). Before long, we have entered a fourth phase of "access contested", which is characterized by more, more diversified and deeper controls, but also by "pushback against some of these controls from civil society, supported in many instances by the resources of major governments, such as the United States and the European Union (Deibert and Rohozinski 2011; Deibert *et al.* 2011b).

The repercussions of these "technologies of disconnection" (Dutton *et al.* 2011: 34) are enormous for freedom of expression worldwide and put the democratizing potential of the

Internet—the "technologies of freedom" (de Sola Pool 1983)—in doubt. The "Great Firewall of China" is the infamous example that swiftly comes to mind, but we have also seen the developments of the "Arab Spring," which more dynamically shows the Internet as a critical space for political action (Roberts *et al.* 2011 and 2011a).

Although filtering increasingly mobilizes new and more sophisticated technological instruments, it is in many ways still an "old" type of control, especially in comparison with regulation by code and architecture:

> The power of filtering lies . . . not primarily in its capacity to encourage behavioural change, alter the impact on harm-generating behaviour, or to prevent harm, but in its ability to detect, identify and thus discriminate between units with prescribed characteristics in a large population. Accordingly, filtering technology is not a modality of control, but a powerful tool of identification and selection
>
> (*Yeung 2008*)

In contrast to the conventional mechanisms of regulating media, Internet filtering as a method of exercising control is neither transparent, nor subject to mechanisms securing legitimacy and accountability (McIntyre and Scott 2008). It is different even from standard surveillance methods, as applied by police enforcement, because Internet filtering is out of judiciary control that may safeguard the rights of the citizens from violations of privacy, freedom of speech or association. The trend of "outsourcing" the enforcement to private entities, often as a precondition for doing business, is particularly worrisome (Graber 2012). Peculiarly, the only legal tool, next to political and diplomatic pressure, that has been mobilized against Internet filtering so far is international trade law (Wu 2006; Hindley and Lee-Makiyama 2009; Gao 2012). In these situations, attempts are made to conceptualize filtering as a trade barrier and to use the sanctions available under the law of the World Trade Organization (WTO) to fight it.[5] It remains to be seen what the outcome of the "access contested" period of the Internet's evolution will be, as all stakeholders (states, civil society, dissidents) on both sides of the battleground are now increasingly aware of its huge potential for political and cultural action.

## Digital rights management systems

Another mechanism to ensure perfect enforcement through technology is found in the so-called digital rights management (DRM) systems. While Internet filtering is a practice that can be carried out in many diverse ways (partial or full sites shutdown, distributed denial of service, content filtering, cyber-attacks, etc.—Deibert *et al.* 2011b; Roberts *et al.* 2011a and 2011b), DRM can be employed for different practices. DRM has mostly been discussed in the field of copyright enforcement, but it may in fact be utilized for many other purposes as a generic, embedded form for controlling access and use of digital content and devices.

Although DRM systems are plainly technical applications, they are problematic in the field of media law and policy because they may unduly restrict access to, and use of, digital content. This has to do first, with the way in which copyright functions, and second, with the way in which DRM can automatically enforce it. Copyright and other types of intellectual property (IP) protection are intended to foster innovation by granting authors a temporary monopoly

5 For example, the US Trade Representative (USTR) has demanded information from China under the WTO rules on the trade impact of Chinese policies that may block US companies' websites in China, creating commercial barriers. See USTR 2011.

over their creations. Copyright has built-in mechanisms, such as fair use, to ensure some balance between the individual rights of the authors and the public interest (Helfer and Austin 2011). This balance becomes very fragile in the digital media environment. Copyright in many sorts of cultural content is now commonly owned by distributors (Ku 2007) and these distributors (normally large media conglomerates) have striven to keep perfect control over "their property" by means of DRM, under the guise of protecting digital content from uncontrolled distribution and unlawful use. In practice, such efforts have eroded some fundamental rights of consumers and restricted usages traditionally allowed under analog/offline copyright (Lucchi 2007). In addition, DRM may, in many situations, deter the full realization of digital content production and distribution, by rendering it illegal or simply by banning it, possibly severely restricting creativity (Cohen 2007; Vaidhyanathan 2007).

The content industries have been very successful in their political efforts to expand the scope and extend the duration of copyright, effectively convincing most governments that strong and enforceable IP rights are the *sine qua non* for a vibrant culture. Through race-to-the-top strategies, this augmented protection has been extended to the international level in the framework of the Agreement on Trade-Related Aspects of Intellectual Property Rights (TRIPS)[6] as an essential part of the WTO structure, and in the even further-reaching free trade agreements (FTAs) (Netanel 2007; Patry 2009), ignoring the checks and balances originally underlying domestic IP systems. Despite grassroots activism, IP issues have remained marginal in key efforts aimed at securing public goods at the international level (Helfer and Austin 2011). For instance, they do not appear in any meaningful way in the 2005 UNESCO Convention on the Protection and Promotion of the Diversity of Cultural Expressions (Burri-Nenova 2009 and Burri 2010), nor do they figure in the World Summit on the Information Society (WSIS) agenda (Ermert 2005). At the same time, the circumvention of technical protection measures, such as DRM, has been prohibited in most jurisdictions, as well as internationally, through the World Intellectual Property Organization (WIPO) Internet Treaties.[7]

It is crucial to stress that, in cyberspace, local decisions have a global impact. As Abdel Latif observes:

> Given the global nature of the Internet, it is also important to take into account that if developed countries, such as the United States, enact restrictive legislation governing the use of digital and Internet content and the manner in which it can be accessed, this has a direct bearing on developing country access to such digital and Internet content.
>
> (*Abdel Latif 2012: 386*)

DRM has repercussions beyond copyright and its problematic interface with citizens' rights. The DRM mechanisms are not transparent and in fact may allow for any type of interference, impacting on the privacy of the person reading an e-book, or watching a film on iTunes; they

6 TRIPS: Agreement on Trade-Related Aspects of Intellectual Property Rights, 15 April 1994, Marrakesh Agreement Establishing the World Trade Organization, Annex 1C, The Legal Texts: The Results of the Uruguay Round of Multilateral Trade Negotiations 320 (1999), 1869 UNTS 299, 33 ILM 1197 (1994).

7 In the United States, anti-circumvention is banned by the Digital Millennium Copyright Act; in the EU, the relevant act is Directive 2001/29/EC of the European Parliament and of the Council of 22 May 2001 on the harmonisation of certain aspects of copyright and related rights in the information society. On DRM, see e.g. Yu 2006; Gillespie 2007; Wheatley 2008. The WIPO Copyright Treaty (WCT) and the WIPO Performances and Phonograms Treaty (WPPT) were concluded in 1996 and entered into force in 2002.

may deprive the individual from making choices between products or services (Lessig 1999) or influence future commercial offers, turning (symbolically put) the user into a product. Ultimately, DRM-like systems can enforce any rule that content or device producers want (Zittrain 2008b), such as making access conditional on a payment. Such developments are aligned with the broader trend of the privatization of content (Drahos and Braithwaite 2002) rather than its democratization. Privileged access to scientific data and knowledge, entertainment, news and archives creates a deep divide, with various implications, between those who can afford to pay and those who cannot. In the discussions of net neutrality (Marsden 2010) and search engines (Chandler 2007; Vaidhyanathan 2007), one can also see elements of the creation of two-tier environments, in which, in exchange for additional payment, one gets either faster access to data and traffic, or becomes more visible on the web. These different modalities are enabled by the different types of architecture in cyberspace.

## Technology as regulation

Internet filtering and DRM are illustrative pieces of evidence that the myths that cyberspace is *un*regulated and that it can*not* be regulated (Johnson and Post 1996) are both dead. It was only at the very onset of the Internet's spread that, as governments grappled with the novelty of the medium, "up until the late 1990s, most states tended either to ignore online activities or to regulate them very lightly" (Palfrey 2010: 2; see also Deibert *et al.* 2011b), especially in comparison with "old" media like telecom and television. As the Internet became more intertwined with everyday life and as its economic, political, social and cultural importance grew exponentially, states increasingly intervened, translating many national and international policies into cyberspace (Goldsmith and Wu 2006). In comparison with the early days, policymakers have also lost their cautious touch both when intervening and when translating existing conceptualizations of space into cyberspace (Price 2001, referring to Lessig 1995 and 1996).

Emerging from the ashes of these two myths of cyberspace regulation is a type of "messy" governance (Mayer-Schönberger 2003) encompassing national and international efforts, as well as private and public–private initiatives (Verhulst 2006; Cave *et al.* 2008). This governance ecology has not yet attained its ultimate shape. Two evolutionary trends can nonetheless be stressed with regard to our discussion. The first relates to Lawrence Lessig's narrative of "code is law," discussed in the following section; the second refers to various models of self- and co-regulation, addressed elsewhere in this volume.

Lessig argued that, in cyberspace, code is overtaking the functions of law (Lessig 1999 and 2006). In contrast to real-space, where architecture is more or less given, in cyberspace, it is "plastic" and open to change (Lessig 2006: 20). Designing cyberspace through software code thus becomes a very powerful regulatory activity (Lessig 2006). This code, which Lessig calls "West Coast Code" (because of the proximity to Silicon Valley), is starkly different from the "East Coast Code" (so-named because of the proximity to Washington, DC) (Lessig 2006: 72). The latter encompasses laws as a product of the conventional legislative processes, which in a democratic state involve highly formalized and complex mechanisms and are subject to a system of checks and balances. Conventional media lawmaking, both in terms of the rules and the institutions that are created, is precisely the product of such a deliberative process; these rules are also transparent, may be discussed, criticized, opposed and, as a result, perhaps modified. But it is arguably not only about the making of law in the public sphere, it is also about the legal system in its entirety, where every single piece of legislation (whatever its place in the legal hierarchy) fits and must be in line with the underlying constitutional principles and values. The US First Amendment case law is strong proof of the practice of testing new media and the ways of regulating them against the high principle of freedom of speech (see e.g. Bellia *et al.* 2007).[8]

"West Coast Code," by contrast, is simply built into the hardware or the software; it is cheaper and faster to create, but also opaque for citizens. In comparison to conventional law, it is also self-enforceable; this enforcement is automatic and not subject to executive or judicial oversight (Zittrain 2008b). While West Coast Code may be an appropriate (and more economical) mechanism to address the pertinent specific and highly technical questions, it lacks the legitimacy and accountability of conventional lawmaking (Koops 2008). In addition, while such code can cater for some narrow policy goals, such as protecting against unlawful use of copyrighted works, it cannot address broader and much more complex objectives that involve a balance between different private and public interests.

The experience gained over the past 12 years, when the first edition of *Code and Other Laws of Cyberspace* was published, has confirmed Lessig's theory and the move from law towards code in creating mechanisms of control in cyberspace. The situation has in many respects only worsened (Lessig 2006; Zittrain 2008a). Indeed, we have seen the deterioration of some principles that initially allowed innovation over the network and have been enshrined in law. A key such principle, for instance, existing in most telecommunications laws, immunized the carriers—(whether broadband companies or Internet service providers (ISPs)—for objectionable material that flows through their channels (Telecommunications Act of 1996). This rule permitted media access by ordinary individuals; as Balkin argues, ". . . in terms of its practical effects, it may be even more important than many aspects of First Amendment doctrine" (Balkin 2008: 111). The Digital Millennium Copyright Act (DMCA) further limited the liability of ISPs for copyright infringements, asking them to react only *ex post* to takedown notices (US Congress 1998).[9] Although the safe harbor rule, as privately administered enforcement, may have had some chilling effects on Internet speech (Seltzer 2010), it may have had positive impact too, because it shielded intermediaries. Balkin believes that:

> [w]ithout these safe harbor provisions, many features of current Internet practice—including the development of Web 2.0 applications that leverage the content contributions of many people—would be legally risky. Indeed, were it not for statutory safe harbors and other limits on copyright liability, the basic practices of search engines, and indeed much of the traffic on the Internet, might be illegal.
>
> (*Balkin 2008: 111*)

Over time, however, some of these important foundational principles have deteriorated in practice. For example, most industrialized countries have severely limited safe harbors and reconsidered intermediaries' responsibilities in copyright enforcement, demanding their active *ex ante* involvement in order to escape liability (de Beer and Clemmer 2009).[10] One can

8 See e.g. *Home Box Office, Inc.* v *FCC* (1977), in which the Court found that "important differences between cable and broadcast television and 'differences in the characteristics of new media justify differences in the First Amendment standards applied to them' " (citing *Red Lion Broadcasting Co.* v *FCC* (1969), which upheld the fairness doctrine on grounds that it implemented the First Amendment). See also Price 2001.

9 ISPs taking care of traffic only were not responsible for copyright violations over their communication channels, as long as the ISPs terminated repeat infringers (17 USC § 512(a) (2000)). Intermediaries that hosted content had more responsibility, and were safe only if they acted swiftly to take down infringing material once they were notified of the infringement.

10 The countries examined in this study were Australia, Canada, China, the EU, France, Germany, Japan, New Zealand, Singapore, South Korea, the United Kingdom and the United States.

observe a shift from "passive-reactive to active-preventive schemes for communication intermediaries" (de Beer and Clemmer 2009: 24) and to a new type of content filtering enabled through the "deep packet inspection" (DPI) technology, which may further erode important users' rights (Katyal 2010; Graber 2012; Mueller 2012).

The efforts by the US legislature to enact the proposed SOPA/PIPA legislation, which has faced immense opposition, is the latest example at the time of writing.[11] In essence, these acts, albeit slightly different in certain aspects, aim to expand the ability of US law enforcement to fight online trafficking, also beyond the US national jurisdiction.[12] Various measures of blacklisting "rogue" websites have been designed, most often enforced through intermediaries, some of them truly far-reaching and almost equal to an "Internet death penalty" (McCullagh 2012). The anticipated dangers of silencing of speech, chilling innovation on the Internet and for the Internet itself are real (Lemley, Levine and Post 2012).

Yet regulatory functions are not simply taken away by code as an inexpensive shortcut to control. Technology is not overtaking society; the relationship between technology and society is much more complex and multidirectional than Lessig suggests (Post 2000; Murray and Scott 2002; Mayer-Schönberger 2008).[13] Both technological determinism and technological skepticism should be viewed with caution. While we pointed more at the dangers, rather than at the opportunities, of digital technologies (perhaps as an intuitive counter-reaction to the many existing elated narratives of their power), it certainly was not our purpose to vilify DRM or other technological measures, because they can be a tool of enhancing access, as well as of limiting it (Armstrong 2006; Mayer-Schönberger 2006).[14] We should just be cautious of the politically endorsed ends that these tools are able to achieve.

Overall, in presenting the above trends, our prime aim was to illustrate that, in the new media space, there are multiple and increasing points of control outside formal legal institutions. The complex and highly fragmented nature of governance threatens the availability of public goods and makes the pursuit of public objectives difficult. This is an important observation, as:

> . . . technological design can be more or less free speech friendly, and more or less participatory. At the same time, the legal rules that regulate technology can promote business practices that encourage media access and democratic participation in mass media or, conversely, practices that seek to limit access and make end users more like passive consumers.
>
> (*Balkin 2008: 110*)

11 Respectively, Stop Online Piracy Act (SOPA), HR 3261, introduced in the United States House of Representatives on 26 October 2011, by House Judiciary Committee Chair Representative Lamar S. Smith (R-TX) and a bipartisan group of 12 initial co-sponsors; and Protect IP Act (Preventing Real Online Threats to Economic Creativity and Theft of Intellectual Property Act, or PIPA), introduced in the United States Senate on 12 May 2011, by Senator Patrick Leahy (D-VT) and 11 bipartisan co-sponsors. On 18 January 2012, the English version of Wikipedia and some 7,000 other websites coordinated a service blackout, or posted links and images, in protest against SOPA in an effort to raise awareness. Many academics, corporations and civil society representatives have also opposed SOPA (see, e.g., the references made available by the Electronic Frontier Foundation online at https://www.eff.org/issues/coica-internet-censorship-and-copyright-bill). Soon afterwards, both the House and Senate Bills were dropped.

12 An essential difference is that PIPA targets domain name system providers, financial companies and advertising networks, but not companies that provide Internet connectivity.

13 ". . . no single innovation and no group of them taken together in isolation from nontechnological elements . . . ever changed the direction in which society was going" (Mayer-Schönberger 2008: 738, citing Daniels 1970).

14 For instance, the creative commons licenses operate on a DRM basis.

## Conclusion

At the outset of this chapter, we briefly sketched the rationales and the basic tools of conventional media law and policy. We also saw that this media regulation (as narrowly construed) has not adopted any forward-oriented reform packages in the face of new technological developments, as brought about by digital media and above all by the Internet, but still very much sticks to old television-like rules. There is some expansion of the scope of regulation to address online media, but the change so far is incremental and not particularly innovative. One reason, certainly, is the strong path dependence within the system. Another reason is that many of the new developments that affect the media seem to unfold outside the bounds of conventional media law; there have been many acts of a diverse legal nature in intellectual property, telecoms, Internet regulation and other governance domains that address (more or less comprehensively) new media implications.

As Sandra Braman so aptly puts it:

> Seeing the media policy trees within this forest [of laws] is difficult. The media policy analyst or law maker is confronted with such questions as: Does the capacity to assert intellectual property rights in modes of doing business affect the media? When does technical standard-setting for the information infrastructure become a matter of media law? What does the controversy about control over domain names on the Internet mean for those with traditional media concerns?
>
> (*Braman 2004: 154*)

Technologically enabled regulation is certainly part of this ever-deeper forest. It can effectively (and very efficiently) influence the production and the flow of information, access to information, and its consumption and reuse. Technology strongly influences both the interactions within the media environment that are to be regulated (that is, the subject of regulation), and on its *regulability* (that is, the possibilities and conditions of regulation).

Increasingly, technology enforces, complements or supplants law. In this process of shifting from law to code, to use Lessig's terminology, the check-and-balance mechanisms of traditional media law may have been lost. In addition, the possibility of defining distinct public goals, which may often require balancing between private and public interests, is compromised. The political economy of the definition of goals and their aggressive pursuit at times, most prominently in the field of copyright enforcement, may be profoundly imbalanced (Patry 2009). The perils of technologically based regulation are all the greater if we bear in mind that there is still a lot of uncertainty as to the effects of the new digital media environment on the intrinsic goals of media policy and how it affects the "appropriate heterogeneity" of the public sphere (Sunstein 2002: 191–2) and the "ecology of freedom of expression" (Dutton *et al.* 2011: 5). This uncertainty is not fully acknowledged, and regulators do not hesitate to intervene, mostly in the IP field, often ignoring the multidirectional effects of their action, and having lost the caution and the lightness of touch of the early Internet days. The overall danger of unintended consequences is augmented by increased policy interdependence and the prevalent messy governance structures. In fact, digital media only accentuates globalness and interdependence, and many of the regulatory advances at the regional and international levels become immediately relevant for media policy design.

## References

Abdel Latif, A. (2012) 'From consensus to controversy: The WIPO Internet Treaties and lessons for intellectual property norm-setting in the digital age,' in M. Burri and T. Cottier (eds.) *Trade Governance in the Digital Age*, Cambridge: Cambridge University Press.

*Abrams* v *United States* 250 US 616 (1919).
Anderson, C. (2006) *The Long Tail: Why the Future of Business is Selling Less of More*, New York: Hyperion.
Armstrong, T. K. (2006) 'Digital rights management and the process of fair use,' *Harvard Journal of Law and Technology*, 20(1): 49–121.
Attentional Ltd (2011) SMART2010/0002. Study on the implementation of the provisions of the Audiovisual Media Services Directive concerning the promotion of European works in audiovisual media services. Report prepared for the European Commission, December. Online. Available HTTP: http://ec.europa.eu/avpolicy/docs/library/studies/art_13/final_report_20111214.pdf
Balkin, J. (2008) 'Media access: A question of design,' *George Washington Law Review*, 76(4): 101–118.
Bellia, P. L., Schiff Berman, P. and Post, D. G. (2007) *Cyberlaw: Problems of Policy and Jurisprudence in the Information Age*, 3rd edn., St. Paul, MN: Thomson West.
Bendrath, R. and Mueller, M. (2011) 'The end of the net as we know it? Deep packet inspection and Internet governance,' *New Media and Society*, 13(7): 1142–1160.
Benkler, Y. (2006) *The Wealth of Networks: How Social Production Transforms Markets and Freedom*, New Haven, CT: Yale University Press.
—— (2011) *The Penguin and the Leviathan: How Cooperation Triumphs over Self-Interest*, New York: Crown Business.
Bennett, J. and Strange, N. (eds.) (2011) *Television as Digital Media*, Durham, NC: Duke University Press.
Braman, S. (2004) 'Where has media policy gone? Defining the field in the twenty-first century,' *Communication Law and Policy*, 9(2): 153–182.
Brynjolfsson, E., Hu, Y. and Smith, M. D. (2006) 'From niches to riches: The anatomy of the long tail,' *Sloan Management Review*, 47(4): 67–71.
Burri, M. (2010) 'Cultural diversity as a concept of global law: Origins, evolution and prospects,' *Diversity*, 2: 1059–1084.
—— (2012) 'The global digital divide as impeded access to content,' in M. Burri and T. Cottier (eds.) *Trade Governance in the Digital Age*, Cambridge: Cambridge University Press.
Burri-Nenova, M. (2007) 'The new Audiovisual Media Services Directive: Television without frontiers, television without cultural diversity,' *Common Market Law Review*, 44: 1689–1725.
—— (2009) 'Trade versus culture in the digital environment: An old conflict in need of a new definition,' *Journal of International Economic Law*, 12: 17–62.
Castells, M. (2009) *Communication Power*, Oxford: Oxford University Press.
Cave, J., Marsden, C. and Simmons, S. (2008) *Options for and Effectiveness of Internet Self- and Co-Regulation*, Cambridge: RAND Europe.
Chandler, J. A. (2007) 'A right to reach and audience: An approach to intermediary bias on the Internet,' *Hofstra Law Review*, 35: 101–142.
Clinton, H. (2010) 'Remarks on Internet freedom,' *The Newseum*, Washington, DC, 21 January. Online. Available HTTP: http://www.state.gov/secretary/rm/2010/01/135519.htm
Cohen, J. (2007) 'Creativity and culture in copyright theory,' *UC Davis Law Review*, 40: 1151–1205.
Council of European Communities (1989) Council Directive 89/552/EEC on the coordination of certain provisions laid down by law, regulation or administrative action in Member States concerning the pursuit of television broadcasting activities, OJ L 298/23, 17 October.
Craufurd Smith, R. (ed.) (2004) *Culture and European Union Law*, Oxford: Oxford University Press.
—— (2011) 'The evolution of cultural policy in the EU,' in P. Craig and G. de Búrca (eds.) *The Evolution of EU Law*, 2nd edn., Oxford: Oxford University Press.
Daniels, G. H. (1970) 'The big questions in the history of American technology,' *Technology and Culture*, 11: 1–21.
de Beer, J. and Clemmer, C. D. (2009) 'Global trends in online copyright enforcement: A non-neutral role for network intermediaries?' *The Journal of Law, Science and Technology*, 49: 375–409.
Deibert, R. (2010) *Access Controlled: The Shaping of Power, Rights, and Rules in Cyberspace*, Cambridge, MA: MIT Press.
—— (2011a) *Access Contested: Security, Identity, and Resistance in Asian Cyberspace*, Cambridge, MA: MIT Press.
—— (2011b) 'Access contested: Toward the fourth phase of cyberspace controls,' in R. Deibert, J. Palfrey, R. Rohozinski and J. Zittrain (eds.) *Access Contested: Security, Identity, and Resistance in Asian Cyberspace*, Cambridge, MA: MIT Press.

—— and Rohozinski, R. (2011) 'Contesting cyberspace and the coming crisis of authority,' in R. Deibert, J. Palfrey, R. Rohozinski and J. Zittrain (eds.) *Access Contested: Security, Identity, and Resistance in Asian Cyberspace*, Cambridge, MA: MIT Press.

—— Palfrey, J., Rohozinski, R. and Zittrain, J. (eds.) (2008) *Access Denied: The Practice and Policy of Global Internet Filtering*, Cambridge, MA: MIT Press.

De Sola Pool, I. (1983) *Technologies of Freedom: Of Free Speech in an Electronic Age*, Cambridge, MA: Harvard University Press.

Donders, K. (2011) *Public Service Media and Policy in Europe*, Basingstoke: Palgrave Macmillan.

Drahos, P. and Braithwaite, J. (2002) *Information Feudalism: Who Owns the Knowledge Economy?* London: Earthscan.

Dutton, W. H., Dopatka, A., Hills, M., Law, G. and Nash, V. (2011) *Freedom of Connection, Freedom of Expression: The Changing Legal and Regulatory Ecology Shaping the Internet*, Paris: UNESCO Publishing.

Ermert, M. (2005) 'Intellectual property issues kept off WSIS agenda,' *Intellectual Property Watch*, 30 November.

European Parliament and Council of Europe (2007) Directive 2007/65/EC of the European Parliament and of the Council of 11 December 2007, OJ L 332/27, 18 December.

Flew, T. (2011) 'New media policies,' in M. Deuze (ed.) *Managing Media Work*, London: Sage.

Gao, H. (2012) 'Googling for the trade–human rights nexus in China: Can the WTO help?' in M. Burri and T. Cottier (eds.) *Trade Governance in the Digital Age*, Cambridge: Cambridge University Press.

Gillespie, T. (2007) *Wired Shut: Copyright and the Shape of Digital Culture*, Cambridge, MA: MIT Press.

Goldsmith, J. and Wu, T. (2006) *Who Controls the Internet: Illusions of a Borderless World*, Oxford: Oxford University Press.

Goodman, E. P. (2004) 'Media policy out of the box: Content abundance, attention scarcity, and the failures of digital markets,' *Berkeley Technology Law Journal*, 19: 1389–1472.

Graber, C. B. (2012) 'Internet creativity, communicative freedom and a constitutional rights theory response to "code is law",' in A. Candeub and S. Pager (eds.) *Transnational Culture in the Internet Age*, Cheltenham: Edward Elgar.

Helfer, L. R. and Austin, G. W. (2011) *Human Rights and Intellectual Property: Mapping the Global Interface*, Cambridge: Cambridge University Press.

Hindley, B. and Lee-Makiyama, H. (2009) 'Protectionism online: Internet censorship and international trade law,' *ECIPE Working Paper*, 12: 1–19.

Hindman, M. (2009) *The Myth of Digital Democracy*, Princeton, NJ: Princeton University Press.

*Home Box Office, Inc.* v *FCC* 567 F.2d 9, 68, D.C. Circ. (1977).

Iosifidis, P. (2007) *Public Television in the Digital Age: Technological Challenges and New Strategies for Europe*, Basingstoke: Palgrave Macmillan.

—— (ed.) (2010) *Reinventing Public Service Communication: European Broadcasters and Beyond*, Basingstoke: Palgrave Macmillan.

Jenkins, H. (2006) *Convergence Culture: How Old and New Media Collide*, New York: New York University Press.

Johnson, D. and Post, D. (1996) 'Law and borders: The rise of law in cyberspace,' *Stanford Law Review*, 48: 1367–1402.

Kalimo, H. and Pauwels, C. (2009) 'The converging media and communications environment,' in C. Pauwels, H. Kalimo, K. Donders and B. van Rompuy (eds.) *Rethinking European Media and Communications Policy*, Brussels: Brussels University Press.

Karppinen, K. (2009) 'Rethinking media pluralism and communicative abundance,' *Observatorio Journal*, 11: 151–169.

—— (2010) 'Making a difference to media pluralism: A critique of the pluralistic consensus in European media policy,' in B. Cammaerts and N. Carpentier (eds.) *Reclaiming the Media: Communication Rights and Democratic Media Roles*, Bristol: Intellect Books.

Katsirea, I. (2008) *Public Broadcasting and European Law: A Comparative Examination of Public Service Obligations in Six Member States*, The Hague: Kluwer Law International.

Katyal, S. K. (2009) 'Filtering, piracy, surveillance and disobedience,' *The Columbia Journal of Law and the Arts*, 32(4): 401–426.

Keller, P. (2011) *European and International Media Law: Liberal Democracy, Trade, and the New Media*, Oxford: Oxford University Press.

Koops, B.-J. (2008) 'Criteria for normative technology: The acceptability of "code as law" in light of democratic and constitutional values,' in R. Brownsword and K. Yeung (eds.) *Regulating Technologies: Legal Futures, Regulatory Frames and Technological Fixes*, Oxford: Hart.
Krotoszynski, Jr. R. J. (2006) *The First Amendment in Cross-Cultural Perspective: A Comparative Legal Analysis of the Freedom of Speech*, New York: New York University Press.
Ku, R. (2007) 'Promoting diverse cultural expression: Lessons from the US copyright wars,' *Asian Journal of WTO and International Health Law and Policy*, 2: 369–398.
Lemley, M., Levine, D. S. and Post, D. G. (2012) 'Don't break the Internet,' *Stanford Law Review*, 64: 34–38.
Lessig, L. (1995) 'The path of cyberlaw,' *Yale Law Journal*, 104: 1743–1755.
—— (1996) 'Reading the Constitution in cyberspace,' *Emory Law Journal*, 45: 869–910.
—— (1999) *Code and Other Laws of Cyberspace*, New York: Basic Books.
—— (2006) *Code: Version 2.0*, New York: Basic Books.
Lucchi, N. (2007) 'Countering the unfair play of DRM technologies,' *Texas Intellectual Property Law Journal*, 16(1): 91–124.
Marsden, C. T. (2010) *Net Neutrality*, London: Bloomsbury Academics.
Mayer-Schönberger, V. (2003) 'The shape of governance: Analyzing the world of Internet regulation,' *Virginia Journal of International Law*, 43: 605–673.
—— (2006) 'Beyond copyright: Managing information rights with DRM,' *Denver University Law Review*, 84(1): 181–198.
—— (2008) 'Demystifying Lessig,' *Wisconsin Law Review*, 4: 713–746.
McCullagh, D. (2012) 'How SOPA would affect you: FAQ,' CNET News, 18 January. Online. Available HTTP: http://news.cnet.com/8301-31921_3-57329001-281/how-sopa-would-affect-you-faq/ (accessed 12 May 2012).
McIntyre, T. J. and Scott, C. (2008) 'Internet filtering: Rhetoric, legitimacy, accountability and responsibility,' in R. Brownsword and K. Yeung (eds.) *Regulating Technologies: Legal Futures, Regulatory Frames and Technological Fixes*, Oxford: Hart.
Murray, A. and Scott, C. (2002) 'Controlling the new media: Hybrid responses to new forms of power,' *The Modern Law Review*, 65(4): 491–516.
Napoli, P. M. (2010) *Audience Evolution: New Technologies and the Transformation of Media Audiences*, New York: Columbia University Press.
—— (2011) 'Global deregulation and media corporations,' in M. Deuze (ed.) *Managing Media Work*, London: Sage.
—— (2012) 'Persistent and emergent diversity policy concerns in an evolving media environment: Toward a reflective research agenda,' in A. Candeub and S. Pager (eds.) *Transnational Culture in the Internet Age*, Cheltenham: Edward Elgar.
Naughton, J. (2006), 'Our changing media ecosystem,' in E. Richards, R. Foster and T. Kiedrowski (eds.) *Communications: The Next Decade*, London: Ofcom.
Netanel, N. (2007) 'Why has copyright expanded? Analysis and critique,' in F. Macmillan (ed.) *New Directions in Copyright Law*, vol. 6, Cheltenham: Edward Elgar.
Palfrey, J. (2007) 'Reluctant gatekeepers: Corporate ethics on a filtered Internet,' in World Economic Forum, *Global Information Technology Report*, Geneva: World Economic Forum.
—— (2010) 'Four phases of Internet regulation,' *Berkman Center for Internet and Society Research Publication*, 9: 1–22.
—— and Gasser, U. (2008) *Born Digital: Understanding the First Generation of Digital Natives*, New York: Basic Books.
Patry, W. (2009) *Moral Panics and the Copyright Wars*, Oxford: Oxford University Press.
Pauwels, C., Kalimo, H., Donders, K. and van Rompuy, B. (eds.) (2009) *Rethinking European Media and Communications Policy*, Brussels: Brussels University Press.
Post, D. (2000) 'What Larry doesn't get? Code, law, and liberty in cyberspace,' *Stanford Law Review*, 52: 1439–1459.
Price, M. E. (2001) 'The newness of new technology,' *Cardozo Law Review*, 22: 1885–1913.
*Red Lion Broadcasting Co.* v *FCC* 395 US 367 (1969).
Roberts, H., Zuckerman, E., Faris, R., York, J. and Palfrey, J. (2011a) *The Evolving Landscape of Internet Control*, Cambridge, MA: Berkman Center for Internet and Society.
—— (2011b) *International Bloggers and Internet Control*, Cambridge, MA: Berkman Center for Internet and Society.

Seltzer, W. (2010) 'Free speech unmoored in copyright's safe harbor: Chilling effects of the DMCA on the First Amendment,' *Harvard Journal of Law and Technology*, 24(1): 171–232.

Sunstein, C. R. (2002) 'The law of group polarization,' *The Journal of Political Philosophy*, 10(2): 175–195.

—— (2007) *Republic.com 2.0*, Princeton, NJ: Princeton University Press.

USTR (2011) 'United States seek detailed information on China's Internet restrictions,' 19 October. Online. Available HTTP: http://www.ustr.gov/about-us/press-office/press-releases/2011/october/united-states-seeks-detailed-information-china%E2%80%99s-i (accessed 29 May 2012).

Vaidhyanathan, S. (2007) 'The googlization of everything and the future of copyright,' *UC Davis Law Review*, 40: 1207–1231.

van Alstyne, M. and Brynjolfsson, E. (2004) 'Global village or cyber-Balkans? Modeling and measuring the integration of electronic communities,' *Management Science*, 51: 851–868.

van Cuilenburg, J. and McQuail, D. (2003) 'Media policy paradigm shifts: Towards a new communications policy paradigm,' *European Journal of Communication*, 18(2): 181–207.

Verhulst, S. (2006) 'The regulation of digital content,' in L. A. Lievrouw and S. Livingstone (eds.) *The Handbook of New Media*, London: Sage.

—— (2007) 'Mediation, mediators and new intermediaries: Implication for the design of new communications policies,' in P. M. Napoli (ed.) *Media Diversity and Localism: Meaning and Metrics*, Mahwah, NJ: Lawrence Erlbaum.

Weinberger, D. (2007) *Everything Is Miscellaneous: The Power of the New Digital Disorder*, New York: Henry Holt.

—— (2012) *Too Big to Know: Rethinking Knowledge Now that the Facts aren't the Facts, Experts are Everywhere, and the Smartest Person in the Room is the Room*, New York: Basic Books.

Wheatley, C. T. (2008) 'Overreaching technological measures for protection of copyright: Identifying the limits of copyright in works in digital form in the United States and the United Kingdom,' *Washington University Global Studies Law Review*, 7: 353–371.

Wu, T. (2006) 'The world trade law of Internet filtering,' *Chicago Journal of International Law*, 17: 263–287.

Yeung, K. (2008) 'Towards an understanding of regulation by design,' in R. Brownsword and K. Yeung (eds.) *Regulating Technologies: Legal Futures, Regulatory Frames and Technological Fixes*, Oxford: Hart.

Yu, P. K. (2006) 'Anticircumvention and anti-anticircumvention,' *Denver University Law Review*, 84(1): 13–77.

Zittrain, J. (2008a) *The Future of the Internet and How to Stop It*, New Haven, CT: Yale University Press.

—— (2008b) 'Perfect enforcement on tomorrow's Internet,' in R. Brownsword and K. Yeung (eds.) *Regulating Technologies: Legal Futures, Regulatory Frames and Technological Fixes*, Oxford: Hart.

# 19

# Are states still important?

## Reflections on the nexus between national and global media and communication policy

*Marc Raboy and Aysha Mawani*

### Introduction

The institutionalization of a global governance environment, the promulgation of a global neoliberal economic regime and widespread claims about the ambivalent role of the nation-state were, up until recently, part of an all-too-familiar equation describing contemporary globalization. It is an equation that has provoked many questions about policy, policy processes and the political actors that mobilize interventions around critical public policy matters. While the contractions currently taking place in the global economy suggest an unequivocal shift in this equation, they also serve to underscore these questions. Media and communication are key issues located at the center of this provocation, both globally and nationally. Who are the principal actors involved in media policy definition and development? Where, and at what, level is policy agenda-setting taking place? In what ways, and using what mechanisms, do various stakeholders choose to influence media and communication policy?[1]

While the development of media and communication systems enjoys a lengthy history with the constitution of the Westphalian nation-state, the purview of media and communication policy emerges increasingly as a global political force—a strategic site for the promotion of a wide array of interests, from public diplomacy and international trade arrangements, to communication rights and social justice across boundaries.

Traditionally, media were among the original anchors for the institutionalization of sovereign territories (Anderson 1983/2006), and were integrally tied to discourses of nationhood, democracy and the public sphere (Curran 2004). National media systems evolved alongside cultural identity, sovereignty and territoriality—all symbolic constructs at the root of the development of nation-states. Public radio and television broadcasting, for example, were strongly associated with these symbols. Media emerged as a primary set of social institutions that would go on to influence democratic practice and participation in the public domain, to facilitate expressions of citizenship and to influence the evolution of rights. Public intervention

1 Embryonic attempts to answer these questions are elaborated at some length in Raboy and Padovani (2010), Raboy and Shtern (2010), and Mansell and Raboy (2011).

to safeguard these institutions and to subsequently influence the development of national media policies became a routine matter in national political and social struggles.

Within a context of contemporary globalization, however, media and communication emerge transformed. Local and national media and communication systems, both in terms of media flows and communication infrastructure, are now subject to *transcultural* considerations and *transnational* policy dimensions that uproot many of the localized and taken-for-granted ideals embedded within a nationally contained framework. To this end, Daya Thussu writes, "the emphasis is moving away from considering the role of media in the vertical integration of national societies, to examining transnational horizontal integration of media and communication processes, institutions and audiences" (Thussu 2009: 3). This trend, among others, has influenced the emergence of a *global* media and communication system that now calls attention to new policy issues, innovative approaches to these issues, and consideration for the assortment of policy actors, processes and structures that direct their governance. Multilateral bodies, transnational corporations and international treaties increasingly attempt to influence nation-state capacity, either limiting or expanding the state's role with respect to media, culture and communication (e.g. through issues such as intellectual property rights, global trade imperatives, privacy and data protection issues, Internet governance and media pluralism), to other key global issues (e.g. poverty reduction, environmental degradation, public health, etc.). These issues represent just a handful of concerns that now mandate policy and governance within, between and across a plurality of jurisdictions, actors and interests.[2]

Thus media and communication issues are progressively subject to broader geopolitical and policy contexts that extend beyond the nation-state. On the one hand, these new contexts challenge the traditional methodology or "business as usual" framework conventionally employed for national policymaking activities. Foreign and domestic policy issues are converging, or are at least "becoming increasingly difficult to disentangle" (Keohane and Nye 2001: ix). On the other hand, media policymaking has been propelled to a global scope and scale influenced by a wider variety of policy actors and issues (Ó Siochrú and Girard 2002; Raboy 2007; Raboy and Padovani 2010).

Notwithstanding these changes, national policy processes remain, in many respects, "the engine rooms of media policy development" (Goldsmith *et al.* 2002: 93). In the field of media and communication, national policy processes also remain at the center of political action. Indeed, collective mobilizations are often developed in national settings to oppose, influence or promote changes in communication policies. Today, these mobilizations often represent the base of transnational political actions that, to a greater extent, focus on and develop further in supranational political spaces. What emerges is a parallel relationship between state and supra-state actors, and state and non-state actors. That is to say, nationally driven mobilizations frequently represent the baseline level of activity for collective transnational and even global actions, with implications for national as well as global media and communication policies. What is more, policymakers and other key stakeholders increasingly attempt to transpose the media and communication policy issues that have, for so long, occupied national agendas to the transnational level.

2 According to Des Freedman, media policy can be defined as the "development of goals and norms leading to the creation of instruments that are designed to shape the structure and behaviour of media systems"; media governance, by extension, is the "sum total of mechanisms . . . that aim to organize media systems according to the resolution of media policy debates" (Freedman 2008: 14).

It is this nexus between national and global media and communication policy landscapes, and an examination of the role of states and state actors in collective political mobilizations in particular, that is our focus in this chapter. Above all, we ask: are states still important in the global media governance environment? What is the point at which state actors effectively intervene in this environment and is their role increasingly relative to or contingent upon a wider sphere of involvement by other policy actors and institutions? Specifically, we assess the weight of state actors who, while having seen their sovereign capacities diminish in certain respects, modify their behavior and forge alliances with non-state actors in order to mobilize and influence an increasingly complex web of international organizations, forums and agreements.

These are critical questions, as both the authority and the legitimacy of state sovereignty were, until recently, regularly called into question in the context of globalization, precipitating claims that the state was experiencing a definitive period of decline. More recent scholarship, however, challenges this conventional wisdom and suggests that the nation-state is not merely an entity in retreat (see, e.g., Morris and Waisbord 2001; Cameron and Stein 2002; Goldsmith *et al.* 2002; Braman 2004; Sassen 2006; Raboy 2007; Randeria 2007; Thussu 2009). This growing body of literature points to the increasingly complex and open-ended relationship between the national and the global—one that is characteristic of a deeper ecology of transformative possibilities, whether to enhance or restrict democratic participation, and, by extension, within which to harness or relinquish the capacity to influence public policy development on media and communication issues.

A key characteristic of this ecology is that the state apparatus has undergone various changes in a context of globalization, notably affecting dimensions of its sovereignty (Reinicke 1998). For example, the increased privatization of public media functions and the sheer density of media and communication infrastructure together impact and complicate the global structure, operation and governance of media and communication today. Concentration of media industries and the rise of global media conglomerates present obstacles for national competition and content regulations (Goldsmith *et al.* 2002; McChesney 2008) and the political economy of communication more generally (McChesney and Schiller 2003; McChesney 2008), stifling the "distribution of communicative power" (Baker 2007: 6; see also Castells 2009). Shifts in the broader geopolitical landscape mark a departure from the conditions and circumstances surrounding both Cold War politics and the 1970s petitions for a New World Information and Communication Order (NWICO).[3] Each of these and many other globalizing tendencies impact nation-states, their media policy agendas, and the opportunities for state actors to publicly intervene and influence communication policies at national and global levels.

The centerpiece of our analysis is the process surrounding the adoption of the UNESCO Convention on the Protection and Promotion of the Diversity of Cultural Expressions (2005). An international communication and cultural policy instrument, the Convention represents an important milestone in the pursuit of communication rights and the promotion of cultural

3 For more details on NWICO, see e.g. Nordenstreng 1984 and Carlsson 2003. Notions reflecting directly or indirectly on communication in society—which, taken together, can be said to constitute a set of acknowledged communication rights—are to be found in the 1948 Universal Declaration of Human Rights and subsequent UN documents. At the same time, however, and especially since the 1970s, experts and activists alike have agreed that the international human rights regime does not go far enough and—with the important exception of freedom of expression—fails to cover most aspects of the "social cycle of communication" (CRIS 2005).

diversity in the global policymaking context. The Convention elevates the issues of cultural development and cultural diversity to the level of global politics and international relations, and, most critically, reinforces the non-commercial value of cultural activities, goods and services in an effort to protect and promote diverse manifestations of culture in a globalized environment. This environment, once predominantly characterized as an arena for cultural homogenization, is today more adequately recognized as a complex space in which culture is not just at risk because of change, but is subject to, and in fact benefits from, change (see UNESCO 2009).

Adopted at UNESCO's General Conference in 2005 and approved by 148 countries, this binding international legal instrument—which some have called the "Kyoto of Culture"—entered into force on 18 March 2007, following its ratification by the requisite number of national legislatures or regional economic integration organizations (UNESCO 2005, Article 29). To date, and with remarkable progress made in the last few years, there are now 125 parties to the Convention, including 124 signatory states as well as the European Union.

While at first glance the Convention may be perceived as an international instrument that weakens state capacity, it actually reaffirms state sovereignty, providing various tools for states to exercise authority in the adoption and implementation of various policy measures deemed necessary for the protection and promotion of the diversity of cultural expressions. The Convention reinforces the position that national governments still wield tremendous leverage both over the territories they govern and as the only legally authorized "rights holders" (Broude 2007) in formal international deliberations. Most notably, the Convention raises important questions about the evolving role of the state relative to multi-stakeholder alliances and the impact of that relationship on the development of a more democratic global media and communication policy environment.

Critical scholarship today increasingly recognizes that, far from becoming irrelevant, states and state actors have emerged as the principal mediating forces in defining the new contexts in which the mobalization of communication rights materialize, and global media and communication systems and their governance develop.[4] The nexus between state and non-state actors, including the state's relationship to, and with, the supranational level is becoming an instrumental feature of global policy and governance activities. This nexus becomes apparent in an examination of the case of the UNESCO Convention, and the processes that resulted in its adoption and subsequent ratification. An examination of the enduring role of the state reinforces the need to try to describe a new understanding of policymaking that embraces the complex nexus between national and global media and communication policy. It situates governance in relation to two crucial dimensions—"new emerging political structures" and the "evolving global media environment" (Raboy 2007: 344)—within which there exists a crucial relationship between the goals and objectives of public policy, policy processes and mechanisms, and political actors and their capacity for agency and action.[5]

4 In an attempt to reinforce the ongoing relevance of the nation-state, some scholars are deliberately returning to discussions that focus on the *international* rather than the *global* dimensions of media studies (see Thussu 2009).

5 Raboy and Shtern (2010) explored how this plays out in a particular national context through a detailed study of the Canadian communication environment, looked at through the prism of communication rights. The study concluded with an appeal to activists and policymakers to recognize the continued critical role of the state in facilitating communication rights and the need to enshrine a formal right to communicate in constitutional law.

## The state as an enabling site for global policy development

The framework for media and communication policy was for many years restricted, at least for the most part, to the enactment of national legislative and regulatory mechanisms governing state intervention in national media policy matters. In Canada alone, a panopoly of policy measures, including content and scheduling quotas in radio and television, support programs for independent book publishing, film production and music, and public service broadcasting, embodied much of the national communication and cultural policy toolkit (Grant and Wood 2004). In recent decades, however, this framework has exploded onto a global landscape where new and old policy issues and actors now intersect with institutional and system-wide changes that cut across a variety of policy domains, governance structures and any number of policy-relevant spaces (Ó Siochrú and Girard 2002; Raboy 2007).

Today's communication environment is seamless, global and apparently boundless in its possibilities. Popular misconceptions and dominant discourses about the end of regulation notwithstanding, activity within this environment is still based on rules and is likely to remain so (Price 2002). The rules are changing, of course, but more significantly, the way in which the rules are made is also changing (Cameron and Stein 2002). New global institutions which as the World Trade Organization (WTO) are the sites of monumental battles between diverse stakeholders. National governments are looking for new ways in which to continue tweaking the influence of communication on their territories (Hallin and Mancini 2004). Corporate strategies are redefining the shape and substance of institutions (Braithwaite and Drahos 2000). Users, the networks they create and the choices they make constitute a perpetual wildcard that makes it hazardous to predict how communication is likely to evolve (Benkler 2006). So what does all of this frenzied activity mean for the state's role in shaping public policy?

We now have a system in which what was once the policy arena of the modern nation-state collapses into a mosaic that encompasses transnational issues, regional considerations, legal complexities and a plurality of actors. Nation-states find their interests and relations intertwined in new ways, with other groups of actors, giving rise to ". . . a world of *overlapping communities of fate*" (Held 1998: 24; emphasis original), where the state emerges simultaneously as both "an agent and an object of globalization" (Randeria 2007: 2). In other words, the state is both an actor instrumental in globalization's evolutionary path and an object subject to its evolution. David Held and Anthony McGrew suggest that this overlapping space is the domain of a "cosmopolitan social democracy," where, at minimum, there is some interest across actors in promoting values such as the rule of law, democratic ideals and social justice. At the same time, there is also recognition that the current political order is "highly complex, interconnected and contested" (Held and McGrew 2002: 130). Ultimately, the test for expanding both legitimacy and accountability within this domain is to cement the adoption of democratic practice as the primary process across governance structures (ibid.).

In an attempt to influence policy and governance outcomes within this domain, states and other actors compete as stakeholders driven by specific interests. Governance encompasses a multidimensional order of power relations between states, as well as negotiations with other major transnational actors—namely, civil society and private industry.[6] Political practice in

6 Civil society is broadly defined in this chapter as "the arena of uncoerced collective action around shared interests, purposes and values" (LSE Centre for Civil Society 2004); see http://www.lse.ac.uk/collections/CCS/what_is_civil_society.htm (accessed 1 September 2010).

such a system becomes "multi-perspectival" (Ruggie 1998: 173) or inclined towards a multiplicity of actors engaged on a variety of issues, operating through diverse mechanisms, and across an array of sovereignties. Needless to say, power is not equally distributed among these actors; disparities are evident and some sites of decision-making are more important and/or carry more significance than others. The role of the state in such a system is nestled somewhere between its capacity to shape national *and* global public policy within domestic and international forums, to reaffirm its authority between dynamics of new, existing and "overlapping sovereignties" (Randeria 2007), and to reinforce social and political legitimacy among its citizens. This shifting political terrain, coupled with the decades-long struggle for the institutionalization of an extensive framework for rights and representation, including appeals to establish a wider basis for public participation, presents new trends, challenges and opportunities for policymaking and governance.

So conceived, the state emerges as a host environment for the cultivation of what we suggest are various adaptive *policy capacities* (or the tools, instruments and resources used to influence policy and policy outcomes), which allow them to mobilize strategically around various policy issues. States become enabling (or constraining) sites where new policy capacities, the range of which have significantly expanded in scope within a context of contemporary globalization, are fostered, harnessed, mobilized and applied to media and communication governance. In this regard, states do not merely respond to the global media and communication policy environment; they are active and enabling participants in its development, formation and governance. Furthermore, conceptualizing the state in this way sheds light on where these capacities are deficient *across* state actors, or where there exists a policy capacity disparity or divide.

Thus there are an array of possibilities for state and non-state actors to build up their policy capacities at the national level in order to effectively mobilize and maneuver politically, to influence policy decision-making and agenda-setting, to undertake advocacy and awareness-raising, and to engage in alliance and coalition-building toward specific public policy goals, or to give policy expression to particular issues. Even weaker states can conceivably combine new methodologies for generating policy capacities around national and transnational policy processes (e.g. by joining multi-stakeholder alliances) both to mobilize and in an attempt to mediate a policy capacity divide. These capacities can be said to influence national policy processes as well as transnational mobilizations, and, by extension, global policy outcomes on media and communication.

The remainder of this chapter returns to the question at the heart of this analysis—whether states are still important—through a case study of the UNESCO Convention and Canada's role in influencing its development. Two parallel narratives emerge from this case study. The first describes Canada's interest in cultural policy and how it moved to adopt a new approach towards public policy in the sphere of media and communication. The second traces the emergence of a transnational policy framework on cultural development and cultural diversity, as espoused by UNESCO. Both narratives eventually converge at the global level to illustrate the instrumental relationship between the state and a receptive supra-state institution, as well as the state and its reliance on non-state actors to further its interests internationally. This case makes clear how the nation-state has reasserted and repositioned itself as an *enabling* site for global policy development and as a resource for communication rights mobilizations, ultimately revealing that states are indeed still important. Their significance is increasingly relative to their ability to coalesce with other actors and institutions in transnational policy contexts.

## The UNESCO Convention on the Protection and Promotion of the Diversity of Cultural Expressions

The trajectory of the UNESCO Convention on the Protection and Promotion of the Diversity of Cultural Expressions (2005) reveals a telling policy story. UNESCO's cultural diversity policy platform was shaped over time, and grew out of a distinct concern for the relationship between culture and development, democracy and dialog, as highlighted in the report of the World Commission on Culture and Development (WCCD), *Our Creative Diversity* (1995), and the *Action Plan on Cultural Policies for Development* (1998) adopted by the Intergovernmental Conference on Cultural Policies for Development in Stockholm.

Although clearly not without shortcomings (see e.g. Magder 2004; Isar 2006; Voon 2006; Crauford Smith 2007), the Convention represents a unique and remarkable accomplishment in international law. It marks a solid effort to crystallize cultural diversity as a human resource and includes a dual concern for both the promotion and protection of culture. The Convention recognizes the special nature of cultural goods and services and reaffirms the sovereign right of nation-states to adopt and implement public policies that favor national cultural industries and other forms of indigenous cultural production, be it through subsidies, public institutions, or fiscal advantages. In this sense, the Convention flies in the face of the worldwide trend of the past twenty years and more, towards freer trade in general and the globalization of culture writ large.

"Cultural development" can be framed in a variety of ways. One understanding is that it is the process by which human beings acquire the individual and collective resources necessary to participate in public life. The treatment of culture, both as a distinct vehicle of development and as a prospect for development itself, reinforces the prominent role of cultural capital in an interdependent world in which media and communication policies come to assume a more prominent role. Adopting such a definition gives meaningful recognition to the social and political character of cultural development. But the issue is both clouded and complicated in a context of contemporary globalization: The global spread of industrial production, the global expansion of a neoliberal ideology, the growing tendency to place priority on the development of cultural enterprise, and the distribution and reception of symbolic goods (i.e. the cultural, artistic and intellectual artifacts that are the raw material of cultural development) affect culture's evolving role and the place of cultural development more generally. Globalization initiates calls to question the traditional basis for state intervention in the cultural sphere (Raboy *et al.* 1994). The fact, for example, that public cultural institutions are in crisis in virtually every sector and in all parts of the world does not inexorably justify a neoliberal or economistic approach to culture. To the contrary, it demonstrates the need for new approaches to public policy in which cultural development, like cultural diversity, is nurtured, promoted and protected.

The call for new approaches to public policy has held a certain currency within specific segments of the Canadian cultural bureaucracy. Canada's new approach to cultural policy emerged as early as 1993 and was grounded in a refined appreciation for the capacity and responsibility of nation-states, the new economic realities of the globalized era, and the social demands expressed by various publics. Around this time, the Canadian government commissioned a series of studies based upon the premise that state intervention in culture is not only legitimate, but also necessary so long as cultural development continues to be a fundamental aspect of democratic public life. About ten years earlier, Canada had decided, as a matter of high policy, to begin investing heavily in the development of a private sector in domestic cultural industries. The bureaucracy moved forward on the assumption that this would not be incompatible with the protection and promotion of national Canadian culture, traditionally promoted by fostering a strong public sector in areas such as broadcasting and film production. Simply put, Canada decisively took the reins on a new approach to public policy, effectively taking stock of existing policy capacities (i.e. investing in culture through the public sector) and developing new tools, instruments and resources with which to influence future cultural policy outcomes (i.e. engaging the private sector as a complement to promote and protect national Canadian cultural industries).

At the same time, Canada also entered into the groundbreaking Canada–United States Free Trade Agreement (1988), in which it successfully insisted on carving out an exemption of cultural industries (although the United States retained the ability to retaliate in other sectors). This exemption was later maintained in the North American Free Trade Agreement (NAFTA) (1994) between Canada, the United States and Mexico, which superseded the 1988 accord between the United States and Canada.[7] Notwithstanding these exemptions for cultural industries, the United States, in a strategic and bold move that would eventually mark a turning point for the regulation of national cultural industries, claimed a few years later that Canada was in violation of existing trade agreements. The issue was split-run magazines[8] (Grant and Wood 2004; Magder 2004).

Early on, the Canadian government had expressed concern about the fate of its own periodical industry if it had to compete with split-run magazines. As early as 1960, the government appointed a Royal Commission on Publications to examine the situation in-depth. The Commission found that 80 percent of Canada's periodicals industry was foreign-controlled and recommended various measures to curb this control, including an outright ban on the import of split-run magazines that advertised directly to Canadian readers (Grant and Wood 2004). The issue resurfaced in the 1990s and has continued with the emergence of new technologies, as US companies now could use digital technologies to circumvent rules preventing the import of split-run magazines into Canada. Canada retaliated by imposing a hefty 80 percent excise tax on Canadian advertising revenue generated from split-run magazines.

In response to these measures, and sidestepping the cultural industries exemption in NAFTA, the United States invoked Canada's commitments under the General Agreement on Tariffs and Trade (GATT) (1947), appealing the matter to the WTO's dispute resolution panel. The case was later transferred to the WTO's appellate body. In 1997, the WTO issued a landmark ruling in favor of the United States with which Canada was forced to comply. The most astonishing part of this case is that magazines were not even mentioned in the GATT, yet the WTO classified them as "goods" (siding with the United States), which, according to the Organization, rightfully fell within the scope of the GATT (Magder 2004).

Dissatisfaction with the WTO outcome and fears about its implications for other fundamental elements of Canadian cultural policy, along with growing concerns surrounding the

7 The cultural industries exemption in NAFTA applies to Canada and the US only, and does not extend to include Mexico (see Raboy *et al.* 1994).

8 "Split-run magazines" are foreign periodicals that also generate a Canadian edition. They typically have little or no Canadian content, and rely on reusing content from the foreign edition as a measure to cut costs. As a result, these publications can sell advertising space to Canadian advertisers at prices well below competitive rates. Popular split-run magazines include *Sports Illustrated*, *Time* and *Reader's Digest*.

subordination of culture and cultural industries to market forces, propelled Canada to once again review its policy capacities in this area.

With fallout from the split-run magazine issue still looming large, the Cultural Industries Sectoral Advisory Group on International Trade (SAGIT)[9] in Canada prepared a report urging the government of Canada to pursue efforts at the international level to develop an international agreement that would promote the importance of cultural diversity and cultural policies. It was increasingly clear that the principle of "cultural exemption [had] its limits" (Grant and Wood 2004: 384). Leading industry actors, through the SAGIT, stressed the importance of developing such an instrument outside the purview of the WTO in order to ensure that the instrument upheld the unique place of culture in a globalized world, independent of its relationship to commerce. The SAGIT recommendations were critical in convincing the Canadian government to take the cause further and remained an invaluable contribution to the later drafting of the UNESCO Convention. Shortly thereafter and following the international circulation of the SAGIT report, Canada assumed a strong lobbying position alongside members of *la Francophonie*,[10] in pursuit of an international cultural promotion and protection instrument.

Meanwhile, the question of cultural development had been emerging in the international arena as well. The earliest explicit links between the notions of cultural development, cultural industry and the role of the state were formulated under the umbrella of a UNESCO conference held in Montreal in 1980. Experts were asked to study "the place and role of cultural industries in the cultural development of societies" (UNESCO 1982). Augustin Girard, a former senior official within the French Ministry of Culture and author of an earlier UNESCO publication, *Cultural Development* (Girard 1972), questioned whether "under certain conditions, cultural industries may provide a new opportunity for cultural development and cultural democracy" (UNESCO 1982: 23; see also Girard 1982a). Girard sketched out a template for national public policy with respect to cultural industries, which, he argued, should aim to meet the following objectives: broaden access to culture; improve quality within the mass media; develop community media and independent media; foster creative work; modernize traditional cultural institutions; strengthen national cultural production; and ensure the country's cultural influence abroad (Girard 1982b: 231).[11]

Implicitly, cultural development was raised during the debates over a New World Information and Communication Order (NWICO). Launched in the 1970s, the NWICO represented a call to resist the hegemonic logic of an emergent global communication order, the dominance of Western media and the one-way flow of information. Countries of the global South, which had previously joined together to form a coalition called the Non-Aligned Movement (NAM),[12] lobbied at UNESCO to influence the development of a "new, more just, and more efficient world information and communication order" (UNESCO 1980; Vincent *et al.* 1999). The heated policy debates of NWICO culminated in the

9 The SAGIT is a group of industry leaders that meets regularly with Canadian government officials to discuss issues of trade. There are advisory groups on various trade issues, cultural industries being one such group. For more information on the SAGIT, see Grant 2011.

10 The international organization of governments with a notable affinity with the French language or culture. *La Francophonie* had fifty-six member states and governments in 2012.

11 This section draws from Raboy *et al.* 1994.

12 The NAM originated at the 1955 Bandung Conference in Indonesia, where twenty-nine heads of state, many from recently decolonized countries in Africa and Asia, met for the first time. It was here that the term "Third World" was first proposed (see Carlsson 2003: 39).

famous "MacBride Report", *Many Voices, One World* (UNESCO 1980), which included a set of recommendations on international communication.

Thereafter, the question of cultural development gained ever-more leverage following the declaration by the United Nations that the years 1988 through 1997 would mark the "Decade of Cultural Development." This was an important move, even if largely symbolic. It catalyzed an array of activities and expanded UNESCO's mandate in support of cultural development. Almost immediately, UNESCO called for the restoration of cultural values in processes of economic and technological development, advancing the idea that human development contained an essential cultural dimension (UNESCO 1987). In 1992, UNESCO, in partnership with the United Nations, launched an international blue-ribbon commission, chaired by former United Nations Secretary-General Javier Pérez de Cuellar. The World Commission on Culture and Development (WCCD), to which Canada became an active participant,[13] issued the path-breaking report *Our Creative Diversity* (1995). The report marked a powerful policy statement in support of culture in all of its guises as a basic dimension of human development. *Our Creative Diversity* established an international agenda and proposed a permanent forum for developing global policy with respect to cultural development. Several chapters and proposals relating to media and new global issues in mass communication were framed by the following question: "How can the world's growing media capacities be channeled so as to support cultural diversity and democratic discourse?" (WCCD 1995). The report reads:

> [C]ommunication in all its forms, from the simplest to the most sophisticated, is a key to people-centred development . . . Yet at whatever level the issues of communication are envisaged, there is a shared challenge. This is the challenge of organizing our considerable capacities in ways that support cultural diversity, creativity and the empowerment of the weak and poor.
>
> (*WCCD 1995: 107*)

While the WCCD admitted that it did not have ready answers to the questions raised by the link between communication, culture and development, the cogency of the report suggested that the answers were best sought through principles of international dialog, diplomacy and global justice. Moreover, many specialists advised the Commission of the importance of arriving at an international balance between public and private interests in the sector of media and communication. To this end, they proposed building a common ground of public interest on a *transnational* scale that combined different national approaches. They further suggested that new international rules could emerge through transnational alliances forged across public and private media spaces (WCCD 1995). Most significantly, the report called for a new and concerted international effort: "An active policy to promote competition, access and diversity of expression amongst the media globally, analogous to policies that exist at the national level" (WCCD 1995: 279).[14]

13 Canada seconded a senior official from the international branch of the Department of Canadian Heritage, Vladimir Skok, to act as programme specialist within the Secretariat of the WCCD.

14 The WCCD's international agenda also contained a series of specific proposals aimed at "enhancing access, diversity and competition of the international media system," and based on the assertion that the airwaves and space are "part of the global commons, a collective asset that belongs to all humankind" (WCCD 1995: 278). At present, this international asset is used free of charge by those who possess both the required resources and technology. Eventually, "property rights" may have to be assigned to the global commons, and access to airwaves and space will need to be regulated in the

Taking the issue of cultural development a step further, in 1998, UNESCO organized the Intergovernmental Conference on Cultural Policies for Development in Stockholm. The Conference objectives were twofold: to contribute to the integration of cultural policies in human development strategies at international and national levels; and to help to strengthen UNESCO's contributions to cultural policy formulation and international cultural cooperation (UNESCO 2004). The major Conference outcome was the adoption of an Action Plan (UNESCO 1998), recommending a series of policy objectives to UNESCO member states.[15] The Action Plan focused on the general philosophical position that communication resources constitute part of the global commons, and explicitly recognized that "in a democratic framework civil society will become increasingly important in the field of culture" (UNESCO 1998: Preamble). The Action Plan made a number of significant contributions, affirming, among other things, that:

> 4. Effective participation in the information society and the mastery by everyone of information and communications technology constitute a significant dimension of any cultural policy. [...]
> 9. Government should endeavour to achieve closer partnerships with civil society in the design and implementation of cultural policies that are integrated into development strategies.
> 10. In an increasingly interdependent world, the renewal of cultural policies should be envisioned simultaneously at the local, national, regional and global levels. [...]
> 12. Cultural policies should place particular emphasis on promoting and strengthening ways and means of providing broader access to culture for all sectors of the population, combating exclusion and marginalization, and fostering all processes that favour cultural democratization.
>
> (*UNESCO 1998: Preamble*)

The Canadian delegation was an active participant in the Stockholm conference. Shortly after the 1998 gathering, then Canadian Minister of Heritage, Sheila Copps, convened a meeting in Ottawa of twenty-two ministers of culture for the first International Meeting on Cultural Policy, which took place in June 1998. Participating ministers represented Armenia, Barbados, Brazil, Croatia, the Dominican Republic, Egypt, Greece, Iceland, Italy, the Ivory Coast, Mexico, Morocco, Poland, Senegal, South Africa, Sweden, Switzerland, Trinidad and Tobago, Tunisia, Ukraine and the United Kingdom (Government of Canada 1998). Notably absent from the invitation list was a representative from the United States.

National representatives at this meeting were brought together by their mutual interest in, and respect for, the will to exercise national sovereignty in the sphere of culture. Many of these countries also held bilateral free trade agreements with the United States, in which they had either explicitly or implicitly ceded a good part of their cultural sovereignty, or were

public interest (WCCD 1995: 278). Just as national community and public media services require public subsidy, internationally, the redistribution of benefits from the growing global commercial media activity could help to subsidize the rest. As a first step, and within a market context, the Commission suggested that the time might have come for commercial regional or international satellite radio and television interests, which now use the global commons free of charge, to contribute to the financing of a more plural media system. New revenue could be invested in alternative programming for international distribution (Ibid.).

15 The WCCD process and subsequent debates also resulted in the adoption, in 2001, of a symbolically important Universal Declaration on Cultural Diversity (UNESCO 2001).

concerned about the possible impact of multilateral agreements on their capacity to make domestic cultural policies (as in the case of Canada and its magazine publishing policies under the GATT). The meeting importantly launched the creation of an International Network on Cultural Policy (INCP), which became a critical catalytic agent to the UNESCO Convention. The representatives also understood that to recapture the *right* to national sovereignty in the realm of culture, it was necessary to foster a *transnational* political force that would involve many other countries—and, crucially, many other non-state actors.

In this regard, the INCP, in collaboration with the Canadian government and well-known Canadian non-governmental organization (NGO) the Canadian Conference of the Arts, jointly convened a meeting of NGOs from around the world interested in countering the effects of the globalization of culture. The resulting International Network for Cultural Diversity (INCD) had member organizations in important countries that were *not* initially part of the INCP network of government ministers; countries such as Germany, Japan and Australia would have to be brought on board if an international policy instrument promoting and protecting culture were to become a reality.

Both the INCP and the INCD met regularly over the coming years, as a plan took shape to develop an international instrument on cultural diversity and to promote its adoption at UNESCO.[16] The goal was to adopt a legally binding convention that would ensure the diversity of cultural expression in the face of the increasing commodification of culture, and to also ensure that culture was recognized in existing trade agreements, including the General Agreement on Trade in Services (GATS 1995), and the Agreement on Trade Related Aspects of Intellectual Property Rights (TRIPS 1994), managed by the WTO.

The United States, meanwhile, was not idle in resisting the Convention's development. It orchestrated a media frenzy reminiscent of the NWICO debate, lobbied its fellow friends and allies (such as the United Kingdom), and attempted to strong-arm many of its smaller trading partners, cautioning them to not join the growing movement of support for the proposed Convention. But by October 2005, when the Convention was presented at the UNESCO General Assembly, only Israel voted with the United States against its adoption. The Convention then came into force on 18 March 2007, three months after ratification by the requisite thirty-five member states.[17]

## Reflections on the nexus between global and national media policy

So what does the story of the adoption of the UNESCO Convention tell us about the nexus between global and national media policy? A good starting point, and perhaps the Convention's most compelling feature, is the process that resulted in and from its development.

16 Both organizations have grown considerably since their inception. In 2012, the INCP had seventy-four members (see http://www.incp-ripc.org/members/index_e.shtml). The INCD, meanwhile, currently boasts a membership base of 500 organizations or individuals from seventy different countries (see http://www.incd.net/membership.html).

17 Since then, a range of activities related to the Convention's implementation have taken place: As of March 2012, three sessions of the Conference of Parties and five sessions of the Intergovernmental Committee (the Convention's two main governance structures) have been held; the International Fund for Cultural Diversity (created under Art. 18 of the Convention) has launched its third round of grant applications; more than ninety signatory countries are preparing to submit their first quadrennial reports; and expert meetings and regional activities are ongoing. Civil society has been involved, to varying degrees, in many of these activities (as per Art. 11 of the Convention).

As a matter of process, the Convention's adoption and subsequent ratification hinged quite forcefully on three key dimensions: the opportunity to develop policy agenda-setting on communication and culture; the establishment of a multi-stakeholder alliance between state and non-state actors; and the use of a receptive venue at the supra-state level, as the site for lobbying and eventual policymaking. In this example, Canada deliberately retooled its domestic capacity vis-à-vis communication policy, outlining a new approach, and, in the process of so doing, became part of a dynamic transnational movement for the development of a binding policy instrument on cultural diversity. Let us consider each of these dimensions.

First, *new opportunities* for agenda-setting around the policy framework of cultural diversity provided an international narrative for national *and* global communication policy. This narrative established a legal counterpoint to the commodification of culture brought on by the dominance of globalization. Internationally, UNESCO's efforts to recognize cultural development as a fundamental value for humanity (e.g. through NWICO, the WCCD, and the Stockholm Conference) were instrumental in laying this groundwork. At the national level, the notion of cultural diversity was introduced as an "integrative" tool to mediate the tensions between economy and culture; in Canada, the SAGIT report, prepared by industry actors, provided a sound rationale for the pursuit of an internationally binding cultural diversity instrument. The introduction of the WTO as an institution in 1993 brought with it resistance in trade deliberations on matters of culture. France and Canada, in particular, wanted to exclude culture (what the French and Quebec governments refer to as *"l'exception culturelle"*), and specifically audiovisual media, as party to the trade agreements of the newly formed institution (Grant and Wood 2004; Isar 2006). Its proponents knew, however, that, as a cultural policy measure, *l'exception culturelle* rang to the tune of protectionism. On the contrary, the cultural diversity narrative enabled states to focus on both the values of cultural protection and promotion and was decidedly much more "neutral" in stance (see Grant 2011). This opened up the possibility and the opportunity for nation-states to "tap into a much broader range of cultural commitments and anxieties in international relations" (Isar 2006: 374).

Second, *new approaches* toward multi-stakeholder and international alliances across conventional geopolitical power blocs (e.g. East–West, North–South, resource rich–resource poor, etc.), and across a constellation of diverse nation-states that traditionally had very little in common, had a catalytic role in the Convention's development. While renewed attention to the advantages and disadvantages of multi-stakeholderism is not new, especially following the World Summit on the Information Society (e.g. Padovani *et al.* 2005; Raboy *et al.* 2010), its use as a tool to bolster state-level policy capacities and to influence global policy outcomes deserves specific attention.

Individual nation-states on their own would have generated very little traction in the international arena without adopting new approaches to alliance and coalition-building with other nation-states interested in achieving like outcomes on cultural protection and promotion. While, traditionally, weaker states may neither have had the opportunity to organize across these conventional power blocs, nor the capacity to lobby the international arena (suggesting a policy capacity disparity or divide), the UNESCO Convention illustrates how effective it was for weaker and stronger states, with a mutual interest in an issue at the *national* level, to strategically combine their policy capacities and to mobilize politically at the *transnational* level. Such state actors effectively modified their behavior by rallying together with others to mobilize collectively, creating new partnerships to shape the Convention's development.

Additionally, a state actor alliance (the INCP)—itself the result of a movement driven in part by non-state actors—supported, both implicitly and explicitly, the development of a non-state, transnational civil society base (the INCD) that would prove vital to the Convention's uptake in international circles. The mobilization of state and non-state actors generated sufficient political force to reclaim the right to national sovereignty in so far as matters of culture and communication were concerned. The transnational alliance forged within and between both the INCP and the INCD, and their mutual interest in protecting and promoting culture, epitomizes David Held's notion of "overlapping communities of fate" (Held 1998: 24). The participation of civil society in the Convention's implementation is one of its unique characteristics (UNESCO 2005: Article 11). This did not go unnoticed: As Broude suggests, even though the Convention primarily recognizes member states as "rights holders," it had an important "indirect effect": "it empower[ed] the stakeholders of cultural diversity, that is the people who create culture and the communities who benefit from it" (Broude 2007: 20).

Finally, the Convention represents a firm example of a multiplicity of policy actors "using" *new spaces and venues* offered by a receptive multilateral agency (in this case, UNESCO) to construct an instrument of global governance that could profoundly affect the way in which culture and communication evolve globally during the next decade. These spaces and venues are revealing themselves with increasing frequency and can be harnessed in creative ways that promote democratic participation in the global policy arena. As April Carter writes: "The sheer existence of international bodies provides an important framework for strengthening global civil society, and . . . participation within that global context" (Carter 2001: 183). At the same time, it is important to note that the motivations and actions of nation-states vary at the supra-state level where states can choose to promote, exclusively, their domestic interests at the global level: "The result, as with the multiplication of the number of international laws and law-making institutions . . . is exacerbation of venue shopping choices and jurisdictional dilemmas" (Braman 2009: 99).

If Canada, France and other participating countries had not aggressively pursued an agenda of safeguarding their respective national cultural industries, and if these countries had refrained from acting as *agents* of governance (Randeria 2007), it is reasonable to suggest that the policy story of the Convention might not exist today, or that it might have unfolded very differently. New opportunities for policy agenda-setting, new approaches toward alliance- and coalition-building, and new spaces and venues for policy deliberations were key parts of the puzzle that enabled states to (re)form and leverage their policy capacities, to make a different set of policy choices, to mobilize transnationally across state and non-state actors, and to locate their struggle within the corridors of a receptive international institution. In this way, the Canadian national policy process, as with parallel processes in other national settings, represented the roots and resources of what became a transnational political mobilization.

As a matter of outcome, the Convention, although still in its early phases of implementation and widely untested as yet, represents a measure to bolster *national* policy capacities to regulate matters of communication and culture within states' own territories. The Convention provides a legitimizing mechanism for states to "flex their muscle," to enact policies and reinforce their authority to regulate aspects of the media and communication environment. It may emerge as an institutional global policy model for developing national policy capacities and mediating policy capacity disparities or divides in order to help to define new contexts for communication rights and global justice.

## Conclusion

The case of the UNESCO Convention uniquely captures the increasingly complex and open-ended nexus that is characteristic of the national and global media and communication policy landscapes. It is clear that the state retains a vital role, whether as an enabling or a constraining influence on the range of policy choices and opportunities available for intervention in a given policy field. In this case, the state emerged as both a vehicle for political mobilization and as an agent for policy activities in the global public policy arena. In order to intervene in this environment, however, the state had to generate adaptive policy capacities. At the same time, the state's capacity to assume a fully actualized role as a policy actor appears to be increasingly relative to the widespread involvement of other state actors, including supra-state institutions and non-state actors, notably civil society, through mechanisms such as multi-stakeholder alliances. These alliances have emerged, in this example, as a critical site for the development and realization of more democratic, inclusive and socially just global media and communication policy processes.

In short, the case illustrates one of the many ways in which the state can modify its sovereign capacity to influence agency and action for communication policymaking in a context of contemporary globalization. States, in this regard, materialize not as static, fixed entities, or merely "objects of governance" (Randeria 2007) and globalization; rather, they become dynamic, fertile landscapes and remain open, flexible and engaged agents.[18]

The case of the UNESCO Convention flies in the face of the view that the nation-state is in a position of inevitable and irreversible demise relative to globalizing forces. Claims about the progressive loss of national sovereignty, economic sovereignty, information sovereignty and cultural sovereignty have indeed warranted calls on the state's diminished capacity and transforming role. Yet many of these claims may have overlooked an enduring attribute of the nation-state—namely, that it retains its domestic capacity to act as a critical reserve and starting point for collective transnational mobilizations.

The nexus between global and national media and communication policy spaces also suggests that international agreements such as the Convention are increasingly becoming strategic sites around which states can derive sovereign authority to pursue their own national interests. States are more and more dependent upon the normative frameworks established in the international arena, including those that impact media and communication policy globally, in order to support and legitimize their activities nationally.

Viewed as such, this perspective on the state enables us to make three conceptual moves. First, it forges a concrete link between national and transnational political mobilizations and global public policymaking. Second, it challenges the oversimplified dualism once pronounced between the national and the global as discrete and separate spheres of policy activity (see Sassen 2006). Third, it helps to unpack the increasingly complex relationship between national and global media and communication policymaking, and the role of the state therein. But this perspective also begs the following question: how, in a context of contemporary globalization, can the state retool itself as a central enabling site for global media and communication policy development?

Notwithstanding the observations presented in this chapter, it is important to note that the specific dynamics brought to light through the example of the process that led to the adoption of the UNESCO Convention may be unique. Certainly, the extent to which these observations can be generalized or to which they are indicative of a broader trend in global media and communication policy and governance, and the role and relationship of the state therein,

18 Indeed, the "spoiler" role played by the United States in opposing the adoption of the Convention at UNESCO stands as a potent counter-example of state power in multilateral fora—but that should be the topic of another examination.

remains less clear. It is too early to tell whether the success witnessed in the Convention's adoption will translate into successful implementation. But, at the very least, the Convention merits attention as a critical moment in the evolving nexus of national and global media and communication policy development.

## References


Anderson, B. (1983/2006) *Imagined Communities: Reflections on the Origins and Spread of Nationalism*, London: Verso.

Baker, C. E. (2007) *Media Concentration and Ownership: Why Ownership Matters*, Cambridge: Cambridge University Press.

Benkler, Y. (2006) *The Wealth of Networks: How Social Production Transforms Markets and Freedom*, New Haven, CT: Yale University Press.

Braithwaite, J. and Drahos, P. (2000) *Global Business Regulation*, Cambridge: Cambridge University Press.

Braman, S. (2004) 'The emergent global information policy regime,' in S. Braman (ed.) *The Emergent Global Information Policy Regime*, Houndsmill and New York: Palgrave MacMillan.

—— (2009) 'Globalizing media law and policy,' in D. K. Thussu (ed.) *Internationalizing Media Studies*, New York: Routledge.

Broude, T. (2007) 'Conflict and complementarity in trade, cultural diversity and intellectual property rights,' *Hebrew University International Law Research Paper No. 11*. Online. Available HTTP: http://ssrn.com/abstract=1001869 (accessed 13 January 2010).

Cameron, D. and Stein, J. G. (2002) 'Globalization, culture and society: The state as place amidst shifting spaces,' in J. G. Stein and D. Cameron (eds.) *Street Protests and Fantasy Parks: Globalization, Culture, and the State*, Vancouver, BC: University of British Columbia Press.

Carlsson, U. (2003) 'The rise and fall of NWICO: From a vision of international regulation to a reality of multilevel governance,' *Nordicom Review*, 24(2): 31–68.

Carter, A. (2001) *The Political Theory of Global Citizenship*, New York: Routledge.

Castells, M. (2000) *The Rise of the Network Society*, vol. 1, 2nd edn., Oxford: Blackwell Publishers.

—— (2009) *Communication Power*, Oxford: Oxford University Press.

Communication Rights in the Information Society (CRIS) (2005) *Assessing Communication Rights: A Handbook*. Online. Available HTTP: http://www.crisinfo.org/pdf/ggpen.pdf (accessed 11 July 2010).

Craufurd Smith, R. (2007) 'The UNESCO Convention on the Protection and Promotion of the Diversity of Cultural Expressions: Building a new world information and communication order?' *International Journal of Communication*, 1: 24–55.

Curran, J. (2004) 'The rise of the Westminster School,' in A. Calabrese and C. Sparks (eds.) *Toward a Political Economy of Culture: Capitalism and Communication in the Twenty-First Century*, Lanham, MD: Rowman and Littlefield.

Freedman, D. (2008) *The Politics of Media Policy*, Cambridge: Polity Press.

Girard, A. (1972) *Cultural Development: Experience and Policies*, Paris: UNESCO.

—— (1982a) 'Cultural industries: A handicap or a new opportunity for cultural development?' in A. Girard (ed.) *Cultural Industries: A Challenge for the Future of Culture*, Paris: UNESCO.

—— (1982b) 'The role of the public authorities,' in A. Girard (ed.) *Cultural Industries: A Challenge for the Future of Culture*, Paris: UNESCO.

Goldsmith, B., Thomas, J., O'Regan, T. and Cunningham, S. (2002) 'Asserting cultural and social regulatory principles in converging media systems,' in M. Raboy (ed.) *Global Media Policy in the New Millennium*, Luton: University of Luton Press.

Government of Canada (1998) *News Release: Ministers From 22 Countries Expected at Ottawa Meeting on Culture*, Ottawa: Department of Canadian Heritage. Online. Available HTTP: http://www.canadianheritage.gc.ca/newsroom/index_e.cfm?fuseaction=displayDocumentandDocIDCd=8NR039 (accessed 5 December 2010).

Grant, P.S. (2011) 'The UNESCO Convention on Cultural Diversity: Cultural policy and international trade in cultural product,' in R. Mansell and M. Raboy (eds.) *The Handbook of Global Media and Communication Policy*, Oxford: Wiley-Blackwell.

—— and Wood, C. (2004) *Blockbusters and Trade Wars: Popular Culture in a Globalized World*, Vancouver, BC: Douglas and McIntyre.
Hallin, D. C. and Mancini, P. (2004) *Comparing Media Systems: Three Models of Media and Politics*, Cambridge: Cambridge University Press.
Held, D. (1998) 'Democracy and globalization,' in D. Archibugi, D. Held and M. Kohler (eds.) *Re-Imagining Political Community*, Cambridge: Polity Press.
—— and McGrew, A. (2002) *Globalization/Anti-Globalization*, Cambridge: Polity Press.
Isar, Y. R. (2006) 'Cultural diversity,' *Theory, Culture and Society*, 23(2–3): 372–375.
Keohane, R. and Nye, J. (2001) *Power and Interdependence*, 3rd edn. New York and London: Longman.
Magder, T. (2004) 'Transnational media, international trade and the idea of cultural diversity,' *Continuum: Journal of Media and Cultural Studies*, 18(3): 380–397.
Mansell, R. and Raboy, M. (2011) 'Foundations of the theory and practice of global media and communication policy,' in R. Mansell and M. Raboy (eds.) *The Handbook of Global Media and Communication Policy*, Oxford: Wiley-Blackwell.
McChesney, R. W. (2008) *The Political Economy of Media: Enduring Issues, Emerging Dilemmas*, New York: Monthly Review Press.
—— and Schiller, D. (2003) *Political Economy of International Communications: Foundations for the Emerging Global Debate about Media Ownership and Regulation*, Technology, Business and Society Programme Paper No. 11. Geneva: UNRISD.
Morris, N. and Waisbord, S. (eds.) (2001) *Media and Globalization: Why the State Matters*, Lanham, MD: Rowman and Littlefield.
Nordenstreng, K. (1984) 'Defining the new international information order,' in G. Gerbner and M. Siefert (eds.) *World Communications*, New York and London: Longman.
Ó Siochrú, S. and Girard, B. (2002) *Global Media Governance: A Beginner's Guide*, Lanham, MD: Rowman and Littlefield.
Padovani, C. *et al.* (2005) 'Multi-stakeholder processes and civil society,' in O. Drossou and H. Jensen (eds.) *Visions in Process II*, Berlin: Heinrich Böll Foundation.
Price, M. E. (2002) *Media and Sovereignty: The Global Information Revolution and its Challenge to State Power*, Cambridge, MA: MIT Press.
Raboy, M. (2007) 'Global media policy: Defining the field,' *Global Media and Communication*, 3(3): 343–347.
—— and Padovani, C. (2010) 'Mapping global media policy: Concepts, frameworks, methods,' *Journal of Communication, Culture and Critique*, 3(2): 150–169.
—— and Shtern, J. (2010) *Media Divides: Communication Rights and the Right to Communicate in Canada*, Vancouver, BC: University of British Columbia Press.
——, Bernier I., Sauvageau, F. and Atkinson, D. (1994) 'Cultural development and the open economy: A democratic issue and a challenge to public policy,' *Canadian Journal of Communication*, 19(3/4): 291–315.
——, Landry, N. and Shtern, J. (2010) *Digital Solidarities, Communication Policy and Multi-stakeholder Global Governance: The Legacy of the World Summit on the Information Society*, New York: Peter Lang.
Randeria, S. (2007) 'The state of globalization: Legal plurality, overlapping sovereignties and ambiguous alliances between civil society and the cunning state in India,' *Theory, Culture and Society*, 24(1): 1–33.
Reinicke, W. H. (1998) *Global Public Policy*, Washington, DC: Brookings Institution Press.
Ruggie, J. (1998) *Constructing the World Polity: Essays on International Institutionalization*, London: Routledge.
Sassen, S. (2006) *Territory, Authority, Rights: From Medieval to Global Assemblages*, Princeton, NJ: Princeton University Press.
Thussu, D. K. (2009) 'Introduction,' in D. K. Thussu (ed.) *Internationalizing Media Studies*, New York: Routledge.
UNESCO (1980) *Many Voices, One World: Final Report of the MacBride Commission*, Paris: UNESCO.
—— (1982) *Cultural Industries: A Challenge for the Future of Culture*, Paris: UNESCO.
—— (1987) 'Qu'est-ce que la Décennie mondiale du développement culturel?' in *Guide pratique de la Décennie mondiale du développement culturel 1988–1997*, Vendome: Presses Universitaires de France.
—— (1998) *Action Plan on Cultural Policies for Development*, Paris: UNESCO.
—— (2001) *Universal Declaration on Cultural Diversity*, Paris: UNESCO.

—— (2004) *The Stockholm Conference*. Online. Available HTTP: http://portal.unesco.org/culture/en/ev.php-URL_ID=18717andURL_DO=DO_TOPICandURL_SECTION=201.html (accessed 13 May 2008).
—— (2005) *Convention on the Protection and Promotion of the Diversity of Cultural Expressions*, Paris: UNESCO.
—— (2009) *World Report, Investing in Cultural Diversity and Intercultural Dialogue*, Paris: UNESCO. Online. Available HTTP: http://unesdoc.unesco.org/images/0018/001847/184755e.pdf (accessed 9 May 2010).
Vincent, R. C., Nordenstreng, K. and Traber, M. (eds.) (1999) *Towards Equity in Global Communication: MacBride Update*, Cresskill, NJ: Hampton Press.
Voon, T. (2006) 'UNESCO and the WTO: A clash of cultures?' *International and Comparative Law Quarterly*, 55(3): 635–652.
World Commission on Culture and Development (1995) *Our Creative Diversity: Report of the World Commission on Culture and Development*, Paris: EGOPRIM.

# 20

# International governance in a new media environment

*Rolf H. Weber**

Because of the far-reaching developments in information and communication technologies (ICTs) within the last two decades, communication practices and the traditional media environment have undergone profound modifications. The established media—including newspapers, books, films and broadcast—are now complemented by the Internet, a valuable tool in everyday life and a phenomenon encompassing social, cultural, economic and legal facets. In light of these developments, existing media governance regulations need to be examined so as to determine whether they are still applicable, and whether changes need to be implemented.

Much has been written about the novelty of the media environment and its challenges to media governance. These changes include the shift from offline to online, from mass communication to individual communication, from verbal and written to visual communication, and from local to global or "glocal." The purpose of this chapter is to look at the response of various institutions to these changes in terms of addressing governance.

## UNESCO: The MacBride Report and mass media declaration

The issues of information flows and the need to introduce principles of governance with respect to information services have been discussion topics for many decades (Weber 2009a). The Internet is a new medium, but traditional media also exercise cross-border information services that have called for an applicable legal framework.

In the early 1970s, a group of developing countries—the so-called "Non-Aligned Movement"[1]—discussed the idea of a "New World Information and Communication Order"

* The author would like to thank Ulrike I. Heinrich (Attorney-at-Law Berlin) for her valuable support in the preparation of this chapter.

1 Founded in 1961, the NAM is a group of states referring to themselves as not aligned formally with or against any major power bloc (Western and Eastern blocs) in the Cold War, with the purpose of ensuring "the national independence, sovereignty, territorial integrity and security of non-aligned countries" (Fidel Castro, Havana Declaration of 1979).

(NWICO), which grew out of the International Economic Order of 1974 (Carlsson 2003). After its launch at the Non-Aligned Summit of 1973 in Algiers—which called for united action in the field of mass communication (Padovani and Nordenstreng 2005)—it soon became obvious that this order would have to be incorporated into a broader concept of a Third World development policy (Hedebro 1982). The NWICO was built on a political approach, and implied far-reaching reforms of the existing order, including all kinds of information, media and forms of communication technologies (Carlsson 2003). The debate did not return the desired results and was later replaced by the activities of the MacBride Commission.

At the same time, the Soviet Union proposed to release a Mass Media Declaration under the auspices of the United Nations Educational, Scientific and Cultural Organization (UNESCO) (UNESCO Doc. 17C/Res.4.113). Aiming at the development of globally acceptable guidelines for the role of mass media in the international system (Carlsson 2003), this attempt provoked the opposition of Western and Northern countries, who were afraid that the principle of the "free flow of information" would be jeopardized. Subsequently, parallel to the negotiations on a possible Declaration, at the 1976 UNESCO Nairobi Conference, the idea prevailed that it would be wise to start inquiries about the factual background of the information and communication regime (Weber 2004).

In December 1977, an International Commission for the Study of Information and Communication Problems, appointed by UNESCO and chaired by Nobel Laureate Sean MacBride, began its work on compiling a report under the title *Many Voices, One World*. During the inquiry process of the MacBride Commission in November 1978, the participants of the UNESCO General Conference had agreed on the Declaration on the Fundamental Principles concerning the Contribution of the Mass Media to Strengthening of Peace and International Understanding, the Promotion of Human Rights and to Encountering Racialism, Apartheid and Incitement to War (UNESCO Doc. 20C/Res.4.9.3/2, 28 November 1978). Agreement on this declaration was achieved in relatively short time owing to the fact that the document proposed that signatory developed countries offer infrastructure support to the developing countries.

In 1980, the MacBride Commission published its report, in which a possible "New World Information and Communication Order" was defined as a process, rather than as a given set of conditions and practices (UNESCO 1980). The MacBride Report addresses a large number of matters, with particular attention paid to aspects such as: strengthening independence and self-reliance of communication capacities; integrating communication into policies on technological challenges and social problems; improving professional integrity and ethical standards; acknowledging communicative democratization (i.e. avoidance of media concentration and realization of media diversity); fostering international cooperation; and providing for more financial resources (Weber 2004).

Despite the controversy that the issue had garnered before, there was only fairly limited discussion within UNESCO after the publication of the MacBride Report; the General Conference of 1980 in Belgrade simply took note of the report without initiating special action, the sole exception being the incorporation of the International Programme for the Development of Communication according to Recommendation 78 of the Report (UNESCO Doc. 21C/Res.4/19). The topic of the NWICO became less relevant in the 1980s because UNESCO was preoccupied with a vital financial crisis. Being charged with "survival plans," UNESCO was unable to concentrate on the NWICO. In the absence of funds to subsidize the communication infrastructure of less developed countries (Weber 2004), the information and communication order disappeared from the political agenda.

## Council of Europe/European Union: From transborder television to tele-media

In the 1980s, there was a relatively limited choice of programs for viewers and most channels were state-owned; other terrestrial "free to air" broadcasters held a dominant position in the market. In this context, the European Commission presented two Green Papers to discuss the regulatory steps needed to establish a competitive open information market: the *Green Paper on the Establishment of a Common Market in Broadcasting, especially by Satellite and Cable* (COM(84) 300) in 1984; and the *Green Paper on the Development of the Common Market for Telecommunications Services and Equipment* (COM(87) 290) in 1987.

Aiming to increase European competitiveness on the global markets (Harcourt 2008), the European Union and the European Commission, respectively, adopted the Television without Frontiers (TwF) Directive (89/552/EEC) in 1989, and the Open Network Provision (ONP) (90/387/EEC) in 1990. Resting on two keynotes, the free movement of European television programs within the internal market and the requirement for television channels to reserve more than half of their transmission time for European audiovisual programs, the TwF Directive was intended to create a single market in television broadcasting by encouraging the exploitation of new technologies (at that time), such as cable and satellite, through deregulation (Harcourt 2008). The document also called for the stimulation of the production and distribution of European works.

The ONP was intended to create harmonizing conditions for open access to telecommunications infrastructure and networks based upon the principle of non-discrimination and the elimination of exclusive rights (Harcourt 2008), by imposing rules or objectives in areas such as tariffs, contracts and billing. These directives are only the beginning of a series of subsequent directives in this field.

After the 1990s, as technological innovations began to blur the boundaries between the traditional telecommunications and the media sectors, the need for a new regulatory framework began to emerge. In 2002, the European Union published a Regulatory Framework for Electronic Communications and Services (2002/21/EC), incorporating a significant range of social and cultural policy objectives (Keller 2011). The document was designed to remodel the existing regulatory framework for telecommunications for the purpose of making the electronic communications sector more competitive.

In 2007, the European Union updated the TwF Directive by adopting the Audiovisual Media Services (AVMS) Directive,[2] which was codified in 2010.[3] With the AVMS Directive, the country of origin principle, in which service providers are only subject to the rules applicable in their own country, remained unchanged, but the coverage increased; the Directive provides a more flexible legal framework than the TwF Directive and covers all audiovisual media services—namely, linear services (traditional radio and television) and non-linear services such as video-on-demand (such as the downloading of films and broadcast programs via satellite, cable and the Internet). According to the AVMS Directive, EU countries, among others, can restrict broadcast of unsuitable on-demand audiovisual content (Article 2) by having recourse to the introduced control mode (Article 4) (see in general Kleinsteuber and Nehls 2011).

2 Directive 2007/65/EC.
3 Directive 2010/13/EU.

## World Summits on the Information Society and Internet Governance Forum

In the late 1990s, discussions on a global regime for an information and communication society were revitalized by the International Telecommunications Union (ITU) (Weber and Grosz 2009a). Taking up the discussions of a global information and communication order (Weber 2003), in 1998, the ITU passed a resolution proposing the idea of organizing a World Summit on the Information Society (WSIS) under the auspices of the United Nations.[4]

The summit's major objectives are summarized in the Geneva Declaration of Principles of the World Summit on the Information Society, held in Geneva in December 2003 (see United Nations 2003), which defines this common vision and a framework for measures to be taken in order to make this vision a reality. The subsequent WSIS in Tunis (WSIS II) in November 2005 was designed to discuss the development of the principles established in Geneva.

The guarantee of the freedom of media and of information is a key issue in the relation between media and democracy that has been reconfirmed in the context of the WSIS II and particularly within the Tunis Commitment (Weber and Grosz 2009a). The strengthening of self-reliance of countries, the democratization of communication and the provision of more extensive financial resources, as proclaimed in the context of the NWICO, have become an actual "digital divide" topic in the WSIS discussions. Despite such developments, however, media and democracy were not key issues of the WSIS, and more attention was paid to the "governance aspects" of the Internet (Weber and Grosz 2009a).

Numerous socio-political transformations have taken place in the period between the NWICO and the WSIS (Padovani and Nordenstreng 2005). Whereas the NWICO predominantly followed a political approach, the WSIS instead was built on an information technology approach that allowed it to reach a broader part of civil society (Padovani and Nordenstreng 2005). Compared to the WSIS, the NWICO and the MacBride Report followed a rather idealistic approach, as they were based on the idea of common values and aims of the countries in the sphere of communications. A typical example can be seen in the objective, in the earlier discussions, to give priority to non-commercial forms of mass communication in expanding information systems; a reduction of the commercialization of communication was even recommended (MacBride Report 1979).

Nevertheless, the outcomes of both the MacBride Report and the WSIS principles underscore the fundamental meanings of the freedom of information and the right to access information (Weber and Grosz 2009a). The reaffirmation of human rights in the WSIS principles can be crystallized around the following goals in an open information society: (1) everyone should be able to receive basic information and electronic education; (2) no-cost access to public data is essential in the information society; (3) affordable access to infrastructure must be guaranteed; and (4) intellectual property rights may not prevail over the right to education and knowledge (Weber 2004).

### *Recent developments*

Apart from the aforementioned developments, new aspects in the creation of an international media governance framework are to be taken into account, especially with regard to the

4 Resolution 73 of the ITU Plenipotentiary Conference. For further details on the historical development of the WSIS, see Malcolm (2008).

increased importance of social networks (e.g. Facebook or Twitter). Social networks and other new technologies provide for an extremely fast spread of information about people and events (Kolb 2011), but involve the risk of infringing personality rights and provoking data abuse. As a result, the call for more transparency about sharing personal data in social networks is growing within the Internet community (Taddicken 2012).

The political relevance of social networks came into the picture with the so-called "Arab Spring," which began at the end of 2010 in Tunisia when Mohamed Bouazizi, disaffected with the Tunis work system, political corruption and increasing poverty, set himself on fire. In the course of the following uprising, citizens of a number of Arab countries, including Tunisia and Egypt, organized demonstrations against the authorities, in large part through social media networks (Meddeb 2011). Although the Egyptian government succeeded in shutting down the Internet and mobile communications for a brief period of time during the demonstrations, people's desire to exchange messages and ideas prevailed.

Further developments in the media landscape bearing challenges for a future media governance framework concern the control of the media: the acquisition of Skype by Microsoft, as well as the acquisition of Motorola Mobility by Google, are worth mentioning. The continuing convergence of media sectors obviously leads to "new" media enterprises offering their services in a broad variety of communications fields.

## Elements of an adequate media governance framework

### *Conceptual and political perspectives of a media governance framework*

In the context of mass media, a distinction is often made between the traditional, hierarchically oriented "government" approach and the "governance" approach, which describes the general process of overcoming problems among the various actors involved (Meier and Trappel 2007). Discussions around the keyword "media governance" deal with the question of how developed governance principles can be used for the regulation of media, especially with regard to the fact that approaches to media regulation range between state control (particularly applied to broadcasting) and self-regulation. "Media governance," encompassing both co-regulation and self-regulation, refers to both private actors and the state that align their media policy and media organizations that develop and implement their own internal regulations (Meier 2011).[5]

According to Denis McQuail (2007), media policy should focus on certain problem areas arising from the nature of communication, such as: the achievement of due accountability for ethical, moral and professional standards of media performance; the protection of both individuals and society from potential harm in the context of communication systems; the definition of positive expectations and goals for public social and cultural communication; the maintenance of essential freedoms of communication under conditions of total surveillance and registration; and the relationship management according to democratic principles between state and political power, on the one hand, and communicative power, on the other.

5 The Interinstitutional Agreement on Better Lawmaking of 16 December 2003 (2003/C 321/01) defines "co-regulation" as "the mechanism whereby a Community legislative act entrusts the attainment of the objectives defined by the legislative authority to parties which are recognised in the field (such as economic operators, the social partners, non-governmental organisations, or associations)."

Journalistic, political, social, economic and legal differences between countries deny the assumption of the existence of only one media market. Media policymaking occurs not only at the national, but also at the regional and international, levels (Meier 2011), for the time being, a universal media governance framework does not exist. Despite the aforementioned efforts of the European Union to regulate elements of the communications industry, media governance is handled differently in various domains in Europe and worldwide, since each national and regional entity has adopted its own regulations.

## *Regulatory issues of a media governance framework*

### Overcoming present weaknesses and incoherencies of media regulations

Given the large number of domestic media regulations and the absence of a universal media governance framework, uniform arrangements regarding many relevant regulatory areas (for example media ownership, Internet filtering and censorship) are missing.

Media ownership refers to a process through which individuals or organizations control increasing shares of the mass media. This development leads to a powerful position of media groups, allowing them to exercise undue influence over media consumers.

Internet filtering,[6] enabling the "controller" to decide which data packages are allowed to be sent, is generally accomplished by Internet programs such as firewalls. For example, programmers of web pages could install filters to restrict employees' access to distracting entertainment sites to ensure the staff's productivity.

Governments engage in online censorship[7] for a range of social, cultural, security and political reasons (EU Parliament 2010). Internet censorship is a subject of growing concern around the world because governments of countries such as China, Vietnam, Iran, or Syria very often use this tool to fight their opponents (Woorkup 2010). During the aforementioned "Arab Spring," governments (often unsuccessfully) tried to silence political opposition by filtering their political statements and barring access to the media.

Given the absence of harmonized rules related to the potential regulatory areas, and in light of the corresponding risks to freedom of expression, a universal media governance framework comprising appropriate regulations is needed to create legal certainty. Public order depends on the given circumstances and the national appreciation of state interests; the term "refers to the preservation of the fundamental interests of a society, as reflected in public policy and law. These fundamental interests can relate, *inter alia*, to standards of law, security and morality" (WTO 2004: 6.467). The focus, as in international private law, is on societal interests. The objective of harmonized rules is not to jeopardize cross-border Internet traffic. For these reasons, it is of the utmost importance to remove the existing democratic deficits that accrue from media ownership, filtering and censorship.

6 "Filtering" describes the process of blocking an Internet user from visiting specific websites, for example by directive numeral simulation (DNS) tempering, URL filtering, Internet protocol (IP) address filtering, deep packet inspection (DPI), HTTP proxy filtering, geolocation filtering, content filtering software and denial of service (DoS) attacks (European Parliament 2010).

7 The term "censorship" characterizes the control or the suppressing of the publishing or accessing of information on the Internet, often undertaken by governments to filter out unwanted information and to prevent the information's spread throughout the World Wide Web.

## Need for increased cooperation between international bodies

In addition, light must be shed on the necessity of the international bodies' integration into a new media governance framework. In that regard, the Internet Society (ISOC) and the Internet Corporation for Assigned Names and Numbers (ICANN) need to be closely examined.

ISOC, founded in 1992, is a global non-profit organization with 130 organizational and more than 55,000 individual members (ISOC n.d.). The organization aims to provide leadership in Internet-related standards, education and policy for ensuring unrestricted access to the Internet for the benefit of all interested parties throughout the world; it does not make any arrangements regarding proper handling of the Internet.

ICANN was established in 1998 as a private non-profit organization headquartered in Marina del Rey, California, aiming at keeping the Internet secure, stable and interoperable, by promoting competition and developing policies on the Internet's unique identifiers.

Although both ISOC and ICANN are part of the media landscape and exercise considerable influence on the Internet, there are practically no points of contact between them and the traditional media environment, since specific regulations regarding collaboration among the two sectors do not exist. This hinders the creation of a coherent and accepted regulatory framework, and raises the question of how, and under what terms, to cooperate.

With regard to the issue of "multi-stakeholder governance" within the ongoing Internet governance discussions (e.g. see Weber 2009a), the cooperation between the aforementioned international bodies and the media landscape could rest upon their involvement in laying down media governance rules including sanctions against violators. Giving the international bodies a "voice" would entail a broader acceptance of the new media governance framework, especially with regard to the scale of influence that they exert on the media environment.

## Necessity of inclusion of private actors (media enterprises and recipients)

A dominant attribute of today's media environment consists in the concentration of media ownership. Over the last century, a large number of independent media enterprises evolved into a small number of dominant media groups regardless of nation state borders or continents (Meier and Trappel 2007). This gave a small number of media owners, such as Rupert Murdoch, significant access to the public (Barnett 2004). As they seek to concentrate their economic and societal power, these media enterprises focus on the enhancement of their productions to arouse the interest of the largest possible amount of receivers, although without giving them a vote.

Currently, consumers are practically voiceless within the whole media area; as such, the inclusion of civil society (e.g. through multi-stakeholderism) needs to be encouraged. The "involvement" of civil society refers to both their possible contribution to the organization and control of media institutions, as well as their participation in the media's "dialog" with the broad public (Eilders 2011).

Multi-stakeholderism is a quite new phenomenon. The inclusion of all stakeholders in the governance and legislation processes has become a hotly debated topic in different areas,[8] since the joint involvement of all stakeholders having the necessary know-how is desirable. The involvement of the general public in decision-making processes strengthens confidence

8 Among others, in the context of Internet governance discussions (Weber 2009a).

(Weber 2008), because the public knows what led to respective decisions. Furthermore, public participation increases the transparency and accountability of the governing bodies (Weber 2009b).

The inclusion of new issues, interests and concerns communicated by civil society can also encourage the bodies responsible for producing media services to look at the specific societal aspects from different angles, therein finding a more adaptable solution for the inclusion of civil society (Steffek and Nanz 2008). However, for the public to participate effectively in decision-making processes, it has to be able to understand and criticize technical issues, must possess sufficient knowledge of the given structures and potentials, and must have the skills necessary to negotiate with more powerful actors (Weber 2009b).

Hence the responsible information providers should concentrate their efforts on getting their audience out of inactivity by offering them more possibilities to actively participate within the media environment (Kleinsteuber 2011). Participation and involvement of civil society can have a legitimizing side effect and allow for higher credibility of the actions taken by competent institutions (Weber 2009a). Public scrutiny—as an indispensable instrument to civil society—based on adequate information mechanisms allows for public intervention in decision-making processes.

## Quality requirements and compliance with framework rules

A further disadvantage of the missing universal media governance framework lies in the fact that, as a consequence, (unified) regulations regarding quality control (see Weber 1999b) and the establishment of compliance with framework rules are still missing. In fact, quality control mechanisms traditionally exist only within domestic law—namely, within areas such as criminal law, civil law and privacy protection—but such rules can also be included in self-regulatory codes of conduct.

The issue of quality control is of particular importance to the Internet because, as the number of producers of information on the Internet expands, there is a corresponding potential for a decrease in quality of information. Eventually, the uncontrolled provision of information through an infinite number of sources negatively impacts the Internet's credibility (Holznagel and Schumacher 2011). In order to ensure that information complies with the respective framework's rules, several control mechanisms need to be introduced. Development and compliance these rules also helps to guarantee individual protection, since it might help to prevent the spread of false insults.

## Special problems related to public service requirements

Since, with regard to the broad impact and suggestive influence of radio and television, most lawmakers still adhere to the principle that a legally described public service shall be provided (following Weber 2007), public interest regulations also need to be integrated into the development of an adequate media framework.

The fundamental idea of public service aims at the establishment of provisions attempting to realize public interest objectives within the electronic media landscape (i.e. placing at the disposal of civil society a minimal offer of audiovisual topics in politically relevant domains, with the goal of building opinions and preserving culture, among other things). With respect to this objective, broadcasting programs shall actively contribute to the development and conservation of a lively culture of communication by imparting knowledge concerning all areas. To address the concern that the broadcasting market alone would be unable to meet public service requirements, official financing guaranteeing public service is provided (Weber 1999a), as part of the state's obligation (Bullinger 1999). In so doing, the dual system of public and private broadcasters and the horizontal model of regulation seems to prevail.

Within the commonly used dual system, one entity is appointed for being mainly responsible for the public service delivery. In return for this fulfillment of tasks, the so-called "public service broadcaster" would be given preferential treatment in its financing by being awarded shares of the broadcast fees. Thus the content mandate would be compensated by gaining an offset from privately financed broadcasters. Compared with this, the less-often-adapted horizontal model is marked by competition of several broadcasters in the region of both public service and simple entertainment.

### Special problems related to visual communication (privacy)

Further difficulties regarding the creation of a new media governance framework concern the nascent problems related to visual communication, especially with regard to privacy, as the quantity of visual information available on the Internet increases. Google's application *Google Street View* has become a controversial application for this reason, particularly in continental Europe. From specially equipped cars used by Google, visual records are taken of individuals, streets, places, traffic means, houses and gardens. Subsequently, those visual data are made ready for publication on the World Wide Web, legally executed by Google, Inc. in the United States (Weber 2011b). Since faces of people and license plates have not been made entirely unrecognizable, the website at least potentially violates the right to privacy and anonymity.

Securing the individual's privacy is of utmost importance, especially because media recipients have the ability to react immediately to the published visual information and can be both receiver and sender of information (Taddicken 2012). In addition, visual information usually has a strong suggestive effect on civil society and an incorrect interpretation might damage someone's reputation. As a result, the development of policy related to protection against undue publicity is an important consideration in the creation of a new international media governance framework.

## Conclusion: Towards legitimacy and accountability

Legitimacy and accountability are persistent considerations. According to Walk (2008), aspects such as competence, power, strategy, transparency and democratization serve as basic guidelines for what key elements must be included in the new media governance perspective.

Media governance, particularly with regard to the Internet, tackles central questions such as: who rules the communication channels, in whose interest, by which mechanisms, and for which purposes? (See also Weber and Grosz 2009b.) Particularly with the growing influence of some international bodies, questions of their legitimacy have arisen (Weber 2009a; Weber and Grosz 2009b). The envisaged realization of a concept of "multi-stakeholder governance," perceived as the new way ahead in favor of the inclusion of the whole society, goes beyond the scope of traditional governance theories, which generally pursue an approach strictly distinguishing the state (public law) from the society (civil law) (Weber and Grosz 2007). With this in mind, an even stronger involvement of "media enterprises," as discussed above, needs to be sought.

Such a development challenges the traditional international legal and political understanding of legitimacy as a concept primarily relevant to sovereign states as subjects of international law.

Can the same criteria for assessing states' legitimacy be applied to international entities in the media field? The development of the World Wide Web has generally led to an increase in influence of the organizations and entities engaged with the Internet. However, with the gradual extension of their operational sphere beyond merely technical questions and towards addressing policy issues, the legitimacy of their actions has been questioned—the debates on ICANN are a conspicuous example. ICANN's performance has failed to meet stakeholder expectations, and the organization undisputedly suffers from lack of accountability (Weber and Gunnarson 2011). ICANN has responded to these issues by initiating different reforms, which attempted to enhance the democratic processes within the corporation by supporting the individual Internet user's participation in ICANN's activities.

The inclusion of accountability measures is central to the development of an effective media governance framework. Accountability, based on the Latin word *computare* ("to calculate"), is a broad concept, encompassing political, legal, philosophical and other aspects; each context casts a different shade on the meaning of accountability (following Weber 2011a). Nevertheless, a general definition incorporating the main elements of accountability is directed to the obligation of a person (the accountable) to another person (the accountee), according to which the former must give account of, explain and justify his actions or decisions in an appropriate way (Weber and Weber 2010). Together with checks and balances, accountability is a prerequisite for legitimacy and an important topic in any discussion about governance. While checks and balances take place by providing mechanisms to prevent the abuse of power, accountability does so by providing for or accessing actions with mechanisms such as non-judicial remedies or judicial review (Kaufmann and Weber 2010).

In particular, accountability implies that the stakeholders who form part of the governance mechanisms should be obliged to answer to anyone. As a fundamental principle, accountability concerns itself with power, and power cannot be divorced from responsibility (Young 1989). Therefore responsibility should be commensurate with the extent of the power possessed (Lastra and Shams 2001). Furthermore, accountability depends on reliable information that needs to be available, accessible (both logistically and intellectually) and based on known sources. Without such mechanisms, civil society will not be informed or able to participate, and decision-making will not be democratic.

Accountability can be framed along the following lines (Weber and Weber 2010: 81): standards need to be introduced that hold governing bodies accountable, at least on an organizational level; such standards help to improve accountability; information should be made more readily available to the concerned recipients, enabling them to apply the standards in question to the performance of those who are held to account; active rather than passive consultation procedures are to be established; and finally, beneficiaries of accountability must be able to impose some sort of sanction, thus attaching costs to the failure to meet the standards. Such "sanctioning" is possible only if adequate participation schemes are devised through direct voting channels and indirect representation schemes.

To be widely accepted and sustainable, a media governance framework should focus on legitimacy and accountability, encompass the participation of civil society, include provisions to protect quality and privacy, and be as international as possible.

## References

Barnett, S. (2004) 'Media ownership policies: Pressures for change and implications,' *Pacific Journalism Review*, 10(2): 8–19.

Bullinger, M. (1999) *Die Aufgaben des öffentlichen Rundfunks*, Gütersloh: Bertelsmann-Stiftung.

Carlsson, U. (2003) 'The rise and fall of NWICO—and then? From a vision of international regulation to a reality of multilevel governance,' Paper presented at EURICOM Colloquium in Venice, May. Online. Available HTTP: http://www.bfsf.it/wsis/cosa%20dietro%20al%20nuovo%20ordine.pdf (accessed 30 May 2012).

Dittler, H. P. (2011) 'Besonderheiten der Internetkommunikation,' in W. Kleinwächter (ed.) *Grundrecht Internetfreiheit*, Berlin: Eurocaribe Druck Hamburg.

Eilders, C. (2011) 'Zivilgesellschaftliche Beteiligung im Medienbereich,' in H. J. Kleinsteuber and S. Nehls (eds.) *Media Governance in Europa: Regulierung—Partizipation—Mitbestimmung*, Hamburg/Haan: VS Verlag.

European Parliament (Directorate-General for External Policies) (2010) *Information and Communication Technologies and Human Rights*. Online. Available HTTP: http://www.europarl.europa.eu/activities/committees/studies/download.do?language=it&file=31731 (accessed 30 May 2012).

Harcourt, A. (2008) 'Introduction,' in G. Terzis (ed.) *European Media Governance: The Brussels Dimension*, Bristol/Chicago, IL: Intellect.

Holznagel, B. and Schumacher, P. (2011) 'Die Freiheit der Internetdienste,' in W. Kleinwächter (ed.) *Grundrecht Internetfreiheit*, Berlin: Eurocaribe Druck.

Internet Society (ISOC) (n.d.) 'Our members.' Online. Available HTTP: http://www.internetsociety.org/who-we-are/our-members (accessed 30 May 2012).

Kaufmann, C. and Weber, R. H. (2010) 'The role of transparency in financial regulation,' *Journal of International Economic Law*, 13: 779–797.

Keller, P. (2011) *European and International Media Law: Liberal Democracy, Trade, and the New Media*, Oxford: Oxford University Press.

Kleinsteuber, H. J. and Nehls, S. (eds.) (2011) *Media Governance in Europa: Regulierung—Partizipation—Mitbestimmung*, Hamburg/Haan: VS Verlag.

Kleinwächter, W. (ed.) *Grundrecht Internetfreiheit*, Berlin: Eurocaribe Druck.

Kolb, A. (2011) 'Internet, Recht, Internetrecht und die Medien,' in W. Kleinwächter (ed.) *Grundrecht Internetfreiheit*, Berlin: Eurocaribe Druck.

Lastra, R. M. and Shams, H. (2001) 'Public accountability in the financial sector,' in E. Ferran and C. A. E. Goodhart (eds.) *Regulating Financial Services and Markets in the 21st Century*, Oxford: Hart Publishing.

Lester, P. M. (2006) *Syntactic Theory of Visual Communication*. Online. Available HTTP: http://commfaculty.fullerton.edu/lester/writings/viscomtheory.html (accessed 30 May 2012).

Malcolm, J. (2008) *Multi-Stakeholder Governance and the Internet Governance Forum*, Perth: Terminus Press.

McQuail, D. (2007) 'The current state of media governance in Europe,' in G. Terzis (ed.) *European Media Governance: National and Regional Dimensions*, Bristol/Chicago, IL: Intellect.

Meddeb, A. (2011) *Printemps de Tunis: La Métamorphose de l'Histoire*, Paris: Editions Albin Michel.

Meier, W. A. (2011) 'Demokratie und Media Governance in Europa,' in H. J. Kleinsteuber and S. Nehls (eds.) *Media Governance in Europa: Regulierung—Partizipation—Mitbestimmung*, Hamburg/Haan: VS Verlag.

——, and Trappel, J. (2007) 'Medienkonzentration und Media Governance,' in P. Donges (ed.) *Von der Medienpolitik zur Media Governance?* Köln: Halem.

Padovani, C. and Nordenstreng, K. (2005) 'From NWICO to WSIS: Another world information and communication order?' *Global Media and Communication*, 1(3): 264–272. Online. Available HTTP: http://www.uta.fi/laitokset/tiedotus/laitos/From_NWICO_to_WSIS.pdf (accessed 30 May 2012).

Press, A. L. and Williams, B. A. (2010) *The New Media Environment: An Introduction*, Oxford: Wiley-Blackwell.

Shamsuddoha, M. (2008) *Globalization to Glocalization: A Conceptual Analysis*. Online. Available HTTP: http://papers.ssrn.com/sol3/papers.cfm?abstract_id=1321662 (accessed 30 May 2012).

Steffek, J. and Nanz, P. (2008) 'Emergent patterns of civil society participation in global and European governance,' in J. Steffek, C. Kissling and P. Nanz (eds.) *Civil Society Participation in European and Global Governance: A Cure for the Democratic Deficit?* Basingstoke: Palgrave Macmillan.

Suresh, K. (2003) 'Theories of communication,' in K. Suresh (ed.) *Journalism and Mass Communication*. Online. Available HTTP: http://www.peoi.org/Courses/Coursesen/mass/mass2.html (accessed 30 May 2012).

Taddicken, M. (2012) 'Privacy, surveillance, and self-disclosure in the social web: Exploring the user's perspective via focus groups,' in C. Fuchs, K. Boersma, A. Albrechtslund and M. Sandoval (eds.)

*Internet and Surveillance: The Challenges of Web 2.0 and Social Media*, New York and London: Routledge.
UNESCO (1980) *Many Voices, One World: Towards a New, More Just and More Efficient World Innovation and Communication Order* (the MacBride Report). Online. Available HTTP: http://unesdoc.unesco.org/images/0004/000400/040066eb.pdf (accessed 30 May 2012).
United Nations (2003) *Declaration of Principles: Building the Information Society—A Global Challenge in the New Millennium*, Document WSIS–03/GENEVA/DOC/4-E. Online. Available HTTP: http://www.itu.int/wsis/docs/geneva/official/dop.html (accessed 30 May 2012).
Van Dijk, G., Minocha, S. and Laing, A. (2007) 'Consumers, channels and communication: Online and offline communication in service consumption,' *Interacting with Computers*, 19(1): 7–19.
Walk, H. (2008) *Partizipative Governance: Beteiligungsformen und Beteiligungsrechte im Mehrebenensystem der Klimapolitik*, Wiesbaden: VS Verlag.
Warschauer, M. (2001) 'Online communication,' in R. Carter and D. Nunan (eds.) *The Cambridge Guide to Teaching English to Speakers of Other Languages*, Cambridge: Cambridge University Press. Online. Available HTTP: http://www.gse.uci.edu/person/warschauer_m/oc.html (accessed 30 May 2012).
Weber, R. H. (1999a) *Neustrukturierung der Rundfunkordnung*, Zurich: Schulthess.
—— (1999b) 'Information und Schutz Privater,' *Zeitschrift für Schweizerisches Recht*, II: 1–86.
—— (2004) 'From "Many Voices One World" to "Information Society",' *Computer Law Review International*, 4: 97–104.
—— (2007) *Media Governance und Service Public*, Zurich: Schulthess.
—— (2008) 'Transparency and the governance of the Internet,' *Computer Law and Security Report*, 24: 342–348.
—— (2009a) *Shaping Internet Governance: Regulatory Challenges*, Zurich: Schulthess.
—— (2009b) 'Accountability in Internet governance,' *International Journal of Communications Law & Policy*, 13: 144–159.
—— (2011a) 'Accountability in the Internet of Things,' *Computer Law and Security Review*, 27: 133–138.
—— (2011b) 'Switzerland: Data protection compliance of Google Street View,' *Computer Law Review International*, 3: 87–89.
—— and Grosz, M. (2007) 'Internet governance: From vague ideas to realistic implementation,' *medialex*, 3: 119–135.
—— and —— (2009a) 'Legal framework for media and democracy,' *Communications*, 34(2): 221–232.
—— and —— (2009b) 'Legitimate governing of the Internet,' *International Journal of Private Law*, 2: 316–330.
—— and Gunnarson, R. S. (2012) 'A constitutional solution for Internet governance.' Online. Available HTTP: http://user.xmission.com/~kirton/images/News_articles/gunnersonsolution.pdf (accessed 30 May 2012).
—— and Schneider, T. (2009) *Internet Governance and Switzerland's Particular Role in its Processes*, Zurich: s.n.
—— and Weber, R. (2010) *Internet of Things: Legal Perspectives*, Zurich: Schulthess.
Woorkup (2010) *Internet Censorship 2010 Report*. Online. Available HTTP: http://woorkup.com/2010/06/27/internet-censorship-report/ (accessed 30 May 2012).
World Trade Organization (2004) *United States: Measures Affecting the Cross-Border Supply of Gambling and Betting Services (US-Gambling)*, WT/DS285/R, Panel report. Online. Available HTTP: http://www.wto.org/english/tratop_e/dispu_e/285r_e.pdf (accessed 30 May 2012).
Young, S. B. (1989) 'Reconceptualizing accountability in the early nineteenth century: How the tort of negligence appeared,' *Connecticut Law Review*, 21: 197–292.

# 21

# Self- and co-regulation

## Evidence, legitimacy and governance choice

*Michael Latzer, Natascha Just and Florian Saurwein*

The combination of globalization, liberalization and the convergence of communications markets have triggered major changes in the governance arrangements of the communications sector, including the growing role of alternative modes of regulation (e.g. self- and co-regulation). These alternatives to traditional statutory regulation are marked by a stronger involvement of non-governmental actors in regulatory processes. Both industry and policymakers consider alternative modes of regulation to have great potential for solving contemporary problems of communications regulation. The increase in alternative regulatory institutions, their potential advantages and disadvantages as compared to state regulation, and challenges of governance choice between available modes of regulation have led to an increasing political and scientific interest in self- and co-regulation. This chapter brings together central findings from research on alternative modes of regulation in the convergent communications sector, focusing on results regarding evidence, legitimacy and governance choice.

### Communications governance in the regulatory state

Traditionally, national governments have played a pivotal role in the development and control of the electronic communications sector. Strong, sector-specific state regulation, particularly monopoly regulations and public property in market-dominant companies, have characterized both the electronic media and the telecommunications sectors in most developed economies worldwide (Noam 1991, 1992; Latzer 1997; Schneider 2001; van Cuilenburg and McQuail 2003; Bauer 2010). In recent decades, this dominant pattern of government intervention in the electronic communications sectors has eroded, and the emerging new pattern of control is leading to a transformation of statehood in the convergent communications sector (Latzer 1999; Just and Latzer 2004). This new pattern of statehood is characterized by changes in content (policy), institutional structures (polity) and processes (politics). With respect to the institutional dimension of communications governance, the transformation of statehood is reflected in several trends (Latzer 2000), among others by a shift from national regulation to international regulation, by the establishment of independent regulatory agencies (IRAs), by an increase in self- and co-regulation, and by a trend from central regulation to decentralized, technology-based self-help by individual users. In sum, these trends lead to a redistribution of regulatory responsibilities in the governance arrangement of the communications sector. However, the changing role of the state in general, and self- and co-regulation in particular, are not unique to the communications sector.

Symptoms similar to those identified with the concept of a transformation of statehood in the communications sector are discussed in various other sectors as well. They are generally dealt with as shifts from government to governance (Rosenau and Czempiel 1992; Rhodes 1996), from hierarchical to a cooperative form of government (Mayntz 2003, 2009), from an interventionist/positive state towards a regulatory state[1] (Majone 1996, 1999; Moran 2002), and even a post-regulatory state (Scott 2004). The trends refer to several changes in the institutional formation and the modes of steering and control, for instance to the emergence of responsive regulation (Ayres and Braithwaite 1992; Baldwin and Black 2007) and to new modes of governance (see Hèritier 2002; Treib, Baer and Falkner 2005) that rely on more indirect approaches for achieving behavioral change (Knill and Lenschow 2005).

Today, the institutional governance approach assists scholars of various disciplines in their efforts to analyze the complex patterns of steering and control in contemporary societies (Mayntz 2008). The governance approach extends the traditional, rather narrow focus on national–hierarchical government to the interplay between various levels of control and to the changing division of regulatory responsibilities (Rosenau and Czempiel 1992). It recognizes varieties in institutional steering and control arrangements—that is, the varieties in rules, organizations and actors in their respective roles as controllers and controllees, and the varieties in control mechanisms (Scott 2004). It describes, for example, the vertical and horizontal extension of government (Engel 2004; Mayntz 2009). At the vertical level, there are changing institutional arrangements of regional, national, supranational and international players toward a multilevel governance structure. At the horizontal level, governance expands from governmental regulation to the inclusion of private/societal actors that take over regulatory tasks and form new regulatory networks beyond, and in cooperation with, governmental actors (Streeck and Schmitter 1995; Ronit and Schneider 1999; Rhodes 1996; Scott 2002; Buthe and Mattli 2011). Scholars have also observed and described these trends for governance in the communications sector (e.g. Holznagel and Werle 2004; Raboy and Padovani 2010; Puppis 2010).

These general governance trends often form the wider background for scientific analyses of self- and co-regulation. More narrowly, their analyses are driven by observations and considerations such as: (1) the growth in attention for and trust in alternative regulatory solutions by politics and industry; (2) an increase in the number of alternative regulatory institutions; and (3) the weighting of potential benefits and drawbacks of self- and co-regulation as compared

1 The emergence of the *regulatory state* is strongly associated with the rise of non-majoritarian institutions (Thatcher and Stone Sweet 2002) in general and independent regulatory agencies (IRAs) in particular. Analyses of the regulatory state therefore focus on the politics of delegation of regulatory powers, the rise of independent regulatory agencies, the state of de facto independence, and the trade-off between efficiency and democratic accountability (Jacint, Levi-Faur and Fernandez 2009; Gilardi 2008, 2007; Maggetti 2007; Hans-Bredow-Institut *et al.* 2011). Independent regulatory agencies, as well as alternative modes of regulation, serve as indicators of the trends from government to governance and from the interventionist to the regulatory state. However, compared to IRAs, self- and co-regulatory arrangements represent a further step away from traditional, politically dominated state institutions towards indirect government.

to state regulation (Latzer, Just, Saurwein and Slominski 2002; 2003). As regards potential *advantages*, alternative regulatory institutions are expected to:

i. overcome the problem of information deficits of state regulation because they benefit from greater expertise and special skills within the industry (e.g. of a technical nature);
ii. be faster and more flexible than state regulation, mostly because they are not bound by statutory procedures to the same extent as state regulation;
iii. reduce regulatory cost to the state and implementation costs in general, especially because profit-driven companies are supposed to carry out the self-regulatory process more cost-efficiently; and
iv. be applicable in areas sensitive to state regulation (e.g. in content regulation, where government intervention may conflict with the principle of freedom of expression).

However, the literature also refers to a list of potential disadvantages of self-regulation as compared to state regulation. Alternative modes of regulation may:

i. provide symbolic policy with weak standards, ineffective enforcement, mild sanctions and limited reach, because they often apply only to those who voluntarily participate and not to all members of an industry;
ii. result in self-service by the industry, with public interests being neglected vis-à-vis private interests—and the outsourcing of regulation may also result in a loss of know-how on the part of regulators, thus exacerbating existing information asymmetries;
iii. entail the danger of cartels and other anticompetitive behavior, resulting from close cooperation between companies in self- and co-regulatory regimes—and the dominance of large, long-established companies in self- and co-regulation may produce solutions that discriminate against smaller enterprises and newcomers; and
iv. decrease the democratic quality of regulation, especially owing to lack of accountability, transparency, legal certainty and the like.

The increase in political and industry attention to alternative regulatory solutions, their sharp increase in numbers, and considerations of advantages and disadvantages are often the starting point for case studies. The numerous issues that are dealt with can be grouped into five fields of analysis.

i. For empirical and theoretical research on alternative modes of regulation, clear definitions and classifications are indispensable. They make it possible to analytically grasp applications and to assess transformation processes.
ii. Research often concentrates on descriptive analyses of empirical evidence of self- and co-regulation. It tries to identify examples, modes of application and patterns of diffusion that contribute to the transformation of the governance arrangement in communications.
iii. The rise of alternative regulatory institutions raises major questions about their implications. The danger of a steadily decreasing democratic quality of regulation is leading to a closer look at democratic standards such as participation and accountability (input legitimacy).
iv. However, legitimacy of alternative regulatory institutions can also derive from valuable contributions to the achievement of public objectives (output legitimacy). Hence performance evaluation is a central, but rather difficult, task for research.

v. Finally, the growing role of alternative modes of regulation gives rise to major questions about regulatory choice between available governance mechanisms. Research is developing approaches for *ex ante* assessments, and is focusing on the identification of factors that should be included in any effort to predict whether alternative regulatory arrangements are likely to emerge and to be effective.

## Definitions and classifications

Despite rising interest in alternative modes of regulation, definitions of self- and co-regulation vary widely. Even for self-regulation—which is well established in practice and has been subject to research for a long time—there is no "clear picture of its properties as a distinctive organizational form" (Porter and Ronit 2006: 42). Porter and Ronit argue that this is in part because:

> . . . existing studies scattered around the social sciences have chosen to examine self-regulation as one variant of a broader spectrum of regulatory arrangements involving mixes of public and private elements (Grabosky 1995; Sinclair 1997) and analyzed under such diverse historical and contemporary names as gentleman agreements, codes of conduct, ethical guidelines, voluntary agreements, standards, certification schemes, guilds, charters, cartels, regimes, syndicates, networks, alliances, self-governments, private governments, private interest governments, partnerships and a vast variety of other forms.
> (*Porter and Ronit 2006: 42*)

On the one hand, there is a common understanding that alternative modes of regulation differ from pure state/governmental regulation, because they are marked by the involvement of non-governmental actors in regulatory processes. On the other hand, alternative modes of regulation are distinct from pure market coordination driven by the private interests of individuals and organizations, because regulation refers to intentional restraints on the conduct of market players with the goal of achieving public objectives. Alternative modes of regulation usually have identifiable institutional forms (norms, organizations) and make use of instruments that relate to at least one of the three stages in the regulatory process: rule-making, enforcement or adjudication. These characteristics constitute alternative modes of regulation as distinctive institutional phenomena.

"Self-regulation" is often referred to as a process in which rules that govern market behavior are developed and enforced by the governed themselves. It is often a collective, voluntary activity, involving market participants who agree to abide by joint rules, much like a club membership (NCC 2000; Gupta and Lad 1983). This standard definition of voluntary industry self-regulation is challenged, because examples point to potential shortcomings of this rather narrow understanding. In practice, not all self-regulatory institutions cover all regulatory stages, from rule-making to enforcement and imposing sanctions. Regulatory responsibilities may be split between state and private institutions along the regulatory process.[2] Alongside collective self-regulation there is also individual self-regulation, which is valid only for single companies. Such individual self-regulation can be referred to as "self-organization" (Puppis *et al.* 2004) and includes, for example, concepts of corporate governance and corporate social responsibility. Other individual forms of self-regulation can

2 Standardization organizations usually do not provide certain enforcement mechanisms. Internet hotlines for reporting illegal content complement state enforcement, but the definition of what kind of content is illegal is defined in legislation, not by the hotline service providers themselves.

be observed at the user/consumer level. Measures are taken by individuals to protect their interests and rights, thus restricting their own behavior as well as the opportunities of suppliers, for example by means of filter software or privacy-enhancing technologies. These growing modes of individual self-regulation can be referred to as "self-help" (Dam 1999; Latzer and Saurwein 2008), and they often make use of technological architectures and their constraining effects, as pointed out by Lessig (1999).

Self-regulation is often a misnomer, because self-regulation by the industry only rarely exists without a contribution from the state (cf. Sinclair 1997; Price and Verhulst 2000). The relationships between the state and private institutions, the hybrid regulatory constellations involving public and private actors, the role of law and the involvement of government in alternative regulatory arrangements are therefore highlighted frequently in the literature (Michael 1995; Cane 1996; Doyle 1997; Gunningham and Sinclair 1999; Baldwin and Cave 1999; Ogus 2001; Black 2001, 1996; Engel 2004; Levi-Faur 2010). Many analytical classifications suggest analysis of alternative regulatory arrangements according to varying modes and degree of state involvement (Gunningham and Rees 1997; Latzer, Just, Saurwein and Slominski 2002, 2006; Bartle and Vass 2007). Many of these classifications are based on the term "self-regulation" but, by means of extensions in terminology, they also take into account forms of governmental involvement, such as enforced self-regulation (Braithwaite 1982; Price and Verhulst 2000), audited self-regulation (Michael 1995), mandated self-regulation (Gunningham and Rees 1997), regulated self-regulation (Hoffmann-Riem 2000; Schulz and Held 2002), or self-regulation in a wide sense (Latzer, Just, Saurwein and Slominski 2002). From an institutional perspective, regulation takes place on a continuum between pure state regulation, on the one hand, and pure self-regulation, on the other; this can generally be understood as a closely interlinked combination of state/public and societal/private contributions (Gunningham and Rees 1997; Sinclair 1997; Lehmkuhl 2008).

Another term that refers to the shared responsibility and partnership between industry and the state is "co-regulation," which is used increasingly, but not consistently, in politics and research. In general, the "co-" points to the involvement of both governmental and private actors in the regulatory arrangement. Definitions of co-regulation sometimes specify the regulatory instruments with which governmental players define the formal basis for cooperation with private actors (e.g. by means of legislative acts and formal delegation of regulatory powers—see Latzer, Just, Saurwein and Slominski 2002). Broader concepts of co-regulation build on the "legal link" between private and state contributions to the regulatory arrangement (HBI and EMR 2006a). Others define co-regulation by structuring the distribution of responsibilities between governmental and private actors within the regulatory process (Ofcom 2006).

These classifications often focus on formal state contributions in alternative regulatory arrangements; they prove useful for the classification of regulatory institutions, for identifying formal state involvement in alternative regulatory arrangements and for monitoring institutional changes. In addition, it is important to consider less formalized state action, which is a more implicit, but nevertheless crucial, ingredient in the formation of governance arrangements. Bartle and Vass (2007: 894) propose a category called "tacitly supported self-regulation," and Birnhack and Elkin-Koren (2003) point to the relevance of "invisible handshakes" between public authorities and private actors. State authorities can draw on a range of instruments to support alternative regulatory institutions, to make active use of them and to control them. These may be applied in a differentiated manner along different stages of the policy cycle, from agenda-setting and problem identification via organization-building and rule-making, to implementation/enforcement and evaluation (Porter and Ronit 2006). Various forms of the "shadow of hierarchy" (Héritier and Lehmkuhl 2008; Héritier and Eckert 2008) are marked by varying degrees of intensity of state involvement, with measures ranging from soft forms of symbolic support to direct control in a co-regulatory framework (Latzer and Saurwein 2008).

## Evidence: Patterns of application

A growing body of literature depicts institutional changes in the governance arrangement to demonstrate evidence for emerging governance patterns. This calls for *descriptive analyses* of where and how alternative modes of regulation are applied in practice (and where not), and how alternative regulatory arrangements emerge, disappear and change over time. For analyses of patterns of application and transformation in communications, the first challenge is the definition of the communications sector. Should analyses be limited to mass communication services or should they also encompass services for individual and group communication? Is the focus on media content or should analyses be expanded to regulatory arrangements for communications infrastructure and transaction services such as e-commerce? Answers to these questions are not a matter of right or wrong, but strongly dependent on research interests and available resources. The convergence of communications sectors (broadcasting, telecommunications, print, Internet) and the changes of the techno-social communication systems toward mediamatics (see Latzer 1997) call for an integrated perspective (Latzer 2009), but comprehensive, all-embracing analyses of alternative modes of regulation in communications are an exception (Latzer, Just, Saurwein and Slominski 2002; PCMLP 2004). A review on mostly sectoral analyses reveals that alternative modes of regulation are applied in many subsectors of the communications market, and that many regulatory challenges overlap. Moreover, one can observe a strong increase of alternative regulatory institutions in communications since the mid-1990s, which is leading to challenging additional questions regarding their legitimacy, performance and governance choice.

In the press sector, the traditional regulatory structure is characterized by self-regulation, on the one hand, and a general legal framework, on the other. For professional ethics, there is a tradition of voluntary self-regulation of the press, while state authorities exert no appreciable influence. For this reason, there are very few co-regulatory systems that have been developed especially for the press (HBI and EMR 2006a; Puppis 2009). The self-regulatory practice has been institutionalized for the press by a large number of ethical guidelines and mediation services. It comprises both self-organization at the company level and collective self-regulation in the form of press councils. With comparative analysis, PCMLP (2004a; 2004c) finds that nine of fifteen EU states have press councils. Puppis (2009) describes twenty-three press councils in EU and European Free Trade Agreement (EFTA) countries. Europe's oldest press council is the Swedish Pressens Opinionsnämn, which was established in 1916. The majority of "press" councils are responsible for journalism in different media (Puppis 2009), and in a reaction to online publishing many councils have extended their scope to online journalism.

Broadcasting is traditionally more strictly regulated by law than the press sector. Of traditional importance in Europe is the regulatory regime for public service broadcasting (PSB). Control of PSB is sometimes referred to as co-regulation, because it combines a legal framework with self-organization in the operational practice intended to foster PSB's independence from politics and state authorities. While collective broadcasting self-regulation was introduced early in the United States by the National Association of Broadcasting (Campbell 1999), it does not have a long tradition in European broadcasting. Only in recent times, with the liberalization of broadcasting in Europe, have self-regulatory institutions for commercial broadcasters emerged. These "self-regulation islands" operate within regulatory arrangements that are traditionally controlled by state regulatory institutions in a narrow sense and, to an increasing extent, by independent regulatory agencies (IRAs). Alternative modes of regulation in European broadcasting more often take the form of co-regulation (e.g. Freiwillige Selbstkontrolle Fernsehen, or FSF, in Germany) than of self-regulation. One of the major fields of application of alternative modes of regulation in broadcasting is parental control, such as by means of program rating (PCMLP 2004a: 29f), combined with watershed regulations or filtering, which was introduced with the V-chip for analog television (Price 1998; Price and Verhulst 2002; PCMLP 2004a: 29f). Forms of alternative regulation in the broadcasting sector are not, however, restricted to programming. Developments on the television market are largely influenced by technical standards that are developed in industrial consortiums and in recognized standards bodies—the standards for digital broadcasting, for example, in the Digital Video Broadcasting (DVB) Project. Moreover, broadcasting governance is also influenced by alternative regulatory institutions in the film and advertising sectors.

The film industry is also controlled by varied regulatory institutions for age classification of movies (rating), which are carried out by public or private regulatory organizations. In the United States, for example, the Motion Picture Association of America has been operating a self-regulatory scheme since 1968. The German Freiwillige Selbstkontrolle der Filmwirtschaft (FSK), in contrast, is embedded in a co-regulatory framework. Many countries have a legal basis for film classification (see Olsberg/SPI *et al.* 2003), but specifications differ, among other things, according to whether they apply to cinema performances only or also include other presentation media (DVD, video, broadcasting). Leeway for self-regulation initiatives is created where downstream opportunities for exploiting the media are only marginally covered by governmental regulation. This flexibility is in some cases used in practice, for example in the UK by the Video Standards Council (VSC), in which a code of practice for promoting higher standards in the video industry has been developed. The Netherlands follows an integrated co-regulatory classification approach, with a rating scheme (*Kijkwijzer*) that covers movies, videos, DVDs and television programs, including music videos and some mobile services (NICAM 2007).

In contrast to the film and broadcasting industry, the electronic games industry (video, console and computer games) is comparatively young. Debates about the need for regulation started correspondingly late, and neither governmental regulation nor self-regulation has a long tradition here. In the United States, the Entertainment Software Association (ESA) established the Entertainment Software Rating Board (ESRB) as a non-profit, self-regulatory body in 1994. It assigns computer and video game content ratings, and enforces industry-adopted advertising guidelines for the interactive entertainment software industry. In many European countries where self-regulation is important, recourse is made to the Pan-European Game Information System (PEGI), launched in 2003 by the Interactive Software Federation of Europe (ISFE). Recently, PEGI has even replaced a few existing national age-rating systems. In Germany, rating of electronic games is carried out by the Unterhaltungssoftware Selbstkontrolle (USK), which is embedded in the co-regulatory arrangement provided by the Youth Media-Protection State Agreement.

Alternative regulatory institutions have also been established at international, European and national levels for advertising, marketing and public relations (PR). There are a large number of ethical guidelines and organizations for collective self-regulation (e.g. advertising councils), some with a long tradition (see Boddewyn 1985, 1988). The Advertising Code of the International Chamber of Commerce (ICC), for example, was adopted as early as 1937. In Europe, advertising self-regulation is coordinated by the European Advertising Standards Alliance (EASA). In many European countries, there is a dual system for advertising regulation, with both legal regulations and self-regulatory advertising codes and councils. But advertising is also one of the subjects recommended for co-regulation (HBI and EMR 2006a) and co-regulation has been applied successfully in the UK (Brown 2006). The diversification of marketing and PR instruments that accompany technological developments in the communications sector (e.g. telemarketing, email marketing, and behavioral targeting) also results in new self-regulatory initiatives. Codes of conduct are developed for email marketing, such as in the German Dialog Marketing Association (DDV). At the international level, the Interactive Advertising Bureau Europe (IAB Europe) recently launched a self-regulatory scheme for better privacy and data protection in online media. In the future, privacy-enhancing technologies (PETs) are also expected to gain importance, and implementation responsibilities will shift to the individual user.

The telecommunications industry in most developed economies was for a long time characterized by strong sector-specific state regulation, particularly monopoly regulations and public property in market-dominant companies (Bauer 2010). Alternative modes of regulation did not play a major role, apart from technical standardization (Werle 2001), for example by the European Telecommunications Standards Institute (ETSI). With the liberalization of telecommunications sectors, the governance arrangement has changed. Alternative modes of regulation have gained in importance for selected governance issues in telecommunications. Examples are the coordination of administration for interconnection, transparency regulations for premium telecommunications services (e.g. ICSTIS in the UK and DVTM in Germany), coordination of decisions on antenna positions, and protection of minors from access to harmful content on mobile devices. Content regulation is a new challenge to the telecommunications industry. The first self-regulatory reactions were observed in the UK and Germany in 2004–05. In 2004, UK mobile operators announced a joint code of practice for the self-regulation of new forms of content on mobile phones and subsequently established the British Independent Mobile Classification Body (IMCB), an independent organization for classifying content that is distributed via mobile phones. The classification system is based on a self-rating procedure implemented by the content providers. The IMCB examines complaints about incorrect assignments. In Germany, mobile operators agreed on a code of conduct for the protection of minors in 2005. One year later, the mobile initiative merged into the Freiwillige Selbstkontrolle Multimedia-Diensteanbieter e.V. (FSM). More recently, at the European level, the European Commission has initiated the European Framework for Safer Mobile Use by Young Teenagers and Children. The framework describes principles and measures that the signatories committed themselves to implement at a national level throughout Europe, including access control for adult content, awareness-raising campaigns for parents and children, the classification of commercial content according to national standards of decency and appropriateness, and the fight against illegal content on mobiles.

Many of these examples show how traditional sectors are expanding into the Internet realm and how established regulatory institutions are extending their scope to Internet issues, which leads to regulatory convergence (Latzer 2009). Internet diffusion has also led to the establishment of new organizations and standards (PCMLP 2004b; Tambini, Leonardi and Marsden 2008). These cannot look back on any historical traditions, but, right at the beginning of the Internet's development, models of self-regulation were strongly promoted to protect "the Net" against interference from governmental institutions and legislative regulation—"Keep your laws off our Net!" was the slogan (Boyle 1997: 189). This normative claim, combined with the need for substantial technical expertise, might have been an important lesson why essential technical standardization of the Internet is carried out by expert bodies such as the Internet Engineering Task Force (IETF), the Internet Architecture Board (IAB) and the World-Wide-Web Consortium (W3C) with hardly any formal governmental involvement. The standardization bodies are characterized as open, collaborative organizations, "resembling a fluid and loosely linked network of individuals and institutions under a common structural framework" (Dutton and Peltu 2005). Stronger (inter-)governmental involvement is evident for regulation of the domain name system by the Internet Cooperation of Assigned Names and Numbers (ICANN). ICANN assumed regulatory responsibilities under a US Department of Commerce contract and established the Governmental Advisory Committee (GAC). Yet the relationship between users at large, governments, and technical and business communities is still a process of continued redefinition of roles, rights and duties (Dutton and Peltu 2005).

Informal social standards for Internet users (Netiquette), formal technical standards (protocols, codes) and organizations for domain-name administration are increasingly being supplemented by other self- and co-regulatory institutions for Internet issues. Since the mid–1990s, for example, national Internet service providers associations (ISPAs) have been set up, which take over self-regulatory tasks and develop codes of conduct (PCMLP 2004a, 2004b). Hotlines for illegal Internet content are also being installed, such as the Meldpunt ter bestrijding van Kinderpornografie op Internet in the Netherlands and the Internet Watch Foundation (IWF) in the UK. They use "notice and takedown procedures" to support governmental agencies in combating illegal content. In addition to the initiatives of cross-industry associations, various sectoral initiatives have been started at the Internet content provider (ICP) level. For example, the mid-1990s saw the foundation of the Health on the Net Foundation (HON) and the adoption of a HON code of conduct for the sensitive medical and healthcare information sector on the Internet (Boyer *et al.* 1998; Boyer and Geissbuhler 2005).

The growth of Internet content and sites and the resulting increase in importance of providers of search services has led to self-regulation. There are forms of individual self-regulation (self-organization) by operators of search engines, such as Google's Code of Conduct (2004) and Yahoo's Corporate Governance Guideline (2006). In 2005, the German search engine providers formed the first worldwide collective initiative. The Selbstkontrolle Suchmaschinen was established under the umbrella of the Freiwillige Selbstkontrolle Multimedia-Diensteanbieter e.V. (FSM) and adopted its Subcode of Conduct for the Search-Engine Providers.

Another major policy field for self- and co-regulatory approaches on the Internet is the protection of children by content rating and filtering (Keller and Verhulst 2001; Lievens, Dumortier and Patrick 2006; Latzer and Saurwein 2008; Lievens 2010). Complex regulatory systems with major industry participation are emerging for rating and filtering digital content. Forms of collective self-regulation are found in both the development of rating systems and in the technical standardization of filter software. However, so far, a couple of more or less ambitious initiatives for content rating have failed, most prominently the Internet Content Rating Association (ICRA) (Archer 2009). Internet rating and filtering models are often based on a self-rating approach in which producers or providers of the content rate it themselves. Here, individual self-restriction sees them comply with the standardized criteria agreed upon beforehand in the context of collective self-regulation. Categorization of content that is possibly harmful or unsuitable for minors, e.g. through rating and labeling in combination with technical solutions, such as filtering and access control, is frequently mentioned in the various alternative regulatory initiatives.

Increasing user-generated content (UGC) and the rapid growth of social network services are accompanied by self-organization and self-regulation. IDATE, TNO and IViR (2008) found eighteen codes and guidelines for UGC in different industries. A frequently addressed issue in the codes and guidelines is the infringement of intellectual property (IP) rights by online services and on UGC platforms. Several initiatives have been set up especially to fight

IP infringements. Many codes also address issues such as illegal content, hate speech and obscenity, as well as unsuitable or undesirable content that is not necessarily illegal. The origin of these codes and guidelines varies from initiatives that have some level of government involvement, to collective self-regulatory initiatives of the industry or individual companies. Thanks to their "wiki" nature, some self-regulatory initiatives even give individual users a hand in making the codes (IDATE, TNO and IViR 2008: 57). At the European level, in 2009 the European Commission initiated the Safer Social Networking Principles for the EU.

Finally, alternative modes of regulation on the Internet are also applied in the context of e-commerce (de Bruin *et al.* 2005). They focus on transactions and they have been established to enhance consumer protection and to increase consumer confidence in e-commerce services (OECD 1999). Alternative regulatory institutions typically operate with codes of conduct, trustmarks/quality seals, or alternative dispute resolution (ADR) systems such as ombudsman schemes. Following the Internet euphoria of the late 1990s, numerous trustmarks and online dispute resolution schemes (ODR) were established, but only a few trustmarks have achieved significance in the marketplace (Calliess 2007) and many ODR systems have already ceased (ibid.). Webtrust and Eurolabel are among the bigger initiatives that operate on an international scale, but quality seals and dispute resolution systems are also offered by many national trade associations and private companies. Transaction-related self-regulation in order to increase consumer trust has also emerged in the field of online gambling. The E-Commerce and Online Gaming Regulation and Assurance (eCogra) operates a control scheme under which more than 140 online gambling services have been certified. The interactive communication capabilities of the Internet have also enabled other alternative modes of governance in e-commerce, such as the establishment of large-scale reputation mechanism systems, including collaborative ratings and personalized evaluation (Zacharia, Moukas and Maes 2000; Dellarocas 2003). These decentralized mechanisms complement both state and industry self-regulation in e-commerce.

This brief overview of examples of self- and co-regulation in communication markets shows a variety of applications and some patterns of diffusion. Self-regulation already has a long tradition in the communications sector. Above all, there is a long history of institutions for technical standardization in communications, as well as ethical guidelines for journalism and advertising (press and advertising codes and councils). In the convergent communications sector, applications were extended to areas such as (mobile) telephony and Internet-based services, and the rapid growth of the Internet, in particular, has led to a significant increase in new self-regulatory institutions. With their wide range of initiatives (codes of conduct, rating/filter systems, hotlines, quality seals), they contribute to the implementation of public interest in the convergent communications sector and complement existing state regulatory institutions. A variety of regulatory goals are being pursued by means of self- and co-regulation, ranging from consumer protection (e.g. e-commerce) to the promotion of effective competition and market development (e.g. Internet domain-name administration), to content-related goals such as the protection of minors from harmful content. The increase in alternative regulatory institutions is leading to questions regarding their legitimacy, performance and governance choice.

## Legitimacy

The rise of alternative forms of regulation is often accompanied by concerns regarding potential risks. One of the dangers is that the growing application of self- and co-regulation may result in a steady decrease in the democratic quality of regulation—that is, a decline in legitimacy, accountability and control of the regulatory arrangement (see Parker 2002). In "free" economies and societies, regulatory institutions that restrict market behavior need to justify their market interventions, legitimacy of authority, and adequate modes of control (e.g. to counter abusive practices). Justifications for market interventions via private or public regulation include usually potential market failures, and the goal of pursuing public social and economic objectives in a sector. Regarding legitimacy and control, the picture is more complex. State regulatory institutions acquire their legitimacy from public elections, political responsibility and parliamentary control. Independent regulatory agencies, as well as co- and self-regulatory institutions, operate at a distance from traditional governmental institutions, and they are not bound by the mechanisms and standards of the traditional parliamentarian-representative model. Hence scholars and politicians alike fear insufficient democratic control, a lack of accountability and an unbalanced representation of interests (e.g. the absence of proper stakeholder involvement in alternative regulatory arrangements). Since parliamentarian representative modes of control are hardly applicable to alternative regulatory institutions, the shift from an interventionist to a regulatory state is accompanied by the search for standards by which the democratic quality of alternative modes of regulation may be assessed.

There is a rich literature on normative democratic standards for regulatory institutions. Measures to promote democratic quality include clear objectives, due process, contestability of decisions and transparency. Adequate stakeholder involvement, in particular, is considered essential to counter self-service and unbalanced representation in an alternative regulatory arrangement. The institutional setting is supposed to ensure that no single institution controls the entire decision-making process. In terms of input legitimacy, relevant stakeholders are to be empowered to express their views and concerns and to participate in the regulatory process on an equal basis. For independence from interference by single interested parties, the rules of appointment and the sources of funding are additional relevant organizational factors that may promote or inhibit the balance of interests.

Assessments of alternative regulatory institutions against these criteria often show deficits in meeting the standards. Empirical analysis of the institutional design of more than twenty organizations in the Austrian convergent communications sector showed that criteria such as openness and stakeholder involvement are met only partly (Latzer, Just, Saurwein and Slominski 2006: 163f.). In particular, there are high barriers to participation, because many alternative regulatory institutions are either fully closed in respect to participation by outsiders, or characterized by significant access barriers (e.g. financial barriers) or narrowly defined target groups, where admission is subject to special criteria (e.g. compulsory industry membership or special expertise). Analysis also shows that the openness to participation in alternative regulatory institutions, as well the as de facto involvement of stakeholders, rises with increasing state involvement. Stakeholders are more often involved in co-regulatory arrangements than in self-regulatory schemes. However, analyses of the Hans-Bredow-Institute and the Institute for European Media Law (HBI and EMR 2006a) point out that openness and stakeholder involvement are considered too weak even in co-regulatory systems. This has to be stressed, because the legal demand for adequate stakeholder involvement is a potential technique in co-regulatory schemes, in which a regulatory organization may not gain accreditation without appropriate stakeholder involvement.

"Multi-stakeholderism" is heavily promoted, especially for regulatory approaches in the Internet realm (e.g. Cave, Marsden and Simmons 2008). However, a more in-depth analysis reveals that the involvement of non-industry members is a highly controversial topic both in theory and practice. The UK National Consumer Council (NCC) recommends that up to 75 percent of a co-regulatory organization's governing body should be made up of independent representatives (NCC 2000). From a theoretical point of view, Ofcom (2004) points out that there is a clear tension between the desirability of achieving independence and the objective of introducing industry expertise.[3] Investigations show that there is no standard pattern for the involvement of non-industry members in alternative regulatory institutions (Latzer *et al.* 2007). The modes of involvement differ depending on the institutional structure of the organizations (involvement in supervisory bodies, governing bodies, complaints boards, appeals units). Adequate involvement of non-industry members does not necessarily depend on significant involvement of non-industry members in each single decision-making unit, but on an appropriate overall mix of industry and non-industry members to allow for the balancing of interests. However, stakeholder involvement is not the only way in which to control alternative regulatory organizations and to counter industry self-service. Under certain circumstances, non-industry groups may fulfill a critical watchdog function (even better) from outside the alternative regulatory institution, for example via criticism of industry schemes and periodic critical review (Latzer, Just, Saurwein and Slominski 2007).

Finally, there are doubts that all alternative regulatory institutions should be measured against the same standards. Not all alternative regulatory institutions are equipped with the same regulatory powers, and it could be argued that the demand for democratic quality increases with the amount of regulatory power that an institution holds. Factors that have to be taken into account are the status of the regulatory institution in the respective branch and policy field, the intensity of intervention in terms of enforcement and sanction powers (Latzer, Just, Saurwein and Slominski 2002), and the impact of regulatory measures on third parties that are not voluntarily participating in the alternative regulatory scheme (Saurwein 2011). The latter is evident (and problematic), for example, for technology-based regulatory solutions that restrict access to particular services and content (Tambini, Leonardi and Marsden 2008; IDATE, TNO and IViR 2008; Marsden 2010; Deibert *et al.* 2008; McNamee 2011). In addition, ICANN illustrates the precarious status of a self-regulatory institution's democratic credentials. As a result of its central status, far-reaching competencies and high intensity of intervention, the institutional design of ICANN has been the target of extensive criticism (Mueller 1999; Weinberg 2000; Froomkin 2000).

If it is unsuitable to judge every small trustmark or ombudsman scheme against the same standards, as, for instance, in the case of ICANN, evaluation schemes should allow for gradual and differentiated adaptations of standards according to relevant factors such as status, intensity of intervention and impact on third parties.[4] In any scheme, transparency forms the *conditio sine qua non* because it is the precondition for *ex post* evaluation of an alternative regulatory solution by any affected or interested third party. Empirical evidence demonstrates that this basic requirement is hardly fulfilled in European co-regulatory institutions (HBI and EMR 2006a).

3 "The former would suggest reliance on expertise drawn from outside the industry being regulated; the latter would clearly work in the opposite direction. Consequently a system involving a mixture of lay and industry members will often be appropriate, if possible allied to a genuinely independent review and appeals mechanism" (Ofcom 2004: 10f).

4 However, even if alternative regulatory institutions lack status, powers of intervention and third-party impact, they may prove meaningful in keeping democratic quality to a high standard, because this not only enhances the legitimacy of a given regulatory measure, but also tends to be enforced more efficiently because of a higher degree of acceptance.

## Performance

Alternative regulatory institutions may also derive legitimacy from their performance and their contribution to the achievement of public goals (output legitimacy). Central questions related to performance include: how can we evaluate performance, output, outcome or impact of alternative regulatory solutions? What is their contribution to the achievement of public goals? Where do self- and co-regulation succeed, where do they fail and how can success and failure be explained?

Research has started to develop assessment approaches, but evaluation of alternative modes of regulation in communications is still in its infancy. Latzer, Just, Saurwein and Slominski (2002) try to identify evaluation indicators for alternative regulatory institutions in the communications sector, but they do not provide performance evaluations. Schulz and Held (2002) distinguish the levels of "adequacy" and "compliance" for the assessment of alternative regulatory institutions. "Adequacy" refers to the question of whether the written law (acts, state agency guidelines, self-regulatory codes) is appropriate and sufficient to fulfill the regulatory tasks. "Compliance" entails the observance of rules enacted, but Schulz and Held do not provide an empirical compliance assessment. HBI and EMR (2006a) develop a cost–benefit approach for evaluation and assess selected performance criteria by means of an expert survey and desk research. Latzer *et al.* (2007) propose a "4A" approach for the assessment of alternative regulatory institutions, under which the performance of regulatory schemes is to be determined by: (1) the processes of adoption of the regulatory scheme; (2) the awareness of the citizens and institutional players; (3) the public attitude towards the scheme, including acceptance and appreciation of the regulatory institutions and their rules/processes; and (4) the actions undertaken by those who regulate, who are regulated or affected by regulations. Performance is thus a nuanced concept, involving both direct impact on the industry and the perceptions of ways in which the various schemes are working. The approach provides basic assessment criteria that can be applied for performance analyses of different cases in various sectors. These, however, have to be complemented by criteria derived from public objectives in the respective policy field.

In general, performance assessments are rather difficult for many reasons (for an overview, see HBI and EMR 2006a). There are no one-size-fits-all evaluation concepts, because every evaluation has to be tailored according to public policy goals in the respective policy field, and according to the particular goals of a regulatory institution. In the communications sector, many regulatory issues, goals and performance can hardly be measured by numeric indicators. Even if a measurement is possible, it is often impossible to isolate the particular contribution of individual institutions to an evident progress in performance. Notwithstanding these difficulties, an increase in evaluations of alternative regulatory institutions can be observed. Many are carried out on behalf of national authorities and the Directorates-General of the European Commission (Cave, Marsden and Simmons 2008), which financially support alternative regulatory institutions. Results of these evaluations are fragmented, however, and hardly provide any general answers on the success and failure of alternative modes of regulation, as a brief overview of selected findings shows.

Significant steps have been taken to grasp the adoption assessment criterion. Descriptive analyses show where alternative regulatory institutions are established in different countries and industries in reaction to a variety of regulatory issues. Recent implementation reports for the European Commission, for instance, analyze the extent to which social network service providers adopted principles and measures in relation to privacy and illegal and harmful content (Donoso 2011). Haraszti (2008) compiles an overview on press councils among the Organization for Security and Co-operation in Europe (OSCE) states. In his analysis, he not only identifies the established councils, but also the countries in which no press councils exist, or where they have ceased to function. Systematic comparative analyses make it possible to identify such gaps and to ask questions regarding the reasons for adoption failures. Haraszti considers political, economic, legal and cultural reasons for the lack of councils.[5]

The awareness performance indicator is more difficult to assess, because it either demands representative consumer surveys, or at least surveys among relevant stakeholders. Cave, Marsden and Simmons (2008) do not conduct such a survey, but suspect significant gaps in public knowledge of even the best-resourced and most well-known examples of information society self-regulation: "Most members of the public appear to continue to believe that content should be reported to the police, government regulator or ISPs, for instance, rather than the various alternative regulatory institutions" (ibid.: 26). Outdated but representative data are available for e-commerce. According to the Special Eurobarometer on issues relating to business and consumer e-commerce (EEIG 2004), only "one in ten EU15 citizens had heard of Internet trust marks" (ibid.: 20). In reaction to awareness deficits, several alternative regulatory institutions in different policy fields are enhancing their attempts to raise outreach.

For the assessment of the attitude performance indicator, it is appropriate to conduct interviews with relevant stakeholders (e.g. members, internal and external experts including critics of established schemes). HBI and EMR (2006a), for instance, conducted an expert survey and found a mixed picture. On the one hand, respondents criticize the lack of transparency of several co-regulatory institutions; on the other hand, they estimate a high level of performance in terms of satisfaction regarding the protection of minors from inappropriate content that seems to be rarely transmitted in film, video and broadcasting in Germany, Austria and the Netherlands. The estimates by internal and external experts are related to compliance, but they are more likely to display the individual, subjective attitudes towards a scheme and satisfaction with interaction within a scheme rather than an impartial/objective compliance indicator.

Cave, Marsden and Simmons (2008) suggest that a test of alternative regulatory organizations' effectiveness must be whether it has "shown its teeth" to a member through some type of sanction (withdrawal of membership, censure for non-compliance, or an increased market use of, and adherence to, the standards of the technique used). However, Cave, Marsden and Simmons (2008) do not provide an enforcement evaluation and state that more extensive quantitative and qualitative research is needed into the methods and techniques used by alternative regulatory organizations. One of the reasons why assessments of action-related criteria such as compliance are difficult is a lack of data (e.g. compliance reports), which partly results from the fact that many alternative regulatory institutions simply have not adopted an enforcement/compliance mechanism. In a comprehensive comparative analysis, IDATE, TNO and IViR (2008) found eighteen codes and guidelines for UGC in different industries, but "only a few initiatives provided for a compliance mechanism including sanctions in the event of noncompliance of a member or signatory of the initiative" (ibid. 58). De Bruin *et al.* (2005) point to deficits in self-regulation in the domain of e-commerce. Comparative analysis of ten trustmark schemes showed that a majority have a negative average evaluation on proactive monitoring measures and the enforcement system.

5 For example, in countries where governments strive to censor the media, or where there are press and electronic media laws dealing with issues of ethics and accuracy; countries where the media are used solely to make money or maintain the interests of business and political elites, or where the media market is too small; and countries where media professionals oppose self-regulation. The reasons mentioned by Haraszti (2008: 49) point to contextual conditions for alternative modes of regulation discussed in the section below.

Finally, the question of the wider social impact of alternative regulatory institutions in communications has, so far, not been assessed at all. For newer institutions in the Internet sector, it seems simply too early to take any meaningful assessments. But even for the well-established institutions in the domain of media accountability, it is stressed that "the impact of media accountability is often debated but rarely studied systematically" (Fengler, Eberwein, and Leppik-Bork 2010: 13f). Only very few small-scale and outdated research projects have at least partly tackled the impact of (established) media accountability institutions on media professionals, but not on the wider implications, for instance, for the public sphere.

The difficulties and lack of large-scale evaluations does not mean that there are no assessments at all. These are, however, often devoted to single organizations, most notably to identifying and describing best practice. The media content-rating system in the Netherlands, Kijkwijzer, run by the Netherlands Institute for the Classification of Audiovisual Media (NICAM), is frequently referred to as a role model and an effective example of co-regulation in the communication sector (COM 2001; HBI and EMR 2006a; Schulz 2007). There is a very high public awareness, understanding and satisfaction regarding Kijkwijzer, and strong industry support in terms of adoption of the rating system. There is a coherent and transparent enforcement process, and complaints procedures are widely used by the public. There is also close involvement and support for NICAM by parliament and the Dutch Media Authority (Latzer *et al.* 2007). Empirical analysis, however, has also revealed that the system fails on the shop-floor level of cinemas, libraries and media vendors when it comes to preventing the sale, rental and display of harmful media to ineligible minors (Dorbeck-Jung *et al.* 2010). Findings suggest that enforcement failures seem to be induced mainly by the wait-and-see attitude of the regulators involved, who do not take responsibility for monitoring and evaluating the performance of regulatory activities (ibid.).

The results of evaluations not only point to the relevance of performance assessments, but also to the fact that different evaluation approaches lead to differences in findings (e.g. expert interviews vs. compliance tests). Moreover, they point to a lack of large-scale evaluations that compare and contrast alternative regulatory solutions. Because research has so far concentrated on established organizations and "best practice" examples, the rich resources of adoption and performance deficits have hardly been exploited so far. The failures of initiatives such as ICRA for content rating on the Internet (Archer 2009)[6] or WebTrader in the e-commerce area could serve as valuable case studies from which to draw conclusions regarding success factors for alternative modes of regulation.

## Governance choice

The increase in alternative regulatory institutions also gives rise to major questions about (rational) governance choice between available governance mechanisms. For the communications sector, Cuilenburg and McQuail (2003) note that the choice of policy instruments is one of numerous dilemmas and unanswered questions for policymakers, but the difficulties of governance/regulatory choice are not unique to communications policies (Schuppert 2005).

6 Also, former efforts to develop Internet content rating schemes either failed or were absorbed by other initiatives. In 1996, the Recreational Software Advisory Council on the Internet (RSACi) announced the launch of a content-labeling advisory system to empower parents and consumers to make informed choices. W3C began to develop the Platform for Internet Content Selection (PICS) in the mid–1990s in response to the Communications Decency Act (CDA) 1996 and the threat of more strict regulatory action against illegal and harmful material on the Internet.

In the last decade, public administrations have increased their efforts to structure regulatory choice processes and policy evaluations by introducing regulatory impact assessments (RIA). The spread of RIA in the context of good governance and better regulation initiatives has been almost universal, although different practices are found under the same label in different countries (Radaelli 2004). RIA guidelines often contain provisions for the assessment of multiple regulatory options, including the zero option of no intervention, market-friendly alternatives to regulation, soft law, voluntary agreements and traditional command-and-control regulation (Radaelli 2005). Altogether, the RIA initiatives aim at more informed, evidence-based policymaking and improved regulatory effectiveness and legitimacy. RIA guidelines typically suggest the assessment of alternative modes of regulation such as self- and co-regulation, but they have—with some exceptions—hardly specified the criteria against which the suitability of alternative regulatory institutions can be scrutinized in the early stages of the regulatory choice process (*ex ante* evaluation) and in the course of performance review once alternative regulatory organizations have been established (*ex post* evaluation).

In academic research, many efforts have been made to identify assessment criteria, but there is no single theory that allows for performance predictions. There are numerous partly complementary, but also contradictory, assessment approaches. This heterogeneity provides a challenge for scholars and for regulators who have to decide on regulatory arrangements in practice. From a public policy perspective, the central questions in the context of governance choice are: (a) whether the adoption of an alternative regulatory solution by private actors is feasible at all; (b) whether a potential arrangement is durable and effective in meeting the public interest; and (c) whether there are needs and options to stimulate adoption or enhance performance of a private regulatory solution by means of state involvement. Economic, institutional/organizational and macro-systemic conceptions are provided to approach the questions (see, among many others, Garvin 1983; Gupta and Lad 1983; Ostrom 1990; Pattberg 2005; Saurwein 2011). These approaches identify a multitude of intertwined factors related to macro, meso and micro levels of alternative regulatory schemes, which have an influence on the success and failure of self- and co-regulatory solutions.

Such influencing factors are frequently mentioned in the academic literature and partly considered in the practice of regulatory governance (e.g. Ofcom 2008). Most are drawn from theoretical analyses on private regulatory regimes and from lessons of *ex post* evaluations of successful and unsuccessful examples of self- and co-regulation. Based on a comprehensive review of the literature, Latzer *et al.* (2007) developed an approach for the systematic assessment of alternative modes of regulation to facilitate governance choice. The approach starts from the basic assumption that the performance of alternative regulatory schemes is influenced by the specific organizational design of a regulatory entity (institutional/organizational success factors) and by the particular market and regulatory environment (enabling contextual factors). The performance of regulatory schemes is determined by the "4A" approach (adoption, awareness, attitude, action). On the one hand, performance is influenced by institutional/organizational success factors that can be designed or modified at the organizational level of self- and co-regulation (endogenous factors). They include, for example, the modes of stakeholder involvement and adequate enforcement powers. On the other hand, performance is influenced by enabling contextual factors that are related to the type of the regulatory challenge, the characteristics of industries involved and the characteristics of the regulatory environment. Contextual factors include the risks and potential impact in case of regulatory failure, and conflicts between public and private interests. In contrast to institutional/organizational success factors, contextual factors cannot be modified at the organizational level of an alternative regulatory institution (exogenous factors). If at all, they can be affected by reforms in the regulatory environment. In combination, they can provide a more or less enabling context for alternative regulatory institutions. They affect the possibilities and probabilities of their adoption (e.g. incentives to cooperate), as well as the performance of already-established institutions (e.g. effectiveness in reducing market failure). Table 21.1 summarizes three dimensions for evaluations and criteria for systematic theoretical or empirical assessments.

*Table 21.1* Template for governance choice: Overview of evaluation criteria

*Performance criteria*

(a) Awareness: Knowledge and understanding of schemes
(b) Adoption: Concurrence with schemes and enduring acceptance of authority
(c) Attitude: Perception in terms of trust, credibility and legitimacy
(d) Action: Compliance with schemes, complaints received, disputes handled, governmental engagement

*Enabling contextual factors*

(a) Direct benefits for the industry
(b) Reputational sensitivity of the industry
(c) Intervention capacity of governmental actors
(d) Impact of regulatory failure and need for uniform and binding minimum standards
(e) Intensity of required regulatory intervention
(f) Conflicts of public and private interests in a regulatory question
(g) Number of market participants and market fragmentation
(h) Intensity of competition
(i) Availability of organizations that could take over regulatory tasks
(j) Support for public policy objectives by the existing industry culture
(k) Involvement of governmental actors

*Institutional/organizational success factors*

(a) Rule-making: Clearly defined remit, intelligible objectives and (measurable) standards that go beyond governmental regulatory requirements
(b) Enforcement: Adequate, proportionate enforcement mechanisms
(c) Adjudication: Adequate sanction power in case of malpractice (effective, credible, commercially significant sanctions)
(d) Review: Periodic internal and external review (control, evaluation, monitoring, auditing)
(e) Resources: Adequate resources to assure that objectives are not compromised
(f) Participation and representation: Balanced representation, involvement of stakeholders, independence from interference by interested parties
(g) Transparency: Transparent institutional design and regulatory processes
(h) International involvement: Appropriate measures to contribute to international efforts for the solution of transnational regulatory problems
(i) Coherence with the established governance architecture
(j) Accountability: Clear distribution of regulatory responsibilities between private/industry and public/state regulatory organizations involved in the regulatory process
(k) Adequate intensity and modes of involvement of governmental actors

*Acknowledgement:* The categories and indicators for empirical analysis are derived from in-depth literature reviews on the evaluation of alternative modes of regulation (Latzer, Just, Saurwein and Slominski 2002) and have been adapted and reapplied to various regulatory issues in communications (see Latzer *et al.* 2003; Latzer and Just 2004; Latzer *et al.* 2006; Just, Latzer and Saurwein 2007; Latzer 2007; Latzer and Saurwein 2008). A comprehensive template for regulatory choice, with numerous indicators for the empirical evaluation of each of these criteria/factors, was developed in an evaluation project for Ofcom (Latzer *et al.* 2007; Saurwein and Latzer 2010). A comprehensive discussion of contextual factors is provided by Saurwein (2011).

Taking into account the interrelations between context, organizational design and performance, the template provides a conceptual framework for *ex ante* assessments and *ex post* evaluations of alternative regulatory arrangements. Application of the approach for empirical *ex post* evaluation makes it possible to assess the performance of an alternative regulatory institution and to explain whether and how success and failure of self- and co-regulatory schemes result from the institutional/organizational design of an alternative regulatory scheme and/or by industry characteristics and the particular regulatory environment. Findings of empirical analysis on reasons for failures may be used as a basis for governance reform, either at the organizational level of an alternative regulatory institution or, if possible, for reforms in the regulatory environment. The application of this approach for *ex ante* assessments cannot start with empirical investigations on performance. It therefore concentrates on analysis of the regulatory challenge/problem and given contextual conditions, and it aims at prognoses on the feasibility of adoption and the effectiveness of an alternative regulatory solution. It makes it possible to derive conclusions regarding the question of whether a problem can be solved by market players or there is the need for governmental involvement. Moreover, it may be used to draw conclusions regarding the adequate and effective institutional/organizational designs in reaction to unfavorable contextual conditions (e.g. to take organizational measures to counter freeriding if assessment of contextual conditions predicts a potential freerider problem). The framework therefore is a helpful tool when it comes to comparing governance options in the framework of a regulatory impact assessment (RIA).

Practical applications of the approach in pilot studies yield a number of interesting findings that demonstrate the value of the analytical approach for research and policymaking. The framework, for example, was applied for an assessment of content rating schemes in the audiovisual industry (Latzer *et al.* 2007; Saurwein and Latzer 2010). Findings of theoretical analyses on contextual conditions suggest the suitability of a regulatory arrangement with significant industry involvement in the rating practice, combined with some degree of public oversight. Freedom of speech concerns, high costs of rating content, and little demand for uniform and binding minimum standards support the suitability of alternative modes of regulation for content rating. However, the lack of direct economic benefits for the industry, sharp conflicts between public and private interests, incentives for freeriders, the potentially major economic impacts of a rating, and increasing fragmentation of the audio-visual market indicate that content rating is not suitable for pure, unlimited industry self-regulation.

Moreover, the body of literature on alternative modes of regulation in communications suggests further lessons on the suitability of self- and co-regulatory solutions, underlining the explanatory strengths of the developed approach. HBI and EMR (2006b) argue that co-regulatory schemes are well suited for advertising content regulation and the protection of minors. According to HBI and EMR, this suitability is caused by the rapid changes in programming and advertising, by the inherent weaknesses of external content control and by the flexibility to adjustments in established alternative regulatory organizations: "New concepts of regulation can tie in with existing professional ethics or even self-regulatory organizations that already deal with media content-matters on a voluntary basis" (ibid.: 123). Moreover, HBI and EMR's findings suggest that co-regulatory schemes perform better in countries that "are known for innovative regulatory concepts which are worked out in collaboration with industry" (ibid.: 119), such as the UK, Netherlands, and, to some extent, Germany. Assessment thus points to the relevance of a regulatory culture/tradition within a state or in the industry within the respective branch. But differences in the applicability of alternative modes of regulation also have to be considered. For broadcasting, industry commitment and incentives for participation are relatively high, because the move towards co-regulation will often entail a relaxation of regulation in a former heavy-handed, state-regulated industry environment. Additional contextual conditions in favor of alternative modes of regulation in broadcasting comprise the small set of well-organized and sufficiently resourced industry actors that are able to enter into joint decisions and who can afford the establishment of co-regulatory structures. For non-linear online services, decentralized solutions may be more effective, because the large number of online services would hamper co-regulatory approaches that require submission of all material for rating to a central organization: "Pre-clearing by the providers themselves—within a regulatory framework—might be an attractive option to cope with the huge amount of fast-changing material in the web" (ibid.: 125). Hence industry fragmentation is one of the reasons why different models of co-regulation for different sectors might be preferable, and why one can also find different approaches in the regulatory practice regarding online services, broadcasting, film and video games.

## Conclusion: Questions and challenges for further research

Empirical analyses show a significant increase in alternative regulatory institutions with a wide variety of initiatives and instruments (e.g. codes of conduct, rating/filter systems, hotlines, trustmarks) in the convergent communications sector. But little is known about the impact of these developments on the governance arrangement for communications as a whole. Do alternative regulatory approaches only complement existing state regulation, or do regulatory powers in fact shift from the state to the private sector? Are we observing the emergence of a more efficient state that exploits the advantages of self- and co-regulation, or a powerless state that is forced to rely on private regulatory initiatives? Only large-scale analyses that comprise and compare state and private regulatory responsibilities and powers would make it possible to answer this general question.

The rise of self- and co-regulation is accompanied by concerns regarding a decrease in the democratic quality of regulation. Alternative regulatory institutions are not bound by the traditional mechanisms and standards of democratic political control. But the standards for evaluation of the democratic quality of alternative modes of regulation are not completely clear. "Multi-stakeholderism" is an oft-mentioned, but not always practicable, principle. A major challenge for research is the development of frameworks that can be applied for assessments in a graduated and differentiated manner depending on the degree of power that an alternative regulatory institution holds. Status, intensity of intervention and impact on third parties are factors that have to be taken in consideration for evaluation. Impact on third parties is of particular relevance, for instance, in the case of technology-based regulatory solutions that restrict access to particular services and contents.

Owing to a range of methodological difficulties, there are major research gaps in the evaluation of performance and outcomes of alternative modes of regulation. Research has started to develop assessment approaches, but the evaluation of alternative modes of regulation in communications is still in its infancy. As a consequence, knowledge about the contribution of self- and co-regulation to the achievement of public goals is limited. Moreover, evaluations focus largely on the analysis of existing "best practice" examples and organizational designs of successful institutions. This scope is too limited to explain and predict when alternative regulatory arrangements are likely to emerge and when they are more likely to fail. The enabling and constraining contextual conditions that shape the adoption of alternative regulatory institutions also need to be taken into consideration. Exploring failed examples ("flop analysis") and the reasons for these failures will contribute to the development of more comprehensive evaluation frameworks comprising organizational success factors *and* enabling contextual factors.

## References


Archer, P. (2009) 'ICRAfail. A lesson for the future.' Online. Available HTTP: http://www.philarcher.org/icra/ICRAfail.pdf (accessed 11 October 2011).

Ayres, I. and Braithwaite, J. (1992) *Responsive Regulation: Transcending the Deregulation Debate*, New York and Oxford: Oxford University Press.

Baldwin, R. and Black, J. (2007) 'Really responsive regulation,' LSE Legal Studies Working Paper No. 15. Online. Available HTTP: http://ssrn.com/abstract=1033322 (accessed 17 August 2010).

—— and Cave, M. (1999) *Understanding Regulation: Theory, Strategy and Practice*, Oxford: Oxford University Press.

Bartle, I. and Vass, P. (2007) 'Self-regulation within the regulatory state,' *Public Administration*, 85(4): 885–905.

Bauer, J. (2010) 'Changing roles of the state in telecommunications,' *International Telecommunications Policy Research*, 17(1): 1–36.

Birnhack, M. and Elkin-Koren, N. (2003) 'The invisible handshake: The reemergence of the state in the digital environment,' *Virginia Journal of Law and Technology*, 8(6). Online. Available HTTP: http://works.bepress.com/michael_birnhack/ (accessed 11 October 2011).

Black, J. (1996) 'Constitutionalising self-regulation,' *The Modern Law Review*, 59(1): 24–55.

—— (2001) 'Decentering regulation: The role of regulation and self-regulation in a "post-regulatory world",' *Current Legal Problems*, 54(1): 103–146.

Boddewyn, J. J. (1985) 'Advertising self-regulation: Organization structures in Belgium, Canada, France and the United Kingdom,' in W. Streeck and P.C. Schmitter (eds.) *Private Interest Government. Beyond Market and State,* London: Sage.

—— (1988) *Advertising Self-regulation and Outside Participation: A Multinational Comparison*, New York: Quorum.

Boyer, C. and Geissbuhler, A. (2005) 'A decade devoted to improving online health information quality,' *Studies in Health Technology and Informatics*, 116: 891–896.

——, Selby, M., Scherrer J. R. and Appel, R. D. (1998) 'The health on the net code of conduct for medical and health websites,' *Computers in Biology and Medicine*, 28(5): 603–610.

Boyle, J. (1997) 'Foucault in cyberspace: Surveillance, sovereignty, and hardwired censors,' *University of Cincinnati Law Review,* 66: 177–205.

Braithwaite, J. (1982) 'Enforced self-regulation: A new strategy for corporate crime control,' *Michigan Law Review*, 80: 1466–1507.

Brown, A. (2006) 'Advertising regulation and co-regulation: The challenge of change,' *Economic Affairs*, 26(2): 31–36.

Buthe, T. and Mattli, W. (2011) *The New Global Rulers: The Privatization of Regulation in the World Economy*, Princeton, NJ: Princeton University Press.

Calliess G.-P. (2007) 'Transnational consumer law: Co-regulation of B2C-E-Commerce,' CLPE Research Paper 3/2007. Online. Available HTTP: http://ssrn.com/abstract=988612 (accessed 11 October 2011).

Campbell, A. J. (1999) 'Self-regulation and the media,' *Federal Communications Law Journal*, 51: 711–771.

Cane, P. (1987) 'Self-regulation and judicial review,' *Civil Justice Quarterly*, 6: 324–347.

Cave, J., Marsden, C. and Simmons, S. (2008) *Options for and Effectiveness of Internet Self- and Co-Regulation*, Research report prepared for the European Commission, DG INFSO.

Dam, K. W. (1999) 'Self-help in the digital jungle,' John M. Olin Law and Economics Working Paper No. 59, Chicago, IL: The Law School of the University of Chicago.

de Bruin, R., Keuleers, E., Lazaro, C., Poullet, Y. and Viersma, M. (2005) *Analysis and Definition of Common Characteristics of Trustmarks and Web Seals in the European Union*, Research report. Online. Available HTTP: http://www.crid.be/pdf/public/5026.pdf (accessed 19 October 2011).

Deibert, R., Palfrey, J., Rohozinski, R. and Zittrain J. (eds.) (2008) *Access Denied: The Practice and Policy of Global Internet Filtering*, Cambridge, MA: MIT Press.

Dellarocas, C. (2003) 'The digitization of word-of-mouth: Promise and challenges of online feedback mechanisms,' MIT Sloan Working Paper No. 4296–03. Online. Available HTTP: http://ssrn.com/abstract=393042 (accessed 11 October 2011).
Donoso, V. (2011) *Assessment of the Implementation of the Safer Social Network Principles for the EU on 9 Services: Summary Report*, Luxembourg: European Commission, Safer Internet Programme.
Dorbeck-Jung, B. R., Oude Vrielink, M. J., Gosselt, J. F., Van Hoof, J. J. and de Jong, M. D. T. (2010) 'Contested hybridization of regulation: Failure of the Dutch regulatory system to protect minors from harmful media,' *Regulation and Governance*, 4(2): 154–174.
Doyle, C. (1997) 'Self-regulation and statutory regulation,' *Business Strategy Review*, 8(3): 35–42.
Dutton, W. and Peltu, M. (2005) 'The emerging Internet governance mosaic: Connecting the pieces,' OII Forum Discussion Paper No. 5, Oxford Internet Institute, University of Oxford.
Engel, C. (2004) 'A constitutional framework for private governance,' *German Law Journal*, 5 (3): 197–237.
European Opinion Research Group (EEIG) (2004) 'Issues relating to business and consumer e-commerce,' EBS 201. Online. Available HTTP: http://ec.europa.eu/public_opinion/archives/ebs/ebs_201_executive_summary.pdf (accessed 11 October 2011).
European Commission (2001) *Evaluation Report from the Commission concerning the Protection of Minors and Human Dignity*, COM(2001) 106. Online. Available HTTP: http://eur-lex.europa.eu/LexUriServ/LexUriServ.do?uri=CELEX:52001DC0106:EN:NOT
Fengler, S., Eberwein, T. and Leppik-Bork, T. (2011) 'Mapping media accountability—in Europe and beyond,' in T. Eberwein, S. Fengler, E. Lauk and T. Leppik-Bork (eds.) *Mapping Media Accountability—in Europe and Beyond*, Köln: Herbert von Halem Verlag.
Froomkin, M. (2000) 'Semi-private international rulemaking: Lessons learned from the WIPO domain name process', in C. T. Marsden (ed.) *Regulating the Global Information Society*, London: Routledge.
Garvin, D. A. (1983) 'Can industry self regulation work?' *California Management Review*, 25(9): 48–63.
Gilardi, F. (2007) 'The same, but different: Central banks, regulatory agencies, and the politics of delegation to independent authorities,' *Comparative European Politics*, 5: 303–327.
—— (2008) *Delegation in the Regulatory State: Independent Regulatory Agencies in Western Europe*, Cheltenham: Edward Elgar.
Grabosky, P. (1995) 'Regulation by reward: On the use of incentives as regulatory instruments,' *Law and Policy*, 17(3): 256–281.
Gunningham, N. and Rees, J. (1997) 'Industry self-regulation: An institutional perspective,' *Law and Policy*, 19(4): 363–414.
—— and Sinclair, D. (1999) 'Integrative regulation: A principle-based approach to environmental policy,' *Law and Social Inquiry*, 24(4): 853–896.
Gupta, A. K. and Lad, L. J. (1983) 'Industry self-regulation: An economic, organizational, and political analysis,' *Academy of Management Review*, 8(3): 416–425.
Hans-Bredow-Institut [HBI], Interdisciplinary Centre for Law and ICT (ICRI), Center for Media and Communication Studies (CMCS) and Cullen International (eds.) (2011) *Indicators for Independence and Efficient Functioning of Audiovisual Media Services Regulatory Bodies for the Purpose of Enforcing the Rules in the AVMS Directive* (INDIREG), Final report, SMART 2009/0001.
HBI and EMR—Hans-Bredow-Institut and Europäisches Institut für Medienrecht (2006a) 'Studie über Co-Regulierungsmaßnahmen im Medienbereich (Endbericht)', Studie für die Europäische Kommission, Generaldirektion Informationsgesellschaft und Medien, Abt. A1 Audiovisuelle Politik und Medienpolitik.' Online. Available HTTP: http://ec.europa.eu/avpolicy/docs/library/studies/coregul/final_rep_de.pdf (accessed 11 October 2011).
—— Hans-Bredow-Institut (HBI) and Institute of European Media Law (EMR) (2006b) 'Study on co-regulation measures in the media sector.' Online. Available HTTP: http://ec.europa.eu/avpolicy/docs/library/studies/coregul/final_rep_en.pdf (accessed 17 August 2010).
Haraszti, M. (2008) *The Media Self-Regulation Guidebook*, Vienna: Office of the Representative on Freedom of the Media—Organization for Security and Co-operation in Europe (OSCE).
Héritier, A. (2002) 'New modes of governance in Europe: Policy making without legislating?' in A. Héritier (ed.) *The Provision of Common Goods: Governance across Multiple Arenas*, Lanham, MD: Rowman and Littlefield.
—— and Eckert, S. (2008) 'New modes of governance in the shadow of hierarchy: Self-regulation by industry in Europe,' *Journal of Public Policy*, 28: 113–138.
—— and Lehmkuhl, D. (2008) 'The shadow of hierarchy and new modes of governance: Sectoral governance and democratic government,' *Journal of Public Policy*, 28: 1–17.

Hoffmann-Riem, W. (2000) *Regulierung der dualen Rundfunkordnung*, Nomos: Baden-Baden.
Holznagel, B. and Werle, R. (2004) 'Sectors and strategies of global communications regulation,' *Knowledge, Technology, and Policy*, 17: 19–37.
IDATE, TNO and IviR (2008) *User-Created Content: Supporting a Participative Information Society*, Final report, SMART 2007/2008.
Jordana, J., Levi-Faur, D. and Fernández i Marín, X. (2009) *The Global Diffusion of Regulatory Agencies: Channels of Transfer and Stages of Diffusion*. Online. Available HTTP: http://poli.haifa.ac.il/~levi/jlx.pdf (accessed 17 August 2010).
Just, N. and Latzer, M. (2004) 'Self- and co-regulation as indicators of a transformed statehood in the mediamatics sector,' in S. Puntscher Riekmann, M. Mokre and M. Latzer (eds.) *The State of Europe: Transformations of Statehood from a European Perspective*, Frankfurt and New York: Campus Verlag.
——, —— and Saurwein, F. (2007) 'Communications governance: Entscheidungshilfe für die wahl des regulierungsarrangements am beispiel spam,' in P. Donges (ed.) *Von der Medienpolitik zur Media Governance?* Köln: Herbert von Halem Verlag.
Keller, D. and Verhulst, S. G. (2000) *Parental Control in a Converged Communications Environment. Self-Regulation, Technical Devices and Meta-Information*, Report commissioned for the DVB Regulatory Group. Online. Available HTTP: http://ec.europa.eu/avpolicy/docs/reg/minors/dvbgroup.pdf (accessed 20 November 2010).
Knill, C. and Lenschow A. (2004) 'Modes of regulation in the governance of the European Union: Towards a comprehensive evaluation,' in J. Jordana and D. Levi-Faur (eds.) *The Politics of Regulation*, Cheltenham and Northampton, MA: Edward Elgar.
Latzer, M. (1997) *Mediamatik: Die Konvergenz von Telekommunikation, Computer und Rundfunk*, Opladen: Westdeutscher Verlag.
—— (1999) 'Transformation der Staatlichkeit im Kommunikationssektor: Regulierungsansätze für die Mediamatik,' in K. Imhof, O. Jarren and R. Blum (eds.) *Steuerungs- und Regelungsprobleme in der Informationsgesellschaft*, Opladen: Westdeutscher Verlag.
—— (2000) 'Transformation der Staatlichkeit: Schlussfolgerungen für die Politik,' in M. Latzer (ed.) *Mediamatikpolitik für die Digitale Ökonomie*, Innsbruck and Wien: Studien-Verlag.
—— (2007) 'Regulatory choice in communications governance, communications,' *The European Journal of Communication Research*, 32(3): 399–405.
—— (2009) 'Convergence revisited: Toward a modified pattern of communications governance convergence,' *The International Journal of Research into New Media Technologies*, 15(4): 411–426.
and Saurwein, F. (2008) 'Vertrauen in die Industrie: Vertrauen in die Nutzer,' in W. Schulz and T. Held (eds.) *Mehr Vertrauen in Inhalte: Das Potenzial von Ko- und Selbstregulierung in digitalen Medien*, Berlin: Vistas.
——, Just, N., Saurwein, F. and Slominski, P. (2002) *Selbst- und Ko-Regulierung im Mediamatiksektor: Alternative Regulierungsformen zwischen Staat und Markt*, Wiesbaden: Westdeutscher Verlag.
——, ——, —— and —— (2003) 'Regulation remixed: Institutional change through self- and co-regulation in the mediamatics sector,' *Communications and Strategies*, 50: 127–157.
——, ——, —— and —— (2006) 'Institutional variety in communications regulation classification scheme and empirical evidence from Austria,' *Telecommunications Policy*, 30(3–4): 152–170.
——, Price, M. E., Saurwein, F. and Verhulst, S. G. (2007) *Comparative Analysis of International Co- and Self-Regulation in Communications Markets*, Research report commissioned by Ofcom, Vienna: ITA.
Lehmkuhl, D. (2008) 'Control modes in the age of transnational governance,' *Law and Policy*, 30: 336–363.
Lessig, L. (1999) *Code and Other Laws of Cyberspace*, New York: Basic Books.
Levi-Faur, D. (2010) 'Regulation and regulatory governance,' Jerusalem Papers on Regulation and Governance No. 1. Online. Available HTTP: http://levifaur.wiki.huji.ac.il/images/Reg.pdf (accessed 11 October 2011).
Lievens, E. (2010) *Protecting Children in the Digital Era: The Use of Alternative Regulatory Instruments*, Leiden and Boston, MA: Martinus Nijhoff Publishers.
——, Dumortier, J. and Ryan, P. S. (2006) 'The co-protection of minors in new media,' *U.C. Davis Journal of Juvenile Law and Policy*, 10(1): 97–151.
Maggetti, M. (2007) 'De facto independence after delegation: A fuzzy-set analysis,' *Regulation and Governance*, 1(4): 271–294.
Majone, G. (ed.) (1996) *Regulating Europe*, New York and London: Routledge.
—— (1999) 'The regulatory state and its legitimacy problems,' *West European Politics*, 22(1): 1–24.

Marsden, C. T. (2010) *Net Neutrality: Towards a Co-regulatory Solution*, London, New York: Bloomsbury Academic.
Mayntz, R. (2003) 'From government to governance: Political steering in modern societies,' Paper presented at the Summer Academy on IPP, 7–11 September, Wuerzburg.
—— (2008) 'Von der Steuerungstheorie zu Global Governance,' in G. Folke Schuppert and M. Zürn (eds.) *Governance in einer sich wandelnden Welt*, Wiesbaden: VS-Verlag.
—— (2009) *Über Governance: Institutionen und Prozesse politischer Regelung*, Frankfurt: Campus.
McNamee, J. (2011) 'The slide from 'self-regulation' to corporate censorship,' Edri Discussion Paper 2011/1. Online. Available HTTP: www.edri.org/files/EDRI_selfreg_final_20110124.pdf (accessed 11 October 2011).
Michael, D. C. (1995) 'Federal agency use of audited self-regulation as a regulatory technique,' *Administrative Law Review*, 47: 171–253.
Moran, M. (2002) 'Review article: Understanding the regulatory state,' *British Journal of Political Science*, 32(2): 391–413.
Mueller, M. (1999) 'ICANN and Internet governance: Sorting through the debris of "self-regulation",' *info*, 1(6): 497–520.
National Consumer Council (NCC) (2000) *Models of Self-Regulation: An Overview of Models in Business and the Professions*, London: NCC. Online. Available HTTP: http://www.talkingcure.co.uk/articles/ncc_models_self_regulation.pdf (accessed 11 October 2011).
NICAM (2007) '*Kijkwijzer*: The Dutch rating system for audiovisual productions.' Online. Available HTTP: http://www.kijkwijzer.eu/upload/download_pc/24_Overview_Kijkwijzer_version_41__eng.pdf (accessed 11 October 2011).
Noam, E. (1991) *Television in Europe*, New York and Oxford: Oxford University Press.
—— (1992) *Telecommunications in Europe*, New York and Oxford: Oxford University Press.
Ofcom (2004) 'Criteria for promoting effective co and self-regulation: Statement on the criteria to be applied by Ofcom for promoting effective co- and self-regulation and establishing co-regulatory bodies.' Online. Available HTTP: http://stakeholders.ofcom.org.uk/binaries/consultations/co-reg/statement/co_self_reg.pdf (accessed 11 October 2011).
—— (2006) 'Online protection: A survey of consumer, industry and regulatory mechanisms and systems.' Online. Available HTTP: http://stakeholders.ofcom.org.uk/binaries/research/telecoms-research/report.pdf (accessed 11 October 2011)
—— (2008) 'Identifying appropriate regulatory solutions: Principles for analysing self- and co-regulation.' Online. Available HTTP: http://stakeholders.ofcom.org.uk/binaries/consultations/coregulation/statement/statement.pdf (accessed 11 October 2011).
Ogus, A. (2001) *Regulation, Economics and the Law*, Cheltenham: Edward Elgar.
Olsberg SPI *et al.* (2003) 'Empirical study on the practice of the rating of films distributed in cinemas television DVD and videocassettes in the EU and EEA member states.' Online. Available HTTP: http://ec.europa.eu/avpolicy/docs/library/studies/finalised/studpdf/rating_finalrep2.pdf (accessed 17 August 2010).
Organization for Co-operation and Development (OECD) (1999) *Guidelines for Consumer Protection in the Context of Electronic Commerce*, Paris: OECD Publishing.
Ostrom, E. (1990) *Governing the Commons: The Evolution of Institutions for Collective Action*, Cambridge: Cambridge University Press.
Parker, C. (2002) *The Open Corporation: Effective Self-Regulation and Democracy*, Cambridge: Cambridge University Press.
Pattberg, P. (2005) 'The institutionalization of private governance: How business and nonprofit organizations agree on transnational rules,' *Governance*, 18(4): 589–610.
Porter, T. and Ronit, K. (2006) 'Self-regulation as policy process: The multiple and criss-crossing stages of private rule making,' *Policy Science*, 39(1): 41–72.
Price, M. E. (ed.) (1998) *The V-Chip-Debate: Content Filtering from Television to the Internet*, Mahwah, NJ: Lawrence Erlbaum.
—— and Verhulst, S. G. (2000) 'In search of the self: Charting the course of self-regulation on the Internet in a global environment,' in C. T. Marsden (ed.) *Regulating the Global Information Society*, London and New York: Routledge.
—— and —— (2002) *Parental Control of Television Broadcasting*, Mahwah, NJ: Lawrence Erlbaum.
Programme in Comparative Media Law and Policy (PCMLP) (2004a) *Self-Regulation of Digital Media Converging on the Internet: Industry Codes of Conduct in Sectoral Analysis*, Research report for the European Commission, Oxford: PCMLP.

—— (2004b) *Internet Self-Regulation: An Overview*, Oxford: PCMLP.

—— (2004c) *Self-Regulation and the Print Media: Codes and Analysis of Codes in Use by Press Councils in Countries of the EU*, Oxford: PCMLP.

—— (2004d) *Self-Regulation and the Broadcast Media*, Oxford: PCMLP.

Puppis, M. (2009) *Organisationen der Medienselbstregulierung*, Köln: Halem.

—— (2010) 'Media governance: A new concept for the analysis of media policy and regulation,' *Communication, Culture and Critique*, 3(2): 134–149.

——, Künzler, M., Schade, E., Donges, P., Dörr, B., Ledergerber, A. and Vogel, M. (2004) Selbstregulierung und Selbstorganisation. Unpublished final report for the Federal Office of Communications (Bundesamtes für Kommunikation, or BAKOM), Zürich: IPMZ. Online. Available HTTP: http://www.mediapolicy.unizh.ch/forschung/selbstregulierung_report.pdf (accessed 11 October 2011).

Raboy, M. and Padovani, C. (2010) 'Mapping global media policy: Concepts, frameworks, methods,' *Communication, Culture and Critique*, 3(2): 150–169.

Radaelli, C. M. (2004) 'The diffusion of regulatory impact assessment: Best practice or lesson-drawing?' *European Journal of Political Research*, 43(5): 723–747.

—— (2005) 'Diffusion without convergence: How political context shapes the adoption of regulatory impact assessment,' *Journal of European Public Policy*, 12(5): 924–943.

Rhodes, R. A. W. (1996) 'The new governance: Governing without government,' *Political Studies*, 44(4): 652–667.

Ronit, K. and Schneider, V. (1999) 'Global governance through private organizations,' *Governance*, 12 (3): 243–266.

Rosenau, J. N. and Czempiel, E. O. (eds.) (1992) *Governance without Government: Order and Change in World Politics*, Cambridge: Cambridge University Press.

Saurwein, F. (2011) 'Regulatory choice for alternative modes of regulation: How context matters,' *Law and Policy*, 33(3): 334–336.

—— and Latzer, M. (2010) 'Regulatory choice in communications: The case of content-rating schemes in the audiovisual industry,' *Journal of Broadcasting and Electronic Media*, 54(3): 463–484.

Schneider, V. (2001) *Die Transformation der Telekommunikation: Vom Staatsmonopol zum globalen Markt (1800–2000)*, Frankfurt and New York: Campus.

Schulz, W. (2007) 'Neue Ordnung durch neues Medienrecht? Modelle der Co-Regulierung im Medienbereich,' in O. Jarren and P. Donges (eds.) *Ordnung durch Medienpolitik*, Konstanz: UVK.

—— and Held T. (2002) 'Regulierte Selbstregulierung als Form modernen Regierens,' Endbericht im Auftrag des Bundesbeauftragten für Angelegenheiten der Kultur und der Medien, Arbeitspapiere des Hans-Bredow-Instituts Nr. 10, Hamburg: Hans-Bredow-Institut.

Schuppert, G. Fw. (2005) 'Governance im Spiegel der Wissenschaftsdisziplinen,' in G. F. Schuppert (ed.) *Governance-Forschung: Vergewisserung über den Stand und Entwicklungslinien*, Baden-Baden: Nomos.

Scott, C. (2002) 'Private regulation of the public sector: A neglected facet of contemporary governance,' *Journal of Law and Society*, 29(1): 56–76.

—— (2004) 'Regulation in the age of governance: The rise of the post-regulatory state,' in J. Jordana and D. Levi-Faur (eds.) *The Politics of Regulation*, Cheltenham and Northampton, MA: Edward Elgar.

Sinclair, D. (1997) 'Self-regulation versus command and control? Beyond false dichotomies,' *Law and Policy*, 19(4): 529–559.

Streeck, W. and Schmitter, C. P. (1985) 'Community, market, state—and associations? The prospective contribution of interest governance to social order,' in W. Streeck and P. C. Schmitter (eds.) *Private Interest Government: Beyond Market and State*, London: Sage.

Tambini, D., Leonardi, D. and Marsden, C. (2008) *Codifying Cyberspace: Communications Self-Regulation in the Age of Internet Convergence*, London and New York: Routledge.

Thatcher, M. and Stone Sweet, A. (eds.) (2002) 'Theory and practice of delegation to non-majoritarian institutions,' *West European Politics*, 25(Special Issue): 1–22.

Treib, O., Bähr, H. and Falkner, G. (2005) 'Modes of governance, old and new: A note towards conceptual clarification,' European Governance Papers No. N–05–02. Online. Available HTTP: http://www.connex-network.org/eurogov/pdf/egp-newgov-N–05–02.pdf (accessed 20 November 2010).

Van Cuilenburg, J. and McQuail, D. (2003) 'Media policy paradigm shifts: Towards a new communications policy paradigm,' *European Journal of Communication*, 18(2): 181–207.
Weinberg, J. (2000) 'ICANN and the problem of legitimacy,' *Duke Law Journal*, 50: 187–226.
Werle, R. (2001) 'Standards in the international telecommunications regime,' HWWA-Institut für Wirtschaftsforschung-Hamburg, Discussion Paper 157.
Zacharia, G., Moukas, A. and Maes, P. (2000) 'Collaborative reputation mechanisms in electronic marketplaces,' *Decision Support Systems*, 29(4): 371–388.

22

# Media governance and technology

## From "code is law" to governance constellations

*Christian Katzenbach*

### Introduction

Social communication has always been realized to a large degree through media technologies. Since the end of the twentieth century, however, information and communication technologies (ICTs) are increasingly tangled up with our everyday social interactions and structures. We no longer turn to distinct media products like newspapers or television channels to experience mediated communication; our everyday life is deeply embedded within media. Krotz (2007) and others have coined the term "mediatization" to describe this process. "Contemporary society," argues Hjarvard, "is permeated by the media, to an extent that the media, may no longer be conceived of as being separate from cultural and other institutions" (2008: 105). Deuze (2012) even speaks plainly of a "media life" that we are living—not *with* media, but rather *in* media.

This deep integration of media technology into our daily life calls attention to an issue that has been discussed for decades in media and communication studies: how do media technologies change and shape the way in which we communicate, both on an individual, as well as societal level? Whereas media theorists such as Marshall McLuhan have long argued for the strong impact of media technology, this thread has been put to one side by constructivist approaches since the early 1980s. Since then, media scholars have either focused on the domestication and usage patterns of technologies (cf. Berker *et al.* 2006), or postulated technology as a black box that triggers change and, in some cases, regulatory adjustments.

This chapter takes a different stance on the relationship between media regulation and technology. Drawing on governance research, regulation is understood as a complex process of ordering, including private and public law, formal and informal means, discursive and material elements. This shift of perspective allows technology to be conceptualized not simply as an external trigger or as a target for regulation, but as an integral and contested part of regulatory constellations.

Taking Lawrence Lessig's (1999) term "code is law" as a starting point, this chapter brings together literature from the fields of governance research and science and technology studies (STS) to tackle the "politics of information and communication technologies" (Mansell and Silverstone 1996), outlining a model of media governance with a special focus on technology.

## Media governance as a concept

In recent years, the general debate within the social sciences on regulatory structures has shifted from viewing the state as the central actor and legislation as the main instrument, towards more heterogeneous regulatory structures. Under the umbrella term "governance," researchers have drawn their attention to the emergence, consolidation and transformation of various structures and processes that facilitate, constrain and coordinate the range of behavior of actors in a specific field. This perspective not only implies a renewed interest in heterogeneous sets of actors (including the state but going far beyond it), but also means dealing with different forms of establishing order and varying mechanisms used to coordinate interdependence between actors; networks, markets, communities, knowledge, "*leitbilder*,"[1] standards, and social norms now supplement statutory regulation in coordinating the behavior of actors in a certain field.

## Media governance revisited: From actors to modes of regulation

In media policy and law, this shift has highlighted various sets of actors involved in media policy processes: research has focused on the varieties of industry co- and self-regulation that have emerged, as well as forms of citizen participation, implying a more inclusive perspective on media regulation. Just and Latzer (2005), for example, identify a general shift from vertical to horizontal regulation in the media sector, a move that increasingly involves private actors across a wide range of communication policy issues. As part of this shift, independent regulatory agencies have taken over operative tasks of regulation from public administration in most Organization for Economic Co-operation and Development (OECD) states (Thatcher 2002; OECD 2005; Latzer 2009). Traditional self-regulatory institutions such as press councils have been rediscovered by research (Puppis 2009). In addition, a whole strand of research is investigating the participation of civil society actors in regulation processes (e.g. Stone 2008; Cammaerts 2011; Hintz and Milan 2011; Padovani and Pavan 2011).

Kooiman (2003), as well as Just and Latzer (2005), argue that this regulatory—and analytical—trend is the result of the increasingly complex, dynamic and diverse communication structures of contemporary societies. Given this context, the efficacy of statutory regulation is seen as limited; thus a more diverse range of stakeholders is included in media governance research, with policymakers acknowledging the contribution that private actors and civil society make in regulative structures.

Additionally, the governance approach is frequently used to cope with the multilevel nature of media policy and its variety of policy arenas. Authors have analyzed the relations between policy processes in international institutions such as the International Telecommunication Union (ITU) or the World Trade Organization (WTO), supranational institutions such as the European Union (EU), and national legislation (Ó Siochrú and Girard 2002; Krasner 1991). Raboy and Padovani (2010: 153) see a "shifting in the location of authority" through which "more and more institutional arrangements to steer communication systems take place at the supranational level." This perspective, focusing on the

1 *Leitbilder* are a core concept of science and technology studies—especially with German scholars—that deal with cognitive elements, shared (or divergent) understandings and visions attached to a technological innovation by the involved actors (cf. Dierkes *et al.* 1996).

pluralization of actors involved in media and communication regulation, views media governance as a horizontal and vertical extension of government (Puppis 2007).[2]

Yet this heterogeneity of actors is only one aspect in the overarching governance discourse. In addition to these changes in the actors involved, the governance literature also discusses novel modes of governance. Since this strand of research has not influenced media policy literature in a comparable way, alternative modes of establishing order and coordination such as private ordering and social norms are discussed in the following sections. This will set the ground for the inclusion of technology into the governance discourse.[3]

## Governance as an analytical concept

If it is not the pluralization of actors, what is it then that characterizes the governance approach? In line with Puppis (2010) and recent governance literature in other fields (Blumenthal 2005; Schuppert 2008), governance is understood here as a rather broad concept that not only covers allegedly new forms and mechanisms of regulation that are characterized by non-hierarchical structures and the inclusion of non-governmental actors, but also the regulatory structure in its entirety—privileging neither statutory legislation nor forms of self-regulation. It is thus not used as a normative notion, but as an analytical concept that draws attention to the emergence, consolidation and transformation of structures and processes that facilitate and constrain, as well as coordinate, the range of behavior of actors in a specific field. The analytical focus can thus be trimmed "to shifts between various forms of regulation" (Hofmann 2011: 3) and their interplays, which is particularly instrumental for analyses in media and communication regulation and the role of technology.

At the analytical core of such an approach to regulatory constellations are "patterns to cope with interdependencies between actors" (Lange and Schimank 2004), referring both to structures and processes. Schuppert (2008) argues similarly that governance research focuses on structures of coordination. These structures of coordination are not only constituted by the "regulative pillar," but also by a "normative" and a "cognitive pillar" (Scott 1995: 35). Norms, values, shared meanings and symbolic systems are seen here as central elements that provide orientation and guidance.[4]

2 Horizontal extension refers to the inclusion of private actors through co-regulation or self-regulation; the growing influence of international institutions can be described as a vertical extension of the traditional mode of rule-making through the nation-state. If both processes are intertwined, regulatory responsibilities are transnationalized.

3 For a theoretically sound description of the governance approach and its adaption in media policy research, see Puppis 2010. For a more detailed discussion and critique of the adaption of the governance concept in media policy research, see Katzenbach 2011.

4 Donges (2007a) and Puppis (2010) have already convincingly linked institutional theories and governance research. In contrast to the argument put forward here, Puppis (2010: 139) sees *rules* as the core concept of the governance perspective: "It is a new way of describing, explaining, and criticizing the entirety of forms of rules that aim to organize media systems." He puts forward the convincing argument that the structure and dynamics of a media system and its actors are not only shaped by collective rules that are obligatory for every actor, but also by internal, organizational rules such as editorial guidelines, codes of conduct or other control mechanisms implemented by single actors or a group of actors themselves.

As convincing as this is, this concept seems to neglect the point that it is not only explicit, codified rules that regulate and coordinate the behavior of actors in a field. Although rules might be the predominant factor (Raboy and Padovani 2010; Price 2002), a perspective restricted to rules fades

These pillars, or rather, dimensions of institutions, interact strongly. Marie-Laure Djelic and Sigrid Quack (2003) argue that the stability, robustness and self-reproducing character of institutions depends on the interplay of regulative pressures and systems of control within normative and cognitive frames. Institutional change occurs "where and when internal challenges and spaces of opportunity combine with and are being reinforced by external triggers and alternatives" (Djelic and Quack 2003: 23). Thus to understand the dynamics of an institutional setting means essentially to understand the "internal" interplay of its compounds—regulative, normative and cultural—and the supposedly "external" changing contexts.

On the grounds of this institutional approach to governance, the perspective applied here understands governance as the processes of establishing (and questioning) order and coordination in a wide sense.

## From laws to discourses, numbers, contracts—and technology

So as not to replicate the existing reviews and discussions on central mechanisms and actors of media governance (Braman 2004; Puppis 2010; Raboy and Padovani 2010; cf. also Schulz in this volume), in the following sections some of the less acknowledged modes of governance, derived from an institutional perspective, are introduced and discussed.

### *Private ordering*

The regulative "pillar" of media governance obviously consists of statutory law on the national and international level. It is also built upon what Puppis (2010: 139ff) discusses under the notion of "rules." In addition to public law, this covers all of the codified rules that organize and frame mediated communication, including rules on an organizational level (e.g. editorial guidelines and codes of conduct).

Another aspect of formal regulation that has not gained comparable attention in research in media policy and law, but is of enormous practical relevance in the ordering of media and communication, is private ordering. Mechanisms of private law such as contracts, licenses and end-user agreements (EUA) are complementing, enforcing or even undermining the traditional mechanisms of public law in some areas, especially concerning copyright, but also in other legal areas such as privacy and consumer rights. Legal scholars such as Bechtold (2002; 2003), Dreier (2000) and Lessig (1999) have long argued that the combination of user licenses with technical protection measures for digital works and their legal protection within copyright law[5] has diminished the relevance of traditional copyright law for individual usage practices because there are several regulative layers built on top of it.

Similar to these phenomena of privatization of copyright through licenses, Niva Elkin-Koren (2008) highlights the importance of contractual elements in her study on the

out the analytical surplus of the governance concept. Common beliefs, mutual expectations and cognitive frameworks of actors in a policy field, as well as those of different publics and of individual citizens, play an important role in shaping and framing media communication—and in some cases again lead to codified rules.

5 The World Intellectual Property Organization (WIPO) Copyright Treaty (WCT) and the WIPO Performances and Phonograms Treaty (WPPT), negotiated within the WIPO, introduced in 1996 the protection of technological measures into the international copyright system. In effect, any circumvention of digital rights management systems should be considered a violation of copyright (Dussolier 1999; Koelman and Helberger 2000).

governance of creative works in the context of social media. Here, the *terms of service*, issued by platforms (e.g. YouTube, Facebook, Twitter, etc.), govern the creative works and the associated usage patterns on the site. In most cases, the agreement of the user is manifested simply through his usage of the service, and thereby authorizes the platform (and the other users) to "use, modify, publicly perform, publicly display, reproduce, and distribute" his content through the site (Elkin-Koren 2008: 12). As in the case of licenses, described above, these contractual elements are often embodied in the software architecture of the service on social media platforms.[6]

This policing of content through terms of services not only affects copyright and privacy issues, but also has a "substantial impact on freedom of expression." Jillian C. York's (2010: 28) analysis of the handling of terms of service violations on different platforms in the context of political activism illustrates this phenomenon. Drawing on Zeynep Tufekci (2010) and her analogy with shopping malls, York sees a trend towards a "privatization of our publics" and their regulation, with corporations drawing the line between free speech and violation of other rights differently from statutory legislation and courts.

These trends towards a growing importance of contractual, bilateral agreements[7] illustrate the enormous impact of private ordering in media communication. Elkin-Korin (2008: 5) concludes that private ordering "has become a dominant source of the norms which govern access to creative works."[8] Thus, in the realm of copyright, the privatization of the regulatory structure is clearly evident—yet less visible.[9] With that, the public negotiation process about the "right" balancing of interests *within* the copyright system is partly displaced by one-sided dispositions through content or platform providers. It is especially the *interplay* between these forms of private ordering with technical measures that changes the mechanisms of media and communication governance broadly.

### Norms and discourses

As argued earlier, it is not only explicit, binding and formally sanctionable regulatory efforts that regulate and coordinate the behavior and relations of actors in a field. Legal scholars are also increasingly pointing to "soft laws," referring mainly to international norms or statements that are not formally binding, but which expand, realign or constrain the scope of possible decisions or actions of actors (Gersen and Posner 2008; Brummer 2010; Saldias 2011). In media policy and law, this is highly relevant in both traditional fields such as broadcasting policy as well as emerging recent fields such as Internet governance.

6 For this interplay between governance by contracts and governance by technology, see the following sections of this chapter.

7 There is an intense scholarly debate on the legal status of EUAs and Terms of Services: are they contracts or "simply unilateral provisions which are held enforceable against third parties." (Elkin-Koren 2008: 19)

8 This privatization of regulatory mechanisms in this realm is not only used to restrict access to creative works, however. Lots of initiatives, like the Free Software Movement or Creative Commons, in fact use license agreements to move creative works into the public domain and to guarantee free access to them (see Reichmann and Uhlir 2003; Dussolier 2007; Dobusch 2011). With Merges (2004: 183), private ordering even accounts for a "new dynamism in the public domain."

9 Braman (2004: 165) hints at a different form of "invisible policy": "Many types of media policy decisions are highly influential but little discussed or even acknowledged, [. . .] such things as presidential executive orders, decisions by federal and state attorneys general and the practice of hiding statutory law directed at one issue within a piece of legislation commonly understood to deal with another."

In this line of argument, Donges (2002, 2007b) argues that, in the field of public broadcasting policy, the EU Commission does not have its greatest impact through legislation, but through considering that the funding of public broadcasting might constitute a state aid that interferes with the common market. With that, the Commission changed the conversation on public broadcasting and the very criteria by which its regulation and legitimacy are being judged. This might be the beginning of a "shifting baseline effect"[10] changing the perception of public broadcasting fundamentally. Whereas public broadcasting was considered the very foundation for broadcasting activities by private companies until the 1980s in numerous European countries, it is now increasingly seen as an exemption that needs to be legitimized.

A shift of conversation has also happened in the realm of Internet governance. Jeanette Hofmann (2007) describes the development of Internet governance and its arenas as an "open-ended, collective process of searching" that has meandered from the Internet Engineering Task Force's (IETF) "technical regime," to ICANN, via the UN's 2003 and 2005 World Summit on the Information Society (WSIS) to the Internet Governance Forum (IGF). With these shifts in its main arena, the whole debate around Internet governance—its very definition and the topics included— has changed. "The result is," argues Hurwitz, "that the world is discovering that Internet Governance embraces many more topics than names and numbers" (2007: 2). As a result, ICANN and the US government have lost their position as dominant actors to a much more heterogeneous constellation: "Thus, definitions of Internet governance, either narrow or broad, always implicitly include preliminary decisions about institutions, constellations of actors, and forms of authority" (Hofmann 2007: 20).

Besides this macro perspective on regional or global norm-setting and the processes that are shifting agendas, it is necessary to zoom in closer to the meso and micro levels using an institutional approach to governance to understand how these discursive modes of governance work. Institutional theorists usually describe the emergence of norms and shared values as a process in three stages (Berger and Luckmann 1966; Tolbert and Zucker 1996). First, regular local interactions and cognitive patterns for specific problems become habitualized. At the second stage, which has been termed "objectification," these "solutions" and cognitive frames become generalized beyond the local context in which they developed; a consensus on their legitimacy is established within a certain range of actors (or not). The third stage has been called "sedimentation": here, patterns become fully institutionalized in the sense that they are internalized, not questioned, and in some cases materialized into formal or structural institutions (Tolbert and Zucker 1996); "It is during this last stage that institutions can potentially acquire the 'quality of exteriority,' that is, become taken for granted and develop a reality of their own" (Djelic and Quack 2003: 22).

So, if shared meanings and common beliefs emerge and stabilize (by undermining and displacing competing dispositifs), they provide frames for situations and policy issues, promoting some patterns of behavior and decisions more than others. This implies that

10 The concept of the "shifting baseline effect" was developed by Pauly (1995) and Saénz-Arroyo *et al.* (2005) in the context of environmental psychology. Here, "shifting environmental baselines are inter-generational changes in perception of the state of the environment. As one generation replaces another, people's perceptions of what is natural change even to the extent that they no longer believe historical anecdotes of past abundance or size of species" (Saénz-Arroyo *et al.* 2005: 1957). Günther Ortmann (2010) has put this concept in the wider context of rules and rule-following; Leonhard Dobusch (2011) has observed a shifting baseline effect in the last thirty years with regard to the relation of copyright and the public domain, rendering unregulated uses of informational and cultural goods an exemption today.

discursive struggles can translate into regulative struggles and vice versa (Göhler *et al.* 2009). Janice Denegri-Knott (2004) has distilled these "governance translations" in the discourse over the labeling of music file sharing in the context of copyright by showing how "power machinates in establishing the parameters between acceptable and unacceptable behaviors," not only by influencing public law directly. Matthias Künzler's (2009) study on the role of ideas and normative principles in the liberalization and privatization of European broadcasting markets illustrates the coordinative force of cognitive and discursive elements. Similarly, yet in a very different case, Christian Pentzold (2010) has sketched the "communicative construction" of Wikipedia as an online community. The study shows that the discursive process of negotiating what constitutes Wikipedia is, in fact, an important element in governing the community as well as the outcome: "[A]utonomous authors are made amenable to administrative actions by a language of 'community' which ties community membership to compliance with a set of norms and values—orthodoxy and orthopraxy" (Pentzold 2010: 717). An intricate interplay between explicit policies and normative obligations lead to "shared actions," so that both "right actions" as well as "right thinking" determine the inclusion in or exclusion from the community.

In this way, normative, cultural and symbolic elements play an important role in regulatory structures that come into focus with a sociologically informed governance perspective.

## How to frame technology in media governance: From "code is law" to governance constellations

The governance approach, as examined here, is interested in looking at diverse forms of regulation and its interplays. As illustrated by mechanisms of private and discursive ordering, rule-setting authority is seen as "decentered" (Bevir and Rhodes 2006; Hofmann 2011) and ontologically flattened. In this chapter, this governance approach is combined with concepts and perspectives developed within the science and technology studies (STS) and actor-network theory (ANT). The resulting perspective provides a stance on technology and its role in media regulation that is considerably different from the traditional view on technology in media policy and law. Along these lines, it is first necessary to open the black box that technology constitutes in many policy studies; this allows the avoidance of a deterministic stance on technology by tracing its social construction. Once in use, technological constellations become a part of the institutional frame in specific situations that facilitates certain practices and controls or constrains others. Lawrence Lessig (1999) has prominently coined this role of technology as "code is law." Finally, the regulatory constellations formed by these different politics of technology and their interplay with other *social* elements are addressed.

## Opening the black box

In most cases, media policy scholars look at technology from a bird's eye perspective.[11] From this analytic altitude, technological elements appear as rather fixed elements that either can be

11 See also Orlikowski *et al.* (1991: 121): "[T]he field of information systems (IT), which is premised on the centrality of information technology in everyday life, has not deeply engaged its core subject matter—the information technology (IT) artifact. [. . .] The outcome is that much IT research draws on commonplace and received notions of technology, resulting in conceptualizations of IT as relatively stable, discrete, independent, and fixed."

a trigger for regulation, or an object for (mostly *ex post*) regulation. In this view, digitalization and connected computer networks have allowed easy, cheap and perfect replication and distribution of music and movies, triggering the need for a reformulation of copyright. Alternatively, online services such as Google's Street View or Facebook have become targets for regulatory initiatives concerned with privacy and citizen rights. Such an account of technology in media governance reflects a view of regulation as an exclusive domain of the state and privileged self-regulating actors. Thus technological arrangements necessarily are seen as objects that are either triggers or targets of formal regulation. In both cases, technology stays (more or less) a black box, as we will discuss later.

Following the line of governance research elaborated here, in deconstructing regulation as a complex process of public and private ordering, of formal and informal norms, it becomes possible to develop a more nuanced view of the role of technology.[12] This is achieved by leaving the bird's eye perspective and zooming in on the intricacies of public and private orderings by which norms are negotiated.[13] Technological configurations, then, do not appear as stable black boxes, but as internal and contested parts of regulatory constellations. Hence technology in this view is neither purely a trigger nor a sole target for external regulation, but one out of multiple "crystallizations of meanings" (Berger 1981) that condensate in ordering processes—and might stabilize, dissolve or transform sooner or later.

In STS, this process is commonly referred to as the opening of a "black box":

> What is needed is an understanding of technology from the inside, both as a body of knowledge and as a social system. Instead, technology is often treated as a 'black box' whose contents and behaviour may be assumed to be common knowledge.
>
> (*Layton 1977: 198*)

So, what Bruno Latour and many others in this field have done has been a metaphorical opening of the black boxes of scientific knowledge (e.g. Latour and Woolgar 1979; Knorr-Cetina 1989) and, later on, of technology and artifacts (Pinch and Bijker 1984; MacKenzie and Wajcman 1985; Latour 1987 and 1999; Bijker and Law 1992; Bijker 1995; Bijker *et al.* 1997). By deconstructing statements, things and institutions, these scholars have demonstrated that the technologies and scientific findings we take for granted are indeed very much contingent on the respective circumstances. For that, researchers in most cases pursue detailed case studies on the deconstruction and "reassembling" of things (Latour 2007), be it refrigerators (Schwartz Conan 1985), bicycles (Bijker 1995), aircraft (Law and Callon 1992) or hotel keys (Latour 1992). When the "interpretative flexibility"[14] diminishes (i.e. if the

12 The argument that there are two different views on the role of technology in media regulation follows and adapts the observation by Niva Elkin-Koren (2004: 252f) that there are two opposing concepts shaping the discourse on the Internet and information governance. In the first, binding rules are set by "centralized institutions of the territorial state"; in the second, mechanisms of private ordering such as contracts are taken into account, yielding a fundamentally different view on regulatory developments (cf. Hofmann 2011).

13 Schuppert (2007) introduced the zooming metaphor to governance research. Similarly, yet differently, Latour (2007: 221) characterizes the actor-network theory (ANT): "When we shift to ANT, we are like lazy car drivers newly converted to hiking; we have to relearn that if we want to reach the top of the mountain, we need to take it one step at a time, right foot after left foot, with no jumping or running allowed, all the way to the bitter end!"

14 For a discussion and elaboration of this central core concept of STS, see Meyer and Schulz-Schaeffer 2006.

competing concepts and meanings attached to an artifact or service converge or if one artifact gains dominance over another), this social arrangement stabilizes. This process yields a technological artifact that can be seen as fixed and "closed" from the outside. In other words, technologies have become a black box:

> . . . made invisible by its own success. When a machine runs efficiently, when a matter of fact is settled, one need to focus only on its inputs and outputs and not on its internal complexity. Thus, paradoxically, the more science and technology succeed, the more opaque and obscure they become.
>
> (*Latour 1999: 304*)

As the media technologies permeating our daily lives become more complex, it is necessary for scholars to look inside successful technologies. The opening of black boxes as a research strategy, developed within STS, can be instructive for governance research in order to bring technology into the "game"—not as purely external trigger or sole target for regulation, but as part of complex governance arrangements in today's highly engineered communication environments.[15]

## The social construction of technology

The first and most obvious step in this process of untangling the relationship between governance and technology is to analyze the social factors that shape the development and use of technology. Researchers in the history of science and STS have shown empirically that technologies do not follow their own "intrinsic" teleological path, but are strongly socially constructed; this constructivist view of technology is currently dominating this research field (Meister *et al.* 2006).

One line of research here is illustrated by the case studies conducted by ANT and STS scholars mentioned above, tracing the "stabilization" and "closure" of artifacts, often with a focus on the "relevant social groups" framing the artifact (see, for an overview, Bijker 2006). Closer to media policy and law are scholars who, drawing on sociological literature, have investigated processes and key determinants in the development of (media) technology. Here, coordination and negotiation between different sets of actors in standardization processes as well as the impact of *leitbilder* on technological development and its regulation come into focus (Schmidt and Werle 1998; Dierkes *et al.* 1996; Bröchler 2008). Other scholars discuss the effects of national or sectorial institutional structures on technological innovations (Porter 1990; Carlsson *et al.* 2002; Freeman 1987), or investigate the causes for different trajectories of a certain technology in different countries (cf. Hughes 1983) or the role of actor constellations and coalitions in the development and diffusion of new technologies (Weyer *et al.* 1997; Castilla *et al.* 2000; Giesecke 2001).

15 A similar approach of analyzing from the inside out is put forward by the emerging field of software studies. Whereas other disciplines focus on "the development of software from an engineering-centered perspective and the [. . .] impacts of software-enabled technologies," software studies aims specifically at the "software that enables such technologies [. . . and] tries to prise open the black box of algorithms, executable files, captabase structures, and information protocols to understand software as a new media that augments and automates society" (Kitchin and Dodge 2011: 245–6). Lev Manovich (2008: 4–5) contends that "if we don't address software itself, we are in danger of always dealing only with its effects rather than the causes: the output that appears on a computer screen rather than the programs and social cultures that produce these outputs."

However, it is not only institutional macro and meso settings in this narrow sense of formal structures and rules that shape the development and use of technologies. Normative and cultural elements also play a role. Harmeet Sawhney (2004), for example, shows, in a stimulating study that compares the diffusion of clocks and computers as decentralized means of synchronization, that technological artifacts do not necessarily foster change. The decentralization of artifacts—from tower clocks to wrist watches, from mainframes to personal computers, laptops and mobile devices—did not lead to greater individual autonomy, but rather to more compliance to general "system rules":

> While the reduction in size and cost of a technology facilitates mass adoption and thereby creates a sense of empowerment, the interconnection process reties the discrete devices together to create a new apparatus for exerting control. [. . .] In the case of the clock [. . .] it was the culture of punctuality that drove individuals to synchronize their watches. Similarly, in the case of computers [. . .] it is the culture of flexibility and teamwork that holds networked organizations together.
>
> (*Sawhney 2004: 371*)

In media and communication studies, this constructivist strand of research has been primarily adapted by scholars with a cultural studies background investigating the integration of technology and media products into our everyday life (e.g. Berker *et al.* 2006; Röser 2007; Silverstone and Hirsch 1992). This "domestication" perspective stresses that technology in use does not follow blindly any inherent logic, but is always appropriated, reinterpreted and domesticated by its users. Social values, financial as well as "moral economies," political and family hierarchies, the material aspects of the household, all essentially shape the use and meaning of technological devices and media products.

In sum, these findings show that technology is neither an artifact outside of politics and society that follows its own teleological path nor simply a flexible object of statutory regulation. It is subject to complex negotiations and politics, and is essentially shaped by both formal institutions and normative, cultural factors.

## Code is law—or society made durable

Scholars in the field of media policy and law might have neglected this constructivist account, but it has—as sketched out—produced a considerable amount of research on the impact of social processes and structures on technology. This is not the case for the opposite perspective. Since the 1980s, a stance that conceives technology less as an object of social shaping or regulation and more as a means of regulation and as an formative element of media structures that causes change has been under the suspicion of technological determinism, and has consequently been marginalized in accounts of technology, media and communication.[16]

However, at the fringes of media policy research there are stances that start from the assumption that the specific design of technology facilitates and constrains certain ways of

16 Winner (1993: 368): "The most obvious lack in social constructionist writing is an almost total disregard for the social consequences of technical choice. [. . .] What the introduction of new artifacts means for people's sense of self, for the texture of human communities, for qualities of everyday living, and for the broader distribution of power in society—these are not matters of explicit concern."

regulation and of using a certain device or service. Such an approach is always in danger of falling into the trap of technological determinism, but it does provide the starting point for tackling the role of technology in governance arrangements.

Such a position was prominently stated in the debate around the regulation of the Internet in the mid-1990s. The architecture of the Internet was conceived to be immune to statutory regulation: "Indeed, the very design of the Internet seemed technologically proof against attempts to put the genie back in the bottle. [. . . It] treats censorship like damage and routes around it" (Walker 2003: 25). Although this view of the net as being regulatory immune has been proved to be naive in retrospect (Goldsmith and Wu 2006), the point that the architecture of the net and the software code itself must be seen as elements that facilitate, norm or constrain social behavior has persisted: "Law and government regulation are [. . .] not the only source of rule-making. Technological capabilities and system design choices impose rules on participants [. . .]; the set of rules for information flows imposed by technology and communication networks form a '*lex informatica*'" (Reidenberg 1998: 554). For this idea, Lawrence Lessig (1999) has coined the catchphrase "code is law": software code or—more generally technical architectures—are seen as one of four constraints regulating social behavior (next to law, market and norms). Lessig also hinted at interdependencies between the constraining forces, but his model remains sociologically under-complex (e.g. it does not deal with the emergence of norms at all, nor the interdependencies with software); also the market is depicted as working under perfect conditions, and it might generally be considered a category mistake.[17]

The structural and individual impacts of emerging and existing technologies on users and social structures have also been addressed in STS, notwithstanding the constructivist dominance. The core assumption here is, similar to Lessig, that the very design of technology facilitates, controls and constrains social behavior (Bijker and Law 1992; Winner 1980) and influences sectorial change (Dolata 2009). Technology is conceived as an integral part of society and social relations; with Latour (1991), "technology is society made durable." Road bumps, bridges, automatic door closers, or heavy hotel keys are the classic examples in this "sociology of things" that illustrate how artifacts have a strong impact on how we move, talk and interact. In this sense, technology is an institutionalized form of social action or structure that itself has an effect on social interactions and structures.

In recent years, scholars from media studies have taken up Lessig's focus on software as a very "plastic" and increasingly important form of technology. With Lev Manovich (2001; 2008), Andrew Mackenzie (2006), Matthew Fuller (2008), Rob Kitchin and Martin Dodge (2011), and others, a field of "software studies" is emerging, focusing especially on the codification of social relations, rules and routines into algorithms and databases. These scholars ascribe a form of agency to technologies as they augment and execute the agency of programmers, corporations, policymakers and users (Mackenzie 2006; Kitchin and Dodge 2011: 5).[18]

## Networks and translations in media policy and law

What we see here—and sometimes forget—is that technologies have their politics (Mansell and Silverstone 1996). This political nature of technologies and artifacts is double-sided.

17 For this reason, Wolfgang Schulz and Niva Elkin-Koren substitute this category convincingly with contracts as part of market transactions.

18 A similar line of argument is brought forward by scholars stressing the importance, yet invisibility, of (technical) infrastructures; here also a new field of "infrastructure studies" seems to emerge (Bowker *et al.* 2010).

They are shapeable elements, developed, used and regulated within existing institutions, norms, cultures and established modes of interactions, while simultaneously existing as essential elements within the institutional environment that facilitates and constrains the range of preferences, behavior and relations of actors.

Sociologists have tried to conceptualize these interplays and mutual relations of impacts with slightly varying concepts such as the "'co-evolution' of technology and institutions" or —referring to Gidden's structuration theory—the "duality"' of technology and society. From a macro perspective, scholars have investigated the "co-evolution" of social structures and technologies in which periods of technological changes and path creations, on the one hand, and of institutional and societal (re-)framing, on the other, alternate and overlap (cf. for an overview, see Dolata 2009; Geels 2004; Nelson 1994). In some cases, a technological leapfrog may lead to "periods of mismatch" in which "the established social and institutional framework no longer corresponds to the potential of a new techno-economic paradigm" (Dosi *et al.* 1988: 11). Along these lines, with several refinements, Ulrich Dolata and Raymund Werle have recently argued convincingly for the need to "bring technology back in" and to look more into the details of structural impacts of technology (Dolata 2009; Dolata and Werle 2007). On a micro-meso level, Schulz-Schaeffer (2000) describes these interrelations as an interplay of resources and routines. In this concept, the social potency and embeddedness of a technology relies on the duality of two structural aspects: the emergence and institutionalization of reliable sets of events that—as a technology—can be used as resources for actions; and the establishment of routines in the use of such events.

Scholars following the ANT approach give this a more radical spin, eschewing any a priori distinction between people and things. Bruno Latour (2007: 1ff), particularly, insists that the "social" is not a "specific type of causality" or domain that differs from other materials or explanations (e.g. technical, economic, legal, organizational). Rather, "'social' for ANT is the name of a type of momentary association which is characterized by the way it gathers together into new shapes" (Latour 2007: 65).

> Machines, architectures, clothes, texts—all contribute to the patterning of the social. And [. . .] if these materials were to disappear then so too would what we sometimes call the social order. Actor-network theory says, then, that order is an effect generated by heterogeneous means.
>
> (*Law 1992: 382*)

Approaching the role of technology in media governance means *shifting the analytical focus* from the "social" construction of technology and supposed "societal" implications of technology to patterns of associations and heterogeneous networks. As a consequence, technological devices and services are, in this view, no less part of the heterogeneous networks that constitutes the social than norms or power—and not an external trigger or target for regulation.

Next to this analytical shift, the deep integration of the technical into the social, ANT also suggests a different research strategy: telling empirical stories about *processes of translation* (Callon 1986; Latour 1991, 1992, 2007). Latour's classic example is that of the hotel key (Latour 1991). His story starts with the hotel manager asking his guests to leave the hotel key at the front desk whenever they leave the hotel. However, this verbal request does not mean that his guests behave according to his wishes. What follows in Latour's telling of the story is a chain of translations wherein the hotel manager's "program of action" (Akrich and Latour 1992) is successively loaded with moral obligations ("please"), visualizations and a reminder (sign), and—finally—the heavy piece of metal that no one wants to keep in his pocket while exploring a city.

Latour's overarching argument is that a study of the fabric of the social essentially means looking at how statements, stances and wishes are more or less successfully translated and loaded with things, words and people. Important here is that these translations always come with shifts of meanings of the individual element *and* of the whole arrangement:

> [W]e are not following a sentence through the context of its application, nor are we moving from language to the praxis. The program, 'leave your key at the front desk', which is now scrupulously executed by the majority of the customers, is simply not the one we started with. Its displacement has transformed it. Customers no longer leave their room keys: instead, they get rid of an unwieldy object that deforms their pockets. If they conform to the manager's wishes, it is not because they read the sign, nor because they are particularly well-mannered. It is because they cannot do otherwise. They don't think about it. The statement is no longer the same, the customers are no longer the same, the key is no longer the same—even the hotel is no longer quite exactly the same.
>
> (*Latour 1991: 105*)

Taken together, the concern of ANT scholars is to open the black boxes of social order, to inspect their ingredients, relations and chains of translations, and to trace how they came to be considered stabilized as an entity in the first place:

> [H]ow actors and organizations mobilize, juxtapose, and hold together the bits and pieces out of which they are composed; how they are sometimes able to prevent those bits and pieces from following their own inclinations and making off; and how they manage, as a result, to conceal for a time the process of translation itself and so turn a network from a heterogeneous set of bits and pieces each with its own inclinations, into something that passes as a punctualized actor.
>
> (*Law 1992: 386*)

For the study of media governance, the actor-networks approach thus complements the analytic focus elaborated from the governance literature. Both emphasize, using different vocabulary, a dynamic perspective that studies the *shifts between various forms of regulation*—instead of focusing on a static arrangement of social order. In combining governance research on "decentering regulation" (Bevir and Rhodes 2006; Hofmann 2011) with STS, regulation can be conceived as a very complex process of ordering, private and public, formal and informal, discursive and material, wherein different sets of institutions and "bundles of entitlements" (Bracha 2007; Hofmann 2011) are stabilized—and contested, transformed and dissolved.

To pursue the necessary steps to integrate technology into these heterogeneous networks that constitute the social order, it is necessary to more closely analyze the elements and processes that constitute it. Technological configurations, then, do not appear as stable black boxes, but as internal and contested parts of regulatory constellations.

## Illustration: The regulation of information goods

This analytical stance on media governance and technology changes the view on several issues discussed in the field of media policy and law quite a bit. The consequence of this shifted theoretical perspective is illustrated in the following for the regulation of information goods—not as a fully fledged case study, but rather a short illustration to show the mutual translation and transformations of different norms and entitlements in this context.

The regulation of information goods is probably one of the most prominent and controversial debates conducted in media policy and law—both academically and politically. This debate is generally framed as follows. Digital networks have radically lowered the costs for the reproduction and distribution of cultural goods, such as music, films and books. This constitutes, on the one hand, an enormous potential for the creation and sharing of culture; on the other hand, it is seen as the basis for copyright infringements on a scale never seen before. Thus copyright holders have—successfully—demanded the adaption and expansion of copyright law for the digital realm. Critical scholars, in turn, argue that this has lead to a paradoxical situation: even as digital technologies support creative uses as never before, citizens are more restricted in their creative work.

> Because every use of creative work technically produces a copy, every use of creative work technically triggers copyright law. [. . .] For the first time, the law regulates ordinary citizens generally [. . .] For the first time, the law reaches and regulates this culture. Not because Congress deliberated and decided that this form of creativity needed regulation, but simply because the architecture of copyright law interacted with the architecture of digital technology to produce a massive expansion in the reach of the law.
>
> (*Lessig 2008: 103*)

In this view, technology is seen as an external trigger that demands copyright reform from international organizations and national states. It is argued here that the stance on media governance and technology shifts this view considerably.

The first aspect of this shift concerns the analytic view on the regulation of information goods. Niva Elkin-Koren (2004: 252f) has convincingly delineated two differing concepts in the discourse on the Internet and information governance: In the first, binding rules are set by "centralized institutions of the territorial state"; in the second, mechanisms of private ordering such as contracts are taken into account. On these grounds, Jeanette Hofmann (2011) articulates, along the case of Google Books, a governance perspective on the regulation of information goods, neither privileging public nor private ordering, which "escapes the narrow debate on whether or not Google Books constitute a copyright infringement and opens up additional analytical avenues for studying the development of such arrangements" (Hofmann 2011: 5).

License contracts play a central role in this regard—being applied both in the back-ends of technological systems as well as in consumer markets. For example, measures to regulate information goods are deeply embedded in consumer electronics devices such as DVD players. Here, bundles of patent rights and licenses effectively rule that every manufacturer must implement a certain kind of content encryption to combat copyright infringement (Gillespie 2004; Grassmuck 2006). In consumer markets for digital information goods, licenses also have become the principal way in which to regulate the access and usage of music, movies and books. In fact, buying a DVD in a retail store is fundamentally different from buying a movie online. In the latter, the movie comes with a license that allows certain uses of the movie and prohibits others. These contracted entitlements might be in line with copyright law, but are not necessarily so. Contracts can limit the use of the purchased product on a certain type or number of devices or prescribe the allowed number of digital copies. In consequence, these regulatory means are not only partly replacing public ordering with private ordering, but are also changing the way in which culture is commoditized by "replacing transfer of ownership with selling access" (Hofmann 2011: 15).

So the first aspect that comes to light with the adjusted view is that statutory regulation is increasingly complemented, and even partly replaced, by other governance arrangements. Relevant actors such as copyright holders, manufacturers, service and platform providers, and users mobilize different forms of norms and entitlements to bring forth their interest. Interestingly, the story that this account of the regulation of information goods yields is not the same as the one told by traditional accounts on copyright regulation. There is a trend towards a commodification, privatization and juridification of culture and knowledge, but this movement is not linear; a governance perspective brings discontinuities and contested trajectories to light (Hofmann 2011). The case of Google Books is one of the areas in which the mechanisms of public and private ordering are being negotiated—with private ordering counter-intuitively allowing for more access to cultural goods, as the proper copyright would do. Also with regard to the online distribution of music, a varied trajectory seems to have been taken. Whereas in the beginning the wholesale distribution of music by online services was strongly dominated by various forms of digital rights management (DRM) systems, today most of the platforms offer music in non-protected formats.[19] The association of usage practices, norms and interests of manufacturers and platform providers appears to have proved more stable than the opposing view offered by the music industry.

The second aspect of the shift in perspective concerns the very role of technology. To limit the view on technology in these governance constellations as an external trigger would mean to miss a constitutive point. In fact, the mechanisms of private and public ordering would probably not exist if technology were not an integral part of this constellation. Especially with regard to licenses and contracts, technology is always almost the entity that enforces it. Gillespie (2004: 241) sees a "technological regime where control depends on the tight coupling of technology and law, each sharing the task of regulation not only copying, but access, use, and purchase." Actually, it is not a technology regime, but an entanglement of contested norms and interests that are being translated from one form into another, in which both technological devices and software play a principal role not as a trigger, but as the very entity of governance arrangements.

## Discussion and outlook

Communication technology is increasingly permeating our daily lives. This chapter argued that whereas technologies are commonly being seen as a trigger for societal change, they are seldom addressed explicitly as elements of our social world. This blind spot in media and communication studies in general, and in media policy and law in particular, is tackled in this chapter with a research perspective that draws upon both governance research and science and technology studies.

The described shift towards a governance perspective in media policy and law allows for the integration of different modes of regulation into a common frame of research by decentering regulation—privileging neither public nor private ordering. This analytic approach to governance arrangements in "mediatized" environments is similar to the one sketched by Lessig (1999) and recently taken up by Wolfgang Schulz and others (cf. Schulz

19 Amazon sells music in the mp3 format, and Apple's iTunes store uses the m4a format, a variation of mp4.

*et al.* 2011). Both approaches take different modes of governance explicitly into account including technology or *code*. They differ slightly in the way in which these different modes are conceived. Whereas Schulz *et al.* ask whether or not these regulative forms coincide, the approach developed here applies a more dynamic perspective, focusing on the *translations* from one form into another.

Instead of focusing on a static arrangement of social order, the combination of governance research on "decentering regulation" (Bevir and Rhodes 2006; Hofmann 2011), and science and technology studies allows us to conceive regulation as a very complex process of ordering—private and public, formal and informal, discursive and material—wherein different sets of institutions and "bundles of entitlements" (Bracha 2007; Hofmann 2011) are stabilized, contested, transformed and dissolved.

The analytical focus on the shifts between various forms of regulation and their interplays is particularly instrumental for analyses in media and communication regulation and the role of technology, because both private ordering as well as technical means of regulation are increasingly relevant in our "media lives" (Deuze 2012). A different and more detailed view of the role of technology is achieved by more closely examining the intricacies of public and private orderings by which norms are negotiated. Technological configurations, then, do not appear as stable black boxes, but as internal and contested parts of regulatory constellations. Hence technology in this view is neither purely a trigger nor a sole target for external regulation, but one out of multiple "crystallizations of meanings" (Berger 1981: 31) that condensate in ordering processes—and might stabilize, dissolve or transform sooner or later.

An analytical view of technology as integral part of the fabric of the social, as unfolded here becomes even more relevant considering the increasing permeation of technology and networks into everyday objects. With location-based services and the "Internet of Things," the "technicity" of our communications environment is increasing, while at the same time becoming less visible. In consequence, media governance needs to develop an interest and analytic frame for an in-depth examination of technologies.

## References


Akrich, M. and Latour, B. (1992) 'A summary of a convenient vocabulary for the semiotics of human and nonhuman assemblies,' in W. E. Bijker and J. Law (eds.) *Shaping Technology/Building Society*, Cambridge, MA: MIT Press.

Bechtold, S. (2002) *Vom Urheber- zum Informationsrecht: Implikationen des Digital Rights Management*, München: Beck.

—— (2003) 'The present and future of digital rights management: Musings on emerging legal problems,' in E. Becker, W. Buhse, D. Günnewig and N. Rump (eds.) *Digital Rights Management: Technological, Economic, Legal and Political Aspects*, Berlin: Springer.

Berger, P. L. (1981) *Sociology Reinterpreted: An Essay on Method and Vocation*, New York: Anchor Press/ Doubleday.

—— and Luckmann, T. (1966) *The Social Construction of Reality: A Treatise in the Sociology of Knowledge*, Garden City, NY: Doubleday & Comp.

Berker, T., Hartmann, M., Punie, Y. and Ward, K. (2006) *Domestication of Media and Technology*, Maidenhead: Open University Press.

Bevir, M. and Rhodes, R. A. W. (2006) 'Interpretive approaches to British government and politics,' *British Politics*, 1: 84–112.

Bijker, W. E. (1995) *Of Bicycles, Bakelites, and Bulbs: Toward A Theory of Sociotechnical Change*, Cambridge, MA: MIT Press.

—— (2006) 'Why and how technology matters,' in R. E. Goodin and C. Tilly (eds.) *Handbook of Contextual Political Analysis*, Oxford: Oxford University Press.

—— and Law, J. (eds.) (1992) *Shaping Technology/Building Society: Studies in Sociotechnical Change*, Cambridge, MA: MIT Press.

——, Hughes, T. P. and Pinch, T. J. (eds.) (1997) *The Social Construction of Technological Systems: New Directions in the Sociology and History of Technology*, Cambridge, MA: MIT Press.

Blumenthal, J. V. (2005) 'Governance—eine kritische Zwischenbilanz,' *Zeitschrift für Politikwissenschaft*, 15: 1149–1180.

Bowker, G. C., Baker, K., Millerand, F. and Ribes, D. (2010) 'Toward information infrastructure studies: Ways of knowing in a networked environment,' in J. Hunsinger, L. Klastrup and M. Allen (eds.) *International Handbook of Internet Research*, Heidelberg: Springer.

Bracha, O. (2007) 'Standing copyright law on its head? The Googlization of everything and the many faces of property,' *Texas Law Review*, 85: 1299–1869.

Braman, S. (2004) 'Where has media policy gone? Defining the field in the twenty-first century,' *Communication Law and Policy Communication Law and Policy*, 9, 153–182.

Bröchler, S. (2008) 'Governance im Lichte der sozialwissenschaftlichen Technikforschung,' in S. Bröchler and H.-J. Lauth (eds.) *Politikwissenschaftliche Perspektiven*, Wiesbaden: VS Verlag.

Brousseau, E., Marzouki, M. and Méadel, C. (2012) *Governance, Regulation, and Powers on the Internet*, Cambridge and New York: Cambridge University Press.

Brummer, C. (2010) 'Why soft law dominates international finance—and not trade,' *Journal of International Economic Law*, 13: 623–643.

Cammaerts, B. (2011) 'Power dynamics in multi-stakeholder policy processes and intra-civil society networking,' in R. Mansell and M. Raboy (eds.) *The Handbook of Global Media and Communication Policy*, Chicester: Wiley-Blackwell.

Carlsson, B., Jacobsson, S., Holmen, M. and Rickne, A. (2002) 'Innovation systems: Analytical and methodological issues,' *Research Policy*, 31: 233–245.

Castilla, E. J., Hwang, H., Granovetter, E. and Granovetter, M. (2000) 'Social networks in Silicon Valley' in C.-M. Lee (ed.) *The Silicon Valley Edge: A Habitat For Innovation and Entrepreneurship*, Stanford, CA: Stanford University Press.

Denegri-Knott, J. (2004) 'Sinking the online "music pirates:" Foucault, power and deviance on the web,' *Journal of Computer-Mediated Communication*, 9. Online. Available HTTP: http://jcmc.indiana.edu/vol9/issue4/denegri_knott.html (accessed 17 January 2012).

Deuze, M. (2012) *Media Life*, Boston, MA: Polity Books.

Dierkes, M., Hoffmann, U. and Marz, L. (1996) *Visions of Technology: Social and Institutional Factors Shaping the Development of New Technologies*, Frankfurt: Campus.

Djelic, M.-L. and Quack, S. (2003) 'Theoretical building blocks for a research agenda linking globalization and institutions,' in M.-L. Djelic and S. Quack (eds.) *Globalization and Institutions: Redefining The Rules of the Economic Game*, Cheltenham: Edward Elgar.

Dobusch, L. (2011) 'The digital public domain: Relevance and regulation,' Draft paper prepared for the *First Berlin Symposium on Internet and Society*, 26–28 October. Online. Available HTTP: http://berlinsymposium.org/session/digital-public-domain-between-regulation-and-innovation (accessed 17 January 2012).

Dolata, U. (2009) 'Technological innovations and sectoral change: Transformative capacity, adaptability, patterns of change—An analytical framework,' *Research Policy*, 38: 1066–1076.

—— and Werle, R. (2007) *Gesellschaft und die Macht der Technik: Sozioökonomischer und institutioneller Wandel durch Technisierung*, Frankfurt: Campus.

Donges, P. (2002) *Rundfunkpolitik Zwischen Sollen, Wollen und Können: Eine Theoretische und Komparative Analyse der Politischen Steuerung des Rundfunks*, Wiesbaden: Westdt. Verl.

—— (2007a) 'The New Institutionalism as a theoretical foundation of media governance,' *Communications*, 32: 325–330.

—— (2007b) *Von der Medienpolitik zur Media Governance?* Köln: Halem.

Dreier, T. (2000) 'Urheberrecht an der schwelle des 3. jahrtausend: Einige gedanken zur zukunft des urheberrechts,' *Computer und Recht*, 16(1): 45–49.

Dusollier, S. (1999) 'Electrifying the fence: The legal protection of technological measures for protecting copyright,' *European Intellectual Property Review*, 21(6): 285–297.

—— (2007) 'Sharing access to intellectual property through private ordering,' *Chicago-Kent Law Review*, 82: 1391–1435.

Elkin-Koren, N. (2004) 'The Internet and copyright policy discourse,' in H. Nissenbaum and M. Price (eds.) *Academy and the Internet*, New York: Lang.

—— (2008) *Governing Access to Users-Generated Content: The Changing Nature of Private Ordering in Digital Networks*. Online. Available HTTP: http://papers.ssrn.com/sol3/papers.cfm?abstract_id=1321164 (accessed 17 January 2012).

Freeman, C. (1987) *Technology, Policy, and Economic Performance: Lessons From Japan*. London and New York: Pinter.

Fuller, M. (2008) *Software Studies: A Lexicon*. Cambridge, MA: MIT Press.

Geels, F. W. (2004) 'From sectoral systems of innovation to socio-technical systems: Insights about dynamics and change from sociology and institutional theory,' *Research Policy*, 33: 897–920.

Gersen, J. E. and Posner, E. A. (2008) 'Soft law: Lessons from congressional practice,' *Stanford Law Review*, 61: 573.

Giesecke, S. (2001) *Von der Forschung zum Markt Innovationsstrategien und Forschungspolitik in der Biologietechnologie*. Berlin: Ed. Sigma.

Gillespie, T. (2004) 'Copyright and commerce: The DMCA, trusted systems, and the stabilization of distribution,' *The Information Society*, 20(4): 239–254.

Göhler, G., Höppner, U. and De La Rosa, S. (eds.) (2009) *Weiche Steuerung: Studien zur Steuerung durch diskursive Praktiken, Argumente und Symbole*, Baden-Baden: Nomos.

Goldsmith, J. L. and Wu, T. (2006) *Who Controls The Internet? Illusions of A Borderless World*, New York: Oxford University Press.

Grassmuck, V. (2006) 'Wissenskontrolle durch DRM: Von Überfluss zu Mangel,' in J. Hofmann (ed.) *Wissen und Eigentum*, Bonn: Bundeszentrale für politische Bildung.

Hintz, A. and Milan, S. (2011) 'User rights for the Internet age: Communications policy according to "Netizens"', in R. Mansell and M. Raboy (eds.) *The Handbook of Global Media and Communication Policy*, Chicester: Wiley-Blackwell.

Hjarvard, S. (2008) 'The mediatization of society: A theory of the media as agents of social and cultural change,' *Nordicom Review*, 29(2): 105–134.

Hofmann, J. (2007) 'Internet governance: A regulative idea in flux,' in R. Kumar and J. Bandamutha (eds.) *Internet Governance: An Introduction*, Hyderabad: The Icfai University Press.

—— (2011) *Private Ordering in the Shadow of Copyright Law: Google Books as a Blueprint*. Online. Available HTTP: http://papers.ssrn.com/sol3/papers.cfm?abstract_id=1898120 (accessed 17 January 2012).

Hughes, T. P. (1983) *Networks of Power: Electrification in Western Society, 1880–1930*, Baltimore, MD: Johns Hopkins University Press.

Hurwitz, J. (2007) *Whois WSIS; Whois IGF: The New Consensus-Based Internet Governance*. Online. Available HTTP: http://papers.ssrn.com/sol3/papers.cfm?abstract_id=954209 (accessed 17 January 2012).

Just, N. and Latzer, M. (2005) 'Self- and co-regulation in the mediamatics sector: European community (EC) strategies and contributions towards a transformed statehood,' *Knowledge, Technology & Policy*, 17(2): 38–62.

Katzenbach, C. (2011) 'Technologies as institutions: Rethinking the role of technology in media governance constellations,' in N. Just and M. Puppis (eds.) *Trends in Communication Policy Research: New Theories, Methods & Subjects*, Bristol and Chicago, IL: Intellect.

Kitchin, R. and Dodge, M. (2011) *Code/Space: Software and Everyday Life*, Cambridge, MA: MIT Press.

Knorr-Cetina, K. (1989) *Die Fabrikation von Erkenntnis*, Frankfurt: Suhrkamp.

Koelman, K. J. and Helberger, N. (2000) 'Protection of technological measures,' in B. Hugenholtz and K. J. Koelman (eds.) *Copyright and Electronic Commerce*, London: Kluwer.

Kooiman, J. (2003) *Governing as Governance*, London: Sage.

Krasner, S. D. (1991) 'Global communications and national power: Life on the pareto frontier,' *World Politics*, 43(3): 336–366.

Krotz, F. (2007) 'The meta-process of "mediatization" as a conceptual frame,' *Global Media and Communication*, 3(3): 256–260.

Künzler, M. (2009) *Die Liberalisierung von Radio und Fernsehen: Leitbilder der Rundfunkregulierung im Ländervergleich*, Konstanz: UVK.

Lange, S. and Schimank, U. (eds.) (2004) *Governance und gesellschaftliche Integration*, Wiesbaden: VS Verlag.

Latour, B. (1987) *Science in Action: How to Follow Scientists and Engineers through Society*, Cambridge, MA: Harvard University Press.

—— (1991) 'Technology is society made durable,' in J. Law (ed.) *A Sociology of Monsters*, London: Routledge.

—— (1992) 'Where are the missing masses? The sociology of a few mundane artifacts,' in W. E. Bijker and J. Law (eds.) *Shaping Technology/Building Society: Studies in Sociotechnical Change*, Cambridge, MA: MIT Press.

—— (1999) *Pandora's Hope: Essays on the Reality of Science Studies*, Cambridge, MA: Harvard University Press.

—— (2007) *Reassembling the Social: An Introduction to Actor-Network Theory*, Oxford: Oxford University Press.

—— and Woolgar, S. (1979) *Laboratory Life: The Social Construction of Scientific Facts*, London: Sage.

Latzer, M. (2009) 'Convergence revisited,' *Convergence: The International Journal of Research into New Media Technologies*, 15(4): 411–426.

Law, J. (1992) 'Notes on the theory of the actor-network: Ordering, strategy, and heterogeneity,' *Systemic Practice and Action Research*, 5: 379–393.

Layton, E. (1977) 'Conditions of technological development,' in I. Spiegel-Rosing and D. J. de Solla Price (eds.) *Science, Technology, and Society*, London: Sage.

Lessig, L. (1999) *Code and Other Laws of Cyberspace*, New York: Basic Books.

—— (2008) *Remix: Making Art and Commerce Thrive in the Hybrid Economy*, London: Bloomsbury.

Mackenzie, A. (2006) *Cutting Code: Software And Sociality*, New York: Lang.

MacKenzie, D. A. and Wajcman, J. (1985) *The Social Shaping of Technology: How the Refrigerator Got its Hum*, Maidenhead: Open University Press.

Manovich, L. (2001) *The Language of New Media*, Cambridge, MA: MIT Press.

—— (2008) 'Software takes command,' Manuscript, November. Online. Available HTTP: http://lab.softwarestudies.com/2008/11/softbook.html (accessed 1 October 2011).

Mansell, R. and Raboy, M. (eds.) (2011) *The Handbook of Global Media and Communication Policy*, Chicester: Wiley-Blackwell.

—— and Silverstone, R. (eds.) (1996) *Communication by Design: The Politics of Information and Communication Technologies*, Oxford: Oxford University Press.

Meister, M., Schulz-Schaeffer, I., Böschen, S., Gläser, J. and Strübing, J. (eds.) (2006) 'What comes after constructivism in science and technology studies?' *Science, Technology & Innovation Studies*, Special Issue.

Merges, R. P. (2004) 'A new dynamism in the public domain,' *University of Chicago Law Review*, 71: 183–203.

Meyer, U. and Schulz-Schaeffer, I. (2006) 'Three forms of interpretative flexibility,' *Science, Technology & Innovation Studies*, 1: 25–40.

Nelson, R. R. (1994) 'The co-evolution of technologies and institutions,' in R. W. England (ed.) *Evolutionary Concepts in Contemporary Economics*, Ann Arbor, MI: University of Michigan Press.

Ó Siochrú, S. and Girard, B. (2002) *Global Media Governance*, Lanham, MD: Rowman & Littlefield.

Organization for Economic Co-operation and Development (OECD) (2005) *Telecommunication Regulatory Institutional Structures and Responsibilities: Report to the Working Party on Telecommunication and Information Services Policies*, OECD: Paris.

Orlikowski, W. J. and Iacono, C. S. (2001) 'Research commentary: Desperately seeking the "it" in IT research—A call to theorizing the IT artifact,' *Information Systems Research*, 12(2): 121–134.

Ortmann, G. (2010) 'On drifting rules and standards?' *Scandinavian Journal of Management*, 26(2): 204–214.

Padovani, C. and Pava, E. (2011) 'Actors and interactions in global communication governance: The heuristic potential of a network approach,' in R. Mansell and M. Raboy (eds.) *The Handbook of Global Media and Communication Policy*, Chicester: Wiley-Blackwell.

Pauly, D. (1995) 'Anecdotes and the shifting baseline syndrome of fisheries,' *Trends in Ecology & Evolution*, 10(10): 430.

Pentzold, C. (2010) 'Imagining the Wikipedia community: What do Wikipedia authors mean when they write about their "community"?' *New Media & Society*, 13(5): 704–721.

Pinch, T. J. and Bijker, W. E. (1984) 'The social construction of facts and artefacts: Or how the sociology of science and the sociology of technology might benefit each other,' *Social Studies of Science*, 14(3): 399–441.

Porter, M. E. (1990) *The Competitive Advantage of Nations*, New York: Free Press.

Price, M. E. (2002) *Media and Sovereignty: The Global Information Revolution and its Challenge to State Power*, Cambridge, MA: MIT Press.

Puppis, M. (2007) 'Media governance as a horizontal extension of media regulation: The importance of self- and co-regulation,' *Communications*, 32(3): 330–336.

—— (2009) *Organisationen der Medienselbstregulierung: Europäische Presseräte im Vergleich*, Köln: Halem.
—— (2010) 'Media governance: A new concept for the analysis of media policy and regulation,' *Communication, Culture & Critique*, 3(2): 134–149.
Raboy, M. and Padovani, C. (2010) 'Mapping global media policy: Concepts, frameworks, methods,' *Communication, Culture & Critique*, 3(2): 150–169.
Reichman, J. H. and Uhlir, P. F. (2003) 'A contractually reconstructed research commons for scientific data in a highly protectionist intellectual property environment,' *Law and Contemporary Problems*, 66: 315–462.
Reidenberg, J. R. (1998) 'Lex Informatica: The formation of information policy rules through technology,' *Texas Law Review*, 76(3): 553–584.
Röser, J. (ed.) (2007) *MedienAlltag: Domestizierungsprozesse alter und neuer Medien*, Wiesbaden: VS Verlag.
Saenz-Arroyo, A., Roberts, C. M., Torre, J., Carino-Olerva, M. and Enrique-Andrada R. R. (2005) 'Rapidly shifting environmental baselines among fishers of the Gulf of California,' *Proceedings of the Royal Biological Society*, 272: 1957–1962.
Saldias, O. (2011) 'Patterns of legalization in the Internet,' Draft paper prepared for the First Berlin Symposium on Internet and Society 26–28 October. Online. Available HTTP: http://papers.ssrn.com/sol3/papers.cfm?abstract_id=1942161 (accessed 17 January 2012).
Sawhney, H. (2004) 'The slide towards decentralization: Clock and computer,' *Media, Culture & Society*, 26(3): 359–374.
Schmidt, S. K. and Werle, R. (1998) *Coordinating Technology: Studies in the International Standardization of Telecommunications*, Cambridge, MA: MIT Press.
Schulz, W. *et al.* (2011) 'Mapping the frontiers of governance in social media,' Draft paper prepared for the First Berlin Symposium on Internet and Society 26–28 October. Online. Available HTTP: http://hiig.de/en/events/1st-symposium-on-internet-society/governance-and-social-media/ (accessed 17 January 2012).
Schulz-Schaeffer, I. (2000) *Sozialtheorie der Technik*, Frankfurt: Campus.
Schuppert, G. F. (2008) 'Governance: Auf der Suche nach Konturen eines "anerkannt uneindeutigen Begriffs,"' in G. F. Schuppert and M. Zürn (eds.) *Governance in einer sich wandelnden Welt*, Wiesbaden: VS Verlag.
Schwartz Conan, R. (1985) 'How the refrigerator got its hum,' in D. A. MacKenzie and J. Wajcman (eds.) *The Social Shaping of Technology: How the Refrigerator Got its Hum*, Maidenhead: Open University Press.
Scott, W. R. (1995) *Institutions and Organizations*, Thousand Oaks, CA: Sage.
Silverstone, R. and Hirsch, E. (eds.) (1992) *Consuming Technologies: Media and Information in Domestic Spaces*, London and New York: Routledge.
Stone, D. (2008) 'Global public policy, transnational policy communities, and their networks,' *Policy Studies Journal*, 36(1): 19–38.
Thatcher, M. (2002) 'Regulation after delegation: Independent regulatory agencies in Europe,' *Journal of European Public Policy*, 9(6): 954–972.
Tolbert, P. S. and Zucker, L. G. (1996) 'The institutionalization of institutional theory,' in S. R. Clegg, C. Hardy and W. R. Nord (eds.) *Handbook of Organization Studies*, London: Sage.
Tufekci, Z. (2010) 'Facebook: The privatization of our privates and life in the company town,' *technosociology blog*. Online. Available HTTP: http://technosociology.org/?p=131 (accessed 17 January 2012).
Walker, J. (2003) 'The digital imprimatur: How big brother and big media can put the Internet genie back in the bottle,' *Knowledge, Technology and Policy*, 16(3): 24–77.
Weyer, J. *et al.* (1997) *Technik, die Gesellschaft schafft—Soziale Netzwerke als Ort der Technikgenese*, Berlin: Ed. Sigma.
Winner, L. (1980) 'Do artifacts have politics?' *Daedulus*, 109(1): 121–136.
—— (1993) 'Upon opening the black box and finding it empty: Social constructivism and the philosophy of technology,' *Science, Technology, & Human Values*, 18(3): 362–378.
York, J. C. (2010) 'Policing content in the quasi-public sphere,' *Bulletin of the OpenNet Intitative*. Online. Available HTTP: http://opennet.net/policing-content-quasi-public-sphere (accessed 10 January 2011).

# 23

# Governing media through technology

## The empowerment perspective

*Antonios Broumas*

### Prologue

From the age of the printing press to that of the next-generation networks, technology has always mediated human communication. Today, both the rapid convergence of information and communication technologies (ICTs) and their widespread effect on the media have upgraded the mediating role of technology on how we communicate, get informed, socialize, engage in political activity, create, consume and play. Such mediation does not come in the simplistic form of merely extending human capabilities (McLuhan 1964), but in the much more sophisticated form of structuring their potential field of action. By this it is meant that the physical and logical infrastructure of the technologies underlying the media eventually determines their architecture. Technology, as the architecture of today's media, enables some human activities, while discouraging others, functioning in this way as a double-edged tool of both empowerment and control.

This chapter deals with the issue of media governance and its interrelation with technology from an empowerment perspective. It supports the view that if governing is defined as the act of structuring the possible field of action for others (Foucault 1983), then the most subtle mode of media governance is the design of media space and time by technological means. Having as a starting point the fact that technology plays an ever-growing role in the media, I proceed by analyzing the concept of technology as media architecture. Furthermore, I attempt to categorize in a coherent manner the ways in which ICTs are developed and utilized for the purposes of individual and collective empowerment, each time structuring the media in corresponding ways. In parallel, I explore the interaction of technological rules with media law and policy, as these are deployed and enforced in practice either in collision, or in harmonious combination, with each other. The main hypotheses employed throughout the chapter are that: (a) technology and society are intrinsically related to each other in a dynamic loop of mutual influence, in which humans shape technology and technology conditions social activity; (b) technological evolution does not follow predetermined trajectories, but rather is influenced by socio-historical relations of power; and (c) research on the social use and effect of technology is meaningful only if it is conducted in connection with specific technologies in specific social contexts. Furthermore, and contrary to certain established lines of thought that emphasize media governance through technology only in relation to regulation and control (Zittrain 2008; Lessig 2006), my central argument is that media can also be governed by technological means in a decentralized and democratic manner to empower access to information, knowledge and culture, to enable creativity and cooperation, and to deepen democracy.

Whether the balance in media governance choices will be tipped towards more empowerment or more control is a matter that ultimately depends on politics in its deepest sense—namely, on political activation, mobilization and participation.

## Designing the media

### *The growing role of technology*

Historically, different media evolved on separate physical and logical infrastructures. As a consequence, different kinds of media content (i.e. data, images, sound and video) have been communicated via distinct networks and service providers. Two disruptive waves of technological achievement in ICTs are currently shifting both the media ecology and its social context in the opposite direction. The gradual transition of media from analog to the digital world has enabled efficient conveyance of any kind of content on multiple infrastructures and delivery platforms. Since the 1990s, digitization has been combined with the development and social diffusion of wireless communication technologies in the forms of mobile telephony, wireless broadband and satellite broadcasting services (Castells 2009). Concomitantly, popularization of the Internet and the user experience of its many-to-many (either in real or chosen time) interactive communication are creating a strong social demand for the implementation of similar characteristics to other media, such as mobile telephony and broadcasting. As a result, media-related technologies, both at the core and at the edges of contemporary media networks, are currently in a state of rapid convergence. At the core—the network physical infrastructure and communication standards—there are signs of convergence between old and new media towards a packet-based general purpose communications medium, capable of being compatible with all kinds of information and services. At the edges, devices are being manufactured with the capacity to connect to multiple networks and technological infrastructure (wired, wireless and satellite) and to deliver all kinds of information and services. The ongoing phenomenon of technological convergence has already proved to have far-reaching socio-economic effects. In the media industry, ownership is accumulated in fewer hands, while corporations strive to acquire horizontal and vertical integration to both incumbent and new media infrastructure and services (Castells 2009). As these effects deepen, changing industries and consumer behavior, the locus of social gravity and the focus of economic activity is transferred from traditional media online.

In the context of this chapter, the phenomenon of technological convergence raises two important points. First, it is empirically self-evident that the significance of technological mediation in human communications is on the rise. This can be determined in both quantitative and qualitative terms. As technological convergence shifts the center of political, economic and cultural activity from traditional media, such as the press, to new media, such as mobile telephony and the Internet, peer-to-peer human communication becomes increasingly dependent on ICTs. This rise in significance also has a qualitative aspect: As contemporary media develops in complexity and sophistication, they become ever more important not only for communication of information, but also for entertainment, socializing, collaboration, work, political activity and cultural creativity. In this way, technological framing now penetrates in multiple ways into a growing variety of human experiences and social activities. The growing role of technology in human communication is having a corresponding effect on media law and policy. Thus technology is now seen as an important component of media governance, while modes of governing media through technology increasingly appear in practice. Second, technological convergence brings Internet governance into the forefront. In the current transitory phase of convergence, the Internet has become the archetypal communication medium of our times. Therefore how this medium is governed and the choices made about its destiny acquire major importance for the media sector as a whole. As the Internet leads the way to a common future for all media, its governance inevitably molds this specific future. For this reason, analysis of how media are governed today through technological means should emphasize Internet governance, taking into account any important aspects of the media ecosystem as a whole.

## *Technology as media architecture*

Architecture, in general, has strong connections with governance. To govern is to "structure the possible field of action of others" (Foucault 1983: 221), and structure places "limits upon the feasible range of options open to an actor in a given circumstance" (Giddens 1984: 177). Therefore architecture both enables and constrains human activity. In the context of media, especially new media, architecture is mainly synthetic, in the sense that the structure and rules defining it are to a large extent man-made using technological means. Rules in this space and time are implanted and, at the same time, enforced through the design of communication networks and devices and through communication standards and software code. Depending on the prevailing choices and aims pursued, the technological structure of the media is designed to enable certain human activities and capabilities and to discourage others. In this way, media-related technology functions as a tool of both individual/collective empowerment and social control.

Media governance refers to the strategies and techniques by which the media ecosystem is rendered governable. The media are constructed as a network: flexible, interactive and gradually borderless. As a result, media governance is ultimately about managing and steering this network. As a network, the media have certain values embedded in it that crystallize in the form of "protocols" (i.e. rules and standards that govern relationships). In the context of new media, protocols are, first and foremost, technological. They are located at the physical and logical layers of their architecture—as components of their physical infrastructure, such as wires, wireless links, backbone network equipment and end-user devices, and as components of their logical infrastructure, such as standards and software. Constituting actual human choices in the design of these technologies, protocols play a key role in the framing of social activity at the content layer of new media.[1] Therefore, as media gradually converge into a general-purpose packet-based communication medium, technology as its architecture is becoming the key to sovereignty within the jurisdiction of this environment, giving to its holders the power to structure media space and time by defining the boundaries of social activity and exploiting such formations as a means either for empowerment or for rule

1 There are several ways in which to conceptualize new media architecture as a layered system (see Zittrain 2008, with further references). The general three-layered model, first introduced by Yochai Benkler (2000), is employed here as more helpful in our context.

enforcement and control. These characteristics render technology as architecture a strategic tool for governing contemporary media in combination with other modes of governance, such as law, markets and social norms (Lessig 2006).

Media governance through technology is not only a static top-down process, in which those who shape technologies are unresponsive to how these are used in societies. Technological design is shaped through a dynamic, dialectical process, in which the social use of technology has an interactive relationship with its fundamental processes.[2] The social use of ICTs influences the architecture of the media in specific ways. First of all, users and user communities influence design choices through their consumer power in the markets of media services. Henry Jenkins (2006) has showed how social demand for interactivity and ubiquitous connectivity has pushed technological convergence in the media sector. Much earlier, David Post (1995) had emphasized the ability of Internet users to switch between "jurisdictions," or regulatory environments, of cyberspace and to choose the rule sets that suit them. Furthermore, the social use of technologies may take forms unexpected by their initial designers, thus wrenching control away from them and released to other social actors and/or society at large (Benjamin 1973). The Internet, which was initially intended to be used as a war technology, gradually evolved through social use into the most developed communication medium of our times (Leiner *et al.* 2003). Most importantly, in the context of ICTs, technological design acquires radically democratic, bottom-up characteristics. The ability of individual users or communities of users to modify, reprogram and redesign existing technologies, or even to create new ones in order to meet their needs, democratizes technological design, influences the media ecosystem as a whole, and, ultimately, plays a central role in the structure and governance of the media.

## *Social processes and modes of technological design in modern media*

If decisions over technological design matter, then special attention should be granted to the social processes and modes of such decision-making as these have evolved throughout the history of new media. Roughly, two general social modes of technological design have emerged and defined contemporary ICT-based media: one based on bureaucratic, hierarchical and formal processes of decision–making; another based on consensus-based and informal modes of collaborative innovation. The best example illustrating the direct collision and comparison in practice of these two modes is the Internet–Open Systems Interconnection (OSI) standards war (Bygrave and Bing 2009).

In 1977, the International Organization for Standardization (ISO) formed a subcommittee in collaboration with the International Telecommunication Union (ITU) to set the ground rules for network interconnection, with the strategic goal of defining the future of emerging ICTs. Decision-making processes on the design of the model were formal, hierarchical and based on top-down commands, reproducing the organizational structure of ISO, an international organization consisting of formal industrial and governmental membership (Russell 2006). The OSI model was gradually adopted by several governments, including the United States, and became popular during the 1980s and the 1990s; at the time, it seemed as if it would replace transmission control protocols (TCP) and Internet protocol (IP) as the prevailing standard for computer networks. Ultimately, however, the pragmatic approach of the Internet engineering community, with the capacity to pool and integrate high-quality,

2 For an analysis of this approach, see Fuchs (2008: 3–4), with further references. For a wider technological perspective, see Pinch and Kline (1996).

specialized knowledge, produced much simpler, more functional and freedom-enabling networking standards that outperformed OSI in practice. Elements of such community-based technological design and decision-making can be traced back to the early days of the Advanced Research Projects Agency Network (ARPANET) and the inception of the TCP/IP suites (Abbate 2000; Leiner *et al.* 2003), but are exemplified in the formation of the Internet Architecture Board (IAB), the former Internet Configuration Control Board (ICCB), the Internet Engineering Task Force (IETF) and the Internet Society (ISOC), the bodies of the Internet engineering community that have governed IPs from 1979 until today. Driven by the motto "We reject: kings, presidents, and voting. We believe in: rough consensus and running code" (Clark 1992: 543), and an informal, open and free, international membership, the community's decision-making processes have led to architectural choices that have rendered IPs the most efficient, innovation-friendly and widely used standards in computer networking.

The historical example highlighted above pinpoints the deep differences between the bureaucratic and the community-based modes of decision-making in ICT design. Bureaucratic modes are governed in the form of formal top-down and "command and control" structures with clearly delineated rules as to who is responsible, who has authority over whom and what sort of accountability is to be expected, and structured mechanisms for monitoring and enforcement of rules. In contrast, communal modes are the product of self-organization, characterized by informal, consensus-based decision-making, structured in more decentralized and multidependent poles of power that constantly evolve according to the needs of the community. Bureaucratic modes refer more or less to social innovation inside relatively small groups of people with a clear division of labor and allocation of power, whereas community-based modes refer to social innovation between large numbers of peers with a strongly developed communal culture and voluntary task allocation based on personal inclination and motivation (Benkler 2005). In relation to informational flows, in the bureaucratic modes, knowledge and innovation (both as input and as output) tend to be treated as property, while in community-based modes the free flow of information inside and outside the community's boundaries is considered to be a prerequisite for an effective peer-review process and collaborative innovation. Holding this last characteristic as central, Eric Von Hippel (2006) categorizes these modes under the terms "private investment" and "collective action" models of innovation.

### *Who controls the architects?*

From a moral standpoint, ICT design can be viewed as an assertion of power by the actors of decision-making (i.e. technology designers) vis-à-vis the actors who are influenced by such decisions (i.e. the users of these technologies). A normative evaluation of the legitimacy of such power can follow either the instrumental/consequential or the deontological approach. Within the instrumental approach, moral justification is related to the degree of effectiveness these modes have in increasing general social welfare. In this context, the nature of innovation is critical. Innovation is invariably a collaborative effort, both because the necessary information, knowledge and talent needed to achieve it are distributed among individuals, and because it is based on a laborious "trial and error" problem-solving process that normally requires extensive human resources. Several authors claim that the characteristics of collaboration between large numbers of individuals, the capacity to pool and to aggregate knowledge and talent, the freely flowing information and the peer-review processes guarantee that communal innovation in ICT design is much more efficient in producing socially beneficial technological innovations than bureaucratic forms of decision-making (Bauwens 2006; Benkler 2006; Sunstein 2006; Tapscott and Williams 2006; Von Hippel 2006).[3] Another approach of normative evaluation, which can be termed "deontological," establishes the moral justification of modes of ICT design in relation to the degrees of participation, equality, accountability and transparency that their decision-making processes afford. Viewed in this way, community-based modes of technological design appear to perform better than bureaucratic ones. Through consensus-based processes of decision-making, they guarantee wider user participation. Even in communities of innovation that do not take decisions by consensus, the decentralized, multidependent structures of power and the voluntary character of their members' contribution result in greater accountability. Finally, community-based modes rely heavily on collaboration, knowledge pooling, peer review and the free flow of information, thus keeping innovations and the rules engraved on them open and transparent to literally everybody. While community-based modes of ICT design are not strictly democratic, since asymmetries of power and lack of peer equality in decision-making are frequent among them, they nevertheless exhibit greater degrees of moral justification than bureaucratic ones.

The relationship between technology and society is interactive: Social actors develop technologies as a means to attain specific aims, and the use of these technologies by societies contributes to social change. ICT design should be considered both as a result of power relations and as a tool to influence and change these relations; social use of ICTs may take forms that were not predicted or expected at the stage of their design, and the social use of existing ICTs may also involve their further development by their users to satisfy arising social needs. Thus exertion of power at the stage of ICT design by certain social actors does not guarantee their sovereignty. Conversely, ICTs designed for specific purposes may be utilized and modified by other social actors to serve completely different aims. Therefore, contrary not only to techno-deterministic beliefs, according to which technological development follows a predetermined trajectory uninfluenced by given social conditions (McLuhan 1964; Bell 1973), but also to techno-reductionist views, according to which technological design and development is a mere mirror of the social conditions (Williams 1985; Harraway 1991), a more balanced approach sees the moment of designing any new technology as a moment of human choice between a wide spectrum of socially constructed and value-laden alternatives (Williams and Edge 1996; Stefik 1999). The effect upon the social domain is, to a certain extent, unpredictable and uncontrollable.

If there is no predetermined form or function of ICTs and, instead, the eventual outcome of the process of ICT-related innovation is determined by the selections and preferences of human actors, not mechanical or digital systems, then who controls the processes of such innovation? In answering this question, it should first be noted that the choices that determine the shape of these technologies are not just the product of individual practices, assumptions and beliefs. ICTs are neither constituted nor utilized by individuals inside a social vacuum, but are in dialectic relationship with their social context (Fuchs 2008). Owing to the fact that our societies are realms in which antagonism prevails over cooperation and, as a result, realms that tend to be extensively hierarchical, stratified and laden by conflict between competing social actors (Mann 1986), ICTs can be more properly perceived as a tool for power, in relation to which social actors engage in antagonistic relationships both to define their design and to control their use according to their own needs and purposes. Depending

3 Eric Raymond has coined the phrase "Given enough eyes, all bugs are shallow," to show the superiority of massive peer-review processes in the context of free software (Raymond 2001: 30).

on which actors dominate these processes, the ways in which ICTs are constituted and utilized may produce and reproduce either existing, or alternative, social conditions and institutions. Structures and institutions, such as states, transnational/international organizations and universities, are also crucial for the processes of ICT design and use, since they play a decisive role in the allocation of resources and the coordination of scientific research; at the same time, states, interstate organizations and transnational law enforcement agencies exercise control on these processes through the enacting and enforcement of legal rules. In addition to incumbent social actors, such as political parties, cultural organizations and private corporations, contemporary ICTs have provided the technological base for an emerging category of collective social action in the media and in society in general, such as grassroots political movements, non-market modes of production and networked forms of social self-organization.

## Information and communication technologies as a tool for empowerment

Baron Haussmann rebuilt Paris after the 1848 Revolution in such a way as to discourage social upheavals (Benjamin 2002). He changed the architecture of public space to regulate collective behavior and to apply social control on a mass scale. Like Hausmann in post-1848 Paris, after the Internet revolution, large private enterprises find themselves in the position in which they can code media space and time, whereas states enhance their capacity to enforce technological choices through law. However, much more than the citizens of Paris during Haussmann's wide-scale project of redesigning public space, media citizens have the tools to autonomously be the architect of media space and time in radically democratic processes and to build a media ecology that can greatly encourage individual and collective empowerment. The term "empowerment" is used here to mean increasing access to, and use of, necessary media resources, of enhancing creativity and cooperation, and of deepening democracy. By exploiting certain properties of modern ICTs, individuals and collectivities are able to effectively manage media infrastructure and resources, to extensively produce and freely disseminate information, knowledge and culture in collaboration with each other, and to participate in, and coordinate, political activity. This capability of collective action steers contemporary media using technological means in the direction of enabling access, empowering creativity and cooperation, and deepening democracy.

### *Enabling access to infrastructure*

Deployment and access to the physical and logical layers of media networks is a prerequisite for accessing media environments. Owing to their significance in contemporary societies, citizen access to media is interwoven with the fundamental human rights to freedom of information and expression (Balkin 2009), and the foundations for individual and collective empowerment—that is, economic opportunity and human development (Benkler 2006).

Post-WWI media policies in Western Europe and the United States were founded on the view of media as a fundamental public service and emphasized tight state control of broadcasting and communications through the establishment of either state or private monopolies in these sectors (Cuilenburg and McQuail 2003). By the 1980s, it was evident that this approach would not allow the rapid deployment and social access to newly developed ICTs, such as the Internet and mobile telephony. During the 1980s and 1990s, media privatization and liberalization proved widely successful in diffusing these new technologies to societies at large. At the same time, these modes tend to create barriers to access new media for those that cannot afford them and they retain media infrastructure under private control.

Today, in parallel with, and supplemental to, the statist and the proprietary, a new commons-based mode of media infrastructure deployment and management has arisen. This mode, which is likely to spread in the future if favored or at least taken into account in public policy, has the potential to increase access for all on an equal footing and to radically democratize control on media infrastructure.

## Spectrum commons

Unregulated or inefficiently regulated access to common scarce resources is bound to lead to their overuse, waste and depletion. Privatization is claimed to be the best solution to the problem of the "tragedy of the commons," because private control (through allocation of exclusive property rights) is supposed to result in more efficient management of scarce resources (Hardin 1968). Applied on radio spectrum management, this school of thought has led to the auctioning of exclusive and long-lasting rights of use of radio frequencies as the most efficient way for states to manage spectrum and avoid overuse and interference (Coase 1959). Today, conventional spectrum management and regulation follow the same mentality, based upon the assumption that radio spectrum is a scarce resource. Yet recent innovations in wireless technologies and mesh wireless equipment, such as "smart radios" and "white space devices" (WSDs), make possible the simultaneous and dynamic sharing of spectrum frequencies by multiple users and operators with low or minimal risk of harmful interference. These technological developments are gradually transforming the radio spectrum from a scarce into a relatively abundant common resource (Lehr and Crowford 2006). This change calls for extensive policy reforms that apply commons-based forms of spectrum access alongside spectrum privatization regimes, and limit regulation only in regard to the devices and uses permitted (Lehr and Crowford 2006). Advantages of such policy reforms are that they diminish the phenomena of privatized spectrum underutilization and spectrum warehousing by incumbent media enterprises, which are widespread under exclusive licensing regimes, and furthermore increase access and open the spectrum to the dynamics of social collaboration, scientific innovation and business creativity (Benkler 2002).

Along these lines, legislators and regulatory authorities around the world have taken cautious steps towards opening the spectrum and managing it as a common public resource. The US Federal Communications Commission (FCC) has adopted rules to make the unused spectrum in the television bands available for unlicensed broadband wireless devices (FCC 2008, 2010). The European Union has enacted spectrum commons provisions in the decision establishing its first radio spectrum policy program, urging member states to open spectrum white spaces and encourage the deployment of wireless mesh networks (European Union 2012). And in the UK, the regulatory agency Ofcom has announced that it purports to allow license-exempt wireless devices to access the television white space spectrum (Ofcom 2011). Arising interest on these issues shows that policymakers are gradually realizing the social and economic benefit of commons-based spectrum management, and are trying to gain a competitive edge.

## Infrastructure commons

The emerging spectrum commons has constituted the base for a growing wireless infrastructure commons. Thus radically decentralized and democratic modes of media governance through technology gradually emerge in rapidly spreading schemes of communal deployment and management of media infrastructure. Social, economic and technological factors, such as the relatively low cost of network equipment and the usefulness of pooling and sharing resources, combined with the easier dissemination of necessary knowledge and information through the media and the social need for autonomous all-to-all connectivity, give rise to self-organized community wireless networks (CWNs), in which individuals deploy nodal equipment at their own cost and connect between themselves to construct and participate in wider networks (Flickenger 2002). Furthermore, with the use of specially equipped mobile devices, such as laptops and cellphones, which have the capacity to let information hop between them and act as radio nodes of a wider network, collectives of individuals are capable of constructing wireless mesh networks on an ad hoc and ephemeral basis.

In CWNs and wireless mesh networks, nodal equipment is individually owned and controlled, but the whole network is managed and controlled collectively by all participants. Therefore such networks can best be described as self-organized infrastructure commons, governed through the participation and collective decision-making of their members.

## *Open standards*

Open standards are a necessary element of open ICT ecosystems, enabling efficiency, innovation and growth (Berkman Center for Internet and Society 2004). The characterization of open in-computer networking and software standards generally refers to participatory, transparent and consensus or majority-based processes of standards development and their unrestrained availability and usage by all interested parties. Indeed, open standards effectively ensure interoperability between machines and software originating between different manufacturers and suppliers and, therefore, enhance product and service efficiency. Furthermore, characteristics of transparency, participatory development of the rules and unrestrained access guarantee flourishing innovation at upper layers of media architecture by both users and businesses. Open standards are the ideal vehicle for ensuring collaboration between competitors at a crucial aspect of the logical layer; this avoids closed-standards wars that result in the inefficient exploitation of social resources. Open standards also boost competition in the upper media layers, thus leading to economic growth (Shapiro 2001; Ghosh 2005). Yet arguments in favor of open standards are not only economic, but also deeply political. Because of the centrality of standards in media ecology, the issue of how one decides upon the rules engraved on them acquires major importance. In contrast to proprietary standardization, in which decisions are privately taken, open standards' processes of development, decision-making and management are participatory, based on the consensus or will of the majority of the communities built around them. Furthermore, the techno-social rules that they implement are transparent to all; they are therefore open to critique and individuals can choose not to use them. Finally, open standards are freely available for use and innovation, thus constructing a vibrant commons at the logical layer of new media and providing momentum to democratic modes of governing media through technology.

Open standards have played a decisive role in the constitution of the Internet's public character and its gradual transformation into the paradigmatic communications medium of our times. Since their invention, the TCP/IP standards were released without usage constraints, while their management and development by the Internet Engineering Task Force (IETF) has always been open, participatory and consensus-based. Accordingly, the World Wide Web set of standards was openly released by Tim Berners-Lee to ensure its universal availability (Berners-Lee 2000) and is today managed by the World Wide Web Consortium (W3C) in a transparent and participatory manner. Open standardization has made the Internet a truly open ICT ecosystem and has become a key factor of its success. Open software standards and formats are also the basis of all free software projects, which are greatly widespread in the new media. Owing to their advantages, open standards' processes of design and management are increasingly employed by international standardization organizations, such as the International Telecommunication Union and European Standardization Organizations (ESOs), and by market consortia, such as the Organization for the Advancement of Structured Information Standards (OASIS). Legislators and regulatory bodies around the globe have focused on policies that encourage open ICT standardization and have made the use of open standards compulsory in the public sector. For example, the WTO has set certain criteria for good standards development, including openness, transparency and consensus (WTO 1994), and the World Summit on the Information Society (WSIS) recommended that open standards implementation constitutes the best practice for e-government applications to enhance their growth and interoperability (WSIS 2005). Accordingly, the Council of Europe has called on its member states to promote "technical interoperability, open standards and cultural diversity in ICT policy covering telecommunications, broadcasting and the Internet" (CoE 2007). Finally, a growing number of countries (e.g. Denmark) have either already legislated for the compulsory use of open standards in their public sectors,[4] or have released action plans for their gradual implementation (e.g. the United Kingdom).[5]

## *Free software*

The free software movement is a prominent example of commons-based peer production at the logical layer of new media. The movement has its historical roots in the hacker culture cultivated among the first programmers' communities in the early stages of the computer revolution (Himanen 2002; Levy 2010; Stallman 2010). It consists of communities of programmers from all around the world who together write and improve software code on a voluntary basis (Von Krogh, Spaeth and Lakhani 2003). Production processes in the movement are held together by a wide variety of governance mechanisms that are in constant flux to meet community needs. Division of labor mechanisms are characterized by flexibility and the constant adaptability to the needs of the project development and the particular characteristics of its participants. Decision-making mechanisms vary, depending on the maturity and the size of the community. Free software project decisions are taken either consensually and democratically among peers (Weber 2004), or hierarchically by individuals that legitimize their authority vis-à-vis the community from their central role as developers in the project and/or from their decision-making skills (Raymond 2001). Larger communities develop pyramidal structures of decision-making (Weber 2004), while communities with more distributed and participatory traditions, such as Debian, have developed a mixture of direct democratic and representative rules of decision-making (Siobhan and Fabrizio 2007). Despite a number of serious setbacks, the production processes of the movement have proven to be successful.

The foundations of the free software movement also feature a crucial socio-legal pillar. Free software communities use a variety of *sui generis* licensing schemes to release their products. Having their legal basis in copyright and contract law, these licenses function as social

4 Denmark (2007) Agreement between the Government, Local Government Denmark and Danish Regions about Open Standards for Software, available online at http://en.itst.dk/it-architecture-standards/open-standards (accessed 4 May 2012).

5 See UK Government Action Plan (2010) Open Source, Open Standards and Re-Use, available online at http://www.cabinetoffice.gov.uk/sites/default/files/resources/open_source.pdf (accessed 4 May 2012).

contracts both for relations inside the community and relations of the community with its user-base. Their philosophy is based on the reversal of the "all rights reserved" logic of copyright law and the release of software code under four basic freedoms: free use and sharing of the licensed work; openness of its source code; freedom to make derivative works; and viral licensing.[6] From an empowerment perspective, the free software movement is important because it acts to democratize the design of the media software infrastructure and to "decommodify" of key software products. The ability of free software communities to modify, reprogram and redesign existing software, or to develop a new software infrastructure, influences the media ecosystem as a whole and, ultimately, plays a central role in the structure and governance of the media. Social processes of design in the movement follow a communal, consensus-based and voluntary mode of collaborative innovation, which guarantees an increased degree of accountability in regard to the design choices being made. The right to redistribute copies unleashes free software products from any restrictions of access that normally accompany commodities, and pushes for-profit activities to fields of services built around their customization or maintenance and support. Thus the production processes of the movement have managed to ensure access for all, at least to the basic media software tools, constituting a significant step forward towards bridging the digital divide.

### *Enabling creativity and cooperation*

Contemporary ICTs have increased to an unprecedented extent both the connectivity between people and devices and the human capability to process and store data (Castells 1996). Simultaneously, the cost of computation, communication and storage has significantly declined, resulting in the diffusion of the material means of information and cultural production to a large portion of the world's population (Benkler 2006). Social exploitation of these technological properties has given rise to widespread patterns of human communication, creativity and cooperation that have been described as mass self-communication and commons-based intellectual peer production. Given the technological tools, multitudes of individuals around the globe increasingly share information, knowledge and culture and engage in cultural creation and information production. Social use of media in the ways mentioned above has a defining, transformative effect on media ecosystems and their governance.

### *Enabling the wider sharing of information*

Intellectual production derives from knowledge and art accumulated from the past. New media have an extensive beneficial effect at the input phase of intellectual production by making available an abundance of information, knowledge and culture to authors, innovators and artists. In particular, media networks enable the wider sharing of information, knowledge and culture between individuals and communities by significantly diminishing the obstacles of space and time and the capacity of control on informational flows. Access is increased in the public domain, as both profit and non-profit initiatives gradually upload and make available on the Internet a growing wealth of intellectual works that are not protected

6 These freedoms are summarized in the GNU Free Software Definition of Free Software Foundation (FSF) and the Open Source Initiative (OSI) Open Source Definition, correspondingly available online at http://www.gnu.org/philosophy/free-sw.html and http://opensource.org/docs/osd (accessed 4 May 2012).

under intellectual property or the protection of which has expired. Widespread social practice has also led towards de facto decommodification and the unencumbered flow of proprietary informational goods (Barbrook 2005). Furthermore, users of the new media have developed cultures of information sharing by offering their own intellectual works online on a non-commercial, access-free basis.

The social use of ICTs in the ways mentioned above results in access to information at marginal or no cost for individuals and collectives. This lowers the social cost of using existing information as input into new information production to close to zero (Benkler 2005). As a result, abundance of information, knowledge and culture at the content layer of new media constitutes the input basis for a thriving cultural creativity and intellectual production based on sharing and cooperation. For these reasons, the global free flow of information is gradually perceived as a vital characteristic of the Internet economy, with international organizations, such as the Organisation for Economic Co-operation and Development (OECD), calling for its promotion and protection in a balanced and prudent manner (OECD 2011).

## *Encouraging cultural creativity*

Cultural production should be viewed as an inherently collective process of constructing and attributing meaning to our natural and social environment. When individuals have a fair opportunity to participate in a self-determining manner in the forms of meaning-making, then cultural production can be claimed to be democratic (Balkin 2004). Technological properties of new media offer the material basis for a radical empowerment of individual and collective cultural expression. Depending on whether and to what extent these properties are exploited in practice by media users around the globe, a new folk culture may possibly flourish and radically influence the entrenched modes of cultural production that dominated the industrial era (Benkler 2006).

Modern ICTs empower users to engage in cultural creativity in multiple ways. I described above how new media facilitate and expand access to prior information, knowledge and culture for individuals and collectivities. As information about art flows down to societies at large in all types of digital format, wide access to prior works of art boosts innovative capabilities of users, communities and social groups. Alongside this, new media provide their users with the necessary technological tools to create art. Equipment relevant to artistic creation, such as personal computers, cameras and microphones, has been made readily available to a large segment of the world population as a result of declining cost along with a variety of free or proprietary software tools. Media users can now create works of speech, music and video individually or collectively in an independent, self-determining manner. In addition, such tools give users the opportunity to manipulate and remix prior works of art, thereby boosting creativity at the domain of derivative art (Lessig 2008). Finally, new media open novel perspectives in regard to the modes of cultural consumption by enabling free communication between creators and their audience and a reduced need for intermediating industries. As a result, the lines between producers and consumers of culture blur and give rise to a more participatory and democratic culture (Benkler 2006; Fisher 2004; Lessig 2004, 2008; Reuveni 2007).

## *Enhancing cooperation*

Innovation and intellectual production are inherently collective, socialized processes, bearing a very close relation with cooperation, collaboration and communication (Hardt and Negri

2004). The capacities of modern ICTs in regard to connectivity, information storage and processing have empowered individuals around the globe to coordinate, cooperate and produce on a voluntary, peer-to-peer basis and offer the intellectual products of their work on non-commercial terms (Bauwens 2006; Benkler 2006). A novel mode of intellectual production, termed "commons-based peer production," is flourishing in the new media, in parallel to traditional for-profit modes. This mode reveals more than anything else the emergence of the multitude, a post-industrial social subject able to democratically produce and reproduce the logical and content layers of new media and to shape wider social change (Hardt and Negri 2004).

The free software movement has already been referred to as a prevalent mode of commons-based peer production at the logical layer of new media. Similar modes flourish at the content layer; the most impressive is Wikipedia, the unrivaled online encyclopedia managed by the Wikimedia Foundation. In numbers, as of October 2012, Wikipedia consisted of 21 million articles in 283 languages, written collaboratively by approximately 100,000 regularly active volunteers and many more contributors around the world (Wikipedia 2012a). The whole project is held together by a complex set of rules governing the generation of its content that has evolved through time by a self-governing process of trial and error inside its collaborative community. Content contributors must follow certain rules of law, verifiability, neutrality and respect among peers, and must follow specific editing policies that ensure content uniformity (Wikipedia 2012b). Dispute resolution in content generation and editing procedures is solved by a series of hierarchically organized community mechanisms (Hoffman and Mehra 2009). In order to control vandalism or other antisocial misuse of content editing, a small number of editors appointed by the community acquire "sysops" (system operators) status and have the powers to "protect, delete and restore pages, move pages over redirects, hide and delete page revisions, edit protected pages, and block other editors" (Wikipedia 2012c). Since 2005, Wikipedians have met annually in open conferences or informal gatherings to discuss, work together and strengthen communal relationships. Licensed under creative commons, Wikipedia content is freely accessed and shared for non-profit purposes, constituting a vast and sufficiently reliable source of knowledge and news. According to Alexa, Wikipedia was the sixth most popular website in 2011. In terms of content quality, at least one scientific comparison of Wikipedia with the world-renowned *Encyclopedia Britannica* has found a similar level of accuracy and rate of errors between the two (Giles 2005). Other commons-based peer production, including online tools such as blogs, forums and wikis, constitute a communication and information ecosystem in which individuals jointly produce and freely share digital content without spatio-temporal co-presence, flooding communication networks with the fruits of their intellectual labor and collaboration (Benkler 2006; Fuchs 2008). Hence, in parallel to growing commercialization, the development, improvement and social use of these technologies of cooperation also steers the new media ecosystem towards a more participatory and democratic mode of intellectual production.

## *Deepening democracy*

Cyber-optimists prophesy that cyberspace will lead to the demise of autocratic regimes around the world and the global prevalence of democracy (Levy 2002). In contrast, cyber-pessimists dismiss the link between democracy and ICTs as hype and stress the potential of new media to cultivate alienation and inability to political commitment (Dreyfus 2008) or to enhance surveillance, to compromise privacy and to reinforce totalitarian forms of power (Morozov 2011). Both utopian and dystopian accounts of the relationship between ICTs and democracy suffer from technological determinism and disorientate scientific analysis on the issue. Indeed, ICTs have certain properties that may be utilized to deepen democracy, while at the same time they can be exploited for the exertion of arbitrary state or corporate power and suppression (Barber 1998). It is purely a matter of relations and correlations of power and political struggle—any given social context which one of these contradictory social uses shall prevail and shape social change. My purpose here is to give a brief overview of certain technological properties that link ICTs with democracy and to provide specific examples of their use by individuals, collectivities and societies at large for political empowerment.

## Towards an alternate public sphere

In industrial societies, the public sphere has been characterized by the accumulation of communication power by commercial mass media corporations, allowing them extensive control over the means of mass communication (Habermas 1989). Today, modern ICTs set the conditions for the emergence of an alternate public sphere, organized on the basis of computer networks, in which end-users become transceivers of messages, views and meanings. The technological design of new media gradually shifts the topology of social communication from the traditional hub-and-spoke model of mass media to a distributed networked architecture with multidirectional connections (Benkler 2006). Furthermore, technological properties of modern ICTs have led to a dramatic reduction in the costs of transmitting messages to a larger audience. Enabled by these technological conditions, social use of new media has given rise to a new form of communication, termed "mass self-communication," which progressively disperses communication power from the center to the periphery of the contemporary public sphere (Castells 2009). These transformations show that, at the edges of mainstream mass media, the post-industrial public sphere features vibrant alternate networks of participatory political communication that empower individuals to freely disseminate information, to autonomously exchange their political views, to form collective meanings about the world around them and to influence corporate mass media practices (Castells 2008).

The empowering effect that the social use of ICTs has on democratic dialog and political participation for individuals and collectivities is best examined along the well-established lines of normative thought in regard to the relationship between media and democracy (Carpentier 2007). Along these lines, the media are considered crucial for democracy, because they are expected to promote informed citizenship and to provide a check on the state and powerful private actors through their public watchdog function. Widespread social practices in the new media, such as hyperlinking, short message service (SMS), email, blogging, Internet forum communities, instant messaging and social networking, enable decentralized, horizontal and autonomous information dissemination and deliberation among individuals (Benkler 2006). Furthermore, the borderless and more censorship-resistant character of the Internet has compressed media space and time and has blurred the boundaries between the public spheres of nation-states, thus increasing awareness of the global character of certain social problems, such as climate change, and multiplying social pressure and mobilization for globalized solutions. With the help of technology, collective projects in citizenship journalism, such as the global indy-media network, non-profit Internet radio stations, web-television projects, and online public watchdog communities, such as Wikileaks, enable direct citizen access and participation in the formulation of the public sphere (Gilmor 2004), and contribute to social accountability and transparency of public authorities and arbitrary private power. In the new media, low or non-existent communication costs allow all voices and opinions an opportunity of being heard. Even though such an environment does not guarantee equal opportunities to be heard, it nevertheless promotes a greater degree of pluralism and fairness in comparison to the public sphere of industrial societies, which has been dominated by corporate mass media.

In the past two decades, the social diffusion of ICTs has brought extensive transformations in the state of the public sphere. At present, new and radically democratic and participatory modes of political deliberation in the new media by end-users coexist at the edges of the incumbent corporate mass media. Hybrid modes of the old and the new can also be observed gradually gaining popularity and significance, pointing a possible way towards the future.[7] As the locus of economic activity and the focus of professional journalism shifts online, the future of such transformations remains uncertain, mostly dependent on the organizational capacity of these social practices to acquire stability, coordination and massive scale, and the capability of social movements and societies in general to shape the debate in the public sphere (Castells 2008).

## From political deliberation to democratic participation and action

Democracy is the polity that can best accommodate social change, by giving the opportunity for political minorities to turn into majorities. It is therefore useful to examine democratic politics in both in a top-down manner (by analyzing the existing correlations of incumbent political forces in order to understand the present) and in a bottom-up manner (by studying the arising dynamics of political counter-power in order to grasp the future). In the age of globalization, top-down political analysis finds democratic institutions of nation-states to have entered a period of severe crisis. On the contrary, bottom-up analysis shows that, alongside economic globalization, new media have reinforced the phenomenon of a radically democratic and globalized political counter-power. The ongoing transformations that are taking place in our semi-globalized public sphere empower individuals and collectivities to coordinate and mobilize themselves in a massive transnational scale for political purposes. In particular, the enhanced capability to constitute and disseminate alternate collective meanings through technological means regardless of space and time limits, along with the increased capacity for grassroots coordination and mobilization through the social use of ICTs, contribute to the formation of powerful social movements demanding social change in a "think global—act local" combination (Castells 2008: 87). Furthermore, technological properties of new media open opportunities for these movements to claim the democratic revival of traditional representative institutions through direct citizen participation.

The use of new media for political purposes reveals a dynamic and dialectical relation between technology and political activity. The properties of contemporary ICTs set the conditions of the political use of technology, whereas at the same time people collaboratively design and develop new technologies to adjust these conditions to their actual needs. It is clear, however, that while technology may be considered to provide certain tools for political deliberation, coordination, organization and participation, it is people that form body politics through collective purposeful action in order to enter the political arena and pursue shared aims. Hence it is when social needs arise and people collectively act for political purposes that contemporary ICTs are brought to the service of grassroots political

7 Characteristic of such hybrids is the commercial collaborative blog *Huffington Post*, ranking as the fourth most popular news website in the world: http://www.alexa.com/topsites/category/Top/News (accessed 30 September 2011).

coordination and mobilization at a massive scale. Despite its open contempt for law and its sometimes irresponsible and antisocial characteristics, the hacktivism of the Anonymous group is an example of such political use that is worth our attention. Being something closer to a subculture of cyberspace rather than a structured social movement of the classic type, Anonymous has managed to effectively utilize ICT capacities to coordinate massive online political protests and direct action events in cyberspace, while at the same time preserving a decentralized, nodal character of decision-making. In the case of Anonymous, this ability to achieve unity in action while preserving multiplicity of its nodes appears to be greatly enabled through technology. Furthermore, contemporary ICTs have enhanced the organizational capacities of grassroots political movements offline, and can rapidly spread their messages and practices irrespective of national borders and continents. The most vivid example of such an effect is the global real democracy movement. Since the eruption of social unrest in Tunisia in December 2010, a massive current of direct democratic peoples' assemblies and uprisings has swept the Middle East and North African region, spreading in Spain, Greece, Israel and the United States. Although wildly dispersed around the world and born in very different social contexts, through use of the new media, this global movement has managed to acquire critical mass, spread its messages and practices of organization and decision-making, and establish common general aims towards more freedom, actual democracy and social justice.

Yet the impact of new media on the political sphere has not been confined to forms of global grassroots political deliberation, mobilization and action; it has also led to ways for direct citizen participation in democratic institutions. The most ambitious example of such democratic restructuring is the recent amendment process of Iceland's Supreme Law. Undergoing a harsh period of economic recession, social unrest and popular demand to deepen democratic rule, the parliament of Iceland has recently been compelled to follow a radical process of deliberative democracy combined with direct electronic citizen participation to amend its Constitution.[8] First, an assembly of 950 randomly selected Icelanders—the National Forum—was convened on 6 November 2010 to deliberate on equal terms for a day regarding the appropriate amendments to the Icelandic Constitution. Then, the findings of the National Forum were condensed into a 700-page report prepared by a special constitutional committee. A twenty-five-member constitutional council was elected by popular vote on 30 November 2010, with the task to make the final decisions about the amendments to the Constitution, based on the submitted report. During the council's activities, which finished successfully in July 2011, all Icelanders were able to participate and offer their views on weekly council meetings via live broadcasts on Facebook or to take part in public discussions on the council's YouTube and Twitter accounts. The end result of the draft Constitution was approved by 66 percent of the constituency in a nationwide referendum in November 2012; the final decision by the Icelandic parliament for it's rejection or approval is still pending.

All of these stories show the growing transformations that the political use of new media brings to political systems on a global level. Utilization of ICTs for political mobilization, organization and action by individuals around the world reveals the emergence of the multitude, a post-industrial social subject able to act for social change while preserving the multiplicity of its participants. In addition, the push for stronger democracy has transformative effects on the character of new media themselves, as they are more and more being viewed, used and redesigned as an invaluable component for grassroots political deliberation and

8 For the official history of the process, see http://stjornlagarad.is/english/ (accessed 4 May 2012).

organization. Finally, modern ICTs are being used as the technological basis for a revival of democratic polities through greater transparency and accountability of public authorities and citizen participation, in both the deliberative and the decision-making political processes.

## Conclusion

In this chapter, I have attempted to show why technology constitutes the key of sovereignty in modern media. I have also tried to describe the strategies and techniques relevant to technology by which the multitude intervenes to influence power relations and correlations in the governance of the contemporary media ecosystem for purposes of individual and collective empowerment. This influence has been manifested in specific ways. In the physical and logical media layers, elements of a nascent, community-based mode of infrastructure and resource management, which enables social access to media on equal terms, have been observed to develop in parallel to bureaucratic and market modes of governance. In the content layer, the phenomena of mass self-communication and commons-based intellectual peer production, which thrive in the new media, enable the wider sharing of information, knowledge and culture, and encourage creativity and cooperation among multitudes of individuals around the globe. Finally, in the political field, the use of ICTs empowers individuals and collectivities to transform the contemporary public sphere and to deepen democratic self-governance, on the one hand, by massive political deliberation, mobilization and participation, and, on the other hand, by reinforcement of democratic institutions.

Taking into account all of these manifestations, the central claim of this chapter has been that the multitude transforms the media ecosystem not only by directly or indirectly intervening in its technological architecture, but also by diverting its social use to purposes other than those embedded in its design. Legislators and policymakers around the world have not been especially receptive to empowering potential of such transformations, at best following a cautious approach and, at worst, producing suppressive effects. Despite the successes, however, the future of such transformations remains uncertain and depends on politics in its deepest sense—namely, on grassroots political mobilization and struggle.

## References

Abbate, J. (2000) *Inventing the Internet*, Cambridge, MA: MIT Press.

Balkin, J. (2004) 'Digital speech and democratic culture: A theory of freedom of expression for the information society,' *New York University Law Review*, 79(1). Online. Available HTTP: http://www.yale.edu/lawweb/jbalkin/telecom/digitalspeechanddemocraticculture.pdf (accessed 4 May 2012).

—— (2009) 'The future of free expression in a digital age,' Faculty Scholarship Series Paper No. 223. Online. Available HTTP: http://digitalcommons.law.yale.edu/fss_papers/223 (accessed 4 May 2012).

Barber, B. (1998) 'Three scenarios for the future of technology and strong democracy,' *Political Science Quarterly*, 113 (1): 573–589.

Barbrook, R. (2005) 'The hi-tech gift economy,' *First Monday*, March. Online. Available HTTP: http://firstmonday.org/htbin/cgiwrap/bin/ojs/index.php/fm/article/view/1517/1432 (accessed 4 May 2012).

Bauwens, M. (2006) 'The political economy of peer production,' *Post-Autistic Economics Review*, 37: Article 3.

Bell, D. (1973) *The Coming of Post-Industrial Society: A Venture in Social Forecasting*, New York: Basic Books.

Benjamin, W. (1973 [1935–39]) 'The work of art in the age of mechanical reproduction,' in W. Benjamin (ed.) *Illuminations*, London: Fontana.

—— (2002 [1927–40]) *The Arcades Project*, R. Tiedemann (ed.) H. Eiland and K. McLaughlin (trans.), New York: Belknap Press.

Benkler, Y. (2000) 'From consumers to users: Shifting the deeper structures of regulation towards sustainable commons and user access,' *Federal Communication Law Journal*, 52: 561–579.
—— (2002) 'Some economics of wireless communication,' *Harvard Journal of Law & Technology*, 16(1): 25–83.
—— (2005) 'Coase's penguin, or, Linux and the nature of the firm,' in R. A. Ghosh (ed.) *Collaborative Ownership and the Digital Economy*, Cambridge, MA: MIT Press.
—— (2006) *The Wealth of Networks: How Social Production Transforms Markets and Freedom*, New Haven, CT: Yale University Press.
Berkman Center for Internet and Society (2004) 'Roadmap of open ICT ecosystems.' Online. Available HTTP: http://cyber.law.harvard.edu/epolicy/ (accessed 4 May 2012).
Berners-Lee, T. (2000) *Weaving the Web: The Original Design and Ultimate Destiny of the World Wide Web by its Inventor*, New York: Harper Collins.
Bygrave, L. and Bing, J. (2009) *Internet Governance: Infrastructure and Institutions*, New York: Oxford University Press.
Carpentier, N. (2007) 'Coping with the agoraphobic media professional: A typology of journalistic practices reinforcing democracy and participation,' in B. Cammaerts and N. Carpentier (eds.) *Reclaiming the Media, Communication Rights and Democratic Media Roles*, Bristol: Intellect Books.
Castells, M. (1996) *The Rise of the Network Society*, Oxford: Blackwell.
—— (2008) 'The new public sphere: Global civil society, communication networks, and global governance,' *Annals, AAPSS*, 616(1): 78–93.
—— (2009) *Communication Power*, Oxford: Oxford University Press.
—— Fernandez-Ardevol, M., Qiu, J. and Sey, A. (2004) 'The mobile communication society: A cross-cultural analysis of available evidence on the uses of wireless communication technology,' Presentation to the International Workshop on Wireless Communication, Annenberg School for Communication, Los Angeles: University of Southern California.
Clark, D. (1992) 'A cloudy crystal ball: Visions of the future,' Plenary Presentation at 24th meeting of the Internet Engineering Task Force, Cambridge, MA. Online. Available HTTP: http://www.ietf.org/old/2009/proceedings/prior29/IETF24.pdf (accessed 4 May 2012).
Coase, R. (1959) 'The Federal Communications Commission,' *Journal of Law and Economics*, 2: 1–40.
Council of Europe (2007) *Recommendation of the Committee of Ministers to Member States on Measures to Promote the Public Service Value of the Internet*, CM/Rec(2007)16. Online. Available HTTP: https://wcd.coe.int/ViewDoc.jsp?id=1207291&Site=CM&BackColorInternet=9999CC&BackColorIntranet=FFBB55&BackColorLogged=FFAC75 (accessed 4 May 2012).
European Union (2012) *Decision No 243/2012/EU of the European Parliament and of the Council Establishing a Multiannual Radio Spectrum Policy Programme*. Online. Available HTTP: http://eur-lex.europa.eu/LexUriServ/LexUriServ.do?uri=OJ:L:2012:081:0007:0017:EN:PDF (accessed 4 May 2012).
Federal Communications Commission (2008) *Second Report and Order and Memorandum Opinion and Order*, ET Docket Nos. 02-380 and 04-186, 23 FCC Rcd 16807.
—— (2010) *Second Memorandum Opinion and Order*, ET Docket Nos. 04-186 and No. 02-380, FCC 10—174. Online. Available HTTP: http://hraunfoss.fcc.gov/edocs_public/attachmatch/FCC-10-174A1.pdf (accessed 4 May 2012).
Flickenger, R. (2002) *Building Wireless Community Networks*, Sebastopol, CA: O'Reilly.
Foucault, M. (1983) 'The subject and power,' in H. Dreyfus and P. Rabinow (eds.) *Michel Foucault: Beyond Structuralism and Hermeneutics*, Chicago, IL: University of Chicago Press.
Fuchs, C. (2008) *Internet and Society: Social Theory in the Information Age*, New York: Routledge.
Ghosh, R. (2005) 'An economic basis for open standards,' University of Maastricht. Online. Available HTTP: http://flosspols.org/deliverables/FLOSSPOLS-D04-openstandards-v6.pdf (accessed 4 May 2012).
Giddens, A. (1984) *The Constitution of Society: Outline of the Theory of Structuration*, Cambridge: Polity Press.
Giles, J. (2005) 'Internet encyclopedias go head to head,' *Nature*, 438(7070): 900–901.
Gilmor, D. (2004) *We the Media*, Sebastopol, CA: O' Reilly.
Habermas, J. (1989/1962) *The Structural Transformation of the Public Sphere*, trans. T. Burger and F. Lawrence, Cambridge: Polity Press.
Haraway, D. (1991) *Simians, Cyborgs and Women: The Reinvention of Nature*, New York: Routledge.
Hardin, G. (1968) 'The tragedy of the commons,' *Science*, 162(3859): 1243–1248.

Hardt M. and Negri A. (2004) *Multitude, War and Democracy in the Age of Empire*, New York: Penguin.

Himanen, P. (2002) *The Hacker Ethic: A Radical Approach to the Philosophy of Business*, New York: Random House.

Hoffman, D. and Mehra, S. (2009) 'Wikitruth through Wikiorder,' *Emory Law Journal*, 59: 151–210.

Jenkins, H. (2006) *Convergence Culture: Where Old and New Media Collide*, New York: New York University Press.

Lehr, W. and Crowford, J. (2006) 'Managing shared access to a spectrum commons,' Massachusetts Institute of Technology Engineering Systems Division Working Paper Series.

Leiner, B., Cerf, V., Clark, D., Kahn, R., Kleinrock, L., Lynch, D., Postel, J., Roberts, L. and Wolff, S. (2003) *A Brief History of the Internet*. Online. Available HTTP: http://www.isoc.org/internet/history/brief.shtml (accessed 4 May 2012).

Lessig, L. (2004) *Free Culture: The Nature and Future of Creativity*, New York: Penguin.

—— (2006) *Code Version 2.0*, New York: Basic Books.

—— (2008) *Remix: Making Art and Commerce Thrive in the Hybrid Economy*, Harmondsworth: Penguin. Online. Available HTTP: http://www.archive.org/details/LawrenceLessigRemix (accessed 4 May 2012).

Levy, S. (2010) *Hackers, Heroes of the Computer Revolution*, Sebastopol, CA: O' Reilly.

Mann, M. (1986) *The Sources of Social Power, Vol. 1: A History of Power from the Beginning to AD 1760*, New York: Cambridge University Press.

McLuhan, M. (1964) *Understanding Media: The Extensions of Man*, London: Routledge and Kegan Paul.

Morozov, E. (2011) *The Net Delusion: The Dark Side of Internet Freedom*, New York: Perseus Books.

Office of Communications Statement (2011) 'Implementing geolocation, summary of consultation responses and self–tests.' Online. Available HTTP: http://stakeholders.ofcom.org.uk/binaries/consultations/geolocation/statement/statement.pdf (accessed 4 May 2012).

Organisation for Economic Co-operation and Development (OECD)(2011) *OECD Council Recommendation on Principles for Internet Policy Making*. Online. Available HTTP: http://www.oecd.org/dataoecd/11/58/49258588.pdf (accessed 4 May 2012).

Pinch, T. and Kline, R. (1996) 'Users as agents of technological change: The social construction of the automobile in rural America,' *Technology and Culture*, 37(4): 763–795.

Post, D. (1995) 'Anarchy, state and the Internet,' *Journal of Online Law, Article 3*. Online. Available HTTP: http://papers.ssrn.com/sol3/papers.cfm?abstract_id=943456 (accessed 4 May 2012).

Raymond, E. (2001) *The Cathedral and the Bazaar: Musings on Linux and Open Source by an Accidental Revolutionary*, Sebastopol, CA: O'Reilly.

Reuveni, E. (2007) 'Authorship in the age of the conducer,' *Copyright Society of the USA*, 54(218): 180–1859.

Russell, A. (2006) '"Rough consensus and running code" and the Internet–OSI standards war,' *IEEE Annals of the History of Computing*, 28(3): 48–61.

Shapiro, C. (2001) 'Setting compatibility standards: Cooperation or collusion,' in R. C. Dreyfuss, D. L. Zimmerman, and H. First (eds.) *Expanding the Boundaries of Intellectual Property: Innovation Policy for the Knowledge Society*, New York: Oxford University Press.

Stallman, R. (2010) *Free Software, Free Society: Selected Essays of Richard M. Stallman*, 2nd edn. Boston, MA: GNU Press. Online. Available HTTP: http://www.gnu.org/doc/fsfs-ii-2.pdf (accessed 4 May 2012).

Stefik, M. (1999) *The Internet Edge: Social, Technical and Legal Challenges for a Networked World*, Cambridge, MA: MIT Press.

Sunstein, C. (2006) *Infotopia: How Many Minds Produce Knowledge*? New York: Oxford University Press.

Tapscott, D. and Williams, A. D. (2006) *Wikinomics: How Mass Collaboration Changes Everything*, New York: Penguin.

Van Cuilenburg, J. and McQuail D. (2003) 'Media policy paradigm shifts, toward a new communications policy paradigm,' *European Journal of Communication*, 18(2): 181–207.

Von Hippel, E. (2006) *Democratizing Innovation*, Cambridge, MA: MIT Press.

Von Krogh, G., Spaeth, S. and Lakhani, K. R. (2003) 'Community, joining, and specialization in Open Source software innovation: A case study,' *Research Policy*, 32: 1217–1241.

Wikipedia (2012a) 'Wikipedia,' in *Wikipedia, The Free Encyclopedia*. Online. Available HTTP: http://en.wikipedia.org/w/index.php?title=Wikipedia&oldid=483567908 (accessed 5 October 2012).

—— (2012b) 'Wikipedia: Policies and guidelines,' in *Wikipedia, The Free Encyclopedia*. Online. Available HTTP: http://en.wikipedia.org/wiki/Wikipedia:Policies_and_guidelines (accessed 4 May 2012).

—— (2012c) 'Wikipedia: Administrators,' in *Wikipedia, The Free Encyclopedia*. Online. Available HTTP: http://en.wikipedia.org/wiki/Wikipedia:Administrators (accessed 4 May 2012).

Williams, R. (1985) *Towards 2000*, Harmondsworth: Penguin.

—— and Edge D. (1996) 'The social shaping of technology,' *Research Policy*, 25(6) : 865–899.

World Summit on the Information Society (WSIS)(2005) *Tunis Agenda for the Information Society*, WSIS-05/TUNIS/DOC/6(Rev. 1)-E. Online. Available HTTP: http://www.itu.int/wsis/docs2/tunis/off/6rev1.html (accessed 4 May 2012).

World Trade Organization (WTO)(1994) *Code of Good Practice for the Preparation, Adoption and Application of Standards*, attached as Annex 3 to the *WTO Agreement on Technical Barriers to Trade*. Online. Available HTTP: http://www.wto.org/english/docs_e/legal_e/17-tbt_e.htm#annexIII (accessed 4 May 2012).

Zittrain, J. (2008) *The Future of the Internet*, Harmondsworth: Penguin.

# Part V

# Media policy and technological transformation

24

# Do we know a medium when we see one?

## New media ecology

*Karol Jakubowicz*

### Introduction

In 2009, the Council of Europe (CoE) devoted an entire two-day conference of ministers responsible for media and new communication services to the subject of "A new notion of media?" The conference decided that fundamental change in mediated communication called for an in-depth analysis of the current understanding of media, including the criteria and assumptions that underlie this conceptual approach (see Jakubowicz 2009, for the background paper prepared for the participants). The conference called for a review of the concept itself, if necessary. In any case, the goal would be to establish criteria for distinguishing "media or media-like services from new forms of personal communication that are *not media-like mass-communication or related business activities*" (Council of Europe 2009: 4; emphasis added).

The Council's interest in all of this is more than theoretical. This all-European intergovernmental organization specializes in formulating and interpreting human rights standards and in the development of normative, policy and regulatory frameworks as concerns, *inter alia*, freedom of expression and of the media. In the interest of legal certainty, it needs to be sure whether the standards it promotes retain their relevance and, if not, what should be done for them to be applicable to new forms of social communication. More broadly, how does all of this change affect the exercise of the right to freedom of expression, information and the media? A focus on the efforts of the C.E and of the European Union to come to grips with the new media ecology permits analysts to go beyond theory and to observe the process of policymaking in action.

These efforts to distinguish or maintain a category for regulatory purposes can be interpreted as the next step after earlier attempts to end what Latzer (2009: 415) has called "disorder in communications policy" (see also Verhulst 2002; Jakubowicz 2012)—that is, the fact that policy and regulation had not caught up with convergence and continued to apply obsolete regulatory models to the mass media and telecommunications.

The C.E.'s follow-up to the ministerial conference has taken the form of *Recommendation CM/Rec(2011)7 on a new notion of media* (with its appendix entitled "Criteria for identifying media and guidance for a graduated and differentiated response"). The Recommendation states in paragraph 7 that media-related policy must take full account of the fluid and multidimensional reality of social communication and should be future-proof. For that purpose:

> All actors—whether new or traditional—who operate within the media ecosystem should be offered a policy framework which guarantees an appropriate level of protection and provides a clear indication of their duties and responsibilities in line with Council of Europe standards. The response should be graduated and differentiated according to the part that media services play in content production and dissemination processes.
>
> (*Committee of Ministers 2011: 2*)

It is accepted that standards for the new media-like service providers "may have to be adapted, or new ones will have to be elaborated" (Council of Europe 2009: 4).

The Council also decided to develop criteria for distinguishing between these media and "media-like" forms of mediated communication (discussed in detail below), so as to be able to decide how its policy and regulatory frameworks should, where appropriate, be adjusted, differentiated and graduated, so as to serve as an appropriate policy tool in each case.

Taking the Council's work as a point of departure, I consider here, in an exploratory way, whether the new media ecology and the emergence of "the new media" do indeed call for a "new notion of media," suitable for the new technological environment. In this chapter, we will consider differences between "the media," "new media," "media-like" activities and new forms of mediated "personal communication." We will then develop the argument by examining possible criteria for distinguishing these three segments of social communication. Then, we will look at policy and judicial efforts to decide whether bloggers are journalists as a case study showing how much confusion and how little legal certainty there is in trying to extend the current conceptual and legal system to new forms of mediated communication. We need to begin, however, with a brief examination of the new media ecology.

## New media ecology and emerging legal and socio-political challenges

The term "media ecology" has a rich and varied tradition, but here we use it simply, after Neil Postman, to mean "the study of media as environments . . . their structure, content, and impact on people" (Postman, *The Reformed English Curriculum*, cited after Strate 2004: 4). In this understanding, these environments consist of techniques as well as technologies, symbols as well as tools, information systems as well as machines. They are made up of modes of communication as well as of media.

CoE documents posit a simple continuum of forms of communication (see Figure 24.1). From the Council's point of view, the key question is how to define and what regulatory regime, if any, to apply in the case of this new category of "media-like services." Below, we will seek to develop this continuum to show how it can be applied for policy and regulatory purposes. It can also help us in developing a conceptual framework for our analysis of the new media ecology, and especially in developing a new notion of media.

A media ecology is a product of social change as much as of technological change. The present chapter adopts an approach close to that of Lievrouw and Livingstone (2006), who view the media system in general and the new media in particular as infrastructures with three components: the artifacts or devices used to communicate or convey information; the activities and practices in which people engage to communicate or share information; and the social arrangements or organizational forms that develop around those devices and practices.

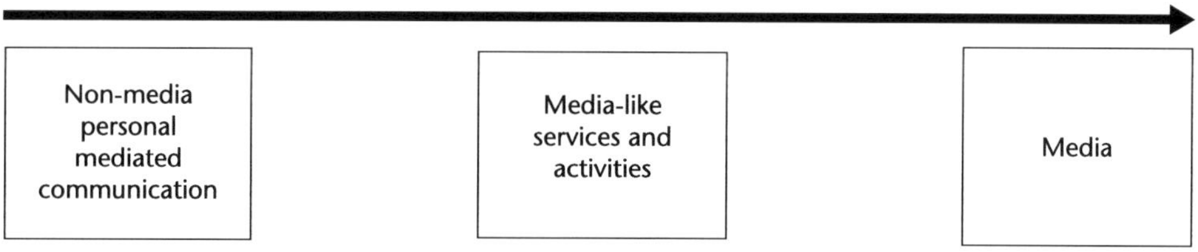


*Figure 24.1* Categories of forms of mediated communication

They add that the new media require us to reconsider the longstanding dependence within media research on theories and phenomena of mass society.

Some basic changes in these three "components" arise out of the process of convergence. Mueller (1999) sees convergence as a takeover of all forms of media by one technology: digital computers, capable of handling multimedia content. Thanks to this, the digital media can process content potentially without any restrictions. Telecommunication networks provide diverse and distant people with connectibility and access to content anywhere.

According to the European Commission (1997), convergence leads to the ability of different network platforms to carry essentially similar kinds of content and services.

Some changes in mass communication stemming from convergence are shown in Table 24.1.

The table shows a fundamental change in mass communication, including, especially, the emergence of new communicators and of the content they provide. This is the driving force behind the appearance of, among other things, "media-like" services and activities.

As a result of convergence, the mass audience and its interrelationship with the media have also changed profoundly (see Table 24.2).

Higher communication competence and a willingness on the part of a considerable segment of the audience to be active participants in the process of mass communication have contributed to the emergence of media-like activities.

*Table 24.1* The mass communication process before and after convergence

| *Before* | *After* |
|---|---|
| Large-scale distribution and reception | Distribution at once global and personalized |
| One-directional flow | Three-way flow: the audience can respond or provide content to be disseminated by the medium, or indeed distribute content themselves |
| Push (allocutory) mode prevalent, as in linear broadcasting | Pull (consultative) mode of reception grows in importance, as in non-linear reception of content |
| Asymmetrical relation | User can respond, offer feedback, engage in dialogue |
| Impersonal and anonymous | Affected by individualization and personalization |
| Calculative or market relationship | User-generated content (UGC) and new communicators change that |
| Standardized content | Highly diversified content |

*Source*: Adapted from McQuail (2005: 56)

*Table 24.2* The mass audience before and after convergence

| *Before* | *After* |
|---|---|
| Large numbers | Full range—from global to individual reception |
| Widely dispersed | Addressability and localization permit reaching clearly identifiable audiences or even individuals |
| Non-interactive and anonymous | Interactive and potentially personalized |
| Heterogeneous | Potentially homogenous, when content is targeted at particular audience groups |
| Not organized or self-acting | Capable of organization, reaction, response |
| An object of management or manipulation | More media literate, resistance to propaganda or manipulation |

*Source*: Adapted from McQuail (2005: 57)

These processes of change have been promoted by a succession of what we have seen as three "generations" of new media technologies that emerged and have developed from the second half of the twentieth century:

i. "New Media 1.0"—cable, satellite, VCR, teletext, etc.—extensions of traditional analog television in the pre-convergence era (1960–70s);
ii. "New Media 2.0"—traditional media technologies transformed as a result of digitization and convergence, so that they acquire the features of digitality, hypertextuality, dispersal and virtuality (Lister *et al.* 2003). The term also applies to the Internet and other digital platforms facilitating different modes of communication: allocution, conversation, consultation and registration, as well as linear or non-linear one-to-one, one-to-many, one-to-few, few-to-few, many-to-many communication (1980–90s); and
iii. "New Media 3.0"—connected TV, smartphone, tablet—all in one (2000s).

There is, of course, much more to the new media ecology, as this chapter will make clear, including primarily, from our point of view, the explosion in the number of active, mediated communicators. We will concentrate primarily here on the structure of this new media environment (i.e. on the types of actor performing different roles in it, especially in creating, assembling and delivering content). The structure is changing for a number of reasons.

First is the multiplication, thanks to satellites and cable, and now to the digital switchover, of professional (public, or—mostly—commercial) electronic media operators. Second, many telecom operators are becoming active in media markets, turning into what the European Audiovisual Observatory (2011) calls "convergent players," and offering media content and services far beyond their usual field of operation, but also beyond forms of content delivery available until now. Third, non-professional (community, civic, citizen) media are a growing sector of the media ecology. The CoE has defined community media, taking the form of broadcasting and/or other electronic media projects, as well as print formats, as sharing some of the following characteristics:

> ... independence from government, commercial and religious institutions and political parties; a not-for-profit nature; voluntary participation of members of civil society in the devising and management of programmes; activities aiming at social gain and

> community benefit; ownership by and accountability to the communities of place and/ or of interest which they serve; commitment to inclusive and intercultural practices.
>
> (*Committee of Ministers 2009: 3*)

Community radio has spread to some 115 countries worldwide (Sanchez 2003).

Finally, and most important, the new media ecology is growing in size and degree of complexity due to the Web 2.0-driven phenomenon known as "user-generated content" (UGC). Technological and social change have promoted the deinstitutionalization of mediated communication: it is possible to be a mass communicator without being part of, or having to rely on, a media institution to develop and distribute content. (Thus we can, in some cases, speak of "one-person media," incidentally involving a considerable amount of multi-skilling for the individuals concerned.) Technologically driven change also facilitates the disintermediation of mass communication, whereby the communicator can reach the audience directly (e.g. online) without a media outlet or other institution (other than a telecom service provider) as the go-between. A third process springing from convergence is the dematerialization of media content (Lister *et al.* 2003). This means that the content of communication is being turned into, or created as, digital files, separate both from its traditional physical form (roll of film, book, tape, etc.) and from the "devices" and technology so far used to deliver it to the public. Digital production of content allows it to be created by many more people than with the use of old technologies and in old institutional settings.

In short, a multiplayer media ecology has emerged, posing many challenges for the existing policy and regulatory system. As telecom operators develop new media services, they operate on the borderline between telecommunications and media regulation. Where broadcasting and telecommunications laws and regulators are separate, these companies may, in different areas of their activities, be subject to different legal regimes and supervised by different regulatory authorities. This has created many headaches for lawmakers and regulators.

In many countries, community/civic media are unregulated or insufficiently regulated, leading to calls for a more precise definition of their status. Both the European Parliament (2008) and the CoE Committee of Ministers (2009) have called on member states to give legal recognition to community media and to adapt legal frameworks to create an enabling environment for them. Still, there is at least no doubt that community media are subject to media legislation.

User-generated content creates perhaps the greatest number of legal dilemmas. Chief among them is the question of whether or not content created and distributed in this way should be classified as media content. This will be in the focus of our attention in this chapter.

This, however, is just the beginning of the policy and legal challenges caused by the new media ecology. Much more is at stake because its impact on society is contradictory and potentially capable of producing societal and political upheaval. On the one hand, Bowman and Willis (2003) view the processes described above as enabling online communities, as well as individuals, to produce participatory journalism, grassroots reporting, annotative reporting, commentary and fact-checking, which the mainstream media feed upon, developing them as a pool of tips, sources and story ideas. The result, as noted by Gillmor (2010: xv), is a "radically democratized and decentralized creation and distribution, where almost anyone can publish and find almost anything that others have published" (see also Gillmor 2004).

Benkler (2006) posits an opposition between what he calls a "social production" approach and a business approach to the Internet. The latter seeks to "colonize" the Internet (Dahlberg 2005a and 2005b) and to "sell you and your clicks" (Kang and McAllister 2011). One of the forecasts of the "future Internet" (Brown *et al.* 2010) envisages four scenarios, of which two precisely match this opposition:

i. "Power to the People"—emergence of the e-demos, a forum for democracy and freedom;
ii. "Commercial Big Brother"—an authoritarian/commercial consumer platform.

If the business approach proves stronger, then the "Commercial Big Brother" option of a system probably consolidated on a global scale and dedicated to serving business interests will indeed come true.

Yet even if it does not, democratization and decentralization of the media ecology may also potentially lead to unwelcome consequences as regards the public sphere and the operation of democracy, including fragmentation and polarization of attention and discourse (see Sunstein 2001a and 2001b). Instead of the one main public sphere of the mass media age, many different public spheres will emerge. There is a danger that the different public spheres can become closed "digital ghettoes," conducive to "nichification," including the development of "enclave" or "niche" mentality (Dahlgren 2010). Multiplication of communicators and potentially far-reaching diversification of the public discourse may undercut political effectiveness and make governance more difficult. A new social and political situation could well emerge, potentially exploding the nation-state and the democratic system from within. Eli Noam (2001) and Benjamin Barber (2002) argue therefore that the Internet may well "destroy" democracy.

In view of all of these dilemmas, the goal of policy and regulation needs to be to secure the best possible societal effects of the emergence of the new media ecology and minimize the risk of negative effects.

## Three forms of mediated communication

We will begin with a general look at definitions of the media and then work backwards to establish differences between the media and "media-like services," on the one hand, and non-media personal communication, on the other. These differences will be explored in more detail when we describe the criteria for establishing them.

### *Media*

Definitions used by different authors variously place emphasis on one or more of different dimensions: material, organizational and functional.

i. "Material" relates to the prerequisites needed for an act of communication to take place (i.e. the physical or other infrastructure that mediates in the process of transmitting or distributing the message or content).
ii. "Organizational" refers to the "media organization" that produces the content, involving the editorial processes required for the development of content to be distributed to a mass audience.
iii. "Functional" refers to the tasks and functions of the media (such as information, education and entertainment, or any combination of them), influence on public opinion (especially in the case of the news media) and availability to all potential receivers or at least significant parts of the public (see Lasota 2010).

The material definition is frequently used. Jeffries (1986: 1) says that "any device that carries messages between people is a *medium*." Similarly, De Fleur and Ball-Rokeach (1982: 4) use the terms "premedia" (pictorial and stylized art forms) and "media" (writing, print, etc.) to describe what Jeffries calls "devices" that—in their words—"bring messages to larger numbers of people."

For their part, Lister *et al.* (2003: 9–10) concentrate on the organizational and functional dimensions. For them, the term "media" encompasses, in the established sense:

> ... the institutions and organizations in which people work (the press, cinema, broadcasting, publishing and so on) and the cultural and material productions of those institutions (the forms and genres of news, road movies, soap operas which take the material form of newspapers, paperback books, films, tapes, and discs).

In other words, the term refers to what the authors call "media production" taking place in those institutions, highlighting the functional aspects of media operation.

Today, these three types of definition need to be reexamined. The usefulness of a "material" definition has largely been vitiated by the increasing dematerialization of media content. Since it is not possible to predict which technology or delivery platform (or how many different ones) will be used to carry content to the users, mass communication research that has traditionally organized itself around a specific communications medium (Morris and Ogan 1996) needs to concentrate on something other than the "device(s)" used to carry the message.

In turn, the deinstutionalization of the media makes the organizational definition largely, but not wholly, ineffective. The institutional (or non-institutional) setting for the development of media content can take many unpredictable forms—from huge transnational media corporations, through community radio and citizen journalism sites, to what Andrew Keen (2008) has called "the pyjama army" of individual bloggers or other UGC providers. Accordingly, the institutional dimension can by no means be taken for granted, and even less, serve as a basis for a definition. Yet, as we will see, some elements—the organization of the process of "media production"—retain their importance.

That leaves the functional dimension (i.e. the process of "media production" of content, the resulting content and its nature) as the only constant feature of media operation and thus the only stable point of departure for the formulation of definitions.

The process of media production of content was the point of departure for the EU Audiovisual Media Services (AVMS) Directive's definition of "audiovisual media service," which sought to modernize the Television without Frontiers (TwF) Directive, which dealt exclusively with television, and to make it technology-neutral. Hence the new term "audiovisual media service."

Most noteworthy is very heavy emphasis in the language of the AVMS Directive on the functional dimension of audiovisual media services ("intended for reception by, and which could have a clear impact on, a significant proportion of the general public"; "the function of the services is to inform, entertain and educate the general public"; an "impact of these services on the way people form their opinions"; "the principal purpose should be the provision of programmes"). There is some focus in the definition on the organizational or institutional dimension of the media ("a service, thus requiring an economic activity, which is under the editorial responsibility of a media service provider"), and the element of "editorial responsibility" is especially important. For the sake of regulatory clarity and legal certainty, an element of the material dimension was also introduced ("A service with audiovisual character . . . provided by electronic communications networks"). Given the Directive's scope of application, this was done partly for tactical reasons, to placate media interests demanding clear demarcation of the scope of the Directive, so that it would not cover online versions of print media.

All of these efforts notwithstanding, old approaches—concentrating on material and/or organizational dimensions—continue to appear. One example is the proposal by Morris and Ogan (1996) to approach the Internet as a mass medium. They say that each point in the traditional model of the communication process can, in fact, vary from one, to a few, to many on the Internet. This view appears to proceed from the assumption that the Internet is an integral and constitutive part of these aspects of the communication process. Fortunati (2005: 35) has no doubt that the Internet *is* a mass medium: "In one unbroken process, the internet is editorial office, newsagent, newspaper library and place of consumption. In the internet the newspaper is produced, distributed, filed and read: the whole chain of information finds its dwelling place on the net."

These concepts are contradicted by McQuail's (2005: 137) view that "the Internet is not only or even mainly concerned with the production and distribution of messages." Noam (2003) goes further by defining the Internet in a way that expressly *excludes* content. The Internet Governance Project explains that the Internet is not a physical infrastructure, but a set of software instructions (known as "protocols") that can operate on many different physical technologies to send data over networks (Mathiason 2004). As such, it would be hard to recognize the Internet as a medium. Noam drives the point home by adding "The Internet is today part of most organizations' activities. To encompass all of them as part of the Internet industry would equate this sector with almost the entire economy" (Noam 2003: 2). This reaffirms the point that a media organization should not be identified with, or defined by, the distribution technology it uses.

Based on these remarks, we need to give serious consideration to Goban-Klas's (2007: 9) argument that definitions of "media" as all technologies for the recording and distribution of information in time and space create only "unnecessary conceptual complications." In his view, the correct definition of "the media" is as "institutions that produce information and entertainment content that is distributed on a mass scale . . . " This is also clear from McQuail's (2005) analysis of "media organizations," which concludes that they are precisely the place where content is produced. They are separate from the means of distribution (such as cable, satellite and the Internet), although new kinds of media organizations may arise to take advantage of the opportunities that these means offer.

In view of all of this, we may, in very general terms, say that it is the nature of content that is the determining factor in deciding whether we are dealing with a mass communication medium. This calls for a technologically and institutionally neutral definition of the term "a mass medium" as a media organization devoted to the production in an editorial process of media content and its periodic distribution to the general public, whatever the organization's institutional and organizational form and legal status, and whatever technology(ies) it uses to produce and disseminate content.

## *Media-like activities*

The term "media-like" was inspired by "television-like," a concept used in the AVMS Directive to mean video-on-demand services. The Directive states in Recital 24 that:

> It is characteristic of on-demand audiovisual media services that they are 'television-like,' i.e. that they compete for the same audience as television broadcasts, and the nature and the means of access to the service would lead the user reasonably to expect regulatory protection.

Taking its cue from this approach, the CoE's ministerial conference coined the term "media-like activities." Compared to audiovisual "television-like services," "media-like activities" naturally also cover text-based content. Obviously, given the fast and unpredictable nature of technological change, it is not possible to compile a list of such "activities," although citizen journalism and citizen journalism sites (see e.g. Bowman and Willis 2003; García-Avilés

2010) can clearly be recognized as "media-like," or perhaps even "media," organizations if other conditions are met. Otherwise, the best that can be done is to identify features either shared by "media-like" activities and traditional media, or features differentiating them. As we will see below, if there are enough features shared by the media and "media-like services," the latter can stay in such a category, or indeed be recognized as media. If not, their status will need to change and they may be classified as non-media personal mediated communication. The latter needs to be defined and classified with special care, given the confusion created by terms such as "social media" (used for social network sites) and the view of some authors who, as we have seen, consider even the Internet as a "medium."

In terms of policy and regulation, the main difficulty is recognizing which new forms of mediated communication can be classified as "media-like," for example, UGC (Le Borgne-Bachschmidt *et al.* 2008; Wunsch-Vincent and Vickery 2007). Table 24.3 shows the various types of UGC.

According to the Council of Europe (2009: 4), both "media" and "media-like activities" pursue the same goals: "to provide or disseminate information, analysis, comment, opinion and entertainment to a broad public." The other underlying objectives are comparable: to set the public agenda; to animate public debate or exert influence on public opinion (Grünwald 2003; Verhulst 2002); to contribute to development or to promote specific values; to entertain; to generate an income; or, most frequently, a combination of the above. Thus the key to recognizing a medium among new forms of mediated communication is knowing which of the above forms of UGC are intended to, and actually can, serve these purposes.

As for differences, they can be found in unprecedented levels of interaction and engagement by users, in their participation in the creation process and in the dissemination of information and content, blurring the boundaries between public and private communication. To

*Table 24.3* Types of user-generated content

| *Type of content* | *Description* |
|---|---|
| Text, novel and poetry | Original writings or expanding on other texts, novels, poems |
| Photo/images | Digital photographs taken by users and posted online; photos or images created or modified by users; photo blogging; remixed images |
| Music and audio | Recording and/or editing one's own audio content and publishing, syndicating, and/or distributing it in digital format; podcasting |
| Video and film | Recording and/or editing video content and posting it; includes remixes of existing content, homemade content and a combination of the two; video blogs and videocasting; posting home videos |
| Citizen journalism | Journalistic reporting on current events done by ordinary citizens, who write news stories, blog posts, and take photos or videos of current events and post them online |
| Educational content | Content created in schools, universities, or with the purpose of educational use |
| Mobile content | Content that is created on mobile phones or other wireless devices such as text messaging, photos and videos; videos and photos of public events, environments such as natural catastrophes that the traditional media may not be able to access; text messages used for political organizing; user-created games are also on the rise |
| Virtual content | Variety of virtual goods that can be developed and sold on Second Life including clothes, houses, artwork |

*Source*: Adapted from Wunsch-Vincent and Vickery (2007: 15)

*Table 24.4* Traditional journalism versus blog journalism

| | *Traditional journalism* | *Blog journalism* |
|---|---|---|
| Narrative style | Detached | Personal |
| | Neutral | Opinionated |
| | "Both" sides | One-sided |
| Approach to audience | Audience as passive recipient | Audience as co-creator |
| Story form | Structured format (e.g. inverted pyramid) | Fragments |
| | Answers basic questions | Incomplete |
| | (Who? What? etc.) | Open text |
| | Closed text | Hyperlinks for credibility |
| | Sources and datelines for credibility | |

*Source*: Wall (2005)

give an example, an examination of current events blogs, dedicated to the provision of news and information, found that these blogs are a new genre of "post-modern" journalism. Table 24.4 shows how blogs differ from traditional journalism.

Media-like activities may be based on institutional arrangements and editorial practices that differ from those of traditional media organizations. What still remains to be considered is what actually constitutes a medium in this context: is it the work of one author or content provider (e.g. a blogger or a citizen journalist) who individually and periodically publishes his or her reports and stories online, or is it the (online or other) publication that contains and aggregates such content produced by many authors of media-like content? We might refer in this context to Banda's (2010) distinction between two types of citizen journalism: *non-institutional* and *institutional*.

In case of "non-institutional" citizen journalism, private citizens use a combination of platforms to generate content and disseminate it as widely as possible, without recourse to any organizational framework of constraints. "Institutional citizen" journalism, on the other hand, has a form of organizational structure or constraining ability, complete with external constraints (gatekeeping, moderation, editorial process), however minimal. Three cases may be identified: professional media organizations, which provide space for citizen journalists; "hybrid" forms, which combine the work of both the professional and citizen journalists (e.g. OhmyNews.com of South Korea); and publications consisting solely of UGC-type content (e.g. AgoraVox, the French citizen journalism site).

## *Non-media personal mediated communication*

New information and communication technologies make possible networked communication on the Internet and other digital platforms that combines many of the modes of communication that previously required different communication tools and delivery platforms. This includes: one-to-one communication; "private" communication (one-to-few, as in Google Circles); group communication (few-to-few); "masspersonal communication" (mass interpersonal communication, such as in the case of blogs, a form of one-to-many communication); mass self-communication (personal self-expression or creativity for general consumption); and general communication (many-to-many). "Allocution" (top-down communication in the one-to-many mode) is being complemented more and more (but not replaced) by interactive "conversation."

It is here that a methodology for setting media and "media-like" activities apart from other forms of mediated communication is most needed, given the ease with which the term "media" is applied, for example, to cellphone messaging (Kalathil 2008) or to "social media." In reality, neither qualifies as media.

"Social media," as properly understood, are defined as "online applications, platforms and media which aim to facilitate interaction, collaboration and the sharing of content" and as consisting of the following "social platforms": blogging; micro-blogging; RSS (Really Simple Syndication); widgets; social networking; chat rooms; message boards; podcasts; video sharing; and photo sharing (Smith 2008). The way in which the "social media" are described suggests that whatever the platform, whether Facebook, Twitter, local community or special interest forums:

> ... there are a lot of the same elements typical of face-to-face *socializing*: discussions, opinions, requests for advice, gossip, chitchat, jokes, jibes, gripes and games. Unlike in most face-to-face interactions, however, social media make it possible to pull in and share media content there and then, such as images, videos, sounds, news stories and product information
>
> (*Euro RSCG Worldwide 2009: 9; emphasis added*).

"Social media" (personal, private, group, mass communication) certainly may include "media-like activities" (blogging, podcasting), provided that such content appears on them on a periodic basis. They may also include media-derived content on social networking sites, for example. From the perspective of the analysis in this chapter, their wholesale identification with the media, as defined in mass communication theory, is unjustified.

## Identifying elements of the media in new players in the media ecology

In its *Recommendation CM/Rec(2011)7 on a new notion of media* (Committee of Ministers 2011), the CoE suggests the following criteria for deciding whether particular content offers should be regarded as media: intent to act as media; purpose and underlying objectives of media; editorial control; professional standards; outreach and dissemination; and public expectation.

Each criterion is accompanied by indicators, and both the criteria and indicators are to be applied in a flexible manner. Not all criteria carry equal weight, says the Recommendation. The absence of certain criteria such as purpose (criterion 2), editorial control (criterion 3) or outreach and dissemination (criterion 5) would tend to disqualify a service from being regarded as media. The absence (or apparent absence) of other criteria, such as intent (criterion 1) or public expectation (criterion 6), should not automatically disqualify a service from being considered media, but may carry considerable weight if they are present.

The Recommendation also says that impact on public opinion should not be considered as a determining factor, since all content provided by media has a potential impact on society and assessing impact is highly subjective.

For reasons explained below, we will discuss a similar, but somewhat different set of criteria.

i. Purpose
ii. Editorial policy and process
iii. Actors involved: journalists and other content creators; management and technical sectors of the organization
iv. Ethical and other standards
v. Periodic dissemination
vi. Public nature of communication

We begin with "purpose." A declaration of intent alone, as required by Council of Europe criteria, while important, may be misleading or unsupported by the activities actually undertaken. "Purpose," as manifested by those activities, is also evidence of actual intent. This is followed by "editorial policy and process." The CoE speaks of "editorial control," but we believe that what is crucial in turning a communication activity into a media activity is the application of editorial policy and process (which may include both editorial control and moderation) in the actual production of the content. The criterion of the "actors" involved is highly pertinent, given the long-running dispute (discussed in this chapter with regards to the Crystal Cox decision) regarding whether bloggers are journalists or not, and whether they should be able to enjoy the same legal treatment as journalists. The CoE's criterion of "public expectation" (with indicators such as availability, pluralism and diversity, reliability, and respect for professional and ethical standards, accountability and transparency) duplicates some of the other criteria and refers more to how the media system should be organized than to the features needed to qualify a particular provision of content as a medium, or a "media-like activity". Finally, the CoE's "outreach and dissemination" criterion appears here as "periodic dissemination" (a key feature, because one-off distribution of media content does not transform the content provider into a medium organization) and as "public nature of communication" (another key criterion, distinguishing "mass" from "group" or interpersonal mediated communication).

This perspective concentrates on functional aspects of the media, with some organizational elements (editorial policy and process) included as well. It is thus technology-neutral, proceeding from the assumption that what really determines a media organization and media or media-like content are "soft" criteria: (i) purpose; (ii) editorial policy and responsibility; (iii) awareness of, and an acceptable degree of conformity with, normative, ethical, professional and legal standards; and finally (iv) periodic distribution. As explained by some commentators, the nature, quality and integrity of the method of reporting is significant in determining whether content should be regarded as media or journalism (see e.g. Rosen 2011; Angelotti 2012).

## *Purpose*

This criterion incorporates those of "intent" and "purpose" in the Council of Europe approach.

So, if the nature of content is the main criterion, then creation and distribution of content serving media-related goals and its periodic distribution are sufficient evidence both of the intent to perform a media role and of the fact that this role is actually performed. The purpose will usually be to pursue some or many of the following goals: to exercise, and enable exercise of, freedom of expression and information; to serve the public interest; to provide a forum for public debate; to influence public opinion; to inform; to educate; to entertain; to operate as a business (where appropriate); to gain social influence and prestige; to maximize the audience (where appropriate); and potentially also to serve sectional interests (political, religious, cultural, etc.).

There is no lack of definitions or statements of intent regarding the media/journalistic nature of "media-like activities."

Bowman and Willis (2003: 9) similarly highlight the intent behind "participatory journalism" (see also Jurrat 2011), their term for citizen journalism:

> The act of a citizen, or group of citizens, playing an active role in the process of collecting, reporting, analyzing and disseminating news and information. The intent of

> this participation is to provide independent, reliable, accurate, wide-ranging and relevant information that a democracy requires.

The American National Association of Citizen Journalists defines the intent of citizen journalists in an almost identical way.

Ultimately, however, it is necessary to analyze the content of a particular form of mediated communication to determine whether it can be classified as "media-like." This is clear in the case of blogs (including audioblogs, videoblogs and photoblogs). As reported by Lomborg (2009), 79 percent of bloggers worldwide self-identified as personal bloggers in 2008, with the personal weblog mostly understood as a private diary or lifelog. In 2004, 17 percent of weblogs in the United States covered news and current affairs (Kenix 2009). Of the two, mainly the latter could qualify as media. According to Matheson (2004), much of the writing on blogs frames them within discourses of journalism and public discussion, such as:

i. weblogs as a space for journalistic thinking for which institutional journalism provides little room;
ii. weblogs as a challenge to corporate journalism; and
iii. weblogs as a democratic, interactive space.

However, the American Electronic Frontier Foundation admits, in its *Legal Rights for Bloggers*, that bloggers can only "sometimes" be classified as journalists (and therefore, by implication, that their blogs can only sometimes be classified as media):

> You can use blogging software for journalism, and many bloggers do. But you can also use blogging software for other purposes. What makes a journalist a journalist is whether she is gathering news for dissemination to the public, not the method or medium she uses to publish.

Categorizing a blogger as a medium on such a tenuous basis ("sometimes") is bound to fail, especially given the wide variety of types of blog (see e.g. Lomborg 2009; Domingo and Heinonen 2008). It has been said that any blogger can "commit journalism" when describing or analyzing an event that they have witnessed (Domingo and Heinonen 2008). However, does such "accidental journalism" (see below) turn a blog into a mass medium, as defined here? Such current events and political blogs (Singer 2005) will usually approximate media functions. Another indicator is the desire to influence public and elite opinion. One study has concluded that American political bloggers, for example, "often portrayed their own and others' blogs as effective tools for changing the world and as prime movers in the world of setting the public and elite agenda" (Park 2009: 261).

This confirms that some bloggers do perform media functions, and others do not.

### Editorial process, policy and responsibility

In the CoE text, the criterion of "editorial control" incorporates as indicators editorial policy and process (as well as moderation and editorial staff), with special emphasis on editorial oversight and control.

The indicator of "editorial staff" introduced in the CoE text may potentially be misleading. We deal with content providers under a separate item, because there may be no "editorial staff" in the usual sense of the term in a one-person operation or in unprofessional, amateur or "pro-am" (see Leadbeater and Miller 2004) media organizations.

We may find the application of the editorial process in the use of journalistic skills and techniques for the actual preparation of content: gathering, processing, researching, reporting, analyzing and publishing news and information.

Editorial oversight, policy and responsibility are reflected, for example, in the routines applied within media and media-like services, but also in moderating and editing content coming from external (non-professional) content creators (for extensive information on such standards for UGC, see Le Borgne-Bachschmidt *et al.* 2008b), especially by services dedicated to publishing or hosting citizen journalism and other media-like content (see Table 24.5).

Moderation may thus be an act of putting editorial policy into effect and of assuming editorial responsibility for the content that is published. For example, AgoraVox, a French citizen journalism site, has announced that it has an "editorial policy," which is to publish verifiable news related to objective events or facts. The submitted information is moderated to avoid any political or ideological drift. AgoraVox publishes around 75 percent of all submitted articles and has a specific list of reasons why it may refuse publication. This is clearly a gatekeeping role. On Ohmynews.com, a South Korea-based online newspaper that relies on citizen journalism for 80 percent of its contents, every article is vetted, copyedited and double-checked before it is published.

*Table 24.5* Content and conduct provisions in terms of service of UGC sites

| | |
|---|---|
| Content regulation and editorial responsibility | Most sites specify that users are solely responsible for the content that they publish or display on the website, or transmit to other members. The sites specify that they have no obligation to modify or remove any inappropriate member content, and no responsibility for the conduct of the member submitting any such content.<br>The sites reserve the right to review and delete or remove any member content that does not correspond to defined standards.<br>Some sites use age and content ratings or have areas for content that is rated mature. |
| Community standards | Most sites have community standards on intolerance (derogatory or demeaning language as to race, ethnicity, gender, religion, or sexual orientation), harassment, assault, the disclosure of information of third parties and other users (e.g. posting conversations), indecency, etc. |
| Actions to enforce standards | Sites specify penalties when users infringe community standards. They range from warnings, to suspensions, to banishment from the service. The creation of alternative accounts to circumvent these rules is being tracked. |

*Source*: Wunsch-Vincent and Vickery (2007)

### *Journalists and other content creators*

In its *Handbook for Citizen Journalists,* the National Association of Citizen Journalists identifies different categories of content creator, with different goals and intentions.

i. "Accidental journalists" are people caught unexpectedly in the middle of an event, who take photos or videos and upload them to either social networking websites such as Facebook, MySpace or Twitter, or news websites such as CNN's iReport or Fox News' iReport. However, the authors explain, that "does not make that person a citizen journalist."
ii. "Advocacy citizen journalists" refers to a genre of journalism that adopts a viewpoint for the sake of advocating on behalf of a social, political, business or religious purpose. It is journalism with an intentional and transparent bias.
iii. "True citizen journalists" are explained as follows: "True—or enthusiastic—citizen journalists work hard at their craft. They are trained. They strive to tell all sides of the story in an accurate manner" (cited after Cormier 2011).

Two other journalistic organizations have displayed contrasting attitudes to this issue. The European Federation of Journalists (2009) is fighting a rearguard action, trying to discredit bloggers and citizen journalists as untrained, potentially unethical and incapable of producing stories of high quality. On the other hand, the Committee to Protect Journalists (CPJ) was guided in 1999, when considering whether to take up the case of six Chinese authors arrested by Chinese authorities, by a different, functional, logic: "None was a journalist in any traditional sense . . . But they were, we reasoned, *acting journalistically. They disseminated news, information, and opinion.* We took up the cases" (Cooper 2008; emphasis added).

That still leaves for consideration the distinction between "advocacy" and "true" citizen journalists. It applies to citizen journalists an outdated concept of professional journalism that is not applicable in this case and is (for better or for worse) falling out of favor also in mainstream media.

### *Conformity with normative, ethical, professional and legal standards*

There is widespread acceptance in the citizen journalism and blogging community of views like those formulated by Gillmor (2008: 23) that when bloggers "do journalism," they should be ethical and respect the values and principles of honorable journalism, such as thoroughness, accuracy, fairness, transparency and independence

The US National Association of Citizen Journalists (n.d.) is aware of the need for standards and when defining citizen journalists said in a segment on its website on "What do citizen journalists do?" that "they act ethically." This means that, in theory at least, they:

> ... are committed to accuracy and context; identify their sources and provide proper attribution; respect the English language and use it properly; do not plagiarize; are always sensitive to those affected by tragedy or grief; retrain from stereotyping by race, gender, age, religion, etc.; are aware that people can be hurt, lives ruined.

Confirmation of this view can be found in the 2006 Pew Internet study of American bloggers (Lenhart and Fox 2006), which found that bloggers' most frequently reported journalistic activities are spending extra time verifying facts included in a posting, and including links to original source material that has been cited or in some way used in a post. One in seven bloggers (15 percent) say that they quote people or other media directly on their blog "often," and another 12 percent say that they often seek permission before posting copyrighted material to their blog. Only 11 percent of bloggers regularly post corrections on their blog.

Normative, ethical and other standards are extensively discussed in the blogging community and various draft codes of ethics have been proposed. The model Bloggers' Code of Ethics, developed by the American portal CyberJournalist.net by "modifying the Society of Professional Journalists Code of Ethics for the Weblog world," includes sections entitled "Be Honest and Fair," "Minimize Harm," and "Be Accountable." However, no such codes have been formally adopted and embraced. In some cases, at least, the blogging community is developing forms of training, self-regulation, editorial responsibility and accountability serving precisely this purpose.

The Electronic Frontier Foundation (EFF) has published a number of documents promoting enhanced professional and legal competence and protection of bloggers, for example *The Bloggers' FAQ on Online Defamation Law* and *The Bloggers' FAQ on Privacy*.

## Periodic dissemination

One-off publication of content, however "journalistic" or "media-like" it might be, cannot transform that content into a "medium," as defined here. Periodic (although not necessarily regular) publication retains its relevance as a criterion of whether a particular case of content provision can be classified as a media service. Periodic dissemination may, in practical terms, mean, in the case of traditional media, very different frequency of publication—from daily (possibly with "extras" of daily newspapers increasing the frequency) to yearly. It can be an altogether different situation in online content services. There, news headlines are sometimes updated hourly, but there is a wide scale of updating frequency. Internet publications can update or revise news items or stories countless times a day, as new information comes in.

Another reason for frequent updating on the Internet is explained by Mauriac and Riché (2009), creators of the French news website *Rue89*: "We know that people visit our site several times a day and they must always find a site that has been updated." This suggests that updating may be done to make the service more attractive, rather than for any substantive reason.

This, then, is a "dynamic" web page (Hellsten, Leydesdorff and Wouters 2006); others may be "static." Archived web pages, such as citation index databases, online archives and postings in discussion groups, usually remain static over time, which excludes them from consideration as media services.

## Public nature of communication via different delivery and distribution platforms

A citizen journalist, blogger and podcaster can periodically self-publish their own content (e.g. online) and the publication could be considered a mass medium, if that content meets the other criteria. Much more often, however, citizen journalism is published or hosted either by an established media organization, or by an Internet site specifically dedicated to this kind of content.

Examples of such sites include OhmyNews (South Korea), AgoraVox (France), Skoeps (the Netherlands), NowPublic (Canada), AllVoices (the United States), The-Latest.com and Blottr (UK).

For regulatory purposes, public communication usually means availability of content to the general public. The determining criterion for recognizing a communication service as a mass medium in this regard must, therefore, be that its contents are intended for reception by, and are accessible (either as a linear service or on demand) to, the general public without discrimination, regardless of the actual number of recipients.

## Blogs: A case study of legal uncertainty in the new media ecology

Ultimately, the whole debate that we are examining here is one about freedom of speech and of the media, and about the role of the media in society and the democratic system. It is perhaps a measure of the social impact of some "media-like" activities that they may meet with official persecution, even in democratic countries. Their unregulated status often leaves them at the mercy of unpredictable and contradictory decision-making by policymakers, officials and the judicial system. This may have a serious "chilling effect" on bloggers.

In June 2011, Jacqui Thompson, author of the blog *Carmarthenshire Planning Problems and More*, was arrested for "breaching the peace" while silently using her phone in the public gallery to record a meeting of Carmarthenshire County Council in the UK. Running battles between local councils and citizen journalists and bloggers regarding whether the latter have the right to cover local council meetings are quite common in the UK. As one of the bloggers explains it: "Bloggers are best at covering local [budget] cuts across the UK: so we're being banned," while "respectable media" are allowed in (Belgrave 2011). In the last instance, the issue is one of public scrutiny over elected officials and of the watchdog role of the media, professional and unprofessional alike.

Without even mentioning what happens to dissident bloggers in undemocratic countries (Reporters sans Frontières, 2011), these and other examples cited below (admittedly coming from different countries with different legal systems, but still conforming to a certain pattern) show that creation of a system of identifying media and "media-like" activities, and outlining a legal and regulatory framework for the latter, really is needed and not only for political reasons. The European Parliament (Mikko 2008: 1) signaled this when it voiced its concerns regarding "the undetermined and unindicated status of authors and publishers of weblogs [that] causes uncertainties regarding impartiality, reliability, source protection, applicability of ethical codes and the assignment of liability in the event of lawsuits."

In some cases, bloggers have been successful in becoming "court-approved journalists" when the authority in question adopted a functional approach to the nature of their occupation. Canadian blogger Charles LeBlanc received a court decision in 2006 "establishing his journalistic credentials," based on the judge's appraisal of the nature of his activity, regardless of any other formal or legal considerations. In the situation in question, the judge decided, the blogger "was simply plying his trade, gathering photographs and information for his blog *alongside other reporters*" (Austen 2006; emphasis added).

A pro-blogger, functional attitude was also displayed by Dutch Minister of Justice, Ernst Hirsch Ballin, in 2008, when he proposed legislation that would give journalists, bloggers and other opinion-makers the legal right to protect their sources. The minister decided not to impose a strict definition of a "journalist" so that other people could join public debates.

A similar tack was taken by the Belgian Constitutional Court when it argued that excluding occasional or amateur journalists from the right to protect their sources would violate press freedom. The Court extended the scope of application of such regulations to "everyone who directly contributes, edits, produces or disseminates information aimed at the public via a medium." Thanks to this functional criterion, Belgian bloggers are no longer necessarily excluded from the right to protection of journalistic sources (Werkers *et al.* 2008).

Elsewhere, however, an organizational/institutional perspective is most often adopted, serving to exclude citizen journalists from among the ranks of officially recognized journalists. In Canada in August 2011, Quebec's Culture Minister Christine St-Pierre floated possible legislation that would define the "status of professional journalists, to distinguish those dedicated to 'serving the public interest' from 'amateur bloggers.' The former would enjoy unspecified 'advantages or privileges,' such as 'better access to government sources' " (Hamilton 2011).

The legal uncertainties of defining a journalist are well illustrated by a recent, controversial US federal court decision in which, in two separate subject areas, the court took two disparate approaches towards its decision that a blogger was not a member of the media. The first approach was legal, but the second was arbitrary.

The case of *Obsidian Finance Group, LLC* v *Cox*, in which an American blogger was sued for defamation, leaves uncertainly as to how and whether laws protecting "journalists" and "journalism" will be applied to bloggers and other amateur reporters.

Much of the attention the case has garnered centers on the court's decision that Crystal Cox, a blogger unaffiliated with any "official" media outlet, fell outside the protections of Oregon's shield law, which affords journalists a privilege against compelled disclosure of certain information and journalistic work product.

In reaching this determination, the court took a legal approach. The judge considered the shield law's terms, which provide that:

> [n]o person connected with, employed by or engaged in any medium of communication to the public shall be required by . . . a judicial officer . . . to disclose, by subpoena or otherwise . . . [t]he source of any published or unpublished information obtained by the person in the course of gathering, receiving or processing information for any medium of communication to the public[.]
>
> (Obsidian Finance Group, LLC v Cox *2011: 3;* amendments in original)

The court recognized that Ms. Cox called herself an "investigative blogger" and defined herself as "media," but focused its attention on whether she satisfied a narrow reading of the "engaged in any medium of communication" element of the statute.

Although acknowledging that the term "medium of communication" was "broadly defined as including, but not limited to, 'any newspaper, magazine or other periodical, book, pamphlet, news service, wire service, news or feature syndicate, broadcast station or network, or cable television system', " the court nonetheless concluded that it did not apply to blogs, the medium employed by Cox (*Obsidian Finance Group, LLC* v *Cox* 2011: 3). The court did not address why Internet-based publications such as blogs could not be analogized to any paper-based counterpart.

Thus, by construing the law more restrictively than its terms required, the court held that Cox failed to demonstrate that she was "affiliated with" one of the media explicitly listed and therefore was "not entitled to the protections of the law in the first instance" (*Obsidian Finance Group, LLC* v *Cox* 2011: 3). This conclusion has been widely criticized.

Elsewhere in the opinion, in the court's analysis of the fault standard to be applied in the defamation claim against Ms. Cox, the court took an arbitrary approach to again determine that Ms. Cox should not be considered a member of the "media." The court stated:

> Defendant fails to bring forth any evidence suggestive of her status as a journalist. For example, there is no evidence of (1) any education in journalism; (2) any credentials or proof of any affiliation with any recognized news entity; (3) proof of adherence to journalistic standards such as editing, fact-checking, or disclosures of conflicts of interest;

> (4) keeping notes of conversations and interviews conducted; (5) mutual understanding or agreement of confidentiality between the defendant and his/her sources; (6) creation of an independent product rather than assembling writings and postings of others; or (7) contacting "the other side" to get both sides of a story. Without evidence of this nature, defendant is not "media."
>
> (Obsidian Finance Group, LLC v Cox *2011: 9*)

This rather detailed examination of the case shows that lacunae in the law provide American (and other) judges unlimited freedom to invent sometimes demanding and unjustified criteria for recognizing a blogger as a journalist. The requirements of education in journalism and of affiliation with any "recognized news entity" are completely unfounded. This would exclude a range of journalistic activities undertaken by both professional and unprofessional journalists without the requisite education or institutional affiliation. According to McQuail (2008), journalism as a process of observing, reporting and publishing about public events must be open to all citizens in a free society, without artificial legal or other barriers.

A number of the other requirements that the court considered to be evidence of "media" are also problematic. This is the case, for example, with requirement (7)—citizen journalists and especially bloggers are often highly opinionated, and attitudes to journalistic objectivity are changing anyway; today "transparency is the new objectivity" (Weinberger 2009). The onus on journalists is not to be objective, but to be transparent (i.e. candid and open about their views, giving the public a clear interpretative framework for assessing the opinions they are expressing and the stance they are taking). Even in broadcasting, the Fairness Doctrine has not been applied for more than twenty years and was eliminated by the Federal Communications Commission (FCC) in 2011 as "obsolete" and "outdated" (FCC 2011: 1).

As we have seen in this case, the procedure leaves a large margin of appreciation. A different court might well have come to a different conclusion. Indeed, if the court had taken "a functional approach and read the terms of the [relevant] statutes to encompass methods of publication that were closely analogous to those listed in the statute," it could have decided that the blog was a "printed periodical" under the retraction statute's definition, and a "periodical" under the anonymous source statute's definition (Hilden 2011). With a different judge and a functional approach, Cox and her publications would have been entitled to greater legal protections, both under the shield law and in the context of the defamation claim against her.

Referring to the many cases in which journalists are sentenced to prison terms in the United States for refusing to reveal their sources, Durity (2006) has called for a functional definition of "journalist" to be formulated, in view of technological change, to shield journalists from compelled source disclosure so as to protect the free flow of information to the public. What she described as a "technology-neutral" approach should perhaps really be called a "communicator-neutral" approach to protecting journalistic sources. This is supported by the opinion of the First US Circuit Court of Appeals that, in an era of changing technology and society, "the news-gathering protections of the First Amendment cannot turn on professional credentials or status" (cited after Kyu Ho Youm 2011).

## Conclusion

The Council of Europe has called for a "new notion of media," but the evidence presented here suggests that the emerging notion of media is not "new," only stripped down to the media's functional essentials, with the elimination in most cases of material and organizational elements. What *is* new is that the long-popular "material" definition, concentrating on the different "devices" for transporting information, is coming to its own "end of history." Only the functional definition—of media, but also, as we have seen, of journalists—can ultimately survive. The convergence-driven realignment of the policy, legal and regulatory frameworks to make them relevant at a time of the integration of telecommunications and the mass media has been, and continues to be, difficult and ridden with controversy. The new process, of readjusting the entire system to this modernized understanding of media and journalism, will be even more complex and prolonged.

The resulting chaos and uncertainty will further exacerbate mounting difficulties as concerns freedom of speech and of the media, resulting from growing tensions at both national and international levels. Efforts to curtail freedom of speech, of the media and of online communication are rife even in democratic countries such as the United States (Reporters sans Frontières, 2011b) and Europe (Reporters sans Frontières, 2011c). So it is all the more important that freedom of expression of online media and media-like activities is safeguarded as effectively as possible, while at the same time required them to comply with professional and ethical standards and to accept greater accountability for their activities.

Returning to the simple Council of Europe continuum of different forms of mediated communication, we can—on the basis of information presented here—adapt it to reflect unfolding processes more fully.

Figure 24.2 shows roughly what types of content fall under each category and what regulatory regime, if any, applies to each category (in the case of the media, it is graduated, as broadcasting is regulated differently from the print media and there are also different degrees of regulation within broadcasting, such as for traditional television channels and for video-on-demand). More importantly, it shows that there is no "natural" progression from one form of mediated communication to a more "advanced" one. As the dotted arrows show, "media-like" activities may join the category of "media" if they meet the criteria presented above. If not, they may remain "media-like," or may ultimately be regarded as non-media mediated

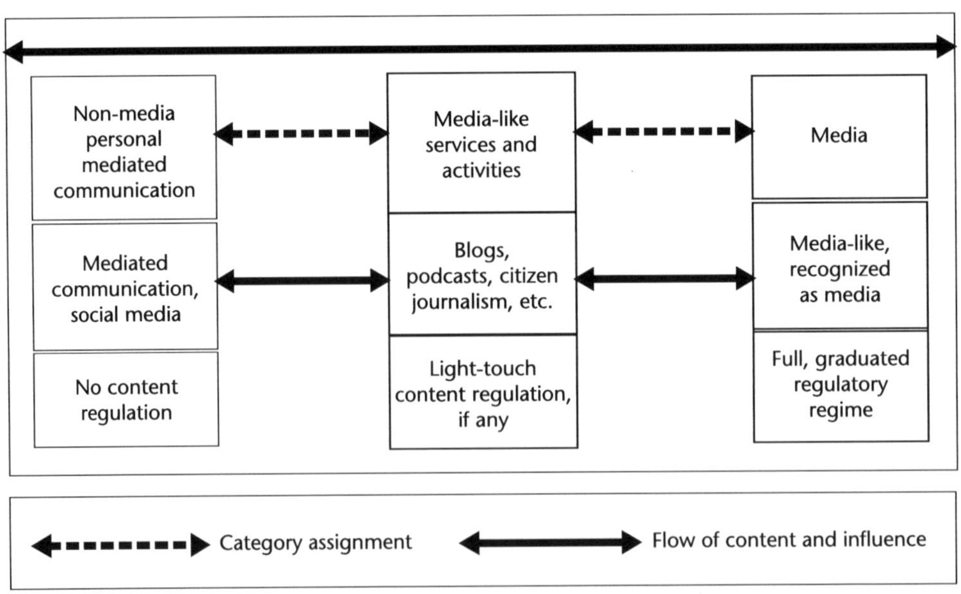


*Figure 24.2* Categories of forms of mediated communication and relations between them

communication. Non-media personal mediated communication can conceivably, if they acquire appropriate features, change into "media-like activities," or even into "media." On the other hand, media outlets may generate "media-like" activities, such as blogs or podcasting, as well as non-media personal mediated communication in the form of social networks attached to a particular media outlet, or a part of its content offer (e.g. a popular television series).

Straight arrows in Figure 24.2 show flows of content and influence, expressive of the interdependence of these three forms of mediated communication. For example, traditional mass media provide most news-related content available on the Internet (Rosenstiel 2011). News organizations are also the biggest contributors of content on Twitter (Wu *et al.* 2011). YouTube, once described as potentially a "post-television" medium (Lister *et al.* 2003), has for some time now been urgently "televising" itself by adding scores of channels of traditional television content (Stross 2010).

As for mutual influence, let us refer only to the fact that bloggers rely on mainstream media for most of the topics they discuss in their blogs, but may perform an agenda-setting function for the media. They may affect political debate by affecting the content of media reportage and commentary about politics. Just as the media can provide a collective interpretive frame for politicians, so blogs can create a menu of interpretive frames for the media to appropriate (Farrell and Drezner 2008: 22).

These increasingly symbiotic relations between the three forms of mediated communication identified in Figures 24.1 and 24.2 (which have been described as the "Internetization of the media" and the "mediatization" of the Internet–Fortunati 2005) obscure dividing lines, and make it harder to identify these forms of communication and to recognize which forms fall under the category of media.

All of this explains why the CoE referred in its *Recommendation CM/Rec(2011)7 on a new notion of media* to a "fluid and multi-dimensional reality of social communication," and points to the necessity of modernizing media-related conceptual, policy and legal frameworks, backed up by appropriate analytical and regulatory tools. Otherwise, it will be increasingly difficult to fully understand the new forms of mediated communication and to know how to approach them in policy and regulatory terms. Council of Europe efforts in this regard are a first step, but a great deal more remains to be done.

## References

Angelotti, E. (2011) 'A broader definition of journalist,' *The New York Times*. 12 December. Online. Available HTTP: http://www.nytimes.com/roomfordebate/2011/12/11/are-all-bloggers-journalists/we-need-a-broader-definition-of-journalist (accessed 11 January 2012).

Austen, I. (2006) 'A blogger who's a court-approved journalist,' *The New York Times*, 27 November. Online. Available HTTP: http://www.nytimes.com/2006/11/27/business/media/27blog.html (accessed 12 September 2011).

Banda, F. (2010) *Citizen Journalism and Democracy in Africa: An Exploratory Study*. Grahamstown: Highway Africa.

Barber, B. R. (2002) *The Ambiguous Effects of Digital Technology on Democracy in a Globalizing World*. Online. Available HTTP: http://www.wissensgesellschaft.org/themen/demokratie/democratic.pdf (accessed 3 January 2012).

Belgrave, K. (2011) 'Bloggers are best at covering local cuts across the UK: So we're being banned,' *OpenDemocracy*, 11 March. Online. Available HTTP: http://www.opendemocracy.net/ourkingdom/kate-belgrave/bloggers-are-best-at-covering-local-cuts-across-uk-so-were-being-banned (accessed 12 September 2011).

Benjamin, S. (2011) 'Rethink shield laws,' *The New York Times*, 12 December. Online. Available HTTP: http://www.nytimes.com/roomfordebate/2011/12/11/are-all-bloggers-journalists/should-we-rethink-shield-laws (accessed 12 September 2011).

Benkler, Y. (2006) *The Wealth of Networks: How Social Production Transforms Markets and Freedom*, New Haven, CT: Yale University Press.

Bowman, S. and Willis, C. (2003) We Media: How Audiences are Shaping the Future of News and Information. Reston, VA.: The Media Center at the American Press Institute. Online. Available HTTP: http://www.hypergene.net/wemedia/download/we_media.pdf (accessed 2 January 2012).

Brown, I. (2010) *Towards a Future Internet: Interrelation between Technological, Social and Economic Trends*, Final Report for DG Information Society and Media. Oxford: Oxford Internet Institute, SCF Associates Ltd.

Committee of Ministers (2009) *Declaration on the Role of Community Media in Promoting Social Cohesion and Intercultural Dialogue*, Strasbourg: Council of Europe. Online. Available HTTP: https://wcd.coe.int/wcd/ViewDoc.jsp?id=1409919&Site=CM&BackColorInternet=9999CC&BackColorIntranet=FFBB55&BackColorLogged=FFAC75 (accessed 2 January 2012).

—— (2011) *Recommendation CM/Rec(2011)7 on a New Notion of Media*, Strasbourg: Council of Europe. Online. Available HTTP: https://wcd.coe.int/ ViewDoc.jsp?id=1835645&Site=CM&BackColorInternet=C3C3C3& BackColorIntranet=EDB021&BackColorLogged=F5D383 (accessed 2 January 2012).

Cooper, A. (2008) 'The bigger tent,' *Columbia Journalism Review*, Sept–Oct. Online. Available HTTP: http://www.cjr.org/essay/the_bigger_tent_1.php (accessed 12 January 2012).

Cormier, S. (2011) 'Not all contributors are citizen journalists,' *Susan Cormier's Blog*. Online. Available HTTP: http://susancormier.com/?p=238 (accessed 12 January 2012).

Council of Europe (2009) *Political Declaration and Resolutions*, First Council of Europe Conference of Ministers Responsible for Media and New Communication Services, 'A new notion of media?' MCM(2009)011, Strasbourg. Online. Available HTTP: http://www.coe.int/t/dghl/standardsetting/media/MCM(2009)011_en_final_web.pdf (accessed 1 January 2012).

Dahlberg, L. (2005a) 'The corporate colonization of online attention and the marginalization of critical communication?' *Journal of Communication Inquiry*, 29(2): 16–180.

—— (2005b) 'The Internet as public sphere or culture industry? From pessimism to hope and back,' *International Journal of Media and Cultural Politics*, 1(1): 93–96.

Dahlgren, P. (2010) 'Public spheres, societal shifts and media modulations,' in J. Gripsrud and L. Weibull (eds.) *Media, Markets & Public Spheres*, Bristol: Intellect.

De Fleur, M. L. and Ball-Rokeach, S. (1982) *Theories of Mass Communication*, 4th edn. New York and London: Longman.

Domingo, D. and Heinonen A. (2008) 'Weblogs and journalism: A typology to explore the blurring boundaries,' *Nordicom Review*, 29(1): 3–15.

Durity, L. (2006) 'Shielding journalist-"Bloggers": The need to protect newsgathering despite the distribution medium,' *Duke Law & Technology Review*, 5: 1–19. Online. Available HTTP: http://www.law.duke.edu/journals/dltr/articles/2006dltr0011.html (accessed 6 September 2011).

Electronic Frontier Foundation (2009) *Bloggers' Legal Guide*. Online. Available HTTP: http://www.eff.org/issues/ bloggers/legal (accessed 5 September 2011).

Euro RSCG Worldwide (2009) *White Paper: Social Life and Social Media*. Online. Available HTTP: http://www.eurorscg.com/flash/pdf/ EuroRSCGWhitePaper_SocialMedia.pdf (accessed 7 January 2012).

European Audiovisual Observatory (2011) *Trends in European Television 2010: Yearbook, Vol. 2*, Strasbourg: EA.

European Commission (1997) *Green Paper on the Convergence of the Telecommunications, Media and Information Technology Sectors, and the Implications for Regulation: Towards an Information Society Approach*, COM(97)623, Brussels: European Union.

European Federation of Journalists (2009) *Trusting Journalism to Make the Best of Democracy*, MCM(2009)020, First Council of Europe Conference of Ministers Responsible for Media and New Communication Services "A new notion of media?", 28–29 May, Reykjavik, Iceland.

European Parliament (2008) *Resolution of 25 September 2008 on Community Media in Europe*, 2008/2011 (INI). Online. Available HTTP: http://www.europarl.europa.eu/sides/getDoc.do?pubRef=-//EP//TEXT+TA+20080925+ITEMS+DOC+XML+V0//EN&language=EN (accessed 6 January 2012).

Farrell, H. and Drezner, D. W. (2008) 'The power and politics of blogs,' *Public Choice*, 134: 15–30. Online. Available HTTP: http://www.danieldrezner.com/research/ blogpaperfinal.pdf

Federal Communications Commission (FCC) (2011) *FCC News*. News Media Information 202 /418-0500. Washington, DC: FCC. Online. Available HTTP: http://transition.fcc.gov/Daily_Releases/Daily_Business/ 2011/db0822/DOC-309224A1.pdf (accessed 13 January 2012).
Fortunati, L. (2005) 'Mediatization of the Net and internetization of the mass media,' *Gazette*, 67(1): 27–44.
García-Avilés, J. (2010) ' "Citizen journalism" in European television websites: Lights and shadows of user generated content,' *Observatorio (OBS*) Journal*, 4(4): 251–263.
Gillmor, D. (2004) *We the Media. Grassroots Journalism by the People, for the People*. Sebastopol, CA: O'Reilly Media, Inc.
—— (2008) 'What ethics should bloggers have?' in D. Gillmor *Handbook for Bloggers and Cyber-Dissidents*, Paris: Reporters sans Frontières. Online. Available HTTP: http://en.rsf.org/IMG/pdf/guide_gb_md-2.pdf
—— (2010) *Mediactive*. Online. Available HTTP: http://mediactive.com/wp-content/uploads/2010/12/mediactive_gillmor.pdf (accessed 13 February 2012).
Goban-Klas, T. (2007) 'Media i medioznawstwo,' in Chudzi ski (ed.), *Słownik wiedzy o mediach*, Warszawa: Wydawnictwo Szkolne PWN.
Grünwald, A. (2003) *Final Report on Possible Options for the Review of the European Convention on Transfrontier Television*, T-TT (2003) 2, Strasbourg: Standing Committee on Transfrontier Television, Council of Europe.
Hamilton, G. (2011) 'Quebec mulls "privileged" professional journalists,' *National Post*, 24 August.
Hellsten, I., Leydesdorff, L. and Wouters, P. (2006) 'Multiple presents: How search engines rewrite the past,' *New Media & Society*, 8(6): 901–924.
Hilden, J. (2011) 'Should bloggers be deemed journalists?' *Counterpunch*, 27 December. Online. Available HTTP: http://www.counterpunch.org/2011/12/27/should-bloggers-be-deemed-journalists/
Hyunjin, K. and McAllister, M. (2011) 'Selling you and your clicks: Examining the audience commodification of Google,' *tripleC—Cognition, Communication, Co-operation*, 9(2): 141–153.
Jakubowicz, K. (2009) *A New Notion of Media? Media and Media-Like Content and Activities on New Communication Services*, Strasbourg: Media and Information Society Division, Directorate General of Human Rights and Legal Affairs, Council of Europe.
—— (2012) 'Battle of the paradigms: Defining the object and objectives of media/communication policy,' in N. Just and M. Puppis (eds.) *Trends in Communication Policy Research: New Theories, Methods and Subjects*, Bristol: Intellect.
Jeffries, L. W. (1986) *Mass Media: Processes and Effects*, Prospect Heights, IL: Waveland Press, Inc.
Jurrat, N. (2011) *Citizen Journalism and the Internet*, Mapping Digital Media Reference Series No. 4. London: Open Society Media Program, Open Society Foundation.
Kalathil, S. (2008) *Scaling a Changing Curve: Traditional Media Development and the New Media*, Report to the Center for International Media Assistance, Washington, DC: Center for International Media Assistance. National Endowment for Democracy.
Keen, A. (2008) *Kult amatora. jak internet niszczy kulture*. Warsaw: Wydawnictwo Akademickie i Profesjonalne.
Kenix, L. (2009) 'Blogs as alternative,' *Journal of Computer-Mediated Communication*, 14: 790–822.
Kyu Ho Y. (2011) 'According to the law,' *The New York Times*, 12 December. Online. Available HTTP: http://www.nytimes.com/roomfordebate/2011/12/11/are-all-bloggers-journalists/according-to-the-law
Lasota, A. (2010) 'Czy media sa nowe: Próba polemiki,' *Studia Medioznawcze*, 1(40): 169–180.
Latzer, M. (2009) 'Convergence revisited: Toward a modified pattern of communications governance,' *Convergence*, 15(4): 411–426.
Leadbeater, C. and Miller, P. (2004) *The Pro-Am Revolution: How Enthusiasts Are Changing Our Economy and Society*, London: Demos.
—— *et al.* (2008a) *User-Created Content: Supporting a Participative Information Society*, Montpellier: IDATE, TNO, IviR.
Le Borgne Bachschmidt, F. (2008b) 'ANNEX 4: Overview of self- and co-regulatory measures for the UCC sector,' *User-Created Content: Supporting a Participative Information Society*, Montpellier: IDATE, TNO, IviR.
Lenhart, A. and Fox, S. (2006) *Bloggers: A Portrait of the Internet's New Storytellers*, Washington, DC: Pew Internet & American Life Project. Online. Available HTTP: http://www.pewtrusts.org/uploadedFiles/wwwpewtrustsorg/Reports/Society_and_the_Internet/PIP_Bloggers_071906.pdf (accessed 10 January 2012).

Lievrouw, L. A. and Livingstone S. (2006) 'Introduction to the updated student edition,' in L. A. Lievrouw and S. Livingstone (eds.) *Handbook of New Media: Social Shaping and Social Consequences*, Rev. edn. London: Sage. Online. Available HTTP: http://eprints.lse.ac.uk/21502/1/ Introduction_to_the_updated_student_edition_ (LSERO).pdf

Lister, M. *et al.* (2003) *New Media: A Critical Introduction*, London and New York: Routledge.

Lomborg, S. (2009) 'Navigating the blogosphere: Towards a genre-based typology of weblogs,' *First Monday*, 14(5). Online. Available HTTP: http://firstmonday.org/htbin/cgiwrap/bin/ojs/ index.php/fm/article/viewArticle/2329/2178 (accessed 10 September 2011).

Matheson, D. (2004) 'Weblogs and the epistemology of the news: Some trends in online journalism,' *New Media & Society*, 6(4): 443–468.

Mathiason, J. (2004) *Internet Governance: The State of Play*, Internet Governance Project. Online. Available HTTP: http://www.internetgovernance.org/pdf/ig-sop-final.pdf (accessed 6 January 2012).

Mauriac, L. and Riché, P. (2009) 'Online journalism: Transposition or transformation?' *Eurozine*. Online. Available HTTP: http://www.eurozine.com/articles/2009–05-22-mauriacriche-en.html# (accessed 9 February 2012).

Mckinley, J. (2006) 'Blogger jailed after defying court orders,' *The New York Times*, 2 August.

McQuail, D. (2005) *McQuail's Mass Communication Theory*, London: Sage Publications.

—— (2008) 'Journalism as a public occupation: Alternative images,' in N. Carpentier *et al.*, (eds.) *Democracy, Journalism and Technology: New Developments in an Enlarged Europe*, Tartu: Tartu University Press.

Mikko, M. (2008) *Explanatory Statement: Report on Concentration and Pluralism in the Media in the European Union*, 2007/2253(INI), Brussels: European Parliament. Online. Available HTTP: http://www.europarl.europa.eu/sides/getDoc.do?type=REPORT&reference=A6–2008-0303&language=EN#title2 (accessed 12 January 2012).

Morris, M. and Ogan, C. (1996) 'The Internet as mass medium,' *Journal of Communication*, 46(1): 39–50.

Mueller, M. (1999) 'Digital convergence and its consequences,' *The Public/Javnost*, 6(3): 11–28.

National Association of Citizen Journalists (n.d.) 'What do citizen journalists do?' Online. Available HTTP: http://nacj.us/ (accessed 12 January 2012).

Noam, E. (2001) *Will the Internet Be Bad for Democracy?* New York: Graduate School of Business, Columbia University. Online. Available HTTP: http://www.citi.columbia.edu/elinoam/articles/int_bad_dem.htm (accessed 3 January 2012).

—— (2003) *The Internet: Still Wide Open and Competitive*? OII Internet Issue Brief No. 1, Oxford: Oxford Internet Institute.

*Obsidian Finance Group, LLC* v *Cox* (2011) No. CV-11–57-HZ, F. Supp. 2d.

Park, D. (2009) 'Blogging with authority: Strategic positioning in political blogs,' *International Journal of Communication*, 3: 250–273.

Reporters sans Frontières (2011a) *Internet Enemies*, Paris: Reporters sans Frantières. Online. Available HTTP: http://march12.rsf.org/i/Internet_Enemies.pdf (accessed 13 January 2012).

—— (2011b) *Domestic Reality Does Not Match Bold Words on Internet Freedom of Expression*, Paris: Reporters sans Frontières. Online. Available HTTP: http://en.rsf.org/etats-unis-domestic-reality-does-not-match-02–11-2011,41324.html (accessed 13 January 2012).

—— (2011c) 2010 *World Press Freedom Index*, Paris: Reporters sans Frontières. Online. Available HTTP: http://www.rsf.org/IMG/CLASSEMENT_2011/GB/C_GENERAL_GB.pdf (accessed 13 January 2012).

Rosen, R. J. (2011) 'Why we should stop asking whether bloggers are journalists,' *The Atlantic*. Online. Available HTTP: http://www.theatlantic.com/technology/ archive/2011/12/why-we-should-stop-asking-whether-bloggers-are-journalists/249864/ (accessed 12 January 2012).

Rosenstiel, T. (2011) 'Five myths about the future of journalism,' *The Washington Post*. Online. Available HTTP: http://www.washingtonpost.com/opinions/five-myths-about-the-future-of-journalism/2011/04/05/AF5UxiuC_story.html (accessed 14 January 2012).

Sanchez, G. (2003) *Legislation on Community Radio Broadcasting: Comparative Study of the Legislation of 13 Countries*, Paris: UNESCO.

Singer, J. (2005) 'The political j-blogger: "Normalizing" a new media form to fit old norms and practices,' *Journalism*, 6(2): 173–198.

Smith, T. (2008) *Power to the People*: *Social Media Tracker Wave 3*, New York: Universal McCann.

Strate, L. (2004) 'A media ecology review,' *Communication Research Trends*, 23(2): 3–48.

Stross, R. (2010) 'YouTube wants you to sit and stay awhile,' *The New York Times*, 29 May. Online. Available HTTP: http://www.nytimes.com/2010/05/30/business/ 30digi.html?th&emc=th (accessed 14 January 2012).

Sunstein, C. (2001a) 'The future of free speech,' *The Little Magazine*, 2(2). Online. Available HTTP: http://www.littlemag.com/mar-apr01/cass.html (accessed 3 January 2012).

—— (2001b) 'The daily we: Is the Internet really a blessing for democracy?' *Boston Review*, Summer. Online. Available HTTP: http://bostonreview.net/BR26.3/sunstein.html (accessed 3 January 2012).

Verhulst, S. (2002) 'About scarcities and intermediaries: The regulatory paradigm shift of digital content reviewed,' in L. Lievrouw and S. Livingstone (eds.) *The Handbook of New Media*, London: Sage.

Wall, M. (2005) 'Blogs of war: Weblogs as news,' *Journalism*. 6(2): 153–172.

Weinberger, D. (2009) 'Transparency is the new objectivity,' *JOHO, The Blog*. Online. Available HTTP: http://www.hyperorg.com/blogger/2009/07/19/transparency-is-the-new-objectivity/ (accessed 12 January 2012).

Werkers, E. *et al.* (2008) 'Ethics and rights for online journalists: Inseparable and obligatory?' Paper submitted for "The End of Journalism?" International Journalism Conference, Centre for International Media Analysis, Luton, UK, 17–18 October.

Wu, S. *et al.* (2011) *Who Says What to Whom on Twitter*, International World Wide Web Conference Committee. Online. Available HTTP: http://research.yahoo.com/ pub3386 (accessed 14 January 2012).

Wunsch-Vincent, S. and Vickery, G. (2007) *Participative Web: User-Created Content*, DSTI/ICCP/IE (2006)7/Final, Paris: Working Party on the Information Economy, OECD.

# 25

# To "be let alone" in social media

## The market and regulation of privacy

*Katharine Sarikakis and Dimitris Tsapogas*

### Introduction

The issue of privacy, often an afterthought in media policy, is becoming much more central to the way in which media are imagined and implemented. Privacy is rapidly becoming inextricably linked to the world of digital communications and social media. As a policy issue, privacy is multidimensional, not only in terms of its regulation, but also in terms of the normative aspects surrounding the *right* to privacy. Political, philosophical and sociocultural terms lie at the core of the privacy debate as it is connected to personal autonomy and democratic practice, personal development and liberty.

Until recently, concerns about privacy were relatively clearly distinguished as "invasions" of privacy across two realms. The most publicly debated aspect has been that referring to the case in which the private sphere is invaded by the media. This is mostly associated with popular media intruding into, or reporting on, the lives and private affairs of celebrities or politicians. This is, for example, the issue that frames the public perception of the role of paparazzi in the death of Diana Princess of Wales. The other dimension is that of state surveillance of citizens' behavior in their private lives, where examples of intrusion into the private sphere of "common" people have marked the 1960s and 1970s in Europe and the United States, and saw a revival in the era of anti-terrorism (e.g. the US Patriot Act). With the end of the Cold War, such phenomena were understood in the public mind to be rendered irrelevant, yet new forms of state risks and crises have framed the agenda of privacy in both law and politics.

In the second decade of the new millennium, privacy occupies a precarious position not only in law, but also in practices in the daily routines of media and related corporations vis-à-vis their users, customers and audiences. Moreover, the issue of privacy no longer affects only elites, but is increasingly important in the everyday lives of ordinary media users. Authorities can, often almost unchecked, monitor citizens in their political and civic lives, putting both legal and legitimate behaviors under surveillance for the purposes of profiling. It is not always clear where the boundaries are, and whether such policies are trying to protect the citizen or protect the state. The US Supreme Court raised such a concern in January 2012 by interpreting the Fourth Amendment against police searches using modern technological tools (Barnes 2012). The ruling in *United States* v *Jones* states that the police cannot use the Global Positioning System (GPS) without having been granted a related warrant from a judge. This decision overturned the conviction of a suspected drug dealer whose car was monitored for twenty-eight days by a GPS device that had been secretly attached by the police. In another case, John Catt and his daughter, peace campaigners with no police records, were placed under surveillance at more than eighty authorized protests by a secretive National Public Order Intelligence Unit. This unit has been logging an extensive national database of thousands of protesters who were classified as "domestic extremists" (Evans and Lewis 2011). Combine this with the recently available high-tech surveillance software and their diminishing cost, and police and governments have now unprecedented power to monitor communicative transactions. Indicatively, the Metropolitan Police, the largest police force in the United Kingdom, has recently acquired state-of-the-art software that is able to map and depict three-dimensional graphic information captured from social networking sites, satellite navigation equipment, mobile phones, financial transactions and Internet Protocol network logs (Gallagher and Syal 2011).

The question of "privacy" has not attracted much attention among media scholars—as compared with legal scholars—with the exception of studies on the law and ethics of journalism practice, and especially around questions of public interest vs. the individual right to privacy. That was the case until recent years, as the increasing popularity of media platforms allows direct connection among users in both semi-private and semi-public ways. What is new is that the possibilities and cultures of self-disclosure are combined with the technical capabilities of media platforms and sites to collect information on their users. These companies do so without always and/or consistently and effectively revealing details about their practices or being monitored about the legality of these practices. New technological capabilities not only facilitate more freedom of connection, association and communication among people, but also leave the personal and individual level of users more vulnerable to intrusion and manipulation. As such, the implications of these two parallel realities in shaping the relation of citizens with the media and the media's role in the democratic process are important for the communication policy scholar.

This chapter seeks to explore the profound shift in the ways in which privacy is gaining a mainstream position in public debate and policy, and the ways in which it is understood, applied or operationalized as a right, regulation, and possibly even as a political claim in relation to the widespread use of social media. It discusses the ways in which social media have challenged public approaches to, and understanding of, privacy by moving away from its original definition as the right to "be let alone." Privacy as a concern is now linked not only to the intrusive powers of the state, of big traditional media, or information technologies, but to media platforms as many-to-many communicative vehicles. In the world of social media, accepted norms and legal boundaries of what constitutes privacy are forcing policymakers to revisit existing regulatory frameworks. The challenges of such a task are inherent in the aim to protect citizens' privacy rights without stifling freedom of expression and association, while at the same time pursuing this protection by regulating what is largely a global issue in national terms. The following pages briefly discuss the concept of privacy, before moving on to explore its market and regulatory dimensions as factors that contribute actively to the construction of a new state of affairs between citizens and communication.

## Privacy as the right to "be let alone"

The concept of privacy has been used to express variations in the role and scope of a sense of the "personal" as an autonomous and emancipated sphere. Philosophical traditions and their translation into politics tend to emphasize certain understandings of "privacy." Political and normative dimensions of privacy, as well as regulatory debates about the nature of the right to privacy, its limitations and possible contexts, demonstrate the centrality and complexity of the concept in the self-imagination and self-governance of human beings and societies. One strong facet of privacy is that of confirming boundaries between an intimate and a more public life for an individual.

For a better understanding of the policy evolution of privacy, it is useful to review four main philosophical traditions that have been correlated with it (Scoglio 1998). Privacy is discussed, in particular, through the principle of "utility" (utilitarianism)—that is, effort for the maximization of pleasure. According to this approach, privacy can only be considered under financial terms, an approach that can frequently be found in the history of privacy policies. Another philosophical position places the "individual" as the core engine of social organization (neoliberalism). Neoliberalism, still highly informed by the centrality of personal or individual needs and interests, considers privacy as the upholding of a sphere within which personal choice aims at sensual and financial gain, and in which intervention is undesirable. Communitarianism, in contrast, treats privacy as useful for the "lower acquisitive, sensual, and sexual nature" of human beings (Scoglio 1998: 33). According to communitarianist moral theory, life should be as public as possible, and privacy can only support the public, without otherwise having a "meaning" of its own. Scoglio notes that these philosophical understandings of privacy fall short of developing a comprehensive understanding of privacy, because they stop at either its "public side" (communitarianism), "property" (utilitarianism), or "personality" (neoliberalism) (ibid.: 35). As Scoglio argues, a "transformational and transpersonal political theory" would understand privacy as the way in which to ethical interiority (ibid.: 38). Warren and Brandeis were directed by the very same transpersonal inspiration when they developed the now widely used privacy concept as "the right to be let alone" (ibid.: 38).

Warren and Brandeis' work has, for more than a century, unquestionably influenced the way in which the right to privacy has been perceived and regulated. The authors noticed the implications that the growth of technology had on media practices, and more specifically, on the press: "Instantaneous photographs and newspaper enterprise have invaded the sacred precincts of private and domestic life and numerous mechanical devices threaten to make good the prediction that 'what is whispered in the closet shall be proclaimed from the rooftops' " (Warren and Brandeis 1890: 195). In particular, they argued for the protection of the right to determine to what extent and under which conditions an individual's thoughts "sentiments, and emotions shall be communicated to others" (ibid.: 198). Privacy law in the United States was directly influenced by this approach, in constitutional and statutory law (Solove 2008). Warren and Brandeis were concerned with the impact of the social world on the space of interiority, deep thought and spiritual connection among people, in particular the space of family and intimacy. In this sense, contemplation and spirituality (as an affair of the mental state of human beings freed from the excesses of materiality—but not asceticism) can only be achieved when individuals are safe in a "quiet" place, by renewing and understanding eternal moral principles (Scoglio 1998: 196). Privacy allows the exercise of judgement and the rule of reason as an aspect of human conduct that promotes democratic deliberation and ethical self-development. Privacy for Warren and Brandeis, as well as for

Scoglio, was not subordinated to property, but the other way around, since, for example, economic and political concentration and "bigness" (of business, of state) insults human dignity and leads to corruption, among other things (Scoglio 1998: 199). The essay on the "right to be let alone" was a profound work that promoted the development of privacy as a concept.

The idea of privacy is related to the desire to act within a zone that is "private," away from the scrutiny of others. Thus it defines an individual's relationship with society and implies the existence of the "public," which is a prerequisite of its existence. Jürgen Habermas has highlighted the importance of the public sphere in forming public opinion in his book *The Structural Transformation of the Public Sphere* (1989). Habermas emphasized that the existence of a private sphere is also necessary to keep important parts of our social lives protected from the control of the ruling powers.

Critics, such as Thomson (1975), reject the value of a specific right to privacy on the basis that all private interests can be explained and protected by other basic rights, such as the right to property and security. Posner (1981) argues that privacy is protected in ways that are economically inefficient, and that it should be defended only when access to information would reduce its value. Bork (1990) argues that, in the US context, the right to privacy does not derive from any pre-existing right or natural law, but instead is a newly created right with no foundation in the Constitution or the US Bill of Rights. More recently, Fuchs (2011) claims that academic analyses of privacy tend to focus only on its positive aspects, ignoring possible negative issues related to its political economy. According to this view, privacy is an "ideological mechanism that helps reproducing and deepening inequality" (Fuchs 2011: 4). As an example, Fuchs refers to the high level of anonymity of bank accounts and transactions that can be found in certain countries, such as Switzerland, and which increase social disparities by allowing money laundering and by hiding wealth.

This chapter views privacy as a realm related to the right of self-governance for individuals and their communities. This right does not extend to institutions or organizations. Despite the rich debate on privacy between philosophers, legal theorists, jurists and academics, it is difficult to describe privacy in a single way or as one single idea, because its meaning and usage have been linked to many individual rights (Solove 2008). Privacy is linked to both positive and negative freedoms. In terms of positive freedom, privacy expresses the set of rights for a person's ability to control four broad areas of legal concern: freedom of personal autonomy; the right to control personal information; the right to control property; and the right to control and protect personal physical space (Mills 2008). As a negative freedom, privacy is understood as the absence of invasion of privacy by the government, business, or other actors into the space considered personal (Debatim *et al.* 2009).

In relation to autonomy and information, privacy is the freedom that allows individuals to make choices without the fear of being scrutinized and judged by others, a process that involves a "safe" place to withdraw and contemplate. For Gibbs, "privacy sensitive" information is therefore information considered "off limits," intimate information, which will not add to the general public interest, but rather would affect personal judgement on the basis of bias (Gibbs 1995, in Doyle and Balgaric 2005: 42). On the subject of privacy and information, Solove's taxonomy of privacy issues (2008) is mainly related to informational privacy. He identifies two ways of collecting information: surveillance and interrogation. For Solove, the processing and dissemination of information are important privacy issues. Finally, Solove identifies two types of privacy invasion: intrusion and decisional interference. Clearly, this taxonomy is concerned with the role of external actors and the process by which they intervene and cancel out claims of privacy from an individual's point of view.

Gibbs's attention to community standards as those setting the bar of interiority and privacy in intimacy provides an important element in the debate on privacy in social media. While Solove's taxonomy problematizes (mainly industrial and state) practices of privacy invasion through informational monitoring and manipulation, the element of what is accepted by the "community"—and perhaps, for this discussion, by the social media community of users, if one can refer to users as a community—is an argument appearing in speeches by powerful social media owners (e.g. the concept and notion of privacy—what is acceptable to observe and what is not, what kinds of personal information are acceptable to collect and which ones are not). This argument is in a somewhat fluid state, particularly because of the voluntary nature of self-disclosure in new communication environments. Nevertheless, the desire for self-disclosure and its facilitation should not be conflated with a desire to reject privacy as a right or necessary element of self-governance on behalf of the "users." The situation is even more complex when it comes to constantly "pushing" the boundaries of privacy-related accepted norms, as the following section on social media strategies briefly discusses. These are all elements that are new in the relationship between citizens and communication, and raise questions about privacy anew and intensively, as they have become present in everyday media use.

## *Privacy and the political economy of socialization*

Social media and social networking sites (SNS) have risen sharply in popularity and widespread use, allowing new forms of socialization, sharing and communication between people. This new state of communication raises new privacy questions. The sheer numbers of users and the fact that their communication is very public are new factors, unknown at the time of Warren and Brandeis.

SNS are discussed in the literature in a variety of ways. Ofcom, the UK's communication regulatory authority, defines SNS as:

> . . .sites, which allow users to set up online profiles or personal homepages, and develop an online social network. The profile page functions as the user's own webpage and includes profile information ranging from their date of birth, gender, religion, politics and hometown.
>
> (*Ofcom 2008: 10*)

The main point about SNS is that they are popular with millions of users worldwide and they promote a self-exhibiting, self-disclosing culture. In that respect, a great deal of personal information becomes public or semi-public without the users entirely understanding the ramifications for their privacy.[1] Given the fact that most users are young people, this means that new conditions and understandings of privacy as imposed or initiated by SNS will become established as the new norm very quickly.[2] It is therefore important to understand what loss of privacy and changing notions of privacy mean in the context of SNS.[3]

1 Friendster was the first SNS launched in 2002, with MySpace and LinkedIn following in 2003, Facebook in 2004 and Twitter in 2006.

2 According to Alexa (2012), at the time of writing, Facebook is the second most popular website in the world. Twitter is positioned as the ninth most visited website in the world, while LinkedIn, a business-related SNS mainly used for professional networking, is sixteenth. Friendster discontinued its SNS in 2011, while MySpace has been facing an ongoing decline, losing approximately 50 million users over the course of 2010 and 2011 (Whittaker 2011).

3 In particular, 25.4 percent of users are between 15 and 24 years old and 24.3 percent of users are between 25 and 34 years old (comScore 2011).

Aimeur (2010: 173–174) categorized privacy risks occurring from SNS usage as follows: (a) SNS users are always subject to *security risks* and may experience different kinds of online attacks, such as *identity theft, phishing, scam, predator* and other *cybercrime*; (b) the *reputation* and *credibility* of users are also threatened by the continuous sharing of data to a wider circle of people; (c) SNS companies are building and maintaining user profiles, which they then sell to third parties for advertising—a procedure that is called *profiling*. As research has shown, although SNS give their users the option to set their own privacy preferences, the settings seem to be long, confusing and complicated (Aimeur *et al.* 2010; Kirkpatrick 2010; Grimmelmann 2009; Stutzman *et al.* 2011). Realistically, only experienced and concerned users will spend the time needed to overcome these difficulties (Aimeur *et al.* 2010). This means that the vast majority of unsuspecting users rely on the system and use its predefined settings, allowing the private corporations of SNS to collect data and to monitor and profile them. The majority of users do not even read the SNS privacy policy (Aimeur *et al.* 2010; Grimmelmann 2009).

Other factors that may influence users' behavior online and shape their disclosure practices include the general understanding of the concept of privacy (Stutzman *et al.* 2010; Livingstone 2008; Livingstone and Brake 2010) and the acceptance of the existence of identifiers—that is, the placement of cookies in their browsers by companies (Cranor *et al.* 1999). The relationship between user attitudes toward privacy and the value and type of content shared can be mediated by informing users about company privacy policy and by empowering their control over personal privacy settings (Acquisti and Gross 2000; Stutzman *et al.* 2010).

Although young people claim, or appear to be, both concerned about and aware of privacy issues (boyd and Hargittai 2010), they usually do not take any precautionary measures to protect themselves (Ngeno *et al.* 2010; boyd and Hargittai 2010; Grimmelmann 2009; Ofcom 2008; Campisi *et al.* 2009). This is what Susan Barnes (2006) calls the "privacy paradox." Livingstone (2008) confirmed that privacy issues were of high importance for most of the young users who participated; in her study she explains that young people's notion of privacy is not about the kind of information provided, but about their need to control who has access to that information.

Lewis *et al.* (2008) demonstrated that there are four predictors of changing privacy settings. A student is very likely to have a private profile when their student friends have private profiles, when they use Facebook regularly, when the student is female, and when the student favors relatively popular music (Lewis *et al.* 2008: 94). Finally, Lewis *et al.* suggested that safety is proposed to be another motivating factor. Young girls are targeted by online predators and this may offer an explanation of the reasons why women apply stricter privacy settings than men. By considering privacy as a safety measure, women's potential for public engagement is possibly affected (boyd and Hargittai 2010). Beyond gender, disclosure evolves into identity construction that is directly associated with popularity: "the people who are most popular are those whose identity construction is most actively participated in by others" (Christofides *et al.* 2009: 343). Therefore, for an individual, access to personal information and thus to popularity may be more important than the risks of disclosure. Still, public disclosure is closely linked with reputation. It is widely known that employers are checking users' profiles in SNS to evaluate their applications (Kirkpatrick 2010). Grimmelmann points out that information shared online will remain there and, as he emphatically describes, "either society will significantly adjust its privacy norms or a lot of people are going to have some lifelong regrets about their youthful Internet indiscretions" (Grimmelmann 2009: 1181). Furthermore, privacy issues not only occur when an individual shares personal data, but also when their online friends reveal personal information about them with or without their consent (Aimeur *et al.* 2010; Squicciarini *et al.* 2010; Kirkpatrick 2010; Grimmelmann 2009).

## *Privacy policies of SNS: The chronicles of Facebook*

SNS companies are, by and large, private, for-profit corporations with a global reach and international profiles. They engage in actively shaping the debate on privacy on digital media through the ways in which they design the technologies of privacy on their sites and the options that they make available to users—the ways in which they revise and revisit these policies often causing strong reactions from users—and through their public discourses around privacy issues. One of the most controversial sites in this regard is Facebook. The company has changed its privacy policy several times in the past, and has combined technological intervention and corporate policy to push the boundaries of acceptable privacy standards. In 2004, Facebook accepted registration by university students from specific campuses. The information provided by its early members was only shared by default within the same campus. As Facebook opened to a wider public and allowed developers to create applications integrated within the site, users' personal data was shared with third-party companies. Facebook then brought out new privacy settings, according to which users would decide which third parties would access their data.

The steady "experimentation" of Facebook with the boundaries of its market—the users and advertisers—continued through a series of technologies developed to manipulate (collect, manage, store, etc.) data provided by its users during their login sessions and participation on its web pages. None of the stages described below were preceded by a warning to users or in consultation with them. A controversial application, News Feed, introduced in 2006, brought to users' screens random shared updates from their listed "friends." Users reacted negatively to a function that they perceived to be of significant difference—that is, between actively visiting someone's Facebook page and automatically receiving updates in the News Feed (boyd and Hargittai 2010). The Facebook group "Students Against Facebook News Feed" listed, at the time of the research, 700,000 users; combined with the public outcry by privacy advocates, the company was forced to redesign privacy settings so that users had more control over what was allowed to appear on their friends' News Feeds (boyd and Hargittai 2010).

One year later, Facebook developed and introduced Beacon, an advertising platform that collected data from external websites visited by Facebook users and published it on News Feed. It did not ask for users' permission to share purchase information to Facebook friends (Kirkpatrick 2010); a small drop-down menu, asking the user if they did not want to share the data, appeared only for a few seconds. A class action lawsuit occurred from exposed users. Four weeks after the introduction of Beacon, Facebook founder and chief executive Mark Zuckerberg admitted publicly: "We've made a lot of mistakes building this feature, but we've made even more with how we've handled them [. . .] we simply did a bad job with this release and I apologize for it" (Kirkpatrick 2010: 251). Facebook abandoned the Beacon platform in September 2009—and introduced a much bigger and more intrusive app, Facebook Connect.[4] This feature allows thousands of websites to interact with Facebook and automatically update users' News Feeds on the site.

4 As of February 2010, more than 80,000 websites were using Facebook Connect, including about half of the 100 most-visited websites in the world (Kirkpatrick 2010).

Controlling privacy settings has become increasingly complex, as each new privacy setting starts from the default position of automatically "sharing" in a broader network. Research has shown that default settings matter, because most people do not change them (boyd and Hargittai 2010; Grimmelmman 2009; Ofcom 2008). In January 2010, Zuckerberg claimed that social norms had evolved and people had become increasingly comfortable with sharing much of their information to a wider audience (Johnson 2010). That statement followed Facebook's change in privacy settings in December 2009 when users were asked to choose between two options: "Everyone" or "Old settings." The first option, to make more content available to the public and to developers, was provided as the default, while the second option was to keep the old privacy settings. Users were asked to choose before continuing on to the site, and it is likely that many users clicked through quickly, accepting the default (boyd and Hargittai 2010). A number of privacy organizations and the Electronic Privacy Information Center (EPIC) complained to the US Federal Trade Commission about this practice.[5] Facebook responded that the way in which the new privacy settings were introduced was successful, citing that one third of users who had never changed their privacy settings had done so after the new settings were introduced (boyd and Hargittai 2010; Kirkpatrick 2010).

Like Facebook, most other SNS platforms do not provide clear information regarding which data they obtain from their users and the ways in which they use it (Aimeur *et al.* 2010). In theory, as Eecke and Truyens (2010) suggest, both SNS platforms and users can decide the fate of personal data, and can thus be considered as both data processors and data controllers. In practice, however, it is clear that SNS platforms see themselves as the owners of that information (Aimeur *et al.* 2010). Grimmelmann (2009) argues that if Facebook's users were to read, and more important, understand Facebook's privacy policy, they would be aware that it actually does not protect their privacy and thus does not pose any restrictions to the company's policies.

Concerns over privacy are not, however, "confined" to the technologies visible by Facebook users. There have been media reports about more sinister and ethically questionable methods of data surveillance and manipulation invisible to the user (Acohido 2011). According to the reports, Facebook tracks Internet users' online behaviors not only while they are using their Facebook accounts, but also when they are logged off, and Facebook also tracks users not subscribed to its service. By placing different kinds of identifiers on Internet browsers, every time users revisit any Facebook.com page or a third-party web page that has embedded one of Facebook's features, such as the "Like" option, the installed cookie "informs" Facebook about the date, time and web address of the website visited, as well as other unique characteristics, such as IP address, screen resolution, operating system and browser version. All of users' Internet activity is saved in a log and kept for ninety days.[6]

## Regulating privacy

The problem with privacy issues on SNS is that these companies are not entirely regulated the same way as Internet service providers (ISPs), both generally and in relation to privacy, on

5 EPIC is a public interest research group based in Washington, DC, and was established in 1994 to focus public attention on emerging civil issues and to protect privacy, the First Amendment, and constitutional values.

6 Whereas if the user is logged in to Facebook, the "session" cookie also keeps records of the user's name, email address, friends and all of the data that can be found on his or her profile.

how they manage the data they collect.[7] It is therefore worth looking at the broader privacy and data protection policy environment in Western societies that shape the possibilities and conditions for data manipulation and protection in the context of digital media. Policies that are designed to regulate privacy focus on the "fate" of personal information and how this is manipulated. The underlying assumption is largely related to the sense of self-governance and control over information about a person that is considered too "personal" to be freely available to third parties, such as information related to the intimate sphere of sexuality and love and relevant "lifestyle" choices, information about one's cultural and political inclinations; intimate details about everyday life and persons related to these aspects. The intimate sphere and the public are not always clearly separated; for example, as feminist activists first declared, "the personal is political," meaning that the private person enters the public arena within which the intimate dimensions of one's life can hinder or encourage her participation in public affairs. Perhaps it is not important that these two spheres be distinctively separate, as communicative habits on SNS demonstrate a blurring of their boundaries. What is at stake is the principle and praxis of controlling the conditions under which intimate details and personal information become public, and to what degree, as a matter of personal autonomy. Moreover, it is of the utmost importance that privacy is considered to be the zone of autonomy of a citizen (in the broadest sense) vis-à-vis the state and state authorities. The implications are, of course, far-reaching and important, which is the reason why the right to privacy is recognized in international legal instruments under the supervision of the United Nations. More specifically, in the International Covenant on Civil and Political Rights (ICCPR) the right to privacy is protected under Article 17, which states:

> 1. No one shall be subjected to arbitrary or unlawful interference with his privacy, family, home or correspondence, nor to unlawful attacks upon his honor and reputation. 2. Everyone has the right to the protection of the law against such interference or attacks.

In our technology-centered times, correspondence takes various forms, from emails to messages on SNS, as well as the generation of computerized information. The United Nations Guidelines on Computerized Personal Data Files provide specific principles to states, and at the same time, define cases in which they may not be valid: These Guidelines "should be made applicable, in the first instance, to all public and private computerized files as well as by means of optional extension and subject to appropriate adjustments, to manual files" (UN 1990: 3). However, as the Guidelines clearly mention, a different approach "may be authorized only if they are necessary to protect national security, public order, public health or morality, as well as, inter alia, the rights and freedoms of others [. . .] provided that such departures are expressly specified in a law or equivalent regulation [. . .]" (ibid.: 2).

In Europe, the European Convention of Human Rights issued by the Council of Europe recognizes the right to privacy under Article 8: "Everyone has the right to respect for his private and family life, his home and his correspondence." There are limitations on this right,

7 For instance, the European Parliament and the Council demands that its member states retain specific kinds of data generated or processed in connection with the provision of publicly available electronic communications services, or of public communications networks (European Commission 2011).

however, in the case of "national security, public safety or the economic well-being of the country, for the prevention of disorder or crime, for the protection of health or morals, or for the protection of the rights and freedoms of others."

The Council of Europe's 1981 Convention for the Protection of Individuals with regard to Automatic Processing of Personal Data (known as "Convention 108") demands that collaborated states respect every individual's right to privacy. The Consultative Committee of the Council of Europe is currently considering updating the Convention to synchronize it with the fast-growing telecommunication technologies (Richter 2011). Furthermore, within the EU Charter of Fundamental Rights, data protection is included as an autonomous fundamental right under Article 8, where "an independent authority" is also responsible for controlling the application of the rules.

The creation of the Data Protection Directive (Directive 95/46/EC) was an effort to harmonize national laws on privacy and data protection. This Directive moved Convention 108 further, by detailing the criteria according to which data processing is legitimate (Richter 2011: 10). It applied to "any operation or set of operations which is performed upon personal data," called "processing" of data. According to Article 3(1), the Directive applied "to the processing of personal data wholly or partly by automatic means, and to the processing otherwise than by automatic means of personal data which form part of a filing system or are intended to form part of a filing system." Personal data were defined as:

> . . . any information relating to an identified or identifiable natural person ('data subject'); an identifiable person is one who can be identified, directly or indirectly, in particular by reference to an identification number or to one or more factors specific to his physical, physiological, mental, economic, cultural or social identity.

However, there are cases in which the restrictions do not apply, in particular in the case of public security, defense and state security. The 2002 ePrivacy Directive[8] was drafted as an extension of the Data Protection Directive to cover certain provisions, such as cookies, spam and the confidentiality of communications.

Within the EU Charter of Fundamental Rights, data protection is included under Article 8:

1. Everyone has the right to the protection of personal data concerning him or her.
2. Such data must be processed fairly for specified purposes and on the basis of the consent of the person concerned or some other legitimate basis laid down by law. Everyone has the right to access to data, which has been collected concerning him or her, and the right to have it rectified.
3. Compliance with these rules shall be subject to control by an independent authority.

The European Data Protection Supervisor (EDPS) is a new "instrument," an independent authority responsible for supervising European institutions and bodies regarding privacy and data protection issues; it has already come into conflict with the European Commission over measures to allow data retention. In particular, the Data Retention Directive[9] demands that all providers of telecommunication services within the European Union retain all of their

8 Directive 2002/58/EC.
9 Directive 2006/24/EC.

customers' traffic and location data for a period of not less than six months and not more than two years from the date of the communication. The European Commission's evaluation of the Directive argues that it is "a valuable tool for criminal justice systems and for law enforcement in the EU" (European Commission 2011). However, EDPS has stated that:

> . . . the retention of telecommunications data clearly constitutes an interference with the right to privacy of the persons concerned as laid down by Article 8 of the European Convention of Human Rights and Article 7 of the EU Charter of Fundamental Rights [. . .] [It] has failed to meet its main purpose, namely to harmonize national legislation concerning data retention.
>
> (*EDPS 2011: 2, 7*)

In 2012, the European Commission announced the forthcoming reform of the EU's data protection policies. A proposal for a new Regulation, "on the protection of individuals with regard to the processing of personal data and on the free movement of such data," was published on 25 January 2012 (EC 2012b). This intends to replace the main EU legislation on personal data protection—Directive 95/46/EC—with a new Directive that provides specific data protection rules for the law enforcement sector. Along with these proposals, the EC released a Communication (EC 2012a) to the European Parliament, the Council, the European Economic and Social Committee and the Committee of the Regions, which explains the reasons for this reform, as well as the contemporary challenges to data protection. In particular, the EC acknowledged the inefficiency of the 1995 Directive to ensure the right to personal data protection and pointed to the fact that there is no harmonization at the level of member state legislation. To address these deficiencies, the new regulation "will do away with the fragmentation of legal regimes across 27 Member States and remove barriers to market entry, a factor of particular importance to micro, small and medium-sized enterprises" (EC 2012a). Its focus on the economic aspects of privacy and data protection policy has a particular stance in the aforementioned documents. Since the announcement of the new reform, several interested parties have welcomed the proposed framework, but have also raised a number of concerns. For example, the EDPS has expressed concern that the regulation provides:

> . . . the possibilities for restricting basic principles and rights; the possible derogation for transferring data to third countries; the excessive powers granted to the Commission in the mechanism designed to ensure consistency among supervisory authorities and the new ground for exceptions to the purpose limitation principle.
>
> (*EDPS 2012*)

On a self-regulatory and voluntary basis, the European Union has pursued the regulation of SNS in relation to vulnerable groups, in particular youth and children, through its Safer Internet Plus Programme. In July of 2008, the Programme initiated a public consultation on child safety and social networking, the results of which were summarized and published in a related report (EC 2008). Following this, the Safer Social Networking Principles (EC 2009) were issued in February 2009, and the first self-regulatory agreement to follow these principles was signed by the main social networks. The Commission assessed the implementation of this agreement on Safer Internet Day in 2010, and again in 2011, and stated its disappointment with the ways in which SNS had failed to protect the privacy of underage users. This is a major blow to many years of efforts to develop self-regulatory regimes for SNS as an answer to the issues raised by the risks faced especially by younger users, who make up the majority of their users.

Within this context, the German *Land* of Schleswig-Holstein proceeded to prohibit all public organizations from appearing on a Facebook fan page and embedding the "Like" option on their websites in an effort to protect logged-off Facebook users and non-users. Privacy in Germany is regulated by the Federal Commissioner for Data Protection and Freedom of Information (*Der Bundesbeauftragte für Datenschutz und die Informationsfreiheit*). Overall, Germany has one of the strictest privacy policies in the world (Privacy International 2011). In August 2011, the Independent Centre for Privacy Protection (*Unabhängiges Landeszentrum für Datenschutz*, or ULD) in the state of Schleswig-Holstein took measures against the appearance of public organizations on Facebook. According to the head of ULD, Dr Thilo Weichert, one of the main reasons for this privacy policy is Germany's past. As he explained: "For almost 40 years, people were under surveillance and it's obvious that this makes people very nervous when it comes to privacy" (Meyer 2011).

Also based on the federal model, privacy in the United States is found in a number of places that deal with contexts and dimensions of privacy. In principle, privacy is regulated by the Privacy Act of 1974, which is the code of fair information practices mandating how federal agencies, such as the Environmental Protection Agency (EPA), maintain records about individuals. The Computer Matching and Privacy Protection Act of 1988 amended the Privacy Act of 1974 by adding certain protections for the subjects of Privacy Act records whose records are used in automated matching programs. In 2006, the US Department of Justice established the Chief Privacy and Civil Liberties Office (CPCLO) and the Office of Privacy and Civil Liberties (OPCL), with responsibility to protect privacy and civil liberties. The main policy tools include the Privacy Act of 1997, the privacy provisions of the E-Government Act of 2002, the Federal Information Security Management Act and further policy directives that are created as extension of these Acts. Certain privacy rights are being protected in the United States by specialized legislation such as the Children's Online Privacy Protection Act (COPPA), which gives parents control over what information websites can collect from their children. The state of California promotes and protects this right in its Constitution.[10] The California Online Privacy Protection Act (OPPA) demands a privacy policy from online services companies that collect personal data from its residents to publish on their websites. This is particularly important, taking into consideration that Facebook and other major online companies are headquartered in California. However, the California Office of Information Security and Privacy Protection adopts a more relaxed approach to what private corporations are allowed to do within their privacy policies.

Canada has taken a leading international role in investigating privacy violations in the context of Facebook, and its approach is closer to the European model. The Office of the Privacy Commissioner of Canada (OPC) was created in 1997 to protect Canadian consumers' privacy rights. It focuses on the resolution of public complaints through public discussion and cooperation. In case of non-compliance, OPC can use a number of available tools and take the issue into the Federal Court. One of those policy tools is the Personal Information Protection and Electronic Documents Act (PIPEDA) 2000, the purpose of which is to:

> . . . establish . . . rules to govern the collection, use and disclosure of personal information in a manner that recognizes the right of privacy of individuals with respect to their

10 In particular, in art. 1, § 1.

> personal information and the need of organizations to collect, use or disclose personal information for purposes that a reasonable person would consider appropriate in the circumstances.
>
> (*PIPEDA 2000, s. 3*)

This applies to private organizations regarding the collection, use or disclosure during commercial activities. Another policy tool is the Privacy Act 1985, which protects the privacy of individuals "with respect to personal information about themselves held by a government institution" (Privacy Act 1985, s. 1). It applies to the federal public sector regarding data collection by public institutions. In 2009, OPC conducted a comparative investigation of five major SNS, focusing on Facebook. Privacy Commissioner Jennifer Stoddart criticized Facebook for raising serious privacy violations in the way in which it operates (OPC 2009a). Facebook was given one month to respond to the findings of the report. The Privacy Commissioner announced later that OPC was satisfied with Facebook's reply and believes that it is on the right path to address the privacy gaps (OPC 2009b). However, a few months later and in response to a new public complaint regarding Facebook's new default settings of December 2009, a new investigation into Facebook's privacy policy was launched (McMullen 2010). Shortly afterwards, the Canadian law firm Merchant Law Group, LLP launched a class-action lawsuit against Facebook targeting its major privacy changes (Goodyear 2010).

## Privacy as challenge and claim

This chapter set out to reflect on the definitions and understandings of privacy, its political economy and relevant policy dimensions. If we consider the citizen as the starting point of a debate, analysis and critique of the current state of privacy policy, then the right to privacy is argued to be closely linked to the exercise of self-governance, autonomy and ultimately associated freedoms such as expression, association and dignity. Seen from this perspective, the right to privacy directly or indirectly implies the need for the protection of a "space" (whether physical, virtual, informational, mental or other) that remains free from the intervention of others. This chapter neither addresses the invasion of privacy by individuals nor the right to privacy of institutions or corporations. Our interest is a discussion of the conditions for privacy for individuals and society against actors with the resources, means and opportunity to invade and violate this right. Our discussion on the philosophical and other analytical perspectives of privacy helped us to contextualize the significance of this right for the exercise of other rights and the integrity of the person.

This chapter argues that, with the popularity and continuous growth of social media, the question of privacy is a matter of significant concern to the average user. As such, it ought to occupy a central place in media scholarship. Privacy is multidimensional and, until recently, was associated with attempts by states and regimes to police and restrict their citizens' freedoms, or, in the context of the media, it was seen as a concern of the famous and the elites. The widespread relevance of privacy and the media to the average citizen is something relatively new; communication technologies have afforded unprecedented access to monitoring practices as a great deal of our everyday affairs now take place through online platforms. Our discussion aims to highlight that privacy-related priorities between different actors are more often than not incompatible. Corporate privacy policy—which is expected to rely on the letter of the law as this applies in its national or other context—has different objectives from those of consumers and users. Facebook remains an important case study because of its ever-increasing popularity and sheer numbers of users around the world. Individuals, companies, causes, groups and even public authorities and institutions, such as schools, maintain Facebook pages. The way in which its usage by all of these different actors is underpinned by the privacy policies of the company is neither known, understood, nor controlled by the users. In fact, the user seems to be constantly at a disadvantage, as Facebook continuously probes for new technologies and policies that push the boundaries of what is considered a commonsense approach to privacy.

Another policy dimension is the regulation of privacy by public institutions and authorities, the state and international organizations, such as the EU. Here again, the situation is complex, incomplete and fragmented. The way in which the law approaches privacy does not entirely reflect the multifaceted dimensions of privacy met in both democratic praxis and debates around the notion and value of privacy, or political claims for the right to privacy to be protected. In the era of digital communications in particular, it seems that our ideas about privacy are being challenged. At the same time, regulatory frameworks are also being pushed to accommodate corporate pressure at a global level amid concerns from the public and even states (e.g. Germany) about the permeability of corporate practices (Chakravartty and Sarikakis 2006). As has been the case with macro-level communication policy, especially where it is driven by global developments in markets and politics, political institutions respond to and normalize a de facto new status quo that arises through corporate practices (Chakravartty and Sarikakis 2006). In the case of global communication, as is the case of SNS, the difficulty of effective national regulation has led nations and governments to collaborative and coregulatory approaches. A large part of this direction is the development of self-regulatory incentives, but these do not always bear fruit. Again, the case of SNS and Facebook is particularly telling. Even though norms, institutions and guidelines were established to deal with new policy questions, a collaborative approach with the private sector of SNS (as they are entirely privately owned) has not brought the desired outcome as far as individual user privacy is concerned.

As we have seen, the largest part of privacy in law is concerned with the fate of data: their collection, processing, and manipulation without the consent—and increasingly even *with* the consent—of the user. While laws, too, erode the sanctity of privacy through exemptions that allow state interference, online technologies can be used for such purposes without warning or user knowledge. There is a sense of uncertainty and fluidity in terms of users' protection that derives not only from the differences between philosophical and normative dimensions of privacy, but also from the difficulty in effectively protecting such a fragile right, as long as users lack the technical, as well as the political and economic, means to provide a counterforce to international (and) corporate actors.

## References


Acohido, B. (2011) 'How Facebook tracks you across the web,' *USA TODAY*. Online. Available HTTP: http://www.usatoday.com/tech/news/story/2011-11-15/facebook-privacy-tracking-data/51225112/1 (accessed 10 January 2012).

Acquisti, A. and Gross, R. (2006) 'Imagined communities: Awareness, information sharing and privacy on the Facebook,' *Data Privacy Lab*. Online. Available HTTP: http://privacy.cs.cmu.edu/dataprivacy/projects/facebook/facebook2.pdf (accessed 30 May 2012).

Aimeur, E., Gambs, S., Ho, A. and Inria, I. (2010) 'Towards a privacy-enhanced social networking site,' *Proceedings of the Fifth International Conference on Availability, Reliability and Security*, IEEE Computer Society, Los Alamitos.

Alexa (2012) 'Top sites.' Online. Available HTTP: http://www.alexa.com/topsites (accessed 10 January 2012).

Barnes, R. (2012) 'Supreme Court: Warrants needed in GPS tracking,' *The Washington Post*. Online. Available HTTP: http://www.washingtonpost.com/politics/supreme-court-warrants-needed-in-gps-tracking/2012/01/23/gIQAx7qGLQ_story.html (accessed 7 February 2012).

Barnes, S. B. (2006) 'A privacy paradox: Social networking in the United States,' *First Monday*. Online. Available HTTP: http://firstmonday.org/htbin/cgiwrap/bin/ojs/index.php/fm/article/view/1394/1312 (accessed 10 January 2012).

Bork, R. (1990) *The Tempting of America: The Political Seduction of the Law*, New York: Simon and Schuster.

boyd, d. and Hargittai, E. (2010) 'Facebook privacy settings: Who cares?,' *First Monday*, 15(8). Online. Available HTTP: http://firstmonday.org/htbin/cgiwrap/bin/ojs/index.php/fm/article/view/3086/2589 (accessed 10 January 2012).

Campisi, P., Maiorama, E. and Neri, A. (2009) 'Privacy protection in social media networks: A dream that can come true?' *Proceedings of the Sixteenth International Conference on Digital Signal Processing*, Santorini.

Chakravartty, P. and Katharine, S. (2006) *Media Policy and Globalization*, Edinburgh: Edinburgh University Press.

Christofides, E., Mulse, A. and Desmarais, S. (2009) 'Information disclosure and control on Facebook: Are they two sides of the same coin or two different processes?' *Cyberpsychology & Behavior*, 12(3): 341–345.

comScore (2011) *The comScore 2010 Europe Digital Year in Review*, comScore White Paper. Online. Available HTTP: http://www.comscore.com/Press_Events/Presentations_Whitepapers/2011/2010_Europe_Digital_Year_in_Review (accessed 7 February 2012).

Cranor, L. F., Reagle, J. and Ackerman, M. S. (1999) 'Beyond concern: Understanding net users' attitudes about online privacy,' in I. Vogelsang and B. M. Compaine (eds.) *The Internet Upheaval: Raising Questions, Seeking Answers in Communication Policy*, Cambridge, MA: MIT Press.

Debatim, B., Lovejoy, J. P., Horn, A. K. and Hughes, B. N. (2009) 'Facebook and online privacy: Attitudes, behaviors, and unintended consequences,' *Journal of Computer-Mediated Communication*, 15(1), 83–108.

Doyle, C. and Bagaric, M. (2005) *Privacy Law in Australia*, Sydney: The Federation Press.

Eecke, P. A. and Truyens, M. (2010) 'Privacy and social networks,' *Computer Law & Security Review*, 26: 535–546.

European Commission (2008) *Public Consultation on Online Social Networking: Summary Report*, Brussels: EC. Online. Available HTTP: http://ec.europa.eu/information_society/activities/sip/docs/pub_consult_age_rating_sns/summaryreport.pdf (accessed 9 February 2012).

—— (2009) *The Safer Social Networking Principles for EU*, Brussels: EC. Online. HTTP Available: http://ec.europa.eu/information_society/activities/social_networking/docs/sn_principles.pdf (accessed 9 February 2012).

—— (2011) *Evaluation Report on the Data Retention Directive (Directive 2006/24/EC)*, Brussels: EC. Online. Available HTTP: http://ec.europa.eu/commission_2010-2014/malmstrom/archive/20110418_data_retention_evaluation_en.pdf (accessed 9 February 2012).

—— (2012a) *Safeguarding Privacy in a Connected World: A European Data Protection Framework for the 21st Century*, COM(2012)9. Online. Available HTTP: http://ec.europa.eu/justice/data-protection/document/review2012/com_2012_9_en.pdf.

—— (2012b) *Proposal for a Regulation of the European Parliament and of the Council on the Protection of Individuals with Regard to the Processing of Personal Data and on the Free Movement of Such Data*, COM(2012)12. Online. Available HTTP: http://ec.europa.eu/justice/data-protection/document/review2012/com_2012_11_en.pdf (accessed 21 March 2012).

European Data Protection Supervisor (EDPS) (2011) *Opinion on the Evaluation Report from the Commission to the Council and the European Parliament on the Data Retention Directive (Directive 2006/24/EC)*, Brussels: EDPS. Online. Available HTTP: http://www.edps.europa.eu/EDPSWEB/webdav/site/mySite/shared/Documents/Consultation/Opinions/2011/11-05-30_Evaluation_Report_DRD_EN.pdf (accessed 9 February 2012).

—— (2012) 'EDPS applauds strengthening of the right to data protection in Europe, but still regrets the lack of comprehensiveness.' Online. Available HTTP: http://www.edps.europa.eu/EDPSWEB/webdav/site/mySite/shared/Documents/EDPS/PressNews/Press/2012/EDPS-2012-07_DPReform_package_EN.pdf (accessed 21 March 2012).

European Parliment and Council (2008) *Decision No. 1351/2008/EC*. Online. Available HTTP: http://ec.europa.eu/information_society/activities/sip/docs/prog_decision_2009/decision_en.pdf (accessed 9 February 2012).

Evans, R. and Lewis, E. (2011) 'Protester to sue police over secret surveillance,' *The Guardian*. Online. Available HTTP: http://www.guardian.co.uk/uk/2011/may/03/protester-sue-police-secret-surveillance (accessed 7 February 2012).
Fuchs, C. (2011a) 'Towards an alternative concept of privacy,' *Journal of Information, Communication and Ethics in Society*, 9(4): 220–237.
Gallagher, R. and Syal, R. (2011) 'Police buy software to map suspects' digital movements,' *The Guardian*. Online. Available HTTP: http://www.guardian.co.uk/uk/2011/may/11/police-software-maps-digital-movements (accessed 11 May 2011).
Goodyear, S. (2010) 'Facebook faces Canadian class-action lawsuit,' *Toronto Sun*. Online. Available HTTP: http://www.torontosun.com/news/canada/2010/07/02/14593546.html (accessed 9 February 2012).
Grimmelmann, J. (2009) 'Saving Facebook,' *Iowa Law Review*, 94: 1137–1206.
Habermas, J. (1989 [1962]) *The Structural Transformation of the Public Sphere: An Inquiry into a Category of Bourgeois Society*, T. Burger and F. Lawrence (trans.), Cambridge, MA: MIT Press.
Johnson, B. (2010) 'Privacy no longer a social norm, says Facebook founder,' *The Guardian*. Online. Available HTTP: http://www.guardian.co.uk/technology/2010/jan/11/facebook-privacy (accessed 9 February 2012).
Kirkpatrick, D. (2010) *The Facebook Effect: The Inside Story of the Company that is Connecting the World*, New York: Simon & Schuster.
Lewis, K., Kaufman, J. and Christakis, N. (2008) 'The taste for privacy: An analysis of college student privacy settings in an online social network,' *Journal of Computer-Mediated Communication*, 14(1): 79–100.
Livingstone, S. (2008) 'Taking risky opportunities in youthful content creation: Teenagers' use of social networking sites for intimacy, privacy and self-expression,' *New Media & Society*, 10(3): 393–411.
—— and Brake, D. R. (2010) 'On the rapid rise of social networking sites: New findings and policy implications,' *Children & Society*, 24(1): 75–83.
McMullen, T. (2010) 'Canada's Privacy Commissioner probes Facebook over users private information,' *abcNEWS*. Online. Available HTTP: http://abcnews.go.com/Technology/canada-investigates-facebook-privacy-settings/story?id=9691133#.TxB2HWNAbtg (accessed 9 February 2012).
Meyer, D. (2011) 'The Schleswig-Holstein question,' *BBC News Technology*. Online. Available HTTP: http://www.bbc.co.uk/news/technology-14859813 (accessed 9 February 2012).
Mills, J. L. (2008) *Privacy: The Lost Right*, New York: Oxford University Press.
Ngeno, C., Zavarsky, P., Lindskog, D. and Ruhl, R. (2010) 'User's perspective: Privacy and security of information on social networks,' *Proceedings of the Second IEEE International Conference on Privacy, Security, Risk and Trust*, IEEE International Conferene on Social Computing.
Ofcom (2008) *Social Networking: A Quantitative and Qualitative Research Report into Attitudes, Behaviours and Use*, London: Ofcom. Online. Available HTTP: http://stakeholders.ofcom.org.uk/binaries/research/media-literacy/report1.pdf (accessed 9 February 2012).
Office of the Privacy Commissioner of Canada (OPC) (2009a) 'Facebook needs to improve practices, investigation finds'. Online. Available HTTP: http://www.priv.gc.ca/media/nr-c/2009/nr-c_090716_e.cfm (accessed 9 February 2012).
—— (2009b) 'Facebook agrees to address Privacy Commissioner's concerns'. Online. Available HTTP: http://www.priv.gc.ca/media/nr-c/2009/nr-c_090827_e.cfm (accessed 9 February 2012).
Posner, R. (1981) *The Economics of Justice*, Cambridge, MA: Harvard University Press.
Privacy International (2011) 'Federal Republic of Germany.' Online. Available HTTP: https://www.privacyinternational.org/survey/phr2003/countries/germany.htm (accessed 9 February 2012).
Richter, A. (2011) 'The protection on privacy and personal data on the Internet and online media,' Strasbourg: Committee on Culture, Science and Education, Parliamentary Assembly of the Council of Europe. Online. Available HTTP: http://assembly.coe.int/Documents/WorkingDocs/Doc11/EDOC12695.pdf (accessed 9 February 2012).
Scoglio, S. (1998) *Transforming Privacy: A Transpersonal Philosophy of Rights*, Westport, CT: Praeger Publishers.
Solove, D. J. (2008) *Understanding Privacy*, Cambridge, MA: Harvard University Press.
Squicciarini, A. C, Shehab, M. and Wede, J. (2010) 'Privacy policies for shared content in social network sites,' *VLDB Journal*, 19(6): 777–796.
Stutzman, F., Capra, R. and Thompson, J. (2011) 'Factors mediating disclosure in social network sites,' *Computers in Human Behaviour*, 27(1): 590–598.

Thomson, J. (1975) 'The right to privacy,' *University of Pennsylvania Law Review*, 154: 477–564.
United Nations (1990) *Guidelines for the Regulation of Computerized Personal Data Files*. Online. Available HTTP: http://www.unhcr.org/refworld/docid/3ddcafaac.html (accessed 9 February 2012).
Warren, S. D. and Brandeis, L. D. (1890) 'The right to privacy,' *Harvard Law Review*, 4(5): 193–220. Online. Available HTTP: http://www.jstor.org/stable/1321160 (accessed 9 February 2012).
Whittaker, Z. (2011) 'MySpace lost 10 million users in a month: Close within the year?' *ZDnet US Edition*. Online. Available HTTP: http://www.zdnet.com/blog/igeneration/myspace-lost-10-million-users-in-a-month-close-within-the-year/9111 (accessed 9 February 2012).

# 26

# Self-regulation and the construction of media harms

## Notes on the battle over digital "privacy"

*Joseph Turow*

This chapter proposes the utility of a social constructionist approach to understand societal struggles around media regulation. It presents as a case study the battles taking place in the United States over whether self-regulation, historically a common activity in certain American media industries, is adequate to protect citizens' privacy online in the face of marketers who want to use their information as a profitable currency of exchange. "Self-regulation" refers to the practice of lawmakers and corporate executives working out arrangements whereby practitioners, rather than Congress or regulatory bodies (e.g. the courts or the Federal Communications Commission), act to provide remedies. Self-regulation developed largely in the context of public ire over objectionable content, such as sex and violence. Supported by policymakers, the approach aims to ameliorate the societal concerns in ways that place fewer burdens on the industry and raise fewer potential First Amendment issues than regulations would. Whether in the movie, radio, television, comic book or recording industries, self-regulation has not solved the problems that ignited angry groups, but it has brought down levels of concern often enough to rescue the businesses involved from unwanted government interference.

The early twenty-first century is witnessing new tensions around regulation and self-regulation with respect to what might be loosely called a new kind of media "content": certain types of "cookie" file on the browsers of people's desktops, laptops, mobile handsets, tablets and other digital instruments. Individuals and organizations are voicing anger that, through these files, digital firms have the legal right to track digital activities of those individuals, to link that knowledge to other information they have about those people, to tailor messages to them based on what they have learned, and then to sell their data to other firms and marketers that have similar aims. The cookies do not search or alter the individuals' computers, nor do they act to identify anonymous individuals. Nevertheless, the fact that all of this data tracking and gathering can be accomplished without the permission of device owners has angered members of the public, social movement organizations and politicians. In response, industry groups have set up self-regulatory regimes in the hope that they might stop tougher government actions that might disrupt revenue streams. Most notably, during 2011, a consortium of data-collection firms and publishers called the Digital Advertising Alliance supported the development of an advertising icon that aims to alert people that an advertisement they see is based on one aspect of the data collection process: the tracking activity that the industry terms "behavioral advertising." Clicking on the icon leads to industry material about this activity and the possibility of opting out from having ads delivered based on tracking.

This chapter sketches the digital media industry's engagement with the tracking-and-targeting issue, particularly with the icon mentioned above. Industry leaders are carrying out self-regulation in ways that exploit the complexity of an arena that the public, advocates and lawmakers do not understand well. The industry is using the self-regulatory regime to get far more than a compromise with authorities aimed at pushing away regulations that threaten current revenue streams. Industry leaders are using their asymmetrical knowledge about marketing technologies to obscure certain industry activities, to disguise others and to keep understanding of the particulars low. Their actions allow them to frame this social problem in ways that allow the digital marketing and media executives much greater power to guide the future of the new media terrain than if regulators and the public had full control of the issue's definition.

## The social construction of issues

Economic theorists have traditionally noted that the purpose of regulation is to carry out two basic tasks: one is to identify the failure of the market, which justifies intervention; the other is to "select the method of intervention which predictably will correct that failure at least cost" (Ogus 2004: 32). Economists and political scientists have put forth a number of frameworks that try to model how this works in a representative democracy. Two that have gained particular traction are *public interest theory* and *private interest theory*. They present different perspectives on the nature of political reality. "Public interest theory" explains the existence and forms of regulation with reference to the extent to which they are justified economically—that is, whether the people implementing them believe they work best (or most efficiently, based often on cost–benefit analysis) in the public interest. "Private interest theory," by contrast, sees regulation as "a commodity made available in the political 'marketplace' and 'supplied' by politicians and bureaucrats by reference to the demand of those who will benefit from its promulgation" (Ogus 2004: 36). Ogus points out flaws in both. He notes: "The public interest approach, which assumes that law is made exclusively to generate aggregate social welfare, is too naïve; and the private interest theory which regulates it entirely to the furtherance of personal and group welfare is excessively cynical." He acknowledges, though, that both sets of theories "have been helpful in focusing attention on how the different institutions of regulatory decision-making can be used either to advance the ostensible goals of regulation or else to subvert those goals to private ends" (Ogus 2004: 42).

Claims of market failure have certainly been plentiful when it comes to media content. Controversies over the past two centuries alleged that publishers of books, movies and television programming were creating materials that were corrupting the morals of society in general, and children in particular. Regulators, sensitive to public furor, insisted that something must be done. But in many cases, and particularly in the twentieth century, they allowed the industry under attack to create a self-regulatory regime rather than submit to direct regulations. Part of the reason for regulators' reluctance to regulate directly may be a fear of trampling the First Amendment's exhortation that Congress should not abridge the press, a clause that the Supreme Court has interpreted increasingly broadly during the past century and a half. Part of the reason may be the "regulatory capture" phenomenon—that is, when commissioners, regulatory staffs and even members of Congress temper their battles against media firms because they hope to join them as highly paid executives or lobbyists when they leave government. Part of the reluctance to regulate may also relate to the success of lobbyists representing large firms such as Time Warner and Electronic Arts, as well as industry groups such as the Recording Industry Association of America. They often persuade officials at all levels of government that placing direct limits on their activities would create more economic losses than social gains, particularly in the increasingly competitive international economy. Self-regulation allows for a least-cost solution, they say, because firms can salve public and advocacy fury without onerous requirements that are extraneous to the problem at hand.

Discussions of media self-regulation typically center on media executives' attempts to press for least-cost solutions that benefit their firms and calm broad publics, while not implementing content changes that satisfy the advocates who brought the complaints to the government. Less attention has focused on a different function of self regulatory efforts that involves playing down and even obscuring emerging industry developments from regulators and the public that might underscore severe limitations in the self regulatory approach. This view is an extension of the notion that industries try to hijack the construction of social problems that impinge on them. Social constructionism is the notion that society's identification and handling of social problems ought to be seen as "activities of individuals or groups making grievances and claims with respect to some putative conditions" (Spector and Kitsuse 1977: 75). The description of a social problem, writes sociologist Joel Best (2012), "always begins with a claim, with someone arguing that some social condition is harmful and needs to be addressed."

Best (2012) notes that "claims-making" is an inherently persuasive activity, and he points out that the rhetoric involves the mobilization of resources by all sides in the debate. The resources may be symbolic—a good reputation, a license to speak over broadcast frequencies—or they may be material—for example, lots of cash and many well-trained lobbyists (see Turow 1996). Social movement organizations (SMOs) that want to urge publics and regulators to define social problems in certain ways use their resources to frame arguments in their behalf. Best's understanding of framing resonates with Entman's definition: selecting "some aspects of perceived reality and mak[ing] them more salient in a communicating text, in such a way as to promote a particular problem definition, causal interpretation, moral evaluation, and/or treatment recommendations for the item described" (Entman 1993: 52). Best (2012) notes that SMOs often create different frames:

> Beyond the interaction between a movement's advocates and those they hope to recruit, movement frames find themselves competing with one another. Different SMOs within a social movement may promote rival frames (e.g. radical vs. moderate), and movements may be divided by *frame disputes* (Benford 1993; Lofland 1993). Moreover, movements encounter direct opposition from *counter movements* that advance their own *counter frames*; in turn, activists may respond to their rivals and their opponents by *reframing* their issues (Benford and Hunt 2003).

Best does not link this idea of frame competition to industry actors. He therefore does not mention the possibility that industry actors might work to obscure developments with the hope of decreasing chances for alarm about the social problem and stricter forms of self-regulation. Connecting industry-SMO competition over frames to media issues, it stands to reason that rhetorical attempts to obscure developments would not be successful in the many media situations in which a range of SMOs and government officials have long been involved in disputation about content issues. Obscuring rhetoric might, however, work in the industry's advantage when government officials and officials confront new developments around content and technology and are trying to think through their implications.

## Data collection as a media issue

Just this sort of situation applies to the collection of information ("content") about consumers in the digital media environment. At the start of the twenty-first century, the American media are undergoing their largest transformation since the rollout of commercial television during the 1950s, and arguably before that. We are at the start of a revolution in the ways in which marketers and media firms learn about their audiences. Every day, most Americans who use the Internet, along with hundreds of millions of others from all over the planet, are being quietly peeked at, poked, analyzed and tagged as they move through the world. The central driving force is the advertising industry's media buying system. Media buying involves planning and purchasing space or time for advertising on outlets as diverse as billboards and radio, websites, mobile phones and newspapers. For decades, media buying was a backwater, a service wing of advertising agencies that was known for having the lowest-paying jobs on Madison Avenue. But that has all changed. The past twenty years have seen the rise of "media agencies" that are no longer part of ad agencies, although they may both be owned by the same parent company, and a wide array of satellite companies that feed them technology and data.

Media-buying agencies wield more than US$100 billion of their clients' campaign funds in the United States alone to purchase space and time on media that they think will advance their clients' marketing aims. But, in the process, they are doing much more: with the money as leverage, they are guiding the media that system toward nothing less than an entirely new way of thinking about audience members, of bidding on the right to reach them based on the value of their profiles, and of defining success in doing that. Traditionally, marketers have used media such as newspapers, magazines, radio, outdoor boards and television to reach out to segments of the population through commercial messages. These advertisers typically learned about audience segments by using data from survey companies that polled representative portions of the population via a variety of methods, including panel research. Less commonly, they sent questionnaires to people they knew to be readers or listeners.

The emerging new world is dramatically different. Instead of large populations and population segments as audiences, advertisers in the digital space expect media firms to deliver to them very particular types of individual—and increasingly particular individuals—by leveraging a level of detailed level of knowledge about them and their behaviors that was unheard of even a few years ago. The new way draws as detailed a picture as possible of particular individuals based in large part on measurable physical acts they perform such as clicks, swipes, mouseovers and even voice commands, as well as through new tools such as cookies and beacons to track those acts, and through hundreds of startup organizations with names like "BlueKai," "Rapleaf," "Invidi," and "Simulmedia". With only the barest nod to people about these activities, these and other companies track them on websites and across websites. The aim is to learn what individuals do, what they care about and whom they talk to. Firms that exchange the information often do ensure that the individuals' names and postal addresses remain anonymous, but not before they add specific demographic data, lifestyle information and "behavioral" information—that is, data about what individuals have done in the digital domain that suggests their buying interests.

Other than firms that track people in various ways and sell data about them are various categories of companies that populate the space between the advertisers who buy ads and the publishers that serve them. There are, for example:

i. data-management firms, which buy individual-level information from the publishers as well as other online and offline sources and merge them with cookie data or other ways of identifying individual computers, individual people, or individual households;

ii. advertising networks, which link publishers and sell the right to advertisers on them;
iii. real-time-buying exchanges, which allow publishers, networks and other holders of cookie data to sell to marketers the ability to reach individuals with particular demographic, lifestyle and/or behavioral characteristics instantly; and
iv. cost-optimization firms, which help digital publishers to decide the best going rate of people with particular characteristics—and far more.

Activities by these and other types of company in the digital marketing space are quite complicated, a new preserve of mathematicians, statisticians, software engineers and specialized digital marketing practitioners who have learned to work with them and speak their language. In fact, at a 2011 Online Media, Marketing and Advertising (OMMA) conference, a keynote speaker (Mandese 2011), as well as several members of one panel, took time to lament that the complexity of their business, and particularly its jargon, is making it difficult for them to explain the work to clients and even to practitioners of the traditional advertising world. The baroque nature of what members of the advertising business have come to call "the new media ecology" has also made learning about it by regulators and advocates quite difficult. More than one person among the public interest sector informants interviewed for this work observed that few people in the Federal Trade Commission (FTC), the US Senate Judiciary Commission, and other areas of the government that relate to digital marketing understand the particulars of its processes. Moreover, there are few SMOs that concentrate on digital media and arguably only one—the Center for Digital Democracy—that sees marketing and new media as a primary focus.

In this environment, it makes sense that advocacy organizations latched onto traditional paradigms to make sense of the new uses of data by the various marketing, publishing and data agencies. From the late 1990s onward, they framed arguments around the idea that marketers in the new media environment were causing "privacy" problems. Typical of this approach was an important 2011 request of the FTC by a coalition including the American Civil Liberties Union, Consumer Action, the American Library Association and the Center for Digital Democracy (EPIC 2011). They urged the FTC to investigate what they alleged was Facebook's secret tracking of users after they logged off, as well as its recent announced changed practices that gave "the company far greater ability to disclose the personal information of its users to its business partners." The first paragraph of the coalition's letter to the commissioners and the chairman stated, "we would like to bring your attention to new privacy and security risks to American consumers," underscoring "the company's failure to uphold representations it has made regarding its commitments to protect the privacy of its users" (EPIC 2011).

Clearly, through this letter, the organizations were intending to raise Facebook's actions to the level of a social problem framed in terms of risks to consumers' privacy and security. Wikipedia's definition of "privacy" reflects an understanding of the term that underpins the claim. (Wikipedia's definition of privacy is one that is constantly evolving as the term and its uses evolve.) "Privacy" it says, "is the ability of an individual or group to seclude themselves or information about themselves and thereby reveal themselves selectively" (Wikipedia 2011a). Wikipedia adds that: "Information or data privacy refers to the evolving relationship between technology and the legal right to, or public expectation of [*sic*] privacy in the collection and sharing of data about one's self." Wikipedia also reflects the common notion—inherent in the coalition's letter—that data security is separate from, but relates to, privacy. Security is a means, Wikipedia states, "of ensuring that data is [*sic*] kept safe from corruption and that access to it is suitably controlled. Thus data security helps to ensure privacy. It also helps in protecting personal data" (Wikipedia 2011b).

The usefulness of these frames to organizations concerned about the Internet tracking of consumers is that perspectives link to longstanding philosophical and legal views. Writings interpreting Internet privacy often relate their thinking to a nineteenth-century *Harvard Law Review* article by Samuel Warren and Louis Brandeis (1890) that itself reflected on changes in people's ability to be "let alone" owing to new technology of that era (the camera). Moreover, advocates know that, by law, policymakers and regulators need to evaluate "harms" when considering whether to act on an issue brought before them. Placing tracking within a privacy frame allows the advocates to make the required case to policymakers that tracking creates harms in ways that have precedence and that are easily understandable—even if the policymakers do not understand the particulars of how the digital environment works. Wikipedia's summary of the harms associated with "privacy concerns" points out that:

> Various types of personal information are often associated with privacy concerns. For various reasons, individuals may object to personal information such as their religion, sexual orientation, political affiliations, or personal activities being revealed, perhaps to avoid discrimination, personal embarrassment, or damage to their professional reputations.
> (*Wikipedia 2011a*)

The article also underscores that the unwanted sharing of medical information may "cause substantial harm to individuals . . . it might affect their insurance coverage or employment," and that financial privacy "is important for the avoidance of fraud including identity theft" (Wikipedia 2011a). Its list reflects the examples that advocates have brought before government officials familiar with how such potential dangers fit into the law. When making the case that tracking exposes people to problems that are unrelated to this list, advocates tend to fall back on deception as an obviously illegal harm. So, for example, in their letter urging the FTC to investigate Facebook, the coalition led by EPIC argues that:

> Facebook's frictionless sharing and post-log-out tracking harms consumers throughout the United States by invading their privacy and allowing for disclosure and use of information in ways and for purposes other than those to which users have consent [*sic*] and relied upon . . . By concealing the company's tracking of users' [*sic*] post-log-out activity and materially changing the framework under which users' share data without providing a clear opportunity for users' to maintain existing privacy protections, Facebook is engaging in unfair and deceptive trade practices.

Although this approach to information privacy may seem obvious and sensible in creating a social problem in the public sphere, it leaves out important alternative frames for understanding harms that marketers and publishers are committing in the digital space. Broadly speaking, many of these perspectives understand the very activity of following someone and recording data about them without their knowledge as inherently problematic. Ideas advanced by Daniel Solove (2008, 2010), Priscilla Regan (1995), Leslie R. Shade (2008), Helen Nissenbaum (2009), and others suggest that at least some activities of the new marketing ecosystem are harmful because they violate the kinds of moral actions that people should expect from each other and from companies that relate to them. Compatible with their approaches is the view (Turow 2006; Turow 2011; Gandy 2010) that tracking individuals in the digital environment for the purpose of sending personalized materials to them is essentially a process of social discrimination. Marketers are increasingly involved in trying to distinguish between people who would and would not be likely (and profitable) consumers of their products. An efficiency-oriented urge to separate populations into "targets" and "waste" is cultivating an industry of data processors and sellers that aim to send "relevant" commercial messages to individuals within contexts of news and entertainment stories. As we move further into the twenty-first century, people with certain reputations among marketers will get "richer" offers, coupons and media fare than others based on what marketers have learned about them—and based on how willing they are to accede to marketers' interests. In this account, the harm is to people's limited vistas on the world based on views of them that they might intuit, but do not know for sure, and over which they have no control. It is also to the larger social polity, which may be riven by tensions as people try to understand where they stand and to get the offers and media views that they see some of their neighbors receiving.

According to several of these alternative frames, the very act of not allowing people control over the selective self-revelation is what is at issue—rather than any physical damages engendered by that loss of control. Compared to concerns about concrete medical, financial and other losses, though, these alternative views of the social meaning of data tracking are rarely mentioned as causes for action among members of SMOs. The reason is their belief that regulatory officials, lawmakers and their staffs feel bound by traditional metrics of harm.

## The industry's self-regulatory approach

The people tagged to protect the digital marketing ecosystem with regulators understand this constraint in the system well. They exploit it to their advantage in two ways. One is to play down the traditional notions of harm that advocates allege. The other way is to camouflage and minimize digital tracking, targeting, and tailoring in their self-regulatory regime so that it is difficult for regulatory officials and even advocates to make the case for harm without significant additional knowledge.

Digital marketing advocacy organizations have been consistent in playing down the traditional notions of harm. Industry representatives have made the case at government hearings and at industry conferences that the real harms to individuals and society have already been tackled. Concerns about the use and sale of personal financial and health information are addressed by the Health Insurance Portability and Accountability Act (HIPAA) and the Gramm-Leach-Bliley Act, respectively. Rules limiting the collection of information from children under the age of 13 are covered by the Children's Online Privacy Protection Act (COPPA). Identity theft, representatives note, is clearly illegal. Bad actors using deceptive advertising practices are warned and even pursued by an increasingly activist FTC as well as a new Consumer Protection Agency. The rest—the recording of individuals' everyday actions and attributes for the purpose of selling them products and serving them material that they are likely to enjoy—is really quite harmless, and may even be useful for the people who are targeted. After all, the goal is to present consumers with materials that they deem relevant. In any event, marketers note, the tracking and targeting activities are particularly harmless when the individuals are anonymous, as they often are in this process.

In August 2010, the president and chair of the US Interactive Advertising Bureau (IAB), Randall Rothenberg, added a twist—the idea of *conspiracy*—to the industry line that the public's negative reactions to being followed and targeted online are misguided. Rothenberg had been an *Advertising Age* columnist and a strategist at the consulting firm Booz Allen Hamilton. Since the mid-1990s, the IAB had helped to bring order to web advertising by creating technical standards that made it possible for publishers, media agencies and technology firms to work together efficiently. Those standards would be irrelevant, Rothenberg implied, if determined attacks on Internet-industry marketing activities were to continue. His call in a *USA Today* op-ed piece was to the newspaper's broad readership. "A wild debate is on," he began, "about websites using 'tracking tools' to 'spy' on American Internet users. Don't fall for it. The controversy is led by activists who want to obstruct essential Internet technologies and return the United States to a world of limited consumer choice in news, entertainment, products and services." Not naming names, Rothenberg stated that the activists "have rebranded as 'surveillance technology' various devices—cookies, beacons and IP addresses—that fuel the Internet." He then asserted that, "Without them, Web programming and advertising can't make its way to your laptop, phone or PC. At risk are $300 billion in US economic activity and 3.1 million jobs generated by the advertising-supported Internet, according to [an IAB-funded study by] Harvard professors John Deighton and John Quelch" (Rothenberg 2010).

Rothenberg went on to note that "thousands of small retailers and sites" depend on the web for a living. After giving a few examples of regular folks' ad-supported sites, he noted the tracking activities that sustain them should raise no alarms because anonymity is the rule: "The information they use to deliver content is impersonal. Unlike newspaper and cable-TV subscription data, it doesn't contain your name or address." Besides, he said, "You already have what you need to control your privacy, by eliminating cookies from your browser. Major websites offer highly visible tools that put consumers in charge of their data" (Rothenberg 2010).

On blogs and in emails, privacy activists disagreed fiercely with Rothenberg's points about consumer power over their data. They noted that his claim about cookies was especially disingenuous. Certainly, web users can eliminate cookies (about a quarter of them say do so regularly), but marketers keep putting them back. There are ways in which to block the insertion of browser cookies—Ghostery.com is a site that helps with that—but there is little evidence that a substantial percentage of the Internet population uses them. Rothenberg undoubtedly also realized that companies have been facing threats to the traditional tracking cookie by figuring out new ways of keeping persistent identities of people they meet online. One tack is to make a third-party "tracking cookie," which is typically the kind that browsers erase, look like a "first party" cookie, so that it will not be zapped. Another involves the use of locally shared objects (LSOs), also called "Flash cookies." LSOs perform the function of cookies, but are harder to erase because they are stored on the user's hard drive in connection with the Adobe Flash program. Rothenberg must also have been aware that the need for persistent identification would push companies in his industry toward new ways of tracking people without erasure. Two months after his piece appeared, for example, a startup called BlueCava announced to the trade that it had begun to provide original equipment manufacturers with technology that would allow a digital device "with the ability to identify itself" and that a website could associate with particular information it would store. *Online Media Daily* reported that the company "has put together a data exchange where businesses can contribute information they know about a device that should make targeting ads more accurate" (Sullivan 2010). Within the same time window, the *New York Times* reported on a technology company called Ringleader Digital with a product called Media Stamp that uses the HTML5 technology, and according to critics "acquired information from plaintiff's phone and assigned a unique ID to their mobile devices" (Vega 2010: B3).

So Rothenberg had to know that he was overreaching in his claims about individual controls. Punctiliousness was not the point, though, because the essay's purpose was really political. It was a salvo in a struggle by what Rothenberg called "the nation's largest media and marketing trade associations" to counter rising ire at the federal and state levels about the tracking and targeting of individual consumers. The larger battle took place over a number of years. It began getting into high gear when the FTC, in 2007, released a preliminary report that urged the industry to follow a set of principles for self-regulation when it came to online behavioral advertising. Intentionally defining behavioral advertising broadly, the FTC said "behavioral advertising means the tracking of a consumer's activities online—including the searches the consumer has conducted, the web pages visited, and the content viewed—in order to deliver advertising targeted to the individual consumer's interests" (Federal Trade Commission 2007: 2). Town hall meetings and petitions from industry groups as well as activists led the FTC to release a 2009 staff report in which it laid out a suggested regulatory framework that fundamentally supported marketers' needs. When the dust settled, it was clear that the staff had written their document in a way that meshed with the views of industry lobbyists.

The new regulatory framework did respond to concerns that non-business interests raised in town hall meetings. It proposed that firms engaging in tracking and targeting provide an explanation, separate from the site's formal privacy policy, about the information they gather. The staff report also encouraged firms to give their audiences the choice of whether to receive targeted ads. It enjoined firms to inform consumers when privacy policies are changed, to receive consent to use the old data in new ways, and to make sure the data are secure and not retained indefinitely. It urged that so-called "sensitive data" (data about finance, health, and sexual preferences) be handled with great care, to the point at which consumers should consent, or affirmatively opt in, to their use. It accepted privacy advocates' contentions that, because of sophisticated linking techniques and data accidents, it made no sense from a privacy standpoint to distinguish between the online collection of personally identifiable information (e.g. a person's name, postal address, email address) and information that was supposedly not clearly identifiable (e.g. the health condition of an anonymous person). Firms should treat all data in the same way.

Most prominently, though, the FTC staff report accepted that tracking and targeting had become part of the digital landscape, important for present and future business opportunities. What particularly upset privacy advocates was the report's agreement with marketers that they could carry out most data collection on an opt-out basis—that is, an advertiser did not have to get permission to collect information from individuals except in highly sensitive areas. In fact, in some areas the staff agreed that companies did not even need to offer an opt-out possibility at all. So, for example, the staff report (Federal Trade Commission 2009) distinguished between "first party" and "third party" tracking. The first involves a company tracking people only on its site and sites with the same brand (e.g. Disney.com and Disney.net). Third-party tracking involves a company that follows people across sites and uses the data to send ads to them. The FTC staff concluded that the two types of tracking involved different consumer expectations:

> After considering the comments, staff agrees that "first party" behavioral advertising practices are more likely to be consistent with consumer expectations, and less likely to lead to consumer harm, than practices involving the sharing of data with third parties or across multiple websites. . . . In such case, the tracking of the consumer's online activities in order to deliver a recommendation or advertisement tailored to the consumer's inferred interests involves a single website where the consumer has previously purchased or looked at items. Staff believes that, given the direct relationship between the consumer and the website, the consumer is likely to understand why he has received the targeted recommendation or advertisement and indeed may expect it. The direct relationship also puts the consumer in a better position to raise any concerns he has about the collection and use of his data, exercise any choices offered by the website, or avoid the practice

> altogether by taking his business elsewhere. By contrast, when behavioral advertising involves the sharing of data with ad networks or other third parties, the consumer may not understand why he has received ads from unknown marketers based on his activities at an assortment of previously visited websites. Moreover, he may not know whom to contact to register his concerns or how to avoid the practice.
>
> (*Federal Trade Commission 2009: 26–27*)

This basic distinction became a key launching pad from which five industry groups—the American Association of Advertising Agencies, the Association of National Advertisers, the Direct Marketing Association, the Interactive Advertising Bureau and the Council of Better Business Bureaus—formed the Digital Advertising Alliance to build their self-regulation policy (Clayburn 2010). The approach solidified around the use of an advertising option icon next to an ad to disclose that behavioral targeting has taken place. The icon would link the site visitor to the kinds of explanations and opt-out activities that the FTC report suggested (Interactive Advertising Bureau 2010). Industry representatives met with the staff intensively to make sure that the emerging industry approach mapped onto the FTC's report and intent. Marketers then worked with two primary organizations, Evidon and TrustE, to serve the Alliance's icon and opt-out procedures.

Guidelines that the five industry groups released in 2009, however, used a narrower definition of online behavioral advertising than the FTC's initial broad take. Online behavioral advertising (OBA), the report said, is:

> . . . the collection of data online from a particular computer or device regarding Web viewing behaviors over time and across non-affiliate Web sites for the purpose of using such data to predict user preferences or interests to deliver advertising to that computer or device based on the preferences or interests inferred from such Web viewing behaviors.
>
> (*AAAA et al. 2009: 2*)

Taking a cue from the FTC staff report's sense of consumer expectations, the Digital Advertising Alliance excludes first parties from even the notion that behavioral advertising is taking place. That means a publisher does not have to display the icon if it buys offline information about its site visitors or if it follows people around on its own site and on "affiliate sites."[1] If a publisher exerts management control over the advertising on 100 sites that have totally different names, it can track people across those domains and not have to show them the icon.

The icon is supposed to be a company's portal to "clear, meaningful" notice about "data collection and use practices." In important ways, though, what it leads to is little different from a web staple that should have helped with such disclosures, but did not: the privacy policy. As Wikipedia notes, a privacy policy "is a legal document that discloses some or all of the ways a party gathers, uses, discloses and manages a customer's data" (Wikipedia 2011a). With the exception of certain information involving health, financial and children, the United States does not have specific regulation requiring companies to explain themselves when they collect and use data about individuals. Nevertheless, in 1995, the FTC published what it called the Fair Information Principles, which set out the proposition that companies ought to follow four fair information practices when collecting personal information from members of the public: *notice* about the activities; *choice* about whether and how the personal

1 "Affiliate sites" are those that the publisher owns or controls even if the names of the sites are so different as to make it unlikely that a consumer could tell. Disney.com and ESPN.com are examples.

information should be used beyond the initial purposes for which it was provided; *access* to the data to be able to judge its accuracy; and reasonable steps for *security*—that is, ensuring that the information collected is accurate and protected from unauthorized use (Federal Trade Commission 2009). The Commission made clear that although no law mandated the principles and practices, they were norms to guide the drafting of privacy policies online.

By the turn of the 2000s, many critics were already pointing out that, overwhelmingly, privacy policies did not fully follow the FTC's principles. Moreover, the legalistic formulations of the policies made them nearly impossible to understand. The FTC, implementing a privacy policy requirement in the Children's Online Privacy Protection Act of 1998, tried to enforce clarity on those texts (see Turow 2001). It did not help. A systematic content analysis of ninety children's websites found major problems with their completeness and complexity (Turow 2001). While there is no similar analysis of children's sites today, we can say with assurance that complexity and incomplete adherence to the Fair Information Principles are hallmarks of websites in general. Just as important from the standpoint of advertiser power is a more subtle phenomenon: Even if you can get through a site's privacy policy, you will find little that is direct and explicit about what advertisers do on the site. Put another way, part of the power advertisers hold over websites is manifested by the way in which the websites cover up how responsive they are to advertisers.

By the late 2000s, the lack of public clicking on, and understanding of, privacy policies led the FTC staff to exhort the industry to help the public to learn about behavioral targeting "outside of the privacy policy" (Federal Trade Commission 2009: 35). Ironically, however, the well-established pattern of cloaking and ambiguity in the privacy policy has served as a model for the approach to the advertising option icon taken by many advertisers and ad networks. They hide their activities behind jargon and rabbit-hole links.

Consider this experience from December 2011. You visit a Yahoo! sports page and see an ad from Target stores that has the advertising option icon on its top right corner. You might not notice the icon: on Yahoo!, for example, it is a tiny gray drawing next to the word "AdChoices," also in gray. But say you do, and you click to learn more. Clicking on the icon next to an ad promoting "One Odd Trick to Stay Asleep at Night" in late 2011 leads to a page served by Yahoo! (not Evidon or TrustE, in this case) that, confusingly, has nothing to do with the ad. It is a Yahoo! Privacy page titled "AdChoices: Learn More About This Ad" (Yahoo! 2011). The page is divided into two parts, one "for consumers" and the other "for advertisers and publishers." The consumer-oriented part presents a preamble about how "The Web sites you visit work with online advertising companies to provide you with advertising that is as relevant and useful as possible." It then has three major bullets: who placed this ad? (The answer: Yahoo!) Where can I learn more about how Yahoo! selects ads? (The answer: a link to a page about Yahoo!'s "privacy and advertising practices.") What choices do I have—about interest-based advertising from Yahoo!? (The answer: a link to see the "interest-based categories" Yahoo! uses to serve you ads as well as to add to the list or opt out.) Click on the link to the choices, and you may see that Yahoo! has tagged you in a few, or several, from among hundreds of interest categories.

Yahoo! is following the rules, and the rules say that it does not have to give detailed explanations about data mining or tracking right after you click on the icon. What Yahoo! actually says may sounds quite innocuous, so a person might not find it worth the time to take additional action. Let us assume, though, that you decide to opt out of the company tracking you. You find a lot of language on the page and successive links that try to dissuade you. A prominent "Learn More!" notice on the AdChoices web page exhorts you to follow a link to "Find out how online advertising supports the free content, products, and services you use online."

Another link takes you to the Network Advertising Initiative (NAI), which tells visitors at the top that allowing cookies is "a way to support the websites and products you care about." Say you still want to stop Yahoo! from tracking you. As it turns out, you cannot do it. The only thing that you can do is link to a part of the NAI site, where you can tell that company and others that you do not want to receive their online behavioral ads. The company can still track you with a cookie so that it can use what it learns about you in statistical analyses of web users. The rules do not allow you to tell it to stop doing that. In fact, when you go to the opt-out area (NAI 2011), the site cautions you that your action to stop the firm's targeted ads will not enable you to stop receiving advertising; it will simply result in ads that are not relevant to your interests. In view of the limitations—that you will be continue to be tracked and have irrelevant ads sent to you—why would many people click to opt out?

That, of course, is exactly what the Internet advertising industry hopes will happen. Advocacy groups voiced indignation that an individual's opting out via the icon meant only opting out from being served "relevant" ads, not from being tracked and having data stored about them. The FTC responded with a report in early 2012 that exhorted the industry to work toward genuine options such as providing do-not-track instructions in browsers as well as through websites (Vega and Wyatt 2012). As of late April 2012, though, the Alliance had not accepted browser technologies that would allow do-not-track. Moreover, a click on an advertising icon next to a Ford ad on Yahoo!'s website led to an Evidon site with the same disclaimers seen in December 2011.

It may be a bit startling that the self-regulatory apparatus is set up to guide people to accept tracking by behavioral marketers. An even deeper concern is that the digital advertising system's reports, websites and leaders weave four propositions into their pronouncements that discourage people from taking seriously what is going on behind their screens. Randall Rothenberg's essay underscores the first proposition: namely, that marketers and regulators have dealt successfully with the real privacy problems of the web so that the only reason why people worry about the use of their data in the new media environment is because it feels "creepy." This view sees the web's real potential for harm as the leaking of information about a person that can damage a person's financial situation, reveal sensitive health information, or cause other forms of embarrassment that might corrode interpersonal or employment relationships. The 2007 FTC report quietly accepts this view of harm. The report does not present a summary of why we ought to be concerned about behavioral targeting, but its strongest statements of concern center on situations in which people may be stung when their anonymity is unmasked without permission. This approach also shows up in the above-noted quote about first- and third-party tracking; the report accepts that some of what worries people may relate to real estimations of misused or abused information and some to the creepiness of being followed.

The Internet industry accepts this framing of harms, although it argues that the FTC follows privacy advocates in overestimating the real dangers that exist. It leads to the second proposition that runs through industry pronouncements: that regulators and the public should thank marketers for promoting anonymity and relevance as the two pillars of acceptable tracking by the advertising system. Marketers and websites reserve the right to learn and use people's names and email addresses, but they typically do not reveal that personally identifiable information to other parties that are using their data. That said, the public and regulators should increasingly know that companies feed on individuals' data if they are to bring them relevant, enjoyable material. Giving up information, even personal information, will increasingly be the price of circulating "free" or inexpensive relevant content on the Internet. But the kind of information requested—and the protections of that information—are such that the worries are merely psychological.

This stream of logic leads to the two other propositions, each of which gives marketers the moral high ground. One argument states that because privacy concerns about Internet advertising are really emotional states not rooted in logical or valid concerns, people's reactions to marketers' data collection is inherently unstable. Individuals may say they want to protect their information, but they will gladly relinquish it for token rewards. This contention has a long history in the trade press and at industry meetings. A 2001 *Advertising Age* article, for example, quoted industry analyst Rob Leathern as saying "flatly" that "Consumers are very schizophrenic. They want their privacy, but they're willing to give out information for entry into an online sweepstakes" (Dobrow 2001). An alternative proposition about audiences, though, sees them as more rational. It argues that, while some Americans are simply unconcerned about their privacy online, most Americans make cost–benefit analyses about whether to release their information. Privacy consultant Alan Westin calls these people "privacy pragmatists." Interpreting survey questions about Americans' attitudes, he noted: "They examined the benefits to them or society of the data collection and use, wanted to know the privacy risk and how organizations proposed to control those, and then decided whether to trust the organization or seek legal oversight" (Westin 2003: 445).

This description of most Americans as aware of their online privacy options supports the industry line that self-regulation through opt-out mechanisms is a logical way to go, and that the small opt-out numbers reflect rational choice. Those who champion the notion that consumers are illogical about privacy would probably agree that opt-out mechanisms cannot hurt, but that in the end their decision not to opt out reflects their fickleness about privacy more than anything else. Either proposition would click with Dave Morgan's suggestion for tempting consumers with quid pro quo value propositions to release data. Morgan is a target-marketing entrepreneur who has founded companies (24/7 Real Media and Tacoda) that have exerted profound influence on the Internet space. "If you're giving medicine to a dog, you put it inside some peanut butter," he advised in 2001. "Tell consumers what you're going to do, but give them something for it" (Dobrow 2001).

Morgan's recommendation that companies offer people something they like in exchange for their information resonates even more so with the needs of marketers today. Publishers are developing new software that tracks people, not via cookies that they can erase, but by reading a unique identifier of the device they are using (e.g. a particular phone or television set). In addition, publishers increasingly will want visitors to register so that they can track them across different devices (e.g. a desktop computer, a laptop, an iPad, a mobile device and a home television set). In the heat of escalating competition, publishers will also want to ask people for information—about their health, their travels, the value of their homes—that can attract advertisers to them, but that individuals may think twice about providing. For some visitors, a gift, kind words and a nod to security will loosen their data. The tactic will escalate among marketers and third-party data providers, as they want to collect their own special data or convince people not to opt out of their ability to carry out behavioral advertising practices. The belief that people are inconsistent about their data, or a belief that people carefully consider their choices, provides the advertising industry with cover for allowing them to show their more giving sides. The industry is particularly off the hook if the public and regulators grant that, because of self-regulation, the risk to them is actually quite low. To hear Randall Rothenberg tell it, the risk may even be non-existent, exaggerated or trumped up by activists.

Issues of social discrimination, the creation of reputations, and the importance of respecting individuals information do not make it into that frame. In the absence of an ability to point to major harms that fit the contemporary frame and the lack of other sophisticated policy frames, policymakers and others who are indignant about the very nature and presence of the web have taken to using words such as "creepy" and "icky" to express their concerns about companies tracking them online. The terminology has even reached the halls of the US Senate. During a 2010 privacy hearing, Senator Claire McCaskill, Democrat of Missouri, said that she found behavioral targeting troubling. "I understand that advertising supports the Internet, but I am a little spooked out," McCaskill said. "This is creepy" (Helft and Vega 2010: A1). Joanna O'Connell of Forrester Research attributed a similar impression to consumers in general during a National Public Radio (NPR) interview. When some marketers consider tracking consumers, she noted, they try to figure out where the negative reactions will start. "There's sort of the human element, the sort of ick factor," O'Connell said. "And marketers are aware of that. Depending on the marketer, there are some that are very reticent about using certain types of targeting" (Sydell 2010).

When lawmakers and analysts confront an issue by invoking an "ick" or "creep" factor as a reason for their distaste, it shows that the self-regulatory strategy is working for the industry. Part of the reason is that industry groups have been successful in foregrounding traditional frames of harm, and using the self-regulatory icon system to disguise what they do so as not to validate alternative frames. In succeeding with this endeavor, they have relied on the unwitting help of regulators, and even some advocacy organizations and regulators, which have found industry activities too abstruse to understand without industry help. Public thought leaders at the highest levels of government and advocacy have not worked through the issue of audience tracking and labeling well enough to be able to present a succinct, logical argument about the harm that it can cause. In a circular argument of their construction, web-marketing leaders exploit this lack of a clear frame as evidence that the use of individuals' data is basically a psychological issue. It is, they say, rooted in consumers' negative emotional reactions rather than in any widespread or genuine threats to society or its members.

This narrow view on the social and personal implications of the new digital-tracking-targeting-and-tailoring universe does not have to be the final frame—nor should it be. As the twenty-first century progresses, tensions centering on data-driven social discrimination and the importance of personal control over reputations may well become clear to policy-makers, social-movement organizations, media firms and even major marketers. The social-constructionist lens applied here can be helpful for crystalizing the dynamics and implications of debates that center on stakeholders in an American context. It is quite possible that the approach can be as helpfully adapted for exploring contestations of media "harms" in other societies, as well.

## References

American Association of Advertising Agencies (AAAA), Association of National Advertisers (ANA), Better Business Bureau (BBB), Direct Marketing Association (DMA) and Interactive Advertising Bureau (IAB) (2009) 'Self-regulatory principles for online behavioral advertising', July. Online. HTTP available: http://www.iab.net/insights_research/public_policy/behavioral-advertising-principles (accessed 26 October 2010).

Benford, R. D. (1993) 'Frame disputes within the nuclear disarmament movement,' *Social Forces*, 71: 677–701.

—— and Hunt, S. A. (2003) 'Interactional dynamics in public problems marketplaces: Movements and the counterframing and reframing of public problems,' in J. A. Holstein and G. Miller (eds.) *Challenges and Choices: Constructionist Perspectives on Social Problems*, Hawthorne, NY: Aldine de Gruyter.

Best, J. (2012) 'Constructionist social problems theory,' in C. Salmon (ed.) *Communication Yearbook 36*, New York and London: Routledge.

Clayburn, T. (2009) 'Ad industry sets seven privacy protection principles,' *Information Week*, 2 July. Online. HTTP available: http://www.informationweek.com/news/internet/search/showArticle.jhtml?articleID=218400278&subSection=News (accessed 4 November 2010).

Dobrow, L. (2001) 'Tread carefully on privacy: Be wary of e-consumer backlash,' *Advertising Age*, 29 October: S6.
Entman, R. (1993) 'Framing: Toward clarification of a fractured paradigm,' *Journal of Communication*, 43(4): 51–58.
EPIC (2011) 'EPIC-led coalition calls for FTC Facebook investigation,' 29 September. Online. Available HTTP: http://epic.org/2011/09/epic-led-coalition-calls-for-f.html (accessed 3 October 2011). Letter available online at http://epic.org/privacy/facebook/EPIC_Facebook_FTC_letter.pdf.
Federal Trade Commission (2007) 'FTC staff proposes online behavioral advertising privacy principles.' Online. Available HTTP: http://www.ftc.gov/opa/2007/12/principles.shtm (accessed 7 October 2011).
—— (2009) *FTC Staff Report: Self-Regulatory Principles for Online Behavioral Advertising*, Washington, DC: PTC. Online. Available HTTP: http://www.ftc.gov/os/2009/02/P085400behavadreport.pdf (accessed 7 October 2011).
Gandy, O. (2009) *Coming to Terms with Chance*, Williston, VT: Ashgate.
Helft, M. and Vega, T. (2010) 'Seeing that ad on every site? You're right. It's tracking you,' *New York Times*, 30 August: A1.
Interactive Advertising Bureau (2010) 'Major marketing/media trade groups launch program to give consumers enhanced control over collection and use of web viewing data for online behavioral advertising,' Press release, 4 October. Online. Available HTTP: http://www.iab.net/about_the_iab/recent_press_releases/press_release_archive/press_release/pr-100410?gko=7b157 (accessed 4 October 2011).
Lofland, J. (1993) *Polite Protesters: The American Peace Movement of the 1980s*, Syracuse, NY: Syracuse University Press.
Mandese, J. (2011) 'WTF? Can the alphabet soup of targeting technology spell "clarity" anytime soon?' OMMA Behavioral Conference, 22 March, New York City. Online. Available HTTP: http://www.mediapost.com/events/?/showID/OMMABehavioral.11.NYC/type/Agenda/itemID/1845/OMMABehavioral-Agenda.html (accessed 3 October 2011).
Network Advertising Initiative (NAI) (2011) 'Opt out of behavioral advertising.' Online. Available HTTP: http://www.networkadvertising.org/managing/opt_out.asp (accessed 20 April 2012).
Nissenbaum, H. (2009) *Privacy in Context*, Palo Alto, CA: Stanford Law Books.
Ogus, A. (2004) 'W(h)ither the economic theory of regulation? What economic theory of regulation?' In J. Jordana and D. Levi-Faur (eds.) *The Politics of Regulation*, Northampton, MA: Edward Elgar.
Regan, P. M. (1995) *Legislating Privacy: Technology, Social Values, and Public Policy*, Chapel Hill, NC: The University of North Carolina Press.
Rothenberg, R. (2010) 'Don't fear Internet tracking,' *USA Today*, 9 August: 10A.
Shade, L. R. (2008) 'Reconsidering the right to privacy in Canada,' *Bulletin of Science, Technology & Society*, 28(1): 8–91.
Solove, D. (2008) *Understanding Privacy*, Boston, MA: Harvard University Press.
—— (2010) *Nothing to Hide*, New Haven, CT: Yale University Press.
Spector, M. and Kitsuse, J. I. (1977) *Constructing Social Problems*, Menlo Park, CA: Cummings.
Sullivan, L. (2010) 'Report: Click fraud reaches new heights,' *Online Media Daily*, 21 October. Online. Available HTTP: http://www.mediapost.com/publications/?fa=Articles.showArticle&art_aid=138061 (accessed 21 October 2010).
Sydell, L. (2010) 'Smart cookies put targeted online ads on the rise,' National Public Radio's *All Things Considered*, 5 October, via Lexis Nexis.
Turow, J. (2001) *Privacy Policies on Children's Websites: Do They Play by the Rules?* Philadelphia, PA: Annenberg Public Policy Center. Online. Available HTTP: http://www.asc.upenn.edu/usr/jturow/Privacy%20Report.pdf (accessed 5 October 2011).
—— (2006) *Niche Envy: Marketing Discrimination in the Digital Age*, Cambridge, MA: MIT Press.
—— (2011) *The Daily You: How the New Advertising Industry is Defining Your Identity and Your Worth*, New Haven, CT: Yale University Press.
Vega, T. (2010) 'Code that tracks users browsing prompts lawsuits,' *New York Times*, 21 September: B3.
—— and Wyatt, E. (2012) 'US agency seeks tougher consumer privacy rules,' *New York Times*, 26 March: A1.
Warren, S. and Brandeis L. (1890) 'The right to privacy,' *Harvard Law Review*, 4.

Westin, A. (1968) *Privacy and Freedom*, New York: Atheneum.
—— (2003) 'Social and political dimensions of privacy,' *Journal of Social Issues*, 59(2): 431–453.
Wikipedia (2011a) 'Privacy.' Online. Available HTTP: http://en.wikipedia.org/wiki/Privacy (accessed 3 October 2011).
—— (2011b) 'Security.' Online. Available HTTP: http://en.wikipedia.org/wiki/Security (accessed 3 October 2011).
Yahoo! (2011) 'AdChoices: Learn more about this ad.' Online. Available HTTP: http://info.yahoo.com/privacy/us/yahoo/relevantads.html (accessed 4 October 2011).

# 27

# Technological innovation, paradox and ICTs

## Challenges for governing institutions

*Robin Mansell*

### Introduction[1]

Transformations in the technological composition of the contemporary communication system raise many questions about whether institutional arrangements for the governance of the system are "fit for purpose." McQuail defines "governance" as the means by which actors are "limited, directed, encouraged, managed, or called into account, ranging from the most binding laws to the most resistible of pressures and self-chosen disciplines" (McQuail 2003: 91). Following this definition, governance issues are the concern of formal institutions of regulation by the state and they arise as a result of the explicit and tacit norms influencing the practices of actors involved in many other institutions.

With the spread of the Internet, the term "network governance" has been coined to describe interactions among multiple public, semi-public and private actors (Sörenson and Torfing 2008). As the number of stakeholders with an interest in the governance arrangements for the communication system increases, debates in this area have become flashpoints for multiple disputes about the need for adjustments to traditional ways in which the telecommunication and broadcasting sectors have been regulated (Mansell and Raboy 2011), as well as to the arrangements for governing the Internet. These disputes tend to be articulated around the interests of stakeholders favoring market-led developments and those favoring opportunities for developments outside the constraints of the market. Two of the most visible flashpoints are concerned with what is referred to as "network neutrality" and with the roles of Internet service providers (ISPs) in enforcing intellectual property rights legislation, both of which are considered in this chapter.

This chapter begins with a consideration of the profile of contemporary debates about the governance of the communication system on the international stage, emphasizing the tension between a market-oriented model of governance and a model that emphasizes non-market relationships. The next section introduces some of the key features of technological changes

1 Some aspects of this chapter draw on Mansell 2012.

in the information and communication technologies (ICT) sector, giving particular attention to their disruptive implications for both industry and government. The focus then shifts to debates about network neutrality and their implications for the technologies for control of the communication system and for the roles of ISPs in managing Internet traffic flows. (For a more detailed treatment of network neutrality issues, see Yoo and Van Eijk in this volume.) This discussion sets the stage for an examination of the implications of technological innovation in contemporary efforts to enforce intellectual property rights on the Internet. The controversies over whether ISPs should be required to serve as gatekeepers on the network, the likely effects of legal requirements requiring them to serve in this capacity, and the challenges faced by those who resist the prevailing view that ICT convergence and the Internet are facilitating the "stealing" of digital information provide the focus for this section.

The penultimate section considers the contrasting perspectives of stakeholders claiming that market-imposed information scarcity is the optimal way in which to foster the production and consumption of digital information and those who claim, instead, that an information commons-based approach is consistent with the same goals. The persistence of conflict over governance arrangements is discussed in the light of the paradoxical features of technological innovation and digital information. The conclusion summarizes the main arguments of this chapter. It emphasizes the need to devise governance arrangements for the Internet that will foster reconciliation of the goals of economic growth and social justice in the face of these paradoxical features and conflicting interests. This applies to matters relating to the future management of the Internet and to the rights of citizens to produce, circulate and reconfigure digital information for a variety of economic, political and social purposes.

## Contemporary governance debates

Controversies over Internet governance, sometimes referred to as "Internet regulation," and over the right to access and use digital information, are prominent in debates in forums at the global level such as the G20, as well as in the institutions formally charged with policymaking and regulation in the media and communication sector (see Maclean 2011 for a review of these institutions). For example, when President Sarkozy argued for tougher Internet regulation at a French government-hosted e-G8 summit in 2011, there were protests from those defending an open Internet. Sarkozy had called for coordinated international regulation to defend the Internet (and the web) against monopoly control, copyright breaches, child pornography, intrusions into personal privacy and security threats associated with rogue software. Addressing an audience that included representatives of the private sector actors such as Google, Facebook, Amazon and eBay, he remarked that "the universe you represent is not a parallel universe. Nobody should forget that governments are the only legitimate representatives of the will of the people in our democracies. To forget this is to risk democratic chaos and anarchy" (Pfanner 2011).

His claim signals the close association between issues relating to the governance of the technological features of the communication system and those concerning the purposes or aims of such regulation, which raise broad questions about social, political and cultural values, as well as about social justice and equality. Governments are far from being united in their approaches to the challenges of governance in the face of technological innovation. The UK government, among others, resisted the French government's initiative in this case since it seemed to suggest stronger (more intrusive) state-led regulation of the Internet.

The Organization for Economic Co-operation and Development (OECD) subsequently issued what it described as a "consensus-based" policy, setting out principles for Internet governance. These had been devised with input from governments, the private sector and civil society representatives (OECD 2011b). Although many of the principles were welcomed by civil society organizations, their representatives refused to sign up to this statement of principles because of the support it gives to the creative industry's bid to achieve stronger enforcement of intellectual property law. A communiqué issued at the time the policy principles were announced noted that "effective protection of intellectual property rights plays a vital role in spurring innovation and furthers the development of the Internet economy." It went on to state that "appropriate measures include lawful steps to address and deter infringement, and accord full respect to user and stakeholder rights and fair process" (OECD 2011a: 3, 6). Thus a key element of the principles envisages that organizations such as ISPs should respect the fundamental rights and freedoms of citizens, but that they should also assist rights holders in reducing the flows of illegal content on the Internet.

In contemporary debates about Internet governance, stakeholders with an interest in the commodity value of digital information tend to encourage governance solutions that privilege the market exchange of information. This relies on the acceptance of private rights of ownership of digital output and the enforcement of intellectual property laws. These stakeholders assume that Internet users express their preferences for digital content in the marketplace and that the role of governments is to ensure that governance arrangements secure the ownership rights of the creative industry firms.

In contrast, the stakeholders who privilege the cultural and social value of digital information tend to emphasize the non-market sharing of information, which they argue is best facilitated by self-governing communities of Internet users that safeguard democratic values, freedom of speech and content diversity. Sassen's (2001: 28) analysis of power dynamics in the emerging network environment suggests that "power, contestation, inequality, in brief, hierarchy" always inscribe electronic space. Disputes about network neutrality and the role of ISPs in intellectual property law enforcement are indicative of power asymmetries of many kinds, which are subject to changes that are partly attributable to the disruptive influence of technological innovation in the ICT domain. The next section summarizes some of the features of technological innovation that are presenting challenges for the governance of the communication system.

## Technological innovation

In the ICT sector, technological convergence refers to the progressive application of digital ICTs for the input, storage, processing, distribution and presentation of information (Hawkins *et al.* 1997). Older generations of these technologies can be distinguished from newer ones by their use of integrated circuitry, the independence of software from hardware and the open configuration of the Internet. Developments in all of these areas mean that hardware, software and content-producing firms need to engage in constant innovation if they are to compete successfully in the market (Cusumano 2010). Changes in these technologies do not occur at a uniform rate, with the result that conflicts are common among the leading firms in the market and between these firms and government and civil society stakeholders. The modularity of technology, network externalities, integrated technology platforms and the architecture of the Internet all conspire to disrupt the stability of market relationships (Fransman 2008), and they lead to substantial changes in the non-market relationships among social actors in all aspects of everyday life.

Instability leads to contests over issues of governance with respect to the production and consumption of digital information because the markets for both ICTs and digital information are substantial. They comprise a growing share of gross domestic product (GDP) in the countries that host the leading firms.[2] Worldwide spending in the ICT sector was estimated at US$ 3,398 billion in 2009, of which 76 percent was in the OECD member countries (OECD 2010). The United Nations Conference on Trade and Development (UNCTAD) estimated the value of the creative industry in 2008 at US$ 407 billion (UNCTAD 2010). In the OECD countries, the output of firms in the creative industry is estimated to account for about 5–6 percent of GDP (TERA Consultants 2010), which is indicative of the growing dependence of the wealthy industrialized economies on intangible services.

Among the many changes in the communication technology landscape are the protocols that comprise the Internet. These are widely regarded as disruptive technologies because of their internetworking capabilities. The Internet can be defined technically as "the global data communication capability realized by the interconnection of public and private telecommunication networks using Internet Protocol (IP), Transmission Control Protocol (TCP), and other protocols required to implement IP inter-networking on a global scale, such as DNS [domain name system] and packet routing protocols" (Mathiason 2009: 11; see also Mueller *et al.* 2007). In the scholarly literature on matters of Internet governance, references to *the* Internet are commonplace. Such references often draw attention to the importance of a decentralized "end-to-end" public network that is blind to the content that flows through it, at least in principle, but they also reach beyond the technical features, suggesting the considerable implications of technological innovation for all aspects of the control and management of digital information.

Radical technological innovations such as the architecture of the Internet can disrupt the stability of earlier industrial relationships (Bresnahan and Trajtenberg 1995; Freeman 2007). The emergence of peer-to-peer (P2P) technologies and services that enable file uploading and downloading on the Internet is implicated in a wide range of disruptive effects that are impacting not only the economics of the markets for ICTs and digital information, but also the social, cultural and political environments in which online participation occurs. The significance of P2P is that, in a P2P network, every network client is a potential server and the reverse is also true. Some networks are centralized (e.g. Napster and Seti@Home), whereas others are decentralized (e.g. Freenet and Gnutella), with a variation being the BitTorrent protocol (EBU 2010). The essential disruptive feature is the relative ease with which interworking can occur without regard to centralized authority or traditional boundaries.

The growth of global IP traffic overall was estimated at a cumulative rate of 32 percent between 2010 and 2015. Estimates vary, but P2P file transfer traffic, which comprised more than 80 percent of all consumer IP traffic in 2010, is set to decline from 58 percent to a smaller share by 2015 as other forms of file transfer grow, indicating that P2P file transfer is not the only technical capability that is disrupting governance arrangements. There is very rapid growth in the transfer of large video files that are far more bandwidth "hungry" than the short-duration connections needed to deliver web pages or email. Some estimates suggest that Internet video will comprise 62 percent of all consumer Internet traffic by 2015 (CISCO 2011). Traffic growth on this scale creates a constant pressure for investment in network capacity and for greater efficiency in the management of this traffic. Some of the traffic is legally transmitted, but the creative industry is concerned about the 24 percent of all Internet traffic (excluding pornography) that is estimated to be copyright infringing (Envisional Ltd 2011).

2 With mergers and acquisitions, the names of the leading firms change over time. For a list of world leaders by revenue in 2010, see IDATE 2010.

Increasing volumes of IP traffic of various kinds must be carried on the open Internet.[3] This is prompting network operators and ISPs to claim that they need the flexibility to shape or control traffic on the Internet for both engineering-related quality-of-service reasons and for financial reasons to ensure that there are incentives for investment in higher bandwidth networks (Mansell and Steinmueller 2013). All of these developments in technology and markets, combined with changes in online social and cultural practices, are presenting major challenges for prevailing governance arrangements, and creating stresses and strains in the relationships among government, private sector and civil society stakeholders. The next section turns to an examination of some of the reasons for contestations over the issue of network neutrality, highlighting the implications for the control of digital information.

## Internet governance and network neutrality

Network neutrality has come to serve as an all-embracing term for policy matters relating to the Internet, but its implications are much more far-reaching than those directly concerned with the technical architecture of the Internet. Network neutrality is a technologically constituted ideal of the Internet as a network that enables the indiscriminate flow of all digital information. Assuming sufficient capacity, the Internet's technical design—its architecture—makes it possible for every digital bit to be treated equally regardless of its originator's wealth, socio-economic status, or other features. In her analysis of Internet governance issues, Denardis comments that "Internet protocols and the resources they create are the least visible but arguably most critical component of the Internet's technical and legal architecture. The development of universal Internet protocols and the management of scarce resources are fundamental Internet governance responsibilities" (Denardis 2009: 188). In the process of managing these scarce resources, ISPs employ a number of techniques, with substantial implications for the way in which the Internet is experienced by its users.

### *Traffic management or citizen monitoring*

ISPs employ traffic management (or shaping) techniques to manage demand for limited network capacity, claiming that they do so independently of the payments they receive for their services. There is a range of possibilities for managing Internet traffic, for instance by limiting the use of encrypted virtual private networks, restricting the operations of those providing certain kinds of information, and excluding high-bandwidth applications such as Voice over Internet Protocol (VoIP) telephony or P2P file sharing (Braman and Roberts 2003). Internet traffic managers have the technical capability to monitor third-party content and to suppress copyright infringing or other "unwanted" content.

The management of traffic flows involves methods for traffic inspection, such as deep packet inspection (DPI). These are used in ordinary traffic control to manage information flows and they include techniques such as those offered by Blue Coat Systems, DtecNet Software, L7-filter, NetScreen-IDP and NetScout Systems, and the use of Packet Details Markup Language (PDML). DPI techniques enable ISPs to give priority to certain content and to speed up data transfers for those willing to pay. Various techniques for filtering online

3 In contrast to "managed IP traffic," which, in the CISCO methodology includes corporate IP wide area network (WAN) traffic and the IP transport of television and video on demand.

content come into play to accomplish a wide range of goals, including the tracing of those who use the Internet for uploading or downloading of copyright infringing content.

These techniques enable ISPs to:

i. ration "bursty demand" and intense baseload demand periods on the network;
ii. choose priorities among different types of traffic, based on "level" criteria, for example constraining all VoIP traffic as opposed to only traffic generated by a particular operator such as Skype;
iii. introduce more "intelligent agent" filtering to produce internationally agreed benefits, for example anti-spam and virus protection, or benefits that are specific to certain national contexts (e.g. anti-pornography or suppression of certain forms of political expression);
iv. allow the extension of techniques to discriminate directly among the traffic on the Internet in a way that gives rise to various forms of "side payments" (non-transparent business arrangements), enabling some originators of traffic to avoid the filtering; and
v. establish a full-blown auctioning of the priority accorded to the traffic generated by suppliers and customers by introducing a market.

Which configuration of these possibilities is adopted by ISPs in the future will set the standard for what is deemed to constitute network neutrality in practice. Each step in the above list represents progress along the road to the "non-neutrality" of the Internet. Thus, despite claims about the need to preserve a neutral open Internet, at present in Western democracies in practice we are somewhere between steps iii. and iv. The rationale for and feasibility of restrictions on further progress are at the heart of network neutrality controversies.

In debates about network neutrality, the technical or engineering features of traffic management have become muddled with proposals to charge for preferential access to the Internet. The former amounts to technological rationing with the possibility for price discrimination (creating incentives to bypass some aspects of traffic shaping by ISPs). The latter involves efforts to create a condition of market scarcity where both suppliers and customers must indicate their willingness to pay for preferential access. Many of the techniques that can be used to pursue a pathway towards a non-neutral Internet have strong synergies with those that are used to pursue Internet users who are suspected of engaging in illegal file sharing of copyright-protected content. As Bendrath and Mueller argue, "if there is no simple 'technical fix' to the problems of the Internet, neither is there a one-way march into the Panopticon. Our findings suggest that the 'end of the Internet' is not pre-determined, nor is its freedom secure; its future rests very much in our own hands" (Bendrath and Mueller 2010: 25). They refer to the choices taken in numerous national jurisdictions and international forums about whether to intervene to limit progress towards a non-neutral Internet, a network that could easily be biased in favor of the corporate interests of the largest firms in the electronic equipment, network and service provider markets.

## *Reasonable or harmful online discrimination*

Debates in this area started to become prominent in the United States when it became clear that network operators and ISPs had incentives that might lead them to block Internet traffic from their competitors, or to charge certain service providers to terminate traffic on their networks, while offering preferential treatment to others (*Comcast Corp.* v *FCC* (2010)). If ISPs were permitted to introduce traffic management practices such as those indicated above, the Internet as it is presently experienced in the wealthy democratic countries would become fragmented, with implications for the sustainability of the open platform that it currently provides, for the costs of services, and for the rights of citizens to access digital information. In other countries as well, as the UN Special Rapporteur's report on the promotion and protection of the right to freedom of opinion and expression makes clear, the grounds for limiting access to information are extremely limited. This is because of "the unique and transformative nature of the Internet not only to enable individuals to exercise their right to freedom of opinion and expression, but also a range of other human rights" (La Rue 2011: Summary).

ISPs claim that, without their control over judgements about the use of traffic management tools, harm to the network will result in the degradation of the Internet user experience. This claim is reminiscent of claims by telecommunication network operators historically that any interference with their network would result in technical harm (Mansell 1993), a claim that proved to be unsubstantiated as the network became a platform for both traffic carriage and information service provision.[4] With respect to the contemporary Internet, the question is whether discrimination among traffic on the network is transparent and justified in the light of the competing goals of providing incentives for investment in network capacity and ensuring the maintenance of an open non-discriminatory network.

With the expansion of IP traffic on their networks, ISPs claim that flat-rate pricing for Internet access encourages excessive consumption of relatively scarce bandwidth resources. Content delivery networks (CDNs) are operated by firms that charge for the reliability and quality of information transmission, substituting data storage for long-distance capacity by using local caches that are located close to users. Those such as Akamai can be used to aggregate content, but this is of little benefit to ISPs because they claim that, under present governance arrangements, they are limited by network neutrality requirements in their means for managing traffic flows. In the United States and elsewhere, large content providers are finding ways in which to reduce their data transport costs and the problems of uneven data transmission rates by using server farms interconnected by private bypass networks. These enable them to avoid paying charges for data transmission on the public network (e.g. using non-Internet fiber for mirroring of content across servers). Google, Yahoo! and Microsoft are reported to be doing this for a growing proportion of their traffic. This has implications for ISPs who argue that their financial prospects are being damaged as a result of their inability to discriminate among sources of traffic and to compete effectively in the market.

While there are many stakeholders who value the neutrality of the Internet, there are very different views about the treatment of ISP traffic management claims. There are those who argue that the network should evolve without intervention by governments, consistent with favoring bottom-up innovation. Zittrain (2003) argues from a civil liberties perspective, for example, that, although it is technically feasible to cordon off areas of the Internet at content source and destination points, "network freedom" means that any intervention, even to mandate content filtering for the protection of children, is akin to the methods used by authoritarian regimes to restrict content. Interventionist regulation is not needed to guide the future development of the Internet.

Resistance to discriminatory traffic management measures aimed at maximizing revenues for the ISP Internet gatekeepers or at supporting the efforts of the creative industry firms to curtail infringing sharing of content comes from those who favor a commons-based peer production model of digital information production and consumption. Benkler and

4 The principle of common carriage is that operators may not "make any unjust or unreasonable discrimination in charges, practices, classifications, regulations, facilities, or services . . . or . . . make or give any undue or unreasonable preference to any particular person, class of persons, or locality" (United States 1996: §202a). See Lentz 2011 for changing definitions of "information service."

Nissenbaum argue, for instance, that information produced with the intention of sharing it on the Internet encourages inclusive virtues that are of great social value (Benkler 2004; Benkler and Nissenbaum 2006). This view is echoed in Lessig's (2008) claims that a remix culture is highly creative. This view finds much favor among those who see the open Internet as a platform for experimentation and collaborative activity (Baym 2010; Burnett 2010; Jenkins 2006). Those who seek to ensure that the Internet is used to preserve an online public sphere and freedom of speech and democracy lobby for regulatory forbearance. They claim that the end-to-end architecture of the Internet must be preserved because "regardless of whether content originates from an individual's server, a non-profit group, or a global corporation, data should be treated with equal priority across the network" (Barron 2008: 90).

However, if resistance is to be effective, it must be backed up by some kind of governance arrangement. For observers favoring both market and non-market approaches, there is a strong tendency to favor reliance on the good behavior of ISPs or that of the members of technical communities, although the rationales differ. Berners-Lee (2010) argues that social networking sites are starting to wall off information, restricting access, and ISPs are discriminating among Internet traffic in ways that are inimical to democracy, but he suggests that we should rely on "good" ISPs that will manage traffic in ways that are transparent to users. Sidak (2007) argues from an economic perspective that any regulatory intervention in the face of uncertainty about the way in which online markets are evolving could be very costly and result in foregone consumer welfare. He, similarly, makes a case against regulatory intervention to preserve an open network.

Many argue that technological innovation will flourish if companies are permitted to adopt business strategies as they see fit, claiming that the likelihood that companies will block or slow traffic on the Internet is low. Market forces can be relied upon to ensure that ISPs do not discriminate among traffic for reasons other than the prevention of technical harm. If they discriminate for other reasons, Yoo argues that cases should be dealt with retrospectively by the courts because "allowing network owners to differentiate their networks can better satisfy the increasing heterogeneity of end user demand" (Yoo 2005: 9). Advocates of non-intervention often argue that the costs and benefits of Internet governance are difficult, if not impossible, to assess. Therefore non-intervention is the optimal strategy. Problems in making such assessments are attributed to the complexity of contemporary networks—that is, to feedbacks and non-linear relationships in a complex technological system. For some, this suggests that government interventions are likely to yield uncertain and potentially damaging outcomes (Bauer 2007).

Even in those instances in which analysts acknowledge that it is likely that firms will use their market power to practice gatekeeping on the Internet, they often opt for industry self-control or self-regulation. Others suggest that "it sometimes happens that the only way to preserve freedom is through judicious controls on the exercise of private power" (Wu 2010: 310; see also Goldsmith and Wu 2006). Rather than call for Internet regulation by the state to limit or curtail the discriminatory practices of firms, however, Wu calls for a "constitutional approach"—that is, a legislative regime "whose goal is to constrain and divide *all* power that derives from the control of information" (Wu 2010: 304). To achieve this in the US context, he argues that the government should mandate a structural separation between the firms that produce information and those who own the network infrastructure or control access to it. Mueller, a strong defender of network neutrality, also is cautious about top-down Internet governance. He calls instead for "networked liberalism," which is to be achieved through the negotiations of "flexible and shifting social aggregations" of actors in a wide variety of forums (Mueller 2010: 269). His objection to governance arrangements from above stems from his concern to prevent states from acting "as information gatekeepers for their populations" (Mueller 2010: 209).

The Federal Communication Commission (FCC) in the United States has been engaged in a long-running debate about network neutrality, especially since its policy statement on the matter in the mid-2000s (FCC 2005). In 2010, it affirmed that the end-to-end architecture of the Internet should be preserved, observing that claims that the open, public Internet is being threatened are "not speculative or merely theoretical" (FCC 2010: para. 35). This view is contested by industry representatives and many economists who argue, as indicated above, that the market incentives for the supply of ISP services make it unlikely that ISPs will act "badly" by discriminating unreasonably among traffic originating from different service providers or from citizens who use the Internet to access and circulate content. Differences in the ISP industry structure in Europe as compared to the United States mean that the network neutrality debate in Europe is somewhat different, but its outcomes are similar (Powell and Cooper 2011). In both cases, network management intended to enhance the quality of service, to promote the development of new services, to secure network stability and resilience, or to combat crime, including illegal downloading, is not regarded as a departure from the principle of network neutrality.

In summary, there is incremental progression towards the use of discrimination among traffic on the Internet in the name of traffic management and this is leading to the emergence of a non-neutral network. Policy assertions by contemporary governing authorities are having relatively little influence on the actual practices of network operators and ISPs. Notwithstanding policy statements upholding the principles of network neutrality, ISPs are moving towards market mechanisms for allocating the use of bandwidth, with counter moves from the content producers to minimize the charges for distributing their content. Policy statements by national and regional governance authorities about network neutrality are achieving less and less traction. The next section examines the way in which the efforts to combat copyright infringing uses of the Internet are pressuring ISPs to manage Internet traffic in the interests of the creative industry rights holders.

## Intellectual property rights and the net

Digital technologies offer many possibilities for the production, distribution and "republishing" of information in terms of format, timing and cost, including nearly costless sharing of information (Mansell and Steinmueller 2011 under review (b)). P2P file-sharing that facilitates legal and illegal information sharing is being targeted by firms in the creative industry in their effort to suppress copyright infringement (Dixon 2009). The industry claims severe revenue losses as a result of this type of file-sharing activity, although the scale of the losses is contested. Whether attempts to suppress infringing activity can be converted into sales that compensate firms in the creative industry for these losses on the scale that is estimated by the rights holders is also contested. The sectors most affected by copyright infringement (film, television, recorded music and software) are estimated to have experienced retail revenue losses of €10 billion in 2008 in Europe, with losses cumulatively by 2015 estimated at €240 billion (TERA Consultants 2010). Experience is uneven, however, since in 2009 there were reports of increasing music sales in some European Union markets (Anderson 2010a). In addition, although growing from a small base, the global market for digital music increased by 1,000 percent between 2004 and 2010 (IFIP 2011), suggesting that there is a growing market for "paid for" digital content, despite copyright infringing activity.

Few would disagree with the goals of intellectual property law, where copyright aims to promote invention and authorship, to safeguard the rights of creators, and to encourage the dissemination of ideas (Bainbridge 1994; HM Treasury 2006). However, increasingly large numbers of online participants either disagree with the manner in which these goals are being pursued, or are unaware of the conflict between their downloading activities and the protections available to authors and publishers provided by copyright law. There is a growing gap between legal and citizen perspectives on what constitutes good online behavior (Meyer and Van Audenhove 2010). Copyright is intended to balance society's interest in the disclosure and dissemination of ideas with the interests of authors in compensation for their efforts, but, as David argues, "the legal institutions of copyright as we know them are properly seen as consequences of 'industrial policy' actions" (David 2004: 5), not as the "natural" balancing of stakeholder interests.

The protection of rights to digital information comes into conflict with the variety of purposes for which information is created, such as the expression and preservation of language, history and culture, the promotion of voluntary associations within networks, and the exchange of useful knowledge. With some fair use or fair dealing exceptions, the right of the information creator to legal protection is absolute. Despite evidence of changing social norms, copyright legislation is unlikely to be rewritten to alter the balance of interests, since the creative industry favors the present approach (Samuelson 2007), governments are upholding existing intellectual property legislation, and they are seeking new means to enforce the law (Hargreaves 2011). As Boyle puts it when he comments on the implications of the Internet, "in the middle of the most successful and exciting experiment in non-proprietary, distributed creativity in the history of the species, our policy makers can see only the threat from 'piracy'" (Boyle 2008: 248).

The creative industry is sponsoring lobbying efforts aimed at encouraging governments to enact additional legal measures aimed at curtailing illegal online activity, and these are intruding into the lives of Internet users, regardless of their guilt or innocence. Even though there are signs of adjustment by the creative industry to the disruptive effects of ICT convergence, the trade associations representing the creative industry have been bringing law suits against individuals suspected of illegal downloading and uploading of digital content, initially in the United States, and there have been numerous high-profile cases (Anderson 2010b; Murtagh 2009). This strategy has been complemented by efforts to tackle the largest websites that facilitate illegal file sharing, such as Baidu in China, IsoHunt in Canada, mp3fiesta in the Ukraine, RapidShare in Germany, RMX4U in Luxemburg and The Pirate Bay in Sweden. The aim is to find effective means of restricting the circulation of digital information in an effort to retain the ability to extract economic value from the online publishing of information. However, the means of restraint comes into direct conflict with the aspirations of those who are influenced by the model of "free" information sharing that privileges the cultural and social value of information.

Within the United States, successful lobbying has encouraged ISPs to reach a voluntary agreement whereby they will send six alerts to their subscribers based on notifications of suspected infringing downloading activity received from content owners, although so far they have not agreed to release subscriber names or to terminate subscriber accounts. They have agreed to use their tools of Internet traffic management as "mitigation measures" (such as temporary reductions in Internet speed, redirecting subscribers to an educational landing page, or other measures determined by ISPs), all of which position ISPs as gatekeepers acting on behalf of the rights holders (Andersen 2011; EFF 2011; Lasar 2011).[5]

5 In 2011, two controversial Bills, aimed at websites used for the distribution of infringing content, were introduced in the US Senate and Congress. The Protect Intellectual Property Act (PIPA) aimed to prevent online threats to economic creativity and theft of intellectual property. The Stop Online Piracy Act (SOPA) aimed to promote prosperity, creativity, entrepreneurship and innovation by combating the theft of US property. Both involved ISPs in combating copyright infringement. After widespread criticism in early 2012—including Internet protests and blackouts—the bills were withdrawn from consideration, although it is likely that alternative intellectual property legislation will be considered in the future.

Outside the United States, lobbying by the International Federation for the Phonographic Industry (IFPI), the International Intellectual Property Alliance (IIPA) and national trade associations aims to promote governance arrangements that will permit them to obtain the names of suspected infringers from ISPs. A "graduated response," or a "three strikes" strategy, is being pursued whereby ISPs are legally mandated to warn their customers that their activities have been monitored and that their ISP accounts show involvement in suspected infringing downloading. After a certain number of warnings, ISPs are being obligated (in most jurisdictions, subject to the permission of the courts) to disclose the identities of customers suspected of copyright-infringing activity (Mansell and Steinmueller 2010). Although representatives of the creative industry acknowledge that "there cannot be a one-size-fits-all approach to the problem" (Fleming 2010), their commitment to involving ISPs in controlling online behavior is clearly illustrated by the following selected examples.

## *ISPs and gatekeeping on the net*

In the United Kingdom, the Digital Economy Act was passed in 2010. This legislation calls for a graduated response strategy to be implemented by the regulator, Ofcom, once a code of practice is agreed with the ISPs. An earlier report on the contribution of the creative industries to the UK economy had acknowledged that "copyright infringement through unauthorized copying and distribution of music and video across the Internet is likened to stealing by some and to sharing by others" (HM Treasury 2006: para. 1.9), signaling that this is contested terrain. However, when the *Digital Britain* report was published several years later, it was clear that the then Labour government was aligning itself with the creative industry's claim that effective means are needed to address "stealing" (BIS and DCMS 2009). The Digital Economy Act 2010 requires the secretary of state to authorize any actions taken by ISPs against their subscribers beyond sending warning letters to suspected infringers, but it presumes that Internet monitoring technologies that are available to creative industry firms and ISPs will be used to identify IP addresses engaged in potentially infringing activity.

Negotiations between the ISPs and the creative industry had been ongoing for some time in the United Kingdom prior to the passage of the Act. Some warning letters had been sent on an experimental basis, but no consensus had been achieved on the specific role of ISPs, the legality of a strategy requiring the release of individual ISP customer identities, or the punishments that should apply. With the legislation in place, ISPs claimed that its implementation would harm their reputations, incur unnecessary costs, and serve as a disproportionate response to the problem created by P2P file sharing. Two of the largest ISPs in the UK market (BT and TalkTalk) were granted a judicial review of the legislation, but the High Court argued that the Act should be implemented (*BTplc and TalkTalk* v *Secretiary of State* (2012)). The judge concluded that it should be for Parliament, not the Court, to decide on how the interests of the creative industry, ISPs, and Internet users are balanced, insisting that the Court must presume that "existing copyright law does strike a fair balance between the interests referred to" (ibid., at [249]). He also argued that an evidence base is needed to evaluate the effectiveness of the graduated response strategy in terms of benefits to the creative industry (revenue recovery) or potential harms to ISPs and their customers (costs and rights of access to information). (See Mansell and Steinmueller 2011 under review (a) for an analysis of this case.)

Ofcom has since acknowledged that the graduated response strategy mandated by the Act requires a degree of confidence in the Internet usage monitoring technology to minimize inappropriate accusations (or false positives). This confidence has yet to be achieved. Ofcom has also encountered difficulties in establishing a workable appeals process (CMU 2011).

Warning letters to ISP customers are likely to be issued in 2012 and an evidence base will then begin to accumulate. However, this leaves advocates of a rollback of the legislation with little alternative than to wait for the evidence of the impact of the strategy.

In France, the HADOPI (The "Law promoting the distribution and protection of creative works on the Internet") was passed in 2009, introducing a graduated response strategy that differs in detail, though not in intent, from the Digital Economy Act 2010 in the United Kingdom. In this case, the role of the court is largely administrative and ISPs are required to suspend or terminate customer accounts on the basis of accusations by the creative industry that might later prove to be unfounded. Although the punishment for illegal downloading is an administrative decision, actual disconnection from the Internet was made a matter for a prosecutor attached to the High Court in the final version of the legislation (Law no. 2009–1311).

In the European Union, strategies for copyright law enforcement are coupled with the wider agenda of promoting innovation and creativity in the European market (European Commission 2001, 2004, 2011). Overall, European Commission policies are favoring enforcement measures that involve surveillance of online activities using DPI and other techniques that are giving the creative industry firms considerable power over ordinary Internet users (Meyer and Van Audenhove 2010). At the international level, industry lobbying has achieved the inclusion of a graduated response strategy in the now abandoned Anti-Counterfeiting Trade Agreement (ACTA). ACTA provided for national authorities "to order an online service provider to disclose expeditiously to a right holder information sufficient to identify a subscriber whose account was allegedly used for infringement, where that right holder has filed a legally sufficient claim of infringement . . ." (ACTA 2010, s. 5, 2.18.4). What constitutes a "sufficient claim" remained to be tested in law, but ACTA, if it had been ratified by the negotiating countries, implicated ISPs in monitoring online activities. Companies backing the ACTA negotiations included Google, eBay, Dell, News Corporation, Sony Pictures, Time Warner and Verizon—that is, most of the large creative industry firms with an interest in securing control over information flows on the Internet. Despite the failure of ACTA, extensive national lobbying continues.

## *Non-neutrality and chilling effects*

The emergence of these governance arrangements aimed at curtailing copyright infringement is consistent with incremental moves towards a non-neutral Internet, notwithstanding policy claims about the importance of maintaining a neutral Internet. Efforts to trace alleged copyright infringers using the tools of network management may affect individuals who are not infringers, or have negative consequences for the organizations providing Internet access because of the threat of actions taken against alleged infringers. These measures could lead to reductions in Internet use—a chilling effect—reducing the potential benefits of online activity and infringing on the rights of citizens.

The technical means of identifying suspected copyright infringers can result in false positive identifications that lead to incorrect accusations of illegal behavior. In addition, the graduated response strategy involves ISPs in contacting their customers, who may need to approach other users of their Internet connections (family, friends, or strangers in the case of public access) to discuss their private actions. Encouraging such behavior on the part of ISP customers involves them in a presumption of the wrongdoing of others and in surveillance that is out of step with norms of good behavior, inconsistent with a culture of online cooperation and information sharing, and contrary to the principle of network neutrality.

Thus far there is little evidence on how ISP customers and others who access the Internet are likely to respond to threats associated with the graduated response strategy. In France, before the introduction of HADOPI, a study by Dejean *et al.* (2010) found a decline in P2P file-sharing infringing activity among those surveyed, indicating an awareness that their behavior is illegal under existing law, but an increase in the use of alternative means of accessing content. There are ambiguous results from studies of the impact of graduated response legislation in Sweden (Lundstrom *et al.* 2010) and, in the United States, research based mainly on college student respondents suggests that a wide range of factors is likely to influence attitudes and behaviors in the face of legal threats aimed at deterring infringing downloading activity (Cox *et al.* 2010; M. David 2010; LaRose and Kim 2007; Liebowitz 2006; Oberholzer-Gee and Strumpf 2010; Plowman and Goode 2009). A study commissioned by the institution charged with implementing the HADOPI in early 2011, after the law's implementation, suggests that the strategy is having little effect on infringing behavior (HADOPI 2011). In fact, the strategy may even prove to be contrary to the interests of the creative industry, since the suppression of sampling of online content may also depress legal sales.[6]

There are signs that the industry is taking steps to introduce business models that go some way towards accommodating social and cultural norms that are consistent with information sharing. Some firms are allowing users to copy digital content, and the content at some sites is serving as advertising to attract users to support services that aggregate, filter and integrate information, generating revenues from those services, rather than from direct access to the content. Apple's launch of its iTunes Music Store in 2003 is a classic illustration. Following the launch of iTunes, Apple's sales rose to 70 percent of the level of infringing downloads by users of Apple Macs. Although initially confining downloading to iTunes subscribers, Apple iTunes later introduced online music without copy protection.[7] The new functionalities and services being offered through packages available with paid services include improved reliability, measures to reduce security problems, faster access, extra features such as celebrity playlists, exclusive music tracks, album art, gift certificates, allowances and audio-streaming capabilities. In addition, some companies are negotiating revenue-sharing arrangements with online communities who want access to their content such as Spotify. Activity in the subscription-based and "free at the point of consumption" markets indicates that there is potential for growth in the variety and scale of such services. Nevertheless, the industry has a huge stake in maintaining the existing copyright regime and is pursuing its campaign to implicate ISPs as its agents.

## *Resisting intrusive strategies*

There is resistance to these and related measures aimed at curtailing copyright infringement on the part of Internet users and in some areas of the state apparatus where greater attention is given to the rights of citizens to access the Internet. When citizens become aware that their online activity is being monitored, some Internet users seek ways of protecting their anonymity using privacy-enhancing technologies such as snoop-proof email programs, anonymous remailers, anonymous web-browsing tools, HTML filters, cookie busters and web encryption tools. Lists of blocked Internet sites are available to protect users from invasions of their privacy, sources of spyware or malicious software, or from government or creative

6 See Karaganis 2011.

7 The initial offer of this service, iTunes Match, had a limit of 25,000 songs with iTunes purchases not counting against this limit. See http://www.apple.com/icloud/features/ (accessed 29 May 2012).

industry monitoring of their activities. For example, the first list indexed by I-Blocklist is named "Anti-Infringement" and there are indications that a significant use of IP blocking software involves attempts to avoid detection of copyright infringement.

Resistance on the part of advocates of the open Internet to these copyright enforcement measures is difficult because they are not nearly as well resourced as the creative industry associations and they are forced to rely on data on economic harm reported by these associations. In addition, the monitoring technologies are already in place to aid ISPs in their existing traffic management activities and to support digital service providers in developing interactive services for their customers. When these are not seen as contravening network neutrality policies, there are few barriers to prevent the extension of these techniques to the copyright enforcement arena even when it is acknowledged that the democratic civil liberties of online participants are threatened in doing so (Cammaerts 2011).

The success of the lobbying activities of the creative industry is visible in the way in which the arguments of those advocating an open Internet in government forums tend to disappear from formal policy texts or to be relegated to the annexes or footnotes. Thus, for example, one European Parliament report on copyright enforcement stated in its initial draft form that "criminalising consumers so as to combat digital piracy is not the right solution" (European Parliament 2007: para. 9). This text was revised to read "criminalising consumers who are not seeking to make a profit is not the right solution to combat digital piracy" (European Parliament 2008: para. 17). The statement subsequently was removed from the final report.

An "Internet Freedom" provision was inserted into a final agreement on telecommunication reform agreed by the European Commission and the European Parliament in 2009. Lobbying by a French activist group, *la Quadrature du Net*, and other groups emphasized that intrusive measures of copyright enforcement abrogate citizen rights (Breindl and Houghton 2010). The "Internet Freedom" provision calls for a fair and impartial procedure to be in place before lawsuits are brought against citizens suspected of illegal file sharing. It refers to the fundamental rights and freedoms of natural persons guaranteed by the European Convention for the Protection of Human Rights and Fundamental Freedoms and general principles of Community law (Directive 2009 136/EC, Art. 1(3)). Others, such as the European Union Data Protection Commissioner, have argued that disclosure of the identity of Internet users to the creative industries should be required only in cases in which infringement seems to be occurring on "a commercial scale" (Hustinx 2010: para. 43).

As country after country takes steps to enhance enforcement of copyright legislation on behalf of the creative industry, the UN Special Rapporteur on Human Rights has expressed alarm about proposals to disconnect users from the Internet, considering that "cutting off users from Internet access, regardless of the justification provided, including on the grounds of violating intellectual property rights law, to be disproportionate and thus a violation of article 19, paragraph 3, of the International Covenant on Civil and Political Rights" (La Rue 2011: para. 49).

In summary, some public institutions and companies are upholding the tradition of private ownership of information and market exchange as the best way of fostering economic growth. It is also important to acknowledge that citizen interests in an open Internet are not homogeneous. Some citizens welcome efforts to enforce the protections afforded by intellectual property legislation. For instance, increasing numbers of online game players have an interest in protecting their intellectual property rights to the virtual objects that they create in their virtual worlds, especially when virtual money can be exchanged for "real" money (Heeks 2010; Lehdonvirta and Virtanen 2010). Others actively promote an information commons in which rights to benefit from the creation of digital information are established in a way that fairly compensates creators while also respecting rights of access. The contests between the proponents of different approaches, as in the case of network neutrality, are engaged in advocacy for governance arrangements that have substantial consequences for the "distribution of wealth and social status" in society (OTA 1986: 11). These conflicts over governance arrangements and strategies persist with little acknowledgement of the paradoxes that are central to technological innovation in the ICT sector. These are considered next.

## Paradox, innovation and governance

The challenges facing governance institutions in the wake of ICT convergence and the spread of the Internet are attributable partly to the opposing views of stakeholders with respect to the underlying dynamics of technological innovation and its outcomes in terms of the stimulus that it provides for economic growth and the way in which the innovation process influences the allocation of resources in society. The prevailing view is that market-imposed information scarcity creates the optimal incentive for the production of digital information. The competing view is that the optimal incentive for information production is created when it is shared freely to maximize its diversity.

On the one hand, information is initially costly to produce and intellectual property rights create the optimal incentives for creativity, diversity and growth. On the other hand, information costs virtually nothing to reproduce and the optimal incentives for creativity, diversity and growth occur when it is freely distributed. This is a paradox of information scarcity that arises because both of these statements are correct. The dilemmas presented by this paradox are associated with several possible outcomes. The first is the continuation of frictions between and resistance to the views of opposing groups who champion the role of the Internet in market-led development and who promote the expansion of the information commons. The second is the emergence of new ways of legitimizing the free circulation of digital information. A third outcome is new ways of garnering economic returns from digital information. Some combination of all three of these is likely, but the relative strength of each is influenced by the way in which contested values are combined in prevailing governance arrangements.

A second paradox is that of technological complexity. The process of technological innovation in the ICT sector is understood by many analysts to be resulting in emergent technological complexity (Arthur 2009). The increasing complexity of the communication system suggests to many stakeholders that interference by the state in the dynamics of the technological system will yield uncertain outcomes. On the one hand, there are intrinsic benefits from the emergent complexity of the technological system that are leading to a loss of hierarchical control of the system by governments and firms. On the other hand, there are intrinsic benefits from the emergent complexity of the technological system that are leading to control that can be achieved through hardware design and software programming, undertaken by decentralized, sharing communities of communication system developers. Again, the paradox is that both these observations are correct.

The network neutrality debate serves as an illustration of the dilemmas created by this paradox of technological complexity. The conflicts among stakeholders also suggest several possible outcomes. The first is friction between those who advocate withdrawal of attempts to govern through formal state measures and those who argue that formal intervention is needed in the name of the public interest to secure an open network. The second is a complex system that maximizes the interests of the firms that seek to profit from the circulation and sale of digital information. The third is a system that maximizes the interests of the state in surveillance. A fourth is a system that favors the interests of decentralized online communities, whatever their values may be. The governance challenge is to determine how these should be combined.

One view of the challenges of governing the Internet, and the communication system generally, privileges market-led development in the interest of economic growth, while another privileges collaborative information production and consumption outside the convention of the market. Progress towards the realization of one view is seen as damaging to the realization of the other. Debates about governance arrangements and measures aimed at reconciling the interests of stakeholders are often blind to the implications of the paradoxes of information scarcity and technological complexity. This may be explained partly by the fact that "the role of subterranean technologies is commonly neglected because the artefacts themselves are hidden from view," an idea that Rosalind Williams was developing at the end of the 1980s, before the Internet had spread globally (Williams 2008: 51), but it is also partly attributable to a prevailing view that sees state governance as invariably irresponsible and anti-democratic. When it is acknowledged that a policy of non-intervention may be problematic, for example, in the case of loss of privacy, proponents of non-intervention argue that, "if undertaken, [it] might ruin the very environment it is trying to save" (Zittrain 2008: 35). The future network environment should be shaped by the generative potential of "technically skilled people of goodwill" (Zittrain 2008: 246), who it is sometimes assumed will develop alternatives to a centralized, market-led information society.

However, advocacy of state withdrawal from governing in this area is also a reflection of a broader vision of how the economy should function that is consistent with neoliberalism and the Washington Consensus on the benefits of market-led economic expansion and free trade (Mansell 2011; Williamson 1990). In this view, the less state governance there is, the better this is for social welfare. Neoliberal advocates of this position oppose regulation of the Internet, emphasizing the potentially negative consequences of intrusive regulations for the dynamics of innovation and for competition in the commercial (global) market.

## Conclusion

The persistent puzzle confronting those with an interest in the governance arrangements for the Internet is how to reconcile the goal of economic growth with the goals of social justice and the equitable distribution of resources. This puzzle is at the core of debates about network neutrality and about the enforcement of intellectual property legislation. It is exacerbated by the paradoxes of information scarcity and technological complexity discussed in the preceding section. In the neoliberal account, it is the self-regulating market for ICTs and information that should "decide" how information resources should be allocated and who should be able to access the communication network. In the commons-based account, it is designers and programmers of the communication network who are charged with this responsibility.

In debates about network neutrality, the governance challenge is to protect citizens from unwanted intrusions into the virtual spaces they deem to be private. Instead of seeing the boundary between public and private information as the outcome of a given trajectory of complex technological innovation, questions need to be raised about whether the firms claiming to depend on intrusive measures really need these technologies to manage their networks. In so far as they do, the issue is whether these uses should be extended to support the interests of creative industry firms, which is a form of governance and regulatory intervention. Online surveillance, privacy intrusions and lack of transparency are becoming increasingly predominant, as is clearly evidenced in the UN report on human rights and the Internet. What is possible today could become excessive in the future, and the right to be free from surveillance should not be seen as an unaffordable luxury in the face of a complex technological system. The persistent contest over the Internet's architecture is around whether the end-to-end architecture of the Internet protocol is sustainable in the face of conflicting interests in controlling digital information for economic gain and for liberating digital information for creative purposes.

However, as the earlier discussion illustrates, the practices of monitoring online activities for various purposes are already well advanced. The issue for governance is how much further along the path towards a more fully non-neutral network we should progress. Acknowledging the reality of the interventions that are already occurring within the communication system and their potential for expansion could help to spark critical reflection on their implications that have consequences far beyond the oppositional debate about preserving (or not) the neutrality of the Internet's architecture.

In addition, some advocates of "free" culture ignore the issue of how creators should make a living, thus appearing to deny them revenue, and this is inconsistent with equitable treatment. When access to information is restricted using a pricing regime, opportunities for creative production are restricted, and this suppresses benefits to society. Conflicts between rights holders' and citizens' interests in information access could be addressed by recognizing that the targeting individuals engaged in file sharing and other means of sharing digital information are unlikely to have the desired impact. Shifting this debate towards ways of broadening opportunities for supporting a flourishing collaborative culture would encourage new means of empowering citizens, while remaining consistent with the values of economic growth and the protection of individuals from potential harms.

In each of these controversial domains of policy debate, a complex matrix of power relationships is at work (Cammaerts 2005; Sörenson and Torfing 2008). As Puppis (2010) reminds us, a particular set of governance choices may not lead to the expected changes in industry structure or to the outcomes envisaged in terms of economic growth, democratic decision-making, or the welfare of citizens. This uncertainty raises questions about the values and principles that should guide decisions in the light of the paradoxical environment in which decisions must be made.

It might be expected that civil society organizations will unite otherwise disparate stakeholder groups to constitute a majority and thus be able to influence the Internet governance process in a direction that favors a shift towards privileging the interests of citizens in being able to exercise their right to access information. However, these organizations may represent vocal minorities with interests that conflict with the mainstream positions of democratically elected governments. The "tyranny of the majority" may systematically exclude dissenting voices. Similarly, governments and their representatives may be captives of corporate interests in the scarcity of information and the neoliberal agenda of market self-regulation. Governments may have been elected undemocratically or they may be unresponsive to the views of their electorates or other social movement organizations. And, as Mueller argues, "participation and representation can give people the feeling that they have a stake in the policy making process, even when they are in fact relatively powerless" (Mueller 2009: 3).

It cannot be assumed that multi-stakeholder approaches to Internet governance in themselves create the conditions for the alignment of governance measures with the goal of promoting the information commons and the goal of securing economic growth. The ever-increasing complexity of the technological components of the communications system, combined with tensions created around interests in access to digital information, are not new phenomena. The paradoxical relationships they give rise to have been central to conflicting interests throughout the history of innovation in the ICT sector. However, the stark opposition between a neutral or non-neutral Internet and between open access to information and the strong enforcement of intellectual property rights on the Internet plays into the features of these paradoxes. It forecloses opportunities to create spaces in which rights to information access can be respected at the same time as the interests of stakeholders in the economic value of information can be catered for. In these highly contested areas of communication system governance, arrangements are needed to encourage a greater diversity of choices involving neither the excesses of state-led governance with its neoliberal ideology of the market, nor naive trust in the governing power of dispersed online communities. Governance measures from both below and above are needed to secure the public interest in a communication system that is fit for economic growth *and* for limiting unwanted intrusions into people's lives.

## References


ACTA (2010) *Anti-Counterfeiting Trade Agreement: Negotiating Parties*. Online. Available HTTP: http://www.mofa.go.jp/policy/economy/i_property/pdfs/acta1105_en.pdf (accessed 28 May 2012).

Anderson, N. (2010a) 'Piracy problems? Music industry grew in 13 markets in 2009,' *Ars Technica*. Online. Available HTTP: http://arstechnicacom/tech-policy/news/2010/04/piracy-problems-music-industry-grew-in-13-markets-in-2009ars (accessed 28 May 2012).

—— (2010b) 'The RIAA? Amateurs. Here's how you sue 14,000+ P2P users,' *Ars Technica*. Online. Available HTTP: http://arstechnicacom/tech-policy/news/2010/06/the-riaa-amateurs-heres-how-you-sue-p2p-usersars (accessed 28 May 2012).

—— (2011) 'Major ISPs agree to "six strikes" copyright enforcement plan,' *Ars Technica*, 5 July. Online. Available HTTP: http://arstechnicacom/tech-policy/news/2011/07/major-isps-agree-to-six-strikes-copyright-enforcement-planars (accessed 28 May 2012).

Arthur, W. B. (2009) *The Nature of Technology: What it Is and How it Evolves*, New York: Allen Lane.

Bainbridge, D. I. (1994) *Intellectual Property*, 2nd edn., London: Pitman Publishing.

Barron, B. (2008) 'The importance of network neutrality to the Internet's role in the public sphere,' *Canadian Journal of Media Studies*, 3(1): 90–105.

Bauer, J. M. (2007) 'Dynamic effects of network neutrality,' *International Journal of Communication*, 1: 531–547.

Baym, N. K. (2010) *Personal Connection in the Digital Age: Digital Media and Society Series*. Cambridge: Polity Press.

Bendrath, R. and Mueller, M. L. (2010) 'The end of the net as we know it? Deep packet inspection and Internet governance,' 4 August. Online. Available HTTP: http://papers.ssrn.com/sol3/papers.cfm?abstract_id=1653259 (accessed 28 May 2012).

Benkler, Y. (2004) 'Sharing nicely: On shareable goods and the emergence of sharing as a modality of economic production,' *Yale Law Journal*, 114(2): 273–258.

—— and Nissenbaum, H. (2006) 'Commons-based peer production and virtue,' *Journal of Political Philosophy*, 14(4): 394–419.

Berners-Lee, T. (2010) 'Long live the Web: A call for continued open standards and neutrality,' *Scientific American*, 22 November: 1–5.

Department for Business and Innovation (BIS) and Department for Culture, Media and Sport (DCMS) (2009) *Digital Britain: Final Report*, London: June, HMSO.

Boyle, J. (2008) *The Public Domain: Enclosing the Commons of the Mind*, New Haven, CT: Yale University Press.

Braman, S. and Roberts, S. (2003) 'Advantage ISP: Terms of service as Media Law,' *New Media & Society*, 5(3): 422–448.

Breindl, Y. and Houghton, T. J. (2010) 'Techno-political activism as ounterpublic spheres: Discursive networking within deliberative transnational politics?' Paper presented at ICA Conference, Singapore, 22 July. Online. Available HTTP: http://canterbury-nz.academia.edu/TessaHoughton/Talks/24893/Techno-political_Activism_as_Counterpublic_Spheres_Discursive_Networking_Within_Deliberative_Transnational_Politics (accessed 28 May 2012).

Bresnahan, T. F. and Trajtenberg, M. (1995) 'General purpose technologies "engines of growth"?' *Journal of Econometrics*, 65(1): 83–108.

*BT plc and Talk Talk Telecom Group plc* v *Secretary of State for Culture, Olympics, Media and Sport and others* (2012) EWCA Civ 232.
Burnett, R. (2010) 'Internet and music,' in R. Burnett, M. Consalvo and C. Ess (eds.) *The Handbook of Internet Studies*, New York: Wiley-Blackwell.
Cammaerts, B. (2005) 'Through the looking glass: Civil society participation in the WSIS and the dynamics between online/offline interaction,' *Communications & Strategies*, 60(4): 151–174.
—— (2011) 'Disruptive sharing in a digital age: Rejecting neoliberalism?,' *Continuum: Journal of Media & Cultural Studies*, 25(1): 47–62.
CISCO (2011) *Cisco Visual Networking Index: Forecast and Methodology, 2010–15*, CISCO White Paper. Online. Available HTTP: http://www.cisco.com/en/US/solutions/collateral/ns341/ns525/ns537/ns705/ns827/white_paper_c11-481360.pdf (accessed 28 May 2012).
CMU (2011) 'DEA three strikes letters won't start until 2013,' *CMU*, 24 October. Online. Available HTTP: http://www.thecmuwebsite.com/article/dea-three-strike-letters-wont-start-until-2013/ (accessed 28 May 2012).
*Comcast Corp.* v *FCC* 600 F. 3d 642 (2010).
Cox, J., Collins, A. and Drinkwater, S. (2010) 'Seeders, leechers and social norms: Evidence from the market for illicit digital downloading,' *Journal of Economics and Policy*, 22(4): 299–305.
Cusumano, M. A. (2010) *Staying Power: Six Enduring Principles for Managing Strategy and Innovation in an Uncertain World*, Oxford: Oxford University Press.
David, M. (2010) *Peer to Peer and the Music Industry: The Criminalization of Sharing*, London: Sage Publications.
David, P. A. (2004) 'The end of copyright history?' *Review of Economic Research on Copyright Issues*, 1(2): 5–10.
Dejean, S., Penard, T. and Suire, R. (2010) *Une Première évaluation des effets de la loi Hadopi sur les pratiques des internautes Francais*, CREM and University de Rennes, 1 March, Paris: Measure & Analyse des Usages Numériques.
Denardis, L. (2009) *Protocol Politics: The Globalization of Internet Governance*, Cambridge, MA: MIT Press.
Dixon, A. N. (2009) 'Liability of users and third parties for copyright infringements on the Internet: Overview of international developments,' in A. Strowel (ed.) *Peer-to-Peer File Sharing and Secondary Liability in Copyright Law*, Cheltenham: Edward Elgar.
Electronic Frontier Foundation (EFF) (2011) 'The content industry and ISPs announce a "common framework for copyright alerts": What does it mean for users?' 7 July. Online. Available HTTP: http://www.eff.org/deeplinks/2011/07/content-industry-and-isps-announce-common (accessed 28 May 2012).
Envisional Ltd. (2011) *Technical Report: An Estimate of Infringing Use of the Internet*, Cambridge: Envisional Ltd. Online. Available HTTP: http://documents.envisional.com/docs/Envisional-Internet_Usage-Jan2011.pdf (accessed 28 May 2012).
European Broadcasting Union (EBU) (2010) *Peer-to-Peer (P2P) Technologies and Services: EBU Technical Report 009*, Geneva. Online. Available HTTP: http://tech.ebu.ch/docs/techreports/tr009.pdf (accessed 28 May 2012).
European Commission (2011) *Communication from the Commission to the European Parliament, the Council, the European Economic and Social Committee and the Committee of the Regions on a Single Market for Intellectual Property Rights — Boosting Creativity and Innovation to Provide Economic Growth, High Quality Jobs and First Class Products and Services in Europe*, COM(2011)287 final, Brussels: European Commission. Online. Available HTTP: http://ec.europa.eu/internal_market/copyright/docs/ipr_strategy/COM_2011_287_en.pdf (accessed 28 May 2012).
European Parliament (2007) *Draft Report on Cultural Industries in the Context of the Lisbon Strategy*, European Parliament Committee on Culture and Education, Rapporteur, Guy Bono, PR/684266EN. Online. Available HTTP: http://www.europarl.europa.eu/meetdocs/2004_2009/documents/pr/684/684266/684266en.pdf (accessed 28 May 2012).
—— (2008) *Report on Cultural Industries in Europe*, 2007/2153(INI), European Parliament Committee on Culture and Education, Rapporteur, Guy Bono, A6-0063/2008. Online. Available: http://www.europarl.europa.eu/sides/getDoc.do?pubRef=-//EP//NONSGML+REPORT+A6-2008-0063+0+DOC+PDF+V0//EN (accessed 28 May 2012).
Federal Communications Commission (FCC) (2005) *Policy Statement*, FCC 05–151, Washington, DC: FCC. Online. Available HTTP: http://www.publicknowledge.org/pdf/FCC-05-151A1.pdf (accessed 28 May 2012).

—— (2010) *Report and Order in the Matter of Preserving the Open Internet, Broadband Industry Practices*, GN Docket No. 09-191, WC Docket No. 07-52. Washington, DC: FCC. Online. Available HTTP: http://www.scribd.com/doc/47905173/FCC-Report-and-Order-In-the-Matter-of-Preserving-the-Open-Internet-Broadband-Industry-Practices (accessed 28 May 2012).

Fleming, M. (2010) 'MPAA urges Japan on pic pirate issue,' *Deadline Hollywood*, 21 October. Online. Available HTTP: http://www.deadline.com/tag/piracy-graduated-response/ (accessed 28 May 2012).

Fransman, M. (2008) 'Innovation in the new ICT ecosystem,' *Communications & Strategies*, 68(4): 89–110.

Freeman, C. (2007) 'The ICT paradigm,' in R. Mansell, C. Avgerou, D. Quah and R. Silverstone (eds.) *The Oxford Handbook of Information and Communication Technologies*, Oxford: Oxford University Press.

Goldsmith, J. L. and Wu, T. (2006) *Who Controls the Internet? Illusions of a Borderless World*, Oxford: Oxford University Press.

HADOPI (2011) *Hadopi, biens culturels et usages d'internet: pratiques et perceptions des internatures francais: Report prepared for Hadopi [Haute Autorité pour la diffusion des œuvres et la protection des droits sur internet]*. Online. Available HTTP: http://www.hadopi.fr/download/hadopiT0.pdf (accessed 28 May 2012).

Hargreaves, I. (2011) *Digital Opportunity: A Review of Intellectual Property and Growth*, Independent report commissioned by UK Prime Minister, London: HMSO.

Hawkins, R. W., Mansell, R. and Steinmueller, W. E. (1997) *Mapping and Measuring the Information Technology, Electronics and Communications Sector in the United Kingdom*, Report prepared for the Office of Science and Technology, Technology Foresight Panel on Information Technology, Electronics and Communications, Version 2.0, Brighton: SPRU.

Heeks, R. (2010) 'Understanding "gold farming" and real-money trading as the intersection of real and virtual economies,' *Journal of Virtual Worlds Research*, 2(4): 3–27.

HM Treasury (2006) *Gower's Review of Intellectual Property*, London: HMSO.

Hustinx, P. (2010) *Opinion of the European Data Protection Supervisor on the Current Negotiations by the European Union of an Anti-Counterfeiting Trade Agreement (ACTA)*. OJ 2010/C 147, Brussels. Online. Available HTTP: http://www.edps.europa.eu/EDPSWEB/webdav/site/mySite/shared/Documents/ Consultation/Opinions/2010/10-02-22_ACTA_EN.pdf (accessed 28 May 2012).

IDATE (2010) *DigiWorld Yearbook 2010: The Digital World's Challenges*, Montpellier, IDATE.

IFIP (2011) *Digital Music Report 2011*, London: IFIP.

Jenkins, H. (2006) *Convergence Culture: Where Old and New Media Collide*, New York: New York University Press.

Karaganis, J. (2011) 'HADOPI says: Let's try cutting off nose to spite face,' *Media Piracy in Emerging Economies*. Online. Available HTTP: http://piracy.ssrc.org/hadopi-says-lets-try-cutting-off-nose-to-spite-face/ (accessed 30 May 2012).

La Rue, F. (2011) *Report of the Special Rapporteur on the Promotion and Protection of the Right to Freedom of Opinion and Expression*, New York: UN General Assembly, Human Rights Council, 17th Session, Agenda Item 3, 16 May. Online. Available HTTP: http://www2.ohchr.org/english/bodies/hrcouncil/docs/17session/A.HRC.17.27_en.pdf (accessed 28 May 2012).

LaRose, R. and Kim, J. (2007) 'Share, steal, or buy? A social cognitive perspective of music downloading,' *CyberPsychology & Behavior*, 10(2): 267–277.

Lasar, M. (2011) 'Big content, ISPs nearing agreement on piracy crackdown system,' *Ars Technica*, June. Online. Available HTTP: http://arstechnica.com/tech-policy/news/2011/06/big-content-isps-nearing-agreement-on-piracy-crackdown-system.ars (accessed 28 May 2012).

Lehdonvirta, V. and Virtanen, P. (2010) 'A new frontier in digital content policy: Case studies in the regulation of virtual goods and artificial scarcity,' *Policy & Internet*, 2(2): 7–29.

Lentz, R. G. (2011) 'Regulation as linguistic engineering,' in R. Mansell and M. Raboy (eds.) *The Handbook of Global Media and Communication Policy*, New York: Wiley-Blackwell.

Lessig, L. (2008) *Remix: Making Art and Commerce Thrive in the Hybrid Economy*, London: Bloomsbury Academic.

Liebowitz, S. J. (2006) 'File-sharing: Creative destruction or plain destruction?' *Journal of Law and Economics*, 49(1): 1–28.

Lundstrom, J., Widriksson, J. and Zaunders, V. (2010) *Changes in Media Consumption and File Sharing: The Impact of Legislation and New Digital Media Services*, Jönköping: Jönköping International Business School.

Maclean, D. (2011) 'The evolution of GMCP institutions,' in R. Mansell and M. Raboy (eds.) *The Handbook of Global Media and Communication Policy*, New York: Wiley-Blackwell.
Mansell, R. (1993) *The New Telecommunications: A Political Economy of Network Evolution*, London: Sage.
—— (2011) 'New visions, old practices: Policy and regulation in the Internet era,' *Continuum: Journal of Media & Cultural Studies*, 25(1): 19–32.
—— (2012) *Imagining the Internet: Communication, Innovation, and Governance*, Oxford: Oxford University Press.
—— and Raboy, M. (2011) 'Introduction: Foundations of the theory and practice of global media and communication policy,' in R. Mansell and M. Raboy (eds.) *The Handbook of Global Media and Communication Policy*, New York: Wiley-Blackwell.
—— and Steinmueller, W. E. (2010) *British Telecommunications plc ("BT") and TalkTalk Telecom Group Limited v Secretary of State for Business, Innovation and Skills ("BIS") in the matter of an intended claim*, Report prepared in connection with Judicial Review of the Digital Economy Act 2010, London: LSE Enterprise.
—— and (2011 under review (a)) 'Copyright infringement online: The case of the Digital Economy Act Judicial Review in the United Kingdom,' *New Media & Society*.
—— and (2011 under review (b)) 'The copyright paradox: Creative destruction, re-publication and the impact of new technologies,' *Industrial and Corporate Change*.
—— and (2013) 'Digital economies and public policies: Contending rationales and outcome assessment strategies,' in W. H. Dutton (ed.) *Oxford Handbook of Internet Studies*, Oxford: Oxford University Press.
Mathiason, J. (2009) *Internet Governance: The New Frontiers of Global Institutions*, London: Routledge.
McQuail, D. (2003) *Media Accountability and Freedom of Publication*, Oxford: Oxford University Press.
Meyer, T. and Van Audenhove, L. (2010) 'Graduated response and the emergence of a European surveillance society,' *Info*, 12(6): 69–79.
Mueller, M. L. (2009) 'ICANN, Inc.: accountability and participation in the governance of critical Internet resources,' *Internet Governance Project*, 16 November. Online. Available HTTP: http://www.internetgovernance.org/pdf/ICANNInc.pdf (accessed 28 May 2012).
—— (2010) *Networks and States: The Global Politics of Internet Governance*, Cambridge, MA: MIT Press.
——, Mathiason, J. and Klein, H. K. (2007) 'The Internet and global governance: Principles and norms for a new regime,' *Global Governance*, 13(2): 237–254.
Murtagh, M. P. (2009) 'The FCC, the DMCA, and why takedown notices are not enough,' *Hastings Law Journal*, 61(1): 233–273.
Oberholzer-Gee, F. and Strumpf, K. (2010) *File-Sharing and Copyright: Music Business Research Files*. Online. Available HTTP: http://musicbusinessresearch.files.wordpress.com/2010/06/paper-felix-oberholzer-gee.pdf (accessed 28 May 2012).
Office of Technology Assessment (OTA) (1986) *Intellectual Property Rights in an Age of Electronics and Information*, Washington, DC: OTA.
Organization for Economic Co-operation and Development (OECD) (2010) *OECD Information Technology Outlook 2010*, Paris: OECD.
—— (2011a) *Communiqué on Principles for Internet Policy-Making*, OECD High Level Meeting on the Internet Economy: Generating Innovation and Growth, 28–29 June. Online. Available HTTP: http://www.oecd.org/dataoecd/40/21/48289796.pdf (accessed 28 May 2012).
—— (2011b) *Shaping Polices for the Future of the Internet Economy*, Paris: OECD. Online. Available HTTP: http://www.oecd.org/dataoecd/1/29/40821707.pdf (accessed 28 May 2012).
Pfanner, E. (2011) 'G-8 leaders to call for tighter Internet regulation,' *New York Times*, 24 May. Online. Available HTTP: http://www.nytimes.com/2011/05/25/technology/25tech.html (accessed 28 May 2012).
Plowman, S. and Goode, S. (2009) 'Factors affecting the intention to download music: Quality perceptions and downloading intensity,' *Journal of Computer Information Systems*, 49(4): 84–97.
Powell, A. and Cooper, A. (2011) 'Net neutrality discourses: Comparing advocacy and regulatory arguments in the US and the UK,' *The Information Society*, 27(5): 311–325.
Puppis, M. (2010) 'Media governance: A new concept for the analysis of media policy and regulation,' *Communication, Culture & Critique*, 3(2): 134–149.
Samuelson, P. (2007) 'Preliminary thoughts on copyright reform,' *Utah Law Review*,3: 551–571.
Sassen, S. (2001) 'On the Internet and sovereignty,' *Indiana Journal of Global Legal Studies*, 5(2): 545–559.

Sidak, J. G. (2007) 'What is the network neutrality debate really about?,' *International Journal of Communication*, 1: 377–388.

Sörenson, E. and Torfing, J. (eds.) (2008) *Theories of Democratic Network Governance*, Basingstoke: Palgrave Macmillan.

TERA Consultants (2010) *Building the Digital Economy: The Importance of Saving Jobs in the EU's Creative Industries*, Commissioned by the International Chamber of Commerce/BASCAP Initiative. Online. Available HTTP: http://www.teraconsultants.fr/assets/publications/PDF/2010-Mars-Etude_Piratage_TERA_full_report-En.pdf (accessed 28 May 2012).

UNCTAD (2010) *Creative Economy Report 2010*, Geneva: UNCTAD. Online. Available HTTP: http://www.unctad.org/Templates/WebFlyer.asp?intItemID=5763&lang=1 (accessed 28 May 2012).

Williams, R. (2008 [1990]) *Notes on the Underground: An Essay on Technology, Society and the Imagination, New Edition*, Cambridge, MA: MIT Press.

Williamson, J. (1990) *Latin American Adjustment: How Much Has Happened*, Washington, DC: Institute for International Economics.

Wu, T. (2010) *The Master Switch: The Rise and Fall of Information Empires*, New York: Alfred A. Knopf.

Yoo, C. S. (2005) 'Beyond network neutrality,' *Harvard Journal of Law and Technology*, 19(1): 1–77.

Zittrain, J. (2003) 'Internet points of control,' *Boston College Law Review*, 44(2): 653–688.

—— (2008) *The Future of the Internet and How to Stop It*, New York: Allen Lane.

# 28

# Net neutrality and audiovisual services

*Nico van Eijk**

## Introduction

Net neutrality is high on the European agenda. New regulations for the communications sector provide a legal framework for net neutrality and need to be implemented at both European and national levels. The key element is not just about blocking or slowing down traffic across communication networks; the control over the distribution of audiovisual services is also a vital part of the problem. This chapter describes the phenomenon of net neutrality, and the American and—in more detail—European contexts are addressed. In the analysis, we refer to the importance of seeing net neutrality as a value-chain issue. Facing the reality that full net neutrality is impossible and that reasonable forms of net management are unavoidable, we conclude that further policy involvement also seems unavoidable.

## Net neutrality: Definition

Discussions about net neutrality in current regulations and policymaking are focused primarily on net neutrality on the Internet. It was Tim Wu who put the subject on the agenda in 2003 with his paper "Network neutrality, broadband discrimination." He described "net neutrality" as "an Internet that does not favor one application (say, the World Wide Web) over others (say, e-mail)" (Wu 2003: 145). For audiovisual services, this would imply the unhindered delivery of, for example, a web-based video-on-demand (VOD) service to consumers.

## Technology

In principle, net neutrality is network-neutral. The call for net neutrality is not restricted to certain fixed or wireless networks, thus lending the subject a high impact. Net neutrality is essential for audiovisual services, which are increasingly distributed in non-traditional ways via terrestrial

* (This chapter is in part based on earlier work published by the European Audiovisual Observatory (EAO).

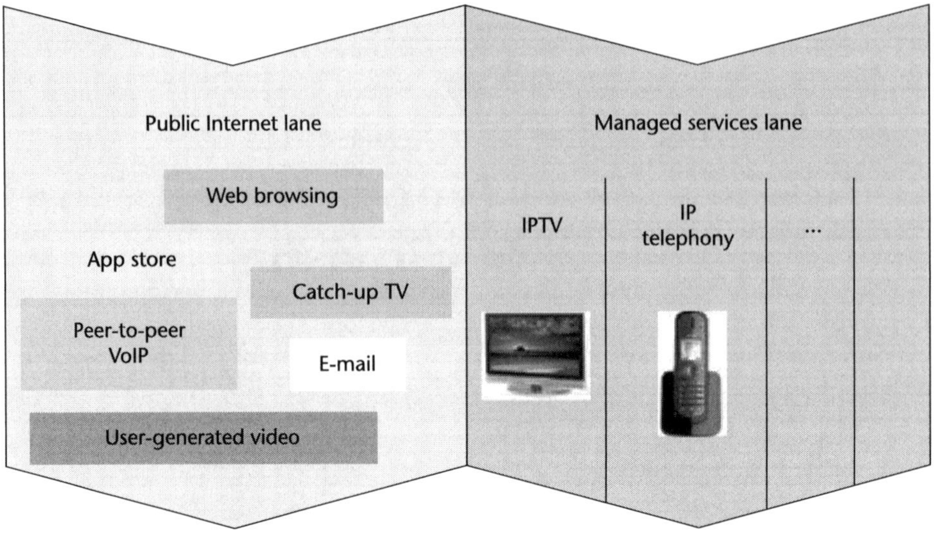


*Figure 28.1* The two-lane model (Marcus *et al.* 2011: 38)

broadcasting networks, satellite or cable television networks. The Internet, accessible through fixed and mobile networks, is also suitable for providing video services, such as linear services consisting of the distribution of television programs via Internet Protocol Television (IPTV) (a service often provided by traditional telecommunication companies, who still own the former telephony network) (Wikipedia 2012), or non-linear services such as video on demand (such as ordering films, time shifting/catch-up television). A certain capacity is usually reserved for such services, part of which is called the "managed service lane" (see Figure 28.1). Both linear and non-linear audiovisual services are increasingly provided "over the top" (OTT), which means that the respective service is "freely" available on the open Internet (the so-called "public Internet lane," or the Internet as the average user experiences it). OTT services are, in principle, similar to those provided via reserved capacity and therefore include "streaming video" services, downloading films, etc. Other examples include the so-called peer-to-peer (P2P) systems that provide access to audiovisual material via file sharing.

Because of capacity demand, the transmission of audiovisual services puts a strain on the network (Marcus *et al.* 2011). The Internet is intended to slow down information temporarily at times of congestion until transport capacity becomes available. For various applications, this deceleration is not relevant. For example, it makes no difference to email if the transfer of messages is delayed by a few milliseconds. In contrast, the delay would be unacceptable for live video or games, because it would have adverse consequences for the end-user's "quality of experience" (QoE). Therefore these services should, in principle, take priority over other services, or they should have a protected status. For video distribution via the Internet, through so-called content delivery networks (CDNs), there is the option of placing video content on servers that are closer to the end-users and of giving priority to particular services over others. Managing the network has always been part of the Internet. In this respect, the idea that "the Internet does not favor one application over others" (Wu 2003: 145) is an idea worth pursuing, rather than something that should be implemented in practice. Proper management can prevent visible deceleration. Of course, available bandwidth is a major factor, and adding sufficient capacity would also help to reduce the problem of scarcity.

Insight into network strain is often obtained by an analysis of traffic flows, either generically or on a highly detailed level. A more generic method is the analysis of the total amount of traffic passing through. Traffic can also be linked to certain "ports" (to which applications can be linked; when these "ports" are managed or switched on and off, the amount of traffic to be transported is increases or decreases respectively). At a detailed level, traffic analysis is possible via "deep packet inspection" (DPI). With DPI, the content of individual data packages can be viewed to determine which applications are used and how much traffic they generate. DPI is widely used, but it is controversial owing to its impact on the freedom of communication and privacy.[2]

## *Economic issues*

Managing Internet capacity is necessary for technical reasons (to prevent congestion), but it can also be relevant from an economic perspective, so as to prevent the cost of adding more capacity from getting out of hand.

Internet traffic management offers some additional interesting options for "optimizing" the business models of Internet service providers (ISPs). The ISP can make strategic use of its position as a bottleneck for Internet access. Both content providers and end-users depend on it. A price can be charged for such privileges as guaranteed bandwidth, or services or end-users using too much bandwidth can be cut off. Limiting competition might be another reason for restrictive measurements. Skype is a classic case in point. Providers of mobile telephony consider Skype a threat to their business model that is based on charging time units, which are a much bigger source of income than the provision of Internet access. Skype, as an OTT service, can set its own rates (or offer its service partly for free). By refusing access to Skype, mobile network providers try to prevent their own business model from being cannibalized. The same is occurring with texting services: With a smartphone application such as WhatsApp (http://www.whatsapp.com), traditional texting services can be bypassed. WhatsApp is an extremely popular cross-platform (iPhone, Android, Blackberry, Nokia) application that allows users to send text messages to each other over the Internet.

A similar situation exists for the distribution of audiovisual media services. Providers of these services (e.g. VOD service providers) can agree with ISPs that priority is given to their traffic and that it is available at a certain quality for end-users. The same applies to end-users: ISPs can offer various quality levels to them at different prices. Last, but not least, ISPs with multiple interests can deploy management to optimize their business model. For example, a cable operator who simultaneously provides open access to the Internet can ensure that the audiovisual services he provides as part of his basic services are also available, at the same quality, on the Internet. If this operator is vertically integrated and has interests in the production of content, management can be used to exclude competing services or to distribute them at a poorer quality.

Net neutrality primarily pertains to these choices to be made with respect not only to the technical, but also to the economic, aspects of network management. What should be the ratio between the free open Internet (the "public Internet lane") and the walled garden part (the "managed service lane")? What priorities can or could be given within either lane to specific services? The perspective of ISPs, as well as the position of the end-user, who is looking for open access to the available assortment of services, play a part in this context and need to be accounted for.

2 In 2008, the European Commission started an investigation on the use of DPI technology in the context of behavioral targeting (European Commission 2009). DPI seems to be an established practice, including the context of video distribution. See the very interesting work on DPI by Bendrath and Mueller (2011).

## Regulatory and policy context

Little by little, net neutrality found its way onto the political agenda, first in the United States, then in Europe. This section summarizes the main aspects of the regulatory and policy context of both jurisdictions.

### *United States*

#### Policy development

In 2005, the Federal Communications Commission (FCC), the US telecommunications and media regulatory authority, issued its Internet Policy Statement. This included four principles with respect to network neutrality, as follows.

i. Consumers are entitled to access the lawful Internet content of their choice.
ii. Consumers are entitled to run applications and to use services of their choice, subject to the needs of law enforcement.
iii. Consumers are entitled to connect their choice of legal devices that do not harm the network.
iv. Consumers are entitled to competition among network providers, application and service providers, and content providers.

Two further principles were subsequently added: non-discrimination and transparency (FCC 2010a).

Several experiences, including audiovisual services, caused the FCC to continue to deal with the topic. Comcast was accused of slowing down traffic (FCC 2008). Google and telecommunications operator Verizon tried to hammer out a deal excluding mobile services from open Internet rules (Van Buskirk 2010). Another conflict arose between Comcast and Level 3 (Kang 2010): Level 3 is responsible for the distribution of the very popular video service Netflix, and Comcast claimed fees from Level 3 because demand for Netflix was leading to the use of too much bandwidth.

#### FCC report and order

The above-mentioned six principles are the core of the FCC *Report and Order*, adopted in December 2010, which for the first time introduced specific regulation for the open Internet and net neutrality (FCC 2010b).[3] The rules focus on transparency, the prohibition of access blocking and the prohibition of unreasonable discrimination. They can be summarized as follows.

Providers of broadband Internet access must publicly disclose accurate information on network management, performance and commercial terms of the provided broadband service. This needs to be done at a level that allows consumers to make informed choices. The Order includes further details as to the type of concrete information to which it refers, without making these details binding. But the use of phrases such as "effective disclosures will likely include" is very telling. It should be noted that the FCC does not regard transparency as a sufficient means to tackle the problem of net neutrality. This is why the two additional rules are set.

3 Implemented 20 November 2011 (Federal Register, Vol. 76, No. 185, pp. 59192–59235, 23 September 2011). It should be noted that the power of the FCC to regulate the matter of net neutrality is questionable. This issue falls outside the scope of this contribution.

Blocking access is not allowed. An Internet provider "shall not block lawful content, applications, services, or non-harmful devices, subject to reasonable network management" (FCC 2010b: 88). This rule applies to providers of fixed Internet access; for mobile providers, the rule is limited to accessing lawful websites. Blocking applications that compete with the providers' voice or video telephony services, however, is not allowed (again "subject to reasonable network management"). This second rule means that end-users are to have free access to the Internet, both to retrieve information and to disseminate it. Although the rules for mobile networks are less stringent, the FCC believes that blocking providers of Voice over Internet Protocol (VoIP) must be prohibited. In addition, in the FCC's view there is no difference between blocking and degradation of traffic. Making non-blocking dependent on the payment of compensation is not allowed under the anti-blocking rule.

The third rule has two elements. First, there is the prohibition for providers of fixed broadband Internet access services to discriminate unreasonably in transmitting lawful network traffic over a broadband Internet access service chosen by the consumer. Second, it is ruled that reasonable network management shall not constitute unreasonable discrimination. According to the FCC, a network management practice is reasonable if it is appropriate and tailored to achieving a legitimate network management purpose, taking into account the particular network architecture and technology of the broadband access services. Next, several examples of legitimate purposes are mentioned, including avoiding congestion of the network.

The FCC's remarks about prioritizing certain traffic over other traffic are particularly important. This is a tricky issue, for there is increasing pressure on certain service providers that generate much traffic to give their traffic priority against payment. Some service providers are also prepared to pay for quality transport. Stating various considerations, the FCC suggests that pay for priority is unlikely to comply with the rule on unreasonable discrimination. From the text, it follows that the rule prohibiting unreasonable discrimination does not, however, apply to mobile services. The argument provided is that mobile Internet use is still under development and that intervention by the FCC therefore remains restricted to "measured steps."

Finally, in the context of reasonable/unreasonable network management, the FCC recognizes the "specialized services" phenomenon (sometimes, including in this chapter, referred to by the term "managed services"). The respective services share capacity with broadband Internet access, such as certain IP-based voice telephony and video services. The development of these services will be monitored closely and, as the FCC notes, the definition of broadband Internet access service also includes services that are functionally equivalent or intended to circumvent the new rules.

## *European Union*

### New regulatory framework

In Europe, the debate on net neutrality coincided with the New Regulatory Framework (NRF). This Framework includes five directives.[4] These directives regulate large parts of the European communications sector and include issues such as access to networks, consumer

4 Framework Directive (Directive 2002/21/EC); Access Directive (Directive 2002/19/EC); Authorisation Directive (Directive 2002/20/EC); Universal Service Directive (Directive 2002/21/EC); and Directive on Privacy and Electronic Communications (Directive 2002/58/EC).

protection, privacy and universal service. Member states must implement the directives into national legislation. The directives were amended in 2009, and included new provisions dealing with net neutrality in the Framework Directive and the Universal Service Directive.[5] The telecommunications network providers were not in favor of the introduction of these provisions and they tried to block them. However, pressure from the European Parliament (influenced by various pressure groups) contributed to setting the new rules.[6]

According to the amended European directives, national regulators have to promote the interests of EU citizens by promoting the ability of end-users to access and distribute information or to run applications and services of their choice (Framework Directive, Article 8(4)(g)). In principle, end-users should be able to decide which content they want to send and receive, and which services, applications, hardware and software they want to use for such purposes (Citizens' Rights Directive, Article 28). The market should provide such a choice, and regulators should support this approach.

Transparency is considered central: operators need to provide their users with information on topics such as limitations on use, including the type of content, applications or services involved. In Article 21(3)(d) of the Universal Service Directive, there is explicit reference to the need to provide users with information on any procedures on shaping traffic and their effect on the quality of the service. This framework assumes that a competitive market will ensure that end-users get the quality of service they want, but also recognizes that, in particular cases, there might be a need to ensure that public communications networks attain minimum quality levels to prevent degradation of service, the blocking of access and the slowing of traffic over networks (Citizens' Rights Directive, Recital 34). In this context, it is recognized that operators apply network management to handle traffic. These practices should be subject to scrutiny by the national regulatory authorities in line with principles set out in the regulatory framework, with a particular focus on discriminatory behavior that would affect competition. If appropriate, the Directive allows minimum quality of service requirements to be set. National regulatory authorities should therefore have the necessary regulatory powers.

Second, as part of the regulations on quality of service, rules can be set by national regulatory authorities with respect to network neutrality (Universal Service Directive, Article 22 (3)). However, before setting such requirements, the relevant national regulatory authorities have to provide the European Commission with a summary of the grounds for action, the envisaged requirements and the proposed course of action. Furthermore, this information must also be sent to the Body of European Regulators for Electronic Communications (BEREC). The European Commission can make comments or recommendations to avoid negative effects on the internal market. Although not binding, the national regulatory authorities are obliged to take account of such comments or recommendations when deciding on specific net-neutrality requirements.

It should be mentioned that the directives as such neither mandate nor prohibit limiting access to, or the use of, particular services or applications; rather, they merely impose an obligation to provide information about it (Citizens Rights' Directive, Recital 29). However, regulators that do want to limit access need to comply with existing fundamental rights including the right to freedom of expression, the right to privacy and rules on due process. It is

5 Citizens' Rights Directive (Directive 2009/136/EC) and Better Regulation Directive (Directive 2009/140/EC).

6 A good overview of the European developments on net neutrality can be found on the website of *La Quadrature du net*: http://www.laquadrature.net/en/Net_neutrality.

for this reason that the amended Framework Directive encompasses a provision on respect for fundamental rights. Article 1(3)(a) makes explicit reference to the European Convention on Human Rights.[7] The wording of this Article is very strong, and the Article itself is of substantial interest for the free flow of information, including audiovisual services. Its creation was strongly influenced by the European debate on illegal downloading of content (Horten 2011).

## *European Commission consultation*

In the context of the implementation of the new regulatory framework for the communications sector, several national regulators and governments have entered into consultations and looked into the matter of net neutrality.[8] The European Commission, too, asked the market for input (European Commission 2010a). The main outcome of the 318 comments was put into a short report by the European Commission (European Commission 2010b/c). According to the general analysis, there seems to be agreement that there are currently no problems with the openness of the Internet and net neutrality in the European Union. However, it is also clear from individual responses that traffic management problems do exist: The BEREC comments indicated several cases of unequal treatment (BEREC 2011). In its response, BEREC gives a list of examples, including the blocking of VoIP, such as Skype, and the slowing down of file-sharing networks (P2P).

Responses from the broadcasting sector also include various issues that have arisen concerning the distribution of audiovisual services.[9] In particular, the European Broadcasting Union (EBU) reports that several of its members and other media organizations have been

7 Article 1(3)(a) states: "Measures taken by Member States regarding end-users' access to, or use of, services and applications through electronic communications networks shall respect the fundamental rights and freedoms of natural persons, as guaranteed by the European Convention for the Protection of Human Rights and Fundamental Freedoms and general principles of Community law. Any of these measures regarding end-users' access to, or use of, services and applications through electronic communications networks liable to restrict those fundamental rights or freedoms may only be imposed if they are appropriate, proportionate and necessary within a democratic society, and their implementation shall be subject to adequate procedural safeguards in conformity with the European Convention for the Protection of Human Rights and Fundamental Freedoms and with general principles of Community law, including effective judicial protection and due process. Accordingly, these measures may only be taken with due respect for the principle of the presumption of innocence and the right to privacy. A prior, fair and impartial procedure shall be guaranteed, including the right to be heard of the person or persons concerned, subject to the need for appropriate conditions and procedural arrangements in duly substantiated cases of urgency in conformity with the European Convention for the Protection of Human Rights and Fundamental Freedoms. The right to effective and timely judicial review shall be guaranteed."

8 For example, the French Autorité de régulation des Communications électroniques et des postes (ARCEP), *Discussion Points and Initial Policy Directions on Internet and Network Neutrality*, May 2010; the British Ofcom, *Traffic Management and Net Neutrality: A Discussion Document*, 24 June 2010; and, more recently, the Italian Autorità per le garanzie nelle comunicazioni (AGCOM), *Delibera 40/11/ CONS, Public Consultation on Net Neutrality*, 3 February 2011.

9 We focus here on responses by the broadcasting sector, but other interested parties also responded, including the producers, distributers and right holders of audiovisual works (FIAD—Fédération internationale des associations de distributeurs de films; MPA—Motion Picture Association; GESAC—European Grouping of Societies of Authors and Composers; and FEP—Federation of European Publishers). These responses addressed similar concerns, but also discussed related issues such as the illegal distribution of audiovisual works.

downgraded because of network congestion and traffic management practices applied by the network operators (EBU 2010). According to the EBU, these practices are particularly significant in the case of live programs, such as coverage of popular sport events. This has created consumer confusion, also owing to the lack of transparency: The quality was less than expected and/or access to video streams was limited because of too high demand. The problems are primarily linked to television because the distribution of video signals demands high bandwidth. Furthermore, the EBU is concerned about discriminatory behavior, which risks undermining the open and neutral character of the Internet, ultimately resulting in consumer harm and citizen detriment. The EBU is of the opinion that sufficient competition is lacking and regulatory intervention is needed to address net-neutrality issues. In this context, IP TV as a managed service is mentioned as a typical example: These services should be open to all interested content providers, contrary to what—at least according to the comments of the EBU—seems current practice by some providers. Elsewhere in its response the EBU refers to "fair, reasonable and non-discriminatory" (FRAND) access as a basic principle for the provision of managed services. The EBU belongs to the group of respondents who emphasize the role of net neutrality in the context of freedom of expression and plurality.

Several of the EBU remarks were supported by reactions from individual broadcasting organizations, such as The Groupe Canal+ (underlining the need for further national implementation), VOD provider Dailymotion (giving an example of its services being blocked) or the Netherlands Public Broadcaster NPO (illustrating congestion when streaming sport events). However, the Association of Commercial Television in Europe (ACT) states that it is not aware of any problems with Internet access to date.[10]

Looking towards the future, respondents to the European Commission questionnaire indicated that new Internet business models might need to be taken into account. Managed services like IP TV could present problems if network operators favor certain services over others. Furthermore, certain content providers signalled the risk that network providers might want to charge them, accusing them of being "freeriders": network providers have to invest in more bandwidth from which the content providers benefit. Such behavior would conflict with the idea of an open Internet and would disregard the investments made by content providers. Network providers argued that such concerns were not justified.

BEREC mentioned three possible issues for the future: (1) the scope for discrimination leading to anti-competitive effects; (2) the potential longer-term consequences for the Internet economy affecting innovation and freedom of expression; and (3) confusion among, or harm to, consumers owing to lack of transparency. However, the general opinion—at least according to the interpretation of the European Commission—was that the new regulatory framework should be able to deal with these future issues and that no immediate further regulation was needed.

The necessity of network management—a concern explicitly expressed by the broadcasting sector (see the response of the EBU mentioned earlier)—was broadly recognized and

10 Groupe Canal+, *Réponse du Groupe Canal+ à la consultation publique sur l'internet ouvert et la neutralité du net en Europe*; Dailymotion, *contribution de Dailymotion à la consultation publique sur l'internet ouvert et la neutralité en Europe*, 29 September 2010; *Response of the Nederlandse Publieke Omroep (NPO: Netherlands Public Broadcasting) to the EC Questionnaire for the Public Consultation on the Open Internet and Net Neutrality in Europe*, 30 June 2010; Association of Commercial Television in Europe (ACT), *The Response of the Association of Commercial Television in Europe to the Net Neutrality Consultation*. The responses can be found online at http://ec.europa.eu/information_society/policy/ecomm/library/public_consult/net_neutrality/comments/index_en.htm

seen as an essential part of the operation of an efficient Internet. Network management was not considered to be incompatible with net neutrality. However, certain respondents addressed privacy issues in relation to network management, such as the use of DPI. With respect to prioritization, various references were made, in line with reactions from broadcasters, to CDNs.[11] Prioritization can help to improve the services delivered to end-users, but does carry the risk of discrimination. Interestingly, content providers also emphasized the need for more clarity about managed services. They underlined the necessity of a level playing field in which managed services are offered to all content and application providers on equal terms and without discrimination. Most comments, however, showed agreement that additional regulation was not yet necessary.

## Communication of the European Commission

Although no direct action has arisen from the consultation, the European Commission issued a communication in April 2011 (European Commission 2011a). The communication included a summary of the current situation and provided some insight into the further steps that the European Commission intended to take. First, in collaboration with BEREC, a study was to be performed exploring practices of blocking, slowing down traffic and equivalent commercial practices, and transparency and quality of service, as well as the competition issues relating to net neutrality such as discriminatory practices by a dominant player. On the basis of these findings, the European Commission would decide if additional guidance with respect to net neutrality is necessary. If significant and substantial problems were to come to light, more stringent measures would be required, for instance in the form of specific regulations on traffic management, including a ban on blocking lawful services. The wording showed that the European Commission was inspired by the United States, where such a ban is already in place. A similar conclusion can be drawn from a statement by the European Council on "the open Internet and net neutrality in Europe" (Council of the European Union 2011).

In March 2012, BEREC presented its first findings (BEREC 2012). These included the fact that DPI, the blocking of VoIP and the slowing down of P2P traffic are common practices in the European Union. Regarding video services, BEREC finds that some operators manage video streaming on the open Internet, and about one third of the fixed operators manage their networks in order to offer specialized services such as television services.

## National implementation

Several EU member states have chosen to put the rules from the New Regulatory Framework on net neutrality into national law without changing the wording, while others have decided to regulate net neutrality in more detail. The Netherlands provides an interesting example in this context.

11 A "content delivery network" or "content distribution network" is a large distributed system of servers deployed in multiple data centers on the Internet. The goal of a CDN is to serve content to end-users with high availability and high performance. CDNs serve a large fraction of the Internet content today, including web objects (text, graphics, URLs and scripts), downloadable objects (media files, software, documents), applications (e-commerce, portals), live streaming media, on-demand streaming media, and social networks. As an example, the Akamai Network, the world's largest CDN, serving about 20 percent of the web traffic and using more than 100,000 servers located in more than 1,000 networks and more than seventy countries (http://en.wikipedia.org/wiki/Content_delivery_network).

The Dutch Parliament voted in favor of an amendment to a newly proposed article of the Telecommunications Act prohibiting service blocking by "[p]roviders of public electronic communication networks which deliver Internet access services and providers of Internet access services must not hinder or slow down applications and services on the internet."[12] Only a limited group of four exceptions is allowed (including reasonable network management). Furthermore, the article forbids providers of Internet access services to make the price of the rates for Internet access services dependent on the services and applications that are offered or used via these services: charging Skype, WhatsApp or Netflix is not allowed.

According to the Explanatory Memorandum, the idea that "Internet service providers will increasingly take measures to hinder or slow down Internet traffic, either at their own initiative or under pressure from third parties, unless this is prohibited" is a main driver behind the new provision. Although congestion may legitimize traffic management, the best solution to congestion is avoiding it by investing adequately in capacity.

## *Council of Europe*

The question of net neutrality also has the attention of the Council of Europe.[13] In 2009, the Council of Ministers adopted a resolution on Internet governance and critical Internet resources in Reykjavik (Council of Europe 2009). The resolution drew attention to the relationship between net neutrality and tools such as the European Convention on Human Rights, and called for further action. In September 2011, the Council of Ministers adopted a Declaration on Internet Governance Principles. One of the principles, about net neutrality, subscribes to the classic point of departure: "Users should have the greatest possible access to Internet-based content, applications and services of their choice, whether or not they are offered free of charge, using suitable devices of their choice" (Council of Europe 2011). The next sentence addresses the traffic management issue:

> Traffic management measures which have an impact on the enjoyment of fundamental rights and freedoms, in particular the right to freedom of expression and to impart and receive information regardless of frontiers, as well as the right to respect for private life, must meet the requirements of international law on the protection of freedom of expression and access to information, and the right to respect for private life.
>
> *(Council of Europe 2011)*

In fact, these more recent activities build on earlier Council of Europe instruments such as the Committee of Ministers' Recommendation on the public service value of the Internet (Council of Europe 2007). This value should be understood as people's significant reliance on the Internet as an essential tool for their everyday activities (including communication, information, knowledge, and commercial transactions), and the resulting legitimate expectation that Internet services be accessible and affordable, secure, reliable and ongoing.

12 For a non-official translation of the provision (Article 7(4)(a) of the Telecommunications Act) and its underlying considerations, see online at https://www.bof.nl/2011/06/15/net-neutrality-in-the-netherlands-state-of-play

13 The Council of Europe unites more countries than the twenty-seven EU member states (http://www.coe.int). The European Convention of Human Rights, enforceable through the European Court of Human Rights, is the most important treaty that binds the forty-seven member states of the Council of Europe.

## Getting the context right

Before further analyzing the US and European contexts of net neutrality, it is important to put relevant policy questions in the right context. More importantly, it should be acknowledged that net neutrality is part of a value chain and that technological questions are not isolated.

### *The value chain and business model*

At the beginning of this chapter, we provided a definition of net neutrality. In a much-quoted article, Lessig and McChesney defined net neutrality as an end-to-end issue: "Net neutrality means simply that all like Internet content must be treated alike and move at the same speed over the network. The owners of the Internet's wires cannot discriminate. This is the simple but brilliant 'end-to-end' design of the Internet that has made it such a powerful force for economic and social good" (Lessig and McChesney 2006). A complex value chain is embedded in such an end-to-end approach, which allows content to travel between users or between content providers and end-users (see Figure 28.2).

The players in this converging value chain have a mutual and permanent dynamic relationship. The telecommunication companies and the access providers, on the one hand, and the content aggregators (such as broadcasters), on the other, are obviously inclined to obtain the value that has been, or can be, realized elsewhere in the value chain.

Every link in the value chain is potentially weak: Every position in the chain can develop into a bottleneck. Should net neutrality obligations restrict Internet service providers in their possibilities to influence (i.e. prioritize) traffic, the problem of potential discrimination of certain services will likely shift to another spot in the value chain. Furthermore, net neutrality issues already exist elsewhere in the chain. Creators take decisions about who will have access to their creations. Platform providers/aggregators and peripheral equipment suppliers try to affect "net neutrality" by granting favors to their own providers by controlling applications and selection systems, e.g. search, recommendation/reputation systems, electronic program guides (EPGs), and apps on devices.

Network providers, particularly cable operators providing Internet access services, themselves discover they have allowed the Trojan horse in: After all, the services that they provided

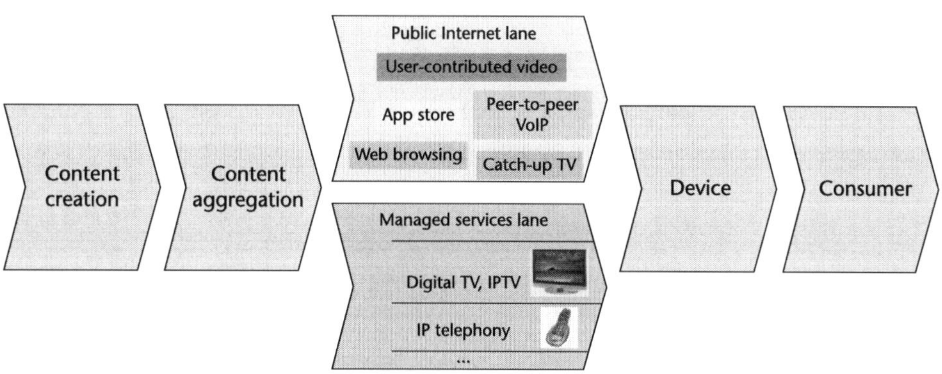


*Figure 28.2* (Nooren, Leurdijk and Van Eijk 2012: 7)

previously (traditional cable TV) can now be substituted by services received via the Internet (e.g. via OTT video services). This explains why various stakeholders prefer to safeguard sufficient space to maneuver with regards to net neutrality. However, solutions that do not take the value-chain dynamics into account fight only the symptoms, not the disease. A value-chain approach is inevitable.

Net neutrality is therefore not only about something "technical," which is only one aspect of a longstanding problem: who takes control of the eyeballs; who takes control of the content? The party taking control of the users and/or content also takes control of the major income flow. From this perspective, the Internet has much in common with the classic broadcasting organizations in terms of its business model.

### *Technological challenges*

This does not mean that technical aspects are unimportant. On the contrary, technology as an enabler/disabler can have a major influence. Scarcity in capacity, whether or not this is artificial, increases the strain on available capacity. Capacity providers can use technology to optimize their business model (by investing more to increase capacity, probably with the result of higher prices for end-users, or by taking advantage of scarcity and making information providers pay). The question about quality guarantees requires technical measures. This applies to the video content distribution described earlier. These types of specialized/managed service change to some extent the architecture of the Internet: services are no longer part of the more or less undefined Internet "cloud," but are more directly supplied by the ISP, based on special agreements with content providers or providers of content delivery networks bringing the content to their front door. Such agreements may also be required to regulate other aspects, such as access to selection systems or payment mechanisms. Yet all of these interventions can be translated into economic or policy-based choices.

## Analysis and conclusions

Net neutrality, both from a policy and regulatory perspective, is becoming further and further concretized. The FCC's pioneering role clearly has had an impact in Europe. The United States is still ahead, but it is likely that new European policies will be consistent, to a large extent, with the US rules. A number of individual EU member states have already taken steps in this direction, without the European Union taking counter measures. This is an indication that these national rules are not infringing on European policies and rules.

As indicated by US regulation, transparency about net neutrality, however important, is not a means in itself. On the one hand, transparency in the context of net neutrality aims at informing users about the service they are getting. On the other hand, transparency also enables the user to make—based on the information obtained—a deliberate choice between staying with one service or switching to another. Practice will probably show that transparency has only a limited effect on switching. Information is definitely not communication and might thus not be endorsed properly by the consumer. The danger is that information overkill may lead to information not being read instead of fully penetrating. The challenge is to provide end-users with clear, precise and relevant information on: (i) the services and applications that they can access through their data transmission services; (ii) the traffic management practices employed on the networks of the providers; and (iii) the technical quality of services offered and their possible limitations. A further challenge is to provide this wide range of information in a form that end-users are able to digest. Whether consumers then actually decide to change providers on the basis of the information obtained depends on many factors. It is not without reason that consumers switching access services in order to reduce costs are receiving more and more attention (BEREC 2010). Various questions are raised, including: is there a genuine choice, or are offers are equally good or rather equally bad? In the event of dissatisfaction about broadband access, how easy is it to change once a bundle of services has been purchased? How complex are the change procedures (red tape, contractual terms, deadlines etc.)? Although European policies tend to overemphasize transparency, a more balanced approach addressing specific measures is more realistic.

Preliminary findings of the European telecommunications regulators indicate substantial practices of blocking services and managing available Internet capacity. Blocking is clearly taking place at the level of mobile networks, and fixed networks are slowing down P2P traffic. Audiovisual services in Europe are not creating issues similar to the United States, but this might change in the near future, taking into account the fact that European developments often follow the US market. The same attractive content is involved and several players are active on both sides of the ocean based on identical business cases. New European policy will concentrate on further developing net neutrality as a means to guarantee the open Internet and to secure reasonable traffic management. This means a no-blocking policy based on non-discrimination is likely to be introduced on a European level. In principle, ISPs might have to make all services provided through the Internet accessible for all users. In this respect, the possibilities to discriminate between different types of service might be limited. It will be interesting to see whether a distinction between mobile and fixed networks will be made, as occurred in the United States, or not, as in the Dutch example.

## Conclusion

Net neutrality is an interesting, complicated phenomenon, and we are currently in an explorative stage in which net neutrality is being mapped out in further detail. It is remarkable how little is known about what is happening in the complex process between providing and purchasing audiovisual media services, in both a technical and economic sense. This should lead to the actual issues becoming more visible. Only then will we get to the heart of the matter. Based on the evidence thus far, it is clear that we have to face the reality that full net neutrality is impossible and that reasonable forms of net management are unavoidable. These are the real questions that need to be addressed.

The regulatory concepts of both the United States and Europe place a great deal of emphasis on reasonableness: Reasonable net management is allowed, while "unreasonable net management" should be forbidden. In the next few years, this basic principle will require further attention—in particular, the role of capacity consumption and the quality of service aspects of audiovisual services. Should capacity be reserved for such services? And if so, how? What would be the position of the "open Internet" in all of this? These questions also have a cultural dimension, and relate to constitutional principles such as the freedom to impart and receive information, freedom of association and the protection of privacy. It is quite clear from the present debate that civil society takes these principles seriously and has been able to influence policymaking.[14] However, part of the net neutrality debate is not new: for instance,

14 For example, the Electronic Frontier Foundation (http://www.eff.gov) in the United States and European counterparts such as EDRI (http://www.edri.org) and *la Quadrature du Net* (http://www.laquadrature.net).

in the past, there have been several showdowns about access to distribution networks. Not surprisingly, a comparison is made in the literature with policy and regulation in the field of cable television networks (Frieden 2010). Countries have introduced must-carry rules, forcing operators to carry specific programs and/or regulation allowing content providers to claim access to analog or digital channels. Other examples include basic practices such as the allocation of frequencies based on content-related criteria, and access rules opening up communications networks and giving service providers a right to claim capacity at regulated conditions. Bringing previous experiences to the task can be useful, but it can also open a can of worms. It requires a cautious approach because previous experiences have shown that results can be negative or can carry a risk of oversimplification. This does not alter the fact that there is unmistakable convergence between the (tele)communications and media domain, and that net neutrality must be discussed within this wider context. Easy solutions in one part of the value chain might lead to the problem popping up somewhere else. The search for the master switch—to control the eyeballs and the connected business model—is ongoing (Wu 2010). In this process, increasing conflicts will probably be the main driver for policymaking and regulation.

## References


Bendrath, R. and Mueller, M. (2011) 'The end of the net as we know it? Deep packet inspection and Internet governance' *New Media and Society*, 13(7): 1142–1160. Online. Available HTTP: http://ssrn.com/abstract=1653259 (accessed 27 April 2012)

BEREC (2010) *Berec Report on Best Practices to Facilitate Consumer Switching*, October, BoR (10)34. Online. Available HTTP: http://www.erg.eu.int/doc/berec/bor_10_34_rev1.pdf (accessed 27 April 2012)

—— (2011) *Response to the European Commission's Consultation on the Open Internet and Net Neutrality in Europe*, September, BoR (10)42. Online. Available HTTP: http://erg.eu.int/doc/berec/bor_10_42.pdf (accessed 27 April 2012).

—— (2012) 'BEREC preliminary findings on traffic management practices in Europe show that blocking of VoIP and P2P traffic is common, other practices vary widely, Press release, 9 March. Online. Available HTTP: http://www.erg.eu.int/doc/2012/TMI_press_release.pdf (accessed 27 April 2012).

Council of Europe (2007) *Recommendation CM/REC(2007)16 of the Committee of Ministers to Member States on Measures to Promote the Public Service Value of the Internet*, Adopted by the Committee of Ministers on 7 November 2007 at the 1010th meeting of the Ministers' Deputies Online. Available HTTP: https://wcd.coe.int/ViewDoc.jsp?id=1207291 (accessed 27 April 2012).

—— (2009) *Resolution on Internet Governance and Critical Internet Resources*, Reykjavik, 29 May. Online. Available HTTP: http://www.coe.int/t/dghl/standardsetting/media-dataprotection/conf-internet-freedom/REYKJAVIK_RESOLUTION_INTERNET_GOVERNANCE.pdf (accessed 27 April 2012).

—— (2011) *Declaration by the Committee of Ministers on Internet Governance Principles*, Adopted by the Committee of Ministers on 21 September 2011 at the 1121st meeting of the Ministers' Deputies. Online. Available HTTP: https://wcd.coe.int/ViewDoc.jsp?id=1835773 (accessed 27 April 2012).

Council of the European Union (2011) *Council Conclusions on the Open Internet and Net Neutrality in Europe*, 13 December. Online. Available HTTP: http://www.consilium.europa.eu/uedocs/cms_data/docs/pressdata/en/trans/126890.pdf (accessed 27 April 2012).

European Broadcasting Union (EBU) (2010) *The EBU Response to the Questionnaire for the Public Consultation on the Open Internet and Net Neutrality in Europe*, 30 September. Online. Available HTTP: http://www.ebu.ch/CMSimages/en/leg_pp_net_neutrality_300910_tcm6-68851.pdf (accessed 27 April 2012).

European Commission (2009) 'Telecoms: Commission launches case against UK over privacy and personal data protection,' IP/09/570, 14 April.

—— (2010a) 'Digital agenda: Commission launches consultation on net neutrality,' IP/10/860, 30 June.

—— (2010b) *Report on the Public Consultation on 'The Open Internet and Net Neutrality in Europe,'* 9 November. Online. Available HTTP: http://ec.europa.eu/information_society/policy/ecomm/doc/library/public_consult/net_neutrality/report.pdf (accessed 27 April 2012).

—— (2010c) '*Digital agenda: Consultation reveals near consensus on the importance of preserving open Internet,*' IP/10/1482, 9 November.

—— (2011a) *Communication from the Commission to the European Parliament, the Council, the Economic and Social Committee and the Committee on the Regions: The Open Internet and Net Neutrality in Europe*, COM(2011) 222 final, 19 April, Brussels.

—— (2011b) 'The Internet belongs to all of us,' Speech by Nelie Kroes, European Commission Vice-President for the Digital Agenda, SPEECH/11/285, Brussels, 19 April.

Federal Communications Commission (FCC) (2005) *FCC Policy Statement on Network Neutrality*, FCC 05-151, adopted 5 August.

—— (2008) 'Formal complaint of Free Press and Public Knowledge against Comcast Corporation for secretly degrading peer-to-peer applications.' Online. Available HTTP: http://hraunfoss.fcc.gov/edocs_public/attachmatch/FCC-08-183A1.pdf (accessed 27 April 2012)

—— (2010a) 'FCC Chairman Julius Genachowski statement on Open Internet Public Notice,' News bulletin, 1 September.

—— (2010b) *Report and Order, In the Matter of Preserving the Open Internet; Broadband Industry Practices*,GN Docket No. 09-191, WC Docket No. 07-52, 21 December (Released 23 December).

Frieden, R. (2010) *Winning the Silicon Sweepstakes: Can the United States Compete in Global Telecommunications?* New Haven, CT: Yale University Press.

Horten, M. (2011) *The Copyright Enforcement Enigma: Internet Politics and the 'Telecoms Package,'* Houndmills: Polgrave Macmillan.

Kang, C. (2010) 'Level 3 Communications calls Comcast fees for Netflix feeds unfair,' *Washington Post*, 29 November. Online. Available HTTP: http://www.washingtonpost.com/wp-dyn/content/article/2010/11/29/AR2010112907024.html (accessed 27 April 2012).

Lessig, L. and McChesney, R. W. (2006) 'No tolls on the Internet,' *The Washington Post*, 8 June. Online. Available HTTP: http://www.washingtonpost.com/wp-dyn/content/article/2006/06/07/AR2006060702108.html (accessed 27 April 2012).

Marcus, J. S., Nooren, P., Cave, J. and Carter, K. R. (2011) *Network Neutrality: Challenges and Responses in the EU and in the US*, Brussels: European Parliament. Online. Available HTTP: http://www.europarl.europa.eu/document/activities/cont/201105/20110523ATT20073/20110523ATT20073EN.pdf (accessed 27 April 2012).

Nooren, P., Leurdijk, A. and Van Eijk, N. (2012) 'Intended and unintended effects of policy measures: An examination of the value chain for video distribution aimed at promoting net neutrality,' Paper presented at EuroCPR2012—27th European Communications Policy Research Conference, Ghent, 25–27 March. Online. Available HTTP: http://www.eurocpr.org/data/2012/Nooren_Leurdijk_VanEijck.pdf (accessed 27 April 2012)

Van Buskirk, E. (2010) 'Here's the real Google/Verizon story: A tale of two Internets,' *Wired.com*, 9 August. Online. Available HTTP: http://www.wired.com/epicenter/2010/08/google-verizon-propose-open-vs-paid-internets/ (accessed 27 April 2012)

Wikipedia (n.d.) 'IPTV'. Online. Available HTTP: http://en.wikipedia.org/wiki/IPTV (accessed 27 April 2012)

Wu, T. (2003) 'Network neutrality, broadband discrimination,' *Journal on Telecommunications and High Technology Law*, 2: 141–176. Online. Available HTTP: http://www.jthtl.org/content/articles/V2I1/JTHTLv2i1_Wu.PDF (accessed 27 April 2012).

—— (2010) *The Master Switch*, New York: Alfred A. Knopf.

# 29

# Network neutrality and the need for a technological turn in Internet scholarship

*Christopher S. Yoo**

## Introduction

Academic scholarship about the Internet now includes a broad array of interdisciplinary perspectives, encompassing such fields as communications, economics, sociology, political science, history, anthropology and law (Nissenbaum and Price 2004). Yet to most social scientists, the technical details of how the Internet actually works remain arcane and inaccessible (Sandvig 2009). At the same time, convergence is forcing scholars to grapple with how to apply regulatory regimes developed for traditional media such as broadcasting, telephony and cable television to a world in which all voice, video and text services are provided via an Internet-based platform. Determining how to reconcile existing law with these changes requires some degree of familiarity with the intricacies of the technology. The required level of technical expertise is likely to continue to increase even further as the Internet matures both as an industry and as a field of study.

This chapter explores the problems caused by the lack of familiarity with the underlying technology by way of illustration. It focuses on the network neutrality debate that has dominated Internet policy for the past several years, beginning with four historical architectural commitments that permit prioritization and then examining ten modern examples of non-neutral, prioritized architectures.

The analysis underscores just how surprising the relative lack of sophistication reflected in the current debate actually is. Unfamiliarity with the Internet's architecture has allowed some advocates to characterize the prioritization of network traffic as an aberration when, in fact, it is a central feature designed into the network since its inception. Moreover, despite the universal recognition of the need to accommodate technical concepts such as network security and congestion management, many people involved in the debate have only the

* This chapter is adapted from comments the author submitted on 4 November 2010, in the Federal Communications Commission Proceeding on "Preserving the Open Internet."

barest notion of how the Internet manages security and congestion. At the same time, the lack of knowledge has allowed advocates to recast pragmatic engineering concepts as supposedly inviolable architectural principles, effectively imbuing certain types of political advocacy with a false sense of scientific legitimacy (Blumenthal 2002; Gillespie 2006).

Lastly, those without an understanding of the network's design will find it difficult to appreciate the significance of changes in the way in which people are using the network. Video is now a significant component of network traffic, with other innovations, such as cloud computing, sensor networks, and the advent of fourth-generation (4G) wireless broadband waiting in the wings. The radical changes in the technologies comprising the network and the demands that end-users are placing on it is creating pressure on the network to evolve in response (Yoo 2012). The absence of some technical grounding risks making the status quo seem like a natural construct that cannot, or should not, be changed.

## Historical examples of prioritization

The current policy debate often tries to depict network owners' recent efforts to prioritize certain traffic as new and aberrant deviations from the status quo. A brief review of the history of the Internet reveals that prioritization is a feature that has been built into the architecture from the beginning. Moreover, the years that followed witnessed sustained and persistent efforts to extend and enhance network operators' ability to engage in sophisticated network management.

### *The type-of-service flag in the original Internet protocol*

The heart of the Internet is the Internet Protocol (IP), which a leading textbook on computer networking aptly describes as "[t]he glue that holds the entire Internet together" (Tanenbaum 2003: 432). IP is designed to provide a single common language that enables a diverse range of different network technologies to interconnect with one another seamlessly (Cerf and Kahn 1974). As a matter of principle, IP was kept as simple as possible, being "specifically limited in scope to provide the functions necessary to deliver a package of bits . . . from a source to a destination over an interconnected systems of networks" (Information Science Institute 1981: 1). IP was thus designed to include only the bare minimum needed for the network to function properly (Leiner *et al.* 1985).

The need to keep IP as simple and robust as possible made the protocol architects' decision to include an eight-bit *type-of-service field* in the IP header particularly telling (Zhu 2007). The type-of-service field was designed to allow networks to attach different levels of priority to particular packets. The first three bits permitted the assignment of three varying levels of precedence to the packet. The next three bits allowed the specification of the three different dimensions of precedence: delay, throughput, and reliability (Information Science Institute 1981; see also Information Science Institute 1979). A separate standard documented how to map the flags in the type-of-service field onto the actual service provided by the networks comprising the Internet (Postel 1981).

This field was included explicitly to "support . . . a variety of types of service . . . distinguished by differing requirements for such things as speed, latency and reliability" (Clark 1988: 108). Indeed, the document establishing IP specifically notes that they included the type-of-service field to "capitalize on the services of its supporting networks to provide various types and qualities of service" (Information Science Institute 1981: 1). The specification later noted: "Several networks offer service precedence, which somehow treats high precedence traffic as more important than other traffic." The decision to include the type-of-service flag in the IP header reflects a belief in the importance in supporting this type of functionality. The protocol designers explicitly recognized that prioritization inevitably gave rise to trade-offs: "In many networks better performance for one of these parameters is coupled with worse performance on another." The existence of such costs counseled in favor of using prioritization judiciously rather than prohibiting it altogether (ibid.: 12).

### *Prioritization of terminal sessions over file transfer sessions on the NSFNET*

One of the earliest examples of prioritized service occurred in 1987 on the Internet predecessor known as the National Science Foundation Network (NSFNET) when end-users first began to connect to the network through personal computers (PCs) instead of dumb terminals. Terminal sessions are an extremely interactive application, in which every key stroke is immediately transmitted and which requires constant, real-time interaction with the network. Any delay causes the terminal to lock up temporarily. File transfers are considerably less interactive. Particularly given the 56 kbps backbone speeds of the time, end-users would typically expect file transfers to last several minutes.

The advent of PCs made it much easier for end-users to transfer files, which in turn increased the intensity of the demands that they were placing on the network to the point at which the network slowed to a crawl. The resulting congestion caused terminal sessions to run agonizingly slowly, and the fact that fixed cost investments could not be made instantaneously created an unavoidable delay in adding network capacity.

NSFNET's interim solution was to reprogram its routers to give traffic running the application protocol associated with terminal sessions (telnet) higher priority than traffic running the application associated with file transfer sessions (file transfer protocol, or FTP) until additional bandwidth could be added. In short, intelligence in the core of the network looked inside packets and gave a higher priority to interactive, real-time traffic and deprioritized traffic that was less sensitive to delay. The network also made wider use of prioritization in the type-of-service field in the IP header (MacKie-Mason and Varian 1994).

This episode demonstrates why forecasting the amount of network capacity is so difficult. The spike in traffic was driven not by any change within the network itself, but rather by a major innovation in a complementary technology (the PC) that changed the way in which people used the network. In this sense, it bears a striking resemblance to the state of affairs in 1995 and 1996, when the simultaneous development of HTML and Mosaic, the first graphically oriented browser, caused Internet traffic to grow at an annual rate of 800–900 percent and to turn the network into what many dubbed "the World Wide Wait" (Yoo 2012). As difficult as it is to anticipate developments within the network correctly, it is even harder to foresee game-changing improvements in complementary technologies.

This episode also demonstrates the beneficial role that network management can play in providing a better end user experience. Indeed, prioritization actually might have been able to offer better service to users of terminal sessions without degrading the experience of file transfer users. This is because the performance of file transfer sessions depends entirely on when the last packet arrives. Interactive applications (particularly streaming applications), in contrast, are very sensitive to the speed and spacing with which intermediate packets arrive. So long as the delivery time of the last packet is not affected, the network can rearrange the delivery schedule for intermediate packets associated with terminal sessions without adversely affecting overall performance of file transfer sessions.

At the same time, this episode demonstrates how core-based solutions that explicitly route traffic based on the application layer protocol with which it is associated can benefit consumers. Although this example represented a short-run solution, in theory such solutions need not be temporary. Indeed, in a technologically dynamic world, one would expect at times that employing network management techniques would be cheaper than adding bandwidth, and vice versa. Moreover, one would also expect the relative cost of these alternative solutions (and the balance that they imply) to change over time.

## *The shift to BGP to enable policy-based routing*

The emergence of border gateway protocol (BGP) also reflects the historic importance of allowing greater control over the way in which certain packets travel over the Internet. Before BGP emerged, the primary routing protocol was known as the exterior gateway protocol (EGP). EGP suffered from a number of shortcomings. For example, it could not accommodate more complex topologies in which a particular network (also called an "autonomous system") was available via more than one route (Rekhter 1989).

In addition, a network running EGP only informed neighboring networks about the length of the path through which it could reach to particular addresses without providing any specific information about the path that particular packets would traverse. A network that was interested only in delivering packets as quickly as possible could simply examine the length of the routes advertised by its neighbors and opt for the shortest option. The problem is that networks are often interested in more than just the length of the path. For example, until 1991, the standard acceptable use policy prohibited using the NSFNET for conveying commercial traffic. As a result, networks sending commercial traffic needed some way to know whether particular advertised routes traversed the NSFNET and sometimes had to forgo a shorter route to comply with the NSFNET's commercialization restrictions (Huitema 1995). Others may prefer certain routes because the existence of peering agreements with particular networks or the need to keep certain traffic within certain ratios may make it more cost efficient to route traffic along a particular path. Still others might prefer to avoid certain paths because of security concerns. A leading textbook gives the following examples of such routing policies (Tanenbaum 2003: 460):

1. No transit traffic through certain networks.
2. Never put Iraq on a route starting at the Pentagon.
3. Do not use the United States to get from British Columbia to Ontario.
4. Only transit Albania if there is no alternative to the destination.
5. Traffic starting or ending at IBM should not transit Microsoft.

Unfortunately, because EGP only provided information about path length without identifying the particular networks traversed, it did not provide sufficient information to support such policies. Instead of following EGP's approach of having routers exchange information only about the length of the path by which they could reach a particular address, routers running BGP notify their neighbors about the precise path used. Every router running BGP examines the advertised routes and uses a proprietary scoring system to calculate the length of the path to each location via every particular neighbor and transmits packets bound for that location via the shortest path.

One advantage of providing complete path information about particular routes is that it provides much stronger support for routing policies. A router conveying commercial traffic during the early days of the NSFNET could easily examine the precise paths comprising particular routes and decline to use any that traversed the NSFNET. Indeed, it is a simple matter to assign any route that violates a policy a score of infinity, thereby guaranteeing that that route will not be used (Tanenbaum 2003); "In nontechnical terms, this means AT&T routers can make discriminatory routing decisions such as treating traffic from Sprint more favorably than traffic from Verizon, or even rejecting Verizon traffic altogether" (Zhu 2007: 635).

The desire to provide better support for routing policies is widely recognized as one of the primary motivations driving the shift from EGP to BGP. Indeed, as the initial standard describing BGP noted, creating a routing system "from which policy decisions at an [autonomous system] level may be enforced" was one of the central design goals underlying BGP (Lougheed and Rekhter 1989: 1). All traffic subject to a routing policy would necessarily have to travel along a longer route (and thus take a longer time) than traffic between the same two points that was not subject to the policy.

BGP is not without its shortcomings. For example, although it allows the advertisement of multiple paths to the same network, it permits only one of those paths to be used at any particular time. When multiple routers connect two networks, BGP does not support balancing the load across all of those routers. Moreover, because route information is exchanged between adjacent networks, information about changes in routes and topology can take time to propagate through the system. During the time when routing information has not yet reached equilibrium, different routers may be referencing routing information that is incorrect or inconsistent (Comer 2006). None of these considerations, however, alters the fundamental fact that BGP was specifically designed to allow individual networks to give preference to traffic associated with particular sources and destinations and to avoid certain networks altogether.

## IETF standards for integrated services, differentiated services and multiprotocol label switching

The development of the IP header and the deployment of BGP did not represent the only way in which the engineering community attempted to support prioritization on the Internet. Over the past two decades, the engineering community has developed a series of potential solutions to provide applications with different levels of quality of service.

The first initiative, developed in 1991, is known as "integrated services" (IntServ). IntServ allows end-users to send a reservation message inquiring whether sufficient resources exist at that time to provide a particular level of service. If the capacity is available, each router notes the reservation and reserves the resources needed to transmit the communication (Braden *et al.* 1994). The principal downside was that implementing IntServ would require substantial changes to the router infrastructure. Specifically, each router would have to be reconfigured to be able to signal the end-user whether the requested resources are available and to have some means for reserving those resources. In addition, the need to set up each flow in advance can be quite complicated, requires routers to maintain per-flow state, and violates the store-and-forward principles requiring that each router route each individual packet independently.

The second initiative, standardized in 1998, is known as "differentiated services" (DiffServ). DiffServ divides traffic into particular routing classes, with each class denoted by a differentiated services code point (DSCP) stored in a reconfigured type-of-service field in the IP header (Blake *et al.* 1998). Disassociating the type-of-service field from the three dimensional, three-level semantics in the original design of the type-of-service field allows DiffServ to support a broader range of quality of service. Many companies have begun to use DiffServ in their internal networks to ensure that delay-sensitive traffic is delivered in a timely manner. For example, Comcast is using DiffServ to prevent delays in its voice service, and AT&T is using DiffServ to ensure that there are no delays in its video service. Unlike the resource reservation and admission control approach employed by IntServ, the prioritization-oriented approach employed by DiffServ cannot guarantee quality of service; it can only increase the probability that a particular packet will arrive within a particular time.

Another solution known as "multiprotocol label switching" (MPLS) incorporates the features of technologies such as "asynchronous transfer mode" (ATM) that were designed to increase routers' forwarding speed. Instead of routing based on IP addresses, MPLS adds a label to the front of each packet and routes on the basis of that label. In addition, each flow (known as a "forwarding equivalence class") is assigned a specific path through the network. Information about the label and the associated route are propogated to other MPLS-enabled routers (Rosen *et al.* 2001). Because labels are shorter than IP addresses, routers can direct traffic more rapidly. The ability to define in advance the route that a particular flow will take gives end-users greater control over security. In addition, MPLS can support load balancing simply by dividing traffic between the same two endpoints into two separate forwarding equivalence classes and assigning them different paths. Most importantly for the purposes of this chapter, in determining the particular path that a particular flow will travel, the MPLS router can match the quality of service demanded by the flow with the resources available along possible paths (Stallings 2001). By establishing what are tantamount to virtual circuits, MPLS exists in considerable tension with many architectural principles that many regard as central to the Internet. That said, MPLS is now being widely deployed by network providers and represents still another way in which the standards comprising the existing architecture are designed explicitly to support prioritizing certain traffic over other traffic.

## Contemporary examples of prioritization

The historical examples enumerated above have been followed by more contemporary examples in which network management is being used to increase the network's functionality or reliability. These examples can serve as useful reference points when determining what constitutes unreasonable discrimination, reasonable network management, specialized services and other key concepts with respect to network neutrality.

### *The 700 MHz auction*

The auction of the spectrum recovered from television broadcasters following the migration to digital transmission (commonly known as the "700 MHz auction") provides another prime example of the benefits of network management. The Federal Communication Commission (FCC) divided the spectrum in this auction into five blocks, labeled "A" through "E." Blocks A and E were the least commercially attractive, as they were subject to interference issues; the E block contained 6 MHz of spectrum, roughly half the amount needed to provide high-quality service.

Of the remaining blocks, which represented the most commercially attractive opportunities, the B block contained 12 MHz of spectrum and was subject to the fewest restrictions. The C block contained 22 MHz of spectrum, but was subject to the requirement that the licensee provide open access to all applications and devices that do not cause harm to the network (FCC 2007).

The D block contained 11 MHz of spectrum subject to the requirement that the licensee build a single network shared both by public safety users and commercial users. Public safety users would be given the unconditional right to pre-empt commercial traffic during emergency situations. Commercial users would operate on a secondary basis that must accept interference from primary users at all times and must not interfere with the primary users. In essence, the rules established two classes of service operating on the same network, with the primary, higher value use being given unconditional priority over all secondary uses (FCC 2007).

The Commission's justification for this decision offers one of the clearest statements of the benefits associated with allowing multiple tiers of service. First, the higher utilization from combining two different types of use can reduce costs by allowing the network to realize economies of scale. Second, sharing spectrum with multiple users promotes more efficient use of spectrum. Third, the addition of secondary uses will help to defray the cost of building out the network without adversely affecting the needs of the higher value, primary uses (FCC 2006; FCC 2007). The FCC's decisions with respect to the D block in the 700 MHz auction provide a powerful exposition of the benefits of allowing networks to give priority to higher value traffic traveling in the same pipe as lower value traffic. Doing so both yields consumer benefits and promotes competition in areas in which broadband is already available. Making it easier for network providers to cover the costs of constructing new networks also promotes entry into areas that are currently not served.

The 700 MHz auction was held on 18 March 2008, with wide variations in the amounts generated by each block. To normalize for the different amounts of spectrum included in each block, the standard practice is to analyze the total price paid on a per MHz basis. In addition, license value is also determined by the size of the population encompassed within its boundaries, since licenses in densely populated areas are more valuable than licenses providing the same amount of spectrum in more sparsely populated areas. Therefore license value is also determined on a per population basis, with the cost of particular spectrum being measured in terms of megahertz/population ("MHz/pop").

The B block, which was the least encumbered by regulatory requirements, proved to be the most valuable, selling for US $2.68 per MHz/pop. The C block, which was encumbered by open access requirements, sold for $0.76 per MHz/pop. The D block, which was required to share spectrum and to give priority to public safety services, failed to meet its reserve price of $1.33 billion (the equivalent of $0.44 per MHz/pop) and thus did not sell at all. In fact, the largest bid for the D block was only $472 million, or roughly $0.17 per MHz/pop. For comparison, the interference-encumbered A and E blocks sold for $1.16 and $0.74 per MHz/pop respectively (Kirby 2008).

The actual results of the 700 MHz auction provide specific empirical evidence of the economic impact of open access requirements. Auction results for specific blocks may reflect variations in the amount of contiguous spectrum in each block, differences in the propagation characteristics of particular portions of the spectrum, disparities in the size of the geographic area being served, and the case-specific dynamics of which firms happen to pursue particular licenses. That said, the fact that the block encumbered by open access requirements (the C block) sold for 72 percent less than the least unencumbered block (the B block) suggests that the reduction in value associated with open access is substantial. Put another way, these prices imply that providers may have to commit up to 3.5 times more spectrum if they are to provide service on an open-access basis. The failure of the D block to meet its reserve price reveals that not all forms of prioritized service are necessarily beneficial. Giving the public safety community the right to interrupt service effectively guarantees that other users will lose connectivity during times of crisis. In the words of one financial analyst, the advertising slogan for such a service would essentially be: "Guaranteed not to work when you need it most" (Bazelon 2008).

## *Load balancing*

When the Internet first emerged, the entities that comprised it interconnected through a relatively simple and uniform set of business relationships. End-users purchased a service from a single last-mile provider. Last-mile Internet service providers (ISPs) exchanged traffic with a single regional ISP. Regional ISPs handed off all of their traffic to a single backbone provider. The one-to-one nature of these relationships caused the network to assume a topology known as a "spanning tree," in which any two endpoints were connected only by a single path. Routing decisions in a spanning tree are relatively simple, because the uniqueness of the path connecting any two endpoints means that there is only a single route that traffic between those points can take.

Over time, the networks that form the Internet began to interconnect with one another in ways that deviated from the spanning tree topology. End-users and ISPs began to *multihome* by purchasing connections to more than one upstream provider. In addition, regional ISPs entered into *secondary peering* arrangements in which they exchanged traffic directly with one another without traversing any backbones (Yoo 2012).

One result of these topological innovations is that many endpoints began to be connected by multiple paths. The presence of multiple paths between endpoints naturally means that someone must decide along which path to route the traffic. Although most networks choose routes that minimize the number of hops, networks may sometimes find it beneficial to route traffic along longer routes in order to satisfy other requirements of their interconnection relationships. For example, a network may seek to reduce congestion and minimize transit costs by balancing the loads between the two available paths. Alternatively, a network may intentionally route traffic over a longer path if doing so will help it to maintain its traffic within the ratios mandated by its peering contract. Some load-balancing systems may also increase the networks' effective performance by testing the throughput rates provided by each path and sending the traffic that is the most sensitive to delay along the faster connection (Yoo 2010).

Again, the effect is to introduce significant variance in the speed with which similarly situated packets will arrive at their destination and the cost that similarly situated packets will have to bear. This variance results not from anti-competitive motives, but rather from networks' attempts to minimize costs and to ensure quality of service in the face of a network topology that is increasingly heterogeneous.

## *AT&T's U-verse*

As the FCC noted when first seeking comment on its "Open Internet" proposal in October 2009, AT&T's U-verse represents an important example of a specialized service (FCC 2009). The benefits provided by prioritization and reserving bandwidth are vividly illustrated by comparing U-Verse with Verizon's FiOS network. Verizon is investing US $23 billion to create a last-mile network, the fiber-based FiOS network, which offers up to 100 Mbps and holds the promise of providing up to 10 Gbps of service. In contrast, AT&T's strategy leverages the existing telephone network by deploying a DSL-based technology known as VDSL. U-verse provides smaller amounts of bandwidth, ranging from 20 to 32 Mbps depending on a particular customer's location, but at the much lower cost of \$6–\$7 billion (Yoo 2012).

The problem is that U-verse does not have enough bandwidth to provide video in the same manner as cable companies and FiOS. Thus, in order to avoid the delays that can render video programming unwatchable, U-verse reserves bandwidth for its own proprietary video offerings and gives its video traffic priority over other traffic.

In many ways, AT&T's practices represent precisely the type of conduct that gives network neutrality proponents pause. It prioritizes a single application (video) from a single source (AT&T) and runs the risk of allowing AT&T to gain a competitive advantage by favoring its own content over others. And yet these practices have allowed AT&T to avoid having to spend an additional US \$17 billion needed to deploy fiber-based solutions such as FiOS.

Given the ever-growing demand for bandwidth and the tightening of the capital markets associated with the ongoing recession, policymakers should avoid regulations that make higher capital investments the only solution to the problem of video-induced traffic growth and should instead permit networks to use prioritization to employ more efficiently the capacity that already exists. Placing regulatory restrictions on network management would not only degrade the service of existing customers; if network providers are not permitted to use network management to ensure adequate quality of service, their only option is to build larger networks to ensure that capacity never reaches saturation. Increasing the amount of capacity needed to support a particular number of customers would increase the per capita expense of building new networks. This de facto increase in cost would limit broadband deployment in rural and other low-density populations, as demonstrated by the large number of filings by public officials and business leaders from rural areas and small towns opposing the Open Internet initiative.

### *The Amtrak Acela*

Another interesting form of network management occurs on the wireless broadband service provided on the Amtrak Acela. Amtrak makes clear in its terms that file downloads are limited to 10 MB. Not only does it block high-volume uses, but it also targets specific applications by explicitly "block[ing] access to streaming media." It does so because "[t]he explosion of the Internet and the use of Wi-Fi have created incredible demands for connectivity." Only by managing its network in this manner can Amtrak "maximize the amount of onboard bandwidth available to all passengers" (Amtrak n.d.).

The use restrictions cannot plausibly be attributed to anti-competitive motives. Indeed, Amtrak provides a free WiFi service in its stations and on many of its most popular routes. Instead, its primary motivation is to promote minimum levels of quality of service by preventing a small group of users from consuming all of the available bandwidth.

### *PlusNet*

The innovative network management techniques employed by British DSL provider PlusNet provide another example of the potential benefits of specialized services. PlusNet uses deep packet inspection (DPI) to divide the data stream into multiple different levels of priority. In so doing, it has served as a model of public disclosure, explaining what it is doing to prioritize traffic, why connection speeds vary in particular cases, and offering meaningful guidance as to expected speeds during different times of day. Prioritizing traffic in this manner has enabled PlusNet to win numerous industry awards for the quality of its network connections and for customer satisfaction (PlusNet 2011a, 2011b, 2011c, n.d.).

In many ways, DPI has generated undeserved criticism. Sometimes denigrated as a deviation from network norms, DPI is widely used by most (if not all) major ISPs to examine samples of traffic to search for security threats. PlusNet provides a particularly telling example of why a reflexive hostility toward DPI is unwarranted.

### *Internet2's interoperable on-demand network (ION)*

One of the central tenets underlying the Internet is that routers should operate on a pure store-and-forward basis without having to keep track of what happens to packets after they have been passed on. This commitment is reflected in the Internet's general hostility toward virtual circuits and the belief that routers should not maintain per-flow state. Opponents of network management often point to the Senate testimony offered by officials of Internet2—a non-profit partnership of universities, corporations and other organizations devoted to advancing the state of the Internet. This testimony noted that, although their network designers initially assumed that ensuring quality of service required building intelligence into the network, "all of [their] research and practical experience supported the conclusion that it was far more cost effective to simply provide more bandwidth" (Bachula 2006: 66).

To a certain extent, this longstanding hostility toward virtual circuits is an artifact of the Internet's military origins that has less relevance for the Internet of today. DARPA protocol architect David Clark has pointed out that the belief that routers operating in the core of the network should not maintain per-flow state derived largely from the high priority that military planners placed on survivability (Clark 1988). Clark notes, however, that survivability does not represent a significant concern for the modern Internet. Moreover, technologies such as IntServ and MPLS, both of which are governed by accepted standards promulgated by the Internet Engineering Task Force (IETF), employ what amount to virtual circuits to enhance quality of service and to increase network efficiency to allow greater control over routing, functions that the original design prioritized below survivability. Although IntServ has not achieved widespread acceptance, interest in MPLS appears to be growing.

These developments can be seen as part of a broader move away from viewing routers as static devices that always operate in a particular way and toward looking at the network as a programmable switching fabric that can be reconfigured from store-and-forward routers into virtual circuits as needed. For example, Internet2 (which, as noted earlier, is often held out as proof of the engineering community's conviction that network management is unnecessary) now offers a service that it calls its "interoperable on-demand network" (ION) that allows researchers to establish dedicated point-to-point optical circuits to support large data transfers and other bandwidth-intensive applications. Internet2 notes that the "advanced science and engineering communities . . . are already straining against the limits of today's network capabilities—and capacities," and that advanced media and telepresence applications often need the type of dedicated circuits previously regarded as anathema (Internet2 2009).

Given the greater flexibility and functionality of today's routers and the increasingly intense demands being placed on them, there seems little reason to require that they always operate in a single, predetermined manner. That said, effective utilization of these new capabilities will doubtlessly require the development of new technical and institutional arrangements. Such innovations and changes may be inevitable if end-users are to enjoy the full range of the network's technical capabilities.

### Peha's real-time secondary markets for spectrum

Another interesting example of a specialized service was proposed by Jon Peha in a paper co-authored with one of his graduate students before he became the FCC's Chief Technologist. The paper takes as its starting point the classic trade-off between licensed and unlicensed uses of spectrum. Because exclusive licensing typically restricts access to a limited number of users, it tends to use spectrum inefficiently when those users connect to the network sporadically and the resource lays fallow whenever those particular parties are not using the network. At the same time, exclusive licensing does enable the network to offer guaranteed levels of quality of service. Unlicensed spectrum reverses this trade-off. The fact that any number of users can share the same spectrum allows the resource to be used more efficiently. At the same time, unlicensed spectrum is unable to provide guaranteed levels of quality of service, in part because the openness of the resource provides little incentive for users to conserve the amount of bandwidth used and in part because there is no way in which to limit the number of devices connected to the network (Peha and Panichpapiboon 2004).

Peha proposed a hybrid system, which "offer[s] both the efficiencies of sharing with the possibility of quality of service guarantees." Under this approach, spectrum is exclusively licensed. Secondary users can request permission to share the spectrum for a fee, but the license holder would be allowed to deny access if the network were already saturated with prior calls. The ability to generate additional revenue without degrading existing sources of revenue makes it easier for networks to break even, which should promote buildout and help to alleviate the digital divide. Although secondary users would receive lower priority, they benefit from paying prices estimated to be only one third of those paid by primary users (Peha and Panichpapiboon 2004).

In essence, this proposal is simply a form of prioritized service, in which the provider divides a single pipe into two tiers, each offering different levels of quality of service and different prices. The addition of a lower quality, lower price tier allows for more efficient use of the spectrum and makes service more affordable by allowing it to be offered at a lower price point. At the same time, it provides consumers who wish to run more demanding applications with the choice of a service able to offer better quality-of-service guarantees.

### Low extra delay background transport (LEDBAT)

Low extra delay background transport (LEDBAT) is a new IETF congestion management initiative that shows tremendous promise. It is designed to address problems caused by applications that transmit large amounts of data over long periods of time. When this traffic passes through routers that forward on a "first in, first out" basis without engaging in any active queue management, it imposes heavy delays on all other applications. LEDBAT is designed to address these problems by allowing this high-volume, low-priority traffic to avoid competing with other best-efforts traffic for its share of the available bandwidth. Instead, LEDBAT permits low-priority traffic to step out of the way whenever it encounters any other traffic (Shalunov *et al.* 2011).

One example of a high-bandwidth, low-priority application would be a service that allows end-users to use the Internet to back up their hard disks to remote locations. The end-user would likely not care if the service took several hours or even several days. Technologies like LEDBAT permit these end-users to run these applications without taking up a disproportionate share of the available capacity or causing network congestion. Peer-to-peer (P2P) applications similarly generate large amounts of traffic over sustained periods of time.

LEDBAT underscores the analytical emptiness of attempting to distinguish between prioritization and degradation. In essence, it provides for a level of priority that is worse than best-efforts routing. Whether or not it is regarded as degradation depends on what level of service is taken as the relevant baseline. While there is a temptation to regard the current level of service reflected in the current status quo as the natural baseline for comparison, the history of the Internet as well as ongoing debates in the engineering community reveal that there is nothing natural about this level. It is instead simply one of many choices made.

Approaches like LEDBAT reduce the cost of networking by allowing providers to offer higher levels of quality of service without having to expand network capacity. It permits a fairer allocation of bandwidth without requiring all providers to reconfigure their routers to actively manage their queues. It does represent a form of tiered service that will almost certainly involve different levels of pricing. Again, it underscores how permitting such differentials can benefit consumers while simultaneously promoting the goals of increasing the amount of network capacity available to all citizens.

## *Internet Protocol Version 6 (IPv6)*

At the time the Internet exploded onto the scene, the unifying protocol was the Internet Protocol version 4 (IPv4). The IPv4 header allocated 32 bits for addresses, which made it possible to assign approximately 4.3 billion unique addresses. At the time, the Internet was viewed as an academic rather than a mass-market phenomenon, and this amount of addresses was considered more than enough to satisfy all future needs. The Internet's commercial success has exhausted the available IPv4 addresses. For this reason, the network is transitioning to a next-generation protocol known as IP version 6 (IPv6), which, by allocating 128 bits to the address field, permits the allocation of 79 nonillion times more unique addresses. This is sufficient to provide a septillion addresses per square meter of the earth and is widely regarded as enough to satisfy the needs for the foreseeable future.

Dealing with IP address exhaustion was only one of the goals of the transition to IPv6. Another explicit goal was to provide greater support for real-time applications. Among the topics listed in the initial solicitation for White Papers was the use of flows and resource reservation to provide better support for time-critical processes, as well as support for policy-based routing (Bradner and Mankin 1993).

Consistent with this emphasis, the document creating IPv6 included within it an 8-bit field for *traffic class* to allow "originating nodes and forwarding routers to identify and distinguish between different classes or priorities of IPv6 packets." IPv6 was thus designed to support differentiated services in the same way as the type-of-service field in IPv4. In addition, the specification included a new field for *flow labels* (a concept developed for the network technology known as "asynchronous transfer mode" and now attached to MPLS). The document describes flow labels as enabling "send requests [for] special handling, such as non-default quality of service or 'real-time' service" (Deering and Hinden 1998: 2; see also Hinden 1996). Although experimental at that time, flow labels were fully specified in a later document (Rajahalme *et al.* 2004).[1]

1 An updated version was proposed in November 2011 and is still pending (Amante *et al.* 2011).

The inclusion of these fields and the supporting documentation makes clear that quality of service is not a relic. Indeed, providing better support for quality of service (particularly for real-time data) was identified as one of the major goals of the transition to IPv6 (Bradner and Mankin 1993).

## *MetroPCS*

Another example of non-neutrality is the new 4G offering by MetroPCS. This example is particularly important, as network neutrality proponents have already indicated their desire to challenge MetroPCS's practices.

MetroPCS is a regional wireless provider in the United States. In January 2011, MetroPCS revised the service plans for its new fourth generation (4G) wireless service. Its US $40 per month plan offered unlimited talk, text and 4G web browsing, including unlimited YouTube access. Its $50 per month plan added additional features,[2] as well as 1 GB of "data access," defined to include multimedia streaming and video-on-demand services. Its $60 per month plan offered unlimited data access (MetroPCS 2011a).

One week later, a consortium of advocacy groups submitted a letter calling for the FCC to investigate whether MetroPCS's proposed service plans violated the FCC's Open Internet order. Their primary complaint was that MetroPCS's $40 and $50 per month plans permitted unlimited access to YouTube, while categorizing other video services, such as Netflix, as data access subject to bandwidth limits (Free Press 2011). Consumers Union (2011) filed a similar letter eleven days later.[3]

Anyone evaluating these claims must take into account several realities. Specifically, MetroPCS controls far less spectrum than its rivals, typically deploying 4G on as little as 1.4 MHz of spectrum, while its rivals typically use 20 MHz of spectrum to offer 4G service. MetroPCS's limited spectrum resources mean that it has to be more innovative in offering a competitive service. For example, consumer requests led MetroPCS to search for ways of making YouTube available despite its bandwidth limitations. Because video delivered to mobile devices do not require the same resolution as full-sized television screens, MetroPCS was able to compress YouTube video so that it would work effectively despite MetroPCS's bandwidth limitations. Moreover, because MetroPCS was already offering unlimited YouTube access on its 1G data plans, it felt it had to include YouTube service in all of its 4G offerings. If new customers were to select 1G over 4G, the increase in 1G traffic would overwhelm its 1G network and force the company to invest in an infrastructure that it was planning to retire. MetroPCS emphasized that it facilitated access to YouTube in response to customer demand and that it lacked any financial arrangements that provided it with any incentive to favor YouTube. It also claimed that no other YouTube competitors had ever sought access to the MetroPCS network (MetroPCS 2011b).

Moreover, according to the most recent FCC data (2011), MetroPCS had 8.2 million subscribers at the end of 2010, which represented less than 3 percent of the market, lagging

2 These features included international and premium text messaging, GPS, mobile instant messaging, corporate email, caller identity screening and WiFi access to its service for full-track music downloads and premium video content (known as "MetroSTUDIO").

3 Some of these organizations also complained that MetroPCS's initial LTE deployments did not support Voice over Internet Protocol (VoIP) because no VoIP clients were available for the application development platform used by MetroPCS. The arrival of an Android-based handset in early February 2011 allowed all MetroPCS 4G LTE customers to access VoIP so long as their handset was technically capable of supporting a VoIP client.

far behind Verizon (96 million), AT&T (94 million), Sprint (50 million) and T-Mobile (34 million), which are the four national providers. It is hard to see how any policy implemented by a firm of MetroPCS's size could hurt consumers or competition.

Lastly, MetroPCS deployed 4G through a device known as the "Samsung Craft," a feature phone that is significantly cheaper and more limited than the typical smartphone. Unlike smartphones, which run open operating systems with open application programming interfaces that anyone can use to write applications, feature phones typically run proprietary operating systems that support a much narrower range of third-party software. Basing its service around feature phones inevitably means that MetroPCS's phones support a more limited range of applications than its competitors. As Tom Keys, MetroPCS's chief operating officer, said, "We didn't build this network or this device to be all things to all people" (Fitchard 2010). In an era in which spectrum is limited, increasing the competitiveness of the market depends on allowing wireless providers such as MetroPCS to experiment with innovative forms of network management, especially for providers like MetroPCS that specialize in offering low-cost plans. Any evaluation of MetroPCS's compliance with the requirements of the Open Internet order must take these technical realities into account.

This brief overview only touches on a few of the innovative ways in which providers are deploying specialized services to use bandwidth more efficiently, to reduce cost and to provide better service. Providers will need to become even more innovative as the universe of end-users continues to become more heterogeneous and as market saturation causes providers to focus on delivering greater value to each customer (Yoo 2012). Most importantly, reducing network costs can help to promote the next generation of capacity expansion and to reduce the digital divide by reducing the number of subscribers needed for an upgrade to the available capacity to break even.

Interestingly, these changes may be just the tip of the iceberg. The US government, the European Union, and university-based researchers are pursuing "clean slate" initiatives exploring how the architecture might differ radically if it were designed from scratch today. Within the scope of these projects are even more extensive usage of specialized services to deal with such emerging functionalities as security, mobility and cloud computing (Pan *et al.* 2011).

## Conclusion

The specific examples recounted above demonstrate how the details of the underlying technology can affect the assessment of a wide variety of types of network management. Far from being an aberration, such practices have been essential features that have been baked into the Internet's design since the very beginning. In addition, they demonstrate how network providers are experimenting with these techniques to provide affordable service in the face of rapid growth in network traffic, widescale deployment of applications that demand increasingly higher levels of quality of service and severe limitations in the spectrum available to support wireless broadband services. Finally, the variety of possible technical solutions reveals the potential benefits of embracing a network diversity principle that permits network providers to experiment with a variety of different forms of network management unless and until the evidence indicates that those practices are harming consumers or competition (Yoo 2005). Internet scholars and regulatory authorities must deepen their appreciation for the technological context surrounding these practices if they are to make an intelligent assessment of their likely impact and whether they represent good policy.

## References


Amante, S., Carpenter, B., Jiang, S. and Rajahalme, B. (2011) 'IPv6 flow label specification,' Network Working Group Request for Comments 6437. Online. Available HTTP: http://tools.ietf.org/pdf/rfc6437 (accessed 15 February 2012).

Amtrak (n.d.) 'Journey with Wi-Fi.' Online. Available HTTP: http://www.amtrak.com/wi-fi (accessed 15 February 2012).

Bachula, G. (2006) 'Net neutrality,' Hearing before the Senate Committee on Commerce, Science, and Transportation, 109th Congress, 2d Session 63–68.

Bazelon, C. (2008) 'Oversight of the Federal Communications Commission: The 700 MHz Auction,' Hearing before the Subcommittee on Telecommunications and the Internet of the House Committee on Energy and Commerce, 110th Congress, 2d Session. 185–210.

Blake, S., Black, D., Carlson, M., Davies, E., Wang, Z. and Weiss, W. (1998) 'An architecture for differentiated services,' Network Working Group Request for Comments 2475. Online. Available HTTP: http://tools.ietf.org/pdf/rfc2475 (accessed 15 February 2012).

Blumenthal, M. S. (2002) 'End-to-end and subsequent paradigms,' *Law Review of Michigan State University Detroit College of Law*, 1: 709–717.

Braden, R., Clark, D. and Shenker, S. (1994) 'Integrated services in the Internet architecture: An overview,' Network Working Group Request for Comments 1633. Online. Available HTTP: http://tools.ietf.org/pdf/rfc1633 (accessed 15 February 2012).

Bradner, S. and Mankin, A. (1993) 'IP: Next generation (IPng) White Paper solicitation,' Network Working Group Request for Comments 1550. Online. Available HTTP: http://tools.ietf.org/pdf/rfc1550 (accessed 15 February 2012).

Cerf, V. G. and Kahn, R. E. (1974) 'A protocol for packet network intercommunication,' *IEEE Transactions on Communications*, 22: 637–648.

Clark, D. D. (1988) 'The design philosophy of the DARPA Internet protocols,' *ACM SIGCOMM Computer Communication Review*, 18(4): 106–114.

Comer, D. E. (2006) *Internetworking with TCP/IP, Vol. 1: Principles, Protocols, and Architecture*, 5th edn., Upper Saddle River, NJ: Pearson Prentice Hall.

Consumers Union (2011) 'Letter from Parul P. Desai and Mark Cooper to Julius Genachowski,' 21 January. Online. Available HTTP: http://fjallfoss.fcc.gov/ecfs/document/view.action?id=7021026388 (accessed 15 February 2012).

Deering, S. and Hinden, R. (1998) 'Internet Protocol, version 6 (IPv6) specification,' Network Working Group Request for Comments 2460. Online. Available HTTP: http://tools.ietf.org/pdf/rfc2460 (accessed 15 February 2012).

Federal Communications Commission (2006) 'Implementing a nationwide, broadband, interoperable public safety network in the 700 MHz band,' Ninth Notice of Proposed Rulemaking, *Federal Communications Commission Record*, 21: 14837–14862.

—— (2007) 'Service rules for the 698–746, 747–762 and 777–792 MHz bands,' Second Report and Order, *Federal Communications Commission Record*, 22: 15289–15575.

—— (2009) 'Preserving the open Internet,' Notice of Proposed Rulemaking, *Federal Communications Commission Record*, 24: 13064–13170.

—— (2011) 'Implementation of section 6002(b) of the Omnibus Budget Reconciliation Act of 1993,' Fifteenth Report, *Federal Communications Commission Record*, 26: 9664–971.

Fitchard, K. (2010) 'LTE launches in the US: MetroPCS style,' *Connected Planet*, 21 September. Online. Available HTTP: http://connectedplanetonline.com/3g4g/news/metropcs-launches-lte–092110/ (accessed 15 February 2012).

Free Press (2011) 'Letter from M. Chris Riley to Julius Genachowski,' 10 January. Online. Available HTTP: http://fjallfoss.fcc.gov/ecfs/document/view?id=7021025490 (accessed 15 February 2012).

Gillespie, T. (2006) 'Engineering a principle: "End-to-end" in the design of the Internet,' *Social Studies of Science*, 36: 427–457.

Hinden, R. M. (1996) 'IP next generation overview,' *Communications of the ACM*, 39(6): 61–71.

Huitema, C. (1995) *Routing in the Internet*, Englewood Cliffs, NJ: Prentice Hall PTR.

Information Sciences Institute (1979) 'DoD standard internet protocol,' Internet Engineering Note 123. Online. Available HTTP: http://128.9.160.29/ien/txt/ien123.txt (accessed 15 February 2012).

—— (1981) 'Internet protocol: DARPA Internet program protocol specification,' Network Working Group Request for Comments 791. Online. Available HTTP: http://tools.ietf.org/pdf/rfc791 (accessed 15 February 2012).

Internet2 (2009) *Internet2 ION*. Available HTTP: http://www.internet2.edu/pubs/200909-IS-ION.pdf (accessed 15 February 2012).

Kirby, P. (2008) 'Verizon Wireless, AT&T big winners in record auction of 700 MHz frequencies,' *Telecommunications Report* 21 April.

Leiner, B. M., Cole, R., Postel, J. and Mills, D. (1985) 'The DARPA Internet protocol suite,' *IEEE Communications Magazine*, 23(3): 29–34.

Lougheed, K. and Rekhter, J. (1989) 'A border gateway protocol (BGP),' Network Working Group Request for Comments 1105. Online. Available HTTP: http://tools.ietf.org/pdf/rfc1105 (accessed 15 February 2012).

MacKie-Mason, J. K. and Varian, H. (1994) 'Economic FAQs about the Internet,' *Journal of Economic Perspectives*, 8(3): 75–96.

*MetroPCS* (2011a) 'MetroPCS new 4G LTE plans offer unprecedented value and choice with prices starting at just $40,' 3 January. Online. Available HTTP: http://www.metropcs.com/presscenter/newsreleasedetails.aspx?id=1 (accessed 15 February 2012).

—— (2011b) 'Letter from Carl W. Northrop to Julius Genachowski,' 14 February. Online. Available HTTP: http://fjallfoss.fcc.gov/ecfs/document/view.action?id=7021029361 (accessed 15 February 2012).

Nissenbaum, H. and Price, M. (eds.) (2004) *Academy and the Internet*, New York: Peter Lang.

Pan, J., Paul, S. and Jain, R. (2011) 'A survey of the research on future Internet architectures,' *IEEE Communications Magazine*, 49(7): 26–36.

Peha, J. M. and Panichpapiboon, S. (2004) 'Real-time secondary markets for spectrum,' *Telecommunications Policy*, 28: 603–18.

PlusNet (2011a) 'Broadband: Your broadband speed—The basics,' 19 April. Online. Available HTTP: http://www.plus.net/support/broadband/speed_guide/speed_basics.shtml (accessed 15 February 2012).

—— (2011b) 'Broadband: Broadband download speeds,' 19 May. Online. Available HTTP: http://www.plus.net/support/broadband/speed_guide/download_speeds.shtml (accessed 15 February 2012).

—— (2011c) 'Broadband: All about traffic management,' 8 July. Online. Available HTTP: http://www.plus.net/support/broadband/speed_guide/traffic_management.shtml (accessed 15 February 2012).

—— (n.d.) 'What we've won.' Online. Available HTTP: http://www.plus.net/press/awards.shtml (accessed 15 February 2012).

Postel, J. (1981) 'Service mapping,' Network Working Group Request for Comments 795. Online. Available HTTP: http://tools.ietf.org/pdf/rfc795 (accessed 15 February 2012).

Rajahalme, J., Conta, A., Carpenter, B. and Deering, S. (2004) 'IPv6 flow label specification,' Network Working Group Request for Comments 397. Online. Available HTTP: http://tools.ietf.org/pdf/rfc3697 (accessed 15 February 2012).

Rekhter, J. (1989) 'EGP and policy based routing in the new NSFNET backbone,' Network Working Group Request for Comments 1092. Online. Available HTTP: http://tools.ietf.org/pdf/rfc1092 (accessed 15 February 2012).

Rosen, E. C., Viswanathan A. and Callon, A. R. (2001) 'Multiprotocol label switching architecture,' Network Working Group Request for Comments 3031. Online. Available HTTP: http://tools.ietf.org/pdf/rfc3031 (accessed 15 February 2012).

Sandvig, C. (2009) 'How technical is technology research? Acquiring and deploying technical knowledge in social research projects,' in E. Hargittai (ed.) *Research Confidential*, Ann Arbor, MI: University of Michigan Press.

Shalnuov S., Hazel, G. and Lyengar, J. (2011) 'Low extra delay background transport (LEDBAT),' LEDBAT Working Troup Internet Draft. Online. Available HTTP: http://datatracker.ietf.org/doc/draft-ietf-ledbat-congestion/ (accessed 15 February 2012).

Stallings W. (2001) 'MPLS,' *Internet Protocol Journal*, 4(3): 2–14.

Tanenbaum, A. S. (2003) *Computer Networks*, 4th edn., Upper Saddle River, NJ: Prentice Hall PTR.

Yoo, C. S. (2005) 'Beyond network neutrality,' *Harvard Journal of Law and Technology*, 17: 1–77.

—— (2010) 'Innovations in the Internet's architecture that challenge the status quo,' *Journal on Telecommunications and High Technology Law*, 8: 79–99.
—— (2012) *The Dynamic Internet: How Technology, Users, and Business are Transforming the Network*, Washington, DC: AEI Press.
Zhu, K. (2007) 'Bringing neutrality to net neutrality,' *Berkeley Technology Law Journal*, 22: 615–645.

# 30

# Regulatory trends in a social media context

*Eva Lievens and Peggy Valcke*[*]

## Introduction

Digitization, convergence, personalization and reintermediation in the media sector have, in recent years, led to a paradigm shift, referred to by media scholars as the shift from mass media and passive consumers to media for mass self-communication and active "prosumers," and by economists as a shift from supply-driven to demand-driven media markets. In the online social media environment, users themselves are distributing enormous amounts of information about their personal opinions, their likes and dislikes, their professional activities, or about others. Whereas social media thus "offer great possibilities for enhancing the potential for the participation of individuals in political, social and cultural life" (Council of Europe 2012a: 2), concerns about infringements on fundamental rights, such as freedom of expression and the right to privacy, on these kind of services have been voiced as well (Council of Europe 2012a). Furthermore, the decentralized, global and interactive nature of these media poses challenges for existing media laws and undermines several of the premises upon which traditional media rules have been based, such as the high threshold to media content production, or the premise of "one (strong) sender—many (weak) receivers."[1]

The objective of this chapter is to discuss a number of the challenges that have arisen in the context of social media, for instance for the protection of minors and for media pluralism, and to assess the potential and the limits of alternative regulatory instruments for new media that have been proposed, developed or reflected upon in previous years. Attention

* The authors wish to thank Pieter Jan Valgaeren for his assistance in preparing parts of the manuscript for this chapter. The chapter presents results of two research projects that are currently being carried out at the Interdisciplinary Centre for Law and ICT (http://www.icri.be): "User empowerment in a social media culture (EMSOC)," (http://www.emsoc.be), funded by the Agency for Innovation by Science and Technology (http://www.iwt.be) and "Risk-reducing regulatory strategies for illegal and harmful conduct and content in online social network sites," funded by the Research Fund Flanders (htpp://www.fwo.be).

1 In this context, "interactive" refers to the fact that content is for a large part requested by the user; hence "pull" instead of "push."

is paid to regulatory trends in the info-communications sector, such as the use of co- and self-regulatory systems, but also evidence- and risk-based regulatory strategies that have been put forward as part of the broader European Union's "Better Regulation" agenda. The central question in the chapter is whether these alternative forms of regulation have the potential for more user participation and accountability in the articulation and enforcement of public interest goals in the new media ecosystem. This question is triggered by the aforementioned observation that the specific nature of social media changes the way in which public interest goals can be enacted and enforced, and urges us to think about new ways, on the one hand, to sufficiently incentivize users themselves to respect certain legal norms, and, on the other hand, to equip them with the necessary tools to react to harmful, false or biased content.

In the first part of the chapter, a number of general regulatory trends are identified, including the adoption of evidence- and risk-based regulatory strategies, the shift from command-and-control regulation to decentered types of regulation or other regulatory options, and the role of participation and consultation in the regulatory process. In the second part, an assessment is made of how users or viewers are addressed in traditional or current regulation, what is expected of them, and how this is changing in an increasingly user-centric media environment.

## Regulatory trends in new media

In 1995, the Organisation for Economic Co-operation and Development (OECD) stressed the necessity of improving the quality of government regulation (OECD 1995). Around the same time, the European Union (EU) started to focus on the adoption of a "Better Regulation" or "Better Lawmaking" policy (Commission of the European Communities 1998; Commission of the European Communities 1999; Senden 2005). Particularly since the beginning of the twenty-first century, the simplification and improvement of the regulatory environment has been an essential item on the EU agenda (European Commission 2006). In 2001, the White Paper on European Governance was adopted as an answer to the increasing loss of confidence of European citizens in the European Union (the so-called "democratic deficit") and dealt with the manner in which this supranational organization uses the power granted by its citizens (Commission of the European Communities 2001). It put forward a number of important regulatory principles, such as the need for cost–benefit analyses or regulatory impact assessments (RIAs), and the consideration of non-legislative instruments to achieve regulatory goals. This approach to improving the quality of regulation was not only adopted at the general EU level, but also strongly endorsed in specific sectors, including the media sector. Throughout the next sections, three specific regulatory trends that can be framed within the Better Regulation discourse will be discussed, as well as their particular significance for (social) media regulation.

### *Assessing evidence, risks and impact as a basis for the adoption of regulation*

In order to avoid unnecessary and/or inappropriate regulation, it has increasingly been stressed that, before adopting regulation, the questions of "whether regulation is necessary" and "what to regulate exactly" are answered in a carefully considered manner. As the OECD put it in 1995:

> Government intervention should be based on clear evidence that government action is justified, given the nature of the problem, the likely benefits and costs of action (based on a realistic assessment of government effectiveness), and alternative mechanisms for addressing the problem
>
> *(OECD 1995: 9)*

A number of trends can be linked with this principle.

In market regulation, *evidence-based approaches* have been promoted for several years, forcing legislators and regulators to consider carefully whether there is a market failure that needs to be addressed and, if so, whether a legislative or regulatory intervention is the best way in which to deal with the concern. In its "Smart Regulation in the European Union" Communication, the European Commission stated that evidence-based policymaking is considered good practice (European Commission 2010).

This trend has also been adopted in the media sector. For example, Ofcom and the Australian Communications and Media Authority (ACMA), the British and Australian media regulators, both claim that their decision-making is evidence-based. One of the regulatory principles to which Ofcom adheres states that "Ofcom will strive to ensure its interventions will be evidence-based, proportionate, consistent, accountable and transparent in both deliberation and outcome" (Ofcom n.d.). The ACMA published an extensive document titled *Evidence-Informed Regulation: The ACMA Approach*, in which it explicitly commits itself to "to develop appropriate, forward-looking regulatory responses which take into account technology, service and market developments and associated changes in consumer behavior and preferences," given "[t]he increasing complexity of policy issues facing governments, public demands for greater government transparency and accountability, and the rise of a knowledge-based society [which] all underscore the importance of continually improving the use of evidence in policy-making" (ACMA 2010a: 1–2). The evidence that is used by the ACMA to develop a balanced and appropriate response to regulatory issues includes industry data, technical information and technology research, social and market research, economic modeling and analysis, consumer complaints data, international approaches to regulation, consultation, and expert knowledge and practice know-how (ACMA 2010a).

Second, *risk-based governance or regulation* has gained importance, because regulation is often developed to respond to a perceived risk (OECD 2012). Although different theories about the role of risk in regulatory processes exist (Black 2010b), we focus on risk-based governance as a "manner of prioritizing activities according to the impact and probability of societal risks" (Rothstein, Huber and Gaskell 2006: 97). The fundamental question in such a regime is what types and level of risk the regulator is prepared to tolerate (Black 2010a). This is a crucial and delicate question that needs to be considered carefully, taking into account both the probability and the impact of the risks.

Proponents argue that risk-based regulation facilitates robust governance, contributes to efficient and effective use of regulatory resources, and delivers interventions in proportion to risk (hence maximizing the benefits of regulation, while minimizing the burdens on regulatees by offering "targeted" and "proportionate" interventions) (Rothstein, Huber and Gaskell 2006). Opponents argue that there are risks associated with risk-based regulatory regimes. Black identifies these risks as follows: (1) not all existing or newly emerging risks may be captured (model risk); (2) the introduction of a risk-based regime implies a necessary change in culture, systems and processes (implementation risk); and (3) choosing which risks (not) to tolerate (taking into account the political context) may result in being accused of over-regulation or may result in failure (political risk) (Black 2010a).

Originally used for matters related to the environment or financial services (Rothstein, Huber and Gaskell 2006), more recently this type of governance has also been adopted in media regulation, more specifically in the field of media pluralism. As part of the debate on media pluralism across the EU, the European Commission ordered a study of indicators for media pluralism, with the aim of developing a:

> . . . robust and multi-faceted monitoring system that may equip policy makers and regulatory authorities with the tools necessary to detect and manage societal risks in this area and provide them with a stronger evidentiary basis to define priorities and actions for improving media pluralism.
>
> *(Valcke 2011a: 189)*

The results of this study, including a prototype for a *Media Pluralism Monitor* (MPM), were presented to the public in June 2009 and are published on the Commission's website (ICRI *et al.* 2009). The Commission stressed that a risk-based approach was chosen to ensure that regulation is applied only where it is needed (de Cockborne 2009).

Third, in deciding whether to make rules, legislators at the EU and often also national levels are required to examine the potential costs and benefits of such an intervention, by means of so-called "regulatory impact assessments" (RIAs). Even though these RIAs can be a part of evidence-based or risk-based regulatory regimes, it is interesting to examine this approach more closely. Carrying out RIAs, which have been defined as "both a *tool* and a *decision process* for informing political decision makers on whether and how to regulate to achieve public policy goals" (OECD 2012: 25), has been advocated at different levels and by different organizations. The OECD, for instance, emphasized in its most recent Recommendation on regulatory policy and governance the importance of:

> Integrat[ing] Regulatory Impact Assessment (RIA) into the early stages of the policy process for the formulation of new regulatory proposals. Clearly identify[ing] policy goals and evaluate if regulation is necessary and how it can be most effective and efficient in achieving those goals.
>
> (*OECD 2012: 4*)

The use of RIAs has been advocated at the EU level as well. In the interinstitutional agreement on better lawmaking (European Parliament, Council and Commission 2003), the use of impact assessments is put forward as positively contributing to the improvement of the quality of Community legislation, and in 2009 the European Commission published its Impact Assessment Guidelines. The Guidelines define an impact assessment as "a set of logical steps to be followed when you prepare policy proposals. It is a process that prepares evidence for political decision-makers on the advantages and disadvantages of possible policy options by assessing their potential impacts" (European Commission 2009a: 4). In the media sector, RIAs were conducted in the preparatory stages of the development of the Audiovisual Media Services (AVMS) Directive, by the Commission (Commission of the European Communities 2005) as well as by national regulators such as Ofcom (Indepen 2005).

## *Decentering regulation*[2]

### From command-and-control regulation to alternative regulation

A second evolution has seen a gradual move from regulation in which the state is the only regulatory actor (traditional "command and control" regulation) to more decentered forms of regulation in which other actors that are considered to add value to the regulatory process

2 Parts of this section are based on Lievens (2010).

are involved, and from the use of traditional legislation to the adoption of alternative regulatory instruments (ARIs). This has also been a very important element of the Better Regulation discourse discussed above.

Command-and-control regulation has lost its luster over the past decade, as it has gradually become clear that this type of regulation suffers from a number of drawbacks (Baldwin 2000). Black identified five shortcomings (Black 2002). The first problem, instrument failure, implies that the instruments that are used (i.e. laws) are "inappropriate and unsophisticated" (Black 2002: 2). Second, the state often does not have enough knowledge or expertise to be capable of identifying the causes of problems, designing adequate solutions and detecting non-compliance (information and knowledge failure). A third issue with command-and-control regulation is its often ineffective implementation (implementation failures). Finally, it has been found that it often does not provide enough incentives for regulatees to comply (motivation failure) and, moreover, that regulators often do not act in the public's interest, but rather in favor of the regulated industry or themselves (capture theory) (Black 2002; Baldwin 2000; Makkai and Braithwaite 1998). Other criticisms directed at command-and-control regulation are that it is slow (Rand Europe 2007), costly, and stifles innovation (Sinclair 1997). On the other hand, as Prosser argued, command-and-control regulation is at least "based on some form of democratic mandate," and the government is in any case "subject to some form of democratic scrutiny" (Prosser 2008: 103). However, owing to the significant pathologies that have been especially strongly felt in complex sectors such as the (digital) media sector (Murray and Colin 2002), a shift from command-and-control regulation to "decentered" forms of regulation has occurred in the past decades.

The use of decentered ARIs, such as self- and co-regulation, has gained importance and has been increasingly referred to in policy documents issued by organizations at different levels. From the mid-1990s onwards, media policy documents, particularly those from the EU and Council of Europe (CoE), started to refer to the use of self-regulation (and later co-regulation) to achieve certain policy goals in the digital media environment. This culminated in the incorporation of an encouragement for the adoption of co- and self-regulatory regimes in Article 4 (7) of the AVMS Directive,[3] an example that was followed by the Council of Europe in its recently adopted Recommendation on the protection of human rights with regard to social networking services.[4]

However, the policy documents that advocate the use of self- or co-regulation have not always provided much clarity on what is really meant when references are made to these types of instrument. In general, we assume that they are an alternative (or, as is sometimes argued, a supplement) to traditional forms of regulation, such as legislation in

3 This was motivated by the fact that "such regimes can play an important role in delivering a high level of consumer protection" (European Parliamnet and Council 2007: Recital 36). According to Recital 36 "[m]easures aimed at achieving public interest objectives in the emerging audiovisual media services sector are more effective if they are taken with the active support of the service providers themselves" (ibid.: Recital 36).

4 This recommendation was prepared by the Committee of Experts on New Media in March 2010, has been finalized by the Steering Committee on the Media and New Communication Services in December 2011, and was adopted by the Committee of Ministers in April 2012. The Recommendation urges member states, in cooperation with private sector actors and civil society, to develop and promote coherent strategies to protect and promote respect for human rights with regard to social media by engaging with social networking providers to carry out a number of actions, such as setting up self- and co-regulatory mechanisms where appropriate.

which the government is the major—and often the only—player. The key characteristic of ARIs is the involvement of non-governmental players, such as the industry and/or users in the regulatory process (Latzer 2007). The required degree of involvement of these different actors is the issue that most often causes controversy or confusion in the ARI debate. Whereas self-regulation is sometimes conceived very strictly, rejecting any kind of interference from the outside, others interpret the concept less rigorously, allowing for some form of involvement of different actors (Verdoodt 2007). It is usually no more clear-cut who exactly can participate in forms of co-regulation and to what extent. In an effort to provide greater clarity to the discussion, both concepts are analyzed in greater detail in the following sections.

## Self-regulation

Self-regulation is by no means a novel phenomenon (Sinclair 1997). The origins of this concept go back to the theories of Max Weber, Emile Durkheim, Niklas Luhmann, Gunter Teubner and John Griffiths (Verdoodt 2007).[5] Self-regulation also has a history within the field of media regulation (Latzer 2007), especially with respect to press and journalist associations (Verdoodt 2007), and in the field of advertising (Boddewyn 1988). In the United States, self-regulatory instruments such as the self-regulatory code of conduct of the Comics Magazine Association of America and the voluntary warning labels of the Recording Industry Association of America ("Parental advisory: explicit content") were adopted to protect minors from harmful content (Kirsch 2006).

However, the rise of the Internet—at its inception, considered by many a "free" social space in which involvement or interference from governments was unwanted and unnecessary[6]—sparked an intensified interest in the use of "self-regulation" (Johnson 1998). In policy documents, "self-regulation" was often presented as the panacea to "regulate" the Internet. At different levels—international and supranational, as well as national—the enthusiasm for the use of this ARI was substantial. This does not mean, however, that there was a uniform, unambiguous understanding of what was meant by "self-regulation."

An endless array of definitions of self-regulation exists, which vary from narrow to very broad (Birnhack and Rowbottom 2004; Mifsud Bonnici 2007; Newman and Bach 2004).[7] Although all definitions contain more or less similar elements, there are slight variations between them. One agreed-upon definition does not exist, but it has been argued that this is not necessary, since self-regulation varies across sectors and states anyway (Price and Verhulst 2000). In this chapter, we assume that self-regulation entails the creation, implementation and enforcement of rules by a group of actors with no—or at least minimal—involvement of actors that do not belong to this group.

The identification of assets and drawbacks of self-regulation is a subject that has been written about extensively by academics over the past decade. It can be noted that most of these advantages and disadvantages counter, in some way or another, the known disadvantages and advantages of government regulation. Often-cited assets of self-regulation are its

5 Teubner built on Niklas Luhmann's theory of autopoiesis. For detailed information on this concept, cf. Teubner (1988); Teubner (1993); Teubner, Nobles and Schiff (2005).

6 The most well-known expression of this idea was the "Declaration of the Independence of Cyberspace," written by John Perry Barlow (1996).

7 For a detailed overview of different classifications of definitions, see Latzer (2007: 38–41).

flexibility (Ofcom 2008; Mifsud Bonnici 2007; Gunningham and Rees 1997; Rand Europe 2008), its capacity to adapt quickly to fast-developing technologies and increasingly global issues (Price and Verhulst 2000; Gunningham and Rees 1997), its higher degree of incorporated expertise (Ogus 1995; Mifsud Bonnici 2007), and its lower cost (Gunningham and Rees 1997; Ogus 1995; Price and Verhulst 2000; Latzer 2007). As a result of the high degree of incorporated expertise, it has been suggested that the rules that are created by self-regulation offer a more suitable solution tailored to the needs identified by the group (Mifsud Bonnici 2007; Gunningham and Rees 1997). It has also been claimed that incentives for commitment and compliance are higher (Price and Verhulst 2000) because the actors themselves are closely involved in the creation of the rules and because of the exercise of peer pressure (Latzer 2007).

The drawbacks of self-regulation are, however, at least as numerous as the assets. One of the most frequent criticisms is that self-regulatory mechanisms often lack effective enforcement (Ogus 1995; Prosser 2008; Gunningham and Rees 1997). Sanctions may be mild, and reluctantly imposed (Rand Europe 2008). Self-regulatory processes also have been known to suffer from a low level of transparency (Latzer 2007; Rand Europe 2008). Compliance with other standard principles of good regulation (accountability, proportionality, consistency, etc.) has been judged problematic (Latzer 2007). Moreover, it has been argued that self-regulation has the potential to establish cartel-like agreements that close markets, thereby infringing competition law principles (Prosser 2008; Latzer 2007). Another crucial objection is the fact that self-regulation does not protect the fundamental rights of users or citizens in an adequate manner—in other words, as adequately as traditional government legislation (Mifsud Bonnici 2007). In addition, self-regulatory mechanisms have been accused of putting the private interest (of the group) before the public interest (Mifsud Bonnici 2007; Gunningham and Rees 1997). Related to this issue is the "legitimacy" or "democratic deficit" argument (Schulz 2008), which implies that, whereas traditional legislation is created by democratically elected representatives and is subject to some form of democratic scrutiny, self-regulatory mechanisms are created by private actors who are not accountable to the public (Prosser 2008; Ogus 1995). Price and Verhulst (2000) argue that, for this reason, self-regulation can never totally replace government regulation in the media sector, since the state ultimately carries the responsibility to safeguard fundamental rights and the public interest.

### *Case study: The Safer Social Networking Principles for the EU*

With regard to social media, an important self-regulatory initiative at the EU level is the Safer Social Networking Principles for the EU (SSNPs) (European Social Networking Task Force 2009), a charter to which a number of social network providers subscribed in February 2009, following a public consultation on online social networking by the European Commission. The pan-European principles have been developed by social networking services (SNS) providers in cooperation with the Commission and a number of non-governmental organizations (NGOs) "to provide good practice recommendations for the providers of social networking and other user interactive sites, to enhance the safety of children and young people using their services" (European Social Networking Task Force 2009: 1).

In order to achieve this, one of the core elements of the SSNPs is multi-stakeholder collaboration (including SNS providers, parents, teachers and other carers, governments and public bodies, police and other law enforcement bodies, civil society and users themselves). The seven principles that are put forward are outlined in Table 30.1.

*Table 30.1* Safer Social Networking Principles

| | |
|---|---|
| *Principle 1*: | Raise awareness of safety education messages and acceptable use policies to users, parents, teachers and carers in a prominent, clear and age-appropriate manner. |
| *Principle 2*: | Work toward ensuring that services are age-appropriate for the intended audience. |
| *Principle 3*: | Empower users through tools and technology. |
| *Principle 4*: | Provide easy-to-use mechanisms to report conduct or content that violates the Terms of Service. |
| *Principle 5*: | Respond to notifications of illegal content or conduct. |
| *Principle 6*: | Enable and encourage users to employ a safe approach to personal information and privacy. |
| *Principle 7*: | Assess the means for reviewing illegal or prohibited content/conduct. |

*Source:* European Social Networking Task Force (2009: 6–9)

In February 2010, the results of an independent evaluation of the implementation of the SSNPs were made public (Staksrud and Lobe 2010). This evaluation analyzed the self-declaration statements of the signatories to the charter, as well a number of services offered by them (Lobe and Staksrud 2010). Overall, the report showed that there was significant room for improvement. As Commissioner Reding stated:

> However, some important measures have not yet been implemented: Less than half of the signatories make minors' profiles visible only to their friends by default; Only half of the tested sites ensure that minors are not-searchable via search engines; Only 9 out of 22 sites respond to complaints submitted by minors asking for help. I expect companies who signed up to the Safer Social Networking Principles to take rapid action to improve this situation.
>
> (*Reding 2010*)

In June and September 2011, the results of a second assessment of the SSNPs again proved to be disappointing: for instance, with regard to the principle of ensuring that minor's profiles are accessible only to their approved contacts by default, only two SNS providers were found to comply (Donoso 2011; European Commission 2011a; European Commission 2011b).

The results of these evaluations seem to confirm the concerns identified above with regard to the effectiveness of this type of self-regulatory initiative: Although the commitment of the SNS providers to take steps to make their services safer is to be applauded, the concrete implementation of such safety measures is, of course, crucial in order to achieve actual protection (Lievens 2011). The text of the SSNPs mentions that "[t]hese Principles are aspirational and not prescriptive or legally binding, but are offered to service providers with a strong recommendation for their use." This neither provides a solid base for enforcement, nor a compelling incentive for compliance. Hence the question of whether self-regulatory instruments provide enough guarantees with regard to the prevention of certain risks and the protection of fundamental rights and values in social media needs to be examined in the near future.

## Co-regulation

Co-regulation has been identified as a regulatory strategy that consists of elements of state regulation and elements of self-regulation (Rand Europe 2007). Different stakeholders are thus involved in the co-regulatory process: the state as well as a number of industry actors, and possibly users, consumers or NGOs as well. This description, however, is deceivingly simple. Over the years, an array of notions and descriptions of regulatory strategies that could be interpreted as "co-regulation" have circulated (Price and Verhulst 2000; Schulz and Held 2001; Palzer 2003; Latzer *et al.* 2003). The quantity of definitions shows that, again, no consensus on the exact scope of the concept of co-regulation exists. It is often not clear where self-regulation ends and co-regulation starts. However, what we can conclude is that there are certain characteristics that can distinguish co-regulation from either state regulation or self-regulation—most importantly, the degree of involvement and participation of the different actors and the roles these actors play.

The fact that many different definitions and classifications regarding co-regulation circulated led the European Commission to commission a study in 2005 to clarify this regulatory concept. The *Study on Co-Regulation Measures in the Media Sector* was carried out by the Hans-Bredow-Institut (HBI) and the Institut für Europäisches Medienrecht (EMR) (HBI and EMR 2006). The study's aim was to clarify the concept of co-regulation, to identify co-regulatory systems and to critically appraise these systems. Co-regulation was defined as "a specific combination of state and non-state regulation" (HBI and EMR 2006: 17). More specifically, the authors took co-regulation to mean "combining non-state regulation and state regulation in such a way that a non-state regulatory system links up with state regulation" (HBI and EMR 2006: 35).

The asset of a co-regulatory system mainly lies in the combination of the advantages of self-regulation—flexibility, fast adaptation, expertise and engagement of the industry—with the advantages of command-and-control regulation—most importantly, legal certainty, democratic guarantees and more efficient enforcement. It is important to be able to fall back on a governmental backbone if private interests threaten to undermine important public policy goals, such as the protection of minors against harmful content.

However, it would not be correct to present co-regulation as a panacea without any drawbacks whatsoever (Prosser 2008). It is important to stress that co-regulatory systems need to be carefully drawn up so as not to lose the advantages of both self-regulation and traditional state regulation (Marsden 2004). Normative requirements or "process values" (Prosser 2008: 103) such as transparency, adequate participation and independence need to be respected and the division of tasks between the different actors needs to be clearly established. Accountability and credibility are crucial requirements for the non-state components of regulation.

## Compliance with the legal framework

It is very important to be aware that the use of ARIs, such as self- and co-regulation, does not occur in a legal vacuum. On the contrary, there are fundamental rights and other legal requirements—stemming from conventions, constitutions, laws, jurisprudence and soft law instruments—that need to be respected when creating, implementing and enforcing ARIs. Research has shown that although there are no legal obstacles that lead to an a priori or absolute exclusion of the use of ARIs to reach public policy objectives, such as the protection of minors, there are a number of requirements that need to be taken into account in order for ARIs to comply with the legal framework (Lievens 2010). ARIs that aim to reach certain normative goals in the new media environment could possibly restrict other fundamental rights, freedoms and principles, especially freedom of expression, the right to privacy, internal market legislation, and competition rules. Yet there are goals of public interest that can, in many cases, be considered to justify restrictions on the abovementioned fundamental rights and freedoms. Measures that interfere with these rights and freedoms, however, should not go beyond what is necessary to achieve their aim. Hence, in balancing the different interests at stake, proportionality will be a very important guiding principle.

On the other hand, the applicability of certain provisions, typically those that are in theory addressed at states or governments, will depend on the level of government involvement in ARIs. This means that a number of provisions will be more likely to apply when there is a degree of government involvement, as is common with respect to co-regulatory systems. Conversely, self-regulatory systems may fall outside of the protection of the legal framework (except, for instance, when theories, such as the "horizontal effect" theory,[8] can be applied). In our opinion, this might be dangerous in delicate areas. Hence the use of co-regulatory systems, for instance to protect minors in social media, might be preferable, because there is an actual symbiosis between the involvement of the government and other actors, and greater guarantees are provided as to the concrete realization of policy objectives. We can also frame this finding within the current general "malaise" with respect to self-regulation or regulation by the market or the sector (for instance, with the financial crisis). As a consequence, in different sectors, the calls for a renewed and more intense involvement of the government have recently grown louder.

## *Participation of users in the regulatory process*

There is no doubt that participation and consultation of different stakeholders in the regulatory process has been increasingly promoted in order to reach policy goals in a more effective way. The OECD, for instance, claims that "adopting a user-centered perspective on regulatory policy should be a goal of government" (OECD 2005: 9), and encourages members to "ensure that regulation serves the public interest and is informed by the legitimate needs of those interested in and affected by regulation" (OECD 2012: 4). The European Commission, in its White Paper on European Governance, also stressed the importance of wide participation from policy conception to implementation, since democracy depends on people being able to take part in public debate (Commission of the European Communities 2001). Consultation of different parties is considered crucial in attaining wider participation in policymaking (OECD 2005). As the European Commission put it: "Consulting citizens and other stakeholders both when developing policies and when evaluating whether they have done what they set out to do is an essential element of smart regulation" (European Commission 2010b: 10). Extensive consultation has, for instance, taken place in the preparatory stages of the so-called "Telecoms package,"[9] as well as the conception of the AVMS Directive.[10]

However, throughout the various policy documents it is not always clear which stakeholders should be consulted or which are considered valuable participants in the regulatory process. The OECD defines those "concerned with and affected by regulation" as "citizens, businesses, consumers, and employees (including their representative organisations and associations), the public sector, non-governmental organisations, international trading partners and other stakeholders" (OECD 2012: 24). This is a broad definition, encompassing a very

8 The complex "horizontal effect" theory entails that if national law accepts the direct effect of the articles of the European Convention on Human Rights (ECHR), individuals or private actors can, in certain circumstances, invoke Article 10 ECHR before the national courts to challenge other individuals.

9 http://ec.europa.eu/archives/ISPO/infosoc/telecompolicy/Welcome.html

10 http://ec.europa.eu/avpolicy/reg/history/consult/index_en.htm

diverse selection of actors within the regulatory process. In the context of this chapter, the actors that interest us the most are the former "viewers," who may be included under an array of labels that are currently used, such as "users," "citizens," "civil society," "public" and "consumers." With regard to media governance, an interesting approach in this respect is being advocated by Hasebrink (2011). Hasebrink argues that "[a]ccountability for media quality and diversity would be significantly improved by expanded public participation in media governance processes" (Hasebrink 2011: 321), and proposes to view media users not only as "consumers" of media products, but also as "owners of rights," meaning "human beings who have to be protected from harm or biased information," as well as "citizens . . . who have specific ideas about how the media could and should serve societal needs" (Hasebrink 2011: 325).

A next question that can be posed in this context is how participation can be organized in order to represent viewers' or users' interest in the regulatory process. As Hasebrink notes, traditionally viewers' interests have been safeguarded through representation in controlling bodies of public service broadcasters or regulatory authorities, through communication platforms, through complaint procedures, through audience research and through civil society actors, such as media users' organizations, consumer organizations or citizens' initiatives dealing with media-related issues (Hasebrink 2011). However, if users are to be included from the very start of the policy process, consultation processes should be organized in order to reach as many stakeholders as possible. As the OECD put it:

> A wide spectrum of consultation tools should be used to engage a broad diversity of stakeholders within the population. Modes of consultation need to reflect the fact that different legitimate interests do not have the same access to the resources and opportunities to express their views to government, and that a diversity of channels for the communication of these views should be created and maintained.
>
> *(OECD 2012: 24)*

Information and communication technologies, such as the Internet, can play a very important role in this (Commission of the European Communities 2001). In this context, an interesting initiative is one taken by the Australian media regulator, the ACMA. It publishes a document on its website titled "Effective consultation: the ACMA's guide to making a submission" (ACMA 2010b), which provides detailed information about how stakeholders and citizens can most effectively present their views for consideration by the ACMA. It is possible to imagine that, in the future, social media could be used to engage a large number of people in policymaking (of course, to the extent that the citizens that are reached through the Internet and social media users can be considered a representative group) (Eurostat 2011).

## User empowerment in new media regulation

Having examined a number of general regulatory trends that have an impact on regulation in a social media context, it is important to explore how "users" (or "viewers" or "consumers") have been and are currently addressed by media regulation, how user empowerment is increasingly advocated and whether non-regulatory instruments can play a role in achieving this.

### *The position of the "user" in media regulation*

Helberger (2008) observes that the traditional role of viewers in audiovisual policy is characterized by a curious mix of absence and omnipresence. On both sides of the Atlantic, the highest courts have stressed that media freedoms are ultimately serving the rights of readers and viewers (seen as "the public" or "the individuals").[11] Yet these readers and viewers have traditionally been protected by obligations that apply to the institutions that inform them—namely, the media companies (in particular broadcasters). Traditional media regulation is characterized by a host of obligations that instruct owners and providers of media products ("provider-oriented regulation"), rather than rules that address readers and viewers directly and give them rights or impose obligations ("user-oriented regulation"). This is the result of the prevailing image of the viewer as a passive, powerless and vulnerable receiver whose ability to exercise choice remained for a long time restricted to switching between different predefined program packages. But not only were those viewers unable to exercise control over their media diet in a technical sense, the idea also reigned that they were unable to do so mentally. The idea of the viewer as a Janus-faced creature, as Helberger calls it, combining the double status of a citizen and consumer whose choices do not always coincide, led to the assumption that even if viewers had a choice, they could not be trusted to exercise it accurately. This made governments and regulators believe, for a long time, that it was their responsibility to safeguard the quality and accessibility of audiovisual services for viewers.[12] The image of the viewer as a set of "powerless eyeballs" (Valcke 2011b: 304) has, however, started to fade as a result of recent technical and market developments that have triggered waves of user empowerment under the form of increasing tools for active choice and selection of content (for instance via pay television, on-demand, pay-per-view, catch-up television and similar services), as well as for active participation in media production and distribution (think of the various Web 2.0 applications and services that seek to integrate user-generated content, or UGC).

In response to these trends, Helberger (2008) notes that the amended Television without Frontiers (TwF) Directive, the AVMS Directive[13] advocates a new image of the viewer: the *responsible or media-literate viewer.* This suggests a corresponding modified regulatory approach that puts more emphasis on the user and makes the role of the user more explicit in achieving certain policy goals. Media-literate people, according to the Directive, are able to exercise informed choices, understand the nature of content and services, and take advantage of the full range of opportunities offered by new communication technologies; they are better able to protect themselves and their families from harmful or offensive material (AVMS Directive, Recital 47; McGonagle 2011).[14] Although media literacy is not part of the

11 Think of the famous quote of Judge White in the US Supreme Court, *Red Lion Broadcasting* v *FCC* 395 US 367, 390 (1969), that "it is the right of viewers and listeners, not the right of broadcasters, which is paramount." The European Court of Human Rights has, on numerous occasions, emphasized that it is incumbent on the press to impart information and ideas on political issues just as on those in other areas of public interest: *"Not only does the press have the task of imparting such information and ideas:* the public also has a right to receive them" (ECtHR, *Lingens* v *Austria*, Judgement of 8 July 1986, Series A No. 103; emphasis added).

12 This is formulated strikingly by Peacock as follows: "While broadcasting is designed to benefit viewers and listeners, they neither know what they want nor where their interests lie" (Peacock, in Veljanovski 1989: 53, cited by Helberger 2008: 129).

13 The AVMS Directive was adopted on 11 December 2007 (Directive 2007/65/EC); the original TwF Directive of 1989 and its subsequent amendments of 1997 and 2007 have been codified in 2010 in Directive 2010/13/EU.

14 The importance of digital and media literacy and skills is also one of the core elements of the European Commission's European strategy for a Better Internet for children (European Commission 2012).

Directive's binding provisions, it plays a prominent role in its recitals. Recital 47 describes media literacy as the "skills, knowledge and understanding that allow consumers to use media effectively and safely," and highlights the importance of promoting and closely monitoring media literacy in all sections of society. Almost simultaneously with the adoption of the AVMS Directive, the European Commission published a Communication on media literacy as a complement to the Directive (European Commission 2007a). In the accompanying press release, the former Commissioner for Information Society and Media, Viviane Reding, emphasized that she "believe[s] that especially with regard to advertising, promoting media literacy is a much more appropriate approach than advocating advertising bans" (European Commission 2007b). In the Communication, the Commission reaffirms the EU's commitment to actively promoting the development and exchange of good practices on media literacy in the digital environment, and adopting a set of recommendations in the future, if necessary.[15] Furthermore, the Commission calls on member states to encourage their regulatory authorities to become more involved and to cooperate further in improving people's level of media literacy.

But the new image of the "empowered" and "media-literate" viewer also had an important second impact on the binding provisions of the Directive itself. The "graduated regulation" approach is the most obvious illustration of this. This approach entails that traditional, linear services are more strictly regulated than on-demand services, which are subject to only some of the rules that apply to traditional broadcasting services—mainly those on hate speech, protection of minors, and relaxed advertisement rules and obligations concerning the share of European works. This "light-touch approach" for non-linear services is justified as follows:

> On-demand audiovisual media services are different from television broadcasting with regard to the choice and control the user can exercise, and with regard to the impact they have on society. This justifies imposing lighter regulation on on-demand audiovisual media services, which should comply only with the basic rules provided for in this Directive.
>
> *(AVMS Directive: Recital 58)*

In other words, the Directive has opted for an approach that is graduated according to the degree of choice and the legitimate expectations of the user, rather than regulating all audiovisual media content in the same way, precisely to take account of greater consumer choice and empowerment.[16]

A third element that illustrates the AVMS Directive's tentative departure from traditional audiovisual law's rather paternalistic approach to a strategy of viewer empowerment is the introduction of a new obligation for all providers of audiovisual services (including broadcasting and on-demand services) to make information on their name, address, website and email easily accessible for consumers.[17] The underlying idea of this "consumer information tool," as Helberger (2008) calls it, is to assist consumers in being responsible for their own choices by providing them with detailed information on the source of their information.

15 Recommendation 2006/952/EC (European Parliament and Council 2006) already contained a series of possible measures for promoting media literacy, such as continuing education of teachers and trainers, specific Internet training aimed at children from a very early age, including sessions open to parents, or organization of national campaigns aimed at citizens, involving all communications media, to provide information on using the Internet responsibly. In 2009, the European Commission adopted a Recommendation specifically dealing with media literacy (European Commission 2009b).

16 For an analysis of this graduated approach, see, amongst others: Valcke and Stevens 2007; Ariño 2007; Craufurd Smith 2007; Valcke *et al.* 2008.

17 Article 5 AVMS Directive.

In other words, the current trend in audiovisual media regulation is a shift in focus towards increased attention to audience empowerment and media literacy (European Commission 2010a; McGonagle 2011). This is welcomed by many as a positive evolution towards breaking with the long tradition of paternalism and belittlement of the media user. However, there is scope for wariness and criticism. Not only does this trend raise many questions about the division of tasks and powers between the regulator, industry and media users, but also the effectiveness of user empowerment tools is still questionable (Livingstone 2009). Moreover, giving more responsibility to the media users to achieve certain policy goals creates major challenges: Whereas, before, a limited number of media actors were controlled with relative ease by means of centralized, top-down regulation, control over the current multitude of content producers is now much more difficult.

In addition, with regard to minors, who have always been protected to a certain extent in all existing media, one can wonder whether the increase of control and choice does warrant lighter regulation. It has been argued that an important element with respect to children's use of new media is that of "context." Contrary to linear media, such as television or film, non-linear technologies permit content to be seen out of its context (e.g. short clips on YouTube, or images received via mobile phone). Other significant differences, which may have an impact on the effects of new media on children and young people, are the facilitated access to (potentially inappropriate) content, the growing element of "choice" and the lowered threshold for content production (making it possible, for instance, to take pictures and disseminate them broadly over the Internet) (Millwood Hargrave and Livingstone 2006). Notwithstanding the fact that young children might, on a technical level, possess the skills to, for instance, circumvent access controls on digital platforms, they are often not mature enough to deal with the content that they consequently encounter (e.g. sexual images, shocking content, content related to suicide). Hence it seems that assuming that on-demand, user-centric media do not need the same guarantees with regard to the protection of minors as traditional media might be premature. With regard to social media, in particular, this was stressed by the Council of Europe in the appendix to the Recommendation on the protection of human rights with regard to social networking services. The Council of Europe argues that since "social networking services play an increasingly important role in the life of children and young people, as part of the development of their own personality and identity, and as part of their participation in debates and social activities" (Council of Europe 2012b: 6), children and young people "should be protected because of the inherent vulnerability that their age implies" (Council of Europe 2012b: 7).

The new enthusiasm for the responsible and sovereign viewer can be seen as part of a broader trend to transfer some of the regulatory responsibility from governments and suppliers to consumers and citizens. This trend can also be observed in general consumer law, but according to Helberger (2008) has to be addressed with the necessary skepticism. While it is certainly to be applauded that regulators pay more attention to the user perspective, it is understandable that they have difficulty getting to grips with the role of the user in regulation. It is an even more open question whether the user will at all be able to take up his role as an empowered media consumer (knowing that the large majority of consumers do not even read the ingredients on food or drinks, or check whether their cosmetics, hair or skin care products contain any toxic or otherwise harmful substances). It is even a more open question whether a higher degree of user empowerment will suffice to guarantee the achievement of public policy goals such as the protection of minors and media diversity. Finally, although users take up a more central position in current media regulation, this has not been the result of an extensive involvement of users in the regulatory process itself. Following

Hasebrink's argument mentioned above, such an involvement could lead to regulation that is better adapted to their expectations and actual use of media, and hence would empower them to an even greater extent.

## *Empowerment-enhancing tools*

Transferring control over content to the user, which, as we have seen above, is currently advocated through regulatory means, may also be facilitated through certain non-regulatory tools—specifically, the use of technology, providing users with certain information, and making reporting mechanisms more available.[18] In an environment that is increasingly difficult to control in a top-down manner, these are instruments that might actually empower users to exercise the control that is put at their disposal.

### Technology

Since the rise of the Internet, and especially during the early years of its rapidly growing popularity, it has often been suggested that technology should be used to deal with emerging problematic issues, such as the protection of minors against harmful content. It was claimed that if the problem originated in the technology, then the answer was also to be found in the technology (Clark 1996). Of course, this was not a new phenomenon uniquely related to the Internet. In the United States and Canada, for instance, the "V-chip" was implemented to protect minors against harmful broadcasting content. This system entailed that a technical device—the so-called "viewer"-chip or "violence"-chip—was built into the television set or into a decoder to enable blocking of inappropriate content according to a specific classification.[19]

Technical tools, such as filtering, embody the trend towards user empowerment (Commission of the European Communities 2004; Helberger 2008), since they can help users to decide what content to receive and block (Mifsud Bonnicci and De Vey Mestdagh 2005). Latzer calls this "self-help by users" or "technology-based self-restriction" (Latzer 2007: 61). Filtering has been used to implement both legislative and alternative regulatory strategies. At the EU level, filtering has long been advocated as a tool to deal with harmful Internet content. The Green Paper on the protection of minors and human dignity (Commission of the European Communities 1996a), the Communication on illegal and harmful content (Commission of the European Communities 1996b) and the 1998 Recommendation (European Council 1998) all suggested the use of filtering. Later documents confirmed this trend (European Parliament and Council 2006). Commissioner Reding also voiced her belief in filtering to protect minors against harmful content when she stated that "[the Commission] firmly believes that rating and labeling of content combined with media literacy and technological solutions, such as user controlled filtering, are key tools to address these important issues" (Reding 2006). The same trend is also noticeable at the Council of Europe level (Council of Europe 2001; Council of Europe 2003; Council of Europe 2008).

18 Whether the use of technology, provision of information and reporting mechanisms are regulatory or non-regulatory options is debatable in theory. Both can implement a regulatory strategy or be the object of individual voluntary initiatives.

19 For more information on the V-chip, see Price 1998; Kirsch 2006; Etzioni 2004. See also http://www.fcc.gov/vchip/ and http://www.cbsc.ca/english/agvot/index.php

Filtering promotes user bottom-up control rather than top-down censorship by state agencies (Commission of the European Communities 1996b), because it shifts control over which content is thought appropriate to watch or consult from governments—who need to be very careful when restricting the distribution of content and therefore the freedom of expression of its citizens, children included—to parents and teachers, who can then decide which content they think is suitable for the children under their care. While this is undoubtedly a positive development, it does require parents and teachers, first, to be aware of the harm certain content may pose, and second, to actually take up their responsibility to guide their children or pupils. In addition, filtering technologies have been the subject of significant criticism owing to their possible "over-inclusiveness" or "under-inclusiveness," their lack of accountability (McIntyre and Scott 2008), and the ease of circumvention (Akdeniz 2004; Ofcom 2007). Therefore it is important to stress that governments should promote, rather than mandate and enforce, the use of filters (Organization for Security and Co-operation in Europe and Reporters sans Frontières 2005; Council of Europe 2001; Möller and Amouroux 2004; Council of Europe 2012b).

## The provision of information

It is often said that "knowledge is power." In order to be empowered, in order to make decisions about the appropriateness or the source of certain content, information and transparency are crucial.[20] In this context, the Council of Europe (2007) stated that:

> The constant evolution and change in the design and use of technologies and services challenges the ability of individual users to fully understand and exercise their rights and freedoms in the new information and communications environment. In this regard, the transparency in the processing and presentation of information as well as the provision of information, guidance and other forms of assistance are of paramount importance to their empowerment.

In its recent Recommendation on the protection of human rights with regard to social networking services, the Council of Europe also stressed the importance of providing clear information about (potentially illegal) content (Council of Europe 2012b).

Information can be provided in a variety of ways. For instance, we have seen above that Article 5 of the AVMS Directive requires providers of audiovisual media services to provide easily accessible information about their identity so that users may form an opinion about the source of the content they are consulting.[21] A second example is content rating or labeling, which has long played a role in the protection of minors. In every EU member state, for instance, a film classification regime is part of the regulatory framework. In the United States, television programs are rated according to the television parental guidelines.[22] The guidelines provide age ratings that can be used to filter content by means of the V-chip.[23] The Dutch cross-media *Kijkwijzer* system, one of Europe's most often praised co-regulatory systems

20 Helberger notes that, in consumer policy, "'empowering' consumers through information has become a singularly important element in the regulatory toolbox" (Helberger 2011: 337).

21 This obligation is comparable to Article 5 of the e-Commerce Directive, which requires information society service providers to make certain information easily accessible.

22 For more information, see http://www.tvguidelines.org/index.htm. See also Hamilton (1998).

23 See also Heins 1998.

aiming to protect minors against harmful media content, also functions on the basis of age classification and content labeling.[24] The *Kijkwijzer* content labels provide parents with information about the content of programs, films or video games and enable them to make more informed decisions about what they find suitable for their children. Notwithstanding the fact that labeling content on the Internet, or social networks, seems to be a Sisyphean task, the "Coalition to make the Internet a better place for kids,"[25] a self-regulatory initiative by a number of companies, including social network providers such as Facebook and Netlog, recently proposed the wider use of content classification as one of its action points. The importance of age rating and content classification across media services was also emphasized by the European Commission in its European strategy for a Better Internet for children, published in May 2012 (European Commission 2012).

## Reporting mechanisms

Whereas the provision of information usually takes place before a choice to consult certain content is made (*ex ante*), reporting mechanisms allow users to complain about certain content or to report about conduct or content *ex post*. An example might be YouTube, where videos can be flagged as "inappropriate" by users or viewers (because they consider the content sexual, violent or repulsive, hateful or abusive, a harmful dangerous act, or spam, or because the content infringes their rights). These videos are then reviewed by YouTube to check whether they violate its terms of use. If they do, they are taken down. As we noted above, given the continually growing number of content delivery methods, it is increasingly difficult to rate or label content on an *ex ante* basis (Olsberg • SPI *et al.* 2003). Hence *ex post* methods with efficient consumer complaint mechanisms may be considered more appropriate in online environments (Olsberg • SPI *et al.* 2003; Reding 2003).[26] With regard to social media, the use of reporting mechanisms is increasingly being promoted. The Council of Europe, for example, has emphasized that, in order to protect children and young people against harmful content and behavior, "while not being required to control, supervise and/or rate all content uploaded by its users, social networking service providers may be required to adopt certain precautionary measures (e.g. comparable to 'adult content' rules applicable in certain member states) or take diligent action in response to complaints (ex-post moderation)" (Council of Europe 2012b). To do this, the setting up of easily accessible reporting mechanisms is actively encouraged (Council of Europe 2012b). The Coalition to make the Internet a better place for kids, mentioned above, also put forward the development of simple and robust reporting tools for users as one of its action points, and the provision of such tools is one of the core Safer

24 For more information, see http://www.kijkwijzer.nl

25 In December 2011, twenty-eight companies voluntarily formed a "Coalition to make the Internet a better place for kids" and published a statement of purpose (http://ec.europa.eu/information_society/activities/sip/docs/ceo_coalition_statement.pdf). This self-regulatory initiative is an answer to a call for action from the European Commission and has been endorsed by EU Commissioner Kroes (European Commission 2011c). To achieve its goal, the coalition has drafted a work plan that runs from December 2011 until December 2012.

26 The YouTube community guidelines state: "We review the video to determine whether it violates our Terms of Use—flagged videos are not automatically taken down by the system. If we remove your video after reviewing it, you can assume that we removed it purposefully, and you should take our warning notification seriously" (http://www.youtube.com/t/community_guidelines).

Social Networking Principles as well. In addition, the European Commission has advocated the establishment and deployment of reporting tools for users, and added that, for children in particular, these mechanisms should be "visible, easy to find, recognisable, accessible to all and available at any stage of the online experience where a child may need it" (European Commission 2012: 10).

## Concluding remarks

Traditional media regulation is increasingly challenged by the growing user-centricity that characterizes today's media environment. Users of different types of fast-changing media, such as digital television, web services, or social networking sites, are not only able to exercise much more control over which types of media they want to consume or consult at any given time or place, but they also actively produce and share different types of content. This stands in stark contrast with the traditional rationales of media regulation (the viewer as "powerless eyeballs") and the manner in which this provider-oriented type of regulation is structured (often rigid instruments with the state or government as the sole actor).

It is thus not surprising that recent initiatives that attempt to achieve certain policy goals, such as the protection of children and young people in the social networking environment, follow current regulatory trends, such as the shift from command-and-control regulation to the use of ARIs, the increasing focus on media literacy and the use of empowerment-enhancing mechanisms. ARIs seem better adapted to fast-changing, complex environments, and hence might be the way forward with regard to the regulation of social networks. In addition, providing users with skills and tools to protect themselves more efficiently may also be the appropriate solution to the challenge of regulating an environment in which every content consumer is potentially also a content producer. Although these evolutions can thus be welcomed, in the near future attention will need to be paid to a number of emerging concerns, such as the potential ineffectiveness of self-regulation to achieve delicate policy goals, the questionable ability of ARIs to offer sufficient guarantees with respect to fundamental rights such as the freedom of expression and the right to privacy, and the successful implementation of user empowerment tools, with sufficient attention for vulnerable groups of users who may need a higher degree of protection.

Two final remarks can be made. First, the shift towards evidence-based and risk-based regulation, which has been a crucial element in the Better Regulation discourse over the past two decades, means that regulating at random is a thing of the past. Over-regulation or "hit or miss" regulation is to be avoided at all costs; assessing whether regulation is necessary or which risks need to be remedied is crucial, as is evaluating the potential impact of different regulatory options. If we transpose this finding to the social media environment, we can conclude that, before adopting regulation, social media risks need to be carefully identified and the impact of regulatory options that are under consideration needs to be thoroughly evaluated.

Second, the suggestion made by Hasebrink (2011) to involve users to a greater extent in media governance processes not only fits in perfectly with the Better Regulation discourse, which advocates a wide participation of stakeholders, but may also provide innovative perspectives and lead to (more) efficient bottom-up regulatory strategies that are better adapted to the new user-centric media environment. Social media may even play a role in facilitating this participatory process.

## References


Akdeniz, Y. (2004) 'Who watches the watchmen? The role of filtering software in Internet content regulation,' in: C. Möller and A. Amouroux (eds.) *The Media Freedom Internet Cookbook*, Vienna: OSCE.

Ariño, M. (2007) 'Content regulation and new media: A case study of online video portals,' *Communications and Strategies*, 66: 115–135.

Australian Communications and Media Authority (ACMA) (2010a) 'Evidence-informed regulation: The ACMA approach.' Online. Available HTTP: http://www.acma.gov.au/webwr/_assets/main/lib311391/acma_evidence_regulation.pdf (accessed 24 February 2012).

—— (2010b) 'Effective consultation: The ACMA's guide to making a submission.' Online. Available HTTP: http://www.acma.gov.au/webwr/_assets/main/lib311391/acma_effective_consultation.pdf (accessed 24 February 2012).

Baldwin, R. (2000) 'Is regulation right?' Carr Launch paper. Online. Available HTPP: http://www.lse.ac.uk/collections/CARR/pdf/IsRegulationRight.pdf (accessed 24 February 2012).

Barlow, J. P. (1996) 'Declaration of the Independence of Cyberspace.' Online. Available HTTP: https://projects.eff.org/barlow/Declaration-Final.html (accessed 24 February 2012).

Birnhack, M. and Rowbottom, J. (2004) 'Shielding children: The European way,' *Chicago-Kent Law Review*, 79: 101–150.

Black, J. (2002) 'Critical reflections on regulation,' Discussion paper. Online. Available HTTP: http://www.lse.ac.uk/collections/CARR/pdf/DPs/Disspaper4.pdf (accessed 24 February 2012).

—— (2010a) 'Risk-based regulation,' in Legal Services Board (ed.) *The Future of the Legal Services: Emerging Thinking*. Online. Available HTTP: http://www.legalservicesboard.org.uk/news_publications/publications/pdf/14_june_conference_papers.pdf (accessed 24 February 2012).

—— (2010b) 'The role of risk in regulatory processes,' in R. Baldwin, M. Cave and M. Lodge (eds.) *The Oxford Handbook of Regulation*, Oxford: Oxford University Press.

Boddewyn, J. (1988) *Advertising Self-Regulation and Outside Participation: A Multinational Comparison*, New York: Quorum Books.

Clark, C. (1996) 'The answer to the machine is in the machine,' in P. B. Hugenholtz (ed.) *The Future of Copyright in a Digital Environment*, The Hague: Kluwer Law International.

Commission of the European Communities (1996a) *Communication to the European Parliament, the Council, the Economic and Social Committee and the Committee of the Regions: Green Paper on the Protection of Minors and Human Dignity in Audiovisual and Information Services*, COM (1996) 347 final.

—— (1996b) *Communication to the European Parliament, the Council, the Economic and Social Committee and the Committee of the Regions: Illegal and Harmful Content on the Internet*, COM (1996) 487 final.

—— (1998) *Commission Report to the European Council: Better Lawmaking—A Shared Responsibility*, COM (1998) 715 final.

—— (1999) *Commission Report to the European Council: Better Lawmaking*, COM (1999) 562 final.

—— (2001) *European Governance: A White Paper*, COM (2001) 428 final.

—— (2004) *Proposal for a Decision of the European Parliament and of the Council on establishing a multiannual Community programme on promoting safer use of the Internet and new online technologies*, COM (2004) 91 final.

—— (2005) *Commission Staff Working Document Annex to the Proposal for a Directive of the European Parliament and of the Council amending Council Directive 89/552/EEC on the Coordination of Certain Provisions Laid Down by Law, Regulation or Administrative Action in Member States Concerning the Pursuit of Television Broadcasting Activities, Impact Assessment, Draft Audiovisual Media Services Directive*, SEC (2005) 1625/2. Online. Available HTTP: http://ec.europa.eu/avpolicy/docs/reg/modernisation/proposal_2005/newtwf_ia.pdf (accessed 24 February 2012).

Council of Europe (2001) *Recommendation REC(2001)8 on Self-Regulation Concerning Cyber Content (Self-Regulation and User Protection against Illegal or Harmful Content on New Communications and Information Services)*. Online. Available HTTP: https://wcd.coe.int/ViewDoc.jsp?id=220387&Site=COE&BackColorInternet=DBDCF2&BackColorIntranet=FDC864&ackColorLogged=FDC864 (accessed 24 February 2012).

—— (2003) 'Declaration on freedom of communications on the Internet.' Online. Available HTTP: https://wcd.coe.int/rsi/common/renderers/rend_standard.jsp?DocId=37031&SecMode=1&SiteName=cm&Lang=en (accessed 24 February 2012).

—— (2007) *Recommendation CM/REC(2007)11 on Promoting Freedom of Expression and Information in the New Information and Communications Environment*. Online. Available HTTP: https://wcd.coe.int/ViewDoc.jsp?id=1188541&Site=COE&BackColorInternet=DBDCF2&BackColorIntranet=FDC864&BackColorLogged=FDC864 (accessed 24 February 2012).

—— (2008) *Recommendation CM/REC(2008)6 on Measures to Promote the Respect for Freedom of Expression and Information with Regard to Internet Filters*. Online. Available HTTP: https://wcd.coe.int/ViewDoc.jsp?Ref=CM/Rec(2008)6&Language=lanEnglish&Ver=original&BackColorInternet=9999CC&BackColorIntranet=FFBB55&BackColorLogged=FFAC75 (accessed 24 February 2012).

—— (2012a) *Recommendation CM/REC(2012)4 on the Protection of Human Rights with Respect to Social Networking Services*. Online. Available HTTP: https://wcd.coe.int/ViewDoc.jsp?id=1929453&Site=CM (accessed 12 April 2012).

—— (2012b) *Appendix to Recommendation CM/REC(2012)4*. Online. Available HTTP: https://wcd.coe.int/ViewDoc.jsp?id=1929453&Site=CM (accessed 12 April 2012).

Craufurd Smith, R. (2007) 'Media convergence and the regulation of audiovisual content,' *Current Legal Problem*, 60: 238–277.

de Cockborne, J.-E. (2009) 'Opening remarks at the stakeholder workshop of the independent study on indicators for media pluralism in the member states: Towards a risk-based approach,' Brussels, 8 June.

Donoso, V. (2011) *Assessment of the Implementation of the Safer Social Networking Principles for the EU on 14 Websites: Summary Report*, Study commissioned by the European Commission. Online. Available HTTP: http://ec.europa.eu/information_society/activities/social_networking/docs/final_report_11/part_one.pdf & http://ec.europa.eu/information_society/activities/social_networking/docs/final_reports_sept_11/report_phase_b_1.pdf (accessed 24 February 2012).

Etzioni, A. (2004) 'On protecting children from speech,' *Chicago-Kent Law Review*, 79: 299–313.

European Commission (2006) 'Better regulation: Simply explained.' Online. Available HTTP: http://ec.europa.eu/governance/better_regulation/documents/brochure/br_brochure_en.pdf (accessed 24 February 2012).

—— (2007a) *Communication from the Commission to the European Parliament, the Council, the European Economic and Social Committee and the Committee of the Regions: A European Approach to Media Literacy in the Digital Environment*, COM(2007) 833 final.

—— (2007b) 'Media literacy: Do people really understand how to make the most of blogs, search engines or interactive TV?' IP/07/1970. Online. Available HTTP http://europa.eu/rapid/pressReleasesAction.do?reference=IP/07/1970 (accessed 24 February 2012).

—— (2009a) 'Impact assessment guidelines.' Online. Available HTTP: http://ec.europa.eu/governance/impact/index_en.htm (accessed 24 February 2012).

—— (2009b) *Recommendation on Media Literacy in the Digital Environment for a More Competitive Audiovisual and Content Industry and an Inclusive Knowledge Society*, COM(2009) 6464 final.

—— (2010) *Communication from the Commission to the European Parliament, the Council, the European Economic and Social Committee and the Committee of the Regions: Smart Regulation in the European Union*, COM (2010) 543 final.

—— (2011a) 'Digital agenda: Only two social networking sites protect privacy of minors' profiles by default', IP/11/762. Online. Available HTTP: http://europa.eu/rapid/pressReleasesAction.do?reference=IP/11/762&format=HTML&aged=0&language=EN&guiLanguage=en (accessed 24 February 2012).

—— (2011b) 'Digital agenda: Social networks can do much more to protect minors' privacy—Commission report', IP/11/1124. Online. Available HTTP: http://europa.eu/rapid/pressReleases-Action.do?reference=IP/11/1124&format=HTML&aged=0&language=EN&guiLanguage=en (accessed 24 February 2012).

—— (2011c) 'Digital agenda: Coalition of top tech and media companies to make Internet better place for our kids [*sic*]', IP/11/1485. Online. Available HTTP: http://europa.eu/rapid/pressReleasesAction.do?reference=IP/11/1485 (accessed 24 February 2012).

—— (2012) *Communication from the Commission to the European Parliament, the Council, the European Economic and Social Committee and the Committee of the Regions: European Strategy for a Better Internet for Children*. Online. Available HTTP: http://ec.europa.eu/information_society/activities/sip/docs/bik/en_comm.pdf (accessed 4 May 2012).

European Council (1998) *Recommendation 98/560/EC of September 1998 on the development of the competitiveness of the European audiovisual and information services industry by promoting national frameworks aimed at achieving a comparable and effective level of protection of minors and human dignity*, OJ, L 270/48.

European Parliament and Council (2006) *Recommendation 2006/952/EC of 20 December 2006 on the protection of minors and human dignity and on the right of reply in relation to the competitiveness of the European audiovisual and on-line information services industry*, OJ, L 378/72.

——, —— and European Commission (2003) Interinstitutional Agreement on Better Law-making, OJ, C 321/01.

European Social Networking Task Force (2009) 'Safer social networking principles for the EU.' Online. Available HTTP: http://ec.europa.eu/information_society/activities/social_networking/docs/sn_principles.pdf (accessed 24 February 2012).

Eurostat (2011) 'Internet access and use in 2011: Almost a quarter of persons aged 16-74 in the EU27 have never used the Internet.' Online. Available HTTP: http://europa.eu/rapid/pressReleasesAction.do?reference=STAT/11/188&format=HTML&aged=0&language=EN&guiLanguage=en (accessed 24 February 2012).

Gunningham, N. and Rees, J. (1997) 'Industry self-regulation: An institutional perspective,' *Law & Policy*, 19(4): 370–380.

Hamilton, J. (1998) 'Who will rate the ratings?' in M. Price (ed.) *The V-Chip Debate: Content Filtering from Television to the Internet*, Mahwah, NJ: Lawrence Erlbaum Associates.

Hans-Bredow-Institut (HBI) and Institute of European Media Law (EMR) (2006) *Study on Co-Regulation Measures in the Media Sector: Final Report*, Study commissioned by the European Commission. Online. Available HTTP: http://ec.europa.eu/avpolicy/docs/library/studies/coregul/final_rep_en.pdf (accessed 24 February 2012).

Hasebrink, U. (2011) 'Giving the audience a voice: The role of research in making media regulation more responsive to the needs of the audience,' *Journal of Information Policy*, 1: 321–336.

Heins, M. (1998) 'Three questions about television ratings,' in M. Price (ed.) *The V-Chip Debate: Content Filtering from Television to the Internet*, Mahwah, NJ: Lawrence Erlbaum Associates.

Helberger, N. (2008) 'From eyeball to creator: toying with audience empowerment in the Audiovisual Media Service Directive,' *Entertainment Law Review*, 6: 128–137.

—— (2011) 'Diversity label: Exploring the potential and limits of a transparency approach to media diversity,' *Journal of Information Policy*, 1: 337–369.

ICRI, CMCS, MMTC and Ernst & Young (2009) *Indicators for Media Pluralism in the Member States: Towards a Risk-Based Approach, Final Report and Annexes—User Guide, MPM, Country Reports*, Study prepared for the European Commission. Online. Available HTTP: http://ec.europa.eu/information_society/media_taskforce/pluralism/study/index_en.htm (accessed 24 February 2012).

Indepen (2005) *Extension of the Television without Frontiers Directive: An Impact Assessment*, Final report for Ofcom. Online. Available HTTP: http://stakeholders.ofcom.org.uk/market-data-research/other/tv-research/tv-without-frontiers/ (accessed 24 February 2012).

Johnson, D. (1998) 'Let's let the Net self-regulate: The case for allowing decentralized, emergent self-ordering to solve the public policy problems created by the Internet.' Online. Available HTTP: http://web.archive.org/web/19990210085611/www.cli.org/selford/essay.htm (accessed 24 February 2012).

Kirsch, S. (2006) *Children, Adolescents and Media Violence: A Critical Look at the Research*, Thousand Oaks, CA: Sage Publications.

Latzer, M. (2007) 'Trust in the industry—Trust in the users: Self-regulation and self-help in the context of digital media content in the EU,' Paper for Working Group 3 of the Expert Conference on European media policy 'More trust in content—The potential of co- and self-regulation in digital media,' Leipzig, 9–11 May. Online. Available HTTP: http://www.leipzig-eu2007.de/en/downloads/dokumente.asp (accessed 21 May 2008; no longer available).

——, Just, N., Saurwein, F. and Slominski, P. (2003) 'Regulation remixed: Institutional change through self- and co-regulation in the mediamatics sector,' *Communications & Strategies*, 50(2): 127–157.

Lievens, E. (2010) *Protecting Children in the Digital Era: The Use of Alternative Regulatory Instruments*, Leiden: Martinus Nijhoff Publishers.

—— (2011) 'Risk-reducing regulatory strategies for protecting minors in social networks,' *Info—The Journal of Policy, Regulation and Strategy for Telecommunications, Information and Media*, 13(6): 43–54.

——, Dumortier, J. and Ryan, P. (2006) 'The co-protection of minors in new media: A European approach to co-regulation,' *UC Davis Journal of Juvenile Law & Policy*, 10: 97–151.

Livingstone, S. (2009) *Children and the Internet*, Cambridge: Polity.

Lobe, B. and Staksrud, E. (2010) *Evaluation of the Implementation of the Safe Social Networking Principles for the EU, Part 2: Testing of 20 Providers of Social Networking Services in Europe*, Study commissioned by the European Commission. Online. Available HTTP: http://ec.europa.eu/information_society/activities/social_networking/docs/final_report/sec_part.pdf (accessed 24 February 2012).

Makkai, T. and Braithwaite, J. (1998) 'In and out of the revolving door: Making sense of regulatory capture,' in R. Baldwin, C. Scott, and C. Hood (eds.) *A Reader on Regulation*, Oxford: Oxford University Press.

Marsden, C. (2004) 'Co- and self-regulation in European media and Internet sectors: The results of Oxford University's study www.selfregulation.info,' in C. Möller and A. Amouroux (eds.) *The Media Freedom Internet Cookbook*, Vienna: OSCE.

McGonagle, T. (2011) 'Media literacy: No longer the shrinking violet of European audiovisual media regulation?' in S. Nikoltchev (ed.) *Media literacy*, Strasbourg: European Audiovisual Authority.

McIntyre, T. J. and Scott, C. (2008) 'Internet filtering: Rhetoric, legitimacy, accountability and responsibility,' in R. Brownsword and K. Yeung (eds.) *Regulating Technologies: Legal Futures, Regulatory Frames and Technological Fixes*, Oxford: Hart Publishing.

Mifsud Bonnici, J.P. (2007) 'Self-regulation in cyberspace,' Unpublished thesis, University of Groningen.

—— and De Vey Mestdagh, C. N. J. (2005) 'Right vision, wrong expectations: The European Union and self-regulation of harmful Internet content,' *Information & Communications Technology Law*, 14(2): 133–150.

Millwood Hargrave, A. and Livingstone, S. (2006) *Harm and Offence in Media Content: A Review of the Evidence*, Bristol: Intellect.

Möller, C. and Amouroux, A. (eds.) (2004) *The Media Freedom Internet Cookbook*, Vienna: OSCE.

Murray, A. and Scott, C. (2002) 'Controlling the new media: Hybrid responses to new forms of power,' *The Modern Law Review*, 65(4): 491–516.

Newman, A. and Bach, D. (2004) 'Self-regulatory trajectories in the shadow of public power: Resolving digital dilemmas in Europe and the United States,' *Governance*, 17(3): 387–413.

Ofcom (n.d.) 'Statutory duties and regulatory principles'. Online. Available HTTP: http://www.ofcom.org.uk/about/what-is-ofcom/statutory-duties-and-regulatory-principles/ (accessed 24 February 2012).

—— (2007) 'Ofcom's response to the Byron Review—Annex 2: Current tools and approaches to protecting children from harmful content online'. Online. Available HTTP: http://www.ofcom.org.uk/research/telecoms/reports/byron/annex2.pdf (accessed 24 February 2012).

—— (2008) *Initial Assessments of When to Adopt Self- or Co-Regulation: Consultation*. Online. Available HTTP: http://stakeholders.ofcom.org.uk/binaries/consultations/coregulation/summary/condoc.pdf (accessed 24 February 2012).

Ogus, A. (1995) 'Rethinking self-regulation,' *Oxford Journal of Legal Studies*, 15(1): 97–108.

Olsberg • SPI *et al.* (2003) *Empirical Study on the Practice of the Rating of Films Distributed in Cinemas, Television, DVD and Videocassettes in the EU and EEA Member States: Final Report*, Study commissioned by the European Commission. Online. Available HTTP: http://ec.europa.eu/avpolicy/docs/library/studies/finalised/studpdf/rating_finalrep2.pdf (accessed 24 February 2012).

Organization for Economic Co-operation and Development (OECD) (1995) *Recommendation of the Council on Improving the Quality of Government Regulation*. Online. Available HTTP: http://www.oecd.org/officialdocuments/publicdisplaydocumentpdf/?cote=OCDE/GD%2895%2995&docLanguage=En (accessed 24 February 2012).

—— (2012) *Recommendation of the Council on Regulatory Policy and Governance*. Online. Available HTTP: http://www.oecd.org/dataoecd/45/55/49990817.pdf (accessed 4 May 2012).

Organization for Security and Co-operation in Europe (OSCE) and Reporters sans Frontières (2005) 'Joint declaration on guaranteeing media freedom on the Internet.' Online. Available HTTP: https://www.osce.org/fom/15657 (accessed 4 May 2012).

Palzer, C. (2003) 'European provisions for the establishment of co-regulation frameworks,' in S. Nikoltchev (ed.) *Co-Regulation of the Media in Europe*, Strasbourg: European Audiovisual Observatory.

Peacock, A. (1989) 'The Future of Public Service Broadcasting,' in C. Veljanovski (ed.) *Freedom in Broadcasting*, London: Institute of Economic Affairs.

Price, M. (ed.) (1998) *The V-Chip Debate: Content Filtering from Television to the Internet*, Mahwah, NJ: Lawrence Erlbaum Associates.

—— and Verhulst, S. (2000) 'In search of the self: Charting the course of self-regulation on the Internet in a global environment,' in C. Marsden (ed.) *Regulating the Global Information Society*, London: Routledge.

Prosser, T. (2008) 'Self-regulation, co-regulation and the Audio-Visual Media Services Directive,' *Journal of Consumer Policy*, 31(1): 99–113.

Rand Europe (2007) *Options for and Effectiveness of Internet Self- and Co-Regulation, Phase 1 Report: Mapping Existing Co- and Self-Regulatory Institutions on the Internet*, Study commissioned by the European Commission. Online. Available HTTP: http://ec.europa.eu/dgs/information_society/evaluation/data/pdf/studies/s2006_05/phase1.pdf (accessed 24 February 2012).

—— (2008) *Options for Effectiveness of Internet Self- and Co-Regulation, Phase 3: Final Report*, Study commissioned by the European Commission. Online. Available HTTP: http://ec.europa.eu/dgs/information_society/evaluation/data/pdf/studies/s2006_05/final_report.pdf (accessed 24 February 2012).

Reding, V. (2003) 'Minors and media: Towards a more effective protection,' Speech at the Workshop of scientists in the field of the protection of minors on media violence, self-regulation and media literacy. Online. Available HTTP: http://europa.eu.int/rapid/pressReleasesAction.do?reference=SPEECH/03/400&format=HTML&aged=0&language=EN&guiLanguage=en (accessed 24February 2012).

—— (2006) 'Freedom of the media, effective co-regulation and media literacy: Cornerstones for an efficient protection of minors in the European Union,' Speech at the ICRA Roundtable Brussels 'Mission Impossible.' Online. Available HTTP: http://europa.eu/rapid/pressReleasesAction.do?reference=SPEECH/06/374&format=HTML&aged=0&language=EN&guiLanguage=en (accessed 24 February 2012).

—— (2010) 'Think before you post! How to make social networking sites safer for children and teenagers?' Speech at Safer Internet Day. Online. Available HTTP: http://europa.eu/rapid/pressReleasesAction.do?reference=SPEECH/10/22 (accessed 24 February 2012).

Rothstein, H., Huber, M. and Gaskell, G. (2006) 'A theory of risk colonization: The spiralling regulatory logics of societal and institutional risk,' *Economy and Society*, 35(1): 91–112.

Schulz, W. (2008) 'Regulating search engines? On the use of self- and co-regulation in the field of Internet search,' in S. Nikoltchev (ed.) *Searching for Audiovisual Content*, Strasbourg: European Audiovisual Observatory.

—— and Held, T. (2001) *Regulated Self-Regulation as a Form of Modern Government*, Study commissioned by the German Federal Commissioner for Cultural and Media Affairs. Online. Available HTTP: http://www.humanrights.coe.int/Media/documents/interim-report-self-regulation.pdf (accessed 24 February 2012).

Senden, L. (2005) 'Soft law, self-regulation and co-regulation in European law: Where do they meet?' *Electronic Journal of Comparative Law*. Online. Available HTTP: http://www.ejcl.org/91/abs91-3.html (accessed 24 February 2012).

Sinclair, D. (1997) 'Self-regulation versus command and control? Beyond false dichotomies,' *Law & Policy*, 19(4): 529–559.

Staksrud, E. and Lobe, B. (2010) *Evaluation of the Implementation of the Safer Social Networking Principles for the EU, Part 1: General Report*, Study commissioned by the European Commission. Online. Available HTTP: http://ec.europa.eu/information_society/activities/social_networking/docs/final_report/first_part.pdf (accessed 24 February 2012).

Teubner, G. (ed.) (1988) *Autopoietic Law: A New Approach to Law and Society*, Berlin: Walter De Gruyter.

—— (1993) *Law as an Autopoietic System*, Oxford: Blackwell.

——, Nobles, R. and Schiff, D. (2005) 'The autonomy of law: An introduction to legal autopoiesis,' in J. Penner, D. Schif and R. Nobles (eds.) *Introduction to Jurisprudence and Legal Theory*, Oxford: Oxford University Press.

Valcke, P. (2011a) 'A European risk barometer for media pluralism: Why assess damage, when you can map risk?' *Journal of Information Policy*, 1: 185–216.

—— (2011b) 'Looking for the user in media pluralism regulation: Unraveling the traditional diversity chain and recent trends of user empowerment in European media regulation,' *Journal of Information Policy*, 1: 287–320.

—— and Stevens, D. (2007) 'Graduated regulation of "regulatable" content and the European Audiovisual Media Services Directive: One small step for the industry and one giant leap for the legislator?' *Telematics & Informatics*, 24(4): 285–302.

——, ——, Werkers, E. and Lievens, E. (2008) 'Audiovisual Media Services in the EU: Next generation approach or old wine in new barrels?' *Communications & Strategies*, 103–118.

Verdoodt, A. (2007) 'Zelfregulering in de Journalistiek: De Formulering en de Handhaving van Deontologische Standaarden in en door het Journalistieke Beroep [Self-regulation in journalism: The formulation and enforcement of deontological standards in and by the journalistic profession],' Unpublished thesis, KU Leuven.

# Index

Printed by PGSTL